The Essential Guide to
Children's Books and Their Creators

THE ESSENTIAL GUIDE TO

Children's Books and Their Creators

Anita Silvey, EDITOR

HOUGHTON MIFFLIN COMPANY • BOSTON • NEW YORK • 2002

For information about permission to reproduce selections from
this book, write to Permissions, Houghton Mifflin Company,
215 Park Avenue South, New York, New York 10003.

Visit our Web site: www.houghtonmifflinbooks.com.

Library of Congress Cataloging-in-Publication Data
is available.
ISBN 0-618-19083-X
ISBN 0-618-19082-1 (pbk.)

Printed in the United States of America

Book design by Robert Overholtzer

VB 10 9 8 7 6 5 4 3 2

FOR MY COLLEAGUES:
the women and men who have created, published,
sold, promoted, and championed children's
and young adult books. They have loved and nurtured
the books described in these pages—and have
taught me all that I know.

Contents

Introduction

"Only the rarest kind of best in anything is good enough for the young."
—Walter de la Mare

LIFE IS A BANQUET—and most of us starve. This adage applies particularly to readers of children's books. Despite the wealth, the complexity, and the beauty of children's books, so few people have the time, or the resources, to experience the full richness offered. *The Essential Guide to Children's Books and Their Creators* brings the banquet to everyone.

For more than thirty years, first as editor of *Horn Book Magazine,* then as a publisher of children's books, I have lectured extensively in the United States and Canada about our most important children's books. Often when seeking basic information, I found myself searching through a dozen reference volumes. Gradually I formed an image of the reference book on children's literature that I frequently reached for but could not find. Such a book, I believed, would concentrate on the literature created for American children over the past fifty years, treat its subjects broadly, offer thoughtful evaluations, contain a wide range of critical perspectives, and allow children's book authors and artists to speak for themselves. With these objectives in mind, I conceived *Children's Books and Their Creators,* published in 1995.

After using *Children's Books and Their Creators* for a few years, I became aware of certain limitations. Because of the size of the volume, I could not adopt it for my college courses. Although extensively covering the history of children's books, it became more outdated with the passing years. Then Susan Canavan of Houghton Mifflin suggested I revise the book for a paperback volume, and I welcomed the opportunity. *The Essential Guide to Children's Books and Their Creators,* alphabetically arranged, contains three types of entries: biographies about the creators; overviews of history, issues, and genres; and "Voices of the Creators," written by thirty of our finest authors and illustrators.

Focusing primarily on contemporary American authors and illustrators, I selected about 375 entries from the 1995 text for this volume. When necessary, I updated certain entries with new information and titles. These essays represent our classic children's literature, the canon of children's books, which continue to be read in the twenty-first century. Although not the only books of merit published, these books motivate children to read. They include captivating stories, compelling characters, and imaginative use of language. They appeal to a wide and diverse audience of children. Because childhood is so brief, we need to expose our children to the best of our literary heritage in their childhood years. That remains the finest—and most poignant—gift we could ever give to the young.

The 1990s proved a particularly exciting time in children's book creation. Thanks to Harry Potter, children's books became front-page news, and some talented writers and illustrators demonstrated their best work during this period. To present information and commentary about these new voices, I added one hundred new essays.

Although I believe that at least one thousand people could be considered essential creators of children's books, I could not offer information about all of them in one volume. In selecting the entries, I considered their historical importance, popularity, current interest in and availability of the books, and the overall contribution of the author or artist; together, the essays provide a thorough and invaluable introduction to children's books. They also reflect the wide variety of cultural backgrounds represented in the field. Those who seek more information should consult the updated electronic version available through Net Libraries and *Children's Books and Their Creators*. Ultimately, I held the quality of artistry as most important for my selections. Because my sympathies lie with those trying to fashion the best children's books, my professional mantra remains those immortal words of Walter de la Mare: "Only the rarest kind of best in anything is good enough for the young."

Like any sane human being undertaking such a massive project, I immediately recognized my limitations. Then I remembered a statement by children's book editor Ursula Nordstrom, one of the great geniuses of the twentieth century. When asked for her job qualifications, she tartly replied, "Well, I am a former child, and I haven't forgotten a thing." Because I haven't forgotten either, this volume contains old — and some-times new — friends, the books of my childhood, my young adult years, and my years of professional work.

Fortunately, I received a great deal of assistance while shaping *The Essential Guide to Children's Books and Their Creators*. About a hundred contributors, passionate about children's books, wrote these entries. The entire staff at Houghton Mifflin, especially Susan Canavan, Becky Saikia-Wilson, Susanna Brougham, and Robert Overholtzer, transformed an ungainly manuscript into a book. My agent, Doe Coover, kept me laughing and working until the end. I am particularly indebted to the two consulting editors, Peter Sieruta and Marie Salvadore. Book people extraordinaire, they helped shape the contents and gave me honest opinions about the works published in the 1990s. And in those final hours, when we had to focus the contents more precisely, they were both clear-headed and consoling. My husband, Bill Clark, provided a clipping service unrivaled on the East Coast and showed admirable patience and humor. Fortunately, the book got finished before he ran out of both. For all of his understanding, I am extremely grateful; every book I have created exists because of his support.

ANITA SILVEY
Westwood, Massachusetts

Getting Started: A Basic Reading List

The books listed here represent some of the finest works produced for children.

Board Books (ages 0–2)
Black on White (1993), White on Black (1993), Tana Hoban
Max's First Word (1998), Rosemary Wells
Sheila Rae's Peppermint Stick (2001), Kevin Henkes
Tickle Tickle (1987), I Touch (1986), Helen Oxenbury

Preschool Books (ages 0–4)
Construction Zone (1999), Tana Hoban
Freight Train (1978), Donald Crews
Goodnight Moon (1947), Margaret Wise Brown, illustrated by Clement Hurd
Have You Seen My Duckling? (1984), Nancy Tafuri
"More More More," Said the Baby (1990), Vera B. Williams
Mr. Gumpy's Outing (1971), John Burningham
Rosie's Walk (1968), Pat Hutchins
The Snowman (1978), Raymond Briggs
Tuesday (1991), David Wiesner
The Very Hungry Caterpillar (1969), Eric Carle
Where's Spot? (1980), Eric Hill

Alphabet Books
Aardvarks, Disembark! (1990), Ann Jonas
Anno's Alphabet (1975), Mitsumasa Anno
Brian Wildsmith's ABC (1963)
Chicka Chicka Boom Boom (1989), Bill Martin Jr. and John Archambault
Jambo Means Hello (1974), Tom Feelings

On Beyond Zebra! (1955), Dr. Seuss
Pigs from A to Z (1986), Arthur Geisert

Counting Books
Anno's Counting Book (1975), Mitsumasa Anno
Moja Means One: Swahili Counting Book (1971), Muriel and Tom Feelings
One Hunter (1982), Pat Hutchins
1, 2, 3 (1985), Tana Hoban
One Was Johnny (1962), Maurice Sendak
Pigs from 1 to 10 (1992), Arthur Geisert
Ten Black Dots (1986), Donald Crews
Ten, Nine, Eight (1983), Molly Bang
Who's Counting (1986), Nancy Tafuri

Nursery Rhymes
Hector Protector and As I Went over the Water (1965), Maurice Sendak
London Bridge Is Falling Down (1967), Peter Spier
Mother Goose's Little Misfortunes (1990), Amy Schwartz
The Mother Goose Treasury (1966), Raymond Briggs
Ring O'Roses (1922), L. Leslie Brooke
The Tall Book of Mother Goose (1942), Feodor Rojankovsky

Picture Books (ages 4–8)
And to Think That I Saw It on Mulberry Street (1937), Dr. Seuss
Andy and the Lion (1938), James Daugherty
Caps for Sale (1947), Esphyr Slobodkina
The Carrot Seed (1945), Ruth Krauss, illustrated by Crockett Johnson
Corduroy (1968), Don Freeman
Crictor (1958), Tomi Ungerer

Crow Boy (1955), Taro Yashima
Curious George (1941), H. A. and Margret Rey
Doctor DeSoto (1982), William Steig
George and Martha (1972), James Marshall
Harold and the Purple Crayon (1955), Crockett Johnson
Harry, the Dirty Dog (1956), Gene Zion, illustrated by Margaret Bloy Graham
A Hole Is to Dig (1952), Ruth Krauss, illustrated by Maurice Sendak
Horton Hatches the Egg (1940), Dr. Seuss
Ira Sleeps Over (1975), Bernard Waber
Lilly's Purple Plastic Purse (1996), Kevin Henkes
The Little House (1943), Virginia Lee Burton
Madeline (1939), Ludwig Bemelmans
Magic School Bus at the Waterworks (1986), Joanna Cole
Make Way for Ducklings (1941), Robert McCloskey
Many Moons (1990), James Thurber, illustrated by Marc Simont
Martha Speaks (1992), Susan Meddaugh
Mike Mulligan and His Steam Shovel (1939), Virginia Lee Burton
Millions of Cats (1928), Wanda Gág
Mirandy and Brother Wind (1988), Patricia McKissack, illustrated by Jerry Pinkney
Miss Nelson Is Missing (1977), Harry Allard, illustrated by James Marshall
Miss Rumphius (1982), Barbara Cooney
Molly Bannaky (1999), Alice McGill, illustrated by Chris Soentpiet
Officer Buckle and Gloria (1995), Peggy Rathman
The Polar Express (1985), Chris Van Allsburg
The Shrinking of Treehorn (1971), Florence Parry Heide, illustrated by Edward Gorey
Snowflake Bentley (1998), Jacqueline Briggs Martin, illustrated by Mary Azarian
The Snowy Day (1962), Ezra Jack Keats
The Story About Ping (1933), Marjorie Flack
The Story of Ferdinand (1936), Munro Leaf, illustrated by Robert Lawson
Sylvester and the Magic Pebble (1969), William Steig
The Tale of Peter Rabbit (1901), Beatrix Potter
The Three Pigs (2001), David Wiesner
The True Story of the Three Little Pigs (1989), Jon Scieszka, illustrated by Lane Smith

Where the Wild Things Are (1964), Maurice Sendak
Yo! Yes? (1993) Chris Raschka

Myths, Legends, Folklore (ages 6–12)

Aesop's Fables (2000), illustrated by Jerry Pinkney
All Night, All Day (1991), Ashley Bryan
The Arabian Nights (1993), Kate D. Wiggin, illustrated by Maxfield Parrish
D'Aulaire's Book of Greek Myths (1962), Ingri and Edgar D'Aulaire
The Girl Who Loved Horses (1979), Paul Goble
The Jack Tales (1943), Richard Chase
Keepers of the Earth (1989), Joseph Bruchac and Michael J. Caduto
The Merry Adventures of Robin Hood (1883), Howard Pyle
The Naked Bear: Folktales of the Iroquois (1987), John Bierhorst
Paul Bunyan (1984), Steven Kellogg
The People Could Fly: American Black Folktales (1985), Virginia Hamilton
The Rainbow People (1989), Laurence Yep
Rumpelstiltskin (1986), Paul O. Zelinsky
Seven Blind Mice (1992), Ed Young
The Stinky Cheese Man and Other Fairly Stupid Tales (1992), Jon Scieszka, illustrated by Lane Smith
Strega Nona (1975), Tomie dePaola
Uncle Remus (1999), Julius Lester, illustrated by Jerry Pinkney
Why Mosquitoes Buzz in People's Ears (1975), Verna Aardema, illustrated by Leo and Dianne Dillon
Zlateh the Goat (1966), Isaac Bashevis Singer, illustrated by Maurice Sendak

Poetry (age 6 and up)

Alligator Pie (1974), Dennis Lee
All Small (1986), David McCord
Bronzeville Boys and Girls (1956), Gwendolyn Brooks
Don't You Turn Back (1969), Langston Hughes
Finding a Poem (1970), Eve Merriam
I Met a Man (1961), John Ciardi
Joyful Noise: Poems for Two Voices (1988), Paul Fleischman

Knock at a Star: A Child's Introduction to Poetry (anthology, 1982), X. J. Kennedy
The New Kid on the Block (1984), Jack Prelutsky
Night on Neighborhood Street (1991), Eloise Greenfield
Peacock Pie (1917) and *Come Hither* (anthology, 1923), Walter de la Mare
The Place My Words Are Looking For (1990), Paul Janeczko
This Same Sky (1992), Naomi Shihab Nye
Side by Side: Poems to Read Together (anthology, 1988), Lee Bennett Hopkins
The Trees Stand Shining (1971), Hettie Jones
A Visit to William Blake's Inn (1981), Nancy Willard
Where the Sidewalk Ends (1974) and *The Light in the Attic* (1974), Shel Silverstein

Easy Readers (ages 7–8)
Amelia Bedelia series, Peggy Parish
The Cat in the Hat (1957), Dr. Seuss
Frog and Toad series, Arnold Lobel
Henry and Mudge series, Cynthia Rylant
Little Bear (1957), Else Holmelund Minarik
Nate the Great series, Marjorie Sharmat

Chapter Books (ages 8–9)
And Then What Happened, Paul Revere? (1973), Jean Fritz, illustrated by Margot Tomes
The Courage of Sarah Noble (1954), Alice Dalgliesh
Encyclopedia Brown series, Donald J. Sobol
Little House in the Big Woods (1932), Laura Ingalls Wilder
My Father's Dragon (1948), Ruth Stiles Gannett
Ramona series, Beverly Cleary
Sarah, Plain and Tall (1985), Patricia MacLachlan
Stone Fox (1980), John Reynolds Gardiner

Middle-Grade Fiction (ages 8–12)
The Adventures of Tom Sawyer (1876/1989), Mark Twain, illustrated by Barry Moser
Anastasia Krupnik series, Lois Lowry
Anne of Green Gables (1908), L. M. Montgomery
Are You There, God? It's Me, Margaret (1970), Judy Blume
Babe: The Gallant Pig (1985), Dick King-Smith

A Bear Called Paddington (1958), Michael Bond
The Best Christmas Pageant Ever (1972), Barbara Robinson
The Black Stallion (1941), Walter Farley
Bridge to Terabithia (1977), Katherine Paterson
Call of the Wild (1903/1999), Jack London, illustrated by Wendell Minor
Charlie and the Chocolate Factory (1964), Roald Dahl
From the Mixed-up Files of Mrs. Basil E. Frankweiler (1967), E. L. Konigsburg
The Great Gilly Hopkins (1978), Katherine Paterson
Harriet the Spy (1964), Louise Fitzhugh
Hatchet (1987), Gary Paulsen
Holes (1998), Louis Sachar
Homecoming (1981), Cynthia Voigt
Homer Price (1943), Robert McCloskey
Humbug Mountain (1978), Sid Fleischman
The Hundred Dresses (1944), Eleanor Estes
Julie of the Wolves (1972), Jean Craighead George
The Jungle Book (1894), Rudyard Kipling
Little Women (1868), Louisa May Alcott
The Man from the Other Side (1991), Uri Orlev
Maniac Magee (1990), Jerry Spinelli
Mary Poppins (1934), P. L. Travers
M. C. Higgins, the Great (1974), Virginia Hamilton
Moffats series, Eleanor Estes
One-Eyed Cat (1984), Paula Fox
Pippi Longstocking (1950), Astrid Lindgren
Rabbit Hill (1950), Robert Lawson
Sounder (1969), William Armstrong
Summer of the Swans (1970), Betsy Byars
Treasure Island (1883/1981), Robert Louis Stevenson, illustrated by N. C. Wyeth
The Westing Game (1978), Ellen Raskin

Fantasy
The Adventures of Pinocchio (1891), Carlo Collodi
Alice's Adventures in Wonderland (1865), Lewis Carroll
Animal Family (1965), Randall Jarrell
The Blue Sword (1982) and *The Hero and the Crown* (1985), Robin McKinley
Borrowers series, Mary Norton

Charlotte's Web (1952), E. B. White

Chronicles of Chrestomanci series, Diana Wynne Jones

Chronicles of Narnia series, C. S. Lewis

Chronicles of Prydain series, Lloyd Alexander

Dark Is Rising series, Susan Cooper

Earthsea series, Ursula K. Le Guin

Five Children and It (1902), E. Nesbit

Green Knowe series, L. M. Boston

Half-Magic (1954), Edward Eager

Harry Potter series, J. K. Rowling

The Hobbit (1938), J. R. R. Tolkien

Incredible Journey (1960), Sheila Burnford

The Mouse and His Child (2001), Russell Hoban, illustrated by David Small

Owl in Love (1993), Patrice Kindl

The Perilous Gard (1974), Elizabeth Marie Pope

Redwall series, Brian Jacques

The Secret Garden (1911), Frances Hodgson Burnett

The Story of Dr. Dolittle (1920), Hugh Lofting

The Sword in the Stone (1938), T. H. White

Tom's Midnight Garden (1958), Philippa Pearce

Tuck Everlasting (1975), Natalie Babbitt

The Wind in the Willows (1908), Kenneth Grahame

Winnie-the-Pooh (1926), A. A. Milne

The Wonderful Wizard of Oz (1900), L. Frank Baum

A Wrinkle in Time (1962), Madeleine L'Engle

Historical Fiction

Across Five Aprils (1964), Irene Hunt

The Borning Room (1991) and *Bull Run* (1993), Paul Fleischman

Caddie Woodlawn (1935), Carol Ryrie Brink

Catherine, Called Birdy (1994), Karen Cushman

Fallen Angels (1988), Walter Dean Myers

The Friendship (1987), Mildred Taylor

Island of the Blue Dolphins (1960), Scott O'Dell

Johnny Tremain (1943), Esther Forbes

Kidnapped (1886), Robert Louis Stevenson

Lyddie (1991), Katherine Paterson

Morning Girl (1992), Michael Dorris

My Brother Sam Is Dead (1974), James and Christopher Collier

Out of the Dust (1997), Karen Hesse

The Slave Dancer (1973), Paula Fox

The Strange Affair of Adelaide Harris (1971), Leon Garfield

The True Confessions of Charlotte Doyle (1990), Avi

The Watsons Go to Birmingham — 1963 (1995), Christopher Paul Curtis

The Witch of Blackbird Pond (1958), Elizabeth George Speare

Information Books

Boys' War (1990), Jim Murphy

Cathedral (1973), David Macaulay

The Endless Steppe (1968), Esther Hautzig

From Hand to Mouth (1987), James Cross Giblin

The Great Fire (1995), Jim Murphy

Harriet and the Promised Land (1993), Jacob Lawrence

My Season with Penguins (2000), Sophie Webb

Neptune (1992), Franklyn M. Branley

Never to Forget: The Jews of the Holocaust (1976), Milton Meltzer

Our Solar System (1992), Seymour Simon

Paddle-to-the-Sea (1941), Holling C. Holling

Sir Walter Ralegh and the Quest for El Dorado (2000), Marc Aaronson

Volcano (1986), Patricia Lauber

The Way Things Work (1988), David Macaulay

The Wright Brothers (1991), Russell Freedman

Science Fiction

Childhood's End (1953), Arthur C. Clarke

The Delikon (1977), H. M. Hoover

Devil on My Back (1984), Monica Hughes

Dragonsong (1976) and *Dragonsinger* (1977), Anne McCaffrey

Enchantress from the Stars (1970), Sylvia Louise Engdahl

Eva (1988), Peter Dickinson

The Giver (1993), Lois Lowry

Moon-Flash (1984), Patricia McKillip

Mrs. Frisby and the Rats of NIMH (1971) and *Z for Zachariah* (1975), Robert C. O'Brien

Pebble in the Sky (1950), Isaac Asimov

Rocket Ship Galileo (1947), Robert Heinlein

Step to the Stars (1954), Lester del Rey

A Wrinkle in Time (1962), Madeleine L'Engle

Young Adult Novels (age 12 and up)

After the First Death (1979), Robert Cormier
The Catcher in the Rye (1951), J. D. Salinger
The Chocolate War (1974), Robert Cormier
The Circuit (1997), Francisco Jimenez
The Contender (1967), Robert Lipsyte
Dark Materials series, Philip Pullman
Deliver Us from Evie (1994) and *Dinky Hocker Shoots Smack!* (1972), M. E. Kerr
The Ghost Belonged to Me (1975), Richard Peck
The Goats (1987), Brock Cole
I Am the Cheese (1977), Robert Cormier
Make Lemonade (1993), Virginia Euwer Wolff
Memory (1988), Margaret Mahy
Monster (2000), Walter Dean Myers
The Moves Make the Man (1984), Bruce Brooks
The Outsiders (1967), S. E. Hinton
The Pigman (1968), Paul Zindel
Skellig (1999), David Almond
Stotan! (1986), Chris Crutcher
Weetzie Bat (1989), Francesca Lia Block

Multicultural Perspectives

African American Literature

The Dream Keeper (1932), Langston Hughes
Every Man Heart Lay Down (1970), Lorenz Graham
My Lives and How I Lost Them (1941) and *The Lost Zoo* (1940), Countee Cullen
Roll of Thunder, Hear My Cry (1975), *Let the Circle Be Unbroken* (1981), and *Road to Memphis* (1990), Mildred Taylor
Stevie (1964), John Steptoe
Walk Together Children (1971), Ashley Bryan
You Can't Pet a Possum (1934) and *Sad-Faced Boy* (1937), Arna Bontemps
Zeely (1964) and *M. C. Higgins the Great* (1974), Virginia Hamilton

Chinese American Literature

City Kids in China (1991), Peggy Thomson
Dragonwings (1975), *Child of the Owl* (1977), and *Star Fisher* (1991), Laurence Yep
El Chino (1990), Allen Say
Fifth Chinese Daughter (1950), Jade Snow Wong

The Five Chinese Brothers (1938), Claire Huchet Bishop
Lon Po Po: A Red Riding Hood Story from China (1990), Ed Young
Tales from Gold Mountain (1989), Paul Yee

Japanese American Literature

Baseball Saved Us (1993), Ken Mochizuki
The Coming of the Bear (1992), Lensey Namioka
Faithful Elephants: A True Story of Animals, People, and War (1988), Yukio Tsuchiya
The Journey: Japanese Americans, Racism, and Renewal (1990), Sheila Hamanaka
Sadako and the Thousand Paper Cranes (1977), Elea Coerr
Samurai of Gold Hill (1972) and *The Bracelet* (1993), Yoshiko Uchida
Tales from the Bamboo Grove (1992), Yoko Kawashima Watkins
Tree of Cranes (1991) and *Grandfather's Journey* (1993), Allen Say
Umbrella (1958), Taro Yashima

Latino Literature

Baseball in April and Other Stories (1990) and *Local News* (1993), Gary Soto
El diablo inglés y otros cuentos (The English devil and other stories, 1969), María Elena Walsh
Un diente se mueve (A loose tooth, 1990), Daniel Bardot
Going Home (1986) and *El Bronx Remembered: A Novella and Stories*, Nicholasa Mohr
Miguel y el pastel (Miguel and the cake, 1992), Maribel Suárez
Teo en un día de fiesta (Teo during a holiday, 1987), Violeta Denou

The Essential Guide to
Children's Books and Their Creators

A

Aesop

Traditional Greek author of fables, b. mid–sixth century B.C.(?) Almost nothing about Aesop is certain except the universal and unfading popularity of the fables associated with his name. We do not know exactly when or where he lived or what he did. We have no evidence that he put any of the fables he told into writing and only a few clues as to which fables are actually his. Twentieth-century research established, moreover, that fables identical to Aesop's in form, and sometimes in substance, existed much earlier, in Mesopotamia. Yet the testimony of Aristophanes, Plato, Herodotus, and other eminent Greeks is firmly in accord on the fame of Aesop as a fable maker, or fabulist.

His life quickly took on legendary dimensions — the eloquent Aesop, it was said, was once a despised, mute slave — and fables from here and there became attached to his name. Originally, they were not meant for children, but first as examples of pithy composition and later as lessons in wise conduct, fables entered the curriculum of young nobles and gentlemen, while young peasants picked up phrases from the fables — "the lion's share," "sour grapes," and "crying wolf," for example — as common wisdom.

The spread of popular education in the nineteenth century, along with advances in printing and graphic reproduction, brought forth schoolbooks and storybooks with selections from Aesop, often vividly illustrated. To parents and pedagogues, fables were instructive tales that children actually enjoyed. Graphic artists appreciated their clear-cut, concentrated action and the scope they allowed for interpretation.

Illustrated collections of the fables especially designed for children became a regular feature of publishers' lists. WALTER CRANE entitled his elaborate, proto–Art Nouveau presentation (somewhat inaccurately) *The Baby's Own Aesop* (1887). In the relatively static, traditionalist world of early-twentieth-century children's literature, Crane's Aesop held its place into the 1950s, along with two other vintage British editions, folklorist Joseph Jacobs's embroidered retelling of the fables (1894), valued for its historical introduction, and the ARTHUR RACKHAM *Aesop* (1912), an odd pairing of Rackham's visual theatrics with lean, shapely new translations by V. S. Vernon Jones.

The one strong American entry was an undisguised artist's showcase, Boris Artzybasheff's *Aesop's Fables* (1933), based on wood engravings and intended for both adults and children. In many quarters, however, a subtler, more far-reaching exploitation of Aesopica was getting under way. Alexander Calder (1931), Antonio Frasconi (1954, 1964), and Joseph Low (1963) produced a motley of broadsides, albums, and portfolios for cultural sophisticates and the occasional questing child.

Early in the picture book explosion, JAMES DAUGHERTY contrived out of Aesop, Roman

Illustration by Thomas Bewick for Aesop's fable "The Crow and the Pitcher," from Bewick's *Select Fables of Aesop and Others* (1784).

legend, and frontier Americana a sentimental blockbuster, *Andy and the Lion* (1938). The widening, unceasing search for picture book texts brought multiple versions of some of the more anecdotal, folktale-like fables ("The Country Mouse and the City Mouse"; "The Miller, His Son, and the Donkey") as well as attention to some little-known ones. There were outright dazzlers, too, most prominently Brian Wildsmith's *The Lion and the Rat* (1963) and *The North Wind and the Sun* (1964), from Aesop via Jean de La Fontaine.

The fables themselves were adapted, grouped, and packaged in a multitude of ways. For beginning readers, Eve Rice retold ten fables in fluent primerese and, under the title *Once in a Wood* (1979), supplied them with emblematic animal close-ups. The single climactic year of 1992 produced, indicatively, two disparate, unorthodox Aesops: Barbara McClintock's rendering of nine *Animal Tales from Aesop* as a courtly theatrical performance and, from Barbara Bader and Arthur Geisert, *Aesop and Company,* which presents the fables in their original terse form (and in a historical setting), with freely interpretive, graphically American illustrations.

At the beginning of the twenty-first century, clearly, there is no end of Aesops in sight. B.B.

African American Children's Books

It is indeed a misconception to believe that little material was published for or about the African American child in the first sixty years of the twentieth century. There were many books by white authors and illustrators whose final products exemplified two schools of thought. There were those whose portrayal of the Negro in words and visuals showed sensitivity to and a respect for this minority culture. Their creations seemed to subscribe to the criteria suggested in 1944 by the noted librarian Augusta Baker:

When considering language, the most important point is to eliminate books which describe Negroes in terms of derision . . . Another language consideration

is the use of heavy dialect. It is too difficult for the child to read and understand and since often it is not authentic, but has been created by the author, it is misleading. The use of regional vernacular is acceptable. . . . [Another] factor is illustrations. An artist can portray a Negro child — black skin, crinkly hair and short nose — and make him attractive.

Among those whose artwork exemplified Baker's criteria was Erick Berry, who illustrated Paul Laurence Dunbar's poetry collection *Little Brown Baby* (1941) and ARNA BONTEMPS's *You Can't Pet a Possum* (1934). Caldecott Medal winner LYND WARD achieved appealing, dramatic figures with which to accompany Hildegarde Swift's stirring biographical sketches in *North Star Shining* (1947). In her novel *Zeke* (1931), set in the area of Tuskegee, Alabama, the white civil-rights activist Mary White Ovington demonstrated her ability to use Negro dialect in a manner that was realistic without being offensive. Florence Crannell Means carved a niche in literary history for the Negro child with her novel *Shuttered Windows* (1938). This appears to be the first novel by a white author in which all the characters are black.

From another perspective, there were those white writers and illustrators who, within a most accepting society, enjoyed great popularity with stories and pictures that would contribute little to the Negro child's self-esteem. Elvira Garner's Ezekiel series, set in rural Florida, Lynda Graham's *Pinky Marie* (1939), with her "ink black" parents, and Inez Hogan's highly praised *Nicodemus* tales, include many of the characteristics against which Baker spoke. The works of these authors — who were not alone — were replete with the exaggerated use of dialect and illustrations that showed the Negro child with heavy lips, bulging eyes, night-black skin, and woolly hair. Too often the "pickaninny" protagonist was portrayed as a youngster who saw his color as less than acceptable.

By far, much of the best literature was created by blacks themselves, some of whom are familiar in contemporary literary history and others, now forgotten, who should be rediscovered.

Arna Bontemps is most often thought of as addressing an adult audience, yet he wrote fun-filled juvenile novels such as *You Can't Pet a Possum* and *Sad-Faced Boy* (1937). In this last title there is one scene to which librarians of any era can relate. The protagonist, Slumber, coming to New York from Alabama, takes his brothers on their first trip to a public library. Slumber reads aloud from a book that sends the group into gales of laughter, and the boys find themselves summarily dismissed by the librarian. As Slumber leaves, he muses about what one is supposed to do with a funny book in the library! With journalist Jack Conroy, Bontemps also wrote a PICTURE BOOK, *The Fast Sooner Hound* (1942), in which a dog outruns a train. In a POETRY anthology for young readers, *Golden Slippers* (1941), Bontemps selected poems from the pens of not only those who had gained name recognition, such as Claude McKay and Sterling Brown, but also pieces from lesser known yet talented writers such as Frank Davis, Beatrice Murphy, and Georgia Johnson. The book was enriched with the inclusion of biographical sketches of each of the contributors.

In these early years, even as today, Countee Cullen was considered to be writing for an adult audience. But at least two pieces were written with young people in mind. Collaborating with his pet cat, Christopher, Cullen wrote *My Lives and How I Lost Them* (1941). The eight rollicking tales describe how Christopher, living gingerly on his ninth life, lost the others. The first life, he relates, was lost almost immediately after birth when out of curiosity he leaned too far over the edge of the top hat in which he was born. The fall to the floor unceremoniously ended life number one. Other lives were lost under circumstances such as an encounter with a rat and trying to survive the results of a fast brought on by a case of unrequited love. As a public school teacher in Harlem, Cullen is said to have written the animal fantasy *The Lost Zoo* (1940) as an innovative way to teach students certain life lessons. He made his point through the poetic description of the misadventures of the animals who never made it onto the ark. He warned against teasing in the tragic tale of the Squilililigee who drowned rather than live with the constant taunting that came as a result of his strange name. The fate of the Snake-That-Walked-Upon-His-Tail was an admonishment against false vanity. Snobbishly proud of his tiny feet, the snake planned to be the last to enter the ark. But those same feet became entangled in a vine. With no help available, the walking snake sank beneath the waters, never to be seen again. The thoughtful reader might well see these humorous images philosophically as more truth than fantasy.

Like many of his peers whose work had a multilevel appeal, the noted poet LANGSTON HUGHES selected from his own works some pieces he felt would speak to young people and put them together in the *Dream Keeper* (1932). The selections were tastefully embellished with black and white illustrations by Helen Sewell. In addition to the poetry, Hughes also wrote a series of "First Books" on topics such as rhymes, jazz, and the history of the Negro, all for early readers. With MILTON MELTZER he organized the still-valuable *Pictorial History of the Negro in America* (1953).

But there were many African American creators whose primary audience was young people. Held in high esteem among those whose novels spoke with quiet forcefulness against racism was Jesse Jackson. He earned a place in the world of children's literature with the publication of two school stories: *Call Me Charley* (1945) and its sequel, *Anchor Man* (1947).

Heartbreak and repeated rejection preceded the acceptance of many African American authors' and illustrators' manuscripts by major publishers. A case in point is the work of LORENZ GRAHAM. It was not until 1958, nine years after the novel had been completed, that Graham's *South Town* was printed. The story, whose basic theme explored the injustices that resulted from racist principles in the Deep South, was considered too controversial. To the surprise of many, however, the book's popularity led to a series continuing the saga of the Williams family in *North Town* (1965), *Whose Town*

(1969), and *Return to South Town* (1976). During the time that Graham served as U.S. ambassador to Liberia, he became enthralled with the rhythmic patois speech of the West Africans. This fascination was translated into a collection of Bible stories in *How God Fixed Jonah* (1946). At a later date some of the selections were published as individual volumes, the most popular of which was the Nativity story *Every Man Heart Lay Down* (1970). Graham's work spanned four decades. His last publication was the biography *John Brown* (1980), nine years before Graham's death.

While Lorenz Graham wrote only one children's biography, his sister, Shirley Graham, was a leader among those who saw the form as a driving force to record with truth and accuracy the story of a Negro so often omitted from or distorted in available texts. Her biography *George Washington Carver* (1944) was the first of several designed to tell African American readers and others about the achievements of figures such as Booker T. Washington, Benjamin Banneker, and Julius Nyerere. Graham's marriage to the often castigated civil rights leader W. E. B. Du Bois unfortunately had adverse consequences for her writing career. But her work may have been inspirational for other writers, such as Chicago librarian Charlemae Rollins, who wrote collections of brief biographies about African American poets, entertainers, and leaders in the world of political action, science, and business.

Just as it is the major job of biography to report life within a historical context, by contrast folklore reports life from the perspective of an ethnic group's social structure. Through the tales of a people passed down from one generation to another, one learns of government structure, customs, mores, taboos, and even something of the language. Early in this century a major folklorist was Alphonso O. Stafford. In addition to his collection of ANIMAL STORIES, Stafford was a regular writer for *The Brownies Book* (1920–1922). In almost every issue he had African stories, riddles, and sometimes, songs. *The Brownies Book*, founded by W. E. B. Du Bois,

was a periodical for "children of the sun." Its contents included, in addition to the folklore, biographical sketches of famous African Americans, poetry, games, and even a bit of international news!

Although the purist might question the inclusion of reading textbooks in a study of children's literature, in this circumstance it seems appropriate. The correlation between relevancy and motivation to learn is not really a new concept. In the early years of the twentieth century many African American educators in public school systems were aware of the exclusion of information about African Americans in material in their general texts. The result was the design of readers that incorporated (along with the techniques for teaching reading) historical, biographical, and cultural information. As an example, Emma Akin, in her primer for first-graders, included a simplified story of the life of Paul Laurence Dunbar. Elizabeth Cannon, in her introduction to *Country Life Stories* (1938), stated that she made no attempt to "check the vocabulary with foundation word lists" because so many of those words were of little meaning to the rural children for whom she was writing. The book goes on to describe the works of the Jeanes Supervisor, the role of the County Agents, and the regulations under which the Rolling Store functioned! Stella Sharpe's photographic reader, *Tobe* (1939), was in answer to a little African American boy's query as to why he never saw anyone who looked like him in a book.

Finally, in this glimpse into the history of literature for the African American child, it seems appropriate to include the contribution not of an author or an illustrator, but of a publishing house. Around 1915 Carter G. Woodson organized the Associated Publishers in Washington, D.C. Through this avenue, many little-known yet capable writers and illustrators found an outlet for their works. Books from Associated Publishers included Helen Whiting's EASY READER folktales, such as the collection *Negro Folk Tales for Pupils in Primary Grades* (1938); Parthenia McBrown's *Picture Poetry Book* (1935), designed with the hope that it would inspire children to love poetry; and Altona Trent-Johns's *Play Songs of the Deep South* (1944), well reviewed in some newspapers.

As the first half of the twentieth century drew to a close, the children's literature world was witness to what some describe as a "literary explosion" of works by African American authors and illustrators. Perhaps outside factors such as the growing voice of the civil rights movement and the legal decision in the *Brown vs. Board of Education* Supreme Court case contributed to this phenomenon. But surely the greatest credit must go to the creative talent of the authors and illustrators whose names at this time were becoming better and better known.

VIRGINIA HAMILTON's ever popular *Zeely* (1964) was only the first in a list of quality books for children and young adults that led to her becoming the first African American to win the Newbery Medal, for *M. C. Higgins the Great* (1974). In *Zeely* Hamilton has crafted a deceptively simple plot with a subtle blend of fantasy and reality. Underlying the quiet action is a deep sense of family, a characteristic that permeates later works by this creative storyteller. Elizabeth Perry, a city-raised child, renames herself Geeder and her brother Toeboy, when they go to spend the summer on a farm with their Uncle Ross. Life changes for Geeder on the day she first sees Zeely. With her fertile imagination, Geeder is *positive* that this stately figure must be a Watutsi queen! Who but a queen could stand "six and a half feet tall, thin, and as deeply dark as a pole of Ceylon ebony"? Talking with Zeely, Geeder learns who Zeely really is, something of the history of slavery, and a bit of African American lore and legend. Through Zeely's wise counsel, Hamilton shows not only Geeder but also her readers the importance of recognizing and accepting one's identity. Hamilton's skillful use in this book of dialect and unusual sentence structures has since become the hallmark of her distinctive writing style. Beyond these technical attributes, other constants in this writer's works are the persistent message about positive self-image and the importance of family history, the unobtrusive inclusion of ethnic history, and the admonition never to give up hope.

In 1975 MILDRED TAYLOR received the Newbery Medal for her book *Roll of Thunder, Hear My Cry* (1975). *Roll of Thunder, Hear My Cry* is a well-crafted story of an African American family surviving in Deep South Mississippi during the Depression years of the 1930s. There is a sense of family unity strongly supported by the father, Mr. David Logan, who never let his children forget the value of ownership: he owned acres of land while others, white and black, struggled to survive as sharecroppers. With quiet deliberation Taylor makes the reader aware of the ravages of racism in education, in economics, in the justice system, and in frequently humiliating social interactions. Deftly woven into the story is an aspect of racism sometimes overlooked — its effect on some young white people, represented here by Jeremy Simms. Stacey Logan asks him, "Why don't you leave us alone? How come you always hanging 'round us anyway?" There is pathos in Jeremy's stammered reply: "C-cause I just likes y'all." The mood is sustained as Cassie reports the end of this meeting: "When we reached the crossroads he looked hopefully at us as if we might relent and say goodbye. But we did not relent and as I glanced back at him standing alone in the middle of the crossing, he looked as if the world itself was slung around his neck."

With purposeful selection of words and clearly delineated characters, with honesty and perception, Taylor has introduced readers to a family whose strength is built on positive self-esteem, courage, and a steadfast belief in holding on to what is yours, no matter what it takes. With Cassie Logan as the protagonist, Taylor continued the saga of the Logan family in two other titles, *Let the Circle Be Unbroken* (1981) and *Road to Memphis* (1990), which through the passage of time show what can be accomplished when a family is determined not to be beaten down by any outside forces.

From an understated beginning in the world of children's literature with the drawings for Joyce Arkhurst's *Adventures of Spider* (1964),

JERRY PINKNEY has gone on to receive many honors for his illustrations, which recognize the beautiful uniqueness and individuality of members of the black race. Among his citations, Pinkney has six times received the Coretta Scott King Award for illustration in books written by both black and white writers. ASHLEY BRYAN's talents as an illustrator were introduced in *Moon, for What Do You Wait?* (1964). As an artist, musician, and historian, Bryan saw the need to preserve for *all* children, but especially for black children, the beauty and significance of the Negro spiritual. Over the years he has illustrated and provided musical notations for several volumes of spirituals, the first of which was *Walk Together Children* (1971). A young JOHN STEPTOE came on the scene with *Stevie* (1964). Over the years Steptoe showed amazing versatility in style and medium, culminating in his achieving both a Caldecott Honor and the Coretta Scott King Illustrator Award for the brilliant paintings in *Mufaro's Beautiful Daughters* (1987).

As one continues to view the world of children's literature, it can be observed that not only are the doors of major publishing houses opening wider to African American authors and illustrators, but smaller houses, minority-owned houses, are providing yet another avenue of visibility for an ever-increasing list of talented African American artists and writers. And surely the primary beneficiaries of these signs of progress are the children and young adults for whom the books are produced. H.M.S.

Agee, Jon

American author and illustrator, b. 1960. There is nothing ordinary about Jon Agee's PICTURE BOOKS. This Brooklyn artist, who was trained in painting and filmmaking at Cooper Union, depends heavily on graphic visual images and short but well-composed texts in books that are witty, ludicrous, and satirical. His most boldly graphic paintings appear in *Ludlow Laughs* (1985), in which the opening vision of a thick, black semicircle — a frown — leads into a story about a mean-spirited man who is mysteriously transformed; thus, the book's last image is another thick, black semicircle — a smile. The illustrations, using large areas of intense, slightly muddied primary colors, and the spare text play off each other expertly, each enlarging rather than repeating the effect of the other. Reflecting an oft-used theme in Agee's work, *Ludlow Laughs* shows a man being used and discarded by society. While this daytime grump laughs infectiously in his sleep, the whole world laughs along as a radio crew broadcasts his guffaws. When Ludlow's funny dreams end, his fickle fans move on to other entertainments.

Ellsworth (1983) centers on a similar theme. Ellsworth, a dog, is quite content to be a stuffy economics professor, well respected by his human "peers." But he cuts loose at night, chasing cars and digging up bones, until he is discovered and fired. He hangs around the park, miserably jobless, until he becomes inspired to be a dog. The absurdity of the fable works on the surface, while the satire of human values works on a slightly deeper level.

The Incredible Painting of Felix Clousseau (1988) also shows the main character turning his back on society. Clousseau, a painter, places his small, stylized portrait of a duck next to the gargantuan, elaborate portraits entered in a Parisian competition. His painting reaps ridicule until the duck quacks and walks away. Clousseau becomes famous, but not for long, because his painted tornado erupts and other such tragedies ensue. In a twist of fate, he is released from prison and quietly "return[s] to his painting" by literally disappearing into the empty streets of the town on one of his canvases. Clousseau's viewpoint is never explored, and he never seems to be more than glasses, beard, and nose. Yet while he appears to be a misfit, the reader knows that it is society's routines and habits that are in question.

Agee's artistic approach has changed to suit each story, but *Clousseau* represents his most familiar style. Using thick black outlines on the stylized figures and few contextual details, the paintings consist of large flat areas of subdued colors, often in murky browns and grays. The muddied palette reflects the darker subtexts of Agee's work, which suggest that all is not as pure — or as funny — as it appears. The flat subjects are given depth through mass, shadow, and perspective. Often objects will have a grainy, almost tactile texture. In *Clousseau* each page is like a cartoon on its own, largely because of the concise text and the unrelenting comedy. In *Go Hang a Salami! I'm a Lasagna Hog!* (1991), Agee moved completely to the single-panel comic format. Filled with palindromes, this book highlights Agee's absurd wit, as his zany pen-and-ink drawings elaborate on statements such as "Elsie's on a nose isle" and "Put Eliot's toilet up." His love of language led to other word books, *Elvis Lives: And Other Anagrams* (2000), *Who Ordered the Jumbo Shrimp? And Other Oxymorons* (1998), and *Sit on a Potato Pan, Otis! More Palindromes* (1999).

Agee's distinctive style and outlook provide for interesting and provocative picture books. His work says to the reader, "Dare to be different." And Agee practices what he preaches. S.S.

Ahlberg, Janet; Ahlberg, Allan

Janet: British illustrator, 1944–1994; Allan: British author, b. 1938. The publication of *Brick Street Boys* (1975), a series of five humorous, comic-strip-style books that describe the activities of a group of multiethnic children in a working-class neighborhood, firmly established the Ahlbergs as creators of highly popular books for young readers. Their body of fresh, lighthearted work includes ingenious toy books, joke books, short stories, and PICTURE BOOKS.

Both Janet and Allan attended Sunderland College of Education. Janet worked as a layout artist and freelance designer before illustrating children's books, and Allan worked variously as a letter carrier, plumber's helper, and teacher before becoming a full-time children's book author. While Janet was primarily the illustrator and Allan the writer of this team, they considered themselves first and foremost bookmakers, deciding together on all aspects of production, from the book size and typeface to the endpapers, cover, and jacket copy. Their ease of collaboration is reflected in books that display a flawless integration of words and pictures.

The Ahlbergs claimed there are "no deep philosophies" in their work, preferring instead to stress the playful elements of their books. They often made use of the conventions of storytelling, including morals and happy endings. "Once upon a time there were three bears" begins *Jeremiah in the Dark Woods* (1977), the story of a boy detective who sets out to find the robber who has stolen his grandma's tarts. Rhyming couplets introduce readers to fairy tale and NURSERY RHYME characters as they search for Mother Hubbard, Cinderella, and others hiding in the whimsical, humorous pictures of the Kate Greenaway Medal winner *Each Peach Pear Plum* (1978). Allowing preschoolers both the fun of an "I Spy" game and the pleasure of reexperiencing the familiar in an inventive new way, the book is considered a contemporary classic. Other books that exhibit the Ahlbergs' keen awareness of the child's psyche are *Peek-a-Boo!* (1981), *The Baby's Catalogue* (1982), and *Starting School* (1988). The innovative *The Jolly Postman; or, Other People's Letters* (1986) again reinforces and builds on previous literary knowledge. Warm, witty illustrations depict a postman cycling on his rounds, delivering letters between fairy tale characters. Each real, removable letter, contained in its own envelope, reveals a different form of correspondence — a post card, a party invitation, an advertisement. Published in eleven countries to critical and popular acclaim, the book is the Ahlbergs' best-known work and received the Emil Award in England, the Book Key Prize in Holland, and the Prix du Livre pour la Jeunesse in France. Its companion book, *The Jolly Christmas Postman* (1991), is a Kate Greenaway Medal recipient.

Warm, entertaining, and involving stories convey a sense of joy in reading and have earned the Ahlbergs a place among the best-loved contemporary children's authors and illustrators.

After Janet's death, Allan continued to write picture book texts, including *The Snail House* (2001), illustrated by Gillian Tyler, and *The Adventures of Bert* (2001), with artwork by Raymond Briggs. C.S.

Aiken, Joan

British author, b. 1924. Versatility and a soaring imagination are the hallmarks of the work of Joan Aiken, an accomplished writer who has few equals in the contemporary children's book world. Aiken is noted primarily for her inventive novels and masterly short stories, but her opus also includes POETRY, PICTURE BOOKS, plays, and retellings of folktales. Aiken was born in Rye, Sussex. As the daughter of the American poet Conrad Aiken and the stepdaughter of the English writer Martin Armstrong, she grew up immersed in a literary environment. At the age of five she made up her mind that she, too, would become a writer. During her schooling at Wychwood, Oxford, Aiken had two poems published by the *Abinger Chronicle*, edited by E. M. Forster and others. Aiken married the journalist Ron Brown; after his death she wrote short stories to augment her income. These stories make up Aiken's first published books, *All You've Ever Wanted* (1953) and *More Than You've Bargained For* (1955).

Her second published novel, *The Wolves of Willoughby Chase* (1962), recipient of the Lewis Carroll Shelf Award, began her loosely linked series of adventures set in a historical time that never was — the imaginary reign of King James III of England. Though making use of real historical detail, the book and its successors — *Black Hearts in Battersea* (1964), *Nightbirds on Nantucket* (1966), *The Whispering Mountain* (1968), *The Cuckoo Tree* (1971), *The Stolen Lake* (1981), *Dido and Pa* (1986), and *Is Underground* (1993) — brim with outrageous improbability, wild exaggeration, lavish melodrama, and humor. These "unhistorical" books are often termed Dickensian for their intricate plots and colorful characters. Feisty, smart, and courageous child protagonists — like the resourceful waif Dido Twite — populate Aiken's fictional world. Aiken has said that her "books are concerned with children tackling the problem of an adult world," but, reassuringly, good always triumphs over evil. Aiken's story collections, many of them horror and suspense, have garnered as much acclaim as her adventures, ably demonstrating the scope and variety of her craft. *The Kingdom Under the Sea* (1971), winner of the Kate Greenaway Medal for JAN PIENKOWSKI's brilliant illustrations, draws together new versions of favorite Russian folktales. Stories ranging from the whimsical to the eerie constitute *Up the Chimney Down* (1984). *Past Eight o'Clock* (1987) meshes traditional and contemporary elements by basing each story on a well-known folktale. The atmospheric stories included in *A Whisper in the Night* (1982), *Give Yourself a Fright* (1989), and *A Foot in the Grave* (1992) portray a modern world in which the fantastic and the supernatural are commonplace. Other notable books include *The Shadow Guests* (1980), a novel with a family curse as its premise, and *Arabel's Raven* (1972), the first of several funny books about preschooler Arabel and her raucous, trouble-making pet raven, Mortimer.

A lively, headlong style energizes Aiken's books, which have been honored with the Guardian Award, the Edgar Allan Poe Award, and the Carnegie Medal Honor. Complete command over, and delight in, language evidences itself in her books through delicious wordplay, sly parody, and vivid imagery. Poetic richness and striking originality aside, Aiken's work is wholeheartedly entertaining. C.S.

Alcott, Louisa May

American novelist, 1832–1888. After considering several careers, including acting, Louisa May Alcott learned that her talent and her earning power lay in writing; and though she had aspirations of writing serious novels for adults, she was in demand for the melodramatic, sensational tales she wrote under a pseudonym and for the hugely successful books for children for which she is best known today.

Alcott had an unusual upbringing. Her father, Bronson Alcott, was a penniless philosopher, one of many New England thinkers who wished to effect social reform. During Louisa's childhood he founded a "consociate family" on a fruit farm, where people came and went, contributing ideas as well as depleting the meager supply of food. Louisa and her three sisters, Anna, Elizabeth, and May, were given linen clothing to wear, because linen did not exploit the slaves who picked cotton or deprive sheep of their wool. The commune was a miserable failure, as were many of Bronson Alcott's other ventures, and the Alcotts often had to rely on the charity of Louisa's mother's wealthy Boston relatives. But the family was a close and loving one, and their neighbors and friends in Concord, Massachusetts, included great writers and activists such as Henry David Thoreau and Ralph Waldo Emerson. The Alcotts were also staunch abolitionists, sometimes harboring escaped slaves making their way north on the Underground Railroad.

Louisa and her sisters were taught from early childhood to read philosophy and to keep diaries, recording their shortcomings and resolving to improve upon them. Louisa saw her faults as her temper and impatient nature — traits she later gave to Jo in *Little Women*. She began writing poetry at age eleven and was soon adapting fairy tales for the dramatic performances she and her sisters produced in their barn. Then followed original plays, stories, and fables. In 1852 she sold her first story and became aware that she might be able to support her family — a lifelong concern of Louisa's — through writing. She invented lurid, dramatic, sensational stories that were published in various magazines under pseudonyms such as A. M. Barnard. Her first book, a collection called *Flower Fables,* which she wrote as a girl to amuse Emerson's daughter Ellen, was published in 1854.

The year 1858 was a difficult one for Louisa. Her beloved younger sister Elizabeth died of scarlet fever after an illness of many months, and her older sister, Anna, announced her engagement. Anna married and left home in 1860. Although Louisa continued to work at her par-

ents' house in Concord, she would occasionally rent a room in Boston, where she could write. It was an invigorating time to be in Boston: there were lectures on social and prison reform, abolitionism, and women's education. Louisa was in favor of women's suffrage and was one of the first women to vote in Concord. It was during this period that she wrote *Moods* (1864). The book departs from the potboiler style of her pseudonymous stories. This was Louisa's first attempt at serious writing. Two other books, also written for adults, like *Moods,* never sold well; they are *Work: A Story of Experience* (1873) and *A Modern Mephistopheles* (1877). She revised and republished *Moods* in 1882 and liked it best of all her work.

During the Civil War, Louisa volunteered to work as a nurse in a hospital in Washington, D.C., but after just a few weeks contracted typhoid and was sent home. She was treated with a mercury-based medicine and as a result suffered ill health for the rest of her life. Over the next few years, however, she wrote a series of lighthearted pieces about her nursing experiences. They were first serialized in a newspaper under Louisa's own name but were so popular that they were published as a book, *Hospital Sketches* (1863). Soon her work was in demand.

In 1867 she was asked to write a book for girls. Part One of *Little Women, or Meg, Jo, Beth, and Amy* was written in two and a half months and published in 1868. Essentially it was the story of her own family, in which the girls enjoy the loving devotion of their thoughtful parents and strive to improve their small faults through their trials and pleasures. The book includes the death of Beth and the marriage of Meg, but Louisa made light of the poverty the family endured. The partner and manager of the publishing house suggested that she take a royalty rather than a flat fee for *Little Women,* and as the book was an immediate and immense success, Louisa's fortune was made.

At the request of her publishers, Louisa wrote the book's sequel the following year, resisting the pressure from the girls who wrote to her by refusing to "marry Jo to Laurie to please anyone." (The two books were later published together in one volume under the title *Little Women*.) Louisa became such a celebrity that her picture was mounted on cards and sold to fans. On more than one occasion, she climbed out of a back window to escape the reporters who hounded her parents' door. She was asked to write more lurid stories under her own name, but she refused and never again wrote this type of story after her success.

Little Women not only brought financial stability to the entire Alcott family but also allowed Louisa to indulge them with comforts and pleasures, including travel to Europe. But while abroad, Louisa received word of Anna's husband's death and immediately began to write *Little Men* (1871) specifically to provide for Anna's children. The book features Jo March as a married woman, running Plumfield School with her husband, Professor Bhaer. In the book, orphaned or abused boys are directed to their home and taken in. A strong, swaggering boy named Dan is sent away after introducing the other boys to poker playing and beer but returns, drawn by his affection for a baby in the household. Though the Bhaers' goodness and love permeate the book, Louisa lent the work a few thrills through her portrayal of the rough Dan and his daring ways. Some of her subsequent books include *Eight Cousins* (1875), *Rose in Bloom* (1876), and *Jo's Boys* (1886).

Louisa hosted her nephews and nieces in Nonquitt, Maine, for the happiest times of her later years, which were plagued with ill health. She died in 1888, only two days after her father's death. Louisa May Alcott saw a million copies of her books sold during her lifetime. *Little Women* remains her most popular and enduring work.

S.H.H.

Alexander, Lloyd

American author, b. 1924. When Lloyd Alexander decided at age fifteen that he wanted to be a writer, he had no plans to write for children; in fact, for seventeen years he wrote books for adults before producing his first work for children, *Time Cat: The Remarkable Journeys of Jason and Gareth* (1963). With the publication of the Chronicles of Prydain series in the 1960s, Alexander emerged as one of the foremost American writers of fantasy for young people.

Based loosely on Welsh mythology, which fascinated Alexander from a young age, the Prydain series consists of five fantasy novels: *The Book of Three* (1964); *The Black Cauldron* (1965), a Newbery Honor Book; the *Castle of Llyr* (1966); *Taran Wanderer* (1967); and *The High King* (1968), winner of the Newbery Medal. The books trace the development of Taran from a headstrong Assistant Pig-Keeper with a desire for adventure to a humble man with a challenging but realistic vision of rebuilding the war-ravaged land. Filled with quests, romance, magic, and humor, the classic tales deal with some of the more difficult matters that challenge every individual, including personal identity, pride, justice, decision making, failure, friendship, and death. Heroic but very human figures face villains ranging from the merely misguided to the purely evil. Each of Taran's faithful companions possesses memorable gifts and peculiarities as well as a distinctive voice: Fflewddur Fflam, whose harp strings break whenever he stretches the truth, puts aside his royal crown to travel as a bard, while Princess Eilonwy scorns traditional feminine activities and insists on taking part in the adventures.

Alexander undeniably possesses a flair for characterization, using lively description and expressive speech patterns in all of his work. Vesper Holly, the brilliant, resourceful protagonist of *The Illyrian Adventure* (1986) and other adventure novels, fairly overflows with vitality. Her less confident, very proper guardian narrates the escapades, a perfect counterpoint to Vesper's unconventional personality. Other noteworthy feisty, intelligent female characters in Alexander's work include Mickle and Voyaging Moon. Alexander's frequent use of feline characters reflects his fondness for cats, which are featured in the Chronicles of Prydain, *The Marvelous Misadventures of Sebastian* (1970), *The Cat Who Wished to Be a Man* (1973), *The Town Cats and*

Other Tales (1977), and *The Remarkable Journey of Prince Jen* (1991). Music, another of the writer's passions, is also a recurrent theme in his work. An amateur violinist, Alexander took pleasure in writing about a gifted musician and his magic violin in *The Marvelous Misadventures of Sebastian*. The Chronicles of Prydain feature a lovable bard, while Voyaging Moon fills *The Remarkable Journey of Prince Jen* with beautiful music from a perfectly crafted flute.

Alexander brings more to his work from his personal life than his joyful preoccupations, however. Having had no idea as a young man of how to go about becoming a writer, he entered the military to pursue adventure. His service gave him the background needed to write *Westmark* (1981), *The Kestrel* (1982), and *The Beggar Queen* (1984), a series of novels recounting the political struggles of a country at war internally and with its neighbors. Alexander spares the reader little of the brutality of war and its effect on the human spirit, but the element of hope — an integral part of his work — remains.

Alexander's fiction challenges all readers to be true to themselves and to face the struggles of life seriously, while maintaining the ability to laugh and enjoy living. A.E.D.

Almond, David

British author, b. 1951. Conjuring up haunting and surreal images, David Almond creates fiction that dares to explore life's greatest mysteries. Born in Newcastle upon Tyne, England, the author grew up in a large family that he recalls with affection in *Counting Stars* (2000), a collection of gemlike vignettes about his childhood in northern England, where a visit to the cemetery, an encounter with a mentally challenged neighbor, or a few moments spent pondering family photographs could be filled with mysticism and hints of wonder. Almond developed an early interest in writing, though he rarely discussed it with others; instead, he covertly jotted down his stories and bound them with needle and thread. He attended the University of East Anglia and worked as a mail carrier, a brush salesman, and a teacher before concentrating full-time on fiction writing. A collection of his short stories for adults was published, but Almond's career didn't take off until the release of his first children's book.

Skellig (1998) is a novel that blurs the edges between the everyday world and the sphere of the unknown. Shortly after the protagonist Michael moves into a decrepit old house with his parents and ailing baby sister, the ten-year-old discovers a strange creature living in the garage. "Filthy and pale and dried out," Skellig resembles a man yet has strange winglike appendages that give him the semblance of a bird . . . or possibly an angel. The creature is initially querulous, but as Michael and his new friend Mina provide medicine, Chinese takeout food, and kindness, Skellig's physical condition begins to improve. As Skellig regains his strength, Michael's baby sister begins to fail, ultimately requiring heart surgery. Simply written, filled with beautiful imagery and stunning metaphors, and laced with the poetry of William Blake, the novel will leave readers with many questions: Who is Skellig? *What* is Skellig? How are the fates of Skellig and the ailing infant entwined? Perhaps there are no "correct" answers to these questions, but nearly every reader will have a strong emotional response to the story. *Skellig* won England's Carnegie Medal and Whitbread Award and, upon publication in the United States, was named an Honor Book for the first Michael L. Printz Award for excellence in literature for young adults.

The following year Almond won the Printz Award for *Kit's Wilderness* (1999), another novel distinguished by its magical realism. Narrated by thirteen-year-old Kit Watson, whose family has come to live with his widowed grandfather in a dying coal town, the story concerns a game called Death that Kit and an enigmatic classmate play in the nearby abandoned mines. This tale of ghosts, friendship, and personal redemption is presented in a haunting text that weaves together imagery of the past and present, of darkness and light.

Another hypnotic tale, *Heaven Eyes* (2000), follows a trio of orphans who run away from a children's home and meet a strange girl named Heaven Eyes who lives with the man she calls her grandfather in an abandoned warehouse. As bizarre occurrences swirl around them, narrator Erin and the other orphans are drawn into the unique, joyful vision of the world that Heaven Eyes shares in her strangely elliptical speech. This book, like all of the author's work, takes readers to a world where the everyday coexists with the fantastic, where ordinary events are interrupted by the paranormal, and where big questions about life and death, spirituality, creation, and imagination are raised, then left for the reader to ponder. Almond's plots are so inventive, the characters — whatever their circumstances — so believable, and the quality of the writing so fine that the journey is never less than mesmerizing. P.D.S.

Alphabet Books

Move the clock back 250 years to colonial America. A few solemn children sit in wooden desks and begin their schoolwork, chanting in unison, "In Adam's fall / We sinned all." Their serious rhyme begins one of the first alphabet books, an early instructional tool that provided youngsters with a formal introduction to reading, coupling the letters and sounds of language with moral instruction.

Compare this scene with a modern classroom. Children in one corner respond to Bert Kitchen's *Animal Alphabet* (1984) by cutting out magazine pictures of creatures whose names begin with particular letters. Others roll their tongues over those glorious words in *Hosie's Alphabet* (1972): the "quintessential quail," the "omnivorous swarming locust," and the "ghastly, garrulous gargoyle." Still another group sprawls on the floor, reciting *Potluck* (1991), Anne Shelby's story of a potluck supper: "Acton appeared with asparagus soup. Ben brought bagels. Christine came with carrot cake and corn on the cob. Don did dumplings." Like their historical counterparts, these youngsters are learning to read with alphabet books, but this time the learning crackles with both excitement and joy.

For more than two centuries, what has remained constant in classrooms and nurseries is children and alphabet books. What has changed is how the number and variety in the latter motivate and educate the former.

Children's greatest growth in language comes during the preschool years. Infants make sounds. These sounds translate into words, the words into sentences, the sentences into stories. When they learn to read, youngsters link their oral language to its written counterpart. Their first alphabet books begin this transition.

The very youngest child needs simple, uncluttered books. Words should represent familiar, concrete objects, with *A* beginning *apple* rather than *atom*. First alphabet books typically pair initial sounds with words, and these associations should depict regular phonographs. Pages that proclaim "K is for knife" or "G is for gnu" bewilder rather than educate. These key words should also have unambiguous names; "B for bow-wow," in a book peopled with nouns rather than verbs, will confuse the child who identifies the animal as a dog.

In addition, illustrations must be obvious and straightforward. Complications in naming lead to misunderstandings. One preschooler, upset because she had read an alphabet book incorrectly, sadly pointed out this problem: "I said, '*R* for *rope*,' but the book meant '*S* for *snake*'!"

While the criteria above represent important considerations in evaluation, they must not create static prescriptions for mass producing similar texts. Artists and authors frequently break traditional rules; often they do so brilliantly. *Brian Wildsmith's ABC* (1963), for example, designates *I* for *iguana*, a word and sound less obvious to youngsters than the more standard *I* for *ice cream*. Yet when readers encounter Wildsmith's iguana, a glorious, multicolored reptile with its quivering, scarlet throat, they simply must know more about this strange and wondrous creature.

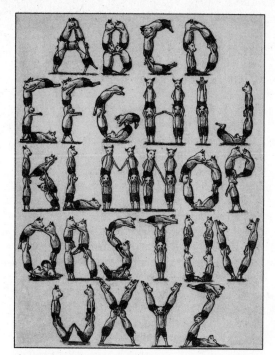

Illustration by Arthur Geisert from his book *Pigs from A to Z* (1986).

Children interacting with their first texts are not reading in the traditional sense of relying solely on the printed word. Instead, they depend on illustrations to create meaning. Consequently, in initial alphabet books, only one or two objects should appear on the page, acknowledging a child's immature perceptual and spatial skills. There's plenty of time later on to hunt for hidden pictures, sort out numerous nouns, or locate obscure objects after letter-sound correspondence has been mastered.

Although text is of less importance than illustrations, it nonetheless deserves attention. Predictable patterns, such as *A* is for *apple, B* is for *bear,* restate a letter-is-for-noun sequence that lets children imitate reading each time they turn and identify an illustration within the established motif. In addition, text that includes both upper- and lowercase letters gives youngsters a true picture of our written language.

Once children familiarize themselves with the basics, they can be challenged to apply their newfound knowledge to other texts. Lucy Micklethwait's *I Spy: An Alphabet in Art* (1992), for example, not only introduces readers to twenty-six handsome reproductions but also directs them to find appropriate symbols on each canvas, alternating the obvious umbrellas from Rembrandt's signature painting to Miró's stars in the more abstract *Woman and Bird in the Moonlight.*

Not all alphabet books concentrate on naming; some deal with the positioning of letters. BILL MARTIN JR. and John Archambault's *Chicka Chicka Boom Boom* (1989) treats youngsters to a jazzy alternative to the traditional "Alphabet Song," which for generations has led children to wonder just what letter "el-em-en-o-pee" really is. Here they chant, "A told B, and B told C, I'll meet you at the top of the alphabet tree." For a show-stopping alternative to reading aloud, pair the book with Ray Charles's classy audiocassette and let children explore the alphabet with a musical master.

In real words, letters appear out of sequence, so children need practice in identifying them without their traditional orthographic neighbors. Laura Geringer's *The Cow Is Mooing Anyway* (1991) combines this skill with a slight story line and more advanced, busy illustrations. A mother initiates a morning ritual when she brings her daughter breakfast. But once she leaves the scene, all sorts of wacky diners join the little girl. First a horseshoe crab "drives up in a taxicab," accompanied by the iguanas, who "come in their pajamas." They are joined, in turn, by other combinations of animals who enter the two-page spreads: a dragonfly/goose, a quail/albatross/x-ray fish, and a kangaroo/eel. Each alphabetic entry is noted in a repeating lettered border that positions the letters in their traditional slots, while frenetic scenes call for multiple readings, since details, such as the wall paintings, change along with the story.

Expanding on letter play, Suse MacDonald manipulated shape rather than position. In *Alphabatics* (1986) each letter is twisted, enlarged, and altered until it becomes a visual representation of a key word. *A*, for instance, turns upside down, adds a watery base, grows two animals, and becomes an ark, while *b* rotates on its side, rounds its former base, and floats across the page as a balloon. ARTHUR GEISERT introduced more text in his *Pigs from A to Z* (1986), while encouraging pictorial detectives to locate the numerous examples of a specific letter, along with both preceding and succeeding ones, hidden in his clever illustrations of swine in motion.

Additional visual and verbal sophistication awaits readers of *Anno's Alphabet* (1975), by MITSUMASA ANNO. Each bordered page introduces a single letter, an improbable Möbius strip of twisted wood, and a full-color, slyly implausible illustration: a typewriter types only *T*s, an umbrella rains inside itself, and a rocking horse rests on crossed runners. Delicate pen-and-ink borders frame the wordless text, introducing animals and plants beginning with the appropriate letter. The naming of these creatures and flora requires, or begins to cultivate, an extended vocabulary, while locating them becomes an optical treasure hunt.

As children's language develops, so does their need for story, and more advanced alphabet books provide simple narration within their familiar pattern. ANITA and ARNOLD LOBEL's *On Market Street* (1981), for example, takes a shop-till-you-drop youngster to Market Street, where he discovers all sorts of wondrous wares to sample. Anita Lobel's unusual illustrations depict each product (from apples to zippers) as a costume, while the simple text provides the sparest of frames for naming the twenty-six objects. Two cumulative pages recap the shopping expedition, first in alphabetic sequence, and second in random order.

ANN JONAS's *Aardvarks, Disembark!* (1990) makes use of this sophisticated narrative pattern. Couching her alphabet book within the story of Noah and the ark, Jonas has outlined events of the Great Flood. As the waters recede, Noah must empty his vessel and, showing a real flair for organization, does so in alphabetical order. His biological roll call allows the most con-

ventional creatures to emerge, but Noah soon discovers all sorts of less familiar animals aboard. He "didn't know their names, so he could only call, 'Disembark, everyone! Everyone disembark!'" They start down Mount Ararat, in familiar alphabetical order, taking an entire day to reach the bottom. Who are these forgotten animals, the aye-ayes, the dingos, the tarpans, and the wombats? Most are either endangered or extinct, and, in an informative appendix, Jonas has given the status and environmental location of each.

This pattern, which uses the alphabet as an organizing structure for presenting like information, defines a subculture of alphabet books that explore finite subjects, introduce concepts, and organize literary forms for older children. LOIS EHLERT's *Eating the Alphabet* (1989), for example, highlights fruits and vegetables, often including the less obvious varieties, such as *X* for *xigua* or *U* for *ugli fruit*, along with nonstandard sounds, such as *J* for *jalapeño* or *jicama*. Intended to introduce subjects rather than letters, this book concludes with a picture glossary, which for many provides an appropriate introduction to the dictionary. Mary Beth Owens's *A Caribou Alphabet* (1988) narrows the subject to one species of animal, including entries such as *lichen*, *predator*, and *xalibu*, the Indian word meaning "one who scrapes or paws snow," from which the word *caribou* derives.

Betsy Bowen introduced a sequential structure along with the alphabet in *Antler, Bear, Canoe: A Northwoods Alphabet Year* (1991). From January to January readers sample activities, terms, and situations native to her Minnesota environment, covering fishing in March, loons in June, and zero temperatures in December.

Many such subject-driven alphabet books cover less concrete, and consequently more sophisticated, topics. Ann Whitford Paul's *Eight Hands Round: A Patchwork Alphabet* (1991), for instance, represents American history through twenty-six quilting patterns. Each highlights a specific characteristic, introducing games (kite flying), handicrafts (Yankee puzzle), living conditions (log cabin), and events (Underground

Railroad). Similarly, Jim Aylesworth's Pennsylvania Dutch alphabet book, *The Folks in the Valley* (1992), outlines a daily way of life that begins with *A* for *alarm clocks,* continues with *H* for *pitched hay,* and concludes with *Z* for "the sound / Of their well-earned rest."

Other alphabet books depend heavily on text and thus expand their audience to older children. Individual volumes, such as *Alligators to Zooplankton: A Dictionary of Water Babies* (1991), resemble mini-encyclopedias, combining the traditional format of letter-word identification with expository text, informative charts, handsome illustrations, a detailed bibliography, and a cross-index. Similar in form but more idiosyncratic in execution, Tim Arnold's *Natural History from A to Z: A Terrestrial Sampler* (1991) employs varied entries (from specific animals such as *C* for *coatimundi* to the more general classifications such as *U* for *ungulates*) as convenient points of departure for all kinds of far-ranging discussions on natural history.

Literary forms, as well as informational subjects, will occasionally depend on ABC order for organization. Sylvia Cassedy's *Roomrimes* (1987) explores twenty-six spaces in verse, taking the reader from attics to elevators to parlors to zoos. Assonance and alliteration appropriately mark Jeanne and WILLIAM STEIG's alphabetic POETRY (*Alpha Beta Chowder,* 1992), introducing memorable creatures such as the irksome and irascible Ivan the Terrible and Adorable Daphne, who dresses divinely, unlike Deplorable Dora, who is "definitely dowdy" in "that dismal dirndl."

Alphabet books not only use the basic structure of language for reading readiness, subject exploration, and organizational patterns, but sometimes introduce early wordplay. Cathi Hepworth's *Antics!* (1992) spotlights twenty-six words, all with "ant" hidden in the syllables. There's the philosophical Kant, the artistic "Rembrant," and the worldly Nonchalant, who appear with several clever linguistic creations: a Xanthophile, worshipping yellow bananas, and Your Ant Yetta, relaxing with tea and bonbons.

But leave it to DR. SEUSS to find the standard twenty-six letters limiting. In *On Beyond Zebra* (1955) his young narrator declares: "In the places I go there are things that I see / That I never could spell if I stopped with the *Z*." His lingua franca includes creatures like Yuzz-a-ma-Tuzz, Umbus, and Jogg-oons, which require letters such as YUZZ, UM, and JOGG just to spell them. A few readings of *On Beyond Zebra!* and a creative child might just agree with the good doctor: "This is really great stuff! / And I guess the old alphabet / ISN'T enough!"   B.C.

American Folklore

Folklore, that combination of myth, legend, folktales, anecdotes, sayings, and songs that have been passed down from one generation to the next, reflects a people's concept of themselves — their beliefs, hopes and fears, courage and humor, sense of delight in the odd, fascination with the supernatural. By its nature, folklore incorporates the traditional with a society's changing view of itself. In America, we are in the midst of great change and an ever-expanding sense of who "we" are. Our understanding of the term *American folklore* has therefore expanded also.

American folklore includes stories and legends that have been so influenced by this land and its peoples' histories that no matter where some of the plot lines originated, they now belong to our own traditions. A ghost story first told in Scotland, for instance, is transformed into a New England story with a Massachusetts setting, common settlers' names, and New Englanders' speech mannerisms. Or a Spanish tale, brought to Santa Fe with a seventeenth-century governor's entourage, is retold by a Pueblo from an entirely different perspective, in his own language, and passed down until it is translated again and printed in a collection of his tribe's stories to be shared in English with a larger audience.

The American experience differed by group and condition from the very beginning. The hundreds of Native American tribes established distinct cultures. Then, with the coming of Europeans and slaves and later immigrants from a broad range of countries, even more variety was introduced. Though we can point to distinct periods in this nation's history and say that major events had an impact on all of its peoples, what that impact was depended on who the people were.

Free men immigrated with the expectation of making their way in the wilderness and told exaggerated tales of pioneer heroism to bolster their courage. Slaves imported talking-beast tales from various African regions and developed a wryly humorous view of their own survival in a foreign land where they were prisoners, unable to follow their own dreams. Certainly, there are distinct philosophical differences between the swaggering of a Paul Bunyan willing to cut down half the trees in the country and Native American lore about humanity's connection with the land it shares with all other living things. Chinese immigrants remained almost invisible because of barriers of language and outlook as they worked in mining camps and on the transcontinental railroad, telling tales that are only now being made available.

This continent's oldest stories, and its only indigenous religions and mythologies, come from the various Native American tribes who crossed the Bering Strait centuries before the first Europeans arrived. But for myths to be vital, they must still be told within the culture. In some places that vitality holds and is being encouraged by a new awareness in the society as a whole, particularly concerning humans' role in the environment. Appreciation of these earliest tales may reflect a more holistic approach to survival in the modern world.

Indian agent Henry Rowe Schoolcraft is credited with being one of the first to purposefully collect and translate Indian myths and stories into English; his two volumes of Chippewa tales (*Algic Researches,* 1839), though romanticized and rewritten, are still mined for folkloric gold. After him came more serious ethnologists and collectors, who convinced tribal traditionalists that their heritage could be preserved in books no matter what happened in their struggle with the U.S. government and white value systems. Franz Boas and others who were creating the science of anthropology at the turn of the century realized that folklore would be one of their greatest resources, and as they collected and compared their findings, the patterns of influence and change among tribes became apparent. But their emphasis on what was common among the tribes was changed in the 1930s by anthropologist Ruth Benedict, who insisted that in spite of commonalities, it was a tribe's specific selection of tales to tell that gave the greatest insights into its culture. Later still, collectors began to showcase individual storytellers. One of the most exciting recent developments has been the growing number of Native Americans who are publishing their own narratives as well as being published as authors and illustrators in the mainstream book trade. The result is a growing respect for sources, an understanding that the rhythms of narrative often differ between the Native American and European models, and that many of the earlier retellings in English have strayed from the heart of the original stories.

In earlier times (and even now where storytellers still pass on a tribe's traditions), some stories served to educate as well as to entertain, teaching what a person needed to know about survival, explaining the natural and spiritual worlds, and reinforcing the culture's sense of order and balance. In some tribes, certain stories are sacred, a reflection of the people's spiritual view of the universe, and told only in certain situations and at certain times of the year.

Native American folklore, as varied as it is from tribe to tribe, includes many similar types of stories, among them a large body of *pourquoi* tales, or "why" stories explaining natural phenomena — why possum has a naked tail, for instance, or why constellations are shaped as they are, or why birds are different colors. There are quest stories or hero tales, transformation tales, and, of course, the popular trickster tales.

The same trickster figures can be godlike or greedy or foolish. In Margaret Hodges's adaptation of *The Firebringer: A Paiute Indian Legend*

(1972) Coyote heroically brings fire to the first men, while in Shonto Begay's rendition of the Navajo traditional story *Maii and Cousin Horned Toad* (1992), he tries to cheat virtuous Horned Toad out of his corn and is soundly beaten. Such tales typically include ghosts, riddles, laughter, and a great many moral lessons.

Among those works available to children, JOHN BIERHORST has provided several impeccably documented collections, including *The Naked Bear: Folktales of the Iroquois* (1987). PAUL GOBLE has written and illustrated some striking PICTURE BOOKS, several of them transformation tales, such as *Buffalo Woman* (1984) and the Caldecott Medal–winning *The Girl Who Loved Wild Horses* (1979), in which a girl finally becomes a fine mare in the herd. More recently, he has published several picture books about the Plains trickster figure Iktomi. Christie Harris's collections — *Once Upon a Totem* (1963), *Mouse Woman and the Vanished Princesses* (1967), and others — highlight tales from the tribes of the North Pacific. JOSEPH BRUCHAC, storyteller and gatherer of his grandfather's Abenaki tales as well as those of many other tribes, has published individual stories and several collections, including his well-known *Keepers of the Earth* (1989), written with Michael J. Caduto.

In the seventeenth and eighteenth centuries, colonists came from northern Europe and Britain to settle the East Coast, bringing their desire for religious freedom and their belief that they must make a community of saints in the wilderness of the New World. Puritans, with their deep resolve to live with clear consciences, hoped to govern themselves through their theology; their culture heroes were godly men. Their storytelling derived from those concerns, emphasizing providences, witchcraft, and diabolical possessions, such as the tales published in Boston by Increase Mather in his 1684 publication *An Essay for the Recording of Illustrious Providences,* in which God sends great storms, saves ships, or destroys sinners according to His divine will. New England is still famous for its witches and ghost stories along with later tall tales about giant codfish and an abiding reputation for retaining a "Puritan conscience" and adding a dry, understated wit.

Southern Appalachia has provided a wonderful opportunity to hear what happened to many of the less religious and lighthearted settlers' tales when they met another way of life. Because some people who moved into this mountain country remained there for generations, virtually cut off from much of the rest of the world, their oral traditions remained strong and their use of language rich and humorous, often mixing down-home dialect with an Elizabethan turn of phrase that delights the ear. RICHARD CHASE produced the first collections of these stories in *The Jack Tales* (1943), and this and his later collection, *Grandfather Tales* (1973), provide endless enjoyment for children and resources for storytellers. Jack the trickster hero outwits his foes with great insouciance, and the combination of giants, unicorns, bean trees, and kings with hams, turkeys, colloquial mountain sayings, and common sense brings laughter and satisfaction to the listener. Gail Haley's collection *Mountain Jack Tales* (1992) gives a fresh voice to the well-known stories, as do her *Jack and the Bean Tree* (1986) and William Hooks's *Three Little Pigs and the Fox* (1989), which have come out as single picture books with unexpected mountain language giving old tales new charm.

While those who stayed in the mountains transformed a group of folktales from England, Scotland, and Ireland, the pioneers who moved on and out into other areas of the new nation in the early nineteenth century began to create a new group of stories. They celebrated their young country with democratic culture heroes who had been willing to stand up to tyranny in the Old World and fight for independence. From George Washington to that true man of the people, Honest Abe Lincoln, legends grew up about political heroes. Side by side came even more exaggerated stories about common folk with great courage, like the woodsman Daniel Boone and daredevil Davy Crockett, as well as one of our quietest heroes, Johnny Appleseed.

Daniel Boone was born in Pennsylvania in

1735, but he and his fast-moving wife, Rebecca — who was first mistaken for a deer by the mighty hunter — moved to Kentucky, where Daniel became a model for the perfect folk hero, his exploits exaggerated into near impossibility as the legends grew. Interestingly, Davy Crockett's wife was also known for streaking through the woods faster than a deer, though Sally Ann Thunder Ann Whirlwind Crockett is credited with much more now that heroines are sought after by anthologists and storytellers. Born in the mountains of Tennessee in 1786, Davy Crockett wrote much of his own press when he ran for Congress. He was known as a sharpshooter, trapper, bear wrestler, humorist, the perfect match for Mike Fink the Keelboatman on the Mississippi, and, at the end, a man who died at the Alamo. The numerous stories about him were collected in the Davy Crockett Almanacks, which began to circulate not long after his death.

Paperbound books, magazines, and newspapers may also have been the source of most of our tall tale heroes, though their creators insisted that they came originally from oral tradition. Wherever they came from, they matched the American mood of the nineteenth century perfectly — and they reflected the nation's rising industries. Here were heroes so much larger than life that they could solve any problem — even physically reshape the land itself, pushing mountains into place and moving rivers where they liked, as the cowboy's hero, Pecos Bill, did. Or, in the case of the Eastern sea salt's answer to pioneer bravado, soap the cliffs of Dover white when Old Stormalong sailed the biggest Yankee clipper in existence through the English Channel. Paul Bunyan, the greatest lumberjack who ever lived, was born in Maine and felled giant forests from there through Michigan and on to the Pacific Northwest, accompanied by the gigantic blue ox, Babe. There was even a consummate Swedish farmer named Febold Feboldson who could make it rain in Nebraska. Steven Kellogg's *Paul Bunyan* (1984) and Ariane Dewey's *Pecos Bill* (1983) are part of a small but growing number of picture book editions available. There are work heroes among the stories coming from the African American heritage as well, such as the great steel-driving John Henry, but he came after the Civil War and the end of slavery (if not racial prejudice).

Brought here against their wills and held prisoner in a land where as slaves they were forbidden to learn to read and given few opportunities for leisure, many African Americans maintained a strong oral tradition, importing African animal stories that were transformed into familiar folk tricksters like Brer Rabbit and passing on secret messages through songs and stories about Moses (Harriet Tubman) and the Drinking Gourd that gave encoded directions on how to flee north to freedom. A legendary trickster hero who could always outsmart the master is presented in Steve Sanfield's *The Adventures of High John the Conqueror* (1989). Virginia Hamilton's beautifully written collection *The People Could Fly: American Black Folktales* (1985) displays the variety and range of African American tales, including as it does talking beast tales, supernatural stories to chill the spine, and moving tales of freedom won. Ashley Bryan selected songs from slavery days for his *All Night, All Day: A Child's First Book of African-American Spirituals* (1991).

Perhaps the best-known animal character is Brer Rabbit, who first appeared in print through the journalist Joel Chandler Harris in the nineteenth century. These stories about talking animals show the underdog's shrewd understanding of human nature and a heartening ability to outwit those who seem more powerful. Harris's original work, though a rich resource, is less accessible than William Faulkner's *The Days When the Animals Talked* (1977) or recent adaptations by Van Dyke Parks in *Jump!: The Adventures of Brer Rabbit* (1986) and its sequels. Julius Lester's four scholarly yet readable editions, beginning with *The Tales of Uncle Remus: The Adventures of Brer Rabbit* (1987), shed new light on the stories' many hidden meanings for the slaves who told and heard them.

Children can now read stories told by Chinese workers who helped lay the tracks for the Central Pacific Railroad across the Sierra Nevada, such as Kathleen Chang's retelling of "The Iron Moonhunter" in compiler Amy Cohn's invaluable resource, *From Sea to Shining Sea: A Treasury of American Folklore and Folk Songs* (1993), and in *Rainbow People* (1989) and *Tongues of Jade* (1991), by LAURENCE YEP. Yep, in his introduction to *Tongues of Jade,* has told about large numbers of men from southern China who could not easily bring their wives and children to this country because of immigration laws and who told each other stories to "show how a wise man could survive in a strange, often hostile land." There it is again: survival, with wisdom and humor.

As the collections and single-picture-book folktales continue to be published, that sense of ourselves continues to grow. We learn a lot about those who came before us by hearing the tales they shared; we learn a great deal about ourselves when we look at which stories most touch our hearts, carry our ideals, or make us laugh out loud today. We add stories to the general storehouse. We subtract — at least in the telling — those that jar our current sensibilities. We change. Stories change. Even now, in this age of print, the author-illustrator-storyteller makes an impact on our folklore, re-visioning an old tale for us in a familiar setting, carrying on the ancient tradition of honing and personalizing a tale to its audience. We are rich — and growing richer. S.M.

Andersen, Hans Christian

Danish poet and writer, 1805–1875. A prolific writer best known for his fairy tales, Hans Christian Andersen wrote and published numerous plays, novels, travel books, and an autobiography. Written between 1835 and 1872, Andersen's fairy tales are among the most anthologized and retold literary works in children's literature. Many of his 156 fairy tales and stories have been translated into more than one hundred languages. What ensured Andersen's fairy tales their widespread popularity was their universality — rags-to-riches themes and characters with recognizable human traits and foibles who overcome adversity through their determination, goodwill, and humor. Yet his tales have been described as paradoxical, revealing a dark side of life and human nature and presenting themes of unrequited love, poverty, selfishness, and vanity.

Andersen's early years influenced his work as a writer. About his works Andersen wrote, "Most of what I have written is a reflection of myself. Every character is from life. I know and have known them all." Like the heroine in "The Princess and the Pea" (1835), Andersen was extremely sensitive. Although he realized his talents, he suffered self-doubt and loneliness. He endured persecution before fame, just like the hero in "The Ugly Duckling" (1845), while "The Little Mermaid" (1837) reflects his unhappy love life and his lifelong struggle as an outsider in society. He has been described as hypochondriacal because of his recurring anxiety that he would suffer the same fate as his mentally disturbed paternal grandfather. But Andersen was witty and considered good company; perhaps these contrasts formed the basis for Andersen's genius as a writer.

Born and raised in Odense, on an island off the coast of Denmark, Andersen was the only child of a poor shoemaker and a washerwoman. Although the Andersen household lacked money, Hans was allowed the freedom to dream, play with his puppet theater, and wander about the countryside at will. His father loved to tell stories and often read aloud from *The Arabian Nights,* La Fontaine, and Danish dramatic works. Andersen's first volume of stories for children, *Fairy Tales Told for Children* (1835), contains four tales, three of which are based on Danish folktales he had heard as a child: "The Tinder Box," "Little Claus and Big Claus," and "The Princess and the Pea." Only "Little Ida's Flowers" is completely original.

Although Andersen's childhood town had a small population of seven thousand, Odense represented a miniature version of Danish society. The crown prince of Denmark lived in Odense. Therefore, royalty and the royal court, merchants and tradesmen lived in close proximity to the unskilled workers and journeymen. Andersen had ample opportunity to observe and even to visit members of the royal court, where he sang songs and recited scenes from the plays of Danish playwright Ludwig Holberg. Later, he used the insights derived from these experiences to write "The Tinder Box" and "The Emperor's New Clothes" (1837). Although Andersen received an uneven education in Odense, he learned to read and developed a passion for books, borrowing them whenever he could. After his confirmation at the age of fourteen, Andersen left home for Copenhagen to seek his fortune, not unlike the hero in his tale "The Traveling Companion" (1836).

Practically penniless but ambitious, Andersen tried unsuccessfully to become an actor and singer. Eventually, friends from the Royal Theater persuaded King Friedrich VI to fund Andersen's education, enabling him to receive a few years of schooling at Slagelse and Elsinore. In 1822, he wrote his first book, *Youthful Attempts* — only seventeen copies sold, and the remaining 283 copies served as wrapping paper for a local grocer. Andersen published a more successful volume in 1829, a fantasy entitled *A Journey on Foot from Copenhagen to the Eastern Point of Amager.* Six years later he wrote his first novel, *The Improvisator,* and, more important to his subsequent career, he published *Fairy Tales Told for Children.* Thereafter he published a fairy tale almost every year until his death. He discovered that the form of the fairy tale, rather than plays or novels, allowed him the freedom to break away from the more staid parameters of Victorian literature.

Andersen enjoyed reading his works aloud, and he infused his fairy tales with an intimacy that quickly pulls the reader into the story. About his first tales, Andersen wrote to a friend, "I have set down a few of the fairy tales I myself used to enjoy as a child and which I believe aren't well known. I have written them exactly as I would have told them to a child." Andersen had an intuitive understanding of children; he conveyed abstract concepts by using straightforward images that children understood. In "The Little Mermaid," for instance, Andersen described the depth of the sea this way: "Many church steeples would have to be piled up one above the other to reach from the bottom of the

sea to the surface." He achieved his realistic style through simple colloquial language. Andersen exploited the characteristics of inanimate objects. He brought to life doorknobs, broomsticks, teacups, darning needles, and fire-tongs, always deriving their attributes from a realistically restricted realm of experience. Among his most famous tales are "The Ugly Duckling," "Thumbelina," "The Nightingale," "The Snow Queen," "The Little Match-Girl," "The Steadfast Tin Soldier," and "The Little Fir Tree."

Continuously popular since the middle of the nineteenth century, Andersen's fairy tales have been translated and illustrated by writers and artists from around the world. The first English translation of his stories was published in 1846. *Wonderful Stories for Children,* rendered by Mary Howitt, featured a selection of ten tales. The Danish translators, however, are often hailed as the most accurate interpreters of Andersen's colloquial diction. Considered highly representative of Andersen's inimitable style, *Hans Christian Andersen's Complete Tales,* translated by the Danish scholar and children's book author Erik Christian Haugaard, was published in 1974. *Hans Christian Andersen's Eighty Fairy Tales* (1976), translated by Danish author R. P. Keigwin, incorporates the classic black-and-white line drawings of Andersen's most notable early Danish illustrators, Vilhelm Pedersen and Lorenz Frolich.

Andersen's words best describe the enduring function of the literary genre he mastered so well: "In the whole realm of poetry no domain is so boundless as that of the fairy tale. It reaches from the blood-drenched graves of antiquity to the pious legends of a child's picture book; it takes in the poetry of the people and the poetry of the artist." S.M.G.

Anderson, Laurie Halse

North American author, b. 1961. One of two daughters of a Methodist minister in Potsdam, New York, Laurie Halse Anderson grew up building athletic prowess, writing in journals, bristling against authority, and editing the sports section of her high school newspaper. Just after she turned five, the family moved to Syracuse, where her father pastored the Syracuse University chapel and she enjoyed what she has called an idyllic childhood. Lifted out of a moderately violent public school and gently placed into a private academy (thanks to scholarship funds), Anderson discovered the true magic of education in eighth grade. But her educational bliss was short lived. When her father had a falling-out with the church, Anderson was ejected from the private school and the parsonage she and her family had called home.

Elements of her new suburban high school life — including a sense of the outsider's isolation — wound up in her gripping first novel, *Speak* (1999), named an Honor Book for the Michael L. Printz Award in 2000. The protagonist, fourteen-year-old Melinda, raped by a popular boy at an unsupervised party, reflects Anderson's angst at being thrust into an environment she didn't understand or fit into. Through a distinctive blend of humor and thoughtful, almost brooding prose, Melinda's character springs to life through Anderson's able craft. Heralded by critics, this authentic voice is not, according to Anderson, autobiographical. Instead, the character Melinda arrived as a dream apparition when the author woke from a deep sleep to the perceived sound of teenage sobbing.

Melinda's tortured revelations became the foundation for Anderson's first YOUNG ADULT NOVEL, but not her first book for children. Earlier, after a stint as a Philadelphia newspaper reporter in the late 1980s and early 1990s, Anderson had written and sold two PICTURE BOOKS, *Turkey Pox* (1996) and *Ndito Runs* (1996). Duties of marriage and motherhood distracted Anderson from producing more books in the next few years. Then another geographic move — this time to accommodate her husband's career — and a bout with mononucleosis bounced Anderson out of her rut.

Speak is considered a book for young readers because of Melinda's age and sensibilities, though Anderson has insisted she never set out to write a "young adult" novel. Instead, the book marks her own professional transition from lighter books for kids to darker explorations of the real world.

In the wake of *Speak*'s critical success, Anderson has written nearly a dozen more books for young readers, including the veterinary series Wild at Heart for *American Girl,* nonfiction books for young readers, and, most notably, *Fever 1793* (2000). In this work of HISTORICAL FICTION, Anderson once again explored life-changing disaster — this time a foxfire of yellow fever that overtakes eighteenth-century Philadelphia — through the eyes of a teenage girl. Fourteen-year-old Matilda Cook learns about loss, survival, and heroics in this well-researched, moving work. As her career continues, Anderson admits she loves her writer's life, though her two daughters and her husband still command the lion's share of her devotion.   K.M.H.

Animal Stories

Nearly every baby shares its crib with an assortment of teddy bears, flop-eared dogs, and calico cats, beginning an association with animals that for many children continues to grow and deepen with the years. Infants, like puppies, kittens, and other young animals, not only share a diminutive size and appealing "cuteness" but are also alike in their innocence and dependency on larger creatures. This early identification between child and animal often leads to a lifelong respect and love for both household pets and the entire animal kingdom. Certainly children's literature reflects this interest, as animal stories are among the most popular and enduring books published for young people. There are folktales in which animals enact universal truths about humanity, PICTURE BOOKS filled with bunnies and mice, child and dog stories, ambitious fantasies about animal communities, and naturalistic portraits of wild animals. Stories about animals cross a wide spectrum of genres and intended age groups, providing evidence that these books are popular with readers of nearly every age and taste.

More than two thousand years ago, AESOP

used animal characters to convey moral lessons in fables such as "The Town Mouse and the Country Mouse" and "The Fox and the Grapes." This tradition predates Aesop, however, and is in reality as old as storytelling itself. Most cultures have folktales and myths in which animals represent human characteristics. Talking animal stories, a staple of FOLKLORE, have also inspired many original books for children. This genre, however, which includes some of the most brilliant works of the twentieth century, also includes some of the worst. Too many authors have tried to make a hackneyed, sugary, or moralistic story palatable to children by slapping a tail, paws, or a cold, wet nose on the protagonist. A prime example is the regrettably popular Berenstain Bears series, created by Stan and Jan Berenstain. These stories of a humanized bear family offer trite, didactic writing and cartoon-like illustrations to an audience of beginning readers. Fortunately, the same age group can enjoy one of the finest talking animal series ever produced: the Frog and Toad books by Arnold Lobel. Beginning with *Frog and Toad Are Friends* (1970) and including the Newbery Honor Book *Frog and Toad Together* (1972), the books follow the pair as they go swimming, bake cookies, and tell each other stories. Distinguished for both their gentle prose and amusing illustrations, the books present a portrait of true friendship accessible to most young readers.

Frog and Toad spring from a literary tradition that allows animal characters to think, behave, and sometimes even dress as human beings, although they remain animals in many other respects. Thus, Lobel's Frog wears a bathing suit and rides a bicycle, yet hibernates all winter. BEATRIX POTTER, beloved by generations of readers for her charming illustrated stories, also utilized this technique. In her classic *The Tale of Peter Rabbit* (1901), the young rabbit wears a jacket and shoes but also has a craving for carrots and a fear of being caught by Mr. McGregor and cooked into a pie.

Humanized animals inhabit a number of important FANTASY novels for intermediate readers. KENNETH GRAHAME's classic *The Wind in the Willows* (1908) contains an evocative portrait of nature as several animals travel through the English countryside. The novel depicts the friendship of Mole and Water Rat, as well as the comic adventures of Toad, who lives in a mansion and covets motorcars. Published near the twentieth century's midpoint, *Charlotte's Web* (1952) immediately established itself as a benchmark by which all later animal fantasies must be measured. E. B. WHITE's unforgettable tale of Wilbur the pig, whose life is saved by the spider Charlotte, is filled with memorable animal characters, features important themes of life, death, and friendship, and is written in crystalline prose. Critics continue to express shock that this distinguished book failed to win the Newbery Medal, but nearly twenty years later, another strong animal fantasy did capture the prize. *Mrs. Frisby and the Rats of NIMH* (1971), by ROBERT C. O'BRIEN, mixes a domestic story of a mouse who must relocate her family with scientific speculation about escaped superintelligent laboratory rats who live in a sophisticated rodent community.

Two British animal fantasies must also be noted. *Watership Down* (1972), by Richard Adams, is an epic novel about rabbits who leave their warren to find a new home. The book succeeds as both an exciting adventure and a wonderfully complex portrait of a rabbit society. Young readers and adults continue to enjoy this lengthy, ambitious novel. Although lacking the philosophical depth of a great animal fantasy, Dodie Smith's *One Hundred and One Dalmatians* (1956) is an immensely popular farce of kidnapped puppies, vicious villains, and harrowing rescues. The style is tongue-in-cheek, but the suspense is real.

While most talking animal stories are presented in a matter-of-fact tone, another type of fantasy, which dates back to the nursery rhyme "Old Mother Hubbard and Her Dog," derives its humor from animals that display human characteristics. DR. SEUSS's time-tested classic *The Cat in the Hat* (1957) uses a minimal vocabulary and bouncing rhyme to tell the story of a boisterous cat who visits two bored children on a rainy day. One of the funniest canines in children's literature appears in *Martha Speaks*, SU-

SAN MEDDAUGH'S 1992 picture book about a dog who develops the ability to talk. At first Martha's family of humans is charmed by her new skill because she can now explain long-pondered questions such as "Why don't you come when we call?" and "Why do you drink out of the toilet?" Less charming is Martha's tendency to tattle, make rude remarks, and tell her life story in excruciating detail. How Martha traps a burglar and learns to control her talking makes a thoroughly delightful story.

A final category of animal fantasy combines everyday behavior with fantastic happenings. RANDALL JARRELL'S *Animal Family* (1965), illustrated by MAURICE SENDAK, features a bear and a lynx. Although perhaps tamer than most wild animals, the pair do not talk, dress up, or emulate human behavior in any way. Yet these animals are integral to the plot of this fantasy about a mermaid who leaves the sea to join a hunter in starting a family. Exploring issues of loneliness, love, and family, this poetic and lyrical story speaks directly to the heart.

Conversely, Catherine Cate Coblentz placed a mystical animal within a fact-based story of colonial history in *The Blue Cat of Castletown* (1949), the beautifully written tale of a cat who inspires a Vermont girl to create a rug that would later be displayed in the Metropolitan Museum of Art. Few modern readers are familiar with this Newbery Honor Book, but it deserves rediscovery as one of the most magnificent depictions of creativity and the power of art ever explored in a children's book.

Realistic fiction that examines the connections between humans and animals is consistently popular with children. Many stories concern a child's longing for a pet or the pleasure that an animal can bring to a young person's life. Meindert DeJong wrote with intensity of Davie's longing for, and eventual attachment to, a small black rabbit in *Shadrach* (1956), an exceptionally sensitive novel highlighted by Maurice Sendak's illustrations. WALTER FARLEY'S *The Black Stallion* (1941) is the exciting story of young Alec Ramsey, who, along with a wild horse, is shipwrecked on a desert island. Alec gentles the horse and, after their rescue, rides him to victory in a race. The boy-and-dog stories of Jim Kjelgaard are also appealing. His best-known, *Big Red* (1945), depicts the relationship between a rural teenager and a neighbor's prize-winning Irish setter. Danny travels to New York for Big Red's dog show, then returns to Smokey Creek, where he teaches the dog to hunt game and track the marauding bear that is killing local livestock. MARGUERITE HENRY has explored the bond between child and animal in a number of realistic novels, including *Misty of Chincoteague* (1947) and *King of the Wind* (1948), which are based on historical horses. The vivid background material provides authenticity to her always exciting story lines.

Many children list animal stories and funny stories as their favorite types of reading. Realistic books that combine the two are especially welcome, as proven by the popularity of BEVERLY CLEARY'S work. Beginning with *Henry Huggins* (1950), in which Henry finds a stray dog and takes him home, through *Henry and Ribsy* (1954), which concerns Henry's efforts to keep his dog out of trouble for two months, the series presents the warm relationship between boy and dog as they become involved in numerous comic situations.

Even in an uncomplicated, humorous story, the relationship between child and animal usually serves as a catalyst for positive change in the young person's life. Similarly, animals often help guide a child through a crisis or personal problem in a serious novel. Lynn Hall's realistic animal stories are written with conviction, integrity, and heart. *Halsey's Pride* (1990) concerns a thirteen-year-old girl who learns to accept her epilepsy through her relationship with a collie. A lonely boy who shoots a stray feline confronts issues of guilt and responsibility in PAULA FOX'S moving and elegantly written *One-Eyed Cat* (1984). Arctic wolves help a troubled Eskimo girl sort out her problems and survive the North Slope of Alaska in JEAN CRAIGHEAD GEORGE'S *Julie of the Wolves* (1972), a Newbery Medal–winning novel distinguished by evocative writing and deep understanding of both human and animal behavior. Another Newbery Medal winner, *Sounder* (1969), by William Armstrong, tells the story of an African American family in which the father is arrested and his "coon dog" is wounded. The dog is both a presence and a metaphor in this stark, Depression-era novel that has the power of an American myth.

Realistic animal stories do not always concern a child's interactions with a pet or wild animal. Some books focus on the animal itself, giving a naturalistic account of its life experiences. Anna Sewell's nineteenth-century novel *Black Beauty* (1877) was a forerunner of this type. Although the reader must first accept the premise of a first-person story narrated by a horse, the text is firmly grounded in the animal's perceptions and observations. Albert Payson Terhune collected a number of stories about his own collie in *Lad: A Dog* (1919), a volume that realistically records a dog's varied adventures. An even better known collie is featured in *Lassie-Come-Home*, by Eric Knight (1940). Knight took assiduous care to avoid humanizing Lassie in this story of her four-hundred-mile journey from Scotland to Yorkshire; the dog's actions are consistently guided by instinct or simple thought processes. *The Incredible Journey* (1960), by Canadian author SHEILA BURNFORD, tells of a lengthy trek made by an English bull terrier, a Labrador retriever, and a cat, and also ascribes few human emotions or thoughts to the trio of animals. Felix Salten's *Bambi* (1926) presents a naturalistic portrait of life in the wild. There is savagery, bloodshed, and fear of the human "He." Bambi grows into adulthood, and an almost ineffable sadness hangs over the story as he begins to behave in instinctive ways he does not completely understand. Yet for all its realism, the animals of this tale converse with one another, making the novel a hybrid between an animal-centered realistic story and a fantasy.

Stories that adopt the viewpoint of a dog or deer are based on the author's perceptions and conjectures and may not be an accurate representation of an animal's experience, yet there is little question that these books increase understanding of the natural world and cause many readers to view animals in a different light. Realistic fiction detailing the love between a child and an animal, whether through comic situations or through personal drama, is also engaging and enlightening. Fantasies in which animal communities symbolize human society or individual animals represent human traits may be the most illuminating of all. Sometimes the most important thing about an animal story is what it teaches us about ourselves. P.D.S.

Anno, Mitsumasa

Japanese author and illustrator, b. 1926. Mitsumasa Anno was a teacher for ten years, and his books reflect an understanding of how children learn. He is both an artist and a mathematician and has won many awards, including the Golden Apple Award given by the Biennale at Bratislava and the First Prize for Graphic Excellence in Books for Children conferred by the jury at the Bologna Children's Book Fair.

The first Anno book published in the United States was *Topsy-Turvies: Pictures to Stretch the Imagination* (1970), and a companion volume, *Upside-Downers: More Pictures to Stretch the Imagination,* appeared the following year. *Topsy-Turvies* is an amazing collection of improbable constructions filled with impossible perspectives and angles in the watercolor paintings peopled by tiny figures in ingenious confusion. There are no words in the trompe-l'oeil first book; its companion volume has a text in which playing-card characters argue about which way is up.

In *Anno's Alphabet* (1975) the letters are shown as solid pieces of rough-grained wood and the facing pages have delicately drawn black-and-white frames filled with plant and animal forms. Centered objects are in strong but muted colors, and the book is as much an art lesson as an ALPHABET BOOK. In *Anno's Animals* (1979) the inventive artist has added a new element: creatures hidden in leafy forest scenes. This is a device used in some other Anno books, deliberately included because of his belief that children are interested in challenges. *The King's Flower* (1979) is one of the few Anno books that has a story line; it's an amusing if minatory tale about a foolish king who wants everything he possesses to be the biggest of its kind in the world.

Several of this innovative author's books focus on mathematics: *Anno's Counting Book* (1977), *Anno's Counting House* (1982), and *Anno's Mysterious Multiplying Jar* (1983), written jointly with his son Masaichiro Anno. The first COUNTING BOOK adroitly incorporates concepts (including "zero") so that they reinforce each other via a landscape in which details accumulate. The second book introduces the first ten numbers, plus concepts such as addition, subtraction, sets, and group theory in the form of a game in which ten little people move from one house to another. The book can be read backward or forward. The third book is for somewhat older readers, as it blends a story with the concept of factorials and moves into fantasy.

One of a set of books about other countries, *Anno's Journey* (1978) moves from an open landscape to a town and then to a city with visual delights everywhere: a Van Gogh bridge or a building marked "Anno 1976." This was followed by *Anno's Italy* (1980) and *Anno's Medieval World* (1980), and to the delight of his fans in the United States, *Anno's USA* (1983). The pictures, meticulously drawn, show familiar landscapes and many historical personages as well as some surprises: Laurel and Hardy, for example, or the ducks from ROBERT McCLOSKEY's *Make Way for Ducklings.*

Anno's draftsmanship and composition are always impressive and his use of color restrained. Both entertaining and informative, he informs with wit and offers his readers both humor and beauty. Z.S.

Aruego, José

Filipino-born American author and illustrator, b. 1932. After being born and raised in Manila and earning B.A. and law degrees from the University of the Philippines, José Aruego moved to New York City to attend the Parsons School of Design. He worked in advertising and graphic design until he started illustrating children's books in 1969.

Aruego has chosen humorous stories aimed at toddlers and preschoolers and has illustrated them with simple line drawings and wash that portray fanciful, endearing animal characters who express the immediacy of children's emotions. Aruego has created books by himself, but the bulk of his work he has illustrated with his former wife, Ariane Dewey (also Ariane Aruego). In their continuing collaborations, Aruego designs the page and draws the outlines and Dewey fills in the wash. The color is often flat, but occasionally shaded or textured, and the palettes range from subtle earth tones to creamy sherbet hues.

Typical of Aruego's story matter is a lesson hidden beneath the rollicking effervescence of the characters' antics. In *Rockabye Crocodile* (1988), written and illustrated by Aruego and Dewey, a mean, selfish boar learns the delights of being kind, but the story is all fun and frolic along the way. The boars, with their dainty, curved tusks, stand on tiny two-toed feet with bulky, fluffy bodies seemingly lighter than air. As in his other books, Aruego's active, almost balletic characters, often buoyed by a flat background, have expressive postures and revealing facial expressions executed with minimal use of line.

Aruego and Dewey have illustrated several of Mirra Ginsburg's simple adaptations of Russian tales. *Mushroom in the Rain* (1974) shows a chain of animals taking shelter under a little mushroom. They all fit because the rain makes the mushroom grow. Aruego designed many of the pages in a frameless comic-strip format, so the reader can follow the struggle as each animal squeezes under the dome. The brown mushroom is lumpy and cushionlike, its form and function implying the softness and caring of a mother. Aruego's curvilinear drawing style imparts this comforting beanbag look to all his characters and landscapes.

Both alone and with Dewey, Aruego has collaborated on many books with ROBERT KRAUS.

Leo the Late Bloomer (1971) has achieved classic status since it was first published. In *Herman the Helper* (1974), a young octopus spends his whole day helping friends and family and then gets to "help himself" to mashed potatoes. This story reflects a common theme in Aruego's books: the animals convey toddler and preschooler traits, such as Herman's eagerness to help and the mastery of language that allows him to enjoy a different kind of helping — helping himself.

The unbounded enthusiasm of toddlers and preschoolers is the crux of the plot in *We Hide, You Seek* (1979), written and illustrated by Aruego and Dewey, in which a young rhinoceros seeks his camouflaged friends. The distracted rhino accidentally startles them out of hiding by sneezing or stumbling or stepping on a tail. His exuberant expressions and jubilant movements reveal the essence of childhood joy. And for children, the recognition of their own spontaneous feelings is what leads them to take Aruego's books into their hearts. S.S.

Ashabranner, Brent

American author, b. 1921. *People Who Make a Difference,* the title of Brent Ashabranner's 1989 book describing the actions of ordinary citizens involved in helping others, is a designation that could well be applied to the author himself, for he has taken on the difficult role of America's conscience. After graduating from Oklahoma Agricultural and Mechanical College, where he helped finance his education by selling stories to Western magazines, Ashabranner found that his interest in people, especially those at risk, resulted in his entering a career in public service. While working for the Agency for International Development and the Peace Corps, Ashabranner continued his writing, but his vocation as spokesperson for the underprivileged did not achieve full stride until his retirement. He was then able to devote all of his efforts to addressing the issues that troubled him.

Having lived in many countries around the globe, Ashabranner acquired an interest in differing cultures, which he went on to apply to peoples of varying backgrounds living largely within the United States. In books such as *To Live in Two Worlds: American Indian Youth Today* (1991) and *Morning Star, Black Sun* (1982), Ashabranner has pondered the concerns of Native Americans. Whether interviewing refugees from Central America or newly arrived young Asian immigrants, he has created complete and sympathetic portraits from his thoughtful, probing conversations. Ashabranner's travels — often in the company of photographer Paul Conklin, whose excellent work illuminates many of his accounts — may take him to Western farms and ranches or to a small town in Florida. But no matter what the destination may be, Ashabranner is there to meet people and to listen. He found that the objective writing style of the investigative reporter is the one best suited to the complicated subjects he examines. Ashabranner's intuitive sense of what makes a good story, coupled with his even-handed approach, allows him to write about hardships and survival and to turn the information into highly readable accounts. Perhaps the best example is *Gavriel and Jemal: Two Boys of Jerusalem* (1984). This journey, which took Ashabranner and Conklin to Israel, provided an opportunity to write about two youths — one Arab, one Jewish — living parallel lives in a city separated by religious and racial barriers. The book stands as a significant statement on behalf of peace and understanding. When Ashabranner turned his attention to national monuments, as in *Always to Remember: The Story of the Vietnam Veterans Memorial* (1988), *No Better Hope: What the Lincoln Memorial Means to America* (2001), or *Remembering Korea: The Korean War Veterans Memorial* (2001), he did far more than recount the history of the structure.

Ashabranner's perceptive investigation has brought to light poignant anecdotes that make his books memorable. His award-winning human interest accounts are concise, balanced, and well documented. But of equal importance is his ability to increase the reader's understanding of others, and this he has done with authority and grace. P.S.

Avi

American author, b. 1937. In 1991, Avi's seafaring adventure, *The True Confessions of Charlotte Doyle* (1990), was first named a Newbery Honor Book and then went on to win the Boston Globe–Horn Book Award for fiction. The following year, his novel *Nothing but the Truth* was chosen as an Honor Book for both those awards. Critics and readers began to re-evaluate this author, who had served a lengthy apprenticeship in children's and young adult books. Although he had long been considered a dependable, solid writer, it had taken twenty years of published work before he was recognized as one of the most talented and inventive authors of his generation.

Born and raised in New York, Avi Wortis was such a poor writer during high school that he required a private tutor. He has credited this tutor with awakening his desire to become a writer. Avi received degrees in theater and history from the University of Wisconsin and attended library school at Columbia University. He worked as a full-time librarian during much of his writing career. Avi began writing for the stage, without great success, but this early experience is evident in his terse, dramatic style. In fact, his novel *"Who Was That Masked Man, Anyway?"* (1992) is written entirely in unattributed dialogue without a single word of conventional narration.

Avi began writing for young people only after he had children of his own. Starting with the publication of *Things That Sometimes Happen* (1970), he has become one of the most prolific creators in the field, producing books for all age groups and spanning numerous genres, including HISTORICAL FICTION (the two-volume *Beyond the Western Sea*, 1996, and *Don't You Know*

There's a War On?, 2001), FANTASIES (his Tales of Dimwood Forest series includes *Poppy*, 1995, which won the Boston Globe–Horn Book Award for fiction), thrillers, light comedies, and even a graphic novel (*City of Light, City of Dark*, 1993). Avi has been acclaimed for his versatility, although his audience has sometimes been limited since his works cannot easily be slotted into a single category.

Despite their diversity, however, Avi's books share a number of common traits. Most begin with a strong, attention-grabbing chapter that immediately captures the reader; they are often written in an episodic style, with short, tightly written scenes; and the multilevel storytelling offers a plot strong in incident and action, yet with a thematically rich subtext. *Wolf Rider* (1986) is a riveting suspense novel in which Andy searches for a possible killer, but the book contains an equally strong subtext about trust and communication in the unfolding of the strained relationship between Andy and his father.

The True Confessions of Charlotte Doyle is a wonderfully entertaining, finely detailed depiction of the 1832 ocean voyage during which Charlotte abandons the principles of her prim background and joins the ship's crew in mutiny. On a deeper level, the novel is about Charlotte's liberation from a family and a society that have very restrictive and rigid expectations for a thirteen-year-old girl.

Perhaps the most innovative novel by Avi is *Nothing but the Truth*. Presented as a pastiche of memos, journal entries, newspaper articles, and dialogue blocks, it is the story of a teenager's disruptive classroom behavior and its snowballing consequences. There are no simple answers in this novel, and each reader may come away with a different perception — but almost every reader will find the novel thought-provoking and the final scene overwhelmingly powerful.

As Avi's books continue to grow in power and depth, readers will continue to await each new book with high expectations. P.D.S.

Awards and Prizes

At least two hundred children's book prizes exist. Awards for children's books — by their sheer numbers, marked increase in recent years, and variety — have sometimes been confusing to parents and others concerned with children's reading. Yet they need not be. By becoming aware of the basic trends and categories in the field, concerned adults can become familiar with the awards that will best serve to lead them to good books for the readers they guide. There are four basic categories: major awards given by organizations, awards selected by children, awards chosen by state or regional groups, and international awards.

In the first category, the Newbery and Caldecott Medals are the oldest, best-known, and most prestigious awards given by an organization in the United States. The Newbery, established in 1922, was donated and named by Frederic G. Melcher, editor of *Publishers Weekly*, as a tribute to the first English publisher of books for children, John Newbery (1713–1767). The award is given annually and is selected by an awards committee of the Association for Library Services to Children (ALSC) of the American Library Association (ALA) to honor the author, a resident or citizen of the United States, who has made the most distinguished contribution to literature for children published in the United States during the preceding year. In 1937, Melcher donated a parallel award for PICTURE BOOK illustration, naming it the Caldecott in honor of the nineteenth-century English illustrator RANDOLPH CALDECOTT. By establishing these two awards, Melcher made an inestimable contribution to the validation and prestige of the field of children's literature.

The Laura Ingalls Wilder Award, also administered by a committee of ALSC, was first awarded in 1954 to the author for whom it was named. From 1960 to 1980 the honor was given every five years to an author or illustrator whose books, published in the United States over a period of years, had made a significant contribution to children's literature. Currently, the bronze medal is bestowed every two years.

In 1966 the ALA established the Mildred L. Batchelder Award to honor a book originally published in a foreign language in a foreign country and translated. In 2000 the first Michael L. Printz Award was given for "literary excellence in young adult literature." In 2001 the first Sibert Award was presented to honor the finest INFORMATION BOOKS published each year for young readers.

Other U.S. organizations offer equally influential awards. Since 1967 the Boston Globe–Horn Book Awards have been awarded annually by the *Boston Globe* and the *Horn Book Magazine*. In 1976 the awards categories were expanded from two (text and illustration) to three; the current categories are Outstanding Fiction or Poetry, Outstanding Nonfiction, and Outstanding Illustration.

The Coretta Scott King Award was established in 1970 to honor Martin Luther King Jr. and his wife. Recognition is given annually to an African American author and to an African American illustrator whose books, published in the preceding year, are inspirational and educational contributions to children's literature. The Social Responsibilities Round Table and the ALSC select the winners and make the presentations.

The Jane Addams Book Award is presented to the author of a children's book that helps to promote peace, social justice, and equality of the sexes and of all races. This award has been given annually since 1953 by the Women's International League for Peace and Freedom and the Jane Addams Peace Association.

The Scott O'Dell Award for Historical Fiction was instituted and donated by SCOTT O'DELL, himself an honored children's book author, in 1981. First awarded by the selection committee in 1984, the O'Dell award is an annual prize for a distinguished work of HISTORICAL FICTION for children or young adults, published in English by a U.S. publisher and set in North, Central, or South America.

An increasing number of awards are selected each year by children. In 1986 there were twenty-eight such statewide awards; in 1992 the number had risen to forty-one. Child-selected awards counter the complaint made by some that the winners of the prestigious children's book awards often appeal to the adult readers who made the selections but not to the very readers for whom the books are intended. Sponsored by state departments of education, universities, or library associations, these awards are usually organized for the express purpose of encouraging children to read more and better books. Candidates for child-chosen awards are most often initially nominated by teachers and librarians before being voted on by young readers. The oldest such program is the Pacific Northwest Young Reader's Choice Awards, established in 1940 and covering students from Alaska, Idaho, Montana, Oregon, and Washington in the United States and from Alberta and British Columbia in Canada. Other awards selected by young readers include the Texas Bluebonnet Award, Minnesota's Maud Hart Lovelace Book Award, and Wyoming's Indian Paintbrush Book Award.

Many state and regional awards recognize the work of resident authors or illustrators or books about or taking place in the specified state or region. These awards are often sponsored by state library associations, as in the case of the Lupine Award, sponsored by the Children's and Young Adult's Services Section of the Maine Library Association (begun in 1990 to recognize an outstanding contribution to children's literature from or about Maine), or by a local organization, as in the case of the Society of Midland Authors Book Awards (established in 1961 to honor the outstanding book of the year written by a native or resident of the Midwest).

Of the awards made in other countries, the most useful for American readers are those from the primarily English-speaking countries, especially Australia, Canada, and Great Britain. The international awards selections are made from candidates from a select list or from all countries

of the world. The Carnegie and Kate Greenaway Medals are major British awards. The former, established in 1937, is presented annually by the British Library Association to the outstanding children's book written in English and first published in the United Kingdom during the preceding year. The Kate Greenaway Medal, also given annually by the British Library Association, honors the most distinguished illustrated children's book of the preceding year.

In Canada the most prestigious award is the Canadian Library Association Book of the Year for Children Award. First presented in 1947, this annual award honors a children's book of outstanding literary merit written by a Canadian. Between 1954 and 1973 two awards were made: one for a work in English and the second for a work in French. The Prix Alvine-Belisle, established in 1975 and administered by the Association pour l'avancement des sciences et des techniques de la documentation, is awarded annually to the author or illustrator of the best children's book by a Canadian national published in Canada in French. The Amelia Frances Howard-Gibbon Medal has been presented annually since 1971 by the Canadian Library Association to honor the outstanding illustrated book published in Canada by a Canadian native or resident.

The Australian Children's Books of the Year Awards, begun in 1946, recognize books in three categories: Book of the Year for Older Readers, Book of the Year for Younger Readers, and Picture Book of the Year. The winners, selected by the Children's Book Council of Australia, must be Australians or residents of Australia. A short list of finalists is announced in March, and these books are the subject of much attention and speculation before the winners are announced at the beginning of Children's Book Week in July or August. The BILBY Awards (Books I Love Best Yearly) are child-selected awards, named for the bilby, a rare species of bandicoot. First presented in 1990, the award has three categories: Read Alone (Primary), Read Alone (Secondary), and Read Aloud.

The world's most prestigious award in children's literature, often referred to as the "little Nobel Prize," is the Hans Christian Andersen Award, the first international children's book award. Established in 1956 by the International Board on Books for Young People (IBBY), the medal is given every two years to an author whose body of work has made an important international contribution to children's literature. Since 1966 an artist's medal has been conferred on the same basis. Winners are selected by a jury composed of the jury president, the president of IBBY, and eight children's literature experts elected by an executive committee of IBBY.

The sheer number of awards and their recent increase express the strength and vitality of children's literature and its place as a major genre in contemporary literature. That so many prize programs, honoring so many titles, are available is a sign of the health of children's literature and the support it receives from readers as well as professionals in the field. Trends toward more child-selected awards, more state and regional awards, and stronger contenders from Canada and Australia serve not to diminish the genre, but rather to enhance it. By learning to navigate the confusing shoals of children's book awards, adults can get good books into children's hands.

C.B.

Azarian, Mary

American illustrator, b. 1940. Born in Washington, D.C., Mary Azarian grew up on a farm in Virginia. While attending Smith College in Massachusetts, she studied printmaking under Leonard Baskin. In the early 1960s, she and her husband bought a small farm in rural Vermont and tried to make a living on the land. Because they needed money, she taught in a one-room school, with few books, and consequently made alphabets to adorn the school walls. Later, when the state of Vermont commissioned alphabet cards to be distributed to its schoolchildren,

Azarian won the commission. These cards came to the attention of a publisher, and *A Farmer's Alphabet* (1981), an oversize ALPHABET BOOK, presented Azarian's elegant designs.

To create her art, Mary Azarian works in a studio surrounded by gardens and fields and uses a cast-iron Van der Cook press. For each illustration, she starts with a fine-grained board of wood, sketches a fairly detailed design in dark ink, and then covers it with a light wash of color. She carves the wood around the black lines. After making each print, she colors it by hand with acrylics.

Although she always works in woodcuts, Azarian is adept at capturing different periods and moods. For Lisa Lunge-Larson's *The Race of the Birkenbeiners* (2001), she re-created medieval Norway, decorating her pages with elaborate borders to help tell the story of how the baby King Hakon lives to ascend to the throne. For *A Gardener's Alphabet* (2000), she brought a bright palette into play. *The Four Seasons of Mary Azarian* (2000), containing fifty hand-colored woodcuts, celebrates the four seasons, snow, gardens, and scenes of Vermont. In Penny Pollock's *When the Moon Is Full: A Lunar Year* (2001), evocative two-page spreads depict each month's full moon.

To date, Azarian's most accomplished works are her illustrations for Jacqueline Briggs Martin's *Snowflake Bentley* (1998). For this volume Azarian combined her passion for snow, the Vermont landscape, and following one's dream. The text of this PICTURE BOOK recounts the life of Vermont's Wilson Bentley, who "marched to his own drummer" and spent many years photographing snowflakes and cataloguing their shapes and characteristics. For this work, Azarian won the Caldecott Medal, both for the excellence of her art and for innovative book design. Many of the spreads include informative details from Wilson's life, set off in sidebars.

In her Caldecott speech, Mary Azarian said, "It is my fervent hope that *Snowflake Bentley* may inspire both children and adults to follow their own unique paths in life." A.S.

B

Babbitt, Natalie

American author and illustrator, b. 1932. With *Tuck Everlasting* (1975), Natalie Babbitt created an enduring classic of American children's literature. The thought-provoking story of ten-year-old Winnie Foster, who discovers a fountain of youth, raises profound questions of morality and immortality. Winnie learns of the magical effects of a spring hidden in the woods on her family's property when she discovers Jesse Tuck, an eternal seventeen-year-old, drinking from it. As she encounters the rest of the Tucks — a gentle pioneering family who haven't aged since drinking from the spring more than eighty years before — she comes to understand the complex combination of blessings and curses their secret holds.

Angus Tuck, the father, provides strength to his family, though he has grown tired of their eternal existence; Mae, the mother, is accepting and wise; Miles, the older brother who had once married, is full of sorrow from having left his wife and children, who aged while he remained unchanged. Only young Jesse, handsome and lively, revels in what he believes is a gift.

A suspenseful interplay comes with the foreboding presence of the villainous "man in the yellow suit," a shady, opportunistic fellow who intends to profit from the power of the spring. The momentum increases when Mae Tuck inadvertently kills this man and faces a death sentence; since she cannot die, this would make their secret public, opening the spring to exploitation. Winnie, showing her inner strength and resourcefulness, chooses to help the Tucks escape, thereby keeping the spring secret. Before the Tucks set off to continue their endless roaming, Jesse leaves Winnie a tempting bottle of the spring water, encouraging her to wait to drink it until she is seventeen and then to come find them.

Babbitt successfully paralleled events in the text with symbolic use of weather to create tension. The writing is economical, straightforward, and unassuming, like the Tucks, yet the result is a mysterious, subtle evocation of emotion for this family and their fate. Here, as in most of Babbitt's fiction, sophisticated ideas are presented with simplicity. Never doubting that her concepts are within the grasp of children, Babbitt has never succumbed to didacticism or condescension.

While some adults have objected to what they consider the unnecessary death of the man in the yellow suit, most young readers focus on Winnie's ultimate decision not to drink from the spring. Her choice is revealed when, many years later, the Tucks again pass through Winnie's town, Treegap, and find a tombstone that reads: "In Loving Memory / Winifred Foster Jackson / Dear Wife / Dear Mother / 1870–1948." Pa Tuck is moved. "Good girl," he says.

Much of Babbitt's work displays a unique combination of folklore, fairy tale, myth, and legend, as in the allegorical tale *The Search for Delicious* (1969). To settle a disagreement among members of the court, a twelve-year-old prime minister's assistant, Gaylen, is sent out to poll the kingdom on the correct definition of the word *delicious*. From its beginnings in folly, the quest develops into a dangerous and politically significant mission. Exposed to a great variety of opinions, and to eccentric characters and supernatural beings such as the worldweller (a tree dweller), a group of dwarfs, and a mermaid, Gaylen is finally faced with the unexpected challenge of saving the kingdom. The main character evolves believably through his mythical quest, and the fanciful, satirical tale is distinguished by Babbitt's lyrical writing, as well as its adventures and humor.

Another beautifully written allegory is *Kneeknock Rise* (1970), a Newbery Honor Book. This story about man's desire to believe in the mysterious is a delightfully entertaining fable of a town's fear of the Megrimum, a mythical creature that resides on the top of a neighboring mountain. A boy, Egan, who is visiting his relatives one day, ventures to seek out the Megrimum and discovers, of course, that there is no such beast. The book's philosophy is conveyed through Egan's itinerant Uncle Ott, who postulates: "Is it better to be wise if it makes you solemn and practical, or is it better to be foolish so you can go on enjoying yourself?"

Though Babbitt's wit is evident in all her stories, nowhere is it more prevalent or immediate than in her collections of short stories about the devil as he attempts to stir up trouble on earth and to increase the population of his southern realm. *The Devil's Storybook* (1974) and *The Devil's Other Storybook* (1987) feature a devil who is less evil and daunting than he is merely mischievous and cantankerous. His plans are often thwarted, and he is frequently outsmarted; the result is folktale-like stories riddled with comical error and whimsy.

Most of Babbitt's works are complemented by her own expressive pen and ink drawings. Her original intention was to become an illustrator, and to that end she studied art at the Laurel School in Cleveland and at Smith College. Her first book, *The Forty-Ninth Magician*, was written by her husband, Samuel Fisher Babbitt, and published in 1966. Babbitt also provided the simple but elegant drawings for several collections of short poems written by Valerie Worth. Babbitt began writing primarily to have stories to illustrate. With the publication of the PICTURE BOOKS *Nellie: A Cat on Her Own* (1989) and *Bub: Or the Very Best Thing* (1994), she came full circle as an illustrator, providing full-color illustrations for her own texts.

Other notable works include *Goody Hall* (1971), a period piece with gothic elements, about young Willet Goody, the heir to the great mansion Goody Hall, who, with the help of his new tutor, Hercules Feltwright, uncovers the mystery of his father's disappearance; and *The Eyes of the Amaryllis* (1977), a FANTASY involving a young girl, Jenny, who visits her grandmother and learns of her romantic and potentially dangerous enchantment with the sea.

Babbitt's work is known for its haunting, ethereal quality as well as its clear, poetic writing. Her stories are infused with ideas from myth, folklore, and legend, and though the concepts they contain are far from simple, they are accessible to young readers while still intriguing to adults. Each is an insightful, wise offering in a timeless body of work. E.K.E.

Voices of the Creators

🎋 Natalie Babbitt

I became a writer more or less by accident. It was certainly not part of my plan, a plan quite settled when I was nine. That year, my mother sent away for a very nice edition of LEWIS CARROLL's *Alice in Wonderland,* and I fell in love at once with JOHN TENNIEL's pictures because they were beautiful and funny both at once. I was used to pictures that were beautiful and sweet, or cartooned and funny, but this was a new combination. It made a deep impression on me. I had already decided to be an artist, and now, thanks to Tenniel, I knew what sort of artist: I would be an illustrator of children's books, and I would draw funny, beautiful pictures in pen and ink.

In this country we believe it is our right to choose the kind of seeds we will plant in the gardens of our lives — a cloying metaphor, but useful. We have the right to choose the seeds, but whether or not they will flourish depends on a lot of things beyond our control: weather conditions, the chemistry of the soil, and whether or not the head gardeners are vigilant. I was lucky. The soil and the weather were adequate, and the head gardeners, my mother and father, were not only vigilant, they were also good role models. My mother was a beautiful, though nonprofessional, artist, and my father was funny.

I don't know how common it is to decide on a future career in the fourth grade and then to stick firmly to that decision and bring it to fruition nearly a quarter of a century later. Most of the people I know changed their minds a number of times while they were growing up. But for me it seemed reasonable, by the age of nine, to settle the question. I had wanted, as a preschooler, to be a pirate, and then, in second grade, to be a librarian. I might have made a pretty good librarian, but with my distaste for heavy exercise, I would probably have made a poor pirate. No matter; an illustrator I soon decided to be, and an illustrator I have, in part, become.

I chose to plant that particular seed in my garden, but my mother planted a few of her own choosing, and it is from these, I guess, that the writing part came. For she read aloud to my sister and me for years, thereby creating a love for stories and reading. My father planted a seed, too, though I know he didn't do so on purpose: he loved the language and used it in the most inventive and hilarious ways, thereby creating in me an ear for words. Plagued as we were by the 1930s Depression, there were many things we didn't have. Looking back, I know now that we had all the things that really matter.

When my first illustrations were published, to accompany a story written by my husband, it felt natural and preordained. But then my husband had other fish to fry, and I had to try to create my own stories. This felt decidedly unnatural. Nothing in my growing up, it seemed, had prepared me to be a professional writer. But now I see that we all have stories to tell and we all use words every day of our lives. And if we have also grown up with books, there's no reason why a writing career shouldn't be possible, assuming we have a taste for the life. The writing I've done — though it's certainly been hard work — has seemed pretty simple. There's always one best word, if you listen for it, and there are always a few ideas about which you feel passionate enough to turn them into stories. Writing is a left-brain exercise, and insofar as ideas come from the subconscious, can

even be seen as a kind of therapy. But picture-making is a right-brain exercise. To me it is mysterious, and I have no idea at all how it can happen, even though I've been doing it all my life. Watching my preschool grandson at work with crayons, I am awestruck to see how, one day, he suddenly does not merely scribble but makes a creature with legs and neck and one large eye. Something has all at once clicked into place in his brain, and a message, sent down to his little hand, has told him how to draw.

All this is not a value judgment on my part about pictures as opposed to stories. I would always rather read a book than visit an art museum. And a PICTURE BOOK with a bad story is a bad picture book, no matter how beautiful the pictures may be. Still, picture-making is a kind of kinetic marvel, poorly understood — and poorly understood marvels are for me the most interesting things in life. 🐟

Bang, Molly

American author and illustrator, b. 1943. Molly Garrett Bang's PICTURE BOOKS draw from the legends of many cultures and reflect her belief in the importance and power of folktales.

Born in Princeton, New Jersey, Bang has lived in Japan, India, and Mali and holds degrees in French and Oriental studies. She has said that she was inspired as a child to become an illustrator by looking at the work of ARTHUR RACKHAM. After illustrating health manuals overseas, Bang began to collect and illustrate folktales. Her first book, *The Goblins Giggle* (1973), is a compilation of stories that she illustrated with frightening black and gray paintings. The stories are filled with mystery and suspense, and the collection is notable for the fluency of its retelling.

Both *The Grey Lady and the Strawberry Snatcher* (1980) and *Ten, Nine, Eight* (1983) were named Caldecott Honor Books. *Grey Lady* is a suspenseful, wordless picture book painted in rich gouache colors. The Grey Lady is pursued through the story by a frightening blue figure who attempts to steal her strawberries. The Grey Lady blends into the gray of the background until at times only her face, hands, and strawberries are discernible. The striking, unusual illustrations are, like Bang's folktales, full of surprises. *Ten, Nine, Eight* is a very different book, a rhythmic bedtime story that has been much compared to MARGARET WISE BROWN's *Goodnight Moon*. Bang wrote the text for her adopted Bengali daughter because she was concerned about the paucity of positive images of brown children in picture books. The gentle countdown to bed stars a happy girl surrounded by people, objects, and love.

Bang's many retellings of folktales have earned her a devoted readership and acclaim for her attention to detail and authenticity. *Wiley and the Hairy Man* (1976), a folktale from the southern United States, is the exciting story of a young boy and his mother who together outwit the frightening Hairy Man. Like *The Goblins Giggle*, it is illustrated entirely in black and gray paint, and Bang skillfully uses white space as another element in the page design. *The Paper Crane* (1988) was awarded the Boston Globe–Horn Book Award for illustration. The Japanese tale of a beggar who rewards a man for his generosity and gives him a magic paper crane is illustrated with remarkable cut-paper collage. The three-dimensional artwork suits the text in which an origami crane turns into a live dancing bird. Bang achieved the same transformation in her art — a folded paper bird becomes a rounded, delicate crane in a series of cut and folded paper images. *When Sophie Gets Angry — Really, Really Angry* (1999), executed in a vivid, bright palette, explores the rage of a young girl. It garnered for Bang another Caldecott Honor Book.

Bang's illustration style always matches the particular story and the sound of the text. Her illustrations for Sylvia Cassedy's collection of Japanese haiku, *Red Dragonfly on My Shoulder* (1992), are created from collages that include objects such as a carrot, a bolt, and grains of rice. Bang's tutorial on design and visual composi-

tion, *Picture This: Perception and Composition* (1992), leads the reader through exercises to understand the art of illustration and how meaning is created through images.

Although she began as an artist, Bang has retold many of her own stories and exhibits an awareness of the sounds of language, so her stories read aloud particularly well. Bang has made a place for herself through her willingness to experiment with illustration, her understanding of the power of traditional stories, and her skills as an artist and storyteller. M.V.K.

Banks, Lynne Reid

See REID BANKS, LYNNE.

Barton, Byron

American author and illustrator, b. 1930. Since 1969, when his ink drawings appeared in Constance Greene's *A Girl Called Al*, Byron Barton has created striking illustrations and PICTURE BOOKS with his skilled use of bold lines and flat shapes. Barton grew up in Los Angeles and studied art at the Chouinard Art Institute. He worked in television animation before becoming interested in children's books.

Most of Barton's excellent picture books are works of nonfiction for the very youngest child. Many of them focus on technology: *Trucks* (1986), *Wheels* (1979), *I Want to Be an Astronaut* (1988), *Machines at Work* (1987), *Boats* (1998), and *My Car* (2001) are just a few of his well-received titles. These books use few words and dramatic line and color to convey the excitement of machines and technology to preschool children. Barton's INFORMATION BOOKS do include a story. For example, they may show the drama of a train arriving and leaving again or the joy of finding a dinosaur skeleton and then reconstructing the dinosaur. Barton has used black line and bold colors and shapes to define his subjects. The people he has drawn are representative rather than realistic, but both objects and people are clearly recognizable, including a multiethnic population of men and women in both conventional and nontraditional occupations. The whole book, including covers and endpapers, is used to create his story.

When illustrating the work of other authors, Barton has varied his style and use of color. In *Truck Song* (1984), written by Diane Siebert, Barton defined objects with shadow and shades of color as well as with his characteristic bold lines. *Gila Monsters Meet You at the Airport* (1980), written by MARJORIE WEINMAN SHAR-MAT, is illustrated with predominantly brown and green tones, suited to the protagonist's imaginary vision of the West. The hilarious story about misconceptions is aptly illustrated with childlike drawings accentuating the ridiculous aspects of the real and mythical West.

In addition to his nonfiction, Barton has also illustrated nursery stories and folktales for very young children. His retelling of *The Three Bears* (1991) received attention for its refreshingly childlike art and spare story. Here, again, Barton's work is exemplary for his use of simple, flat shapes and for his ability to capture the essence of a story or subject for very young children.

Barton approaches his subject matter first from a visual perspective; illustration is more important than text in his books, which have gained a wide readership among young children who are attracted to his powerful images and simple stories. His books embody an understanding of the drama inherent in information, making nonfiction subjects available and attractive to the youngest readers. M.V.K.

Bauer, Joan

American author, b. 1951. The protagonists in Joan Bauer's books are invariably endowed with unusual talents and interests. One is obsessed with growing pumpkins. Another is a history buff. Others view selling shoes and waiting tables not as after-school jobs, but as true vocations. Born and raised in River Forest, Illinois, Bauer also had an uncommon childhood ambition: she wanted to become a comedian or comedy writer. She eventually fulfilled this goal by writing humorous YOUNG ADULT NOVELS — after working in sales and advertising for several publishers, selling articles to newspapers and magazines, and trying her hand at writing for television and film.

After settling with her husband and daughter in Darien, Connecticut, Bauer was involved in a serious car accident after which she required surgery and months of recuperation. During this time she began writing *Squashed* (1992). The winner of the Delacorte Prize for a First Young Adult Novel, this hilarious, heartfelt story concerns sixteen-year-old Ellie Morgan's efforts to win the Rock River Pumpkin Weigh-In and Harvest Festival with her prize squash, Big Max. Whether fattening Max with a specially concocted booster solution or pulling an all-nighter to protect him from a downpour, Ellie remains a likable, wise-cracking heroine, whose obsessive concern for her pumpkin is balanced by more typical teenage issues: self-esteem, a rocky relationship with her widowed father, and her romantic interest in another agriculturally minded classmate.

Squashed is a prototype for Bauer's subsequent novels, which also feature funny narrators with out-of-the-ordinary interests. *Backwater* (1999) concerns teenage Ivy Breedlove, whose fascination with history and genealogy marks her as different from members of her extended family, most of whom practice law. A winter trek up the Adirondack Mountains to meet a mysterious aunt helps Ivy better understand both her family and herself. The highly popular *Rules of the Road* (1998) features a teenager with a gift for selling shoes. Jenna's job, driving a wealthy shoe-store owner cross country, becomes a journey of self-discovery.

Somewhat less successful is *Thwonk* (1995), a novel that includes elements of FANTASY, as a cupid doll comes to life and helps A.J. turn the tables on the boy she has long secretly adored. What keeps the volume anchored in reality is A.J.'s interest in photography, presented with intensity and enthusiasm. Pool playing is the passion of ten-year-old Mickey in *Sticks* (1996), the first Bauer novel written for younger readers and the first to feature a male protagonist. Although the story is entertaining, Mickey lacks the verve and personality typically associated with the author's heroines.

In *Hope Was Here* (2000), a very satisfying novel, a teenage girl with a unique gift — waitressing — moves from New York to rural Wisconsin to help her aunt run the Welcome Stairways diner. The indominatable Hope gets to know a cast of eccentric townspeople, campaigns for a seriously ill man running for mayor, and finds time for a little romance, all the while serving up maple corn bread, buttermilk fried chicken, and Big-Hearted Stew. This warm and funny story about community and finding one's place was named a Newbery Honor Book, an unusual selection considering Hope's age — sixteen — but a measure of the esteem in which this book is held. P.D.S.

Bauer, Marion Dane

American author, b. 1938. Through absorbing stories, Marion Dane Bauer has confronted her own internal conflicts while engaging young people in comparable psychological and moral challenges. In her insightful *What's Your Story: A Young Person's Guide to Writing Fiction* (1992), she emphasized that "the secret is to find that place within yourself where feelings are strong and then to ask, What if . . .?"

Having struggled through her own maturing years with a father who was "argumentative and neurotic" yet brilliant and a mother who tried to keep her socially isolated, Bauer has frequently focused her writing on young adolescent characters who face various harsh realities of growing up. It is no surprise that adult-child relationships are the frank focal point in a number of her works. Although Bauer's characters must take personal responsibility for their own decisions and actions, in doing so they inevitably move toward some meaningful connection with others. *On My Honor*, a widely acclaimed novel chosen as a 1987 Newbery Honor Book, epitomizes the best of Bauer's work. Here she has provoked the reader to explore with twelve-year-old Joel a myriad of emotions, including fear, guilt, and blame, and reconciliation with his father, as Joel struggles with the drowning of his friend, Tony, and with his own decision on whether to tell the truth about his part in it. *Shelter from the Wind* (1976), Bauer's first published novel, brought her immediate positive attention and was selected as an ALA Notable Book. Praiseworthy are Bauer's respectful, straightforward writing and her forceful, precise imagery in describing a young adolescent's quest for her mother in the hot, desolate Oklahoma panhandle.

A fine-tuned sense of place and time characterizes this and other of the author's novels set primarily in her native Midwest. Powerfully evoking her own experience in central Illinois of the 1940s, *Rain of Fire* (1983), the revealing exploration of a young boy's shame and his lies to cover up his soldier brother's refusal to claim heroism in World War II, earned Bauer the Jane Addams Book Award. Bauer's experiences as both a biological and a foster parent provided background for her novel *Foster Child* (1977), recipient of the Golden Kite Honor Award of the Society of Children's Book Writers. Through her straightforward treatment of sexual abuse in this novel, psychological abuse in *Face to Face* (1991), gay and lesbian issues in her short story collection *Am I Blue? Coming Out from the Silence* (1994), and similar candor in other works, Bauer has demonstrated the courage she expects of her characters. On occasion she explores her themes through FANTASY as well as realism, especially when her intended audience is the preadolescent child, as it is in *Ghost Eye* (1992).

Forthright in life as in fiction, Bauer has openly discussed reasons she considers some of her works less effective than others. Her keen analysis of the art of writing reflects the many years she has taught writing to adults. The impact of Bauer's literature has been extended through the *ABC Afterschool Special* "Rodeo Red and the Runaway," loosely based on *Shelter from the Wind*, and the videocassette *On My Honor*.

E.T.D.

Voices of the Creators

🌺 *Marion Dane Bauer*

"But how," the teenage boy demanded to know, "can you write for kids when you yourself are so old?"

No, that's not quite the way he put it, but that is exactly what he meant. I gave him, basically, Ursula Nordstrom's famous answer: "I am a former child, and I haven't forgotten a thing." But I could see he was not convinced. And the truth is, I wasn't entirely convinced either, because maintaining a long career as a children's writer is difficult, but difficult in very different ways than that young man can guess.

When I was young and starting my career I had a mission. I was a truth teller. Which meant, of course, not only that I was determined to tell the truth, whatever that might be in any given situation, but that I was confident the truth was mine to tell. If maturity brings any gift at all, however, it is the gift of knowing that "the truth" is seldom so easy to know . . . let alone to convey.

I tell my students that the best fiction writing rises out of our own deepest questions, not out of our answers. And I believe that. But the energy that lies behind most good fiction comes from the conviction that the answers are, at the very least, worth seeking. Maturity brought for me a willingness to settle for half answers, a comfort with not attempting to answer many of the questions at all. And with the loss of that determination to discover and tell "the truth," I began to find myself running out of the energy required to sustain stories.

But life changes are never simple. Often a blessing comes tucked in beside a loss. And one of those blessings was, for me, the gift of grandchildren. In response to the appearance of my first grandson, I found myself going to the library and bringing home books about birth, every kind of birth, then writing a celebration of the births of kittens, sea horses, porcupines, whales, and this one-of-a-kind, absolutely outstandingly fantastic child. *If You Were Born a Kitten* launched a new and utterly delightful arm of my career.

It is a curious fact that a four-hundred-word picture book can give a writer more space to play with language than a novel is apt to do. In writing a novel, I am always pushing the story through the consciousness of my main character. Language becomes a secondary concern, and language that I love can sometimes even get in my way. In small books I move into the world of rhythm, sometimes of rhyme, of the perfectly chosen word like someone being freed to fly. And when I take wing as a three-year-old, a five-year-old, even a seven-year-old, I find the questions — and consequently the answers — both simple and profound.

But writing that picture book did something else for me. It turned me on to research. I have always done some research for my novels, investigating aspects of a story for validation, but the stories themselves came entirely from my imagination. Many of the picture books I have written since *If You Were Born a Kitten* — and early readers and even novelty books — were born very directly from research. Piles of books brought home from the library to glean a few facts which can be put into even fewer words. And once I began discovering how much fun research could be, it was a short step to researching topics that were brand-new to me in order to write novels.

As I write this, I am just completing the final work on two novels: *Runt,* a story set in the fascinating world of a wild wolf pack, and an addition to the Dear America series, *Land of the Buffalo Bones,* based on my own family history. The work on each novel began with months of research, but when I sat down to write, both stories flowed out of me like water from a pitcher. The research, a very different kind demanded for each story, seemed to provide not just information but a new energy too.

What lies ahead . . . beyond accumulating more years, more of the gentle sadness of maturity? Beyond trying to explain to more slightly bored, slightly incredulous, slightly superior teenage boys how it is that I, a woman of "a certain age," can dare to write for children?

I hope the answer will be more fun verses such as this one, which has yet to find its home in a book: "A pelican's mouth / makes a fine picnic basket. / If you don't agree, / just ask it." And more explorations into worlds I never dreamed before — wolves, family history, sod houses, weather, the animal world. Into whatever lies waiting around the next corner. I'm wide open. ⚏

Baum, L. Frank

American author, 1856–1919. With more than 150 books, plays, songs, poems, and essays to his credit — many written under pseudonyms — Lyman Frank Baum is best known as the creator of *The Wonderful Wizard of Oz* (1900), which has been called "America's first fairy tale." His place in the history of children's books is firm; in the realm of children's literature it is less so. Whatever strengths the best of his work for children possesses, whatever flashes of humor and storytelling genius shine through, however popular his books may have been, his prose style remains ordinary. It is not his words but the land of Oz and its characters that endure in the affectionate memories of long-ago readers and that are immortalized in the classic 1939 film *The Wizard of Oz*, an ironic yet fitting tribute to Baum's own theatrical vision.

Baum was a man of many talents and accomplishments whose direction in life took many turns before ending in the world of books. Born and raised in upstate New York, he lived briefly in South Dakota and for many years in Chicago and finally in Hollywood. In his lifetime he was a journalist, poet, playwright, actor, composer, salesman, business manager, theater manager, filmmaker, showman, master storyteller, prodigious author, and happy family man who has been compared to P. T. Barnum, Walt Disney, and his own creation, the Wizard of Oz.

It was to amuse his children that Baum elaborated on familiar Mother Goose rhymes, resulting in *Mother Goose in Prose* (1897), illustrated by MAXFIELD PARRISH and the first book for both men. *Father Goose, His Book* followed in 1899 to become the best-selling book of the year. Baum's friend W. W. Denslow did the colored illustrations that appeared on every page — an innovation in children's books of the time, author and artist sharing the high cost of production.

Baum much admired the work of the cartoonists of his day, wanting the pictures for his books to be colorful and humorous. Denslow also illustrated *The Wonderful Wizard of Oz*, which tells of practical, honest, kind-hearted Dorothy Gale (her name itself typical of Baum's penchant for punning), who is swept away by a cyclone from her beloved Kansas home into the magical land of Oz and who journeys to the Emerald City to seek the wizard's help in getting home again. In a land filled with magic, talking animals, witches good and bad, winged monkeys, and friendly characters such as the Scarecrow, the Tin Woodman, and the Cowardly Lion, Oz the Great and Terrible turns out to be merely a humbug wizard whose "magic" is based on technology and psychology. In the end, magical silver shoes take Dorothy and her dog, Toto, back home to Aunt Em and Uncle Henry, while a real gas-filled balloon carries the wizard off to his native Omaha and Dorothy's friends remain behind, happy to believe that through the wizard's magic they now possess the things they thought they had lacked: a brain, a heart, and courage. *The Wonderful Wizard of Oz* is not a literary masterpiece, but it is a highly original, imaginative, and enduring story for children, laced with humor and excitement.

Baum's approach to writing was strongly visual, and after the publication of *The Wonderful Wizard of Oz*, his theatrical bent took over. His musical extravaganza of 1902, *The Wizard of Oz*, was a great success, but it was written and staged for adults. The writing of the thirteen Oz sequels (all illustrated by John R. Neill) was influenced by Baum's simultaneous absorption with the stage and the new technology of film. It was through his investment in film that he lost the modest fortune he had earned with his early books, forcing him to concentrate on turning out SERIES BOOKS for children. Written under various pseudonyms, these included *The Boy Fortune Hunters in Alaska* (1908) by "Floyd Akers," *The Flying Girl* (1911) and *Mary Louise* (1916) by "Edith Van Dyne," and *Sam Steele's Adventures on Land and Sea* (1906) by "Capt. Hugh Fitzgerald."

The best books in the Oz series — after the first — are considered to be *The Marvelous Land of Oz* (1904), *Ozma of Oz* (1907), and the last one, *Glinda of Oz* (1920), which some regard, along with his 1901 story for boys, *The Master Key: An Electrical Tale,* as early SCIENCE FICTION. His wildly popular series of ten adventure stories for girls (1906–1915), which began with *Aunt Jane's Nieces,* was written under the pseudonym Edith Van Dyne and, like the Oz books, was continued by others after his death.

Baum set out to do two things in his writing for children: to entertain them and to write "modern" fairy tales, merging magic with technology in a world without violence or any emphasis on romantic love — a world solidly based on American idealism, virtues, and homely realism. In this he succeeded. S.L.R.

Bellairs, John

American mystery novelist, 1938–1991. The American MYSTERY writer and master storyteller John Bellairs has enthralled countless fans with his intriguing tales that pit ordinary characters against extraordinary situations. Bellairs's stories include all the trappings of the genre — haunted houses, coffins, bones, ghosts, and wizards — but they are distinguished by the use of what Bellairs calls "the common ordinary stuff — the bullies, the scaredy-cat Lewis, the grown-ups, the everyday incidents." Drawing from his own experience, Bellairs found that "writing seems to be a way of memorializing and transforming my own past. I write about the things I wish had happened to me when I was a kid."

Born in the small town of Marshall, Michigan, Bellairs turned his hometown into the setting of New Zebedee in *The House with a Clock in Its Walls* (1973), the novel that started his first series. Other places where he has lived are used as settings for later books. His characters, like the author, are intellectual, bookish loners who worry about finding friendship, and his protagonists are helped by an older relative or friend who offers wisdom, understanding, and more often than not a dose of eccentricity.

Bellairs's first frolicsome novel was the popular, well-received FANTASY *The Face in the Frost* (1969), which recounts the tale of two magicians and their attempt to stop a third sorcerer who has acquired a deadly book of spells.

With *The House with a Clock in Its Walls,* Bellairs achieved even greater popularity and established himself as one of the most compelling mystery writers for children. The book introduces Lewis, who goes to live with his Uncle Jonathan after his parents die in an accident. From the moment of his arrival, Lewis suspects that there is something strange about his uncle and Mrs. Zimmermann, the kindly next-door neighbor. When he discovers they are both witches, Lewis experiments with some magic forces, setting in motion a wild chase with two dead wizards that threatens to bring about the end of the world. In subsequent books, a common feature is the protagonists' accidental mishandling of magical properties.

Lewis returns in *The Letter, the Witch, and the Ring* (1976), which also features Mrs. Zimmermann and Lewis's cohort, Rose Rita Pottinger. With his second series, the Blue Figurine series, Bellairs introduced Johnny Dixon, his grandparents, and the cantankerous Professor Childermass, who confront a slew of ghosts and evil sorcerers. Johnny Dixon and Lewis reappear in a number of his books, which have some of the qualities of a series without repeating the same format.

When asked why he chose to write for children, Bellairs responded, "I have the imagination of a ten-year-old." Bellairs's work is marked by an adroit balance between tension and humor. Spooky tales move between the insecurities and foibles of his protagonists and the chilling descriptions of apparitions and evil enemies, providing one of the key dynamics in Bellairs's writing.

Bellairs's books will forever be linked with the distinctive black and white artwork of ED-WARD GOREY, whose illustrations capture perfectly the subtle humor and eerie nature of the author's mysteries. C.L.

Bemelmans, Ludwig

American author and artist, 1898–1962. Throughout his life, Ludwig Bemelmans saw himself, first and foremost, as a painter, despite his considerable success at writing for both children and adults. He wrote short stories, novels, articles, essays, POETRY, and reminiscences of all sorts, and he always wrote about what he *saw* — usually with great wit, charm, and honesty. He was forty-one years old when *Madeline* was published in 1939, but everything in the book was drawn from a child's point of view — the enormously tall and energetic teacher Miss Clavel, the twelve identically shaped little girls, the color, splash, and joy of the streets of Paris. Best of all were the simplicity and directness of his line.

Bemelmans emigrated to the United States from Germany in 1914, when he was sixteen. He had been raised in the Austrian Tyrols and in Bavaria and learned to speak French and later German. During his early childhood he lived in a hotel his father owned and managed, and later, in New York, he worked his way up in the hotel business to support himself. On the side he pursued what gave him the greatest pleasure — painting and drawing.

Bemelmans's first children's book, *Hansi* (1934), recounts a young boy's visit to his uncle's mountain home in the Austrian Tyrols; *The High World* (1954) is also an adventure set where Bemelmans grew up. These long storybooks, with half-page illustrations throughout, were similar in format to *The Golden Basket,* which was a Newbery Honor Book in 1937. In this story, two girls tour Bruges with their father, encountering one day twelve little girls out for a walk, one of whom is called Madeline. Bemelmans was an inveterate traveler, and it was a visit to Belgium with his wife, Madeline Freund, that inspired *The Golden Basket.*

His great success as an artist is that he con-veyed much childlike joy, energy, and spontaneity in his work. *Madeline* (1938), a Caldecott Honor Book, was followed by five other stories in a similar large, spacious format about the fearless little girl who always stepped out of line and found her way to adventure. *Madeline's Rescue* (1953) won the Caldecott Medal in 1954, and after that came *Madeline's Christmas in Texas* (1955), *Madeline and the Bad Hat* (1956), *Madeline and the Gypsies* (1959), and *Madeline in London* (1961). Of all Bemelmans's books for children, these are the ones that have stayed in print and won the loyalty of countless readers.

The original inspiration for *Madeline* was the convent where Bemelmans's mother was educated as a child, along with the author's own experience in boarding school, where he walked with his classmates in two straight lines. The story itself grew in Bemelmans's imagination as he recuperated from a biking accident in France; a little girl in the same rural hospital had just had her appendix out. The text for *Madeline* is brief, written in rhyming couplets, and the memorable opening lines are found in other Madeline books: "In an old house in Paris / that was covered with vines / lived twelve little girls in two straight lines."

Bemelmans wrote more than fifteen children's books and more than twenty for adults, including anecdotal collections about his years in the hotel business, diaries of his World War I experiences in the U.S. Army, and, later, writings about Paris, which he loved and which became his second home.

When Bemelmans was becoming established as a painter in New York, his work was exhibited and sold in galleries, and he found the public role of a gallery artist very unpleasant. But eventually he discovered a way to maintain his privacy and still have a wide audience for his work. In his Caldecott acceptance speech for *Madeline's Rescue,* he explained:

I looked for another way of painting, for privacy; for a fresh audience, vast and critical and remote, to whom I could address myself with great freedom. . . . I wanted to paint purely that which gave me pleasure

... and one day I found that the audience for that kind of painting was a vast reservoir of impressionists who did very good work themselves, who were very clear-eyed and capable of enthusiasm. I addressed myself to children. K.M.K.

Bierhorst, John

A merican folklorist, editor, and adapter of American Indian literature for children; linguist and translator, b. 1936. John Bierhorst has held a unique and respected position in the field of children's literature as an editor and a translator of stories, poems, and songs of American Indians. His reverence for his material and penchant for accuracy result in the impeccable presentation of the culture of a people in all its beauty, mystery, and humor.

Bierhorst was born in Boston, Massachusetts, and grew up in Ohio. He never encountered American Indian culture in any of the books he had as a child. In fact, his boyhood passion was his study of botany, and he spent countless hours classifying plants. He discovered he wanted to write when he was at Cornell University. His first writing job eventually earned him the money to travel, and it was in Peru that he heard the Quechua language and became aware of American Indian life and FOLKLORE. He began to study native cultures of America and was encouraged by his wife, Jane, a children's book designer, to edit his first collection of stories. The material in the book, *The Fire Plume* (1969), was collected by Henry Rowe Schoolcraft. One of his early books, *In the Trail of the Wind* (1971), is an anthology of songs, prayers, orations, and chants from forty languages of tribes of the Americas. As always, Bierhorst provided admirable notes on the tribes and languages represented.

In *The Hungry Woman: Myths and Legends of the Aztecs* (1984), his versions of the myths and legends are taken directly from the Nahuatl texts or from the earliest Spanish or French adaptations. Bierhorst compiled an Aztec-English dictionary in the course of his research on Aztec lit-erature. He also translated *Spirit Child: A Story of the Nativity from the Aztec* (1984). In 1985, *The Mythology of North America* was published, delineating the mythology described into eleven regions in the Americas. Bierhorst also concentrated on the Mayan people, in *The Monkey's Haircut and Other Stories Told by the Maya* (1986); and he published a source book on South America in *The Mythology of South America* in 1988. He concentrated on the Iroquois in *The Woman Who Fell from the Sky: The Iroquois Story of Creation* (1993), a PICTURE BOOK; and on the Pueblo in *Is My Friend at Home? Pueblo Fireside Tales* (2001), illustrated by WENDY WATSON.

Bierhorst is a member of the American Folklore Society and the American Anthropological Association. He has published scholarly articles in publications such as the *Journal of American Folklore* and the *Bulletin of Research in the Humanities*. He has also received grants from several agencies, including the National Endowment for the Humanities. His translation of eight tales of CHARLES PERRAULT from the 1697 text, in *The Glass Slipper* (1981), was praised as another example of accuracy in translation, research, and documentation. He has also written a study of American Indian music, *A Cry from the Earth* (1992). S.H.H.

Biography

C arlyle observed that "a well-written Life is almost as rare as a well-spent one." Emerson maintained that "there is properly no history; only biography." And George Eliot commented that "biographies generally are a disease of English literature." All three quotations could well describe the evolving nature of biography for children.

Probably the earliest biographical efforts were inscriptions on some type of monument, still a popular device, carried to gargantuan proportions on Mount Rushmore. Later, storytellers, minstrels, and poets celebrated heroes through the oral tradition. Commemorating greatness dictated certain conventions in style and content: repetition of key phrases is typical of ballads; preternatural circumstances of the subject's birth, lack of information about his adolescence, and mysterious elements attendant on his demise are characteristic of hero stories. Although one of the precursors of biography, the art of storytelling — of narrative construction — often ignored in formulaic treatments, is a significant element in literary biography.

The move from commemoration to didacticism seems inevitable. If legends of heroes indicated virtues peculiar to a particular nation, legends of saints, recorded in medieval monasteries, offered scope for teaching ethical concepts and numerous subjects for emulation. The Victorian period saw renewed emphasis on exemplary lives and avoidance of the unseemly — a view that dominated selection of subjects for children's books until after the 1960s. These two impulses, the commemorative and the didactic, are still functioning, particularly in the children's book field.

Until the mid-1970s, biography was the stepchild among the genres of children's literature. Not that there were too few but rather that there were too few that qualified as literature, let alone as good biography. In various manifestations such as fictionalized accounts of famous childhoods, encyclopedic compilations of facts about "worthy" lives, or cut-and-paste versions of books written originally for adults, these so-called biographies enjoyed a kind of half-life. Adults found them useful; children read them. After all, they were harmless — or so popular theories had it — and they were inspirational. But as children's literature came under scrutiny as an academic discipline in the 1960s, shortcomings in biographical writing for the young became more apparent. In 1973, writing in *Top of the News*, Patrick Groff entitled an article on the misuses of biography for educational or bibliotherapeutic purposes "Biography: The Bad or the Bountiful." Emphasis on nonliterary applications of biography, he maintained, encouraged the proliferation of contrived, poorly written books, unacceptable as literature. Earlier, in 1972, in *A New Look at Children's Literature*, written with William Anderson, Groff not

only critically examined biography but also included an annotated bibliography, complied by Ruth Robinson, of acceptable books. Among these were *Abraham Lincoln* (1939), written by INGRI and EDGAR PARIN D'AULAIRE, a PICTURE BOOK and winner of the 1940 Caldecott Medal; Aliki Brandenberg's *A Weed Is a Flower* (1965), an introduction to the life of George Washington Carver for the primary grades; *The Walls of Windy Troy: The Biography of Heinrich Schliemann* (1960), written by Marjorie Braymer; *Tom Paine, Revolutionary* (1969), written by Olivia Coolidge; *George Washington's World* (1941), a comparative history written by Genevieve Stump Foster; and *Langston Hughes: A Biography* (1968), written by MILTON MELTZER. William L. Shirer's *The Rise and Fall of Adolf Hitler* (1961) was included, a World Landmark biography that demonstrates that not all books in a series should be categorically dismissed. Absent from Robinson's compilation were two Newbery medalists: Cornelia Meigs's *Invincible Louisa* (1933), considered dull by some critics because it failed to re-create the subject's personality, and *Daniel Boone* (1939), written by JAMES DAUGHERTY and criticized for stereotyping American Indians. Among the selections, however, were two titles criticized by others for racist elements, both Newbery Medal winners: *Amos Fortune, Free Man* (1950), written by Elizabeth Yates, the story of an eighteenth-century New England slave who later bought his own freedom, and *I, Juan de Pareja* (1965), written by Elizabeth Borton de Trevino, a fictionalized account of the relationship between the Spanish painter Velázquez and the slave who longed to be an artist.

Most titles on the bibliography in Groff's book were for older readers; some, such as Ann Petry's *Tituba of Salem Village* (1964), might be more accurately classified as HISTORICAL FICTION. Clearly, there were not many examples of well-written biography, particularly for younger readers. Few books for this audience approached the integrity of ESTHER FORBES's *America's Paul Revere* (1946), illustrated by LYND WARD, a reconstruction of her Pulitzer Prize–winning work.

Then came JEAN FRITZ, and the picture changed dramatically. Already praised for her historical novels *Brady* (1960) and *The Cabin Faced West* (1958), Fritz combined the storyteller's art with the discipline of the historian in writing biography for preadolescents as well as for readers in their early teens. She launched a new era in approaching the past — not as a maker of myths or perpetuator of stereotypes — but as a joyous explorer, keenly interested in the human condition, certainly a prime requisite for a biographer and historian. In books such as *What's the Big Idea, Ben Franklin?* (1976) and *Traitor, the Case of Benedict Arnold* (1981), she provided examples in books for children not only of what biography is but of what it could be. That biography has now become one of the more exciting genres in children's book publishing is due in large part to her influence. We still have the made-for-school projects, textbook-style accounts of famous lives, but there is now a considerable body of biographical writing worthy to be examined by literary standards and in relation to the historical development of the genre.

Another factor may be renewed interest in and heightened standards for biography in general. Because children's books tend to reflect rather than originate literary trends, quite likely the art of biographical writing as practiced by Lytton Strachey in *Eminent Victorians* (1918), further developed by Leon Edel in his study *Literary Biography* (1973), and manifested in books such as David McCullough's *Truman* (1992) has created a climate in which writers like RUSSELL FREEDMAN, Jean Fritz, and Albert Marrin can be appreciated. Biographies such as Tamara Hovey's *A Mind of Her Own: A Life of the Writer George Sand* (1977) would have been considered too risqué in the 1940s and 1950s. VIRGINIA HAMILTON's *Paul Robeson: The Life and Times of a Free Black Man* (1974) required a freer political climate than prevailed in earlier decades.

To reach a wider audience while acknowledging differences in experience and interest as well as the relatively limited number of competent practitioners, Jo Carr in her essay "What Do We Do About Bad Biographies?" (1982) advocated,

among other approaches, using autobiographies, historical fiction, diaries, and journals. From a practical perspective, she is correct. But strictly speaking, these are not biographies. Discussion of literary genres as literature requires that definitions be clear and distinctions drawn. There are many forms of writing related to biography, including autobiographies, diaries, and letters — and yet they differ from the observations and interpretations of a third person. Wonderful as they are, books such as Erik Blegvad's *Self-Portrait* (1979); *The Endless Steppe* (1968), ESTHER HAUTZIG's memoirs of growing up as an exile in Siberia during World War II; and Ferdinand Monjo's *Letters to Horseface: Being the Story of Wolfgang Amadeus Mozart's Journey to Italy, 1769–1770, When He Was a Boy of Fourteen* (1975) require somewhat different criteria for evaluation than Albert Marrin's *Unconditional Surrender: U. S. Grant and the Civil War* (1994). Although biography and its associated forms are frequently treated as equivalent to historical documents, this blurs valuable distinctions and is a disservice to young readers.

A brief overview of format, subject, text components, and style affords insight into some of the current trends in biography for children. Picture book biographies focusing on a specific event and brief, copiously illustrated lives appeal to a generation accustomed to visual presentations. Both *The Glorious Flight: Across the Channel with Louis Blériot* (1983), written and illustrated by ALICE and MARTIN PROVENSEN, and *Flight: The Journey of Charles Lindbergh* (1991), written by Robert Burleigh and illustrated by Mike Wimmer, stress pivotal episodes in the subjects' lives. DIANE STANLEY's *Peter the Great* (1986) and, with Peter Vennema, *Shaka, King of the Zulus* (1988) present accessible portraits of personalities not usually found in children's books. Collective biographies, the best of which have a thematic organization, are exemplified by Russell Freedman's stunning *Indian Chiefs* (1987). Already mentioned are the proliferation of series on specific themes. Although many are poor, others deserve attention. Particularly interesting are a number of series about artists. The series Portraits of Women Artists for

Children includes Robyn Montana Turner's *Mary Cassatt* (1992), a picture book biography; the series First Impressions: Introductions to Art, for preadolescents, such as Avis Berman's lively *James McNeill Whistler* (1993), incorporates a considerable amount of art history into readable narratives; and the series A Weekend With . . . features diverse personalities such as Picasso, Renoir, and Velázquez. The Weekend books weave factual material into imagined monologues with which the subject entertains a young visitor; not strictly biography in the classic sense, they offer creatively constructed interpretations of their subjects' lives. As these series indicate, the range of topics for biography has expanded considerably since the 1970s.

Given the possibilities in form and content, what should be expected of biographies? While biographies for children may be selective in the years of a life to be chronicled, certainly accuracy, honest interpretation, and insight should be no less in biographies for the young than in those for adults. Softening reality to the point of distortion is unacceptable. Nor should these works be stylistically inferior. Given the resources available, we expect documentation as thorough as Albert Marrin's; we applaud the skill with which Russell Freedman has allowed details to reveal the subject, as in *Lincoln: A Photobiography* (1987); and we celebrate Jean Fritz's remarkable ability to transform facts into an engrossing narrative. Above all, the biography, whatever the subject, should suggest that it was written with passionate attention and intense curiosity for, as Jean Fritz has stated: "We cannot afford to forget that the past is not just a series of events; it is *people* doing things."

M.M.B.

Blake, Quentin

British illustrator and author of fiction and poetry, b. 1932. Quentin Blake began drawing for *Punch* and other British magazines while still in his teens. After attending Downing College in Cambridge and the London University Institute of Education, he took life classes at the Chelsea School of Art and soon after began to illustrate children's books. As an award-winning illustrator of two hundred books, Blake is a visiting tutor at the Royal College of Art in London, where he was head of the illustration department for ten years.

Among the many esteemed writers and poets whose books Blake has illustrated are JOAN AIKEN, RUSSELL HOBAN, MARGARET MAHY, EDWARD EAGER, Michael Rosen, and John Yeoman. Blake and Hoban received the Whitbread Literary Award for *How Tom Beat Captain Najork and His Hired Sportsmen* (1974), in which Blake's jaunty illustrations perfectly suit the story about Tom, whose aunt summons Captain Najork and his hired sportsmen to teach the boy to stop fooling around. Another made-in-heaven pairing was Blake's illustrations and Margaret Mahy's text in *Nonstop Nonsense* (1989), a collection of comic poems and stories enhanced by Blake's madcap drawings. In Yeoman's *Wild Washerwomen* (1979), Blake's art extends the understated humor of the narrative about seven discontented washerwomen who go on a rowdy rampage until they meet their match in seven woodcutters. They all then marry and share a contented life in which both men and women wash clothing and cut wood with gusto.

Blake is perhaps most widely recognized among young readers for his long-term collaboration with the popular but sometimes controversial author ROALD DAHL, with whom he produced a number of books, including *The Enormous Crocodile* (1978), *The Twits* (1980), *The B.F.G.* (1982), and another Whitbread Award winner, *The Witches* (1983).

Blake's accomplishments as an author-illustrator have also been highly praised by critics and appreciated by children. The Kate Greenaway Medal was given to *Mister Magnolia* (1980), in which the utter absurdity of Blake's nonsense poem about a man with one shoe is further magnified by his hilarious color illustrations. In another PICTURE BOOK, *Mrs. Armitage on Wheels* (1987), Blake has told a cumulative story about an elderly woman who continues to add accessories to her bicycle until, inevitably, it crashes in a riotous ending. The art depicts a proper-looking Mrs. Armitage, who sits primly atop her bike and then, following its sad demise, dons a pair of roller skates.

The unique appeal of Blake's art lies in his ability to create pictures that provide information not explicit in the story. The physical stances, facial expressions, and actions of his characters go beyond the text to tell the reader even more about their individual attitudes and personalities. Blake's spare sketches are deceptive, for their appearance of having been hastily scribbled in a helter-skelter manner conceals the many hours spent in their planning. The exaggerated and zany sense of humor conveyed in all of Blake's art is something no reader, child or adult, can fail to see and appreciate.

J.M.B.

Block, Francesca Lia

American author, b. 1962. Called one of the "coolest people in L.A." by *Buzz* magazine, California-born author Francesca Lia Block consistently draws material from her glitzy Hollywood background. Growing up a would-be writer in this fantasy-driven world — with a poet and a painter for parents — Block learned to create fresh, cinematic characterizations and stories to which young urban readers could relate. Studying the novelist Gabriel García Márquez and the poet Hilda Doolittle (HD) at UCLA and UC–Berkeley, she fine-tuned her sophisticated style. Discovered by legendary editor/author Charlotte Zolotow shortly after Block graduated from Berkeley, Block produced her first YOUNG ADULT NOVEL, *Weetzie Bat*, in 1989. Through the eyes of Weetzie, a spirited young Los Angeles native, and her gay friend Dirk, this quirky novel thoughtfully examines the hopes and dreams of young people perceived as "different" yet who nevertheless yearn for purpose and true love, as most everyone does. Block has since crafted several sequels: *Witch Baby* (1991), *Cherokee Bat and the Goat Guys* (1992), *Missing Angel Juan* (1993), and *Baby Be-Bop* (1995). She has also addressed edgy topics such as drug addiction and eating disorders in the novel *The Hanged Man* (1994) and in her signature anthologies, including *Girl Goddess #9* (1996).

Unflinching in her depiction of real teens in surreal scenarios, Block has acknowledged that her books are often censored. But she doesn't let this issue limit her creativity. If parents feel her books are not appropriate for their children, Block can respect the decision, especially since becoming a parent herself in 2000. But such decisions don't influence what she writes; instead, she considers her readers and supporters, who communicate through letters and e-mail. Though called a writer for young adults, Block resists such categorization, and the crossover appeal of her books is evident in the many letters she receives from readers in their twenties and thirties. Her loyal readers are drawn to the special atmosphere Block creates: a blend of gritty realism (such as the chain-smoking high school senior, middle-aged drag queen, and rock star in *Violet and Claire*, 1999), FANTASY elements including fairies and myths (as expressed in *I Was a Teenage Fairy*, 1998, and *The Rose and The Beast: Fairy Tales Retold*, 2000), and the voices of quirky narrators (such as Barbie and My Secret Agent Lover Man). And though each book has been heralded as a true original, Block believes that her works exhibit common themes from her personal philosophy: the importance of love, acceptance, kindness, and facing both darkness and light, as well as the power of personal expression. Whispered between the lines, these messages connect Block's wildly original pop literature to universal concerns. K.M.H.

Bloor, Edward

American author, b. 1950. Edward Bloor is one of the most exciting new voices to emerge in YOUNG ADULT FICTION. Born in Trenton, New Jersey, he played soccer there from the age of eight until he entered college at Fordham. A former middle school and high school teacher, he lives in Florida with his wife and two children, where he works as an editor. His books, *Tangerine* (1997) and *Crusader* (1999), are distinguished by their suburban Florida settings, underdog protagonists, and a plethora of social and environmental concerns. His books juggle myriad subplots — almost too many — but he sustains interest by creating a brooding atmosphere of danger, menace, and mystery. His plots inexorably lead to a stunning series of revelations and climaxes.

Tangerine tells the story of Paul Fisher, a legally blind seventh-grader who has just moved to Tangerine, Florida. There, his family confronts an assortment of natural disasters — lightning storms, underground muck fires, and giant sinkholes (one of which swallows his school). But freaky environmental problems are the least of Paul's concerns. At his new school, he must fit in with a tougher crowd and find his place on the championship soccer team. At home, his parents are too preoccupied with their own (often petty) concerns to notice what Paul has known for years: his older brother, Erik, is out of control. As Erik begins to terrorize Paul's new friends, not only does the truth about Erik come out, but so does the secret of Paul's blindness. *Tangerine* is chock full of issues for further thought and reflection, such as class and ethnic divisions, the unchecked sprawl of suburbia, and family dysfunction.

These concerns also figure prominently in Bloor's second novel, *Crusader*. Fifteen-year-old Roberta Ritter's mother was murdered seven years ago, and though Roberta still lives with her father, she doesn't see much of him. She spends much of her time working in her uncle's arcade in a failing shopping mall. But her life is not empty. She enjoys her journalism class with a passion, and she has diverse friends and acquaintances, including an elderly Holocaust survivor and a young Arab American. Hate crimes accompany the arrival of a violent new virtual-reality game at the mall, and as Roberta investigates the situation, she ultimately finds more than she bargained for: the shocking truth about her father's role in her mother's death.

Disturbing family secrets, smoldering like embers, lie at the heart of these novels, and as their protagonists come to learn these painful truths, they also gain a greater understanding of their own identities. Bloor successfully juggles numerous subplots, external action, and psychological insight in stories that interweave two series: MYSTERY thrillers and coming-of-age stories. Edward Bloor truly is a writer to watch.

J.H.

Blumberg, Rhoda

American nonfiction writer, b. 1917. When *Commodore Perry in the Land of the Shogun* (1985) received the Boston Globe–Horn Book Award for nonfiction, Rhoda Blumberg recalled how her job as scriptwriter and researcher for CBS radio had developed her taste for information: "Nonfiction proved to be as gripping as fiction — a fantastic discovery."

When Blumberg started writing INFORMATION BOOKS for children as well as for adults, her books covered a wide variety of subjects. A series of professional travel guides eventually led to the publication of two children's books — *The First Travel Guide to the Moon* (1980) and *The First Travel Guide to the Bottom of the Sea* (1983) — both of which gained recognition from science educators. Blumberg then began to focus on history. *Commodore Perry in the Land of the Shogun* traces U.S. efforts to make contact with Japan in the mid–nineteenth century, a time when the Japanese and the Americans knew very little about each other. Part of a general trend toward engaging, eye-catching nonfiction, this Newbery Honor Book was followed by *The Incredible Journey of Lewis and Clark* (1987), an account of the expedition to the Pacific Coast headed by the two explorers from 1804 to 1806. In *The Great American Gold Rush* (1989), Blumberg wrote about the people who flocked to California from 1848 to 1852 in search of riches. *The Remarkable Voyages of Captain Cook* (1991) chronicles the British explorer's three journeys to the Pacific Ocean between 1768 and 1780; *Full Steam Ahead: The Race to Build a Transcontinental Railroad* (1996) tells the exciting story of the development of the American railway system.

Blumberg's work reveals her fascination with topics that straddle the boundary between fiction and fact; her history books show how travel and exploration have helped establish facts where only legend and speculation existed before. For instance, in Patagonia, South America, Captain Cook met normal humans, not the expected twelve-foot giants. Lewis and Clark came across numerous animals unknown to them, but they never did sight the giant sloths or live mammoths they thought they might find.

Good design is a prominent feature of Blumberg's large-format history books, which have uncluttered pages abundantly illustrated with historical material selected by Blumberg herself; for example, more than seventy pictures from fourteen collections enhance *The Remarkable Voyages of Captain Cook*.

The books also demonstrate other qualities vital to good information books. Striving for a balanced presentation, Blumberg has displayed an increasing sensitivity to the viewpoints of the peoples encountered by the explorers and travelers she describes. Her passion for research sends her to numerous primary and secondary sources, all recorded in thorough bibliographies and chapter notes. She has said, "I . . . willingly endure monotonous diaries and poorly written manuscripts when they reward me with surprising information about people." For *The Great American Gold Rush*, she dug through letters and diaries for more than a year. Blumberg complements her research with skilled use of the storyteller's art; she enjoys language and has the ability to select and tell audience-pleasing stories. As she remarked, upon receiving the John and Patricia Beatty Award for *The Great American Gold Rush*, "Stories are enchanting, and for me true stories — from history — are the most enchanting." M.F.S.

Blume, Judy

American novelist, b. 1938. Few authors have equaled Judy Blume's popularity, whether one judges by the sales of her books, all of which seem to stay in print *ad infinitum*, or by the number of awards chosen by children, primarily in statewide contests.

Her first two books, *The One in the Middle Is the Green Kangaroo* (1969), which deals with the problems of being a middle child, and *Iggie's House* (1970), the story of a black family that moves into a white neighborhood, were lightly humorous despite the fact that they dealt — realistically — with serious problems. Blume's third book, *Are You There, God? It's Me, Margaret* (1970), brought her national attention: some raves, some disparaging frowns. It was in this story that her readers first saw the author's compassion and sympathy and her conviction that the universal problems of adolescents should be reflected, with dignity and understanding, in the books they read.

"I think I write the kind of books," she said in a statement for *Something About the Author*, "I would have liked to read when I was young." This followed a comment about the fact that there were no books that mirrored her own interests and feelings when Blume was a child. Certainly eleven-year-old Margaret, in *Are You There, God?*, is a prototypical preteen, worried about how long it will be before she develops breasts and begins menstruating. She is, as the title indicates, devout — but she's not sure exactly how she should worship, with one parent who's Jewish and one who's not. The religious conflict incurred no observable wrath; the inclusion of sexual and physical concerns did upset many adults. Girls tended to be delighted at finding topics about which almost all preteens are concerned.

The same kind of percipient concern for the problems of teenage boys appears in *Then Again, Maybe I Won't* (1971). It describes thirteen-year-old Tony's adjustment to change, his realization that his parents are social climbers, and his embarrassment at showing sexual arousal (he drapes his coat over his arm and holds it in front of him — just in case). While the book deals with specific problems, it addresses Tony's growing sensitivity and maturity.

In *Deenie* (1973) and *Blubber* (1974) Blume explored young people's intense concern with their physical appearance and their reactions to their own physical limitations and those of others. Deenie's mother wants her pretty twelve-year-old daughter to become a model, and she's appalled when a test reveals the reason Deenie moves oddly, a peculiarity spotted by an agency interviewer. Deenie is also upset at learning that she has scoliosis and will have to wear a back brace for four years. She finds that her friends won't desert her just because she's "different," a predictable and happy conclusion to the secret fears of being unpleasantly set apart. But the author is realistic about the fact that such acceptance doesn't always happen, as is evident in her next story. *Blubber* is painfully honest in showing how cruel children can be to each other and in illustrating group dynamics. Linda is the fifth-grade scapegoat, even though she's not the only fat girl in the class. One classmate is sympathetic, but she's one of the few who stop persecuting Linda. In this book Blume decided to include the sometimes rough language that she heard fifth-graders using. But the author yielded to compromise: "bad" language stayed in if it contributed to plot or character development; otherwise it was removed.

Certainly Blume's most controversial book has been *Forever . . .* (1975). Those who objected were not impressed, as were many critics and parents (and young people), by the author's advocacy of sexual responsibility and her recognition of developmental and physical needs. The characters Katherine and Michael are in love; their feelings are passionate and romantic, and they become lovers. Kath, who tells the story, feels wholly committed — but she finds, when she takes a summer camp job at her parents' insistence, that she is attracted to another man. That's the end of "forever." Moralists felt that the lovers should have been punished; some of them felt that the book encouraged sexual activity. Other critics praised the candor of the story and its dialogue, characterization, and depiction of familial relationships.

In two novels, Blume's protagonists are affected by their parents' marital problems. In *Just as Long as We're Together* (1987) Stephanie's parents have begun a trial separation, and she's therefore particularly vulnerable when she runs into a problem with peer relationships. Parental separation also causes grief in *It's Not the End of the World* (1972), but the main character here admits to herself that the hostility would still be there if Dad did come back. Always concerned about personal relationships, Blume has told a touching and credible story of loss, adjustment, and the slow healing process that can be helped by friendship, love, and patience in *Tiger Eyes* (1983), in which the father has been shot in a robbery at his convenience store.

While most of her books for teenage readers have moments of humor even when they deal with serious issues, it is in her books for younger readers of MIDDLE-GRADE FICTION that Blume is at her amusing best. Many of the titles for this age range are linked: *Tales of a Fourth Grade Nothing* (1972) is a chapter-by-chapter wail of comic despair from Peter, whose two-year-old brother, Fudge, is his greatest trial — for example, Fudge gulps down Peter's turtle. The sequels, *Superfudge* (1980) and *Fudge-a-Mania* (1990), are equally ebullient and equally popular. In the last, Peter's parents share a summer house with the parents of Sheila, Peter's archenemy and the protagonist of *Otherwise Known as Sheila the Great* (1972).

For Blume fans, there is a special appeal in *Starring Sally J. Freedman as Herself* (1977) because it seems so clearly a reflection of the author's childhood. The wildly imaginative, highly histrionic heroine is both beguiling and amusing; the book's episodic structure makes it less cohesive than most of Blume's writing, but readers have been captivated. In Sally they see the seeds of the writer who has been their advocate, who has broken barriers of taboos about what subjects and what language are appropriate for children's books. "Perceptive, funny, sad, and honest," one reviewer said. It is all those aspects that have made Judy Blume loved and defended by her readers. Contributing to her own long record of defending the right to better access to information on serious issues, she established The Kids Fund in 1981; the organization has made many grants each year to nonprofit organizations for the development of programs that address such needs. It is for that courageous honesty that she was given the Carl Sandburg

Freedom to Read Award in 1984 and the American Civil Liberties Union Award in 1986. Z.S.

Board Books

Board books are a relatively new phenomenon in the world of children's trade publishing. Responding to a perceived need for books suitable for babies and toddlers, the first of a modern generation of cardboard-paged books appeared in 1979 with the publication of ROSEMARY WELLS's series about a rabbit named Max. One in a set of four, *Max's Ride* is a disarmingly simple story about Max's thrilling adventure the day his baby carriage careens out of control. The strong visual appeal of the uncluttered illustrations, which are placed on bright, solid-colored backgrounds, grabs children's attention, and the understated, economically phrased text adds humor and suspense that guarantees requests for repeated readings.

In the 1980s the trickle of board books turned into a flood, astutely timed to coincide with the decade's baby boom, when many affluent, highly educated professionals who had postponed childbearing until later in life and had a strong interest in the future success of their children put much of their considerable disposable income into educational materials and books. A number of award-winning children's authors and illustrators, such as LEO LIONNI, PETER SPIER, and ERIC CARLE, produced board books during this time.

A large number of new titles continued to appear in the 1990s, although most resemble successful books from the plethora of board books that appeared in the previous decade. The format continues to be popular with public libraries and the book-buying public because the books can withstand repeated abuse at the hands of very young children. Echoing an earlier phenomenon, authors and illustrators who have already established their reputations in other arenas of children's book publishing continue to try their hand at board books. Martha Alexander (Lily and Willy Board Books, 1991), Frank Asch (Moonbear Books, 1993), Lucy Cousins (Animal Board Books, 1991), and CYNTHIA RYLANT (The Everyday Books, 1993) are among the writers who have made recent contributions of note to this popular field.

A new and sensible trend that began in the early 1990s is the publication in board book format of titles that were originally successful as traditional books. Interest by babies and toddlers in books such as RUTH KRAUSS's *Carrot Seed* (1945, 1993), MARGARET WISE BROWN's *Goodnight Moon* (1947, 1991), Charles Shaw's *It Looked like Spilt Milk* (1947, 1993), and BILL MARTIN JR.'s *Chicka Chicka Boom Boom* (1989, 1993) has resulted in welcome board book versions of these titles. Alexandra Day's nearly wordless stories about a Rottweiler named Carl, such as *Carl's Masquerade* (1993), have also been released as board books.

Some of the most frequently encountered physical features of cardboard books include rounded page corners for the safety of small children who are often unsteady on their feet and might fall while holding the book; pages that are coated so they can be wiped clean; and small size for the comfort of the tiny hands that carry them. A typical book measures no more than 6 inches square, although some titles have appeared that are as large as 8½ by 9½ inches.

Many board books are wordless, so that adults can use the pictures to stimulate discussion with a child. TANA HOBAN's wordless *What Is It?* (1985) offers elegant color photographs of familiar objects — such as a shoe, a spoon, and a set of keys — for a child and adult to name and talk about together. Hoban has made use of recent research in the field of child development in her stylish illustrations for *Black on White* (1993) and *White on Black* (1993), which showcase high-contrast black or white shapes against the opposite color background; scientists indicate that children are able to focus on high-contrast pictures at a very young age. Other titles, such as Valerie Greeley's set about animals, feature delicate but realistic painting of animals in naturalistic settings. In *Field Animals* (1984), for example, squirrels and rabbits appear amid flowering plants and trees and provide a first introduction to nature for a young child.

Some board books for this audience do include words and a simple plot, as seen in Wells's Max series. Caldecott Honor recipient NANCY TAFURI's successful introduction to colors, *In a Red House* (1987), features a narrative that is a model of economy: "A purple chair / an orange ball / a brown bear / a yellow dog / a white duck / green blocks / a pink bunny / and a gray truck / are all in my own blue room!" The uncomplicated, brightly colored objects outlined in black take up most of the space on the book's white pages. In *I Hear* (1986), HELEN OXENBURY introduced the concepts of listening and sounds as a round-faced, overall-clad toddler experiences a bird's song, a baby's wail, and a telephone's ring. One word, such as *bird, telephone,* and *baby,* accompanies each two-page spread. *Tickle, Tickle* (1987) is one in a set of four books by Oxenbury that features a multicultural cast of toddlers, a growing trend in children's books. Four young children with a variety of skin colors cavort in the mud and clean up in the bath; a delightful rhyme accompanies joyous illustrations that pulse with the energy generated by toddlers playing.

Recent research demonstrates the importance of children's early years in their future educational success. Parents, teachers, and librarians who embrace these findings begin sharing books with children when they are infants. Their continued quest for high-quality board books — books that match content with format by limiting text and using developmentally appropriate illustrations or photographs — keeps publishers, authors, and illustrators searching for fresh ideas. This push toward providing materials for infants and toddlers has also influenced traditional hardcover publishing. Books by author-illustrators such as Jim Arnosky and Douglas Florian incorporate some of the genre's best stylistic features, such as large print, uncomplicated illustrations, and brief stories, in books for slightly older children. Adults who choose children's books can expect to see a continuing trend of cross-fertilization among books for various ages of children, as those who produce board books heed the needs of very young children. E.G.F.

Bond, Felicia

American author and illustrator, b. 1954. Felicia Bond was a preschooler when she decided to become an artist. She liked to draw houses, animals, and people in her family. Her parents encouraged her to draw, but it was a beam of sunlight that became her motivation and inspiration.

When I was five . . . I was standing in the doorway of my bedroom in the late afternoon. The room was dark, except for a brilliant but soft beam of sunlight filtering through the window . . . the red leather window seat glowed a rich, dark color. I was moved somehow, and decided I had to capture that feeling of poignancy and time passing. Art seemed to me to be the best way to do this. My feelings about light and what it represents have not changed.

The second child in a family of four brothers and two sisters, Bond was born in Yokohama, Japan, where her father, an American civil engineer, worked. Two years later the family moved to Texas, where Bond earned a degree in fine arts from the University of Texas at Austin in 1976. After graduation she moved briefly to Canada, where she became interested in illustrating folk and fairy tales. She studied books with illustrations by Edmund Dulac, Kay Nielsen, and ARTHUR RACKHAM, which her mother, an English teacher, had given her. Fascinated with their art and that of Errol Le Cain, JEAN DE BRUNHOFF, and LUDWIG BEMELMANS, Bond put together a portfolio of her own work, including botanical illustrations from her seven years of work for the Spring Branch Science Center in Houston. Only weeks after she moved back to New York City a few years later, she had a contract to do a science PICTURE BOOK.

The portfolio grew, as did offers to illustrate more books, but Bond was interested in inventing stories of her own. With encouragement from an editor of the publishing house where she was working, in 1980 Bond wrote and illustrated her first book, *Poinsettia and Her Family,* a childlike story about an engaging family of porcine characters. The experience was so engrossing that Bond found she was hooked — on children's books.

In 1985 Bond illustrated an amusing story about a mouse and a cookie, *If You Give a Mouse a Cookie,* written by Laura Joffe Numeroff. The huge success of the book sparked three more animal/food stories: *If You Give a Moose a Muffin* (1991), *If You Give a Pig a Pancake* (1998), and a spinoff, *If You Take a Mouse to the Movies* (2000). Perhaps the ultimate measure of popularity is the number of times a book title appears in a favorite comic strip. Twice Charles Schulz featured *If You Give a Mouse a Cookie* in his *Peanuts* comic strip, a true compliment to Bond, who describes Schulz as "the artist whose work influenced me early on. His work is precise, alive, and very specific in its movements and expressions of the characters' bodies and faces. I devoured all his books from first grade on and I have to credit Schulz as one very specific and powerful influence."

The success of *If You Give a Mouse a Cookie* didn't keep Bond from writing and illustrating more of her own books, which include *Poinsettia and the Firefighters* (1984), *Wake Up, Vladimir* (1987), *The Halloween Play* (1983, 1999), and *Tumble Bumble* (1996). When collaborating with Numeroff, Bond's capricious, brightly colored, cartoonlike drawings form a perfect foil for the whimsical, energetic narratives. Together they delight children and adults with their puckish humor and improbable scenarios. J.C.

Illustration by Peggy Fortnum from *Paddington Abroad* (1972), by Michael Bond.

Bond, Michael

British author, b. 1926. It is almost impossible to think of Michael Bond without also thinking of his most famous character, Paddington Bear, so inescapably linked are the two. Bond's first published writing, however, was not for children.

Born and raised in Berkshire, England, Bond began writing while serving with the British army in the Middle East. His first short story published, Bond decided to become a writer. As he has said, "I amassed a vast quantity of rejection slips but also had articles published. I turned to writing radio plays, then television. At my agent's suggestion, I began to write things for children." Such "things" turned into a collection of short stories about a small bear named Paddington, published in 1958 in England as a book, *A Bear Called Paddington,* which chronicles the discovery by the Brown family of an English-speaking bear from Darkest Peru at the Paddington train station and Paddington's gradual assimilation into the Browns' London household.

Paddington's appeal came not only from the hilarious situations and mishaps in which he found himself — from being buried under groceries on his first supermarket trip to discovering cheese soufflés and pickled onions at a fancy restaurant — but also from Peggy Fortnum's pen and ink sketches, which capture Paddington's bewitching charm and combination "little boy/ small bear" character.

Paddington's adventures continued with the publication of *More About Paddington* (1961), *Paddington Helps Out* (1961), *Paddington at Large* (1963), *Paddington at Work* (1967), *Paddington Goes to Town* (1968), *Paddington Takes the Air* (1971), *Paddington Abroad* (1972), and *Paddington on Top* (1975). In each book — actually a compilation of seven distinct stories joined by a general theme — Paddington Bear bumbles delightfully from one absurd escapade to the next. While Bond believes his bear to be a typical English character — as English as Mary Poppins and Peter Pan — the books have been translated into more than ten languages. "Obviously," Bond has said, "Paddington-type situations happen to people all over."

In 1967 Bond introduced a new series and a new character in *Here Comes Thursday.* Thursday, an orphaned mouse, enters the lives of the Cupboardosities, a family of mice who live in the church organ loft and run the cheese store. His adventures continue in *Thursday Rides Again* (1969) and *Thursday in Paris* (1971). The Thursday series — noted for its fluent style and light humor — lacks the contrast between engaging animal behavior and realistic human behavior that adds a nonsensical note to the Paddington Bear stories.

Continuing with his tradition of orphaned animals and adoptive families, Bond introduced the guinea pig Olga da Polga in *The Tales of Olga da Polga* (1972) and continued her story in *Olga Meets Her Match* (1975), *Olga Carries On* (1977), and *Olga Takes Charge* (1983). Olga was, in fact, a real member of Bond's family — she arrived as a birthday present for Bond's daughter — and he has claimed that while some of Olga's tales are partly based on actual events, "others are figments of Olga's imagination." Olga's appeal lies in her exuberant zest for life, her penchant for inventing stories, and her complacent confidence in her own charms.

The enduring popularity of Bond's characters may be due to his philosophy about writing children's books: if you plan to write *for* children, "you run the risk of writing down." Rather than condescendingly treating his readers to quaint animal stories, Bond's books, specifically the Paddington Bear series, recognize the everyday worries of small, accident-prone children and treat their fears with compassion, wit, and laughter. M.I.A.

Bonsall, Crosby

American author and illustrator, 1921–1995. Beginning readers have cheerfully and enthusiastically embraced the work of Crosby Barbara Newell Bonsall, most notably her I Can Read MYSTERIES, for many years, and her books continue to appeal to new generations of young readers.

Born in New York City, Bonsall received her professional training at the American School of Design and the New York University School of Architecture before beginning a career in advertising. Later she was to say, "All that commercial art, advertising copy, and the year I spent at New York University of School of Architecture struggling with sculpting and design were not lost. Writing copy to space teaches you a discipline which I find handy in writing books for children just learning to read. I've never used a controlled vocabulary — I just keep the consumer in mind." It is this focus on the child that has allowed Bonsall's books to retain their appeal. Her characters are real children — children who interact with humor and charm but also with a certain amount of temper, rivalry, and frustration so commonly found at the preschool age. Whether writing about a young boy trying to overcome his fears (*Who's Afraid of the Dark?*, 1980), or the gang of investigators in her I Can Read titles, Bonsall clearly has kept her "consumer" in mind.

Prior to her work in the beginning-to-read field, Bonsall collaborated on a series of books featuring the photography of Camilla Koffler, who uses the pseudonym Ylla. In works such as *Polar Bear Brothers* (1960), *Look Who's Talking* (1962), and *I'll Show You Cats* (1964), Bonsall created stories that provided a framework for a series of beautiful black-and-white animal photographs. When illustrating her own work, Bonsall used finely detailed, expressive ink drawings to capture her characters' actions. Bonsall relied primarily on black, browns, and grays, adding one or two muted shades, such as green or blue, and let the black line dominate. She used detailed cross-hatching to add dimension or to differentiate skin tones.

Bonsall's entries in the I Can Read series are appropriate for the beginning reader and can be enjoyed as read-aloud stories. Even the simple text of *Mine's the Best* (1973), which features a brief conversation between two young boys about their newly purchased balloons, sparkles with the kind of obvious humor and sight gags that young children love. The background illustrations are particularly effective. As the two boys argue, a procession of young children, all carrying identical balloons, pass by and add their own amusing antics to the scene. *The Day I Had to Play with My Sister* (1972) is equally engaging, as a young boy tries, unsuccessfully, to teach his little sister the finer points of hide-and-seek. Bonsall captured perfectly the interaction between these siblings, especially the sister's inability to follow even the simplest directions. Many young readers with younger siblings of their own will find themselves on familiar ground.

The four young crime fighters featured in Bonsall's many "Case" mysteries also capture the young reader's interest. In the first book, *The Case of the Hungry Stranger* (1963), a defiant NO GIRLS sign appears on the boys' clubhouse door. As the boys, led by Wizard, the chief private eye, go about their business of solving difficult crimes — the disappearance of a blueberry pie, a lost pet, and an invisible doorbell ringer — young readers will notice that these detectives could use a little help. In *The Case of the Double Cross* (1980), the boys have joined forces with Marigold and her friends, and the NO GIRLS sign has been replaced with a new clubhouse logo that combines *Wizard* and *Marigold* into the *Wizmars*. Bonsall's mysteries are excellent for

beginning readers, with intriguing plots and the evidence of boy-girl rivalry that so often appears at this age.

In all Bonsall's books, her conversational style, appealing illustrations, and delightful young characters combine to entertain young readers. E.H.

Bontemps, Arna

American author, editor, and anthologist, 1902–1973. Through difficult times and into the postsegregation Second Reconstruction, Arna Bontemps worked to bring African American history and everyday black life into the mainstream of American children's books and the standard school curriculum — with almost no company, for years, save that of his great friend and occasional collaborator, LANGSTON HUGHES.

Born in Louisiana, Bontemps grew up in Los Angeles and in the nonracial Seventh-Day Adventist Church, where his father was a minister. Spared institutional segregation, he was sensitive to other, subtler, potentially more corrosive forms of marginalization. As a boy, Bontemps wondered "why the slave never fought for freedom" and, digging away, he discovered that they had — unbeknownst to the history texts — in Haiti and elsewhere in the Caribbean and in the antebellum South. When he was just short of twelve, he read about the celebration of the centennial of the Battle of New Orleans, "exclusively by white soldiers, white orators, and white schoolchildren," with no recognition of the role of black troops, extravagantly praised by General Andrew Jackson, which he learned about from the black press. In a milieu and a household indifferent to black culture, Bontemps became a bookish rebel with a cause.

At twenty-three Harlem beckoned — a Harlem recently launched, in 1924, on its celebrated Renaissance. Bontemps, who had entrée as a fledgling poet, quickly met Countee Cullen, the latest poetry sensation, and through him met Hughes and other writers and intellectuals. But he was also living a stable, diligent, down-to-earth personal life that set him apart — as a teacher at Harlem Academy, an Adventist high school, and as a husband and a father of the first of an eventual brood of six children. Throughout most of his subsequent career as a writer, Bontemps would have one foot in the big world of black culture, and one in the small world of teaching (or other regular employment), child-rearing, and pragmatic child study.

For Bontemps, displaced from Harlem by the Depression — teaching for three unhappy years in Alabama, taking refuge under the paternal roof in Los Angeles, recouping during a Chicago stay, then settling in as librarian at Fisk University (1943–65) — the chief conduit between the two worlds was his buddy Hughes. In a constant flow of correspondence, Bontemps and Hughes swapped literary ideas and publishing tips, discussed joint projects, and proposed one another for assignments. Back from Haiti with the nub of a children's book, it was only natural for Hughes to turn to Bontemps for help in getting it into shape. Set in a pristine, paradisiacal Haiti of naked tykes and soap from trees, *Popo and Fifina, Children of Haiti* (1932) revolves around the delight a small boy and his older sister take in moving from the countryside into town, where carefree days of kite flying on the beach calmly give way to apprenticeship in a wood-working shop and the pride of accomplishment. Disarmingly illustrated by E. Simms Campbell, *Popo and Fifina* met with an appreciative reception.

In their later collaborations, Bontemps and Hughes functioned as coeditors, not coauthors, and Hughes, though the designated literary person of the pair, attempted no further fiction for children. Bontemps, on the other hand, had published one adult novel of black folklife, *God Sends Sunday* (1931), and was only just turning to HISTORICAL FICTION and historical writing, his area of expertise in the division of labor with Hughes. And while writing for children was mainly a welcome source of additional income for Hughes, it was that and more for Bontemps,

who saw in children's books a way to let in light and sweep away misconceptions.

In the early 1930s, that called for ending the monopoly of jocose tales like *Epaminondas*. With that view Bontemps wrote a sunny story of a barefoot Southern black farm boy and his "ole, yellow, no-nation" dog, *You Can't Pet a Possum* (1934), which was undone by near caricature illustration; a picaresque yarn about three Alabama boys amid the perils, temptations, and golden opportunities of Harlem, *Sad-Faced Boy* (1937); and the haunting tale of a dreamy young trumpet player, *Lonesome Boy* (1955), which came later and endured. To Bontemps *Lonesome Boy* was "prose in the folk manner," a designation that fits all three works. As such they are akin to Gwendolyn Brooks's stories about Maud Martha and Hughes's famous anecdotes of "My Simple Minded Friend," and unique in American children's literature of the period.

Bontemps's other juvenile projects fell into more conventional categories. But just about everything he did has application elsewhere, as fodder or reinforcement. Two works of adult historical fiction, *Black Thunder* (1936), about the Gabriel Prosser insurrection, and *Drums at Dusk* (1939), about the 1794 Haitian revolt, prepared him to write antebellum African American history, notably *Story of the Negro* (1948), a landmark volume that lays out the truth about the African past and the distortions about slavery.

They Seek a City (1945), written in collaboration with proletarian writer Jack Conroy (and issued in a revised edition in 1966 as *Anyplace but Here*), drew on research into black migration, from DuSable's Chicago trading post to World War II Detroit, that Bontemps and Conroy conducted on the Chicago WPA Federal Writers' Project. That research was also utilized in a Bontemps-Hughes crossover compendium, *The Book of Negro Folklore* (1958), as well as in Bontemps's all-age history, *One Hundred Years of Negro Freedom* (1956), which re-creates the immediate gains of Reconstruction and the ensuing setbacks and years of struggle through the interwoven lives of Booker T. Washington, W. E. B. Du Bois, and other principals.

From industrial AMERICAN FOLKLORE Conroy gathered for the WPA, Bontemps fashioned three tall tales that appeared under joint authorship: *The Fast Sooner Hound* (1942), a longtime favorite bouncily illustrated by VIRGINIA LEE BURTON; *Slappy Hooper, the Wonderful Sign Painter* (1946); and *Sam Patch, the High, Wide, and Handsome Jumper* (1951). To suit the first to children, Bontemps toned down the ending — but, "I expect the truth will out." (See B. A. Botkin, *Treasury of American Folklore*, 533–36.) The body of black literature, familiar to Bontemps from childhood, furnished him with classics and fresh discoveries for *Golden Slippers* (1941), the first anthology of African American POETRY for children.

True stories of triumphing over odds lay to hand. With typical World War II expansiveness, Bontemps wrote *We Have Tomorrow* (1945), profiles of twelve young blacks succeeding at a variety of occupations "as Americans, not as heroes." On the Fisk campus he could not help but be inspired by the Jubilee Singers, subjects of *Chariot in the Sky* (1951).

There was also a call, of course, for individual BIOGRAPHIES of noted African Americans. Bontemps's *Story of George Washington Carver* (1954) differs from other early biographies, juvenile and adult, in making less of white encouragement to the budding scientist and more of aid and comfort from the Midwest's scattered blacks. Twice Bontemps directly took on the protean figure of Frederick Douglass. In *Frederick Douglass: Slave, Fighter, Freeman* (1958), a book for younger readers, it is the boy's effort to get an education and the youth's resolve to gain his freedom that hold center stage. In *Free at Last: The Life of Frederick Douglass* (1971), a full-length portrait for teenagers and adults, the focus is justifiably on Douglass the abolitionist.

But Bontemps, who knew his subjects inside out, did not leave off quite there: in *One Hundred Years of Negro Freedom* he took Douglass through to his controversial remarriage, late in life and long past his heroic prime, to his young white secretary. A fascinating, fine-screened chapter baldly titled "The Second Mrs. Douglass" carries the newlyweds around the British Isles and across the European continent, attended by an odd lot of old admirers, to Egypt and the Great Pyramid, which the aged Douglass, mindful that Egyptians are persons of color by American definition, cannot but climb. "One view of the Sphinx, the River Nile, and the desert was reward enough for three score and ten years of pain and effort."

As African American history by an African American author, Arna Bontemps's books were exceptional in his time. As authoritative history, thoughtfully presented and stirringly dramatized, they are exceptional for any time. B.B.

Boston, L. M.

British author, 1892–1990. Of all the rich crop of mid-twentieth-century books, Lucy Maria Boston's Green Knowe stories are notable for their perfect portrayals of a sense of place. Using her own home in rural England as a model — a place she called a "miracle" to own — Boston set her novels in a twelfth-century manor house beside a river. Its magical grounds include a maze and topiary yew trees representing various animals and a huge, vaguely human figure known as Green Noah.

Boston did not begin writing for children until she was in her sixties, stimulated by her fascination with the history of her ancient house. Using a complex story structure, she intertwined multiple themes seamlessly, allowing her stories to unfold in the dramatic climaxes that characterize her novels. Boston did not moralize. She said of writing: "In a work of art every word . . . has a reference to every other. . . . They interrelate, foreshadow, recall, enlarge, and play all over each other to produce a specific feeling — *not* a moral. . . . A word arbitrarily changed . . . could change a book." Such meticulous attention to words never became an end in itself, however, and never interfered with Boston's sense of story.

Boston not only respected the written word, she respected her audience, the children. She believed they "react to style with their whole being. . . . Style has an irresistible authority." She abhorred writing down to children and felt that "the young of the race continue to be born with their hope intact. . . . I would bring two gifts [to them] — veneration and delight, because you can't have one without the other."

Combining the realistic with the fantastic, Boston never asked readers to believe more than they could believe. The joyousness of the characters and the curiosity of the children in the stories bring the mansion's secrets and history to life and breathe story into its history. In *The Children of Green Knowe* (1954) and *The Chimneys of Green Knowe* (1958), young Toseland, known as Tolly, and old Mrs. Oldknowe experience a time gone by through the lively ghosts of three young children; in *The Stones of Green Knowe* (1976), Roger, the son of the twelfth-century builder of the mansion, slips through time to meet other children living in the mansion in centuries to come; and in *A Stranger at Green Knowe* (1961), a child named Ping, in an entirely realistic though surprising story, meets an escaped gorilla.

Boston's smooth prose is ideal for reading aloud to younger children, and children of all ages respond to the dramatic setting and characters revealed in these stories. Although Boston's own story of finding and meticulously restoring the house may be a miracle, it is her Green Knowe stories for children that best preserve the manor and disseminate its history. J.B.

Brett, Jan

American illustrator, b. 1949. A book illustrated by Jan Brett is many things: vivid, rich, lavish; filled with attention to detail; often humorous. Indeed, each page created by this artist is so lush with colorful objects, large and small, that it tells an entertaining story by itself.

Born and raised in Massachusetts, Brett goes to a cabin in the Berkshire Mountains of western Massachusetts, where she finds inspiration for her children's books. Using no models, she designs her intricate pages from memory, recalling objects from her past and transferring them to paint on paper.

The majority of Brett's most successful picture books find their subjects in folklore, whether traditional or modern. Those she has written herself are based on established motifs, such as holiday stories, ANIMAL STORIES, or FANTASY, and often employ a cumulative structure. Brett's adaptation of the Ukrainian folktale *The Mitten* (1990) is perhaps the best example of this format. Using an elaborate series of borders, the artist has framed the action detailed in the text with small pictures suggesting both a simultaneous and a future event, a foreshadowing that provides the child observer with a delicious sense of anticipation. Brett played similar artistic games in her rendition of EDWARD LEAR'S *The Owl and the Pussycat* (1991), where a pair of fish carry on their own courtship in the waves under the pea-green boat.

While always maintaining the same recognizable style of illustration, Brett has remained true to each story's individual traits, such as nationality, class, time period, and character. She is known in particular for her illustrations of Scandinavian characters and settings. For her fairy tales she has carefully clothed her subjects in an accurate rendition of traditional folk costume, often including jewelry, braid, embroidery, lace, feathers, and other finery when appropriate. Dramatic backgrounds filled with tapestries, variegated outdoor landscapes, and complex architectural structures frequently reflect a specific setting or theme, but fade at moments of high drama in favor of close-ups or silhouettes.

Brett has met with occasional criticism from those reviewers who embrace a "less is more" artistic philosophy; her illustrations fall under the category of realism, and, indeed, they leave little to the imagination. Brett is seen as less gifted with words than with pictures, and her adaptations of folktales and her illustrations for books by other authors are generally considered to be the most successful of her works. Praise for her own writing, however, has been just as frequent as criticism. *The Mitten*, Brett's finest book, was named one of *Booklist*'s Best Books for the 1980s, and a number of other works have received similar well-deserved acclaim. C.C.B.

Bridwell, Norman

A merican author and illustrator, b. 1928. *Clifford, the Big Red Dog* first appeared as an unpretentious paperback in 1962 but grew into an extremely popular series of books for preschool readers. Clifford's creator, Norman Bridwell, was born in Kokomo, Indiana, and educated at the John Herron Art Institute and Cooper Union Art School. He worked for a filmstrip company, designed fabrics, and was a freelance artist before publishing his first book.

Clifford, the Big Red Dog is narrated by Emily Elizabeth, a little girl whose pet is so large that he bathes in swimming pools and lives in a doghouse that dwarfs his owners' home. Despite the bland writing and cartoonlike red and black illustrations, children were enchanted by this oversized, good-natured, but sometimes clumsy canine; further volumes include *Clifford Gets a Job* (1965), *Clifford's Halloween* (1966), and *Clifford's Tricks* (1969). Bridwell has published a series about a young witch, including *The Witch Next Door* (1965) and *The Witch's Vacation* (1973), and a few individual titles such as *Kangaroo Stew* (1979), but he is best known for the Clifford books, which later included pop-up editions and nonstory items such as *Clifford's Sticker Book* (1984). When Clifford graduated to hardcover in the 1980s, some of the earlier volumes were reissued with full-color illustrations. The Clifford, the Small Red Puppy series of BOARD BOOKS concerns the dog's early years and includes *Clifford's Animal Sounds* (1991) and *Clifford Counts Bubbles* (1992).

From a critical perspective, Bridwell's contributions to children's literature appear slight. Yet the books are undeniably popular with beginning readers, who appreciate the antics of Emily Elizabeth's dog and who may use the stories as steppingstones to more challenging, rewarding reading. P.D.S.

Briggs, Raymond

B ritish author and illustrator, b. 1934. Raymond Briggs has been providing comic joy for young readers since he first began his career in book illustration in the early 1960s. Children laugh out loud at his balding, grumpy Father Christmas, his nearsighted, stubble-faced giants, and a host of other traditional characters he has brought to life in anthologies of NURSERY RHYMES and fairy tales.

Among his early works are two brief collections, *Ring-a-Ring o' Roses* (1962) and *Fee Fi Fo Fum* (1964), which received a commendation for the Kate Greenaway Medal. These were followed by *The Mother Goose Treasury* (1966), which won the medal. This collection of over four hundred nursery rhymes includes almost nine hundred of Briggs's drawings and paintings. What makes the illustrations in all three books unique is Briggs's irreverent attitude. Rather than use the pastel colors and romantic treatments of earlier nursery rhyme collections, Briggs employed contemporary settings and comic, working-class characters. His plump Mother Goose has a prominent chin, a perpetual grin, and sensible shoes, and many of his characters wear rough clothes, day-old beards, and bemused expressions. The red-cheeked, redheaded giant featured in *Treasury* foreshadows the giant in his later work, *Jim and the Beanstalk* (1970). With this book Briggs came into his own as an author as well as an illustrator of children's books. This fractured tale of a giant who needs love and understanding, glasses, a wig, and false teeth appeals to young readers who wish that they, like Jim, could rescue a giant.

Another sassy, original tale, *Father Christmas*, was published in 1973 and received the Kate Greenaway Medal. While some adults were shocked at Briggs's portrayal of Santa, who punctuates almost every sentence with the word "blooming," many were delighted by the down-to-earth story, which features comic-book frames and dialogue bubbles. Briggs has said that Father Christmas's job was probably much like his father's job as a milkman, with all the early-morning deliveries. He has created a working-class Father Christmas who does not dislike his work but goes about it with a certain grouchy style. In a sequel, *Father Christmas Goes on Holiday* (1975), Father Christmas gets fed up with the cold North Pole and takes off to visit warmer climes in a caravan flown by his reindeer.

Two of Briggs's books use a similar comic-book format but appeal to older readers. *Fungus the Bogeyman* (1977) features clever language and is set in the green-and-brown slimy underground world of the bogeys. *When the Wind Blows* (1982) is Briggs's darkest work and reflects his involvement in the British Campaign for Nuclear Disarmament. Here, he has told the story of a working-class couple who don't believe that nuclear war is possible and quietly die of radiation sickness after a nuclear explosion. This book, which Briggs has rewritten for radio, the stage, and an animated film, has deeply affected young adult readers, who come to it expecting a cartoon and find themselves moved by its message. Briggs's best-known book, *The Snowman* (1978), a wordless PICTURE BOOK, features soft watercolor paintings rather than the pen and ink outlines and bright colors of his earlier books. In this gentle story, a boy's snowman comes to vivid life for one long blissful night of fun, but the boy awakes to find him melted and gone in the morning. The book, which features the author's own house and garden, has a bittersweet quality missing from his earlier works.

Briggs has said that he doesn't necessarily write and illustrate books for children, but he writes and draws to please himself. In pleasing himself Briggs uses sly humor and serious themes, twitting the world and beliefs of adults to the delight of children of all ages. B.C.

Brooke, L. Leslie

British illustrator and author, 1862–1940. Leonard Leslie Brooke, whose droll pen-and-ink line drawings, enchanting watercolor illustrations, and beloved books about Johnny Crow and his friends have delighted generations of children and the grownups who read to them, was educated in his native Cheshire and later in London at the Royal Academy. He received the Academy's Armitage Medal in 1888 and began his artistic career as a watercolorist and portrait painter, but when he succeeded WALTER CRANE in 1891 as illustrator of Mrs. Molesworth's Victorian novels for children, his career took a different course.

With the publication of *The Nursery Rhyme Book* (1897), edited by ANDREW LANG, Brooke found his niche among children's book immortals. The pictures he drew with such skill and humor, that he painted with such warmth and color for his lovely books of Mother Goose rhymes and traditional nursery tales, class his art with that of Walter Crane, BEATRIX POTTER, KATE GREENAWAY, and RANDOLPH CALDECOTT and his gently absurd humor with that of EDWARD LEAR and LEWIS CARROLL. *Johnny Crow's Garden* (1903), the first book he both illustrated and wrote, earned a Lewis Carroll Shelf Award in 1960.

Johnny Crow, ever courteous, solicitous, and unassuming, plays quiet host to an intriguing assortment of fellow birds and animals in his beautiful garden. Rhymed couplets introduce his individual friends and their antics. The accompanying pictures reveal further details of their stories until at last "they all sat down together in a row in Johnny Crow's garden."

The roots of this appealing classic for young children and of its companion books, *Johnny Crow's Party* (1907) and *Johnny Crow's New Garden* (1935), lie in childhood: Brooke's own childhood, that of his sons, and that of his grandson. The clever rhyming game shared among four generations produced three books equal in wit, beauty, and spirit that are filled with the character and personality of their creator. Brooke was a kind and gentle man who loved and understood children. His sense of fun, his feelings for the English garden and countryside, and his affection for animals are apparent in all his work.

Brooke lavished his attention on portraying animals, not as an animal artist, but as a friendly observer of his fellow man. His humanized animals, though true to their kind, express in their faces and bodies an enormous range of mostly sunny human emotions that children can instantly recognize. Whether from farm or jungle, they are happy, funny, silly, serious, surprised; coy, bored, sick, embarrassed, proud, crestfallen. To admire his animals, however, is not to slight his humans. The young kings and queens who grace his books are as royal and as beautiful as one could wish, the children as charming and innocent, but none would be recognized in the face of a neighbor. It is the lined and worn faces of his old folk that are a reminder of the artist's early interest in portraiture.

The height of Brooke's picture book creativity was from the turn of the century to about 1916. During this period — besides the first two books about Johnny Crow — he created new illustrations for the nonsense rhymes of Edward Lear, retold and illustrated four classic nursery tales that appeared both separately and later together in *The Golden Goose Book* (1905), and illustrated a series of Mother Goose rhymes that were published in omnibus form in 1922 under the title *Ring O' Roses*.

During the 1920s Brooke illustrated several books for adults. In the thirties the world received the gift of two more inspired children's books from his hand. *A Round-about Turn* (1930), written by Robert Charles, had originally appeared as a poem in *Punch* and, like Lear's nonsense verses, was in perfect tune with Brooke's own whimsical art. *Johnny Crow's New Garden* (1935), written for his grandson, was the astonishing equal of its two predecessors, written thirty years before.

In an age when humor, playfulness, and pictorial detail in books for the young have reached a new level of appreciation, there is much to appreciate in the world of Leslie Brooke. S.L.R.

Brooks, Bruce

Amerman author, b. 1950. Since making an explosive debut in YOUNG ADULT NOVELS with *The Moves Make the Man* (1984), Bruce Brooks has published a succession of challenging, complex, and brilliantly crafted novels.

Born in Richmond, Virginia, the author spent a childhood divided between his divorced parents' homes in Washington, D.C., and North Carolina. From his first day of school, Brooks created alternate plots for the stories he read in textbooks and soon began writing original fiction. He attended the University of North Carolina at Chapel Hill and the prestigious University of Iowa Writers' Workshop. He was employed as a teacher, a letterpress printer, and a journalist before his first book won the Boston Globe–Horn Book Award for fiction and was named a Newbery Honor Book.

The Moves Make the Man concerns the friendship between two thirteen-year-old boys in 1950s North Carolina. Jerome is a smart and savvy African American; Bix is a troubled white boy with a mentally ill mother and malevolent stepfather. Jerome teaches Bix how to play basketball, and the game serves as a stunning metaphor on several levels throughout the novel. Jerome's first-person narration is exceptionally fine, and Brooks extended his mastery of the first-person voice in *Midnight Hour Encores* (1986), whose narrator is a sophisticated sixteen-year-old cello prodigy. The story artfully explores the bonds between parent and child as Sibilance T. Spooner and her father travel from Washington, D.C., to San Francisco, where Sib meets her mother for the first time and makes some momentous decisions about her life.

Family relationships are also at the center of *No Kidding* (1989), in which fourteen-year-old Sam is forced to take on adult responsibilities in a twenty-first-century society ravaged by the effects of alcoholism. Although the book includes an unnecessary subplot involving clerics and the omniscient narration lacks the immediacy of the author's previous novels, Brooks has presented a thoughtful, intriguing look at the future.

An unnamed Southern boy confronts issues of mortality and love after his grandfather suffers a heart attack in *Everywhere* (1990), a small gem of a novel, which, like each of Brooks's books, departs from his previous work in style and content. What all the novels have in common are protagonists who, despite their vastly different backgrounds and speech patterns, share a keen awareness of their own intelligence. A particularly shrewd yet open-hearted character is portrayed in *What Hearts* (1992), a volume of four short stories focusing on crucial events in young Asa's life, such as leaving home at age seven and falling in love at age twelve. Rich in emotion and challenging in vision, this Newbery Honor Book contains wonderful writing but seems to be directed at adult readers rather than children. The author has also written several IN-FORMATION BOOKS. The Knowing Nature series includes *Predator* (1989) and *Making Sense: Animal Perception and Communication* (1993). Collections of essays written especially for young readers are rare, but in *Boys Will Be* (1993), Brooks, the father of two sons, has written about baseball caps, dangerous friends, sports, and other boyhood concerns in spirited, compassionate prose.

As an author of well-received nonfiction and novels distinguished by their integrity, superb characterizations, and inspired use of language, this versatile stylist has proved himself a writer of nearly limitless possibilities. P.D.S.

Brooks, Walter R.

American author, 1886–1958. Born in Rome, New York, Walter R. Brooks became an orphan at an early age. After being sent to a military academy, he attended the University of Rochester. His interest in homeopathic medicine led him to New York City, where he studied at a homeopathic college. After working for the Red Cross, he turned his hand to magazines, writing for *Outlook,* the *New Yorker,* and *Scribner's Commentator.*

In 1927, Brooks created the first book of a series that would make him famous, *To and Again* (later retitled *Freddy Goes to Florida*), one of twenty-six books to star Freddy the pig. Although Freddy seems an unlikely hero — he oversleeps, overeats, daydreams, and has a pronounced streak of laziness — he proves to be a Renaissance pig: he writes poetry, paints, edits the *Bean Home News,* runs a successful detective agency, works well with his fellow barn animals — Mrs. Wiggins the cow, Jinx the cat, Charles the rooster — and even knows how to communicate with Martians.

Along with the Freddy books, Brooks also wrote more than 180 short stories for adults, many of which appeared in *Forum,* the *Saturday Evening Post,* the *Atlantic Monthly,* and *Esquire.* Twenty-five of these starred Ed, a talking horse, the inspiration for the 1960s television series *Mr. Ed.*

The Freddy books find devotees equally among children and adults who remember them from their childhood. Frequently selected by families as titles to read aloud, the books contain gentle humor and appealing animal characters. Freddy even has a dedicated fan club, Friends of Freddy Club. The recent success of the reissues of these books proves that talking ANIMAL STORIES, delivered with panache, can stand the test of time. A.S.

Brown, Marc

American author and illustrator, b. 1946. The name Marc Brown is well known to most elementary school children. The author and illustrator of the beloved Arthur books as well as many other successful works of fiction and nonfiction, Brown has secured for himself a sparkling reputation among both child readers and adult reviewers — certainly no easy task. An awareness of contemporary children and issues, combined with a bright, captivating visual artistry, are the signatures of his large and diverse body of work; a television series, based on the Arthur books, only increased the visibility of an already popular author.

Born in Erie, Pennsylvania, Brown showed an early artistic talent that flowered under the guidance of an encouraging grandmother and uncle. Trips to area museums became favorite excursions, and he went on to receive a B.F.A. in painting at the Cleveland Institute of Art. He has worked as a television art director, a professor of mechanical drawing, and a freelance illustrator.

Brown has created in several media, but he prefers pencil with watercolor, and he uses a variety of papers to produce different visual effects. Strong lines and bold colors characterize his recent work; such strong artistic statements capture the attention of young audiences without sacrificing a highly expressive quality that makes believable characters out of dinosaurs, monkeys, cats, and other winsome creatures.

During the mid-1970s, Brown began writing his own material. His first effort, *Arthur's Nose* (1976), began a series that would span two decades and introduced one of the most popular characters in picture book history. Starring the enormously appealing anteater, Arthur, and his diverse and likable group of friends and relatives, each of the titles addresses a child-relevant theme or situation with an easy-to-read text, colorful illustrations, and plenty of humor. A spinoff series featuring Arthur's irrepressible sister, D.W., makes use of the same down-to-earth style and has also met with success.

Brown's ability to keep a long series fresh and innovative is a rare gift. In addition to the Arthur books, he has created several other notable series. The Rhymes series — *Finger Rhymes* (1980), *Hand Rhymes* (1985), *Play Rhymes* (1987), and *Party Rhymes* (1988) — is a joyfully illustrated set of fingerplays, jump-rope games, and other movement activities suitable for use with children of all ages. Aside from these books' popularity with parents, their ability to hold the attention of young children has made them indispensable tools for librarians and preschool teachers. For information on timely topics such as divorce, safety, and the environment, children and adults turn to Brown's nonfiction Dinosaurs series. Created in collaboration with his wife, psychologist Laurene Krasny Brown, appealing and useful books such as *Dinosaurs, Beware! A Safety Guide* (1982), *Dinosaurs Divorce: A Guide for Changing Families* (1986), *Dinosaurs Travel: A Guide for Families on the Go* (1988), and *Dinosaurs to the Rescue! A Guide to Protecting Our Planet* (1992) feature a set of charismatic green dinosaurs that cavort across the pages while they convey their important dos and don'ts. Unlike many unsuccessful theme books, the Dinosaur guides take a humorous but sincere approach that avoids stereotypes or saccharine characterizations. They are as accessible to their young audiences as are any of Brown's other favorites, and readers continue to clamor for more. Whether it's an Arthur book, a favorite seen on television, or a special fingerplay, children are always ready to revel in the words and pictures of Marc Brown. C.C.B.

Voices of the Creators

Marc Brown

The first drawing I remember being really excited about was one I created in second grade at Jefferson Elementary School. It was a Nativity scene on blue construction paper, and I used a silver crayon for the stars. Something very special happened in my reaction to that drawing; I knew then that drawing was something I could do well. I had feelings of elation and great self-satisfaction.

As a child, I loved telling stories and had a friend who did, too. We would find quiet places away from everyone else, where we could tell stories. Each of us might talk for an hour or so, and we would listen patiently to each other. We were good listeners; I don't know if we were good storytellers.

My parents didn't think it was a good idea for me to study art; they wanted me to do something more respectable. My art teacher surreptitiously took me to apply to art school. The most remarkable person I have ever known, my grandmother, gave me money to start college; then, after my first year, I had to get scholarships.

To support myself in college, I took a job at a television station. My first assignment was to make more people want to watch the weather report. The station wanted something different. I gave it my best shot. I decided to dress up the weather reporter, Shirley, as a weather fairy; she'd swing onto the set on a big swing with her gossamer wings flapping behind her. My boss didn't see the humor: he gave me a free Christmas ham — and fired me.

After school I started teaching and illustrating textbooks. When I began illustrating PICTURE BOOKS, my first son was born. In sharing books with Tolon and later with my son Tucker, I could see the kinds of things they looked for in a book. I changed my ideas about illustrating because of the way they looked at the world. They had this wonderful fresh vision that I had lost. I wanted to recapture that view. I worked hard in joining them in their childhood and in their vision.

Arthur's Nose evolved out of a bedtime story I was telling my son. My editor, Emilie McLeod, at the Atlantic Monthly Press, thought it needed a lot of revision but was willing to work with me. The hardest thing for me at the beginning was to learn how to say something in a sentence or in a few words. I thought I needed three paragraphs. Emilie helped me understand how to use the pictures to do what they could do best and how to use the words to do what the pictures could not do.

Usually my story ideas come from something that is happening in real life. My sons were eating dinner one night, and they were having mashed potatoes and little peas, or rather *heaving* mashed potatoes and little peas. This prompted me to look for a good book on manners at the library. The ones I found were very stale, and I wanted a manners book that would be fun. Consequently, Stephen Krensky and I collaborated on *Perfect Pigs: An Introduction to Manners.*

When I begin working on a book, I always struggle with the writing at first and read the story aloud to hear how it sounds. I often create thirty versions of a manuscript before I show it to anyone. Sometimes I will put a manuscript away for a year before I finish it. I use pencil and paper and cut and paste. Once I have the right sequence, I start to think of picture possibilities.

For me the most satisfying part of the process is how children feel about the books. I never tire of hearing that children like what I am creating. It is also wonderful to have a partner who shares the same interests, and my wife, Laurie, and I sometimes collaborate. We are always looking for picture book subjects to help inform children about their world, because they are increasingly thrust into complex situations and premature independence.

Every morning when I walk into my studio, I feel so lucky to be able to make a living doing what I really love. 🐾

Brown, Marcia

American author and illustrator, b. 1918. Of the thirty books Marcia Brown has written, translated, and illustrated, three have won Caldecott Medals and six have been named Caldecott Honor Books, an unprecedented achievement and proof of her success in portraying the spirit of a story. Brown always wanted to illustrate children's books, particularly individual folk and fairy tales. After graduating from the New York College for Teachers in 1940, she taught English and drama for three years before deciding to immerse herself in children's literature. At a time when the Central Library in New York was the seminal hub of children's literature, she was hired into the New York Public Library system. Brown worked as an assistant librarian from 1943 to 1948, telling stories, mounting exhibits, and meeting people involved in children's books from all over the world. During her tenure there, she continued taking art lessons with the hope of becoming a writer and an illustrator. This, plus her love of art, reading, and travel, provided the foundations for her stories.

Her first book, *The Little Carousel* (1946), focuses on a child's loneliness when he is left at home by himself. Barbara Bader has noted that at a time when picture books addressed "archetypes and universals," Brown's book saw the "personal and circumstantial." *Stone Soup,* winner of the 1948 Caldecott Medal, was the first of many folk and fairy tales Brown would illustrate. Brown firmly believes in the power of story as one of the building blocks children need in defining their personalities and in the power that pictures have in making tales memorable. Because she believes that children need heroes with whom they can identify, she has presented ordinary people who achieve extraordinary feats: a poor boy becomes Lord Mayor of London (*Dick Whittington and His Cat,* 1950); a penniless son becomes the Marquis of Carabas (*Puss in Boots,* 1952); a stepdaughter goes to the prince's ball (*Cinderella, or the Little Glass Slipper,* winner of the 1955 Caldecott Medal).

Further, Brown believes that "fairy tales are revelations of sober everyday fact. They are the abiding dreams and realities of the human soul." She also believes that an illustrator must feel the rhythm of the story in order to "interpret . . . and intensify its meaning." Brown has always been faithful to this creed; her hallmark is the originality she brings to her art. She has used wash and line, pastels and ink, gouache and watercolors, and linoleum cuts in her interpretations: each time, she let the story dictate the medium. To evoke the endurance and spirit of fable, Brown turned to woodcuts for stories such as *Once a Mouse,* winner of the 1962 Caldecott Medal, *Backbone of the King* (1966), and *The Blue Jackal* (1977). Because she believes in the vital importance of passing down folklore from generation to generation, she was enthralled by a poem by the Swiss-born French writer Blaise Cendrars, which became *Shadow,* winner of the 1983 Caldecott Medal and her most powerfully illustrated book. This tale, inspired by African storytelling, reaches back and taps man's primal fear of the dark, hauntingly pulling ghosts, past and present, in and out of the subconscious. Through *Shadow,* Brown has created the dance of the eternal spirit of man, again, successfully weaving timelessness through her work. In 1992

she won the Laura Ingalls Wilder Award for the body of her work. S.R.

Brown, Margaret Wise

American writer, 1910–1952. In a brief, many-faceted, and remarkable career, Margaret Wise Brown pioneered the writing of books for the nursery school ages; authored more than one hundred volumes including the classic *Runaway Bunny* (1942) and *Goodnight Moon* (1947); and served as a bridge between the worlds of publishing, progressive education, and the experimental arts of the 1930s and 1940s.

Born in the Greenpoint section of Brooklyn, New York, on May 23, 1910, Brown grew up the second of three children in suburban Beechurst, Long Island. Her father, Robert Bruce Brown, was an executive of the American Manufacturing Company, makers of rope and bagging for the maritime trade. Her mother, born Maude Johnson, had been Robert's childhood playmate in Kirkwood, Missouri. Both parents traced their American ancestry to pre–Revolutionary War Virginia, where Robert's forebears had distinguished themselves in church and government service. It was a great thing to be born a Brown, as young Margaret soon learned; and in the perfectionistic, emotionally chilly world of the Brown household, each child vied for attention.

Margaret's older brother Gratz was a shrewd problem solver like their father. Their younger sister Roberta's intellectual prowess was more broadly based. Always a brilliant scholar (and dutiful daughter), Roberta would skip two grades of school (and become Margaret's unwelcome classmate) on her triumphant march to Vassar. Wedged uncomfortably between these daunting paradigms of achievement, Margaret carved out a dubious niche for herself as the family daydreamer, prankster, and storyteller.

At the girls' preparatory school Dana Hall, "Tim" Brown (as Margaret was known for the golden color, like timothy, of her long, flowing hair) at last met teachers capable of channeling her free-form, intuitive style of learning. As an undergraduate at Hollins College, she received her first encouragement to write. Brown graduated from Hollins in 1932, however, without either definite goals or plans. Three more years passed before, for lack of an alternative, she enrolled in the teacher training program of New York's progressive Bureau of Educational Experiments (called "Bank Street" for its Greenwich Village location). There, as part of the experientially based training routine, Brown wrote her first stories for children and found her vocation.

Brown's inspired teacher, Bank Street founder Lucy Sprague Mitchell, taught the new arrival important lessons in professionalism and craft and gave her a thorough grounding in her own then highly controversial ideas about writing for the very young. Mitchell's research into early childhood development, begun in the 1910s, had prompted her to ask whether there were not certain types of stories and poems that corresponded most closely to the specific needs and interests of children at each developmental stage. Mitchell's findings impelled her to reject the library establishment's basic assumptions about literature for the younger ages. Children under the age of six, Mitchell concluded, had no special affinity for fantastic "once upon a time" tales about castles and kings, or for traditional nursery nonsense, as the librarians supposed. Mitchell believed that the very young were more at home with stories about the modern world, which to them was both fantastic and real. Mitchell laid out this and several other equally arresting ideas in the introduction of her *Here and Now Story Book* of 1921, an age-graded anthology that provoked a lively debate on publication and later served as a model for Brown and others.

By the mid-1930s, with a talented protegée — now called "Brownie" by friends — to assist her, Mitchell felt ready to advance her children's literature project several steps further. She began, in 1936, by enlisting Brown and a small group of others to collaborate with her on a sequel anthology, *Another Here and Now Story Book* (1937), which reaffirmed in somewhat more flexible terms Mitchell's critique of the librarians' unscientific and, as she thought, essentially sentimental point of view. Then, in 1937, Mitchell established the Bank Street Writers Laboratory as a training workshop for writers in the here-and-now vein (Brown was a charter member). The following year, Mitchell helped launch the small publishing firm of William R. Scott, Inc., with Brown as editor, as a vehicle for sending here-and-now-style books out into the world.

As Scott's editor, Brown was in a position to publish her own writings as well as to champion the innovative work of others. She did both with abandon. "I submitted it," she later recalled of her *Noisy Book*'s (1939) origins. "We" — that is, Brown again — "accepted it." From the start, her own books led the list of the fledgling firm's critical and commercial successes (limited as those successes were by the reluctance of the library establishment to accept books hatched in the laboratory of progressive education). The roster of Brown's editorial discoveries — illustrators CLEMENT HURD, author-artists ESPHYR SLOBODKINA and Charles Shaw, and others — was also impressive. Her most spectacular coup, however, came with the publication of Gertrude Stein's first FANTASY for children, *The World Is Round* (1939), which Scott commissioned at Brown's prompting. Stein's robust delight in wordplay and fascination with the expressive possibilities of rhythmic repetition were features of the voluble expatriate's avant-garde work that Brown found distinctly "childlike" (as defined by Mitchell's research) and thus adaptable to writing for the young.

Steinian echoes reverberate throughout Brown's own Noisy Book series (which grew to eight volumes), *Red Light, Green Light* (published under the name Golden MacDonald, 1944), *The Important Book* (1949), *Four Fur Feet* (1961), and many others. Brown's affinity for modernist experimentation and her appreciation of its relevance for children's literature are equally apparent in the styles of illustration art she favored as an editor. Slobodkina and Shaw (both charter members of the American Abstract Artists group of painters), Hurd (who had studied in Paris with Fernand Léger), Jean Charlot (a dazzling printmaker with links both to the Paris avant-garde and to the Mexican muralists), and Weisgard (an illustrator influenced by Stuart Davis and the Constructivists) all created children's book art that eschewed the anecdotal realism of the day for a bolder, more graphic, and deliberately contemporary vision. Starting with elements of the modern artist's stock-in-trade — the purely expressive use of color, the ideographic distillation of representational forms, the free-flowing reorganization of pictorial space — these illustrators produced vibrant, accessible art aimed at heightening the here-and-now sensory enjoyment of young children. Inspired by their author-editor friend, Hurd, Weisgard, and the others joined Brown in an impassioned quest to make the PICTURE BOOK new.

Bumble Bugs and Elephants (1938), *The Little Fireman* (1938), *A Child's Good Night Book* (1943), *They All Saw It* (1944), and *Where Have You Been?* (1952) are among the many books in which, sentence by sentence or stanza by stanza, Brown presented young children with simple, gamelike structures in which to frame their own rhymes, thoughts, and perceptions. In thus extending to readers an open invitation not to hold solemnly to the author's word as final, these books epitomize the Bank Street view that children are best approached as full collaborators in learning.

The Noisy Book series and *SHHhhh . . . BANG* (1943), which ask readers to produce a variety of amusing sound effects; *The Color Kittens* (1949), which offers a winsome introduction to color theory; and *Little Fur Family* (1946), in its original snuggly-soft fur dust jacket, reflects the Bank Street belief in the centrality of sensory experience for the development of children under the age of six. In *Goodnight Moon,* the one- and two-year-old's here-and-now world is shown to consist in large measure of his or her own home surroundings. *Five Little Firemen* (coauthored by Edith Thacher Hurd under the joint pseudonym Juniper Sage, 1948) is one of several books to survey a somewhat older child's expanding here-and-now awareness of modern towns and cities and their myriad doings. Mitchell had argued that once

children acquired an understanding of their present-day world, a grounding rooted primarily in firsthand observation, they were ready to study the past. In *The Log of Christopher Columbus' First Voyage to America in the Year 1492* (1938) and *Homes in the Wilderness* (1939), the latter of which contained excerpts from the diaries of William Bradford and other Plymouth Colony settlers, Brown provided readers of eight and older with opportunities to glimpse the past through the firsthand observations of participants.

Mitchell's influence on Brown's writings and editorial work was thus both wide-ranging and profound. But Brown had too incisive an imagination, and was too fine a writer, not to have searched out the limits of her mentor's ideas and ventured beyond them. Mitchell's model of here-and-now development focused on the child's changing capacity for cognition and perception. Brown's first published book, *When the Wind Blew* (1937), a melancholy tale about a solitary old woman, signaled its author's interest in exploring the emotional realm. In *The Runaway Bunny, Little Fur Family, The Little Island* (published under the name Golden MacDonald, 1946), *Wait Till the Moon Is Full* (1948), and *Mister Dog* (1952), Brown fashioned poignant fables about the shifting internal balance between the child's deep-seated yearnings for security and independence. In books like *Little Fur Family, The Little Island, Fox Eyes* (1951), and *The Dark Wood of the Golden Birds* (1950), she took further exception with here-and-now orthodoxy through her whole-hearted embrace of fairy-tale elements of magic and mystery. Brown, who from early childhood had relished ANDREW LANG's Rainbow Fairy collections and the rhymes of Mother Goose, was never fully convinced that such open-endedly imaginative material could be inappropriate for children of *any* age.

In 1942, the year of *The Runaway Bunny's* publication, Brown ended both her editorial work for Scott and her regular participation in Bank Street activities, including the Writers Laboratory. As an extraordinarily prolific author, she continued to publish some of her books with Scott and to begin new associations with other houses. But from the early 1940s onward, Harper and Brothers, under the editorship of the boldly receptive Ursula Nordstrom, was Brown's creative home.

As the titles of several books — *Big Dog, Little Dog* (1943), *Night and Day* (1942), and *The Quiet Noisy Book* (1950) — suggest, Brown delighted in the play, and contemplation, of opposites. In *Goodnight Moon,* the book for which she has long been best known, she achieved her most compelling synthesis of the opposing tendencies within her imaginative vision. Brown furnished the "great green room" not only with the chairs and clocks of Bank Street actuality but also with fanciful images (the three little bears, the cow jumping over the moon) of classic make-believe, and with the tantalizing nonpresence of "nobody." In so doing, she expressed the basic insight that from a young child's point of view the here-and-now and the land of pretend are largely overlapping territories.

On November 13, 1952, Margaret Wise Brown died suddenly, at the age of forty-two, while vacationing in the south of France. The cause of death was an embolism following a routine operation. Brown never married or had children of her own. Her private life was a whirl of glamorous friends, eccentric houses, and adventurous travel, but also of torturous bouts with self-doubt and inconclusive, more than occasionally painful relationships, most notably a ten-year-long on-again, off-again affair with Michael Strange, the celebrity-socialite-poet and former wife of John Barrymore. Strange, who died in 1950, was old enough to have been Brown's mother; James S. Rockefeller Jr., to whom Brown became engaged just months before her death, was almost young enough to have been her son. The striking reverse symmetry of these two relationships, whatever its significance as a clue to Brown's own internal dynamics, hints at the source of the lasting power of her work. Brown had the ability to write both from a child's perspective *and* from that of the good provider of comforting fables and luminous, clarifying perceptions. In *Goodnight Moon,* it is the godlike good provider who gently leads the listener into the great green room. But it is the child who then takes up the litany of "goodnights," and is thus granted a satisfying role in the scheme of existence. L.S.M.

Browne, Anthony

British author and illustrator, b. 1946. With the publication, in 1983, of his PICTURE BOOK *Gorilla,* Anthony Browne firmly established his ranking as one of the most highly original creators of picture books to arrive on the scene in recent years. By 2000 he had won the prestigious Hans Christian Andersen Award for illustration.

Gorilla tells the story of a child whose loneliness is assuaged when her toy gorilla comes to life one night and provides the kind of companionship that has so far been unavailable from her usually preoccupied father. The winner of numerous awards in the United States, Britain (where it won a Kate Greenaway Medal), and elsewhere, the book exemplifies many of the qualities characteristic of Browne's work: forceful, strongly narrative watercolors that blend near-photographic realism with fantastical touches and that exert a strong emotional, often unconscious pull; the skillful use of color, pattern, and background detail to convey mood and meaning; ingenious visual puns and surprises that frequently point to serious, often disturbing, underlying themes; and an exquisite empathy for the concerns of lonely, sensitive children.

Browne was born in Sheffield, England, where his parents ran a pub — a circumstance he credits with his affinity for simian characters, since his father, he has said, was "like a gorilla, big and potentially aggressive during his pub days." He has described himself as having been "a kid with terrors" and can recall "a lot of dark furniture which looked very menacing to me," reminiscences that open fascinating windows onto the symbolic and suggestive ways in which he has employed ordinary household objects, such as a couch or a television, in his art. Although Browne's family was not especially bookish, his father was a frustrated painter and helped spark his son's artistic interest — one that, Browne has said, manifested itself from the start in storytelling pictures and in visual jokes, such as a decapitated talking head he drew as a child.

Browne obtained a degree in graphic design from Leeds College of Arts. He then worked as a medical artist at the Royal Infirmary (a stint that developed his gift for visual narration, for he learned to "tell the story of an operation in pictures"), as a teacher, and as a greeting card designer before publishing his first book, *Through the Magic Mirror*, in 1976. Many notable works followed, among them the deceptively simple but unsettling *Bear Hunt* (1979) and the more ominous *Bear Goes to Town* (1982); *Willy the Wimp* (1984), a hilarious tale that spoofs the physical fitness craze by profiling a chimpanzee who remains as timid as ever despite a beefed-up physique, followed by *Willy the Champ* (1985) and *Willy's Pictures* (2000); *The Visitors Who Came to Stay* (1984), written by Annalena McAfee, another title that demonstrates his remarkable ability to plumb an unhappy child's inner world; and a version of *Hansel and Gretel* (1981) that was, variously, praised for its effective use of symbol to suggest both external and psychic realities and excoriated for its grimly contemporary setting. As the controversy attending this last title implies, Browne is a boldly unconventional artist whose striking images rarely fail to elicit a powerful response. A.J.M.

Bruchac, Joseph

A merican author, b. 1942. Joseph Bruchac III, partially descended from Abenaki Indians, has drawn on his Native American heritage throughout his writing career. Born in Saratoga Springs, New York, Bruchac attended Cornell and Syracuse University and received his doctorate from Union Graduate School. He has taught literature and writing in West Africa, at American universities, and in a prison school.

His first adult book, *Indian Mountain and Other Poems* (1971), was followed by many volumes of POETRY and by novels such as *Dawn Land* (1993).

His early works for children include AMERICAN FOLKLORE such as *Turkey Brother, and Other Tales: Iroquois Folk Stories* (1975) and *Stone Giants and Flying Heads: Adventure Stories of the Iroquois* (1978). These retold tales are written with authority but were published in unfortunately mediocre editions. Two oversize volumes, *Keepers of the Earth: Native American Stories and Environmental Activities for Children* (1988) and *Keepers of the Animals: Native American Stories and Wildlife Activities for Children* (1991), both written with Michael J. Caduto, interestingly combine stories, crafts, and scientific experiments but are directed at an adult audience of parents and educators.

Bruchac is best known for his PICTURE BOOK texts. Written with Jonathan London, *Thirteen Moons on Turtle's Back: A Native American Year of Moons* (1992) is a collection of evocative, yet mysterious poems, each celebrating a different Native American nation. *The First Strawberries: A Cherokee Story* (1993) is a moving folktale about marital respect. *Fox Song* (1993) weaves elements of Native American culture into the story of a contemporary child's grief over her great-grandmother's death. Two picture books for older children, *The Boy Called Slow: The True Story of Sitting Bull* (1995) and *Squanto's Journey* (2000), present historical figures from the point of view of a Native American.

Illustrated by distinguished artists, these accessible, emotionally satisfying texts prove Bruchac to be a formidable talent in the field of multicultural books for children. P.D.S.

Bryan, Ashley

A merican author and illustrator, b. 1923. Born in the Bronx, New York City, Ashley Bryan was artistic from childhood. He considers his work as an illustrator to be a "natural outgrowth" of his love for drawing and painting and makes no distinction between the fine arts and fine illustration, "since, through the ages, artists have used themes from tales or books as a basic resource for expression."

Bryan majored in philosophy at Columbia University and also graduated from two art schools, the Cooper Union Art School and Columbia. He taught drawing and painting at Queens College, Lafayette College, the Dalton School, and other institutions around New York. He has also worked in the Head Start program and within organizations such as churches, teaching art to children. He had the idea of illustrating folktales years before he illustrated his first book, *Fablieux,* in 1964; after illustrating one more book, he began to create his own works. His first, *The Ox of the Wonderful Horns and Other African Tales* (1971), contained four tales of trickery. Bryan has done extensive research into source material and adapted it for his authentic tales. Many of his books are illustrated with paintings made to resemble woodcuts; with this technique, the art in the finished book bears a closer relation to the original art.

Bryan's next book, *Walk Together Children: Black American Spirituals* (1974), grew out of an interest in that music while he was growing up. In this case, he used block prints, inspired by early block-print religious books, to illustrate the book. Music, language, and art converged again in *Beat the Story-Drum, Pum-Pum* (1980), a collection of folktales told with humor and a rhythmic, poetic use of language. The book won the 1981 Coretta Scott King Illustrator Award. In addition to his books of spirituals and folktales, Bryan illustrated and introduced a volume of POETRY by Paul Laurence Dunbar, *I Greet the Dawn* (1978). In a critical article for the *Horn Book Magazine* in 1979, he not only discussed Dunbar's poetry in dialect and in standard English but gave an overview of African American poets that is as elegantly written as it is informative. Bryan has also written poetry; in his *Sing to the Sun* (1992), twenty-three original poems are depicted in illustrations that are composed of color blocks stylized somewhat like stained glass windows.

Ashley Bryan began an association with Dartmouth College in the early 1970s, and after serving as chairman of the art department, he became professor emeritus of art and visual studies. Bryan exhibits his work on the island in Maine where he lives. He is known for his dramatic readings of his own and others' works, using different voices and grand gestures. He creates puppets using driftwood, shells, and bones, which he uses when telling stories on the island. Bryan has exhibited his paintings in many one-man shows and has lectured extensively on his own work and on African American poets. He was invited by the American Library Association to deliver the 1990 May Hill Arbuthnot Lecture.

S.H.H.

Bunting, Eve

American writer, b. 1928. Eve Bunting, born in Ireland, has told of the tradition of the Shanachie, who "went from house to house telling his tales of ghosts and fairies, of old Irish heroes and battles still to be won." The author has said, "Maybe I'm a bit of a Shanachie myself, telling my stories to anyone who'll listen." With more than one hundred titles to her credit, this prolific author has shared her unique storytelling talents in PICTURE BOOKS, MIDDLE-GRADE FICTION, and YOUNG ADULT NOVELS. Her stories explore the imaginary worlds of giants and ghosts as well as contemporary themes that reflect the adolescent world.

Bunting's writing career began in 1958, when she moved to California with her husband and three children. Several years after the transition to a new country, she enrolled in a writing-for-publication class at her local junior college. "All doubts vanished when I had my first published story and then my first published book," she recalled.

The sheer range and volume of Bunting's work make one speculate as to how the author generates so many new ideas. "I would definitely say that 90 percent of my story seeds come from something I've read in my daily paper or in my weekly periodical . . . and the other 10 percent from what I see happening around me." Bunting's books have tackled homelessness, in the picture book *Fly Away Home* (1991); the Japanese internment camps in *So Far from the Sea* (1998); mixed-up identities in *Sharing Susan* (1991); and responsibility in *Our Sixth-Grade Sugar Babies* (1990). In *Babies*, Bunting, with a light touch, looked at the perils of a classroom experiment in which each sixth-grader is expected to look after a five-pound bag of sugar as if it were a baby. For the character Vicki this is a chance to try to prove to her mother that she can be trusted to baby-sit her half sister. But when a handsome seventh-grader asks her to go bicycling, Vicki is faced with some uncomfortable choices about her charge.

Bunting's stories are well paced and engaging. *Coffin on a Case* (1992) introduces Henry Coffin, the twelve-year-old son of a private investigator who spends part of the summer helping an attractive high school student track down her missing mother. Appealing even to reluctant readers, the lighthearted book won the Edgar Award for Best Juvenile Mystery in 1993. In addition to this award, Bunting has received the Golden Kite Award from the Society of Children's Book Writers and Illustrators, the Southern California Council on Literature for Children and Young People 1993 Distinguished Body of Work Award, and the Regina Medal of the Catholic Library Association. Reaching a variety of readers is an important part of Bunting's work. She has said, "One of my greatest joys as a writer is the knowledge that I do reach older, reluctant readers."

Bunting's characters wrestle with the choices that face them, and their responses are believable and genuine. Yet without becoming didactic, the author can skillfully guide her readers to responsible choices. Her adult as well as her child characters are not immune to problems or mistakes. In *The Wednesday Surprise* (1989), the father is illiterate and tries to hide the fact from his young daughter. In *Sixth-Grade Sleepover* (1986), Janey's parents help her overcome her fear of the dark, which resulted from a negative experience with a harsh baby sitter. Bunting has dealt with compelling issues. Her protagonists often face difficult situations and choices because, as she has said, "That's life." C.L.

Burnford, Sheila

Scottish-born Canadian writer (1918–1984). Critical debate goes on over whether *The Incredible Journey* (1961) is a model of the realistic animal novel or whether it is, like Anna Sewell's *Black Beauty*, another sentimental and anthropomorphic ANIMAL STORY for children. Ironically, Burnford did not even conceive the novel as a children's book.

Sheila Burnford wrote just six books, only two for children. But *Mr. Noah and the Second Flood* (1973), which she intended for children, is not read today; *The Incredible Journey*, which has been claimed by them, outshines work by more prolific writers for children. The fictional story tells of a treacherous 250-mile journey through the Canadian wilderness made by three animal friends — an old bull terrier, a Siamese cat, and a Labrador retriever. While their owners vacation, the trio are left in the care of a family friend, but they escape and embark on the trek home. They struggle against wild animals, interfering humans, and rugged terrain, all the while fighting their domestication in order to survive and protect each other. The animals — and their relationships — were taken from life.

Born in Scotland and privately educated in England and Europe, Burnford lived in Sussex during World War II, when her children were young. She once recalled, "I came to rely upon [Bill, my English bull terrier] for comfort and security far more than one would in normal times." She talked to him, even read aloud to him for long stretches at a time. After they moved to Canada, a Siamese kitten, Simon, was added to the family "as companion and consolation for Bill, when the children were away all day at school. They were closer than any other cat-and-dog relationship I have seen." When Burnford's husband later acquired a Labrador, the aging bull terrier and young Lab developed an interdependent relationship as well. It was at this time that Burnford started writing for magazines, and, when Bill died, *The Incredible Journey* began to take shape.

The novel turns on one of Burnford's longstanding interests, the "individual and original communication that exists even between animals of diversified species when they live harmoniously with common domestic background." *The Incredible Journey* has been translated into over twenty languages and made into two Walt Disney films, the first (1963) using the same name, and more recently (1993) as *Homeward Bound: The Incredible Journey.* It has received numerous awards, including the Canadian Library Association's 1963 Book of the Year for Children Award, the counterpart to the Newbery Medal. It was placed on the 1964 IBBY Honor List, named an ALA Notable Book, and in 1971 received a Lewis Carroll Shelf Award.

Fans point to the highly dramatic third-person point of view and to Burnford's care in keeping the animals true to their breeds. Critics point out the plot's heavy reliance on coincidence and the animals' human motivations. Although flaws exist, the strengths far outweigh them and the body of children's literature has no finer example of realistic animal fiction than *The Incredible Journey.* S.A.B.

Burningham, John

British author and illustrator, b. 1936. John Burningham is one of the most respected author-illustrators of books for the very young. His books convey a message that children love: though dependent on their parents in many ways, they have a rich life of their own apart from them.

Burningham was born in Farnham, Surrey, England, and his family — which included his two older sisters — moved frequently while he was growing up because his father was a salesman. Burningham attended ten different schools, including A. S. Neill's Summerhill, well known as a place where nonconformism was the norm. Burningham was an indifferent student at every school he attended — although he loved art — and he preferred to be out of doors. A conscientious objector for two years during the 1950s, Burningham worked on farms, in hospitals, and on forestry projects. After his alternative service, he attended London's Central School of Art and Craft, where he met his wife-to-be, illustrator HELEN OXENBURY. After he finished art school, London Transport gave him an assignment designing posters. After a brief time in New York, Burningham returned to London and was teaching part-time in art school when his first book sold.

This first attempt at writing and illustrating was accepted when an editor saw a rough draft of *Borka, the Adventures of a Goose with No Feathers* (1963). The book won the Kate Greenaway Medal and encouraged Burningham to pursue a career in children's books. In 1973 he wrote and illustrated *Mr. Gumpy's Outing,* the story of a man who goes out for a Sunday afternoon ride on the river and ends up with a boat full of children and animals. For this book he once again won the Kate Greenaway Medal, which secured him a respected place in Great Britain's children's literature world. His version of *Around the World in Eighty Days* took him on the path of Jules Verne; the real-life charting of a fictitious journey was so hectic that Burningham had no time at all to draw and had to reconstruct the trip back home in England. *Come Away from the Water, Shirley* (1978), a favorite of many readers, exhibits his customary triumph in depicting a child's imagination, in this case, one who sees herself on a pirate ship rather than at the beach in her parents' dull, prosaic world. *Would You Rather . . .* (1978) presents choices that make children laugh and wonder at the same time.

Burningham has worked in a variety of media, including crayon, charcoal, India ink, gouache, and pastel. The Burninghams have three children, Lucy, William, and Emily, and though John did not consciously seek their opinions, the offhand critiques of his readership were available to him while he worked at home. Burningham has won many awards, including the *School Library Journal's* Best Book Award, the Child Study Association of America's Children's Book of the Year, the Deutscher Jugendliteraturpreis (the German Youth Literature Prize), a New York Times Best Illustrated Book award, and the Boston Globe–Horn Book Award for illustration. A.C.

Burton, Virginia Lee

American author and illustrator, 1909–1968. The undiminished reputation of Virginia Lee Burton is embodied in a lifework of seven books of her own creation and her illustrations for seven books by other writers. Taking her cue from her small sons, Aristides and Michael, Burton chose subjects that would intrigue children: Choo Choo, the runaway engine; Mary Ann, the steam shovel who helped Mike Mulligan; Katy, the brave snowplow; the Little House, who survived a city burgeoning about her; Calico, the wonder horse of a Western adventure told in a comic-strip format. All are characters who have

survived for generation after generation of readers. What also survives is the quality of the art: the strong drawings in *Choo Choo* (1937) and *Calico the Wonder Horse* (1941), full of liveliness and motion; the small telling details that children enjoy finding on the pages of *Mike Mulligan and His Steam Shovel* (1939); the satisfying integration of shaped text areas and pictures in *The Little House* (1942); the decorative borders that enhance *Katy and the Big Snow* (1943).

Elements that most distinguish Burton's work are her intricate theory of design, which she used in all her books but which was particularly effective in Anne Malcomson's *The Song of Robin Hood* (1947), and her sense of the wholeness of the book, that is, the relationship of successive pages, which she showed by reprising each page in a sequence of tiny drawings on the endpapers of the 1950 edition of *Calico* and of *Maybelle the Cable Car* (1952). Over the years she kept refining her theories of design and became unhappy with her art for the 1941 edition of *Calico*. Her zeal for perfection led her to redraw every illustration, sharpening details and using subtle gradations of black and white, and, happily, to use the word she originally wanted, *Stinker* instead of *Slinker*, in the title: *Calico the*

Endpaper illustration by Virginia Lee Burton for her book *The Little House* (1942).

Wonder Horse, or the Saga of Stewy Stinker. In *Life Story* (1962) she used the device of a stage on which various characters — an astronomer, an explorer, a lecturer, an author, and an artist (herself) — dramatically pull the curtains to reveal scenes showing the history of the universe and the development of life. Act V relies on the seasonal themes and setting of *The Little House,* but far from being repetitious, the familiar scenes fit into her overarching scheme — the story of life from cosmic bang to her own backyard.

Although she illustrated several tales by ARNA BONTEMPS and her favorite HANS CHRISTIAN ANDERSEN story, "The Emperor's New Clothes," Burton's long labor of love was *The Song of Robin Hood.* Using with virtuosity a black-and-white scratchboard technique, she designed full-page illustrations with vignettes for each ballad verse that are vigorous, witty, and intricately designed and detailed. *The Song of Robin Hood* was named a Caldecott Honor Book in 1948, and *The Little House* won the 1943 Caldecott Medal.

Born in Massachusetts, Burton was brought up in California. Her father was the first dean at Massachusetts Institute of Technology; her mother was a poet and painter who called herself Jeanne D'Orge. Burton intended to make dance her career, but on coming to Boston in her late teens, she studied drawing with George Demetrios, a well-known sculptor whom she married in 1931. At her home in Folly Cove, part of Gloucester, Massachusetts, she taught her theories of design to friends and neighbors. Together they organized the Folly Cove Designers, a guild-type group that for over thirty years was internationally famous for its hand-block-printed textiles.

Burton never considered herself a writer, and her ideas and their subsequent development into art provided the impetus for her texts. Once her sons were grown her inspiration to create books for children waned, and she spent her time block-printing textiles and working on *Design and How!,* a book presenting her theories of design, which she had not finished at the time of her death. Her stories may be simple and straightforward; but her books have heroes and heroines children can understand and enjoy, ingenious and satisfactory endings, and lively illustrations. The books survive because they exhibit so effectively the elements most basic to children's literature. L.K.

Byars, Betsy

American author, b. 1928. Reading a Betsy Byars book is like talking to a good friend: ideas and problems are taken seriously, but laughter is sure to follow. Betsy Byars has written PICTURE BOOKS, EASY READERS, FANTASIES, and HISTORICAL FICTION, but she is best known for her realistic fiction in which splashes of humor brighten serious subjects. Byars started writing when her children were young, first magazine articles and then children's books. Her children's books began to receive critical mention after several years, and she has won numerous awards, including the Newbery Medal for *The Summer of the Swans* (1970).

In *The Summer of the Swans,* Sara, a young girl at odds with herself and her family, discovers the strength of both when she locates her mentally handicapped younger brother, who had become lost in the woods. Byars's protagonists are usually likable preadolescents who are seeking a sense of belonging or connection to alleviate loneliness. In *The Midnight Fox* (1968), Tom, a nonathletic city boy, is sent to his aunt and uncle's farm for the summer while his parents travel in Europe. He feels lonely and out of place until he discovers a black fox and is distracted from his sadness by her wild beauty and by the fierceness with which she protects her one remaining cub.

Byars is particularly adept at making her protagonists come alive, giving vivid form to their sadness and joy. The reader is privy to much of the characters' thoughts, and the frequent use of memory and fantasy provides further illumination of character. When we first meet Byars's characters, they are frequently being pulled along by a tide of events, with little control over the direction of their lives. But from their inevitable and brave attempts to swim the current, wisdom and maturation result. When the three children in *The Pinballs* (1977) are sent to a foster home, they initially see themselves as pinballs: they simply go wherever the adult world sends them. But as they begin to care about one another, they discover that they can make choices — and take responsibility.

Unusual families are typical in Byars's books and are often significant, if not central, to the protagonist's difficulties. Frequently one or both parents are absent, due to divorce, death, or even, as in *The Two Thousand Pound Goldfish* (1982), because they are wanted by the FBI. The remaining parent or guardian is often distracted by trying to earn a living or simply gives way to selfishness. In *The Night Swimmers* (1980), while Retta's father is consumed by his attempt to become a successful country singer, Retta must be a mother to her younger brothers — with anger and sadly predictable failure as the result. Byars's Blossom Family series and Bingo Brown series, both for younger children, are lighter; in them the humor mingles with simpler problems than appear in her other books. The enduring popularity of Byars's books attests to her knack for connecting with the emotions and experiences of her readers. A.E.Q.

C

Cadnum, Michael

American author, b. 1949. Michael Cadnum was already known as a poet and author of adult suspense novels when he began writing a story with a particularly intriguing premise: a teenage alcoholic accidentally kills his best friend and then constructs an elaborate cover-up, which includes periodically telephoning his friend's parents and impersonating the dead boy. Although Cadnum assumed the book would be published for adults, *Calling Home* (1991) was instead released as a YOUNG ADULT NOVEL — an auspicious debut followed by many more psychological thrillers featuring teenage protagonists.

Born in Orange, California, the author moved frequently with his family when he was growing up, an experience that inspired his 1997 picture book, *The Lost and Found House*. He attended the University of California, received a master's degree from San Francisco State University, and, at various times, worked as a shipping clerk, ran a suicide prevention center, and was employed as teacher. Now living with his wife in Albany, California, he writes full-time, with his pet Amazon parrot keeping him company.

Cadnum's suspense novels always place teenagers in edgy, dramatic situations. Sometimes these young people have created their own predicaments. In *Breaking the Fall* (1992), Stanley enters homes and steals small objects while the occupants are sleeping; Jennifer falsely reports an attack by a serial rapist in *Rundown* (1999). Other protagonists are thrust into situations over which they have no control: Clay's sister mysteriously disappears in *Zero at the Bone* (1996); *Edge* (1997) concerns a teenage boy whose feelings of security are destroyed after his father is shot during a carjacking.

Using the first-person narrative voice, Cadnum creates character studies of often-disturbed teenagers. Some verge on being unlikable, yet the reader eventually comes to understand their anxiety and reasons for acting out. In *Taking It* (1995), a seventeen-year-old kleptomaniac, Anna, is alienated from her family and, in the final pages, reveals a secret that adds emotional viability to her increasingly uncontrolled actions. Cadnum excels at this type of sleight-of-hand. Though his lean prose style is coolly introspective, tension and emotion bubble beneath the surface. With a poet's eye for detail, he records precise observations — the "bright, beautiful burst" of a bottle hitting the pavement, the sandpaper surface of a diving board, the eye-watering tartness of lime sorbet — many of which contribute to the disquieting atmosphere of unease and anxiety.

This gift for memorable detail and imagery is also evident in the author's HISTORICAL FICTION. *In a Dark Wood* (1998) is a violent account of the Robin Hood legend, written from the perspective of the sheriff of Nottingham. Also set in the Middle Ages, *The Book of the Lion* (2000) follows Edmund, an apprentice metalworker, as he travels to the Holy Land on the Crusades; this novel was a finalist for the National Book Award. *Raven of the Waves* (2001) contrasts the experiences of seventeen-year-old Lidsmod, a Viking warrior on his first raid, with those of thirteen-year-old Wiglaff, a monk's apprentice with a gift for healing. Though likely to appeal to a different audience than his thrillers do, Cadnum's historical novels — with their gory battle scenes and naturalistic accounts of drunken brawls and pestilence — are less subtle, but no less memorable, than his contemporary young adult books.

P.D.S.

Caldecott, Randolph

B ritish illustrator and author, 1846–1886. Along with WALTER CRANE and KATE GREENAWAY, Randolph Caldecott was one of the three great illustrators to work under the auspices of the English printer Edmund Evans and to usher in a golden age of book illustration for children. His style, livelier than Crane's and more robust than Greenaway's, is still held up as a model for illustrators of children's books, for his pictures are full of energy and humor as well as mischief, and they speak to a real rather than an idealized world of childhood.

Caldecott showed an early talent for drawing and for remodeling in clay and wood, but unlike Crane and Greenaway, whose artist fathers encouraged their talents, Caldecott's father steered him away from a career in art and into banking. Caldecott continued to draw the farms and animal life of his beloved countryside in his spare time, however, and banking colleagues recall finding sketches of horses and dogs among his bills and ledgers. When he moved from the Shropshire countryside to Manchester, he took classes at the school of art and developed a group of friends among the artists of that community. By 1872 he had had several drawings published, and when he moved to London he continued to study art and sculpture. Here, too, he established close friendships with artists and publishers who encouraged his talents. Indeed, throughout his life Caldecott's warm and unassuming manner endeared him to a wide circle of friends who sought eagerly to assist his endeavors and protect his well-being. In fact, it was because of his ill health, thought to be the result of a bout with rheumatic fever when he was a child, that his good friend, editor Henry Blackburn, suggested that he illustrate travel books. This occupation would allow him to travel to milder climates and avoid English winters. One of the first of these books, *Harz Mountains: A Tour in the Toy Country* (1872), exhibits his unique and lively view of life that would so delight children and helped to establish his reputation as an illustrator.

Following a great success with the illustrations for several chapters of Washington Irving's *Sketch Book* called *Old Christmas* (1878) and the commission for a second Irving book, *Bracebridge Hall* (1878), Caldecott began to think seriously about illustrating children's books. He knew of Walter Crane's success with his books for children and admired their quality; he turned to Crane for advice. At about the same time, the printer Edmund Evans, having seen Caldecott's illustrations for the Irving book, called upon him to propose a collaboration. Although at this point in his career Caldecott had not done much color work, Evans's success in color printing and Crane's recommendations must have convinced him to consent. Eventually, the two agreed to produce the first of sixteen PICTURE BOOKS for children, *The Diverting History of John Gilpin* (1878) and *The House That Jack Built* (1878). In these and others, such as *The Queen of Hearts* (1881) and *Three Jovial Huntsmen* (1880), Caldecott's delight in life, his eye for the odd detail or the ludicrous incident, and his warmth and playfulness found their true home. He was a skilled draftsman, and the exceptional and lively quality of his work can be seen in his outline sketches as much as in his full-color illustrations. Caldecott was able to bring individual characters to life, giving each their own personality. Drawn with a careful sense of composition and with as much care for the empty spaces as for the little details, Caldecott's illustrations do not simply mirror words in the text, they extend them in unique, humorous, and surprising ways. His books have offered delight to readers of all ages in his time and our own.

B.K.

Carle, Eric

American illustrator and author, b. 1929. The artist and author of one of America's most popular contemporary PICTURE BOOKS, *The Very Hungry Caterpillar* (1969), works in a studio filled with large drawers of colored tissue paper on which he has splashed, painted, or dabbed acrylic paints to create special textures and effects. Eric Carle cuts tissue paper into the desired shapes, then pastes them in layers on cardboard. He then takes full-color photographs of the artwork, to be reproduced in a picture book format. "Ninety-nine percent of the illustration is made of paper," Carle has said, "but sometimes I use a crayon or a bit of ink to accent small details."

Born of German parents in Syracuse, New York, in 1935, Carle and his family returned to Germany, where he disliked the rigid school system except for his art classes, in which he was free to exercise his creativity. At age twenty-two, Carle returned to the United States and worked as a graphic designer for the *New York Times*. He began freelance work in commercial art in 1963.

It never occurred to Carle to write and illustrate children's books until BILL MARTIN JR., an editor at Holt, Rinehart and Winston, asked him to illustrate *Brown Bear, Brown Bear, What Do You See?* in 1967. Shortly after the publication of

Brown Bear, Carle met Ann Beneduce, and she became his editor, a relationship that lasted almost twenty years. Carle has said, "We discussed picture books and agreed they should be fun, bright, bold, and educational without being heavy-handed." Carle's first book for Beneduce, the COUNTING BOOK *1, 2, 3 to the Zoo* (1968), won first place at the Bologna International Children's Book Fair. Said Carle, "Suddenly, at age forty, I was an illustrator and author! And I knew what I wanted to do for my life's work."

The Very Hungry Caterpillar is the story of a winsome caterpillar who eats his way through holes in the book while introducing themes of counting, days of the week, and the life cycle of the butterfly. Carle was one of the first illustrators intrigued with the idea of introducing natural science concepts to young children. *The Very Hungry Caterpillar* has remained in print, attesting to its popularity with preschool and elementary-age children. Since that book, Carle has illustrated more than seventy books for preschool and primary school children, which have sold over fifty-five million copies worldwide.

The underlying purpose behind the brightly colored pictures and hidden surprises in Carle's books is, he has said, "to combine learning with fun and to bridge the gap for youngsters making the transition between home and school." His approach to making picture books is exemplified in *The Grouchy Ladybug* (1977), a cumulative tale about an impolite ladybug who becomes happier when she is better behaved. Here Carle works the themes of appropriate social behavior and telling time into the entertaining plot. Also representative is *The Very Busy Spider* (1984), a story about persistence that features a raised spider web, enabling visually impaired children to feel the story's progression. In *Animals Animals* (1989) and *Dragons Dragons* (1991), the artist's vivid collages illustrate poems describing a variety of real and imagined creatures. *Today Is Monday* (1993) bears all the earmarks of its popular predecessors. The energy of its pictures combined with its spirited traditional verses offers a rollicking, good-humored romp for young listeners and readers. With each decade the list of his fine books has increased; in *Dream Snow* (2001), Carle used bright, textured collages and a clear plastic sheet to show the creatures that lie beneath the snow.

In 2001 Carle received the Officer's Cross of the Order of Merit of the Federal Republic of Germany. In the same year construction began on the Eric Carle Museum of Picture Book Art on the campus of Hampshire College in Amherst, Massachusetts, which will house his art and the work of other children's book artists.

A young child once called Carle "Mr. Picture Writer," a title he enjoys and one that seems highly appropriate for an illustrator whose picture books continue to entertain, teach, and spark a child's imagination. S.L.

Voices of the Creators

Eric Carle

One day in kindergarten, in Syracuse, New York, my teacher stamped a cow and a rooster into my workbook. I then drew a barnyard scene around the oddly placed animals. I harnessed the cow to a wagon loaded with hay and added a farmer with a pitchfork. Then I surrounded the rooster with a hen house, which I attached to a barn with a sliding door. It seemed to me that these two forlorn animals needed to be "explained."

My teacher asked my mother to come to school for a conference. My mother was convinced that I had behaved badly or worse. Walking down the hallway, she noticed many pictures taped to the wall; they were signed "Eric." The teacher told her that her son had drawn them, that he was good at art, and that she should nurture this talent. My mother promised that she would. A door opened that day. I formed the unshakable conviction that drawing and making pictures would be the core of my life. My teacher opened the door; my mother kept her promise; my father gave the promise shape.

My father had wanted to become an artist, but his strict father would not have a starving artist in the family. My father loved nature and animals, especially small ones. He and I, hand in hand, would walk across meadows and through the nearby forest. On our explorations, he would lift rocks to show me a worm or a salamander; he taught me that it was easier to catch a slow lizard in the cool morning than a quick lizard in the hot afternoon.

My parents went back to Germany in 1935. Because of a grade-school teacher who inflicted corporal punishment, I felt physically and emotionally so devastated that I hated school for the next ten years — until I went to art school. But while I was in Gymnasium — high school — I discovered a love of classical music. My Latin teacher, a short man with a goatee, was a lover and practitioner of classical music. He and his wife and six children each played an instrument, and some Sunday afternoons they performed at his home. From these occasions he would ask his pupils to join his friends and family for a round of Beethoven, Mozart, and Schubert.

In a strange way a door had opened again. Later I learned that PICTURE BOOKS, too, need rhythm, that a book must flow like a symphony or quartet or duo; that it must have movements, adagios, and fortissimos. Books, like music, must be held together by a beginning, a middle, and an end.

My art teacher soon discovered my love for drawing and painting. There were few who liked art, and Herr Kraus was grateful to have found someone who took his classes seriously. As a young man he had been a socialist and follower of the German expressionist movement. Socialists and expressionists, however, were out of favor under Hitler. Abstract artists were "degenerate" and forbidden to paint or show their work; often it was confiscated and even destroyed.

One day Herr Kraus asked me to his home. There he pulled from the rear of his linen closet a large box. "I like your drawings," said my art teacher. "I like their loose and sketchy quality. Unfortunately, I have instructions to teach naturalistic and realistic art. But I want to show you something else." He reached into the box and pulled out a reproduction of one of the forbidden paintings. At first I was shocked and repulsed. Never had I seen anything like this. But Herr Kraus stood there, unruffled and unafraid; he was proud of his kind of art, and his love for it shone in his eyes. He opened one more door at a most appropriate moment.

My childhood during World War II was gray. The buildings in the cities and towns of Germany were camouflaged in dull greens, dull grays, and dull browns. Clothing, now utilitarian, was cheerless and without color. Even the weather in central Europe is often gray. In art school after the war I learned about the joys of color. Ever since, I have striven for bold colors in order to counteract the grays and dark shadows of my youth. I want to celebrate color and push the range of colors to ever new heights.

Not too long ago, a child wrote to me: "We are alike in the same way; you like colors and I like colors." Another one wrote, "Dear Mr. Carle, you are a good picture writer." I would like to be remembered as a picture writer and as someone who has opened a door for children to the world of pictures and words. 🎨

Carrick, Carol; Carrick, Donald

Carol: American writer, b. 1935; Donald: American illustrator, 1929–1989. For more than twenty years writer Carol Carrick collaborated with her husband, Donald, to create thirty-seven outstanding children's books. Their career together began when Donald, a portrait and landscape painter who had studied in Spain, was asked by Robert Goldston to illustrate his children's history book *The Civil War in Spain* (1966). As Donald went on to illustrate other books, an editor suggested that he write and illustrate a PICTURE BOOK of his own. He asked Carol to help. In Vermont, Don drew sketches of a beautiful barn; Carol researched animals that lived in barns and wrote a text for his drawings. *The Old Barn* (1966) was published and was soon followed by a number of nature books, in-cluding *The Brook* (1967), *Swamp Spring* (1969), and *The Pond* (1970), which captures in poetic imagery and watercolor the atmosphere of a summer pond and the creatures that depend upon it.

Both Donald and Carol grew up playing in woods and ponds, Donald in Michigan, Carol in Queens, New York. Donald drew, and Carol collected cocoons, identified wildflowers, and wrote poems and stories. Their shared deep appreciation for nature, balanced with their conscientious concern for accuracy, makes their books richly sensitive and substantial and has earned them many awards, including the Outstanding Science Trade Book for Children from the National Science Teachers Association and the Children's Book Council for *The Blue Lobster* (1975) and *The Crocodiles Still Wait* (1980). Carol imagined these books visually, choosing the concepts for Donald's art. When she got an idea for a book, she would first ask Donald what he thought of it. Later, she would show him a draft of the manuscript and again ask for his opinion. They worked independently, save for their research. As Donald always worked from life, this involved crayfish living in the turkey roaster, turtles in the bathtub, and a vole and a lobster in captivity.

With the birth of their sons, Christopher and Paul, Carol rediscovered emotions from her own childhood and began to write from family experiences. The family moved from New York City to Martha's Vineyard, and she wrote numerous picture book adventures starring Christopher and his dog on the island: *Sleep Out* (1973), *Lost in the Storm* (1974), *The Accident* (1976), and *The Foundling* (1977). In these adventures, as in all her work, the child is portrayed as an independent thinker, making important decisions alone. The writing is simple and heartfelt, sincere, with the right balance of drama and tension.

Carol's sensitivity found its fullest expression in her books for older readers. *What a Wimp* (1979), *Some Friend* (1979), and *Stay away from Simon* (1985) deal with the idea of outsiders and explore inner feelings with deep insight. *Stay away from Simon,* set in the nineteenth century, is a powerful adventure story of a retarded boy, feared and shunned, who rescues two children lost in a snowstorm. Here, where lives are at risk, Carol demonstrated the great importance of understanding between people, compassion, and the ability to see beneath appearances.

During their years of collaborating, Donald was always open to opportunities for new directions for his work. He especially enjoyed writing and illustrating his own books, the first of which were *The Tree* (1971) and *Drip Drop* (1973), and he illustrated numerous books by other writers. Since her husband's death in 1989, Carol has continued writing: *Whaling Days* (1993), *Patrick's Dinosaurs on the Internet* (1999), and a book illustrated by Paul Carrrick, *Mothers Are Like That* (2000).

In all their work together Donald and Carol's unique insight into the child's experience made them a strong creative team. Donald's skillful drawing conveys a tenderness and sensitivity that complements Carol's intuitive grasp of the child's vision, her empathy, and the strong value of human kindness. L.L.H.

Carroll, Lewis

British author and mathematician, 1832–1898. The English masterpiece *Alice's Adventures Under Ground* had a modest beginning: it was handwritten and charmingly illustrated by Charles Lutwidge Dodgson as a Christmas gift for a child friend, Alice Liddell. Three years later, in 1865, at the insistence of Mrs. George MacDonald, the manuscript, retitled by the publisher *Alice's Adventures in Wonderland,* was published under the pen name of Lewis Carroll, adorned with illustrations by SIR JOHN TENNIEL. The book's droll illustrations, exuberant fun, and lunacy combined with logic captivated children, and this revolutionary FANTASY achieved immediate and rousing success. Its influence was widespread, inspiring other writers, including GEORGE MACDONALD and E. NESBIT, to write stories for children unfettered by the didacticism that had previously been the norm in British children's books. Carroll followed *Alice* with *Through the Looking Glass and What Alice Found There,* also illustrated by Tenniel. Children so eagerly awaited the second book that 15,500 copies were presold before the book's release in 1871. Carroll's other major contributions to children's literature include the poems *Jabberwocky* (1855) and *The Hunting of the Snark: An Agony in Eight Fits* (1876).

Alice's Adventures in Wonderland begins with a bored Alice who is suddenly mesmerized by the appearance of a fully clothed white rabbit running toward a large rabbit hole and repeating "Oh dear! Oh dear! I shall be too late!" Without a moment's thought, Alice follows the rabbit down the hole and finds herself in a veritable wonderland where nothing seems to follow the logic she has learned during her proper British upbringing. So powerful has been the book's influence that memorable characters, such as the Hatter, March Hare, Dormouse, and Cheshire Cat, to name a few, have become inextricable parts of our popular culture.

Dodgson, a shy and obscure mathematician and deacon at Christ Church, Oxford, was horrified to discover that his alter ego, Lewis Carroll, was famous, praised, and sought after, even by Queen Victoria. Dodgson attempted to dissociate himself from Lewis Carroll, and he wrote, "Mr. Dodgson neither claims nor acknowledges any connection with the books not published under his name." Although Dodgson wrote mathematical treatises and invented many games of mathematics and logic under his own name, his fame was reserved for his children's books and poems written as Lewis Carroll.

Carroll's books have been analyzed by critics, and his inner life has been scrutinized by psychologists. Originally reviewed simply as nonsensical fairy tales, the stories came to be seen as symptoms indicating a disturbed mind. More likely, Carroll retained his playful and childlike perspectives as a result of a happy childhood.

Apparently he was more comfortable with children because with them he did not stammer, as he did when in the company of adults. He avidly read fairy tales and nonsense rhymes and even as a boy had entertained other children with games, stories, puzzles, plays, and drawings. Carroll recognized the child's inner fears, wishes, intelligence, and imagination. He unleashed thousands of children's minds and imaginations and invited them to laugh.

His stories and poems have been translated into many languages and adapted to stage, film, television, and even rock music. In 1991–1992, the British Museum exhibited Carroll's original writings and photographs in celebration of the 125th anniversary of *Alice's Adventures in Wonderland* and of the talented man who changed children's literature. B.J.B.

Catalanotto, Peter

American illustrator and author, b. 1959. Peter Catalanotto burst onto the PICTURE BOOK scene with his very first book and continues to receive well-deserved attention. He grew up on Long Island, one of five children, four of whom went to art school. He recalls being amazed that everyone didn't draw all the time, as his family members did. Catalanotto attended the Pratt Institute, earning a B.F.A. in 1981. After college he tended bar, worked as a custodian, and did illustration work for magazines including *Woman's Day* and *Reader's Digest* before he began painting book jackets in 1984. His painting for the cover of JUDY BLUME's *Just as Long as We're Together* (1987) led to his first job illustrating a picture book, CYNTHIA RYLANT's *All I See* (1988). Its luminous watercolors are the hallmark of Catalanotto, using light to convey emotion. *Publishers Weekly* designated him "most promising new artist" in 1989. Catalanotto immediately tried writing his own manuscript, and the result was *Dylan's Day Out* (1989), the story of a Dalmatian and a soccer ball.

Catalanotto's illustrations are particularly well suited to the work of poet and author GEORGE ELLA LYON, and he has illustrated several of her books, including *Cecil's Story* (1991), *Who Came Down That Road* (1992), and *Dreamplace* (1993). In these books and others, Catalanotto painted one event right on top of another. For example, in *Dreamplace* a child is exploring an Anasazi ruin. The native people of the past are depicted in the illustration with the child but appear less substantial, as if they are shadows or spirits. This is a tremendously effective technique for a book about exploring and imagining the past.

Not all of Catalanotto's books have the introspective feel of the Lyon collaborations. SuAnn Kiser's *The Catspring Somersault Flying One-Handed Flip-Flop* (1993) is much more lighthearted, and Catalanotto's palette suits the romping mood of the text. *Mr. Mumble* (1990), which Catalanotto both wrote and illustrated, is also funny although somewhat poignant, a story of a man who is misunderstood. It reflects Catalanotto's own experience as a shy child.

In *Celebrate!: Stories of Jewish Holidays* (1998), written by Gilda Berger, Catalanotto used light and shadow effectively. Moses' face is lit from below, by the light from the burning bush, glorifying him. Each watercolor painting is suffused with golden light, imparting a feeling of holiness appropriate to stories from the Hebrew Bible.

Catalanotto used an entirely different palette for the illustrations in *Circle of Thanks* (1998), written by Susi Gregg Fowler. Focused on the interconnection of animals and human beings in the Arctic, the book is illustrated in soft, pale blue — you can almost feel the cold. As in all of his work, Catalanotto's translucent layers of color give depth and texture to his scenes. Brush strokes define movement, and light illuminates the focus of each illustration.

Getting Used to the Dark: 26 Night Poems (1997), written by Susan Marie Swanson, is illustrated with pencil. Catalanotto used shading to develop the depth and layering that characterize his watercolor works. His glowing, light-filled illustration enhances poetry and nostalgic stories equally well. M.V.K.

Chapter Books (Transitional Readers)

Nothing is more satisfying to a new reader who is six, seven, or eight years old than the ability to read a book independently. Chapter books are intended to motivate these young readers by providing transitional reading that falls between controlled vocabulary books and fully developed novels. In the best of these books, the vocabulary is not limited but is clear and natural and the writing spare but rich. Relatively large type and plenty of white space create unintimidating pages; the books are usually slim, with a minimum of subplots, and the chapters often episodic. Novels attempt to be simple enough not to daunt the tentative while offering sufficient detail of character and plot to allow readers space to lose themselves in the story.

The Little House in the Big Woods (1932), written by LAURA INGALLS WILDER, has long been one of the first choices of a child attempting a chapter book for the first time. Its homey details of pioneer life, the independent spirit of its main character, and the resourcefulness of the Ingalls family are remembered affectionately by readers long after they have moved on to more difficult books. Almost as popular are the two Betsy series: MAUD HART LOVELACE's Betsy-Tacy titles, first appearing in 1940, and Carolyn Haywood's series, beginning with B Is for Betsy (1939). Both series feature fully developed characters who grow with each succeeding book. Another perennial favorite is The Hundred Dresses (1944), ELEANOR ESTES's poignant story of prejudice that introduces Wanda Petronski, a Polish girl from the wrong side of the tracks who is the butt of her classmates' jokes.

Based on a true story, Alice Dalgliesh's The Courage of Sarah Noble (1954) describes the ad-ventures of an eight-year-old girl who travels with her father to the Connecticut wilderness of the eighteenth century, where they build a home in the woods. Sarah stays behind with Indian neighbors while her father leaves to collect the rest of the family. The sensitive treatment of the Native Americans in this book, as well as Sarah's plucky determination to be brave, renders it timeless. The hero in JOHN REYNOLDS GARDINER's Stone Fox (1980) displays courage of another kind. In order to earn enough money to pay the back taxes on his and his grandfather's farm, Willy pits himself and his dog Searchlight in a dogsled race against Stone Fox, the best racer in the country. The heartbreaking ending of this exciting story is alleviated by Stone Fox's gesture of tribute to the dog and the boy.

That simplicity and brevity need not be synonymous with skimpiness in either characterization or plot was made manifestly clear in Sarah, Plain and Tall (1985), which won the Newbery Medal. The poetry of PATRICIA MacLACHLAN's language, rich in metaphor and imagery as it describes Sarah's attempts to acclimate herself to the prairie landscape, coupled with Anna and Caleb's palpable yearning for Sarah to become their mother, gives the book the undiluted power of a small masterpiece.

Stories about pioneers have always been popular with younger readers. One that combines that theme with the equally cherished subject of horses is Elizabeth Shub's White Stallion (1982), in which a young girl traveling west in a covered wagon finds herself in the midst of a herd of wild horses. Also set in the past, but in a different era entirely, is Riki Levinson's Dinnie-AbbieSisterr-r! (1987), an endearing story about a Jewish family living in Brooklyn during the Depression. LUCILLE CLIFTON's The Lucky Stone (1979) takes a longer, symbolic view of history as it tells the story of a pebble first found in the cotton fields by Miss Mandy during slavery days. The stone rescues, in some way, all those who possess it.

While most younger children find it comforting to read stories about everyday experiences, more adventurous readers seek to have their imaginations captured by fantasies that bridge the gap between the familiar and the exotic. An early animal FANTASY still enjoyed by children is *My Father's Dragon* (1948), written by RUTH STILES GANNETT. Also much admired is *A Toad for Tuesday* (1974), written by Russell E. Erickson, with appealing line drawings by Lawrence Di Fiori depicting the comically perilous relationship between Warton the toad and his owl captor. Maxine Chessire's black-and-white wash drawings add depth and mystery to *My Friend the Monster* (1980), written by Clyde Robert Bulla, with its themes of friendship and tolerance. Even SCIENCE FICTION is occasionally represented in transitional novels, one of the most notable being Lee Harding's dramatic account of an alien who falls to Earth in *The Fallen Spaceman* (1980).

For the pure, unadulterated silliness that children love, however, few can compete with the books of DANIEL PINKWATER. One of the most accessible to newly independent readers is *Blue Moose* (1975), which describes in five brief, hilarious episodes the doings of a blue moose who appears unannounced one day at the door of Mr. Breton's restaurant. More recent novels in the same nonsensical vein are JAMES MARSHALL's *Rats on the Roof and Other Stories* (1991) and JON SCIESZKA's books about the Time Warp Trio, beginning with *Knights of the Kitchen Table* (1991). Only slightly less outlandish is *Hilary and the Troublemakers* (1992), Kathleen Leverich's amusing cautionary fable about a girl who has trouble keeping her imagination in check.

Like well-worn shoes, SERIES BOOKS are appreciated by tentative readers for the easy comfort of the instantly recognizable characters and settings. While many are unremarkable, some remain spontaneous in plot and consistently strong in style and characterization. Among the best of these are Johanna Hurwitz's books about the rambunctious and curious boy described in *Rip-Roaring Russell* (1983). Other popular series characters include Adam Joshua, from Janice Lee Smith's series beginning with *The Monster in the Third Dresser Drawer* (1981), and Julian from Ann Cameron's heartwarming series about an African American family that originated with *The Stories Julian Tells* (1981). Two well-drawn characters with special appeal to girls are Angel (*Back-Yard Angel*, 1983, written by Judy Delton) and Jenny (*A Job for Jenny Archer*, 1988, written by Ellen Conford). Slightly more sophisticated in tone is Sheila Greenwald's *Give Us a Great Big Smile, Rosy Cole* (1983). As the potential subject of a children's book written by her famous uncle, Rosy might find herself glorified, but her instincts are appealing and natural.

Books that focus on the familiar world of the classroom are especially popular, and some of the most widely read are Patricia Reilly Giff's stories about the Polk Street School. A strikingly independent character is the feisty heroine of *Muggie Maggie* (1990), written by BEVERLY CLEARY, a writer who understands well how small issues can loom large in childhood. An especially endearing story in the younger range of transitional novels is BETSY BYARS's *Beans on the Roof* (1988), in which the Bean family becomes involved in Anna's school poetry project. This little treasure by an author who usually writes for older children portrays a loving, hardworking family in a few well-chosen words.

Some notable chapter books have been set in foreign countries. Ann Cameron's *The Most Beautiful Place in the World* (1988) is about a boy who lives with his grandmother in a small village in Guatemala, where in spite of the intense poverty he experiences, he manages to find a way to go to school. In Margaret Sacks's *Themba* (1992) a boy leaves his small South African village and embarks on a journey to the city to meet his father, who is returning from the gold mines of Johannesburg. Miriam Schlein's *The Year of the Panda* (1990) introduces an environmental theme in her story of a Chinese boy who finds and raises an abandoned baby panda.

Clearly, self-imposed limitations of vocabulary and length have not prevented the authors of chapter books from expressing largeness of imagination, feeling, and spirit. N.V.

Charlip, Remy

American author and illustrator, b. 1929. Drama, originality, and a vibrant design sense permeate Remy Charlip's entire body of work, which engages and entertains children and adults.

As a highly creative PICTURE BOOK author and illustrator, Charlip first entered the field of children's literature in the mid-1950s and has since crafted over thirty books, which differ extensively in pictures and words. Charlip's artwork, a peculiar pastiche of media, clearly demonstrates his penchant for colorful, kinetic, graphic innovation in picture book illustration. He successfully employs line drawings, naive art, and watercolors to produce imaginative and noteworthy works. As diverse as his illustrations, Charlip's texts include an EASY READER, jokes, POETRY, a jump-rope rhyme, plays, and a retelling of a legend.

Born in Brooklyn, Charlip has brought to children's literature a diverse background especially rich in theatrical experience, which translates specifically into a unique understanding of the dramatic turning of the picture book page. His second self-illustrated book, *Where Is Everybody?* (1957), succeeds because of such drama. Starkly simple in design and execution, the book introduces beginning readers to vocabulary as it places a word or words directly on a black-outlined image the word denotes. *Sky, bird, sun, river,* and *cloud* — each labels its respective image on separate pages; each word picture compels the reader to turn the page to reveal yet another. With this onward thrust the narrative unfolds to tell of an afternoon rain shower, a story easily grasped by novice readers.

Charlip most frequently has used naive art, a childlike style of drawing characterized by simplicity and devoid of sentimentality, to illustrate children's books, as he did for two of MARGARET WISE BROWN's titles. In *The Dead Bird* (1958), one of the first American picture books about death for very young children, Charlip's superb naive drawings, in predominant hues of green, blue, and yellow, convey the childlike fascination the young protagonists have for the dead bird they find, bury ceremoniously, and eventually forget. Simply and directly, Charlip's illustrations capture perfectly the text's tone; Charlip's whimsically naive pictures for Brown's cheerful poem *Four Fur Feet* (1961) cleverly show only the bottom half of a furry, four-legged, nameless animal who ambles around the world. To accompany the creature on his global circumnavigation, the reader literally turns the book completely around, an innovative design technique choreographed by Charlip. For *Baby Hearts and Baby Flowers* (2002), he used bright watercolor art to illustrate a sweet poem, celebrating babies of many species.

Fortunately (1964), written and illustrated by Charlip, contains alluring naive artwork and page-turning drama. Alternating colorful two-page spreads with black and white ones — which coincide with his humorous usage of "fortunately" and "unfortunately" — Charlip has told of the good luck and bad luck that befall a young boy en route to a birthday party. He solemnized and softened his naive style of art when he illustrated *Harlequin and the Gift of Many Colors* (1973), which he wrote with Burton Supree. Set in rural Italy, the legend retells how penniless Harlequin acquired his patchwork carnival costume from compassionate, generous friends and quietly glows with the love and sacrifice Harlequin's peers offer him. Equally resplendent are Charlip's naive watercolor drawings, rendered in delicate pastel hues of lavender, peach, and blue. More realistic than his previous illustrations, the drawings for *Harlequin* include details, shadows, and perspective that emphasize an exquisiteness the tender tale imparts.

A long collaboration with Jerry Joyner resulted in *Thirteen* (1975), Charlip's most intriguing, ingenious, and complex work. Winner of the 1976 Boston Globe–Horn Book Award for Outstanding Illustration, the book develops thirteen individual graphic stories simultaneously in an equal number of two-page spreads. The barest of text accompanies lovely pastel watercolors, and each image possesses narratives over which readers can pore. Brilliant in concept and form, *Thirteen* further establishes Charlip's dramatic propensity to craft picture books that distinctively dance alone.   S.L.S.

Chase, Richard

American folklorist, 1904–1988. Richard Chase was a collector and teller of tales that had been handed down from generation to generation in the Appalachian regions of the United States. His forte was the ability to combine scholarly research on the origins of AMERICAN FOLKLORE and patient editing of the many versions of the stories he collected with his passion for encouraging their oral tradition of being told *spontaneously.* "Reading the printed

Illustration by Berkeley Williams, Jr., for "Jack and the Bean Tree," from *The Jack Tales* (1943), edited and retold by Richard Chase.

word," he wrote in a preface to *Grandfather Tales* (1948), "is, indeed, not the same as the sound of your own voice shaping a tale as it wells up out of your memory and as your own fancy plays with all its twists and turns." His advice to storytellers was not to worry about dialect but to tell the tale in their natural common speech and let the surge of the story prevail. By the 1930s folk singers and country dancers had found a rich heritage in the songs and ballads, the steps and tunes, of Anglo-American folk music. Chase was among them, and his *Old Songs and Singing Games* appeared in 1938.

He also found that the Appalachian regions of Virginia and North Carolina were a repository of folktales, such as "Jack and the Beanstalk" and "Jack and the Giant Killer," in which the hero is a stock figure, a lad generically known as Jack. But in the few generations since the tales had been brought over by emigrants from England and Scotland, the eponymous Jack, according to Chase, had been transformed from "the cocksure, dashing young hero" of the fairy tale to "an easy-going, unpretentious" rural boy, and even though mysterious forces sometimes aided Jack, he remained a "thoroughly human . . . unassuming representative of a very large part of the American people." Chase first learned the tales from R. M. Ward and his kin, descendants of Council Harmon, a renowned storyteller, and edited them into *The Jack Tales* (1943).

Chase traced stories and traditions on both sides of the Atlantic. When *Grandfather Tales* was published, the collection included Appalachian versions of European tales: Robin, in "The Outlaw Boy," learns his bow-and-arrow techniques from the Indians; in "Ashpet" the heroine goes to a church meeting instead of a ball; "Like Meat Loves Salt" is a version of King Lear's story; and Hansel and Gretel, abandoned in a primeval wilderness, become Buck and Bess in "The Two Lost Babes." Chase also researched the Uncle Remus stories first collected by Joel Chandler Harris and was the editor and compiler of *The Complete Tales of Uncle Remus* (1955). His retellings of *Jack and the Three Sillies* (1950),

Wicked John and the Devil (1951), and *Billy Boy* (1966) were published as PICTURE BOOKS. Chase is termed the compiler, rather than editor, of *Billy Boy,* and his rhythmic retelling echoes the many rhymed versions of Lord Randall's tragic tale.

For many years Richard Chase, born in Alabama, lived near Henderson, North Carolina, and was closely associated with the Appalachian Center at Mars Hill College in Mars Hill, North Carolina. He played the recorder, enjoyed leading children and adults in songs and "play-party" games, taught American folk songs and dances, and took part in many storytelling and folk festivals. Chase has been called the man "most responsible for the renaissance of Appalachian story-telling." L.K.

Chess, Victoria

American author and illustrator, b. 1939. Born in Chicago and raised in Washington, Connecticut, Victoria Chess lived for fifteen years in Manhattan and traveled extensively before returning to rural Connecticut, where she now lives with her husband and pets. When Chess attended the Boston Museum School for art training, she was asked to leave due to her lax work habits, but she later found that the promise of money would help keep her productive through more than thirty children's books.

Chess renders her illustrations in a cartoon style with clean outlines and pages busy with pattern, decoration, and detail. She uses colored pencils, liquid watercolors, technical pens, and waterproof inks in a distinct and recognizable style. Her characters have ample, pink flesh, and although they are stocky, the flat outlines filled in with light wash make them appear almost weightless. Long, toothy grins and close-set, circular eyes surrounded by heavy cross-hatching create intense expressions often bordering on mania, a technique quite appropriate for some of the bizarre books Chess has illustrated. Even when the subject matter is wild, however,

Chess's controlled line and stable composition grant the book a mainstream acceptability, and the renegade themes hold great child appeal. For example, when a careless girl breaks all her toys in *Fables You Shouldn't Pay Any Attention To* (1978), written by FLORENCE PARRY HEIDE and Sylvia Worth Van Clief, she gets replacements, while her good siblings, who still have their old toys, receive nothing. In *Poor Esmé* (1982), written and illustrated by Chess, Esmé learns a harsh lesson when she wishes for a playmate and ends up with a hair-pulling, diaper-soiling baby brother. David Greenberg's verse in *Slugs* (1983) describes kids torturing slugs until the creatures take revenge. Chess's drawings allow the reader to feel no sympathy for the amorphous slugs, who let themselves be victimized, or for the mean people, who are as bulbous as the slugs. According to Jim's parents in Hilaire Belloc's *Jim, Who Ran Away from His Nurse, and Was Eaten by a Lion* (1987), another gruesome book, Jim gets what he deserves. The punishment seems severe, but thanks to Chess's portrayal of Jim as mean-eyed and disgustingly roly-poly, the amused reader knows Jim won't be missed.

As in *Jim* and *Slugs* and in several collaborations with JACK PRELUTSKY, many of Chess's books contain texts written in light verse. The combination of singsong text and comic art can defuse a scary situation, so the story is harmless yet titillating, and children can feel scared and secure simultaneously. Such is the case in Florence Parry Heide's *Grim and Ghastly Goings-on* (1992), where even the cheerful colors belie the grisly content.

With little variation in style, Chess has successfully adapted her techniques to suit a range of manuscripts. With vivid colors and her strong line, Chess helped Verna Aardema retell a Mpongwe folktale in *Princess Gorilla and a New Kind of Water* (1992). In *A Hippopotamusn't* (1988) the quietly joyful illustrations capitalize on J. Patrick Lewis's witty animal POETRY. For *The Beautiful Butterfly: A Folktale from Spain* (2000), Chess added a madcap atmosphere to Judy Sierra's more serious text.

Whatever the theme of the book, always present is Chess's sense of humor, as her illustrations ask the reader not to take life too seriously. S.S.

Chinese American Children's Books

Published in 1950, *Fifth Chinese Daughter,* written by Jade Snow Wong, attracted a great deal of attention; the story of a second-generation Chinese American girl growing up in San Francisco's Chinatown in the 1930s was soon translated into several languages and won worldwide acclaim. Never before had there been such an intimate account of a Chinese American family as it struggled to retain and pass on its culture, while bearing hardship and discrimination and learning the many lessons necessary to become part of its new country.

Until *Fifth Chinese Daughter* children's books were mainly about China, the country left behind, and they were written by people outside the culture. Books such as Newbery Medal winner *Young Fu of the Upper Yangtze* (1932), written by E. F. Lewis; *The Story About Ping* (1933), written by MARJORIE FLACK; *The Five Chinese Brothers* (1938), written by Claire Huchet Bishop; and Caldecott Medal winner *Mei Li* (1938), written by Thomas Handforth, represented almost all that was available about China in children's fiction books.

It was puzzling to Chinese American children that the clothing, food, and customs depicted in these books were not what they knew about the land from which their parents emigrated. Imagine the confusion when, each year, at Chinese New Year, well-meaning teachers and librarians read *Mei Li* to their students and talked about how the new year was celebrated in China in walled cities where people rode on camels on the frozen ground. America's largest group of Chinese immigrants came from Guangdong (Canton) province in the south of China, where the weather was temperate and where camels and snow existed only in stories.

The concepts of the vastness of China and the diversity of its population are difficult to comprehend. Language, as well as local customs, food, and clothing, reflect regional differences and differences of social class, occupation, religion, and diverse ethnic traditions. In 1949, China experienced a great upheaval that changed the lives of all the people at every level and in every region. For the first time in its long history, China was united under one government and its people shared a common language. But the China found in America's children's books continued to be exotic and anchored to the past, and the experiences of Chinese Americans continued to be overlooked and underrepresented.

The success of Wong's *Fifth Chinese Daughter* was not to be followed by another such story for twenty-seven years. In *Dragonwings* (1975) LAURENCE YEP combined the elements of life in turn-of-the-century San Francisco Chinatown, the 1906 earthquake and fire, and the reunion of a young man with his father into a compelling story. It is based on a true account of a Chinese immigrant who built a flying machine and flew it off the Oakland hills in 1909. *Dragonwings* was selected as a 1976 Newbery Honor Book. Yep's *Child of the Owl* (1977), imbued with Chinese tradition, is the story of a young girl who is sent to live with her grandmother in San Francisco's Chinatown. The child grows to love and accept herself as a "child of the owl," akin to the dark, negative *yin* elements of the universe. A more recent book, *Star Fisher* (1991), is based on Yep's family's experiences when they moved from Ohio to West Virginia in the 1920s. In an autobiographical work, *The Lost Garden* (1991), Yep wrote about his own experiences of growing up in San Francisco.

Stories of early Chinese in America include *Chang's Paper Pony* (1985), written by Eleanor Coerr, in which an immigrant boy's wish for a pony is fulfilled in the gold mining country; Ruthanne Lum McCunn's *Pie Biter* (1983), a fable of success of a hardworking young Chinese pioneer; and McCunn's *Thousand Pieces of Gold* (1981), which chronicles the life of a Chinese slave girl who overcomes adversity to become a respected and loved member of her Idaho community.

By far the richest stories of early immigrants are to be found in the anthologies by Paul Yee and Laurence Yep. The stories in Yee's *Tales from Gold Mountain* (1989) are stories of the Chinese in the New World. The tales are full of humor, irony, and optimism, qualities that gave strength to these early adventurers. Yep's two collections, *The Rainbow People* (1989) and *Tongues of Jade* (1991), were selected from sixty-nine folktales gathered and translated by Jon Lee as part of a WPA project in the 1930s. These stories, brought by the Chinese from their homeland, were told and retold to help sustain their bonds with the country they left. Ghost stories and tales of luck, cunning, heroism, and magic have entertained generations of Chinese immigrants and their children. These folktales, adapted to their New World settings, not only passed on the stories from China but also included the stories of the immigrants.

Since folklore continues to account for much of what is considered "multicultural literature," demand for culturally diverse materials has resulted in the recent publication of more and more folktales; many are filtered through the minds of writers and illustrators outside the culture. Among the more successful Chinese folktales written from outside the culture are Marilee Heyer's *The Weaving of a Dream* (1986); ARNOLD LOBEL's *Ming Lo Moves the Mountain* (1982); MARGARET MAHY's *The Seven Chinese Brothers* (1990); Doreen Rappaport's *The Journey of Meng* (1991); Robert San Souci's *The Enchanted Tapestry* (1987); and Diane Wolkstein's *The Magic Wings* (1986).

But the most important contributions to the literature have been made by those inside the culture. Few Chinese authors and illustrators have been as successful as ED YOUNG, who has illustrated Diane Wolkstein's *White Wave* (1979), Ai-Ling Louie's *Yeh Shen: Cinderella Story from China* (1982), Margaret Leaf's *Eyes of the Dragon* (1987), Margaret Hodges's *The Voice of the Great Bell* (1989), and Robert Wyndham's *Chinese Mother Goose Rhymes* (1968). Young's personal knowledge of China not only lends authenticity to these works, but his elegant artwork enhances the stories as well. Like Chinese calligraphy, Young's illustrations are simple and complex at the same time. Young has been the recipient of many awards for his work. The most prestigious have been the Caldecott Honor Award for his illustrations for JANE YOLEN's *Emperor and the Kite* (1968), the Caldecott Medal for *Lon Po Po: A Red Riding Hood Story from China* (1990), and a Caldecott Honor Award for *Seven Blind Mice* (1992).

Frances Carpenter's *Tales of a Chinese Grandmother* (1937) and *Chinese Mother Goose Rhymes* (1968), compiled and edited by Robert Wyndham, continue to find new audiences as teachers, librarians, and parents, searching for material on China, encounter them in library collections and in bookstores. The stories and the translated NURSERY RHYMES reveal much about the lives of children in China.

Biographies written about Chinese Americans have been scarce, since few have achieved national notoriety in fields traditionally selected for biographies for children: sports, entertainment, and government. *Tiffany Chin: A Dream on Ice* (1986), written by Ray Buck, was published at the height of interest in the Olympic ice-skating medalist. In *El Chino* (1990) ALLEN SAY chronicled the life of Bill Wong, who chose an unusual sport for a young Chinese American when he sought to become a bullfighter in Spain. Mary Malone's *Connie Chung: Broadcast Journalist* (1992) traces the life of Ms. Chung as an immigrant to her current role as one of the nation's leading television journalists.

In China, three-year-old Yani started painting and won international acclaim when she became the youngest artist to exhibit at the Smithsonian Institution. Yani's work and her early years are featured in Zheng Zhensun's *A Young Painter* (1991). There have been several biographies of Mao-Zedong and Chou En-Lai, two of China's revolutionary leaders, but few others have been selected as subjects of biographies.

JEAN FRITZ's *Homesick* (1982) is an account of what it was like to grow up as a child of American missionaries in a troubled China of the 1920s. When the family moved back to America, Fritz had to learn about living in a new country. When she was living in China she was homesick for America, and she often felt like an outsider. Once in America, she felt homesick for China, and so still felt like an outsider. On her first day at school in America, she was called "Chinaman" by a boy. Fritz tried to explain to her classmates that the Chinese were not called "Chinks" or "Chinamen," and, in any event, she was an American. Her turmoil parallels the experience of many immigrant children, who feel that they are strangers in both the land of their birth and the land where they live. This perspective of an outsider is valuable to share with young readers who often think they are the only ones who feel alienated.

In *The China Year* (1991), written by Emily Cheneyl Neville, a thirteen-year-old girl spends a year in Beijing after her father accepts a job teaching there. Without the usual amenities vital to the welfare of the typical American teenager, she finds her life difficult until she meets a Chinese student who speaks English. The observations of life in China through the eyes of this young girl are fresh, tough, and compassionate.

There have been few titles published about children living in modern China. Miriam Schlein's *Project Panda Watch* (1984) is a story of a Chinese boy who finds a baby panda and becomes a part of his country's organized effort to preserve the nearly extinct animal. These Chinese, dressed in contemporary clothing and concerned with contemporary issues such as the environment and endangered animals, enable young readers to understand that China is not a land of mythical dragons, pagodas, and people wearing elaborate silk robes.

City Kids in China (1991), written by Peggy Thomson with photographs by Paul Conklin, shows the daily lives of the children of Changsha in posed and candid black-and-white pictures. Depicted are poignant unguarded moments as well as the usual events that give readers insight into a culture — perhaps quite different from their own. *City Kids in China,* an album of one city, is not to be taken as typical of all of China, where cultural and geographical diversity is at least as extensive as that of the United States.

Children's books about this diverse group of Americans need to include more than folktales. There should be more stories that focus on their experiences as immigrants, more stories that recognize the contributions of Asian Americans to the growth and strength of America, and many more stories that include Asian Americans in the fabric of American life. Only then will young readers be able to discover the remarkable wholeness in the intricately woven tapestry of American society and learn to appreciate and embrace the unique variety brought by many cultures to that intriguing fabric. M.L.

Christelow, Eileen

American author and illustrator, b. 1943. Eileen Christelow delights readers with her romping, humorous stories and illustrations. Christelow grew up in a family that valued books. She received books as gifts for every holiday and recalls lending them to friends and even charging overdue fines. She majored in architecture at the University of Pennsylvania in Philadelphia and discovered photography. Upon graduation she earned a living by photographing buildings. While raising her daughter and reading aloud countless picture books, Christelow worked as a freelance graphic designer and then decided to try her hand at writing a children's book. She struggled with an ALPHABET BOOK, an effort that was rejected by publishers, but she received enough encouragement to continue trying. Her first book, *Henry and the Red Stripes* (1982), was well received, and Christelow has since written more than eighteen books and illustrated more than twenty others.

Many of Christelow's books feature ANIMAL STORIES. *Jerome the Babysitter* (1987) is the funny story of an alligator who survives his first babysitting job and even triumphs over his twelve troublesome charges. Readers can see themselves in both Jerome and the troublemakers, and Christelow's illustrations are as lively as the story. The lumpy, bright green alligators are quite expressive. Jerome appears again in *Jerome and the Witchcraft Kids* (1988) and *Jerome Camps Out* (1998). Each is a strong story, full of childlike details.

Many of Christelow's books have an element of mystery or suspense, making them especially popular with children. *The Robbery at the Diamond Dog Diner* (1988) is a mystery and comedy of errors in which a foolish hen finds herself kidnapped by diamond thieves. As in Christelow's other mysteries, the tension is just right for young audiences, always offset by humor and the brightly colored cartoon illustrations, which seem to assure readers that nothing too terrible can happen in a world of bright yellow, pink, and green.

Christelow adapted and illustrated the familiar toddler song *Five Little Monkeys Jumping on the Bed* (1989) with tremendous success. Her sketchy monkey children, with their long limbs and mischievous smiles, insist upon ignoring their mother's pleas with very funny and only slightly disastrous results. The success of this book led Christelow to tell other stories about the monkeys, including *Don't Wake Up Mama: Another Five Little Monkeys Story* (1992) and *Five Little Monkeys Wash the Car* (2000).

Christelow has also illustrated PICTURE BOOKS and short CHAPTER BOOKS for other authors, including Sue Alexander, Jim Aylesworth, and EVE BUNTING. The books *What Do Authors Do?* (1995) and *What Do Illustrators Do?* (1999) mark a departure for Christelow. The books follow two writers and two illustrators as they start with the same material and transform it into entirely different books. Christelow used comic-book-style panels to tell these entertaining yet informative stories. Children learn about not only the mechanical steps an author and illustrator take to develop a children's book but also the infectious sense of fun that Christelow brings to the process. M.V.K.

Christopher, John

British science fiction and fantasy writer, b. 1922. John Christopher, a pseudonym for Christopher Samuel Youd, was born in Lancashire, England. As a young boy he loved science but performed poorly in his science classes. At sixteen he left school to work in a government office and spent many years working in industry before turning his full-time attention to writing. His early novels — written under the pseudonyms Hilary Ford, William Godfrey, Peter Graaf, Peter Nichols, and Anthony Rye — were for adult readers. Then a publisher asked him to write a SCIENCE FICTION series for boys. In 1967, as John Christopher, he wrote the enormously popular novel *The White Mountains,* the first book in the Tripods trilogy (1967–68) and Christopher's first work for young readers. Christopher thus began a new phase in his writing career and has since said of writing for children that "it is the form of writing which I can now least imagine giving up."

In the futuristic Tripods trilogy, Earth has been invaded and conquered by an alien species from outer space. Human beings are controlled by the mysterious tripods through the ritual of "capping," the implanting of metal caps on people's heads. But thirteen-year-old Will Parker and his companions Henry and Beanpole struggle to escape capping and search for a community of free, uncapped people living in the White Mountains. Eventually, the companions' goal becomes freedom not only for themselves but for all humankind. Masquerading as a capped slave, Will manages to enter the aliens' secret city and discovers their plan to eradicate the human race. Henry, Beanpole, and Will lead the tiny band of free people in a courageous and ultimately successful attempt to rid the planet of the alien menace.

With the publication of the Tripods trilogy, science fiction for children — previously the home of hack or uncreative writing — came into its own and was finally taken seriously. The high quality of Christopher's writing, his emphasis on character development, and the difficult, often troubling questions he has raised in his novels make it impossible to dismiss his work as simple action/adventure stories for children.

The Guardians, published in 1970, won the Christopher and Guardian Awards. Set in the year 2052, the novel describes a world divided into two rigidly controlled social classes: one class lives in overpopulated, violence-ridden cities, while the select few of the other class maintain a privileged existence reminiscent of traditional English aristocracy. The Sword of the Spirits trilogy (1970–72) is set in the unspecified future, in a world profoundly changed by the aftereffects of a nuclear holocaust, and combines elements of medieval chivalry and the Arthurian legends with advanced technology. As in many of his other books, technology is portrayed as a double-edged sword, capable of benefiting humanity in important ways, but equally capable of wreaking destruction upon the world. In the Fireball trilogy (1981–86), Christopher has combined fast-paced adventure with a playful exploration of an alternative history when two cousins are transported to a parallel world in which the Roman Empire never fell.

A recurring theme in Christopher's books is the importance of free will. His protagonists must choose between a life of contentment and happiness and the ability to think and act freely, with all the difficulties and responsibilities this freedom entails. His protagonists are primarily young boys on the brink of manhood, but boys and girls alike respond to their courage, curiosity, and determination. His heroes, far from perfect, wrestle with and often surmount their all-too-human flaws in a way that makes them appealing to young readers. Christopher has explored serious issues, giving his books added substance and interest, but he is also justly appreciated for his consistent ability to tell a good story. In a straightforward narrative style, he has recounted fantastic yet strangely plausible adventures that always leave his readers spellbound from start to finish. K.T.

Cleary, Beverly

American author, b. 1916. Henry Huggins. Ramona Quimby. Ralph S. Mouse. Ribsy. For many, the names of Beverly Cleary's best-known characters read like a list of very special friends. Since the publication of *Henry Huggins* in 1950, Cleary has been entertaining readers with simply written books filled with some of the most endearing characters in children's literature.

Born Beverly Atlee Bunn in McMinnville, Oregon, the author spent her earliest years on a farm in nearby Yamhill before moving to Portland at the age of six. Although her school-teacher mother had organized the first library in Yamhill, Cleary did not enjoy reading. In her outstanding autobiography, *A Girl from Yamhill* (1988), Cleary has related how a difficult first-grade teacher made her fear the written word. Even though she loved looking at books and hearing stories read aloud, Cleary found reading a laborious and unpleasant activity. Things changed one rainy Sunday afternoon during the third grade. Out of boredom, Cleary picked up a copy of Lucy Fitch Perkins's *The Dutch Twins* to look at the pictures but suddenly found herself reading; she was enthralled by the experience. She became a voracious reader, although she always questioned why the juvenile books of that era were predominantly set in historical times or dealt with children in foreign countries; she further wondered why events usually centered on mysteries or wild adventures. Cleary wanted to read funny stories about everyday children.

Soon after discovering the joy of reading, Cleary wrote a book review that was published in the Oregon *Journal* and later won a two-dollar prize for an essay about a beaver. A school librarian suggested that Cleary should someday write books for children. This goal was put on hold while she attended the University of California at Berkeley and library school at the University of Washington, worked as a children's librarian, married, and became the mother of twins.

Inspired by a brief job selling children's books in a department store, Cleary began writing *Henry Huggins,* the story of a third-grade boy who lives on Klickitat Street in Portland. Early on, Henry discovers a stray dog and names him Ribsy; the relationship between boy and dog is at the heart of this book and all the books that follow in the Henry series. With *Henry Huggins,* Cleary achieved her goal of writing an amusing book about an ordinary child. The episodic plot touches on problems that sometimes seem overwhelming to Henry. Cleary's skill as an author makes the reader sympathize with

Henry's concerns, but the events are also hilariously recounted. There is the time Henry's pet fish begin to multiply, resulting in "gallons of guppies." Another time Henry dusts Ribsy with talcum powder before a dog show and Ribsy turns pink from head to toe. In a moving final chapter, Ribsy's original owner appears and Henry must face the possibility of losing his pet. Later volumes are equally percipient and humorous but more cohesively structured around a particular event in Henry's life — his first paper route, an upcoming fishing trip, a backyard clubhouse.

As the series grew in popularity, Cleary wrote books about Henry's friends. *Ribsy* (1964) is presented from the point of view of Henry's dog. *Beezus and Ramona* (1955) concerns Henry's friend Beatrice Quimby — always known as Beezus — and her mischievous little sister. Ramona receives scant mention in *Henry Huggins,* but she can be glimpsed on the very last page of the book. In one of Louis Darling's superb illustrations, she appears as a small, ghostlike figure in overalls, standing apart from the other children as they gather around Ribsy. But as the series progresses, Ramona assumes a greater role in each of the books — destroying birthday cakes, upsetting checkerboards, following Henry on his paper route. It was almost inevitable that Cleary would publish a series of books about this boisterous yet appealing character.

Beginning with *Ramona the Pest* (1968), the stories follow Ramona from kindergarten through the third grade and contain a depth of emotion only hinted at in the Henry books. The reader laughs at Ramona's antics but also empathizes with the imaginative, often misunderstood girl. Cleary has shown that even a child from a happy family has a strong need for understanding and love. Ramona is Cleary's most developed characterization, a child at once ordinary and extraordinary. This is most evident in *Ramona the Brave* (1975), in which the character can be viewed as both a typical first-grader and an exceptionally creative, artistic child. *Ramona Forever* (1984), the last volume in the series, deals with monumental events such as a wedding, a new baby in the Quimby family, and the death of a pet.

Cleary has written a variety of other books. *The Mouse and the Motorcycle* (1965) begins an extremely popular FANTASY series about interactions between a boy and a talking mouse. Cleary's four teenage romances were published in the late 1950s and early 1960s; though they are dated, they continue to be read. Several PICTURE BOOKS have been generally well received but lack the freshness of the author's other works. Cleary is most adept at writing simple CHAPTER BOOKS that can be enjoyed by even the youngest readers yet are so sharply observed that readers of all ages respond to the material.

For much of her career, the stigma connected with SERIES BOOKS prevented many from recognizing Cleary's remarkable achievements. The author labored in the field for over a quarter century before *Ramona and Her Father* (1977) and *Ramona Quimby, Age 8* (1981) were selected as Newbery Honor Books. Cleary finally won the Newbery Medal in 1984 for a book completely different from anything she had previously written. Employing the first-person voice in a series of letters and journal entries, *Dear Mr. Henshaw* depicts a boy's growing self-awareness and maturity, brought about through his correspondence with a favorite author. Leigh Botts is a well-rounded character in a book that contains humor, but it is a sadder, more complex work than most Cleary novels, and it marks the first time the author has dealt with children of divorce. Cleary received the Laura Ingalls Wilder Award for the body of her work and remains one of those rare authors who are both critically acclaimed and immensely popular with young readers. P.D.S.

Voices of the Creators

Beverly Cleary

I recall my pleasure upon entering the first grade at seeing above the blackboard a reproduction of Sir Joshua Reynolds's painting *The Age of Innocence.* I was filled with admiration for the pretty little girl who was wearing, to my six-year-old eyes, a white party dress. I loved that little girl, but by Thanksgiving my love had changed to resentment. There she sat under a tree with nothing to do but keep her party dress clean. There I sat itching in my navy blue serge sailor dress, the shrunken elastic of my new black bloomers cutting into my legs as I struggled to learn to read.

My first grade was sorted into three reading groups — Bluebirds, Redbirds, and Blackbirds. I was a Blackbird, the only girl Blackbird among the boy Blackbirds, who had to sit in the row by the blackboard. Perhaps this was the beginning of my sympathy for the problems of boys. How I envied the bright, self-confident Bluebirds, most of them girls, who got to sit by the windows and who, unlike myself, pleased the teacher by remembering to write with their right hands — a ridiculous thing to do, in my six-year-old opinion. Anyone could see that both hands were alike. One should simply use the hand nearer the task.

To be a Blackbird was to be disgraced. I wanted to read, but somehow I could not. I wept at home while my puzzled mother tried to drill me on the dreaded word charts. "But reading is fun," insisted my mother. I stomped my feet and threw the book on the floor. Reading was not fun.

By second grade I was able to plod through my reader a step or two ahead of disgrace. Although I could read if I wanted to, I no longer wanted to. Reading was not fun. It was boring. Most of the stories were simplified versions of folktales that had been read aloud to me many times. There were no surprises left.

Then, in third grade, the miracle happened. It was a dull rainy Portland Sunday afternoon when there was nothing to do but thumb through two books from the Sunday school library. After looking at the pictures, I began out of boredom to read *The Dutch Twins,* by Lucy Fitch Perkins. Twins had always fascinated me. As a small child, I had searched through magazines — my only picture books — for pictures of the Campbell Soup twins. To me, a solitary child, the idea of twins was fascinating. A twin would never be lonely. Here was a whole book about twins, a boy and girl who lived in Holland but who had experiences a girl in Portland, Oregon, could share. I could laugh when the boy fell into the Zuyder Zee because I had once fallen into the Yamhill River. In this story, something happened. With rising elation, I read on. I read all afternoon and evening, and by bedtime I had read not only *The Dutch Twins* but *The Swiss Twins* as well. It was one of the most exciting days of my life. Shame and guilt dropped away from the ex-Blackbird, who had at last taken wing. I could read and read with pleasure! Grownups were right after all. Reading was fun.

From the third grade on, I was a reader, and when my school librarian suggested that I should write children's books when I grew up, I was ecstatic. Of course! That was exactly what I wanted to do. By now I had gone on from the twin books and was reading everything on the children's side of our branch library. I had grown critical. Why couldn't authors write about the sort of boys and girls who lived on my block? Plain, ordinary boys and girls I called them when I was a child. Why couldn't authors skip all that tiresome description and write books in which something happened on every page? Why couldn't they make the stories funny?

And so I grew up to try to create the books I had wanted to read as a child — books to make reading exciting and interesting and, most of all, enjoyable. It is my fondest hope that readers will finish a book of mine, close it, and think, "Well! Grownups are right after all! Reading is fun!"

Clemens, Samuel Langhorne

See TWAIN, MARK.

Clements, Andrew

American author, b. 1949. Some people just can't seem to get enough of school; perhaps Andrew Clements is one of them. After attending Northwestern University and receiving an M.A. from National-Louis University, he taught elementary, middle, and high school in the Chicago area before moving east to take a series of jobs in publishing. He now lives in Massachusetts with his wife and four sons.

Clements first entered the field of children's literature with PICTURE BOOKS, most notably *Big Al* (1988), *Temple Cat* (1991), and *Billy and the Bad Teacher* (1992). He has also written the Jake Drake series. But it is his school stories that have made him wildly popular among middle-grade children. With gentle humor and unexpected poignancy, these works of MIDDLE-GRADE FICTION portray school as a place where life lessons are learned along with academic subjects. His characterizations of adult-child relationships are particularly remarkable. While the adults in these novels recognize children's capacity for creativity, curiosity, and caring, the children understand that adults are only human and learn to deal with that awareness. A healthy sense of equality, respect, and passion for learning coexists with the authority inherent in a teacher-student or a parent-child relationship.

Clements's first novel, *Frindle* (1996), won the Christopher Award for affirming the highest values of the human spirit; it proved equally popular among younger readers, winning an overwhelming number of children's choice awards. In the story, mischievous Nick Allen finally meets his match in his fifth-grade language arts teacher, Mrs. Granger. Their struggle over a made-up word — *frindle* — has unexpected consequences when it becomes local news and then hits the national media. Eventually the word is absorbed into the English language and appears in the dictionary. Only then do Nick and Mrs. Granger truly realize the profound influence they have had on each other.

Freedom of the press and the responsibility entailed in that freedom — that is, the need to balance truth and mercy — are the central themes of *The Landry News* (1999). Cara Landry takes the initiative to start a class newspaper, and her first editorial takes aim at her burned-out teacher, Mr. Larson, who then rises to the challenge and reinvigorates his teaching. The newspaper article, however, gets him in trouble with the principal, and when the issue is brought before the school board, Cara, now one of Mr. Larson's staunchest supporters, testifies on his behalf. *The Janitor's Boy* (2000) reminds us that the true measure of a man is not his job, but rather his heart. Fifth-grader Jack Rankin feels humiliated that his father is the school janitor. As revenge for his father's public acknowledgment of their relationship, Jack sticks a wad of bubble gum under his desk. Caught, and sentenced to help his dad after school, Jack comes to see his father in a new light.

In *The School Story* (2001), the character Natalie is such a good writer that her best friend Zoe thinks she should try to get a story published. Natalie's mother is a children's book editor, but Natalie wants her story to stand or fall on its own merits, not her mother's influence. With the help of a young teacher, the two sixth-graders submit the manuscript under a pseudonym and anonymously shepherd the book through the entire editing process to publication. This improbable, endearing story features smart, headstrong kids, perceptive teachers, and a well-realized educational setting — hallmarks that have elevated Clements into the first tier of "school story" writers, along with LOUIS SACHAR and BARBARA PARK. J.H.

Clifton, Lucille

American author of fiction and poetry for children and adults, b. 1936. Lucille Clifton was born Lucille Sayles in Depew, New York, near Buffalo. Her father told stories about her African ancestors, including her great-great-grandmother, born of Dahomey people but captured and forced into slavery. There was POETRY in the household as well — her mother wrote poetry and read it aloud to her children. Later in life, Clifton wrote a memoir about her family, *Generations* (1976). When she was sixteen years old, Clifton won a full scholarship to Howard University. After spending two years there, she transferred to Fredonia State Teachers College, where she banded together with a group who liked to read and perform plays. She met the novelist Ishmael Reed, who showed her poetry to LANGSTON HUGHES. He included some of her poems in an anthology.

In 1969 Clifton won an award for her poetry and had her first book of poems published. *Good Times,* poems for adults, was chosen as one of the ten best books of the year by the *New York Times.* She went on to write several other books for adults.

Her first work for children, *Some of the Days of Everett Anderson,* was published in 1970. It chronicles the life of a six-year-old black child who lives in the city, each day of the week described in a poem. *Everett Anderson's Christmas Coming,* which followed a year later, describes the anticipation and joy of the five days before Christmas. EVALINE NESS illustrated both books. Several other Everett books followed, illustrated by Ann Grifalconi. Clifton won the 1984 Coretta Scott King Award for *Everett Anderson's Goodbye.*

In addition to these well-loved PICTURE BOOKS, Clifton wrote *All Us Come Cross the Water,* a children's book about people being brought into slavery, in 1973. *The Time They Used to Be* (1974) is an example of her fiction for children. It is a story told in the first person, describing a period of time in 1948 in the life of two girls who observe the people around them, some of whom are recovering from the war, some who see ghosts. It ends when President Truman ends Jim Crow laws in the military. A poet's touch and a storyteller's art combine in the language and the narrative pacing to capture a moment in history and some unforgettable memories. Clifton continued to portray black experiences in *Amifika* (1977), which tells of a small boy, again a city dweller, who is fearful about his father's return from the army, since the boy does not remember him. *The Black BC's* (1970) is an ALPHABET BOOK that contains information on black history.

Clifton has turned her storyteller's background and her lyrical use of language into the basis for realistic and full-dimensional African American characters. She was poet laureate of the state of Maryland and has been poet in residence at Coppin State College in Baltimore, Maryland. She has held positions at Columbia University School of the Arts, at George Washington University, and at the University of California at Santa Cruz. S.H.H.

Cofer, Judith Ortiz

Puerto Rican–born American author, b. 1952. In Judith Ortiz Cofer's adult novel *The Line of the Sun* (1989), the teenage Puerto Rican–American narrator describes herself as "living in a state of limbo, halfway between cultures." This also describes the way Cofer felt during her own childhood as she shuttled between Paterson, New Jersey, and her native Puerto Rico, never completely fitting into either place. Her ability to vividly convey an outsider's perspective draws teenagers to her writing, which has taken various forms, including memoirs, poetry, and short story collections for YOUNG ADULTS.

Cofer's father, a navy officer, made a relatively comfortable salary that kept her family at a certain distance from the other residents of Paterson's El Building, the Puerto Rican tenement where her family lived for a while and the setting for many of her stories. Yet whenever she went back to Puerto Rico with her mother and younger brother while her father was at sea, she was told she spoke Spanish like a *gringa.* Cofer explored both the isolation and the richness of this paradoxical existence in the autobiographical *Silent Dancing: A Partial Remembrance of a Puerto Rican Childhood* (1990). Through evocative vignettes interspersed with poems, she pieced together parts of her family history, using a commanding storytelling style passed along to her by her maternal grandmother. Exotic images of life on a tropical island are woven together with situations familiar to many adolescents, such as the frustration of dealing with overprotective parents and the heartbreak of an unrequited crush.

An Island like You: Stories of the Barrio (1995) examines Puerto Rican–American life from numerous teen perspectives. Cofer's first book written specifically for young adults, it takes its title from a line in her poem "Day in the Barrio," suggesting that even in a bustling immigrant neighborhood, surrounded by blasting stereos, traffic noise, and gossip, it is not unusual to feel "alone in a crowd." In the story "The One Who Watches," the character Doris would like to go one step beyond isolation and become invisible. She shadows her brash, risk-taking friend Yolanda from one New York City store to another, assuming she can just fade into the background if Yolanda gets caught shoplifting or doing something else crazy. But even the fearless Yolanda turns out to have a vulnerable side in "Don Jose of La Mancha." Her widowed mother has taken up with a *jibaro,* a man fresh from the island, and Yolanda struggles to accept her mother's newfound happiness while remaining faithful to her father's memory. All of the stories in *An Island like You* are interrelated and celebrate the vibrancy and resilience of Paterson's Puerto Rican community. In 1996, the book received the American Library Association's first Pura Belpre Medal for work by a Latino/Latina writer.

A second evocative collection for young adults, *The Year of Our Revolution* (1998), combines new and selected poetry, short stories, and autobiographical vignettes. It ends with a poem called "*El Olvido*" (Forgetfulness) that warns "It is a dangerous thing / to forget the climate of / your birthplace." Through her writing, Cofer has assured readers that she won't forget while also giving them the privilege of delving into her unique cultural heritage and perhaps better appreciating their own, whatever it may be.

C.M.H.

Cole, Brock

American author and illustrator, b. 1938. Formerly a philosophy instructor at the University of Wisconsin, Brock Cole is a self-taught illustrator who has created a number of fine PICTURE BOOKS. His texts recall the simplicity and dignity of folktales, and the matter-of-fact tone of his smoothly flowing narratives lends plausibility to even the most extraordi-nary happenings. Cole's skillful art successfully portrays action, emotion, and humor through the facial expressions and body language of his characters. The protagonists in his picture books often find that appearances are deceiving. Jessie McWhistle, in *No More Baths* (1980), envies animals until she learns that, like humans, they have their own disgusting bathing practices. Preston the pig, in *Nothing but a Pig* (1981), discovers that "fine clothes do not make a man." In *The Winter Wren* (1984), young Simon finds that Spring is not, as he had believed, simply "a princess all dressed in green and gold."

Deceptive appearances are also a theme in Cole's YOUNG ADULT NOVELS. In *The Goats* (1987), a girl and a boy at a summer camp are labeled social misfits by their camp mates, stripped of their clothing, then left on a small island as a prank. Laura and Howie manage to swim back to land, but instead of returning to the camp, they decide to stay in the woods together, and, using survival skills they didn't know they possessed, they find clothing, food, and shelter. On leaving the island, Laura and Howie no longer see each other as social outcasts but begin to see each other as they truly are: intelligent, caring, and honest individuals. Though in the end they return to their old world, Laura and Howie are not their old selves, having found a measure of self-worth that emboldens and empowers them. Certainly controversial when it was published, *The Goats* was hailed by some as a rare and significant publication and was criticized by others for its portrayal of adults as unconcerned or unable to help the children. But the novel found a readership and has proved especially effective as a book to spark classroom discussion. The raw emotion in the novel is well balanced. Cole counterposes pain with joy, shame with pride, ostracism with friendship, and impotence with competence. Primary and secondary characters are fully drawn; Laura and Howie, on the cusp of adolescence, are particularly believable, and their transformation is realistic and touching.

Cole's second young adult novel, *Celine* (1989), is quite different but just as arresting, juggling tragedy and comedy. It is narrated by sixteen-year-old Celine, a young artist and a true individual. The adults in Celine's world are greatly lacking in maturity and honesty and seem mainly concerned with escaping from their present lives and responsibilities. As in *The Goats,* adults often fail children, but it is ultimately heartening to witness Celine and her young neighbor, Jacob, help each other compensate for the sad lack of adult assistance. In *The Facts Speak for Themselves* (1997), Cole has presented a different kind of protagonist, a raw young woman whose story is gritty and violent.

In Cole's novels the young protagonists initially appear to be lacking in maturity but eventually prove themselves more responsible than many of the adults. With the publication of these novels, Cole has earned himself a place among the gifted few who have multiple talents as artists and as writers of both picture books and novels.   J.M.B.

Cole, Joanna

American author, b. 1944. As the author of almost sixty fiction and nonfiction books for children, Joanna Cole is undeniably a versatile and accomplished writer. In her case, quantity is also quality. In 1991 Joanna Cole received the Washington Post–Children's Book Guild Nonfiction Award for her contribution to IN-FORMATION BOOKS for children.

In recent years she has given the term *nonfiction* new meaning with the Magic School Bus series. A masterly combination of scientific facts, humor, and FANTASY, these books turn science class into story hour. Whether traveling through the city's waterworks as raindrops in *The Magic School Bus at the Waterworks* (1986) or coursing through a human body as red blood cells in *The Magic School Bus Inside the Human Body* (1989), Miss Frizzle, the strangest teacher in school, and her sometimes disbelieving but always eager class learn firsthand about what they are studying. In the Magic School Bus books, illustrator BRUCE DEGEN's lively artwork and comic-strip-style word balloons fully engage the reader and humorously extend Cole's fascinating text.

Her highly praised series on animals' bodies, with stunning black and white photographs by Jerome Wexler, is a noteworthy illustration of Cole's unique approach to her subject. Beyond merely describing and explaining the different parts of, for example, a snake's body, Cole has taken the reader a step further to show how a snake's particular form relates to its environment. As she has said, the books are a study of "adaptation and morphology, that is, the form and structure of a living animal as they relate to the animal's way of life."

Science has been a lifelong passion with Cole: as a child growing up in East Orange, New Jersey, she spent hours wandering around her backyard, studying insects and plants. She loved school and particularly enjoyed writing reports for science class. Her love of learning is evident in all of her work. As Cole has said, "I see it as my job to learn about something that fascinates me, to filter all I've learned through my own mind, to tell the story in the simplest, clearest way possible and then to present it as a gift to the reader." After graduating from the City College of New York with a degree in psychology, Cole began her career as a librarian in a Brooklyn elementary school. It was during that time that the idea for her first book, *Cockroaches* (1971), came to her. Many other award-winning nonfiction titles were soon to follow, and in 1980 Cole decided to become a full-time children's book writer. She has written books on parenting for parents and children to share, such as *How You Were Born* (1984; revised edition, 1993), *Your New Potty* (1989), *My Big Boy Potty* (2000), and *My Big Girl Potty* (2000), which clearly and matter-of-factly deal with topics to which children are sensitive.

Always keeping in mind the emotional level of her audience, Cole has presented information in a reassuring, caring tone, with great respect for children. She has also retold a number of folktales; they appeal to her because the hero's quest parallels the child's struggle to exist in an adult world. Cole has said that she considers it a privilege to be doing as an adult the very thing she loved doing as a child; it is, also, a privilege for her readers that she is able to share her enthusiasm for learning and for childhood in her many exciting and absorbing books. K.F.

Collier, Bryan

American author and illustrator, b. 1967. With a distinctive artistic style, Bryan Collier combines watercolors and collage to create textured, deeply hued, semiabstract illustrations. He began painting at age fifteen while growing up in Pocomoke, Maryland; winning his first national contest, the Congressional Competition in 1985, he exhibited his work in the U.S. Capitol. That year he was awarded a scholarship to the Pratt Institute in Brooklyn, New York, where he received his B.F.A. four years later. He now lives in New York City and directs the Harlem Horizon Art Studio at the Harlem Hospital Center, a program to encourage children and youth to express themselves through art.

Collier's style and use of color and form in mixed media effectively convey story and emotion. The patterns, texture, and vivid color in his first book, *These Hands* (1999), written by Hope Lynne Price, evoke what engages a child's hands daily. In 2001, Collier's art was recognized in two awards: the Coretta Scott King Illustrator Award and a Coretta Scott King Illustrator Honor Book award. The award book, *Uptown* (2000), launches readers on a fast-paced journey through the vividly colored sights and sounds of Harlem. In *Freedom River* (2000), written by Doreen Rappaport, the honor book, Collier's signature style lends a reflective, tense, yet hopeful tone to this chronicle of the life of a former slave who becomes a successful conductor on the Underground Railroad. Collier's textured illustrations augment the powerful emotional impact of *Martin's Big Words* (2001), written by Doreen Rappaport, which introduces the life of Martin Luther King Jr. through words and images.

In 2001 Collier also received the Ezra Jack Keats New Illustrator Award for *Uptown,* which he both wrote and illustrated. He has the ability to create myriad moods in a unique and vital style. M.B.S.

Collodi, Carlo

Italian author, journalist, editor, and translator, 1826–1890. *The Adventures of Pinocchio* is a children's classic, but Carlo Collodi's life was ordinary and his skills unremarkable. Born in Florence, Italy, Carlo Lorenzini (his mother's village provided his pen name, Collodi) grew up in poverty. His wide-ranging knowledge was gained through self-education. Collodi became a hack journalist, an undecorated soldier, and a low-level government official; he began two different idealistic magazines — which folded — and wrote a series of stiff educational texts.

Collodi's fame rests solely on *Pinocchio,* a thirty-five-episode children's serial story begun in 1881 and published as a book in 1883. In the rambling tale a disobedient marionette comes to life as he is being whittled and immediately sets about making trouble. After being lectured by a talking cricket, Pinocchio agrees to behave and attend school but runs away instead, meeting with the first of many unsavory characters. Eventually a kindly puppet master gives Pinocchio five gold pieces and tells him to go home, but the naive puppet stumbles upon one trouble after another as he struggles to return to Gepetto, his "Daddy."

The Adventures of Pinocchio has been translated into over one hundred languages; it has been adapted for movies and filmstrips, plays, musicals, and television. James T. Teahan maintains, in *Twentieth-Century Writers for Children,* that the story has been so "bowdlerized, expurgated, abridged, adapted, dramatized, trivialized, diluted, and generally gutted" that it no longer resembles the original. In its original form (and in faithful translations), *Pinocchio* is full of inconsistencies and contradictions, evidence of careless writing. What sets it apart is not the craftsmanship but the conception. A bachelor, Collodi was clearly at his creative apex when he invented the mischievous boy-puppet and the tale's fifty-odd imaginative creatures. Of Collodi's large body of writing — liberal journalism, translations of PERRAULT's fairy tales, technical books for adults, and numerous stories for children — only *Pinocchio* survives for readers. Scholars have found complex symbolism, classical references, and ties to traditional folklore; religious parallels, political allegory, social morality, and psychological quest. *Pinocchio* has been variously considered an animal fable, literary folktale, FANTASY, and didactic tract. The episodic series of escapades has been favorably compared to Jonathan Swift's *Gulliver's Travels* and LEWIS CARROLL's Alice books. It is often declared superior to L. FRANK BAUM's *Wizard of Oz*, J. M. Barrie's *Peter Pan,* and even E. B. WHITE's *Charlotte's Web*. Scholarly assessment aside, the tale is notable for its universality, its blend of imagination and humor, its lively pace, and its ethereal charm. But it has a dark side — its honest depiction of children's fears. *Pinocchio* has been criticized for its didacticism, a characteristic of nineteenth-century children's literature, but it has also been praised for its refreshingly modern, highly pragmatic morality. *Pinocchio* delicately balances fantasy and reality, and therein lies its source of greatness.

It is ironic that Carlo Lorenzini, a man of middling talent, died in 1890, while his tale was only a middling success. He never saw its international popularity or knew he was the creator of a classic. S.A.B.

Coman, Carolyn

American author, b. 1951. An increasingly well known author of YOUNG ADULT NOVELS, Carolyn Coman has a propensity for clear language and incisive characterization, which illuminate her stories. Throughout her career, Coman has tackled difficult territory in her writing; though she emphasizes that she does not seek to write about specific issues, she has contributed several portraits of brave protagonists to the young adult canon. She is unapologetically candid in her portrayal of characters in traumatic and cathartic circumstances.

Born in Chicago, Illinois, Coman grew up in an Irish Catholic family and dreamed of a career as a writer from an early age. Many of the emotional elements of her novels reflect the thoughtful, observant nature she had as a child. "I wanted to understand things clearly enough to be able to say what they were," she has said, "and that same desire I felt as a child impels my writing now." Coman was a member of the first graduating class of Hampshire College in Amherst, Massachusetts. After college, she worked as a bookbinder, an editor at an educational publishing company, and later, an instructor at the Harvard Extension and Summer schools. However, the dream of writing her own books continued, and she came to realize that such jobs, no matter how close to writing, would not satisfy her. She continues to teach, however, in the M.F.A. program at Vermont College.

Coman's first novel, *Tell Me Everything,* was published in 1993. The story of Roz, a girl who seeks out the last person to see her mother alive, bears Coman's trademarks as a writer: clear, concise language and vivid descriptive passages, as well as a refreshingly honest characterization of an adolescent who has borne an extreme burden and survived. *What Jamie Saw* (1995) features a very young boy who has witnessed the abuse of his mother at the hands of her boyfriend and the consequences of her decision to leave him. Told through Jamie's voice, this relatively short story achieves astonishing depth. A Newbery Honor Book, *What Jamie Saw* was also a National Book Award finalist.

Perhaps Coman's most controversial novel, *Bee and Jacky* (1998) deals with incest between an adolescent sister and brother. Bee and Jacky are intense and delicate characters, raised in a family haunted by the father's traumatic experience in Vietnam. When their parents leave them home alone one Labor Day weekend, the house takes on a mystical atmosphere as Bee recalls the games she and Jacky played in an effort to understand their father, and the way the games evolved into a desperate reach for comfort. As Coman's protagonists invariably do, Bee draws on enough inner strength to survive her situation, grow out of it, and emerge a more mature and resilient young woman.

Coman's fourth novel, *Many Stones* (2000), was a National Book Award finalist and was named a Michael L. Printz Honor Book. With each successive novel, Coman has continued to hone her craft and distinguish herself as one of the most crystalline voices in children's literature today. Her advice to aspiring authors reveals her own greatest gift: "Listen carefully to everything. Watch closely, practice choosing the perfect words — your own words, in your own voice — for what you have seen and heard and imagined." H.F.R.

Conly, Jane Leslie

American author, b. 1948. The daughter of author ROBERT C. O'BRIEN, Jane Leslie Conly entered the field of children's books indirectly, helping to write a modern classic for which she received no public credit. She has gone on to publish a number of books under her own name, winning critical acclaim and awards.

Conly was born in Virginia, where her family lived on a small farm before moving to Washington, D.C. She attended Smith College and the Writing Seminars Program at Johns Hopkins University. Upon her father's death, Conly completed his unfinished manuscript about a teenage girl struggling to exist in a post-apocalyptic world. An outstanding survival story that continues to be read and enjoyed, *Z for Zachariah* (1975) was credited solely to O'Brien upon publication. Conly didn't return to writing until a few years later, after she had married and become a mother. Her first book was a continuation of her father's Newbery Award–winning

Mrs. Frisby and the Rats of NIMH (1971), a talking-animal FANTASY about a community of intelligent laboratory rats. Using his premise and many of the same characters, Conly wrote *Racso and the Rats of NIMH* (1986), which concerns a field mouse and a young rat who help save the rodent settlement from being destroyed by developers. Conly's second sequel, *R-T, Margaret, and the Rats of NIMH* (1990), features the first significant human characters in the series, as a brother and sister get lost in the woods and are befriended by the rat community. The novel contains adventure and humor but is not quite as focused as its two fine predecessors.

Conly's first completely original work, *Crazy Lady!* (1993), tells the well-crafted story of Vernon, a lower-class Baltimore boy who is failing seventh grade and grieving over his mother's death. Vernon's relationship with an alcoholic neighbor and her retarded son helps him appreciate the strength of his own family's unity. Selected as a Newbery Honor Book, this novel features sharply defined characterizations, honest emotions, and a developing sense of self and community.

All of Conly's novels have dealt with children who are, in one way or another, separated from a parent, and her subsequent books also follow this pattern. In *Trout Summer* (1995), a brother and sister befriend an elderly neighbor while living in a rural cabin during their parents' separation. A Boston Globe–Horn Book Honor Book, *While No One Was Watching* (1998) is the story of three abandoned siblings and their involvement with a missing pet rabbit. Set in 1958, *What Happened on Planet Kid* (2000) concerns twelve-year-old Dawn, staying on a Virginia farm with relatives and creating a fantasy world with a new friend.

After getting her start working on an archetypal survival story, Conly has continued to write survival stories of a somewhat different sort, in which often poor or disenfranchised young characters try to get along in a sometimes confusing world. Thus Conly has charted her own territory as a strong and distinctive voice in contemporary children's fiction. P.D.S.

Conrad, Pam

American author, 1947–1996. In PICTURE BOOKS, stories for young readers, and YOUNG ADULT NOVELS, many of Pam Conrad's characters experience loss of some kind. At times the loss results from the ordinary trials of everyday existence. Eight-year-old Nicki moves to a new house and misses her old neighborhood in *I Don't Live Here!* (1984). In a sequel, *Seven Silly Circles* (1987), Nicki worries about losing her dignity: playing with the suction cup on a toy arrow has left her with red circles on her face. Heather, the protagonist of *Staying Nine* (1988), does not want to forsake the familiar life of a nine-year-old, so she decides to ignore her first double-digit birthday.

Conrad's books for older readers usually deal with graver losses. Simone, haunted by guilty memories of the death of her beloved caretaker, attempts suicide in *Taking the Ferry Home* (1988). Despairing over the truth about her dead father, Darcie literally follows the charismatic but deeply disturbed Roman into a lion's den in *What I Did for Roman* (1987). *Holding Me Here* (1986) shows how Robin's unresolved feelings about her parents' divorce lead to her disastrous interference in another family's problems. In *My Daniel* (1989) Julia, now an old woman, recalls her childhood on the prairie and the death of her brother, to whom she was completely devoted.

In these deeply felt books, however, loss is seldom the end of the story. An accidental fire destroys the meager possessions of the solitary castaway in the picture book *The Lost Sailor* (1992), illustrated by RICHARD EGIELSKI, yet this fire attracts the ship that finally rescues him. Another picture book, *The Tub People* (1989), also illustrated by Egielski, shows how two toy parents cherish their toy child even more after he has been lost and found. In the suspenseful Edgar Award–winning *Stone-words: A Ghost Story* (1990), Zoe Louise travels back in time and saves the life of the girl whose ghost has been her playmate for years. While doing so, she uses her mixed feelings about her absent, nonnurturing mother to summon the strength and love she requires to overcome her fear. She loses her ghostly companion, but she begins to heal herself. Louisa, the narrator of the evocative, highly acclaimed HISTORICAL NOVEL *Prairie Songs* (1985), witnesses the mental breakdown of a fragile newcomer to the frontier, but she also gains a new appreciation for her family.

In *Prairie Visions: The Life and Times of Solomon Butcher* (1991), Conrad has demonstrated that her storytelling skills extend to nonfiction writing as she explores the life of a traveling photographer who took pictures of frontier families in Nebraska. It comes as no surprise that Butcher's story caught her eye, since he employed photographic images to preserve his visions of prairie people. Conrad, too, is concerned with capturing moments. In an "Author's Note" for *Pedro's Journal: A Voyage with Christopher Columbus, August 3, 1492–February 14, 1493* (1991), she has stated her main reason for writing the novel: "to sail through a brief period of history inside the mind and heart of a young boy."

Using her considerable command of language, including her talent for creating effective imagery, Conrad has told the stories of characters who stand poised at turning points in their lives. M.F.S.

Cooney, Barbara

American illustrator and author, 1917–2000. In a career begun in 1940, Barbara Cooney created more than one hundred PICTURE BOOKS for children. She twice received the Caldecott Medal: in 1958 for *Chanticleer and the Fox* (1957), her retelling of the Chaucer tale, and in 1979 for DONALD HALL's *Ox-Cart Man* (1978), a celebration of the cycle of working and growing on a nineteenth-century New Hampshire farm. Cooney's work reflects a strong sense of place and a love of small living things — an awareness, in her words, of "the beauty of humble flowers or tiny, peering animal faces."

Born in Brooklyn, New York, Barbara

Cooney was brought up on Long Island and spent her summers on the Maine coast. Introduced to art as a child by her artist mother, Cooney became an artist herself because she had "access to materials, a minimum of instruction, and a stubborn nature." She majored in art at Smith College, graduating in 1938, and then studied lithography and etching at the Art Students League in New York. It was at this point that she began illustrating books for children — her first was Carl Malmberg's *Ake and His World* (1940) — and illustrated continuously for almost sixty years. She lived most of her life in New England, first in Pepperell, Massachusetts, where she and her physician husband, Charles Talbot Porter, raised four children, and later — like the heroine of what is possibly her best-loved book, *Miss Rumphius* (1982) — in a house overlooking the sea in Damariscotta, Maine.

Cooney's choice of media changed over the years. She used scratchboard frequently in the first two decades of her career, notably in books such as MARGARET WISE BROWN's *The Little Fir Tree* (1954) and her own *The Little Juggler* (1961) and *Chanticleer and the Fox*. Cooney's etchings are clean yet intricate, set exquisitely against white space and full of authentic detail. But after the success of *Chanticleer* — "I had always thought: once you succeed, change" — she tried a variety of media, including pen and ink, collage, watercolor, and acrylics, fitting her technique to the spirit of each book she took on. In later years she worked almost exclusively in acrylic, now filling up the whole page with her luminous paintings. In the 1980s Cooney produced a trilogy of picture book biographies featuring strong, self-determining characters — *Miss Rumphius*, about a venturesome woman who at the end of her peripatetic life returns to live by the sea and fulfills her grandfather's charge to do something to make the world more beautiful by planting lupines everywhere; *Island Boy* (1988), a historical account of Matthais Tibbetts, who grew up with his family on a remote Maine island and chose to spend his life there; and *Hattie and the Wild Waves* (1990), set in the opulent world of turn-of-the-century

Brooklyn and based on the childhood of Cooney's mother. Each of these encapsulated biographies features Cooney's distinctive style and palette — flat, spacious, luminous landscapes in cool, chromatic blues and greens; quiet, detailed, warm interior scenes; children with small, pixieish faces. Cooney's gift became even more finely honed in the 1990s, as evident in books such as Alice McClerran's *Roxaboxen* (1990), an exploration of the imaginative play of a group of children in the desert of the Southwest; *Emily* (1992), written by Michael Bedard, the story of a young girl's unforgettable encounter with Emily Dickinson in Amherst, Massachusetts; and *Eleanor* (1996), the saga of Eleanor Roosevelt's childhood and coming of age.

All of Cooney's work, as critic Ethel Heins has noted, exudes "an atmosphere of calm and composure that reflects the strength and serenity" of the stories she illustrated. As the artist said, "I draw from life whenever possible, and I do not invent facts. . . . In spite of this, my pictures don't look realistic; they always look like me, which bothers me. However, they are the truth — as I see it — and my attempt to communicate about the things that matter to me." Like Miss Rumphius, who must "do something to make the world more beautiful," Barbara Cooney adorned the world of children's books with her elegant, life-affirming illustrations.

M.V.P.

Voices of the Creators

✦ *Barbara Cooney*

My life is in my books, in thousands of pictures, in hundreds of words. It's all there — well, at least all that I care to tell — for anyone who is interested. The places that I love are there — the fields and the hills, the mountains and the desert and the sea; the seasons are there, with snow and clouds and fog; and above all there are people, adults and children, always children. I never went to the hospital to have my babies without a sketchbook. Almost before they opened their eyes,

I made pictures of them. In my many books I tried to hold on to all these wonders. But the three books, the ones I call my trilogy — *Miss Rumphius, Island Boy,* and *Hattie and the Wild Waves* — come as close to any autobiography as I will ever get.

Like my character Hattie, I was "always making pictures" on any scraps of paper that were handy. "Some of [my] happiest times were when [I] had a bad cold and Mama kept [me] in bed for two or three days running. Then [I] could make pictures from morning until night, interrupted only by bowls of milk toast and chicken broth."

Like little Alice in *Miss Rumphius,* I "got up and washed [my] face and ate porridge for breakfast. [I] went to school and came home and did [my] homework. And pretty soon [I] was grown up."

At two I had fallen in love with the coast of Maine. My heart still skips a beat when I look at the sea's horizon. Adventure, magic, all possibilities lie beyond it. Nearer at hand the sun and the moon sparkle on the water, and its reflections dance on my studio walls. I made *Island Boy* as my hymn to Maine.

How I happened into the field of illustration I cannot say. Perhaps because I am a bookworm. Shortly after college the long career of illustration began. In the beginning I worked in black and white, that being the most economical for the publisher. I yearned for color. "But," said my editor, "you have no color sense." Still yearning for color, I accepted the discouraging pronouncement. Eventually a little color was allowed — sometimes two colors, sometimes three. But each color had to be painted on a separate sheet of paper. These were called "overlays." One art director hoped to convince me that working with these separations was "the purest form of illustration." But I found it tedious.

After roughly twenty years I made a book called *Chanticleer and the Fox.* I had found the story in Geoffrey Chaucer's *Canterbury Tales.* Because I had taken a fancy to a particular hen yard full of exotic chickens glowing in late afternoon October sunlight and because I was fond of the Middle Ages, I thought to combine these in a PICTURE BOOK. For this I was allowed *four* color overlays plus the black key drawing. And the book won a Caldecott Medal. The first thing I did was buy a huge old second-hand Smith-Corona typewriter for thirty dollars. The second thing was to order a wooden skiff, $185, complete with two sets of oars. A third thing happened: my editor offered me a lovely book, with a French setting, and in *full color!* So I packed up the family and went to France. My apprenticeship was now half over.

The French period was a happy one. Now with full color I could create *ambiance.* My people and animals and buildings and plants were no longer isolated in space. They became part of the scene. They were placed in landscapes and seascapes, on farms and in villages and cities and inside buildings; they were placed in Spain and in Ireland and Greece, in the Spice Islands and in New England.

Another change began to come into my work during this period: I fell in love with the art of painting with light — with photography. I even considered changing careers. I sat at the drawing table in Hermit Wood, my new studio/house in Maine, and watched the reflections from the water tremble on the white walls. And light began to flood my artwork. Twenty years after *Chanticleer,* I was illustrating DONALD HALL's *Ox-Cart Man* and wondering about my career. When *Ox-Cart Man* won the Caldecott, I figured my apprenticeship was over at last. I would not change careers, after all. Still, a change was in order. I decided to write the stories for my illustrations. And in 1981 I sat down and wrote *Miss Rumphius.* Twelve years have gone by, during which some of my best work has been done. For four or five of the books I was simply the illustrator. But I have written the trilogy, which is my heart.

I can't end without saying that I started out like Hattie, making pictures simply for the delight it gave me. It was selfishness. And it has brought me rewards beyond measure. Recognition is gratifying, but the love is far, far better. ꙮ

Cooper, Susan

British author residing in the United States, b. 1935. Raised on the ancient stories of legend and folklore, Susan Cooper instinctively turned to them when writing *Over Sea, Under Stone* (1965), her first book for children, which relates the adventures of three siblings on a quest to find the Holy Grail. A journalist, Cooper decided to try her hand at fiction when she saw a press release for a prize offered by a publishing company. Though she has produced several PICTURE BOOKS and novels for children in addition to her award-winning FANTASY sequence — The Dark Is Rising — Cooper has not limited her audience to young readers; her achievements include newspaper columns, a biography, and plays for theater and television. Nevertheless, the power of her fantasy for children places Cooper firmly among the best of children's authors.

Challenging but accessible, the Dark Is Rising series draws from the legends surrounding King Arthur and other figures rooted in the mythology of Britain and Wales and depicts the struggle between the powers of the Light and the Dark. Will Stanton, who discovers on his eleventh birthday that he is one of the Old Ones, the servants of the Light, joins forces with the three siblings introduced in *Over Sea, Under Stone* and Bran Davies, who has been raised in the modern world, though he is the son of King Arthur and Guinevere. Possessing varying degrees of understanding, step by step, and with the help of Merriman Lyons — Merlin — the children fulfill the prophecies that strengthen the Light for the final defense against the Dark. Set in modern England and Wales, the sequence depicts the epic struggle with depth and brilliance but also conveys the message that the potential for evil is embedded in human nature; hence, the fight for that which is right is eternal. Often compared to TOLKIEN's work, Cooper's fantasy series is intricate and intriguing; by involving ordinary characters as well as those with supernatural powers, she has explored the relationship between acts that are humane and those that are good.

Cooper has brought her love of the ancient literature of her native land into all her work. *The Silver Cow: A Welsh Tale* (1983) and *The Selkie Girl* (1986) are fluid picture book retellings of British folktales, while the novels *The Boggart* (1993) and *The Boggart and the Monster* (1997) explore the collision of the Old World and the New, as two children accidentally transport a mischievous sprite called a "boggart" to Canada from the castle in Scotland that is his home.

A child of World War II who left her family and country at age twenty-seven to marry and move to Cambridge, Massachusetts, Cooper has invested in her characters her feelings of displacement. The Boggart yearns intensely for home; Bran Davies is torn between his birthright as King Arthur's son and his place among modern friends and family; Will Stanton rarely forgets that he is more than an ordinary boy. In *Seaward* (1983), Cally and West travel through an unknown land, fleeing from terrors behind them and facing the uncertain future. Filled with images of life and death, the story is an allegory and more; like all of Cooper's fiction, it is deeply symbolic, multifaceted, and rewarding. The tremendous scope and intensity of Cooper's work mark her as a modern master of the high-fantasy genre. A.E.D.

Cormier, Robert

American author, 1925–2000. In 1974 Robert Cormier entered the field of young adult fiction with *The Chocolate War*. Although the title suggests an innocuous, even humorous story, the novel's first line establishes a very different tone: "They murdered him." With these stark, uncompromising words, the reader is plunged into a dark tale of tyranny and evil played out against the background of a boys' parochial school. With its challenging themes and taut, suspenseful writing, the book made a shattering impact on the world of the YOUNG ADULT NOVEL. The author's subsequent books enhanced his reputation as one of the outstanding creators in the field.

Cormier was born and raised in the French Hill section of Leominster, Massachusetts, a small, close-knit community of French Canadian immigrants. Renamed Monument, Massachusetts, his hometown is featured in several of his books, including *Fade* (1988), which evocatively describes a neighborhood where all the fathers work at the town plastics factory, all the children attend the local Catholic school, and grandparents, aunts, and uncles live just down the block. As a teenager, some of Cormier's early poems were published in the Leominster *Daily Enterprise.* He attended nearby Fitchburg State College for one year but left school to make his living as a writer. He worked for a radio station and a newspaper before settling at the Fitchburg *Sentinel,* where he spent more than twenty years as a writer and editor. The married father of four also published stories in magazines such as *Redbook* and the *Saturday Evening Post.* His powerful first novel, *Now and at the Hour* (1960), concerns an elderly man facing death. Cormier wrote two more adult novels before his teenage son's experiences with a school candy sale inspired a new story.

Although published as a young adult book, *The Chocolate War* is written with a complexity seldom associated with the genre. A mosaic of short, tightly written scenes, the book centers on Jerry Renault, a freshman at Trinity, a New England Catholic school. Insecure and still grieving over his mother's death, Jerry asks himself the question printed on his favorite poster: "Do I dare disturb the universe?" Archie Costello, the amoral leader of the Vigils, Trinity's secret society, gives Jerry the assignment of refusing to sell chocolates for the school fundraiser. In turn, Brother Leon, an evil and power-hungry teacher, pressures Archie into revoking Jerry's assignment. But Jerry continues not to sell the chocolates, resulting in an inevitably brutal conclusion. The novel is an explosive examination of evil and the corruption of power; each of the many characters is brilliantly defined and the writing is stark and fast-moving, yet contains penetrating images and metaphors.

In Cormier's next two books, social and political problems alter the lives of contemporary teenagers. *I Am the Cheese* (1977) is extremely complex in structure, interpolating three connected stories: Adam Farmer's first-person, present-tense account of a mysterious bicycle journey, a third-person description of his past, and a transcript of his interrogation by a strange man named Brint. The plot, which hinges on a witness-relocation program, comes to a breathtaking conclusion that causes many people to reread immediately the entire novel, looking for the clues that foreshadow the disheartening outcome. *After the First Death* (1979) also contains riveting suspense, an unusual structure, and a grim theme. The story concerns a busload of small children held hostage by terrorists, and its young adult appeal results from its focus on three teenage characters, including Kate, the young bus driver. Cormier's first female protagonist is particularly memorable for her courageous actions in this exquisitely written novel of suspense, betrayal, and bravery.

The author received the 1991 Margaret A. Edwards Award for his first three young adult novels, which remain unforgettable in their storytelling and devastating in their impact. Among his other young adult books are *Eight Plus One* (1980), a collection of short stories that is somewhat uneven due to the frequent use of adult protagonists; *The Bumblebee Flies Anyway* (1983), a chilling tale of terminally ill teenagers; *Beyond the Chocolate War* (1985), a strong sequel, with an even greater suspense quotient; and *We All Fall Down* (1991), a well-written story of urban violence that includes few appealing characters. One of Cormier's most talked-about novels is a vast departure from his previous works. *Fade* contains elements of the supernatural, as young Paul Moreaux discovers his ability to become invisible and, a generation later, must stop his troubled nephew from abusing the power that he, too, has inherited. The work's raw violence and sexuality push the envelope of adolescent fiction and may disturb readers of all ages. But few will deny the power of this compelling novel, which is notable for its autobiographical descriptions of 1930s "Frenchtown," its shifting viewpoints, and its terrifying plot and themes. In *Tenderness* (1997) Cormier explored the mind of a psychopathic teen killer. In *The*

Rag and Bone Shop (2001) he found fresh fictional forms for his favorite themes: guilt, forgiveness, misuse of authority, and the corruption of innocence.

Much of the author's work was informed by his strong Roman Catholic faith, a topic he addressed directly in *Other Bells for Us to Ring* (1990), his first book for younger readers. This story of Darcy, who moves to Frenchtown during World War II and becomes friends with a Catholic girl, is very well written but may seem simplistic and sentimental to fans of Cormier's earlier novels. *Tunes for Bears to Dance To* (1992) explores the subject of evil for a juvenile audience, as a loathsome employer bribes young Henry into committing a destructive act against an elderly Holocaust survivor. Although flawed by insufficient character motivation and a truncated plot, the author's fine writing and descriptive skills remain in top form.

Cormier's novels have been adapted for films, taught in secondary schools, studied by critics, and continue to be popular with young readers. Like all important books, they have elicited controversy. The author's unwillingness to sugarcoat his themes or compromise the integrity of his stories by providing unrealistic happy endings has caused some to criticize the bleak, pessimistic view of humanity displayed in his work. Do the books portray a universe filled with only defeat and despair? Yes, they often do. But is this actually the overriding theme of the writing? No. Half of each reading experience involves the emotions and attitudes of the reader. Cormier's readers come away from his books asking serious questions of themselves. Do I have the courage of Kate in *After the First Death*? Do I have the resolve of Jerry in *The Chocolate War*? What would I do if I were one of his classmates? Do I dare disturb the universe? In his brilliantly crafted novels, Cormier presented important ethical issues and asked tough questions. The reader is left to ponder the answers.

When Cormier died, hundreds of his readers, friends, and young people gathered in Leominster to pay tribute to the man who had not only vitalized the field of young adult literature but touched their personal lives as well.   P.D.S.

Voices of the Creators

Robert Cormier

In a single paragraph of an article dealing with *The Chocolate War, I Am the Cheese,* and *After the First Death,* a writer listed these topics as central to the books: brutality, sadism, corruption (religious and governmental), insanity, murder, torture, personality destruction, terrorism, child murder, and suicide.

What kind of person writes about those terrible things? And why?

The name on the novels is Robert Cormier, and my name is Robert Cormier. But sometimes I don't recognize myself, either in what others say about my work or when I face questions from an audience about the violent nature of the books that bear my name.

I am a man who cries at sad movies, longs for happy endings, delights in atrocious puns, pauses to gather branches of bittersweet at the side of a highway. I am shamelessly sentimental: I always make a wish when I blow out the candles on my birthday cake, and I dread the day when there may be no one there to say "Bless you" when I sneeze. Although I aspire to be Superman, I am doomed to be Clark Kent forever, in an endless search for that magic telephone booth. I wear a trench coat, but nobody ever mistakes me for Humphrey Bogart. I hesitate to kill a fly — but people die horrible deaths in my novels.

But, of course, it's easy to kill off characters in novels or assign them tragic roles, because they are only figments of the imagination. People in books are made of print and paper, not flesh and blood, after all. They are creatures who live and die only between the covers of a book. Right?

Wrong. They also live in my mind and imagination and have the power to disturb dreams and to invoke themselves at odd, unguarded moments. Kate Forrester in *After the First Death* was a very real person to me. I cheered her brave actions as they unfolded on the page. I was moved by her sense of responsibility toward the children who were hostages on that hijacked bus. I loved the way she refused to concede defeat. And yet, I sensed a doom descending on her, a foreshadowing of failure. She was an amateur at deceit and intrigue. And amateurs often make mistakes, fatal miscalculations. In going to the limit of her dwindling resources to protect the children and then to escape, it was inevitable that she would go too far. I saw her moving in that direction with the horror that a parent feels watching a child dash into noonday traffic on a busy street, helpless to avert what must happen.

Fiction must follow an internal logic. Given the circumstances I had created, Kate had to die. That doesn't mean I didn't mourn — or that I don't wish to write happier stories, with strolling-into-sunset endings, the cavalry arriving at the last minute. How I loved the sound of bugles and those thundering hooves at Saturday movie matinees.

But I've come to realize that Saturday matinees have nothing to do with real life, that innocence doesn't provide immunity from evil, that the mugger lurking in the doorway assaults both the just and the unjust.

It is possible to be a peaceful man, to abhor violence, to love children and flowers and old Beatles songs, and still be aware of the contusions and abrasions this world inflicts on us. Not to write happy endings doesn't mean the writer doesn't believe in them. Literature should penetrate all the chambers of the human heart, even the dark ones.

A fifteen-year-old high school sophomore sat in my living room recently and asked me, "Why do people get upset by your novels?" She is a lovely person, tender toward small animals, and she tries to be a good kid. But she knows that people like Kate Forrester don't always survive or that a boy like Adam Farmer in *I Am the Cheese* can become a victim of the times in which he lives. That doesn't mean that she is cynical or that she is not idealistic. But she has faced realities.

It's sad, of course, to face realities. But not to face them is to live in a never-never land, where

struggle and growth and the possibility of triumph are absent.

This essay may not tell you what kind of person writes about terrible things — but, perhaps, it tells you why. ⚏

Counting Books

The toddler calls out "one, two, fwee" and is immediately greeted with smiles, applause, and exclamations of approval by her adult audience. Their response is so satisfying that she adds this performance to her repertoire even though she does not yet know that these sounds form part of a sequence that can be expanded and reversed, can reveal a one-to-one correspondence, can be represented orthographically and symbolically, can be manipulated to reveal insights about the objective world, can be a stimulus for aesthetic experiences, and, best of all, can be a continuing source of fun and pleasure. Children's counting books help this toddler and countless others discover the possibilities inherent in the world of numbers.

Ostensibly a category of books with limited possibilities, counting books have attracted some of the most prominent names in the field of children's literature, revealing surprisingly varied approaches in content as well as aesthetics. For the youngest child, there are simple, direct books that typically employ easily identifiable, familiar objects in limited quantities. TANA HOBAN's *1, 2, 3* (1985) is a BOARD BOOK for the nursery set that features a birthday cake with a single candle, two baby tennis shoes, three building blocks, and, finally, ten infant toes. There is no text other than the names of the numbers, which are accompanied by numerals and a corresponding quantity of dots. Equally suitable for the preschool child is *Who's Counting*, by NANCY TAFURI (1986), which follows a puppy past one squirrel, two birds, and the like until he reaches home, where his nine siblings join him for dinner.

In *Ten Black Dots* (1986), DONALD CREWS

transmuted five black circles into "buttons on a coat or the portholes of a boat." This handsome little book, with its vibrant colors, clear, uncluttered images, and rhyming text, is a work of charm as well as practicality. MOLLY BANG has counted, in *Ten, Nine, Eight* (1983), a serene bedtime book featuring an African American child and her loving father counting backward from "ten small toes all washed and warm" to "one big girl all ready for bed." *One Was Johnny* (1962), from the incomparable Nutshell Library, is anything but a bedtime book. MAURICE SENDAK's young hero is invaded by a succession of rowdies whom he evicts by counting backward until he reestablishes his preferred solitary state.

In *One Hunter* (1982), PAT HUTCHINS has dispatched her totally incompetent hunter on a safari. He marches obliviously past nine sets of wild creatures, who are only imperfectly camouflaged, finally fleeing in panic when all are assembled together. In Peter Pavey's *One Dragon's Dream* (1979), it is again the objects to be counted that are camouflaged. Embedded in busy and complex illustrations, the elements of the sets may vary in form, be partially obscured or viewed from differing angles, complicating the identification process but expanding the understanding of what may constitute a set. Brushes, all elements of a single set, are variously suitable for artists or house painters; of the three tigers, two are real and one paper. Employing both visual puns and linguistic games, the book's intellectual challenge extends far beyond just counting. Joy Hulme's *Sea Squares* (1991) can be either a simple counting book or an exercise in multiplication and division or even in squares and roots.

MITSUMASA ANNO's books are the work not only of an artist but also of a mathematician. Beginning with zero and proceeding through twelve, each page of *Anno's Counting Book* (1975) reflects a different month and different hour of the day. More complicated is *Anno's Counting House* (1982), which extends beyond sets and correspondence to comparison, conservation, subsets, position, addition, and subtraction.

Kveta Pacovska's *One, Five, Many* (1990) de-fies categorization. Using cutouts, accordion foldouts, paper doors, and even a silver mirror, this spiral-bound book is more a celebration of the joys and possibilities of numbers than a straightforward counting book. It invites the child to consider, ponder, and play with numbers for the sheer glory of the experience.

Some authors have used popular media characters to introduce number concepts. Considering the emphasis on counting in *Sesame Street,* it is not surprising to see *Little Bert's Book of Numbers* (1992), by Anna Ross, utilizing the popular television muppet to introduce a simple sequence. *One Hundred and One Dalmatians* (1956), by Fran Manushkin, employs these favorite film canines to lead young readers in counting just past one hundred.

In some books, the counting aspect may be equaled or eclipsed by other elements. *Animal Numbers* (1987), by Bert Kitchen, is little more than an excuse for some stunningly beautiful illustrations. A child could certainly count the three baby squirrels or the ten Irish setter puppies, or even the twenty-five garter snakes, but such usage is mere *lagniappe*. The pictures alone more than justify this lovely book. BRUCE MCMILLAN's expertly photographed wildflowers in *Counting Wildflowers* (1986) are more a celebration of nature than an excuse to move from one to twenty, and Jan Thornhill's *The Wildlife 1, 2, 3: A Nature Counting Book* (1989) reveals in its title its dual purpose. This beautifully designed book features handsome illustrations, intriguingly framed on each page, a pleasure to contemplate and incidentally offering objects to count. A notable book of this type is *Moja Means One* (1971), by Muriel and TOM FEELINGS. Primarily a book to introduce aspects of East African rural and village life and evoke a sense of rootedness in African American children, it is secondarily a Swahili counting book. The eponymous heroes of ARTHUR GEISERT's *Pigs from 1 to 10* (1992) embark on a quest to locate "a lost place with huge stone configurations." In each two-page spread, the numerals from 0 to 9 are embedded. Some are readily spotted, but others take considerable study to unearth. This challenge, the sophisticated language, and the witty illustrations suggest that the intended audience is well past toddler age.

Counting is a fundamental behavior. Its exploration in children's books would seem to be relatively limited and constrained, but such is not the case. The twentieth century witnessed an astounding variation in children's counting books, and the past few years have produced a truly surprising array of works. Just when it seems every possible aspect of this topic has been explored, a genuinely unique work appears. There is no reason to suspect this process will not continue indefinitely. K.H.

Craig, Helen

British illustrator and author, b. 1934. With the publication of *Angelina Ballerina* in 1982, illustrator Helen Craig and author Katharine Holabird introduced a spunky, winning heroine in the form of an anthropomorphic mouse. Angelina's debut heralded the beginning of a SERIES that currently boasts a multitude of volumes and is extremely popular with young children. The success of these books results from their breadth and variety; Craig took some of the stories away from the ballerina's dance floor and grounded them in the ordinary, everyday experiences of a child's world. *Angelina Goes to the Fair* (1985) finds Angelina disgruntled because she must take her cousin Henry to the fair; her annoyance turns to fright when she loses the youngster and then to joyous relief upon finding him. *Angelina's Birthday Surprise* (1989) features Angelina on an old bike that crashes and sends the heroine sprawling, so Angelina must start a vigorous campaign to earn money for a new bike. In *Angelina Ice Skates* (1993), the protagonist shows the neighborhood boys that girls are able to move as quickly on skates as boys.

One aspect of the Angelina books' appeal to all youngsters is their agreeable gender balance within text and illustrations. Although Angelina's personality is clearly the force that moves the stories within the series, the real thread that binds them securely together is Craig's artwork. Craig has delineated character and expression with the slightest line. The illustrations are energetic, humorous, and alive with movement that sends the eye across the page.

Craig began illustrating children's books in 1970; the first book she both wrote and illustrated was the ALPHABET BOOK *The Mouse House ABC* (1977). Another character created by Craig, with author Sarah Hayes, is Bear, a beguiling teddy bear who stars in three charming books that the youngest listeners have taken to heart. The appeal of the predictable stories is in the interaction between the three main characters: Bear, the young boy devoted to Bear, and a naughty, lovable dog who thinks Bear gets too much attention. *This Is the Bear* (1986) introduces the series; it is followed by *This Is the Bear and the Picnic Lunch* (1988) and *This Is the Bear and the Scary Night* (1992). The text, written in rhythmic, cumulative verse, is accompanied by word balloons that allow the Bear, the dog, and other creatures to speak as they proceed through their amusing adventures. Executed in watercolor and ink, the illustrations, perfectly attuned to a child's world, create relationships among the characters that are believable, warm, and reassuring.

Craig has illustrated books of her own: *The Night of the Paper Bag Monsters* (1984), *The Knight, the Princess, and the Dragon* (1985), and *A Welcome for Annie* (1986). The stories' appeal rests in Craig's imaginative integration of text and pictures. Susie and Alfred, two close friends who happen to be piglets, cavort through simple plots laced with good-natured humor.

Whatever the text, Craig's gentle, detailed watercolors and perceptive interpretations visually celebrate the wonders of friendship and the commonplace events of childhood. S.L.

Crane, Walter

British illustrator and author, 1845–1915. Walter Crane was the first of the grand triumvirate in children's book illustration who worked under the tutelage of the English printer Edmund Evans. Crane, the son of an artist, developed his artistic talents from an early age and at seventeen exhibited at London's Royal Academy. As a young teenager, he apprenticed himself to the engraver William James Linton for three years before setting out on his own to earn a living as an artist. His early books were illustrated anonymously, but he soon met Evans, who had developed and perfected a method of color printing and was looking for talented illustrators to produce books for children. Crane's first children's books, *The House That Jack Built* and *Dame Trot and Her Comical Cat,* were published in 1865 when he was twenty and were followed by more than forty books for children over the course of his career. Many of these were toy books, so called because of their small length and size.

In addition to illustrating and painting, Crane worked as a teacher and as a designer of wallpaper, textiles, ceramics, and interiors. He was a disciple of William Morris and a member of the Arts and Crafts movement, which at-

tempted to provide an alternative to the ugliness that resulted from the industrial revolution by seeking to bring beautiful design and craftsmanship to everyday things. The influence of this movement can be seen in Crane's concern for the overall design of his books. He was one of the first illustrators to be concerned with the appearance of the two-page spread and often planned the entire book design, including the endpapers, title page, and lettering.

Crane took readily to illustrating for children. His strengths as an illustrator lay in his strong sense of composition and design and in his use of color, which was influenced by Japanese prints. In books such as the *Absurd ABC* (1874), the contrasting values set up by the use of large areas of black set against red and yellow convey a feeling of lively movement in spite of the flatness of the figures that resulted from his use of uniform color. In this book, the breakup of some pages into panels depicting the different letters creates an alternative rhythm to the two-page spreads and further energizes the overall effect. The illustration style is also reminiscent

Illustration by Walter Crane for "Beauty and the Beast," from Crane's book *Beauty and the Beast and Other Tales* (1875).

of the Japanese wood-block prints that Crane found so appealing. At times, Crane's admitted concern with design and detail made him lose sight of his child audience, and the storytelling qualities of his illustrations are sometimes overwhelmed by decoration. But the range of his talent as an illustrator for children is most evident in works like *The Baby's Opera* (1877) and *The Baby's Bouquet* (1879). *First of May: A Fairy Masque* (1881) has surprisingly delicate drawings and restrained page design. Another book that demonstrates Crane's versatility is *Household Stories* (1882) by the brothers GRIMM. Here we see his true talents in the small drawings used to illustrate the beginnings and endings of the chapters. In these small spaces there is no room for fussy details, and Crane's vitality of line and composition is particularly evident.

Over the course of his career Crane set himself many artistic challenges by choosing to illustrate a variety of texts, from ALPHABET BOOKS and brief rhymes to fully developed fairy tales, and he strove in all of these works to bring coherence to the overall appearance of the individual book. In addition to his books for children he created illustrated books for adults and several textbooks about book design and illustration. When Crane died in 1915 he had become internationally known and admired, and his contributions to children's book illustration can still be seen in children's books at the beginning of the twenty-first century. B.K.

Creech, Sharon

American author, b. 1945. Versatile and gifted in her use of language, Sharon Creech tells stories that speak to the hearts and souls of her readers. She has translated her almost unparalleled understanding of the human experience into books for readers of all ages. Though best known as a writer of YOUNG ADULT NOVELS, she has extended herself into the genres of PICTURE BOOKS and MIDDLE-GRADE NOVELS and succeeded with every effort.

Sharon Creech grew up in what she has consistently termed "a big, noisy family" outside of Cleveland, Ohio. She first learned the advantages of vivid storytelling while competing with her sister and brothers for attention at the dinner table; furthermore, she learned the importance of hoarding pens, pencils, and paper so they were always close at hand. A voracious reader, Creech has fondly recalled the magic of reading, "of drifting into the pages and living in someone else's world, the excitement of never knowing what lay ahead." Creech studied writing at Hiram College and went on to various jobs that utilized her gift for words and love of books: editorial assistant, indexer, researcher at the Library of Congress. Sometime after obtaining a graduate degree from George Mason University, Creech decided to pursue a teaching career and moved with her children to Surrey, England. After she remarried, the family moved to Lugano, Switzerland, and then returned to England, where Creech taught American and British literature.

Her first novel for young readers was *Absolutely Normal Chaos* (1990). The book (like her previous two for adults) was published in England and did not find its way to the United States until 1995. Meanwhile, Creech authored *Walk Two Moons* (1994), which won the 1995 Newbery Medal. The novel's heroine, Salamanca Tree Hiddle, embarks on a cross-country journey with her grandparents and along the way regales them with the story of another girl, Mary Lou Finney, a character who previously appeared in *Absolutely Normal Chaos*. In addition to layering her characters in this way, Creech layers the narrative so that, in speaking about Mary Lou, Salamanca reveals a great deal about herself and her feelings about losing her mother. *Walk Two Moons* reveals Creech's most remarkable talents in an inspiring, poignant story.

Creech's extensive catalogue of books includes another Newbery Medal winner, *The Wanderer* (1999), which features another thoughtful and storied girl on a passage both literal and figurative: crossing the Atlantic on a sailboat, Sophie comes to terms with tragedy in her past and the promise of a new future. The novel was highly praised for its true adolescent voices, both male and female, and for its gentle yet honest approach to the issue of death. Creech effected the same tenderness in her book for younger readers, *Love That Dog* (2001), in which a boy named Jack learns to appreciate poetry and use it to express his sorrow about the loss of his dog.

Again and again, Sharon Creech creates books that embody the very best of literature for young people: stories finely told with humor, honesty, and wisdom. H.F.R.

Cresswell, Helen

British author, b. 1934. Born in Nottinghamshire, Helen Cresswell won her first literary prize at age fourteen. "I do not remember a time when I did not know that I was to be a writer," she has recalled. Cresswell is the author of more than sixty books, including books written for early readers, such as *Rainbow Pavement* (1970) and the Two Hoots series, beginning with *Two Hoots* (1974), as well as original scripts for television.

Cresswell is perhaps best known, however, for her MIDDLE-GRADE and YOUNG ADULT FICTION, from the hilarious chronicles of the eccentric but lovable Bagthorpe family, introduced in *Ordinary Jack* (1977), to the complex FANTASY of *The Night Watchman* (1969) and the contemporary drama of *Dear Shrink* (1982), in which three young siblings face the challenges of living on their own. Her work has been critically acclaimed throughout Cresswell's career, and four books — *The Piemakers* (1967), *The Night Watchman* (1969), *Up the Pier* (1971), and *The Bongleweed* (1973) — were runners-up for the top British children's book award, the Carnegie Medal. Her many other honors and awards include five titles selected as ALA Notable Books.

Cresswell's trademark style — an exaggerated, often slapstick humor; comedic timing; and a keen appreciation of the absurd — has garnered a devoted following among many young readers. "I have a very strong sense of childhood," she has explained, "and like to be talking to human beings before they have become capable of pose

or hypocrisy or prejudice." Cresswell delights in the unexpected and unpredictable; events often unfold at a dizzying pace. In *The Piemakers,* the Roller family decides to create the "biggest pie that's ever been made in the whole history of the world," enlisting the aid of the entire town of Danby Dale. They commission a pie dish so big it has to be steered, like a barge, down the river, to which they add sensational seasonings, crust, and filling — and are rewarded by winning the King's contest. When a wild weed starts growing at a remarkable rate in *The Bongleweed,* Becky Finch and her sensible father, a gardener, find themselves defending a plant that threatens to overtake their village. The Wilks family, servants in London in 1887, enjoy an unusual vacation one hundred years in the future, in *Time Out* (1990). The Pontifexes are brought from 1921 into 1971 by a magic spell in *Up the Pier,* and in *Moondial* (1987) young Minty Kane tries to rescue the spirits of abused children from long ago.

Cresswell offers an affectionate, nostalgic view of an unspoiled English countryside and memorable characters. Even their names are evocative: the proper housekeeper Mrs. Fosdyke, desperately trying to keep order among the unruly Bagthorpes; Gravella Roller of *The Piemakers;* the title character of *Lizzy Dripping* (1973). Often eccentric, always determined and spirited, these charming characters lead the reader on a "magical mystery tour" that is quite exhilarating — or sometimes just plain silly. Cresswell has celebrated the value of creativity and of the individual, who is often at odds with a more stodgy society. In the more subtle and subdued fantasy of *The Night Watchman,* the offbeat characters of Josh and Caleb, two tramps who inhabit an underworld of hidden reality, transform the boring and lonely life of young Henry. Turning this theme topsy-turvy in the six-part Bagthorpe saga, the hero of *Ordinary Jack* despairs of ever fitting into his frenetic, unconventional, talented family. In the end, Jack learns to accept himself as he is, reinforcing the Cresswell creed that "family" is a place where solace and comfort can be found, no matter how unusual that family might be. Like Jack, the reader inevitably emerges refreshed and satisfied at the conclusion of Cresswell's lively and boisterous novels. C.J.

Crews, Donald

American author and illustrator, b. 1938. Donald Crews was born in Newark, New Jersey. Long interested in drawing and sketching, he attended Arts High School, which had special classes in music and art, then went to Cooper Union School for the Advancement of Science and Art in New York City. While serving in the military in Germany, he worked on a design portfolio. There he designed his first book for children, *We Read: A to Z,* which was published in 1967. He next wrote a book called *Ten Black Dots* (1968), a companion to the first. He has illustrated many books by others, such as *Rain* (1978) and *Blue Sea* (1979), written by Robert Kalan, and *The Talking Stone: An Anthology of Native American Tales and Legends* (1979), retold and edited by Dorothy de Wit.

When he turned back to creating his own texts, Crews captured the imagination of critics and judges with *Freight Train* (1978). The spare text labels the different freight cars, shown in bright colors and bold shapes, and depicts the train moving across trestles and passing by cities. At first stationary, it begins to pick up speed until it is a blur, an effect achieved with airbrush technique. Crews based the book on childhood memories of travels south to his grandparents' farm in Cottondale, Florida, where he watched and counted trains that passed near the house. The book was named a 1979 Caldecott Honor Book by the American Library Association, and its success allowed Crews to devote himself to PICTURE BOOKS.

Crews's next work, *Truck,* also has a simple text, in which the journey of a brightly colored tractor-trailer displays the intricate shapes of highways and geometric signs. In 1981 the American Library Association named *Truck* a Caldecott Honor Book. *Harbor* (1982) shows an active city harbor, with all manner of shipping vessels, ocean liners, and tugboats. Crews worked the names of some family members into the illustrations as the names of boats, as he often has worked messages into his artwork in the form of signs and other lettering. In *Carousel* (1983) Crews varied his technique by photographing the artwork, which depicts children on a carousel, moving the camera so that the image appears blurred to signify movement. He explored other aspects of a child's world in books such as *Light* (1981), *Parade* (1983), and *School Bus* (1984). He returned to the setting that inspired *Freight Train* in *Bigmama's* (1991), in which he portrayed a trip his family made to visit his grandmother in Florida. *Shortcut* (1992) tells the sobering tale of a group of children who take a route home via some railroad tracks. They come so close to being struck that it frightens them deeply. Thus Crews has evolved from the creator of *Freight Train,* bold, simple, and devoid of human characters, into the author of a book that re-creates an incident that has lasting emotional reverberations for its protagonists.

This innovative artist continues to experiment; he applies his fascination with elements such as light, movement, photography, and collage to invent new ways of creating a picture book. Crews has been recognized by the American Institute of Graphic Arts in several of its exhibits. S.H.H.

Crutcher, Chris

American author, b. 1946. Chris Crutcher was born at Ohio's Wright-Patterson Air Force Base. Six weeks later, the family moved to the remote and sparsely populated logging community of Cascade, Idaho, that became the heart of, and inspiration for, so many of his stories. Based on the recurring sports themes within his fiction, one might assume Crutcher grew up an avid athlete, but he was actually forcefully recruited. In a town so small, every boy played — like it or not — just to guarantee ample numbers to form a team. Humor was Crutcher's calling as a boy. He made his mother, his teachers, and his classmates laugh with such regularity that he once considered standup comedy as a possible trade. He joined that comedic edge with journalism in "Chris's Crumbs," a column for his high school newspaper, though he never contemplated writing as a profession.

Crutcher graduated high school with anemic grades and headed for Eastern Washington State College (now Eastern Washington University) in 1964. He swam competitively with teammates who would inspire his second YOUNG ADULT NOVEL, *Stotan!* (1986), and studied psychology and sociology between meets. After earning a teaching certification, he taught at several schools, including one in Kenniwick, Washington, with fellow EWU graduate Terry Davis — the start of a pivotal friendship for both novelists. Crutcher was promoted from teacher to director at the Lakeside School in Oakland, California, a "last chance" academy for troubled kids. Seven years later, after he had watched Davis write and publish *Vision Quest* (1980), Crutcher's own stories started to emerge.

Resigning his position at Lakeside, Crutcher packed his VW and headed back to Spokane with enough money saved to write for one year. *Running Loose* (1983) was complete by the time Crutcher's bank account dwindled, but not yet published. So he again sought employment, landing a job with Spokane's Child Protection Team. Though almost immediately he became an intuitive child advocate, Crutcher never imagined his life would take that turn. He went on to become a child and family therapist with the Spokane Community Mental Health Center and later with a private therapy group, also in Spokane. Working with severely troubled teens and families had a powerful impact on the balance of Crutcher's work. *The Crazy Horse Electric Game* (1987), *Chinese Handcuffs* (1989), *Staying Fat for Sarah Byrnes* (1993), *Ironman* (1994), and *Whale Talk* (2001) all explore the crushing impact of human struggle and the triumph of survival. They celebrate loyalty, friendship, and diversity. But mostly, they herald the healing power of inclusion — connection, as Crutcher has called it. "There is very little about life that isn't about connection," he has said. "Being inside rather than outside can change any individual's life."

The message has clearly been received, as Crutcher has been awarded some of the industry's top honors, including back-to-back ALAN Awards from the Assembly on Literature for Adolescents of the National Council of Teachers of English (1994, 1995), the NCTE's National Intellectual Freedom Award (1998), and the ALA's Margaret A. Edwards Lifetime Achievement Award (2000) for his commitment to serving young adults. K.M.H.

Cummings, Pat

American illustrator, b. 1950. Variety has been a common thread in both the personal life and the work of artist Pat Cummings. She experienced variety during her years as an army brat; although born in Chicago, she spent her childhood in many places both in and out of the United States. Cummings began drawing as soon as she could hold a crayon, desiring, even then, to be an illustrator. Her parents encouraged her by keeping her well supplied with artists' materials. In 1974 she graduated from Pratt Institute and began her career as a freelance illustrator.

Cummings's interest in illustrating children's books sprang from her work with children's theater groups. Her duties ranged from creating the ads, posters, and flyers to designing the sets and even some of the costumes. The fantasy and imagery of children's theater appealed to her, and she has continued to rely upon this background in creating her book illustrations. She has incorporated her personal experiences into books in other ways as well, by including people she knows, household items she uses, and places she has been.

Cummings's first children's book was *Good News* (1977), written by Eloise Greenfield. In 1982 her drawings for Jeannette Caines's *Just Us Women* made it a Coretta Scott King Honor Book. Recognition of her artistry began to grow.

She has since won the Coretta Scott King Illustrator Award in 1984 for *My Mama Needs Me* (1983), written by Mildred Pitts Walter, and received two additional Coretta Scott King honorable mentions for *C.L.O.U.D.S.* (1986) and for MARY STOLZ's *Storm in the Night* (1988). Cummings both wrote and illustrated two books: *Jimmy Lee Did It* (1985), which draws on children's everyday use of their imaginations; and *C.L.O.U.D.S.*, in which she returned to her love of FANTASY.

In three Talking with Artists volumes, Cummings compiled BIOGRAPHIES of outstanding artists and illustrators by using a series of questions similar to those which she is asked by students. She conveyed insight into the importance of art in the lives of her subjects and introduced her readers to the variety of careers that one may pursue with an art background. Much emphasis is placed on the art created by each artist during childhood, and the text is accompanied by examples of this art as well as by their illustrated work in children's books. Through the combination of biographies, interviews, and artwork, Cummings has provided a text that encourages children to appreciate their own artistic talent and to consider art careers, while it feeds the curiosity of adult readers interested in the backgrounds of these artists. Cummings has illustrated a number of other books, which vary in theme from child molestation, in *Chilly Stomach* (1986), to hugging, in *Willie's Not the Hugging Kind* (1989).

Whether the stories deal with fantasy or reality, are humorous or serious, Pat Cummings's signature of colorful illustrations and a zest for life infuse the pages of her books. C.H.S.

Curtis, Christopher Paul

American author, b. 1953. The encouragement of a supportive wife helped Christopher Paul Curtis make the giant leap from aspiring writer to published author of award-winning books. Born and raised in Flint, Michigan, Curtis was an avid reader as a youth but, like many minority children, complained that he couldn't find books that reflected his own life experiences. After graduating from high school he began working the assembly line at Fisher Body while attending the University of Michigan–Flint at night. Laboring at the factory, he devised time-saving methods that allowed him extra minutes away from the assembly line to pursue his writing. Some of these early efforts were honored with the University of Michigan's prestigious Avery and Jules Hopwood Awards. In 1993, his wife, Kaysandra, volunteered to financially support the family, which includes a son and daughter, while Curtis took a year off to finish his first book. Writing every day at a table in the children's department of the Windsor Public Library, on the Canadian side of the Detroit River, he completed *The Watsons Go to Birmingham — 1963* (1995).

When it was published, the novel was an immediate sensation, earning both critical acclaim and wide popularity. Narrated in a fresh and appealing voice by ten-year-old Kenny Watson, the story concerns the everyday experiences of a close-knit African American family living in Flint during the early 1960s. The tone is initially laugh-out-loud funny as Kenny describes the layers of clothing that his Southern-born mother insists he and his little sister wear to school in the wintertime and the escapades of his thirteen-year-old brother, Byron, who gets his lips stuck to the frozen surface on their car's side-view mirror and defies his parents by having his hair straightened. But the mood turns darker when the family travels south to visit Grandma Sands in Alabama — a trip that coincides with the historic firebombing of the Sixteenth Avenue Baptist Church. The novel's splendid blending of fiction and historical fact, as well as its broad emotional range, made it one of the most arresting debut novels of the decade, and it was named a Newbery Honor Book and a Coretta Scott King Honor Book.

Curtis also visited the past with his next novel, *Bud, Not Buddy* (1999), the picaresque tale of orphaned Bud Caldwell searching for his father in Depression-era Michigan. Humor again plays a role in the narrative, as the precocious narrator puts a comic spin on events as potentially unsettling as his escape from the home of a ghastly foster family. Armed with his own "Rules and Things for Having a Funner Life and Making a Better Liar Out of Yourself," a good share of tenacity, and the few clues his deceased mother shared about his father's identity, Buddy travels from Flint to Grand Rapids, Michigan, in search of band leader Herman E. Calloway, the man he believes to be his father. Even food lines and Hoovervilles don't thwart the likable orphan in this genial, well-paced novel, which won the Newbery Medal, making Curtis the first African American man to receive the award. P.D.S.

Cushman, Karen

American author, b. 1941. "As a writer, I whisper in children's ears. And they talk back." Karen Cushman's intimate connection with her audience grew out of a childhood devoted to reading, writing, and telling her own stories. Life experiences, which include a classics degree from Stanford, a family, and teaching museum studies, were all preparation, she has said, for a return to writing that coincided with her daughter's departure for college.

Although discouraged from writing HISTORICAL FICTION, the author persevered for three years with her first book, *Catherine, Called Birdy* (1994), a 1995 Newbery Honor Book. "Birdy is my favorite character. She is the way I would have liked to have been as a child: assertive, imaginative, stubborn, brave, kind, funny, and determined to be who she was and not who other people wanted her to be, yet still retaining the ability to grow and change." Described in a series of diary entries, Catherine, a knight's daughter, tries to find a way out of her arranged marriage by devising pranks and schemes. The tone of Cushman's Newbery Medal winner, *The Midwife's Apprentice* (1995), is set by an unforgettable opening image — Alyce burrowing into the dung heap to escape the cold. When Alyce emerges, she must overcome not only physical deprivation but also her own self-doubts. In *Matilda Bone* (2000) the sheltered and otherworldly protagonist has an uncompromising attitude that is nearly her undoing, for none of the inhabitants of Blood and Bone Alley can meet her narrow standards of religious piety. *The Ballad of Lucy Whipple* (1996), set during the California gold rush, is a departure in time and place for the author. Lucy's adventures in the primitive mining camp, Lucky Diggins, are told to her Massachusetts grandparents in a series of letters. The story has personal resonance for Cushman: at the age of ten the author's family relocated from Chicago to California, and Cushman has admitted that her mixed feelings about this move are echoed in Lucy's resistance to her plight.

Cushman has created enduring young heroines and complex mature women. Alyce and Matilda are apprenticed to women who function less as surrogate mothers than as professionals who model how to live and work independently in a society dominated by men. Catherine learns that her mother has initiative and hidden strengths not always apparent to her willful daughter. And Lucy's widowed mother is the risk taker, prepared to move on when the next opportunity presents itself.

The stories' authentic settings are a testament to the author's meticulous research into the artifacts, social customs, and language of a particular time and place. Cushman immerses the reader so completely in the setting that tastes and odors seem sharply realistic, and physical discomforts experienced by the characters become almost tangible. Each character's voice reflects the language of the period, such as the medieval use of Latin, archaic swear words, and fifty-one different words for *liquor*. Names are integral to all of Cushman's works, defining the protagonists' relationships with other characters and their function in society. The author skillfully weaves humor into her narratives to provide relief from the unrelenting difficulties and challenging environment each protagonist must face. These strong characters offer young readers a guide to finding their own place in the world. M.B.D.

D

Dahl, Roald

British author, 1916–1990. The creator of what many claim to be the most popular children's books of all time, Roald Dahl is a legend despite the enormous campaigns that have been mounted against him by the adult world. For children, to read one Dahl book is reason to read them all, and to read them all is reason to read them all again. Born in South Wales to Norwegian parents, Dahl's early life was not without difficulties. When his father died of pneumonia in 1920, the family was left with a large estate and moved to Kent, England. At age eight, Dahl was shipped off to boarding school, where he learned to cope with disciplinary procedures that bordered on the torturous. He remained there through his early teens, when he transferred to a renowned British private school. Dahl's experiences in boarding school, summer vacations in Norway, and other anecdotes from his childhood years are the subject of his first autobiography, *Boy* (1984).

Dahl joined the Royal Air Force in 1939 and suffered severe injuries when his plane was shot down over Egypt. Even after his recovery, the resulting ailments plagued him for the rest of his life, necessitating numerous spinal operations as well as a hip replacement. In 1941, while still serving in World War II, he wrote his first fiction, a collection of short stories for adults based on his experiences in the air force that were published in 1946 as *Over to You*. Dahl and his famous wife, actress Patricia Neal, had four children. The first, Olivia, died of measles at the age of seven; their only son, Theo, developed hydrocephalus after a severe car accident but was cured several years later. The well-known couple and their various misfortunes have been the subject of much fascination and scrutiny, and in 1969 a biography, *Pat and Roald*, was published and later made into a TV movie.

Dahl's first book for children, *The Gremlins*, appeared in 1943 and was later purchased by Walt Disney for a feature film, which was never completed. After 1943 Dahl penned numerous other children's favorites, creating for himself a reputation rivaled by none. These books include *James and the Giant Peach* (1961), *Charlie and the Chocolate Factory* (1964), *Danny: The Champion of the World* (1975), *The BFG* (1982), and *The Witches* (1983). Most of Dahl's stories revolve around a strict portrayal of good versus evil, and the child who embodies good is always triumphant. Evil, whether it is represented by landowners, witches, giants, or nasty children, is always severely done away with in the end by a means appropriate to the character involved, evoking a bizarre and often gruesome sense of justice that empowers the child hero and, in turn, the child reader.

The reasons for children's attraction to Dahl's books can also be found in the author's horrific descriptions of evildoers: the Twits, possibly the most disgusting couple in all of children's books (*The Twits*, 1980), the colossal creatures wreaking havoc in *The BFG*, and Dahl's version of witches (who appear to be ordinary people until they reveal their toeless feet, bald pimpled heads, teeth stained by blue saliva, and hideously long claws — all hidden by high-heeled shoes, wigs, closed-lip smiles, and gloves) are just a few of his fanciful freaks whose attempts to rid the world of goodness are repeatedly denounced and foiled. His heroes, in turn, are generally bright, patient, selfless children who are suffocating under the misguided protection of delinquent caregivers or burdened by some other penalty such as poverty, dyslexia, or shyness. By heroic effort, and sometimes some assistance from a sympathetic adult figure, they are destined to overcome their difficulties in a miraculous manner and to have plenty of deliciously harrowing escapes along the way. Using a remarkable skill with words, Dahl combined likable children, nasty villains, plenty of action, a large dose of nonsense, and deftly constructed plots to create one extraordinary tale after another.

But not all agree that Dahl's work merits praise. Critics, reviewers, teachers, and parents the world over have looked at the events of Dahl's early life and labeled them the cause of the black, violent side found in nearly all his books; whatever the cause, this blackness is most certainly present with a vengeance. Characterized by racial stereotyping; violent, gruesome deaths; negative portraits of parents, teachers, and other adults; extreme depictions of right and wrong; and crude and vulgar language, the books certainly provide ample material for his detractors. Dahl's *Charlie and the Chocolate Factory,* one of the most popular children's books of all time, also ranks among the most controversial. The story of a young, impoverished boy whose selflessness and luck eventually win him the coveted Willy Wonka Chocolate Factory, *Charlie* earned for its author a cult following among child readers as well as critical condemnation for the book's racist overtones, age discrimination, and excessive violence. Leading the crusade has been Eleanor Cameron, a well-known author of fantasy for children and a respected critic. In her 1972 essay "McLuhan, Youth, and Literature," Cameron lashed out against *Charlie and the Chocolate Factory,* calling it "one of the most tasteless books ever written for children." Cameron's remarks drew a flurry of outrage and united Dahl's fans, young and old, in a war of words. Most of his books, in turn, came under similar attack, but they did not remain undefended in the realm of professional critics.

Dahl has been called a literary genius; his books have been considered modern fairy tales. But whether or not adults approve of them, Dahl's fiction has found a devoted readership in children, and despite his significant contribution to adult literature (*Kiss Kiss, Switch Bitch*) and screenwriting (*You Only Live Twice; Chitty Chitty Bang Bang*), his name will be forever associated with the peaches, chocolate, and Big Friendly Giants of the children's book world that he changed forever. C.C.B.

Danziger, Paula

American author, b. 1944. As a teenager, Paula Danziger read *The Catcher in the Rye* repeatedly because it reassured her that she "wasn't alone." As an adult, her best-selling YOUNG ADULT NOVELS have engendered that response in junior high–age readers since the publication of the popular *The Cat Ate My Gymsuit* (1974). Several years as a junior high school English teacher, along with a vivid recall of her own painful adolescence, helped Danziger forge this successful connection with her audience. Her narrators, typically female, with a first-person narrative voice, fight for their rights within their less-than-perfect families and schools, while simultaneously suffering the typically teenage blights of acne and awkwardly emerging sexuality. Through it all, they keep intact a sharp, occasionally pun-laden, sense of humor.

The therapeutic role literature played in her own life fostered Danziger's commitment to write about difficult situations her young readers commonly face. Her books don't shy away from ugly emotions, such as the anger Phoebe harbors for her materialistic mother in *The Divorce Express* (1982) or Cassie's comic but real fear that her dictatorial homeroom teacher will make her remove her sunglasses, exposing her overly tweezed eyebrows in *The Pistachio Prescription* (1978). Along with her best-selling status, Danziger has received numerous regional awards as well as two Parents' Choice Awards for Literature. Some critics, however, have faulted her for offering teens easily digestible clichés about themselves. Thirteen-year-old Marcy Lewis in *The Cat Ate My Gymsuit,* Danziger's self-proclaimed autobiographical novel, provides a counter to this criticism when she points out that "middle-class kids have problems too." Most of Danziger's heroines' problems stem from adults more concerned with exercising authority than with listening, although one or two sympathetic teachers or parents usually surface in each book to act as mentors, encouraging young people not to conform but to stand up for themselves. Danziger herself found such a mentor in the poet John Ciardi, who nurtured her appreciation for literature and gave her the courage to believe she could actually become a writer.

Not only issues of self-esteem but political concerns such as women's rights, the rights of young people, education reform, and environmentalism thread their way through Danziger's stories. She has taken a traditionally liberal stance, mobilizing her teenage characters to work together within the system for change. Though sticking to the same types of main characters and issues, her writing has evolved over the years: her perspective has become less black and white and her humor less angry. *Everyone Else's Parents Said Yes* (1989) marks a switch to third-person narration and a male protagonist — eleven-year-old Matthew, also featured in succeeding books. But as with all of Danziger's stories, the Matthew books exist firmly within the often tumultuous realm of the everyday.

First appearing in 1994, Amber Brown soon became Danziger's most popular character. In each of the books devoted to Amber, the first-person narratives develop an issue important to young readers. Excellent CHAPTER BOOKS for the beginning reader, the books have been enhanced by Tony Ross's art.   C.M.H.

Daugherty, James

American illustrator and author, 1889–1974. James Daugherty is primarily remembered for his inspired expression of the American spirit in both visual and literary form, a spirit characterized by appreciation for the heroes of democracy and the affirmation of Manifest Destiny. Daugherty confessed that his first reading of the poet Walt Whitman, when he was a young art student in England, was life-changing for him: "I took fire from his vision of America." This fire inspired murals in public places and, later, book illustrations with swirling lines, energetic rhythm, humor, and a compassionate view of humanity. Whitman's inspiration also found expression in Daugherty's carefully composed dedicatory pages, his popular

Illustration by James Daugherty from his book *Andy and the Lion* (1938).

Random House/Landmark volumes, and lively biographical accounts of American heroes. His BIOGRAPHIES include the winner of the 1940 Newbery Medal, *Daniel Boone* (1939); *Poor Richard*, about Benjamin Franklin (1941); *Abraham Lincoln* (1943); and *Of Courage Undaunted*, about Lewis and Clark (1951). Some readers of *Daniel Boone* have commented on what they perceived as offhand treatment of American Indians and African Americans; in fact, the historical times were accurately reflected.

Daugherty began to create art for young people in the mid-1920s when Doubleday's May Massee suggested he illustrate *Daniel Boone, Wilderness Scout* (1926), written by Stewart E. White. He subsequently became one of the best-known American illustrators of children's books, illustrating more than forty books by other authors. One of his most felicitous collaborations was with CARL SANDBURG in *Abe Lincoln Grows Up* (1928), which remains an outstanding example of the book as art form, a seamless integration of subject, word, and image. For Daugherty, line and design were foremost and to simplify was "the first of all the commandments." His work was exhibited in many one-man shows and is represented in a number of art collections.

Daugherty's writing career did not begin until after he was well established as an illustrator. He first created text to go with his drawings in *Andy and the Lion* (1938), an original version of the Androcles tale, which was a Caldecott Honor Book. LYND WARD praised it as a model PICTURE BOOK worthy of study by other writer-artists: "The interlocking relationship between the word and picture . . . has been carried several steps farther than I have seen it in any other place."

Nearly twenty years later, Daugherty's illustrations for *Gillespie and the Guards* (1957), written by Benjamin Elkin, was also a Caldecott Honor Book. This story with folktale elements is about a boy who cleverly outwits the king's sharpsighted guards. In the turbulent 1960s, Daugherty chose to illustrate his own selections from the writings of Whitman and Thoreau for young people: *Walt Whitman's America* (1964) and *Henry David Thoreau, A Man for Our Time* (1967).

Daugherty's art and texts combine gusto, exuberance, and rich detail — singing, with Whitman, a song of America. In his Newbery acceptance speech in 1940, Daugherty summed up the spirit of his major lifework: "Wit and taste, beauty and joy are as much a necessary part of the democratic heritage as economics and the utilities . . . Children's books are a part of that art of joy and joy in art that is the certain inalienable right of free people." E.C.H.

D'Aulaire, Edgar Parin; D'Aulaire, Ingri

Edgar: American author and illustrator, 1898–1986; Ingri: American author and illustrator, 1904–1980. The D'Aulaires established the picture book BIOGRAPHY for younger children as a valued staple of library book collections; for nearly fifty years they produced more than twenty books of outstanding craftsmanship. Their favorite subjects were heroes of American history and Norwegian culture. For their biography *Abraham Lincoln* (1939), they won the Caldecott Medal. Both D'Aulaires received early art education and worked with the abstract expressionist Hans Hofmann in Munich. Edgar, who was born in Munich, had illustrated German books, and Ingri Mortenson was a portrait artist. They met in Paris and were married in 1925; immigrating to the United States in 1929, they began to create PICTURE BOOKS together.

The style of their large, colorful, impressionistic illustrations was intended to appeal to a child's eye. The figures have a large paper-doll quality, resembling folk art. To some the illustrations in *George Washington* (1936) appear stiff and lifeless, but the artists' intention was to offer drawings that would remind children of rocking horses and toy soldiers. They included a wealth of authentic detail in their books, and their pictures have the integrity of originals with their unusual depth and richness of color. The D'Aulaires employed the lithographic process of early craftsmen, who without cameras had worked carefully by hand. This process requires that each picture be completely drawn (with no erasing possible) on a large stone, with separate drawings made for each color. Their detailed illustrations expand their carefully developed texts. One thousand hours of research in the Louvre, the New York Public Library, and the University of Norway might be compressed into one book. Extended camping and "tramping" trips enabled them to see and feel the prairies for *Abraham Lincoln,* the clear waters of the West Indies for *Columbus* (1955), and the hills of Virginia for *George Washington* and *Pocahontas* (1946).

The biographies were inspired by the imaginative heroic tales Edgar had been told by his American mother in Germany, including some about his grandfather, who had enlisted in Lincoln's army. Some critics have seen excessive idealism in the Lincoln pictures; some have criticized the mention of George Washington's slaves, who "kept everything spic and span."

Others note that biographies reflect the times in which they were written and provide useful information about the ideals and legends that were valued. In fact, the D'Aulaires presented balanced information for young children. Columbus must face disappointment in his failure to find a passage to India, while others succeeded. In *Benjamin Franklin* (1950) a selection of Poor Richard's wise sayings adorns each page, but the reader is told that Franklin was lucky not to be electrocuted during his experiments with lightning.

The D'Aulaires' Norse culture books, which include translations of folktales and two bright, oversize books, *Norse Gods and Giants* (1967) and *D'Aulaires' Trolls* (1972), are authenticated in the stories and experiences of Ingri's childhood in Norway. The large, humorous, detailed illustrations complement the subjects. A companion book to *Norse Gods and Giants* is *Ingri and Edgar Parin D'Aulaire's Book of Greek Myths* (1962).

The D'Aulaires, who were once described as "one unity with two heads, four hands, and one handwriting," received the Regina Medal in 1970.

E.C.H.

de Brunhoff, Jean; de Brunhoff, Laurent

Jean: French author and illustrator, 1899–1937; Laurent: French author and illustrator, b. 1925. If there is a universal symbol for childhood, Babar the elephant is probably it. Created by Jean de Brunhoff in the 1930s, continued by his son, Laurent, in the following decades, and available now in every manner of merchandise, the character has enthralled generations of children all over the world with his Victorian rectitude and pachyderm panache.

The inspiration for Babar came from Madame de Brunhoff, Jean's wife, who told stories about a little elephant to amuse her young children. Their enthusiasm for the tales encouraged their artist father to shape them into illustrated books, beginning with *The Story of Babar* (1933). Six more Babar books by Jean de Brunhoff followed quickly, including *Babar and His Children* (1938) and *Babar and Father Christmas* (1940), which were published after his death.

The original Babar books were oversize in format, with the text printed in script. Subsequent editions have taken every imaginable shape and form, but the luxuriously large volumes are still the best way to fully appreciate Jean de Brunhoff's mastery of the PICTURE BOOK form. His books, as MAURICE SENDAK once observed, "have a freedom and charm, a freshness of vision, that captivates and takes the breath away. . . . Between 1931 and 1937, he completed a body of work that forever changed the face of the illustrated book."

The elder de Brunhoff's Babar books were kind-hearted portrayals of family and community life, yet at the same time, unflinchingly direct in their depiction of tragedy. Within the first few pages of *The Story of Babar* the little elephant sees his mother killed by hunters. He cries but does not tarry in his mourning, fearful that he too might be shot. The plot then proceeds briskly, compelling the elephant and perhaps readers as well to go forward and get on with their own lives. Jean de Brunhoff's tuberculosis was diagnosed in the early 1930s, as he was beginning the books. His failing condition and the fact that he created the books with his own children in mind may well have inclined him to present sorrow in as straightforward a manner as possible, artfully offering consolation to his young audience by showing that even the cruelest blows can be survived.

Laurent de Brunhoff was only twelve years old when his father died. He studied art and in 1945 decided that he wanted to continue the series his father had begun. "Babar was a friend to me," he once remembered. "I had lived with him for years. It occurred to me that I could follow a tradition that had been cut off too early." Over the decades, the younger de Brunhoff has written and illustrated dozens of additional Babar stories, creating new characters and often putting the elephant in the service of helping young children sharpen their skills in counting, cooking, color recognition, and the like. His books, though often more pedestrian than inspired, have indeed accomplished what he set out to do: they have kept Babar alive for children who, like Laurent de Brunhoff himself, think of the elephant as part of their family. A.Q.

Degen, Bruce

American author and illustrator, b. 1945. Armed with a sense of joy, an appreciation of silliness, a love of nature, and a passion for children's books, Bruce Degen has illustrated dozens of books since 1977. Having first started to draw in elementary school, he later earned a B.F.A. at the Cooper Union and an M.F.A. at Pratt Institute and began a multifaceted artistic career. When he turned to children's book illustration, he chose a variety of manuscripts to illustrate, from POETRY to PICTURE BOOKS, from EASY READERS to INFORMATION BOOKS. Degen's artwork has received occasional awards, including children's choice awards for *Little Chick's Big Day* (1981), *Jamberry* (1983), and *The Forgetful Bears Meet Mr. Memory* (1987), and a Boston Globe–Horn Book honor for *The Magic School Bus at the Waterworks* (1986). However, this artist's work has contributed most to children's literature not by drawing attention to itself but by providing strong accompaniment to the texts.

Degen has generally used pencil or ink line with watercolor, but his pencil work is also strong. His artwork in JANE YOLEN's Commander Toad series and Clyde Robert Bulla's *Dandelion Hill* (1982), for instance, displays a sinuous, almost voluptuous line and a decorative sense of design. Many of Degen's pages employ creative borders, and his illustrations can be strongly narrative. They are nearly always delightfully full, if occasionally overfull, of details extending the text. Degen's cartoon-style people tend to be stiff, but this style perfectly suits the successful Magic School Bus series. Usually, his main characters are animals, and bears are featured in some of his best work, such as those

who prance at the nonsense verse in *Jamberry* and to the joyous rhymes in Nancy White Carlstrom's Jesse Bear series. Although all the bears resemble one another, Degen has provided individual and endearing characteristics through facial expressions, posture, and attire. Visual gags that go beyond the literal text commonly appear in Degen's books. In the Commander Toad series, a takeoff on space quests like *Star Wars*, a humanoid toad and his frog crew eat "hop-corn" and drink green tea. In his strongest self-authored book, *Jamberry*, Degen depicted a boy wallowing blissfully in a train-car loaded with berries — "boys-in-berries." For that matter, the main character is a bear, an animal that not only eats berries but whose name is a shortened aural version of *berry*. Degen's appealing treatment makes these jokes fresh and funny.

Collaborating with JOANNA COLE on the Magic School Bus series, Degen epitomized visual silliness. The straight-faced teacher, Ms. Frizzle, wears outlandishly thematic clothes, such as a dress printed with frogs eating flies and coordinating shoes decorated with Venus's-flytraps. The children's usual grade-school antics accompany "The Friz's" unusual teaching methods, as they travel by bus through the earth or through a child's circulatory system. The crowded pages are absorbing as they display action, text, bubble-dialogue, and school reports. The result is an endlessly entertaining set of books with a wide and loyal readership — a remarkable achievement for a science SERIES. No doubt these books, like many of Degen's efforts, will retain their child appeal perennially. S.S.

de la Mare, Walter

British poet, anthologist, storyteller, and writer, 1873–1956. Walter de la Mare was the most distinguished lyric poet writing for children in the first half of the twentieth century. His fresh original voice, noted for its astute perception and subtle imaginative vision, was elegantly balanced by his mastery of language and of the many melodies of rhythmic pattern. De la Mare's apparent indifference to "writing for the market" kept his work from period limitation, and thus it has maintained a place in the canon of children's literature. The ethereal loveliness of "Silver" in *Peacock Pie* (1913) still finds delighted listeners.

While POETRY for both children and adults was his most natural channel of expression, de la Mare was also a master of prose. He produced retellings of traditional tales and Bible stories, original stories with folkloric elements, anthologies with remarkable prefaces and notes, a play, one long FANTASY, criticism, collections of essays, and award-winning novels. De la Mare maintained the same high standard of artistic integrity whether writing for children or adults; he lived by his own dictum: "Only the rarest kind of best in anything can be good enough for the young."

Childhood was the primary topic for de la Mare, but never one for fond sentiment. Children as well as adults were to be considered authentic individuals. "The acorn is the oak . . . in mind and spirit we are most of us born . . . the age at which for the rest of our lives we are likely to remain." He observed his own four children, but more important, he retrieved many of his own childhood memories, dreams, and fantasies. He often fused the imaginative and the commonplace in his poems, effecting a haunting eeriness. There are glimpses of phantom children, spellbinding dreams, or dilemmas such as that of poor Jim Jay who "got stuck fast in yesterday"; there are unanswered questions posed in "Someone" and "The Little Green Orchard."

The masterpiece of anthologies is *Come Hither* (1923). An illuminating, allegorical preface introduces a collection of more than 483 poems by 260 poets, covering approximately 600 years of literature in English; the poems are accompanied by 300 pages of fascinating notes that disclose the wisdom, humanity, and scholarship of its editor. *The Three Royal Monkeys* (formerly *The Three Mulla Mulgars*, 1919) is a fantasy adventure story about the loyal and intrepid Nod Nizzaneela Ummanodda, his broth-

ers, and the wonderstone. Inventive language, a fully realized secondary fantasy world, well-crafted suspense, and numinous poetic vision combine to create an enthralling experience. Many children today find it difficult reading, but when it is read aloud by an appreciative reader, entire classrooms may be brought under its spell.

De la Mare received the Carnegie Medal of the Library Association for *Collected Stories for Children* (1947). The British Crown made him a Companion of Honor in 1948 and awarded him the Order of Merit in 1953. In a rare tribute by the *Horn Book Magazine,* the June 1957 issue was devoted to an appreciation of the art of Walter de la Mare. E.C.H.

dePaola, Tomie

American illustrator and author, b. 1934. Tomie dePaola is one of the country's most popular illustrators for children, who greatly enjoy his recognizable characters and clean, stylized art form and respond to the energy and empathy expressed in both his ink and watercolor art and in his lively storytelling.

Thomas Anthony dePaola was born in Meriden, Connecticut, into a mixed Irish and Italian family. His artistic talent developed early, encouraging him to pursue a bachelor's degree in art education at Pratt Institute in Brooklyn and a master's degree at California College of Arts and Crafts in Oakland. During his years in graduate school, he worked as a stage set designer and muralist, painting murals for a number of New England churches. This experience is reflected in the architectural and friezelike qualities of many of his books.

Tomie dePaola has written more than 180 books since his first publication in 1965. He has drawn on his Italian and Irish backgrounds for many folktales and for his series of autobiographical stories. His best-known book, *Strega Nona* (1975), is a retelling of the folktale of a magic pot that stops boiling only with the proper magic spell. In his version the pot spews pasta all over an Italian village square when Big Anthony fails to master Strega Nona's magic. DePaola has always been completely at ease with folktales, whether it is *Fin M'Coul: The Giant of Knockmany Hill* (1981) from Ireland, *The Legend of the Bluebonnet* (1983) from the Comanche of Texas, or his many Italian stories.

He has written several autobiographical stories in which he has shared childhood experiences that are sometimes amusing, as in *Watch Out for the Chicken Feet in Your Soup* (1974), but more often deeply personal and serious, as in *Nana Upstairs and Nana Downstairs* (1973). The poignancy of these books is also present in his series of religious stories. *The Clown of God* (1978) and *Francis, the Poor Man of Assisi* (1990) have formal compositions and serious-faced characters reminiscent of medieval Italian church paintings.

DePaola began a series of anthologies in 1985 with *Tomie dePaola's Mother Goose*, an exuberant, brightly illustrated book that has become one of the standards of the genre. It was followed by collections of nursery tales, poems, Bible stories, and Christmas carols. In addition to his own books, he has illustrated many works by other writers, most notably Tony Johnston (*The Quilt Story*, 1985) and JEAN FRITZ (*Shh! We're Writing the Constitution*, 1987). Recently, he broke out of his simple PICTURE BOOK mold with *Bonjour, Mr. Satie* (1991), a spoof of Gertrude Stein's literary salon. It received mixed reviews, and its visual jokes appealed mainly to dePaola's adult audience.

DePaola has garnered many awards from children's literature professionals during his career: he received a Caldecott Honor Award in 1976 for *Strega Nona*, the Kerlan Award of the University of Minnesota in 1981, the Regina Medal by the Catholic Library Association in 1983, and in 1990, he was the United States nominee for the Hans Christian Andersen Award for illustration. In 1999 Barbara Elleman chronicled his life in *Tomie dePaola: His Art and Story*.

Tomie dePaola's popularity and volume of work assure him prominence in the world of children's books. The variety, wit, and child ap-

peal of his books should make a lasting contribution to the field. J.S.

Voices of the Creators

Tomie dePaola

When I was a student at Pratt in the 1950s, studying illustration, I remember a fellow student asking one of our instructors, "When do we learn about style?" "We won't learn about style," he replied. "Style happens naturally. If you keep on working, eventually the way you can and want to express yourself will surface. Meanwhile, do the assignments, listen to the critiques, don't miss your drawing classes, painting classes, design classes and, by all means, look at everything. Go to the galleries and the museums. Your own style will surface." Another instructor, the wonderful Richard Lindner, told us, "Observe. Observe everything around you. Observe what *you are* interested in. Observe what kind of objects you surround yourself with. That will give you the clue to your *own* vision." During the summer of 1955, I was studying at Skowhegan School of Painting and Sculpture in Maine. I was fortunate enough to work with Ben Shahn, who was an idol of mine. The wise words from this great man were similar. Style evolves. He also spoke to me at length about "the shape of content." It was Shahn's thought that "a point of view conditions the paint surface which the artist creates."

So, being a "good student," I listened to my mentors. I noticed how my devotion changed from Jon Whitcomb, who did "pretty girl" illustrations, to Shahn, Picasso, Bonnard, and Rouault. How the "candy box" religious art from my Catholic boyhood was replaced by Cimabue, Fra Angelico, Giotto, and Botticelli and all those unknown sculptors and fresco painters of the Romanesque period. How over the years my love of folk art from all cultures became and still is close to obsessive.

All these things added up and my style began to emerge. And it hasn't really changed in over thirty-five years. The roots are there in my early drawings and paintings — things done way before I began illustrating books. There are white birds, pink tiled roofs, arched doors and windows. My early love of line and strong design and stylization has grown and been refined over the years, but the seeds are all there in the early work.

My work is recognizable. I've chosen to follow my own vision rather than switch around and try what is fashionable or "au courant." It thrills and pleases me when teachers, parents, and librarians tell me that young children know when they are looking at one of my books or a piece of my art. My style is purely an outward expression of my own inner vision, further determined in its nuances by the content of the piece being visualized.

At Pratt Institute, students were also exposed to a myriad of technical skills — representational drawing, rendering, perspective, stylized drawing, use of nonrepresentational color, various painting techniques — and mediums. Success was measured by how well one could use the various techniques and skills when called upon. But, finally in junior and senior year, favorite mediums and favorite ways of applying them became very individual and personal. Even to this day, I can do a photographic rendering if I have to. (I'd rather give up popcorn or use a camera.) Those skills and techniques are just that — methods to be called upon when needed. My preference is for strong line and design, using the medium and technique appropriate to the piece.

I personally use one of several techniques for my work. The first is very straightforward — a dark brown line with the color applied within the line. For this, I use Rotring Artists Colors, which is a liquid transparent acrylic paint. I use it because it is color-fast and permanent and totally intermixable. It reduces with water and is waterproof when dry, so I can build up thin "skins" of color. *The Art Lesson* was done in this technique.

The second technique is more painterly. I use acrylic paints opaquely. I lay down a base color, usually a golden shade. Next, I do a line drawing, again with a dark brown line. Then, I begin painting, building up layer after layer. *Bonjour, Mr. Satie* is a good example of this technique.

The third technique I employ is a combination of the two — both transparent and opaque, with the occasional use of colored pencils as well. I used this technique in *Hark!*

Unfortunately, technique can mask bad composition and bad drawing. Flashy, rendered photographic art can overwhelm the untrained eye so that mediocre expression gets undeserved attention. The personal expression that style hinges on is just that — personal. And after thirty years of illustrating books, I'd need several volumes to pass on all that I think about when I create my books.

Design and Typography

Most readers express surprise when told that all books, including those for children, are designed. While perhaps dismaying to the practitioner of the craft, this response is really quite understandable. For, ironically, book design and typography are at their most successful when not immediately apparent to the reader. It can even be said that book design is a kind of "invisible" art.

In her book *The Crystal Goblet* (1956), British typographer Beatrice Warde likened good bookmaking to a crystal goblet of wine: "Everything about it is calculated to *reveal* rather than to hide the beautiful thing it was meant to *contain*." As she further pointed out in her metaphor, to pour wine into a solid goblet would be to disguise the drink — one would appreciate the vessel itself perhaps, but that is all. And so it is with good bookmaking — good design provides the form or framework within which words and images can shine through. The child who reads to herself or the adult who reads to her surely senses the feeling of delight — of appropriateness — that the fully realized book can bring. Each book — whether PICTURE BOOK, POETRY, fiction, or nonfiction — has a personality as distinct as the individual who will read it or appreciate its illustrations. It is the special job of the designer to assemble the many diverse elements which make up a book and bring them together into a whole that is much more than the sum of its parts. It is the author who provides the words, but it is the designer, along with the illustrator, who must give the text a visual shape while remaining true to the spirit of the author's message.

The designer first encounters a book accepted for publication in the form of typewritten pages, handed over by an editor who has been working with the author to bring it to this stage. Much transpires at this initial "meeting" with the manuscript. While the designer reads the text carefully, many thoughts begin to surface as he or she tries to visualize the physical properties of the future book. Most designers are prepared for this moment by their training in several fields of the graphic arts. A children's book designer must have a thorough working knowledge of illustration and photography, graphic design, typography, printing, paper, and binding techniques. It is also most important for anyone involved with bookmaking to love to read and to be excited by the prospect of bringing the elements of a new book together, a process that can take anywhere from six months to two years to complete. It is not unusual to work simultaneously on as many as fifty projects in various stages of completion. An ability to see the larger picture, while focusing on a myriad of details, is important.

In a true picture book, there should be a seamless mesh of words and images — one could not exist without the support of the other. Picture books are like little plays, and the illustrator must bring the characters to life, moving them across the thirty-two pages most commonly allotted the form, to tell a story that reflects and extends the author's words. Some authors are also illustrators, but if the author has provided just the words, the designer and editor look for an artist who can successfully visualize and execute illustrations for the text.

Once the illustrator is chosen, the designer suggests a shape or trim size for the book. Here form most surely follows content — a book on a snake, for instance, begs to be long and horizontal to accommodate the special shape of that animal. A book for a very young child lends itself to a small trim size, perfect for tiny hands to hold. After a general trim size is agreed on, the designer, in consultation with the production manager, confirms that this is a size that fits well on the large sheets of paper, printing press, and binding machinery that are necessary to produce the book in multiple editions for publishing.

With the trim size and page count confirmed and with manuscript in hand, the illustrator can now begin work on the dummy, or rough-sketch version of the book. The illustrator considers not only which images to create but also how to break up the text and pace the story to create drama and interest. With the help of the designer, the illustrator decides which images to make large and which to make small, providing variety and tension on the page.

Frequently, at this stage, it is necessary to have the words set into type galleys, to plan out how much actual space will be available for the illustrations. The selection of a typeface is another of the key decisions a designer must make, whether the book is illustrated or not. There are many typefaces from which to choose, and the widespread use today of the computer for typesetting has further expanded the number of types available to the designer. The challenge is to find the appropriate one for the book at hand. As with all other decisions in the design process, the clues to selecting the right typeface lie within the manuscript itself. A careful reading will yield a strong suggestion of the "feel" of the story. The designer then pores over type specimen books, searching for the style of type that fits the concept of the book in hand. Classic or modern, heavy or light, condensed or expanded — the choice can seem daunting at times. In selecting a typeface, however, there are rules and models to follow.

Legibility is the most important consideration. In keeping with the *Crystal Goblet* theory, the designer is trying to create a sense of order and clarity, making it easy for the reader to enter the world of the author. A designer, through study and experience, learns which faces look best in the larger sizes common to children's books and how certain type designs give a better fit between the letters and words when set on specific typesetting equipment. For a picture book, the text must be large enough for legibility, yet still leave plenty of room for illustrations. In a novel, on the other hand, much care must be given to the proportions of the page. Size of type, length of line (type measure), number of lines on the page, and the space between lines (leading) are only some of the elements to deal with at this stage. As elsewhere, much of the problem solving that occurs is a fine balance between the real and the ideal. While the best possible page design is surely the goal, reality dictates that the designer also be responsible for making the book come out to an acceptable number of pages. The number of characters in any given text must be counted and translated into an actual number of typeset book pages. Restrictions such as these are very much part of the collaborative process of producing a commercial product and can actually enhance and refine the process when looked on as challenges rather than as limitations. When positioning the type on the page, consideration is given to the amount of area or margin to leave around the type block. Books are read while opened out to two-page spreads — the inner, or gutter, margin should be the narrowest because it doubles in size when the book is opened. The outer margin must leave sufficient room for thumbs to rest and not cover up text. Likewise, folios or page numbers should be placed for discreet visibility, far enough from the curve of the gutter or the edge of the page.

Basic utilitarian decisions such as these are always influenced by both historic models for page design and current design styles. Classical proportions refer back to the golden rectangle, devised from the golden section, a system first used in ancient Greece for designing architecture. Many early printed books reflected these proportions. This is, however, but one of many historic models learned when studying book design. In the end one must trust one's own instincts to determine what appears pleasing or appropriate on the page. In fact, the uniqueness

of designing books for children is that all of the rules can be broken if necessary. *The Stinky Cheese Man* (1992) takes all of the elements of book design and turns them upside-down, spoofing the form in the same way that the text skews traditional fairy tales. While this is rather unorthodox, it is certainly appropriate for the subject matter.

After the proper text has been designed, the other elements of the book must be addressed. All books have title pages and copyright pages, and type for these has to be specified and arranged. If necessary, specifications must be made for a table of contents, index, and bibliography — whatever the author has written, the designer must style typographically. A display, or larger size, type must be chosen to feature the book's title on the title page and jacket. This display type must at once complement the text type and be bold enough to attract attention. A book title is made up of only a few words, and a book jacket must be read at considerable distance and often by someone moving past a bookstore window or library shelf. The number of display types available far exceeds that of text faces, but with the opposite effect. While a designer tends to rely on a relatively small number of dependable text types, there never seem to be enough display faces to satisfy the wide variety of subjects dealt with on children's book jackets. There are many times when either the style of the artwork itself or lack of just the right face dictates the use of hand-drawn lettering or calligraphy, usually to wonderfully creative results. The use of the computer has also made it possible for designers to create their own display (and sometimes text) faces, and this has opened up very interesting possibilities, particularly in jacket design.

A book jacket is a small poster and must convey at a glance the essence of the story. In many cases the appeal of the jacket alone will be what first entices a prospective reader to pick up a book and examine it further. A children's book jacket might portray the main characters in the story in a representational way or be more abstract and convey primarily the mood of the story. Many jackets accomplish both. Some jackets are entirely typographic, and on them typography, color, size, and arrangement have to do the whole job. Most commonly, art and typography appear together, in all manner of styles. While some books are successfully designed with art and type complementing each other, another approach is to contrast typographic form with illustration style, juxtaposing a humorous illustration with a more formal type, to create a bit of tension or surprise.

After the artwork is completed and reproduction proofs of the type are in hand, the designer creates a mechanical, or camera-ready version of the book, for the printer to photograph. With the help of the production department, the book now goes through several stages of proofing, where everyone involved can preview what the artwork and text will ultimately look like when reproduced with ink on paper. In the collaborative world of children's books, illustrator, editor, designer, and production manager all have a role to play in choosing the materials used to produce the book. The production manager will suggest certain printing stocks that might produce the desired effect and the designer will make the final decision. Color proofs of the pages of a picture book arrive, and the designer and illustrator will comb them carefully, comparing the results to the original art, making adjustments where necessary. They must then rely on the expertise of the production manager to let them know if their desired corrections can be carried out by the printer. Blueprints arrive from the printer and are checked by editor and designer to make certain all type and artwork are where they should be and that nothing is missing or misspelled. The moment of truth arrives when the book goes on press, and final press sheets are checked by the designer and production manager. A sigh of relief can usually be heard when the first press sheet is okayed, and the press is activated to print the thousands of copies that will make up the edition.

But the book still must be bound, and the designer is involved in specifying cover materials for the binding, colors for the endpapers, and typographic styling for the title on the spine and front cover if warranted. After the final specs are delivered, all involved eagerly await the exciting moment when bound copies of the book arrive. The designer examines the object of his or her labors and usually experiences a combination of pride and regret — how beautiful the title page looks, but if only the folios were handled differently! Fortunately, the publishing process, unlike life, offers in the second edition a chance to correct serious errors, although usually of an editorial nature.

Much has been written recently concerning the possible demise of the book as we know it, with the CD-ROM and electronic book relegating ink on paper to the archival corner now occupied by the medieval manuscript. Without question, the new technology is influencing all facets of the book design and production process, and this will change forever the way that books are made. There is certainly room for both the traditional and electronic book forms to coexist comfortably, each one borrowing stylistically from the other. Indeed all books — in whatever form — will need to be designed. And any designer still doubting the ultimate survival of the book has only to refer to that most ancient of books — the Bible — to contemplate the wise and reassuring proverb in Ecclesiastes, "of making many books there is no end."   C.G.

Diaz, David

American illustrator, b. 1958. Little could have prepared illustrator David Diaz for the wild success of his first children's PICTURE BOOK, *Smokey Night* (1994), written by EVE BUNTING. Just two years earlier, Diaz's sole contribution to the world of children's books had been a series of modest, black and white drawings to accompany GARY SOTO's *Neighborhood Odes* (1992), a book of poems for young people. But with the publication of *Smokey Night,* a story inspired by the 1992 Los Angeles riots, Diaz unveiled an innovative style that combined bold brush strokes, bluesy acrylic colors, and mixed-media collages. Since Diaz had never before illustrated a picture book, he wasn't inhibited by conventions or tempted to "draw down" for kids. Instead, he approached the assignment as if it were an illustration for the *Atlantic Monthly* or one of his other longtime clients: he simply tried to make the images as interesting as possible. *Smokey Night* earned Diaz the 1995 Caldecott Medal and was later named one of the most significant children's books of the twentieth century by *School Library Journal.*

Yet as superb as *Smokey Night* is, Diaz's art for *Wilma Unlimited* (1996) is even better. Written by Kathleen Krull, *Wilma Unlimited* tells the inspiring story of track star Wilma Rudolph, an American sprinter who overcame childhood polio on her way to winning Olympic gold. In *Wilma Unlimited,* Diaz refined the style he introduced in *Smokey Night*. But this time out, he muted the background collages, relying on sepia-toned photographs to convey a sense of history. Diaz also added watercolor and gouache to his repertoire and softened his color palette — scattering rusty reds, olive greens, and deep blues throughout the scenes of Rudolph's extraordinary life. The result is a perfect marriage of collage and illustration.

Diaz was born in New York City. A few years later, his family moved to Fort Lauderdale, Florida. The epiphany moment, when young David first realized he wanted to become an artist, occurred in first grade. His teacher had handed out a worksheet with simple line drawings and corresponding words, each missing a vowel. When Diaz came to the word *nose,* he correctly supplied the missing *o* and transformed his answer into a face. He suddenly knew that he wanted to become a "draw-er."

Diaz attended Hollywood Hills High School, where his art teacher, Sandra Tobe, encouraged him to enter competitions. Tobe also introduced Diaz to Duane Hanson, a prominent sculptor with whom Diaz apprenticed throughout high school and art school. After studying at the Fort Lauderdale Art Institute, Diaz headed to San Diego, California, in 1979, to try to make it as an illustrator.

One of his first jobs was doing spot illustrations for a local newspaper. Diaz later worked as a designer, creating annual reports, textbooks, logos, and book covers. During a trip with his brother down the Amazon River in 1992, he perfected the fluid, seemingly effortless drawings that would surface two years later in *Smokey Night.*

Reflecting on his career, Diaz, who now lives north of San Diego, has said that he doesn't want to be pigeonholed. There's little chance of that. In *The Little Scarecrow Boy* (1998), MARGARET WISE BROWN's long-lost tale about a straw boy who struggles to emulate his father, Diaz put away his collages and used watercolor and pencil to create a daffy farmscape of bright, cheery creatures, unlike anything he had done before. In *Roadrunner's Dance* (2000), a mythic story written by Rudolfo Anaya, Diaz created computer-generated images of archetypal birds and beasts. And in *Angel Face* (2002), written by Sarah Weeks, he used pastels to tenderly depict a mother in search of her missing child. R.M.

Dickinson, Peter

British author, b. 1927. Sometimes referred to as a FANTASY or SCIENCE FICTION writer, Peter Dickinson is a difficult author to characterize. Amazingly prolific and versatile, he has published over twenty books for children, with settings ranging from contemporary England to the Byzantine Empire. Although his subject matter varies considerably, critics and young readers alike appreciate the consistently high quality of his writing and his unerring ability to tell exciting stories rich with detail. Born in Zambia, Peter Dickinson was educated at Eton and Cambridge, where he received his B.A. in English literature. He worked for seventeen years on the editorial staff of *Punch,* the British humor magazine, and didn't begin writing until he was in his forties. He has been writing steadily ever since, alternating books for children with adult thrillers.

His first novel for children, *The Weathermonger* (1968), eventually became part of The Changes trilogy, which explores the time of The Changes, when the people of England have been possessed by a mysterious aversion to machines.

The Changes trilogy received critical acclaim, and both *Heartsease* (1969) and *The Devil's Children* (1970) were nominated for awards. Although Dickinson's full power as a writer of YOUNG ADULT NOVELS isn't fully realized in these first books, his gifts as a writer are apparent. His mastery of the English language sets him apart from many other children's book authors. His flawless prose can be heart-stoppingly beautiful, with an unusual attention to landscape. Dickinson's characters are unusual, fascinating, and despite their eccentricity, utterly believable and lovable.

Dickinson has said that "the intricate exploration and development of character play no great part in my stories." Yet it is the remarkable people one finds between the covers of his books that make them unforgettable. His protagonists tend to be quiet, self-contained personalities whose inner strengths are drawn out by the remarkable situations they find themselves in. In *Emma Tupper's Diary* (1971) Emma finds herself on vacation at a remote Scottish loch with four flamboyant cousins. When her cousins dream up a scheme to fake the appearance of a Loch Ness–type monster, sensible Emma plays along with them. But when the young people find real prehistoric creatures living in the loch, Emma reveals her deeply passionate nature in her efforts to protect the secret of the animals' existence. *The Dancing Bear* (1972), a HISTORICAL NOVEL set in the Byzantine Empire, follows the adventures of the young slave Sylvester. When Sylvester's beloved mistress and childhood friend is captured by invading Huns, Sylvester sets out to rescue her, accompanied by Holy John, a decrepit prophet, and Bubba, a dancing bear.

Many of Dickinson's characters are intensely spiritual or possessed of paranormal abilities. Set in an imaginary world, *The Blue Hawk*, which won the Guardian Award in 1977, tells the story of a young priest whose true religious calling leads him to defy the priesthood that holds his country in an iron grip of servitude and stagnation. In *Tulku*, which won the Carnegie Medal and the Whitbread Award in 1979, the devoutly Christian son of an American missionary killed in the Boxer Rebellion is befriended by an unconventional British botanist and her Chinese lover and travels with them to Tibet, where they eventually find themselves virtually imprisoned in a Buddhist monastery, awaiting the birth of Mrs. Jones's child, believed to be the next Tulku. In *Eva* (1989) Dickinson explored what might happen when a human's brain is grafted onto a chimpanzee's body; in *The Ropemaker* (2001) he combined fantasy with a compelling coming-of-age story.

Dickinson's work resonates with affection and pity for the human condition, with its startling capacity for both cruelty and compassion, stupidity and intelligence. His books are infectiously joyful in their celebration of humanity and love for all living creatures. K.T.

Dillon, Leo; Dillon, Diane

Leo: American illustrator, b. 1933; Diane: American illustrator, b. 1933. The lives of Leo and Diane Dillon have been blended into one for more than three decades. Only eleven days separate their births, but many miles and worlds initially separated their lives. Born in Brooklyn, New York, Leo was a loner who turned to art for pleasure and self-expression. His parents encouraged his talent yet planned a future for him in law or medicine. In school, and later in the navy, Leo used his artistic talent as a means of coping with racial discrimination. Upon leaving the navy, he worked briefly for the family business and then enrolled in Parsons School of Design.

Diane, born in Glendale, California, moved with her family thirteen times within southern California while growing up. She knew at an early age that she wanted to be an artist and found, during her childhood, that her family and her art were the only constants in her life. Her parents encouraged her talent but did not value it, expecting her to get married and become a housewife. She worked to put herself through two years of school at Los Angeles College and later attended Skidmore College for one semester before moving to Parsons. Diane and

Leo became rivals at Parsons, and even after they fell in love, their rivalry continued. Upon marrying, and after holding individual jobs in advertising, they decided to collaborate on freelance work to avoid the rivalry and competition of their college days. This work included collaboration on album covers, advertisements, magazine artwork, movie posters, and book covers for paperbacks.

When they began illustrating children's books, however, the Dillons found freedom. Not all of their children's book illustrations have been in PICTURE BOOKS. Many of their earlier illustrations appeared in novels and short stories written for juvenile readers, most of which were legends or folktales. For all of their work they spend much time researching the stories, time periods, cultures, settings, and artwork of these eras, incorporating their findings in their illustrations. Their early work used woodcuts, which the Dillons found to be a nearly universal art form, used by many cultures and during many time periods, and a style conducive to collaboration. From the mid-1970s their work has been noted for its diversity. Their illustrations for *Whirlwind Is a Ghost Dancing* (1974), an ALA Notable Book written by Natalie Belting, brought them to the attention of the children's book establishment through the felicitous combination of art and folklore and FANTASY themes and the inclusion of decorative motifs from the traditions of various Indian nations. They followed *Whirlwind* with woodcuts in *Song of the Boat* (1975) and the bleaching of dark brown watercolors in *The Hundred Penny Box* (1975).

In the same year, the Dillons won the Caldecott Medal for their illustrations for Verna Aardema's *Why Mosquitoes Buzz in People's Ears*. Acting on their philosophy that the role of the illustrator is not simply to duplicate the text but to enlarge on it, to restate the words in their own graphic terms, they used the African style of batik to create the lively fragmented forms. Their next book, *Ashanti to Zulu* (1976), written by Margaret W. Musgrove, became their second Caldecott Medal winner and made them the first illustrators to win this award in consecutive years. Their research skills helped them create accurate, authentic depictions of the twenty-six different African tribes introduced in the book, including distinctively representative artifacts, animals, dwellings, and a costumed person for each group. They also illustrated Leontyne Price's retelling of *Aïda* (1990), in which their son Lee collaborated in producing borders with the appearance of carved gold frames. Among the varied devices in the Dillons' work are marbleized paper, electrifying colors, and bas-relief decorations. For a reissue of MARGARET WISE BROWN's *The Little Trains* (2001), they moved to a much simpler, more graphic style.

Leo and Diane Dillon have progressed from being two distinct artists who work separately, passing artwork between them, to becoming a "third artist," with thoughts and styles so blended that the resulting art could not have been produced by either working alone.   C.H.S.

Drescher, Henrik

Danish-born American author and illustrator, b. 1955. When Henrik Drescher decided to become an illustrator at the age of fifteen, he did not choose to follow the route of formal art training. Instead, he traveled the world equipped with a drawing book, pen and ink, and an open mind. When he came to the United States in 1977, his drawing quality and freshness of vision landed him jobs as a political illustrator, and he contributed to *Rolling Stone* and the *New York Times Book Review*.

In 1982 Drescher published his first work for children, *The Strange Appearance of Howard Cranebill Jr.* (selected as a New York Times Best Illustrated Book), an amusing allegory of a childless couple who discover an odd-looking child on their doorstep. Though this work shares with all of Drescher's later books a visual richness of design elements, such as a frenetic, energetic quality of line, a playful use of intricate decorative borders, splotches of color, and a lively combination of fantasy and humor, a distinct progression can be noted from this book to his later books. Offbeat and unique in story and presentation, *The Strange Appearance of Howard Cranebill Jr.* is visually more subtle than his later work. The softer, more muted pastel colors and subdued action that remains within borders surrounded by white space provide a constrained feeling.

In 1983 the book that defines Drescher's style was published. *Simon's Book* (a New York Times Best Illustrated Book, a Reading Rainbow selection, and Parents' Choice Award winner) tells a great tale involving a boy, a beast, a drawing pad, and three unlikely heroes — two pens and a bottle of ink! Only an illustrator could spin this tale, as only an illustrator would think of pens and ink as heroic. In this adventure the drawings take over and almost leap off the page as they mirror the written action of the tale. Colorful backgrounds pulsing with rich color, borders that move and shift with colors and shapes, and unusual characters that jump from one page to the next enhance the high-speed pacing of this fantastic romp.

Though all of Drescher's books are filled with adventure and drama, their great humor prevents them from being threatening to his young readership. For instance, when the beast chasing Simon leaps forward, he plants a wet sloppy kiss rather than a painful blow on the boy's cheek. The adventures *Looking for Santa Claus* (1984) and *Look-alikes* (1985) may have less interesting plots, but visually the adventures equal the sophistication and imagination of *Simon's Book,* and all seem to draw from Drescher's travel experiences. Maggie, the heroine in *Looking for Santa Claus,* travels around the world with Blossom the cow in search of Santa. *Look-alikes* tells of a boy and his pet monkey as they retreat to their playhouse to follow the antics of dolls that look like themselves. Both books make playful use of every element of the book, from the jacket flaps to the endpapers. In *Look-alikes,* Drescher used trompe l'oeil techniques borrowed from M. C. Escher and Salvador Dali. Stairs travel up and down simultaneously while a waterfall falls nowhere at all. A solid bird's egg in one picture turns into a hole in the ground in the next. Drescher's unique body of work includes two

INFORMATION BOOKS, *Whose Scaly Tail? African Animals You'd Like to Meet* (1987) and *Whose Furry Nose? Australian Animals You'd Like to Meet* (1987). Not quite scientific references, the books provide a fun introduction to a variety of animals and include an informative two-page spread on the important habits of each animal. Drescher's work includes a wordless two-color adventure, *The Yellow Umbrella* (1987), the highly acclaimed *Poems of A. Nonny Mouse* (1989), selected by JACK PRELUTSKY, and *No Plain Pets!* (1991). He also teamed up with Ken Nordene for *Colors* (2000), a book that reveals the quirky personalities of colors.

Inventive in both writing and depicting his stories, Drescher continually explores the boundaries of storytelling and the PICTURE BOOK format. J.A.S.

du Bois, William Pène

American author and illustrator, 1916–1993. For more than fifty years, the works of William Pène du Bois have delighted audiences and critics with their original, fantastic stories and illustrations. Born in Nutley, New Jersey, du Bois moved with his family to France at the age of eight. Du Bois credited the French schools he attended with instilling in him a sense of order and meticulousness, which he applied in his work. Du Bois moved back to the United States at age fourteen and won a scholarship to Carnegie Technical School of Architecture, but he soon sold his first book, *Elisabeth the Cow Ghost* (1936), and never returned to school.

As a child, du Bois, whose family included many artists, was fascinated with Jules Verne and pored over the illustrations of mechanical devices. He also loved the circus and claimed to have visited the circus an average of thirty times a year. His passions for France, the circus, and Jules Verne are all evident in du Bois's work for children. *The Twenty-one Balloons* (1947), winner of the 1948 Newbery Medal, recounts the fascinating story of Professor Sherman's unexpected visit to the Pacific island of Krakatoa, where the sophisticated islanders, with unlimited resources of diamonds, have invented complex work-saving and entertainment devices. The inventions, which recall those predicted by Verne, are rendered clear to readers through the precise text and beautiful, detailed illustrations.

Story and illustrations, perfectly integrated, are equally important to the reader's understanding and enjoyment of the story. *Lion* (1956), named a Caldecott Honor Book in 1957, also reflects du Bois's interest in invention. In it an angel invents the king of beasts, trying feathers, stripes, and fish scales before discovering just the right combination of attributes for a lion: a charming, accessible metaphor for the process through which artists create a thing of beauty. In keeping with its theme, *Lion* was handsomely produced; its design, type style, color, and delicate line all contribute to a visually striking, emotionally satisfying whole.

In all of his books, du Bois's stories and pictures combine humor, fantasy, and adventure with elegant simplicity. Beginning with the familiar, they take the reader from there to the absurd. *The Giant* (1954) explores the chaos that develops when a baby grows to enormous size, and the isolation and loneliness of a child outside of the norm. Along with eccentricity, du Bois wrote about morality. *The Twenty-one Balloons* explores human greed, and *Lazy Tommy Pumpkinhead* (1966), one of du Bois's series of books about the seven deadly sins, examines the ramifications of sloth.

Du Bois received critical acclaim for both his writing and his handsome, delicate artwork. Each illustration, painstakingly created in pencil, is traced with ink, a process that lends his art a draftsmanlike quality that suits his clear and direct writing style. Du Bois also illustrated works by other writers, including CHARLOTTE ZOLOTOW's *William's Doll* (1972) and Claire Huchet Bishop's *Twenty and Ten* (1952). In each book, his style is unmistakable but tailored to suit the individual story. William Pène du Bois's enormous talent and consistent inventiveness have earned him an important place on children's bookshelves. M.V.K.

Duvoisin, Roger

S wiss-born American author and illustrator, 1904–1980. The internationally popular books by Roger Antoine Duvoisin are praised for the author's skillful art and writing and his sure sense of what delights children. A prolific children's book creator, Duvoisin created over forty of his own books and illustrated more than 140 written by others. He was one of the few who understood and mastered the unity found only in the finest children's literature.

As a child, Roger Duvoisin loved to draw, laboring to make his images lifelike. He was encouraged by his father, an architect, and his godmother, a well-known painter of enamels. After art school he began to paint murals and stage scenery, to make posters and illustrations. He became manager of an old French pottery plant, then turned to textile design, the occupation that brought him to the United States. When the textile firm folded during the Depression, Duvoisin decided to remain in the United States, turning his diverse skills to children's books and magazine illustration.

Duvoisin's books all have a compelling graphic quality. The hallmarks are fine craftsmanship, a strong sense of composition and design, and humor. Of the books he illustrated for other writers, he is probably best known for the popular Happy Lion series, written by his wife, Louise Fatio. Equally notable is his 1948 Caldecott Medal–winning art in *White Snow, Bright Snow,* by Alvin Tresselt, part of a SERIES about weather. Every book provided new challenges, which Duvoisin eagerly embraced.

In addition to his artistic mastery, Duvoisin was a skilled writer. He is respected for his translation and illustration of medieval European folktales, such as *The Crocodile in the Tree* (1973), and for his ALPHABET BOOK, *A for the Ark* (1952). But his homely ANIMAL STORIES established him as a premier bookmaker. His delightfully original characters — personable animals such as Petunia the goose, Veronica the hippo, and Donkey-Donkey — are drawn with an economical humorous line and graced with understated color. Their escapades, the way they strut, poke, and race across the page, create drama and capture the sympathy of the reader. And Duvoisin's text is part of the book's unity, reinforcing the rhythm and pacing of the page. It is this consummate professional bookmaking, from sketch to text, from layout to jacket design, that sets him apart from many other children's book creators. Duvoisin believed that "a beautiful book is a beautiful object which the child may learn to love."

More recent illustrated books use fewer pages and employ tighter plots, so Duvoisin's stories can seem both overly long and repetitive. And, unfortunately, Duvoisin felt it important to do more than "merely entertain." He valued "that little sneaking desire to teach and to moralize, to pass on to children what we think of our world," a trait now dismissed as didactic. Still, Duvoisin's art remains fresh, and his work has lasting appeal, largely because of his affection and respect for his audience. Children still respond to his sense of freedom, friendly humor, and playfulness, and his characters remain some of the best loved of all time. **S.A.B.**

E

Eager, Edward

American author, 1911–1964. Good old-fashioned magic and the adventures it brings never go out of style, especially in Edward Eager's books. Although the last was written more than three decades ago, Eager's stories are still full of humor and excitement as he interweaves the commonplace with the extraordinary. Ordinary children in cities like Toledo, Ohio (where

Eager grew up), and Baltimore, Maryland, hungry for adventures like those they read about in books and see in movies, unexpectedly find themselves with magical powers. The magic doesn't always work the way they want it to, however, and that's when the adventures really begin.

A playwright and lyricist with several Broadway productions to his credit, Eager began writing children's books to entertain his young son, Fritz. Both father and son loved magical adventures, especially those by British author E. NESBIT, and Eager borrowed many conventions from these tales and acknowledged Nesbit's books in his own. Besides being full of wordplay and literary allusions, Eager's books are continually surprising; the reader and the characters never know where or when the magic will turn up next. What looks like a coin on the sidewalk turns out to be a talisman in Eager's first and most popular book, *Half Magic* (1954). Figuring out the true nature of the coin and trying to master its powers before its magic wears off save a family from an otherwise boring summer. The same family encounters a magical turtle that turns an ordinary lakeside vacation into a time-traveling extravaganza in *Magic by the Lake* (1957).

A strange toadlike creature rules over a magic thyme garden in *The Time Garden* (1958). A wishing well grants children's wishes — or are the fantastic happenings mere coincidence? — in *Magic or Not?* (1959) and *The Well-Wishers* (1960). A mysterious library book on a week's loan provides magic each day in *Seven-Day Magic* (1962). *Knight's Castle* (1956) brings the time and characters of *Ivanhoe* to life, with a time-traveling group of children meddling in the story's development. Eager's magic books empower the young protagonists; once they discover the magic, they are responsible for learning how to control it. In most cases, the assorted children must cooperate so they can all have turns before the magic runs out, and they must right any mistakes they've made along the way. The episodic chapters are perfect for reading aloud, and the books have the appeal of a SER-

IES, as characters reappear in a variety of ways. The two children appearing in *Half Magic* and *Magic by the Lake* are the parents of the children featured in *Knight's Castle,* and with all this time travel, adventures eventually overlap and characters from different books literally bump into each other while adventuring.

Time has treated these books well; the pacing and plot easily keep young readers entertained and intrigued. There are a few unfortunate racial references that reinforce stereotypes and slightly date the books: the Arab the children meet in the desert in *Half Magic* is described as "crafty," "unpleasant," and "unattractive," and the children address him in mock Chinese; the dark-skinned natives in *Magic by the Lake* are illiterate cannibals speaking Pidgin English. Otherwise, the adventures in these books are still fresh and will spark plenty of imaginative trips in young readers' minds. A.M.D.

Early Literacy

W here does it all begin? When does a child begin to form patterns that will lead to reading for pleasure as well as for information? What creates a lifelong reader?

When a toddler points to a picture of a cow in a book and says, "Moo," the parent, caregiver, or librarian responds, echoing the child's delight: "Yes! The cow says, 'Moo!'" The adult recognizes that the child is making a connection between a picture and what it represents. The adult may also realize the positive connection being made between adult and child. What the adult may not fully appreciate is the significance of this seemingly simple interaction — this interchange, and countless others like it, is laying the foundation for literacy.

In recent years what parents and educators have known instinctively is now confirmed by neuroscience. The development of brain-imaging technologies allows the growth of the human brain to be measured and literally mapped. These images have revealed that, contrary to popular belief, the human brain is not fully de-

veloped at birth. In fact, the infant and young child's brain is much more active and complex than previously assumed, more like an absorbent sponge than a blank slate. Experiences and sensory inputs (what is seen, heard, touched, smelled, and tasted) organize patterns of communication between the neurons (cells) of the brain. These patterns determine how we think, feel, and behave. Since most synapses, or neural connections, are formed during the first three years of life, early experiences are crucial.

These first years provide infants and young children with valuable stimulation and positive experiences that will literally last a lifetime. All young children need nurturing, consistent, secure relationships; individualized and responsive attention and care; and a stimulating learning environment that includes exposure to good language models.

Creating a language- and literacy-rich environment is an effective way to fulfill all these essential needs while strengthening and building a literacy base. Books and reading certainly build positive connections between adult and child. Sharing books contributes to a nurturing relationship and provides individualized and responsive attention. It also offers "sensory input," the foundation upon which other language skills are built.

Sharing PICTURE BOOKS, such as *Goodnight Moon* (1947), written by MARGARET WISE BROWN, with young children, is an auditory experience ("Listen now, 'In the great green room there was . . .'") and a visual experience ("Look at the red balloon! What else can you see in the room?"). (Sometimes books provide a tasty experience as a young child directs the book to his or her mouth.) Through these sense experiences, sharing books with young children literally helps create the neural connections that support literacy.

Research suggests that the growth of literacy involves several specific areas of knowledge and skill. First, children must develop an understanding of the alphabetic system to identify printed words as well as the ability to associate letters with sounds. They must gain knowledge in order to associate meaning with spoken or printed words. And children must achieve the capacity to read fluently, with ease. After all, children — or adults — tend to avoid painfully arduous activities. The final but no less critical component is motivation.

What motivates a child to want to read? Perhaps it is the desire to enter a more grown-up world, to please a cherished adult, to take pleasure in a story, to share an enjoyable experience, or to emulate a significant adult.

Of course, parents play a central role in a child's early experience and education, yet many influences outside the parents' domain play a crucial part as well. A 1996 study by the National Center for Education Statistics revealed that three out of five children in America under the age of six received nonparental child care and education. Also, families come in many configurations, including those headed by grandparents or other relatives. The experiences parents and, increasingly, other caregivers share with young children during the earliest years are among the most important in life. Therefore, early literacy efforts must engage parents and other significant adults. It is as important to introduce adults to books that are appropriate for and appealing to children as it is to present them to children. Books for the very young are often a child's first introduction to art and literature. They can inspire both adult and child and provide a shared experience that bridges generations, time, and place.

Consider the range of children's books available both in presentation and content. Most are intended to attract the adult to share with children. BOARD BOOKS were developed for the young child, even the newborn, though the content reflects adult tastes as well as the adult's perception of a child's world. TANA HOBAN's *Black on White* (1993) and *White on Black* (1993) were created for infants. Based on research about an infant's vision, shapes of familiar objects are placed on a page of the opposite color (for example, the shape of a baby's bottle in white on a black page). Board books are appropriate for slightly older children as well, as the sturdy format is more likely to hold up in young hands.

Babies and toddlers can see themselves in the faces of HELEN OXENBURY's chubby-cheeked children in *Tickle, Tickle* (1987) and *I Touch* (1986). Both celebrate the simple joys of babyhood, perhaps reminding adults of the pleasure in these celebrations while allowing them to share it again with a young child. Max and Ruby of ROSEMARY WELLS's board books, including *Max's First Word* (1979, 1998), achieve a similar effect. Max says only "BANG!" in spite of his sister Ruby's prodding — that is, until he's ready to say more. This behavior is readily recognizable to those familiar with babies and toddlers.

Comparable child-centered topics can also be presented through highly realistic visuals. Glossy, full-color photographs often illustrate board books. *Baby's First Words* (1985), with photos by Lars Wik, couples a crisp photograph of a child with one word describing the object or activity. Highly realistic illustrations are used to examine a cherry tree and its animal visitors on a journey through *The Four Seasons* (2001), by Gallimard Jeunesse, described as "a first reference book for toddlers and preschoolers, with a pictorial tab index to 'look up' simple facts."

Books for slightly older children continue to build language and formative sensory experiences. In *Goodnight Moon*, simple rhyming text combines with meticulously crafted illustrations by CLEMENT HURD to create a cozy bedtime story and a naming game as pages are examined many times. *Ten, Nine, Eight* (1983), written by MOLLY BANG, is similar to *Goodnight Moon* in theme and tone as a little girl counts down to bedtime. Incidental to the emotional warmth and comfort is the depiction of the child and her father with brown skin. Also, *Ten, Nine, Eight* provides another naming or counting game in addition to a tender nighttime tale.

Language is gained through conversation, through the process of asking questions and giving answers (and vice versa), and through the exploration of concepts and ideas. Books provide an opportunity to share conversation while investigating a wealth of concepts with children of many ages. For example, adults may gain as much vocabulary as the children with whom they share Tana Hoban's *Construction Zone*

(1999), as together they look at and name the construction equipment placed on each page. *Look! Look! Look!* (1988) and *Look Again!* (1971), also by Hoban, challenge readers to examine seemingly familiar objects from a new perspective, again creating guessing and naming games as well as an opportunity for much conversation and entertainment.

In addition to helping children name objects and other tangibles, books help name and validate emotions. And because they are shared, books can provide common experiences that may become a point of reference for adults and children while building the secure relationships, responsive attention, and stimulating environment so crucial to early literacy. For example, KEVIN HENKES's picture books authentically represent the emotional world of a young child. In *Wemberly Worried* (2000), Wemberly constantly worries about things, virtually everything, but especially starting school. Lilly of *Lilly's Purple Plastic Purse* (1996) is self-centered and becomes angry when her teacher reminds Lilly that she is part of a school community. The main character in *Owen* (1993) is concerned about giving up his security blanket before starting school. Though these characters are depicted as mice, readers relate to their ultimate triumph, which usually involves caring adults. Each book is illustrated in Henkes's signature style, using line and white space with dramatic effect and genuine emotion.

Though seemingly simple, these and countless other books for children are rich in the language of words and illustration. When shared with children, they not only lay but also strengthen the foundation for early literacy, leading to a lifetime of reading. M.B.S.

Easy Readers

Forty years ago books for the child just learning to read tended to be dull — lacking excitement and originality. Written to reinforce existing reading skills, they failed to introduce reading as a pleasurable experience. At the point when it is essential to maintain a child's interest in reading, these books deadened it.

Then in 1957 two wonderfully unexpected books appeared. Although intended for the child with limited reading skills, they were far from simply utilitarian; they were well written and imaginative, offering stories and illustrations attractive not only to their intended audience of beginning readers but also to children not yet able to read. DR. SEUSS's *Cat in the Hat* (1957) offered children a zany story, inspired wordplay, and a glimpse of a fantasy world outside adult control. Seuss showed children just how much fun language and reading could be. The same year saw publication of *Little Bear* (1957), a collaboration between ELSE HOLMELUND MINARIK and illustrator MAURICE SENDAK, consisting of a series of comforting stories about a childlike bear cub and his family and friends. Although the story lines and vocabulary were clear and appealing enough to be read aloud to younger children, beginning readers knew that *Little Bear* was not a "baby book" — it had chapters. *Cat in the Hat* and *Little Bear* not only set the standard for quality publishing for early readers, they marked the beginning of two highly successful publishing series for children: Random House's Beginner Books and Harper's I Can Read series. Writers, illustrators, and publishers produced a number of fine books that have already been made classics by their devoted readers: Dr. Seuss's *Green Eggs and Ham* (1960), PEGGY PARISH's *Amelia Bedelia* (1963), ARNOLD LOBEL's *Frog and Toad Are Friends* (1970), and Stan and Jan Berenstain's *The Bike Lesson* (1964). The timeless quality of these books speaks to conflicts and joys shared by most six- to eight-year-olds, generation after generation.

Thanks to the success of these groundbreaking books, children beginning to read today have a panorama of enticing books: books on the sciences; a wide selection of POETRY; histories and HISTORICAL FICTION; books with simple science experiments, recipes, and arts and crafts projects; and stories from all the genres that their older siblings enjoy, including SPORTS STORIES, MYSTERY, adventure, and SCIENCE FICTION.

In fact, there are so many books that the wise adult learns to turn to a knowledgeable children's librarian, teacher, or children's bookstore clerk for guidance in selecting the books that will most appeal to a particular beginning reader.

The challenge to today's writers, illustrators, and editors is to produce appealing, well-written, and factual books, often only thirty-two pages long, on a level easily read by the beginning reader. Confined to a brief text and simple language, an author's talents, strengths, and weaknesses become obvious. Because a child is not yet an accomplished reader and may be new to books, illustrations are essential: they must not only be accomplished, creative, and have child appeal, they must offer clues to the text — and not stray from it. When writers, illustrators, and editors successfully collaborate to create fine easy readers, children respond. Further, with the emergence of the "whole language" classroom in the 1980s and its demand for quality trade books to supplement or replace textbooks, libraries have seen a tremendous increase in the demand for books in all areas — including math, science, history, and poetry — for beginning readers.

Humor books are among the most popular easy readers. Illustrated collections of riddles and jokes such as *Bennett Cerf's Book of Riddles* (1960) and Joseph Low's *A Mad Wet Hen and Other Riddles* (1977) can rarely be found on the shelf in public libraries. A seven-year-old delights in the same jokes that mom and dad or grandma and grandpa told when they were the same age, and they delight even more in finding them in books they can read themselves.

One of the funniest and most popular series of stories involves Peggy Parish's Amelia Bedelia. When the good-natured but literal-minded maid carefully follows instructions to "draw the drapes" by getting out a pencil and paper, children not only have something to laugh about but they are also gaining familiarity with English language idioms.

Among the many Seuss favorites, children especially relish two: *Wacky Wednesday* (1974) (written under the pseudonym LeSieg) uses Seuss's zany rhyming to challenge children to find mistakes in the illustrations as they follow the hero from scene to scene; *Fox in Socks* (1969) pits Mr. Knox against Fox as poor Mr. Knox is almost overwhelmed by Fox's barrage of tongue twisters. No lover of humor should miss the hilarious books of author and illustrator JAMES MARSHALL. In his comic stories about Fox, *Fox and His Friends* (1982), *Fox on Wheels* (1983), *Fox on the Job* (1990), and so on, the lazy and conniving, yet basically decent, character all too often falls victim to his own schemes.

Although humor is the genre most popular with young readers, mysteries intrigue these children as much as they do their older siblings and parents. MARJORIE WEINMAN SHARMAT's perennially popular books about Nate the Great, boy detective, and his bedraggled, woebegone dog, Sludge, are a great introduction to mysteries. Each story about Nate and his friends involves children — and adults — in a good time, reading aloud in Joe Friday *Dragnet*-style voices as they try to solve Nate's latest case. The characters in the series live in a diverse urban area, a plus for families and schools trying to reinforce ethnic and racial understanding. Included among the popular titles in the series are *Nate the Great and the Stolen Base* (1992), *Nate the Great Goes Down in the Dumps* (1989), and *Nate the Great and the Sticky Case* (1981). Also in the mystery genre, Kin Platt's *Big Max* (1992) tells of a diminutive detective who travels by umbrella — not always the best means of transportation but definitely one of the silliest.

Children beginning to read often enjoy suspenseful, slightly spooky stories. Few are able to resist ALVIN SCHWARTZ's ghostly folklore collections, especially *In a Dark, Dark Room and Other Stories* (1984). The stories are perfect for reading aloud or retelling at Halloween or summer camp-outs, and the illustrations offer a humorous touch that is reassuring to the ready-to-believe child reader.

Stories from the folklore of many nations of the world are also represented in books for this age group. JOANNA COLE's *Bony Legs* (1983) is a retelling of a Russian Baba Yaga story. It is just scary enough for a first- or second-grader. An almost-scary AMERICAN FOLKTALE, MOLLY

BANG's *Wiley and the Hairy Man* (1976), transports readers and listeners to Alabama's Tombigbee River and its swamp. There they meet young African American Wiley and cheer him on as he three times bests the hairy man, a comical yet slightly frightening conjurer.

Some of today's best writers and illustrators create books of FANTASY and fairy tales specifically for the beginning reader. JANE YOLEN's fractured fairy tale *Sleeping Ugly* (1981) pits the beautiful but nasty Princess Miserella against poor but nice Plain Jane. In *Commander Toad in Space* (1980), Yolen had fun parodying the *Star Trek* television series. The characters and adventures of the amphibian crew of *Star Warts* are made even more humorous and vivid by the illustrations of BRUCE DEGEN. SYD HOFF's *Stanley* (1992), set in a definitely imaginary time of cavemen and dinosaurs, is a good example of fantasy. The story humorously demonstrates how one nonconformist can make a tremendous difference to society. An appealing addition to the books of original fantasy or fairy tale stories is the Dragon series by DAV PILKEY. Generous, kind, comical, and not always patient, the little blue dragon is chronicled in brightly illustrated stories that begin with *A Friend for Dragon: Dragon's First Tale* (1991).

To children, family and friends are not just important parts of their lives but two of their favorite subjects for stories. Whether humorous or serious, books about families and friends offer young readers opportunities for affirmation, growth, or escape into a safer and more secure world. Frog and Toad appear in four books by Arnold Lobel, starting with *Frog and Toad Are Friends,* each containing several gently comical stories about the best friends and their adventures. Lobel's fine writing and illustrations earned his books both Newbery and Caldecott Honor Awards as well as a multitude of fans.

Mandy and Mimi, who debuted in Pat Ross's *M and M and the Big Bag* (1981), are best friends who manage to get each other into trouble — and out of it. The two little girls are curious, adventurous, often silly, and very real. In Joan Robins's *Addie Meets Max* (1985), fear of a new neighbor's dog nearly stops a friendship from developing. Addie, like so many children, has mixed feelings about her new neighbor. With her mother's help, Addie not only makes a new friend but overcomes her fear of Max's dog.

FAMILY STORIES vary as much as families do. The protagonist of Barbara Porte's series is a young boy who lives with his widowed dentist father. Harry is shy, worries too much, and wants the same things other children want: acceptance, love, a pet, and to be good at sports. Porte and illustrator Yossi Abolafia have created a realistic and very appealing series that offers a positive portrayal of a single-parent family.

Jean Van Leeuwen's *Amanda Pig and Her Big Brother Oliver* (1982) is one of a series of books about a model "pig" family: a stay-at-home mother, loving father, adoring grandmother, and brother and sister who usually get along. Though there are occasional rivalries between the brother and sister, problems at school, or misunderstandings of one kind or another, family love keeps them secure. Another kind of idealized family can be found in CYNTHIA RYLANT's *Henry and Mudge: The First Book* (1987). The boy and his big mastiff dog are the stars, but Henry's easygoing, loving parents unobtrusively watch over things, helping the little boy through difficult moments.

Since the late 1960s, exciting historical fiction has been a staple in publishing for children learning to read. Aware of the careful research and fine writing of authors such as Nathaniel Benchley and F. N. Monjo, teachers and librarians have enjoyed recommending these books to children. In Barbara Brenner's *Wagon Wheels,* the Muldie boys and their father head west to Kansas territory to get a homestead of their own. Based on a true story, the book shows the courage and resourcefulness of this real African American family of pioneers. A little girl and an amazing wild horse are the heroes of another pioneer story, *The White Stallion* (1982), written by Elizabeth Shub. Set in Texas in 1845, the book tells how little Gretchen, separated from her family's wagon train, is miraculously rescued by the leader of a herd of wild horses. Based on historical accounts, the seemingly fantastic story is quite believable.

Another pioneer story, set in California during the gold rush, tells of Chang, a Chinese immigrant child, who spends his days working and occasionally dreaming of having a pony of his own. *Chang's Paper Pony* (1988), written by Eleanor Coerr, gives children an idea of the prejudice the Chinese encountered, as well as the rare moments of kindness.

Nonfiction is another popular easy-reader category. Excellent, well-written, and enticing books have been published about math, dinosaurs, astronomy, human biology, and much more. Today's young readers are curious about many of the same subjects as are older children and adults. Fortunately, there are usually carefully written, well-illustrated easy readers available to satisfy that curiosity. Among the more prolific authors are Paul Showers and Franklyn M. Branley. Showers most often has written about aspects of human biology; two of his titles are *The Listening Walk* (1991) and *A Drop of Blood* (1989). Branley has written many books on earth science and astronomy, including *The Planets in Our Solar System* (1987) and *Tornado Alert* (1988). Both authors have presented information clearly and provided opportunities for children to try simple experiments in testing scientific concepts.

Other areas of nonfiction are also popular with young children. Two biblical stories, *Noah and the Flood* (1992), written by Barbara Brenner, and *David and the Giant* (1987), written by Emily Little, offer children just honing their reading skills the opportunity to read on their own about these biblical heroes. For children curious about magic, Rose Wyler and Gerald Ames have offered simple but fascinating instructions for fooling friends or for putting on a magic show in their two books, *Magic Secrets* (1990) and *Spooky Tricks* (1968). Young sports fans can find books about their heroes and instructions for improving their playing in books such as Chuck Solomon's *Our Little League* (1988) and *Our Soccer League* (1988).

Among the several good poetry collections available are Lee Bennett Hopkins's *Surprises* (1984) and *More Surprises* (1987), which contain an assortment of poems, some thoughtful, some funny, and all accessible to the young reader. Karla Kuskin's *Soap Soup* flows from one poem to another, each about a child's world and the child himself. Kuskin's deceptively simple poems are sure to inspire children to try writing their own poetry. A well-known and popular poet for older children, Jack Prelutsky has also published poetry for beginning readers. His collections describe the seasons, holidays, and all the disappointments that the title *Rainy, Rainy Saturday* (1980) implies.

Libraries today are busier than ever, and in any children's department, books for beginning readers continue to be popular and in demand. Despite concern about the negative impact of television on reading habits, children in the primary grades seem as excited as ever about the first word and the first book they read. Most important, these children are constantly being offered not just the wonderful classic titles such as *Little Bear, The Cat in the Hat,* and *Amelia Bedelia,* but they are being encouraged to remain readers by new works of fiction and nonfiction written, illustrated, and produced with the care and sensitivity that young minds deserve. The response of today's children to these wonderful books bodes well for their future as readers in a literate world. B.M.B.

Edmonds, Walter D.

American writer, 1903–1998. Walter Edmonds was born in Boonville, New York, a small town in the Mohawk Valley. He spent winters in New York City but considered his real home the family dairy farm in Boonville, where he spent summers. Edmonds was educated at St. Paul's School and the Choate School and graduated from Harvard University in 1926. As a junior he took an advanced composition course and was persuaded to send a short story to *Scribner's Magazine.* It was accepted for publication, and Edmonds was on his way to a writing career.

Edmonds claimed he never wrote a book specifically for children: "The criterion of any child's book should be whether it has enough stuff, humor, reality, wisdom, excitement to be interesting to an adult mind." He wrote about unusual topics, such as the plight of a young Confederate aeronaut in the Civil War story *Cadmus Henry* (1949), and told a tall tale with humor and wit, as shown in *Uncle Ben's Whale* (1955). More often than not, however, Edmonds would return to his roots: the history of the Mohawk Valley region. Edmonds felt strongly about the continuity and relevance of American history and delved deeply into the history and the lives of the people who lived, worked, and struggled to survive on the frontier. A sense of possibility and adventure permeates these tales of quietly determined individuals who persevere against insurmountable odds. In his Newbery Medal–winning book, *The Matchlock Gun* (1941), young Edward defends his mother and small sister against a savage Indian attack with an antique, unwieldy gun. Based on an actual incident, this story reflects Edmonds's preference for conducting research using original sources rather than formal history and immersing himself in the period about which he writes.

Two Logs Crossing (1943) relates the story of John Haskell, the son of a recently deceased ne'er-do-well father, who proves himself by supporting his family and repaying his father's debts through two hard winters of fur trapping. Edmonds's most accomplished work is *Bert Breen's Barn*, winner of the 1976 National Book Award. This lyrical ode to perseverance spans several years of young Tom Dolan's life, from the time he sets the goal of acquiring the barn through earning the money to buy it to its eventual erection and consequent impact on his family. Like John in *Two Logs Crossing*, Tom lives with the legacy of a lazy, shiftless father, but through diligence and hard work, both boys elevate their family's social and economic stature. Edmonds's considerable skills come together in *Bert Breen's Barn*. It has fine characterization, spare, eloquent prose, and a compelling plot with elements of mystery and adventure. In all

of his books, Edmonds illuminated history with colorful characters and dynamic, accurately drawn historic episodes.

Edmonds also wrote many books for adults, including *The South African Quirt* (1985), *The Night Raider and Other Stories* (1980), and *Drums Along the Mohawk* (1936). M.O'D.H.

Egielski, Richard

American illustrator, b. 1952. At one time a student of MAURICE SENDAK at the Parsons School of Design, Egielski shares his teacher's devotion to idiosyncratic and highly personal PICTURE BOOKS. In collaboration with ARTHUR YORINKS, as well as with other writers, he has created some of the most quirky and original children's books of recent decades.

Born in New York City, Egielski was an artistically inclined boy, but it was his desire to escape from parochial schools and not his interest in making a career of art that encouraged him to apply to the city's High School of Art and Design. Once there, however, his talent found root, and he later studied art at the Pratt Institute and Parsons. Upon graduating, he showed his portfolio to children's book publishers who, as he recalled, decided his work was a bit too strange and "sophisticated" for a young audience. Sendak thought otherwise and introduced him to another young man starting out, writer Arthur Yorinks.

Together, Egielski and Yorinks forged an unusually intimate collaboration, each critiquing the other's work and going through many phases of design before presenting a project to a publisher. In their first notable success together, *Louis the Fish* (1980), Egielski's illustrations capture the long shadows and dingy hues of his native city as well as the edgy tension that marks all true New Yorkers. His Louis, the butcher who loves fish, has a constantly bewildered air about him. His customers, even when they are pictured as fish, maintain a harried, belligerent posture.

A later Egielski and Yorinks collaboration,

Hey, Al, won Egielski the 1987 Caldecott Medal. Here the depressingly claustrophobic apartment of Eddie, a janitor who lives alone with his dog, Al, is mostly rendered in shades of brown. Details that break out of the pictures' frames — a newspaper dropped outside the front door, a suitcase half in and half out of the bathroom — emphasize just how cramped a place it is. When Eddie and Al take flight to a seeming paradise in the sky, the art explodes with lush, tropical colors. Once again, details break through the frame, but the effect now suggests expansiveness and the island's amazing fecundity. When paradise sours, Al and Eddie struggle back to their old home, but in the last picture, gentle and triumphant, they find a more agreeable way to add color to their lives.

Egielski insists that provocative and wry texts interest him most as an illustrator, an assertion that has been borne out by his work for PAM CONRAD's first-person narrative from the point of view of a meteorite, *Call Me Ahnighito* (1995), or Marjorie Palatini's spoof of *Dragnet, The Web Files* (2001). *The Tub People* (1989), *The Tub Grandfather* (1993), and *The Tub People's Christmas* (1999), written by Pam Conrad, tell the story of a family of wooden tub toys who manage to stay together despite perilous trials. Egielski's illustrations endow these stiff toys with subtly powerful personalities, so much so that in *The Tub Grandfather* there is one double-spread picture of the Grandmother dancing with her newly found husband that is almost heartachingly tender. This astonishing picture, like all of Egielski's best work, reflects the singular vision, emotional urgency, and technical mastery of an artist at the top of his form. A.Q.

Ehlert, Lois

American author and illustrator, b. 1934. Lois Ehlert's background as a designer and graphic artist is apparent in her many acclaimed PICTURE BOOKS.

The Wisconsin native was encouraged by her parents to pursue the arts at a very young age, and they provided her with a private work space, scraps of cloth, and pieces of wood for her creations. After attending the Layton School of Art and the University of Wisconsin, where she received a B.F.A., Ehlert worked in the graphic arts as a production assistant, designer, and freelance illustrator. She began to illustrate children's books but was disappointed with the final production quality and stopped working on books to focus on other graphic design work. After several years she returned to children's book illustration because she felt that publishers were paying more attention to details of design and production.

Ehlert's illustrations for *Limericks by Lear* (1965) reflect her interest in design. Each illustration is created as a black print with overlays of shapes of color. The effect is bold and whimsical, suited to Lear's humorous limericks.

Ehlert turned to writing and illustrating her own books with *Growing Vegetable Soup* (1987) and *Planting a Rainbow* (1988). These books use flat shapes and bright colors combined with a simple text about gardening to convey both information and a story. Ehlert's success with these books led her to experiment further with color and form. *Color Zoo* (1989), a Caldecott Honor Book, was much lauded for the skill of the design. Each page is a different bold color and a shape is cut out of the middle. The combination of shapes and colors created by several pages overlaying the others reveals an animal's head. For example, a circle, a square, and a triangle form a tiger. The reader uncovers a new animal with the turn of each page. The book ends with a review of all the animals introduced earlier. *Color Zoo* is about concepts — shapes, colors, and animals — but also about looking at the world in a new and creative way.

Each of Ehlert's successive books explores the effects of shape, color, and form within her subject matter. Her books convey information to the youngest readers, allowing them to explore a subject through dramatic visual presentation. The ALPHABET BOOK *Eating the Alphabet* (1989) introduces the reader to fruits and vegetables beginning with each letter of the alphabet, and the glossary gives additional information about the foods, which include the ugli fruit and the jicama. *Feathers for Lunch* (1990) is the story of a cat who is unable to catch a bird for lunch, and each page introduces the reader to a different life-size bird in a garden setting. Ehlert labeled each bird and plant, using the typography as part of the overall design. In *Fish Eyes: A Book You Can Count On* (2001) a child imagines what she would see if she were a fish. Ehlert has played with color and size of typography in all her books, which have been well received by critics and lauded by teachers and parents for their educational value. Many of her books conclude with a glossary or a chart summarizing the information therein.

Ehlert's books are visually exciting and bold. Each is an experiment with form and a discovery for the reader. M.V.K.

Voices of the Creators

Lois Ehlert

Although I've been a graphic designer and illustrator for many years, it was in 1984 that I first began to experiment, joining my own text and art in children's books. I think of these books as little love notes to children, records of things I care about, ideas and feelings I want to pass on to the next generation. I don't think of myself as doing things in a particularly conventional way, and none of my books has been very easy, simple, or just fallen into place. If a book ever just fell into place for me, that would probably mean that I was repeating myself. I'm interested in the book as a whole, not just the illustrations. I choose the size for the book, select the type style and size, and integrate all elements on the page. That's the graphic designer part of me at work.

I feel comfortable with multiple subjects for my books, both fiction and nonfiction, sometimes blending the two. I try to extend the age range of my readers by adding extra things, such as small labels, a glossary, or information so that the older reader can choose part or all of the book, while

the younger child may just "read" the art. Depending on reading ability, the child may notice something new tucked into a composition that was missed at the first reading. I always liked those books best myself, when I was learning to read — the ones with the little surprises to test my reading and observation skills.

Getting ideas for my books comes about in a variety of ways. Children always ask me where my ideas come from. I cannot fully understand it myself; I usually don't even know how an idea will work until I do a little bit of it. I've been known to do three or four dummies for one idea and usually change the text a dozen times, or more. Even the size and shape of the book continue to change as I move along. The beginning of an idea may come in the writing (sometimes only a title); other times it starts with the art style or subject matter.

Once I get one little glimmer of the book, I begin a dummy. If I can get one page right, it seems that things open up more easily from that point on. I go back and forth between the text and picture. If I say something in the picture, I can eliminate it in the text.

It's like a play, with stage directions — once the performance begins, the directions aren't needed anymore. I write the text in longhand, then type it, and begin to read it aloud to find the rhythm and music of the language. With a sparse text, each word has to work hard.

Once the idea for the book is decided upon, I begin research. I love doing the research for a book. I get to go to interesting places: museums, nature centers, aquariums, anywhere I can get the information or inspiration I need. I talk to experts in the field about details, such as the formulation of a vegetable soup recipe, what one calls a young sugar maple tree sprout, the origins of a Chinese fruit, or the many uses of a squirrel's tail.

I try to maintain a feeling of freshness in my work, and usually roughly sketch out the concept of what I want to do in pencil, including the type. I then collect or observe the objects I want to paint (I do as much as I can from real models). Then I begin to work with gay abandon. My art looks impressionistic rather than realistic. I work in collage, cutting paper and pasting, which allows me to be very spontaneous. I use a variety of papers (some of which I paint), watercolors, ink, and real objects and start to cut and paste. I have been an art teacher over the years and use some of the same materials the children use. I glue all of these pieces together on bond paper to form the illustrations, and then begin to move the art around on the page, adding to it or deleting a part, until I find the right composition. I try not to censor myself at this point, nor limit myself because of some preconceived idea. That's the beauty of collage. The "un-fun" part of it is painting all those cut edges so they won't show when the art is photographed for reproduction.

If there is a single thread that weaves its way through all of my books, it is a colored thread. I love color. When I'm painting in color, I'm in my most heavenly mood. I always hope that time will go on forever, although I know it won't and can't. There is an unearthly quality about this part of the creative process, impossible to describe. It commands my total being. It's as if I had stepped into the book and walked around in it.

I like to think that if I create a book properly, the hand of the designer does not show. If I do my work successfully, it will look very simple. With paper and glue, and my trusty scissors, I express the simple things of life — the homely, ordinary subjects that I love. ☝

Emberley, Michael

American artist, b. 1960. Michael Emberley grew up outside Boston in a home filled with art and children's books. His mother, Barbara, is a writer, and his father, Ed, is a respected children's author and illustrator. After high school Emberley attended the Rhode Island School of Design and the California College of Arts and Crafts, and he worked with his father. Emberley's first book, *Dinosaurs! A Drawing Book* (1980), gives the reader step-by-step instructions for drawing ten dinosaurs. The book follows the pattern of many of his father's drawing instruction books, but Emberley's style is his

own. The dinosaurs are ferocious and, although simplified, somewhat realistic. *More Dinosaurs! And Other Prehistoric Beasts: A Drawing Book* (1983) followed soon after. Emberley's PICTURE BOOK *Ruby* (1990) marks a decided shift in style. *Ruby* is a variant of the Red Riding Hood story and concerns a mouse who must make her way through rough city streets to deliver triple-cheese pies to her grandmother. Emberley put his own spin on a traditional tale by playing up the suspense of the cat-mouse relationship and injecting sly humor throughout text and art. Emberley's cartoon-style watercolor illustrations, with sketchy, broken outlines and plenty of curves, suit the humor of the story. Emberley followed *Ruby* with *The Present* (1991), the endearing story of lovable Arne Hanson who delivers the perfect gift for his nephew's birthday. Emberley's watercolor illustrations and palette are as gentle and homey as the story.

Emberley used a more realistic style to illustrate *Welcome Back Sun* (1993). Set in a mountain village of Norway, this is the tale of a little girl who, with her parents, climbs the nearest high mountain to call the sun back at the end of a long winter. The story is quiet and well told. Through the pictures and words, readers feel how very dark and depressing the *murketiden* (murky time) is in Norway. Emberley's dark colors fill his pages with the sense of winter until the sun returns and a gold light suffuses his art.

Emberley collaborated with author Robie Harris on several books addressing childbirth and sexuality for young people. Two picture books, *Happy Birth Day!* (1996) and *Hi, New Baby!* (2000), give very young children an idea of what to expect with the birth of a new baby. Emberley's large, sketchy watercolor paintings focus on the devotion and wonder of a family celebrating new life. Emberley used several different styles of art in the critically acclaimed INFORMATION BOOKS *It's Perfectly Normal* (1994) and *It's So Amazing: A Book About Eggs, Sperm, Birth, Babies, and Families* (1999) to convey different aspects of the complex subject of sex education. In both books, a cartoon bird and bee express the curiosity and trepidation with which children and their parents approach the subject. Realistic watercolor paintings convey information and augment the helpful, friendly tone of the book. Whether telling and illustrating his own stories or those of others, such as Mary Ann Hoberman's *You Read to Me, I'll Read to You* (2001), Emberley has provided readers with warmth and a sense of fun.   M.V.K.

Enright, Elizabeth

American author and illustrator, 1909–1968. Since Elizabeth Enright's mother was an illustrator and her father a political cartoonist, it was perhaps inevitable that Enright would follow in her parents' footsteps and become an artist. But after illustrating several books, Enright discovered she had an even greater talent for writing, and she produced a number of memorable children's books.

Although born in Oak Park, Illinois, the daughter of Walter J. Enright and Maginel Wright Barney, Enright was raised in New York. Her parents divorced when she was eleven, and Enright spent her teenage years attending boarding school in Connecticut and studying dance with Martha Graham. She trained at the Art Students League in New York and later spent a year at the Parsons School of Design in Paris. When she returned to the United States, she married, started a family, and began illustrating children's books. One day while doodling, Enright sketched a series of pictures with an African motif. She later wrote a text to accompany the drawings, and *Kintu: A Congo Adventure* was published in 1935. This least-known of the author's works is well designed but has an inconsequential story and caricatured illustrations of African children, which modern readers might deem offensive. Yet it is an important book in the author's career because it awakened Enright's latent talent for writing. In fact, many of the book's reviewers mentioned that the text was stronger than the illustrations. From then on, Enright included fewer and fewer illustrations in her work, to the point where her later books were illustrated by other artists.

Enright wrote her second book while spending the summer on a Wisconsin farm owned by her uncle, the famous architect Frank Lloyd Wright. *Thimble Summer* recounts the experiences of nine-year-old farm girl Garnet Linden as she helps with harvesting, visits a fair, and gets locked in the town library, among other adventures. The book won the Newbery Medal in 1939, making Enright one of the youngest winners in Newbery history. Although Enright's gifts for description and character are evident in this fine book, her later work is even more impressive.

Perhaps her best-known books are FAMILY STORIES concerning the Melendy children — Rush, Mona, Randy, and Oliver — who live in a New York brownstone with their writer father and much-loved housekeeper, Cuffy. These cosmopolitan children are intelligent, artistic, affectionate, and, most of all, interesting. In their first book, *The Saturdays* (1941), the Melendys pool their weekly allowances so that each of them can spend one Saturday a month having an adventure. Later volumes, *The Four-Story Mistake* (1942) and *Then There Were Five* (1944), move the Melendys to the country and add an adopted son to the family. The last book in the series, *Spiderweb for Two* (1951), disappoints only because the older Melendy children have left home, though the writing has the usual Enright percipience and charm.

Gone-Away Lake (1957), the story of two siblings and their cousin spending the summer in the country, where they discover an abandoned resort, may be Enright's finest achievement. Her descriptive powers and unique ability to observe the world through the eyes of a child were never stronger than in this unusual novel. Other notable Enright books include a sequel, *Return to Gone-Away* (1961), a pair of fairy tales, *Tatsinda* (1963) and *Zeee* (1965), and several volumes of adult short stories that also contain keen observation in their evocative prose. Although these adult works are largely forgotten, Enright's children's books are still enjoyed for their vibrant characterizations and fine writing. P.D.S.

Estes, Eleanor

American author, 1906–1988. With her rare gift for depicting everyday experiences from the fresh perspective of childhood, Eleanor Estes based many of her stories on memories of growing up in a poor but loving family in West Haven, Connecticut. Following high school graduation, the author worked at the New Haven Public Library, then won a scholarship to the Pratt Institute Library School in Brooklyn, where she met her husband. She worked as a children's librarian at the New York Public Library until her first book was published.

The Moffats (1941) is a charming, humorous FAMILY STORY about a fatherless family in Cranbury, Connecticut. Older siblings Sylvie and Joey are well-defined characters, but the book usually focuses on the most original-thinking members of the family, eight-year-old Janey and five-year-old Rufus. In a series of loosely related episodes, the children attend dance school, frighten a school bully, and worry about moving to a new house. Although the events are commonplace, Estes perfectly captured children's observations, logic, and speech patterns in prose notable for its immediacy and insight. *The Middle Moffat* (1942) and *Rufus M.* (1943) are equally percipient and even stronger in portraying the World War I period. The latter book closes as the war ends, and the Moffats dream about the future — a comforting scene for World War II–era readers and a beautiful conclusion to a wonderful trilogy.

Nearly forty years later, Estes surprised everyone by writing another volume about the Moffats. *The Moffat Museum* (1983) includes episodes such as Sylvie's wedding and Joey's first job; the writing style proves the author's ear was still well tuned to the language and thoughts of children. Although the Moffat books celebrate a happy family, there is a realistic note of sadness behind many of the scenes, as when poverty forces the family to move and Joey to quit school. Much sadder in tone is *The Hundred Dresses* (1944), the haunting story of a poor girl teased by two classmates. Childhood cruelty has seldom been as effectively explored, yet the overriding theme is one of forgiveness and understanding, demonstrated by the final kind gesture of the victimized girl. Like *The Middle Moffat* and *Rufus M.*, the story was named a Newbery Honor Book. Estes won the Newbery Medal for *Ginger Pye* (1951), which concerns Jerry and Rachel Pye's six-month search for their missing puppy. The sensitive depiction of the children's conversations, memories, and emotions adds to the novel's warm appeal.

Illustration by Eleanor Estes from her book *Ginger Pye* (1951).

Estes's books were usually illustrated by fine artists such as Louis Slobodkin and Edward Ardizzone. For *Ginger Pye,* Estes illustrated her own story in a primitive, amusing style. Among the author's other books are a sequel, *Pinky Pye* (1958); literary fairy tales such as *The Sleeping Giant and Other Stories* (1948); and *The Witch Family* (1960), an artful blend of FANTASY and reality best appreciated by older readers, who unfortunately may not be interested in reading about six-year-old protagonists. Some of the same characters appear in Estes's last book, *The*

Curious Adventures of Jimmy McGee (1987). The author also wrote *The Alley* (1964), which concerns the children of a small New York neighborhood, and its sequel, *The Tunnel of Hugsy Goode* (1972).

The author's clear-eyed, original view of childhood shines through all of her work, particularly her classic books about the Moffat family. P.D.S.

F

Family Stories

"**H**appy families are all alike," Tolstoy told us, but "every unhappy family is unhappy in its own way." A century and a half of family stories in the United States bear him out, to a great degree. From LOUISA MAY ALCOTT's March sisters of 1867 to BETSY BYARS's Blossom family of the 1980s and 1990s, the strength children draw from loving parents, siblings, and other relatives and the guiding principles set forth by elders for youngsters to follow remain constant, however different the principles or the family structure may have become. The things that cause unhappiness, pain, confusion, and angst, however, vary greatly, reflecting changes in the composition of the family and in society.

Only a handful of Alcott's immediate successors are still read, and their readership diminishes with each new wave of electronic competition. *Little Women* (1867), *The Peterkin Papers* (Lucretia P. Hale, 1880), *Five Little Peppers and How They Grew* (Margaret Sidney, 1881), *Rebecca of Sunnybrook Farm* (Kate Douglas Wiggin, 1903), and Dorothy Canfield Fisher's *Understood Betsy* (1917) are among the few pre-1930s survivors. While many later stories are set in times past, their writers speak a language that is closer by decades to our own — a language understood by children whose world turns at an increasingly rapid pace.

Beginning in the 1930s, American writers began to show rather than to tell children about their country's past, putting history in terms not of great men and dates, but of the ordinary people, and especially the children, who lived through it. LAURA INGALLS WILDER's *Little House in the Big Woods* (1932) and its sequels and Carol Ryrie Brink's *Caddie Woodlawn* (1935) vividly describe family life on the frontier — not the life of the solitary trapper or trailblazer, but that of the family making a home at the edge of civilization and bringing to it values from "back home," mingled with the venturesome spirit that carved paths through the wilderness. Both are still widely read. Doris Gates's Janey Larkin, in *Blue Willow* (1940), is an only child who struggles, with her migrant parents, to find a way to make a home amid reduced circumstances. Alice Dalgliesh introduced, in *The Courage of Sarah Noble* (1954), a protagonist strong enough to accompany her father into the wilderness to build a new cabin for their family and to remain there alone when Father goes back for the rest of the family. Whatever its composition, the family circle supports the child's growth and discovery.

Beginning in the late 1930s and early 1940s, a variety of stories focused on the individual among siblings. The wise parent of Alcott's day remains in the background, ready when support is needed. (Like the Marches' Marmee, some of these are, in effect, single parents.) ELIZABETH ENRIGHT introduced Garnet in *Thimble Summer* (1938), set amid rural farm life of the Depression-era Midwest, and the four Melendys in *The Saturdays* (1941), who live in New York with their father and a housekeeper. ELEANOR ESTES added *The Moffats* (1941) of Cranbury, Connecticut, a quartet of independent spirits who tumble into adventures within sight of home, never too far from the watchful eye of their indomitable mother. The Moffats and the Melendys are followed by a flood of characters whose friends and fellow adventurers are their siblings: the Pyes (*Ginger Pye*, 1951, and *Pinky Pye*, 1958, by Eleanor Estes); the four sisters of SYDNEY TAYLOR's *All-of-a-Kind Family* (1951); EDWARD EAGER's Jane, Mark, Katharine, and Martha of *Half Magic* (1954); and Portia and Julian of Elizabeth Enright's *Gone-Away Lake* (1957). In Jennie Lindquist's *Golden Name Day* (1955) it is cousins, rather than siblings, who become fast friends. JOHN D. FITZGERALD, in *The Great Brain* (1972) and its numerous sequels, rang the changes on an intense sibling relationship in which an older brother skillfully manipulates situations so that his little brother gets the blame for most of his pranks.

Despite the number of parents who are absent in these stories — due to war, illness, or death — tragedy is seldom in the foreground. Little by little, however, the darker side of life begins to appear as a realistic element in the stories of the 1950s and 1960s. In Meindert DeJong's *House of Sixty Fathers* (1956) the young protagonist is separated from his family by the vicissitudes of war. Virginia Sorensen's *Miracles on Maple Hill* (1956) portrays a family struggling to put their lives back together after World War II, as does Margot Benary-Isbert's work *The Ark* (1953). In MADELEINE L'ENGLE's *Meet the Austins* (1960) the rhythms of a happy family must be adjusted to make room for a child orphaned when her father is killed in an airplane crash, while Julie in Irene Hunt's *Up a Road Slowly* (1966) must learn to live without her mother, who dies, or her father, who cannot cope alone and sends Julie and her brother to live with their aunt. Dave, Emily Cheney Neville's protagonist in *It's Like This, Cat* (1963), expresses typical adolescent angst in his rejection of his father's advice. Harriet, in LOUISE FITZHUGH's *Harriet the Spy* (1964), identifies and interacts more closely with her nanny, Ole Golly, than with her busy socialite parents. Sara, in Betsy Byars's *Summer of the Swans* (1970), is responsible for her younger brother, who is mentally disabled, and suffers great guilt and anxiety when he becomes lost.

As the more realistic, less romanticized aspects of family life became more common in children's fiction, a parallel development was the increasing presence of stories reflecting America's ethnic diversity, often from firsthand experience. Among the early voices whose resonance has lasted are VIRGINIA HAMILTON, first heard in *Zeely* (1967), in which the young protagonist leaves her family in the North to spend a summer of self-discovery with relatives in the South; Yoshiko Uchida, whose semi-autobiographical novel of a Japanese American family interned after Pearl Harbor (*Journey to Topaz*, 1971) was followed by her trilogy about a Depression-era Japanese American family in California (*Jar of Dreams*, 1981; *The Best Bad Thing*, 1983; *The Happiest Ending*, 1985); LAURENCE YEP, whose *Dragonwings* (1975) and *Child of the Owl* (1977) explore the experience of Chinese Americans; and MILDRED TAYLOR, whose Newbery Award–winning *Roll of Thunder, Hear My Cry* (1976) follows the fortunes of an African American family determined to hold on to their land during the Depression. Both Taylor, in her Logan family saga and in *The Gold Cadillac* (1987), and Yep, in *The Star Fisher* (1991), have explored the pain of segregation and the struggles of families to survive its cruelty. Hamilton, in *Cousins* (1990), probed the conflicts within families: the pain caused by differences of financial status, the struggle of a single parent to steer a family through rocky waters, and the fierce love between grandparent and grandchild that overcomes fear, guilt, and sorrow.

In 1968 BEVERLY CLEARY's *Ramona the Pest* appeared, and for twenty-five years Ramona and her family have been well known and loved by children everywhere. Readers have lived with the Quimby family through Ramona's entry into school, Mr. Quimby's loss of his job, and Ramona's determined efforts to help him quit smoking. Young readers can readily identify with Ramona's life or yearn to trade places with her. She has sympathetic parents with realistic human shortcomings; a sibling who alternates between caring and aloofness, rivalry and frustration; and a family circle in which the bonds are firmly knit with love and concern for one another and for others. Ramona has close kin in Peter and Fudge (*Tales of a Fourth Grade Nothing*, 1972), brothers whose creator, JUDY BLUME, has an unerring ear for the nuances of children's conversation and for their concerns of the moment; Johanna Hurwitz's Aldo (*Much Ado About Aldo*, 1978), whose busy mother juggles work and parenting with skill and care; and *Anastasia Krupnik,* LOIS LOWRY's 1978 creation, whose comfortable only-child status is upset by the impending arrival of a much younger brother but whose family circle widens easily to admit Sam. Each of these authors, in her own way, creates a family rich in traditional values, if not so rich in material things. Ann Cameron, in *The Stories Julian Tells* (1981), introduced a father whose fearsomeness in his sons' eyes takes on mythic proportions, but who is reliably loving and forgiving despite his forbidding sense of humor.

Side by side with these secure middle-class family circles, an extensive literature sprang up reflecting the less-than-secure lives of many other American families. In *The Pinballs* (1977), Betsy Byars introduced a group of foster children whose lives had been damaged either by parental abuse or neglect or by other circumstances beyond their control. The warm, wise foster parents manage, against considerable odds, to create a stable environment that helps these shaken youngsters to begin to trust in life again and to consider themselves part of a "family," albeit not a biological one. Byars, understanding the importance in a child's life of adult support that is wise and strong without being authoritarian, went on to create the Blossom family (*The Not Just Anybody Family*, 1986, and sequels), whose frequently absent mother is replaced, on a day-to-day basis, by Pap, a grandfather whose easygoing philosophy has plenty of backbone. The Blossoms live on the edge of poverty, a fact seldom stated but implicit in their surroundings; but there is nothing poor about their caring for one another, despite frequent rivalries among the siblings.

Close cousin to the "Pinballs" is KATHERINE PATERSON's Gilly in *The Great Gilly Hopkins* (1978), a foster child whose mother, a would-be movie star, is off "finding herself" while her daughter grows up with only a series of foster families for support. In nearly all of Paterson's work the links and supports of family are important, though they are perhaps most evident in *Jacob Have I Loved* (1980), focused on sibling rivalry and misunderstanding, and *Park's Quest* (1988), a son's search for information about his father, killed in Vietnam, and his family history, hidden by the mother who can't bear to explore her pain.

CYNTHIA VOIGT created one of the most memorable family sagas in *The Homecoming* (1981) and its sequels. The Tillerman family consists of four children, abandoned by their mother at a suburban shopping mall in New England, whose long journey in search of their grandmother becomes an odyssey of almost mythic proportions. Once they are reunited with their crusty but caring grandmother, the strength of Dicey, the take-charge sister, and of the family bond slowly heal the children's wounds. Voigt explored deep anger and distrust, guilt and denial, but she rooted the Tillermans firmly to the home they find with their grandmother, and all of them, children and grandmother alike, grow as they are nourished by their relationship.

Like Byars, Paterson, and Voigt, PATRICIA MACLACHLAN has explored a wide range of family relationships. From the very simple story lines of *Seven Kisses in a Row* (1983), in which loving parents leave their children with an uncle and aunt while on vacation, to the bittersweet pioneer story of motherless children whose father advertises for a new wife from back East in *Sarah, Plain and Tall* (1985), MacLachlan has shown an understanding of the child's feelings in a world where all is not right. In *Arthur, for the Very First Time* (1980), a boy spending the summer with relatives while his parents await the birth of another child gradually develops the courage to explore his own fears — of losing his mother, of being displaced by the baby, of change — helped by the wise aunt and uncle who have become his "temporary" family. *Journey* (1991) explores the complex relationships among two children and their grandparents, surrogate parents for the mother who, like Gilly Hopkins's mother, has left them to "find herself." Journey's grandfather helps the boy discover not only who his family is, but that parents are not necessarily the perfect creatures children would like them to be. In *Baby* (1993), Sophie's mother takes the risk of leaving her year-old daughter on the doorstep of a family she has watched, judging by their closeness that they will care for her child while she weathers a crisis. In the process, Sophie's presence helps her adoptive family come to terms with the death of their own second child, a loss they have not been able even to discuss.

PAULA FOX, in *Monkey Island* (1991), told the story of a family that simply disintegrates in the face of poverty and insurmountable challenges, leaving the son to survive on the streets of New York. Like Virginia Hamilton's Buddy in *The Planet of Junior Brown* (1971) and the eponymous hero of JERRY SPINELLI's *Maniac Magee* (1990), this boy finds a "family" to help him survive, taking shelter with others on the street who respond to his need and teach him how to survive on his own. EVE BUNTING, in *Fly Away Home* (1991), used the PICTURE BOOK format to tell the brief but powerful story of a boy and his father who live in an airport, carefully disguising their comings and goings so that they appear to be travelers, but hoping each day for a change of fortune that will allow them to find a home to go to, as the others who pass through the airport do.

Lois Lowry, whose families are generally strong and supportive, painted a grim picture in *The Giver* (1993) of a future in which families are carefully composed by community rules. Jonas, the twelve-year-old protagonist, is assigned the role of Receiver of Memory at the community's coming-of-age ceremony. In his year of tutelage with the elder who gives him, for the first time, knowledge of the world outside, where not all hills have been smoothed out nor wars eliminated, where disease and death await, he is horrified to learn the truth about his "perfect" family and the world in which he has grown up.

It is his response to the concept of love, and his concern for Gabriel, an infant foster child whom his family has been nurturing, that gives him the courage to run away with Gabriel in search of another life — and a true family.

Families disintegrating and re-forming are part of life for today's children, and the candor with which authors address painful issues such as death, divorce, intolerance, abuse, and neglect in the early twenty-first century reflects an awareness that children feel the pain of such changes as deeply as adults do. Yet for children, family is still a crucial factor in survival. The bonds of affection and concern; the warmth and shelter of home and its inhabitants, be they many or few; the depth of love and the tenacity that hold families together through hard times; and the thread that ties one generation to the next — these are themes that resonate through much of our best fiction and that keep stories alive from one generation to the next. D.B.C.

Fantasy

F antasy is the ultimate literature of the imagination. Since humans acquired the capacity to reason and imagine, fantastic tales have been told. Transcending the here and now, such tales relate larger-than-life deeds set in a moral landscape that both evokes and transforms the known world.

Engagement with a work of fantasy requires of the reader a willing suspension of disbelief: the reader must be willing to accept the premise of the fantasy. The secondary, altered world of the successful fantasy, according to J.R.R. TOLKIEN, is one "into which both designer and spectator can enter, to the satisfaction of their senses while they are inside." This requires of the writer extraordinary skill, in that the story must be so seamlessly written, the imaginary world so real, that the reader cannot help but accept it. The story cannot "clank," jarring the reader back to reality. As the children's fantasy writer SUSAN COOPER has said, "Fantasy, like the butterfly, flies without knowing how."

Although the origins of fantasy as a genre can be traced to the nineteenth-century revival of interest in traditional folk- and fairy-tale material, fantasies are distinguished by being manifestly the work of an individual sensibility. *Alice's Adventures in Wonderland* (1865), written by LEWIS CARROLL, for example, noted for its playfulness with words and logic, displays its author's quirky personality, perspective, and preoccupations. Seizing on the popularity of the form, many works followed that use genre to gently point a moral lesson; rather than proving didactic bores, however, some of these works — including GEORGE MACDONALD's *At the Back of the North Wind* (1871) and C. S. LEWIS's Chronicles of Narnia (seven volumes, 1950–1956) — went on to become great classics. Perhaps influenced by *Alice,* a distinct strain of humorous fantasy also emerged, with distinguished exemplars such as L. FRANK BAUM's *Wizard of Oz* (1900), E. NESBIT's *Five Children and It* (1902), HUGH LOFTING's *Story of Doctor Dolittle* (1920), and P. L. TRAVERS's *Mary Poppins* (1934).

Given their origins in the oral tradition — from folktales to Homer — it is not surprising that many successful fantasies make overt use of traditional material. Legends of King Arthur and his court and the tales of the Welsh Mabinogion, in particular, have engendered a wealth of creative and captivating fantasies. SUSAN COOPER used elements of both in her Dark Is Rising quintet, in which her storytelling prowess engages readers through episodes of suspense, even terror, before light triumphs over dark. *Over Sea, Under Stone* (1965) introduces Merriman — who just might be Merlin. *The Dark Is Rising* (1973), the most powerful of the books, brings Merriman together with Will, the seventh son of a seventh son just turned eleven, in an effort to defeat evil. *Greenwich* (1974), *The Grey King* (1975, which won the Newbery Medal), and *Silver on the Tree* (1977) followed, with King Arthur himself appearing at last. Also drawing on Arthurian legend, JANE YOLEN sparked the imagination with her tale *The Dragon's Boy* (1990). Artos, an orphan raised by Sir Ector, gains wisdom from Old Linn, and,

subtly, the reader is led to understand that this is a story of Arthur and Merlin. LLOYD ALEXANDER's classic Chronicles of Prydain were inspired by Welsh myth. Taran, an assistant pigkeeper, appears in *The Book of Three* (1964), beginning a quest that will lead him to combat evil in *The Black Cauldron* (1965) and *The Castle of Llyr* (1966), on a search for self in *Taran Wanderer* (1967), and finally to triumph in both defeating evil and knowing and accepting himself in *The High King* (1968), which won the Newbery Medal.

The most developed secondary worlds appear in works termed *high fantasy.* Moved by their commitment to the themes and concepts that inspired them, the authors of these often multivolume works may create not only dramatic plots and fully developed characters, but geographies, languages, mythologies, histories, and traditions that may bear only an indirect relation to their stories but that immeasurably deepen their meaning, impact, and appeal. Other characteristics of high fantasy include an "Everyman" protagonist, female or male, who comes from humble beginnings to achieve great ends. The protagonist typically pursues a quest, often with the direct or indirect goal of searching for his or her own true nature. The struggle between good and evil pervades these tales, and events are tied to universal human values and ideals.

J.R.R. Tolkien's *The Hobbit* (1938), a favorite since its publication, is an outstanding example of high fantasy. Bilbo Baggins, the endearing main character, undertakes a dramatic quest for adventure and treasure and attains generous amounts of both, as well as a deepened appreciation of himself and his quiet life in the Shire. Although deeply steeped in the myths and legends of northern Europe, *The Hobbit* bears its author's preoccupations lightly. Lewis's Chronicles of Narnia are weighted with the author's search for and desire to represent in allegory the deepest meaning of the Christian faith. His inventiveness; his skill with character, language, and plot; and his compelling theme of the conflict between love and hate have ensured the se-

The Hall at Bag-End, Residence of
B. Baggins Esquire

Illustration by J.R.R. Tolkien from his book *The Hobbit* (1938).

ries many devoted readers. *The Lion, the Witch, and the Wardrobe* (1950), the first of the series, remains the most popular. Ursula K. Le Guin's Earthsea trilogy (*A Wizard of Earthsea,* 1968; *The Tombs of Atuan,* 1971; and *The Farthest Shore,* 1972) focuses on Ged, who in the course of the three novels metamorphoses from callow boy to Archmage, a position accorded the highest respect in his world. A much later Earthsea book, *Tehanu* (1990), returns to Tenar, the young high priestess of the Nameless Ones in *The Tombs of Atuan,* and follows her to her own maturity as a simple village woman with the power to redeem others through her belief in life and love.

The 1980s saw the emergence of strong female protagonists in fantasies as full of adventure as those with male protagonists. Exploring similar themes of coming of age, apprenticeship, and the nature of courage, these books, not surprisingly, deal forthrightly with the issues of gender bias and expectation. In *The Blue Sword* (1982) and *The Hero and the Crown* (1985), the Newbery Medal–winning Robin McKinley

presented two rousing tales of the land of Damar, replete with myth and magic. Meredith Pierce's Darkangel trilogy introduces Ariel, who in the first book, *The Darkangel* (1982), confronts a vampyre to rescue her mistress and ends up saving him from his evil past. As *A Gathering of Gargoyles* (1984) and *The Pearl of the Soul of the World* (1990) unfold, Ariel continues to vanquish the many evils threatening her land and becomes its acknowledged savior. The protagonist of *Alanna* (1983), written by Tamora Pierce, is a young girl who wishes to become a knight. Hiding her gender, she trades places with her brother, who wants to be a sorcerer. How each attains her or his wish is entertainingly told in a series of five books. The supernatural intrudes into a realistic contemporary setting in Margaret Mahy's *Changeover* (1984), in which fourteen-year-old Laura wrestles with both evil and her own nature in this quintessential — if unusual — coming-of-age novel.

Time, an obvious source of fascination to the

young, has provided a theme for several major fantasies, beginning with E. Nesbit. An outstanding example from more recent years, *Tuck Everlasting* (1975), written by NATALIE BABBITT, links the exploration of elusive time and the balance between life and death with provocative results. PHILIPPA PEARCE refined the thematic use of elusive time travel in *Tom's Midnight Garden* (1958), examining the transience of experience and the persistence of memory through this story of a boy who, when the hall clock strikes thirteen, joins a child of the past in a secret garden. L. M. BOSTON's Green Knowe books use the catalyst of an ancient, unchanging house to bring together its child residents of past and present to confront equally enduring evils and human dilemmas. Anne Knowles, in *The Halcyon Island* (1980), explored similar themes in this story about Ken, who is deathly afraid of water and learns to overcome his fear with the help of Giles, a friend whom he meets along the river; only at the very end does the reader learn that Giles drowned several years earlier and has returned to help another child in need.

A major category of fantasy is the animal fantasy. With origins in AESOP, animal fantasies have taken divergent turns, from the somber elaboration of *Watership Down* (1972), written by Richard Adams, to the elegiac familiarity of *The Wind in the Willows* (1908), written by KENNETH GRAHAME, to the gentle celebration of life in *Charlotte's Web* (1952), written by E. B. WHITE. Related to animal fantasies are stories (owing much to HANS CHRISTIAN ANDERSEN tales such as "The Steadfast Tin Soldier") that personify toys and machines. Among the classics in this subgenre are domestic tales, such as A. A. MILNE's *Winnie-the-Pooh* (1926) and Margery Williams's *Velveteen Rabbit* (1922), and more satiric near-epics, such as *The Mouse and His Child* (1967), written by RUSSELL HOBAN. A more contemporary tale is Elizabeth Winthrop's *Castle in the Attic* (1985), in which a boy enters a medieval world through the device of a lead knight.

Fantasy allows authors to create extraordinary worlds and to people them with characters who challenge and expand our sense of the norm. Yet writers of fantasy use their imagined worlds to explore the basic truths of this world: good fantasy puts readers more closely in touch with reality. Ursula Le Guin has said that fantasy is truth — not factual, but true. "Fantasy's truth challenges, even threatens, all that is false, all that is phony, unnecessary, and trivial in life." Fantasy expresses reality through the universal language of the inner self. M.J.G.

Farley, Walter

American author, 1915–1989. Whether fans are introduced to Walter Farley's Black Stallion in the original novel form, as it was abridged for a younger audience, or on the screen in the highly successful film version, they are meeting one of the most enduring and popular animal characters ever created. Farley became one of the most respected authors of books for young readers because he consistently provided his audience with stories that maintain their sense of adventure while remaining true to the development of characters introduced over the course of many books.

Farley was born in Syracuse, New York. As a city boy he was interested in sports and horses, and the racetracks at Aqueduct and Belmont, as well as Central Park, gave him the opportunity to watch and be around the animals. Farley also enjoyed writing and even as a teenager felt there weren't enough good horse books for children. While still attending Erasmus Hall High School, Farley began to write the story that would become *The Black Stallion*. The novel was published in 1941 while Farley was a student at Columbia University and over the years was joined by many sequels.

It has thus been more than sixty years since the Black Stallion and Alec Ramsey first appeared together on board the tramp steamer *Drake,* Alec bound for his New York home after a summer visit with his uncle in India. The dramatic storm at sea, the sinking of the *Drake,* and Alec's desperate battle for survival on the tiny deserted island with only the Black Stallion for company are all familiar elements of this ANIMAL STORY — it is this time together on the island that allows Alec and the mighty stallion to forge the bond that will keep them together throughout Farley's SERIES of novels.

Farley varied his pattern. He introduced another equine character, the equally imposing stallion Flame, in *The Black Stallion and Flame* (1960), and even introduced a female character in *The Black Stallion and the Girl* (1971), in memory of his teenage daughter, who died in an accident. But part of Farley's appeal comes from the fact that he was a series author. For young readers with an interest in a subject, there is reassurance in knowing that after the first book, there are twenty or more waiting to be devoured! Farley's particular skill lay in the fact that his stories in no way feel churned out as do so many contemporary series — although his books are linked by character and story, each can stand alone as a fine adventure tale. Alec and the Black Stallion, and their counterparts Steve Duncan and Flame in the Island Stallion adventures, remain interesting, vital characters in each book.

Farley also produced some fine books for younger readers, especially those featuring the Little Black Pony. In Little Black's first adventure, *Little Black, a Pony* (1961), the young narrator's special relationship with the little black pony is threatened when the stallion Big Red proves to be more enticing. Little Black, understandably jealous of the attention his master gives to Big Red, tries valiantly to compete but always falls short, until the climactic scene in which his small size enables him to save his young friend from an icy mishap. In other stories Little Black races (and naturally wins) and performs in a circus. Farley's readers immediately come to love this small star; this is especially noteworthy considering the beginning-to-read format with which Farley communicated his love of horses to a much younger audience.

Middle-grade readers can enjoy titles such as *The Horse That Swam Away* (1965) and *The Great Dane, Thor* (1966). It is the Black Stallion, however, that remains Farley's greatest creation, and devoted horse fans will continue to cheer as the Black Stallion and Alec thunder down the home stretch for many years to come. E.H.

Farmer, Nancy

American author, b. 1941. As a scientist in Mozambique in the 1970s, visiting remote villages to monitor water supplies, Nancy Farmer gained an appreciation for the complexity of African culture. She has passed this appreciation along to young readers in highly acclaimed novels such as the futuristic Newbery Honor Book *The Ear, the Eye, and the Arm* (1994) and the epic survival narrative *A Girl Named Disaster* (1996), also a Newbery Honor Book as well as a National Book Award finalist.

Farmer grew up on the Arizona-Mexico border, where her family operated a hotel. After serving in the Peace Corps in India and working as a chemistry teacher, she went to southwest Africa to work as an entomologist and stayed for seventeen years. Farmer started writing when her son was four, publishing a few children's books in Zimbabwe before moving with her family to California. Her first book for American readers, *Do You Know Me?*, appeared in 1993. Although she has written two PICTURE BOOKS with non-African settings, *Runnery Granary* (1996) and *Casey Jones's Fireman: The Story of Sim Webb* (1998), her novels all take place in Mozambique and Zimbabwe and creatively mix elements from that region's past and present.

A recurrent topic in Farmer's stories is the difficulty of reconciling traditional African customs and beliefs with modern society. *Do You Know Me?* presents a humorous but nonetheless provocative exploration of this subject. When young Tapiwa's Uncle Zeka moves from his traditional village to his brother's contemporary Zimbabwe home, the life skills he learned in the bush often don't translate well into his new environment. Yet Farmer has endowed this comic character with a certain indestructible dignity, leaving readers with the sense that the new ways are different but not necessarily better than the old.

Set in Zimbabwe in the year 2194, *The Ear, the Eye, and the Arm* offers an exciting hybrid of science fiction and ancient African spirituality as it follows three kidnapped siblings from one evocative locale to another, expertly weaving in the history and belief systems of the "ancestors" with images of robots, holophones, and anti-grav pads. Both the siblings and the three mutant detectives hired to find them receive help from a *mhondoro,* or lion spirit, to ultimately vanquish the evildoers and win freedom. This extraordinary adventure moves at a brisk pace that is never less than gripping.

All Farmer's novels contain a story-within-a-story. In *The Warm Place* (1995), a poignant, magical tale about a baby giraffe trying to return home after being shipped across the ocean to a zoo, a rat regales his literally captive audience with the animals' perspective on the Tower of Babel and other biblical events. In *A Girl Named Disaster,* the main character is alone for so long she must tell stories to stave off crushing loneliness. It is 1981, but Nhamo's village in Mozambique still lives by ancient rules. To avoid being forced into a miserable marriage, the motherless girl steals away in an abandoned boat, toward Zimbabwe, where she has been told her father lives. It seems Nhamo has always had a *shave,* or spirit, for storytelling, and, without a human audience, she practices her talent on the spirits. Nhamo spends months on her own, drifting from one uninhabited island to another, before reaching her destination. Farmer pays meticulous attention to Nhamo's surroundings and her methods of survival in this rewardingly complicated novel documenting a journey not only from place to place but from childhood to adulthood as well. C.M.H.

Feelings, Tom

American illustrator, b. 1933. In his life and work, Tom Feelings has tried to expose the reality of life for African Americans while depicting the beauty and warmth of black culture. In his autobiography for children, *Black Pilgrimage* (1972), he spoke of his struggles growing up in Brooklyn, New York, his years and growth in Africa, his return to the United States, and his success as an artist. As a student studying car-

tooning, Feelings was warned that the comic strip must not include the personal emotions of its creator. Unable to relinquish self-expression, he stopped working in that form. In the 1950s, however, his first printed work, "Tommy Traveler in the World of Negro History," was carried by the *New York Age.* Through this comic strip Feelings shared his childhood quest to learn African American history, and he found an outlet for both his artistic interests and his sensibilities.

In the early 1960s, while on assignment for *Look* magazine, Feelings was struck by the uninhibited warmth and dignity of the children of the South as compared to the withdrawn attitudes and negative self-images of the children of the North. His discouragement over the situation of the northern children led him to Africa. There he found himself surrounded by physical and human beauty, and he worked on producing books with the Ghanaian government. Through his illustrations he tried to show what he saw in the faces of the people, what he described as "a glow that came from within, from a knowledge of self, a trust in life, or maybe from a feeling of being part of a majority in your own world. I had seen this same glow in the faces of very young Black children in America, the ones who hadn't yet found out that they were considered 'ugly.'" This environment encouraged him to alter his black and white illustrations to include bright, vivid colors to represent the inner light that radiated from the faces of the Ghanaians.

When he lost his job in Ghana, he returned to the United States and continued to illustrate in the manner he had developed. He sought black writers with whom to collaborate, and the result was *To Be a Slave* (1968), recipient of a Newbery Honor citation, and *Black Folktales* (1969), both written by JULIUS LESTER; *Daydreamers* (1981), written by Eloise Greenfeld; *Something on My Mind* (1978), with Nikki Grimes; and *A Soul Looks Back in Wonder* (1994), edited by Maya Angelou. The theme of African life and the beauty of its people continued to present itself in his work in *Tales of Temba: Traditional African Stories* (1969), written by Kathleen Arnot, and

African Crafts (1970), written by Jane Kerina. From 1970 until 1974, he collaborated with his wife, Muriel Feelings, to create PICTURE BOOKS about their experiences in Africa, *Zamani Goes to Market* (1970) and two Caldecott Honor Books, the COUNTING BOOK *Moja Means One: Swahili Counting Book* (1971) and the ALPHABET BOOK *Jambo Means Hello: Swahili Alphabet Book* (1974). Following these successful books, Feelings worked for years on the artwork for *The Middle Passage* (1995), a powerful, dramatic narrative picture book about the African slave trade.

Today Feelings's work is widely embraced for its beauty and authenticity. He has accomplished what he set out to do: to portray positive images of black people and to convince black children of their worth. C.H.S.

Feiffer, Jules

American author and illustrator, b. 1929. Of the numerous children's authors known for irreverent humor, Jules Feiffer is perhaps the most versatile. The creator of the comic strip *Feiffer,* which ran in the *Village Voice* from 1956 to 1997, Feiffer received the Pulitzer Prize for editorial cartooning in 1986. He also won an Academy Award for the animated version of his short story *Munro* in 1961, and his 1967 play, *Little Murders,* received a number of prestigious awards, including an Obie. Since 1993, however, Feiffer's main creative outlet has been writing and illustrating books for young readers.

Feiffer was the middle child in a Jewish family from the Bronx; raised during the Depression, he grew up under difficult circumstances and turned to art for comfort at an early age. Even now, he has said, when he writes specifically for children, he is writing to the kid inside himself. Not until after many years of writing, however, did Feiffer seriously consider the idea of creating books for children. He illustrated NORTON JUSTER's *The Phantom Tollbooth* in 1961 because Feiffer and Juster were roommates and friends. Feiffer enjoyed the venture but decided afterward that he wasn't interested in illustrating anyone's work but his own: "the last thing I wanted to do in those years, being a bachelor and having no intention of having children, was kids' books." So he concentrated on editorial cartoons and other projects.

Then Feiffer became a father. Suddenly he was encountering authors and illustrators he would later cite as influences: MAURICE SENDAK, JAMES MARSHALL, CHRIS VAN ALLSBURG, TOMIE DEPAOLA. "You read these books and — if you are a writer — you can't help but start thinking about writing one of your own." Feiffer's first novel for children, *The Man in the Ceiling* (1993), features Jimmy Jibbett, a boy with an abiding love of cartooning, and his Uncle Lester. Jimmy is a middle child in a family insensitive to art, and Lester is an artist who is happiest creating and who, like Jimmy, encounters failure repeatedly. Feiffer deems the lesson valuable for young people: it's not failure itself but what you learn from it that counts.

Feiffer went on to publish several other children's books, including *I Lost My Bear* (1998) and *Bark, George* (1999). Both feature Feiffer's characteristic loose lines. Everything about Feiffer's artwork is animated and full of motion — he envisions drawing as a form of dance. The little girl in *I Lost My Bear* is based on one of Feiffer's three daughters, who inspired him to write a story to express a child's fluid sense of time. Though he clearly dislikes what he calls "thesis books for children," each of Feiffer's books communicates something about his philosophy of life, yet without didactic language or illustrations, giving his readers the chance to benefit from his experience. H.F.R.

Fine, Anne

British author, b. 1947. Anne Fine has explored the complexities of human relationships with dark humor and keen perception in her award-winning novels for young readers. Born in Leicester, England, Fine entered elementary school early, when her family's size suddenly increased with the arrival of triplets. She attended the University of Warwick, taught school, worked for a famine relief organization, married, and spent time living in Canada and the United States before attempting her first novel. *The Summer-House Loon* (1978), the story of a teenager involved in the romantic entanglements of her adult friends, was followed by a sequel, *The Other, Darker Ned* (1979). Fine has since written a wide range of fiction, from PICTURE BOOKS to adult novels.

Two of her books for a younger audience show a special interest in social problems. *Bill's New Frock* (1989), a comic examination of sexism, is one of Fine's most popular titles in Great Britain. *The Chicken Gave It to Me* (1992) is a humorous story of little green men who arrive on Earth with a taste for human beings; a chicken saves the day in a book that promotes free-range grazing for farm stock. Fine also has used humor and social concerns in her well-received YOUNG ADULT NOVELS. In *The Granny Project* (1983), four children band together to prevent their grandmother from entering a nursing home. Some readers may be put off by the book's unflinching realism, indelicate humor, and cold adult characters.

Adults play a central role in several of the author's books, including the 1987 farce *Madame Doubtfire* (published as *Alias Madame Doubtfire* in the United States), which concerns an actor who, disguised as a woman, gets a housekeeping job in his ex-wife's home so he can spend time with his children. The novel was made into a popular 1993 film, *Mrs. Doubtfire*, starring Robin Williams. Children of divorce are also the focus of *Goggle Eyes* (1989), which was published in the United States as *My War with Goggle Eyes*. The novel, which won both the Carnegie Medal and the Guardian Award, presents Kitty's first-person account of the anger she feels toward her mother's new boyfriend, a conservative businessman with old-fashioned ideas about child-rearing. The theme of war also permeates *The Book of the Banshee* (1991), in which Will Flowers relates how his sister's tumultuous adolescence has thrown the family into an uproar. Human

dynamics are well portrayed in both novels; every moment of humor, anger, and reconciliation rings true.

The young people in Fine's novels are unusually intelligent, with interests in reading, theater, school projects, and social issues. But the characters in *Flour Babies* (1992) are very different. These mildly delinquent, unmotivated students are unwilling participants in a science fair project that involves caring for sacks of flour as if they were babies, in order to learn parenting skills. The topic has been fictionalized in other children's books, most notably EVE BUNTING's *Our Sixth-Grade Sugar Babies* (1990), but never with the depth of sympathetic insight that Fine demonstrates in her second Carnegie Medal–winning novel. Her hulking teenage protagonist, Simon Martin, reaches new levels of self-awareness and is perhaps the most appealing character to be found in any of the author's books. *The Tulip Touch* (1999), a study in malevolence, explores a darker vein.

Fine's books are popular with young readers in both Great Britain and the United States. As her funny, contemporary novels have grown in depth and percipience, her characterizations have become warmer, displaying a generosity of spirit that makes the books richly rewarding.

P.D.S.

Fitzgerald, John D.

American author, 1907–1988. John D. Fitzgerald is best known for his loosely autobiographical series of books that chronicle the adventures of Tom D. Fitzgerald, known to friends and family as "The Great Brain." Tom, modeled after the author's older brother, enjoys a well-earned reputation for swindling and conning other children in Adenville, Utah, during the early part of the twentieth century. The seven novels in the series are narrated by his younger brother John, Tom's regular victim and cohort.

These humorous, lively stories continue to appeal to a wide range of readers because they are FAMILY STORIES full of exaggerated humor, outlandish adventure, and insight. They are stories about the dynamics of a family of three unruly but sympathetic boys who compete for status and attention. Tom and his brothers describe growing up Catholic in an overwhelmingly Mormon town, when the tug of war during the annual town picnic is a contest between the Mormons and the Gentiles. In Fitzgerald's stories an indoor water closet is unheard-of and worth the attention of an entire town, and a girl who dons a pair of dungarees is scorned by children and adults alike. The stories are also solid adventures, filled with excitement and tension. Tom is bold enough to try to fool the Jesuit priests at his strict boarding school, and John is foolish enough to face an armed outlaw with just a lariat. Fitzgerald told a sensational tale grounded in enough truth and details of everyday life to be convincing. The novels are filled with facts from his own childhood, and readers recognize the authenticity.

Fitzgerald, a journalist, wrote for adults for many years before his wife suggested he write down some of the stories from his childhood, which he told so well. His series of stories about the Great Brain, which began with *The Great Brain* in 1967, continue to be read and loved.

M.V.K.

Fitzhugh, Louise

American author and illustrator, 1928–1974. Although she published only a few works, Louise Fitzhugh left a permanent mark on children's literature. Or perhaps Harriet M. Welsch, Fitzhugh's greatest literary creation, left the permanent mark, for *Harriet the Spy* (1964) is acknowledged as one of the most original and groundbreaking books published during the 1960s. Harriet is a privileged, upper-class eleven-year-old who lives in a New York brownstone with her somewhat distant parents and an eccentric nursemaid, Ole Golly. An aspiring writer, Harriet goes on a daily spy route and records her devastatingly honest observations in an ever-present notebook. Harriet is saddened when Ole Golly leaves to get married, but faces her greatest challenge when she is ostracized after her classmates read the caustic comments she has written about them in her secret notebook. Harriet M. Welsch represents a new kind of protagonist for children's literature. She is spoiled, self-absorbed, and often rude. She curses and throws tantrums but is also vulnerable and touching.

This refreshing, fully realized character is very much a New York native, but Fitzhugh was born in Memphis, Tennessee, where she spent an unhappy youth. She was the only child of a wealthy family; her parents divorced early and custody was granted to her father. Fitzhugh was educated in private schools and attended several colleges before dropping out a few credits short of graduation. She then moved to New York, where she lived off a trust fund and trained as a painter.

Fitzhugh illustrated two PICTURE BOOKS, *Suzuki Beane* (1961) and *Bang, Bang, You're Dead* (1969), both cowritten with Sandra Scoppettone. But it was the publication of *Harriet the Spy* that made her famous. Early reviews were mixed; some critics praised the book, but many others denounced it. Children, however, recognized its honesty and made it a bestseller. *Harriet the Spy* is now considered a landmark novel, which many believe signaled the true beginning of modern realistic fiction for children. Harriet M. Welsch also plays a role in Fitzhugh's follow-up novel, *The Long Secret* (1965), but the focus of this book is Harriet's friend Beth Ellen Hansen. Many children enjoy this novel, and reviewers have praised its frank discussion of sexual development, but from a critical perspective it is not as successful as *Harriet the Spy*. Because she behaves so passively throughout most of the book, Beth Ellen is not a strong enough character to be the center of an entire novel. The biting satire about her jet-set family seems directed toward an adult audience rather than children, and some of the humor is too broad, resulting in caricatures rather than characterizations.

Fitzhugh did not live to see her next novel published; she died unexpectedly of a brain aneurysm just a week before the release of *Nobody's Family Is Going to Change* (1974). This book is a humorous but angry story about two black children who do not conform to the upper-class lifestyle of their parents. Nonconformity is a theme that runs throughout Fitzhugh's writings and seems to be a trait she values, despite the costs; another theme in the books is the almost palpable sense of loneliness in her young people. Several of Fitzhugh's picture book manuscripts have been published posthumously, as well as a farcical novel, *Sport* (1979), about Harriet's friend Simon Rocque. *Nobody's Family Is Going to Change* was adapted as a mediocre after-school television special; in another incarnation, it was a thoroughly enjoyable Tony Award–winning Broadway musical, *The Tap Dance Kid*. Reportedly, Fitzhugh left behind other manuscripts that may eventually find their way into print, but she will be best remembered as the creator of the inimitable *Harriet the Spy*.

P.D.S.

Flack, Marjorie

American author and illustrator, 1897–1958. "Once upon a time there was a beautiful young duck named Ping." With these words familiar to generations of American children, Marjorie Flack began *The Story About Ping*, a book continuously in print since its publication in 1933. Flack had a gift for creating books for the very young child. Born in Greenport, Long Island, she considered storytelling an intrinsic part of her personality. "As far back as I can remember, pictures were always an important part of my life. I can remember drawing pictures in the sand, pictures on the walls (and being punished for it), and pictures on every piece of paper I could find. For every picture there would be a story, even before I could write." At the age of eighteen, she enrolled at the Art Students League in New York City, where she met artist Karl Larsson. They married in 1919, and the following year their daughter, Hilma, was born.

Flack's first book, *Tak Tuk, an Arctic Boy* (1928), was written in collaboration with Helen Loman, who had lived most of her life in Alaska. Flack wrote and illustrated a story based on Loman's factual accounts of the lives of Eskimo children. *All Around the Town* (1929) came next, the story of a boy enjoying the sights and sounds of New York, inspired by the author's own experiences exploring the city with her young daughter. In 1930, Flack wrote and illustrated *Angus and the Ducks*. The first of five books in a series about "a very young little dog" who is "curious about many places and many things," the book is a "true story about a real dog and some real ducks," Flack noted. "The other Angus books are also built around real incidents. The cat was Hilma's cat, and she really did hide on the roof. Wag-Tail Bess was our own Airedale." Although a highly competent writer and illustrator, Flack's true genius lay in her overall storytelling ability and in the graphic pacing of words and images, and nowhere is that talent more fully realized than in her Angus books. Like ROBERT LAWSON and JAMES DAUGHERTY, she used word and image repetition, type layout, and page design to control timing and add drama. Preschoolers are drawn to her use of bright colors, forthright drawing style, and clear rhythmic prose. They also identify with the inquisitive Angus, who ventures out into unknown territories but always returns to the security of his own home.

Flack had the remarkable ability of instilling personality into her animal characters without denying their outward natural behaviors. While writing *Angus and the Ducks,* Flack became so interested in Peking ducks that she began a thorough investigation of the species, discovering that their ancestors lived in China on the Yangtze River. This fascination led her to write *The Story About Ping*, which Flack asked artist Kurt Wiese to illustrate because he had lived and worked in China. His rich zinc lithographs became as integral to the story as Flack's own lyrical prose, and their successful collaboration created one of the most beloved PICTURE BOOKS in all of children's literature. Flack collaborated with many talented authors and illustrators, including her second husband, Pulitzer Prize–

winning poet William Rose Benét, but it is the story about Ping and his home, the beautiful wise-eyed boat on the Yangtze River, which remains her greatest contribution to children's literature. M.B.B.

Fleischman, Paul

American author and poet, b. 1952. Since the publication of *The Birthday Tree* (1979), a fanciful PICTURE BOOK in which a boy shares an uncanny relationship with a tree planted to celebrate his birth, Paul Fleischman has established himself as a writer of extraordinary originality and versatility. Fleischman's picture books, novels, short stories, and POETRY are written with consummate skill, and his stylistic range is as varied as is his choice of format. The awards and honors Fleischman's books have garnered testify to his literary accomplishments.

Paul Fleischman was born in Monterey, California, the son of SID FLEISCHMAN, a well-known children's book author. Fleischman has credited his father as a literary influence; while growing up he served his story apprenticeship listening to his father read rollicking tall tales and adventure stories aloud. Since music has also been a strong force in Fleischman's life, it comes as no surprise that an astute attention to the power of sound and the musicality of words permeates his work. The harmonious melding of word and sound finds resonance in *Rondo in C* (1988), a mellifluous PICTURE BOOK in which a young girl's piano recital stirs a personal response in each member of the audience. Fleischman's colorful stories, often set in the past, reflect a keen interest in American history, and many are rooted in actual historical events. *Bull Run* (1993) weaves together the voices of sixteen individual characters, each of whom has a unique reason for participating in the Battle of Bull Run. Set during the Philadelphia yellow fever epidemic of 1793, *Path of the Pale Horse* (1983) makes evident the limitations of medicine and explores the relationships among science, religion, and superstition. *Saturnalia* (1990) presents a vivid, multifaceted picture of life in colonial New England for a Narragansett Indian captive-turned-printer's-apprentice. In these books, and in all of Fleischman's fiction, characters grapple with moral and psychological issues, but wry humor and unexpected plot turnings temper sobriety. Rich in figurative language, Fleischman's short story collections, *Graven Images* (1982), a Newbery Honor Book, and *Coming-and-Going Men* (1985), have been compared to the masterly tales of Hawthorne and Poe for their suspense, macabre tone, and ironic twists of plot.

Fleischman's work contains myriad images of bird and insect life. *Townsend's Warbler* (1992), the lyric chronicle of naturalist John Kirk Townsend's discovery of a new specimen of bird, draws directly on Fleischman's enthusiasm for natural history, as do the companion volumes of poetry *I Am Phoenix* (1985) and *Joyful Noise* (1988). Sound and word again dovetail to create poems "to be read aloud by two readers at once," the two parts "meshing as in a musical duet." *I Am Phoenix* features birds, from the passenger pigeon to the cormorant; *Joyful Noise,* the 1989 Newbery Medal winner, celebrates the "booming / boisterous / joyful noise" of the insect world. Keen observation and skilled imagery ensure that the birds and insects retain their true nature, providing a fascinating glimpse into the natural world. These inventive books of verse take their rightful place as some of this wordsmith's most remarkable work. C.S.

Fleischman expanded his exploration of choral verse, offering poems about ghosts and middle school gossip in *Big Talk: Poems for Four Voices* (2000.) Novels such as *Seedfolks* (1997) and *Whirligig* (1998) also utilize a multivoice format as numerous narrators with diverse speech patterns each contribute small pieces to larger stories. Several of the author's books are well suited to reader's theater — particularly *The Mind's Eye* (1999), in which the relationship between a teenage paraplegic and an elderly woman is presented using only dialogue and stage directions. This technique is employed even more effectively in *Seek* (2001), as Rob, searching for the disc jockey father who abandoned him, creates a senior thesis composed solely of dialogue, radio broadcasts, and bits of music. In both verse and prose, Fleischman has continued to reveal the lyricism in everyday language and the poetry of the spoken word. P.D.S.

Fleischman, Sid

American author, b. 1920. When humorist Albert Sidney Fleischman wrote *The Whipping Boy* (1986), he deviated from his usual American tall-tale humor, a hallmark of many of his novels, and created a broadly comic tale, with an Old World flavor, set in an undefined time and place. It won the 1987 Newbery Medal. A whipping boy was "a young boy kept by royal households, educated with a prince, and punished in his stead." In the tale, a bored Prince Brat forces Jemmy, his whipping boy, to escape the castle confines with him. They immediately fall into the hands of the villainous Hold-Your-Nose Billy, "who smells like a ton of garlic," and his sidekick. While the boys are catapulted through adventures and hair-breadth escapes — all richly spiced with comedy — they become friends. As in much of Fleischman's writing, beneath the surface of the rapid, hard-fire entertainment, the story resonates with important universal themes such as trust, friendship, courage, justice, and — above all — humor in the face of disaster.

Few contemporary writers have infused comedy into children's books as successfully as Fleischman. He has tapped into the deep, rich vein of American frontier humor, adding his own brand of engaging, convoluted plots, peppery language, and a cast of picturesque characters dubbed with outrageous names. One of the finest examples he so facilely created is *Humbug Mountain* (1978), winner of the 1979 Boston Globe–Horn Book Award. The hilarious story features a family down on their luck, roaming the West looking for Grandpa. While searching, they find a ghost-haunted riverboat, inadver-

tently start a gold rush, discover a petrified man, and straighten out the villains who plague them. Fleischman, a skillful writer, has handily combined history with adventure and serious statements with fast-paced plots, and he has laced his tales with delightful doses of wild humor, as in *Chancy and the Grand Rascal* (1966) and *Jim Ugly* (1992). Although Fleischman's novels are exactly right for middle school readers, his McBroom series ranks as high humor with early elementary children. During his thirty years as a writer, Fleischman has seen "the status of humor in children's novels change immensely. In my first story, *Mr. Mysterious and Company* (1962), about a family of traveling magicians, I was asked to take out some of the humor, because editors were afraid reviewers would dismiss the book as a joke. Today, humor is enjoyed and no longer regarded as literary brummagem."

Fleischman grew up in California, where, before becoming an author, he pursued many lines of work. In *The Abracadabra Kid: A Writer's Life* (1996), he recounted some of the events that finally led to his writing career — including his stint as a magician. Prestidigitators often find their way into his books. *The Midnight Horse* (1990) is a story about an orphan, a blacksmith, a thief, and the ghost of the Great Chaffalo, a once-celebrated magician. Fleischman's son, PAUL FLEISCHMAN, himself a children's book author, paid an appropriate tribute to his father's books when he wrote, "When [my father] gave up being a magician, he became a prestidigitator of words, palming plot elements, making villains vanish, producing solutions out of thin air. He knows how to keep an audience guessing, how to create suspense, how to keep readers reading." This is why new generations continue to discover and delight in the surprises found in Sid Fleischman's books. S.L.

Fleming, Denise

American author and illustrator, b. 1950. As a child, Fleming was always making things: clothespin Pilgrims, huge treasure eggs that opened, and a school report on George Washington in the shape of George's head. These projects were a portent of her future.

She grew up in a middle-class family in Toledo, Ohio. Her father spent his free time building furniture, and her mother was active in local theater; she and her sister divided their time between "making things" and neighborhood productions of plays, complete with commercials. In the third grade she was chosen to participate in classes at the Toledo Museum of Art. When she was eleven or twelve, one of her paintings appeared on the cover of a teachers' magazine.

Fleming began her career as an illustrator in the 1980s, successfully working in advertising and the toy and craft market as well as illustrating mass market children's books by other authors, including licensed characters such as Care Bears and Charmkins. She describes her first books as her "rikki-tikki" style, using colored pencil and watercolors. Even though she tried different materials and techniques, her paintings ended up looking "rikki-tikki."

A serendipitous discovery changed that. When Fleming enrolled in a papermaking class, she became was so fascinated that she took another course, which led her to develop her own method of painting with paper pulp. Fleming's signature technique involves pouring colored paper pulp through hand-cut stencils. She applies her "paper paint" with squeeze bottles in place of brushes. The layered pulp creates dimension. The resulting scenes and images are bold, colorful, and childlike. She has described the process as cathartic, "wet, messy, and wonderful."

Fleming debuted this medium with *In the Tall, Tall Grass* (1991), which illustrates a caterpillar's point of view of other creatures in the yard, emboldened with the intense colors of a hot summer day. The unique book garnered immediate attention and a Boston Globe–Horn Book Award. Samples from her papermaking class became her next book, *Lunch* (1992), a tale of a greedy mouse who eats its way through a vegetarian feast. It was quickly followed by *Count* (1992), an introduction to numbers. Next came *In the Small, Small Pond* (1993), a com-

panion to *In the Tall, Tall Grass*, which offers a frog's-eye view of nature and was chosen as a Caldecott Honor Book. Fleming continued her charming ANIMAL STORIES with *Barnyard Banter* (1994), *Where Once There Was a Wood* (1996), *Time to Sleep* (1997), and *Mama Cat Has Three Kittens* (1998).

With *The Everything Book* (2000), Fleming switched her focus from nature stories to children. This lively collection of toddlers' favorite things includes words, numbers, poems, and concepts, illustrated with dazzling color-drenched pictures. The book was an instant favorite. *Pumpkin Pie* (2001) evokes the spooky delights of Halloween with clever couplets.

Fleming's exuberant art combines fluid design, precision, and exceptional compositions with evocative language. Completely integrated, her writing and artwork immerse children in a wonderful realm of creativity. J.C.

Folklore

See AMERICAN FOLKLORE.

Forbes, Esther

American historical novelist, 1891–1967. Esther Forbes, an important historical novelist, secured a permanent place in children's literature with the publication of *Johnny Tremain* (1943), winner of the Newbery Medal. Praised by the *New York Times* as a "novelist who wrote like a historian and a historian who wrote like a novelist" and noted for her understanding of human nature, Forbes presented the events behind the American Revolution through the eyes of a young boy. The story spans two years in the life of Johnny Tremain, a young orphan and arrogant silversmith's apprentice. While casting the handle of a sugar basin for John Hancock, he burns his right hand as a result of the actions of the despicable young Dove and must give up his beloved craft. Crippled and bitter, Johnny endures difficult days before finding work as a horse-boy riding for the patriotic newspaper the

Boston *Observer* and as a messenger for the Sons of Liberty. His new work brings him in touch with Rab, an aloof and intriguing young printer who becomes his closest friend. The historical figures Sam Adams, James Otis, Dr. Joseph Warren, and General Thomas Gage are important to the plot and are brought engagingly alive in Forbes's treatment.

Though she was not a professional historian, Forbes won a Pulitzer Prize in history in 1942 for the adult book *Paul Revere and the World He Lived In.* As a result of her research, she became interested in the lives of the apprentices in and about the shops and wharves of Boston during the eighteenth century. As she explained, "It was a horse-boy who brought word to Paul Revere that the British intended to march out of Boston on the night of April in '75. This little incident teased my mind." In her Newbery Medal acceptance speech in 1944, Forbes drew parallels between the Revolutionary War and Pearl Harbor: "In peace times countries are apt to look upon their boys under twenty as mere children and (for better or worse) to treat them as such. When war comes, these boys are suddenly asked to play their part as men. I knew I wanted to show the boys and girls of today how difficult were those other children's lives by modern standards. They were not allowed to be children for very long."

Forbes's vision of the Revolution is clearly reflected in her young protagonist's vision. In presenting some of the economic motivations behind the war, the author asked, "Weren't the Americans after all human beings?" Johnny, however, discovers with James Otis that revolution is "for something more than our pocketbooks." Johnny discovers a dying Rab and later reflects, "True, Rab had died. Hundreds would die, but not the thing they died for." Johnny's stance on the war is not based on the rhetoric that surrounds him. Although he is a patriot who believes in the cause, he also recognizes the personal sacrifices and loss involved, and Forbes indeed evoked with sympathy for both sides the common heritage of the British and the Americans.

What is remarkable about this vividly drawn work are the details that make the characters and the drama of the Revolution so real. Woven throughout the historical aspects of the historical tale is Johnny's own odyssey. In the beginning Johnny's talent and status in a household of less skilled and duller boys have made him arrogant and disdainful. His plunge into humiliation and an uncertain future ultimately changes the course of his development and destiny. In the end Johnny never receives the great fortune or success he hopes for. When Dr. Warren offers to operate on his hand, it is so the boy can hold a musket and fight among the ranks of young men serving their country and their beliefs, not to achieve the high honor and distinction accorded the famous patriots who appear in the novel. Yet Johnny becomes a hero, an emblem of sacrifice and spirit, both inspiring and real to generations of young readers. C.L.

Fox, Mem

Australian writer, b. 1946. Teacher, writer, and storyteller, Mem Fox was born in Melbourne, Australia, but spent only six months there before her missionary parents whisked her away to Rhodesia (now Zimbabwe). There she grew up happily, riding donkeys, climbing trees, writing stories, and reading voraciously. She had every intention of becoming a writer until the age of about thirteen, when the bright lights of the stage caught her eye. In 1965 she set off for drama school in London. She spent three years "learning how to act, being forced to learn how to teach, and accidentally learning how to write." Although the experience eventually cured her of her interest in acting, it also, she has claimed, bestowed on her an "important and lasting gift . . . the gift of language." When she did finally return to Australia in 1970, her English husband accompanied her, and they settled in Adelaide, where their daughter was born. Teaching — "my real occupation, about which I'm passionate and about which I never throw tantrums" — began in Adelaide, where she taught drama in secondary schools and eventually became a senior lecturer in drama and language at Sturt College.

But in 1975 Fox also enrolled as a student at Flinders University. There she began studying children's literature. In its most embryonic stages, *Possum Magic* (1983), Fox's first book, went by the title of *Hush, the Invisible Mouse* and was written as an assignment for a children's literature course. The intrepid student/author then wrote to illustrator Julie Vivas, asking her to illustrate the hefty 1,400-word manuscript. Nine publishers rejected the result. Then, on the condition that it be rewritten and reillustrated, with the mice changed to possums, the setting altered to Australia, and the text cut by two-thirds, the small independent publisher Omnibus Books accepted and published *Possum Magic*. Since this magical "bush" story was first published, it has sold hundreds of thousands of copies in various forms — a phenomenon in Australian publishing. Mem Fox has proceeded to create a number of effervescent PICTURE BOOK texts, including *Hattie and the Fox* (1986), illustrated by Patricia Mullins; *Night Noises* (1989), illustrated by Terry Denton; *Time for Bed* (1993), illustrated by Jane Dyer; and the well-loved *Wilfrid Gordon McDonald Partridge* (1985). In this book, illustrated by Julie Vivas, a little boy comes to appreciate the meaning of memory through his visits to an old people's home.

In addition to her children's books, Mem Fox is also the author of works such as a guide to teaching drama to children and an autobiography that fizzes and sparkles with her enthusiastic personality. She has endeared herself to readers worldwide. But her wonderful storytelling abilities, her legendary teaching style, and her writing have made her a truly extraordinary figure in her native country. As a salute to her remarkable contributions, she received the 1990 Dromkeen Medal, Australia's prestigious award for an overall contribution to children's literature.   K.J.

Fox, Paula

American author, b. 1923. Paula Fox, born in New York City, was educated at schools in Cuba and Canada as well as in the United States, a childhood she has described in her memoir, *Borrowed Finery* (2001). She has been a student at the Juilliard School, a teacher, a journalist, and a writer for television as well as an author. She is married to Martin Greenberg and has two sons by a previous marriage. Among her many honors are a Guggenheim fellowship and a National Institute of Arts and Letters Award in 1972, the Newbery Medal in 1974, and — in the same year — an award from the National Endowment for the Arts. In 1978 she won the most prestigious of awards in the field of children's literature, the Hans Christian Andersen Award, given for the author's body of work.

Paula Fox is a writer of distinction, producing four adult novels and many children's books, from such early stories for younger readers as *Maurice's Room* (1966), her first book, to more intricate and equally moving novels for older children. She attracted from the start devoted readers and appreciative reviews. When, in *Maurice's Room,* Maurice withstands parental wiles and continues to amass "things," young readers recognize a kindred spirit. His room is a collector's joy and a mother's despair. As is often the case in Fox's books, Maurice is an only child, a fact that focuses the story on adult-child relationships.

Also without siblings, Lewis in *A Likely Place* (1967) has been left in the care of delightfully peculiar Miss Fitchlow when his loving parents go off on a brief trip. Lewis is tired of being directed by adults, however loving, who want to help him improve, so his meeting in the park with elderly Mr. Madruga brings instant rapport. Like Lewis, the older man craves independence, and he asks the boy to write to his children, who have forced him into a life of ease. Both of these books have a quiet humor; both are written with fine-honed simplicity.

Of all the early books, perhaps *How Many Miles to Babylon?* (1967) drew the most attention. This was due in part to the drama and suspense of the story line and in part to the fact that the central character is a child who — unlike Maurice and Lewis — is coping with disruption and loss. James is ten, living with three aunts because his disturbed mother is in custodial care. Imaginative and lonely, the small, shy African American boy encounters a gang that is stealing dogs; the gang members force James to go with them to Coney Island as their prisoner. Both his escape and his reunion with his mother are believable, a satisfying conclusion to the reader's suspense.

In *The Stone-Faced Boy* (1968), Gus, who is shy and withdrawn, takes refuge from his boisterous family by maintaining an impassive façade. Only one elderly relative sees the sensitivity behind the stoic mask. The same empathic relationship between a child and someone out of his habitual environment is used in a book for older readers, *Portrait of Ivan* (1969). Here there is a special understanding between motherless Ivan and the man who is painting his portrait, and both of them have confidence in an elderly woman companion. Through the strength gained from their support, Ivan finds the courage to approach his busy, remote father.

The insight and compassion that illuminate Ivan's story are equally apparent in *Blowfish Live in the Sea* (1970) and *One-Eyed Cat* (1984). In the former, the bonds of family love are exemplified in a young girl's acceptance of her half-brother's frailties. Carrie goes with Ben to meet his father, an irresponsible man, weak but lovable, whose absence and garrulous mendacity have embittered his son. Ben, nevertheless, decides to stay with his father. Astutely — and effectively — the author did not *tell* the reader but let Ben's love and acceptance *show* in his words and deeds. The fact that the story is told by Carrie produces a convincing picture of the several relationships and of the maturation that leads to tolerance.

One-Eyed Cat is outstanding for the depth of its insight, the nuance of its writing style, and the many-layered development of its characters. Although Ned has been told not to use an air rifle, he sneaks out one night to try it, then fears he has shot something that moved. He is racked by remorse and guilt. His shame and regret are the core of a sensitive story that develops smoothly and powerfully.

In *The Moonlight Man* (1986), Fox showed

the anguished ambivalence of a child's love for an alcoholic father. Like Ben in *Blowfish*, Catherine grows in understanding through the love and patience that enable her to see past her father's manipulative behavior to his pain. A child also deals with the effects of alcoholism in a family member, albeit more obliquely than does Catherine, in *The Village by the Sea* (1988). Because her father is having heart surgery and her mother is staying with him, Emma has been sent to her aunt's home. Aunt Bea, who has a history of alcoholism, is an unhappy, angry woman whose pervasive hostility includes her niece; she demolishes the miniature village Emma and a friend have painstakingly constructed of found objects on the seashore. The characterization has depth and consistency, and both motivation and relationships have an intricacy that never impinges on the clarity and focus of the story.

In *Monkey Island* (1991) Fox created one of the most touching and trenchant stories of homeless people that has been written for young readers. Clay is eleven; his father has decamped and now Clay's pregnant mother has abandoned him in their dingy hotel. Clay takes refuge with an odd couple of street people — an elderly alcoholic man and a young African American man become Clay's family. There is a reunion, at the end, between mother and son, but the message is that all love is sustaining.

The Slave Dancer (1973) is Fox's only work of HISTORICAL FICTION; in her acceptance speech for the Newbery Medal, she spoke of slaves as "pioneers of the human condition in inhuman circumstances." Fourteen-year-old Jessie is horrified to discover that he's been impressed into service as a "slave dancer," playing his fife to keep slave-ship captives active and more salable. The book is a powerful indictment of the horrors of the slave trade as well as a somber, moving story.

In all her writing Paula Fox has addressed the resilience of the human spirit; her special gift is that she sees the child's viewpoint while feeling the sympathy of an adult and the detachment of an observer. Her children move us because they are so true. One of the finest stylists writing for children today, Fox has the rare ability to create worlds that involve her readers, yet she never comes between the book and the reader. z.s.

Freedman, Russell

American nonfiction author, b. 1929. Born in San Francisco and educated at the University of California, Berkeley, Freedman is best described by the term *Renaissance man*. His résumé is long and varied: newsman at the Associated Press, television publicity writer, editor, and instructor at the New School for Social Research. But it is when he wears his hat as writer of over forty INFORMATION BOOKS that he truly embodies the concept.

Freedman's books can be divided into two general areas: science and social studies, specifically American history. In each book, regardless of its topic, he has carefully combined text and black-and-white photographs to create a medium in which the words reveal something hidden in the pictures and the pictures illuminate the unspoken words. The actions, behaviors, and peculiarities of the animal kingdom serve as the focus for the majority of Freedman's science books. From his first animal book, *How Animals Learn* (1969), to his twenty-third, *Sharks* (1985), Freedman has continued to present facts in a straightforward fashion. Not merely an encyclopedic catalogue, his books also possess a writing style that conveys a subtle sense of drama that intrigues as well as instructs. Two of his books have received national awards: *Hanging On: How Animals Carry Their Own* (1977) was honored by the New York Academy of Science, and *Animal Superstars* (1984), by the National Science Teachers Association.

In order to immerse himself fully in the history of his social studies subject, he often has gone on location with a book, traveling across the country to search for archival photographs that complement the text. A number of Freedman's books focus on the nineteenth-century American West. *Children of the Wild West* (1983), winner of the National Cowboy Hall of Fame's Western Heritage Award and a Boston Globe–Horn Book Honor Book, recounts the experiences of children traveling in covered wagons across the country and the American Indian children they meet along the way. *Cowboys of the Wild West* (1985) looks at the men who inspired the legends without belittling the real place the cowboy has in history and fiction. *Indian Chiefs* (1987) tells the story of six Indian chiefs who served during a critical point in their tribe's history; the tone, while always nonjudgmental, betrays an underlying sympathy for the American Indians' resistance. *Buffalo Hunt* (1988) follows as a logical extension of the three previous works, chronicling American Indian lore and hunting practices. *An Indian Winter* (1992), based on the journal of German prince Maximilian, describes the winter of 1833–34, when the prince and his party lived with American Indian tribes in North Dakota.

Of all his books, it is his BIOGRAPHIES — which include bibliographies and lists of places to visit — for which Freedman has become best known. Winner of the 1988 Newbery Medal, *Lincoln* is a chronological examination of the times and the life, personal characteristics, and career of Abraham Lincoln, with an emphasis on the politics of slavery and the Civil War. There have been more books written about Lincoln than any other American. Freedman's portrait, however, does not just repeat the myths that surround the Lincoln persona; rather, his Lincoln is a man of integrity, deeply troubled by the evils of slavery and by the overwhelming human loss of the Civil War. *Franklin Delano Roosevelt* (1990), winner of the Orbis Pictus Award for outstanding nonfiction books, traces the personal and public events in the life of Roosevelt and tells the story of the era in which he was president; *Eleanor Roosevelt: A Life of Discovery* (1993) was named a Newbery Honor Book. *The Wright Brothers: How They Invented the Airplane* (1991), a Boston Globe–Horn Book Honor Book and a 1992 Newbery Honor Book, tells both the story of Orville and Wilbur Wright and the history of flight. Freedman won the Washington Post–Children's Book Guild Nonfiction Award, the Regina Medal, and the Laura Ingalls Wilder Award for the body of his work. His personal hope that his books "will be read willingly, read from beginning to end with a sense of discovery and with a feeling of genuine pleasure" is being fulfilled. M.I.A.

Voices of the Creators

Russell Freedman

My father was a great storyteller. The problem was, we never knew for sure whether the stories he told were fiction or nonfiction. He was also a dedicated bookman. In fact, my parents met in a San Francisco bookshop. She was a sales clerk, and he was a sales representative for a big publishing house. They held their first conversation over a stack of bestsellers, and before they knew it, they were married. I had the good fortune to grow up in a house filled with books and book talk.

As a young man, I worked as a journalist and later as a television publicity writer before discovering my true vocation. One day I happened to read a newspaper article about a sixteen-year-old boy who was blind; he had invented a Braille typewriter. That seemed remarkable, but as I read on, I learned something even more amazing: the Braille system itself was invented by another sixteen-year-old boy who was blind, Louis Braille. That newspaper article inspired my first book, a collection of BIOGRAPHIES called *Teenagers Who Made History* (1961).

I hadn't expected to become a writer of nonfiction books for children. I had wandered into the field by chance and immediately felt right at home. I couldn't wait to get started on my next book. It was as if I had found myself — even though I hadn't really known that I had been lost.

The term *nonfiction* has always seemed unfortunate to me, because it is so negative. Fiction implies art, imagination, creativity. We take it for granted that good fiction will be a pleasure to read. Nonfiction is supposed to be utilitarian. It's expected to do its duty — to inform, instruct, enlighten. And yet a hard-working, nose-to-the-grindstone nonfiction book should be just as absorbing as any imaginary story, because it is, in fact, a story, too.

After all, there's a story to almost everything. The task of the nonfiction writer is to find the story — the narrative line — that exists in nearly every subject, be it the life of a person or the life of a cell.

Writers of nonfiction have traditionally been storytellers. The word *history,* remember, is made up mostly of the word *story;* it derives from the Greek *historein,* "to inquire"; a *histōr* was a learned man. Going all the way back to Homer and beyond, historians have been storytellers sitting around the fire inside the cave, holding their audience spellbound on a winter's night.

When I begin a new book, that's the tradition I like to remember. I think of myself first of all as a storyteller, and I do my best to give dramatic shape to my subject, whatever it is. I always feel that I have a story to tell that is worth telling, and I want to tell it as clearly, as simply, and as forcefully as I can.

By storytelling, I do not mean making things up, of course. I don't mean invented scenes or manufactured dialogue or imaginary characters. As a writer of nonfiction, I have a pact with the reader to stick to the facts, to be as factually accurate as human frailty will allow. What I write is based on research. And yet there are many storytelling techniques that I can use without straying from the straight and narrow path of factual accuracy. Facts in a literal sense do not rule out art, imagination, or creativity.

When I speak of nonfiction storytelling, I'm using the word *story* in the sense of igniting the reader's imagination, evoking pictures and scenes in the reader's mind. Storytelling means creating vivid and believable people, places, and events — creating a convincing, meaningful, and memorable world. It means pulling the reader into that world. And it means using a narrative framework, a storytelling voice, that will keep the reader turning those pages.

As I work on a book, I'm hoping to change the landscape of the reader's mind — to leave the reader with a thought, a perception, an insight that he or she did not have before. If I write about sharks or rattlesnakes, I want the reader to come away from my book with a greater appreciation of these remarkable living creatures and their place in nature. If I write about frontier children, or Abraham Lincoln, or the Wright brothers, I want to leave the reader with a deeper understanding of our nation's history and a feeling of kinship with people of another era. But most of all, I want to write a book that will be read from beginning to end with a mounting sense of anticipation and discovery — read willingly, with a feeling of genuine pleasure. ⚑

Freeman, Don

American illustrator and author, 1908–1978. Born in San Diego, California, Don Freeman relocated to New York City in the late 1920s to make a living as a musician. A talented amateur artist, Freeman also studied at the Art Students League. Ironically, his permanent career in illustration began by accident. Traveling home one evening, he was so engrossed in sketching his fellow passengers that he left his trumpet lying on the seat as the train sped away. Freeman eventually found work as a freelance graphic artist covering the New York theater scene and contributing to the *New York Times,* the New York *Herald Tribune,* and numerous theater publications.

Then he discovered an outlet for his flair for the dramatic in writing and illustrating original PICTURE BOOKS for children. *Pet of the Met* (1953), a collaboration with his wife, Lydia, tells the story of a mouse maestro named Petrini who works as a page turner at the Metropolitan Opera. His nemesis, Mefisto the cat, lives in the basement, detesting mice and music with equal measure. The commotion that results when cat meets mouse is illustrated in wild, colorful chase scenes that culminate in a glorious finale as Mefisto falls under the spell of the music and is transformed.

Norman the Doorman (1959) relates the tale of Norman, a basement doorman in a large city museum who gives guided tours of the treasure-filled basement and dabbles in art and sculpture in his free time. After Norman's mousetrap masterpiece wins a prize in the museum's contest, Norman's talent is unveiled, and he receives a long-awaited tour of the museum upstairs. In *Bearymore* (1976) Freeman turned to the circus, where a performing bear must cope with both hibernation *and* developing a new act before spring. Using simple yellow-wash and pencil drawings, Freeman captured the animation of the circus and the sleepy activity of hibernation.

Freeman's work is extremely popular among very young children, to whom his basic texts and gentle messages are highly appealing. Both *Mop Top* (1955), the tale of an ornery redhead who refuses to get his hair cut, and *Dandelion* (1964), the story of a lion who remodels himself to the extent that nobody recognizes him, offer mild cautions against pretentiousness and stubbornness within deceptively simple, humorous tales. The most enduring of his books, *Corduroy* (1968), is the tale of a plain department-store bear badly in need of a home. In order to present his best appearance, Corduroy searches the store after hours to replace a missing button on his overalls. Children responded so well to this unpretentious story that Freeman was persuaded to revive the bear in *A Pocket for Corduroy* (1978), his last work. There is a cosmopolitan aspect to Freeman's books that comes from years of observation. *Inspector Peckit* (1972), for example, a Parisian pigeon private eye, bears an uncanny resemblance to another famous French detective, and Freeman's subtle illustrations take anthropomorphic expression to amusing heights.

Despite the subtle humor of some of his allusions, Freeman never lost sight of the childlike. His understated artwork and his creative treatments of his themes led to charming books that feature an unmistakable sincerity. M.O'D.H.

Fritz, Jean

American author, b. 1915. The publication of the refreshing and unconventional biographical vignettes *And Then What Happened, Paul Revere?* (1973), *Why Don't You Get a Horse, Sam Adams?* (1974), *Will You Sign Here, John Hancock?* (1976), and *What's the Big Idea, Ben Franklin?* (1976) in the 1970s clearly established Jean Fritz at the forefront of a handful of authors who have mastered the art of writing BIOGRAPHIES for children. Her distinctive style continues to enliven history and make the complicated lives and events of the past accessible to younger readers.

Fritz has been writing HISTORICAL FICTION for children since 1958, when *The Cabin Faced West,* a pioneer story about her great-great-grandmother, was published. Her earlier books, although not biographies, are firmly grounded in historical events. *Brady* (1960), for example, is set just before the Civil War and tells a runaway slave's story; its depth and drama are the result of vivid characterization and an honest depiction of the moral issues surrounding the abolitionist movement. In *I, Adam* (1963) and *Early Thunder* (1967), both set in New England, strong protagonists come of age against the background of turbulent periods in American history.

When Fritz began writing her "question biographies" (so named because the titles ask questions) for young readers, her irrepressible sense of humor and unique talent for "turning history inside out" was a breath of fresh air for younger minds who, upon reading the short biographies, discovered that learning about history could be fun. Fritz explained her purpose for writing these stories about several leaders in the American Revolution: "My objective was modest. I simply wanted to persuade children that these men were once truly alive, that history is made of the same stuff as our own lives. I hoped children would understand people and their paradoxes, without passing judgment or dividing them up into good and bad."

For thirty years her books have earned awards and honors and are always on best-books lists for young readers. Her autobiography, *Homesick: My Own Story,* was a Newbery Honor Book, and in 1983 *The Double Life of Pocahontas* won the Boston Globe–Horn Book Award for nonfiction. In 1986 Fritz was honored with the Laura Ingalls Wilder Award, which is presented to an author whose books have made an enduring contribution to children's literature.

Jean Fritz's reputation for bringing history to life rests on her ability to combine humorous and humanizing details with factual material. There are many humorous touches about the famous patriot from old Boston in *And Then What Happened, Paul Revere?* Children delight in the fact that Revere was not only a secret agent and express rider for the American Revolutionary forces, but he also made false teeth. And they will discover he was in such a hurry to make his famous ride that he forgot his spurs and sent the dog home with a note so his wife could attach the spurs to the dog's collar. Mistrusting reverence and emphasizing the human side of heroism, Fritz revealed in *Where Do You Think You're Going, Christopher Columbus?* (1980) that the explorer was a hot-tempered, stubborn man, who died thoroughly convinced he had discovered the Indies and China.

Her books have lasting popularity because she has written with directness and integrity while speaking unpatronizingly to young people. Commenting on her unconventional, often humorous approach toward writing, Fritz has said: "I realized when I started doing research for my first book that history wasn't what I'd been taught in school. History is full of gossip; it's real people and emotion. I kept being surprised by the real people I met in the past. They all had their foibles and idiosyncrasies."

Though humor often peppers her stories, in books for older readers Fritz has not sidestepped exploring serious issues or exposing the darker side of characters and events. The highly acclaimed *Traitor: The Case of Benedict Arnold* (1981) is a gripping historical thriller that reveals examples of Arnold's twisted personality from his childhood through his betrayal of the Revolutionary forces. Nor will readers find a typical history-book account of Chief Powhatan's daughter in *The Double Life of Pocahontas*. The thought-provoking story clearly shows the young girl as a pawn of history, trapped in the terrible dilemma of living between two cultures.

Fritz has not gone looking for ideas. "A character in history will suddenly step right out of the past and demand a book. Once my character and I reach an understanding," she has explained, "then I begin the detective work." Accuracy and meticulous research are hallmarks of her writing. "I want to get inside my characters and to do this I have to, first of all, get into their times." She has read old books, letters, and newspapers and has visited places where her subjects lived.

Fritz has attributed her preoccupation with research and writing about American history to her own personal search for roots. As a child of missionary parents, she lived in China for the first thirteen years of her life, where, she has admitted, she spent a great deal of time "wondering what it was like to be an American."

For many years, she wanted to write about life in China, but not until her father's death did she feel an urgency to record her childhood. In 1982 *Homesick: My Own Story*, which combines her early personal search for her imagined homeland with a child's view of the poverty and political turbulence in China in the 1920s, was published. "I needed to write *Homesick* before I returned to China," Fritz commented, "so I wouldn't mix up the present with memories." Fifty-five years after she left China she returned to see what Mao Tse-tung and the Cultural Revolution had wrought. In 1985 she wrote *China Homecoming*, which was followed by *China's Long March* (1988), an excellent introductory volume about Mao's legendary march through China and the beginning of the Cultural Revolution.

Whether she is writing for younger children or for young adults, Fritz's tactics for revealing her characters have always been brilliantly conceived; her knack for effectively highlighting each character's personal eccentricities successfully hooks even reluctant readers. The difficulty for the biographer is to develop not only an accurate picture of the subject at hand but an accurate sense and representation of historical facts, all set within a lively text that does not appear to teach or preach. Many biographers falter. Narratives that successfully mix humor, humanism, and history are rare. But Jean Fritz has found the appropriate blend, and her remarkable style enables her to extract the essence of her protagonists' accomplishments and characters and to place them firmly within the context of their times. S.L.

Voices of the Creators

❧ Jean Fritz

If I arrange the books I've written chronologically on a shelf according to where they fit into American history, I am surprised at how much time they cover — from Columbus to Teddy Roosevelt. I didn't do this deliberately. I have just dropped in on people where and when I've found them — people whose lives seemed to fall into a story shape and whose stories I felt an urgency to tell.

There are over twenty books of nonfiction dealing with American history on my shelf, and as I look at it, I think — well, that's where I've always wanted to be, right in the middle of what's happening. It is not that I am sentimental about the past, but ever since childhood I've wanted to be where it's *at*. The heroine of my first historical book, *The Cabin Faced West* (1958) — which happened to be HISTORICAL FICTION — expresses my feeling. She complains that she is stuck in an out-of-the-way place where, as she says, "nothing ever happens." Although in reality there are few places where nothing ever happens, I longed to be at the center — not of textbook history, but of *real* history.

I would be pleased if this shelf of books turned

out to be useful to teachers, but I am not thinking in curriculum terms. I feel more like a journalist covering my beat. I am in no position to penetrate current history with the same depth as I can the past, where the record has come in, where the story can be examined as a whole. My beat may lie in another time, but my approach is that of a reporter, trying for a scoop, looking for clues, connecting facts, digging under the surface.

Most important, I am tracking down people. As far as I am concerned, there can be no understanding history without coming to terms with the makers and shakers, the oppressed and the oppressors, and seeing how they have been shaped by their times and in turn have shaped them. Enough of their personal record must be available so that I can attempt to figure out why they became who they were. In most instances, their childhood has been of primary importance to me. I could never have understood Stonewall Jackson, for instance, or Benedict Arnold or Teddy Roosevelt or, more recently, Harriet Beecher Stowe without meeting them first as children. In each case the central problem they struggled with their entire lives was the one they were dealt in childhood. It is at the heart of the interplay between their personal and public lives.

I like to think of a historian or a biographer as an artist who has made a compact with the past to be true to it. As an artist, the historian has to use his or her imagination to penetrate the record, to dig deep down into the past to the place where life emerges. At its best, the imaginative process is an electrical experience: the writer comes to the place where sparks fly, and, if all goes well, the excitement is passed on to the reader. The kind of imagination that is required is one that shakes up the twenty-first-century mindset, transports the reader and writer alike into another world of place and time and rules and habits. The purpose and reward both of reading and writing BIOGRAPHY, it seems to me, are to gain insight into the human condition. It is invigorating to step out of the limitations of one's own self and time and to experience life as someone else.

I've been asked if I always *like* my characters. It goes deeper than that. I have to *understand* them. There may be something of a love-hate relationship, but at the very least I have to feel compassion. I expect there is a certain amount of chemistry at work as I take on a character. Moreover, the chemistry has to work both ways. I feel that the character steps up to speak to me. When James Madison spoke (in a whisper, of course, as he always spoke), I thought he'd got me wrong. I didn't see his story possibilities, but he was insistent, and he was right. He was such a committed man that his story and the country's ran on the same path, with the same emotional ups and downs. I ended up admiring him more than anyone I've written about.

In my books for younger children, I've tried to catch my characters quickly, on the fly. The books are shorter; the style is brisker and, wherever possible, humorous. Indeed, throughout my work, when there is a hint of humor in the material, I pounce on it.

It is not surprising that biography should lead to autobiography. *Homesick: My Own Story* (1982) does not fit on my American history shelf, yet it belongs near it. The story of my childhood in China establishes, I think, why I am so preoccupied with America.

G

Gág, Wanda

American author and illustrator, 1893–1946. Ernestine Evans, editor for a new publisher, was determined to make children's books using the best fine-art artists in America. She knew the art of Wanda Gág — Gág's pictures, she recollected, were "beautiful, and very simple, and full of the wonder of common things." So Evans made an appointment to meet her at the Weyhe Gallery in New York, where Gág was having a one-woman show. Out of that meeting came the classic favorite *Millions of Cats* (1928). Evans said, "When we had in the office the marvelous manuscript of *Millions of Cats,* I hugged myself, as children all over the country have been doing ever since."

The simple story, with its roots grounded in folklore, tells of a lonely old man and a lonely old woman who just want a kitten to love. So the old man trudges over hills and valleys until "he came to a hill which was quite covered with cats." And with this, Gág introduced the silly, lyrical lines that have delighted children for more than sixty years: "Cats here, cats there, Cats and kittens everywhere. Hundreds of cats, Thousands of cats, Millions and billions and trillions of cats." Of course, when the old man tries to choose among them, he ends up liking them all, for each one is as pretty as the next. When he brings these hundreds of cats back home, he and the old woman have to choose just one. The cats fight over who is the prettiest, and when they are done, only one very ugly kitten is left. The ending, as the kitten turns into the most beautiful cat in the world through loving care, is shown primarily through Gág's soft, round illustrations, lively with humor. The entire book is done in black and white — "small, sturdy peasant drawings," Gág called them, and the hand-lettered text, done by her brother, is as solid and round as the pictures.

The strength of *Millions of Cats* is that it has its roots in a compelling childhood. Wanda Gág was the eldest of seven children in a German family in New Ulm, Minnesota. Both her parents were artists; her father, in particular, had talent that was frustrated by the needs of providing for a large family. When he died of tuberculosis, his last coherent words were whispered to his fifteen-year-old daughter: "Was der Papa nicht thun konnt', muß die Wanda halt fertig machen." — "What your Papa could not do, Wanda will have to finish." This directive en-

flamed the girl's passion for art. She studied, all expenses paid, at the St. Paul Art School, and in 1926 her first major show opened in New York. After this exhibit, Gág focused on printmaking, an art that lent itself to the bookmaking she was one day to do.

The year after *Millions of Cats,* Gág came out with *The Funny Thing* (1929), artistically distinguished but with a disappointing story, and two years later *Snippy and Snappy* (1931), the story of two young mice. She used the same technique for refining the story line in all three books: she told it again and again to all the children she knew until the words sang with rhythm and internal rhyme.

Gág worked in lithograph for the ALPHABET BOOK *The ABC Bunny* (1933), a technique of wax crayon on zinc plates that allowed for no mistakes. The medium provided her with a rich gray scale, and she played this off brilliant red capital letters. The book is a simple story of a bunny, set outdoors. The location gave Gág a framework to work out the artistic principles with which she was grappling. Especially on the page "V for View / Valley too," Gág created the rolling hills with a series of tightly formed contour lines, similar to Van Gogh's. She wrote: "Just now I'm wrangling with hills. One would never guess [they] could be composed of such a disturbing collection of planes. The trouble is each integral part insists on living a perspective life all its own." Far from the disturbing emotional quality Van Gogh projects, Gág's drawings fill the page with a sense of safe wonder.

As a children's book artist, Gág became interested in the old German *Märchen,* the folk and fairy tales of her childhood. She studied the GRIMM stories in the original German and read them in English translation. Often they felt flat, affected, and artificial to her, lacking the lively vigor of a storyteller's voice. So Gág decided to retranslate the stories, a "free" translation that would be truer to their native spirit. She found most of her childhood favorites among the Grimms' collection, but one of the funniest was missing. Gág retold from memory the story that became *Gone Is Gone; or, The Story of a Man*

Who Wanted to Do Housework (1935). A few years later she did a similar single-story volume of Snow White and the Seven Dwarfs (1938) to coincide with the release of the first Walt Disney movie, which she and many others felt had trivialized, sterilized, and sentimentalized the potent old story. In her first collection, Tales from Grimm (1936), Gág created a mesmerizing mood by using straightforward Anglo-Saxon words in rounded, repetitive lines: "A fiery dragon came flying along and lay down in the field, coiling himself in and out among the rye-stalks."

At last, by 1945, Gág felt that her life was in order: her younger brothers and sisters were all well situated; her career was blooming with awards — she had won two Newbery Honor Awards, for Millions of Cats and ABC Bunny, and two Caldecott Medals, for Snow White and Nothing at All (1941), a story about an invisible dog. She was ready to do her final volume of Grimm tales when she went to visit the doctor. Her husband, Earle Humphreys, hid the news from her: she had lung cancer and had only three months to live. They went to Florida for the warm air, and she continued working on the books from her bed. Defying all predictions, Gág lived another seventeen months, returned to her beloved home, All Creation, in the Musconetcong Mountain region of New Jersey, and very nearly completed the final volume of Grimms' tales. She left clear notes and instructions for her editor, and except for a few unfinished drawings, More Tales from Grimm (1947) was published, in the form she had planned for it, after her death.

The works that Wanda Gág created in the first half of the century are still cherished today, for in her strong, homey pictures and singing text she produced classic books that children will return to time and time again. J.A.J.

Gammell, Stephen

American illustrator, b. 1943. Every line in Stephen Gammell's distinctive illustrations is imbued with emotion. Every color and change of value creates mood. Child and adult alike will find themselves shivering, chilled by his illustrations in ALVIN SCHWARTZ's Scary Stories to Tell in the Dark (1981). His colored-pencil drawings in the Caldecott Medal–winning Song and Dance Man (1988) emanate warmth and joy. Together with Karen Ackerman's prose, they set one's feet tapping. In the Caldecott Honor Book Where the Buffaloes Begin (1981), one feels the vastness of the Western plains, the earth shuddering underneath the heavy hooves of the buffaloes. Gammell's illustrations capture the emotional impact of a story: "The first time I read a manuscript I can immediately tell whether I want to illustrate it. I may not know how the illustrations will look, but I get a certain feeling for the text. I respond to the words, and, if I can respond to a story, I can illustrate it."

Stephen Gammell was reared in Des Moines, Iowa. His father, an art editor for consumer magazines, brought home a variety of periodicals, and Gammell was impressed with the illustrations, cutting them up to make scrapbooks. His father also gave him pencils and stacks of paper, which Gammell has said were better than any toys. "My father was very encouraging. He would help me draw, supply the paper and pencils, but he would never coach me or tell me how to work. I picked up the interest on my own; my parents never pushed me. It got me through elementary school. If you could draw, the big kids were more hesitant about beating you up. I tried to make this work for me."

Gammell continued drawing on his own while attending high school and college in Iowa. In the late 1960s, in Minneapolis, he began drawing small ads for friends' neighborhood businesses. While his commercial freelance work expanded, he became interested in children's book illustration. His first book illustration contract was for A Nutty Business (1973), written by Ida Chittum. Gammell will do research for stories only if absolutely necessary, preferring to draw directly from his own imagination. He believes that trusting his own feelings and imagination results in more expressive drawings. "I am inspired by a text which gives me freedom to interpret. I don't like being tied to a specific historical time period, style of architecture or costume. I enjoy elements of fantasy in a story and turn down anything that is too literal." In the rollicking *The Relatives Came* (1985), written by CYNTHIA RYLANT, Gammell's free interpretation communicates both the exuberance and exhaustion of a family reunion.

Gammell and his wife, Linda, make their home in St. Paul, Minnesota, where he enjoys solitude and works in his studio every day. Although he has authored several of his own stories, he has found writing terribly difficult. "I think of myself as an artist — admittedly a basic term that can mean almost anything. One of the forms my art takes is book illustrations. . . . In a deep sense, I am my work — what you see on the page is really me." M.B.B.

Gannett, Ruth Chrisman; Gannett, Ruth Stiles

Ruth Chrisman: American illustrator, 1896–1979; Ruth Stiles: American author, b. 1923. Ruth Chrisman Gannett and her stepdaughter Ruth Stiles Gannett are best known for their collaboration as illustrator and author of the children's book trilogy about nine-year-old Elmer Elevator and a baby dragon.

Ruth Chrisman was born in Santa Ana, California, and began drawing at an early age. She received bachelor's and master's degrees from the University of California at Berkeley and also attended the Art Students League. She taught art in California public schools, then moved to New York, where she worked for *Vanity Fair* magazine and did freelance artwork. Among the art books she illustrated were *Sweet Land* (1934), which was written by Lewis Stiles Gannett, who became her second husband, and the Modern Library edition of John Steinbeck's *Tortilla Flat* (1937). She received a Caldecott Honor for illustrating Rebecca Reyher's *My Mother Is the Most*

Beautiful Woman in the World (1945), and her finely detailed illustrations perfectly complement the text of the Newbery Medal–winning *Miss Hickory* (1946), written by Caroline Bailey. The artist was especially good at drawing animals that are realistic yet reflect the individual personality described within the text. This talent was particularly important in drawing the cats, lions, canaries, and other animals included in the books of Ruth Stiles Gannett, who, like her stepmother, began practicing her craft at an early age.

Ruth Stiles was born and raised in New York and attended City and Country School, where creative writing was encouraged. She continued her education at a Pennsylvania boarding school and received a bachelor's degree in chemistry from Vassar College. She worked as a medical technician, waited tables, and was employed at a ski lodge. Between jobs, she spent two weeks writing a children's story, which relatives urged her to publish. *My Father's Dragon* (1948) is the entertaining tale of Elmer Elevator, who travels to a distant island to free a baby dragon enslaved by a group of wild animals. Using his wits and the contents of his knapsack — which includes chewing gum, lollipops, and hair ribbons — Elmer outwits the dragon's captors in a series of humorous episodes. Although this talking animal story reads as a whimsical fairy tale, the young hero follows his quest bravely and soberly. Gannett used the interesting technique of referring to nine-year-old Elmer as "my father" throughout, which gives the story an added dimension and also makes it a perfect choice for reading aloud. This popular title was named a Newbery Honor Book.

Ruth Stiles Gannett continued the story with *Elmer and the Dragon* (1950), which follows boy and baby dragon on their flight from the island, and *The Dragons of Blueland* (1951), which tells how Elmer helped save the dragon and his family from a new set of captors. Though these two books lack the unfettered creativity and mythic structure of the first volume, both are thoroughly enjoyable. All three are profusely illustrated by Ruth Chrisman Gannett, whose charming and funny pictures perfectly capture the tone of the writing. The author also wrote two minor children's books, *The Wonderful House-Boat-Train* (1949) and *Katie and the Sad Noise* (1961), but will be best remembered for writing the whimsical trilogy that her stepmother illustrated. P.D.S.

Gantos, Jack

American author, b. 1951. With wry and exuberant style, Jack Gantos has skillfully constructed complicated tales, both hilarious and poignant. Born in Mount Pleasant, Pennsylvania, Gantos moved frequently with his family to places such as Florida, Barbados, and Puerto Rico. This nomadic childhood led to an early devotion to keeping journals, in which Gantos found privacy, a way to cultivate his powers of observation, and a place to store his insect collection.

While attending Emerson College in Boston, Gantos met Nicole Rubel, with whom he collaborated on his first book for children, *Rotten Ralph*. Published just after Gantos graduated in 1976, the PICTURE BOOK features Ralph, a wildly mischievous cat whose owner, Sarah, always manages to forgive him no matter how badly he misbehaves. Ralph's behavior, juxtaposed with Sarah's unconditional love, appealed to young readers, and the book quickly evolved into a substantial series and, eventually, an animated television show.

Gantos remained at Emerson College to complete a master's degree in creative writing and subsequently taught there. During this time he authored a number of picture books, including *The Werewolf Family* (1980), *Sleepy Ronald* (1976), and *Fair Weather Friends* (1977), all illustrated by Nicole Rubel. Gantos's teaching expanded to the graduate level, and he became a seminal creator of master's programs in children's book writing, first at Emerson College

and later at Vermont College in Montpelier. He remained on the faculty at Emerson until 1994, when he moved to New Mexico.

Subsequent to his success as a picture book author, Gantos began to establish himself as a novelist for middle-grade and young adult audiences. His series of fictionalized memoirs feature a protagonist named Jack Henry, whose knack for bizarre explorations and creative problem solving are unmistakably reminiscent of Gantos's own childhood. In the first installment, *Heads or Tails: Stories from the Sixth Grade* (1994), Jack Henry receives a diary from his mother and begins to chronicle his year, interweaving themes of sibling rivalry, parental authority, and a child's need to forge his own identity. Further adventures in *Jack's New Power: Stories from a Caribbean Year* (1995), *Jack's Black Book* (1997), and *Jack on the Tracks: Four Seasons of Fifth Grade* (1999) incorporate autobiographical elements, placing Gantos at the forefront of the burgeoning genre of memoirs for young readers. He further explored this arena in his YOUNG ADULT NOVEL, *Desire Lines* (1997); its plot is derived from an incident Gantos recalled from high school.

Like Jack Henry, the character Joey Pigza has the best of intentions and an unfortunate talent for finding trouble. In *Joey Pigza Swallowed the Key* (1998), Gantos explored the perils of ADHD (attention deficit/hyperactivity disorder). The novel was a 1999 National Book Award finalist and a critical and popular favorite. In a rapid-fire first-person voice, Joey chronicles his efforts to subdue himself enough to seem "normal." Joey's mother, a devoted but harried single parent, and his grandmother, a darkly comic figure, are vivid supporting characters who reappear in *Joey Pigza Loses Control* (2000), a Newbery Honor Book. Joey's father, having returned from a long absence, convinces Joey to abandon his medication and try, once again, to control his condition through willpower. The experiment fails dismally, but the ensuing chaos is thrillingly portrayed with Gantos's signature thoughtful observation and unfettered hilarity. The story

reveals Gantos's talent for creating complex protagonists who, despite their flaws and mistakes,
manage to educate their audience without didacticism or condescension. H.F.R.

Garden, Nancy

American author, b. 1938. Though Nancy
Garden has published a broad range of
work, she is best known for her groundbreaking
1982 novel, *Annie on My Mind,* later the center of
an important legal case settled in federal district
court.

Born in Boston, the author was an only child
in a family that moved frequently; an interest
in reading and writing remained constant
throughout her youth. In high school she became fascinated with drama and began working
professionally as an actress in summer stock. She
attended Columbia University's School of Dramatic Arts, but the vagaries of a theatrical life
led her to seek other employment. After receiving a master's degree in speech from Columbia
Teacher's College, she taught at Hunter College,
worked as an accountant, and served as a book
and magazine editor.

Garden published her first two works for
young readers in 1971 — a nonfiction book called
Berlin: City Split in Two, and a novel about race
relations in a small town, *What Happened in
Marston.* Since that time she has proved her versatility by continuing to write both INFORMA-
TION BOOKS (*Fun with Forecasting Weather,* 1977;
The Kids' Code and Cipher Book, 1981) and
YOUNG ADULT NOVELS, including *Dove and
Sword* (1995), compelling HISTORICAL FICTION
written from the perspective of Gabrielle, Joan
of Arc's girlhood friend. She has also written the
five-volume Monster Hunters series and several
stories, including *Fours Crossing* (1981), *Waters-
meet* (1983), and *The Door Between* (1987), all of
them about a village in New Hampshire that follows Celtic traditions from the past.

Garden's most well known novel is *Annie on
My Mind,* in which high school senior Eliza
Winthrop describes her growing friendship —

and eventual love for — another girl, Annie
Kenyon. Set in New York City, the intense yet
tastefully written story records the pair's first
meeting at a museum, their growing romantic
involvement, and the public revelation that
nearly destroys their relationship and ultimately
causes two lesbian teachers to lose their teaching
positions at Eliza's private school. This highly
praised novel was named an ALA Best Book for
Young Adults and has appeared consistently on
ALA retrospective Best of the Best lists. However, because of its controversial subject matter,
the book has also been challenged by censors
and even burned outside the Kansas City School
Board building. When the Olathe, Kansas,
school district banned the book, a group of students and parents, supported by both the ACLU
and the American Library Association, filed suit
against the school board in the U.S. District
Court. Nancy Garden testified during the trial,
and a 1995 decision ultimately returned the book
to library shelves.

No doubt influenced by Garden's own experiences, *The Year They Burned the Books* (1999) is
a somewhat heavy-handed novel of a small-
town high school facing issues of journalistic
freedom; Garden was commendably fair in creating well-rounded characterizations of those
who support censorship. The author has also
dealt with the subject of homosexuality in *Lark
in the Morning* (1991), *Good Moon Rising* (1996),
and *Holly's Secret* (2000), a MIDDLE-GRADE
BOOK about a seventh-grader who is sometimes
embarrassed to have "two moms." In writing
about an issue that has only recently been explored in children's and young adult fiction,
Garden has created a unique body of work.
P.D.S.

Gardiner, John Reynolds

American author, b. 1944. Best known for
Stone Fox (1980), one of the most popular
and acclaimed adventure stories in recent decades, John Reynolds Gardiner is, in many ways,
unlike most contemporary children's writers. He

doesn't publish very much: *Stone Fox* is the first of only three books he has written. He doesn't have the traditional educational background of a writer: his degree is in engineering, and he has spent much of his adult life in southern California, working on projects such as the space shuttle. He did, however, take writing classes at night and worked for a while adapting children's stories for television. He also invented a plastic necktie filled with water and guppies, although that sideline proved to be less enduring than his writing.

Stone Fox is, by far, Gardiner's most successful book. Inspired by a Rocky Mountain legend the author once heard when he was visiting Idaho, this short novel chronicles a young boy's determination to win five hundred dollars in the National Dogsled Race. Set in some indeterminate time in the Old West, the story in outline is pure melodrama: Plucky little orphan Willy needs the prize money to save the farm of his ailing grandfather from the grasping hands of the tax collector; in order to win the race, he and his little dog, Searchlight, have to beat the great Stone Fox, a giant and silent Indian, who has five massive Samoyeds pulling his sled. Somehow, however, in the simple prose and relentlessly compelling plot, characters that could be merely clichés are drawn instead as archetypes, not perfectly defined like real people, but still satisfying and emotionally rich all the same. This is, in the end, a morality play in which good and bad, joy and sorrow all have their spotlighted solos on stage. Yet it is so moving and so thrillingly paced that readers of every age — no matter how jaded or cynical or tired of being preached to they may be — feel their hearts stopping when the story comes to its climax.

Gardiner's subsequent novels are *Top Secret* (1984) and *General Butterfingers* (1986). In *Top Secret,* a nine-year-old whiz succeeds in turning sunlight into food for humans, but nobody listens to him — until he catches the ear of the president. *General Butterfingers* tracks a little boy's efforts to keep three grizzled World War I veterans from being thrown out of a home that is rightfully theirs. Though both of these books are genial and high-minded entertainment, neither is as accomplished or as appealing as *Stone Fox.* A.Q.

Geisert, Arthur

American illustrator, b. 1941. From the top floor of the house that Arthur Geisert and his wife, Bonnie, built in a deserted rock quarry, they can see for miles. The lovely pastoral landscape includes the town of Galena, Illinois, and the Mississippi River Valley stretching from Dubuque to Bellevue, Iowa. The massive stone walls of the first floor of the house shelter the 2,500-pound etching press that Geisert uses to make his prints. Clipped to lines overhead are prints of the copperplate etchings for his latest book. The tools that Geisert uses daily are the same ones that etchers have used since the sixteenth century: copperplates coated with a waxy compound, Dutch mordant (an acid that eats away unprotected areas of the plate), and a variety of burins, or incising tools. Although Geisert is working in the same classical etching style as Canaletto and Piranesi, his subject matter reflects his own dry humor, his passion for building, and the pig-plentiful rural landscape around him. Many of Geisert's PICTURE BOOKS feature the busy activities of pig families, and his finely detailed scenes depict the charm of their domestic arrangements as well as the intricate gears and pulleys needed for their building projects.

Born in Dallas, Texas, Geisert took degrees from Concordia College, Nebraska, and the University of California at Davis. He studied at the Chouinard Art Institute, the Otis Art Institute, and the Art Institute of Chicago. A full-time artist, he was awarded a 1978 Purchase Award by the Seventh International Print Biennale in Kraków, Poland. He has participated in many group and one-man shows, and his work is represented in university and museum collections. Geisert has long been fascinated with the structure and beauty of arks, and it was his intricate ark prints, especially in cross section, that built his early reputation. In his third picture book, *The Ark* (1988), he carefully detailed the complex geometric interior of the ark, then filled all the spaces with the "organic chaos" necessary to the care and feeding of assorted animals.

This farm life is a part of the daily fabric of life around Galena, and Geisert even conducts life drawing classes of animals at various farms. It is rather unusual to see black-and-white picture books for children, but Geisert's work is very appealing to young readers, partly because children, like Geisert, are builders. They can enjoy the wonderful tree house in *Pigs from A to Z* (1986) and the suspension bridge in *Pigs from 1 to 10* (1992). Then, too, there is the game of finding the hidden letters and numerals that Geisert has cleverly concealed on each page. Geisert's pigs have immense charm: no roly-poly cherubs, these pigs are long-legged, lean, and canny, and endowed with vision and initiative. The strong storytelling quality of Geisert's pictures makes words seem almost superfluous. In *Oink* (1991) Geisert's mother pig expresses a wide range of emotions including panic, indignation, anger, and reassuring love with just one word — *oink* — when her piglets slip away to go exploring by themselves. In 1991 Geisert teamed up with scholar Barbara Bader to create *Aesop and Company: With Scenes from His Legendary Life*. In this handsomely designed book, the animal fables are all set in and around Galena, and the views are the ones Geisert sees every day.

Geisert's books have been recognized in many ways. He received a New York Times Best Illustrated Book Award for *Pigs from A to Z*, and he has heard howls of laughter when *Oink* is read aloud. His readers — both adults and children — are always entertained by the droll humor Geisert combines with his beautiful, classic etching style. P.H.

George, Jean Craighead

American author, b. 1919. More than any other author, Jean Craighead George has brought to American children an awareness of the rich diversity of nature and the complex relationship that humans have with it.

The daughter of a naturalist and a sister to the Craighead brothers, known for their research on grizzly bears, George grew up in a family in which exploring the natural world, raising orphaned wild creatures, and learning about the behavior of animals were everyday activities. In her autobiography, *Journey Inward* (1982), George wrote, "For years I would be encountering wild birds and beasts, living with them, seeing myself in them, and all the while trying to understand what the experience meant to me."

George's earliest works were articles written for magazines and short INFORMATION BOOKS about animals. In 1959 she published her first novel for children, *My Side of the Mountain*, about a young boy's experiences of living alone in the woods, which was named a Newbery Honor Book and has been so popular with children that George finally produced a sequel to it, *On the Far Side of the Mountain* (1990).

George's novels are set in a variety of regions and generally focus on human interactions with animals and the natural environment. *Julie of the Wolves*, recipient of the Newbery Medal in 1973, is set in Alaska and describes a young Eskimo girl's efforts to survive on the frozen tundra by learning about the behavior of a pack of wolves and becoming one of them. In *Water Sky* (1987) George contrasted the concerns of environmentalists with those of the Eskimo people, who rely on whale hunting for their living. *The Talking Earth* (1983), set in Florida, tells of a young Seminole girl who spends time alone with the wildlife of the Everglades as she learns to listen to the earth. In addition to these and other novels, George has written three "ecological mysteries," *Who Really Killed Cock Robin?* (1971), *The Missing 'Gator of Gumbo Limbo* (1992), and *The Fire Bug Connection* (1993).

As with her novels, George's nonfiction books for children reveal her love of the creatures and places she describes. The Thirteen Moons series was originally published from 1967 to 1969 and was re-released in 1991 with new illustrations. In each of the thirteen volumes in this series, George focused on the life of an animal in a different region. The One Day series includes books such as *One Day in the Alpine Tundra* (1984), set on a mountain in Wyoming. These books are brief studies of ecological niches in which the interactions of geology, weather, animals, birds, and humans on a given day are portrayed. Others of George's nonfiction books explore specific aspects of nature. Her *Wild, Wild Cookbook* (1982) introduces children to native plants and ways they are used. *How to Talk to Your Animals* (1985), *How To Talk to Your Dog* (2000), and *How to Talk to Your Cats* (2000) show how pets communicate through body language, behavior, and sounds. She has collaborated with illustrator WENDELL MINOR on a series of books, including *Snow Bear* (1999) and *Morning, Noon, and Night* (1999).

George carefully researches her subjects through natural observations and reading. The data she collects often appear in several formats. Her research on wolves, for example, led not only to *Julie of the Wolves* but also to a PICTURE BOOK, *The Wounded Wolf* (1972), and *The Moon of the Grey Wolves* (1969, 1991), a volume in the Thirteen Moons series. Material about the Everglades appears in *The Talking Earth* (1983) and *The Moon of the Alligators* (1969, 1991), a Thirteen Moons title, as well as in *The Missing 'Gator of Gumbo Limbo*.

George has been an eloquent advocate for the environment. Although she has lovingly described nature, she has also shared some hard truths about it with young readers: that creatures die or need to be wild, that creatures must be true to their natures as hunters or as prey, and that humans sometimes do more harm than good when they interfere in animals' lives. She has also rewarded readers with true stories of behaviors that endear animals to us, stories in which animals act in ways that seem loving or compassionate, loyal or courageous. In these stories George has helped us see ourselves in the creatures with whom we share the world.

B.A.C.

Giblin, James Cross

American author, b. 1933. Born in Cleveland, Ohio, James Cross Giblin was an only child. His father, a lawyer, also wrote poetry, and his mother, a former teacher, studied but did not practice law. Growing up in the company of adults, with few children in the neighborhood, Giblin has said that he enjoyed the conversations he heard among his parents and their friends.

Giblin wrote articles for the student newspaper in high school and college and acted in school plays in both places. He majored in English and dramatic arts, graduating from Case Western Reserve University in Cleveland with a B.A. in 1954. Because of his affinity for theater, he wrote a one-act play, *My Bus Is Always Late* (1954), which was his first published work. He studied playwriting at Columbia University, receiving an M.F.A. in 1955.

At age twenty-four, he began a career in book publishing at the British Book Centre. In 1962, after deciding to work with books for children, he joined Lothrop, Lee & Shepard Books as an associate editor; in 1967, he became editor-in-chief of a juvenile list at Seabury Press, which became Clarion Books. He still enjoyed writing, so he became a contributor to publications such as the *Horn Book Magazine* and *Cricket,* a magazine for children. An article for *Cricket* grew into *The Skyscraper Book* (1981), a photo-essay for which he wrote the text.

Giblin's forte is INFORMATION BOOKS about unusual, mostly historical, subjects that capture his fancy. For example, in *From Hand to Mouth: Or, How We Invented Knives, Forks, Spoons, and Chopsticks and the Table Manners to Go with Them* (1987), Giblin began with a description of a Stone Age man using a flint knife to spear a piece of meat from the cooking fire. He then described utensils and customs through the centuries and throughout the world, generously illustrating the text with photographs of museum pieces, reproductions of illustrations of dining scenes throughout history, and drawings. The book's design is inviting, which is typical of

Giblin's works, and, also typical, it garnered its share of awards and honors. A joint committee of the Children's Book Council and the National Council on Social Studies named it a Notable Children's Trade Book in the Field of Social Studies, and more of Giblin's books received that honor, including *The Skyscraper Book, Chimney Sweeps: Yesterday and Today* (1982), and *The Truth About Santa Claus* (1985). The latter was named a nonfiction honor book in the 1986 Boston Globe–Horn Book Awards. *Santa Claus* is a factual account of the original Saint Nicholas and of how he became a patron saint of sailors, maidens, and children. The evolution of the saint from a gift-giving person to the figure of our present-day Santa Claus legend is explained in Giblin's usual thorough and entertaining manner and illustrated by the fruits of his extensive research. The American Library Association has named many of Giblin's books Notable Books. Giblin has also written some BIOGRAPHIES for young readers — *The Amazing Life of Benjamin Franklin* (2000) and *Thomas Jefferson: A Picture Book Biography* (1994) — as well as other superb titles, including *Milk: The Fight for Purity* (1986), *Let There Be Light: A Book About Windows* (1988), *Charles A. Lindbergh: A Human Hero* (1997), *The Life and Death of Adolf Hitler* (2002), and a book for adults, *Writing Books for Young People* (1990). S.H.H.

nia and the Columbia University School of the Arts. Professionally, she has been a college professor, an editor, and a respected author of essays and fiction. Her first book for adults, *Black Feeling, Black Talk* (1968), is a collection of angry, somewhat militant poems addressing racial problems of the era. Some of these poems are included in her children's book *Ego-Tripping and Other Poems for Young People* (1973), a volume occasionally bogged down by rhetoric but highlighted by poems such as the title piece, which draws on black history to instill racial pride.

Giovanni's books for children illuminate the African American experience even when addressing more generic topics. *Spin a Soft Black Song* (1971) includes poems about basketball, friendship, mothers, and springtime written from an African American perspective. The unrhymed poems contain evocative images and fairly accessible themes, although the book is perhaps too broad in scope, focusing on children of all ages, including infants. *Vacation Time* (1980) includes more traditional rhyming verse. The selections are rhythmic and appealing, even though some of the rhymes are forced.

Giovanni's work is notable for providing an authentic African American voice for modern children's poetry. P.D.S.

Giovanni, Nikki

American author, b. 1943. Racial pride informs the work of Nikki Giovanni, best known for writing poems that explore her African American heritage. Although primarily recognized for her adult books, the author has published several volumes of POETRY for young readers, including *Knoxville, Tennessee* (1994), which draws on summertime memories of her hometown.

Born Yolande Cornelia Giovanni Jr., she entered Fisk University in Nashville at age sixteen and later attended the University of Pennsylva-

Goble, Paul

British-born American author and illustrator, b. 1933. Paul Goble's fascination with the Indians of the Great Plains began when his mother read aloud the complete works of Grey Owl and Ernest Thompson Seton during his youth in Surrey, England. After graduation from London's Central School of Arts and Crafts, he acted on his passion by traveling to the United States to visit some Indian reservations and was adopted by the Sioux and Yakima tribes. Goble returned to England, where he taught and practiced industrial design, but after establishing his career in creating PICTURE BOOKS, he moved to the Black Hills of South Dakota. Sioux, Cheyenne, and Blackfoot beliefs provide the core of all his stories.

In order to tell the Indian side of the Battle of the Little Bighorn, Goble and his first wife, Dorothy, created *Red Hawk's Account of Custer's Last Battle* (1969). In a seamless text, they alternate a fictitious Indian boy's view with historical commentary in an eye-opening tale. The pictures dramatically chronicle the events in a stiff, stylized manner taken from narrative drawings on tipis, buffalo robes, and the ledger-book drawings made while the Indians were held prisoner. The watercolor figures with ink outlines appear in profile on a white background, their featureless faces allowing the viewer to imagine their expressions. Here, as in his whole body of work, Goble's thorough research provides the foundation for his stories, and he almost always includes extensive references and notes.

After publishing two more accounts of HISTORICAL FICTION with Dorothy, Goble retold and illustrated *The Friendly Wolf* (1974), thus beginning a succession of myths and legends that are his most recognized work. In tales like *Buffalo Woman* (1984), in which the Buffalo Nation sends a wife to a kind-hearted hunter, Goble strengthened his artistic vision, fusing his strong design and technique with Indian symbols and artistic traditions. The pages are filled with bold, flat watercolors amid prodigious amounts of white space, producing striking compositions full of motion despite the deliberately stiff, stylized figures. The animals, plants, clothing, and tipis are highly detailed records of the Great Plains environment and Indian folk art. Sometimes white space instead of ink line appears as outline to re-create the clear Plains air or sparkling beadwork, as in *Her Seven Brothers* (1988), a legend about a young woman who decorates clothing with porcupine-quill beadwork for her new family.

In recent years, Goble has retold four tales of the spider trickster Iktomi. These hilarious stories, often *pourquoi* tales explaining why an animal looks a certain way, teach lessons in living. In *Iktomi and the Boulder* (1988), the clever but egotistical trickster insults a boulder that chases him and pins him down. Iktomi's utterances flow cartoon-style from his lips, and the text interjects leading comments in italicized asides. Goble's retellings are contemporary in picture and word: Iktomi wears athletic socks beneath his ceremonial garb and on one title page says, "There goes that white guy, Paul Goble, telling another story about me." Yet Goble still remains solidly in the Plains Indian tradition, for though the storytellers never vary from a story's theme, they freely adapt the details to suit their listeners.

Goble's understated, formal sentence construction and plain wording also reflect Indian storytelling. Often included are songs or chants, adding further cultural richness. Goble has won numerous awards, including a Caldecott Medal for *The Girl Who Loved Wild Horses* (1978). And although he creates books with his Indian friends in mind, perhaps the greatest value of his work is making available to everyone these Plains Indian stories, with their focus on the interconnection of all living things. S.S.

Gorey, Edward

American author and illustrator, 1925–2000. As an illustrator of books for adults, Edward Gorey had a distinctive, instantly recognizable style: intricately detailed pen-and-ink drawings captured characters, fur-coated, turtlenecked, or dressed in 1920s or Edwardian garb, frozen in moments of stoicism. Somewhat Gothic and ostensibly grim, these images were usually accompanied by macabre stories of death, dread, and gore or by humorous verses detailing situations of horror. Gorey's unique character was most pervasive in the works of which he was both author and illustrator. Though largely out of print, many of his books have been made available in the collections *Amphigorey* (1972), *Amphigorey, Too* (1975), and *Amphigorey Also* (1983).

Born in Chicago, Gorey attended the Art Institute of Chicago, served a short time in the U.S. Army, and received a B.A. in French from Harvard. After working in Boston at various jobs, including bookstore clerk and book jacket designer, he moved to New York in 1953 to become a staff artist at Doubleday. That same year, his first book, *The Unstrung Harp*, was published. It was followed by a succession of books, many of which were published under a variety of humorously anagrammatic pseudonyms such as Mrs. Regera Dowdy, Ogdred Weary, and Dreary Wodge.

Though critics and fans were apt to analyze the dark humor in his work, Gorey maintained that his stories were simply entertainments in the nonsense tradition of LEWIS CARROLL and EDWARD LEAR. His attraction to this genre is perhaps more evident in his work for children. In addition to illustrating a few of Edward Lear's poems, including *The Dong with the Luminous Nose* (1969), Gorey wrote and illustrated *The Wuggly Ump* (1963), a story in verse about a group of care-free children who end up in the belly of an obscure dragonlike creature. Gorey's ability to bring visual humor to a text has made him the appropriate illustrator of several collections of POETRY, such as *The Monster Den* (1966) and *You Read to Me, I'll Read to You* (1962), written by John Ciardi. His intuitive illustrations and graphic design add a narrative dimension to the witty text of FLORENCE PARRY HEIDE to create the award-winning *The Shrinking of Treehorn* (1971). With expressive visual detail, Gorey's line drawings add further dimension to parallel the story of an endearing, if slightly odd, only child who independently and rather ably copes with his mysterious condition of shrinking while his emotionally aloof parents carry on their trivial tasks with devout attention, ignorant of his diminishing stature. In a more traditional vein, Gorey produced illustrations for two versions of classic fairy tales: *Red Riding Hood* (1972), retold in verse by Beatrice Schenk de Regniers, and *Rumpelstiltskin* (1974), retold by Edith Tarcov.

Reaching a wide audience through book jackets and the theater — one of the passions that he cited as among his main influences —

Edward Gorey created books that appeal to a mainstream audience as well as to devotees; he brought a lighthearted quality to dark humor.

E.K.E.

Graham, Lorenz

American author, 1902–1989. A pioneer African American writer for children, Lorenz Graham explored both the African and the black American experience in several trailblazing books. The son of a minister, he was born in New Orleans and spent his childhood in a succession of parsonages throughout the country. While still in college at the University of California at Los Angeles, he went to Liberia to teach. That experience, which showed him the wide disparity between the American idea of the "Dark Continent" and the reality of what he observed there, sealed his lifelong dedication to writing books that honestly portrayed African life.

Despite his conviction that books were needed, his early writing career was filled with disappointment. Publishers of the 1920s, he felt, were interested in stories only about African savages, and he put aside his writing ambitions to concentrate on a career in social work, doing graduate work at the New York School for Social Work and at New York University. In time, he and his wife settled in California, where they raised their family while he worked as a social worker and probation officer.

It wasn't until 1946 that his first book, *How God Fixed Jonah*, was published. A collection of Bible stories written in the cadences of authentic African oral tradition, it featured an introduction by the legendary black activist W. E. B. Du Bois, who later became Graham's brother-in-law. Several African tales followed, among them *Song of the Boat* (1975), illustrated by Caldecott medalists LEO and DIANE DILLON. The story of a father and son's search for the perfect tree from which to carve a canoe, it was written in the English that villagers in West Africa often used. Vividly poetic, the prose captures the strong rhythms of the region's folk speech.

His best-known novels form a series that follows David Williams, a young African American, from adolescence through adulthood: *South Town* (1958), *North Town* (1965), *Whose Town?* (1969), and *Return to South Town* (1976). Simply written and deeply felt, *South Town* tracks the ordinary and finally grotesque insults that an ambitious young man and his hardworking family endure in a small Southern town in the mid–twentieth century. A portrait of ordinary people, not heroes, the book and its sequels were inspired by the kind of people Graham said he knew best — people, he once explained, who "feel pain but do not stop to complain, who want to make life better but hesitate to act for fear they will make things worse." Infused by hope and tempered by sorrow, *South Town* and the other novels in the series have lost little of their power even after three decades of profound social change. They ring true now as both a stirring affirmation of human kindness and a clear-eyed reckoning of the cost of racial bigotry. A.Q.

Graham, Margaret Bloy

C anadian American author and illustrator, b. 1920. Margaret Bloy Graham began her career as a children's book artist with considerable success. Her very first book, *All Falling Down* (1951), written by her then husband, Gene Zion, was a Caldecott Honor Book. The following year, *The Storm Book* (1952), written by CHARLOTTE ZOLOTOW, was also selected as a Caldecott Honor Book.

Each book is illustrated in a quite different style. In *All Falling Down*, a satisfying survey of things that fall down (leaves, petals, rain) and things that don't (children caught in their father's arms), the two-page spreads are softly hued. There is a sweetness, arguably a bit too much, in each of the scenes. In contrast, and in keeping with its subject, *The Storm Book* generally has a darker palette, mostly grays and black. The sky looms large, crackling with energy and fury. The text and art never share a page, allowing sweeping pictures of the storm to dominate the two-page spreads unchallenged.

Graham's subsequent work went in another, more humorous direction. In 1956 *Harry the Dirty Dog* made its debut. It was the first in an enduringly popular series that also includes *No Roses for Harry!* (1958), *Harry and the Lady Next Door* (1960), and *Harry by the Sea* (1965). Written by Gene Zion, the Harry stories follow the escapades of an endearingly crafty dog who knows what he likes (his independence) and what he doesn't (washes, sweaters with roses, bad singers). Filled with oranges and greens, the art is loose and spaciously composed. The characters are rounded and simply drawn, wonderfully genial in appearance and attitude. There is a droll, seemingly effortless union of art and text in the Harry stories, a delicious mastery of everyday foolishness.

Born and brought up in Toronto, Graham spent most of her childhood summers in either England or the United States. She came to New York in the 1940s to establish her career as a commercial artist and worked for a time for the Condé Nast magazine empire, where Zion was also employed. They married in 1948, and she and editor Ursula Nordstrom of Harper and Brothers persuaded him to try writing for children. Their collaboration flourished for years, ending with their divorce in 1968.

On her own, Graham illustrated several more books, including some she wrote herself. *Be Nice to Spiders* (1967) dramatizes the value of staying on the good side of arachnids. She also created Benjy the dog, who starred in *Benjy and the Barking Bird* (1971) and *Benjy's Dog House* (1973). Like Harry, Benjy lives an agreeable suburban life and has a strong will. His antics are gently amusing but somehow lack the frisky wit of his canine predecessor. A.Q.

Grahame, Kenneth

B ritish novelist, 1859–1932. A. A. MILNE, author of the Winnie-the-Pooh stories, once called Kenneth Grahame's *Wind in the Willows* a "household book." And so it has become, with more than a hundred editions and countless numbers in print, treasured by their owners and passed on to the upcoming generation as a children's classic.

Its creator was an unlikely candidate for this elevated status in the world of children's literature. Born in Edinburgh, Scotland, Grahame was taken to England to live with his grandmother after his mother's death. His father, unable to deal with the grief of loss, disappeared onto the Continent. While Granny Ingles provided all the necessary physical comforts, there was not much warmth and affection shown toward the Grahame children. Grahame, however, was captivated by the Berkshire Downs where they lived and eventually made them the backdrop for his beloved story of Rat, Mole, Toad, and Mr. Badger.

Grahame attended St. Edwards School in Oxford, where he began dabbling in writing but was forced by family pressure to apply for a clerkship at the Bank of England. Much of his early writing expressed resentment toward the ethic that revered the "real work" of a bank clerkship over the work of an artist. In 1879, at age thirty-nine, Grahame became one of the youngest secretaries in the history of the Bank of England. He was, however, ever rebellious as he pursued his social life in the various restaurants of Soho populated with the literary stars of the times. It was here that he fortuitously met with the great literary scholar F. J. Furnwall and the poet W. E. Henly. During this period he was introduced to neopaganism, the literary cult of Pan, which reinforced his own views on organized religion and pastoral escape. His first gathering of essays, *Pagan Papers*, was published in 1894. In 1895, *The Golden Age*, written in nostalgic praise of childhood, became the bible for children's writers and eventually an important source for the ideas in *The Wind in the Willows*.

In 1899, Grahame married. Although the marriage was not a happy one, the Grahames' son, Alastair, was the inspiration for the wonderful stories told at bedtime or, when he and his father were apart, in letters. In 1907, these stories were first published as *First Whisper of the Wind in the Willows*. Grahame then wrote out the stories as a novel, adding the two mystical chapters, "Pipers at the Gates of Dawn" and

"Wayfarers All." Much of Grahame's own life can be seen in *The Wind in the Willows*. Some say that Mole was Grahame trying to relocate the child within himself. *Willows* reflects the townsman's nostalgic view of country life. The adventures of Mr. Toad, the part written especially for the adventure-hungry Alastair, serve as the main plot device. Mole is allowed his philosophical musings when Mr. Toad is flying off to follow yet another scheme. Each character is always anxious to return to his home, but Rat's home seems to be the most appealing, a reflection of Grahame's own propensity toward the peace and tranquillity of river life. He himself, like Rat, was especially happy just "messing about in boats."

Early in the 1930s E. H. SHEPARD (illustrator also for all of Milne's writings about Christopher Robin and Winnie-the-Pooh) visited Grahame to discuss Shepard's ideas for illustrations for the book. He was urged by an elderly Grahame: "I love these little people, be kind to them." Since Grahame's death in 1932, numerous editions have appeared, illustrated by artists including E. H. Shepard, ARTHUR RACKHAM, Tasha Tudor, and Michael Hague.

Even though *The Wind in the Willows* has been criticized for its old-boys'-club atmosphere, the writing is rich and the sense of place genuine, as is the expression of fondness for each of the characters, their sense of friendship, and the exaltation of nature. It is truly one of the classic read-aloud books that should not be missed by any family.   A.I.

Greenaway, Kate

British illustrator and author, 1846–1901. Born Catherine Greenaway, Kate Greenaway became one of the most important and influential illustrators for children of the late nineteenth century, despite her shyness and avoidance of publicity. Indeed, a whole industry, which included china, fabrics, wallpaper, children's clothing, and dolls, grew up around her books, such as *Under the Window* (1879), *The Language of Flowers* (1884), and *A Day in a*

Illustration by Kate Greenaway for "A Romp," from *A Day in a Child's Life* (1881), with music by Myles B. Foster.

Child's Life (1881). The fascination with the innocent childhood world she pictured continues to this day.

Greenaway's father, a wood engraver, had worked as an apprentice with Edmund Evans, the man who would have such an influence on children's book publishing in the late nineteenth century. Like Kate, John Greenaway was a gentle soul who loved children but who was not financially astute. When the family finances suffered, Kate's mother, Elizabeth, responded by opening a children's clothing shop stocked with designs she made and sewed herself. The loose-fitting, flowing garments she created were meant as an antidote to the tightly fitting fashions of the day, and Elizabeth's ideas about dress were reflected in the clothing Kate would make famous through her illustrations.

As a child, Kate loved to work beside her father, and in view of his profession in publishing and Kate's love for drawing, the family encouraged her to consider art as a career. At that time, with the periodicals market increasing, there was a need for trained engravers' assistants, and this was considered a suitable job for women. Kate began formal art training at the age of twelve and eventually studied at the Finsbury School, where artists were trained in crafts such as ceramics and textiles as well as in painting. While she attended school, she prepared for art exhibits, and her work began to be published in magazines. She came to be more widely known both in Britain and in America for her greeting card designs, in which her attention to detail of costume, stemming from her work as a clothing designer and seamstress, was highly valued. Eventually, John Greenaway introduced Kate to Edmund Evans, who by then had achieved success in color printing and was working with WALTER CRANE and RANDOLPH CALDECOTT.

Evans was struck by Kate's sense of color and line as well as her detail of costume and setting, and he persuaded George Routledge to publish *Under the Window* in 1879. This was followed by many other books of rhymes, songs, and stories, which firmly established her reputation around the world.

Greenaway's children, with their heart-shaped faces, their large eyes, and their rather somber expressions, represented life in an idealized world where the countryside was always lovely, the weather fine, and the children clean and well fed. Her delicate lines and soft watercolor washes, her careful page design and layout, and her eye for every detail of costume and setting conveyed an almost mystical reverence for the world of children. Perhaps this was meant as an antidote to the gloomy and somber settings of the Gothic-revival period her books followed. More likely, however, the world she pictured was the world Kate remembered so lovingly from her own childhood. She frankly admitted that she didn't want to grow up and leave that happy time, and it was her artistic skill combined with her memory and imagination that appealed to her contemporaries as well as to the many generations since who have loved her books. B.K.

Grimm, Jacob Ludwig Carl; Grimm, Wilhelm Carl

Jacob: German author, 1785–1863; Wilhelm: German author, 1786–1859. The brothers Jacob and Wilhelm Grimm, German scholars, philologists, collectors, and editors, are best remembered for *Kinder- und Hausmärchen*, translated under the titles *Nursery and Household Tales* or *German Popular Stories* and commonly known in English as *Grimm's Fairy Tales*. Originally, these stories were not published for children; the Grimms began collecting them as part of a scholarly study on the history of the German language and oral traditions. The first volume (1812) was not illustrated and included numerous scholarly notes; in the six editions that

followed, tales were added and revised. Not until the Grimms saw the first English translation (1823), with its famous illustrations by George Cruikshank, did they design an edition for younger readers. Their second volume (1814) represents a collection of over two hundred stories and legends. In these editions are favorites such as "The Frog Prince," "Hansel and Gretel," "Rapunzel," "The Musicians of Bremen," "Snow White and the Seven Dwarfs," "Rumpelstilskin," and "The Twelve Dancing Princesses." The publication of *Kinder- und Hausmärchen* caused no particular stir in literary circles. In fact, several critics labeled the stories boorish and declared them an insignificant pursuit for serious scholars. In spite of such criticism, the tales were enthusiastically received in Germany and abroad.

A unique relationship existed between the Brothers Grimm, who remained remarkably close throughout their lives. Although their personal temperaments and intellectual pursuits differed, they worked together their entire lives, collecting stories for their book of fairy tales. Born near Frankfurt, they attended the same gymnasium and university, and both taught at Göttingen University. Jacob studied language, but Wilhelm was more interested in collecting folktales. Sources for these tales were often close to home. Wilhelm's wife and sisters were fluent storytellers; "Hansel and Gretel" was among the stories they contributed. A family nurse recounted the tale of "Little Red-Cap," a version of "Little Red Riding-Hood," and "Little Briar-Rose," an analogue of "The Sleeping Beauty." Wilhelm's research included letters to friends asking about folktales, songs, and legends in the oral tradition. The Grimms' tales have all the elements of popular literature: the characters are universally appealing, and plots are recounted with spellbinding quality. The children in the stories, though often dispossessed, fend for themselves and eventually find love and happiness. In these stories, foolhardy souls and humbled heroes accomplish impossible tasks while retaining — or regaining — humility, moral standards, and tenderness. A unique combination of FANTASY and reality, the stories have stood the tests of taste and time; not only do they entertain, but they activate imagination, offer solutions to problems, promote confidence, and generally enrich their readers' lives.

Numerous versions of the fairy tales exist, but several are exceptional. *The Juniper Tree and Other Tales from Grimm* (1973), edited by Lore Segal and translated by Segal and RANDALL JARRELL, is illustrated with some of MAURICE SENDAK's finest work. European and American artists have illustrated individual stories: Nancy Ekholm Burkert's *Snow White and the Seven Dwarfs* (1972) and Gennady Spirin's *Snow White and Rose Red* (1992) are mesmerizing in mood, meticulous in detail, and vibrant in color. S.L.

H

Haas, Jessie

American author, b. 1959. Born and raised in Vermont, Jessie Haas had a childhood filled with gardens, animals, farming chores, and, when time allowed, reading, most especially "all the horse stories ever written." While a student at Wellesley, she wrote her first novel, *Keeping Barney,* (1982), a story that draws upon her childhood life on a farm and her love of horses and family. In fact, familial themes set within a strong sense of place permeate Haas's books and are the hallmark of her writing style.

In a series of PICTURE BOOKS, including *Following Mowing* (1994), *No Foal Yet* (1995), *Sugaring* (1996), and *Hurry!* (2000), Haas has evoked the rhythms and routines of rural life, highlighting the relationship between the character Nora and her grandparents and their intricate relationship to the landscape. Joseph Smith's water-color and pencil illustrations depict the quiet drama and dignity of farm life.

Haas's illustrated CHAPTER BOOKS, *Beware the Mare* (1993), *A Blue for Beware* (1995), *Be Well, Beware* (1999), and *Beware and Stogie* (1998), focus on the protagonist Lily's relationship with her mare, Beware. Haas's characters are well rounded and authentic; the present-tense narrative offers a sense of immediacy that pulls the young reader into the moment. Her attention to detail in riding and horse-keeping will appeal to older horse enthusiasts as well.

In *Unbroken* (1999), difficult issues surrounding grief and life's struggles are gently handled. *Will You, Won't You* (2000), a coming-of-age story, sails through issues of self-identity, ecology, and complex mother-daughter relationships. In *Runaway Radish* (2001), an illustrated chapter book featuring nostalgic pencil illustrations by Margot Apple, Haas tackled the difficult inevitable changes of growing up. Simple lyrical prose tells the humorous yet poignant story of a pony whose riders outgrow him.

Haas varied her pattern somewhat in her most personal book, *Fire!* (1998). About a night fire that destroys a family home, Haas tells the true story of her parents, presenting a profound story of a restoration and the hidden strengths of family. Haas's characters are genuine to their times, vocation, and emotion; her gentle style offers a highly accessible story that ultimately celebrates family.

In addition to her fiction, Haas has written several INFORMATION BOOKS for young riders.

B.M.

Hall, Donald

American poet, author, and anthologist, b. 1928. Born in Connecticut, Hall began writing POETRY at age fourteen in order "to be loved by women." His opinion of poetry has altered slightly over the years; now he hopes that his listeners, both male and female, will "take [the poem] into [their] ears and be moved by it."

Hall attended Harvard University, where he

was editor of *The Harvard Advocate Anthology* (1950), and Oxford University, where he was awarded the Newdigate Prize for his poem "Exile" (1952). During the 1950s, Hall served as poetry editor of the *Paris Review*, editing numerous anthologies that highlighted the younger contemporary poets. He taught at the University of Michigan for almost twenty years before quitting in 1975 in order to devote his time to writing at his family's farm in New Hampshire. Hall made use of his early editing experience when he edited *The Oxford Book of Children's Verse in America* (1985). The anthology presents poetry in chronological order according to the birth date of the poet; the material ranges from indigenous tribal songs and didactic Puritan poems to the lighter verse of more current NURSERY RHYMES. Hall's preface, a minihistory of American children's poetry, speaks of the long relationship children and poetry have had and explores even some earlier poems for which the texts have been lost. An underlying theme running through Hall's poetry and prose is the exploration and celebration of the continuity between generations. Living in the same house that his great-grandfather first occupied in 1865, Hall cannot help but be influenced by the memories that house inspired. *String Too Short to Be Saved: Childhood Reminiscences* (1961) is a collection of prose narratives inspired by Hall's childhood summers; *Kicking the Leaves* (1978) is a collection of poems that reflects his feelings on returning to the farm.

The spirit of the farm and the land is best seen in *Ox-Cart Man* (1979), the illustrations for which earned BARBARA COONEY the Caldecott Medal. The book is based on a family tale: "I heard the story from my cousin, who had heard it when he was a boy from an old man, who told him that he had heard it when he was a boy, from an old man. I was thrilled with it, thinking of man's past life described in cyclical fashion." The story is deceptively simple. In October a farmer journeys from his home to Portsmouth Market, where he sells wool, potatoes, maple sugar, and his ox and cart and carries home a kettle, needle, knife, and two pounds of winter-

green peppermint candies to his hardworking family for use and pleasure during the winter. The cycle of this rural nineteenth-century New England family never changes; it is calm, methodical, and precise. We watch them spend their winter and spring preparing their goods to sell once more in the fall, and we are led to believe that this process will continue each year without change. By using the poetic devices of alliteration and repetition to draw in the reader, Hall's prose becomes poetry. The dignity of the words is matched by the eloquence of Cooney's illustrations, which capture the seasonal landscapes — the lush fall foliage, the crisp, clean winter snow, the pink and white springtime blossoms — and the hustle and bustle of Portsmouth Market.

Hall has also collaborated with illustrator Michael McCurdy to create books about a young girl, Lucy, set in 1910 in New Hampshire: *Lucy's Christmas* (1994) and *Lucy's Summer* (1995). These books, like many of Hall's poems and stories, are characterized by a nostalgic yearning for lost values and a strong respect for the cyclic nature of life. M.I.A.

Hamilton, Virginia

American author, 1936–2002. Born in Yellow Springs, Ohio, Virginia Hamilton studied at Antioch College, Ohio State University, and the New School for Social Research in New York. She and her husband, Arnold Adoff, poet and anthologist, had two children. Among the awards Ms. Hamilton received are the Mystery Writers of America Edgar Allan Poe Award in 1969 for *The House of Dies Drear;* the National Book Award in 1975 for *M. C. Higgins, the Great,* which also won the Newbery Medal; the Regina Medal in 1990; the Hans Christian Andersen Award in 1992; and the Laura Ingalls Wilder Award in 1995.

Hamilton's first two books — *Zeely,* the story of a young black girl's crush on a tall, regal black woman, and *The House of Dies Drear* — were published in 1967 and 1968. *Zeely* was touching but not wholly convincing; but the author's second book gave evidence of increasing control of narrative and a remarkable handling of mood and setting. It is the story of an African American family's frightening experiences when they move into a house which, a century earlier, had been a station on the Underground Railroad. Different as they were, both of the first two books presaged Hamilton's later statement that "Time, place, and family are at the heart of the fictions I create."

It was not until her third book, *The Time-Ago Tales of Jahdu* (1969), that the fluency and inventiveness of this author's style and the distinctive way in which she could use and — occasionally — invent words, became apparent. Here the narrator is a storyteller, Mama Luka, who tells a story each day to a young boy, Lee Edward. The stories came "from a fine good place called Harlem," and "she told them slow and she told them easy." "Woogily!" says the hero Jahdu. The book is an example of, and a tribute to, the power of folk literature, and it is a moving presentation of a folk hero who is a role model for a black child. The same lyric quality emanates from the sequels and from the new tales added to the older ones in a fourth volume, *The All Jahdu Storybook* (1991).

Although many of Hamilton's books have memorable characters and settings, few have had a greater impact than *The Planet of Junior Brown* (1971). It was one of the first books about homeless children, and there is a chiaroscuro quality about the contrast between the bleak reality of Buddy's protective nurturing of a group of younger boys and the almost-fantasy of the mock solar system he and another eighth-grader, Junior, create in the school basement. What has been created here is a family: Buddy says, "We are together because we have to learn to live for each other."

Equally trenchant, *M. C. Higgins, the Great* (1974) is as quintessentially rural as *Planet* is urban. Thirteen-year-old M.C. sits atop his forty-foot pole to survey the mountain his family owns, pondering the encroachment of detritus from strip-mining and worrying about whether

his mother will leave the mountain. The vivid creation of setting and the establishment of mood are remarkable. Hamilton's style is both graceful and intricate, with nuances that may be appreciated by mature readers but that will not come between other readers and the story.

The eponymous protagonist of *Arilla Sun Down* (1976) is twelve, daughter of an African American mother and a father who has both black and Native American origins; overshadowed by a brilliant and articulate brother, Arilla is slow to gain confidence. She is the narrator and, in incorporating flashbacks to her early childhood, Arilla uses language in an odd way: "Can't seeing his face, brown shade." Because of Hamilton's deftness with words, however, the reader, once accustomed to the pattern and cadence of this device, hears its singing quality. The recurrent theme of strong family bonds appears also in *A Little Love* (1984), in which Sheema and her lover go hunting for the father she has never known and finds that it is her grandparents who sustain and comfort her. In this book, too, Hamilton used dialect like poetry. It is a grandfather also in *Junius over Far* (1985) who is the catalyst for family love; Grandfather has returned to the Caribbean island of his youth, and his confused letters worry his grandson Junius so much that the boy and his father go to the island to see what is happening. The story alternates between the boy's and the old man's viewpoints, and the writing, while deliberate in pace, is clear and is richly rewarding for its subtlety and warmth.

There is an impressive variety in other realistic FAMILY STORIES, which range from the sober *Sweet Whispers, Brother Rush* (1982) to the lively and often humorous *Willie Bea and the Time the Martians Landed* (1983), an amused and affectionate look at the response of an extended African American family to the news, taken at frightened face value by so many in 1938, that the Orson Welles broadcast of disaster was genuine. Hamilton wrote diverse stories such as *A White Romance* (1987), which deals with four people from broken homes and their participation in the drug culture, and *Drylongso* (1992), the taut story of a family whose drought-threatened crops are saved by an itinerant stranger. The family is even more the focus in *The Bells of Christmas* (1989), a warm, nostalgic look at the Christmas reunion of an extended family that gathers on an Ohio farm, and in *Cousins* (1990), an intricate and subtle exploration of family relationships that focuses on girl cousins who carry on the hostility that exists between their mothers.

As one might expect of so proficient a fiction writer, Hamilton added a compelling narrative flow to the meticulous research she did for her several BIOGRAPHIES. In *W.E.B. Du Bois* (1972) Hamilton concentrated on Du Bois's career as a writer, teacher, and activist, and showed clearly in this study, as she would do in her work *Paul Robeson: The Life and Times of a Free Black Man* (1974), the importance of both figures in African American political and cultural history. *Anthony Burns: The Defeat and Triumph of a Fugitive Slave* (1988) is both fictional and factual, offering a trenchant depiction of slavery and of those who struggled to escape or abolish it.

Equally adept at writing realistic and fantastic fiction, Hamilton has been both originator and adapter of the latter. As she did with the Jahdu stories, she continued the auspicious start made in *Justice and Her Brothers* (1978) by adding *Dustland* (1980) and *The Gathering* (1981). In this stunning SCIENCE FICTION trilogy, four time travelers combine their psychic forces to defeat, in classic high fantasy tradition, the forces of evil. This is potent stuff: the improbable made credible, the dramatic seamlessly fused with the mystical. *The Magical Adventures of Pretty Pearl* (1983), an inventive blend of history, FANTASY, and African and AMERICAN FOLKLORE, posits the arrival of a young African god, Pretty Pearl, and her brother John de Conquer to the United States during the Reconstruction era — and when they cross the river into Ohio, they take the name of the author's ancestors, Perry.

Retelling or adapting folk material, Hamilton produced three fine collections: *In the Beginning: Creation Stories from Around the World* (1988); *The People Could Fly: American Black Folk Tales* (1985); and *The Dark Way: Stories from the Spirit World* (1990). All are impressive for their range of material and for the effectiveness with which they are told.

In her Andersen Award acceptance speech, Virginia Hamilton spoke of her desire to mark the history and traditions of African Americans; she did this with integrity and distinction. She has given all children a gift for all time. Z.S.

Voices of the Creators

Virginia Hamilton

I call myself a storyteller, and I work alone. I spend large amounts of time in my study, which has expansive glass areas or "lights" which allow me to look out on a hundred-year-old hedgerow (my west property line) and corn fields beyond. The row of twisted osage orange trees is bare and black against the cold blue Ohio sky. The land, the last part of my family's farm, has been in my family for generations. The fields have the corn stubble showing, washed in pale winter sunlight. Those same fields have not changed their size and produce in more than a century.

In my tiny bailiwick of an Ohio village, I, of course, have aged, but life for me here is as it's always been. I was born here; I have lived most of my life here. Everybody knows who I am, and they leave me alone to do my work. Within, I have not changed much. I am still my mother's youngest daughter, still Dad's Baby, which is what he called me for far too long. Time inside my study, however, passes, changing quickly. My working and book process have literally exploded, as has multiculturalism across the American hopescape.

Working alone has to do with insights and outsights and my process of writing. A writer must not only have insight — that is, awareness through intuition — but she must also have the ability to see and understand externals, what we call outsight. Readers, too, are part of this process. Without readers, adults and children, I feel I am blind-sided. Writing without an audience is thus inconceivable, since I write for readers to read and to have them know my process for making fiction and nonfiction. I believe deeply that I have something original to say.

My approach to creating narrative has to do with memories from my childhood, which fit within a creative process. This is my way of solving problems of experience and memory. It is the way I retain some essence of my past, perhaps for future generations. My fiction and most of my nonfiction writing have some basis in reality of a large or small experience, although they are rarely autobiographical. For instance, the making of *Many Thousand Gone: African Americans from Slavery to Freedom* grew out of personal family history. The fact that my own grandfather was a fugitive from slavery gave me the impetus to research two centuries of slave narratives and recast thirty of them for the collection.

Storytelling is my way of sharing in community. It is the method my own parents used to define the boundaries of their living. My mother and father were fine storytellers; they drew me close by their stories. When I was a child, the story lady at the library read stories to us children as we sat around her on what came to mean to me a magic carpet. Somewhere along the way I realized that peoples use story as a means to keep their cultural heritage safe, to save the very language in which heritage is made symbolic through story.

I write my stories down, just as did those authors whose story books my story lady read to us. In *The People Could Fly,* there is the old story called "A Wolf and Little Daughter," a black variation on "Little Red Riding Hood." In my version these words are sung by Little Daughter: "Traybla, traybla, cum qua, kimo." The wolf asks his would-be victim to sing that "sweetest, goodest song again." To escape the wolf, Little Daughter sings again, and she is saved. In the plantation era, African words in stories almost always were meant to empower the teller while saving some aspect of the mother language. Thus, the sung words of Little Daughter are magic and have the power to *save* her — that is, to save the African heritage.

I see my books and the language I use in them as empowering me to give utterance to the dreams, the wishes, of African Americans. I see the imaginative use of language and ideas as a way to illuminate a human condition. All of my work, as a novelist, biographer, creator and compiler of stories, has been to portray the essence of a people who are a parallel-culture society in America. I've attempted to mark the history and traditions of African Americans, a parallel culture people, through my writing, while bringing readers strong stories and memorable characters living nearly the best they know how. I want readers, both adults and children, to care about who the characters are. I want readers to feel, to understand, and to empathize. I want the books to make a world in which characters are real.

There is an essential agreement between us, the writer and reader. We are not without the other. Our bond is our common language, books, schools, teachers, students, libraries, children, reading and writing, and our experiences as Americans. Ours is a multicultural nation of the world village, where in community we enter into the bond of learning together. ✸

Hautzig, Esther

Polish-born American author, b. 1930. Esther Hautzig is best known for *The Endless Steppe: Growing Up in Siberia* (1968), the affecting personal narrative of her life between the ages of ten and fifteen, which she spent as a deportee in a barren, impoverished Siberian village.

Nothing in her early childhood prepared Hautzig for the harrowing experiences she endured and chronicled in her book. She was born into a family of wealth and prestige in Vilna, Poland. As a young girl, her governess instilled in her a love of books and learning, and Hautzig once said, "What I always wanted and loved to do was write." In 1941 her idyllic childhood ended when her family, accused of being capitalists, was arrested by Russian soldiers and shipped by cattle car to Rubtsovsk, Siberia.

Hautzig has credited Adlai Stevenson for inspiring her to write *The Endless Steppe*. After going to Russia in 1959, Stevenson wrote a series of articles, including one on Rubtsovsk, about his trip for the *New York Times*. When Hautzig wrote him a letter about her experiences there, he encouraged her to write about those years. Nine years later, her autobiography was published, and it has remained in print ever since. The story of her family's survival, despite a multitude of hardships that included near starvation, hard physical labor, cramped living conditions in barracks and dung huts, arctic winters and scorching summers, and disease, pays tribute to the resilience of the human spirit in the face of overwhelming odds. While she vividly related her particular privations, the tale Hautzig told remains essentially a universal coming-of-age story. She grew from childhood to adolescence under daunting circumstances but approached her experiences with the buoyancy and optimism of youth. Ultimately she recognized and celebrated the positive aspects of her time in Siberia, noting the kindness she found in unexpected places, her development of a passion for great Russian literature, an appreciation for the desolate beauty of the steppes, and, most important, the sustaining love of her family. After five long years in exile, Hautzig finally returned to Poland only to discover that Siberia truly had become her home. Among its many honors, *The Endless Steppe* was nominated for a National Book Award, won the Lewis Carroll Shelf Award as a book "worthy enough to sit on the shelf with *Alice in Wonderland*," and was named a Boston Globe–Horn Book Honor Book.

Hautzig also authored a number of books on crafts and cooking, such as *Let's Cook Without Cooking* (1955), *Let's Make Presents* (1962), and *Make It Special* (1986). *A Gift for Mama* (1981) draws on memories of Hautzig's childhood to tell the warm and gentle story of a girl who takes on mending to earn money to buy her mother a gift; in *Riches* (1992) an old Eastern European couple follow a rabbi's sage advice to discover the joy in giving of themselves to help others. Works for younger readers describe a child's day at home, in school, and at a park. All contain text in English, Spanish, French, and Russian.

While all of Hautzig's books have been well received, *The Endless Steppe* remains a rare and powerful reading experience, as popular today as when it debuted. C.S.

Hawkes, Kevin

American illustrator, b. 1959. From Sherman, Texas, where he was born (the son of a military officer) to Peaks Island, Maine, where he lives with his family, Kevin Hawkes has acquired a humorous way of looking at things. His imaginative perspective and innovative whimsy have jelled into a signature style of illustration in picture books.

When he was a child, his family lived in France for a time, and Hawkes and his brothers climbed castle stairs, adventured into forests, and explored museums. Many of those childhood images find their way into his work: "It seems that all of my characters come from places where the lampposts are never straight, the hills impossibly steep, and the skies impossibly blue. I love to tell stories through my artwork and transport young readers to new and unusual places."

As a child he loved to draw, paint, and play with modeling clay. He experimented with all types of media and in ninth grade he built a life-size mountaineer, complete with climbing ax, out of papier-mâché. He modeled the figure in a sitting position so he could take him home on the school bus — much to everyone's surprise.

After earning a degree in illustration at Utah State University in 1985, Hawkes worked as an animator's assistant, a photographic retoucher, and a portrait painter. But the two years he spent working in the children's department of a Boston bookstore ultimately launched his career. He spent his lunch hours poring over the artwork in picture books, studying and absorbing styles, looks, and effects. During that time he took his portfolio to publishers in Boston and New York City; he made his debut as a PICTURE BOOK creator with *Then the Troll Heard the Squeak* (1990), which he both wrote and illustrated. The limerick-style verse bounces along as a little girl jumps on the bed, disrupting everyone and everything in the house. The wonderful mock-ghoulish artwork embellishes the naughtiness, playful scariness, and drollness of the tale. Hawkes's second picture book quickly followed. *His Royal Buckliness* (1992) was another rhyming story with charming, humorous illustrations.

Hawkes's talent for matching his artwork to the mood and content of a story quickly made him a favorite with publishers: his tone can range from serious, as in *The Librarian Who Measured the Earth* (1994), written by KATHRYN LASKY, to capricious, as in *My Little Sister Ate One Hare* (1996), written by Bill Grossman. For PAUL FLEISCHMAN's *Weslandia* (1999), Hawkes designed and rendered a new world created by a young boy. His clever images for JACK PRELUTSKY's *Imagine That! Poems of Never-Was* (1998) exactly match each poem's level of exaggeration.

By working primarily in acrylics, Hawkes renders a feeling of elasticity in his illustrations. His combinations of vivid color, perspective, and exaggeration for comic or gross effect are instantly appealing. To get the right feel for a story, he pretends to be a fly, "buzzing around the scenes, flying high and low to see what catches his eye, especially the light and shadow." His use of dramatic shadows can heighten plots, underscore character reactions, and add nuance, achieving the effect that is precisely right for the book at hand. J.C.

Heide, Florence Parry

American author, b. 1919. Florence Parry Heide, with over eighty books to her credit, is a prolific and versatile writer. From PICTURE BOOKS to YOUNG ADULT NOVELS, from humorous to serious, Heide has written in numerous genres. "There are so many ideas waiting out there, so many unwritten stories," she has said. "What an adventure!" Yet a common theme runs through her books: young people take control of their lives in some way. Heide recalled as a child making a conscious decision to face cheerfully what life had to offer. Her father

died when she was three, and Heide and her brother lived with their grandmother until their mother was able to support the family.

Heide grew up in Pittsburgh, and after graduating from the University of California, Los Angeles, she returned to the East and worked for several years in advertising. Then she married, moved to Wisconsin, and raised five children. Once her children were in school, Heide wanted something more in her life. She and her friend Sylvia W. Van Clief tried to start a hot fudge sauce company, but since neither liked cooking, they quickly abandoned the project. Instead, they wrote, collaborating on songbooks, picture books, and MYSTERIES. After Van Clief's death in the early 1970s, Heide worked with her own daughter Roxanne on the Spotlight Club Mystery series, which she had started with Van Clief.

Of her humorous books, perhaps the best known are those about Treehorn, *The Shrinking of Treehorn* (1971), *Treehorn's Treasure* (1981), both ALA Notable Books, and *Treehorn's Wish* (1984), all of which are illustrated by EDWARD GOREY. Treehorn lives in a world in which the adults are wrapped up in their own concerns and interact with him only superficially. When he begins shrinking, for example, his teacher says, "We don't shrink in this class." With deadpan humor, Heide poked fun at the serious adult world and created a young boy who admirably takes care of himself. Gorey's line drawings complement the text delightfully. In *Tales for the Perfect Child* (1985), the children get what they want by perfecting skills such as whining and stalling. Again, Heide used understated humor to create wonderful and wacky situations.

Heide also has written in a more serious vein. Primarily for young adults, these novels provide portraits of young adolescent girls coming to terms with themselves and making choices about their lives. Sara, in *When the Sad One Comes to Stay* (1975), must choose between the friendship of a run-down, warm, older woman and her mother's cold, calculating plan for social success. Though her mother is a somewhat one-dimensional character, Sara's dilemma is real and painful.

When writing the picture books *The Day of Ahmed's Secret* (1990) and *Sami and the Time of the Troubles* (1992), both illustrated by TED LEWIN, Heide teamed up with another daughter, Roxanne's twin, Judith Heide Gilliland, who spent five years in the Middle East prior to working on these books. Ahmed lives in Cairo, and his book is filled with the sounds and sights of this modern yet ancient city. Sami lives in war-torn Beirut and must cope with the daily terrors of war while he hopes for a brighter future. Whether Heide's characters, like Ahmed and Sami, populate highly realistic books, or, like Treehorn, inhabit fanciful stories, they are all strong, believable, and engaging. P.R.

Henkes, Kevin

American author and illustrator, b. 1960. Kevin Henkes is best known for his warm, lively, humorous PICTURE BOOKS, distinguished for their remarkable understanding of the true world of young children. Peopled, for the most part, with expressively drawn mouse characters who are completely human in their feelings and relationships, these picture books sound almost as if the author has been eavesdropping on children at play, so realistic and believable are they. Henkes is also the author of MIDDLE-GRADE FICTION — including the innovative (one chapter is told entirely in pictures), easy-to-read *Margaret and Taylor* (1983), *Return to Sender* (1984), and *Words of Stone* (1992) — that focuses on the strength of family and children's struggles with emotional issues.

Henkes was born in Racine, Wisconsin, one of five children, and much of his work reflects his secure childhood and Midwestern upbringing. From an early age, he knew that he wanted to be an artist and was greatly influenced by the picture books of his childhood, books illustrated by greats such as CROCKETT JOHNSON and GARTH WILLIAMS. He never outgrew his love and appreciation for picture books, and with encouragement from his family to pursue his drawing and from a high school English teacher to continue to develop his writing, he put those two skills together and became a creator of picture books himself.

Henkes finished a draft of what became his first published picture book before the end of his senior year in high school. *All Alone,* an introspective mood piece in which a little boy thinks about all the things he can do when he is alone, was published in 1981; it was followed by *Clean Enough* (1982), an intimate, quiet portrait of an imaginative boy's bathtime; both feature human protagonists, rendered realistically.

A Weekend with Wendell (1986) was the first picture book in which Henkes's now familiar mouse characters — with their marvelously expressive ears and tails — appeared. Executed in pen-and-ink and watercolor, *A Weekend with Wendell* also introduces one of Henkes's favorite themes: friendships between bold, bossy children and meeker, quieter ones. Sophie's weekend guest is having all the fun — when they play hospital, Wendell is the doctor, the nurse, *and* the patient, and Sophie is the desk clerk. But when Wendell plays one too many tricks on Sophie, she instigates a game of firefighter in which she is the fire chief and Wendell is the burning building — and soon they are having so much fun that they are both sorry when it's time for Wendell to go home. In *Sheila Rae, the Brave* (1987), boastful, good-at-everything Sheila Rae finds herself lost one day, only to be rescued by her timid little sister, Louise, who consequently discovers some of her own strengths. Sheila's adventures continue in *Sheila Rae's Peppermint Stick* (2001). In *Wemberly Worried* (2000) Wemberly worries constantly about everything, especially starting school.

Chester's Way (1988), an ALA Notable Book, introduces Henkes's favorite character, the spunky, extroverted, original-minded Lilly. Cautious, routine-loving best friends Chester and Wilson find their lives turned upside-down when Lilly moves into the neighborhood with her crown ("I am Lilly! I am the Queen! I like everything!"), her red cowboy boots, and her jaunty red tail ribbon. Lilly also stars in *Julius, the Baby of the World* (1990), a hilariously funny, realistic portrayal of sibling jealousy. In *Lilly's Purple Plastic Purse* (1996) Lilly becomes angry when reminded by her teacher that Lilly is part of a school community. Henkes received his first major award — a Caldecott Honor Award — for *Owen* (1993), in which a little boy foils a nosy neighbor's attempts to make him give up his beloved fuzzy yellow blanket.

Henkes is the creator of true picture books — in which text and illustrations work together to make a seamless whole — that exhibit an innate understanding of children and always contain a strong element of security and comfort. M.V.P.

Voices of the Creators

🌿 *Kevin Henkes*

I think of my life as an ordinary one — and I sense that my books reflect this. I've also come to believe that by careful and loving observation, the ordinary reveals its complex nature. Take a simple life, a common experience, and render it precisely with words and images — build it with details — and if you're lucky you have an interesting story. A story that is rich enough to say something about the human condition.

I've written and illustrated books about things I know: sibling rivalry, making a new friend, getting lost, the arrival of a new baby. And whether I've chosen to use a PICTURE BOOK format or a CHAPTER BOOK format, whether I've chosen to render my characters as animals or humans, all my stories and protagonists are linked very closely to the life I led as a child.

I don't always remember specific events from my childhood, but I often remember the feeling, and I often remember certain tiny, tiny details very closely — what I wore on the first day of kindergarten, for example. I was very introspective, which I think helps intensify what I do remember.

As a child, my love of art defined me. And although I've had other interests at various times in my life, it was always art that I came back to. And I also loved to read.

My family made regular trips to the local public library. I remember stepping up onto the big wooden stool so I could watch the librarian check out my books. I remember wanting to carry my books all by myself, no matter how many I had chosen. And I remember how much I loved the way books from the library smelled. I'm certain that all those visits to the library had something to do with my becoming an author and illustrator.

More often than not, I chose books because I was drawn to particular illustrations. My favorite book as a child was *Is This You?* written by RUTH KRAUSS and illustrated by CROCKETT JOHNSON. Interestingly enough, it is essentially a guide for making a book of your own. I was lucky enough to own that book, and I still have it. It is as important to me now as it was to me when I was a child. Other favorite books of mine included *The Carrot Seed,* also by Ruth Krauss and Crockett Johnson, and *Rain Makes Applesauce* written by Julian Scheer and illustrated by Marvin Bileck. As I grew up, and the books I read grew longer, I was still inclined to choose books because of their illustrations. I admired GARTH WILLIAMS's art and often looked for novels that he had illustrated.

When I was young, I often drew at the kitchen table. I am one of five children, so there was often a lot of activity going on around me while I worked. But it didn't seem to bother me. Now I work in a spare bedroom in my own house. Sometimes it feels odd to have an entire room to myself for drawing and writing. And there isn't very much noise in the house while I'm working. Sometimes I turn the radio on.

I hope that my books convey a sense of joy and delight. I hope that they are thickly textured. I hope that there is something about my books that connects with children and something that connects with the adult reader. Even if something traumatic happens to one of my characters, I like to have my stories end on a hopeful note. That's my gift to the reader.

I can still remember coming home from school after something awful had happened. I can still remember how simply stepping inside the back door lifted the weight of my emotions. I was home, and it smelled good, and it felt good. I'd put on my play clothes, and everything would be okay. Which doesn't mean that when I walked out the door the next morning — or ten minutes later — something else wouldn't go wrong. I know that this sense of comfort doesn't exist for every child, but I write about what I know. And I want to share this sense of hope through my books. 🐚

Henry, Marguerite

American author, 1902–1997. Marguerite Henry was one of the twentieth century's finest writers of horse stories. Her books depict the close bonds between horse and human, exciting races, and many other standard elements of the genre, but what sets Henry's work apart is the historical authenticity of her plots and the vigor of her writing.

Readers may be surprised to learn that the author grew up in a home without any pets. Born in Milwaukee, Wisconsin, Henry discovered early that her interest in books and writing could be profitable. She sold a magazine story at age eight and shortly thereafter found employment mending books in the local library. She attended the University of Wisconsin at Milwaukee, married at age twenty-one, and pursued her dreams of a writing career and owning lots of pets. She sold a few articles to magazines such as the *Saturday Evening Post* and wrote a number of very minor stories and INFORMATION BOOKS for children, including the sixteen-volume Pictured Geographies series, published between 1941 and 1946.

Henry's breakthrough book, *Justin Morgan Had a Horse* (1945), tells the true story of an eighteenth-century Vermont colt noted for his power and speed who fathered a new breed of American horse, the Morgan. Rich in drama and vivid historical detail, the prose of this Newbery Honor Book is perfectly complemented by the artwork of Wesley Dennis, whose beautiful drawings and watercolor illustrations add great appeal to most of the author's works.

Henry received a second Newbery Honor designation for *Misty of Chincoteague* (1947), the story of two children living on an island off the Virginia coast who long to own one of the wild horses from nearby Assateague Island. Every year some of the horses are captured and brought to Chincoteague, where they are sold to raise funds for the fire department. Paul and Maureen save money to buy the horse and colt that Paul captured on Pony Penning Day. Although the older horse becomes tame enough to win a race, she eventually escapes to her home island, leaving the children with their much-loved colt, Misty. Steeped in salty East Coast atmosphere, Henry's best-known book is a particularly vivid re-creation of real people and events on Chincoteague Island during the 1940s. Misty was an actual Assateague horse and came to live with the Henrys for several years. The author continued writing about Chincoteague in *Sea Star: Orphan of Chincoteague* (1949), *Stormy, Misty's Foal* (1963), and *Misty's Twilight* (1992).

Henry won the Newbery Medal for *King of the Wind* (1948), the story of a Moroccan colt cared for by a mute stableboy. Presented to the young king of France, the horse is rejected by the royal court and forced to perform hard labor before achieving fame as the sire of the Thoroughbred line. The book is compelling for its historical setting and almost mythical portrait of a great creature brought low before rising in triumph.

In addition to her excellent horse stories, Henry wrote an acclaimed story of a burro, *Brighty of the Grand Canyon* (1953), and a non-fiction guide to horse breeds, *Album of Horses* (1951). Several generations of young lovers of ANIMAL STORIES have thrilled to Henry's well-written stories about some very memorable horses. P.D.S.

Hentoff, Nat

American author, b. 1925. *Passion* is no ordinary word, and Nat Hentoff's books for young adults prove that point. Hentoff's well-documented passions for jazz music and social causes have made their way into his YOUNG ADULT FICTION. *Jazz Country* (1965), marketed as a juvenile novel, was a forerunner of modern young adult literature as it dealt earnestly and honestly with subjects such as race relations. His next young adult novel, *I'm Really Dragged but Nothing Gets Me Down* (1968), rode the crest of the realistic fiction wave, inspired by S. E. HINTON. Not as successful as *Jazz Country*, and now somewhat dated, the novel demonstrated that Hentoff, unlike other writers for teens, cared not just about social realism but social reform, as his protagonist wrestles with the draft issue. Hentoff's next two young adult novels, *This School Is Driving Me Crazy* (1975) and its sequel, *Does This School Have Capital Punishment?* (1981), involve a young man (Sam Davidson) enrolled in a private school where his father is headmaster. Sam comes out fine on his own in the first novel, but in the second it takes an adult, a jazz musician, to help him out of his dilemma. In both novels Hentoff's social concern about teenagers' legal rights and his ability to capture the nuances of teen dialogue are at their peak.

Two more books, *The First Freedom: The Tumultuous History of Free Speech in America* (1980) and the young adult novel *The Day They Came to Arrest the Book* (1982), were written at a time when book banning and censorship were on the rise. *The Fist Freedom* is a nonfiction work documenting the history of free speech and challenges to it, while *The Day* puts the subject in a fictional context and concerns an attempt to ban MARK TWAIN's *The Adventures of Huckleberry Finn* from a school. *American Heroes: In and out of School* (1987) is a nonfiction work about teenagers fighting for their legal rights.

While Hentoff has never achieved the popularity among teens or the critical acclaim that authors such as S. E. Hinton have, his contribution is considerable. His books are not polemics, but they have a political edge to them which is missing in most teen fiction. Hentoff is also a dedicated advocate for the rights of teenagers — all of his books in one way or another explore the freedoms allowed and disallowed teens. Finally, Hentoff is a writer with many credits to his name and has chosen, on occasion, to bring his passionate and liberal voice directly to teens.

P.J.

Hesse, Karen

American author, b. 1952. Writing about a broad range of topics in a variety of styles, Karen Hesse has distinguished herself as one of today's most notable creators. Born and raised in Baltimore, Hesse grew up considering herself an observer of life. She attended Towson State College and graduated from the University of Maryland. Although she had held several jobs related to books, including working as a proofreader, as a typesetter, and in a library, she didn't discover the field of children's books until she settled in Brattleboro, Vermont, and began to read to her two young daughters.

Her first published book was *Wish on a Unicorn* (1991), the story of a sixth-grader and her brain-damaged sister, growing up in an underprivileged yet happy family. An empathy for society's poor and disenfranchised has informed several of Hesse's other works, such as *Just Juice* (1998), which concerns a chronically truant girl repeating third grade while her out-of-work father and pregnant mother struggle to make ends meet for their large family.

Hesse's works include insightful PICTURE BOOKS about topics such as death (*Poppy's Chair*, 1993) and personal courage (*Lester's Dog*, 1993), gentle EASY READERS (*Lavender*, 1993; *Sable*, 1994), and a powerfully haunting YOUNG ADULT NOVEL, *Phoenix Rising* (1994), about a nuclear accident and its effects on Nyle and her grandmother as they take in two strangers, including a fifteen-year-old boy suffering from radiation poisoning.

Some of Hesse's most memorable books experiment with form. *Letters from Rifka* (1992), drawn from the memories of the author's aunt, is composed of letters that a young Jewish girl writes to her cousin as she emigrates from Russia to the United States. *The Music of Dolphins* (1996) is the story of feral girl, Milan, found living in the ocean with dolphins and taken for study to a scientific research center. The way Mila relates her own experiences shows her gradual acquisition of language. Her initial words, printed in a large typeface, are limited to simple, declarative sentences; the typeface becomes smaller as Mila's vocabulary improves and her language skills grow more complex. Torn between joining human society and returning to live with the dolphins, Mila must make a crucial decision in a unique book, remarkably told.

Hesse surpassed herself with her next work, *Out of the Dust* (1997), a novel presented completely in free-verse poems. Though many authors have since attempted novels told in verse, Hesse was one of the first, and *Out of the Dust* remains among the best. Set in 1930s "Dust Bowl" Oklahoma, the story concerns fourteen-year-old Billie Jo, whose life is forever changed by her mother's accidental death. Spare poems — notable for their variety of form, haunting imagery, and deeply personal voice — reflect Billy Jo's loss, longing, and eventual healing in a book that deservedly won the Newbery Medal. Hesse used verse to tell a later story, *Witness* (2001), about race relations in 1920s Vermont.

Hesse continues to move between genres, producing a contemporary urban picture book (*Come on, Rain!,* 1999), adding an entry to the Dear America series (*A Light in the Storm: The Civil War Diary of Amelia Martin,* 1999), and crafting a seafaring adventure (*Stowaway,* 2000). Readers eagerly await each surprising development from this talented stylist. P.D.S.

Hest, Amy

American author, b. 1950. Amy Hest grew up in East Meadow, Long Island, in a quiet neighborhood and was fortunate in having an extremely close extended family. This family has found its way into all her books; in fact, Hest maintains that her books are all about her and that she writes, directs, produces, and stars in her own stories.

Hest knew she would become a writer when she was seven, though even after more than thirty books she is still modest about calling herself one. She earned a master's degree in library science at C. W. Post and worked as a children's librarian. In 1975, she began working in children's publishing. In 1977 she met her husband, a lawyer, and when their first child was born in 1979, Hest left publishing and began taking writing workshops. Her first novel, *Maybe Next Year,* was published in 1982.

Hest was paired with illustrator AMY SCHWARTZ for Hest's first PICTURE BOOK, *The Crack-of-Dawn Walkers* (1984). In an emotionally resonant story, Sadie and her brother take turns going on special Sunday morning walks with their grandfather. Other successful collaborations by Hest and Schwartz included *The Purple Coat* (1986), which won the Christopher Award, and *Fancy Aunt Jess* (1990).

All of Hest's books feature a child who is cared for and protected. Whether pouting, demanding, or curious, Hest's children are well loved. Many of her stories are written in first-person present tense, which creates a sense of immediacy and timelessness. Specific sensory details such as the feel of warm sheets, the swishing sound of ball gowns, or the smell of fresh coffee further ground her work. Stories often revolve around recurring events such as birthdays. *Kiss Good Night* (2001) is one such universal good-night tale, told with sweetness and gentle humor; it won the Christopher Award. Equally notable is Hest's focus on defining events in the life of a child, such as the first day of school, a first pair of glasses, or a first haircut. For example, in *Mabel Dancing* (2000), a child who wants to participate in her parents' fancy dance party is allowed one whirl around the floor before being tucked in again.

Much of Hest's work reflects a Jewish sensibility in language, character, and theme. *When Jessie Came Across the Sea* (1997), winner of the Christopher Award and the Kate Greenaway Medal for illustrations by P. S. Lynch, is based on family stories, but Hest breathed fresh life into the familiar story of Jewish immigration. In *The*

Friday Nights of Nana (2001) a grandmother and grandchild prepare for the Sabbath celebration, enjoying the comforting rituals.

When an editor suggested that Hest try shorter texts, she began a series about Baby Duck, an often-cranky duckling whose insufferably cheerful parents fail to understand her problems. Fortunately, Grandpa Duck comes to the rescue. These large-format, funny books resonate with parents as well as children; *In the Rain with Baby Duck* (1995) won the Boston Globe–Horn Book Award.

Beginning with *Love You, Soldier* (1991), Hest wrote three CHAPTER BOOKS about the character Katie Roberts. Katie loses her father in World War II, and eventually her mother remarries and they move to Texas. *Love You, Soldier* is a poignant, spare gem; it has won several state awards, including the Nutmeg Award.

Hest has created a notable body of work reflecting childhood concerns about home and family, with specific details that illuminate universal truths. L.D.S.

Hill, Eric

British author and illustrator, b. 1927. Eric Hill is the ingenious creator of the most popular puppy in children's books, the tawny-colored dog named Spot. Spot made his debut in the best-selling *Where's Spot?* (1980), a lift-the-flap book that shows mother dog Sally searching for her son. As Sally and the reader look under the bed, in the closet, and even in the grand piano, they find a different animal behind each flap. Finally, mischievous Spot is discovered hiding in a basket and is sent off to eat his dinner. The inspiration for the book came when Hill, working as a freelance artist and designer, noticed that his two-year-old son was amused by the flaps and hidden pictures on an advertising novelty. He combined the flap idea with his love for dogs and created a book for his son. On publication, the title was an immediate success, and Hill gave up his graphic work to pursue a career in children's books.

Like a child, Spot progresses from playing close to home to venturing farther away. He steps outside on his own, briefly but eagerly, in *Spot's First Walk* (1981), and in *Spot's Birthday Party* (1982) he plays hide-and-seek with his new friends. He finds that school is "great!" in *Spot Goes to School* (1984) and learns about siblings in *Spot's Baby Sister* (1989). In other books he visits the beach and the circus and stays overnight with his friend Steve Monkey. The lovable pup is also featured in the Little Spot BOARD BOOKS, a series geared toward children too young for lifting flaps; titles such as *Spot's Toy Box* (1991) are plotless, naming objects and actions that are easy for toddlers to recognize. Another board book series created by Hill — the Baby Bear Storybook series — features a friendly brown bear who shows readers a collection of familiar items in titles such as *At Home* (1983) and *The Park* (1983).

Where's Spot? and the many books that followed it are favorites with children and adults for a variety of reasons. The flaps, in the form of different objects, have the appeal of pop-ups but are sturdier and less complicated in design and therefore easier for small hands to manipulate. Integral to the story rather than mere gimmicks, the flaps allow children to help tell the tale, making story time more interactive. The simple texts are brief, and Spot's small adventures are fun and familiar to children. The well-designed ink and watercolor illustrations and the bold type are uncluttered, both standing out clearly against the white backgrounds. This art style is a result of the only art training Hill ever received; leaving school at age fifteen, he was hired as a messenger for a commercial art studio, where a newspaper cartoonist encouraged him and taught him how to draw in the cartoon style.

Though some of the books following *Where's Spot?* have been criticized as having harsher colors, a less precise style, and a more anthropomorphic Spot, the books are still praised as gentle, imaginative stories with universal appeal for young children. World renowned, the Spot books have been translated into fifty languages in one hundred countries. J.M.B.

Hinton, S. E.

American author, b. 1950. Young adult author Susan Eloise Hinton's career is one of firsts: from writing what is widely recognized as the first important contemporary YOUNG ADULT NOVEL, *The Outsiders,* in 1967, to being honored twenty years later with the first Margaret A. Edwards Lifetime Achievement Award by the ALA's Young Adult Services Division and *School Library Journal.* The award seems fitting because Hinton's adult lifetime has been spent writing young adult literature, a field she helped create. *The Outsiders,* her first novel, was written while she was a junior in high school and published two years later. It created a sensation, controversy, and a new realism in fiction for teenagers.

It is difficult to imagine a better young adult novel than *The Outsiders.* Everything works: the characters are real, the plot intriguing, the themes engaging, and the writing simple yet powerful. As the title reveals, *The Outsiders* is a book about feeling left out and seeking desperately to be accepted. In Hinton's world, the gang provides the missing family and an opportunity to establish identity. From the minute Pony Boy steps onto the page, the novel becomes his search to find a place in the world: to both grow up and to remain innocent, or as the book says, to "stay gold." A marketing decision was made to put "S. E. Hinton" as the author to disguise the fact that the writer of a book with primarily male characters and a lot of violence was, in fact, a young woman. The book received rave reviews. Shortly after, Hinton wrote an article for the *New York Times Book Review* called "Teen-Agers Are for Real," and her place in literary history was assured before she had even graduated from college.

Three years later, *That Was Then, This Is Now* was published. A more complex work, the book received favorable reviews as Hinton continued to write about boys and violence. *That Was Then* moves away from the gang setting to tell a tale of friendship and betrayal. *Rumble Fish* (1975) and *Tex* (1977) followed, mining the same territory: an Oklahoma setting, tough talk, missing or ineffectual adults, and the hard choices with often violent outcomes made by a young, sensitive male protagonist. All four books are told in the first person, with Hinton's voice being among the purest in capturing teenage dialogue, inflection, and attitudes. None of these books could be mistaken for those of any other author.

The second phase of Hinton's career found her involved in translating her novels into film. Oscar-winning director Francis Ford Coppola made two Hinton films, *The Outsiders* and *Rumble Fish,* both released in 1983. *Tex* became a Walt Disney production in 1982, and *That Was Then, This Is Now* was released in 1985. Hinton was not involved with *That Was Then,* and it proved to be the weakest of the four films. Hinton made cameo appearances in *The Outsiders* and *Tex,* increasing the films' realism. The translation of Hinton's novels to film was natural, as her writing has a cinematic quality: it is loaded with strong characters, plenty of conflict, lots of action meshed with stinging dialogue, and the struggle between reality and idealism.

The third phase of Hinton's career began in 1988 with the publication of *Taming the Star Runner.* Although the landscape and characters are similar to those in her earlier novels, important changes occurred. The first-person voice is gone, yet the novel is more autobiographical than her others in its story of a young man writing and publishing a novel while still a teenager. After a nine-year hiatus from publishing, Hinton proved in *Taming the Star Runner* that she had lost none of the power in her writing or in her ability to provide insight into the lives of adolescents.   P.J.

Historical Fiction for Children

Historical fiction as a genre sometimes appears to be self-consciously searching for definition as well as justification and approval. It is a hybrid and a shape-shifter: it combines history with fiction; it has been adapted to a number of forms, from PICTURE BOOKS to novels. It is a field that has attracted many of the finest writers for young people, including K. M. Peyton, Rosemary Sutcliff, and Jill Paton Walsh in England and SCOTT O'DELL, KATHERINE PATERSON, and ELIZABETH GEORGE SPEARE in the United States. Given the number of awards garnered by historical novels, the genre impresses critics, as the following selective sampling of Newbery Medal winners indicates: *Caddie Woodlawn* (1935), written by Carol Ryrie Brink; *Adam of the Road* (1942), written by Elizabeth Janet Gray; *Johnny Tremain* (1943), written by ESTHER FORBES; *Island of the Blue Dolphins* (1960), written by Scott O'Dell; *The Slave Dancer* (1973), written by PAULA FOX; and *Roll of Thunder, Hear My Cry* (1976), written by MILDRED TAYLOR. Yet popular opinion holds that, despite the appeal of individual titles, as a genre it does not excite the majority of young readers. Debates continue not only over presentation but also over content, plot, and setting. For example, just when does the past become historical? It seems as if historical fiction poses as many problems as history itself.

One problem is definition. It seems to be a common assumption that the term *historical fiction* refers to the historical novel, the classic conventions for which were established by Sir Walter Scott early in the nineteenth century. As adapted from the commentary on the historical novel in Thrall and Hibbard's *Handbook to Literature* (revised and enlarged by C. Hugh Holman, 1960), these conventions include setting the story in a time when differing cultures are in conflict, placing fictional characters in situations in which they encounter actual historical figures, and using these fictional characters to demonstrate the effects that opposing views had upon those then living. Many of these conventions have been modified. Not all contemporary historical fiction, for example, features encounters between fictional and historical characters. Nor is the blending of fact and fiction confined to longer works, particularly in books for children. All of this explains why the term *historical novel* seems preferable for use in general discussion. But it is surprising how frequently one traditional requirement — that the story be set in a time when differing cultures are in conflict — appears in works by noted writers for children; for example, the late Rosemary Sutcliff set many of her major works in Britain during the last years of the Roman occupation.

Regardless of modifications in the classic conventions, serious historical fiction is more than a story set in the past. Setting must be integral to the plot; otherwise the tale is simply a "costume romance" that exploits rather than explores history. Yet at its best, most critics agree, historical fiction can illuminate the past so that history becomes vital and exciting, experienced rather than studied. There is also general agreement that a book that deliberately re-creates an earlier time is different from one written in that time. LOUISA MAY ALCOTT's *Little Women* (1868–1869), despite its references to the Civil War, is not historical fiction, in contrast to Irene Hunt's *Across Five Aprils* (1964).

Whether a picture book, a book for beginning readers, or a novel, the historical story is composed of two elements. To be taken seriously, it must fulfill the requirements for both good history and good literature. To be truly successful, it must become more than merely the sum of its parts. Ideally, it must be honest, balanced, and enticing, the product of serious scholarship, a distinctive style, and fervent interest in the subject. Unfortunately, old attitudes and stereotypes can be overtly or covertly persistent. Historian Allan Nevins commented: "The facts of the past do not change, but our view of them does." Consequently, reevaluating history as presented in books for children has become a significant aspect of critical analysis — particularly with regard to portrayals of minorities and Native Americans. And writers such as VIRGINIA HAMILTON, Mildred Taylor, and LAURENCE YEP, who write from minority perspectives, have become important contributors to a fuller understanding of times past.

Writers of historical fiction, like conscientious historians, must work within certain restrictions: accuracy (what is fact as opposed to speculation), consistency (establishing and maintaining a thesis and point of view), and selectivity (eliminating the relatively unimportant from the essential, otherwise defined as solving the problem of too little versus too much). Emphasis on scholarship, however, should not eliminate laughter. The past, like the present, could be ridiculous and amusing as well as grim or noble as demonstrated in British writer Leon Garfield's period piece *The Strange Affair of Adelaide Harris* (1971), a comedy of errors set in eighteenth-century Brighton, England, where a certain Dr. Bunnion has established his Academy for the Sons of Gentlefolks and Merchants.

Given the origin of the genre with Sir Walter Scott and the popularity of SURVIVAL STORIES such as Defoe's *Robinson Crusoe* (1719), it is not surprising that classic examples of historical fiction written for children during the Victorian period tended to emphasize adventure, although the best of them, like Robert Louis Stevenson's *Kidnapped* (1886), also evoked political and social concerns. While adventure stories set in the past, as exemplified by AVI's *True Confessions of Charlotte Doyle* (1990), with its strong female central character, are still a significant subgenre of historical fiction, domestic dramas such as PATRICIA MACLACHLAN's *Sarah, Plain and Tall* (1985) — the poignant tale of a mail-order bride and her new family — are firmly established not only as a continuing theme in American literature for children but also as one of its more enduring contributions. Like the Little House books (1932–1943) crafted by LAURA INGALLS WILDER, Elizabeth Coatsworth's *Away Goes Sally* (1934), and Alice Dalgliesh's *The Courage of Sarah Noble* (1954), they draw significance from the lives of ordinary people. Similarly, the plight of Native Americans, overlooked and misunderstood, has made considerable impact on works such as Scott O'Dell's *Sing Down the Moon* (1970), the story of the tragic displacement of the Navajos in 1864, and Michael Dorris's *Morning Girl* (1992), a touching, ironic depiction of the first encounter between the Tainos and Columbus.

Recent historical fiction has a broader scope than that of its nineteenth- and even twentieth-century antecedents. But whether a novel, a book for beginning readers, or a picture book, certain criteria are equally applicable: a sense of history, a sense of story, a sense of audience. These three phrases not only provide common ground for evaluation but also indicate the directions toward which contemporary historical fiction has moved.

First: a sense of history. Many of today's outstanding writers of historical fiction not only possess a sense of the past, they are also aware, as Allan Nevins remarked, that each era tends — and perhaps needs — to reevaluate history in the light of its own experience. One significant example is *My Brother Sam Is Dead* (1974), written by James and Christopher Collier. In an article written for the *Horn Book Magazine,* Christopher Collier observed that *Sam* presents a view of the American Revolution more attuned to twentieth-century historiography than did Esther Forbes's classic *Johnny Tremain* (1943). Implicit in the Colliers' work, written during the Vietnam era, is the idea that war may not be the solution to political problems, that issues underlying the American Revolution — or any major historical event — are never simple. In contrast, *Johnny Tremain,* written at the time of World War II, deplores loss and suffering but subordinates that idea to the sacrifices demanded by such glorious causes. This is not to say that the latter is inaccurate in detail, but rather that it examines the past through a different lens.

Prominent writers emphasize the necessity of research in order to create the sense of place that informs their plot and their characters. Explanatory prologues of appended notes, such as those addressed to young audiences by the late Patricia Beatty, draw the audience into the historian's worldview. Today's historical story may also include a bibliography of sources or suggestions for further reading.

But scholarship is not a substitute for a good tale well told. *History,* after all, is rooted in the French word *histoire,* which means "story." Therefore, the second criterion, a sense of story, requires that the books withstand analysis according to literary standards. Although thinly

Illustration by Michael McCurdy from *Johnny Tremain* (1943), by Esther Forbes.

disguised textbooks have not entirely disappeared, there is now a considerable body of historical fiction that is as compelling as it is illuminating, whether drawn from family reminiscences, as in Mildred Taylor's *The Friendship* (1987), a dramatic novella of the black experience in 1930s Mississippi, or from research, as in Jill Paton Walsh's elegantly crafted *Grace* (1992), based on the story of the British heroine who, in 1838, assisted her father in rescuing the survivors of a shipwreck. It can employ elements of FAN-TASY, as in Nancy Bond's *Another Shore* (1988), in which a contemporary young woman is transported back into the Nova Scotia of 1744, or in Elizabeth Marie Pope's *Perilous Gard* (1974), which blends a scholar's knowledge of Tudor England with a believable variation on the old ballad of Tam Lin. Or, as in PAUL FLEISCHMAN's *Bull Run* (1993), it can introduce the many facets of one historic event through a series of dramatic monologues.

Whatever the era or source of inspiration, the author must create a palpable setting with believable characters whose diction suggests the time in which they live. In contrast to adults who, it seems, buy books by the pound, today's youthful audiences generally prefer their encounters with the past to be of shorter duration than did their nineteenth-century counterparts. Consequently, writers have little opportunity for digressions that interrupt the primary narrative flow. Only the most skilled can evoke significant issues while observing the limits imposed by a young audience — the third sense which the writer of historical fiction must develop.

Nowhere is this skill more in demand than in the writing of a picture book text or a book for beginning readers. Consequently, those working in these genres must narrow their focus, restricting the size of the canvas but not the intensity of emotion, a balance successfully struck in GEORGE ELLA LYON's *Cecil's Story* (1991). Illustrated by PETER CATALANOTTO, the book explores a child's universally recognizable fears during wartime, and only through the pictures is the Civil War setting revealed. Picture book versions of history require illustrations that are as accurate as the text, for there is a symbiotic relationship between them. BARBARA COONEY, for example, deserves acclaim for the research that informs her illustrations in books such as *Ox-Cart Man*, written by DONALD HALL (1979), set in the New Hampshire landscape of 1832.

The more successful historical stories for beginning readers offer vignettes of events or figures as perceived by a child. Exemplified by F. N. Monjo's *One Bad Thing About Father* (1970), a fictionalized view of Theodore Roosevelt's presidency as narrated by his son, this approach demythologizes history without diminishing it. Heroes become approachable; the past becomes comprehensible in human terms.

Influenced by the social upheavals of the 1960s and awareness that today's young readers, conditioned by a media-dominated environment, are less easily shocked than those of previous generations, contemporary historical fiction has changed not only in selection of subject and theme but also in the language and details through which these are conveyed. Although very different in style, novels such as WALTER

Dean Myers's *Fallen Angels* (1988), a devastating look at the Vietnam conflict, and Katherine Paterson's *Lyddie* (1991), the story of a Vermont girl's efforts to gain independence by working in the mills of Lowell, Massachusetts, during the 1840s, are woven from tougher fiber than books written before 1960. Advances in technology have encouraged the production of lavish picture books. But whether designed as a chapter book for beginning readers or a young adult novel, it is desirable that the perspective be compatible with the experience of the intended audience, which perhaps explains the proliferation of first-person narratives.

No artificial boundaries should be set in searching for "the right book for the right reader," as the old maxim states. Many books speak to all ages, like Patricia MacLachlan's *Sarah, Plain and Tall*; others, because of vocabulary or length, may be restricted to an older audience. Some, like Christophe Gallaz and Roberto Innocenti's *Rose Blanche* (1985), a grim story of the Holocaust in picture book format, have engendered lively debates about appropriate readership. More such controversies will undoubtedly occur.

If written with passionate attention to story, scholarship, and audience, tales of times past can awaken in many children the idea that they are part of history. They will have experienced it as lively, significant, and engrossing, for, as Erik Haugaard, the author of many fine historical novels, observed in an article written for the *Horn Book Magazine*, "No one as yet, that I have heard of, has been bored into wisdom." M.M.B.

Hoban, Lillian

American author and illustrator, 1925–1998. Lillian Hoban studied art at the Philadelphia Museum School of Art and worked as a dancer and dance instructor before beginning her career in children's literature. In 1961 she illustrated *Herman the Loser* (1961) for her husband, author Russell Hoban. After several years as an illustrator, she began writing her own books while continuing to illustrate the work of others.

Hoban's many picture books and easy readers have been praised by critics and the public. With a few pencil lines, she can give her people and animals a wide range of expressions and emotions, and her work is characterized by realism, even when she writes or illustrates animal stories about animals who live like humans. Especially well known are Hoban's illustrations for the several stories written by Russell Hoban about Frances, the cheerful, childlike badger, who overcomes familiar childhood traumas — including the addition of a new baby sister — with humor and poetry. Lillian Hoban gave Frances the same honest, childlike attributes and expressions that she has given to all her animal characters: Frances is more child than badger when she takes a school bus or pulls a wagon down the sidewalk with her friends. Both adults and children sympathize with the universal dilemmas presented in the Frances stories and recognize themselves in the cozy relationships of the badger family. In the delightful critical and popular success *Bread and Jam for Frances* (1964), for example, Frances insists on eating only bread and jam. But guided gently by her parents, she decides for herself that she would rather eat a variety of foods.

Equally popular have been Hoban's Arthur books, which she both wrote and illustrated. In each, Arthur, a young monkey, encounters a very real childhood dilemma. In *Arthur's Honey Bear* (1974), Arthur has a yard sale to get rid of the toys he has outgrown, but he is not yet ready to sell his Honey Bear, the only toy his younger sister wants to buy. The tension is resolved through compromise, however, and Arthur becomes Honey Bear's uncle. As in the Frances books, Arthur and his sister behave entirely like humans. Readers recognize themselves in Hoban's animals but are able to laugh at Arthur's foibles because he is, after all, a monkey. Hoban has often used wash and pencil for her illustrations, although she has illustrated her later books with watercolor. In each, the soft colors are well suited to the story's tone and subject.

Hoban again exhibited her interest in the ordinary events in children's lives in her artwork of chubby, cheerful children for Miriam Cohen's books about an elementary school class. Each book in the series focuses on an everyday event or turning point for young children. *Will I Have a Friend?* (1967) concerns Jim's first day of school, and the later books cover themes of fear, friendship, and growing independence. Hoban's children, like her animals, are fully realized characters, although defined by very few lines.

Hoban's cheerful style and her attention to the emotions of young children give life to the books she has written and illustrated. Her books appeal to adults because they present a world in which adults nurture and instruct children, and at the same time, children recognize and respond to her sympathy with the common experiences of childhood. M.V.K.

Hoban, Russell

American author, b. 1925. Whether writing of humble domestic childhood dilemmas or spinning FANTASY tales of courageous survival, Russell Hoban instills his work with pathos and humor so that both children and adults find his stories equally absorbing. His rhythmic prose paints such colorful descriptions of both characters and settings that it is not surprising to learn that he began his creative career as an illustrator. In Lansdale, Pennsylvania, he was the only son and youngest of the three children born to Abram and Jeanette Hoban. His father, an advertising manager for the *Jewish Daily Forward,* rewarded his children with nickels for clever remarks and exceptional drawings. "As a child I drew very well and was expected to be a great artist when I grew up," Hoban has recalled.

Fulfilling parental expectations, and the predicament children often find themselves in when those expectations and their own needs conflict, is a recurring theme in Hoban's life and work. His father died when he was eleven, and after graduation from high school at sixteen, Hoban turned down a scholarship offered by Temple University and enrolled at the Philadelphia Museum School of Industrial Art. He served overseas in the armed forces and in 1944 married fellow illustrator LILLIAN HOBAN. Fulfilling his father's expectations, he became a successful freelance illustrator, and his work appeared in noted publications such as *Time, Sports Illustrated,* and the *Saturday Evening Post.* Although he wrote and illustrated his first book for children, *What Does It Do and How Does It Work?* (1959), others illustrated his work after 1960. Lillian Hoban noted, "Russ and I have completely different feelings about illustration. It was always a heavy thing for him — he used to sit at the easel groaning and yawning, and he was glad to give it up when he did."

Bedtime for Frances (1960), the first of several Frances stories, evolved from Hoban's observations of his own four children. In *Bread and Jam for Frances* (1964), Frances, a small badger, sings soliloquies expressing her fondness for bread and jam and her disdain for all foods which are not bread and jam, most especially soft, runny boiled eggs. She refuses to eat anything but jam sandwiches, which her parents then give her on every occasion — morning, noon, and night. Frances soon yearns for spaghetti and meatballs, acknowledging that variety is indeed the spice of life. The Frances books are delightful to read aloud. Hoban's words skip across the pages, and the characters and the situations in which they find themselves are so simply truthful that any family would maintain that the author had been secretly observing the goings-on in its own household.

The Hobans collaborated on many projects, including *The Little Brute Family* (1966), *Charlie the Tramp* (1967), and *Emmet Otter's Jug-Band Christmas* (1971). In 1967 Hoban published *The Mouse and His Child,* his first children's novel. Illustrated by Lillian, it was acclaimed in England, but American critics were not markedly impressed. Children rarely, if ever, read literary critics, however, and they soon discovered *The Mouse and His Child.* Among preteens and adolescents it has become a cult classic. In this many-layered novel, two clockwork toy mice —

father and son — are bought and taken from the warm comfort of their toy store. Years later a tramp finds them broken and discarded in a trash heap. He does his best to repair them, then winds them up and lets them go. "Be tramps," the tramp declares, and he walks away. The mouse and mouse child begin their journey, and Hoban did not hesitate to portray the cutthroat nature of survival in an evil world in which the villainous Manny Rat plots to enslave the toys. Hoban also, willingly and winningly, showed the great love that exists between the mouse, his child, and the true friends they discover on their journey. Readers admire the courage of the mouse child who yearns for home and family, love and self-determination. English critic John Rowe Townsend wrote, "There's hope as well as pain in this pilgrimage; and, significantly, it's the child who hopes, the child who perseveres when the father would give up. This is a book which can be returned to at many times, at many ages, and there will always be something new to be found in it." Caldecott Medal winner DAVID SMALL brought a vigorous new rendition of the book to readers in a reissue of *The Mouse and His Child* (2001).

After divorce and remarriage, Hoban moved to England and began writing adult novels, most notably *Riddley Walker* (1980). His work continues to reflect his own deeply felt personal experiences: "Life is a continuous presentation of sensation and event. Faced with that presentation and faced with himself facing it, the artist represents it. Why? He can't help it . . . Art, like babies, is one of the things life makes us make."

M.B.B.

Hoban, Tana

American photographer, author, and illustrator, b.? Tana Hoban has presented children with brilliant photography in beautifully designed PICTURE BOOKS. Critics praise her energetic, graphic skill and her ability to fuse photography and objects with the child in mind.

Hoban's photographs, by presenting difficult concepts through familiar objects and surroundings, allow children to look at their world with fresh eyes. The minimal texts keep readers focused on the pictures. Her strong, deceptively simple images usually portray shapes, sizes, or other concepts in subtle ways. Hoban's first concept book, *Shapes and Things* (1970), for example, presents simple black and white photograms without captions. The forms, though familiar to young children, are made to appear abstract through the photogram technique. No other photographer extends a child's world or expands imagination through everyday experiences as does Hoban. Her works are often recommended for a variety of ages and for bilingual children.

Hoban's photographs speak for themselves. Lively and spontaneous, they often provide emotion along with concepts — a child in a silly hat, adult and child hand in hand. Most of her work portrays urban settings, and since moving to Paris in the mid-1980s, her pictures have displayed a subtle combination of Parisian and American city life.

Impressive camera work provides unexpected viewpoints, but Hoban's artistic content remains within the realm of the child's familiar landscape. Her titles often stand as the only books available to children on that subject. *I Read Signs* (1983), *I Read Symbols* (1983), and *I Walk and Read* (1984) provide parent and child with a leisurely look at signs encountered on a walk. Through these books, children can study everyday settings that in reality receive only a quick look. Hoban's titles appeal not only to sight. Her book *Is It Rough? Is It Smooth? Is It Shiny?* (1984) provides photographs that appeal to the sense of touch.

Design is an important aspect of Hoban's success. *Look Again!* (1971), *Take Another Look* (1981), and *Look! Look! Look!* (1988) are original concept books. First, objects are presented through a cutout allowing a partial view; then, by turning the page, the entire object can be seen. The object in its environment appears on the following page. The books are delightful guessing games and invite close examination. Hoban's *26 Letters and 99 Cents* (1987) is a clever two-in-one book. One half of the book presents the alphabet in glistening, brilliantly colored upper- and lowercase letters with photographs of one object for each letter. The other half depicts coins arranged to make up sums from one to ninety-nine cents. Each sum is photographed as if for "making change" — for example, ten cents is presented as one dime, as a nickel and five pennies, and as ten pennies — allowing small fingers to count the change coin by coin. By separating the concepts on each page through four lined blocks of color, Hoban achieved a cohesive design. *Construction Zone* (1999) provides young viewers with thirteen construction machines at work.

Hoban has attributed her ideas for successful picture books to an experiment at the Bank Street School in Manhattan in which teachers provided children with cameras. The children found new perspectives and fresh ways of looking at their world through the camera lens. The experiment made a lasting impression on Hoban, and she began to look at her urban landscape with new eyes. Hoban has said of her photographs, "I try to say, 'Look! There are shapes here and everywhere, things to count, colors to see and always, surprises.'"

Hoban's work includes filmmaking, and her photographs have appeared in numerous national magazines and are part of the permanent collection of the Museum of Modern Art. J.B.

Hoff, Syd

American cartoonist, author, and illustrator, b. 1912. Noted for his books for children just learning to read, Syd Hoff has written and illustrated more than fifty EASY READERS as well as several PICTURE BOOKS and a children's novel. He has created uncomplicated, humorous stories and illustrated them with cartoon drawings.

Hoff began his career as a cartoonist. After dropping out of high school, he attended the National Academy of Design in New York City.

He entered as a fine arts student but received little encouragement from his instructors because of the humorous quality of his work. He turned to cartooning, sold his first cartoon to the *New Yorker* at age eighteen, and became a regular contributor to that and other magazines. Later, he created his own syndicated comic strips: *Tuffy*, which ran from 1939 to 1949, and *Laugh It Off*, running from 1958 to 1977.

Hoff's career took a major turn in the mid-1950s, however, when his daughter was ill and he made a series of drawings to take her mind off her treatment. These drawings evolved into *Danny and the Dinosaur* (1958), perhaps his most popular book for beginning readers. When Danny goes to the museum, a dinosaur miraculously comes to life, and he and the boy set out on a day's adventures. Although they engage in simple and predictable activities, Hoff's humor comes through, making the events funny and appealing. For example, the dinosaur plays hide-and-seek with the children but finds nothing large enough to hide behind. When he gets discouraged, the children pretend they can't see him so he won't feel bad. The illustrations are classic Hoff: simple cartoons with a minimum of background and details. While a number of his books are about animal characters who leave their natural habitat and enter the world of humans, such as *Sammy, the Seal* (1959) and *Chester* (1961), a carousel horse, others feature children facing common situations.

Hoff has said that the best humor springs from the familiar. Drawing on his own experience with relatives, Hoff wrote *My Aunt Rosie* (1972), about an overbearing aunt who praises the character Sherman indiscriminately and greatly embarrasses him. When she gets sick and Sherman doesn't see her for a while, he realizes he misses Aunt Rosie and her "baloney." In *The Horse in Harry's Room* (1970), Hoff dealt with the importance of a child's imagination. Although no one else can see it, Harry keeps a horse in his bedroom. To discourage his fantasy, his parents take him to the country to see real horses. But the plan backfires when Harry, realizing that horses need freedom, offers to let his horse go. The horse, however, stays, and Harry knows he can keep him as long as he wants.

Hoff has tackled historical themes in some of his more recent books. He introduced children to Thomas Nast's cartoons and the role they played in bringing Boss William Marcy Tweed to justice in nineteenth-century New York City in *Boss Tweed and the Man Who Drew Him* (1978). Although the beginning-reader format demands that much of the information is greatly simplified, Hoff included Nast's cartoons to add to the book's authenticity. Although Hoff's plots are not complicated and his characters are not highly developed, his simplicity and his humor are great achievements. **P.R.**

Hogrogian, Nonny

American artist and writer, b. 1932. Nonny Hogrogian is a two-time winner of the Caldecott Medal. The first award was for her illustrations in Sorche Nic Leodhas's *Always Room for One More* (1965), a rollicking Scottish folk song, and the second was for *One Fine Day* (1971), an Armenian folktale she learned from her family. Comparing the two books reveals the range of Hogrogian's versatility as an artist. In *Always Room for One More,* the figures are drawn in pen-and-ink line and crosshatch, and the background combines a gray wash with lavender and green pastels. In *One Fine Day,* she used oils in bold, simple compositions of vigorous, warm colors.

Hogrogian has a remarkable ability to vary the medium or technique in her illustrations to reflect the text's mood. Her exquisite and nuanced sense of design can be broken down into geometry and shape. Her illustrations spill across the page, often regardless of margins: they may have borders, not have borders, or go through the borders.

Hogrogian illustrated her first children's book, *King of the Kerry Fair* (1960), with woodblocks. She led the way in putting expression on the faces of animals and bringing heart and emotion to her animal characters, as in *Carrot*

Cake (1977). In her Caldecott Honor Book *The Contest* (1976), she overlaid her rich texture and controlled color with skeletal pencil studies of two rogues. Her work is childlike in its creation of wonderful, joyful, playful characters who always have depth, and it is recognizable by its richly colored folk illustrations, depth of heart, and humor. Her illustrations for Rumer Godden's *Candy Floss* (1991) are grand and have a romantic sense of color. When using pastels, she has created rich texture and color, but she has used watercolors for her most recent illustrations, such as those in *Feathers and Tails: Animal Fables from Around the World* (1992), one of several books written by her husband David Kherdian for which she has supplied the art.

Hogrogian is a native New Yorker of Armenian heritage who majored in art at Hunter College, then studied the art of the woodcut with Antonio Frasconi at the New School for Social Research in New York City. Her first job in children's book publishing was as a book designer and art buyer, an experience that has contributed to the deft design of her own books. For each manuscript, after careful research, she has created the entire design for the book, including cover, endpapers, and typography.

Hogrogian led the way in children's book illustration with innovative design, the use of mixed media, and the introduction of folk characters with Mediterranean features rather than the more commonplace northern European countenance so familiar in earlier illustrated folktales. Her influence on children's literature has been significant and has been recognized by two Caldecott Medals. **B.J.B.**

Holling, Holling C.

American author and illustrator, 1900–1973. In 1941 Holling C. Holling won instant acclaim and made a lasting impression with *Paddle-to-the-Sea,* a big, handsome geohistory of a hybrid sort not seen before. *Tree in the Trail* (1942) and three other, somewhat lesser successors demonstrated that *Paddle* was not a one-

MINN   THE ALLIGATOR SNAPPER, CALLED   THE REAL LOGGERHEAD OF THE SEA
                       "LOGGERHEAD"

Illustration by Holling C. Holling from his book *Minn of Mississippi* (1951).

shot phenomenon. In fact Holling and his collaborator and wife, Lucille Holling, had been working on children's books of one kind and another, mostly to do with Indian life and lore, since the mid-1920s, and two of those books were distinctive in ways of their own.

The open spaces of the passing frontier were Holling's native landscape as a Michigan farm boy, a sailor on the Great Lakes, an anthropological researcher in New Mexico, a zoological observer in the Rockies, and a muralist in Montana — roles in which he had been securely trained at Chicago's Art Institute and Field Museum of Natural History and in private study with anthropologist Ralph Linton. Among the first products of these exploratory years, when the Hollings also camped on Indian reservations and attended tribal ceremonies, was a story of early conflict between the Chippewa (or Ojibway) and the Sioux, *Claws of the Thunderbird* (1928). The mid-1930s, in turn, yielded an immensely popular mass-market pair, *The Book of Indians* (1935) and *The Book of Cowboys* (1936), which convey a great deal of information via detailed illustrations, large and small, and semifictional narratives. Such a narrative, *The Book of Indians*, includes Otter-Tail, a Woodland Indian, and Buffalo-Calf, an Indian of the Plains. Shortly after its appearance, the education division of the U.S. Indian Service hailed *The Book of Indians* as "one of the few books for children about Indians which we can whole-heartedly recommend," adding that it was "almost unique [in] having no misstatements, either in the text or in the pictures." Some fifty years later a prominent anthropologist, passing over hundreds of books from the intervening years, singled out for praise *Claws of the Thunderbird* and *The Book of Indians*, along with *Paddle-to-the-Sea*.

Claws is an exciting, even hair-raising story about two young Indians, an evenly matched boy and girl, who together are crucially involved in tribal conflict — not conventional pap about prototypical Indians, a description that fits adult as well as juvenile fiction published at that date.

In *Paddle-to-the-Sea* the story line is also a travel route as a tiny carved Indian-in-a-canoe, launched by an Indian boy in the melting snows north of Lake Superior and bearing the words "Please put me back in the water," makes its way through the Great Lakes and down the St. Lawrence River to the Atlantic, cheered on by the intent reader (and assisted by an occasional human hand) past the perils of sawmill and fishing net, of fire and ice and Niagara Falls. Marginal line drawings, a Lucille Holling specialty (though she is not publicly credited in every volume), demonstrate exactly what happens and precisely how; full-color paintings on every facing page make the setting and the drama vividly present. In the illustration as well as the narrative, fact and fiction balance out — the book cannot be said to be more one or the other. Younger children naturally respond more to the story and to the corresponding paintings; at an older age the factual details in text and pictures tend to hold greater interest.

Tree in the Trail features a lone cottonwood on the Great Plains where the Santa Fe Trail eventually goes through — a tree that, dying, sends its "best part" traveling westward as an ox yoke to the end of the trail. The narrative is something of an artificial construct, the paintings are smooth and slick in the period manner of popular magazines, but the intermesh of time and place, of people and natural forces, again captures the imagination. "It opened my eyes at age eight to social and ecological history," a Harvard professor of landscape architecture attested, nominating *Tree* as the most influential book of his childhood.

Holling's books have a way of passionately engaging their readers. Unlike *Paddle-to-the-Sea*, which taps into the historic romance of America's inland waterways, and *Tree on the Trail*, which evokes legendary markers on the wagon trails, *Seabird* (1948), *Minn of the Mississippi* (1951), and *Pagoo* (1957), pegged respectively on the life story and geographic range of a seagull, a snapping turtle, and a hermit crab, are informational make-believe with pictures of varying effectiveness; *Minn* is the beauty and the encyclopedic treasure of the three. Both *Seabird* and *Minn* were Newbery Honor Books. But all have their articulate fans.

Paddle-to-the-Sea continues to inspire American fathers and sons to launch wooden replicas. Like many juvenile authors and some illustrators, Holling made the kind of books he had found lacking as a child — in his case, books that would tell him what he wanted to know about Indians. He achieved his aim with fidelity and imagination and, at least once, a transcending vision. B.B.

Holt, Kimberly Willis

American author, b. 1960. Kimberly Willis Holt was born during a hurricane and has led somewhat of a whirlwind existence ever since. As the daughter of a naval officer, Holt grew up in far-flung places such as France, Guam, Washington, and Virginia. However, in her fiction she revisits her childhood home in Louisiana and her current home in Texas (where she lives with her husband and daughter). Holt has convincingly evoked a warm nostalgia for recent decades through economical prose, gentle Southern voices, first-person narratives, and coming-of-age themes. Her stories are especially noteworthy for their acute awareness of those on the fringes of society, marginalized by disability, physical appearance, race, ethnicity, or class.

Her first novel, *My Louisiana Sky* (1998), a Boston Globe–Horn Book Honor Book, tells the story of twelve-year-old Tiger who, upon her grandmother's death, must choose between remaining in a small town with her mentally handicapped parents or living with her glamorous aunt in the big city. *Mister and Me* (1998), an engaging CHAPTER BOOK, is likewise set in a small Louisiana town at midcentury. Jolene, a young African American girl, resents the attention paid to her widowed mother by a handsome suitor and tries to thwart their marriage plans before coming to accept the situation. Holt won the National Book Award for *When Zachary Beaver Came to Town* (1999), which vividly encapsulates the thoughts and feelings of thirteen-year-old Toby during the summer of 1971 as he copes with the disappointments in his life — the agony of his first unrequited love, the absence of his mother from the family as she aspires to a singing career — while his friends contend with their own problems, including abandonment and the death of a brother in Vietnam. The improbable baptism of Zachary Beaver, the "world's fattest boy," serves as a powerful climax to the story and a perfect metaphor for faith, hope, renewal, and resilience.

Dancing in Cadillac Light (2001) traces the special relationship between eleven-year-old tomboy Jaynell and her grandfather, who has come to live with her family. Grandpap dies midway through the novel and strangely bequeaths his house to a poor, lower-class family. As Jaynell uncovers the family secret, she better understands his motivation and takes his lesson to heart.

Holt knew she wanted to be a writer ever since reading *The Heart Is a Lonely Hunter*, by Carson McCullers, when she was twelve, and her stories tend to come to her in the voices of young adolescents: "I don't think I've ever really gotten over being twelve." Holt has drawn on her own life in creating her stories. While riding with her mother at age nine, they passed a mentally retarded woman who, her mother revealed, had a lot of children with her mentally retarded husband; the incident haunted Holt and eventually inspired *My Louisiana Sky.* Talking with her father about the sawmill town where two of her great-grandfathers had worked led her to interview people in that town; though *Mister and Me* is not based on any of those stories, the setting is. Holt paid two dollars to see the world's fattest boy at the Louisiana State Fair when she was thirteen. *Dancing in Cadillac Light,* which started out as a short story, is her only novel to have begun with the characters rather than the setting. She drew on her own relationship with her sister and the humble childhoods of her parents. The remarkable quality of her writing, her productive pace, and two major awards mark Holt as a writer to reckon with. J.H.

Hopkins, Lee Bennett

American author and anthologist, b. 1938. When asked to speak, Lee Bennett Hopkins has been far more comfortable talking about his mission than his books, which number more than seventy. His mission, about which he has spoken with passion, is to recognize quality children's POETRY, bring such work to the attention of teachers and librarians, and nurture conversation and dialogue among children about poetry.

Hopkins was born and spent the first ten years of his childhood in Scranton, Pennsylvania. He has recalled, "I was Dick straight out of *Dick and Jane,* the basals that taught me to read." Life changed dramatically in 1948 when his family moved to Newark, New Jersey. Turmoil struck again when Hopkins was fourteen and his parents' marriage collapsed. Money was tight and life uncertain. Officially, Hopkins was enrolled at the South Eighth Street School, although by his own admission he spent more time out of than in school: "I hated school and

everything associated with it, including books and reading." Luckily, a teacher introduced him to the magic of books and the theater. Hopkins graduated from high school and went on to college and graduate school.

Hopkins's first book, *Let Them Be Themselves: Language Arts Enrichment for Disadvantaged Children in Elementary School* (1969), was reissued in its third edition in 1992. Other books include YOUNG ADULT FICTION, anthologies, and nonfiction for adults. *Mama* (1979) and *Mama and Her Boys* (1981) are semiautobiographical remembrances of life in the Hopkins home. His anthologies represent a number of influences. *Surprises* (1984), *Best Friends* (1986), *More Surprises* (1987), *Good Books, Good Times* (1990), and *Questions* (1992) celebrate the exuberance of youth. The world surrounding children is the subject of several collections, including *On the Farm* (1991), *Still a Star: Nighttime Poems* (1990), and *To the Zoo* (1992). *Marvelous Math: A Book of Poems* (1997) and *Spectacular Science: A Book of Poems* (1999) present poetry centered on these subjects. As an anthologist, Hopkins has collected poetry he admires. On two occasions, this admiration resulted in anthologies devoted solely to one poet, *Rainbows Are Made: Poems by Carl Sandburg* (1982) and *Voyages: Poems by Walt Whitman* (1988). "Good poetry," he has noted, "is by a master craftsman who knows the rules of his craft. He/She gets the maximum impact from a minimum number of words."

Over the course of two decades, Hopkins has also been the voice of social warning. *Wonder Wheels* (1980) was one of the first young adult novels about teen suicide. *Pass the Poetry, Please!* (1972) exposed elementary classrooms for the dreary places they were in the late 1960s — rooms of potentially creative youngsters lacking rhyme. Now in its second edition, the book continues to challenge educators. *Through Our Eyes* (1992) also contains a plea of sorts. In sixteen short poems, Hopkins has presented the hopes, fears, and observations of today's youth. The anthology is honest, hard-hitting, and revealing.

Hopkins closed the third edition of *Let Them*

Be Themselves with the hope that we — the collective society responsible for children — begin to value their words. If we do this, then perhaps "they will begin to think more about thinking."

B.A.M.

Horvath, Polly

American author, b. 1957. Long before she learned to write, Polly Horvath pulled boxes and cans out of the kitchen cupboards to use as characters while making up stories on her family's kitchen floor in Kalamazoo, Michigan. Perhaps this experience accounts for the persistent presence of food in her highly imaginative MIDDLE-GRADE FICTION. Casseroles and cakes provide opportunities for expressing togetherness and individuality in *When the Circus Came to Town* (1996). Betty Grunt tends to munch cookies when pondering her options and her future in *The Happy Yellow Car* (1994), and not surprisingly, cereal plays an important part in *No More Cornflakes* (1990). *An Occasional Cow* (1989) provides the Reinstein kids with the versatile, all-occasion threat "I shall leave the nuts out of my banana bread!" The indelible scene of Aunt Sally savoring her vegetables in *The Trolls* (1999) will spring to the mind of readers any time they face a plate of green beans; others will strike off in search of fiddleheads.

Horvath's tour-de-force anecdotal food book is *Everything on a Waffle* (2001). A seaside village comes together to care for Primrose Squarp, whose parents have been lost in a storm at sea. Primrose finds solace and good advice at a restaurant called The Girl on the Red Swing, where everything is served on a waffle — meat, potatoes, and even waffles. The reader is treated to a recipe at the end of each chapter as Primrose is nourished by the memory of her parents through her memories of their meals. It is no surprise that Horvath enjoys reading books by M. F. K. Fisher and Laurie Colwin.

Though she wrote steadily from ages nine through eighteen, Horvath paused for many years to pursue a career in dance and studied at the Canadian College of Dance in Toronto and the Martha Graham School of Contemporary Dance in New York City. Her six novels (so far) are a feast for the intellect, and each has a unique flavor. Quirky characters are folded into outlandish episodic plots, blended with very real settings and universal themes. Though the conclusions of her stories are not always the ones readers might want, they have integrity. Sophisticated words and phrases mix with colorful colloquialisms to make a lively voice that resonates long after the cover is closed. As Horvath has said, "It's like I have a flock of sheep, and I want to make a tapestry. First, I have to shear the sheep then spin the wool into yarn, then dye the yarn and then weave it. So, is that thing on the wall the flock of sheep? Well, yes and no."

Everything on a Waffle and *The Trolls* both received Boston Globe–Horn Book honors. *Everything on a Waffle* was also named a Newbery Honor Book, and *The Trolls* was selected as a finalist for the National Book Award. S.L.T.

Houston, James

Canadian author and illustrator, b. 1921. In 1948, having made it to the northeast coast of Hudson Bay, James A. Houston decided to forgo his return flight and stay at an Eskimo settlement with only his sleeping bag, sketching materials, and a can of peaches. Fourteen years later, after working as civil administrator of West Baffin, Northwest Territories, where he introduced printmaking to the Inuit and established the West Baffin Eskimo Co-operative to help them market carvings and prints, Houston left the Arctic for New York City and a job as associate director of design for Steuben Glass. He still works for Steuben, as master designer, but now he and his wife, Alice, divide their time between homes in Connecticut and the Queen Charlotte Islands.

The North, which he visits regularly, continues to serve as inspiration for Houston's books and much of his art. Almost five decades after first setting foot in the Arctic, he introduced readers of all ages to a way of life most will never experience themselves. Some of those books — beginning with *Nuki* (1953), illustrated by Houston and written by his first wife, Alma — have been labeled children's literature, although, as Houston pointed out, "the Inuit made no difference between children's stories and adult stories; children stayed around and were aware of everything at all times."

The Toronto-born author has admitted he was relatively clueless when first in the Arctic — he managed to fall through the sea ice five times during the first year he was there — but the Inuit shared their knowledge and their stories, which he in turn shared with his readers. The first book he both wrote and illustrated was *Tikta'liktak: An Eskimo Legend* (1965), which won the Canadian Library Association's Book of the Year for Children Award. He also won the prize for two other volumes: *The White Archer: An Eskimo Legend* (1967) and *River Runners: A Tale of Hardship and Bravery* (1979).

In all his books, whether Inuit or Native American stories, Houston is at his best when recounting tales of traditional nomadic life. *Drifting Snow* (1992), for example, about a girl who returns to the North in search of family she lost when she was sent south for tuberculosis treatment as a toddler, is most riveting when it involves the girl's experiences camping on an island with an Inuit family but stalls when dealing with contemporary issues. Houston himself seems to breathe easier when his characters are away from civilization; it is there that his writing is most evocative. In books like *Akavak: An Eskimo Journey* (1968), *Wolf Run: A Caribou Eskimo Tale* (1971), *Frozen Fire: A Tale of Courage* (1977), and *The Falcon Bow: An Arctic Legend* (1986), he has made readers feel bone-numbing cold, mind-altering hunger, the joy of a successful hunt, and gratitude for that first hot meal. The author has explained how to build an igloo, how to stave off frostbite, how to help and rely on others. He has described a life among people of great generosity, respect, and ingenuity.

Houston's tales of adventure are captivating in short form — *Long Claws: An Arctic Adventure* (1981) at thirty-two pages is hardly a tome, but it tells a thrilling story about children who save their family from starvation. His full-length novels such as *Whiteout* (1988), the story of a rebellious teenager sent north for a year of community service, are also compelling. The author, meanwhile, has carved himself a solid niche in the history of Canada's Arctic. At a time when cultural appropriation has become a hotly debated subject, Houston's books about the Inuit stand as testimony to the fact that cultures *can* be bridged — and that stories from an oral tradition can be respectfully retold in print. B.G.

Howe, James

American author, b. 1946. If any common features define James Howe's MYSTERIES and PICTURE BOOKS, novels and INFORMATION BOOKS, they are the author's respect for and understanding of children and childhood. He has remembered well what it is like to be small and powerless, and his books all strive, in different ways, to connect with his readers through those feelings. One of his most successful and effective devices is humor, "the most precious gift I can give my reader."

Although Howe grew up telling stories, writing plays, and editing *The Gory Gazette,* the official newspaper of his Vampire Club, his first desire was to be an actor. After graduating from Boston University in 1968 with a degree in theater, Howe moved to New York City to pursue his acting career. In 1981, after the success of his first three children's books, he left his job as a literary and theatrical agent and turned to writing full-time. Howe and his late wife, Deborah, had no idea, however, when they began writing their first book, *Bunnicula* (1979), just for fun, that it would be as popular as it was or that it would launch his career as a children's book author. But their mystery was embraced by middle-grade readers and won more than twenty state awards. *Bunnicula* and its sequels, which Howe wrote after Deborah's death, are all infused with generous doses of humor and wordplay. Having trained as an actor and a director, Howe understands how to build suspense, and he has a fine sense of dramatic timing.

Bunnicula is a little black and white rabbit who, in the first book, comes to live with the Monroe family. The human members of the household don't notice anything strange about their new pet, but Chester, the family cat, who has a vivid imagination, is convinced that Bunnicula is a vampire. The story of Chester's hilarious attempts to warn the Monroes of this evil in their midst is told by Harold, the family dog. In *Howliday Inn* (1982), Harold and Chester are boarded at Chateau Bow-Wow when the Monroes go on vacation. They soon find themselves caught up in a suspicious chain of events that Chester believes must involve murder. Bunnicula returns in *The Celery Stalks at Midnight* (1983), which introduces the newest Monroe pet, Howie, the dachshund puppy. Howe has explained his belief that his series of picture books featuring the popular Bunnicula characters are a suitable introduction to mysteries for younger children. This particular genre speaks directly to children because, Howe has written, in addition to being fun to read, "mysteries allow us mastery and control." To children, this desire for control is fundamental. "Through reading," Howe has said, children "gain some measure of control. They are able to see something through to a neat resolution; and perhaps through the children in the story, gain a sense of themselves as human beings who are valid and powerful."

Howe's concern for his readers' empowerment is evident in his other books as well. *The Hospital Book* (1981), a sensitively written nonfiction photo-essay, helps children anticipate what a hospital stay is like — from the staff, to the equipment, to the feelings with which they may have to cope. Howe's series for beginning readers, featuring best friends Pinky and Rex, celebrates childhood friendships. As with all of Howe's characters, Pinky and Rex appeal to children because they know the challenges and rewards of being best friends. With them children learn something about what it means to be a friend while maintaining individuality. Howe's stories are funny, but they are also about the joy and pain of being human.   K.F.

Hughes, Langston

American poet and author, 1902–1967. Primarily known for his POETRY, James Langston Hughes also wrote fiction, drama, autobiography, and INFORMATION BOOKS. Born in Joplin, Missouri, he spent his formative years in Kansas and Cleveland. His childhood was not easy. An only child, Langston began to read books to escape his deep loneliness. In his first autobiography, *The Big Sea* (1940), he referred to his second-grade year: "Then it was that books began to happen to me, and I began to believe in nothing but books and the wonderful world in books." Among the books he enjoyed were the Bible and the works of W. E. B. Du Bois, MARK TWAIN, and Paul Laurence Dunbar; he also avidly read news articles about race relations. His eighth-grade class in Lincoln, Illinois, elected him class poet, and during his sophomore year at Central High School in Cleveland, his first poems appeared in print. In his senior year, he wrote the appealing commentary on black beauty, "When Sue Wears Red." Two rarely cited poems for children — "Winter Sweetness" and "Fairies" — were published in *The Brownies Book* in 1921, and in the same year the *Crisis* published one of his most popular poems, "The Negro Speaks of Rivers."

Travel, adventure, and a move to Harlem influenced the style and content of his work. Simple and informal, his poems were composed in free verse and rhyme. His works flourished during the Harlem Renaissance in the 1920s. Hughes drew his inspiration from urban black life, managing to capture its essence and at the same time express in language the rhythm of the jazz and blues music that meant so much to him. The ability to write about ordinary people and the accessibility of his lyricism contributed to the popularity of his poetry with children. A literary descendant of Dunbar, Hughes sometimes wrote in dialect. Despite his despair about racial injustice in America, he was able to imbue much of his creative output with a sense of humor, an affirming spirit, a love for the natural world, and optimism. Although many of his poems were not specifically intended for young people, he published his collection *The Dream Keeper and Other Poems* (1932) especially for them. Many of his poems appeared in anthologies, and in 1967 Lee Bennett Hopkins compiled for children *Don't You Turn Back,* a selection published in 1969 after the poet's death. A poet of the people, Hughes was properly dubbed the poet laureate of Harlem.

Hughes explored several genres, including autobiography, novels, short stories, drama, and nonfiction. For children, he coauthored with Arna Bontemps a story about poor people in Haiti titled *Popo and Fifina* (1932). Among his books that introduced young readers to various topics are *The First Book of Rhythms* (1954), an engaging look at rhythm around us, and *The First Book of Jazz* (1955). Through his collective biographies *Famous American Negroes* (1954) and *Famous Negro Heroes of America* (1958), young readers were introduced to outstanding persons. These short informative books highlight the lives of black achievers at a time when few sources on black history were available. In 1956 Hughes published, with Milton Meltzer, an enlightening overview, *A Pictorial History of the Negro in America.* His last work was a book of aphorisms for children, *Black Misery* (1969), published after his death.

Hughes had great pride in his race. His works continue to inspire readers seeking a voice against injustice. L.F.A.

Hughes, Shirley

British author and illustrator, b. 1927. Sit down with a pile of Shirley Hughes books and come away certain that this woman loves children. Invite her to tea, and there is no reason to send the dog to the cellar and the kids off to play; she will revel in whatever comes. Her characters are dressed to play; she has elevated scruf-

finess to an art form. And if her children do not look steamed and pressed, they do look well loved.

Hughes has illustrated more than two hundred books and written more than a dozen of her own, several of them about one of her outstanding characters, a mischievous little guy named Alfie. In *Alfie Gets in First* (1981), Alfie squeezes through a window when the family's locked out; in *Alfie Gives a Hand* (1983), he takes his blanket to a birthday party; in *An Evening at Alfie's* (1984), he comforts baby sister Annie Rose when the pipes spring a leak. The first book Hughes illustrated was Doris Rust's *Story a Day* in 1954. Since then, she has illustrated dozens of others, including Louisa May Alcott's *Little Women* in 1960 and books by Margaret Mahy, Nina Bawden, Helen Cresswell, and Alison Uttley.

Her own first book was *Lucy and Tom's Day,* the first in the Lucy and Tom series, in 1960. *Dogger* (1977), which she also both wrote and illustrated, won for her the Kate Greenaway Medal, Great Britain's highest picture book honor.

Born in Holylake, England, near Liverpool, Hughes married an architect, and they have three grown children. She had a childhood full of acting out plays with her older sisters and of writing. Plenty of books were always around, so she got to know the work of illustrators such as Arthur Rackham and Edmund Dulac. After attending the Liverpool Art School and Ruskin School of Drawing and Fine Arts in Oxford, she taught at Oxford.

Hughes compares picture books to a small theater production, in which the illustrator is the stage manager, lighting specialist, playwright, and costume designer. She did, in fact, take classes in costume design, thinking she might go into that field, but her devotion to writing and illustration turned her toward children's books. Another push toward children's books as a career choice was Hughes's family life itself, her observation and participation in the day-to-day chaos. She knew, too, from her own children how a book needs to be strong enough to withstand the test of repeated readings. In all her books Hughes's generous spirit shines through, providing a warm place from which all small readers can explore their world. A.C.

Hurd, Clement

American illustrator and author, 1908–1988. Clement Hurd's career lasted from 1939 to 1980, during which time he illustrated over seventy books, five of which he also wrote. He is best known for *Goodnight Moon* (1947), written by MARGARET WISE BROWN, a frequent collaborator. He also illustrated nearly fifty books written by his wife, Edith Thacher Hurd.

Hurd was born in New York City and spent his childhood in New York and Locust, New Jersey. He started drawing in boarding school at age thirteen. After graduating from Yale University, he spent one year at the Yale School of Architecture before traveling to Paris, where he studied painting under Fernand Léger for two years, developing his style of bold, well-defined shapes and clean, flat colors. Returning to the United States, he found work painting murals and doing small design jobs. In the late 1930s, Hurd joined the Writer's Laboratory at the Bank Street College of Education, the program that so influenced Margaret Wise Brown's successful method of writing for small children. Edith Thacher was also a member of this group, and in 1939 they married, beginning their prolific professional collaboration. Nineteen thirty-nine also brought Hurd's first published illustrations: two wordless books for William R. Scott, *Town* and *Country,* and Gertrude Stein's *The World Is Round.* Hurd died of pneumonia in 1988, and now his son, THACHER HURD, continues the family's creative tradition, writing and illustrating children's books.

Goodnight Moon, a picture book classic, continues to mesmerize the very young. Of his collaboration with Brown, Hurd said, "Maybe collaboration on a creative level is always difficult, and maybe the more creative a person is, the more difficult he or she is to work with; but I do feel that all Margaret's main illustrators did their best work on her books. . . . [W]orking with Margaret was difficult but at the same time stimulating and satisfying." The collaboration of text and art is integral to *Goodnight Moon*'s success, with the minimal, carefully chosen list of objects and nearly the same picture on each color spread. Like the mouse hidden on each spread, the child experiencing the story is allowed to explore both the familiar and the unknown, saying, "Goodnight nobody," "Goodnight air," and finally to set aside fears by facing them, saying, "Goodnight noises everywhere." Hurd's increasingly darkened room with dark green walls, red balloon, and cozy yellow lights in the doll's house has become a symbol of comfort and safety for thousands of children.

Hurd's style of flat, bold colors that bleed off the page, as in *Goodnight Moon, The Runaway Bunny* (1942), and *The Little Brass Band* (1955), all written by Brown, was well suited to the color separations he used at the beginning of his career. But he enjoyed experimenting with a variety of media, particularly creating hand-pressed prints combining wood grains, plants, and linoleum cuts, which he printed on a variety of papers. Some of his favorite books use these methods, including *Christmas Eve* (1962) and *The So-So Cat* (1965), both written by Edith Thacher Hurd. In the three-color Johnny Lion books and other I Can Read books his wife wrote, the loose, expressive line drawings take center stage. The other two colors are added simply, using a texture or visible brush strokes when appropriate, liveliness prevailing over accuracy.

Perhaps Hurd's most remarkable accomplishment is his use of bright colors in vibrant combinations that nonetheless convey a sense of comfort through sympathetic characterizations, care-free lines, and page designs that show both playfulness and order. L.R.

Hurd, Thacher

American author and illustrator, b. 1949. Thacher Hurd's books are filled with exuberant energy and vibrant color. Remembering what delighted him as a child, he has tried to make his stories alive and funny.

Hurd grew up in a household where the creation of children's books was commonplace; his mother, Edith Thacher Hurd, was a writer and his father, CLEMENT HURD, an illustrator. As a young child living in Vermont and later in California, he often spent time in his father's studio, where he was given paints and encouraged to experiment. It was not until he was in college, however, that he began to study art formally. He then transferred to California College of Arts and Crafts and earned a B.F.A.

His early PICTURE BOOKS, gentle mood pieces, were influenced by his parents' style. In *The Quiet Evening* (1978), Hurd described how a household settles down for the night, with alternating scenes of activities at home and those far away. His illustrations reflect the hushed and peaceful text, using appropriately dark colors.

Gradually, however, Hurd found his own voice and colors, and his stories became more exuberant. The settings shifted from home to the larger world, and he began using animals for characters. For example, rats populate *Mystery on the Docks* (1983). After his favorite opera singer has been kidnapped, Ralph, who runs the diner on Pier 46, helps rescue him. The colors are bolder and the cartoon-like pictures are in keeping with the fast-paced story.

Hurd has described himself as a frustrated musician and has said that music often creeps into his books. At the end of *Axle the Freeway Cat* (1981), for instance, Axle and his newfound friend watch the sunset and play a duet for harmonica and auto horn. Music has also been the direct inspiration for several other stories. While listening to a jazz program on the radio, Hurd heard an unusual song, "Mama Don't Allow." Suddenly he had images of a swamp, alligators, and a band. But it took several years before he finally worked out how to put all the parts together. The resulting book, *Mama Don't Allow* (1984), received the Boston Globe–Horn Book Award for picture books. When the town sends Miles and his loud band to the swamp, the alligators invite them to play for their Saturday night ball. Hurd's spirited story line, his loose drawing style, his strong colors — rich greens and blues — and the occasional use of balloons to provide dialogue all give the book its boisterous energy. Both *Mama Don't Allow* and *Mystery on the Docks* have been adapted for television.

The *Pea Patch Jig* (1986) was also inspired by music, this time by an old fiddle tune. While her family prepares for a party, Baby Mouse wanders off and gets into all sorts of trouble. Baby Mouse is a delightful character, and Hurd created a wonderful sense of orderly chaos as she romps through her adventures in this and the other two books about her: *Blackberry Ramble* (1989) and *Tomato Soup* (1991).

Little Mouse, the star of another SERIES, worries that his friends have forgotten his birthday and goes off skiing in *Little Mouse's Birthday Cake* (1992). Using a more controlled composition and quieter colors in these snow-filled pictures, Hurd explored Little Mouse's emotions. In other picture books, he has used dogs as his main characters, as in *Art Dog* (1996) and *Zoom City* (1998), where a group of dogs drives through the city.

Besides the many wonderful picture books he has created, Thatcher Hurd and his wife Olivia founded Peaceable Kingdom Press, a publisher of fine posters, which celebrate the work of many other artists. Thatcher Hurd has been as generous in his praise of the work of others, as he has been talented in developing his own books. P.R.

Hutchins, Pat

British author and illustrator, b. 1942. With the publication of *Rosie's Walk* in 1968, Pat Hutchins became established as a gifted creator of PICTURE BOOKS for young children. The clean, white background of the pages and large type size make the book open and inviting; textured patterns used for fox and chicken and flowers and trees have the wonderfully appealing symmetry of patterns found in nature. But the look of the book was not its only strength; a great joke unfolds in the pictures as a fox tries fruitlessly to pounce on Rosie the hen — a joke never mentioned in the minimal text but one that even very young readers appreciate enormously.

In Hutchins's first book lie the qualities and strengths that characterize much of her work: a great sense of humor, a brilliant graphic design, and a simple, logical story line. Hutchins went on to create many other books with animal characters, including *The Surprise Party* (1969), *Good-Night Owl!* (1972), and *What Games Shall We Play?* (1990), to name a few.

Hutchins has credited her early years as one of seven children with giving her the time and freedom to roam the woods and fields surrounding her home in northern England, where she developed a love of woodland creatures. Her books are always childlike in their worldview, taking seriously the things that matter to children. In *Happy Birthday, Sam* (1978) she showed how only a gift from Grandpa allows Sam to reach the things he *thought* he'd be tall enough for on his birthday. *The Very Worst Monster* (1985) and *Where's the Baby?* (1988) are about sibling rivalry in a monster family. *Changes, Changes* (1971) is another groundbreaking title, with Hutchins's trademark balance of bright, bold colors, clean line, and lots of white space. Here, two wooden figures arrange and rearrange colorful blocks to make all sorts of shapes: a house, a fire truck, a boat, and more. There is not a word of text, but a delightful story emerges from the pictures. The Weston Woods film studio did a filmstrip adaptation of *Changes, Changes* — using all wooden instruments in the soundtrack — as well as of *Rosie's Walk* and other picture books by Hutchins.

Hutchins clearly intended some of her books to teach, but they are never dull or preachy. *One Hunter* (1982) is an ingenious COUNTING BOOK in which the hunter can't find any of the animals, although readers see them on every page. Hutchins has written longer books as well — beginning novels full of tongue-in-cheek humor, fast-moving action, hilarious characters, and outlandish situations. Most of them, including

The House That Sailed Away (1975), *The Mona Lisa Mystery* (1981), and *The Curse of the Egyptian Mummy* (1983), were illustrated by her husband, film director Laurence Hutchins. Overall, she has written more than twenty picture books as well as several novels, demonstrating a great breadth of talent.

Hutchins began drawing at an early age and earned a scholarship to art school at sixteen. After graduating, she worked for an advertising agency in London, where she met her husband. They lived in New York for a brief time, and there she showed her work to American publishers. An editor's suggestion that she write her own text resulted in *Rosie's Walk*. Her work has been widely praised by critics on both sides of the Atlantic, not only for illustration and story but for the buoyant warmth and gaiety that emerge from every page. Many titles have been named ALA Notable Books and have received illustration honors. *The Wind Blew* (1974), a humorous, rhyming picture book about people chasing after possessions that have been whipped away by the wind, was the 1974 winner of the Kate Greenaway Medal. K.M.K.

Hyman, Trina Schart

American illustrator, b. 1939. Trina Schart Hyman has been hailed as one of the great romantic illustrators of our time, and her gloriously illustrated fairy tales — the best known of her many works — are a true testament to this high praise. The gifted creator of many of the most beautiful princesses, gallant knights, gruesome monsters, and frightful hags ever to grace the pages of a PICTURE BOOK, Hyman has brought brush to paper and captured the essence of fantasy.

Born in Philadelphia, Hyman studied art in Philadelphia, Boston, and Stockholm and served as art director of *Cricket* magazine for seven years. Her first publication, the Swedish tale *Toffe och den lilla bilen* (Toffe and the little car, 1961), took longer to decipher than to illustrate, but it nonetheless launched a highly successful career. Since then she has illustrated more than 130 books, many of which she wrote herself.

Hyman can recall being disappointed with picture books as a child; the beautiful princesses were simply not beautiful enough. Indeed, while very precise and technically skilled, her illustrations are remarkable primarily for their great beauty. Hyman won the Caldecott Medal in 1985 for her work on Margaret Hodges's retelling of *Saint George and the Dragon,* an excellent example of her technique. Using an elaborate series of borders that enclose one page of text and one page of illustration per double spread, Hyman created the illusion that each scene is being viewed through a window. Every text page is enclosed by a different border of flowers indigenous to the story's setting; illustration pages, however, are framed simply so as not to interfere with the depicted scene. The child observer is therefore given a special glimpse through the window of history, turning a book with a universal message into a very personal experience. In less structured books, Hyman's work is notable for other design features, including accommodation of text. Rather than create a painting into which words must be placed, she designs her pages to flow around the story, forming a visually dynamic and unified whole. Striving for the perfect integration of text and artwork, she is an illustrator in the classic Caldecott mode.

While Hyman is best known for her fairy tales, she has illustrated many other important books as well, including a rendition of *Swan Lake* (1989) retold by Margot Fonteyn; the Caldecott Honor Book *Hershel and the Hanukkah Goblins* (1989), with text by ERIC KIMMEL; LLOYD ALEXANDER's original folktale *The Fortune-Tellers* (1992), set in the exotic country of Cameroon; *King Stork* (1973), written by HOWARD PYLE and a Boston Globe–Horn Book Award winner; and a picture book autobiography, *Self-Portrait: Trina Schart Hyman* (1981).

Hyman is as proficient with pen and ink as with the richly hued colors of her most recent illustrations and considers her work for Norma Farber's *How Does It Feel to Be Old?* (1979) to be

her best. In this quiet glimpse into the lives of a thoughtful girl and her grandmother, Hyman's softly rendered sketches capture the reflective mood and broaden the themes of love and loss to create a book that is genuine in its emotion and message. Regardless of subject matter or medium, Hyman's illustrations have a special impact on children, who respond positively to their sensitivity and beauty. C.C.B.

I

Information Books

"There are such excellent informational books available for children today in so many fields that no adult who guides children's reading can afford to be ignorant of them." May Hill Arbuthnot's enthusiastic assessment appears in the first edition of her highly regarded *Children and Books* (1947). By the time of her writing, many such books had established nearly all the trends in the crafting of children's nonfiction that would flourish through the remainder of the twentieth century. Some of them continued as library staples and popular children's reading for several decades. Yet it would be another twenty-five years before critical writers really began to argue that nonfiction works for children should be accorded the same depth of value and scrutiny as PICTURE BOOKS, fiction, POETRY, and folklore.

English critic Margery Fisher summed up the problem in her 1972 book *Matters of Fact: Aspects of Non-Fiction for Children:* "Because of an unexpressed feeling that information books are not 'creative,' they are far more often viewed for their content than for their total literary value." MILTON MELTZER, already established as a writer of children's nonfiction, took the critics further to task in an eloquent and oft-cited *Horn Book Magazine* article, "Where Do All the Prizes Go?" (Feb. 1976). Making a well-argued case for the literary artistry of good nonfiction, Meltzer questioned why so few books had been granted the stature of Newbery honors.

Several other critics and writers of children's nonfiction added new perspectives in a group of essays created and collected by educator Jo Carr in *Beyond Fact: Nonfiction for Children and Young People* (1982). Another major champion of nonfiction, classroom teacher Beverly Kobrin was speaking and writing widely throughout the 1980s. Her book *Eyeopeners!: How to Choose and Use Children's Books About Real People, Places, and Things* (1988) addressed a particularly wide audience of parents, grandparents, teachers, and librarians. Calling children's nonfiction "literature non grata," Kobrin joined the complaint that a lack of prizes, literary consideration, and even bookstore sales characterized the very books that most appeal to some children.

By the 1990s many more writers and teachers were building on the work of this small band of founding critics. Books and journal articles on evaluating and selecting nonfiction books, utilizing them in classrooms, and reading them aloud broadened considerably the stream of thinking and writing about books of information, now published in quite large numbers and in a broad array of forms.

The arguments for stronger consideration of nonfiction in the granting of book awards gained ground in the 1980s and 1990s. The Newbery Medal was given to RUSSELL FREEDMAN's *Lincoln: A Photobiography* in 1988. This remains only the sixth nonfiction book to receive the award since its 1922 inception, following the previous such winner by thirty-two years. A half dozen nonfiction works were designated Newbery Honor Books in these two decades, and at the end of this period the Caldecott Medal, given for distinction in illustration of a picture book, was given twice to works of nonfiction, first to MARY AZARIAN in 1999 for *Snowflake*

Bentley, written by Jacqueline Briggs Martin, and then to DAVID SMALL in 2001 for *So You Want to Be President?*, written by Judith St. George. The small number of nonfiction titles honored by these best-known of all book awards fueled arguments to establish an award devoted solely to nonfiction, and two such awards were created.

In 1990, the National Council of Teachers of English began awarding the Orbis Pictus Award for Outstanding Nonfiction for Children. Named for Johannes Amos Comenius's 1657 work *Orbis Sensualium Pictus,* usually considered the first information book actually planned for children, the award was first given to JEAN FRITZ for *The Great Little Madison* (1989). In 2001 the Association for Library Service to Children announced the winner and honor books of the first Robert F. Sibert Informational Book Award. Named in honor of the longtime president of Bound to Stay Bound Books Inc., the first medal was awarded to Marc Aronson for *Sir Walter Ralegh and the Quest for El Dorado* (2000), with four books named for honors.

Several other organizations recognize the creation of fine nonfiction. Established in 1977, the Washington Post–Children's Book Guild Nonfiction Award honors a nonfiction writer for her or his body of work. In 1976 the Boston Globe–Horn Book Award added a nonfiction category to its previously established fiction and picture book awards. Since 1977 the Society of Children's Book Writers and Illustrators has also given its Golden Kite Award for nonfiction. Several children's choice awards, usually given at a statewide level, include an award for nonfiction. And finally, in 2001, Milton Meltzer, credited with best arguing the merit of awarding nonfiction writing, received the Laura Ingalls Wilder Award, also administered by the Association for Library Service to Children. Given for a body of work in any genre, the Wilder award had been given only one other time to a distinctive creator of nonfiction — Russell Freedman.

The growing body of critical literature and the criteria for the various awards have differed little over the years in valuing certain qualities in nonfiction. Accuracy always tops the list, and sometimes the notion of authority or authenticity is stated as part of this requirement. Some writers of children's nonfiction, such as astronaut Sally Ride and botanist Carol Lerner, are actually subject specialists. Others do copious research, even traveling to relevant sites to assemble information. Having manuscripts checked by authoritative readers is a common practice. Even quite simple books may reveal a depth of scholarship by stating the author's background and work process, acknowledging the experts consulted, or providing endnotes and source lists.

Clarity is usually very high on the criteria list. No simple matter, clarity involves choice of language, well-presented explanations, logical organization of the material, and understanding of the intended audience. Writing for young people may tempt authors to oversimplify technical information, which may mislead or confuse the reader.

Also, good nonfiction books are expected to both inform and engage readers, and so content should be delivered in an interesting writing style. Skill in the use of language, an unusual or imaginative view of the subject, or humor can contribute to such a style. Some critics search for passion or enthusiasm about the subject. Milton Meltzer has summed up the matter of style with panache: "Style . . . is not a trick of rhetoric or a decorative daub. It is a quality of vision."

Pictorial material is essential to most nonfiction works for children. Through long tradition, attractively designed pages of related text and illustration have become a critical requirement. Well-chosen artistically rendered pictures (photos, drawings, diagrams, etc.) complement the words, which together make up a package of information. Page design can enhance or weaken the effect.

Other features add usefulness and appeal to a nonfiction book. Access tools — a table of contents, index, chapter or section titles in longer books — are now common in even short, simple books of information. The body of the book

may be framed with other ancillary materials: introductory notes, a time line, glossary, informative captions, sidebars (framed commentary adding bits of information to the main discussion), or endnotes. Some books add a relevant map, while others create confusion by omitting one. A few children's books do supply bibliographies with reasonably up-to-date children's books on their subject. Many others provide bibliographies of adult materials — ostensibly sources the writer consulted in preparing the book. A few writers of substantial books based on scholarly research and primary sources provide commentary on the scope and qualities of the listed materials.

The critical considerations of artistry, content, structure, and book features are capped with a final, equally important requirement: appeal to children. While many informational books are written and published to serve school curriculum requirements or to explain topics that adults feel are important for children to understand, those books considered superior must be both immediately appealing to children and

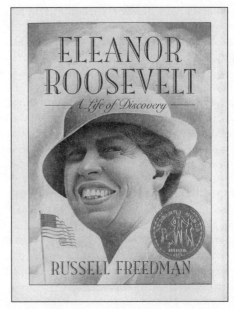

Jacket illustration by Wendell Minor for *Eleanor Roosevelt* (1993), by Russell Freedman.

also capable of touching their hearts or stimulating their curiosity and imagination.

While children's nonfiction books have long appeared in a wide array of forms, the durable practice of using fictional story as a basis for conveying information has always had a mixed reception among critics. Fictionalizing in the writing of biography, once more widely practiced, has been largely denounced by critics, children's book authors, and teachers. Here, however, the terms *fiction* and *story* must not be used synonymously, for the shaping and some of the conventions of story (theme, characterization, setting) are often capably rendered in biography and other works of nonfiction. Story, sometimes in a more fictional form, continues as a popular tactic for conveying information to very young children and even those in the primary grades. Information distilled into story form sometimes achieves a simple, enduring introduction to a subject. TOMIE DEPAOLA's *Charlie Needs a Cloak* (1982) continues to be a staple on library shelves, just as Elsa Beskow's *Pelle's New Suit* (1929) on a similar theme did for many years. JOANNA COLE and BRUCE DEGEN created a memorable cast of characters who take preposterous trips to explain very factual information in their widely read Magic School Bus books of the 1980s and 1990s.

Informational stories are but one strand of nonfiction in picture book form. Many artists and writers have chosen to present factual material to children in this format, sometimes in straightforward explanations and sometimes in imaginative and playful approaches. Gail Gibbons, a master of the matter-of-fact approach, packed considerable information on the life cycle and behavior of honeybees and the work of beekeepers into her well-designed *Honeymakers* (1997), with its bright, well-labeled drawings and framed text. In a bolder vein, LOIS EHLERT blended vivid collage views of plants and animals on pages differing in size to introduce the butterfly life cycle in *Waiting for Wings* (2001).

Though picture book presentations — from very simple to quite sophisticated in subject and shaping — flourish, drawings and paintings are now usually the chosen illustration of just a few of the notable longer nonfiction works each year. In Sophie Webb's slim volume *My Season with Penguins* (2000), one of the first Sibert Honor Books, journal entries accompany watercolor sketches to describe both the work and everyday life of scientists in Antarctica and the Adelie penguins the author was observing. A much longer volume, Joan Dash's *The Longitude Prize* (2000), winner of the Boston Globe–Horn Book Award for nonfiction, chronicles the invention of a seagoing clock by John Harrison in a deeply researched text and handsome black and white drawings by Dasan Patricic. In *Asteroid Impact* (2000) Douglas Henderson employed paintings, some of his own and some that are computer generated, to supply drama and realism in his detailed explanation of the probable event that destroyed much life on Earth some sixty-five million years ago.

Photographs, common in children's informational books by the 1940s, are the most typical form of illustration and sometimes the dominant feature in a book. Photo-essays, in which a continuous text and photographs usually have an equal share in conveying information, have long been popular. Often the photographs have been made specifically for the book, though images are often selected from commercial services or archival collections. George Ancona, Christopher Knight, and Sandra Markle have each documented many subjects in fine photography. SEYMOUR SIMON began using the essay form with well-chosen, bold, full-page photographs in 1984 with *Moon*. This format became a model for many more books.

Careful selection of photographs, drawings, and other illustrative materials is also usually a hallmark of the many fine, longer books for older children that combine scholarship and good writing. Milton Meltzer, Russell Freedman, JAMES CROSS GIBLIN, and JIM MURPHY have each explored many subjects in handsome, intelligent books that have set high standards for other writers today.

Publishers' series have gained momentum over the decades. Some have been thoughtfully conceived and produced. The First Book series begun by Watts in 1944 offered useful books of science, the popular Landmark series begun by Random House in 1950 featured biography and history titles by notable writers of adult books, and the Let's Read and Find Out series launched by Thomas Y. Crowell in 1960 paired work of established science writers and illustrators. Series, of course, wax and wane, and these trend-setters were followed by numerous others of varying quality and success.

Noted for their abundant illustration, the Eyewitness Books, introduced by Dorling Kindersley in 1988, set trends and spawned numerous other series for the company. Featuring a wide range of appealing subjects, from baseball to ancient Egypt, the slim volumes mass a sumptuous array of photographs, art, and graphics across two-page spreads, with bits of expository text and informative captions. Although extremely popular, some of the books become incoherent masses of miscellany.

Some Dorling Kindersley series became ever larger in format, even extending the dimensions of earlier popular oversize series such as the Giant Golden Books and the Wonderful World Books begun in the 1950s. The ratio of printed text to pictorial material has shifted over the decades in nearly all nonfiction published for children, giving modern books a slimmer, sleeker appearance. Many stand tall, and giant volumes of irregular size, awkward in the hands and on bookshelves, continue as a common publishing choice.

As nonfiction book sizes and shapes have taken on ever greater variety, so too has subject matter extended its range. History, science, and the arts continue expanding foundations laid by the early twentieth century. Before the winds of social change of the 1960s, however, many subjects had not been covered much, if at all, in books for children. Among books on the human body, a few did include the physical changes of puberty and human reproduction. No books, however, told children about death, divorce, adoption, or how to deal with bad feelings, mental illness in the family, or substance abuse. But

as society has grown larger and more complex and popular media ever more frank and pervasive in covering human issues, few subjects remain taboo for children. Objective, straightforward discussion, mindful of the level of children's understanding yet unsettling to some parents, abounds in children's information books. For example, noted picture book creators Laura Numeroff and David McPhail collaborated with Dr. Wendy S. Hapham in *The Hope Tree: Kids Talk About Breast Cancer* (2001), presenting a congenial cast of animal characters who discuss experiences common among real children whose families are dealing with this challenge. As with all subject areas of nonfiction, some discussions are utilitarian and others crafted with skill and insight.

Changing styles in writing, art, and book design; evolving technology in photography and printing; developing theories in teaching and curriculum design; the expanding body of knowledge; and shifting social issues all contribute to the content and shaping of nonfiction published for children. There can be no doubt that the best books, in their great variety, feed children's interest in the real world, offer aesthetic pleasure, and stimulate curiosity and imagination. Many books offer information; some even misinform. But finally, at the beginning of the twenty-first century, nonfiction has found its rightful place in the pantheon of children's literature. M.B.

Isadora, Rachel

American author and illustrator, b. 1953. Rachel Isadora's life has had an enormous impact on her art. Born in New York City, she grew up wanting to be a ballerina and began dancing professionally at age eleven. When an injury forced her to give up dancing, she turning to writing and illustrating. Not surprisingly, many of her books are about dance.

Her first book, *Max* (1976), about a boy who uses ballet exercises to warm up for his baseball games, was named an ALA Notable Book. In *My*

Ballet Class (1980), a young girl explains the essence of ballet lessons, and the illustrations, soft black-and-white line drawings with just a hint of color, demonstrate the various ballet steps and capture the intensity of the young dancers. As is typical in her books, this class is well integrated and includes African Americans, Asian Americans, and a few boys. Isadora's attraction to the subject of ballet also has informed other titles: *Lili at Ballet* (1993), *Lili on Stage* (1995), *Lili Backstage* (1997), and a companion volume about figure skating, *Sophie Skates* (1999).

Isadora's early illustrations are predominately in black and white. But her rich use of patterns, created by composition, shading, and cross-hatching, make lush pages that don't need color. Nowhere is this more evident than in *Ben's Trumpet* (1979), a Caldecott Honor Book. Ben dreams of playing a trumpet like the musician at the local jazz club and practices on an imaginary horn. The book's design is striking. Starting with the endpapers, Isadora used a zigzag line to represent Ben's music. As he delights in his melodies, this line grows to create more and more elaborate patterns until they fill an entire page. When other children ridicule Ben, the line suddenly goes flat. Isadora does not describe Ben's feelings; the picture and design tell the viewer everything.

In the mid-1980s Isadora added full color to her books. She created two series for toddlers: *I See*, *I Hear*, and *I Touch* (all published in 1985) and *Babies* and *Friends* (both published in 1990). Using bright, simple pictures and minimal text, the books portray the everyday activities of a young child, capturing natural body postures and delightful facial expressions, thus making real little people to whom the youngest reader can relate. Spending time in South Africa with her second husband, Isadora was struck by the beauty of the landscape and the plight of the blacks. *At the Crossroads* (1991) and *Over the Green Hills* (1992) are simple yet moving stories. In the first, children wait at the crossroads for their fathers to come home for the first time in ten months, while the other describes a family's long walk to visit their grandmother in a coun-

try where blacks have few conveniences. Isadora's vibrant watercolors capture the energy and joy of the people as well as the results of apartheid.

In general, Isadora has used simple language to create uncomplicated plots and straightforward characters, enriched and brought to life with her illustrations. Using gesture, expression, composition, and now color, she has created delightful and vigorous stories and people. P.R.

J

Jacques, Brian

British author, b. 1939. A series of FANTASY novels about the animals that live in and around Redwall Abbey has propelled author Brian Jacques to international success with readers of all ages.

Born in Liverpool, England, Jacques attended local Catholic schools until he became a sailor at age fifteen. He also worked as a longshoreman, truck driver, radio broadcaster, and professional comedian. His first book was written to entertain the students at a school for the blind. *Redwall* (1986) concerns a community of field animals that join together to fight off an invading army of rats. The plot contains many standard fantasy elements, including the quest for a legendary sword, an awkward young hero who discovers the secret of his heritage, and the omnipresent war between good and evil. The second book in the series, *Mossflower* (1988), goes back in time to tell the story of Martin the Warrior, the original mouse hero of Redwall Abbey. *Mattimeo* (1989), *Mariel of Redwall* (1991), *Salamandastron* (1993), and *Martin the Warrior*

(1994) record the history of preceding and succeeding generations. Some readers may find the novels too long and involved, but fantasy fans enjoy every page of the often thrilling adventures, which include detailed descriptions of battles and sumptuous feasts.

Jacques's Redwall stories have become a publishing phenomenon; each new volume is released to much publicity and fanfare, and sales instantly place it on bestseller lists. Although the author has proved his diversity with a collection of scary stories, *Seven Strange and Ghostly Tales* (1991), as well as *Castaways of the Flying Dutchman* (2000), a richly textured reimagining of the famous "phantom ship" legend, he remains best known for his impressive multivolume fantasy. P.D.S.

Janeczko, Paul

American poet, anthologist, and author, b. 1945. Since the publication of his first anthology, *The Crystal Image* (1977), Paul B. Janeczko has been more responsible than any other individual for putting POETRY into the hands of young adult readers. Dissatisfied with the poetry collections available to him as a high school English teacher, Janeczko collected, mimeographed, and shared with his students contemporary poetry that spoke directly to them. From those mimeographed pages came the first of nearly a dozen anthologies that have captured the imaginations of young readers and gratified their teachers. Several of the collections — including *Don't Forget to Fly: A Cycle of Modern Poems* (1981), *Poetspeak: In Their Work, About Their Work* (1983), *Strings: A Gathering of Family Poems* (1984), *Pocket Poems: Selected for a Journey* (1985), and *The Place My Words Are Looking For* (1990) — have been named to the ALA's annual list of Best Books for Young Adults. Janeczko's second anthology, *Postcard Poems* (1979), set a standard for the compilations that followed, a thematic collection of carefully selected poems, distinctive for their vivid imagery and economy of language, diverse in style and tone, skillfully organized, and representing both acknowledged masters of the craft and fresh new voices.

Janeczko's particular skill is in selecting poems with themes that touch and move young adults, then deftly ordering them so that each poem lures the reader on to read one more. With each anthology Janeczko has taken a unique and fresh approach. *Pocket Poems* reflects life's journey as well as actual departures and returns and can be carried comfortably in a back pocket — the very image chosen for the book's cover art. He presented concrete poetry in *A Poke in the I* (2001) and alternating voices in *I Feel a Little Jumpy Around You: Paired Poems by Men and Women* (1999), a collection he created with NAOMI SHIHAB NYE. For *Poetspeak* and *The Place My Words Are Looking For*, Janeczko asked poets to share not only their poems but their thoughts and feelings about poetry, their sources of inspiration, and their own writing processes. Several of Janeczko's articles, original poems, and stories have appeared in magazines. Only occasionally has he included one of his own poems in the anthologies.

A work of nonfiction, *Loads of Codes and Secret Ciphers* (1981), teaches readers how to write and decode secret languages. His first novel, *Bridges to Cross* (1986), portrays the pivotal summer between eighth grade and high school for a boy and his closest friend. In his first book of original poetry, *Brickyard Summer* (1989), Janeczko revisited the themes, setting, and some significant events from *Bridges to Cross*. Both books are colored by the author's childhood experiences in a small New England mill town and his strict Catholic education. The poems evoke the essence of the setting and its inhabitants with poignancy, sensitivity, and narrative unity. After twenty-two years of teaching, Janeczko left the classroom in 1990 to devote more time to his own writing and to the compilation of yet another poetry anthology. Ever committed to sharing his enthusiasm for poetry, he frequently conducts workshops for teachers, visits classrooms, and serves as poetry editor for *English Journal*. D.M.L.

Japanese American Children's Books

Since the groundbreaking folktales and fiction of Yoshiko Uchida began to appear in the 1950s, many children's books about Japan and Americans of Japanese descent have been published. Seeking to both inform and entertain young readers, the authors and illustrators of these books have presented the distinct, intriguing culture and people of Japan and of Japanese Americans through folktales, HISTORICAL FICTION and nonfiction, and contemporary fiction.

Editions of folktales dominate the field of Japanese American children's books, providing children with a good introduction to — though an incomplete picture of — the land and culture of Japan. Some of the many noteworthy PICTURE BOOK editions of Japanese folktales, produced by those inside and outside the culture, include Japanese woodcut artist Tejima's *Ho-limlim: A Rabbit Tale from Japan* (1990); Sheila Hamanaka's *Screen of Frogs: An Old Tale* (1993); Dianne Snyder's *The Boy of the Three-Year Nap* (1988), illustrated by ALLEN SAY; and *The Tale of the Mandarin Ducks* (1990), retold by KATHERINE PATERSON (who spent four years in Japan studying the language) and illustrated by LEO and DIANE DILLON, who modeled the art on *ukiyo-e*, a style of Japanese woodblock prints. Authoritative folktale collections include *Tales from the Bamboo Grove* (1992), collected by Japanese American author Yoko Kawashima Watkins, and *The Shining Princess and Other Japanese Legends* (1989), collected by Eric Quayle.

Historical fiction set in Japan helps create the context for appreciating books on the Japanese American experience. Most historical fiction set in Japan offers tales of action and intrigue that tell exciting stories while informing readers about Japan's history. One of LENSEY NAMIOKA's mystery-adventure novels set in feudal Japan, *The Coming of the Bear* (1992), focuses on two cultures that learn to coexist despite their differences. Katherine Paterson's well-researched novels of feudal twelfth-century Japan are highly acclaimed, as is her National Book Award winner *The Master Puppeteer* (1975), which takes place in eighteenth-century Japan. Erik Christian

Illustration by Allen Say from his book *Grandfather's Journey* (1993).

Haugaard immersed himself in Japanese life, history, and culture before writing his novels set in sixteenth-century Japan, which include the picaresque epic *The Boy and the Samurai* (1991).

Several books about Japan's modern history tell true stories about the tragedy of war. In Yukio Tsuchiya's picture book *Faithful Elephants: A True Story of Animals, People, and War* (1988), Tokyo zookeepers mourn the death by starvation of three elephants that were among the many animals killed during World War II to prevent their escaping and endangering people if the zoo was bombed. Toshi Maruki's *Hiroshima no Pika* (1980) and Junko Morimoto's *My Hiroshima* (1990) are personal, wrenching picture-book accounts of the day the bomb was dropped on Hiroshima. Two brief novels on the use of the atomic bomb are Eleanor Coerr's *Mieko and the Fifth Treasure* (1993), about a girl injured during the bombing of Nagasaki who overcomes her bitterness, and *Sadako and the Thousand Paper Cranes* (1977), the true story of a girl who died of leukemia as a result of radiation from the atom bomb. Coerr's *Sadako* (1993), a picture book version of the novel, features illustrations selected from ED YOUNG's artwork for the film of the book. Yoko Kawashima Watkins's autobiographical novel *So Far from the Bamboo Grove* (1986) is a moving account of the Japanese author's childhood escape from war-torn northern Korea to Japan.

Historical fiction about Japanese Americans instills in children of Japanese descent a sense of pride in their identity and teaches all children about American history. Yoshiko Uchida's *Samurai of Gold Hill* (1972) tells about the first Japanese immigrants to California in 1859, while her novels *A Jar of Dreams* (1981), *The Best Bad Thing* (1983), and *The Happiest Ending* (1985) focus on eleven-year-old Rinko, a Japanese American girl growing up during the Depression. Picture books on the 1942 imprisonment of Japanese Americans are Uchida's *The Bracelet* (1993), in which a seven-year-old girl is strengthened by the power of her memories, and Ken Mochizuki's *Baseball Saved Us* (1993), about a boy whose father organizes baseball games to help fellow prisoners deal with their feelings of anger and boredom. Uchida's *Journey to Topaz: A Story of the Japanese American Evacuation* (1971) and its sequel, *Journey Home* (1978), are novels based on the author's family's experiences during and after their internment in the prisons; a memoir of her childhood and her time in the camps is told in *The Invisible Thread* (1992). Sheila Hamanaka's *The Journey: Japanese Americans, Racism, and Renewal* (1990) is a picture book for older readers that depicts the entire history of Japanese Americans, focusing in particular on the so-called relocation centers. The book was inspired by a mural that the artist, a third-generation Japanese American, painted "to open the past, hoping to help chase away the demons of prejudice and injustice."

Contemporary stories about Japan allow readers to explore the differences and similarities between Japanese and American culture. Picture books set in twentieth-century Japan include Takaaki Nomura's *Grandpa's Town* (1991), featuring a bilingual text about a boy's day with his grandfather, and Allen Say's *Tree of Cranes* (1991), in which a boy is introduced to the Christmas holiday celebrations his mother enjoyed in her American childhood. A beautifully crafted YOUNG ADULT NOVEL set in modern Japan is Kyoko Mori's *Shizuko's Daughter* (1993), about a girl's long journey toward hope and acceptance following her mother's suicide. Allen Say's autobiographical novel *The Ink-Keeper's Apprentice* (1979) relates his experiences as a young apprentice to a Japanese cartoonist, and his picture book *Grandfather's Journey,* winner of the 1994 Caldecott Medal, depicts the love for two lands — the United States and Japan — felt by his grandfather and himself.

Books set in the contemporary United States and featuring Americans of Japanese descent are few in number. Taro Yashima's picture book *Umbrella* (1958) tells a story featuring Momo, his Japanese American daughter, who was born in New York and whose name means "peach" in Japanese. Ina R. Friedman's picture book *How My Parents Learned to Eat* (1984), illustrated by Allen Say, is narrated by a biracial girl whose parents met when her American father was stationed in Japan. In Hadley Irwin's novel *Kim/Kimi* (1987), a half Japanese, half Caucasian adolescent's search for information about the Japanese father she never knew leads her to the site of an American concentration camp.

Almost nonexistent prior to the 1950s, Japanese American children's books are now available in a variety of genres. Although some of this literature aims at pure entertainment, many of these books seek to pass on important historical lessons about war and racism, impressing upon readers of all backgrounds the necessity for mutual respect among people of different cultures. Closer understanding between Japanese Americans and American children of other ethnic backgrounds continues to be enhanced by publication of these works.   J.M.B.

Jarrell, Randall

American poet and author, 1914–1965. Randall Jarrell came to the creation of children's books late in his writing career. By the time he published his first work for children in 1964, he was already a novelist, a well-known critic, and an award-winning poet for adult audiences. Yet these same poetic gifts led him into writing for children. He had been asked by Michael di Capua, the noted editor, to translate a GRIMM brothers fairy tale for a collection of new versions of the stories that di Capua was planning to publish. Jarrell's retelling had such stylistic grace and evocative power that di Capua urged him to try writing his own original works for children.

The result of that first effort, *The Gingerbread Rabbit*, with illustrations by GARTH WILLIAMS, was a revision of the traditional story "The Gingerbread Man." The familiar character made from cookie dough has a happy fate in Jarrell's version; rather than being devoured by the foxes of the world, he is adopted into a family of real rabbits, where he at last finds a home and safety from the threats of death that have kept him running throughout the book.

A similar quest for a loving community provides the emotional foundation for Jarrell's second children's book, *The Bat-Poet* (1964), illustrated by MAURICE SENDAK. In this story about a young bat who cannot sleep during the day and follows his own individual and isolating creative lights, Jarrell offered his young readers what many consider to be one of the best statements about the plight of the artist in his search for creative independence on the one hand and his longing for acceptance on the other.

In *The Animal Family* (1965), which is generally regarded as one of the classics of children's literature, Jarrell once again found an unusual subject and succeeded in transforming it into a work of breathtaking imaginative and emotional beauty. His narrative brings together a lonely hunter, a mermaid, a shipwrecked boy, a lynx, and a bear in an unlikely family that takes up loving, harmonious, timeless residence in the hunter's cabin, "where the forest runs down to the ocean."

Jarrell's last children's book, *Fly by Night*, published posthumously in 1976 with Sendak's haunting illustrations, again expressed one of Jarrell's abiding interests: the mysterious overlapping of the worlds of dream and waking. David, the young hero of the story, floats through the house and around the countryside, observing the dreams of those he encounters in his own dream state — his parents, the dog, the sheep, and an owl family, whose tale of loss and rescue, of isolation and loving adoption, sounds themes that lie at the heart of this and all Jarrell stories.

Though his writing for children spanned only a few years and a handful of works before his untimely death in 1965, Jarrell left classic works for children that are distinguished by their numinous poetry, their imaginative energy, and their transcendent vision. One wishes there had been dozens more such books, but because they are so few and so unique, they are all the more rare. J.O.C.

Jeffers, Susan

American illustrator, b. 1942. Starting with *Three Jovial Huntsmen* (1973), her first book to receive wide attention, Susan Jeffers's art has gone on to enchant and inspire countless children and adults. After graduating from Pratt Institute in Brooklyn, New York, Jeffers worked "behind the scenes" in children's book publishing in the art departments of several publishers. As she worked on other artists' children's books, she "began to feel again the love I had for them as a child . . . and I became more and more eager to do my own." She quit the security of her publishing day job and plunged into the life of a full-time artist, sharing studio space with ROSEMARY WELLS, who also went on to great success in children's books. Jeffers has occasionally referred in her own work to this early partnership, as in the picture of a Wells character hung in the room of the little boy who is afraid of the dark in *Midnight Farm* (1987), written by Reeve Lindbergh. She published her first book, *Buried Moon*, an English folktale retold by Joseph Jacobs, in 1969. Her first version of *Three Jovial Huntsmen*, a traditional poem, she submitted soon thereafter, but it turned out to be so unsatisfactory for both Jeffers and her publisher that it was abandoned before going to print. She revised it and resubmitted it, and in 1974 it was named a Caldecott Honor Book.

Jeffers's interest in and knowledge of the natural world shows in her finely detailed drawings of animals and forests, skies, meadows, and farms. Her eloquent illustrations for Robert Frost's 1923 poem *Stopping by Woods on a Snowy Evening* (1978) demonstrate this aspect of her work quite well. Often unabashedly sentimental, Jeffers's work is tempered by a sly humor, which peeks through in the hidden images she often employs and in the visual commentary she makes on the texts, as in the three jovial huntsmen's bumbling unawareness of the teeming animal life around them or the harried father's attempts to put his energetic son to bed in *Close Your Eyes,* written by Jean Marzollo (1976). In addition to skillfully rendering animals in their natural habitat, Jeffers has often integrated fantastic imagery in her work, merging the natural world with a dream world that, she has indicated, exists just outside the perception of our senses. It is this spiritual aspect of nature that Jeffers has most fully realized in *Brother Eagle, Sister Sky* (1991), a heartfelt elegy to modern man's lost sense of kinship with the earth. While criticized by some for an overly romanticized, factually inaccurate portrayal of American Indian culture, *Brother Eagle and Hiawatha* (1983) — Jeffers's illustration of a portion of Henry Wadsworth Longfellow's poem — can be viewed as highly personal meditations on the American Indian legacy in modern American culture. *Brother Eagle, Sister Sky,* with Jeffers's own adaptation of the words attributed to Chief Seattle, spent time on the *New York Times* Best-Seller List, one of the few children's books ever to do so, a testament to the eloquence and timeliness of both the words and the pictures.

Jeffers has usually started her pictures with a precise pencil drawing that is then rendered in ink, before dyes and washes for color are added. This technique gives her work a sense of clarity that grounds it in reality and a glowing color that transcends the everyday. Strong use of perspective and foregrounds with large, bold images give her readers a feeling of immediacy — of being surrounded and enveloped by her world. S.G.K.

Jenkins, Steve

American author and illustrator, b. 1953. Steve Jenkins's science books combine his love of natural history with his beautiful and informative collage illustrations. Although he was born in North Carolina, Jenkins has also lived in Panama, Virginia, Colorado, and Kansas. His family moved a great deal as they followed his father's career as a college physics professor. As a child, Jenkins collected all kinds of small animals and insects, memorized the periodic table of the elements, and kept notes on the hardness and color of rocks he found. He always assumed that he, like his father, would study science. Instead he decided to attend design school because he always liked to draw and paint, and art students "looked like they were having a lot more fun" than the chemistry majors. He earned a B.A. and an M.A. from the School of Design at North Carolina State University in Raleigh, where he also met his wife, Robin. Together they moved to New York City, and Jenkins worked as a designer at the firm of Chermayeff & Geismar. In 1982 he and his wife opened their own studio. In 1994 they moved to Boulder, Colorado, where they continue to work together in corporate design.

Jenkins came to children's book illustration when doing book design for a publisher. Jenkins volunteered to illustrate the books he was designing. This suggestion led to his first children's book projects, including *Cock-A-Doodle-Doo! What Does It Sound Like to You?* (1993), written by Marc Robinson. In this book and in subsequent projects, Jenkins has given his collages depth and interest by using papers with a variety of textures and patterns. The first book he both wrote and illustrated is elegant in its simplicity: *Duck's Breath and Mouse Pie: A Collection of Animal Superstitions* (1994) features a simply stated superstition, placed opposite a handsome visual interpretation of it. For example, the admonition to "drink milk in which a fish has been swimming to cure whooping cough" is illustrated with a bewildered fish, tail hanging over the lip, trapped in a small glass of milk. *Biggest, Strongest, Fastest* (1995) is the first of many IN-FORMATION BOOKS about science, in which Jenkins has chosen a subject with tremendous child appeal and presented information in a clear and visually striking way. Some of his books, including *Hottest, Coldest, Highest, Deepest* (1998) and *Making Animal Babies* (2000), also simultaneously present more than one level of information on the page. Large type gives basic facts, such as the name of the coldest place on earth. More information is presented in smaller type and inset maps. A collage of heavily textured white, pink, blue, and gray papers gives the reader a sense of just how cold the coldest place might feel.

Jenkins's books have tremendous visual appeal and have received many awards. *To the Top of the World: Climbing Mount Everest* (1999) won the Boston Globe–Horn Book Award for nonfiction. His illustrations are particularly remarkable, using cut paper to convey the majesty and human challenge of Everest. Jenkins's lucid texts show a respect for audience and a solid grounding in science. Exploring subjects he claims are suggested by the questions his own children ask about the natural world, his books offer the exciting prospect that there is always more to know about every scientific topic. M.V.K.

Jimenez, Francisco

Mexican American author, b. 1943. The work of Francisco Jimenez marks an important addition to depictions of the immigration experience in multicultural literature for children. Jimenez has been a tireless advocate for literacy and bilingual education in California, drawing from his own experiences and those of children with whom he grew up. Above and beyond the success of his books, Jimenez has lived a life that can inspire his readers, a testament to the power of education and will.

Born in Tlaquepaque, Mexico, Jimenez was named for his father, a farm laborer. The elder Francisco and his wife, Joaquina, immigrated to the United States with their children in 1965, an experience that would define Jimenez's childhood and provide the foundation for his first collection of semi-autobiographical stories, *The Circuit* (1997). As illegal immigrants, the family in the stories have no opportunities for legal employment and thus are forced to earn a living by picking crops, moving every few months as one job ends and another has to be found. Panchito, Jimenez's protagonist, struggles to reconcile necessity and his hopes for himself — to stay in one place long enough to receive an education. Panchito's narrative voice is truly that of an observant, wondering child and effectively communicates the frustration and dogged optimism that Jimenez himself felt as a boy. *The Circuit* quickly won acclaim for its accessible and realistic portrayal of the migrant worker experience. The book received the 1998 Boston Globe–Horn Book Award for fiction.

Panchito's story continues in *Breaking Through* (2001), which begins, "I lived in constant fear for ten long years, from the time I was four until I was fourteen years old." Panchito's fear is realized when he and his family are deported to Mexico; eventually they obtain visas to return to the United States, but the trauma of being torn from his classroom and identified as an outsider has set the stage for Panchito's teenage years. Like Jimenez, Panchito must make great sacrifices to fulfill his obligations to his family, working before and after school as a janitor. He takes pride in hard work, as his father taught him to, yet never allows his dreams of a better future to fade.

Two episodes from *The Circuit* have been adapted as PICTURE BOOKS, expanding Jimenez's audience to include younger readers. *La Mariposa* (1998) recounts Jimenez's days in elementary school, when he could not understand his teacher's instructions because she spoke only English. The feelings of isolation and despair communicated in the story are emotions to which many children can relate. *The Christmas Gift* (2000) features text in both English and Spanish, a device that further expands the readership of the story. A young couple, reminiscent of the Holy Family, appears on the doorstep of Panchito's family and asks if Panchito's father will buy their belongings, as they are expecting a baby and desperate for money. When he hears his father say that there is no money to spare, Panchito worries that he will not get the red ball he wants for Christmas. His longing is so palpable and real that readers cannot help but join their own hopes to his.

Despite obstacles, Jimenez earned his undergraduate degree from Santa Clara University and went on to receive a master's degree and a doctorate from Columbia University. This, then, is the rare gift of Jimenez to his readers: the chance to see that life experience is both individual and universal, and nothing is impossible. Though he writes specifically about his own life, his work embraces the larger story of the Mexican American experience, and beyond that, the universal emotions and realities of childhood.

H.F.R.

Johnson, Crockett

American author and illustrator, 1906–1975. Best known as the creator of Harold and the Purple Crayon Books and as illustrator of RUTH KRAUSS's *The Carrot Seed,* Crockett Johnson was a cartoonist whose simplest, sparest, and boldest outlines produced unforgettable, gently humorous, and always endearing caricatures in the world of American children's PICTURE BOOKS. Johnson's natural gift for drawing and writing from a young child's viewpoint enabled him to craft more than twenty juvenile books, two of which have entertained children for more than four decades.

Johnson, whose real name was David Johnson Leisk, was born in New York City and studied art at Cooper Union and New York University. He worked as an art editor of several periodicals, in advertising and design, and as a cartoonist. First recognized in 1942 for his syndicated newspaper comic strip, *Barnaby,* Johnson gained national acclaim when the strip's characters, five-year-old Barnaby Baxter and his imaginary Fairy Godfather, Mr. O'Malley, appeared in the tabloid *PM.* Four years later, *Barnaby* appeared in more than fifty newspapers with a total circulation of over five million. Two cartoon books that contained selected episodes, *Barnaby* (1943) and *Barnaby and Mr. O'Malley* (1944), were among Johnson's first books published; though not intended for children, *Barnaby* and his books delighted young and old alike.

Johnson made his picture book debut in 1945 when he illustrated *The Carrot Seed,* written by his wife, Ruth Krauss, a respected author of children's books for the very young. Johnson's simple cartoon drawings seamlessly match Krauss's poetic, imagistic text of a young boy whose green thumb and self-confidence triumph over his naysaying family. The boy plants the tiniest of carrot seeds and lovingly nurtures it, while his parents and older brother insist that nothing will grow from it. Throughout the entire book, organic browns and tans of the paper, illustrations, and typeface amplify the story's warmth and lend a rich earthiness to the boy's expectant patience. Then, to convey the boy's feat of faith and the tremendous flurry of the ground's activity, Johnson added a dash of luxuriant green for the towering carrot top and an even bolder splash of bright red-orange for the colossal carrot. Still in print, *The Carrot Seed* continues to entertain young audiences.

Johnson alone wrote and illustrated the enormously successful *Harold and the Purple Crayon* (1955), a small book about a little boy's nighttime jaunt that he, with the aid of his purple crayon, draws for himself. Together, Harold and his purple crayon trek through woods, encounter a ferocious dragon, sail the high seas, and conquer mountaintops; together, they wend their way home, with Harold finally safe, sound, and comfortable in bed. With the fewest of lines, Johnson depicted Harold as a toddler clad in sleepers, his chubby hand gripping a fat plum-colored crayon. From page to page, the thick, firm, purple mark delineates Harold's actions against the stark white background so effectively and ingeniously that the crayon is as much a character as Harold. The same economy that informs Johnson's art permeates his text; he wrote so concisely of Harold's moonlight stroll that his style perfectly echoes the clarity of his boldly outlined cartoon illustrations. Johnson created five other Purple Crayon Books that take Harold to places such as a castle, outer space, the North Pole, the circus, and on a clever trip through the alphabet; an additional book, *A Picture for Harold's Room* (1960), is an EASY READER. But none succeeds as well as Johnson's never-out-of-print *Harold and the Purple Crayon.*

Two other notable books, *Ellen's Lion* (1959) and *The Lion's Own Story* (1963), further established Johnson's talent for writing from a child's point of view. Both titles feature brief, witty stories and gloriously pure and simple cartoon illustrations about a charming duo: Ellen, a garrulous, egocentric preschooler, and her sagacious, realist stuffed lion, with whom she has conversations. Ellen and the lion, her alter ego, cavort through escapades exclusively reserved for the world of very young children, a world that few picture book author-illustrators have captured as superbly as Johnson. S.L.S.

Jonas, Ann

American illustrator and author, b. 1932. A keen graphic eye and dramatic sense of design give Ann Jonas a perspective that is not bound by traditional PICTURE BOOK formats or viewpoints. From the simple curiosity of toddlers in *Holes and Peeks* (1984) to the fascinating presentation of endangered animals in *Aardvarks, Disembark!* (1990), Jonas has used a preciseness of line, a uniquely appropriate style, and subtlety of image to convey visual treats.

Growing up in suburban, semirural Long Island, Jonas and her brother spent a lot of time outdoors. Her family attached great importance

in knowing how to do as many things as possible, from car repairs to cabinet building. While everyone worked on numerous projects, drawing was considered to be an incidental skill, only necessary for the planning phase. Jonas's enjoyment in designing and making objects carried over into adulthood. She didn't seriously consider college following high school, but after working a few years in a department store's advertising department, she felt the need to build an art career. While studying at Cooper Union, she met her husband, DONALD CREWS. Following his military stint in Germany, they returned to the States and started a freelance design business. Years later, when Crews had illustrated a number of children's books, his publisher urged Jonas to try her hand at one. The result was a charming preschool book, *When You Were a Baby* (1982).

Her background as a designer has enabled Jonas to approach each book individually, using different styles and techniques. Almost all involve some visual activity or game, with a story line carefully designed into the experience. It was the publication of her third book, *Round Trip* (1983), that generated awards for its stunning graphic design; the black and white book can be read forward and then turned upside-down and in reverse as a day trip to the city becomes a return trip to the country. The next visual game was *The Quilt* (1984), which effectively evoked the transitions in the patterns of a young girl's quilt into a dream sequence. Jonas's love for the hidden picture puzzles in children's magazines led to *The Trek* (1985). On her way to school a girl sees a myriad of zoo animals camouflaged in the scenery. In *Aardvarks, Disembark!* Jonas changed the format to fit the topic; hundreds of endangered animals leave the ark, descending down the pages in Z-to-A order. A magnifying glass on the cover invites the reader to pick up *The 13th Clue* (1992) to follow the heroine on a merry chase from the attic through the woods to a surprise ending.

Each of Jonas's books explores new ways to stretch children's imaginations and encourages them to look at familiar things in different ways.

The clue to her creativity is her designer's eye, her love for graphic challenges, and her ability to shape and illustrate the experience of discovery for children. J.C.

Jones, Diana Wynne

British author, b. 1934. Diana Wynne Jones has recalled that she chose to write FAN-TASY "because I was not able to believe in most people's version of normal life." Jones grew up in Britain during the disruptions of World War II, and her parents' devotion to their work as educators often left her and her sisters to fend for themselves. As an adult, she discovered that her children enjoyed the same sort of books she had missed having as a child, and she has continued to try to create such stories, "full of humour and fantasy, but firmly referred to real life." Writing for children and young adults, she has produced YOUNG ADULT NOVELS, short stories, plays, and a PICTURE BOOK called *Yes, Dear* (1992). In her Dalemark novels — *Cart and Cwidder* (1975), *Drowned Ammet* (1977), and *The Spellcoats* (1979) — Jones explored the connections between magic, folklore, and real life for the citizens of Dalemark, a land she invented.

She has frequently invoked a broader version of reality, one that extends beyond the boundaries humans normally perceive. In *The Homeward Bounders* (1981), beings known only as "They" play a vast game with a whole range of worlds. *A Tale of Time City* (1987) describes a city "that exists outside time and history" from which residents can influence events on Earth. For her Chrestomanci books — *Charmed Life* (1977), a Guardian Award winner; *The Magicians of Caprona* (1980); *Witch Week* (1982); and *The Lives of Christopher Chant* (1988) — Jones envisioned a universe of parallel worlds. From one of them, the Chrestomanci, a magician with nine lives strives to regulate the use of magic.

The Chrestomanci novels and a number of her other books feature gifted but as yet unrecognized protagonists who finally come into their own. While humor is prevalent, true disaster often threatens. In *Archer's Goon* (1984), young Howard realizes that he is actually a wizard, just in time to prevent his siblings from attempting to conquer the world. *Aunt Maria* (1991) takes place in the village of Cranbury, where traditional divisions between men and women, carried to extremes, have resulted in a serious imbalance of magical powers. *Dogsbody* (1975) tells how the "luminary" inhabiting Sirius the Dog Star, unjustly banished into a dog's body on Earth, must remember his identity and find the mysterious Zoi before someone else misuses its power. Frequently Jones's characters must not only recognize their gifts but also learn to control them. The Wizard Howl in *Howl's Moving Castle* (1986) almost comes to grief because he has overexploited his talents by trading his own heart in a magical bargain.

Well known for her ingenuity, Jones may begin with elements from folklore or mythology, such as the tales of Tam Lin and Thomas the Rhymer for *Fire and Hemlock* (1984) or the Norse gods who appear in the contemporary world of *Eight Days of Luke* (1975), but in the end her stories, with their unusual twists, are all her own. Following those twists may occasionally present a challenge, but readers who choose to share her vision will have an uncommon imaginative experience. M.F.S.

Joyce, William

American author and illustrator, b. 1959. J. R. R. TOLKIEN spoke of the "cauldron of story." If ever there were a "cauldron of illustration," William Joyce would be its master chef.

Joyce, who resides in Louisiana, was educated at Southern Methodist University and sold paintings through galleries before discovering that children's book illustration provided the ideal mode of expression for the ideas simmering in his imagination. His creations are a subtle blend of a lifetime of accrued American interests and influences, and each offers something for nearly everyone's tastes.

Every art aficionado will savor the rich, Edward Hopper–like paintings of *Dinosaur Bob* (1988). The minimalist text and expressive illustrations recount the story of the family Lazardo and Bob, the dinosaur they befriend and bring home to New York from their safari in Africa. Add a few futuristic elements to the nostalgia of *Dinosaur Bob* and you have *A Day with Wilbur Robinson* (1990), in which a spaceship is parked on a lawn that, judging by the garb sported by those gracefully relaxing on it, one would think belonged to Gatsby. Wilbur's eccentric extended family is a surrealist's cup of fur: an uncle who blasts himself from a cannon, a robot, a cousin who floats with the aid of an antigravity device, and some yodeling frogs. The pokerfaced text relies on the visual punch lines to complete this story, in which Wilbur's visiting friend joins in the family search for Grandfather's missing teeth. After they are found — in a frog's mouth — everyone celebrates with a pillow fight.

Joyce, a fan of cartoons, television, and movies (from science fiction and horror to classic), maintains that a career goal is to see one of his stories produced as a feature-length film. His enthusiasm for this medium is evident in *Santa Calls* (1993), which is the closest thing on paper to an animated film production and is the movie buff or FANTASY lover's dream. Spiced with moments of Wild West adventure and bravado, the story includes a trip to the North Pole by Art Atchinson Aimesworth; his little sister, Esther; and his best friend Spaulding, a young Comanche. Unbeknownst to Art and Spaulding, the adventure has been arranged by Santa in an effort to meet Esther's only Christmas request: her brother's friendship. The wish is fulfilled when Art rescues Esther from the terrible Dark Queen.

Another book of movie influence is Joyce's first book as both author and illustrator, *George Shrinks* (1985), which Joyce has referred to as "King Kong in reverse." A young boy, George, awakes to find himself about the size of a mouse. On his night table is a list of chores left for him by his parents, which he manages to complete with comic ingenuity.

Joyce has even concocted something for the

sentimentalist. *Bently and Egg* (1992), rendered in gentle pastels, contains a playful use of language. The affectionate story of Bently, who is asked to egg-sit for his friend, Kack Kack the duck, turns to adventure when the egg, beautifully painted by Bently, is mistaken for an Easter egg and heisted. Bently, however, successfully tracks it down and saves the day, not to mention the egg.

Joyce's work reached an even wider audience when the characters from *Rolie Polie Olie* (1999) became the stars of their own TV show. Joyce created several books about this buglike robot family, *Snowie Rolie* (2000), *Sleepytime Olie* (2001), and some BOARD BOOKS, *Olie* (2001), *Zowie* (2001), and *Spot* (2001).

Joyce's interests and influences blend so creatively in his work that, though detectable, they subconsciously meld to produce a completely original flavor. The results, the books that are "vintage Joyce," present a talent that pleases a great variety of tastes and satiates even the most finicky connoisseur.   E.K.E.

Juster, Norton

American author, b. 1929. Norton Juster's *The Dot and the Line* (1963), a small allegorical book detailing the precarious romance of a straight line and a round dot who learn to accept their differences and adapt in order to get along, has always been popular with adults and children. *Alberic the Wise and Other Journeys* (1965) contains three brief FANTASY stories about searching for fulfillment in life. Juster is best known, however, for his first book, *The Phantom Tollbooth* (1961), which is a favorite fantasy among children.

When young Milo, bored with life and its possibilities, drives his small electric car past the toy tollbooth that has mysteriously appeared in his room, he enters a world ruled by words and numbers. An architect by trade, Juster has displayed considerable skill in building with words; by depicting common sayings, phrases, and clichés literally, he has thrown a spotlight on the idiosyncrasies of human behavior and created a believable, though absurd, secondary world. Populated by an unforgettable cast of characters, including Tock the Watchdog, whose body is an alarm clock; Kakofonous A. Dischord, Doctor of Dissonance, and his assistant, the awful Dynne; and two unique, oversize insects called Humbug and the Spelling Bee, the Kingdom of Wisdom has problems so outrageous that Milo becomes determined to help. His journey to rescue Rhyme and Reason, twin sisters banished by their feuding brothers, King Azaz of Dictionopolis and the Mathemagician, ruler of Digitopolis, takes him from one fantastic region of the land to another. The broad humor and magnificent wordplay carry the reader swiftly through a text that possesses a strong thematic base. Although perhaps too directly stated at times, the stress on communication and cooperation — the elements obviously lacking in this fantasy world — and on the importance of continually seeking knowledge for its own sake will always be pertinent. Highlighting the pitfalls into which individuals so easily fall, the fabulous farce ultimately reaffirms creativity, inquisitiveness, and optimism. A.E.D.

K

Kalman, Maira

American author and illustrator, b. 1949. Maira Kalman, born in Tel Aviv and raised in Riverdale, New York, studied music at the High School of Music and Art and turned to illustration after majoring in English at New York University. Her work is a harmonious blending of her talents and education. With music as her educational foundation, it is appropriate that her first book, *Stay Up Late* (1987), was a collaboration with David Byrne, of the rock group Talking Heads, to illustrate his song of the same title.

In subsequent books Kalman has provided illustrations for her own lyrical texts, which are often enhanced by typography that rhythmically follows suit. Stanzas of text blocks form an Eiffel Tower or fill a swimming pool or a zigzagging sidewalk. Tiny staccato words crescendo into larger, louder letters, guiding a reader's speech as they convey the lively adventures of Max, the Bohemian beagle poet who authors a book in *Max Makes a Million* (1990), finds love in Paris in *Ooh-la-la (Max in Love)* (1991), and attempts to direct a movie in *Max in Hollywood, Baby* (1992). Though some of Kalman's literary and artistic asides are undoubtedly beyond the very young reader's comprehension, the cadence of her verse is more than aurally palatable and makes for melodious, poetical reading aloud. While in Paris, Max meets eccentric characters with names such as Peach Melba and Crepes Suzette and stays in a little hotel run by the aromatic Madame Camembert of whom he says, "I adore her and she adores me. It's not always that simple in this town of Paree."

Of all Kalman's work, *Sayonara, Mrs. Kackleman* (1989) speaks most directly to children. The story is told from the perspective of siblings Lulu and Alexander, who journey to Japan, escaping Lulu's piano lesson with the dreaded Mrs. Kackleman. Alexander creates the brutally childlike poem "Hey Hiroko, / are you loco? / Would you like / a cup of cocoa?" and eats at a restaurant where they are served "oodles and poodles of noodles."

Kalman's stories are often of fantastical journeys narrated in stream of consciousness — as in *Next Stop Grand Central* (1999). Her energetic illustrations visually parallel the text, providing a fluid, dreamlike quality. Predominantly void of perspective and reminiscent of Chagall, Matisse, and Picasso, the impressionistic paintings are visual fantasies full of crazy, colorful details that either fascinate or overwhelm the young reader. Although young readers are unlikely to pick up on all of Kalman's ever-present visual and verbal punnery, such as an exhibit of amazing hairdos at the Pompadour Museum, this sometimes criticized technique creates the very quality that garners such enthusiastic devotees of varying ages. In wild and whirling words and images, Kalman has melded her talents with unique synergy to successfully entertain at many levels. E.K.E.

Keats, Ezra Jack

American author and illustrator, 1916–1983. Whether Ezra Jack Keats used Matisse-colored collages or expressionistic blends of dark acrylic paints, he successfully illustrated the emotive landscape of an urban child's life, reflecting both its exuberance and squalor. Boldly stylistic, Keats's early work was marked by strong graphics and vibrant colors and his later work by intense and dramatic contrasts of lights and darks. His PICTURE BOOK portrayal of the city moved it beyond mere setting into the realm of characterization so that it, too, grew and changed along with his stock company of characters.

Born in Brooklyn, Keats, the son of Polish immigrants, was himself a child of the city. He began drawing at the age of five and remembered covering the enamel-topped table in his mother's kitchen with doodles and drawings. He expected his mother to react in anger, but instead she exclaimed with obvious delight. Keats remembered, "She got out the tablecloth which we used only on Friday nights, and she covered the whole little mural, and every time a neighbor would come in, she'd unveil it to show what I had done." His father, Benjamin, warned his son, "Never be an artist; you'll be a bum, you'll starve, you'll have a terrible life." Despite his father's criticism and ridicule from the neighborhood toughs, Keats taught himself to paint. Upon graduation from public high school, he won three scholarships to art schools. After serv-

ing in the Air Force in World War II, he worked as an illustrator, receiving his first assignment from *Collier's* magazine. He spent a year in Paris, came home, and began illustrating adult and children's book jackets, which quickly led to a career in children's picture books.

Keats illustrated nearly a dozen books before writing his first, *The Snowy Day*, which won the 1963 Caldecott Medal. A celebration of color, texture, design, and childhood wonder, *The Snowy Day* is significant in that it was one of the first picture books in which a minority child is seen as Everychild. Years before, Keats had come across photos of a young boy, and he recalled that "his expressive face, his body attitudes, the very way he wore his clothes, totally captivated me." This boy was to become Peter, who, in his red snowsuit, discovers the joys of dragging sticks and making tracks in the snow. After its publication, Keats found out that the photos had come from a 1940 *Life* magazine — he had retained the images for over twenty years.

With solid and patterned paper as wedges of color, Keats used collage to create endearing characters and energetic cityscapes, not only in *The Snowy Day* (1962) but also in *Whistle for Willie* (1964) and *Peter's Chair* (1967). In *Whistle for Willie*, Keats took the act of learning to whistle and, with his superb designing ability, created a book that delights the eye and engages the senses. In his later books, *Goggles!* (1969), *Hi, Cat!* (1970), *Pet Show!* (1972), and *Dreams* (1974), Keats allowed Peter and his friend Archie to grow up and explore the city. Keats's palette grew darker as his characters' experiences broadened, and his use of patterned papers became accents in illustrations thick with paint. *Apt. 3* (1971), with its somber and unflinching view of urban apartment life, prompted some critics to ask, "For whom do we create children's picture books and why?"

For Keats, honesty was the priority; reality was beautiful. His philosophy remains with us: "If we all could see each other exactly as the other is, this would be a different world. But first I think we have to begin to see each other."

M.B.B.

Kellogg, Steven

American illustrator and author, b. 1941. Steven Kellogg has loved "telling stories on paper" his whole life. As a boy growing up in Darien, Connecticut, he used that phrase to describe a favorite activity: he entertained his younger sisters by telling them stories and drawing illustrations to accompany them. He has said that he would happily continue to make up these tales "until my sisters were too restless to sit there any longer or until they were buried under pieces of paper." This is an apt image for this prolific artist, who was awarded the Catholic Library Association's 1989 Regina Medal for the body of his work.

His early years greatly influenced his future work as a PICTURE BOOK illustrator. Young Steven loved any kind of ANIMAL STORY and spent much of his free time drawing animals and birds. In addition to the childhood interests that inspired his adult work, a year in Italy studying the work of Florentine Renaissance artists was an important influence. But it was his honors fellowship from the Rhode Island School of Design that inspired him to pursue seriously his desire to become a professional artist. He graduated from RISD in 1963 with a major in illustration, and in 1967 he illustrated his first book, *Gwot! Horribly Funny Hair-Ticklers*, written by George Mendoza.

Kellogg's early fascination with animals was good preparation for his series of Pinkerton books, based on his experiences with his rambunctious but lovable Great Dane puppy. The first book in this series was *Pinkerton, Behave* (1979). Pinkerton and the chaotic situations he inadvertently creates are the perfect vehicles for Kellogg's unrestrained and humorous style of illustration. In *A Rose for Pinkerton* (1981), the combination of the energetic Great Dane and Rose, an ornery cat, leads to a typical Kellogg scenario — the characters become embroiled in a commotion of such hysterical proportions that, like an exploding pressure cooker, they invariably end up in an out-of-control mass of animals and people.

Kellogg has used a variety of techniques in his full-color artwork; in his later books he has usually employed a combination of colored inks, watercolor, and acrylics. Not all of Kellogg's books have a design line; especially with his early books, publishers didn't always use his work to the best advantage. Of Kellogg's more than eighty picture books, the retellings of tall tales and folktales achieve the best match of story and illustration. In *Pecos Bill* (1986), his energetic style is perfect for depicting this larger-than-life hero whose exploits embody the raw American pioneering spirit. The art crackles with vitality, and the characters almost whirl off the pages. *Paul Bunyan* (1984), *Johnny Appleseed* (1988), *Mike Fink* (1992), and *Sally Ann Thunder Ann Whirlwind Crockett* (1995) also perfectly blend dramatic retellings and vibrant illustrations. Quiet, incidental pictures would not do for these lively tales about the frontier days.

Kellogg has said that he approaches the picture book as a child's introduction to art and literature and believes the text is as important as the art. He made *Chicken Little* (1985) and *Jack and the Beanstalk* (1991) fresh for readers by adding humorous twists to the texts that complement his illustrations. Steven Kellogg's artwork captures the true spirit of childhood, in all its limitless energy and zest for life. K.F.

Kendall, Carol

American author, b. 1917. Best known for her FANTASY novels, Carol Kendall has also demonstrated a sure hand in writing realistic fiction for children. Born in Bucyrus, Ohio, the author attempted her first novel in fourth grade. Although this early effort was disparaged by a teacher, Kendall continued writing for newspapers in high school and at Ohio University, where she met her husband, an English professor who shared his wife's literary interests. Her first book resulted from a love of MYSTERY novels and her belief that she could write a better story than some she had read. *The Black*

Seven (1946) was published for adults, but it features a twelve-year-old detective who solves a second mystery in *The Baby-Snatcher* (1952).

Writing about children was so appealing that Kendall decided to create a story especially for them. *The Other Side of the Tunnel* (1957) is a mystery about four children who discover a diary written in secret code. They crack the code, then tunnel to a nearby mansion, where they find a new friend. Although it takes place in the United States, the story has a vaguely British atmosphere — perhaps because the book was first published in that country. The novel contains sparkling dialogue and strongly individualized characters, some of whom appear in *The Big Splash* (1960), a sequel in which a group of young friends build a parade float for a local charity contest. Long out of print, this comic adventure is fresh, exciting, and delightful from start to finish; it deserves to be rediscovered by a new generation of readers.

Kendall's Newbery Honor Book, *The Gammage Cup* (1959), continues to be read and enjoyed by children, many of whom develop a deeply personal attachment to this intriguing fantasy about the Minnipins, a group of little people who live in a series of villages in the Land Between the Mountains. When a contest is held to determine the finest village, the residents turn against a small band of villagers who do not live in typical Minnipin fashion. These nonconformists have never married, do not wear the usual village apparel, and refuse to paint their front doors a uniform green. Banished from the village, they travel to the wilderness to create a new home, only to become heroes when they rally the villagers to fight off an invading army. The theme of nonconformity is beautifully woven into the story, particularly with the character of Muggles, who moves from distant admiration for the local eccentrics to become a full-fledged nonconformist with a strong sense of her own worth. The book is also memorable for providing an interesting historical background for the Minnipins, for its enjoyable wordplay, and for including female characters among its heroes. A sequel, *The Whisper of Glocken* (1965),

examines the origins and nature of heroism and is written in an equally winning style. Both Minnipin stories were adapted for television. Kendall has also written *The Firelings* (1982), an ambitious fantasy about a civilization living on the edge of a volcano; *Sweet and Sour: Tales from China* (1978), a collection of retold stories from various historical eras; and *The Wedding of the Rat Family* (1988), another Chinese folktale.

Ancient China, contemporary America, and fantasy worlds filled with little people are all brought vividly to life in Kendall's deeply satisfying works. P.D.S.

Kennedy, X. J.

American poet and anthologist, b. 1929. X. J. Kennedy, poet, teacher, anthologist, textbook author, and humorist, has claimed to be "one of an endangered species: people who still write in meter and rime." Kennedy has written or compiled more than forty books for young people and adults. He began to write POETRY for children because, he has said, he "has a tremendous respect for children's intelligence" and has found that adults often underrate a child's ability to understand and enjoy poetry. The anthology *Talking like the Rain: A First Book of Poems* (1992), for which Kennedy and his wife, Dorothy, selected more than a hundred entries, is his most popular juvenile anthology. It includes contemporary and traditional selections for preschoolers as well as poems for older, more sophisticated readers. The verbal feast served up by the Kennedys is brilliantly enhanced by delicate and expressive watercolor illustrations by artist Jane Dyer. The book design is outstanding, as it invites readers to enjoy this unique partnership of words and pictures as they work together to portray universal events and experiences in the life of a child.

Kennedy, a native of New Jersey, wrote his first book of poems for adults, *Nude Descending a Staircase*, in 1961. Kennedy's first volume published for children, *One Winter Night in August and Other Nonsense Jingles* (1975), successfully blends contemporary subject material with traditional verse form to produce some hilarious absurdities. In this book, Kennedy's juxtaposition of humor and seriousness, reality and fantasy sets the tone for subsequent books he has written for young people. When it comes to children and their penchant for nonsense verse, Kennedy is right on target. His original poetry recalls the dexterous rhythms, sparkling imagery, and unexpected rhymes of masters of nonsense such as EDWARD LEAR and LEWIS CARROLL. Particularly representative of this style are the Brats books: *Brats* (1986), *Fresh Brats* (1990), and *Drat These Brats* (1993). Children love Kennedy's outrageous characters and the zany, sometimes slightly blood-curdling verses these books feature. The quirky rhymes, with unexpected twists and bizarre protagonists, are bouncy and eminently recitable.

In *The Forgetful Wishing-Well: Poems for Young People* (1985), some verses are funny, but here the poet has balanced humor with experiences that are serious and poignant. Adding further depth to the content of this particular collection are different verse forms, varied rhyme schemes, and infectious rhythms. Distinguished by fresh, colorful imagery, Kennedy's poems for children stimulate the mind, delight the ear, and echo the natural playfulness and imagination of the young. Not surprisingly, they are popular features in anthologies. S.L.

Kerr, M. E.

Amer: American author, b. 1927. With the publication of *Dinky Hocker Shoots Smack!* in 1972, M. E. Kerr moved to the forefront of the field of the YOUNG ADULT NOVEL and has remained there for more than two decades. The story of Dinky — the wisecracking overweight daughter of a Brooklyn Heights do-gooder, her emotionally damaged cousin Natalia, and their friend Tucker — is written in a style that combines laugh-out-loud humor with moments of wrenching poignancy. Critics marveled that a first-time novelist could produce such an accomplished work. Few knew that M. E. Kerr was the pen name of Marijane Meaker, who had been writing adult books for over twenty years under a variety of pseudonyms.

Meaker was born in Auburn, New York, and educated at a Virginia boarding school. She later shared autobiographical vignettes from her early years in *Me, Me, Me, Me, Me: Not a Novel* (1983). After obtaining a degree in journalism from the University of Missouri, Meaker moved to New York, where she had a succession of clerical jobs before beginning her career as a professional writer, using the name Ann Aldrich for paperback nonfiction, and Vin Packer for suspense novels. Unwittingly, she was already preparing for her career as a young adult author since many of the Packer novels touched on issues and themes that would subsequently find their way into the M. E. Kerr books. The author's ability to write about teenagers was already evident in her suspense titles *The Evil Friendship* (1958) and *The Twisted Ones* (1959).

Meaker had two primary reasons for entering the young adult field. One was the encouragement of her friend LOUISE FITZHUGH, author of *Harriet the Spy*; the other was her admiration for PAUL ZINDEL's novel *The Pigman*. At the time, Meaker was a visiting writer at a New York high school, where she met a student who inspired the character of Dinky Hocker. These three factors led to the creation of her first young adult work. Since then, her novels have won critical acclaim and a legion of readers; she was presented the Margaret A. Edwards Award in 1993. Her books are distinctive for their breezy, economical writing style; razor-sharp dialogue; humor that ranges from subtle to wild, yet is never mean-spirited; and a keen understanding of the human heart. Major and minor characters are brilliantly conceived, and there is a special empathy for loners and outsiders. While many young adult novels falter under the weight of important issues, Kerr's best books often deal with serious topics, such as the revelation that a beloved grandfather was once a Nazi in *Gentlehands* (1978) and the boarding school story *Is That You, Miss Blue?* (1975) in which a teenage girl gains empathy and maturity through her relationships with a number of offbeat characters, including a mentally unbalanced teacher. In *Deliver Us from Evie* (1994) Kerr explored the issues in a Missouri farm family, with a teenager who is a lesbian and her younger brother. *Night Kites* (1986) was the first young adult novel to deal with AIDS and remains one of the best. The books that take place in the fictional community of Seaville, New York, based on Meaker's home in East Hampton, provocatively explore the issue of class differences. She has also focused on one of her most interesting characters, John Fell, in a series of teenage suspense novels and has written MIDDLE-GRADE FICTION under the name Mary James, including *Shoebag* (1990), the story of a cockroach who is transformed into a human boy. Although the Mary James books are FANTASIES, they, too, contain the trademark Kerr wit and style. P.D.S.

Kimmel, Eric

American storyteller, b. 1946. Born in Brooklyn, New York, Eric Kimmel is the product of a culturally diverse neighborhood. "Puerto Rican, Hispanic, Yiddish kids were running around together all on the same block," he has recalled. For fifteen cents, he could take the subway to Rockridge or Greenwich Village, wherever his endless curiosity led him. An avid reader as a child, Kimmel grew up with his parents, a younger brother, Jonathan, and his Yiddish grandmother, from whom he acquired his storytelling knack.

"Nana," Kimmel has said, "always told us stories. Ghost stories, Bible stories, stories of mysterious trickery." His favorite was the "bitza" story, about a bear that tried to eat the grandchildren in Grandma's house when she was out, but Granny always managed to fool the shaggy creature. As an adult on a trip to Montreal, Kimmel learned that there was an original Yiddish version of that story, which, translated, means "Grandma and Her Grandchildren." "Many of my books," the author has said, "began as stories which I told to audiences for years before writing them down." Now, in addition to preserving the oral tradition, this professor of education at Portland State University in Oregon is penning his stories for posterity. "It's the rhythm of the language that makes a good book," he has explained. "If a story reads aloud well, there's a good chance it'll be a winner." In *Nanny Goat and the Seven Little Kids* (1990), he combined the bitza story with a classic from the brothers GRIMM, "The Wolf and the Seven Kids," sometimes called "The Wolf and the Seven Goats." A frequent contributor to *Cricket* magazine, Kimmel also has taken readers to distant places through his books. Journey to the Caribbean with *Anansi and the Moss-Covered Rock* (1988), to Russia in *Bearhead* (1991) and *Baba Yaga* (1991), to Japan via *The Greatest of All* (1991), to Norway through *Boots and His Brothers* (1992), and, in order to witness a traveler rid a village synagogue of goblins by outwitting them, to Eastern Europe with *Hershel and the Hanukkah Goblins* (1989), named a 1990 Caldecott Honor Book for TRINA SCHART HYMAN's illustrations. In one of his most popular titles, *Gershon's Monster: A Story for the Jewish New Year* (2000), he retold a traditional Hasidic legend about a selfish baker, set during Rosh Hashanah.

In 1989 the Oregon Reading Association presented this storyteller with the Ulrich H. Hardt Award for his contributions to reading and literacy throughout the state. But Kimmel does not believe that awards are enough to entice children to read. Frequent visits to classrooms in the Portland area have taught him that what young audiences often want from a book is "a vacation from civilization." That's one of the reasons he enjoys the folktale genre: it allows characters to do things ordinary people could never accomplish. "And, in the end, they make a point," he has said.

Kimmel is constantly searching for good stories that will expand young imaginations, improve children's reading skills, and open new worlds of enjoyment for them. He generally portrays the underdog overcoming enormous odds, often through cleverness or trickery, and gets a positive message across with a generous dose of wit. C.S.

Kindl, Patrice

American author, b. 1951. Truly unique teenage girl narrators distinguish Patrice Kindl's three FANTASY novels for young adults. One narrator is a shape-shifter, a high school student by day and a barn owl by night. Another is so shy that she has lived for seven years in secret rooms she constructed behind the walls of her house. The third might be a typical fairy tale heroine if only she wanted to marry the prince and live happily ever after. Instead, she would prefer to get back to the unglamorous business of tending geese.

Born in Alplaus, New York, Kindl was raised in nearby Ballston Spa. She attended Webster College in St. Louis, Missouri, and then moved to New York City to pursue an acting career. After a couple of television commercials and a lot of waitressing, she returned to her hometown and worked as a secretary. She now lives with her husband and son in Middleburgh, New York, where she writes, raises and trains capuchin monkeys to assist quadriplegics, and tends her "big old house with creaking floorboards, a haunted closet, peculiar little rooms with no apparent purpose, and a huge stone cistern in the basement that looks exactly like a crypt."

Kindl grew up in a large Victorian home that she also adored, as it gave her imagination space to expand. This is just the kind of house Kindl creates for fourteen-year-old Anna in *The Woman in the Wall* (1997). Not counting Anna's behind-the-scenes living quarters, her family's Queen Anne Victorian mansion contains twenty-two rooms — perfect for someone with a desire to disappear. Anna has inherited her "retiring disposition" from her father, who left home years earlier for a job at the Library of Congress, where he apparently got lost in the stacks, never to resurface. Little more than a dream or a questionable memory to her mother and two sisters after seven years in hiding, Anna plays out many a shy person's fantasy of complete escape from social contact. Yet as Kindl's ingeniously envisioned scenario develops, it becomes obvious that self-imposed isolation has its drawbacks. The more Anna matures, both physically and emotionally, the more confining her hidden existence becomes.

Both *Owl in Love* (1993) and *Goose Chase* (2001) also feature protagonists who find it a challenge to function in conventional society. When Owl Tycho, narrator of *Owl in Love,* is introduced to a classmate's pet hamster, Owl initially assumes she's being offered a snack. Hers is a one-of-a-kind voice in YOUNG ADULT FICTION, and her revelations about the differences between human nature and owl nature are fascinating. Though *Goose Chase* presents a familiar cast of charactres — hideous ogres, enchanted geese, a wicked king, a good-hearted prince, and a fair maiden locked in a tower — its narration sets it apart as well. Fourteen-year-old Alexandria Aurora Fortunato dispenses with the traditional once-upon-a-time format, saying "'Tis my own story I am telling and I will tell it as I please." By the same token, she would prefer to go it alone on her journey rather than travel with a prince she considers a dunderhead. Like Anna and Owl, Alexandria comes to revise her outlook a bit. She realizes there might be some value in companionship after all. C.M.H.

King-Smith, Dick

British author, b. 1922. Dick King-Smith has drawn on his twenty years as a farmer and experience as a primary school teacher in England to write his popular, humorous, outrageous farmyard stories, which combine elements of FANTASY with concrete details of farm life as they follow the adventures of remarkable animals who try to overcome natural obstacles.

Pigs Might Fly (1982) is the story of the young pig Daggie Dogfoot, the runt of a litter, who escapes from the farm each day and turns his disability — poorly formed front feet — into an advantage. He learns to swim, and his skill saves the farm from a terrible flood. Daggie is followed by Babe and Ace, King-Smith's other heroic pigs, who each find fame by developing unusual talents and firmly establish the author's belief in pigs' intelligence. Babe, the only pig on a sheep farm, is sure to end up on the breakfast table, but the hero of *Babe the Gallant Pig* (1985) unwittingly controls his destiny and makes himself indispensable by learning to herd sheep. The novel, published as *The Sheep Pig* (1983) in England, won the Guardian Award and a Boston Globe–Horn Book honor citation. It also served as the basis for a very popular movie for children.

Each of King-Smith's carefully crafted fantasies is well grounded in reality, using the physical details of the rural surroundings to create a credible base. The farm scenes are authentic and detailed, and the animals behave characteristically, so the reader is required to accept little on faith. Babe lives in a barnyard and eats slop, so the reader must only accept that he can communicate with other animals to believe the story of his triumph at the Sheep Dog Trials. *Pretty Polly* (1992) begins with the premise that many of the peeps young chickens make are remarkably similar to human speech. It is a short step, therefore, to teaching one talented chicken, Polly, to say "Eat Wheaties." From there, it is another small step to believing that Polly learns other human words. The reader knows that parrots can learn to talk, so why not chickens if they receive the same attention? *The Fox Busters* (1978) chronicles the successful efforts of three chickens who, due to the ineffectual methods of their farmer, must protect themselves from clever foxes. The traditional farmyard battle between foxes and chickens is elevated to riotous levels when the Fox Busters prepare a dangerous new weapon — hard-boiled eggs. Once again, King-Smith asserted that the underdog is able to succeed with cunning and perseverance and that the silliest animal is more clever than a human.

King-Smith has used humor to tell his stories and create memorable characters. His dialogue is full of wit and humor, and broad slapstick pervades his plots. His well-developed human characters are as funny and unusual as his farm animals, but the novels remain centered on the animals, and, inevitably, the animals are the ones to solve the problems that arise. King-Smith's novels combine elements of fantasy and humor with themes of survival and achievement, and his protagonists accomplish great things with their skills. King-Smith has incorporated these universal themes into rollicking adventure stories with sympathetic, memorable characters to create novels that are popular with readers and critics.   M.V.K.

Kirk, David

American author and illustrator, b. 1955. When David Kirk was three years old, his big brother Daniel got an interesting Christmas gift: a toy robot daddy, who carried a baby robot on a swing. That little family caused David's imagination to soar beyond the suburbs of Columbus, Ohio, where he grew up. Unlike many writers, Kirk was not an avid reader as a child but turned to toys, art, and the natural world to nourish his creativity. Ultimately all four members of the family migrated to the arts — David and Daniel have become successful picture book creators and their parents are professional puppeteers.

Kirk's aptitude for art was recognized while he was still in high school. Upon graduation in 1973 he was accepted into the Cleveland Institute of Art. Following his studies at CIA he spent a year in England, where he came to realize that his dream of being a painter in the pre-Raphaelite style might not be practical in today's world.

He moved to New York City and began his toy-making career. His tremendously original handmade, brightly colored wooden toys are highly sought after by collectors. Through his toys — and especially their packaging — Kirk came to the attention of publishers. Having left his New York City loft for an upstate farmhouse, Kirk turned to nature for inspiration — this time his daughter Violet's abiding affection for bugs. He found the world of insects and arachnids the perfect subject for his rich, intensely colored palette and luminous style of oil painting.

A publisher encouraged him to pursue the project that ultimately became *Miss Spider's Tea Party* (1994). Tremendously popular with both children and adults, Miss Spider has spun her way into sequels, an ALPHABET BOOK, BOARD BOOKS, and a series for younger children based on Miss Spider's childhood. The books' blend of sweetness and sophistication accounts for much of their appeal. The fantastic settings and characters are expansive and engaging, and Kirk's environments invite the reader to look for the magic in nature. Yet Kirk does not shrink from sinister elements in nature; instead, he exploits them to maximize the tension and pathos of the stories. His lifelong love of contraptions appears in the ingenious vehicles of *Miss Spider's New Car* (1997).

The Little Miss Spider series chronicles early childhood experiences from Miss Spider's foundling days to her life with Betty, a benevolent beetle. The books in this series are warm, reassuring, and big-hearted, without the sometimes darker tone of Kirk's other books.

Nova's Ark (1999) departed from Kirk's established style and subjects. Working with a team of computer experts at EAI in Ames, Iowa, Kirk created an intricate science fiction world of robots, mechanical creatures, cityscapes, and landscapes in brilliant colors. The unrhymed text is much longer than Kirk's earlier writings, providing detailed descriptions of the young robot Nova's quest to find his missing father.

Kirk has said, "I am still inspired by what I loved when I was seven — robots, toys, and bugs." An avid lover and observer of nature, he rescues toads from roadways and lives with his wife and daughters in the Finger Lakes region of New York State. S.L.T.

Knight, Hilary

American artist, b 1926. Although the possessive phrase "Kay Thompson's Eloise" appears on the front cover of the Eloise books, it would be hard to imagine the stories of the little girl who lives in New York's Plaza Hotel being half as successful without the contribution of Hilary Knight. Knight is the son of artist-writers Clayton and Katharine Sturges Knight, active in the 1920s and 1930s. A 1930 painting by Knight's mother, showing a young girl with a saucy attitude and stance, influenced Knight's own artistic creation of Eloise.

Kay Thompson created the idea of Eloise, a bratty, loquacious six-year-old, but it was Knight who gave Eloise form. After meeting Thompson in the mid-1950s, Knight sent her a Christmas card of a little girl named Eloise riding with Santa. Soon Thompson and Knight were collaborating on four books about Eloise and her adventures with her nanny, her dog, and her pet turtle. The success of *Eloise* (1955), *Eloise in Paris* (1957), *Eloise at Christmastime* (1958), and *Eloise in Moscow* (1959) led to a big blitz in Eloise merchandising. Knight was even commissioned by the Plaza Hotel to paint a picture of Eloise that to this day adorns the first floor (albeit a second edition, as the original painting vanished after a rowdy fraternity convened at the hotel). The collaboration between author and artist ended, however, after Thompson withdrew a fifth Eloise book because she felt the Eloise phenomenon had become too big. Knight would sometimes come into the studio in the morning and find his rough sketches meant for a fifth volume, *Eloise Takes a Bawth*, destroyed by Thompson. Soon after, the three sequels to the Eloise books were withdrawn from publication, and only the first book could clearly demonstrate Knight's talent in personifying the spoiled little girl.

Knight may be best known for his black-and-white line drawings with limited color for Eloise (pink, blue, and yellow — all used separately for the different books) or for his illustrations in several of the Mrs. Piggle-Wiggle books by Betty MacDonald, yet his full-color artwork showcases Knight's full talent. His ability to capture the childlike fairy world is most notable in *The Owl and the Pussycat* (1983), in which two children gradually are transformed into the title characters. Although he effectively conveyed a sense of landscape in the Eloise books, with the swirling snow in *Eloise in Moscow* and the quiet splendor of the sidewalk cafés in *Eloise in Paris*, the books that Knight has authored introduce fictional landscapes most children can appreciate more than the daily life of a rich girl let loose in the Plaza Hotel. In Knight's landscapes and drawings, adults are relegated to the fringes and the child's imagination holds sway. The full-color art in Knight's *Where's Wallace?* (1964), *The Twelve Days of Christmas (1981)*, and *Cinderella* (1981) trace his artistic development.

In the late 1990s, the estate of Kay Thompson released the three Eloise sequels, which had been out of print for more than thirty-five years. *Eloise at Christmastime* was reprinted with a new cover by Knight, as well as some additional new illustrations within the book. The reprints renewed Knight's popularity, and many of his other books were also re-released, bringing his artwork to a new generation. E.M.A.

Koertge, Ron

American author, b. 1940. Between 1973 and 1986, Ronald Koertge (pronounced KUR-chee) published fifteen books, mostly of POETRY. In 1986 he entered the field of children's literature with the highly successful YOUNG ADULT NOVEL *Where the Kissing Never Stops.* This was followed by *The Arizona Kid* (1988), *The Boy in the Moon* (1990), *Mariposa Blues* (1991), *The Harmony Arms* (1992), *Tiger, Tiger, Burning Bright* (1994), and *Confess-O-Rama* (1996), all of which have been equally well received. Koertge's stories are set in areas with which he is familiar: the fictitious Bradleyville, Missouri, based on Koertge's hometown; Tucson, Arizona; and Los Angeles, California. Raised in Colinsville, Illinois, near the Missouri border, he studied English, first at the University of Illinois, earning a B.A., and later at the University of Arizona, where he earned his M.A. Koertge now teaches English at City College in Pasadena.

Events in Koertge's stories usually take place during summer vacation. His protagonists are not handsome hunks; they are ordinary teenage males who stand on the precipitous edge of sexual awakening. They are boys who are unsure of themselves, who are easily embarrassed, whose skin breaks out, whose voices crack. They are too short, thin, heavy, or just too average to be noticed. They have no siblings. Koertge always keeps the safety net of love and support in place for his protagonists, even though parents may be sorting out problems of their own. He delves into the sensitivity and self-centeredness the average teenager experiences. Shyness, moodiness, concern about appearance, establishing self-confidence and self-identity, and the need for friendship are all part of the tumult of growing up that his characters must sort through. "Who am I?" — the question he has Mr. Evars in *The Boy in the Moon* assign the class as their end-of-semester essay — is the thematic question he asks with wit and empathy in all his novels. His format may seem pat since themes of sexuality and self-identity are integral to many young adult novels, but Koertge has put spin on his stories by intertwining quirky subplots and using an eclectic supporting cast of characters, few of whom are what they seem. This cast serves to evoke the underlying theme of encouraging tolerance or acceptance of people whose appearances, lifestyles, and backgrounds are unlike the norm. Although never heavy-handed or didactic, Koertge is clear and candid when addressing sexual issues like AIDS and the use of condoms. His openness about the average teenage boy's sexual arousal and confusion puts Koertge's writing on the cutting edge, which some adults may find objectionable. Yet sex is not gratuitous in his books; it is a natural part of life to be discussed and dealt with openly.

Ron Koertge's warm and witty honesty and understanding in addressing all aspects of the teen experience make his books refreshing and popular. S.R.

Konigsburg, E. L.

American author and illustrator, b. 1930. Elaine Loeb Konigsburg's entry into the field of children's literature was a dramatic one. In 1968 she won the Newbery Medal for her second novel, *From the Mixed-Up Files of Mrs. Basil E. Frankweiler* (1967), and that same year her first novel, *Jennifer, Hecate, Macbeth, William McKinley, and Me, Elizabeth* (1967), was named a Newbery Honor Book. Both novels are remarkable for their inventive plots and strong characters. Both are urban stories, and both are concerned with the lives of intelligent, nonconformist children.

Konigsburg is herself a creative, original writer. Born in New York City, she grew up in a small town in Pennsylvania and studied chemistry and taught science before leaving work to have three children of her own. While her children were young, she became interested in writing and art. In her writing Konigsburg was drawn to the urban experience, and many of her books are set in and around New York. She has illustrated her own novels in ink and has published several PICTURE BOOKS, which she has written and illustrated.

Konigsburg's novels, short stories, and picture books are imaginative, unpredictable, and peopled with individuals. Elizabeth, the heroine of *Jennifer, Hecate,* allies herself with Jennifer, the newcomer and only African American child in her class. The two loners find friendship through a complex relationship, which shifts from inequality to balance. Jennifer teaches Elizabeth to be independent and a strong nonconformist.

Konigsburg has developed this theme of independence in all her novels. Claudia, the heroine of *From the Mixed-Up Files,* learns to rely on herself and to celebrate her strengths when she and her brother run away from their family and live in the Metropolitan Museum of Art. During their stay at the museum, they discover the secret of a new acquisition and meet the eccentric Mrs. Basil E. Frankweiler. The novel succeeds because it is filled with unusual details, strong characters, adventure, and mystery. The Met is a perfect fantasy setting, in which the children wash in the fountain and sleep in luxurious antique beds. The museum setting fosters the intellectual and personal explorations of the characters and reflects Konigsburg's own interest in fine art. This fascination with artistic creativity appears again in the HISTORICAL NOVEL *The Second Mrs. Giaconda* (1975), in which Konigsburg

used an artist's apprentice to tell the story of the life and motivations of Leonardo da Vinci. After writing many novels and short stories, Konigsburg published her first picture book, *Samuel Todd's Book of Great Colors* (1990). Samuel Todd, like Konigsburg's other characters, is a gifted child able to see possibilities in the world around him. Twenty-nine years after winning her first Newbery Medal, Konigsburg won her second for *The View from Saturday* (1996), a novel about a group of sixth-graders who become the champions of the state Academic Bowl.

Throughout her writing, Konigsburg has emphasized the importance of taking risks, and her own writing is a tribute to that philosophy. She has experimented with writing style, point of view, and structure, taking chances and achieving varying success. Her inventiveness is her greatest strength but makes the quality of her books unpredictable. In (*George*) (1970), for example, Konigsburg explored the schizophrenic behavior of a young boy who believes himself to have a concentric twin, but the voice of the narrator is not clear or direct and the plot is more contrived than that of Konigsburg's other works. Although her writing is not uniformly excellent, Konigsburg has exhibited a playful love of words, and her best writing is some of the finest available for children. M.V.K.

Kraus, Robert

American author and illustrator, 1925–2001. Unlike his beloved character Leo, Herman Robert Kraus bloomed at an early age, and his work still continues to delight his young fans. He was born in Milwaukee, where he pursued his love of drawing by following suggestions he found in books about cartooning. By age ten he had sold one of his cartoons to a local barbershop, and after this early success his first published cartoon appeared on the children's page of the *Milwaukee Journal.* During high school Kraus drew for *Esquire,* the *Saturday Evening Post,* and other magazines, and after graduating he headed for New York and the Art Students'

League. During this time Kraus began his association with the *New Yorker,* contracting for fifty
cartoons a year. He also began to write and illustrate children's books, and his first, *Junior the
Spoiled Cat,* appeared in 1955.

Kraus founded his own publishing house,
Windmill Books, in 1965, and began writing stories illustrated by his friends at the *New Yorker,*
including Charles Addams and WILLIAM STEIG.
Windmill earned "an enviable reputation," according to *Publishers Weekly,* for its variety of
children's books, including some award winners.
Unfortunately, financial and distribution problems forced Kraus to sign over the company to
Simon and Schuster in the early 1980s. At various times Kraus also wrote under the pseudonyms Eugene H. Hippopotamus, E. S. Silly, and
I. M. Tubby, the last as author of the Tubby
books. These books, with their vinyl "pages" and
ability to float, have been many a toddler's first
bathtub toy.

Kraus's animal characters are sure to bring a
smile of recognition to parents of young children, and titles such as *Leo the Late Bloomer*
(1971), *Owliver* (1974), and *Herman the Helper*
(1974) deserve space on any parenting shelf,
along with Spock, Leach, and Brazelton, for their
on-target insight into toddler behavior. With
gentle humor, Kraus poked sly fun at Leo's worried father: "A watched bloomer doesn't bloom."
Leo's reassuring "I made it!" at the end delights
young listeners who may also have been scrutinized for early blooming by well-intentioned
moms and dads. Owliver must overcome his
dad's wishes that he become a doctor or a lawyer, and his wise mom recognizes Owliver's theatrical talent and insists he be allowed to follow
his dream. Kraus surprises his readers with a
gently humorous ending, as Owliver fulfills
every young boy's fantasy and grows up to become a fireman!

Many of Kraus's successful PICTURE BOOKS
have resulted from a collaboration with illustrators JOSÉ ARUEGO and Ariane Dewey. With simple lines and bold, vibrant colors, the pictures
perfectly complement the text. With simple
statements such as "Herman liked to help. He
helped his mother. He helped his father" and

brief questions and answers such as "Whose
mouse are you? Nobody's mouse. Where is your
mother? Inside the cat," Kraus evoked universal
childhood experiences. In *Where Are You Going,
Little Mouse?* (1986), his young protagonist feels
unloved by his family and goes off in search of
new parents and siblings. Any toddler who has
ever had a predawn adventure will sympathize
with the title character in *Milton the Early Riser*
(1972), although not many would share Milton's
sense of responsibility as he cleans up the mess
he's made. Nonetheless, Kraus always placed his
characters in a reassuring family scene, and this
sense of family pervades his work. Many of these
toddler favorites are accessible to beginning
readers, who can appreciate on their own these
stories told with limited vocabulary and appealing illustrations. E.H.

Krauss, Ruth

A merican poet and author, 1901–1993. Inspired by the experimental atmosphere in
child development circles during the 1940s and
1950s, Ruth Krauss created simple stories and
POETRY for young children. Best known for her
classic PICTURE BOOK, *The Carrot Seed* (1944), illustrated by her husband, CROCKETT JOHNSON,
Krauss went on to publish more than thirty
books over the next four decades. Among them
were eight picture book collaborations with illustrator MAURICE SENDAK. Their fortuitous beginning resulted in the publication of *A Hole Is
to Dig: A First Book of First Definitions* (1952), the
small innovative picture book that established
Sendak as a formidable figure in children's book
illustration.

During the early 1940s, Krauss was a member
of the experimental Writers Laboratory at the
Bank Street School in New York City, a program
that fostered the talents of other great picture
book writers, such as MARGARET WISE BROWN.
Krauss incorporated the "here and now" philosophy originated by educator and author Lucy
Sprague Mitchell, founder of the Bank Street
School, who maintained that "young children
live in the 'here and now' world around them,

which they use as a laboratory for their explorations." Krauss furthered Mitchell's ideas by incorporating psychologist-pediatrician Arnold Gesell's theories on the acquisition of language to create her own playful perspective on a young child's reality. She adopted Mitchell's concept of "direct observation" and went to the children themselves to glean her text for *A Hole Is to Dig.* She queried the young students to determine their meanings for words and in doing so created one of the first concept books for young children. Definitions like "Dogs are to kiss people" or "A lap is so you don't get crumbs on the floor" reflect a child's pragmatic approach to language.

In her books Krauss often used a child's natural word forms and expressions, most notably in *A Very Special House,* the Caldecott Honor Book in 1954, in which the young narrator pontificates in an unselfconscious, child-centered stream of thought. Krauss's imaginative and humorous use of language in the form of invented words and nonsensical rhymes inspired the first books for young children reflecting the child's inner life. Widely acclaimed as "the little book with the big idea," *The Carrot Seed,* which masterfully builds tension by using repetition in its short, 101-word text, has remained in print since 1945. Unflappable and confident, a little boy weeds and waters his precious carrot seed even though his parents and brother believe "it won't come up." With the simplest word *and,* Krauss paces the story while Johnson intensifies the climax by introducing bold color and oversize scale to picture the boy's huge red carrot topped with bushy green fronds — a carrot so big the boy needs a wheelbarrow to hold it. In *The Happy Day,* selected as a Caldecott Honor Book in 1950, Krauss's word patterns create rhythm in the simple text. Following a linear progression, several woodland animals sleep, sniff, and run to discover a bright yellow flower growing in the snow. Repetition and rhythm allow Krauss to seamlessly introduce five different species to the youngest listeners and readers.

Ruth Krauss's intuitive ability as a writer to capture the free-spirited thought processes and language of young children ensures her books' widespread acceptance and timeless appeal.

S.M.G.

Kuskin, Karla

American poet, author, and illustrator, b. 1932. Karla Kuskin's long, varied, and acclaimed career was presaged by the immediate success of her first book for children, published before she was twenty-five. *Roar and More* (1956), which Kuskin wrote, illustrated, designed, typeset, printed, and bound as part of her academic course work at Yale University, was

Illustration by Marc Simont from *The Philharmonic Gets Dressed* (1982), by Karla Kuskin.

instantly hailed for its original use of typography to represent an array of animal sounds. She revisited this technique in *All Sizes of Noises* (1962), in which the size, shape, and placement of letters convey the multitude of sounds — "HONNNNNNK," "THUDthudTHUDthud," "Hurryuphurryhurryup" — a child encounters in the course of a day. This book, with its urban focus, reflects the many years its creator spent in her native New York City as a child, wife, and mother.

Kuskin is a prolific author and illustrator who has created the text or artwork or both for more than thirty-five books. She is most often cited for her ability to craft nimble verses whose musical lilt and graceful internal and end rhymes all but demand they be read aloud. She has demonstrated, as well, an intuitive feeling for a child's perspective, whether addressing children's concerns about their size (*Herbert Hated Being Small*, 1979), their unshakable attachment to favored possessions (*A Boy Had a Mother Who Bought Him a Hat*, 1976), or, as in so many of her poems, their love of whimsy and gift for imaginative projection. Her child's-eye view of the world can also be seen in her characteristically small, precisely drawn illustrations, with their clean, uncluttered design and close attention to detail. In two books, *Near the Window Tree* (1975) and *Dogs and Dragons, Trees and Dreams* (1980), Kuskin paired her poems with autobiographical notes detailing the inspiration for each one in an effort to inspire children's own poetic undertakings.

Kuskin has won many honors over the years, including several citations from the American Institute of Graphic Arts. In 1979 the National Council of Teachers of English recognized her with their Award for Excellence in Poetry for Children, given for her body of work. Soon thereafter she garnered new accolades for the brilliantly simple, meticulously executed *The Philharmonic Gets Dressed* (1982), which brings a symphony orchestra to life by recounting the preparations, from showering to setting up on stage, undertaken by its 105 musicians in anticipation of an evening's performance. Illustrated by MARC SIMONT, this work was named a Notable Children's Book by the American Library Association and the *New York Times* and was designated a Library of Congress Children's Book. In addition, it was nominated for an American Book Award, a rare honor for a children's book and one that testifies to the breadth and endurance of Kuskin's appeal. A.J.M.

L

Lang, Andrew

British man of letters, editor, and reteller of traditional tales, 1844–1912. At the brink of the twentieth century, *The Blue Fairy Book* (1889) appeared, the first of twelve fairy tale books designated by color (blue, red, green, yellow, pink, gray, violet, crimson, brown, orange, olive, lilac) and edited by Andrew Lang. Publication of *The Blue Fairy Book* marked a return to respectability for the imaginative traditional tale, which had been largely rejected in Victorian England in favor of realistic, didactic children's stories. In *The Green Fairy Book* (1892), Lang explained respectfully to his child audience that though some adults believe fairy tales are harmful to children, Lang himself had faith that his readers "know very well how much is true and how much is only make-believe." Lang clearly aligned himself with those who support children's literature for delight rather than for instruction.

Immersed in NURSERY RHYMES and folktales as a young child, Lang took lifelong pleasure in this literature, a pleasure that took an academic turn when he discovered Homer and later studied classics at Oxford; his subsequent scholarly work in anthropology, particularly mythology, further developed the groundwork for his fairy book series. *The Blue Fairy Book* brings together thirty-seven well-known tales, carefully chosen by Lang from the best of collectors such as the brothers GRIMM from Germany and CHARLES PERRAULT from France.

Initially Lang had no intention of establishing a series, but the immense popularity of each volume seemed to demand another. Lang felt that his careful assembly of tales in *The Blue Fairy Book* was superior to subsequent volumes, but the harder-to-locate tales from around the world make the later books even more appealing to some. It is important to note, however, that Lang heavily edited tales from cultures outside of western Europe to remove elements he believed offensive or boring to his young readers. Interspersed throughout the Lang volumes are tales with active heroines, possibly reflecting the influence of Lang's wife, Leonora Blanche Alleyne Lang, whom he credited with much of the translation and revision of the stories.

The irony of Lang's life and work is that although he wrote for a profession — literary criticism; fiction; poems; books and articles on anthropology, mythology, history, and travel; original stories for children, including *The World's Desire* (1890), a continuation of Homer's *Odyssey* — he is best recognized for the books he did *not* write. Although many people mistake Lang for an original recorder of tales, like the Grimm brothers, his great contribution was, instead, overseeing the gathering of others' collected tales and providing for their wide dissemination. In *The Lilac Fairy Book* (1910), the last in the series, Lang lamented that "in the nurseries of Europe and the United States of America" he was regarded "as having written the tales."

Children through the years have continued to delight in the original editions of Lang's fairy books, illustrated by H. J. Ford, as well as in other editions. Lang's collection *The Nursery Rhyme Book* (1897), illustrated by L. LESLIE BROOKE, and his literate retellings of the *Arabian Nights* (1898) and *Tales of Greece and Troy* (1907) also remain childhood favorites. Lang further enriched children's literature by discovering and encouraging other authors, including E. NESBIT, Robert Louis Stevenson, Rudyard Kipling, and Arthur Conan Doyle. E.T.D.

Langton, Jane

American novelist, b. 1922. Jane Langton has been an inspired and inspiring author for three decades. Having immersed herself in the "layers of history" bordering her home near Walden Pond, she likes to write about contemporary children in real settings "littered with the past." Her fascination with Henry David Thoreau and the nineteenth-century transcendentalist movement provided the backdrop for FANTASIES such as *The Diamond in the Window* (1962); *The Astonishing Stereoscope* (1971); *The Fledgling* (1980), a Newbery Honor Book; and *The Fragile Flag* (1984).

Born in Boston, Massachusetts, Langton was intrigued by the colors of her crayons and paints at an early age. She can vividly recall the children's room of the library in Wilmington, Delaware, where her family moved in 1930. It was there that she plucked from the shelves works by ARTHUR RANSOME, E. NESBIT, A. A. MILNE, and KENNETH GRAHAME. Not only can she still quote passages from these authors, but she also has credited them with fortuitously teaching her how to form sentences and dialogue, how to create characters and plot. Her interest in art, combined with a bestseller she had read about Marie Curie, determined her totally diverse choice of courses in astronomy and art history at Wellesley College. After her sophomore year, she transferred to the University of Michigan, where she met and married Bill Langton. Reading PICTURE BOOKS to the first two of their three sons stirred up memories of her childhood crayons and paints, and Langton began to think about writing and illustrating a book of her own.

Langton's earliest attempts were "under the spell of those remembered English stories of gardens and kings and castles," but it was ELEANOR ESTES's Moffat stories that set her on the right path. "Reading about the Moffats," Langton has said, "I understood that children's books didn't have to be about princesses in imaginary countries. They could be about ordinary people here and now." This realization launched her first book, *The Majesty of Grace* (later retitled *Her Majesty, Grace Jones*), in 1961. After that she turned her attention primarily to writing for both children and adults, and she has been creating memorable American protagonists ever since. Langton's characters often find themselves in the midst of mysterious situations that transport them to other places and times. In *The Diamond in the Window*, Eleanor and Eddy Hall enter a frightening dream world to search for relatives who had disappeared and a lost treasure. With the help of a Canada goose in *The Fledgling*, Georgie Hall fulfills her longing to fly. And by carrying "the fragile flag" from Concord, Massachusetts, to Washington, D.C., Georgie tries to stop the president from launching his "peace" missile.

Good versus evil, right versus wrong, justice versus injustice — these values permeate Langton's books. Like the transcendentalists, her characters are willing to risk personal well-being in their pursuit of more idealistic goals. C.S.

Larsson, Carl

Swedish artist, 1853–1919. It is difficult to believe that the Swedish artist whose paintings are the embodiment of delightful family life could have grown up in the squalor of the slums of Stockholm. He wrote, "If I say that the people who lived in these houses were swine I am doing those animals an injustice. Misery, filth and vice . . . seethed and smoldered cozily." Larsson went to a "poor school," where, when he was thirteen, a teacher recognized his talent and encouraged him to attend Stockholm's Royal Academy of Fine Arts. When he was twenty-two, one of his paintings won the Royal Medal. Two years later, he moved to France; there he fell in love with another painter, whom he had met earlier in Stockholm. Within a few days Karin Bergöö and Larsson were engaged. Feeling holed up in his studio, Larsson switched from painting in oils to watercolors; he then joined the movement of "open air" painters. "I looked at Nature for the first time," he said. "I chucked the bizarre into the trash-heap . . . I have now given Nature a wide embrace, no matter how simple it may be. The pregnant, lusty earth is going to be the theme of my painting."

Larsson and Bergöö married in 1883, and his painting of her as a bride was the first in his lifelong series of family portraits. Carl Larsson had been in and out of France for the better part of eight years when this occurred to him: "Why in the name of all that's blue-green not paint Swedish nature in Sweden itself!" Then Karin's father left them a cottage — Little Hyttnäs — and at last they had a place to call home in Sweden. Scraping together what money they could, they took the tumbledown shack on a pile of slag and added a room here and there, built some furniture, and of course painted everywhere, creating a monument to everyday beauty.

This home at Sundborn is celebrated in Larsson's own book *Ett Hem* (1899). Lennart Rudström has written a BIOGRAPHY for children based on Larsson's book: *A Home* (1968, trans. 1974) was a New York Times Best Illustrated Children's Book. Rudström's series continued with *A Farm* (1966, trans. 1967) and *A Family* (1979, trans. 1980). The books are all illustrated by Larsson's paintings of rooms in his home, the fields of the farm, the river, and the island. But most of all they are filled with his seven children.

"The first picture in the whole series is the one [of] Pontus, who . . . had been impertinent at the dinner table and been ordered out of the room." Larsson found the boy sulking in a corner and "noticed how the rebellious lad stood out sharply against the plain background." Most often the paintings are of happy, cherished children, in daily life or ritual festivals, articulated by Larsson's characteristic curling lines. It was as if by creating the home for them to live in, and then painting his children in this idyllic setting, he was banishing all the ghosts of his miserable childhood. And in doing so, he gave people the world over enduring images of home. J.A.J.

Illustration by Carl Larsson from his book *Ett Hem (A Home)* (1899).

Lasky, Kathryn

American author, b. 1944. Kathryn Lasky is a prolific writer with a widely varied range of interests. Born in Indianapolis, Indiana, her gift as a "compulsive story maker" surfaced in private at an early age. It was only after sharing her work with her parents years later, and sensing their support, that she considered writing a reputable career. Since then her contributions to the literary world have included numerous books for children and adults.

Lasky has written many popular books, using the diary or journal format — such as *Christmas After All* (2001), *The Journal of Augustus Pelletier* (2000), *Elizabeth I* (1999), and *A Journey to the New World* (1996). She is also known for her YOUNG ADULT NOVELS and her juvenile INFORMATION BOOKS, many of which are about traditional crafts and have been illustrated with photographs by her husband, Christopher Knight. In *The Weaver's Gift* (1981), for which she won a Boston Globe–Horn Book Award, the pair combined their talents to show how wool is sheared from sheep and made into a child's blanket and other products. *Dollmaker: The Eyelight and the Shadow* (1981) and *Puppeteer* (1986) similarly reveal the intricacies of these skills as well as the professional and artistic concerns of the craftspeople involved. Lasky and Knight themselves participated in the process of turning sap into maple syrup and recorded their experiences in *Sugaring Time* (1983), which was a Newbery Honor Book; the book was later adapted to a filmstrip. In order to gather research for *Dinosaur Dig* (1990), the entire Knight family — including children Maxwell and Meribah — left the comfort of their home in Cambridge, Massachusetts, to go on a fossil hunt in Montana. Lasky's capacity to draw readers into their journey stems from her eloquent storytelling knack. Along with Lasky and her family, readers stumble down rocky slopes, feel the blistering heat of the sun, and share the excitement of unearthing ancient bones.

History plays a major role in many of Lasky's novels. *The Night Journey* (1981) moves back and forth in time, between Nana Sashie's stirring tale of her Jewish family's perilous flight from czarist Russia and Rachel's comparatively commonplace life in present-day America. *Pageant* (1986), which begins on the eve of the 1960 presidential election, is the humorous yet poignant story about a Jewish teenager at an exclusive Christian school for girls. In *The Bone Wars* (1988), an orphan hired as a Harvard scout encounters adventure while on a search for fossils in the Badlands of Montana in the late 1800s. In each case, ethnic or societal challenges provide character conflict, and underlying all of these fictional accounts is fact. But Lasky wrote in *The Horn Book,* "I really do not care if readers remember a single fact. What I do hope is that they come away with a sense of joy — indeed celebration — about something they have sensed of the world in which they live." Conflict for her stalwart protagonists is ultimately resolved by their discovery of the importance of continuity in life. Recognition of the link between past and present is, in the end, the most essential element in finding contentment. C.S.

Latino Children's Books

The current renaissance in books for and about Latino children is a source of joy and satisfaction to those who serve the reading needs of young Latino readers. In contrast to the situation just a few years ago, young Latino/Hispanic/Spanish-speaking readers can now select from an increasing number of insightful, well-written books — in English and Spanish — that will entertain them, inform them, and enrich their lives in numerous ways.

But numerous problems still persist. Foremost among these is the controversy surrounding bilingualism in the United States. On one hand are those who believe that the United States should be an English-only country. English-only supporters believe that Spanish (or other languages) may be spoken at home but that educating children in languages other than English results in cultural and linguistic barriers. On the other hand are numerous researchers and educators who believe that developing literacy in the first language can make a substan-

tial contribution to literacy development in the second language. Moreover, supporters of bilingualism (and multilingualism) believe that free speech in the United States should not be limited to speakers of English.

Despite the controversy, the good news is the increasing number of books about Latinos now being published for young readers in English in the United States. The best of these possess all the qualities of well-written fiction — honesty, integrity, and imagination.

Foremost among these are the delightful stories, novels, and poems by two Latino authors, GARY SOTO and Nicholasa Mohr. The trials and tribulations of growing up are beautifully depicted in Gary Soto's ever-popular collections of short stories, *Baseball in April and Other Stories* (1990) and *Local News* (1993). Mexican American neighborhoods come alive in Soto's heartfelt poems included in *A Fire in My Hands: A Book of Poems* (1990) and *Neighborhood Odes* (1992).

Family squabbles and misunderstandings with a strong Puerto Rican flavor are honestly portrayed in Nicholasa Mohr's sensitive novel *Going Home* (1986). Mohr's depictions of strong, lovable characters, beautiful warm personalities, and happy Puerto Rican families will be enjoyed by younger readers in *Felita* (1979). And adolescents will be moved by Mohr's collections of poignant short stories, *El Bronx Remembered: A Novella and Stories* (1975) and *In Nueva York* (1977), which reflect the sad, depressing, and difficult lives of many Puerto Ricans in New York City.

Selectors also will note the increasing number of INFORMATION BOOKS that will satisfy young readers' curiosity about Latino people and cultures. The exemplary ones can answer questions on particular aspects of the Latino experience or satisfy the reader's desire for broader knowledge.

The bad news is that many recently published books continue to provide a very limited, one-sided, or even incorrect view of Latinos. They either foster the stereotypes of fiestas, piñatas, and other "artsy-craftsy" views of Latino people or abound in sensationalistic information that distorts specific aspects of Latino cultures — for instance, the Aztec civilization is depicted as if the Aztecs were barbarians involved in gory practices of human sacrifice, disregarding their many wonderful achievements.

Another important issue that selectors should note about books in Spanish published in the United States is the inferior quality of the texts of many of the translations from English into Spanish as well as of works originally published in Spanish: incorrect lexical constructions, unclear phrases, and numerous grammatical, spelling, and typographical mistakes. Some U.S. publishers are indeed starting to pay attention to their Spanish publications; others, however, show a complete disregard for the Spanish language.

The most important feature regarding recently published books in Spanish for young readers is the increasing number of distinguished books that have a high potential for reader involvement or interest. These books — published either in the United States or abroad — can appeal to a wide variety of young readers' interests, backgrounds, and ages. Many are truly outstanding books that provide Spanish-speaking children and adolescents with a sense of wonder and satisfaction that is enjoyed by readers everywhere.

Some noteworthy authors from the Spanish-speaking world are the Argentine María Elena Walsh, whose delightful rhymes and amusing stories provide children with endless joy as they read about their treasure collections in *El reino del revés* (The upside-down kingdom, 1989) or the King of the Compass who searches for his round flower in *El país de la geometría* (Geometryland), which is included in *El diablo inglés y otros cuentos* (The English devil and other stories, 1969). *El diablo inglés* tells about the English devils that appeared in Argentina in 1806.

Maribel Suárez and Laura Fernández, two young Mexican authors and illustrators, truly understand children's sensitivities and interests. *Miguel y el pastel* (Miguel and the cake, 1992), written by Suárez, shows how Miguel's baking experiences can result in a joyous, unexpected

treat, and *Luis y su genio* (Luis and his genie, 1986), written by Fernández, is a delightfully honest story about a boy's real dilemma — should Luis do his math homework or enjoy a day with his genie?

The Venezuela author Daniel Bardot has depicted children's fears about losing their first tooth in the amusing story *Un diente se mueve* (A loose tooth, 1990–1991), and Rosaura, a hen, enjoys a bicycle as a special birthday gift in *Rosaura en bicicleta* (A bicycle for Rosaura, 1990).

Children of all ages enjoy Violeta Denou's amusing, colorful illustrations of small children in contemporary Spanish settings. Her numerous, profusely illustrated stories thrive with the activities common to young children, such as *Teo en un día de fiesta* (Teo during a holiday, 1987), *La familia de Teo* (Teo's family, 1991), and *Vamos al zoo, Teo* (Let's go to the zoo, Teo, 1991).

There is no question that young Latino readers will benefit from the efforts of teachers, librarians, publishers, parents, and others who wish to entice them into the world of reading through insightful books that they can read and understand. The challenge, however, is to ignore long-standing myths that have discouraged young Latino readers from the pleasure of books and to concentrate on books — in English and Spanish — that appeal to the universal likes, wishes, dreams, and aspirations of children everywhere. I.S.

Lauber, Patricia

American author, b. 1924. Patricia Lauber's INFORMATION BOOKS provide a tour of the universe in time and space, making the wide natural world as real and immediate as opening one's eyes. Through her descriptions, readers see small organisms growing in the aftermath of a forest fire; bits and pieces of fossilized bone that reveal the nature of long-dead mammals; geologic formations on the moon and distant planets; and the drama of flowers living and dying in an ordinary backyard. In Lauber's skillful prose, earthquakes form the Rocky Mountains, dinosaurs prowl the forests, and seeds begin their journey through the cycle of life. Her powerful words spark the imagination to accept the reality found through a microscope or a telescope, and even the titles of her books suggest an awaiting ringside seat on the action.

Lauber's *Journey to the Planets* (1990) alerts readers to an orbit alteration that makes Neptune the farthermost planet until 1999. Seen from space, Earth, she has written, resembles a big blue marble, unusual in the amount of water available and the atmosphere retained by the planet's gravity. The fossilized records she described in *Dinosaurs Walked Here* (1987) show the passage of huge creatures who left an earthly diary marked with questions for scientists to explain. Lauber herself answered some questions by describing life 75 million years ago in *Living with Dinosaurs* (1991), placing her readers in a world where Montana exists on the banks of an ocean, seabirds squabble in the dim light, earthquakes rock the ground, and the Great Plains rest at the bottom of an inland sea. She described another world in *From Flower to Flower* (1987), in which industrious honeybees, bumblebees, bats, birds, moths, and butterflies contribute to growth by pollinating trees, flowers, and grasses. And further adventures take place in *Seeds: Pop, Stick, Glide* (1981), as tiny packages of life move through oceans (like the coconut), on an animal's fur (like burdock burrs), or on a fickle wind (like the dandelion) and so propagate their species. Even natural disaster takes on a new light in Lauber's description of the 1988 Yellowstone National Park conflagration in *A Summer of Fire* (1988). Following the disaster, animal and plant life grow and become rejuvenated. The thousands of acres blackened by summer fires produce lush green meadows in the fall and riotous colors and remarkable diversity in the spring.

Throughout her work, Lauber has described nature's eminently sensible way of maintaining order and promoting prosperity — a natural direction she has followed in her writing. Encouraged to express herself in words even as a child — "Being born wanting to write," she has said — she began reading and later experimented with putting words on paper. Since 1945, her writing and editing have evolved into fiction and nonfiction books, essays, and short stories on topics ranging from natural history to humor, from cowboys to the forest, from outer space to backyard gardens. Lauber has retained a childlike excitement about these myriad subjects and the whole world. "I like to stand and stare at things," she has said, "to talk with people, and to read a lot." Along the way, this well-respected researcher and author travels, having fun and "doing research" for her next book. For over sixty books and almost fifty years, she has expressed her enjoyment of the world around her in ways that gently force thousands to experience the great and small, the distant and personal, the beauty and reality of the world. B.W.C.

Lawson, Robert

American author and illustrator, 1892–1957. One of the most prolific and notable figures in American children's literature during the first half of the twentieth century, Robert Lawson achieved distinction both as an illustrator and as an author, winning the Caldecott Medal in 1941 for *They Were Strong and Good*, a PICTURE BOOK tribute to his forebears, and the Newbery Medal in 1945 for *Rabbit Hill*, the story of an animal community and its relationship to the New Folks who come to the neighborhood. This feat, which no one has as yet duplicated, makes his work particularly significant in the context of American culture as well as in the history of publishing. Lawson's contributions ranged from endpapers for T. H. WHITE's *Sword in the Stone* (1939) to illustrations for Ginn's *Mathematics for Success* (1952). By 1957, when *The Great Wheel* was published posthumously, he had written and illustrated twenty books and illustrated forty-six for other authors, in addition to the considerable number of drawings and etchings published before his success as a writer and illustrator for children.

Born in New York, Lawson grew up in New Jersey, graduated from art school in 1914 at the beginning of World War I, and worked as a free-lance artist for several popular magazines, including *Harper's Weekly* and, after the war, *Delineator* and *Designer*. In 1917–1918 he served in France with the Fortieth Engineers, Camouflage Section. In 1922, he married artist Marie Abrams, and in 1923 they moved to Westport, Connecticut, where they designed Christmas cards — one a day for three years — to pay off the mortgage. Like DR. SEUSS, Lawson worked extensively as a commercial artist. Then his collaboration with MUNRO LEAF for *The Story of Ferdinand* (1936), although not his first venture into children's books, brought him national and ultimately international recognition. In 1939, with *Ben and Me*, the story of Benjamin Franklin as told by the irreverent mouse Amos, he became a writer as well as an illustrator. Three more similarly iconoclastic historical fantasies followed, each featuring a talkative pet who presents an insider's view of its famous owner: *I Discover Columbus* (1941), *Mr. Revere and I* (1953), and *Captain Kidd's Cat* (1956). Of these three, *Revere*, closest in comic tone to *Ben and Me,* is probably the most successful, with the fewest unfortunate stereotypes.

As a writer, Lawson was essentially a raconteur, creating characters through dialogue rather than description. As an illustrator, he was, as critics have remarked, a traditionalist in composition and style. The demands of commercial art and his prize-winning work as an etcher made him a master of line — fluid and expressive — emphasizing his talent for visual storytelling characteristic of American art and attuned to American aesthetic sensibilities. He was so clearly of his times that he captured both its strengths and its weaknesses. His love of his country and its heroes is contagious, but his depictions of women and minorities are clichés. But then, most of his human characters were singularly one-dimensional, in contrast to un-forgettable animal creations such as Ferdinand, perhaps the first flower child, and the varied denizens of Rabbit Hill, where there is indeed "enough for all." M.M.B.

Leaf, Munro

American author and illustrator, 1905–1976. During his forty-year career in children's literature, Munro Leaf wrote and illustrated nearly forty books. He is best known as the creator of *The Story of Ferdinand* (1936), a modern juvenile classic that has charmed children worldwide for more than half a century. Unforgettably paired with ROBERT LAWSON's black and white etchings, Leaf's beloved tale of a peaceful Spanish bull ranks significantly in the field of American children's literature as the first PICTURE BOOK to be labeled subversive, as well as an exemplary, seamless union of text and art.

Born in Maryland, Leaf obtained degrees from the University of Maryland and Harvard University. He taught secondary school, then worked as editor and director for Frederick A. Stokes Company, a publishing firm in New York. His first children's book, *Grammar Can Be Fun* (1934), came about because he overheard a mother lecturing her young son about the inappropriateness of saying "ain't." Using stick figures, Leaf illustrated the didactic yet humorous text, which is meant to entertain as well as edify. *Grammar Can Be Fun* earned critics' acclaim; it also launched Leaf's Can Be Fun series, in which he wrote and illustrated nine equally successful titles whose topics range from health, safety, and manners to classroom subjects such as arithmetic, history, and science.

Leaf garnered universal fame when he wrote *The Story of Ferdinand,* his most successful and finest work. He penned the brief text on a yellow legal pad in less than an hour for Lawson, his illustrator friend. Viking's gifted juveniles editor, May Massee, immediately accepted the collaboration and, in the fall of 1936, published the story of gentle Ferdinand, a young bull in rural

Spain who prefers solitude and smelling flowers to the company of his fellow ruffian bulls. When he is stung by a bee, Ferdinand's antics are misinterpreted by scouts as belligerent behavior, and they quickly transport him to Madrid for a bullfight. In the arena, sanguinary spectators watch a phalanx of banderilleros, picadors, and the chivalrous matador readying for battle. But once in the ring, Ferdinand sees only the floral decorations adorning the ladies' hair and tranquilly succumbs to his favorite pastime: smelling flowers. Taken home to his pasture, Ferdinand returns to the quietude and contentment that his special cork tree and flowers offer him.

Ferdinand created a global controversy overnight. *The Story of Ferdinand* was denigrated and banned in civil war–torn Spain, scorned and burned as propaganda by Hitler, and labeled in America as promoting fascism, anarchism, and communism. Others heralded the innocent bovine as an international emblem of pacifism. Leaf rebutted the attacks, stating that he wrote the story simply to amuse young children. With more than sixty foreign-language translations, the never-out-of-print title still enjoys widespread popularity. Leaf's ability to establish a strong character and comic situation with so few words is extraordinary; so, too, is Lawson's gift at interpreting Leaf's understated humor with spirited images that accurately reflect the emotions portrayed in the text. Both talents combined inseparably to craft a perfect picture book.

Leaf and Lawson's second collaboration, *Wee Gillis* (1938), also received wide critical acclaim. A small, orphaned lad who lives neither in the Highlands of Scotland nor in the Lowlands, but halfway between, Wee Gillis warms children's hearts just as humorously as Ferdinand does. Lawson's black and white etchings won the critics' hearts, too, and they named *Wee Gillis* a 1939 Caldecott Honor Book. The third of Leaf's notable collaborations — this time with illustrator LUDWIG BEMELMANS — produced *Noodle* (1937), a happy moral tale about a dachshund who, even after a visit from a magical wish-granting dog-fairy, judiciously chooses to remain exactly the same size and shape he is.

Leaf once said, "Early on in my writing career I realized that if one found some truths worth telling, they should be told to the young in terms that were understandable to them." Few, if any, characters in American children's picture books are better understood or more loved by multitudes around the world than Ferdinand, Leaf's reluctant hero who likes "to sit just quietly and smell the flowers." S.L.S.

Lear, Edward

British writer of nonsense, 1812–1888. Born the twentieth child of twenty children, Edward Lear experienced an early life of hardship, loss, and sadness. Even though Lear never had any formal artistic training, by the age of twenty his drawings of animals and birds were well enough known that he was invited by Lord Stanley to make drawings of the animals that were kept on his estate. It was here that Edward Lear first began writing his ingenious limericks to amuse the children of the household. Lear actually viewed himself as a landscape artist and at the age of twenty-five set off on travels to pursue his artistic career. He described himself as a "Nartist who drew pigchers and vorx of hart."

Lear spent a good part of his early artistic career attempting to become established as a landscape artist and traveled extensively, returning to England to facilitate the publication of his verse, which in turn supported his travels. But success came from the publication of his nonsense verses and sketches, not his work as a landscape artist. *The Book of Nonsense* was published in 1845 under the pseudonym Derry Down Derry. It was a critical and commercial success and is commonly regarded as a pivotal work in children's literature. The continuing popularity of this first edition convinced him to publish under his own name in a 1861 reissue, followed by *Nonsense Songs* (1871), *More Nonsense* (1872), and *Book of Limericks* (1888). There have been numerous books containing individual story poems published since then, both with Lear's illustrations and those of other artists, including *The Owl and the Pussycat, Quangle Wangle's Hat, The Scroobious Pip, The Nonsense Alphabet,* and *The Jumblies.*

Edward Lear appeals as much to the children of the early twenty-first century as he did to the children of his own day. Because of his unhappy childhood, Lear was determined to bring joy and amusement into children's lives. He saw nonsense as a means of escape from life's harsh realities. His poems avoided the strong didactic strain then common in books for children. Lear never moralized; his only purpose was entertainment. Some adults, however, objected to Lear's approach and to his use of misspellings and incorrect grammar as well, fearing their influence.

Lear applied his peculiar blend of artistic and poetic talent and playfulness to create a narrative as well as a visual form for his nonsense. His ingenuity in the invention of new words and sounds created an audible feast.

> E was once a little eel
> Eely
> Weely
> Peely
> Eely
> Twirly, Tweely
> Little Eel.

Lear's alliteration and rhythmic patterns are flawless, and he was at his best when writing verse that combined invented words with conventional poetic meter. But to fully enjoy Lear's poems, one must see and appreciate the illustrations with which he accompanied them. Their humor enhanced by their spontaneity, many were apparently done as Lear recited his limericks to a roomful of children. The inventive yet spare ink drawings, rendered with just a few lines, make no attempt at realism in their depictions of fantastic beasts and birdlike humans.

Lear reveled in upsetting the expected social patterns, maintained that anything is possible,

and advocated that all experience should be peppered with humor. The poet Myra Cohn Livingston wrote of Lear: "And you laugh, and through that laughter grow and recognize that the nonsenses abiding in the real world can be overcome by your belief in yourself and your imagination." Lear's delightful humor, inventiveness, alliteration, and illustrations continue to entertain and tickle the imagination — just as Lear desired. A.I.

Le Guin, Ursula K.

American writer, b. 1929. Ursula Kroeber Le Guin, daughter of the anthropologist Alfred L. Kroeber and the writer Theodora Kroeber, was born in Berkeley, California. After attending Radcliffe College and Columbia University, she spent a year as a Fulbright scholar in Paris, where she met and married the historian Charles A. Le Guin. She began publishing SCIENCE FICTION stories in the early 1960s and has since written numerous novels, short stories, plays, poems, and essays. Widely known for her innovative, award-winning science fiction for adults, Le Guin also wrote the intimate yet epic children's FANTASY the Earthsea cycle, consisting of the original trilogy — *A Wizard of Earthsea* (1968), *The Tombs of Atuan* (1971), and *The Farthest Shore* (1972) — and later volumes, *Tehanu* (1990), *Tales from Earthsea* (2001), and *The Other Wind* (2001).

Earthsea — a collection of archipelagoes amid a constantly changing sea — is as fully developed a fantasy world as J. R. R. TOLKIEN's Middle-earth, with which it is often compared. Le Guin has created a setting both familiar and dreamlike, a pervasive metaphor for life as a perilous yet rewarding journey. Again like Tolkien, Le Guin strengthened readers' belief in and commitment to her created world by interweaving her plot with references to Earthsea's geography, languages, flora and fauna, histories, mythologies, traditions, and superstitions.

A Wizard of Earthsea tells the story of Ged's

apprenticeship as a wizard. While still a boy on Gont, Ged reveals a gift for magery when his spell saves his village from Karg invaders, and, as a consequence, Ogion, the local mage, teaches him to read and write in the Old Speech, the language of magic and dragons. Ogion also tries to teach him the observant patience of mages, but Ged, restless and proud, wants more knowledge, faster. His training accelerates at the School of Wizards on Roke, where he learns skills such as shape-changing, summoning, and naming, but, still proud, Ged takes a dare and rends the fabric of being, unleashing an unknown beast from the realm of the dead to which his fate is thenceforth tied. Chastened and driven to conquer the protean, elusive beast, Ged earns his staff and leaves Roke. His subsequent journeys and adventures — including confrontations with a zombielike creature, a beguiling witch, and an ancient dragon — satisfyingly complete this bildungsroman, written with a wry nod toward the process of a legend in the making.

The Tombs of Atuan depicts Ged as a mature man, with clear goals and full control of his powers. The story focuses not on Ged, however, but on Tenar, a priestess of the Nameless Ones, powers ostensibly worshipped by the rulers of the warlike Kargs, but in reality the focus of an ancient cult in which few believe but which none dare to deny. Consecrated to the Nameless Ones from early childhood, Tenar has been stripped of her name, her past, and any future. She is Arha, the Eaten One, the ever-reincarnated priestess of the Tombs, living only for the endless repetition of the cult's dark, arid rites, which she has killed to uphold. Ged interrupts this sentence of death in life. Searching for the lost fragment of the ring of Erreth-Akbe, a talisman of peace that if made whole would presage the return of a King to Earthsea, Ged finds his way into the forbidden labyrinths of the Nameless Ones. Trapped by Arha, Ged breaks through her indoctrination and, using his genius for discovering true names, returns Tenar to Arha. Only then, acting together, can they fulfill his quest.

The Farthest Shore takes Ged beyond the limits of his powers. The springs of magery are running dry, and a seductive, cruel decadence is spreading from the islands of the outer reaches toward the heart of Earthsea. Ged, now Archmage of Roke, undertakes a final journey to discover and eliminate the source of the contagion. He takes with him a young man, Arren, Prince of Enlad, of the lineage of the old kings, and together through many trials of body and spirit they achieve a greater end than they had hoped: Earthsea is restored to wholeness and peace, and a King is restored to the long-empty throne.

The trilogy thus forms an elastic cycle, combining epic deeds and human qualities. In it we see a young hero grow to manhood as perhaps the greatest of Earthsea's many great mages; we see unfolded the most significant achievement of his prime; and we see him complete his life's work, both as a man and as a mage. Further, each volume describes Ged's exploration of a distinct realm of being and knowledge: the personal in A Wizard of Earthsea, the social in The Tombs of Atuan, and the spiritual in The Farthest Shore. Le Guin has described the three themes as coming of age, sexuality, and death, further underscoring the completeness of the whole. Successfully combining Jungian concepts, such as the shadow, and concepts from Eastern philosophy, such as equilibrium of opposing forces, with the Western tradition of the hero-tale, Le Guin has created a fantasy epic with contemporary yet enduring resonance.

This self-containment makes all the more surprising the author's decision to return to Earthsea in Tehanu. Set contemporaneously with the events in The Farthest Shore, Tehanu provides a closer look at the nature and consequences of the dissolution of civilizing bonds chronicled there. Many years after the events in The Tombs of Atuan, Tenar, a widow, lives alone on a farm on Gont. Accepted and yet always a Karg stranger, she is immediately drawn to a severely abused and abandoned young girl and takes her into her home. Thus embroiled in the ebb and flow of power and evil that mark a lawless time, Tenar struggles to protect and nurture first her damaged young charge, Tehanu; later, the weary and emptied Ged who has returned to find oblivion on Gont; and ultimately, herself. The book's focus on sexuality, cruelty, and violence; the closely paced plot; and the use of Tenar's thoughts to establish point of view, all clearly differentiate it from the three earlier, more sweeping and traditional fantasy volumes. *Tehanu* tells a fascinating story, built on the compelling theme of differences between men's and women's ways of being and knowing and the possibility of somehow, someday synthesizing these. Yet it is a story with more appeal and meaning for adults than for children. *Tehanu* disturbs rather than completes the reader's understanding — and enjoyment — of the Earthsea cycle.

Le Guin's other books for children include a realistic YOUNG ADULT NOVEL, *Very Far Away from Anywhere Else* (1976), and, for younger readers, two brief, dreamlike tales, *Catwings* (1988) and *Catwings Return* (1989). In *A Ride on the Red Mare's Back* (1992) a fairy tale reminiscent of HANS CHRISTIAN ANDERSEN, a brave and resourceful young girl rescues her brother from trolls, with the help of a magical red mare lovingly carved and painted for her by her father. Simple objects — bread, knitting needles, woolen scarf, each made by her for others or by others for her — and the homely virtues of perseverance and kindness also help her in her quest. Through this skillful union of the fruits of simple domestic labor with the strength of family love, Le Guin created a story from the magic of making and doing for the benefit of others, a story she told first and most satisfyingly in the Earthsea cycle. S.B.

L'Engle, Madeleine

American author, b. 1918. Madeleine L'Engle's life is as interesting and inspiring as her books — if not more so. From the high points of winning the Newbery Medal for *A Wrinkle in Time* (1962), garnering a Newbery Honor mention for *A Ring of Endless Light*

(1980), and obtaining a position as writer-in-residence at the Cathedral of St. John the Divine (Episcopal) in New York City through the lows of her "dry decade," when nothing she wrote was accepted for publication, and the wrenching agony of watching her beloved husband of forty years die from cancer, L'Engle has struggled with her often conflicting roles of wife, mother, artist, and Christian. She has also struggled to place herself in time, both in Kronos — eternal time, in which God moves — and Chairos, "clock time," in which man lives. It is from these struggles that her work derives, and it has been a fruitful struggle: nearly twenty books for children and nineteen for adults, including essays, POETRY, fiction, and two plays.

L'Engle began the struggle early, writing her first story at age six. "All about a little 'grul,'" she has said, "who lived in a cloud," something that could be said of many of her time-traveling, space-bending, star-talking protagonists in the books she would write as an adult. L'Engle led an isolated, if somewhat romantic, existence as the only child of sophisticated older parents. Her father had been gassed during a stint as a war correspondent during World War I and subsequently "spent eighteen years coughing his life away." During most of L'Engle's childhood, her mother was occupied with caring for her failing husband. L'Engle has said she felt very loved by her parents but completely apart from their world. She created her own world as an escape and a solace, which was especially important during a series of painful school experiences — first at a "really repulsive New York–type school," where she was labeled "the unpopular one," then at a boarding school in England, where she was sent after her father's ill health forced the family to relocate to the Swiss Alps. "It was absolutely splendidly horrible," she has written. "I still get books out of it." Indeed, her awkward, intense, oddly brilliant heroines are not unlike the author's descriptions of herself. Faith and family are two important themes in her work, as they are in her life: "My own lonely childhood is very likely the reason why family is so important to me — my own present family of children and grandchildren and the families in my stories."

Her first book to be published to wide acclaim was *Meet the Austins* (1960), a FAMILY STORY in the classic mold: the large, noisy, happy Austin family teaches unhappy orphan Maggie the meaning of life and love. This book drew heavily on L'Engle's own life at Crosswicks, the Connecticut country home where she and her husband, actor Hugh Franklin, and their three children retreated in the 1950s, the period the author has termed her dry decade. After modest initial success as a young author fresh out of Smith College — three books and one play published — she was unable to get one piece published for nearly ten years: "The only thing I was selling during this decade was stuff from the store," the store being the general store she and her husband bought, renovated, and ran to support their young family. The publication of *Meet the Austins* ended the drought and established two of her three most important themes: a distinctly spiritual element in the lives of her protagonists, explicitly Christian in most of her books, and a strong belief in the healing power of love, most significantly the love between family members.

The third element in L'Engle's thematic trinity, the world of scientists and scientific exploration, makes its appearance in L'Engle's next work, *A Wrinkle in Time,* in which a physicist's large, cozy family battles Evil in order to save their father and their world. Myopic, coltish Meg Murry and her precocious little brother Charles Wallace join forces with three delightful entities — Mrs. Whatsit, Mrs. Who, and Mrs. Which — to save their scientist-father from the clutches of IT, a giant pulsating brain that wishes to control all thought and action. At once a SCIENCE FICTION story, a philosophical meditation on the nature of Evil and Love, and a coming-of-age novel, *Wrinkle* broke new ground in what was considered appropriate for young readers. Rejected by several publishers for being too complex, this title has amply proven L'Engle's belief that "children are excited by new ideas" and has been credited with bringing science fiction into the mainstream of children's literature. This is L'Engle's best work, with deft, appealing characterizations and a well-crafted plot balancing the strongly stated thematic elements that often overwhelm her later work. *Wrinkle* has received the highest critical acclaim in a career that has been liberally rewarded with praise and condemnation. In the Time Fantasy series L'Engle followed the Murry family, most notably in *A Wind in the Door* (1973) and *A Swiftly Tilting Planet* (1978), which won the American Book Award. All of the Murry family books have elements of FANTASY and science fiction to link them, as well as an apocalyptic struggle between Good and Evil. The Austin family saga, on the other hand, which the author has continued in books such as *The Moon by Night* (1963) and *The Young Unicorns* (1968), includes reality-based, coming-of-age novels in which the adolescent protagonist is tempted by the seductive wiles of cynicism and despair — often personified by a love interest — but is ultimately won over to the side of good by the warmth and decency the Austins exhibit. She was given the Margaret A. Edwards Award in 1998 for the Austin family series.

L'Engle's thematic concerns are her forte as well as the aspect of her work that has brought on the most controversy. Her ability to give face and voice to abstract ideas such as Love, Good, Despair, and Evil and to make the struggle among them believable in her characters' lives have made her work timeless and important to generations of readers. L'Engle has understood that it is of these things that adolescent angst is made, not simply immediate concerns such as pregnancy, AIDS, and gang violence. L'Engle has placed her characters and her readers in a larger context, one in which individual actions have universal implications, or what the author calls "the butterfly effect": the death of a butterfly has an effect in a galaxy light-years away. But this dominating thematic element in her work has caused some critics to term her books didactic, and the religious implications of her themes have caused some schools to remove her books from library shelves for their "anti-Christian" message. For while some may find her overt Christianity an artistic detriment, fundamentalist Christian groups have found it "contrary to biblical teaching." For the author, who has several books of essays published by Christian presses, this sort of thing is nonsensical: "People are reading with a list of words, they're not reading for content." L'Engle has written about what she most strongly believes in: a universe of randomness and chance but one in which everything is completely interdependent. "To hurt a butterfly," she has said, "is to shake the universe."

S.G.K.

Lent, Blair

American author and illustrator, b. 1930. Self-described as "fat and clumsy at sports," Blair Lent, an only child in a family of limited means, grew up in an affluent suburb of Boston. He felt himself an outsider in a town where, he has stated, "money, appearance, and athletic prowess were considered one's most important attributes." Lent's father, an engineering student, shared his love of literature and books with his young son, and this love of story provided Lent with a healthy escape from the peer rejection he experienced. Lent was soon writing and illustrating his own stories.

"When I look back on my childhood," Lent wrote for an autobiographical sketch, "I realize that although I was unhappy growing up in that atmosphere, it was partly the reaction against it that gave me the determination to stick with what I really wanted to do. And without this determination, I might not be writing and illustrating today." Upon graduation from high school, Lent briefly studied economics, then worked at odd jobs, which included a stint as a short-order cook. He decided to act on his dreams and enrolled in the Boston Museum School, where he studied graphics and design. Graduating with honors in 1953, he received a traveling scholarship for additional study in Europe. When he returned to Boston, Lent took a position as a window-dresser in a department store after an unsuccessful search for a job as a graphic designer. He eventually landed a job as a creative designer in a major Boston advertising firm. His day job increased his knowledge of design and provided him with the money to support his real passion, writing and illustrating PICTURE BOOKS.

His hard work and dedication paid off, for in 1964, *Pistachio*, a book he wrote and illustrated, and *The Wave*, a Japanese folktale adapted by Margaret Hodges, which he illustrated, were published. Pistachio is an unusually talented green cow who wants nothing more than the taste of fresh country hay, while her beloved friend, Waldo, yearns for the excitement of a circus life. Overcoming rejection, both eventually get their wishes. *The Wave* is a powerful story in words and pictures. Lent used a limited palette of rich siennas, warm ochers, and cool blacks and grays to illustrate the tale of an old farmer who burns his rice fields to warn his village of an oncoming tidal wave. The illustrations were made from prints from cardboard cuts; Lent studied them and then he selected the best sections from numerous prints to cut and piece together for his finished artwork. Lent feels that cardboard is a perfect medium for the illustrator because it creates unusual textures, and since cardboard is less resistant than wood or linoleum, ideas can be realized much sooner. He also enjoys working with cardboard because, as a child, it was the material he used most often to create his own toys.

Lent went on to produce a number of picture books, including *Tikki Tikki Tembo* (1968), a Chinese folktale retold by Arlene Mosel. Lent's page design, use of white space, and choice of viewpoint and type placement are as important to the pacing of the story as Mosel's crisp prose. Younger brother, Chang, runs for help to save his older brother from drowning in a well, and Lent's illustrations of the distances Chang travels are the visual equivalent of the older brother's dangerously long name.

Always taking creative risks, Lent produced illustrations that became less graphic and more drawn, as he experimented with various mediums, from pen and ink to wash drawings and full-color paintings. His Caldecott Medal–winning book, *The Funny Little Woman* (1972), written by Arlene Mosel, was produced after many years of such experimenting. Lent has said about his work, "Books were important to me as a child, and it is for that little boy that I am working. I can never know other children's innermost thoughts as well as I can remember my own."

M.B.B.

Lester, Julius

American author, b. 1939. Julius Lester has honored the rich, varied, sometimes sad history of African Americans in his prose for children. His award-winning books include IN-FORMATION BOOKS, story collections, and volumes of folktales that reflect the traditions of the author's heritage. Although he later embraced the Judaic religion, as related in his memoir, *Lovesong: Becoming a Jew* (1988), the author was the son of a Methodist minister. Born in St. Louis, Missouri, he was raised in Kansas City, Kansas, and Nashville, Tennessee, where he attended Fisk University. In addition to writing, Lester has worked as a musician, an editor, a college professor, and a radio and television host. His earliest adult books, including *Look Out, Whitey! Black Power's Gon' Get Your Mama!* (1968), reflect the more radical aspects of the civil rights movement, although the author never considered himself a militant figure.

Lester's editor suggested that he try writing for children, and his first major effort, *To Be a Slave* (1968), was selected as a Newbery Honor Book and remains a towering achievement in children's literature. Composed mostly of first-person narratives by former slaves, which were collected by the Federal Writers' Project, the volume provides a multifaceted, painful overview of the slavery experience and includes recollections of the journey from Africa to America, life on the plantations, slave insurrections, and the United States after emancipation. Lester's ac-

companying text provides continuity and places the material in historical perspective.

Although he has written one adult novel, *Do Lord Remember Me* (1985), Lester has utilized the short story format in writing fiction for young readers. His stories are based on actual incidents and characters from the slavery era, but he does not write about widely known historical figures, preferring to tell the stories of ordinary people who have done great things. *Long Journey Home: Stories from Black History* (1972) contains six fictional tales suggested by interviews and previously published accounts. "Satan on My Track" is the story of a rambling blues musician who observes how slaves are kept in servitude even after emancipation; "The Man Who Was a Horse" relates the feelings of an ex-slave cowboy as he captures a herd of wild mustangs. The title story is a monologue concerning dozens of slaves who walk into the ocean, hoping they will be carried home by their gods, a powerful incident diluted by the negativity of the narrator. A later volume of stories, *This Strange New Feeling* (1982), concerns three eighteenth-century African American couples who fall in love; the book works well as both historical and romantic fiction.

Lester has also received acclaim for retelling African American folktales, including *The Knee-High Man and Other Tales* (1972) and *How Many Spots Does a Leopard Have and Other Tales* (1989), which also contains some Jewish legends. His volumes about Brer Rabbit, the well-known trickster from African American folklore — *The Tales of Uncle Remus: The Adventures of Brer Rabbit* (1987), *More Tales of Uncle Remus: Further Adventures of Brer Rabbit, His Friends, Enemies, and Others* (1988), and *Further Tales of Uncle Remus: The Misadventures of Brer Rabbit, Brer Fox, Brer Wolf, the Doodang, and Other Creatures* (1990) — are notable for their humor, breezy storytelling, and distinctive use of language and are especially enjoyable when read aloud. Lester also decided to retell the "Little Black Sambo" story in *Sam and the Tigers: A New Telling of Little Black Sambo* (1996). In these folktales, as in all his works, Lester has recorded and celebrated African American history for today's young readers. P.D.S.

Levine, Gail Carson

American author, b. 1947. Born in New York City, Gail Carson Levine grew up a confirmed city dweller. She earned a bachelor's degree at City College of the City University of New York, married, and embarked on a career in welfare services for the New York State Departments of Labor and Social Services. As employment interviewer and welfare administrator, she liked the direct contact involved in helping people who were "extraordinarily decent — under terrible circumstances." In 1997 she gave up this long-standing career to devote herself to full-time writing.

Strongly influenced by her parents' nurturing belief in creativity, Levine had begun writing early and developed interests in theater and art. Her love for painting led her to a class in illustrating and writing children's books. She discovered she enjoyed writing far more than illustrating. *Ella Enchanted* (1997) was created in a writing class when, unable to think of a plot, she decided to write a Cinderella story, because, she has said, "Cinderella already had a plot." When the book appeared, it quickly achieved widespread acclaim; young readers loved it, and reviewers praised it. The book was named a Newbery Honor Book in 1998.

Levine wove ingenious new threads into the classic fabric of the Cinderella story. At Ella's birth the foolish fairy Lucinda bestows the gift of obedience on the baby. Ella's mother knows the gift will be a curse. When Ella is fifteen, her beloved mother dies, and she is left to struggle along with her "gift." Plagued by commands, Ella perseveres to undo the curse. A friendship with the prince brightens her life, but when he proposes, Ella knows the curse will endanger his kingdom. High drama fills the final scene in this rich story.

The Princess Tales, a quartet of retold fairy tales (*The Fairy's Mistakes*, 1999; *The Princess Test*, 1999; *Princess Sonora and the Long Sleep*, 1999; and *Cinderellis and the Glass Hill*, 2000), showcase Levine's ingenuity and clever humor. Combining a touch of fantasy with contemporary fiction, *The Wish* (2000) features Wilma, an eighth-grader, whose unhappy school life is drastically changed by a witch who grants her a wish. Wilma's new popularity is laced with humorous wisdom. Hoping to create a truthful story, Levine followed a class of eighth-graders for days to get their dialogue, appearances, and behavior right.

Dave at Night (1999) was drawn from the boyhood experiences of Levine's father in Hebrew Orphan Asylum in Harlem. Since her father would not talk about the orphanage, she recreated it in her imagination as the Hebrew Home for Boys and expanded the story with highlights from the vibrant, lively culture of the Harlem Renaissance in 1926. The characters in *The Two Princesses Of Bamarr* (2001) are devoted sisters. Addie is gentle and timid; Meryl, fearless. Their destinies are reversed when Meryl becomes fatally ill. An unforgettable monster, the ancient she-dragon Vollys, stalks this FANTASY. All of these books reflect Levine's characteristic themes: personal freedom, nonconformity, perseverance, friendship, and loyalty. P.W.

Lewin, Betsy

American author and illustrator, b. 1937. Betsy Lewin's love of drawing emanates, she contends, from a childhood filled with books and reading. Her mother, a kindergarten teacher, read regularly from storybooks filled with pictures by KATE GREENAWAY, RANDOLPH CALDECOTT, E. H. SHEPARD, and BEATRIX POTTER, and Lewin was soon covering paper bags, napkins, and margins of her own books with self-styled renditions of animals and caricatures of friends and family. Before long, her creations included stories to match the images on the page.

While Lewin was encouraged by her parents in her artistic endeavors — she entered and won several art competitions and at age fourteen sold her first painting — they discouraged her from pursuing such an impractical career. Nevertheless, she persevered, leaving her Pennsylvania home to attend Pratt Institute of Art in New York City. Following graduation, she found work as a greeting card designer and then began writing and illustrating stories for children's magazines. Her first breakthrough in the children's book field was *Cat Count*. A poem, which had originally appeared in *Humpty Dumpty's* magazine, was expanded into a thirty-two-page PICTURE BOOK with black-and-white brush line drawings. Long out of print, the book was re-released when Lewin agreed to enliven its appearance with full-color illustrations.

The title that brought Lewin her first widespread attention was Karen Ackerman's *Araminta's Paintbox* (1990). Lewin's frothy watercolors added warmth and appeal to the going-west tale. Lewin continues to provide illustrations for other author's stories while also writing tales of her own. Often her subjects are the result of travels to far-flung places with her illustrator-husband Ted Lewin. *Booby Hatch* (1995) is based on experiences in the Galapagos Islands, *Chubbo's Pool* (1998) on a visit to Botswana, *What's the Matter Habibi?* (1997) on travels to Egypt and Morocco. Sometimes these journeys have culminated in producing a book together for the peripatetic husband and wife. *Gorilla Walk* (1999) for example, features Betsy's field sketches alongside Ted's watercolor illustrations of the huge magnificent beasts they saw in Uganda.

The loose strokes Lewin uses give her images a natural expression, energizing the page, and her smoothly integrated colors add gentleness. Humor filters through most of the artist's work. In 2000, she teamed with author Doreen Cronin to create *Click Clack Moo: Cows That Type*. This hilarious spoof on modern technology and labor relations received a Caldecott Honor award. Farmer Brown's cows' unusual typing skills set off a tale that rings with hilarity and ends with an unexpected — and even funnier — twist. Lewin has also collaborated with Mary Skillings Prigger in two jocular stories — *Aunt Minnie*

McGranahan (1999) and *Aunt Minnie and the Twister* (2002) — about an irrepressible spinster. Whether illustrating a lively schoolyard story (*Recess Mess*, 1996, written by Grace Mac-Carone) or collaborating with Elizabeth Winthrop to create a book about a dancing pig (*Dumpy La Rue*, 2001), Lewin can always find the humor in a story. B.E.

Lewin, Ted

American artist, b. 1935. Ted Lewin was born in Buffalo, New York, and received a bachelor of fine arts degree from the Pratt Institute of Art, where he was awarded the Dean's Medal at his graduation in 1956. A freelance illustrator since then, he supplemented his income by wrestling professionally until 1965. He has illustrated more than seventy books by other authors and has written and illustrated three books for the series World Within a World, entitled *Everglades* (1976), *Baja* (1978), and *Pribilofs* (1980).

Lewin has described himself as an "artist-illustrator" and noted that his writing grew as a result of his interest in the natural world. He is an ardent environmentalist and conservationist who travels "around the world for graphic and literary material." In 1978 Lewin presented a one-man exhibit at the Laboratory of Ornithology at Cornell University. Lewin's regard for birds is demonstrated in *Listen to the Crows* (1976), written by Laurence Pringle, an INFORMATION BOOK about the language of crows, and *Bermuda Petrel: The Bird That Would Not Die* (1981), written by Francine Jacobs, the fascinating story of an ancient bird's near extinction. Both are enhanced by Lewin's sympathetic black and white drawings. In a different genre, Lewin's meticulously drawn watercolors amplify and enrich JANE YOLEN's collection of POETRY, *Bird Watch* (1990).

Many of the books Lewin has illustrated fall into the MIDDLE-GRADE READER or YOUNG ADULT categories, and his illustrations punctuate important events in the story. *Grandma Didn't Wave Back* (1972), written by Rose Blue, is a moving story about advancing senility. In black and white drawings that have a density reminiscent of watercolors, Lewin has conveyed emotion through the expressive faces detailed for Blue's characters. Similarly, Lewin's subtle gradations of black and white complement Rita Micklish's novel about an interracial friendship, *Sugar Bee* (1972), and Brenda Seabrooke's *Judy Scuppernong* (1990), a series of poetic narratives highlighted by Lewin's quirky illustrations from various points of view. Leon Garfield's *Young Nick and Jubilee* (1989) allowed Lewin to experiment with historical illustration. His accurate, finely detailed costumes are in perfect harmony with this Dickensian adventure story.

Two books, both coauthored by FLORENCE PARRY HEIDE and Judith Heide Gilliland, spotlight the strength and beauty of Lewin's talent. *The Day of Ahmed's Secret* (1990) takes place in the busy streets of Cairo, which Lewin captured in all their movement and color with intense blues, tones of white, and his renderings of colorful mosaics. *Sami and the Time of the Troubles* (1992) is a story set in modern Beirut. Lewin juxtaposed larger-than-life, vibrant watercolors portraying the colorful carpets, flowers, and lush bounty of pre-war Beirut with the devastation, crumbling buildings, and twisted metal wrought by repeated bombings. These foreign streets come alive in Lewin's capable hands, yet the reader perceives a stillness, a tranquillity in the face of much commotion that captures the essence of both cultures. *Peppe the Lamplighter* (1993), written by Elisa Bartone, demonstrates Lewin's superb ability to illustrate historical PICTURE BOOKS. This Caldecott Honor Book is set in New York's Little Italy around 1900.

Lewin is a talented artist, fortunate in his ability to create luminous works of art that form a perfect complement to an author's text, regardless of format, subject, or medium.

M.O'D.H.

Lewis, C. S.

British author, 1898–1963. A scholar and teacher at Oxford and Cambridge in England, Clive Staples Lewis wrote fiction, SCIENCE FICTION, POETRY, literary criticism, and books of Christian apologia. It was his seven FANTASY books for children, however, that made him one of the most successful and well-loved writers of the twentieth century. Widely read, the Chronicles of Narnia are considered classics of children's literature.

Growing up in Northern Ireland, Lewis and his brother were surrounded by books and even wrote and illustrated their own stories about invented lands. The citizens of Animal-Land, Lewis's imaginary world, were chivalrous animals — forerunners of his Narnian Talking Beasts. In the autobiography *Surprised by Joy* (1955), which describes his conversion to Christianity, Lewis spoke about influential books from his early life, and it is the authors GEORGE MACDONALD and E. NESBIT whose impact is most clearly seen in his children's books.

In the first book in the Narnia series, *The Lion, the Witch and the Wardrobe* (1950), four siblings find their way into another world through a magic wardrobe. Peter, Susan, Edmund, and Lucy meet Aslan, the lion who has come to free the land of Narnia from the evil spell of the White Witch. Aslan sacrifices his life to save Edmund after the boy is lured into treachery by the Witch, but the noble lion comes back to life again through an older magic; after the Witch is defeated, the four children are crowned kings and queens of Narnia. When they return to England after many Narnian years, they find that only minutes have passed in their own time. The book received the Lewis Carroll Shelf Award in 1962.

Prince Caspian (1951) relates the foursome's adventures on their second visit to Narnia, where they learn that hundreds of years have gone by since they were last there. Prince Caspian has used a magic horn to call the long-ago rulers to help him take Narnia back from the Telmarines and restore it to the Old Narnians — the Fauns, Centaurs, Talking Beasts, and others. With Aslan's help, Caspian's evil uncle, King Miraz, is defeated, and the children again return home.

Edmund and Lucy, along with their spoiled cousin Eustace, return to Narnia and find themselves on board a ship with Caspian in *The Voyage of the* Dawn Treader (1952). They help King Caspian search for the seven lords whom his evil uncle had sent away, sharing several adventures before going home, including one involving a dragon that changes Eustace forever.

In *The Silver Chair* (1953), Eustace, along with his classmate Jill, is whisked away to Narnia, called by Aslan to help the aging King Caspian find his missing son. Guided by a pessimistic but likable creature known as a Marsh-wiggle, Jill and Eustace brave giants and the cold northern winter to free Prince Rilian and hundreds of gnomes enchanted by the evil Emerald Witch. Aslan then returns the children to their school in a dramatic, satisfying ending.

The story told in *The Horse and His Boy* (1954) takes place during the long reign of Peter, Susan, Edmund, and Lucy, beloved Narnian rulers. In the land of Calormen, a boy named Shasta meets Bree, a Talking Horse originally from Narnia, and together they decide to run away to that land. Joined by Hwin, another Talking Horse, and a girl named Aravis, the group reaches its destination — with Aslan's help — in time to warn the Narnians of an impending attack, after which Shasta learns he is of Narnian royal blood.

The creation of Narnia is described in *The Magician's Nephew* (1955). Two children, Digory and Polly, are sent out of their world by Digory's magician uncle and then return to London with an evil queen, Jadis. Attempting to take Jadis back, the children stumble into an empty world where Aslan is about to create Narnia. Digory and Polly triumph over temptation and doubt when Aslan sends them on a quest to right the wrong they committed by allowing evil to enter Narnia.

The Last Battle (1956) takes place during Narnia's final days. Jill and Eustace come to help good King Tirian after an Ape named Shift disguises his poor donkey friend Puzzle as Aslan. The resulting chaos signals the end of Narnia but the beginning of something even better; soon Jill and Eustace are joined by all the friends of Narnia — Peter, Edmund, Lucy, Digory, and Polly. The unusual book provides an intense and joyful depiction of life after death. *The Last Battle* was awarded the Carnegie Medal in 1957.

The stories are unforgettable not only for the excitement and suspense of the adventures but also for the strong emotions they describe so well, especially the deep despair and fear caused by death and the unspeakable joy when death is conquered. Aslan is killed by the witch, but deeper magic brings him back to life; Narnia is taken by the Telmarines, then Aslan returns to claim it back; Digory's mother is dying, but Aslan gives him a magic apple that will heal her; and in *The Last Battle,* the children discover that death is merely a door to another, more beautiful world.

The imaginative and emotive stories are further enriched by Lewis's skillful use of language. Much is expressed in names: Cair Paravel and Aslan are regal, beautiful names; humorous names fit the characters of Puddleglum and Dufflepuds; and Jadis, Shift, and Miraz have harsh-sounding names that reflect their evil natures. Lewis's inventive characters also add appeal to the books. Among the many memorable Narnians are tender-hearted Tumnus the faun, the kindly Mr. and Mrs. Beaver, Reepicheep the valiant mouse, Puddleglum the pessimistic Marsh-wiggle, and the loyal dwarf Trumpkin.

Though most readers go through the books in the order in which they were published, Lewis agreed with an American child's preference — written in a letter to the author — for reading them in chronological order according to Narnian time: *The Magician's Nephew; The Lion, the Witch and the Wardrobe; The Horse and His Boy; Prince Caspian; The Voyage of the* Dawn Treader; *The Silver Chair;* and *The Last Battle.*

Though some adults dislike the heavy Christian allegory contained in the books, children — even those aware of the symbolism — enjoy the books because they are good stories first and allegory second. If the symbolism took precedence over the stories, the books would never have had such a large audience: millions of copies have been sold. Lewis, who claimed he wrote stories he would have liked to read as a child, said that the Chronicles of Narnia began with pictures he had in his mind. It is the magic and wonder of these images that readers remember years after encountering the books. J.M.B.

Lewis, E. B.

American illustrator, b. 1956. As early as the third grade, Earl Bradley Lewis displayed artistic talent, but throughout grade school he was known as the class clown. He announced one day in sixth grade that he wanted to be a lawyer, and everyone laughed, thinking he was wisecracking. Lewis realized that he did not want to get attention that way. Inspiration for his career came from two uncles, who were artists, and he decided to follow in their footsteps. After finishing sixth grade, he attended Saturday classes at the Temple University School Art League, run by his uncle. He began his formal art training under the tutelage of a noted painter in Philadelphia, which set him on a direct path to a career in art.

During college, at the Tyler School of Art at Temple University, Lewis majored in graphic design and illustration and art education and discovered his medium of choice — watercolors, which remain his forte. Upon graduation in 1979, Lewis went directly into teaching, along with freelancing in graphic design and painting. His fine art brought critical acclaim, is sold in galleries nationally, and is held in major private collections.

In 1994 Lewis decided to try his hand at illustrating children's books. His debut, *Fire on the Mountain* (1994), written by Jane Kurtz, received enthusiastic reviews. Exceptional watercolor renderings of Ethiopian mountains and people articulate emotion powerfully. More books quickly followed. Lewis has cited his next book, *Down the Road* (1995), written by Alice Schertle, as "a great vehicle to display watercolor at its best. Light, shadow, and the transparency of the medium allow the creation of an atmosphere that no other medium conveys. This classic American tale is one of my favorites."

Lewis's talent for portraying realistic characters with depth and beauty has earned him several awards, including three Coretta Scott King Honor Awards. In *The Bat Boy and His Violin* (1998), written by Curtis Gavin, a father urges his musical son to trade his talent for baseball by joining the Negro National League. A Tanzanian boy resists the temptations of the market to save money for a bike in *My Rows and Piles of Coins* (1999), written by Tololwa M. Mollel. A post–Civil War story, *Virgie Goes to School with Us Boys* (2000), written by Elizabeth Fitzgerald Howard, relates how Virgie proves her brothers wrong, that she can walk the seven miles to school. Other books that evoke a strong sense of place and a rich cultural context include *Only a Pigeon* (1997), written by Jane and Christopher Kurtz, *Dirt on Their Skirts* (2000), written by Doreen Rappaport, and *The Other Side* (2001), written by Jacqueline Woodson. Whether portraying contemporary or historical tales, African or African American cultures, Lewis has created illustrations that imbue stories with life. J.C.

Lindgren, Astrid

Swedish author, 1907–2002. Best known for her books about the irrepressible heroine Pippi Longstocking, internationally acclaimed author Astrid Lindgren was born in Vimmerby, Sweden, and grew up on a farm just outside of the village. She was one of four children and described her own childhood as being much like those depicted in her Noisy Village books. She and her siblings were allowed many freedoms and spent a great deal of time at play, although they were also expected to help with work on the farm. Lindgren read a great deal as a child but declared, when a teacher suggested she might become a writer when she grew up, that she would never write books.

After finishing school, Lindgren worked as a secretary and had children of her own. *Pippi Longstocking* (1950) came out of the stories she told her own daughter. She decided to write down the stories as a gift to her daughter and sent the completed manuscript to a publisher. The story was rejected, but the following year Lindgren submitted *Pippi Longstocking* to a contest at another Swedish publishing house and won first prize. *Pippi* became an international success and led to Lindgren's long and prolific career writing well over one hundred books for children, more than half of which have been translated into English. Astrid Lindgren won the Hans Christian Andersen Medal in 1958, presented by the International Board on Books for Young People (IBBY) for her outstanding contribution to the field of children's literature.

Lindgren's many books include MYSTERIES, FANTASIES, adventures, and realistic stories of family life in Sweden. She wrote both PICTURE BOOKS and novels, and her work appeals to children from preschool through elementary school. Pippi, the heroine of *Pippi Longstocking, Pippi Goes on Board* (1957), and *Pippi in the South Seas* (1959), lives without parents in the middle of a small town in Sweden. Pippi is amazingly strong, able to pick up her own horse, and leads the life she chooses. She refuses to go to school until she hears about vacations and "pluttification" but quickly decides that the rules and structure are not for her. She is an outrageous heroine, anarchic and clever, continually inventing ways to amuse her more traditional friends Tommy and Annika. *Pippi Longstocking* is a perfect fantasy, a way for readers to revel in the possibilities of life without parents but with an endless supply of time and gold coins. Lindgren firmly grounds her story in reality through the characters Tommy and Annika, children who, like her readers, must go to school and observe strict bedtimes but who can also enjoy the larks invented by their neighbor Pippi.

Lindgren wrote many books based on her own childhood in a safe, warm Swedish village. *The Children of Noisy Village* (1962) and *The Children on Troublemaker Street* (1964) are two such novels. Each consists of episodic chapters that tell of the small adventures in the lives of children nurtured by close families and communities. Her characters go on picnics, invent games, and celebrate traditional Swedish holidays. Unlike the larger-than-life Pippi stories, these are tales of the excitement that everyday life can hold for children.

Bill Bergson, Master Detective (1952) and the subsequent adventures of Bill Bergson bridge the distance between Lindgren's impossible fantasies and her concrete FAMILY STORIES. Bill and his friends live in a typical Swedish village and play games much like their counterparts in Noisy Village, but Bill hopes to be a detective and finds himself solving crimes and becoming involved with bandits and thieves. The satisfying mysteries appeal to the reader's sense of adventure while remaining firmly planted in reality. *Rasmus and the Vagabond* (1960) is another mystery complete with thieves, stolen jewels, and a chase through an abandoned town, but it is also the story of an orphan, Rasmus, who runs away from an orphanage to find himself a family. Rasmus discovers a gentle, loving vagabond, and the two tramp through the summer countryside, singing and working for sandwiches. Again Lindgren convinced her readers that a child who goes looking for parents will certainly find them. Lindgren recognized the central yet conflicting longings of childhood — to have the security of a loving family but also a measure of adventure and excitement. In *Brothers Lionheart* (1973), two brothers die young but continue to have heroic adventures together in Nangilyala, an imaginary country invented by the author. Lindgren hoped that, while the book may disturb some adults, it will comfort young children wondering about death.

Astrid Lindgren recognized and wrote about the needs, dreams, and fantasies of children. Her characters, always strong and well defined, are remembered long after readers finish each book. Her range was tremendous, from the quiet, mysterious picture book *The Tomten* (1961) to the hilarious, exaggerated adventures of Emil in *Emil in the Soup Tureen* (1963). Lindgren's vivid writing and imaginative stories achieve a timeless quality that will ensure them an appreciative audience for many years to come. M.V.K.

Lionni, Leo

American author and illustrator, 1910–1999. In Leo Lionni's *Frederick* (1967), a shy, poetic field mouse refuses to help harvest food for the approaching winter because he is busily gathering the warmth of the sun, the colors of the summer, and words to describe the seasons. Late in the winter, when it is dark and the mice are cold and hungry, Frederick's words spark the imagination of his fellow mice so that they can see colors and feel the sun's warmth. In *Frederick,* as in his other PICTURE BOOKS, Lionni used evocative words and expressive art to kindle the imagination so that the reader, too, can dream.

Although he wrote more than thirty books for young children, Lionni did not start writing until he was a grandfather. The inspiration for his first book came during a train ride, when he was trying to entertain his grandchildren by telling them a story with pieces of paper that he had torn from a magazine. From this experience came *Little Blue and Little Yellow* (1959), the story of two small circles of color who are best friends and one day hug each other until they turn green. The strong design and marvelous color in Lionni's work reflect his lifelong career as an artist and graphic designer.

Born in Amsterdam, Lionni spent his childhood living and traveling throughout Europe. Although he earned a Ph.D. in economics, he pursued a career in graphic arts instead and worked as a freelance designer before coming to the United States in 1939. In the States he worked for several corporations as an art director and was also the head of the graphics design department of the Parsons School of Design. His contributions to the field of graphic design resulted in his receiving an American Institute of Graphic Arts Gold Medal in 1984.

Given such a distinguished career, Lionni's contribution to the world in his books for children is even more remarkable. Filled with small animal characters, these picture books unapologetically champion individuality and quietly celebrate the beauty of the natural world. Quite simple, the story lines assume the form of fables, and they almost always have more than one level of meaning. Most often he used collage — although he sometimes relied on other media — to create a rich, lively, and textured art. These bold colors and designs make his books particularly suitable for reading aloud to a group. Lionni is one of the few artists to have four books designated as Caldecott Honor Books — *Frederick, Inch by Inch* (1960), *Swimmy* (1963), and *Alexander and the Wind-Up Mouse* (1969). His stories often treat serious subjects — war, friendship, and honesty — although generally the tone is playful. In *Swimmy,* a tiny fish encourages the other small fish to form collectively a giant fish so the larger fish won't eat them. The tale works as a simple story, although most adults see an underlying message in this book as well as in his others. Probably the only criticism of his work comes from those who find his messages and morals a bit too pointed. But what emerges most clearly is his consistent invitation for the reader to imagine, to experiment, and most of all, to feel good about being an individual. A.Q.

Lipsyte, Robert

American author, b. 1938. As a child, Robert Lipsyte, a confirmed book junkie and "voracious, addicted word snorter," never considered himself a sports fan and hardly ever read SPORTS STORIES. Ironically, his first job upon graduating from the Columbia School of Journalism was as a copy boy for the sports section of the *New York Times.* He quickly advanced to become a prize-winning sports columnist and host of the PBS late-night talk show *The Eleventh Hour,* for which he won an Emmy. During a discussion with boxing manager Cus D'Amato, Lipsyte learned about the narrow, dark, twisting flights of stairs that led to D'Amato's Manhattan gym. Lipsyte was fascinated by the type of boy who would climb the stairs, alone and afraid. This image, along with a request by a publishing house for Lipsyte to write a novel using the boxing ring as its milieu, led to Lipsyte's first novel, *The Contender* (1967). Winner of the Child Study Association Best Children's Novel, *The Contender* tells the story of Alfred Brooks, a high school dropout from Harlem who is struggling to become "somebody," to become a "contender." As the discipline he learns from training crosses over into other parts of his life, Alfred's metamorphosis begins. He decides to start night school, rescues his best friend James from descending into drug-induced oblivion, and recognizes his potential outside of the boxing ring. The book was a commercial and critical success but left most readers with questions and a strong desire to journey further with Alfred.

Thinking that he was meant for something other than just being an author of YOUNG ADULT NOVELS, Lipsyte waited ten years before he picked up his pen to write another young adult book, this one based on his own experiences of growing up fat in the 1950s. *One Fat Summer* (1977), recognized by the *New York Times* as an Outstanding Children's Book, chronicles one summer in the life of overweight fourteen-year-old Bobby Marks. It is a turning-point summer in which he learns to stand up for himself, gaining self-esteem as he loses pounds in a realistic transformation. The response to Bobby Marks was so overwhelming that Lipsyte continued Bobby's story in *Summer Rules* (1981). Losing weight had not solved all of Bobby's problems. At age sixteen he has to deal with an unwanted camp counselor job, his first loves, and the repercussions of his decision to remain loyal to old friends. The trilogy concludes with *The Summerboy* (1982). Spending his last summer before college working at the local laundry brings Bobby unrequited love and confronts him with prejudice; rallying the workers to demand better conditions, he learns the importance of standing up firmly for principles. "Boys are afraid of being humiliated, of being hurt, both emotionally and physically," Lipsyte has said. Bobby Marks, the scared, obese boy who grows into a responsible, mature young man, shows that a hero isn't always strong, that a hero

can have fears. Bobby's humanity has led some critics to call Lipsyte the adolescent male's answer to JUDY BLUME.

Again Lipsyte took a ten-year break from the world of young adult novels to pursue his career as a television journalist. Nevertheless, the questions about Alfred Brooks's future kept coming; a generation of readers wanted his story to continue. A midnight discussion with a Native American boy who felt trapped on the reservation enticed Lipsyte to confront the dark stairs once more. *The Brave* (1991) follows the journey of Sonny Bear, half Indian, half white, from his upstate New York reservation to the seedy, drug-infested underworld of Manhattan. Unable to control his rage and feelings of alienation, Sonny finds himself in jail. He is rescued by Officer Alfred Brooks, who befriends him, recognizing Sonny's hunger to become "somebody." The protagonist in *The Chemo Kid* (1992), Fred Bauer, is an ordinary, unremarkable high school student who often questions his own existence. Fred's life dramatically changes when he develops a cancerous lump on his neck. His chemotherapy drugs appear to give him unexpected surges of superhuman strength, allowing him not only to rid the town of its toxic waste and its drug dealers but also to change his own image from wimp to warrior.

Generally, books that feature male protagonists and sporting activity tend to attract an overwhelmingly male and sports-oriented audience, but Lipsyte's characters — Alfred, Bobby, Sonny, and Fred — speak to all readers, regardless of sex or race. Lipsyte has successfully transcended the genre, smashing sexist myths of manhood while losing none of the excitement and vivid imagery of a sports book. In 2001 he was given the Margaret A. Edwards Award for his lifetime achievement. M.I.A.

Little, Jean

Canadian author, b. 1932. Although Jean Little was born with scarred corneas that severely impair her vision, she has always loved to read and to write stories and POETRY. She had a book of her poetry published when she was seventeen, and she received a B.A. in English and literature from the University of Toronto in 1955. After college Little worked as a camp counselor for disabled children, and for several years following this, she taught in a special school for motor-disabled children. While teaching, Little discovered that when she read classics such as *The Secret Garden* and *Little Women* to her students, they were puzzled by the plight of the disabled characters, who either died or were miraculously cured. None of these characters ever remained physically handicapped, and they grew into self-sufficient, happy individuals who loved life and took on its challenges. This insight inspired Little to write about Sally, a little girl with cerebral palsy. Sally, who had attended a special needs school, comes home to live with her family and enter into the mainstream of regular school. Little's story is insightfully written, never sentimental, and depicts Sally with all the same basic fears and insecurities that the other students in her class have. She needs to learn how to manage everyday routines by herself, she needs family support, she needs friends, and she needs to learn how to reach out to help others.

In 1961 Little entered this story in a Canadian writing contest sponsored by the publisher Little, Brown. She won the competition, $1,000, and the guarantee that her book, *Mine for Keeps* (1962), would be published the following June. Elated by this success, she persevered to make her dream to write full-time come true. Among her books are several stories about children with various handicaps, including cerebral palsy (*Mine for Keeps*), visual impairment (*From Anna*, 1972, and *Listen for the Singing*, 1977), and mental retardation (*Take Wing*, 1968). In these, she gives voice and recognition to children who live with physical and mental challenges. Because she writes from personal experience, she can tackle these once delicate issues honestly, with compassion and humor.

Little is also well known for her Kate books about friendship and self-discovery — *Look Through My Window* (1971), *Kate* (1971), and *Hey World, Here I Am!* (1984) — as well as her Anna books (*From Anna*, 1972, and *Listen for the Singing*, 1977), which have been cited as two of the few Canadian books that give a perspective on World War II.

Other themes she has explored include conquering fears (*Different Dragons*, 1986, and *Stand in the Wind*, 1975), the death of a sibling or parent (*Home from Far*, 1965, and *Mama's Going to Buy You a Mockingbird*, 1984), and lying (*One to Grow On*, 1969). In all her books, strong parental and family support, plus friendship and love of life, prevail.

Little writes with a voice-activated computer, SAM, and travels widely with her Seeing Eye dog, Zephyr. She has written fifteen books of MIDDLE-GRADE FICTION, a book of poetry, a PICTURE BOOK, and a two-part autobiography.

S.R.

Lobel, Anita

American author and illustrator, b. 1934. The folk tradition and designs of Poland and Sweden, where she grew up, have provided inspiration for Anita Lobel's art and writing, which is often either a retelling of old tales or an original story clearly influenced by folklore. Lobel feels particularly drawn to folktales because the main character usually ends up living happily ever after, while the villain gets his just deserts. For example, in *A Birthday for the Princess* (1973), the young princess longs for personal attention from her parents, the King and Queen, but they are too busy to attend to her. After befriending an organ-grinder and his monkey, she saves them from prison and they escape together. She loves her new life, but the final picture shows her parents looking miserable without her.

Lobel was born in Cracow, Poland, and during World War II she and her brother were hidden with a Catholic family. In 1944 the Germans captured them and sent them to a concentration camp in Germany. After the war, they were rescued by the Swedish Red Cross and went to

Stockholm, where they were eventually reunited with their parents. In 1952 she and her family immigrated to the United States. While attending Pratt Institute in Brooklyn, New York, she met ARNOLD LOBEL, whom she married when she finished school. Initially, she worked as a textile designer while her husband wrote and illustrated children's books. Then his editor encouraged her to try a book herself, and she created *Sven's Bride,* which was named one of the New York Times Best Illustrated Books of the Year for 1965.

Lobel is also an actress, and her love of theater is reflected in her PICTURE BOOKS. As she starts working on a book, she often thinks of it as staging a play: each page is a scene. In some cases this can be seen directly. In her husband's *How the Rooster Saved the Day* (1977), her pages are bordered by curtains, and the rooster and a robber are clearly performing on a stage. The title page of her own *The Seamstress of Salzburg* (1970) is also a stage with the curtain closed. As the story begins, we see the curtain opening on a young woman sewing an elegant gown. In the end, after the seamstress marries the prince, all the members of the cast appear for a final bow and the curtain is closed. In other cases the theatrical device is more subtle. There are no curtains in *The Troll Music* (1966), but the pages have the feel of stage sets. The simplified backgrounds are reminiscent of stage scenery, and each detail has been carefully placed on the set.

Lobel often collaborated with her late husband, illustrating his texts. For their joint venture, *On Market Street,* a Caldecott Honor Book in 1982, Lobel was inspired by seventeenth-century French engravings for her illustrations of a young boy's shopping spree. With a wonderful sense of humor, she created each merchant the boy visits out of the items he or she sells — from apples to zippers. In another ALPHABET BOOK, *Alison's Zinnia* (1989), which she wrote and illustrated, Lobel concentrated on flowers. For each letter of the alphabet, a girl picks a flower starting with that letter for a friend whose name starts with the next letter. Lobel uses a more painterly style for these illustrations, moving away from her earlier reliance on pen and ink. As Lobel's work has evolved, it has retained a freshness and a strong appeal for children. P.R.

Lobel, Arnold

American author and illustrator, 1933–1987. Arnold Lobel's creation of a kinder, gentler world, where laughter, happy endings, and the return to a snug home are the norm, have become his signature in the I-Can-Read, EASY READER, and PICTURE BOOK annals of children's literature. Lobel wrote and polished his stories before illustrating them. In his art, he established mood by setting cartoon animals in pastoral and Victorian surroundings. Dressing his animals in formal Victorian attire allowed Lobel to incorporate "amiable incongruities," as critic George Shannon noted, thereby pushing human foibles humorously and inoffensively to their extremes. While this playful sense of the ridiculous abounds in Lobel's work, his stories and pictures examine the human condition with warmth and compassion. Lobel unified text and art in his I-Can-Read books by limiting the use of color. Other books, however, display a full palette. Pen and ink detailing adds depth and dimension to his watercolors, fleshing out characters and background.

Although he wrote and illustrated twenty-eight of his own books and illustrated over seventy for other authors, Lobel is probably best remembered for his four award-winning touchstone I-Can-Read stories: *Frog and Toad Are Friends* (1970), *Frog and Toad Together* (1972), *Frog and Toad All Year* (1976), and *Days with Frog and Toad* (1979). They are considered classics because they exemplify friendship, acceptance, and reliability in a timeless setting. They take place in an idyllic world, free from outside intrusion and adult supervision. Frog and Toad's world is self-contained and secure: a child's paradise. Frog and Toad are complementary personalities: Frog, more adult, practical, and self-directed, is sometimes bossy, but with his energetic optimism, he always knows how to cheer up Toad. Toad, more passive and pessimistic, is truer to his hibernating nature. He likes his bed and his naps. He needs guidelines, like his list of things he must do daily; he is very cautious; he needs encouragement and assurance, especially the assurance that Frog is, and will always be, his friend.

In other books — such as *Gregory Griggs and Other Nursery Rhyme People* (1987); *Fables,* the 1981 Caldecott Medal winner; *The Book of Pigericks* (1983); and *Whiskers and Rhymes* (1985) — Lobel, an admirer of EDWARD LEAR, incorporated nonsense verse, used Victorian settings and clothing, and pushed the improbable to its limit, humorously exposing the pretentious absurdities of societal and self-imposed values with which people shackle themselves. Delightful examples of Lobel's collaborative work with his wife, ANITA LOBEL, are the two folktales he wrote for her to illustrate: *How the Rooster Saved the Day* (1977) and *A Treeful of Pigs* (1979).

Lobel's fascination with books and illustration began at an early age. When he was six months old, his parents divorced, and he was raised by his grandparents. Ill health caused him to miss a year of school and, when he returned to third grade, he felt excluded. Telling and illustrating stories for his classmates eased this isolation. His fascination with children's stories and illustrations continued throughout high school. Lobel attended Pratt Institute, majored in illustration, and graduated with a B.F.A. in 1955. While at Pratt, he met Anita Kempler, whom he married after graduation. Lobel illustrated more than twenty books for other authors during the 1960s. His own career as a children's picture book author/illustrator began in 1962 with *A Zoo for Mister Muster* and its sequel, *A Holiday for Mister Muster* (1963). During his career, Lobel received numerous awards, culminating with two citations for his body of work: the University of Southern Mississippi School of Library Science Silver Medallion in 1985 for distinguished service to children's literature and the Laura Ingalls Wilder Award nomination in 1986 for his distinguished, enduring contribution to children's literature. S.R.

Lofting, Hugh

British author and illustrator, 1886–1947. Hugh Lofting is best known for creating Doctor Dolittle, one of the most enduring characters in children's literature.

Lofting was born in Maidenhead, Berkshire, England, and attended a Jesuit boarding school. Although he was interested in books and writing as a child, Lofting studied civil engineering and architecture in college. He attended Massachusetts Institute of Technology but finished his degree at London Polytechnic. Lofting traveled to Canada as a surveyor and prospector, then worked for railroad companies in West Africa and Cuba before settling in New York, where he wrote humor stories and journalism pieces. During World War I, he joined the British army. While serving in Flanders and France, Lofting began to write and illustrate stories about a kindly animal doctor, which he mailed to his children in the United States. On his voyage home from Europe, Lofting met a novelist who suggested he publish these children's stories as a book.

The Story of Doctor Dolittle (1920) was an instant success. Nineteenth-century English physician John Dolittle lives in Puddleby-on-the-Marsh. When Doctor Dolittle's many pets drive away his human patients, he becomes an animal doctor and naturalist. With the help of Polynesia, an abrasively humorous parrot, the doctor masters a variety of animal languages, then travels to Africa to fight a mysterious illness that is killing off the monkey population. The episodic book is memorable for its entertaining adventures, whimsical animal dialogue, and, above all, the unflappable and humane title character.

Lofting's second book, *The Voyages of Doctor Dolittle* (1922), is narrated by Tommy Stubbins, a ten-year-old aspiring naturalist who becomes the doctor's assistant on a lengthy ocean voyage. Awarded the 1923 Newbery Medal, it remains one of Lofting's finest books due to its sustained humor and imagination. The author continued to publish Dolittle books in rapid succession, with Stubbins returning as narrator several times. The quality of the series is uneven, but critics have cited some of the later titles, including *Doctor Dolittle in the Moon* (1928), as among the author's best, owing to their inventiveness and thought-provoking philosophical content.

Lofting's other writings include PICTURE BOOKS that are similar to the Dolittle stories in their anthropomorphic treatment of animals; *The Twilight of Magic* (1930), a serious, traditional FANTASY; and his only adult work, *Victory for the Slain* (1942), a book-length war poem.

Lofting's greatest achievement, however, is the Doctor Dolittle series, which also inspired a 1967 movie musical. The books remain popular, although their relative length can be daunting to younger readers. The most serious charge leveled against the stories is that they contain racist writing and illustrations. Polynesia uses a number of racial epithets in speaking of Africans, while Lofting's illustrations of black characters are grotesque caricatures. Several episodes, including one in which an African prince wishes he were white, are also deemed offensive. Certain scenes in Lofting's books have been rewritten, and the offending epithets and illustrations have been removed from later editions. Literary purists may disagree with this tampering, but others argue that the books would not otherwise be purchased by libraries or sold in bookstores. Young readers of the edited volumes continue to find the stories appealing, and Doctor Dolittle remains a delightful character. P.D.S.

Lovelace, Maud Hart

American author, 1892–1980. The fact that Maud Hart was born in Mankato, Minnesota, was important to her writing. After graduation in 1910 from Mankato High School, she attended the University of Minnesota, traveled in Europe, and in 1917 married Delos W. Lovelace, another writer. In *Black Angels,* her first novel, published in 1926, Lovelace wrote of a Minnesota family of traveling theater folk in the 1800s.

She wrote other HISTORICAL NOVELS set in Minnesota, the best known of which is *Early Candlelight* (1929), about the early days of Fort Snelling. With Delos she wrote other historical novels, including *Gentlemen from England* (1937), again set in Minnesota. Although these novels were for adults, they are interesting reading for adolescents as well.

It is her children's books for which Lovelace is best known and remembered, however. After telling her daughter stories about the fun she had growing up, she began what are known as the Betsy-Tacy stories. The setting, Deep Valley, Minnesota, is Mankato, and many of the characters and events are drawn from Lovelace's life and from the people she knew. The first four books take Betsy and Tacy and their friend Tib from age five to age twelve and have the naiveté of childhood at the turn of the twentieth century. In the six later books in the series, the characters are in high school or older. The focus in all of the stories is on the fun of being children and young adults. Betsy, patterned after Lovelace herself, sometimes seems almost silly, from an adult's perspective, in what she worries about, but that is typical of and appealing to many young people.

Despite the focus on fun, each book deals with serious issues. In the first, *Betsy-Tacy* (1940), Tacy's baby brother dies, and Lovelace portrayed well the way in which five-year-olds try to cope with such a loss. In later books, Lovelace tackled problems of prejudice, dealing with the community's views about Little Syria, an area outside of town settled by Syrian immigrants. In *Over the Big Hill* (1942), Betsy, Tacy, and Tib make friends in Little Syria, and in another Deep Valley story, *Emily of Deep Valley* (1950), concern about the Syrians and pleasure in their culture are part of the plot. Three books about other Deep Valley characters and another five books for children were published between 1942 and 1966.

The first of the ten Betsy-Tacy books appeared in 1940, more than a half century ago. The books were enjoyed by children, mostly girls, throughout the country. Today there is a wave of nostalgia for the books, evidenced by the formation of a national and several local Betsy-Tacy societies in the early 1990s. After some years of being out of print, several of the books have been reissued. Although dated in some ways, such as in the use of certain racial or cultural terms, and set back almost a century ago in time, the characters and the events are still of interest to many of today's young readers.

Lovelace won few prizes during her lifetime, but now the Minnesota Young Readers Award is named for her, societies to study and admire her work have come into being, and it is likely that her work will continue to be read and enjoyed well into the twenty-first century. B.J.P.

Lowry, Lois

A merican author, b. 1937. Lois Lowry is well known as the author of the books about Anastasia Krupnik and her precocious younger brother, Sam. Always getting herself in trouble, Lowry's irrepressible heroine has a good-natured sense of humor that has made popular titles such as *Anastasia at Your Service* (1984), detailing her first job, and *Anastasia's Chosen Career* (1987), tracing her search for a profession. The first book about Anastasia's brother, *All About Sam* (1988), tells his life story from Sam's own comical point of view, beginning with his first impressions of the world as a newborn. Other popular titles of MIDDLE-GRADE FICTION are the amusing books about siblings Caroline and J. P. Tate. In *Switcharound* (1985), Caroline and J. P. make separate plans to get back at their father and his wife, who invited them for the summer only to stick them with some heavy responsibilities. The normally feuding siblings join forces when they realize at the last minute that they must help each other undo their awful plans.

Lowry is equally adroit at telling stories in a more serious vein, as evidenced by *A Summer to Die* (1977), which marked her debut as a children's book writer. In this novel, winner of the International Reading Association's Children's Book Award, thirteen-year-old Meg's friendship with an elderly but lively and active neighbor gives her strength through the summer during which her older sister suffers a serious illness and eventually dies. The sensitive and moving account also portrays the hope and joy of a new life when Meg witnesses the birth of a neighbor's baby.

In *Autumn Street* (1980), Lowry's finest piece of writing, the narrator looks back on the year she was six, when her father left to fight in World War II. The story begins with the care-free innocence of Elizabeth's close friendship with Charles, an African American boy, and ends with the violence and shock of his murder. When Elizabeth's father is injured and subsequently returns home, he and his young daughter make an "impossible promise" to each other that their separate fears and hurts will go away, knowing that sometimes hope is more important than truth. The flawlessly crafted prose is only one of the reasons the story lingers in the reader's mind long after the book has been closed.

In *Rabble Starkey* (1987), twelve-year-old Rabble Starkey's mother serves as housekeeper and baby sitter for the family of a woman eventually hospitalized for mental illness. When Mrs. Bigelow recovers and returns home, Rabble and

Illustration by Jenni Oliver from *A Summer to Die* (1977), by Lois Lowry.

her mother move on, saying goodbye to people who have become their friends and family. The first-person narrative is written in an authentic-sounding down-home voice, and the characters, learning the joys and sorrows of loving and of leaving, are especially well drawn.

Number the Stars (1989), winner of the 1990 Newbery Medal, tells about ten-year-old Annemarie Johansen, who lives in Denmark in 1943. When her family help smuggle their Jewish neighbors, including the young protagonist's best friend, into Sweden, something goes wrong and Annemarie must exhibit a kind of bravery she never knew she had. The suspenseful, unforgettable novel is geared toward a young audience but does not oversimplify the story of the multitude of people forced to flee their homeland.

Lowry won a second Newbery Medal in 1994 for her innovative novel *The Giver* (1993). Set in a futuristic world that seems to have solved all of humanity's problems — poverty, unemployment, inequality, the loneliness and insecurity of the aged — the story recounts the coming of age of twelve-year-old Jonas. Jonas's gifts of clear sight and empathy earn him the apprenticeship to the Giver, the community's reclusive keeper of all that it has given up — the good and the bad — to achieve its stable placidity. Jonas, in seeing both sides, learns to question the bargain struck, and his responses to his discoveries make *The Giver* a provocative, moving, haunting work.

In *Looking Back* (1998), Lowry explored her life, using both prose and photographs, and how it has influenced her writing. Lowry, who as a child moved from Hawaii to Pennsylvania, then to Japan, is an author who writes from experience. The act of leaving is repeated several times in her books as characters pull up roots and move away, end painful relationships, or lose loved ones to death or distance. The author's experience as a journalist and photographer has provided her with an eye for detail, a skill manifested in her clear, vivid descriptions of place and time. Called the new JUDY BLUME, Lowry has lived up to that description with her tremendous popularity among middle-grade readers.

J.M.B.

Voices of the Creators

🎌 *Lois Lowry*

My grandson, James, nine years old when he visited me in Boston in the summer of 1992, had really outgrown the traditional Swan Boat ride that he had enjoyed as a wide-eyed toddler. We went anyway, for nostalgia's sake; and we watched idly as gleeful children tossed chunks of bread to the ducks that swam beside the boat.

"Have you ever noticed," James asked me casually, "that when people think they are manipulating ducks, actually ducks are manipulating people?"

It is not often, if ever, that a casual remark haunts me and that I can, later, connect it to the origin of a book. But my grandson's perceptive and somewhat cynical words that summer coincided with my awareness of a rapidly changing world. A presidential election was looming and was much on my mind. The Berlin Wall, which I had rejoiced to see topple not long before, now appeared to have been the perching point for all the Humpty Dumpties of eastern Europe, and it was frightening to realize that they might not ever be put back together again.

Maybe it was simply that my parents, both in their mid-eighties, were dying that summer. They were, in essence, turning over the world to my generation; it was a world I didn't understand, and suddenly time seemed to be passing so quickly. I was beginning to feel responsible for what I would eventually turn over to kids like James, who at nine could already see through so much sham. I began then to write *The Giver* (1993). It would be my twenty-first novel for young people.

Looking back seventeen years to the writing of my first, *A Summer to Die* (1977), I can see that I began with the smallest and most personal of themes. Critics would not agree with that, pointing out rightly that the life-death continuum which is central to that book is hardly a "small" theme. But for me, writing it then, it was no more than a retelling of a personal experience: the gathering together of the details and fragments that accompanied a time of saying goodbye in the lives of two sisters.

My succeeding books, for some years, followed the same pattern, I think. As a former photographer, I have sometimes likened writing to a choice of lenses and apertures. The writer, after all, utilizes focus in the same way that a photographer does. I can come in close on the details, open up to get it good and sharp, and blur the background into oblivion. I did that in my first book: focused sharply on those sisters, on that family, and that house. And I blurred the greater world that lay behind and around them. The reader does not know, or need to know, exactly where or when *A Summer to Die* takes place.

Gradually, often without any awareness of it myself, I have changed my lenses. A book called *Rabble Starkey* (1987) stepped back a bit. Now there was not only a house but a town and a state. Now there were social issues: still seen through a personal and subjective eye, but social issues nonetheless.

Number the Stars (1989) went much further. Although intermittently, still, I was writing books that gently examined family life, *Number the Stars* was the first of all my books to expand from that domestic scene out into the much greater scope of world concerns.

Finally, in writing *The Giver,* I looked through a panoramic lens with the f-stop all the way down. It was frightening to do that, as a writer: to try to scrutinize everything that was there, to give it meaning and depth. I was dealing with an entire *world,* after all; it was a long distance from the cozy country house, purposely isolated, which I had created seventeen years before when I wrote my first book.

And now? I will go back, inevitably, to re-create the close-focused glimpses of family life, which I love. Children will always need those as part of their literature. But having now created a world, I will revisit and reexamine it, as well. My grandson and his friends are getting older, and the world will be theirs before we know it. I think all of us should be responsible for helping them see it — people and ducks; ducks and people — crystal clear, with its sparkles and its flaws.

Lynch, Chris

American author, b. 1962. Chris Lynch grew up in an Irish enclave of Boston, in a large working-class family. He graduated from Suffolk University with a degree in journalism, and after working at odd jobs for several years, he enrolled in a master's course in editing and publishing at Emerson College. At Emerson, where he studied with JACK GANTOS, Lynch began his first novel, *Shadow Boxer* (1993), and has been writing prolifically ever since, with more than fifteen novels to his credit. He now lives with his family in Scotland.

Lynch is known in particular for his tough, gritty, sometimes violent YOUNG ADULT NOVELS, such as *Whitechurch* (1999) and *Gypsy Davey* (1994). But just as memorable are his more humorous novels, including *Slot Machine* (1995) and *Extreme Elvin* (1999), and those for younger readers — *Gold Dust* (2000) and the He-Man Woman-Hater series. Although his style has been called fast paced and episodic, his novels are primarily driven by character. Even in his toughest stories, Lynch has focused on the inner battles of his characters and their search for identity.

One way Lynch has approached the search for identity is through issues of race in his native Boston. Mick of the Blue-Eyed Son trilogy (1996) rebels against his bigoted, controlling brother, and Richard in *Gold Dust* tries desperately to befriend his African American classmate by introducing him to baseball. Through Richard and Mick, Lynch has explored what happens when a young person questions the values of his community and tries to define himself against them. The struggle proves much more complicated than either Richard or Mick has first imagined.

Sports is another means by which Lynch has explored identity, particularly male identity and the relationships that influence it. *Slot Machine, Shadow Boxer, Ice Man* (1994), and *Gold Dust* could all be categorized as SPORTS STORIES, yet sports are merely a vehicle for his characters' inner drama. As part of his orientation for high school, Elvin Bishop of *Slot Machine* tries, or is forced to try, every sport imaginable, but he finds he fits none of them. Meanwhile his best friends veer in different directions, leaving him to wonder what high school will hold for them. In *Shadow Boxer*, Monty wants to follow in the footsteps of his late father by pursuing boxing, but his boxing brings the family's loss to the surface and aggravates tensions with his older brother, George.

Lynch has experimented with form in much of his work. *Free Will* (2001) is written in the second person, with limited information on the protagonist, and *Gypsy Davey* is told alternately from first- and third-person points of view, first person being Davey's fluid but mentally challenged perspective. In *Whitechurch*, short stories and poems together form a cohesive novel, and the Blue-Eyed Son trilogy is a serialized novel written in three installments. Lynch has handled all of these forms skillfully, pushing the structural boundaries of fiction for young people. He has received many awards for his work; his ability to balance action and emotion gives his work universal appeal. E.S.

Lyon, George Ella

American author, b. 1949. In George Ella Lyon's work, which includes many fine PICTURE BOOKS and novels for older children, the reader can sense the importance of family and the mountain heritage on which Lyon frequently draws. Born in Harlan, Kentucky, Lyon published his successful first work, *Mountain*, a poetry chapbook, in 1983. It was followed by plays and poetry for adults.

Lyon's background as a poet is evident in many of her works for children, as her texts feature a rhythmic, lyric cadence. Lyon has said, "Being a poet was a great help to me in learning about picture books. As NANCY WILLARD pointed out in a talk I heard . . . poems are the closest genre to picture books, with their use of sound, rhythm, economy of language, and

surprise." Lyon also has drawn on her own children's questions in her work for young readers, attempting to provide answers in books such as *Together* (1989) and *The Outside Inn* (1991).

Lyon began writing for children in 1984, when her letter to poet PAUL JANECZKO led his editor to approach Lyon about writing for children. *Father Time and the Day Boxes* (1985) resulted, as well as a short story that later became the novel *Borrowed Children* (1988). *Father Time* excites a young child's imagination: "Now I expect you've been wondering how the days go by and all that." In *Together* the delightful rhythm of lines such as "You cut the timber and I'll build the house. You bring the cheese and I'll fetch the mouse" lead to the reassuring refrain "Let's put our heads together and dream the same dream." The interconnectedness of family is clearly portrayed in works such as *Who Came Down That Road* (1992), the result of a young child's question about the history of a nearby mountain path, and *Come a Tide* (1990), in which the grandmother's experience of the floods of Spring gives the young narrator a sense of being involved in the cyclical effects of the weather. *A Sign* (1998) focuses on Lyon's own life and how she became a writer.

In her two YOUNG ADULT NOVELS, Lyon's belief in the importance of family pervades the text. In *Borrowed Children*, Amanda Perritt questions her role in the family during her mother's difficult recovery from childbirth. Sumi in *Red Rover, Red Rover* (1989) also has a strong sense of her place in the family, but events such as the death of her beloved grandfather and her older brother's departure for boarding school challenge her understanding of that world. Both novels sensitively explore the transition from child to young woman. It is easy for the reader to become involved in these stories. As Lyon has said, "Books are a collaborative enterprise, not just between author, editor, and illustrator but between those folks and the reader." Readers willing to experience this collaboration should come to Lyon's work expecting to be amply rewarded. E.H.

M

Macaulay, David

British-born American author and illustrator, b. 1946. Born in Burton-on-Trent, England, David Macaulay, like many young boys, found himself fascinated with technology. But unlike most youngsters, he would later take that interest and create the kind of books that he would have loved as a boy. Macaulay has credited his parents with his interest in making things; everyone in the family fashioned items and used their hands — from sewing to wood-carving. Eleven when his parents left England to move to Bloomfield, New Jersey, Macaulay continued drawing and enrolled in the Rhode Island School of Design. After receiving his bachelor's degree in architecture, he spent a fifth year studying in Rome, an experience that would eventually be used in his books *City* (1974), in which he explored the development of a Roman city, and *Rome Antics* (1997), a graphic tribute to Rome's streets and buildings.

After a short stint as a junior high school teacher, Macaulay began instructing art students at the Rhode Island School of Design, and he has continued to teach at various institutions throughout his career as a bookmaker. While teaching, he became intrigued with the process of creating his own books. His first book idea undoubtedly was not his most inspired; this PICTURE BOOK depicted a gargoyle beauty pageant. Fortunately, the book never saw the light of day. What it did do was land on the desk of an editor who was impressed by a picture depicting a gargoyle against the backdrop of Notre Dame. After talking over his enthusiasm for cathedrals in general, Macaulay was inspired to create an INFORMATION BOOK that focused on the building of a cathedral. One of the freshest, most innovative information books to appear in decades, *Cathedral* (1973) was to completely alter the face of this genre for children.

If one looks back over the past fifty years, one can see that there are certainly those who created information books with the skill and artistry that David Macaulay has brought to them — EDWIN TUNIS and HOLLING C. HOLLING being two fine examples. But in *Cathedral* Macaulay crafted a visually stunning information book that worked equally effectively with adults and children. Easily shared and enjoyed on many levels, it is truly a book for all ages. Since both words and pictures are integral to the information shared, *Cathedral* is as interesting to look at as it is to read — and that combination had rarely before been applied to the field of children's nonfiction.

Many of the titles to follow *Cathedral* would employ the same oversize format Macaulay chose for his first book; executed in black and white, they show the structures of various edifices and the human communities that work around them. For the books are not only testaments to the ways things are built, but they also provide a vision of a whole society: social hierarchies, rituals, and lifestyles play as active a role in the books as do tools, materials, and techniques. *City* demonstrates the construction of a Roman city; the building of the monuments to the pharaohs is explored in *Pyramid* (1975); the evolution of a nineteenth-century New England mill is featured in *Mill* (1983); the life that goes on underneath the surface of modern city streets forms the theme of *Underground* (1976). In *Unbuilding* (1980), Macaulay has hypothetically demonstrated how the Empire State Building might be demolished. As critic Barbara Bader has noted, Macaulay in his books has combined "a rare historical imagination, a keen eye, a gift for topographical structural delineation, and a deep sense of the human condition."

Macaulay's sly sense of humor also led him to craft some light and farcical books — *Great Mo-*

Illustration by David Macaulay from his book *Pyramid* (1975).

ments in *Architecture* (1978), *Motel of the Mysteries* (1979), and *Why the Chicken Crossed the Road* (1987) — all of which exhibit Macaulay's freewheeling sense of humor. His Caldecott Medal book, *Black and White* (1990), part of this whimsical series of titles, explores cause and effect. A continuation of the theme explored in *Why the Chicken Crossed the Road, Black and White* contains four stories that can be read in four different ways; in them Macaulay played with the concept of time, simultaneity of events, and one story impinging on another. In this free-spirited book, Macaulay also played with the form of a book itself and what can be done in designing one.

By far Macaulay's most comprehensive, most ambitious, and most creative use of the book form came in *The Way Things Work* (1988); in it he demystified a veritable smorgasbord of me-

chanical and electrical machines. He showed himself equally at ease explaining simple principles — such as the inclined plane — and intricate processes, such as nuclear fission and fusion. From the zipper to the atom bomb, from the plow to the microcomputer, Macaulay focused, distilled, organized, and explained hundreds of items. That he managed to do so and remain funny at the same time is an unparalleled accomplishment. Ten years later he expanded the subjects and redrew and improved an already magnificent book in *The New Way Things Work* (1998).

Macaulay has garnered an impressive number of awards: the Caldecott Medal and Honor Awards, the Boston Globe–Horn Book Award, the Christopher Award, an American Institute of Architects Medal, the Washington Children's Book Guild Nonfiction Award, a nomination for the Hans Christian Andersen Award, the Deutscher Jugendliteraturpreis, the Dutch Silver Slate Pencil Award, and the Bradford Washburn Award, presented by the Museum of Science in Boston for an outstanding contributor to science.

Time magazine once wrote of David Macaulay, "What he draws he draws better than any other pen and ink illustrator in the world." A superb craftsman, a dedicated bookmaker, Macaulay has no contemporary equals in the art of the information book. He knows how to clarify, to make the difficult simple, to communicate, and to make the process of learning enjoyable. It is in the latter that he particularly succeeds. When it comes to nonfiction, no one can equal David Macaulay in his ability to keep readers turning the pages, eager for more. A.S.

Voices of the Creators

🌿 *David Macaulay*

I am frequently asked where I get my ideas. I always answer by saying "from everywhere" — or "by keeping my eyes and ears open." Although vague, both responses have always seemed to serve the needs of the moment. But it is a good question. Where *do* I get my ideas?

First of all, what are ideas? I think of them as living, breathing critters. Offspring if you will, created by and in people's minds from all sorts of fragments and sensations which are everywhere all the time. You go for a walk or a bike ride and bam, you've picked up at least half a dozen just by keeping your eyes and ears open. Once aboard and often even before the journey is over, these seemingly disconnected bits and pieces have begun to organize themselves through some sort of internal dating service developed by, and unique to each of us, into ideas. These ideas then grow into all shapes and sizes. And, like their owners, they begin to show a variety of distinct characteristics ranging from whimsical, intriguing, and even inspiring to demanding, stubborn, and insidious.

Not surprisingly, some of what turn out to be the best ideas are more heavily imbued with the latter characteristics. They have no choice if they are to reach adulthood. There is only so much available cerebral real estate, so competition can get fierce.

It is not always easy to recognize a potentially good idea in its early stages because it rarely looks anything like the idea into which it might eventually develop. Some ideas are fairly modest, satisfied to gently nudge their unwitting host from time to time but otherwise quite willing to hang around and wait their turn. Other ideas stomp around day and night, just looking for attention, desperate to see themselves in print. Regardless of their personalities, though, once aboard, ideas have a tendency to stay. The reclusive ones often remain locked up for years, while their gregarious counterparts hang out the windows, shouting back and forth across the folds of the cortex as they put out their wash.

At least one good idea, and preferably one only partially formed, is necessary if creative thinking is to be undertaken. Without it, the would-be creator is on very thin ice. *Castle* was an easy book to make but a very difficult one to stay with because the idea behind it was already a *fait accompli*, having been developed in *Cathedral* and thoroughly tested in *City* and *Pyramid*. There was no new ground to break. The most important result of that often-frustrating undertaking was that it forced me onto another track. *Great Moments in Architecture* was a collection of little ideas, some of which, farther along that same track, became the basis of *Motel of the Mysteries*. Ideas beget ideas. You just never know which will blossom and which will wither on the vine.

Shortly after completing *Unbuilding*, I began to entertain the notion of a book about a journey. I wanted to use a journey as subject matter. All books are journeys, although not all are interesting journeys. The best books take us to places we've never been, be they distant lands or uncharted internal realms. Many others can accurately be described as dead ends. Over the next ten years, I found myself on this path often, although it never seemed to lead anywhere. I have several sketch-books filled with what look like twisted triptychs from some demonic travel agent. While I could never complete a journey, I also couldn't get off the road. I would return to my sketchbooks between each published effort and look again for ways of identifying and hopefully satisfying my quest. With each visit, the path grew increasingly convoluted until finally there emerged *Why the Chicken Crossed the Road,* a simple cause-and-effect tale of a chicken and an accidental hero named Hooper. After working on the relentless *Way Things Work* for almost four years, I returned with considerable relief to those old ideas and set off on another journey. *Black and White* emerged comparatively quickly — after a mere ten years of aborted liftoffs — as four distinct journeys juxtaposed to create a fifth. *Ship* was finally launched after only three years of false starts. It is also a journey book: first, that of the historian attempting to understand the design and construction of a sixteenth-century caravel from its scattered remains; second, the story of the ship itself, a product of the historian's scholarship, common sense, and informed imagination.

No matter how aggravating or impossible some ideas may seem, no matter how reluctant or uncooperative they are, you can't throw them away carelessly — not that they'd leave even if you tried. Ideas are a necessary fact of my life; and, while sometimes I can barely live with them, I could certainly never live without them. Perhaps the answer to the question "where do I get my ideas?" should be "I don't. They get me." 🔧

MacDonald, George

Scottish author, 1824–1905. Experts in children's literature consider George MacDonald's FANTASIES both enlightening and entertaining. Children often think they are just plain fun. Fantasy writers have often turned to his books for inspiration. Whatever the audience, one thing is certain: the author's stories contain highly adventurous plots, carefully constructed characterizations, and plausible fantastic elements that are accessible to a wide range of readers.

In *The Princess and the Goblin* (1872), Mac-Donald used the typical bipolar fairy-tale structure of opposite lands inhabited by very different characters, one human and one fantastic. The subterranean fantasy world is occupied by goblins who earlier rejected the human king's rule and have established a continual battle with the people on earth. Above ground, the king's daughter, Princess Irene, meets a commoner, the youthful miner Curdie. Throughout the story Curdie and Princess Irene travel and strive together in an effort to defeat the evil goblins.

MacDonald employed common fantasy motifs found in earlier myth and folklore, among them the deviousness and mean-spiritedness of the goblins; the innocence and purity of the princess; and the courage and resourcefulness of Curdie. The plot follows the traditional fairy tale structure: A princess, entering a secret passage, finds her mysterious great-great-grandmother. Initially, she cannot return to her grandmother's tower because she does not believe in her own earlier experiences. The goblins hope to capture the princess and marry her off to their son so they can rule both the earth and the underworld. A poor boy saves the kingdom from disaster and gains the king's blessing. In the second Princess book, *The Princess and Curdie* (1883), the action centers more on Curdie's acceptance of the great-great-grandmother as "real." In the end, Curdie once again helps save the king, and Curdie and Princess Irene are married.

While in many ways the stories resemble fairy tales, MacDonald created unusual fantasies that were lighthearted and entertaining. MacDonald's trusting youths could enter a fantasy world and survive only when they believed that earthly logic must give way to innocent faith. MacDonald depicted a world in which children become heroes because they believe in the mythic, supernatural, righteous spirits they encounter. MacDonald sent these heroes (and their readers) on a journey through fantasy lands in order to promote his own beliefs in religious spirituality. MacDonald wanted to entertain and to educate children at the same time. He sought to develop a style that placed children as "believers" within a context of religious allusions.

In addition to the Princess series, MacDonald's audiences continue to read and enjoy his earlier mystical story, *At the Back of the North Wind* (1871). *North Wind* contains the familiar home/away/home journey of the folkloric hero, but in this tale the hero returns to the mystical country, an ending more fitting to religious parables. Thus, the story is both a tale of the hero's welcome return in his own society and his acceptance of the ways of a new world.

MacDonald has been called the father of modern children's fantasy. His literary patterns were imitated by later fantasy writers. J. R. R. TOLKIEN read MacDonald and credited him as a mentor. C. S. LEWIS also read MacDonald and admired his talent. In his anthology of MacDonald's work, Lewis wrote, "I have never concealed the fact that I regarded him as my master; indeed I fancy I have never written a book in which I did not quote from him." J.P.M.

MacLachlan, Patricia

American author, b. 1938. Born in Cheyenne, Wyoming, Patricia MacLachlan graduated from the University of Connecticut and taught English and creative writing. Married and the mother of three children, MacLachlan has revealed herself in her MIDDLE-GRADE FICTION and PICTURE BOOKS to be a keen observer of the complexity of familial relations. The family, in its various forms and moods, is at the center of all her stories. MacLachlan is best known for her Newbery Medal–winning book, *Sarah, Plain and Tall* (1985), considered by many critics to be the great American children's novel of the 1980s. Written in simple, understated prose, the brief novel tells the story of a young brother and sister who fear that their father's newly arrived mail-order bride will decide to leave them and their prairie home and return to her beloved Maine coast. Their fears melt away in a heartwarming but decidedly unsentimental conclusion.

Children in MacLachlan's books often face a major change in their lives, and from fear and worry at the outset they move toward courage and acceptance. The eleven-year-old boy in *Journey* (1991) struggles to understand his mother's desertion and is helped to reach a slow acceptance of it by his sister and loving grandparents.

Seeing through another's eyes is also a common theme in MacLachlan's books. In *Arthur, for the Very First Time* (1980), ten-year-old Arthur Rasby spends the summer with his eccentric great-aunt and great-uncle and their pet chicken. Arthur worries about the baby his mother is expecting but learns to see a point of view other than his own and comes to believe, as he writes in a letter home, that "things will work out." Many of MacLachlan's characters are artists: musicians, painters, writers, and photographers. In *The Facts and Fictions of Minna Pratt* (1988), Minna is a promising young cellist whose struggle with her music parallels her struggle with her family, particularly with her mother. MacLachlan's protagonists often come to a new understanding and a deeper acceptance of themselves and their families. They are suddenly made aware of the love that exists in their family and the strength and courage that the power of that love grants them. The protagonist in *Cassie Binegar* (1982) envies her friend's calm, conventional parents and their clean, uncluttered house and resents her own loud and loving family, with their messy home and casual ways. With help from a visiting writer and her Gran, Cassie discovers how deeply she loves her raucous family. Willa, in *Unclaimed Treasures* (1984), believes that life is for doing extraordinary things and insists that her mother, who is about to have a baby, is doing a very ordinary thing. An emergency helps bring Willa to a realization of the love that lies within her truly extraordinary family.

MacLachlan's works are peopled with the young and the old, and her stories delineate the affinity that exists between these two groups.

Animals, too, find themselves an accepted part of the family, from cats and dogs to pigs and chickens. The humor in MacLachlan's books is gentle, a perfect match for the true tenderness in her entertaining and highly accessible stories.

J.M.B.

Voices of the Creators

Patricia MacLachlan

I was not born a writer. I didn't actually put words on paper until the age of thirty-five. "Pretty old," one of my children commented. I made a conscious and fervent decision at the age of eight not to become a writer because I read all the books I could find, many of them over and over, and I believed that writers had all the answers. Since I did not have the energy, inclination, or expertise to go out into the world and find the answers, I decided to become an actress or a symphony conductor.

The only story I remember writing in school was part of a school assignment. "Write a story for tomorrow," said my teacher. "It must have a beginning, a middle, and an end, and it must be about your pets." I wrote a story on a three-by-five card: "My cats have names and seem happy. Often they play. The end." My teacher was not impressed. I was discouraged, and I wrote in my diary: "I shall try not to be a writer." I was very fond of *shall* at age eight. I find the word *try* interesting. It did not occur to me then that everything in my diary was fiction, carefully orchestrated and embroidered tales of an exciting life — an unreal life. Or was it? The question of what was real and what was not fascinated me, and I spent lots of time asking people, becoming a general annoyance.

Like my character Cassie in *Cassie Binegar,* I spent hours in hidden places, listening to conversations I was not meant to hear and often did not understand, yet found fascinating. Sometimes I sat under the dining room table out of sight, viewing and listening to the world — the same thing that Cassie does in the book. I never realized how close this book was to me, to my life, until I sent my mother the manuscript to read. Several days later a package arrived for me in the mail. It contained a huge tablecloth, rather worn, that I'd forgotten. It was white with windy swirls of green — exactly like the one I had described in the book, in a work of fiction.

I now believe that writing is for me like tending a garden. There are plants that come up every year, perennial plots and themes and characters. There are the seeds you plant that never flourish, that become bits and pieces of people or places you set aside for later. Then there are what my father has always referred to as volunteers, which come from somewhere unknown, from someone else's garden: "Look, right there in the compost heap. A volunteer!" And we would smile.

Sarah of *Sarah, Plain and Tall* was from a volunteer from long ago. The facts of it haunted me. There once was a woman — an "unclaimed treasure," as my mother called older, unmarried women — who lived by the same sea where I spent my summers. She traveled to the prairie where I was born. My mother loved her.

So the idea of *Sarah* was one I had had for many years. My need to complete it, however, became personal and urgent. My mother, we learned, had Alzheimer's disease. Her recent memory began to fade, although her great humor remained. Soon, I knew, she would have only past memory, then none. In the book I wanted to write the story of a woman who left her roots and the story of children who needed her to preserve theirs. It is now clear that I also needed to preserve this piece of my mother's past for her, for me, and for my children.

Years ago, when I first began to write, wondering all the while whatever I could write about, something happened that made it clear. At the age of five my daughter Emily complained that she could not sleep at night because in her closet there lived a giant shadow that came out only at night to threaten her. My husband went upstairs, and engaged in a dialogue with the shadow. A few weeks later when I lay in bed with Emily, trying hard not to fall asleep before she did, I asked her about the shadow. "Oh," she said happily, "I named that shadow. He's Henry, and he visits at night when the moon is out. See?" And I did see.

For now, as in the past, I can only write about the questions and the issues that confront me, that trouble me — the ones that whisper in my ear or, like Emily's shadow, threaten me. It is my way, whether by fact or fiction, of naming my own shadows.

Maguire, Gregory

American author, b. 1954. Gregory Maguire has claimed that he was unaware he was writing for children until he reread his first book, *The Lightning Storm* (1978), a year after publication. Since then, he has written books that span all age groups — from preschoolers to adults. Born in Albany, New York, Maguire earned a doctorate in children's literature from Tufts University and has taught at the Simmons College Center for the Study of Children's Literature. In 1986, he cofounded the Children's Literature of New England Council.

Maguire's early efforts, such as *Daughter of the Moon* (1980), are somewhat overwritten, but the author found his voice with *The Dream Stealer* (1983). Set in Russia and combining elements of traditional Russian folktales — the legendary witch Baba Yaga has a key role — this story of two children trying to stop a beast from terrorizing their village has a cohesive linear structure.

Following several additional well-regarded novels, Maguire published the first volume in the humorous Hamlet Chronicles series. *Seven Spiders Spinning* (1994) effectively uses contemporary settings. The series centers on the adventures of a class of fifth-graders in the town of Hamlet, Vermont, and their wise and understanding earth-mother teacher (with the not-very-subtle name Miss Earth). *Six Haunted Hairdos* (1997), *Five Alien Elves* (1998), and *Four Stupid Cupids* (2000) continue the stories of this multicultural group of children as they battle otherworldly visitors.

Lacking the supernatural or FANTASY elements of Maguire's previous works, *Oasis* (1995) is the story of Mohandas (Hand), a young man who must reconcile with his mother, as well as deal with his uncle's HIV status, in the year after his father's sudden death. The writing is more subdued than that of Maguire's previous works, but it successfully portrays the confused emotions of an adolescent whose world has suddenly changed. The author also contributed the short story "The Honorary Shepherds" to the collection *Am I Blue? Coming Out of the Silence* (1994), an anthology of short stories about gay, lesbian, and bisexual young adults.

Maguire has shown mastery over the PICTURE BOOK form in *Crabby Cratchit* (2000), illustrated by Andrew Glass. Basing his storybook rhyme on "Old McDonald Had a Farm," Maguire presented the story of a farm woman, one annoying chicken, and their prickly relationship, which takes an unexpected turn when a hungry fox enters the picture.

Maguire's foray into novels for adults did not entirely leave behind the world of children's literature. *Wicked: The Life and Times of the Wicked Witch of the West (1995)* recounts the life story of the famous witch from *The Wizard of Oz.* Rather than a classic story retold from a different perspective, *Wicked* details the rocky political climate of the Land of Oz from the point of view of the ultimate outsider and campus radical, the green-skinned Elphaba. *Confessions of an Ugly Stepsister* (1999) retells the Cinderella story and is set in seventeenth-century Holland at the height of tulip fever. Although the traditional elements of the tale are present (the stepsisters, the beautiful girl, the stepmother), Maguire deconstructed the story, rebuilding it as a novel in which the romantic ideals of love and redemption are revealed to be only a fairy tale.

The author lives in Concord, Massachusetts, where he continues to write for both adults and children. E.M.A.

Mahy, Margaret

New Zealand author, b. 1936. A masterful storyteller who has captivated audiences young and old, former children's librarian Margaret Mahy has successfully written YOUNG ADULT NOVELS, MIDDLE-GRADE FICTION, and

PICTURE BOOKS. Her characters are memorable; she is adept at combining humor, suspense, and imagination; and underlying all her work is an obvious and abiding love of language, which manifests itself in a distinct and dexterous style. The first of Mahy's picture books was published in 1969. One that exemplifies her unique brand of humor is *The Great White Man-Eating Shark: A Cautionary Tale* (1990), in which a young lad's greedy plan to keep a lovely cove to himself backfires when a female shark finds him irresistible in his clever — and convincing — shark disguise. Mahy's first middle-grade novel, *The Haunting* (1982), which received the Carnegie Medal, showcases her talent for weaving tales of suspense that remain grounded in the realities of contemporary family issues. Eight-year-old Barney Palmer's mother died at his birth, and his concerns about his stepmother's pregnancy are compounded by his fear that he may possess powerful psychic abilities. Mahy's gift for nonsense writing is revealed in all its glory in the middle-grade novel *The Blood-and-Thunder Adventure on Hurricane Peak* (1989). The complex plot involves two children, a sorcerer, a variety of zany characters, and a school with the motto "Always Expect the Unexpected."

Mahy's storytelling ability is also apparent in her books for young adults, as is her perceptive understanding of adolescent minds and emotions. In *Memory* (1988), a nineteen-year-old struggling with the vivid but incomplete memories of her sister's accidental death meets up with an elderly woman also wrestling with memory — the almost complete loss of her own. *The Catalogue of the Universe* (1986), another realistic novel, is an intelligent story of young love. Short and brainy Tycho has always loved his childhood friend, the beautiful and popular Angela. The feeling is mutual between the unlikely pair, though it takes a crisis for Angela to find that she loves Tycho, who is her main source of comfort in a mixed-up world.

Mahy's greatest skill is her ability to enrich a story rooted in realism by adding an element of the supernatural. Her novels are given verity by the detailed descriptions of the New Zealand surroundings and her clearly delineated characters; thus, when the supernatural world begins to impinge on the natural one, both reader and protagonist are astonished by these strange events and find they have no choice but to accept them as real. In *The Changeover: A Supernatural Romance* (1984), fourteen-year-old Laura Chant is preoccupied with her mother's dating life until a more dangerous threat poses itself. She seeks help from a strange young man when a demon, disguised in human form, begins draining the life from her three-year-old brother, Jacko. Not at all the tale of horror it may seem, the novel is a touching coming-of-age story in which Laura undergoes a moving, and irreversible, transformation. In *The Tricksters* (1987), another enchanting blend of realism and FANTASY, seventeen-year-old Ariadne, called Harry, seems to have conjured three strange visitors out of thin air, for the young men bear a strong resemblance to characters in the romantic fantasy she has been writing. Incredibly complex, *The Tricksters* is a demanding novel that, in turn, rewards readers willing to fall under the spell of its intricate and richly layered narrative.

A prolific writer, Mahy has contributed significantly to children's literature with her exquisitely crafted and compelling stories that continually prompt readers to "Always Expect the Unexpected." J.M.B.

Marcellino, Fred

American designer and illustrator, 1939–2001. Brooklyn-born Marcellino graduated from Cooper Union and began his career in the early 1970s, designing record album covers, which was then a fertile ground for innovative design. A prolific artist, he designed more than four hundred effective book jackets for adult titles before moving into children's books.

In an audacious decision, Marcellino created a wordless dust jacket front for *Puss in Boots* (1990), featuring not even the entire cat but rather an overpowering headshot, so large that there's only room for a bit of the plumed hat and neck ruff. He placed the title and other customary jacket information on the back. This Caldecott Honor Book features art in a rich array of pastels and colored pencils. Marcellino set his illustrations above, below, and between the words, providing a variety of viewpoints from which to survey the action: one picture, for instance, presents the cat looking down on the granary mice from an exaggerated perspective. The text is printed in gray rather than black — an interesting touch.

In *The Story of Little Babaji* (1996), Marcellino rehabilitated Helen Bannerman's much-maligned *Little Black Sambo,* giving her 1899 story a beautifully fresh look. Little Babaji, in elegant clothes, rides confidently atop a tiger on the dust jacket — the bright, clear colors are enhanced by the stark white background. Heavily textured dark green endpapers suggest a jungle setting without any overt images. The small format echoes the size of Bannerman's original and served Marcellino well. Watercolors evoke effectively, but minimally, the interior and exterior settings, showing that less is sometimes more.

In his first foray into creating both words and pictures, Marcellino turned to a French satire by an unknown nineteenth-century author. The lead character of *I, Crocodile* (1999) is first celebrated and then ignored by a fickle public in search of ever new amusements. Napoleon's plunder of Egyptian artifacts, including the crocodile, provides ample opportunity for Marcellino's decorative treatment of the pyramids and Paris, including that city's sewers. The droll final illustration shows Crocodile picking his teeth with the feather from the hat of his unfortunate meal. An oversize horizontal format stretches two-page spreads to a full twenty-two inches, allowing Marcellino to place as many as five independent vignettes on an opening, without crowding. Though there's less white space here than in *The Story of Little Babaji,* the watercolors sparkle with white flecks; the lightness pervades even the dankness of the sewer scene.

In longer works for older readers, Marcellino has elegantly crafted worlds in black and white. In *A Rat's Tale* (1986), written by Tor Seidler, the full-color jacket opens to an interior of black, white, and a range of grays, an understated treatment for the whimsical FANTASY about a young rat and his artistic parents. *The Wainscott Weasel* (1993) combines full-color interior art with black and white drawings to depict realistic yet lyrical animal forms. In contrast to the urban setting of *A Rat's Tale,* a rural environment sets the scene for the weasel's determination to survive despite human encroachments. Elegance amid the unexpected summarizes this book — and all of Marcellino's work. J.W.S.

Marshall, James

American author and illustrator, 1942–1992. Born in San Antonio, Texas, James Marshall never planned to become a children's book author and illustrator. He studied at the New England Conservatory of Music and played the viola. But a physical accident ended his career, and he then studied French and history, receiving a master's degree at Trinity College.

For a time Marshall supported himself by teaching French and Spanish in a Boston school. Although he himself would eventually teach students at Parsons School of Design in New York City, he was untrained as an artist. Meanwhile he doodled, placing eyes and lines to create characters. Eventually those doodles reached an editor, who gave Marshall his first illustrating assignment, *Plink, Plink, Plink* (1971), written by Byrd Baylor, probably Marshall's only uninspired book. His next book, which came out the following year, was to demonstrate to adults and children the potential that Marshall possessed; *George and Martha,* a collection of five vignettes about two hippopotamuses who have a unique friendship, was a critical success and enthusiastically received by children. As Marshall was later to say, he knew with this book that he had found his life's work. That life's work was to last for twenty years and bring about the creation of dozens of PICTURE BOOKS and novels, including six more George and Martha books, Harry Allard's *Miss Nelson Is Missing!* (1977), and

Ogden Nash's *Adventures of Isabel* (1991), as well as his own *The Stupids Die* (1981), *Fox and His Friends* (1982), and *The Cut-Ups* (1984).

Marshall's talent was wide-ranging; he had an intuitive grasp of how to reduce a visual object to its most basic elements, the type of genius found in the sculptures of Alexander Calder. Marshall's most famous characters, George and Martha, were created with two dots for eyes, a nose, and a mouth. Marshall's compositions depended on line rather than color; he began publishing books when artists were still required to create color separations, and even in his later books he always retained his strong black line, which was filled with verve.

From Marshall's notebooks, available at the De Grummond Collection at Hattiesburg, Mississippi, and the University of Connecticut at Storrs, Connecticut, it is immediately apparent that he drew with great spontaneity and energy. But unlike many artists who lose this spontaneity in the books themselves, Marshall kept it in abundance. His sketches in his books maintain a vitality rare in contemporary children's picture books; his final drawings were not studied or finished but still feel like exuberant sketches.

Marshall's greatest contribution to the children's book field was his ability to develop character. He captured the foibles and idiosyncrasies of his characters; his humor was always gentle; lessons about life were present but never heavy-handed, as when George pours his split-pea soup into his shoes so as not to hurt Martha's feelings. The Marshall canon of characters is legendary: Viola Swamp, George, Martha, the Stupids, Emily Pig, Fox, the Cut-Ups. After reading books about a Marshall character, children believe he or she truly exists as an individual.

Marshall was equally brilliant as a writer. Even in those books that bear other authors' names, Marshall worked and reworked text to achieve that perfect combination of text and art. His own writings, *A Summer in the South* (1977) and *Rats on the Roof and Other Stories* (1991), demonstrate his abilities as a storyteller and what he could accomplish with words alone.

As brilliant as Marshall's work was, as devoted a readership as he found, he won few major awards. The University of Mississippi presented him with its Silver Medallion in 1992, and *Goldilocks* (1988) was a Caldecott Honor Book. His greatest number of awards were those children voted him.

In the late twentieth century, there were many fine practitioners of the art of the picture book, but James Marshall was one of the finest. His books are classics that have endured. A.S.

Martin, Ann M.

American author, b. 1955. Baby-sitting has proven to be a fun and profitable business for Ann Martin, author of the incredibly successful Baby-Sitters Club SERIES. A children's book editor, Martin had already written some children's novels when the concept for the series was suggested to her. Like series character Kristy Thomas's idea for a baby-sitting club, the idea for the series was "simple but brilliant." The first books about a group of girls who form a child-care cooperative were so popular that the original plans for a four-part series were quickly forgotten. The series, begun in 1986, has 100 million books in print, has been translated into nineteen languages, and boasts a fan club of more than sixty thousand members. Super Special editions feature the series characters away from home on trips, MYSTERY books have been added to the series, and younger readers have their own series, Baby-Sitters Little Sister.

Martin has based the characters and events on her childhood friends and experiences. Memories of her own phase of lifeguard-watching created *Boy Crazy Stacey* (1987), and *Claudia and the Sad Good-bye* (1989) contains feelings about her own grandmother's death. The stories, each told from the point of view of a different club member, involve problems such as divorce, deceased or strict parents or stepparents, and occasional fights between club members — interspersed with frequent trips to the mall. But Martin has cleverly latched on to very specific interests of girls ages eight to twelve. Most obvious is the obsession with hairstyles and clothing: readers are provided with lengthy, detailed descriptions of what each character, adult or child, is wearing, from socks to earrings. Stories about baby-sitting are tailor-made for the fascination preteen girls have with large families, especially those that include twins and triplets. Martin has combined the appeal of the impeccably dressed Nancy Drew with that of the multiply cute Bobbsey Twins and added to these the attractive ideas of clubs and earning money. The main ingredient that hooks readers, however, is the empowering stories of girls calmly solving problems on the job and at home. At work they handle a variety of baby-sitting difficulties, including emergencies, and back home they learn to act maturely, bargaining instead of arguing with Mom and Dad.

Growing up in Princeton, New Jersey, Martin loved to baby-sit and to read, passions she has passed on to her fans. Though adults may wish preteens were reading something other than formulaic series books, most are grateful that their children are reading at all. The books have also created an interest in business, and girls nationwide are starting their own baby-sitting clubs, a far more practical venture than that of earlier generations of series-crazed girls who lurked about looking for clues and crooks.

Martin is also the author of MIDDLE-GRADE FICTION and YOUNG ADULT NOVELS, including *Me and Katie (the Pest)* (1985), *With You and Without You* (1986), *Ten Kids, No Pets* (1988), *The Doll People* (2000), with Laura Godwin, and *Belle Teal* (2001). Martin's entertaining novels about family life are praised for the gentle humor and fast pace of the light, upbeat, easy-to-read stories. J.M.B.

Martin, Bill, Jr.

American author and educator, b. 1916. Bill Martin Jr. has purposely written books to be read aloud, paying attention to, as he has said, the "rhythms, melodies, and sounds of language" to create stories that delight both the ear and the tongue of young children, who ask to hear them over and over again.

Perhaps part of his insistence on read-alouds goes back to his own early reading days. As a child growing up in Kansas, he was basically a nonreader. What saved him was a storytelling grandmother and a fifth-grade teacher who read aloud to his class twice a day. From them, he learned to savor the rich and varied quality of language. In spite of his reading problems, he graduated from Kansas State Teachers College (now Emporia State University) and taught high school. In 1945 Martin wrote *The Little Squeegy Bug*, illustrated by his brother, Bernard, which he published himself. When Eleanor Roosevelt mentioned it on her radio program, his writing career was launched. Bill and Bernard continued to collaborate until 1953, publishing a total of seventeen books. After receiving his Ph.D. from Northwestern University in 1961, Martin became an editor at Holt, Rinehart & Winston, creating numerous educational reading programs. He originally wrote *Brown Bear, Brown Bear, What Do You See?* (1967) for one of these, and after several incarnations, it was reissued as a trade book in 1983. Enhanced by ERIC CARLE's illustrations, its simple but melodious repetitions delight children and encourage them to participate. Using a similar formula, *Polar Bear, Polar Bear, What Do You Hear?* (1991), also illustrated by Carle, plays with animal sounds in patterned repetitions. Although Martin introduced words that may be unfamiliar to preschoolers, such as "fluting" flamingos and "braying" zebras, the words themselves are appealing and fun to say.

Martin maintains it is not essential that children understand every word "so long as they . . . assimilate the sounds, the music, the poet's vision." Teaming up with John Archambault, a poet, journalist, and storyteller, Martin has written nine other books, most of which are illustrated by Ted Rand. Using a combination of rhyme and narrative, *The Ghost-Eye Tree* (1985) describes a scary evening's walk past a haunted tree. Again, the sound of language draws the reader into the story, but in this book the characters of the young boy and girl hold one's attention. The sibling rivalry and affection create a nice counterpoint to the delicious fear they experience on their trip. In *Barn Dance!* (1986) Martin and Archambault used the rhythm of a square dance to recount the adventures of the "skinny kid" when he goes to a midnight hoedown in the barn. *Knots on a Counting Rope* (educational series edition, 1966; trade edition, 1987) tells of an American Indian boy's courageous efforts to overcome his blindness. Martin and Archambault use two voices, a dialogue between the boy and his grandfather, to recount the child's growing ability to negotiate his dark world. The result is poetic and moving. In *Chicka Chicka Boom Boom* (1989), illustrated by Lois Ehlert with bright, bold graphic shapes, Martin and Archambault created a delightful alphabet chant in which the letters become characters participating in a rambunctious romp up a coconut tree. Rhythm and rhyme once again encourage the reader to join in, snapping fingers and celebrating the joy of playing with and appreciating language. P.R.

Martin, Rafe

American author, b. 1946. Rafe Martin grew up in a family of storytellers. As a child, his mother read fairy tales and Aesop's fables to him, filling his dreams with images of princes riding through dark forests. His father, a pilot who flew intelligence and rescue missions during World War II, told tales of Odyssean quests and the strange twists of fate that shape people's lives. His grandmothers told harrowing tales of courage and faith about fleeing the Russian Revolution and coming to America, alone and penniless. With the birth of his children, Martin continued the tradition of storytelling. As he began to understand the process of story for himself, Martin realized its powerful ability to "pass on archetypal dramas of cause and effect, and to make values an integral aspect of emotional and imaginative thinking."

Martin began telling stories professionally during the 1970s, discovering the expressive and sometimes unpredictable effect of voice and gestures and the vital role of the audience. Since his first book was published in 1984, Martin has remained true to the voice and the audience implicit in each tale. Drawn especially to ancient myths of faraway places and tales of courage and inexplicable twists of fate, he has touched upon the mysteriousness of life in his books. In *Mysterious Tales of Japan* (1996), illustrated by Tatsuro Kinchi, poetic cadences evoke the eerie beauty of ancient Japan. Martin and Kiuchi brought to life the landscape of the Arctic Circle in *The Eagle's Gift* (1997). Martin's retelling of the traditional Inuit tale, coupled with Kiuchi's powerful illustrations, sweep the audience into a quest to bring song, dance, and story — the sounds of joy — to joyless parents.

In his award-winning book *The Rough-Face Girl* (1992), illustrated by David Shannon, Martin's spare, understated retelling of the Algonquin Cinderella story echoes the oral tradition faithfully. Martin and Shannon teamed up again in *The Boy Who Lived with the Seals* (1993), a poignant retelling of a myth of the Chinook people of the coastal Northwest, reminiscent of the selkie tales of Scotland. In *The Shark God* (2001), against the backdrop of Shannon's explosive illustrations, Martin has explored themes of cruelty and compassion in the Hawaiian tradition, drawing on several regional tales to create the story of a couple's struggle to save their children from a terrible fate. In each book, notations explain sources and changes to traditional stories and FOLKLORE.

In *The Storytelling Princess* (2001), Martin redefined the fairy tale tradition with an original tale of a high-spirited princess and a prince who loves to read. In *Will's Mammoth* (1989), illustrated by Stephen Gammell, and the CHAPTER BOOK version, *The Boy Who Loved Mammoths* (1996), Martin explored a child's imagination in original tales of a boy who believes that mammoths exists. Through story, Martin has said, we share that "deeply human archetypal realm. Every time I tell a story, or write a new book, the mystery lives for me again." B.M.

Mathers, Petra

American artist and author, b. 1945. Petra Mathers's deceptively simple stories offer characters whose comical pathos and quiet courage strike a chord of recognition in her readers. Her work is fresh and original and, best of all, straight from the heart.

Mathers was born in the Black Forest and grew up in postwar Germany. Before beginning her career in children's books, Mathers built on her childhood love of books with an apprenticeship in a bookstore. With her then husband and her child, Mathers immigrated to America, living in Portland, Oregon, where she painted in her spare time, exhibiting her work in several gallery shows while helping to support her family with a series of waitressing jobs. In 1980 Mathers left the United States for a time to dive for treasure in the South China Sea.

Her first children's book, *How Yossi Beat the Evil Urge* (1983), written by Miriam Chaikin, featured black and white illustrations. Though her buoyant artwork has graced several PICTURE BOOKS, including *The Block Book* (1990), *Frannie's Fruits* (1989), and *Molly's New Washing Machine* (1986), Mathers is best known for her own books, which are marked with her distinctively elegant style and wit. Her debut with *Maria Theresa* (1985), about a hen who literally flies her otherwise happy coop in Manhattan to find fulfillment as a member of a circus act in the country, surprises readers with an ending that is laced with a little romance and the notion of finding one's rightful place in the world, themes that recur in Mathers's other work.

Mathers's gentle endings remind us that not everything is a perfect fit at first, although with a little courage and openness people can find their right match. This idea is cleverly pursued in *Theodor and Mr. Balbini* (1980), in which Mr. Balbini wants only a simple canine companion. Instead, he finds himself saddled with a cantankerous and talkative dog with a taste for French and a litany of complaints. It is with the help of Theodor's French tutor, a woman whose own dog eschews all forms of sophistication, that a solution is found with resulting new friendships for all concerned.

In *Sophie and Lou* (1991), recipient of the Boston Globe–Horn Book Award, readers meet Sophie, a mouse so shy that she can only shop during the slow hours. Then Sophie becomes entranced by a dance studio that opens across the street and is pulled into the world of tangos and rumbas, which she practices alone in her living room until one day she is asked to dance by Lou, a debonair mouse who has been shadowing her all along. Mathers is also the author and illustrator of *Aunt Elaine Does the Dance from Spain* (1992); *Victor and Christabel* (1993); and a charming group of books about a chicken, duck, and dodo — *Lottie's New Friend* (1999), *A Cake for Herbie* (2000), *Lottie's New Beach Towel* (1998), and *Dodo Gets Married* (2001).

The charm of Mathers's work lies in her bold, fresh pictures with their flat perspective and clean, spare lines. Mathers's unerring eye for detail, whether it is a plumber's car sporting a leaky faucet as a hood ornament or Sophie's winged alarm clock, lends a warmth and subtle humor. Mathers's simple watercolors combine tenderness and humor. Of her creations, the author has commented, "The characters I invented now live their own lives. They are quietly minding their own business — none of them will set the world on fire. But they are decent, a little comical, and open to love." C.L.

Mazer, Norma Fox

American author, b. 1931. One of three sisters, Norma Fox Mazer grew up in Glens Falls, New York, a small town near the Adirondack Mountains. Her father drove a bread truck, and her mother was a saleswoman. Her grandparents were all from Europe, and Mazer has said that for her the "whole weight of the past" was of immigrants who struggled and were poor. As a child Mazer was imaginative and intelligent and aspired to be a teacher or social worker. Married at eighteen, after a short time at Antioch College in Ohio, she began to raise the first of four children and started to fit writing into her daily life. She began with descriptions, letters, and short stories. Her husband, Harry Mazer, also wanted to be a writer, so the two set early-morning hours and began years of intense, disciplined work, writing for magazines in order to break into the field. Mazer still writes every day and still begins in the early hours of the morning.

Though most of Mazer's more than twenty books are YOUNG ADULT NOVELS, her first, *I, Trissy* (1971), was for a younger audience. Its protagonist, like most of Mazer's, is a strong girl coming to terms with the real problems in her life and facing them with courage. The novel was an experiment with literary devices such as epistolary fiction, an early example of Mazer's interest in varying her style. Mazer wrote two collections of short stories, *Dear Bill, Remember Me?* (1976) and *Summer Girls, Love Boys* (1982). These two books contain fine examples of a genre that is rarely as successful when attempted by most young adult writers.

Mazer has the feeling of being an outsider, which she has said may come from being Jewish but also may be from being bright and female as she grew up. "It just wasn't the thing to be," she has stated. The themes of being an outsider and of having a working-class background are often apparent in her fiction. In *Mrs. Fish, Ape, and Me, the Dump Queen* (1980), the protagonist's father runs the town dump, and the two of them live in a trailer. Mazer also has written about current issues that intrigue her. In *When We First Met* (1982), a Romeo and Juliet story, a child is killed by a drunk driver. *Up in Seth's Room* (1979) is a thoughtful treatment of the quandary of whether a girl should sleep with her boyfriend. Mazer has also written FANTASY; *Saturday, the Twelfth of October* (1975), one of her own favorites, is a time-travel fantasy in which Mazer created a matriarchal society, including its religion, folklore, speech, and rituals. A suspense novel, *Taking Terri Mueller* (1981), won the Edgar Allan Poe Award for the Best Juvenile Mystery. She has also written a series of light-hearted novels, starting with *A, My Name Is Ami*

(1986), and has collaborated with her husband on two books. She has written two books about the character Sarabeth Silver, *Girlhearts* (2001) and *Silver* (1993). Many of Mazer's books have been named ALA Best Books for Young Adults. *After the Rain* (1987) is the story of a teenage girl who learns that her unpleasant, overcritical grandfather has only a few months to live. A better relationship slowly develops between them as she gives up her free time to help care for him until his death. The ALA named this novel a 1988 Newbery Honor Book. S.H.H.

McCaffrey, Anne

Irish author, b. 1926. As a child, Anne McCaffrey was determined that one day she would be a famous author; the large number of her books that have become bestsellers is a testimony to her success in achieving that goal. Born in Cambridge, Massachusetts, McCaffrey resides in Ireland in a home she calls Dragonhold. Her SCIENCE FICTION has received numerous prizes, including the Hugo Award, the Nebula Award, and the Margaret A. Edwards Award, and is widely read by adults and adolescents.

Best known are her novels set on Pern, a planet colonized by and later isolated from Earth. With genetic engineering, the inhabitants of Pern adapted a beast native to the planet to fight with fire the invasive, sporelike Thread that jumps from the Red Star to Pern during certain periods of its orbit. Each of these massive, sentient creatures, called dragons because of their similarity to the mythical Earth creatures, forms at hatching a lifelong, telepathic attachment, called Impressing, to one human, who becomes its dragonrider. Upon this complex but fully developed premise, more than a dozen tales have been founded. Three — *Dragonsong* (1976), *Dragonsinger* (1977), and *Dragondrums* (1979), together known as the Harper Hall of Pern series — were written specifically for young readers. Although the dragons are featured as an integral part of Pernese life, the trilogy focuses more closely on the role of the harper in Pern society.

McCaffrey, who studied voice for nine years and for a time was involved in the theater, has brought her love of music to her fiction by exploring its importance to culture, not only as entertainment but as a way of transmitting knowledge and history from generation to generation. In *Dragonsong*, Menolly, an extremely gifted musician, runs away from her native fishing community because her father believes girls have no right to compose or play music in public. Accidentally, Menolly Impresses nine fire lizards, miniature cousins of the dragons, when she seeks refuge in a cave sheltering the eggs from which they hatch. Unbeknownst to her, the Master Harper of Pern has been seeking her after hearing two songs she wrote, and *Dragonsinger* relates her adjustment to being apprenticed to him at Harper Hall, where she learns about the demands, difficulties, and joys of life as a harper. *Dragondrums* features the adventures of Piemur, a young friend of Menolly's, as he succeeds Menolly as Master Harper Robinton's special apprentice and finagles his way into Impressing his own fire lizard.

Because of McCaffrey's in-depth exploration of character in her works and her smooth integration of the necessary technical information into the backdrop of her stories, some people term her writing "science fantasy" rather than "science fiction." Certainly, her stories have wide appeal among many who eschew the high-technology focus of most science fiction, but McCaffrey never neglects the careful research that backs up the scientific aspects of the novels. By creating well-rounded characters who must overcome numerous setbacks and challenge the restrictions of tradition to achieve their goals, McCaffrey has developed an atmosphere in which those who are thought to be weak prove themselves strong and in which female characters, in particular, find fulfillment.

In her works for adults, McCaffrey has sculpted many other scenarios that push back the boundaries of the known universe and open the reader to new possibilities, but her books about the dragons and people of Pern have found an overwhelming number of fans. Drag-

ons hold great appeal for many FANTASY lovers; in the series, McCaffrey has redefined the beast and thereby added depth to any understanding of the mythical creatures. Her work draws in readers of fantasy and science fiction as well as those who simply love adventurous stories with strong, determined characters. A.E.D.

McCloskey, Robert

American author and illustrator, b. 1914. Probably best known for his PICTURE BOOKS, including two Caldecott Medal winners, *Make Way for Ducklings* (1941) and *Time of Wonder* (1958), Robert McCloskey is also loved for his contemporary tall tales for older children, including *Homer Price* (1943), and for his illustrations for the Henry Reed books, written by Keith Robertson.

McCloskey was born in Hamilton, Ohio, where he spent his youth in a town very much like the ones he later described in *Lentil* (1940) and *Homer Price*. As a boy, his interests included drawing, music (harmonica and oboe), and inventing gadgets. After high school, he won a scholarship to the Vesper George School of Art in Boston and continued his studies at the National Academy of Design in New York City. His first book, *Lentil*, was published in 1940, the same year he married Margaret Durand, the daughter of children's book author Ruth Sawyer. Though he had been awarded the Prix de Rome in 1939, World War II prevented his study abroad until 1949. He spent the war in the United States, putting his inventing skills to use by making visual aids. With characteristic humor and modesty, he has said, "My greatest contribution to the war effort was inventing a machine to enable short second lieutenants to flip over large training charts in a high breeze." In 1946, after the birth of their daughter, Sally, the McCloskeys moved to an island on the Maine coast, which provided inspiration for most of his subsequent books. These include *Blueberries for Sal* (1948), about a bear cub and its mother looking for blueberries on the same hill as Sal and her mother; *One Morning in Maine* (1952), in which Sal spends the morning with her father and loses her first tooth; and *Time of Wonder*, with its misty watercolors and evocative text, which shows both the beauty of Maine and the variety of activities undertaken there.

McCloskey has described how he created his stories. "The book starts with an idea/ideas inside my head. I imagine a lot of pictures. I almost have the book planned before I first put pencil to paper. . . . It usually takes about two years from the first time I write the story until it ends up being a completed book. The first drawing has changed, but the text reads almost exactly as it did in my first draft." Each of his books is a gem, and each accomplishes a different goal, though they are alike in their innocent, homey humor and the best kind of patriotism. *Blueberries for Sal*, printed with blue ink, is sweet and cozy. *Journey Cake, Ho!* (1953), written by Ruth Sawyer, is appropriately bombastic with its red-brown brush line and blue-green litho crayon showing bold areas of pattern and white space. *Time of Wonder* describes a summer in Maine, using paintings with a gentle and joyful color sense and with people depicted in a sketchy yet realistic way that is always kind. And *Burt Dow, Deep-Water Man* (1963) is brighter and more caricatured, with pinks, greens, reds, blues, and daring white space.

While he was working on the illustrations for *Make Way for Ducklings*, in which a family of mallard ducks walks through Boston's streets to the Public Garden, McCloskey realized he needed live models. He bought four mallard chicks at a market and brought them home to his New York City apartment. When he went to Boston to sketch backgrounds, he brought back six more ducks. "All this sounds like a three-ring circus," he has said, "but it shows that no effort is too great to find out as much as possible about the things you are drawing. It's a good feeling to be able to put down a line and know that it is right."

In his career, McCloskey wrote and illustrated eight books and provided illustrations for ten more. Though he chose to stop illustrating in 1970, his combined skills as humorous storyteller and illustrator ensured the longevity of his books. L.R.

McCord, David

American poet, essayist, editor, and teacher, 1897–1997. Among twentieth-century writers for children, David McCord undoubtedly had one of the more extensive and distinguished résumés. Sampling his honors demonstrates not only remarkable achievement but also the breadth of experience distilled in his POETRY for young readers. Ranging from numerous honorary degrees to appointment as Benjamin Franklin Fellow of the Royal Society of Arts, from exhibitions of his watercolors to service on the usage panel of the *American Heritage Dictionary*, his achievements indicated understanding of disciplines as varied as history, literature, art, education, and medicine. In 1977, the year in which he read his "Sestina to the Queen" at ceremonies marking the state visit of Elizabeth II to Boston, he received the first award for excellence in poetry for children given by the National Council of Teachers of English.

Born in New York City, David Thompson Watson McCord spent his early years on Long Island and in New Jersey and his adolescence on a ranch in Oregon near the Rogue River. After graduating from Lincoln High School in Portland, Oregon, he came east to Cambridge, Massachusetts, receiving his A.B. (1921) and A.M. (1922) from Harvard University. Except for service as second lieutenant in the U.S. Army (1918), almost his entire life was intertwined with the university, primarily as the executive director of the Harvard Fund Council. He was already known as a poet, essayist, and editor when, in 1952, *Far and Few*, his first collection of verses selected for children, was published. Ten more would follow.

An only child, afflicted with recurring attacks of malaria, he was solitary but, as he remembers, never lonely. Solitude permitted time for reading, experimenting, observing, listening — and for developing the sense of wonder that infuses his poetry. Sensitivity to the sounds and rhythm of language, appreciation of nature, and knowledge of writers such as William Blake, EDWARD LEAR, and LEWIS CARROLL informed his mind and influenced his theories of what poetry for children should be. McCord acknowledged and wrote perceptively about the contributions of these and other poets to his development. Among those he cited were Blake for emphasizing the child's need for joy and laughter; Lear and Carroll for introducing nonsense and word-play; Robert Louis Stevenson for recognizing the significance of ordinary experiences; and Elizabeth Madox Roberts for capturing the authentic voice of the child. As the poet Myra Cohn Livingston commented, McCord could "remember, extract, and discern the best of the past, reshape and apply it to the present, and in the process offer others a generous share of his unique celebration of life."

John Rowe Townsend, in citing McCord's work for the "light, dry humor and a good deal of technical virtuosity" typical of contemporary American poetry for children, singled out his instructions for composing varied verse forms using the forms themselves. And yet, while these are dexterous examples of his genius, children are probably better acquainted with his onomatopoeic "Pickety Fence," with its infectiously rhythmic instructions.

Equally remarkable is the subtlety that frequently transforms his verses into epiphanies for all ages. M.M.B.

McCully, Emily Arnold

American illustrator and author, b. 1939. Emily Arnold McCully illustrated her first book for children — *Sea Beach Express,* written by George Panetta — in 1966. In this book young readers are introduced to the first of hundreds of distinctively "McCully" children. Drawn in a sketchlike style with lots of line to create small faces, halos of hair, and childish movements, McCully's illustrations have a spontaneous qual-ity that brings to life the characters in books of realistic fiction. From her first book to the present, McCully has been a prolific illustrator, providing pictures for several books a year for authors of novels, PICTURE BOOKS, POETRY, and nonfiction. Her illustrations for novels such as Meindert DeJong's *Journey from Peppermint Street* (1968) and Barbara Williams's *Mitzi and the Terrible Tyrannosaurus Rex* (1982) are done in pen and ink. In her earlier picture books, such as BETSY BYARS's *Go and Hush the Baby* (1971), she used pen and ink with a wash of a single color. An exception is Mildred Kantrowitz's *Maxie* (1970), in which McCully's dark, subdued colors and striking textures capture the tone of this story about a lonely old woman.

McCully's more recent picture books feature the same lively pen-and-ink characters as her earlier books but are enhanced with watercolor washes reflecting the mood and setting of each story. For KATHRYN LASKY's *My Island Grandma* (1979), for example, McCully's pictures make use of the pale blues and greens of its seaside setting. For *Dinah's Mad, Bad Wishes* (1989), written by Barbara M. Joosse, she used bright aqua, chartreuse, and pink to evoke the strong anger felt by the mother and daughter.

In 1984, McCully published *Picnic,* the first picture book in which she created both the story and the pictures. This book introduces children to a new and delightful set of McCully characters. A wordless book, *Picnic* recounts through pictures the story of a little mouse who falls from the back of the family truck on the way to a picnic, becomes lost, and is then reunited with its family. Grandpa mouse, with his glasses, cap, and cane, Mama with her distinctive kerchief, and the small lost mouse with its own stuffed pink mouse — not to mention a small mouse with a very large watch — all become familiar to children in further volumes in this series. These include *First Snow* (1985), *School* (1987), *New Baby* (1988), and *Christmas Gift* (1988), a delightful Christmas story about the warm relationship between the grandfather mouse and the youngest mouse.

In 1988 McCully wrote and illustrated her

first I Can Read book. Called *The Grandma Mixup*, it features realistic human characters, two grandmas of very different styles and temperament. *Grandmas at the Lake* (1990) and *Grandmas at Bat* (1993) have followed the grandmas through several more adventures. McCully has also produced a trilogy of picture books about a theatrical family of bears, with longer texts and bright illustrations. *Zaza's Big Break* (1989) and *The Evil Spell* (1990) were followed by *Speak Up, Blanche!* (1991), in which a winsome, shy sheep comes to work at the Farm Theatre with the bears. McCully's use of tiny print for Blanche's shy dialogue strikes young readers as hilarious. In *The Orphan Singer* (2001), McCully used paintings to tell the tale of a singer in eighteenth-century Venice.

For *Mirette on the High Wire* (1992), McCully used human characters, but she took on a new setting and a vivid new style. In this Caldecott Medal winner, she used lush paintings filled with the details of life in turn-of-the-century France as she told the story of a young girl who heartens a faltering man, an aerialist who has lost his courage, with her ambition to be a high-wire performer. She returned to Mirette again as a character in *Starring Mirette and Bellini* (1997). McCully, in her Caldecott speech, acknowledged Mirette as a highly personal metaphor for the risks that one takes as an illustrator and writer for children. After nearly thirty years of work in this field, McCully continues to take chances and to show her versatility as she shares her thoughts and images with children. B.A.C.

McCurdy, Michael

American illustrator and author, b. 1942. Michael McCurdy is a "Renaissance artist," a master of engraving, woodcuts, and scratchboard, with a multifaceted career that includes children's books. At a time when computerized illustration and mass production dominate children's book publishing, McCurdy's skills and techniques set him apart.

With a grandmother and father who were artists, McCurdy began drawing as a child. He first became interested in wood engraving as a student at the School of the Museum of Fine Arts in Boston. Two other children's illustrators were a serendipitous influence at that time: David McPhail was his roommate for one year, and Wallace Tripp shared the printmaking department with them. McCurdy was drawn to wood engraving as an "honest medium" with no room for error, and he created his first one in 1962. He also graduated with an M.F.A. from Tufts University where, as a student of the poet X. J. KENNEDY, he realized his interest in contemporary literature. In 1965 he began his career in illustration, and in 1966 he was awarded a traveling scholarship from the Museum School. After working as an art instructor at Concord Academy and Wellesley College's book arts program, he devoted himself to engraving and bookmaking.

In 1968 McCurdy became the publisher of Penmaen Press Books, which produced significant small-press first editions of the work of leading American and European writers and poets, such as William Saroyan, Joyce Carol Oates, Lawrence Ferlinghetti, Anthony Hecht, and Vicente Aleixandre. He continued at Penmaen until 1985. When he left, he applied the same quality of excellence and dedication to his fiction and nonfiction for children.

McCurdy's woodcuts have enhanced the beauty of many books — he has illustrated more than 180 — many of them historical in focus. McCurdy is equally deft at working in black and white and in color. Outstanding examples of his color illustrations can be found in *Hannah's Farm: The Seasons on an Early American Homestead* (1988); *Lucy's Christmas* (1994) and *Lucy's Summer*, written by DONALD HALL (1995); *The Sailor's Alphabet* (1998), with irresistible scratchboard drawings; and *The Beasts of Bethlehem* (1992), written by X. J. Kennedy, which comprises nineteen poems in the voices of animals present at the Nativity.

McCurdy's exceptional compositions in black and white include dramatic effects in *Giants in the Land* (1993), written by Diana Appelbaum, a history of logging in pre-Revolutionary New England; Lincoln's *The Gettysburg Address* (1995); *Signers of the Declaration of Independence* (2000), written by Dennis Fradin and containing 113 drawings and portraits; the haunting images of *The Bone Man: A Native American Modoc Tale* (1997), written by Laura Simms; *An Algonquian Year: The Year According to the Full Moon*; and *American Fairy Tales* (1996), compiled by Neil Philip.

The rustic look of McCurdy's woodcuts has a special affinity with folktales, capturing both their somberness and liveliness, as in *The Devils Who Learned to Be Good* (1987), which he wrote and illustrated, and *The Old Man and the Fiddle* (1992). Twice his work has garnered a New York Times Best Illustrated Book award, for *The Owl-Scatterer* (1986), written by Howard Norman, and for *The Seasons Sewn: The Year in Patchwork* 1996), written by Ann Whitford Paul. An example of the range of McCurdy's work is the poster he designed for the 1988 production of David Mamet's Broadway play *Speed the Plow*.

McCurdy's distinguished style is characterized by a crispness of line, delineation of texture, and dramatic composition. All told, McCurdy is an extraordinary illustrator and a master craftsman of the art of the book. J.C.

McDermott, Gerald

American illustrator and author, b. 1941. Gerald McDermott's bold graphic designs interpret folktales in a dramatic style. But his unique approach of balancing modern art and traditional folk design did not occur by happenstance but came via his work in another visual form — film.

At age four, McDermott began taking classes at the Detroit Institute of Art. In high school, his focus on art continued as he received formal training in Bauhaus principles. His silk-screen prints and watercolors gained him a National Scholastic Scholarship to Pratt Institute. Once in New York, he pursued a dual interest in graphics and filmmaking; he also toured Europe and exchanged ideas with filmmakers. Returning to Pratt, McDermott began to produce and direct a series of animated films on mythology. Meeting Jungian scholar Joseph Campbell was a milestone in McDermott's career. Campbell consulted on McDermott's films, making the artist aware of the psychological depths of mythology and the potential for integrating cultural symbols into his art.

McDermott's first book, *Anansi the Spider* (1972), was written and adapted from his own animated film. The transition from film to print form was not easy, as he ended up rendering all new art for the PICTURE BOOK to "retain the bold, graphic feeling of the film and carry over its visual rhythm to the printed page." *Anansi* was a Caldecott Honor Book in 1973. Two years later, McDermott's second book, *Arrow to the Sun* (1974), was awarded the Caldecott Medal, establishing him as a contemporary children's book creator. McDermott continued exploring myths and traditional tales and retelling them with dramatic flair and strong strokes. *Sun Flight* (1980), *Daughter of Earth* (1984), and *The Voyage of Osiris* (1977) are boldly drawn and glowingly colored. His only black and white rendition is *The Knight of the Lion* (1978), the twelfth-century Arthurian legend, which was appropriately foreboding in tone.

Switching from the archetypal mythology of Egypt, Greece, and Rome, McDermott chose a pair of sprightly Irish stories. In *Tim O'Toole and the Wee Folk* (1990) and *Daniel O'Rourke: An Irish Tale* (1986), he playfully depicted his characters with a befitting lilt and bounce, a departure from his previously assertive lines.

McDermott's fascination with the trickster motif in folklore led him to the West African story of *Zomo the Rabbit* (1992), the Pacific Northwest tale of *Raven* (1993), and the American Southwest tale of *Coyote* (1994). Inspired by the traditional designs of both areas, his artwork combines textile patterns and totems with vivid colors and vigorous lines. McDermott assimilated the patterns and designs of various cultures to shape his representation of the story. In his Caldecott acceptance speech, he said, "The role of the artist is that of the shaman, penetrating surface reality to perceive a universal truth, drawing out the essence of an idea." His visual expressions of modern telling of myths and trickster tales have successfully achieved that role. With his stylized perspective, his vibrant colors, and his rhythmic energy, he has become an original interpreter of multicultural tales.

J.C.

McKay, Hilary

British author, b. 1959. In Hilary McKay's novels, children never cease to appall their parents. They come home on the last day of school, two years in a row, splattered in unwashable paint or dig up a pet dog's grave to check if he's gone to heaven. It's a new atrocity every day, sometimes every hour; and while their persistent incorrigibleness often causes their parents to throw up their hands, it is pure exhilaration for McKay's readers.

One of four sisters, McKay has described her own mother and father as loving but careless. A favorite family story recalls the time her father lost his grip on her infant sister Bridget during a walk in the marsh, and Bridget plunged head-first into the mud, emerging unscathed except for a ruined sunbonnet. McKay's father was much more careful about his daughters' mental enrichment, forbidding television and filling the household with storytelling and books. McKay has credited her lifelong career as a reader with fostering her career as a writer. After obtaining a science degree from the University of St. Andrew in Scotland, she worked in a laboratory and at various other jobs before a friend suggested that her knowledge of books might lead her to write one herself.

Reviewers have compared the four Conroy sisters in McKay's first MIDDLE-GRADE NOVEL, *The Exiles* (1992), to BARBARA ROBINSON's Herdmans and HELEN CRESSWELL's Bagthorpe family. But no one could accuse Ruth, Naomi, Rachel, and Phoebe Conroy of lacking their own distinct charms and failings. Perhaps they inherited their individualism from Big Grandma, to whose house they are banished for the summer while their parents oversee renovation jobs at home. Big Grandma wears men's pajamas, drinks whiskey at bedtime, and hides her vast personal library from her granddaughters to prevent them from "skulking in corners reading books all day." Given the dire shortage of reading material, the girls occupy themselves with ghastly natural history projects, one-armed gardening, a diary recording the food eaten at every meal, and fishing in a bucket. They also accidentally set fire to their grandmother's storage space. Sequels *The Exiles at Home* (1994) and *The Exiles in Love* (1998) recount further unconventional escapades and exude the same blend of wit and warmth as the first book.

A second trio of novels, beginning with *Dog Friday* (1995), centers on young Robin Brogan and his neighbors, the Robinsons. Porridge Hall, the seaside bed-and-breakfast owned by Robin's mother, provides the setting for misbehavior to rival anything the Conroys could dream up. This series also weaves in supernatural elements, with the appearance of a mysterious ghost girl in *The Amber Cat* (1995) and rumors about an ancient wish-granting Viking sword in *Dolphin Luck* (1999). Magic seems almost taken for granted by Sun Dance, the middle Robinson child, whose consistently unique logic prompts those who don't know him well — and even those who do — to wonder if he's "bats." He might very well be, but his eccentricities are what make him, along with all of McKay's characters, so thoroughly entertaining. C.M.H.

McKinley, Robin

American fantasy writer, b. 1952. Robin McKinley first received recognition as an important writer of FANTASY fiction for young adults with the publication of her first novel, *Beauty*, in 1978. A retelling of "Beauty and the Beast," *Beauty* brings a tremendous vibrancy to the original fairy tale. Beauty's relationships with her friends and family, her heroic determination to do what is honorable in spite of her fear, and, most important, the love that develops between her and the mysterious beast are all explored with sensitivity and depth. McKinley's astute "reading between the lines" of this classic brings the story to unforgettable life.

Born in Warren, Ohio, McKinley grew up traveling around the world with her parents since her father was a naval officer. She has frequently said she keeps track of her life by what books she was reading at a given time. An avid reader since her earliest childhood, she has a perception of the world that was heavily influenced by classic fantasy literature for children: L. FRANK BAUM's Oz books, ANDREW LANG's collections of fairy tales, and works by J. R. R. TOLKIEN and Rudyard Kipling. These influences are apparent in her writing and in her ability to create worlds of wonder and magic resonant with the elements of a child's imagination, yet McKinley has managed to use the traditional format to create stories wholly her own.

Although *Beauty* was critically acclaimed and extraordinarily popular with young readers and adult fantasy buffs alike, writing it was simply a diversion from the project nearest to McKinley's heart, the writing of the Damar stories. McKinley first introduced her readers to Damar, an imaginary desert kingdom, with *The Blue Sword* (1982), a Newbery Honor Book, and *The Hero and the Crown*, a prequel to *The Blue Sword*, which won the Newbery Medal in 1985. The Damar books combine adventure and romance with elements of mythological symbolism to weave two epic tales of the timeless struggle between good and evil. Their special significance is that they explore this struggle from a feminine perspective. In *The Blue Sword*, Hari, a young "outlander" woman, comes to the kingdom of Damar in its time of greatest need and leads the Hill Folk to victory in their battle against the dark forces from the North. *The Hero and the Crown* is the story of Aerin the Dragon Slayer, the original wielder of the Blue Sword, and her struggle to wrest the hero's crown from a wicked enchanter. With the creation of Hari and Aerin, McKinley has added to the ranks of literary heroes two remarkable young women more than able to hold their own with their male counterparts.

The trademark McKinley characters — strong, competent young women who distinguish themselves through courageous acts of leadership — are also found in *The Outlaws of Sherwood* (1988). In this distinctively contemporary version of the Robin Hood legend, female characters aren't neglected, and Maid Marian and the surprising Lady Cecily take on roles as glamorous and challenging as those of the rest of Robin's Merry Men.

In addition, McKinley has also published other novels based on fairy tales — *Rose Daughter* (1998), a "Beauty and the Beast" retelling, and *Spindle's End* (2000), a Cinderella story. She has also written *The Door in the Hedge* (1981), a book of short stories, including several retellings of fairy tales, which highlights her profoundly personal connection to the fantasy genre, and she has edited an elegant collection of original stories by prominent fantasy writers, *Imaginary Lands* (1987), which received a World Fantasy Award in 1986. With her beautiful adaptations of *Jungle Book Tales* (1985), *Black Beauty* (1986), and *The Light Princess* (1988), McKinley has passed on to a new generation of young readers the priceless gift of classic children's literature.

K.T.

McKissack, Frederick; McKissack, Patricia

Frederick: American author, b. 1939; Patricia: American author, b. 1944. Patricia McKissack feels strongly that all young people need good literature by and about African Americans. An African American writer, McKissack is committed to producing strong, accurate, and appealing stories. Alone and with her husband, Frederick, she has written more than fifty books, including PICTURE BOOKS, EASY READERS, INFORMATION BOOKS, BIOGRAPHIES, and Dear America SERIES books.

McKissack grew up in a storytelling family in Tennessee. Her picture books draw on this rich heritage and continue the tradition. *Flossie and the Fox* (1986), illustrated by RACHEL ISADORA, derives from a story her grandfather told her, and an old photograph of her great-grandparents inspired *Mirandy and Brother Wind* (1988), a Caldecott Honor Book and winner of the Coretta Scott King Award for JERRY PINKNEY's illustrations. The settings are the rural South, and the tales are told in an easily readable Southern dialect. McKissack has frequently picked strong heroines who outsmart their adversaries, but in *A Million Fish . . . More or Less* (1992), illustrated by Dena Schutzer, she wrote of a young boy who learns the art of telling tall tales. All her picture books demonstrate her sense of humor and joy in sharing a tale.

After McKissack graduated from what is now Tennessee State University, she moved to St. Louis, Missouri, with her husband and taught English to junior high school and college students. Her teaching experience gave her a genuine appreciation of the needs of young people, inspiring both her books for beginning readers and her information books. She has written biographies about important African Americans, such as Frederick Douglass, W. E. B. Du Bois, Mary McLeod Bethune, Martin Luther King Jr., Michael Jackson, and Jesse Jackson, for a variety of grade levels from the newly independent reader to middle school students. She has coauthored many nonfiction and a few fiction books with her husband. Frederick was originally a civil engineer; now, he has said, he "builds bridges with books."

McKissack has tried to present an even-handed picture of her biography subjects, including both positive and negative details. For example, in *Jesse Jackson: A Biography* (1989), she discussed many of the criticisms leveled at Jackson after Martin Luther King's assassination.

Together the McKissacks have also written histories of the African American experience. They feel that to put the civil rights movement of the 1960s in perspective, one must go back and understand the events that followed the

Civil War. *The Civil Rights Movement in America from 1865 to the Present* (1987) covers these events, focusing on African Americans, but it also touches on the experiences of other minorities. In *A Long Hard Journey: The Story of the Pullman Porter* (1990), which received the Coretta Scott King Award and the Jane Addams Book Award, the McKissacks presented a fascinating account of the Pullman porter, his struggles with racism, and the rise of the first all-black union. As usual, the McKissacks have researched their subject well, drawing on primary sources including personal interviews, to make this a very readable history. Their *Sojourner Truth: Ain't I a Woman?* (1992) won the Boston Globe–Horn Book Award for Nonfiction and a Coretta Scott King Honor Award. They also received the Regina Medal of the Catholic Library Association in 1998.

Patricia McKissack has stated a dual goal of improving the self-image of African American children and encouraging an open attitude in all children toward cultures different from their own. By telling engaging stories, both fiction and nonfiction, her books clearly move us in this direction. P.R.

McMillan, Bruce

American photographer and author, b. 1947. Bruce McMillan's enthusiasm is contagious. Neither the children nor the adults who pore over the photographs in his stunning books for the very young can help but share his obvious enjoyment of his subject and his medium. A school visit from this energetic writer and photographer sparks excitement as he shares with students and teachers his process of creating a book and his unique way of seeing. With no formal training in photography, McMillan has produced images that are technically superb, outstanding for their clarity, vivid color, and consistently interesting composition.

Born in Boston but a resident of Maine for most of his life, McMillan drew upon his experience, with his wife and young son, as caretaker of a small island to produce his first book, *FinestKind o' Day: Lobstering in Maine* (1977). Another early work, *The Remarkable Riderless Runaway Tricycle* (1978), was inspired by his rescue of an old tricycle from the Kennebunkport dump. The book, illustrated with black and white photographs, remains popular today and has been adapted into a highly acclaimed film. Two books of visual puns published for an adult audience reflect McMillan's quick sense of humor and foreshadow the wit and wordplay that appear in his later full-color PICTURE BOOKS for children: *One Sun* (1990) and *Play Day* (1991), collections of images illustrating pairs of rhyming words ("wet pet") that the author terms "terse verse." McMillan is perhaps best known and most highly regarded for his photographic concept books such as *Counting Wildflowers* (1986), *Dry or Wet?* (1988), and *Time to . . .* (1989), in which events in the small child's daily routine — waking up, eating breakfast, going to school — illustrate both the passage of time and the measurement of time in hours by the clock. In one of his most popular books, *Nights of the Pufflings* (1995), he told a narrative story about the nights when the youngest puffins take flight on an island off the coast of Iceland.

Particular strengths of McMillan's books are the various methods he has used to reinforce the concept presented in the illustrations or to extend the book's appeal and usefulness for older readers. *Eating Fractions* (1991), for example, shows two winsome children preparing and eating food they have divided into halves, thirds, and fourths. Recipes for four of their appetizing creations appear at the end of the book. *Super, Super, Superwords* (1989) demonstrates the grammatical concept of comparison: positive, comparative, and superlative. Colorful images of energetic kindergartners illustrate concepts such as "small, smaller, smallest" and "loud, louder, loudest." McMillan used every element of the book's design to reinforce the concept — the graduated size of the images, the size and darkness of the printed text, the intensity of hue. Gorgeous photographs of baby kittens, cubs, and lambs in *The Baby Zoo* (1992) will charm the smallest child. In addition, each of the animals selected represents a rare or endangered species, and McMillan provided detailed information and habitat maps for older readers. The simplicity of McMillan's picture books belies the meticulous attention he has paid to the smallest detail and the painstaking care he has given to the composition of each picture. The resulting images convey an air of exuberance and spontaneity.

The prolific McMillan has continued to sustain freshness and high quality while producing new titles each year, earning high praise from reviewers, teachers, and librarians. McMillan's conviction that photography was under-utilized in books for children launched a career in which he has ably demonstrated the creative power and charm of photography for children's picture books. D.M.L.

Meddaugh, Susan

American author and illustrator, b. 1944. By happy accident, Susan Meddaugh, creator of the widely acclaimed *Martha Speaks* (1992), the hilarious PICTURE BOOK about a painfully honest talking dog, is now doing professionally what she first began doing as a ten-year-old in Montclair, New Jersey — telling herself stories with pictures. And they are highly original, humorous stories, illustrated with a confident and spontaneous line that is as personal as handwriting.

In the years between childhood desire and adult accomplishment, Meddaugh was a student of fine arts at Wheaton College in Massachusetts, where she painted in a representational style. Upon graduating, she worked briefly for an advertising agency in New York City and then moved to Boston, where she worked for ten years with a major publishing company, first as a designer of children's books and later as art director for children's books. During this time, Meddaugh rediscovered *Curious George*, by H. A. REY, and had the powerful experience of seeing the art again as she had for the first time as a child. Her response to this revelation was a conviction that art that is meaningful to a child cannot be judged in the same way as art for adults. Meddaugh's philosophy and her enjoyment of the whole process of bookmaking soon encouraged her to write and illustrate her own books. Her distinctive color and dramatic use of shadow and light create tension in *Beast* (1981). At this time Meddaugh also began designing jackets for YOUNG ADULT novels and was the designer and main artist for the *New Boston Review*. When illustrating the work of other authors, Meddaugh has looked for "humor, an unusual story, a story worth doing." She has illustrated several of EVE BUNTING's stories, including *In the Haunted House* (1990) and *A Perfect Father's Day* (1991), as well as a POETRY collection, *The Way I Feel . . . Sometimes* (1988), written by Beatrice Schenk de Regniers, and books by Verna Aardema and Jean Marzollo.

Meddaugh is a very visual storyteller whose books can often be summed up by just one of the images. For example, in *Martha Speaks*, the significant illustration shows the alphabet soup going up to Martha's brain rather than down to her stomach, an idea suggested by Meddaugh's young son, Niko. Suddenly Martha can talk, and her proud owners can ask the questions dog owners have always wanted to ask. They ask, "Why don't you come when we call?" And Martha answers, "You people are always so bossy. COME! SIT! STAY! You never say please." But Martha is as honest as a child, and when her candid opinions cause trouble, she quietly sulks until her owners appreciate her volubility once more.

Meddaugh's texts can be admirably economical because so much of the story is carried in her very expressive artwork. Her readers will find more humor the closer they look. In *Witches' Supermarket* (1991), the grocery shelves are filled with everything from "Shake 'n Bake Snake" to "Apples with Worms" (more expensive than without). The dog in *Witches' Supermarket* is the same dog who subsequently stars in her own book, *Martha Speaks*. Martha captivated readers and reviewers alike, and the book was named one of the New York Times Best Illustrated Books of 1992 as well as an ALA Notable Book. Martha, a stray adopted by the family and "so drawable with her big chest," has taken her fame in stride. Once again Meddaugh has created a book with illustrations that appeal directly to children and humor that is irresistible to all. Because of the popularity of Martha, Meddaugh created several books about her. *Martha and Skits* (2000) introduces a new dog Skits, who appears to have star quality of his own. All of Meddaugh's books indicate her ability to tell compelling stories, with humor, that children will want to return to again and again. P.H.

Meltzer, Milton

American historian and biographer, b. 1915. Milton Meltzer is one of the preeminent historians writing for young people. His first book, *A Pictorial History of the Negro in America* (1956; reprinted in 1983 as *A Pictorial History of Black Americans*), which he coauthored with LANGSTON HUGHES, was published for adults, but he felt compelled to write for a younger audience after surveying the lifeless textbook synopses of history they were usually fed. Over seventy books followed, most dealing with Americans and their history and all informed by Meltzer's conviction that children will find the past meaningful only if they see it as a human drama and not a litany of dates and battle names. Whenever possible Meltzer lets excerpts from letters, diaries, newspapers, speeches, and other original documents tell the story. His readers hear voices they may have never heard before, voices of ethnic minorities, women, and the poor.

In *The Black Americans: A History in Their Own Words, 1619–1983* (1984), both famous and "ordinary" black Americans, from ex-slaves to modern civil rights leaders, chronicle their struggle against oppression. Books on the Great Depression, the American labor movement from 1865 to 1915, the American Revolution, and the Civil War tell about these events from the perspective of those who lived through them. Meltzer has always connected the different voices with his own remarks, believing the historian must provide context for the moments in the past he or she reveals.

Growing up in Worcester, Massachusetts, the son of Austrian-Jewish immigrants who suppressed their heritage in an effort to become Americanized, Meltzer thought little about the context of his own life. As he said in *Starting from Home* (1988), an autobiography of his childhood and adolescence, "[My parents] never talked about life in the old country and I never asked them about it. . . . Now I think how stupid I was, how self-centered, not to be curious about the origins of my own family." Later in life he made up for his lack of curiosity not only by researching his family history but by delving into the history of the Jewish people in several books. The winner of numerous awards and honors, *Never to Forget: The Jews of the Holocaust* (1976) combines Jews' eyewitness accounts of the atrocities committed against them by the Nazis with Meltzer's tracing of the origins of anti-Semitism and bureaucratization that made these atrocities possible. A companion book, *Rescue: The Story of How Gentiles Saved Jews in the Holocaust* (1988), recognizes the individuals who staked their lives against institutionalized evil.

From high school, when his favorite English teacher introduced him to Thoreau and antislavery poets and his history teacher encouraged him to find out about Worcester abolitionists, Meltzer has admired activists. He has written biographies of such pioneers of human rights such as feminist Betty Friedan, abolitionist Thaddeus Stevens, and nineteenth-century author and reformer Lydia Maria Child. His biographies of historical icons such as George Washington, Thomas Jefferson, Benjamin Franklin, and Christopher Columbus seek to reveal the human beings behind the myths and monuments. As he has done with all his subjects, Meltzer put the life of each man or woman into context, trying to explain their considerable strengths and weaknesses in light of the world that helped shape them. In 2001 he won the Laura Ingalls Wilder Award for his contribution to books for children and young adults. C.M.H.

Middle-Grade Fiction

While children's varying development makes it difficult to define exactly the term *middle-grade fiction,* the genre is intended for pre- and early adolescents, roughly speaking, those in the upper elementary and middle school grades. Works of literature for these young people assist them in understanding themselves, empathizing with others, learning about the complexities of human relationships, and finding their own special voice. Novels can be viewed as cultural artifacts that simultaneously reflect and create society's values and concerns. Changes in society influence children's books and are mirrored in them. As young adolescents have grown in sophistication, with exposure to a media-dominated world, they have voiced their awareness of current social problems. Authors and publishers have responded with books that, instead of presenting ideal images of children and families, mirror the sometimes rough realities of the contemporary scene — dealing with the position of blacks and women in society, various kinds of abuse, ecological problems, pollution, alcoholism, treatment of the elderly, and death. These honest images are tempered with hope, thereby empowering children to find solutions to their own concerns.

Realistic fiction has shown more change over the past several decades than any other kind of children's book. This change manifests itself not only in the subject matter but in the style in which it is handled. One need only compare the nearly ideal families of novels written in the 1940s and '50s with the diminishing appearances of the image of the perfect parent and the nuclear family in later novels for middle-level readers. ELEANOR ESTES's Moffats in *The Moffats*

(1941), its two sequels, and other books and ELIZABETH ENRIGHT's series on the Melendy children, which began with *The Saturdays* (1941), portray children playing in safe, loving environments. The four Moffat children and their mama represent the noble poor; they live a fun-filled and satisfying life even in the face of, or perhaps especially because of, their poverty.

The works of BEVERLY CLEARY serve as a microcosm of the change in subject matter and tone of novels for middle-level readers. The early Cleary works are pure, nostalgic Americana, all barbecues and supermarkets. *Henry Huggins* (1950) is the story of a typically mischievous small boy who, much like ROBERT MCCLOSKEY's Midwestern child in *Homer Price* (1943), finds himself in humorous predicaments at home and at school. Cleary's title character in *Ellen Tebbits* (1951) is a third-grader concerned with braces and ballet lessons. Her biggest secret is her woolen underwear, and her greatest satisfaction derives from her realization that her new friend is similarly adorned. Cleary's books about Ramona begin with five-year-old Ramona being a trial to her older sister in *Beezus and Ramona* (1955). In the ensuing years, to 1977, Ramona reaches only the age of seven; much else, however, changes in the books. In *Ramona and Her Father* (1977), Ramona's dad finds himself unemployed, does housework, and is a nurturing role model whose smoking habit worries Ramona. By the 1980s, Cleary's families look even less like the models of perfection of the 1950s, a clear reflection of the families of her middle-reader audience. Ten-year-old Leigh Botts, the protagonist in Cleary's Newbery Medal–winning *Dear Mr. Henshaw* (1983), writes letters to a favorite author to help him adjust to his parents' recent divorce and his father's absence.

The social upheaval of the 1960s had a dramatic impact on middle-level fiction. Longstanding taboos were broken in a trend toward more controversial themes handled with candor. Indeed, if one year can be isolated as singularly significant in heralding the arrival of the new realistic fiction, it would be 1964. This year was made important in the history of children's fiction in America by two significant books: *It's Like This, Cat*, written by Emily Neville, won the Newbery that year, and *Harriet the Spy*, written by LOUISE FITZHUGH, was published. Neville's book is about a white fourteen-year-old boy growing up in the New York City neighborhood of Gramercy Park. Not only is its urban setting a change from more rural ones, but its fresh, honest exploration of the inner feelings of an adolescent is also unique. Dave's relationship with his parents, particularly his father — whose desire for him to be a "Real American Boy" Dave rebels against — is uneven at best, yet realistic in its very complexity.

Harriet the Spy is also a boundary-breaking story, candid and perceptive, about an unhappy yet irresistible female whose parents are too busy with their social life to notice their eleven-year-old. The novel's depiction of urban life and the power structure of the sixth grade from the perspective of the loner signaled a change in realistic fiction for middle-level readers. Its sequel, *The Long Secret* (1965), is remarkable for the discussions Harriet and her friends have about the long-taboo subjects of menstruation and developing breasts. Fitzhugh's 1974 novel, *Nobody's Family Is Going to Change*, challenges assumptions of race, gender, and parental wisdom. In a middle-class black family, eleven-year-old Emma's aspiration to be a lawyer meets with parental disapproval as does her younger brother Willie's yearning to be a dancer.

Harriet was the harbinger of one notable development in novels for young readers: lively, independent, strong female protagonists. In response to the feminist movement and paralleling contemporary society, girls play more active roles in later novels. Certainly one of the strongest and most memorable heroines is Mary Call Luther in Vera and Bill Cleaver's *Where the Lilies Bloom* (1969). When her sharecropper father dies, the fourteen-year-old becomes the head of a household that includes a gentle, mentally challenged sister. Mary Call secretly buries her father and tenaciously fights to ensure the family's survival. Divorce is the theme of the

Cleavers' first novel, *Ellen Grae* (1967), while *Grover* (1970) tells of a young boy's attempts to deal with his mother's suicide. *I Would Rather Be a Turnip* (1971) is the poignant story of an illegitimate child's attempts to find acceptance. Clearly there is a trend in young readers' novels written after the early 1960s toward confronting concerns with directness, creating potentially real rather than ideal images.

JUDY BLUME has been astute in her choice of contemporary concerns and direct in her handling of them with humor, natural dialogue, and believable characters. Her *Are You There, God? It's Me, Margaret* (1970) is the story of a twelve-year-old girl, the child of a Jewish-Protestant marriage, and her emotional, physical, and spiritual ups and downs as she expresses her confusion about all sorts of things, ranging from religion to menstruation. Blume's *Then Again, Maybe I Won't* (1971) contains candid treatments of a boy's first sexual stirrings and teenage shoplifting.

BETSY BYARS similarly has acknowledged the variety of children and families and the concerns they share. Byars's quiet, understated humor and her compassion and understanding are evident in her 1971 Newbery Medal–winning *The Summer of the Swans,* one of the early books about a mentally challenged child. Fourteen-year-old Sara is jolted out of her self-pity when her little brother, Charlie, disappears while trying to find some swans he had previously seen. *The Pinballs* (1977) is the story of three children, deeply scarred by parental neglect and abuse, who come together in a caring foster home. In *The Night Swimmers* (1980), Retta, whose mother is dead, tries to be both mother and sister to her two younger brothers while their father works at night. In 1985, in *Cracker Jackson,* Byars explored wife battering and child abuse through the eyes of young Jackson and his attempts to help his former, yet still much-loved, baby sitter.

Other authors have similarly displayed an increased sensitivity to a wide variety of children: loved or neglected, bright or slow, rural or urban, homeless or wealthy, and representing many races, classes, and religions. The concerns that touch these young people, such as alcoholism, drug abuse, sexual abuse, death, divorce, handicaps, and abandonment, are reflected in contemporary realistic fiction for middle-level readers. The best authors present these situations with dignity and honesty, creating characters that evoke readers' understanding.

The civil rights protests of the 1960s exposed the dearth of real rather than stereotypical blacks in children's books. Socially aware authors responded promptly. E. L. KONIGSBURG's 1968 Newbery Honor Book, *Jennifer, Hecate, Macbeth, William McKinley, and Me, Elizabeth,* is the story of an interracial friendship between two fifth-grade girls, one of whom is the first black child in a middle-income suburb. John Neufeld's *Edgar Allan* (1968) is a tersely told depiction of the reactions of a family and a community to a white family's adoption of a three-year-old black boy. Alice Childress's novel *A Hero Ain't Nothin' but a Sandwich* (1973) uses Black English to describe the seesaw battle with drug addiction experienced by thirteen-year-old Benjie. *M.C. Higgins, the Great,* written by VIRGINIA HAMILTON, is the story of a young black boy's dream of saving his family's home from an Ohio strip-mining slag heap. M.C. finds the answer to his dream by coming to terms with his heritage and his own identity. *M.C. Higgins* was the first book to win the Newbery Medal, the Boston Globe–Horn Book Award, and the National Book Award.

Death of a sibling or young friend is sensitively handled by several fine authors. Constance Greene's *Beat the Turtle Drum* (1976) tells of eleven-year-old Joss's sudden death from a broken neck in a fall from an apple tree and the resulting trauma to his family. Kate, older by two years, is left to her own resources as their mother turns to tranquilizers and their father to alcohol to numb the pain. LOIS LOWRY's *A Summer to Die* (1977) recounts Meg's difficulty in coping with her older sister Molly's degenerating illness and eventual death. *Bridge to Terabithia,* KATHERINE PATERSON's 1978 Newbery Medal winner, tells of the sudden death of a ten-year-old boy's new friend as she tries to reach their secret hide-away in the midst of a storm. Paterson is also the author of *The Great Gilly Hopkins* (1978), a National Book Award winner about a tough foster child whose protective shield dissolves as she learns to give and receive love.

The impact of divorce on young people and the variety of the new family arrangements it engenders are the subjects of many novels for middle-grade readers. GARY PAULSEN's *Hatchet*, a 1988 Newbery Honor Book, tells not only of Brian's struggle to survive in the Canadian wilderness following an airplane crash but of his inner struggle to accept his parents' recent divorce and the crushing secret that a love outside the marriage precipitated the separation.

Marlene Fanta Shyer's *Welcome Home, Jellybean* (1978) conveys with convincingly painful honesty how difficult a young adolescent finds living with a profoundly mentally challenged sibling. *Do Bananas Chew Gum?* (1980), written by Jamie Gilson, realistically exposes the anguish, fear of discovery, and damaged self-esteem of a learning disabled sixth-grader. The gifted student's difficulties with socialization are vividly described in ZILPHA KEATLEY SNYDER's *Libby on Wednesdays* (1990). The homeless and acts of violence against them are a theme in Marilyn Sachs's *At the Sound of the Beep* (1990). Sexual abuse against children is Becky's concern in Laura Nathanson's *The Trouble with Wednesdays* (1986), as the girl dreads her weekly appointment with her orthodontist, who is becoming increasingly sexually aggressive.

Critics of the trend toward the realistic inclusion of adolescent concerns and societal ills in books of fiction for middle-level readers feel that this realism has gone so far in its quest for truth that it has drained children of their hopes and dreams. This clearly is not the case; in fact, the opposite is true. Truth is more cruel than fiction, for fiction can offer hope as well as honesty. Good novels have moved away from didacticism, and capable authors write books that empower children, from the protagonist's beginning steps, through his or her growing aware-ness of available options, and finally to some form of resolution. Parents are no longer portrayed as all-wise, and families are defined in a myriad of configurations. But the children featured in modern realistic fiction are young people of strength who, in the best of these books, grow, change, and take responsibility for their futures, regardless of gender, race, or class. What could be more reassuring and empowering to the abused, disabled, neglected, or ridiculed young child or to any child who is struggling with adolescent concerns of identity, independence, and maturation? In *The Fragile Flag* (1984), JANE LANGTON's protagonist is a nine-year-old girl who leads a march on Washington to protest a new missile capable of destroying the world. The very power of books is their ability to enlarge the reader's world, allowing deeply involved yet vicarious experiences. Readers can test their beliefs and their values without consequences, for good literature ultimately is about values, one's own and those of the story's characters.

Realistic fiction for middle readers continues its trend of reflecting society's concerns and changes and being sensitive to the variety of children. Books with multicultural themes demand a shift in our notion of the United States as a melting pot, an image that negates cultural uniqueness and works against a respect for and celebration of diversity. Furthermore, the continued trend to reflect contemporary society will produce more books dealing with the issues of the day. A danger is that the trend will produce something akin to "docunovels," works that will diminish in the quality of writing precisely as the presentation of controversial materials increases. Yet good writers will continue to write with respect for their young readers. Their concerns will be contemporary, their style direct, their dialogue natural, and their characters believable. Finally, the increasing trend toward the child-protagonist's point of view will enhance the notion of voice, that readily discernible yet difficult-to-define quality that distinguishes the best writing. C.B.

Milne, A. A.

British writer, poet, and playwright, 1882–1956. One would have to search far and wide to find fictional characters as beloved to so many readers as Winnie-the-Pooh, Piglet, Christopher Robin, and their many animal friends. Although Alan Alexander Milne wrote novels, short stories, POETRY, and many plays for adults, in addition to his work as assistant editor of *Punch* from 1906 to 1914, it is his writings for children that have captured the hearts of millions of people worldwide and granted Milne everlasting fame.

Published in 1926 and 1928 respectively, *Winnie-the-Pooh* and *The House at Pooh Corner* introduced the stuffed-animal friends of Christopher Robin, Milne's small son. Dorothy Milne, Christopher Robin's mother, had given each toy a voice, and Christopher Robin engaged in active, imaginative play with them. According to Christopher Milne's account of his life with his father, A. A. Milne's role in his son's life was as an observer and a chronicler more than a participant, and as Christopher grew older and began school, the boy came to resent the world's perception of him as merely a storybook character. Although it caused his son some grief, Milne's depiction of the sweet child who acts as a kind of parent to the animals of the Hundred Acre Wood while maintaining a childlike artlessness has created a lasting tribute to the dignity and joy of childhood.

Milne's lighthearted prose, periodically interspersed with simple verses composed by Pooh, is a joy to read and displays Milne's mastery of the English language. The reader responds not only to the story but to the words themselves; Milne capitalized various words and phrases to stress their importance to the characters, which provides the narrative with a distinctive charm and emphasizes the characters' naïveté. Stylistically, the books shine. The animals of the Hundred Acre Wood possess endearing traits that allow them to be quickly described, but they are far from simple caricatures. At various moments, readers can identify with fearful Piglet, bossy Rabbit, single-minded Kanga, glum and underappreciated Eeyore, the irrepressible and energetic Tigger, or Winnie-the-Pooh himself, a lovable, "hummy" sort of bear, who, more than anything, loves "a little something" at eleven o'clock. Whether building a trap for Heffalump; planning an Expotition to the North Pole; staging the kidnapping of baby Roo in order to scare his newcomer mother, Kanga, into moving out of the Wood; or playing Poohsticks on the bridge over the river, Pooh Bear and his friends make their adventures memorable with their silly observations, calculations, and deductions.

Milne framed *Winnie-the-Pooh* with scenes showing Christopher Robin, faithful teddy bear in hand, requesting and listening to his father's stories about Pooh, which sets the stage for the other tales by making clear that they are — however completely fleshed out and believable — mainly stories. Although *The House at Pooh Corner* contains similar charming tales about the "Bear of Very Little Brain" and his companions, Milne carefully depicted Christopher Robin's gradual separation from his toys and his attraction to school and the opportunity to learn. Indeed, Owl and Rabbit consider themselves more educated than the other inhabitants of the forest, but their unintentional silliness and innocent ignorance, as well as Owl's secret insecurity about his own wisdom, allow the young reader to feel comparatively knowledgeable. Simultaneously, they highlight Christopher Robin's need to step away from the security and authority of his childhood world in order to embark on the adventures involved in growing up. Even as Milne was celebrating childhood, he subtly prepared both characters and readers for the inevitable need to forge ahead.

E. H. SHEPARD's illustrations, modeled after the actual toys, show character and movement in simple line vignettes, which add so much to the books that most people consider them to be inseparable from the texts. Shepard's artwork also graces *When We Were Very Young* (1924) and *Now We Are Six* (1927), which contain poems that are, regardless of their simplicity, flawless in rhyme scheme, meter, and general composition. Many feature or are spoken by Christopher Robin; all reveal Milne's superior understanding of the world as viewed through a child's eyes. Verses about toys, Nanny, friendships, ridiculous scenarios, and ordinary aspects of daily life represent the concerns of Christopher Robin's boyhood. Despite the fact that the poetry depicts what is, in modern eyes, an overly idealized childhood and that some critics have suggested they are sentimental, the verses remain extremely popular with children and adults alike.

Publishers and producers have capitalized on the enduring success and appeal of the four books by making widely available countless cartoons, pop-up books, and condensed and colorized versions of the stories. Unfortunately, many of these efforts involve tampering with or completely changing the artwork and text to something incalculably inferior to the inimitable collaboration of Milne and Shepard; at best, these versions lead at least some children back to the classic editions.

Milne's contributions to the world of children's literature include a FANTASY entitled *Once on a Time* (1917 in England, 1922 in the United States) and *Toad of Toad Hall,* a play based on *The Wind in the Willows,* written by KENNETH GRAHAME. But best loved are those books, set in the Hundred Acre Wood, that touch a chord in the hearts of readers of all ages. Expert characterization, a care-free pastoral setting, and Milne's precision of language and style put *Winnie-the-Pooh* and *The House at Pooh Corner* in a class of their own. Winnie-the-Pooh's adventures are not only arguably the greatest toy fantasies ever written for children, but they are also, simply and undeniably, great literature.

A.E.D.

Minarik, Else Holmelund

American author, b. 1920. When she first arrived in the United States from Denmark at the age of four, Else Holmelund Minarik hated the English language. Since that time, however, she has not only learned English but grown to love it, and she has translated that love into warm and entertaining books for young readers, much to the delight of two generations of children.

After getting degrees in education and psychology, Minarik taught first grade for many years. An avid gardener, she often found inspiration for her books as she worked in the garden. She wrote for beginning readers to answer the needs of not only her students, who were just learning to read, but also her young daughter, who started reading very early. In the mid-1950s there were few EASY READERS. Ursula Nordstrom, her editor at Harper and Row, was so delighted with her first book, *Little Bear* (1957), that she used it to launch the highly successful I Can Read series. Although the language in *Little Bear* is simple and the sentences are short, Minarik created a truly lovable character. Little Bear's escapades are filled with humor and the right mix of FANTASY and realism. But the emotional tone of the book, which speaks to the universal needs for love, acceptance, and independence, is particularly captivating. The relationship between Little Bear and his mother is especially respectful, warm, and playful. In one story, Little Bear decides to fly to the moon. After jumping off a little tree on a little hill, he imagines himself on the moon and marvels at its similarities to Earth. Mother Bear plays along with Little Bear's fantasy, and, pretending not to recognize him, invites him in for lunch. When Little Bear tires of the game, he tells his mother, "You are my Mother Bear and I am your Little Bear and we are on Earth, and you know it." Mother Bear gathers him into her arms and reassures him that he is indeed her little bear and "I know it." What Minarik did not put into words, illustrator MAURICE SENDAK more than ably added in the illustrations.

Four more books about Little Bear followed over the next eleven years. *Little Bear's Visit* was named a Caldecott Honor Book in 1962 for Sendak's illustrations, and *Father Bear Comes Home* and *A Kiss for Little Bear* were both cited as New York Times Best Illustrated Books, in 1959 and 1968, respectively.

Although Minarik's language is easily accessible to beginning readers, her humor and character development keep the books from becoming dull or monotonous. Liking the device of a story-within-a-story, she used it not only in *Little Bear's Visit,* in which Little Bear's grandmother tells him about his mother as a child, but also in *No Fighting, No Biting!* (1958). In this book two children want to sit beside their older cousin Joan as she is reading. They squeeze and push to be next to her. To calm them down, Joan finally tells them a story about two young alligators who always fight and bite. More recently, Minarik has turned her skills to PICTURE BOOKS. In *It's Spring!* (1989) two kittens vie to see who can imagine jumping the highest as they celebrate spring. Here, as in her other books, humor is an important ingredient. But what comes through most strongly in all of Minarik's work is her skill in using simple but expressive language to create delightful and memorable characters.   P.R.

Minor, Wendell

Amerian illustrator, b. 1944. Born in Aurora, Illinois, Wendell Minor grew up close to the edge of town, near corn fields and the country. Because he suffered from dyslexia as a student, he found school difficult. But in fourth grade he began to realize he had a special talent for drawing. Eventually he attended Ringling School of Art and Design in Sarasota, Florida, and came to New York to pursue a career in the graphic arts.

In 1968 Minor finished his first cover illustration, for a book by Jessamyn West. After twenty-five years as a cover artist, he has completed more than fifteen hundred jacket designs; his art has graced the jackets of some of the greatest books of the era — including the historical works of David McCullough, Harper Lee's *To Kill a Mockingbird,* and Pat Conroy's *The Great Santini.*

While continuing to create jackets, Minor be-

gan to provide the artwork for children's picture books. After painting pictures of corn fields, lush pastures, and barns for *Heartland* (1989), written by Diane Siebert, Minor knew that he had discovered his true vocation. In his words, "Children's book illustration is the last frontier of creative freedom for an artist. You can still contribute to young minds in a way no other art can."

After designing a new jacket for *Julie of the Wolves,* Minor finally met JEAN CRAIGHEAD GEORGE, and they began to collaborate on a series of books, including *Everglades* (1995), *Snow Bear* (1999), *Arctic Son* (1997), and *Morning, Noon, and Night* (1999). They worked together from the research stage to the final production stage, visiting sites together and exchanging information and ideas.

His years of jacket illustration have given Minor a particular strength when reillustrating classic novels, such as Jack London's *The Call of the Wild* (1999) or Jack Schaeffer's *Shane* (2001). Like a good jacket image, each illustration in the book works as a poster. Each could stand separately on the jacket of the book, and yet all move the story forward. The illustrations for *The Call of the Wild* capture the dignity of Buck, the dog, but also show the tundra and snow-covered landscapes of Alaska that dwarf man and dog. The illustrations for Shane re-create the West of the 1880s, and the book features particularly compelling portraits of the protagonist and the man called Shane.

Known for thorough research and meticulous work, Minor works in pencil form, often to scale, to craft initial illustration ideas for a book. So detailed and thorough are these compositions that they have been shown in galleries and could almost be published as final pieces. Yet Minor subtly and deliberately reworks them to get the final images as perfect as possible. Minor's knowledge of book printing — what happens when the ink actually hits the paper — contributes to the precision of his artwork.

With roots in the images of the American Midwest and in classic American book illustration created by N. C. WYETH, Winslow Homer, and Edward Hopper, Minor has brought the art of twentieth-century illustrators into the twenty-first century. A.S.

Voices of the Creators

❧ Wendell Minor

I really feel that 1986 was the beginning of my true calling as an artist. That is when I started illustrating Diane Siebert's *Mojave* (1988). I had been designing and illustrating book jackets for almost twenty years. As it turned out, those years were essential in helping me refine and perfect my craft, and they prepared me for children's books, the epitome of craft. I remember CHRIS VAN ALLSBURG being a real inspiration to me; he brought a fine art perspective to picture books. I have also been very much influenced by late-nineteenth- and early-twentieth-century illustrators and painters, such as HOWARD PYLE, N. C. WYETH, Winslow Homer, and Edward Hopper.

American illustrators have created a very unique art form; they made it their own in the way that American jazz and baseball have become icons of American culture. David McCullough once told me that American illustration tells the story of America, starting with Paul Revere's engraving depicting the Boston Massacre at the beginning of the American Revolution. Children's literature and children's book illustration in America are a major part of a rich heritage. I believe children's book illustration is the last frontier of creative freedom for an artist. It is an art form that still contributes to young minds in a way no other can.

I grew up in the Midwest, learning about nature from my father. I've heard it said that 75 percent of American children live in an urban environment; most can't tell an oak from a maple, or a robin from a sparrow. That's a tragedy. When we lose touch with nature, we lose touch with our humanity. When my father took me trekking through the woods and corn fields of Illinois, I didn't realize what a gift that was. It was while illustrating *Heartland* (1989), in my Greenwich Village studio, with only a view of brick wall, that I had an epiphany: you can take the boy out of the country, but you can't take the country out of the boy. It took me a very long time to come full circle as an artist, to know that my heartland roots help me express truth in the images I paint. I have to be faithful to that; it has become my chosen course.

I met JEAN CRAIGHEAD GEORGE for the first time in 1990 at the twentieth anniversary of Earth Day at the United Nations. *Everglades* (1995) was our first PICTURE BOOK for a younger audience, followed by *Morning, Noon, and Night* (1999), *Arctic Son* (1997), *Snow Bear* (1999), and *Cliff Hanger* (2002). We are currently working on a number of new picture book projects that will bring a new generation of children closer to nature, just as her books for young adults have done so beautifully.

My love of America and my narrative style, with a sense of time and place, first came together in *Heartland.* All the subjects that interested me as a child — natural history, science, biology, American history — and love of the outdoors have come together in my work. My interest in so many subjects can now be funneled through the vehicle of a picture book. I hope that my passion for these subjects will create a spark of interest in many young readers that will help them find a path in their own lives.

When I talk to children today, I tell them that as a boy I had to attend special reading classes and didn't take tests very well. I tell them that if they are having trouble keeping pace with their classmates, things will be fine eventually if they persist. We don't all learn as easily as others. At some point each child will find his or her own pace. Every child has a special talent that can be developed, if encouraged. I was very fortunate to have a few terrific teachers who fostered my artistic talents and persisted in helping me develop my reading skills. My world, at the time, was visual, not verbal. What I couldn't put into words, I could put into pictures.

If a child is having difficulty with reading or writing, I often recommend to teachers that they encourage their students to tell a story by drawing a picture and then encourage them to write about what is in their pictures. Get them to think visually as well as verbally. It made a world of difference in my life. 🐾

Montgomery, L. M.

C anadian author, 1874–1942. Born with what she called "an itch for writing," Lucy Maud Montgomery began her literary apprenticeship at a young age. Eleven when she started submitting manuscripts to magazines, she was fifteen when her first poem appeared in a small Canadian newspaper. By age twenty-one she was earning her living in the thriving periodical market of turn-of-the-century North America. International acclaim came in 1908 with the publication of her first novel, *Anne of Green Gables,* which instantly became — and remains — a bestseller. By the end of her life, Montgomery had produced twenty-three books of fiction, a short autobiography, and an estimated five hundred poems and five hundred stories written for popular magazines. Selections from her ten volumes (more than five thousand pages, including photographs) of personal diaries, chronicling in compelling detail her life from 1889 to 1942, have also been edited and published.

Writing served several purposes in Montgomery's life. She was raised in the small Prince Edward Island town of Cavendish by dour Scots-Presbyterian grandparents. They were ill equipped to handle a high-strung child, and as a young girl she channeled repressed energies into creating stories and poems. She lived most vividly in the book worlds of Bunyan, Bulwer-Lytton, Scott, Tennyson, Austen, and the Brontë sisters, writers whose influence is evident in her work. As an adult woman living with her widowed grandmother and, later, as the frustrated wife of a depressive Presbyterian minister, she again turned to writing as an outlet for pent-up emotion. A restorative process itself, writing also earned Montgomery accolades from a world literary community that too seldom honored its female members. In 1923, she became the first Canadian woman to be appointed a member of the Royal Society of Great Britain; in 1935, she was made an officer of the Order of the British Empire and was selected for the Literary and Artistic Institute of France.

No less important to Montgomery were the financial rewards of being a successful writer. She savored the social standing and legitimacy that money brought with it. Unwilling to jeopardize her status as a best-selling author, she produced what the market demanded: romantic stories with "happy endings" that were, perhaps simply because they were popular, often dismissed by the arbiters of literary taste as shallow formula fiction.

Were that an adequate assessment of Montgomery's work, it would be difficult to explain her enduring popularity. Even more difficult to account for would be the profound, lasting effect her writing has had on readers of all ages, from countries as diverse as Canada and Japan, Poland and Sweden. For example, one of Canada's most celebrated writers, Alice Munro, has spoken of the empowering model for female authorship she found in Montgomery's autobiographical Emily of the New Moon trilogy of novels. Interesting thematic comparisons have been drawn between Montgomery's writings and those of Canadian Margaret Atwood. And Sweden's ASTRID LINDGREN — whose own red-headed heroine, Pippi Longstocking, is beloved by readers worldwide — cited Montgomery as a powerful literary influence.

In part, what Montgomery's readers respond to so deeply and with such emotion are the same things that elevate her writing above the sentimental fiction of other popular writers of her day: lively storytelling seasoned with equal parts realism, folklore, and Celtic mythology; a tart sense of humor and a deft comedic touch; and a richly detailed evocation of setting. All but two of her novels are set on Prince Edward Island, and the tiny Canadian province today counts Montgomery-inspired tourism among its major industries. The exceptions are *The Blue Castle* (1926) and *Jane of Lantern Hill* (1937), both set at least partly in Ontario, where Montgomery lived from 1911 until her death.

But there is energy of another type that animates Montgomery's books, which retain a strong hold on adult readers. It is the energy of social critique, and it operates just below the surface of many of her novels. Anne and Emily, her two best-known and best-developed heroines, may fulfill their womanly duty by marrying the saccharine-sweet boy next door, but not before each voices loud and angry criticisms of the way in which girls, orphans, and other disempowered members of society are ignored and trivialized. In the later of the nine Anne books, the popular redhead capitulates to social convention and becomes the matronly, submissive Mrs. Gilbert Blythe. Out of the mouths of secondary, marginalized characters like Leslie Moore in *Anne's House of Dreams* (1917), however, come caustic comments that subtly undercut the artificially blissful Blythe household.

Of course, not everything Montgomery published in her long, prolific career was entirely successful. Many of her short stories do not reward repeated readings, and her ear-pleasing poetry is little more than that. But recent critical reevaluation of Montgomery's literary output, prompted largely by the publication of her journals, has reversed some earlier assessments of her work. For example, *Rilla of Ingleside* (1920), once considered a lesser light in the Montgomery canon, is now recognized as a valuable fictional account of the Canadian experience on the World War I homefront, one of very few such records.

Much of the historical detail in *Rilla of Ingleside* is drawn from Montgomery's long, anguished diary entries during the tumultuous war years. The impassioned tone of these entries is typical of the journals, which combine to form a lively and riveting narrative of a remarkable woman's life. Uniquely valuable documents of social history, they provide crucial insight into the conditions of women's lives during an era of radical social change. In writing and recording her own life, L. M. Montgomery created a character as engaging and memorable as Canada's most famous fictional heroine, Anne of Green Gables. M.C.C.

Moser, Barry

American illustrator and designer, b. 1940. The first books Barry Moser illustrated were literary classics, mostly for adults, such as *Moby-Dick*, issued in a limited edition by a small press. Since the 1980s, he has also applied his artistry to the field of books for children.

Born in Chattanooga, Tennessee, Moser was raised in a loving environment and introduced to diverse cultural experiences such as Italian opera, musical comedy, and the music of Fats Waller. But he also has recalled that he was "taught to be a racist, to be anti-Catholic, anti-Semitic, and xenophobic." He hated school but had a talent for drawing, which was encouraged, and he benefited from the direction of an uncle who had a woodworking shop and worked with him there, giving Moser a drawing table. At age twelve, Moser was sent to military school; in 1958 he attended Auburn University and had his first instruction in drawing and design. He then attended and graduated from the University of Chattanooga as a painting major in 1962. He found a mentor there who led him to study the works of Cézanne, Braque, and Shahn, among others. After teaching in Tennessee, he and his family moved to Williston Academy in Easthampton, Massachusetts. For fifteen years, he taught himself the skills of making etchings and wood engravings, working with type, life drawing, art history, book design, and calligraphy.

In 1969 Moser met illustrator Leonard Baskin, who helped him improve his drawing and also made an introduction to a pressman who taught Moser how to improve his skills in printing wood engravings. He designed and printed his first book in 1969. Since then, Moser has illustrated more than 120 books, and his work is represented in many museums and collections, such as the Library of Congress, Harvard University, the London College of Printing, the British Museum, and Cambridge University.

His powerful watercolors for Dante's *The Divine Comedy* (1980) are typical of his style. In black and white wash, he delineated the gnarled roots of a tree and so mimicked the tangled veins and blood vessels imposed on the bodies of tortured souls. His use of light and dark shading is dramatic and powerful, and his exquisite calligraphy is an instantly identifiable aspect of his books. In 1982 his illustrations for LEWIS CARROLL's *Alice's Adventures in Wonderland* were published. The book won an American Book Award for pictorial design. Moser illustrated classic Joel Chandler Harris tales, adapted by Van Dyke Parks and Malcolm Jones, in *Jump!: The Adventures of Brer Rabbit* (1986). Another example of his fine work in books for children is *In the Beginning: Creation Stories from Around the World* (1988), retold by VIRGINIA HAMILTON, which was named a Newbery Honor Book by the American Library Association. Moser has applied his distinctive style, coupled with his trademark calligraphy, to a great number of works of classic literature for adults and for children, including Kipling's *Just So Stories* (1996) and ELIZABETH GEORGE SPEARE's *The Witch of Blackbird Pond* (2001). With an amazing body of work to his name, he has distinguished himself as a major American book illustrator. S.H.H.

Munsinger, Lynn

American illustrator, b. 1951. There is no mistaking Lynn Munsinger's interest in creating visually memorable characters. Smug llamas, disgruntled porcupines, and bemused kangaroos fill the pages of her books. A close observer of the emotions that play over the human face and figure, Munsinger has applied these same expressions to animals with extremely effective and often humorous results.

Munsinger was born in Greenfield, Massachusetts, graduated from Tufts University, studied illustration at the Rhode Island School of Design, and continued her study of art in London. Munsinger began her career using black-and-white line illustration. One of her first book

Illustration by Lynn Munsinger from *A Zooful of Animals* (1992), by William Cole.

assignments was *An Arkful of Animals* (1978), a collection of POETRY selected by William Cole. Munsinger's whimsical drawings of animals are a perfect complement to the poems and made her a natural choice to illustrate *Hugh Pine* (1980), a short novel by Janwillem van de Wetering. Her scratchy, prickly black-and-white line work was admirably suited to the illustration of Hugh Pine, a scratchy, prickly porcupine. Hugh dresses like his human friend, Mr. McTosh, in order to avoid the hazards of the highway, which too frequently result in flattened porcupines. Yet even when there is little to be seen of Hugh between his pulled-down hat and turned-up overcoat, his posture can be clearly read as dejected, cunning, or self-satisfied in Munsinger's drawings.

Munsinger has illustrated books by Pat Lowery Collins, Ann Tompert, and Sandol Stoddard, and while she is adept at working from the inspiration of each author's text, she has also worked very effectively as a collaborator. Helen Lester as author and Munsinger as illustrator have worked as a team to create books that are great favorites with young children. Their first book, *The Wizard, the Fairy, and the Magic Chicken* (1983), is full of the droll expressions

Munsinger has used to establish character and is enhanced with soft watercolor. Many other books followed, each marked with the duo's mischievous, joke-filled humor. *Tacky the Penguin* (1988) is particularly popular and has won the California Young Reader Medal (1991), the Colorado Children's Book Award (1990), and the Nebraska Library Association's Golden Sower Award (1991). *Hooway for Wodney Wat* (1999), the story of a rat with a speech impediment, also has become enormously popular with young readers.

More than ten years after *An Arkful of Animals,* William Cole chose a new selection of witty and wise animal poems for illustration. *A Zooful of Animals* (1992) stands as tribute to Munsinger's development as an artist, for this volume is a lavishly produced showcase of her work. The large trim size gives plenty of room for a toe-dancing, ballerina giraffe to stretch overhead and for a quizzical, gift-wrapped elephant to fill a spread. Munsinger has added to the book's appeal by using a variety of presentations. Some of the art is enclosed in charming borders, while some exuberantly runs off the page. A nice rhythm is established by the llamas moving down, across, and up the mountain crags that surround their poem. The changes in scale, the placement of spot art, and the effective use of soft background color keep the reader's eye moving from poem to poem. Munsinger's watercolor is clean and fresh, and ample white space sets off her ever-expressive line. From her smartly sleek seals to her lonely platypus, Munsinger has matched and extended the poetic animals in Cole's collection. P.H.

Murphy, Jim

American author, b. 1947. Growing up in Kearny, New Jersey, Jim Murphy became interested in history as a child, although he originally found schoolwork in history difficult. As taught in textbooks and the classroom, history was a string of facts and not the passionate pursuit he fancied; eventually Murphy took up writing the kind of books he would have liked as a child.

After several years of publishing books for children, Murphy decided to write his own. Although he has created more than twenty-five books, most of them INFORMATION BOOKS about American history, he has approached each volume in a different way. His works allow readers to experience the situation, to step into the middle of it. Murphy's books range dramatically in topic and scope, but he always has managed to bring a different perspective to each one. In *The Great Fire* (1995), a Newbery Honor Book, the Great Chicago Fire itself becomes the main character. In *Blizzard* (2000) the great snowstorm of 1888 stalks victims almost like a wild animal, so palpable is its force. In *Across America on an Emigrant Train* (1993), Murphy used the story of Robert Louis Stevenson, who is taking a train trip across the United States, as a means to discuss important social issues — the plight of Native Americans and Chinese workers. In *The Long Road to Gettysburg* (1992), he detailed the Battle of Gettysburg and the Civil War by recounting the experience of two specific soldiers — one Union and one Confederate — who fought at Gettysburg.

One outstanding feature of Murphy's books is the photographs and images that illustrate the text. Fanatical about the details of research, he will seek out a wide range of contemporary photographs, drawings, maps, and illustrations, from a wide variety of sources, to supplement the information in a particular text. In titles such as *The Boys' War* (1990), the evocative vintage photographs of young boys who went off to fight in the Civil War speak as eloquently as the text about how war affected the young.

Several of Murphy's books focus on a relatively unknown individual. In *A Young Patriot* (1996), the war experience of Joseph Plumb Martin, who enlisted in the Revolutionary War at the age of fifteen, explains the battles of the Revolution to young readers. *Pick and Shovel Poet* (2000) presents the biography of an obscure figure, Pascal D'Angelo, an Italian construction worker who wrote poetry. Both books demonstrate how Murphy can work from a journal written at the time and then expand upon it to develop a book.

Because of the excellence of his work, Murphy's books have garnered many prizes: he has won the Washington Post–Literary Guild Award and received honor awards from Newbery, Sibert, and Boston Globe–Horn Book.

A.S.

Myers, Christopher

American illustrator and author, b. 1974. After Christopher Myers graduated from Brown University, he collaborated with his father, WALTER DEAN MYERS, on *Harlem* (1997), a visually striking, oversize PICTURE BOOK for older readers. The two celebrated this unique place in different, complementary ways. In a poetic text, Walter Dean Myers captured Harlem as a touchstone of African American aspiration and a culture that reverberates with music. Chris Myers used collage illustrations to create a cityscape that vibrantly resonates with feeling and rhythm. Myers's distinctive style is as graceful as it is powerful. His pictures strongly connect readers to the spirit of Harlem's music, art, literature, and history. The artwork in *Harlem* immediately gained national recognition; the book was designated a 1997 Caldecott Honor Book and a Coretta Scott King Honor Book.

Collage art has appealed to Myers for two reasons. As an artist, he has been interested in taking images and "mixing them, reformulating them, and making them into pictures that convey what I feel and reflect my experiences." Second, collage can be created from readily available, inexpensive materials such as magazines and photographs. "One time I needed a scrap of yellow paper. I went outside and there was the color yellow I needed on a discarded envelope — on my doorstep."

In *Black Cat* (1999), Myers's artwork remains modern, powerful, and surreal, but it is softened by an element of charm. The story, written by the artist for a younger audience than *Harlem*

was, trails a black cat as it explores city spaces. A simple refrain — "Black cat, black cat, we want to know / where's your home, where do you go?" — unifies the text and tantalizes the imagination.

Wings (2000), written and illustrated by Myers, features a contemporary boy, Ikarus Jackson, who is mocked because he has wings and can fly. Then a young friend is awed by his flight and speaks out. Others then see Ikarus from a new perspective and view him with respect, a strong statement about daring to be different and accepting differences in others. S.L.

Myers, Walter Dean

American author, b. 1937. Walter Dean Myers has recalled that when he submitted *Where Does the Day Go?* (1969) to a PICTURE BOOK competition sponsored by the Council on Interracial Books for Children, "it was more because I wanted to write *anything* than because I wanted to write a picture book." Myers won and went on to publish several picture books, as well as two works of nonfiction; he later focused on YOUNG ADULT NOVELS, beginning with *Fast Sam, Cook Clyde, and Stuff* (1975), which chronicles the adventures of a group of friends in Harlem. It reflects, as Myers has said, "the positive side" of his childhood in New York City. Other books in a similar vein include *Mojo and the Russians* (1977), *The Young Landlords* (1979), and *Won't Know Till I Get There* (1982). *Me, Mop, and the Moondance Kid* (1988) and *Mop, Moondance, and the Nagasaki Knights* (1992) follow the fortunes of two adopted brothers, a white girl named Mop, and their Little League ball team. Though these novels have serious moments, they display the engaging sense of humor that also surfaces in Myers's Wild West tale, *The Righteous Revenge of Artemis Bonner* (1992), with its exaggerated, flowery language, and in the clever wordplay in *The Mouse Rap* (1990).

Myers, a versatile writer, has also written powerful, hard-hitting books about contemporary young African Americans. In *Motown and*

Didi: A Love Story (1984), Motown has made surviving on the street into an art, while Didi longs to escape the city. Jamal becomes entangled in an inner-city gang and finds himself in possession of a gun in *Scorpions* (1988). The young soldiers in *Fallen Angels* (1988), a gripping novel about the Vietnam War, must fight to preserve their humanity as well as their lives. *Somewhere in the Darkness* (1992) skillfully explores a troubled father-son relationship. The rhythm of life within one city block in Harlem is honestly portrayed in *145th Street: Short Stories* (2000).

In Myers's landmark novel *Monster* (1999), the story of sixteen-year-old Steve Harmon, accused of felony murder, is told through a personal journal and a screenplay to create an internal and an external perspective, both created by Steve. This innovative approach let Myers explore complex issues and themes authentically. The inaugural Michael L. Printz Award for "literary excellence in young adult literature" was presented to Myers for *Monster* in 2000.

Prior to creating the illustrations for *Monster*, CHRISTOPHER MYERS had collaborated with his father, the author, on another award-winning book. POETRY and image combine in *Harlem* (1997) to present a place, its history, and its people. In *Brown Angels: An Album of Pictures and Verse* (1993), Myers's poetry accompanies turn-of-the-twentieth-century photographs of African American children, collected by the writer himself. Photographs also appear in *At Her Majesty's Request: An African Princess in Victorian England* (1999). Intrigued by nineteenth-century letters available from a London book-and-ephemera shop, Myers created an engaging portrait of a young West African who came under the protection of Queen Victoria.

Careful research characterizes Myers's work. An advocate of looking back in order to progress into the future, Myers has explored history and biography to clarify the present. *Now Is Your Time!: The African American Struggle for Freedom* (1991) combines historical survey, biography, storytelling, and family history. Myers's *Malcolm X: By Any Means Necessary* (1993) and *Malcolm X: A Fire Burning Brightly* (2000) present this complex man to diverse audiences. *The Greatest: Muhammed Ali* (2001) takes an appreciative and candid look at an outstanding athlete. Personal pain and triumphs are shared in Myers's fascinating self-portrait, *Bad Boy: A Memoir* (2001).

Over the years, the prolific Myers has continued to improve his craft, garnering numerous honors. The forthrightness of *Bad Boy*, the unique structure and power of *Monster*, and the emotional honesty of the poetry in *Harlem* provide evidence not only of his commitment to young readers but also his willingness to broaden his scope as a writer. M.B.S.

Voices of the Creators

Walter Dean Myers

When I was a kid in Harlem, I used to imagine that there were two kinds of life, one the life that we kids had, and the other the life of adults. The street life of kids was, to me, especially wonderful. All we needed was an old ball, a piece of chalk, or a tin can, and we would have a game going. We usually played in front of the church, running into the church offices to get a cool drink or a Band-Aid. Away from the streets I would still spend time daydreaming about being a cowboy, or a great ballplayer. Sometimes my imaginary wanderings would be inspired by my grandfather's Bible-based stories or by the scary stories of my stepfather.

Somewhere along the line I discovered that books could be part of a child's world, and by the time I was nine I found myself spending long hours reading in my room. The books began to shape new bouts of imagination. Now I was one of "The Three Musketeers" (always the one in the middle), or participating in the adventures of Jo's boys. John R. Tunis brought me back to sports, and I remember throwing a pink ball against the wall for hours as I struggled through baseball games that existed only in the rich arena of invention.

As a teenager I quickly realized that the world of imagination had its limitations. I wanted a *real* girlfriend, and I wanted more of a social life. Yet I seemed drawn to the life of the mind, and to books. After leaving school and a stint in the army, I bounced around in a series of jobs, none very satisfying, until I finally reached a point where I was writing full time. I was writing fiction primarily, putting my world on paper, exploring the real and imagined lives that comprise my existence. I had found that my real life, the life in which I found my truest self, was the life of the mind. And this life is the one I would use to write my books.

Sometimes, as in *The Revenge of Artemis Bonner,* my imagination has free rein, and I allow it to go where it will, enjoying the journey, delighting in the characters I meet along the way. It is both creation and discovery. The creative process seems to be a synthesis of present thought and the memory of those thoughts and feelings long past. A book like *Somewhere in the Darkness* deals more with imagined feelings and encounters that might have been. Although I did meet my real father, I had never had an intimate moment with him, had never seen him in that wholeness of being with which we get to know people.

Oddly enough, it is my imagination, my novelist's freedom to create characters and situations, that fuels my nonfiction as well. To write *Malcolm X: By Any Means Necessary,* a BIOGRAPHY of the fiery black leader, I played his taped voice constantly, surrounded myself with pictures of him as a boy and as a young man, walked down the same Harlem streets that he walked down, and tried to put myself in his classroom when a teacher said that it wasn't practical for him to be an attorney because of his race. In seeing what Malcolm saw, in allowing his voice to fill my imagination, by touching upon those instances of racism that touched my life and mirrored his, I re-created Malcolm as surely as I have created fictional characters. As I wrote, I felt him looking over my shoulder, and so I could write with a sureness of voice, with an authority that went beyond the factual material.

When my son comes home from college, he finds it amusing to walk into a room to discover me in conversation with imaginary companions, or to see in my face the reflection of some inner dialogue, some adventure of the mind. He has forgotten that the world of the mind has always been my landscape. The stories I told him as a child are the ones that eventually ended up in books and magazines. The broccoli space people that he still remembers have always been important to me, even if they grow less so to him.

What I do with my books is to create windows to my world that all may peer into. I share the images, the feelings and thoughts, and, I hope, the delight. ✄

Mysteries

Suspicious strangers, strange occurrences, secret codes, stashed treasures — few armchair sleuths can resist the challenge of matching their wits alongside those of the protagonists of mysteries for young readers. This strong involvement of readers certainly contributes to the widespread appeal of the genre. Furthermore, mysteries allow young people to experience, vicariously, pulse-quickening elements such as danger, intrigue, and suspense. And mysteries usually place the child investigator, like DONALD J. SOBOL's Encyclopedia Brown, in a position of power by solving crimes that may baffle adults.

The emergence of the mystery genre for young people is a relatively modern phenomenon, dating to the first part of the twentieth century. It owes its existence more to the writings of Wilkie Collins and Agatha Christie than to a traditional juvenile literature. One of the first mysteries written specifically for children, *Emil and the Detectives,* by Erich Kästner, came from Germany in 1930. In the tradition of the youthful detectives who would later emulate him, Emil and his band of friends use their determination and ingenuity to catch a thief, to the great admiration of the Berlin police force. In the past thirty years, the preoccupation of television and other media with mystery and crime detection has resulted in an outpouring of junior whodunits.

Aspects of mysteries cut across the boundaries of many types of juvenile fiction. For example, mysteries occur regularly in LLOYD ALEXANDER'S FANTASIES, such as *The Illyrian Adventure* (1986), and Eleanor Cameron wove a mystery into her contemporary novel *The Court of the Stone Children* (1973). Even those books categorized specifically as mysteries vary greatly in flavor, from the detective novel to stories of the supernatural to HISTORICAL FICTION. The range of mysteries now available for young people is rich and varied enough to suit every taste. These types include the formulaic or plot-driven mystery, which is usually strong on action and suspense; clever and sophisticated puzzles; tests of deduction and problem solving; and multilayered novels in which an element of mystery may simply be a catalyst motivating other themes.

While most children's mysteries are written for the eight- to twelve-year-old group, more and more are being published each year for PICTURE BOOK readers or those who are just beginning to read. Standard mystery conventions such as clues, sidekicks, setbacks, and solutions can all be found, but the plots tend to center on one strand, are not very frightening, and fit understandably into the world of the four- to seven-year-old. Many also have a humorous or witty side. For example, *Piggins* (1987), written by JANE YOLEN and illustrated by Jane Dyer, introduces the upstairs/downstairs world of the very proper Reynard family. When Mrs. Reynard loses her diamond lavaliere at an elegant dinner party, it is Piggins, the portly and imperturbable butler, who saves the day with his clever deductions. Elegant and detailed, the illustrations do their part not only to describe the Edwardian milieu but to give sharp-eyed readers pertinent visual clues.

Aimed at beginning readers, *Nate the Great* (1972), written by MARJORIE WEINMAN SHARMAT and illustrated by MARC SIMONT, features a self-styled detective, who, along with his faithful dog, Sludge, has built a reputation among his peers for finding lost objects. Dressed in the garb of Sherlock Holmes, Nate delivers his pithy observations in the deadpan voice of a young Sam Spade. This terse style works well with the simple vocabulary.

Female detectives, full of ingenuity and spirit, are well represented in mysteries for the youngest. *Something Queer at the Library* (1977) is one of a series of lively mysteries written by Elizabeth Levy and illustrated by Mordicai Gerstein, featuring two exuberant girl sleuths, Gwen and Jill. The zesty style of the story is complemented by humorous line drawings that make the most of every situation. In *Jane Martin, Dog Detective* (1984), written by EVE BUNTING and illustrated by AMY SCHWARTZ, the young female sleuth finds two missing dogs and clears the name of a third whose reputation has been wrongfully sullied. Jane charges twenty-five cents a day to do her sleuthing, while her mother tails the suspects at night. But true to the junior mystery convention, it is Jane who always solves her case. *Encyclopedia Brown, Boy Detective* (1963) and the many other books in the series by Donald J. Sobol have long been a staple for new independent readers who wish to match their wits with a genius who has an encyclopedic memory. With the publication of David Adler's *Cam Jansen and the Mystery of the Dinosaur Bones* (1981), readers were introduced to Encyclopedia Brown's counterpart, a female sleuth, who with a photographic memory remembers facts as if she had taken pictures of them.

For those who enjoy observation and deduction, Sherlock Holmes still lives in a number of juvenile spinoffs. Robert Newman's *The Case of the Baker Street Irregulars* (1978) is the first in a series featuring a group of poor London neighborhood children who do special errands for Holmes. Using techniques modeled after the feats of reasoning found in Conan Doyle's original stories, the plot combines a group of sinister characters to be outwitted and a series of seemingly disparate strands that keep the suspense high until Holmes ties it all together. Also, in a humorous parody of Holmes for younger children, Eve Titus developed a series featuring Basil the English mouse detective, who studied at the feet of Holmes. In *Basil of Baker Street* (1958), his friend and associate Dr. Dawson tells how Basil solves a baffling kidnapping case, restores the children to their parents, and brings the dangerous kidnappers to justice.

Animal characters such as Basil can be marvelous detectives. Acting like humans, they are part of a familiar tradition within children's literature that borders as much on animal fantasy as on mystery. With the publication of *Bunnicula, a Rabbit Tale of Mystery* (1979), Deborah and JAMES HOWE achieved new levels of sophisticated wit in their combination mystery/animal fantasy. When the household vegetables are drained of their juices and turn white overnight, Chester (the family's bookish cat who sits up nights reading Edgar Allan Poe) is convinced that the family's new pet rabbit, which popped up in the local theater one night, is actually a vampire bunny. Chester enlists the help of the dog, Harold, in getting to the bottom of the mystery. With an abundant dose of puns, slapstick humor, and wild chases, the mysterious adventures of Harold and Chester are continued in *The Howliday Inn* (1982) and *Nightly Nightmare* (1987).

JAMES MARSHALL is another writer who had a grand time placing animal characters in mysterious situations. In his first novel, *A Summer in the South* (1977), a hilarious spoof set at a resort, a ghostly figure tries to frighten the tender actress Marietta Chicken. Readers will discover that it is one of the hotel guests, the renowned detective Eleanor Owl (a Miss Marple lookalike), who exposes the culprit with the aid of the hotel's assortment of zany guests.

Humor can serve as both a tension reliever and a source of entertainment, and when authors such as Marshall and the Howes combine humor and mystery, they create a winning combination of the two most sought-after subjects by children. Newbery Medal winner PHYLLIS REYNOLDS NAYLOR also used humor to provide

comic relief in *The Bodies in the Bessledorf Hotel* (1986). As Bernie Magruder saves his father's job as hotel manager by nabbing the person who has been planting dead bodies throughout the hotel, Naylor used standard mystery conventions such as cliff-hanging chapter endings and a number of red herrings to keep the well-constructed story moving. Another Newbery Medal–winning author, SID FLEISCHMAN, dabbled in lighthearted, easy-to-read fare in a series created for the Children's Television Workshop, featuring the Bloodhound Gang. In *The Case of the Cackling Ghost* (1981) the gang is hired by rich Mrs. Fairbanks to sort out the curse of the Darjeeling Necklace. Ranging in ages from ten to sixteen, the gang acts believably in a professional manner, entirely without the benefit of adults (payment for the services is never mentioned), and Fleischman, himself a professional magician, added a touch of hocus-pocus to the solution.

There is humor, too, in Eve Rice's *The Remarkable Return of Winston Potter Crisply* (1978), but it is the setting that distinguishes this mystery romp through Manhattan. When Becky and Max discover that their older brother is not at Harvard but is skulking about the Big Apple in a black cape, they trail him. Based on pieces of evidence, they suspect he is the central figure in a CIA case, but after many twists and turns of the plot, they discover a far different truth.

Setting not only provides a rich backdrop but is crucial to the plot of *The December Rose* (1987), a historical mystery written by the British novelist Leon Garfield and set in Victorian London. Barnacle, a chimney sweep, mistakenly falls down the wrong flue, tumbling headfirst into a skullduggerous plot involving international intrigue. The authentic British dialect gives the flavor of the period, and the memorable images, unusually well drawn characters, and hair-raising escapades make this picturesque novel both a page-turner and a literary delight. Another historical mystery with an equally strong sense of place is Avi's complex novel *The Man Who Was Poe* (1989). Drawing upon historical facts known about the time Edgar Allan Poe spent in Providence, Rhode Island, the author spun the story of young Edmund, who in 1848 finds himself alone after both his aunt and sister mysteriously vanish. Seeing a possible story in Edmund's predicament, Poe promises to help the boy. Cryptic clues and Poe's brilliant, if at times irrational, behavior sustain the high suspense in this engrossing novel.

While set in present-day Ohio, VIRGINIA HAMILTON's modern classic *The House of Dies Drear* (1968) adroitly blends history, mystery, and lost treasure in a beautifully taut story. Moving into the Drear house has had a profound effect on Thomas Small and his family. It is a former station on the Underground Railroad, filled with a labyrinth of tunnels, concealed closets, springs and locks, and the ghosts of former slaves. Hamilton's absorbing story is filled with delicious tension as well as meaningful personal relationships, and the dramatic denouement is highly satisfying. Almost twenty years later, Hamilton concluded the Dies Drear chronicle with *The Mystery of Drear House* (1987). Another mystery that makes important historical connections to a present-day black community is Eleanora E. Tate's *The Secret of Gumbo Grove* (1987). Twelve-year-old Raisin Stackhouse is full of gumption and community spirit, so it is not surprising that Miss Ellie (the aging church secretary out to save the cemetery) selects Raisin to help her make the black community recognize their history. The portrait of the town characters and several subplots involving sibling and family relationships serve to make this more than just a mystery.

Like the writers of historical mysteries who use facts for the foundation of their tales, writers of informational mysteries draw upon pertinent research to authenticate their novels. At the height of the fight to ban DDT, naturalist JEAN CRAIGHEAD GEORGE wrote a unique ecology mystery titled *Who Really Killed Cock Robin?* (1971; reissued with a new introduction in 1991). When the town's prized robin dies on the mayor's front lawn, environmental detective Tony Isidoro, assisted by his sidekick, Mary Alice

Lamberty, uses scientific methods and determination to describe and trace the ecological imbalances that caused the bird's death. George, who "sees all of nature as a mystery," works a good deal of sound ecological information into her novel and humorously delivers it in the manner of a hard-boiled detective. Another mystery laced with ecology information for younger readers is *Elisabeth and the Marsh Mystery* (1966) written by Felice Holman. Elisabeth, her father, Mr. Threw from the wildlife museum, and Elisabeth's friend Stewart search for the source of spooky sounds coming from the marsh. Through their humorous efforts they find that the culprit is a sandhill crane that has become lost while migrating.

Some juvenile mysteries border on novels of the occult and the supernatural. JOHN BELLAIRS, for one, has been particularly skillful at blending mystery, sorcery, and the macabre, while adding a touch of humor to the cauldron. In the first novel featuring the orphan Lewis, *The House with a Clock in Its Walls* (1973), Lewis discovers that his Uncle Jonathan is a wizard, that the next-door neighbor is a witch, and that there is a magic clock hidden in the walls of his uncle's mansion, ticking away the hours to doomsday. Here the time element is used as an effective device in maintaining suspense. Betty Ren Wright's novels also contain satisfying touches of the supernatural. In *The Dollhouse Murders* (1984), Wright gave an added dimension to the spooky story by melding twelve-year-old Emily's family concerns with the solution to a mysterious murder that happened long ago.

Wright, like many mystery writers for the young, conveniently has relegated her murders to the past. While crimes such as shoplifting, kidnapping, dope smuggling, and terrorism do occur in juvenile novels, violence is kept at a minimum and murder is usually avoided or committed "off-stage." A novel that broke with this tradition is *The View from the Cherry Tree* (1975), written by Willo Davis Roberts. Here eleven-year-old Rob witnesses the murder of the old lady next door, and because no adult will pay attention to his story, he narrowly misses becoming the killer's next victim. There are some implausible plot elements, but it is still a chilling tale with real suspense and danger.

Readers are told that a murder has been committed in ELLEN RASKIN's unparalleled mystery puzzle, *The Westing Game* (1978), but the crime here is more cerebral, for all is not what it appears to be in this Newbery Medal–winning novel. Offering the ultimate challenge for those who love to reason through a highly intricate plot, Raskin assembled an unconventional group of sixteen characters who are possible heirs to Samuel Westing's fortune. In the Christie tradition, the heirs are isolated, then paired off and given clues to a puzzle they must solve, but "some are not who they say they are, and some are not who they seem to be." Admitting her "strong aversion to the obvious," Raskin indulged in developing shifting identities, enigmatic clues, and a surprisingly sympathetic set of eccentric characters in this complex tour de force.

While Raskin's novels represent the height of sophisticated mental games, few books intertwine mystery and imaginative play with as much originality as ZILPHA KEATLEY SNYDER's *The Egypt Game* (1967). Fascinated with Egypt, an ethnically diverse group of neighborhood children re-create the ancient world in a deserted storage yard, a world complete with hieroglyphics, oracles, evil gods, and ceremonies. But a murderer is terrorizing the neighborhood and, in a frightening climax, it is the Egypt game that leads to his capture. But beyond the mystery, the importance of the make-believe world is evident. "It had been a place to get away to — a private lair — a secret seclusion meant to be shared with best friends only." It was a game "full of excitement and way out imagining" that greatly affects the lives of the children.

Many juvenile novels contain imaginative writing with mystery as the underpinning, providing a rewarding literary experience for readers. *The Way to Sattin Shore* (1983), written by the distinguished British writer PHILIPPA PEARCE, is a beautifully crafted FAMILY STORY with rare emotional depth; the element of mystery simply propels the plot. Kate Tranter, the youngest in her family, discovers some incongruities about her father's death and sets out to learn the truth. The elegant prose and the understated pace of the unfolding events belie the mounting tension as Kate slowly uncovers each piece of her family's hidden secret.

Another skilled stylist, the American writer NATALIE BABBITT, placed mysterious elements in many of her highly regarded novels. But in *Goody Hall* (1971), the mystery is unabashedly full-blown. This witty gothic mystery involves ten-year-old Willett Goody and his tutor, the erstwhile actor Hercules Feltwright, in an Odyssey-like search for the whereabouts of Willett's father. Impersonation, robbery, stolen jewels, empty coffins, gypsy seances, and a cast of characters with names like Alfresco Rom keep the unpredictable plot boiling. The climax is dramatic and satisfying, with all the loose ends tied together and a moral on human behavior thrown in for good measure.

Like *Goody Hall*, Vivien Alcock's novel *The Mysterious Mr. Ross* (1987) is often described as a gothic mystery, but it has an unusual twist, for here the mystery is never solved. Twelve-year-old Felicity, who is clumsy and insecure and can never manage to get things right, becomes a heroine overnight when she rescues a young man from a dangerous tide near her English seaside home. Cleverly, Alcock never revealed the man's identity but allowed his presence to irrevocably change the lives of Felicity and her family. Alcock has a knack of imbuing commonplace situations with mysterious touches, and her characters, even the minor ones, are fully realized.

The popularity of the mystery genre continues unabated, and many are published each year for children. The majority tend to fall into the comforting familiarity of a series format or to rely heavily on action-filled plots. Few match the inventive game playing of Ellen Raskin. Occasionally an author comes along, like Annette Curtis Klause, with a totally fresh approach to the mystery genre. Klause's novel *Alien Secrets* (1993) playfully integrates a mystery and a ghost story into a SCIENCE FICTION setting. Novels like this satisfy the necessary thrills of the mystery genre, while providing originality of narrative, fully developed characters, and a stylistic wit and grace that places them alongside the finest novels written for young people. C.W.

N

Namioka, Lensey

Chinese American author, b. 1929. When Lensey Namioka began writing fiction in the 1970s, she didn't realize she was writing for children. She just wrote what she liked to read: adventure stories filled with action, mystery, and suspense. As a child she found such stories in her mother's collection of Chinese pulp novels, and she and her sisters made up their own tales of valiant sword-fighting outlaws to amuse one another after the family's move to the United States during World War II.

Later, after she had been a freelance writer and translator for a number of years, her Japanese father-in-law introduced her to Japanese adventure stories about *ronin,* unemployed samurai, who wandered the country, getting into scrapes. He also told her the ghostly legends surrounding the castle in his hometown of Himeji. Both provided the inspiration for *White Serpent Castle* (1976), the first of Namioka's samurai books, which take place in feudal Japan and feature Zenta and Matsuzo, a duo of *ronin* with a relationship not unlike that of Sherlock Holmes and Dr. Watson. Master swordsman Zenta can usually solve a mystery before anyone else has sorted out the clues. And Matsuzo, the more romantic of the two, remains loyal to his teacher even when he questions his actions. Besides

fighting sinister villains such as the one murdering young girls in *Village of the Vampire Cat* (1981) or discovering the men behind the supposed monsters in *Island of Ogres* (1989), Zenta and Matsuzo teach readers by example about the honor code of the samurai.

Each of Namioka's samurai books acts as a window into ancient Japan, revealing the food, dress, customs, and lifestyle of the different social classes, from peasants to royalty. In *The Coming of the Bear* (1992) Zenta and Matsuzo come to accept, if not wholly embrace, a foreign culture when they are shipwrecked on the northern Japanese island of Hokkaido and rescued by the Ainus, hunter-gatherers who once inhabited all of Japan.

When Namioka's editor suggested that she try her hand at realistic fiction, she drew upon her own experience in adapting to a foreign culture. Set in the 1950s, *Who's Hu?* (1981) recounts the sometimes humorous dilemmas of Emma Hu, a Chinese teenager trying to fit in at her high school in Massachusetts. As a girl who likes math, Emma gets hassled by the other students, who think she should spend less time working equations and more time preparing for the prom. Namioka received similar treatment in high school but went on to major in math in college and to teach math at the college level before turning to writing. She believes her mathematics background lends a thriftiness to her writing, born of a desire not to waste a word or, in her MYSTERY stories, a clue.

Yang the Eldest and His Odd Jobs (2000), *Yang the Second and Her Secret Admirers* (1998), and *Yang the Youngest and His Terrible Ear* (1992) continue the theme of tolerance. In *Yang the Youngest,* Yang's whole family is musical, and Yang's parents push him to continue his violin lessons, hoping that with practice he will learn to carry a tune. But Yang feels more at home on the baseball diamond than at a recital and finally convinces his father to let him trade his violin for a bat in a prank gone comically awry, a scene consistent with Namioka's belief that the more important an author's message, the more fun her book should be. C.M.H.

Napoli, Donna Jo

American author, b. 1948. Donna Jo Napoli, author of close to forty books for young people, is also head of the linguistics department at Swarthmore College and mother to five children. She grew up in and around Miami, Florida, in a home devoid of books until she herself discovered the library in second grade. She became an avid reader and scholar, thriving in school. Napoli went on to Harvard University, where she studied mathematics and Romance linguistics.

After college, she taught mathematics, Italian, and philosophy as well as linguistics. She did not begin to write fiction for children until years later. Her first published book was *The Hero of Barletta* (1988), a brief, humorous retelling of an Italian folktale about a giant. Napoli had mixed feelings about its success because she feared she was capable of telling only traditional tales, not stories of her own. She has since written several original stories. One of these, *The Bravest Thing* (1995), tells the touching and funny tale of a ten-year-old girl's attempts to breed rabbits. In another, *Stones in Water* (1997), the character Roberto, an Italian boy, is taken by Nazis during World War II and forced to work in a military camp.

Like most of Napoli's books, *Stones in Water* deals with linguistic as well as emotional issues. Nazis separate the Italian boys in the work camp into groups in which no two boys come from the same town; without a common local dialect, the boys are kept at a distance from each other. Roberto eventually runs away from the camp and manages to build relationships with people who do not share his language at all. Napoli's exploration of the power of language is thought provoking and organic to the story.

Still, Napoli is best known for adapting fairy tales. She adds depth and history to these stories, making them entirely her own. In *Zel* (1996), she has crafted a mature, multilayered retelling of the story of Rapunzel, alternating points of view among Rapunzel (called Zel), the witch, and the prince. The witch plays the part of a desperate, overinvolved mother who can't accept her daughter's coming adolescence and their inevitable separation. *The Magic Circle* (1993) also deals with mother-daughter relationships. Here Napoli has told the story of Hansel and Gretel's witch, a woman who uses magic to heal others. She summons demons away from the bodies of sick people until one of them curses her with a desire to eat children. She is forced to leave her beloved daughter and hide in the woods. Then Hansel and Gretel arrive, seeking shelter, and she develops a twisted, motherly relationship with Gretel, as she longs for her own lost daughter. When Gretel finally pushes her into the oven, it is at the witch's urging — a suicidal redemption.

Not all of Napoli's fairy tales are dark; one of her first books, *The Prince of the Pond (Otherwise Known as De Fawg Pin)* (1992), tells of a prince turned frog, learning the ways of the pond. In this book she again demonstrated her passion for nuances of language use — the frog prince has a speech impediment that reflects how a human might speak if dealing with an unfamiliar frog's tongue.

Recently, Napoli has written books for younger children. The Angelwings series of CHAPTER BOOKS features angels who earn their wings helping children through rough times. In each story, the angel, as well as the child, has a lesson to learn.

Rich in its own language as well as in language-based themes, each new book by Napoli presents complicated characters who show us new ways to look at the world. J.P.

Naylor, Phyllis Reynolds

American author, b. 1933. Because she had always been an avid writer, Phyllis Reynolds Naylor was delighted when, as a teenager, some of her works were published in a church paper. Bolstered by this success, she submitted short stories to children's magazines, only to have them rejected. She quickly realized that writing was a demanding business. Naylor married when she was eighteen, received an associate degree from Indiana's Joliet Junior College in Illinois, and moved to Chicago, where her husband planned to pursue a master's degree. She worked as a clinical secretary, taught third grade, and wrote. When the onset of her husband's illness created the need for additional money to cover living expenses and the cost of his treatments, she accelerated her submissions to various magazines. After she and her husband divorced, she married Rex Naylor and returned to college to become a clinical psychologist. Although she received a B.A. in psychology from American University, she realized that writing full-time was her greatest desire.

Since the publication of her first children's book, *What the Gulls Were Singing* (1967), Naylor has produced one to two books annually, encompassing a broad range of topics. Acute sensitivity to childhood and teenage experiences has made her the successful author of over seventy books, both fiction and nonfiction. Naylor loves variety but has admitted to being partial to suspenseful tales. She has spiced her MYSTERIES with numerous seasonings: the Besseldorf SERIES, with humor; the York series, with FANTASY, time travel, and the search for a cure for hereditary Huntington's disease; and the compelling six books of the Witch series, with fantasy and the occult. Naylor's serious topics include coping with parental divorce (*The Solomon System*, 1983); crib death and loss of religious faith (*A String of Chances*, 1982); living with a mentally ill father, based on the ordeal of her first marriage (*The Keeper*, 1986); teenage rebellion (*No Easy Circle*, 1972); watching a mother die from cancer (*The Dark of the Tunnel*, 1985); and the anguish of being a middle child (*Maudie in the Middle*, 1988). On the lighter side, experiments in an annual school science contest, in *Beetles, Lightly Toasted* (1987), result in unusual lunches for unsuspecting classmates, and *Eddie, Incorporated* (1980) explores the trials and tribulations of an eleven-year-old's attempts to start his own business. The delightful Alice series focuses on a spunky preteen girl's search for a female role model.

Naylor's acute observations of human nature make her books touching, comical, and uplifting. While facing one's fears is the underlying theme in Naylor's narratives, family issues, getting along with others, and moral values are also strong elements. Naylor has allowed her characters to evolve intellectually, socially, and morally. She has focused on those first moments of awareness young people experience and also examines the parameters of right and wrong, placing her protagonists in situations where they must rely on their own judgments. Naylor has portrayed life as a series of compromises and offers her readers a view of life as a multifaceted, unfolding adventure, a growing experience, and a challenge.

Naylor is the recipient of many awards, including the Edgar Allan Poe Award from the Mystery Writers of America for her children's thriller *Night Cry* in 1985, and a Creative Writing Fellowship Grant from the National Endowment for the Arts (1987). In 1991 she received the Newbery Medal for *Shiloh*, the compelling story of a boy's attempt to save an abused dog while discovering that life is not fair, no one is perfect, and compromise is a necessary art. S.R.

Nesbit, E.

British author, 1858–1924. One wonders if Edith Nesbit was at all aware of just how unconventional her children's novels were and that they would determine the direction for both realistic FAMILY STORIES and FANTASY in the twentieth century. What set her books apart from those that preceded them was that Nesbit did away with the didacticism prevalent in Victorian children's books, which sought to "improve" young readers. Nesbit's narrators don't talk down to children; Nesbit spoke to her readers as respected and admired equals. Her characters — imaginative, intelligent, strong-willed individuals — are well intentioned if not always well behaved: they are real children with whom readers identify and empathize. Nesbit's fantasy novels combine her successful formula for the realistic family story with the added enticement of magic. Unlike fantasies of the past, her stories take place in the everyday world of Edwardian

England, not in a make-believe fairyland. Nesbit did not sentimentalize children and childhood. She once wrote: "When I was a little child I used to pray fervently, tearfully, that when I should be grown up I might never forget what I thought, felt, and suffered then."

As a child, Nesbit was said to have been a rebellious tomboy with a great imagination and a passion for reading and writing. Her father, who ran a London agricultural college, died when she was three, and she was raised by her mother along with four older brothers and sisters. When she was fifteen years old, a newspaper published some of her verses, and she began to dream of becoming a poet. A few years later, soon after her marriage to businessman Hubert Bland, her comfortable Victorian life took a turn when Bland, seriously ill with smallpox, lost his money when his partner absconded with the business's funds. It fell to Nesbit to support her small family. For the next nineteen years, she poured out a stream of novels, essays, articles, poems, greeting card verses, and short stories. Most of her work during that time was not memorable and today would be judged as highly sentimental.

Nesbit's first successful book for children was published in 1899, and nothing she had written before anticipated it. *The Story of the Treasure Seekers* essentially launched her career as a children's author. In this book, the motherless Bastable children decide to search for treasure to restore the family fortune after the failure of their father's business, and their attempts result in many humorous disasters. Two sequels, *The Wouldbegoods* (1901) and *The New Treasure Seekers* (1904), continued the comic misadventures of the Bastable children. Of the three, *The Wouldbegoods* is the best tribute to a theme in many of Nesbit's books: the power of literature and the imagination. The Bastables are well read and highly imaginative. Their delight in pretending and make-believe, as inspired by stories, is contagious. In *The Railway Children* (1906), reality, merely a device lending credibility in the Bastable stories, has a darker side. Bobbie, Phyllis, and Peter have to move with their mother to a smaller house in the country because not only has the family fallen into financial difficulties, but their father is in prison. Through their adventures at a nearby railroad station the children are able to amuse themselves and cope valiantly with their situation.

Five Children and It (1902) was the first of Nesbit's fantasy novels. Set in contemporary England, this book must have been enchanting fare for young readers who solemnly believed magic was all around them, if only they knew where to look. The children in the story discover not a beautiful fairy godmother but an ill-tempered, odd-looking creature called a Psammead. The Psammead (often unwillingly) grants their wishes — not without short-lived, comic results — and the children learn that getting what one wishes for is not the key to happiness. In the sequels *The Phoenix and the Carpet* (1904) and *The Story of the Amulet* (1906), the fantasy and humor are more and more refined. *The Enchanted Castle* (1907) is in many ways the most sophisticated achievement of Nesbit's career. It shares the same elements of Nesbit's other successful fantasy novels, yet the magic in this book is more mysterious and, at times, terrifying. The children's wishes produce unexpected and often undesirable results, and their attempts to understand the rules of the magic are frustratingly in vain.

Nesbit continued writing until her death from a bronchial illness. While her children's stories brought her fame and wealth, ironically, her true ambition was to be a poet, and she always regretted that she had not spent more time on her poetry. Nevertheless, her influence on twentieth-century British and American children's literature has been widely acknowledged; perhaps it was the naiveté of her own genius that freed her to produce such lasting and beloved classics. K.F.

Ness, Evaline

American illustrator and author, 1911–1986. Evaline Ness, author and illustrator of the 1967 Caldecott Medal–winning *Sam, Bangs, and Moonshine,* was a well-established studio artist and a highly paid commercial artist when she was first asked to illustrate a children's manuscript. She recalled, "[It was] so unlike the frantic hot-air environment of advertising production [that] I never went back to the 'rat-race' again." She found that every manuscript — like Sorche Nic Leodhas's *All in the Morning Early* (1963) and Rebecca Caudill's *A Pocketful of Cricket* (1964) — offered new challenges, new opportunities to strengthen existing skills and experiment with new techniques. But this outpouring of originality was a far cry from her youthful efforts in Pontiac, Michigan: "As soon as I was able to read and write, I copied down my favorite stories on the hundred-yard rolls of white paper that backs ribbons. . . . And with that same critical industry, I searched through magazines to find appropriate pictures to illustrate stories . . . [a] sister turned out daily. It never occurred to me to compete with ready-made words and pictures."

It was only as a young woman that Ness decided, on a whim, to be a commercial artist. She took several wrong turns — most notably enrolling in the fine arts department of the Art Institute of Chicago instead of the commercial art department because she didn't know the difference — before beginning a limping artistic career. There followed years of apprenticeship, course work, and learning fundamentals, in Chicago, New York, and Washington, D.C.; but as her skills grew, so did her ambition. Eventually the effort paid off: Ness got her break back in New York illustrating for *Seventeen* magazine and then fashion drawing for Saks Fifth Avenue department store. She became successful and her work was very well paid, but it was grueling. No wonder she found such relief in children's books.

Ness began writing when she created a text for some woodcuts set in Haiti: *Josefina February* (1963) is the simple tale of a girl's search for a lost burro. *Sam, Bangs, and Moonshine* began with some portfolio drawings, one of a "shabby misplaced child" and several of fishing boats. The story came from nowhere: the tale of a girl whose "reckless habit of lying" almost causes a tragedy. The daughter of a fisherman, motherless Samantha ("always called Sam") lives in a fantasy world with her talking cat, Bangs. But her announcement that a pet kangaroo is visiting her mermaid-mother at Blue Rock almost causes the drowning of her gullible young friend, Thomas. The scare finally enables Sam to distinguish between reality and "moonshine." Some Ness texts, such as the English folktale retellings *Mr. Miacca* (1967) and *The Girl and the Goatherd* (1970), are criticized for their weak plots, but she gets praise, especially with her original tales, for economical language, sprightly storytelling, and skillful interweaving of art and words. A Ness hallmark is the uncanny match between story and technique — whether in the woodcuts of *Josefina February*, set in the Caribbean; the ink and color wash of *Sam, Bangs, and Moonshine*, with its Mediterranean setting; or the contemporary world of Lucille Clifton's *Some of the Days of Everett Anderson* (1970). Ness's selection of medium is skillful whether she is working with her own text or the words of others. The child once content to play with copied words and pasted pictures became an artist admired for her range of skill and craftsmanship, her continual experimentation and growth, and her freshness and originality.

S.A.B.

Newberry, Clare Turlay

American author and illustrator, 1903–1970. Clare Turlay Newberry always lived with and loved cats. As a child, she included them in all her drawings. Born and raised in Eugene, Oregon, Newberry attended the University of Oregon for one year, then pursued but never completed her academic studies in art, finding that she worked best alone. In 1930, on the eve of her departure to study in Paris, Newberry wrote a story about a little girl, Sally, who adamantly wanted and received a lion for her birthday. In order to earn return passage, Newberry illustrated the story. *Herbert the Lion* (1931), Newberry's first PICTURE BOOK for children, met with immediate popularity and acclaim. While living in New York City, Newberry's original plan to make her fortune in portraiture failed, but not her determination to make art her life's endeavor.

In 1934 she turned to the subject that had fascinated her all her life and that became her hallmark: cats. Her ownership, observation, and love of felines naturally led to her incorporating their antics and poses in her books: the tucked paws and pure contentment of a dozing cat; the irritable tail twitch of a harried one; the ornery, mischievous glare in a feisty cat's eyes; the frisky romping and tumbling of kittens. Her cats looked so alive, they could have stepped out of her books. In 1936, *Mittens*, the first of many books in which Newberry relied on her own cats and children as models, introduced her as an artist-illustrator who knew how to appeal to both young children and the parents who read to them. Her subtle humor, straightforward dialogue, and simple plots were elemental to her success. Four of her works were named Caldecott Honor Books: *Barkis* (1938), about a sister's spiteful antics, which endanger her brother's new puppy; *April's Kittens* (1940), about a family who must resolve how they will keep an extra kitten in a one-cat apartment; *Marshmallow* (1942), about a baby rabbit who endears himself to a confirmed bachelor cat; and *T-Bone the Baby-Sitter* (1950), about a usually reliable cat who experiences spring fever. *Mittens*, Newberry's bestseller about a six-year-old boy whose ad for his lost kitten brings unexpected results, was chosen as one of the Fifty Books of the Year by the American Institute of Graphic Arts. While the body of Newberry's work involves cat protagonists, the puppy in *Barkis* and the baby rabbit in *Marshmallow* are equally unforgettable.

Although Newberry took her subjects from real life and customarily worked in watercolors, pencil, or Conté crayons, two of her books stylistically depart from this format. Both *Herbert the Lion* and *Lambert's Bargain* (1941), a wonderfully funny story about the problems that ensue when a brother is talked into accepting a hyena

as a birthday gift for his little sister, are fantasies drawn in line figures. For Newberry, daily life with its ironic humor and challenges between parents and young children who want pets provided inspirational grist for seventeen stories, most of which were about or included cats. In the field of children's literature, Clare Turlay Newberry and cats have become nearly synonymous. S.R.

Newell, Peter

American humorist and illustrator, 1862–1924. Peter Newell drew like no one else and created PICTURE BOOKS like no others. A humorist famously sober of mien, he was a true original.

Two anecdotes are always told about Newell — stories that, poker-faced, he liked to tell about himself. As a young tyro in a small Illinois town, he sent a humorous drawing to the editor of *Harper's Bazaar* with a note asking if it showed talent. "No talent indicated," came the reply, but a check was enclosed. Sales to other magazines took him to New York and a few months' formal study before he decided to remain unschooled and unassimilated, or, to his way of thinking, himself.

He was, however, a thoroughgoing professional. Capitalizing on the new method of halftone reproduction, he introduced in America the technique of drawing in flat halftone washes developed by the French illustrator Maurice Boutet de Monvel, and, for maximum effect at minimum cost, he planned many of his illustrations to be printed in black and white with a single second color each, a practice that later became common. His plain-as-plain style, with its moon-faced, popeyed, goblinlike figures, looked decidedly spooky to some and like no style at all to many. But as the graphic arts connoisseur Philip Hofer pointed out, "He used simple means because he liked simple subjects. Probably he chose both because he was thinking of his audience: children, and grown-ups who retain their youth."

Illustration by Peter Newell from *The Rocket Book* (1912).

Much of Newell's work has that dual appeal. His first big success was an illustrated nonsense jingle, "Wild Flowers," which appeared in *Harper's* magazine in August 1893. A solicitous schoolmaster bends over a trembling little girl: "'Of what are you afraid, my child?' inquired / the kindly teacher. / 'Oh, sir! the flowers, they are wild,' / replied the timid creature."

At the same time he illustrated books: nonsense for all and sundry by Guy Wetmore Carryl and Caroline Wells; the absurdist humor of John Kendrick Bangs's *Houseboat on the Styx* (1896) and its sequel, *The Pursuit of the Houseboat* (1897); and, following LEWIS CARROLL's death in 1898 and the end of his copyright control, *Alice's Adventures in Wonderland* (1901) and *Through the Looking Glass* (1902).

Newell's *Alice,* the most prominent of four new American editions issued between 1899 and 1904, was roundly denounced and just as firmly if less widely defended, with Newell himself taking the lead in favor of fresh interpretations. Today, after a century of *Alice in Wonderland*

makeovers by artists of every bent, Newell's formalized compositions and histrionic airs look considerably less peculiar and often quite aptly comical.

His third major sphere of activity, the making of picture books, came about by chance, though given his inventiveness, hardly by accident. As the cherished Newell anecdote goes, he spotted one of his offspring looking at a picture book upside down and determined to produce a book that could be turned around. The result was *Topsys and Turvys* (1893), which is reversible page by page. Thus, "In sandy groves Adolphus swings when Summer zephyrs blow" reverses to become "And slides headforemost down the hill when Winter brings the snow." Acclaim was immediate, and a second series of *Topsys and Turvys* appeared the next year.

How *The Hole Book* (1908) came about we do not know, or need to. Of picture book inventions, it comes close to sheer, ungimmicky inspiration; among novelties, it is one of the few with perennial appeal. The fun starts on the cover, as a procession of boys and girls approaches a tantalizing hole straight down into the interior; who, then, can resist the invitation to "OPEN THE BOOK AND FOLLOW THE HOLE." Inside a boy accidentally shoots off a gun and the bullet makes a flying entrance into scene after peaceful scene, cutting the rope of a backyard swing, shattering a goldfish bowl, sending a high silk hat a-sailing via a hole cut in each page. An instantaneous hit, so to speak, *The Hole Book* led Newell into other innovations in format. *The Slant Book* (1910), in the shape of a parallelogram, with pictures and verses on the diagonal, has a runaway baby carriage spilling the contents of a pushcart, tumbling a painter from his ladder (with messy results for a passer-by), literally slicing through a watermelon patch — all to the intense delight of the infant passenger. *The Rocket Book* (1912) repeats the pattern of *The Hole Book* on the vertical, as a rocket set off by the janitor's son Fritz in the basement shoots up through the twenty-one stories of the apartment house, causing predictable and unpredictable havoc among the social types en route.

Philip Hofer, a Newell fan, saw in his work

admirable, all-American slapstick. American-art historian Edgar Richardson discerned in Newell a forerunner of "the gentle humor of the absurd" later cultivated in the *New Yorker*. Both, of course, were right. B.B.

Nonfiction

See INFORMATION BOOKS.

Norton, André

American author, b. 1912. A prolific writer of SCIENCE FICTION and FANTASY for children and adults, André Norton has more than a hundred books to her credit, many of them still in print. Her first, *The Prince Commands,* came out in 1934; a historical fantasy, it was the third novel she had written, and she was not yet twenty-one when it was published. Because female adventure/science fiction writers were not being published at the time, she legally changed her name from Alice Mary Norton to André Norton.

When she began writing it was taboo to use female protagonists, so she developed strong male characters with rough, dynamic personalities. When she ventured into the realm of women as main characters (a vanguard in sci-fi publishing), they were equally powerful, inventive, curious, and courageous. Indeed, in the best of her books, it is the characters and their internal, interpersonal, and intercultural conflicts that become the life force of the story, rather than the more technical scientific aspects that dominate much science fiction.

Norton is one of the first writers for young people who casually used characters of many nationalities and races in her stories. One fantasy novel for younger readers, *Lavender-Green Magic* (1974), is about a black family that is relocated from its integrated Boston neighborhood into an all-white suburb. Magic from the witches of the past helps Holly accept herself and allow people to accept her. Although the portrayal of racism is simplistic, it is admirable

that Norton attempted it when she did. Norton did not set out to write books in a series, though many have continuous plots and characters, as in the Witch World books that began in 1963, a series of nearly twenty sword-and-sorcery fantasies, the most recent of which is *Flight of Vengeance* (1992). Most of the science fiction titles are, if not siblings, cousins. Norton used the same language and the same assumptions about the universe, so when one enters a book, the territory is familiar. But the invented galactic logic is grounded by a rich base in Western mythology and history, and familiar stories are rewoven in stellar patterns. In her short book *Outside* (1974), the pattern is based on the tale of the Pied Piper, as a magical minstrel gathers up the children and leads them outside the enclosed city sphere. The air inside is becoming fouled, and the outside, which once was hazardous due to nuclear fallout, now has regenerated itself into a green and promising land.

Norton has centered her stories on familiar, human themes. Her characters are often loners who, through the events of each book, reach a certain maturity. In *The Time Traders* (1958), one of several books in the Time Travel series, Ross Murdock is arrested and, instead of getting a jail sentence, is given over to an experimental process. Steeped in a cold war atmosphere, the book depicts brave men traveling through time into prehistory and discovering alien spaceships among Bronze Age peoples.

Norton's later novels become more sophisticated, crossing myth with history and a projected future. In *Forerunner Foray* (1973) Ziantha is a young woman trained in the sensitive arts of telepathy and psychometry. She discovers a rock that conceals a gem that has gathered power for centuries by being used as a focus point for energy. This stone takes her on an intergalactic journey and thrusts her back through time to encounter the women who were the stone's keepers, one a human sacrifice for a warlord's tomb, another a mermaid priestess.

Living alone with her cats, Norton has created characters who hearken to a universal longing: finding one's path through the stars. Among many other awards and honors, Norton received the Nebula Grand Master Award for her life's achievement in 1984.   J.A.J.

Norton, Mary

British author, 1903–1992. An actress and one-time member of London's Old Vic Theatre Company, Mary Norton used her tremendous stagecraft and vivid imagination to create classic works of FANTASY that continue to captivate young audiences. *The Magic Bed-Knob,* her first book, was published in the United States in 1943, and its sequel, *Bonfires and Broomsticks,* was published in England in 1947. A combined edition of the two, *Bed-Knob and Broomstick* (1957), inspired the 1971 Disney film *Bedknobs and Broomsticks,* starring Angela Lansbury. Norton's story tells of three siblings who, when they discover that a neighbor is secretly training to be a witch, offer to keep quiet in return for some magic. The children's subsequent adventures, traveling by bed through space and time, are exciting and memorable, though one episode is marred, by contemporary standards, by a racist depiction of "cannibals." The amusing portrayal of the ladylike Miss Price primly studying the dark arts and trying in earnest to be more wicked firmly established Norton as a master of comedy.

Norton is best known for the series that begins with *The Borrowers* (1953), a book that earned its author the Carnegie Medal and the Lewis Carroll Shelf Award. Equally popular are the books that followed: *The Borrowers Afield* (1955), *The Borrowers Afloat* (1959), and *The Borrowers Aloft* (1961). Scientists have yet to provide a better explanation than Norton's for the mysterious disappearance of small household objects such as safety pins, crochet hooks, pencils, stamps, and matchboxes. Norton posited that these items are "borrowed" by a race of small people who stay hidden away, living in old, quiet houses. The stories have the appeal of the cozy, miniature world of dollhouses, pixies, and talking mice, but without the magic and whimsy. There is nothing cute about the Victorian-era Clock family — Arrietty and her parents, Pod and Homily — who are very human in their thoughts, actions, and appearance and who struggle daily for their survival while being careful never to be "seen." Readers can easily sympathize with the young, high-spirited Arrietty, who longs to satisfy her intense curiosity about humans and the world outside. Both fairy fans and adventure lovers can appreciate the Borrowers' ingenious use of human-scale objects and their execution of numerous escapes: through a drain in a soapbox lid, down a river aboard a cutlery tray, and out an attic in a homemade hot-air balloon. Readers care deeply about what happens to these characters, but the suspense is always tempered by humor and wit.

After a gap of ten years, Norton published *Poor Stainless: A New Story About the Borrowers* (1971). The brief tale is told to Arrietty by her mother and describes a young Borrower who disappears and spends a freewheeling week in a village shop on his own. Next came a whimsical story, unrelated to the Borrowers, entitled *Are All the Giants Dead?* (1975), about a boy who travels to the land of fairy tales. In 1982 fans and critics were pleasantly surprised by the unexpected publication of a fifth Borrowers novel, *The Borrowers Avenged.* The acclaimed book features the illustrations of Beth and Joe Krush, whose depictions of the Clock family had added a further dimension to the previous books. Norton's well-loved stories continue to instill in audiences a sincere desire for a magic bed-knob or a glimpse, at least, of a Borrower.   J.M.B.

Nursery Rhymes

The infant gurgles and coos, smiles and wiggles; the adult reaches out, grabs the little hands, and brings them together, reciting "pat-a-cake, pat-a-cake, baker's man," as indulgent predecessors have been doing for centuries. The rhyme, stored unused by the adult for decades, springs unhesitatingly to the lips. Humpty Dumpty, Georgie Porgie, Little Miss Muffet, Old King Cole and company, dormant, unretrieved for years, can be called back just as effortlessly while other more newly acquired literary acquaintances have faded and disappeared.

Nursery rhymes, both in the culture and in individual consciousness, have been remarkably durable. Some verses were already aged when Shakespeare was a lad, a few finding a home in his plays. Even without so august a setting, the rhymes persisted, carried on initially through the oral tradition but now increasingly in written form. Although most are firmly within the province of the nursery — lullabies, counting rhymes, fingerplays, and the like — many derive from adult sources: peddlers' cries, street chants, tavern songs, or ballads.

Whatever the source, students of language development have convincingly demonstrated the causal relationship between early familiarity with Mother Goose and subsequent linguistic competence. Internal and end rhymes, assonance, onomatopoeia, alliteration, and repetitions sensitize toddlers to the sounds and patterns of language and help them make distinctions that they will later employ in correlating phonemes and letters. The best preparation infants can have for their later role as readers and spellers is to be immersed in nursery rhymes.

But such academic purposes are irrelevant to the young child, who finds in these rhymes only an enduring source of pleasure. The baby's first encounter with Mother Goose provides a visual and sensory feast. He sees the adult's approving, smiling face, hears the rhythmic sounds, and feels his arms or hands moved in synchronization. It is the best possible introduction to a lifelong involvement with books.

Although Mother Goose is sustained by the oral tradition, illustrators have found the challenge of interpreting these familiar verses irresistible. In the many, many editions of Mother Goose published, there is a virtually limitless choice of style, quantity, and selection. In fact, it is possible to chart the history of juvenile illustration in the twentieth century through an examination of editions of nursery rhymes alone.

In the first quarter of the twentieth century, British editions dominated the American nursery. KATE GREENAWAY's Victorian children, RANDOLPH CALDECOTT's lively and spirited characters, and ARTHUR RACKHAM's porcelain-faced youngsters and wittily rendered adults appear in books that show every indication of surviving well into the twenty-first century. A persisting favorite is L. LESLIE BROOKE's *Ring O'Roses* (1922). His ability to give human expression to animals remains unsurpassed, as seen in the poor befuddled pig going to market who is clearly on a mission beyond his limited abilities. Later editions chronicle the changes in children's book art: Byam Shaw's Pre-Raphaelite art; Jennie Harbour's art deco pictures; Mabel Attwell's evocations of images from 1930s advertising and movie cartoons; FEODOR ROJANKOVSKY's *The Tall Book of Mother Goose* (1942), with its benign realism and political allusion (Humpty Dumpty as Adolf Hitler); Marguerite De Angeli's *Book of Nursery and Mother Goose Rhymes* (1954), with its charming and serene drawings; and the exciting use of color in *Brian Wildsmith's Mother Goose* (1964).

Contemporary titles offer a cornucopia of

Illustration by Randolph Caldecott from *The Diverting History of John Gilprin* (1878), by William Cowper.

choices of artistic styles, format, size, and individual rhymes. Everything from huge compendiums of use to scholars to profusely illustrated single-rhyme editions are available.

Styles range from sweet, serene, delicately colored pictures suitable for bedtime reading to raucous, witty drawings more appropriate for the fully energized toddler — as found in AMY SCHWARTZ's depictions of characters on the verge of catastrophe in *Mother Goose's Little Misfortunes* (1990). For those who cannot favor one artist over another, there are collections such as *The Glorious Mother Goose,* by Cooper Eden (1988), which recapitulates nursery rhyme interpretations from 1870 to 1933, or *Tail Feathers from Mother Goose* (1988), which offers illustrations by sixty-two contemporary British artists.

At one end of the spectrum is *The Mother Goose Treasury* (1966), by RAYMOND BRIGGS, which offers slightly over four hundred verses, and ARNOLD LOBEL's superlative *Random House Book of Mother Goose* (1986), featuring over three hundred rhymes. At the other end are the single-rhyme PICTURE BOOKS such as SUSAN JEFFERS's delicate, detailed *Three Jovial Huntsmen* and PETER SPIER's *London Bridge Is Falling Down* (1967). Beyond the simple verse, Spier's illustrations depict a history of London Bridge from the first Roman span to its 1970s reconstruction.

For children who have outgrown the nursery, Kevin O'Malley's *Who Killed Cock Robin?* (1993) uses the familiar rhyme to provide a frame for a MYSTERY replete with clues as to the deceptive and "fowl" practices of birds. MAURICE SENDAK has several credits in this genre, most notably *Hector Protector and As I Went over the Water* (1965), *I Saw Esau* (1992), and *We Are All in the Dumps with Jack and Guy* (1993), in which his interpretation and illustrations comment on poverty and homelessness among children in America.

Mother Goose in this century has gone from innocence to experience: initial images of a gentle, serene, bucolic world have been gradually supplemented by more worldly ones. There are still many volumes for the infant and toddler, but these have been joined by new titles for the more mature reader, offering varied choices and more opportunities for pleasurable exploration of this elastic genre. K.H.

Nye, Naomi Shihab

Palestinian American poet, essayist, book author, anthologist, and teacher, b. 1952. Naomi Shihab Nye was born in St. Louis, Missouri, of Palestinian American heritage. Nye's childhood was influenced by her American mother, a Montessori teacher who was artistic and musical, and her Palestinian father, a journalist and spectacular teller of Middle Eastern folk tales. She learned from them the value of free expression and poetry. At fourteen the family moved to Jerusalem where she met her Palestinian grandmother — her adored Sitti. The Six-Day War caused their return to the States, to settle in San Antonio, Texas.

After graduating summa cum laude from Trinity University, Nye began working in the Texas Writers-in-the-School project. As a visiting writer, she held hundreds of POETRY workshops for children across the United States. She taught at several universities, traveled abroad for USIA arts tours, and won both a Library of Congress and a Guggenheim fellowship. She has received national recognition and honors for her adult poetry. *Never in a Hurry: Essays on People and Places* (1996) includes thirty-nine previously published essays of extraordinary breadth. In a fine crossover collection, she shared her hometown life, encounters with strangers, and startling adventures in the Middle East and other lands.

Elegant, uncommon language flows naturally through Nye's PICTURE BOOKS. In *Come with Me: Poems for a Journey* (2000), friendly meanderings ask questions, capture thoughts, or prompt a journey. *Lullaby Raft* (1997) was created from Nye's original song. A child and her companion animals are lulled to sleep on a floating moon raft. Her son's description of a dream bottle inspired *Benito's Dream Bottle* (1995), about a boy whose magical efforts recapture memories for his grandmother. In *Sitti's Secrets* (1994) a little girl travels far to meet her Palestinian Sitti — her grandmother. Smiles and pantomime bridge language and custom. This exquisitely written, poignant story won the Jane Addams Children's Book Award. *Habibi* (1997), Nye's autobiographical novel, follows fourteen-year-old Liyana Abboud as her family moves from St. Louis to Jerusalem, her father's birthplace. The author's knowledge of the area, customs, and people contributes to a riveting story, full of emotional tension.

Nye has produced six excellent poetry anthologies, distinctive in theme and style, for a broad range of tastes, ages, and sophistication. *This Same Sky: A Collection of Poems from Around the World* (1992) reflects Nye's belief that America's children must hear voices from other countries. *The Tree Is Older Than You Are: Bilingual Poems and Stories from Mexico* (1995) was praised for design and beauty. Handsome art accompanies the side-by-side text in original Spanish and translated English. *The Space Between Our Footsteps: Poems and Paintings from the Middle East* (1998) begins with Nye's plea to look beyond regional stereotypes for universal themes. Poets from nineteen countries have contributed poems about childhood, families, friendship, and longing for home. In *I Feel a Little Jumpy Around You: Paired Poems by Men and Women* (1996), compiled by Nye and PAUL JANECZKO, paired poems show different ways in which men and women see the world. The book is timely and both serious and comic, a stimulus for conversation. *What Have You Lost?* (1999) is filled with knowledge that loss is infinite. *Salting the Ocean: 100 Poems by Young Poets* (2000) features poems written by children from Nye's workshops.

In all of Nye's work, childhood influences, poetry, the importance of place, imagination, subtle insights and observations, pleasure in people, and belief in the power of connecting with others reach through and touch readers.

P.W.

O'Brien, Robert C.

American author, 1918–1973. During his brief career as a novelist, Robert C. O'Brien earned great acclaim but remained an enigma. What little personal information he released to the public was often incomplete or confusing. At the time of his greatest professional triumph, O'Brien did not deliver his own Newbery Medal acceptance speech but asked that his editor speak in his place. Perhaps one reason behind these mysteries was that, under his real name, Robert Leslie Conly, he worked as an editor of *National Geographic,* a publication that discouraged any outside writing by its staff. Born in Brooklyn, the author was raised in Amityville, New York. After receiving a degree in English from the University of Rochester, he worked as a reporter for *Newsweek* and several other publications before joining *National Geographic* in Washington, D.C. O'Brien began writing fiction in the mid-1960s.

His first novel, *The Silver Crown* (1968), is a FANTASY about a girl who finds a magic crown, loses her family, then undertakes an arduous journey. The writing style is promising, with an intense aura of danger and violence, but while the novel contains many exciting scenes, the pace occasionally lags. There are also a few loose ends in the plot. Some later editions include an alternate final chapter, which clears up a key plot question, but the reader may remain unsatisfied.

In *Mrs. Frisby and the Rats of NIMH* (1971), the author successfully combined an old-fashioned talking-animal story with futuristic scientific speculation. When a widowed field mouse named Mrs. Frisby learns that her home and family may be destroyed by a farmer's plow, she seeks assistance from a group of superintelligent laboratory rats. The core of the book is a lengthy first-person account in which Nicodemus relates how he and the other rats were captured by the NIMH labs, treated with steroids, and taught to read, before eventually escaping to form an advanced rat society. Structurally, this long story-within-a-story disrupts the narrative flow of Mrs. Frisby's tale, but the material is fascinating and raises many questions about what constitutes intelligence and civilization. With its interesting plot and fine blend of scientific and nature writing, this unique fantasy would surely have built a large audience eventually, but it was helped immeasurably by winning the Newbery Medal in 1972. The book continues to be extremely popular with young readers and was the basis for an animated feature film, *The Secret of NIMH* (1982).

O'Brien published an adult novel in the early 1970s and was working on *Z for Zachariah* at the time of his death. Completed by his wife and one of his daughters and published in 1975, this YOUNG ADULT NOVEL is a compelling first-person account of a teenage girl surviving alone after a nuclear war and the ominous stranger she meets. All of O'Brien's novels concern characters trying to make the best of a terrible situation, with a threat of danger lurking in the background. In these intriguing, unusual books, the fantastic exists side by side with the mundane. The children in *The Silver Crown* deal with magic in twentieth-century suburban America. Mrs. Frisby receives assistance from intelligent rats in fighting a common garden plow. Masterfully written, Robert C. O'Brien's novels show a love of nature and raise thought-provoking questions. P.D.S.

O'Dell, Scott

American author, 1898–1989. Scott O'Dell wrote his first novel for young people at an age when many Americans consider retirement.

Published in 1960, *Island of the Blue Dolphins* is based on the true story of an Indian girl who spent eighteen years living alone on an island off the California coast. Using the few facts known about this incident, O'Dell created a riveting survival story that speaks to the heart. Karana's tribe is permanently departing from the island when the girl realizes her young brother, Ramo, has been accidentally left behind. Since weather conditions will not permit their ship to turn around, Karana jumps overboard and swims back to join her brother. After Ramo is killed by a wild dog, the girl must survive alone on the island. Karana's haunting first-person narrative records her triumph over adversity and loneliness. She builds a home, survives an earthquake, and tames wild birds. Although she initially vows to kill the dog that murdered her brother, he eventually becomes her devoted companion. The beautifully cadenced prose sings with courage, dignity, and an appreciation for nature. This modern classic received the 1961 Newbery Medal.

Scott O'Dell spent part of his childhood living in a seaport town near the island where the real Karana once lived. The Los Angeles–born author attended a number of colleges, including Stanford University, the University of Wisconsin, and the University of Rome, but never received a degree. He found work in the motion picture industry, wrote for magazines and newspapers, labored on a citrus ranch, and served as book editor for the Los Angeles *Daily News*. He also wrote several books for adults, including historical novels about California. But O'Dell found his greatest success writing for children. Three of his novels were named Newbery Honor Books. *The King's Fifth* (1966) concerns sixteenth-century Spanish adventurers seeking gold in the American Southwest; *The Black Pearl* (1967) is based on a California legend; *Sing Down the Moon* (1970) tells of Bright Morning, who joins her Navajo tribe on the three-hundred-mile Long Walk enforced by the U.S. government in 1864. All are first-rate HISTORICAL NOVELS, strong in character, plot, and incident.

O'Dell drew on events both famous and little known in his novels about the American Revolution, the Civil War, and a slave revolt in the West Indies. Francis of Assisi, Pocahontas, Sacagawea, and William Tyndale are among the historical figures featured in his books. *The Captive* (1979), *The Feathered Serpent* (1981), and *The Amethyst Ring* (1983) comprise a trilogy about sixteenth-century Central and South American cultures. *Zia* (1976), a sequel to *Island of the Blue Dolphins*, concerns Karana's niece. O'Dell occasionally made forays into contemporary fiction. Two of his best, *Child of Fire* (1974) and *Kathleen, Please Come Home* (1978), are arresting problem novels, despite the author's questionable use of adult narrators.

O'Dell's use of the first-person voice, however, has proven to be particularly apt for his historical narrators, whose distinctive language and speech patterns always reveal their culture and background. The author's novels are also notable for their strong female protagonists; this unspoken yet impassioned statement about women's rights is particularly impressive coming from a male author.

Scott O'Dell received the international Hans Christian Andersen Award in 1972 for the body of his work. He later established the Scott O'Dell Award for Historical Fiction, an annual prize that continues to reward outstanding works of historical fiction for young people. O'Dell's ability to bring the past alive through the words and experiences of his unforgettable protagonists established his work as a touchstone by which all children's historical fiction can be measured.

P.D.S.

Opie, Peter; Opie, Iona

Peter: British author and folklorist, 1918–1982; Iona: British author and folklorist, b. 1923. An article in *Research Update* was headed: "Peter and Iona Opie: Patron Saints of Children's Literature," and their contribution has indeed been both prolific and unique. Both are British, although Peter was born in Egypt; both saw military service during World War II; they married in 1943, and their interest in NURSERY RHYMES and the folklore and games of children was sparked by a chance discovery that they remembered the same verse about "Ladybird" or "Ladybug."

Thus, because of their own passionate interest, the Opies began their long career of gathering, sorting, comparing, validating, analyzing, and interpreting. Neither had had formal training in folkloric theory or in research methodology; yet as all who have been the beneficiaries of their findings know, their knowledge of the body of folklore is vast, their research skills impeccable. Both have received an honorary degree of master of arts from Oxford University, and together they were awarded the Chicago Folklore Prize in 1970. In 1988 the American Folklore Society established the Peter and Iona Opie Prize in memory of Peter, who had died six years earlier.

Although the Opies had published a small

Jacket illustration by Evaline Ness for *Island of the Blue Dolphins* (1960), by Scott O'Dell.

and saucy selection of nursery rhymes, *I Saw Esau*, in 1947, it was not until 1951 that their first major work appeared, *The Oxford Dictionary of Nursery Rhymes*. It is an exhaustive and scholarly study of the origins of nursery rhymes, of their earliest recordings, and of variations over the years. Other books of and about nursery rhymes are *The Oxford Nursery Rhyme Book* (1955), *A Family Book of Nursery Rhymes* (1964), and *Tail Feathers from Mother Goose* (1988). *A Nursery Companion* (1980) contains reproductions of early-nineteenth-century booklets of folktales and nursery rhymes, with erudite commentary on their history and use.

The Lore and Language of Schoolchildren (1959) includes rhymes, riddles, childhood customs, and beliefs and is rich in perceptive commentary; a series based on the book was broadcast by the BBC. *Children's Games in Street and Playground* (1969) is based on the Opies' observation of more than ten thousand children in England, Scotland, and Wales; it excludes party games, organized sports, and team games, focusing on what children of about ages six to twelve play "of their own accord when out of doors and usually out of sight." The book is voluminous, illuminating, and detailed. The last two books the Opies worked on together were *The Classic Fairy Tales* (1974) and *The Singing Game* (1985), which won several awards, including the Children's Literature Association Book Award.

A 1989 volume, *The Treasures of Childhood: Books, Toys, and Games from the Opie Collection*, catalogues the products of their years of collecting. In 1992 a new edition of *I Saw Esau* appeared, revised by Iona Opie and illustrated by MAURICE SENDAK. *The People in the Playground* (1993) shows how children change folk material and pass it on. Iona Opie and illustrator ROSEMARY WELLS collaborated together on some very attractive volumes of Mother Goose rhymes, *My Very First Mother Goose* (1996), *Here Comes Mother Goose* (1999), and *Humpty Dumpty and Other Rhymes* (2001).

In 1986 a public appeal was made so that the Bodleian Library at Oxford could accept Iona Opie's generous offer to sell it the Opie book collection at half its value of one million pounds. In less than two years, the goal of the Opie appeal was met. This wealth of primary sources and the integrity of its collectors led a London newspaper to refer to the Opies as "the pioneer anthropologists of the previously uncharted world and lost tribes of childhood."

Z.S.

Oxenbury, Helen

British illustrator and author, b. 1938. Nowhere have the ups and downs of baby and toddler life been more accurately depicted than in Helen Oxenbury's many books. A former set designer for theater, television, and film, Oxenbury began to illustrate books after the birth of her children and had her first book published, in England, in 1967. Though her husband, John Burningham, was already a well-known author-illustrator, she made her own name as a keen observer of the preschool-age experience. As a parent, Oxenbury noticed a lack of books created specifically for preschoolers and became one of the first author-illustrators to design BOARD BOOKS. These durable volumes — made to fit in little hands and to withstand serious teething — were a hit with toddlers and parents alike, as were the simple pictures with little or no text.

Small domestic events are the subjects of Oxenbury's beloved books and round-faced babies and sturdy toddlers the unassuming stars. The series of wordless books that include *Beach Day and Mother's Helper* (both 1982) trace a toddler's daily life, and *I Can, I Hear, I See*, and *I Touch* (all 1986) comprise a series highlighting the objects and actions of the toddler world. Another series, featuring babies at play, includes *Tickle, Tickle* (1999), *Clap Hands* (1999), *All Fall Down* (1999), and *Say Goodnight* (1999). Small-sized books such as *The Checkup* and *The Dancing Class* (both 1983) are for children just past the board book stage who are beginning to venture into the world outside the home.

Oxenbury's popular series about toddler Tom and his companion, a stuffed monkey named Pippo, is presented in a bigger, PICTURE BOOK format. Titles such as *Tom and Pippo and the Washing Machine* (1988), *Tom and Pippo Go Shopping* (1989), and *Tom and Pippo at the Beach* (1993) follow the stalwart child as he and the monkey brave a number of miniadventures, narrated in the authentic-sounding voice of young Tom. Oxenbury's talent for subtle humor is revealed in the expressions on the toy monkey's face as ever-patient Pippo silently endures the capricious friendship of his pre-schooler pal.

An award-winning illustrator, Oxenbury garnered Kate Greenaway Medals for her art in ED-WARD LEAR's *The Quangle Wangle's Hat* (1969) and MARGARET MAHY's *The Dragon of an Ordinary Family* (1969). *We're Going on a Bear Hunt* (1989), Michael Rosen's version of the well-loved song, is another of Oxenbury's highly acclaimed picture books. In it, her black and white sketches, alternating with watercolor paintings, capture the high spirits of the family setting out on a cross-country search for a bear. The illustrations offer readers a glimpse of the Suffolk countryside, where the artist spent her childhood, and a chance to admire Oxenbury's atmospheric use of landscapes, a skill not usually employed in board books. A picture book for older readers, *The Three Little Wolves and the Big Bad Pig* (1993), written by Eugene Trivizas, reverses the roles established in the traditional tale; the amusing text is well matched with Oxenbury's art. One illustration depicts the wolves demurely playing croquet, and when the big bad pig approaches their brick house, the threesome are shown nervously trotting out the back, clutching their beloved china teapot.

Gentle humor and warmth are the hallmarks of this author-illustrator, whose down-to-earth stories provide young children with both amusement and comfort. J.M.B.

P

Parish, Peggy

American author, 1927–1988. When children first become independent readers, humor is an important ingredient for them, and Peggy Parish is one of the authors to whom they turn. Parish wrote close to fifty books, most of them for beginning readers. Best known for her Amelia Bedelia series, Parish also wrote a number of other EASY READERS, some nonfiction and craft books, and a MYSTERY series for the middle grades.

Amelia Bedelia, that wacky, literal-minded housekeeper, constantly misinterprets instructions in the dozen or so books about her. She sketches the drapes when asked to draw them in *Amelia Bedelia* (1963); she shouts, "Roll. Hey, roll!" as she calls the roll in *Teach Us, Amelia Bedelia* (1977); she uses tea to make tea cakes in *Amelia Bedelia Helps Out* (1979); and when her employers suggest she invite everyone to a party in *Amelia Bedelia's Family Album* (1988), she does just that — she stands in the middle of the street and invites everyone. Parish seems to know exactly what will tickle children as she plays with the ambiguities of the English language.

Parish was born in South Carolina and after college began teaching third-graders, first in Kentucky, then in Oklahoma, and finally in New York City. Her teaching experience provided her with an appreciation of newly independent readers. She said, however, "I don't try to teach anything in my stories — I write just for fun."

And most of her books can indeed be described as fun.

She frequently wrote of the foibles of adults with childlike qualities. In addition to Amelia Bedelia, she created Granny Guntry, Miss Molly, and Aunt Emma. In the three Granny Guntry books, Granny, an independent pioneer woman with a gun that doesn't shoot, appears naive and helpless. Yet in the end she manages to get just what she wants. Although the story lines are slight, the action and humor provide amusing tales for young readers. Miss Molly is terribly forgetful, so forgetful, in fact, that in *Be Ready at Eight* (1979) she forgets her own birthday. In *The Cats' Burglar* (1983) Aunt Emma's neighbors try to tell her what to do. They insist she has too many cats, but when the cats save her from a burglar, Aunt Emma feels justified in keeping them. Young readers easily identify with these characters and, at the same time, feel in charge as they laugh at the adults' mistakes.

Parish also wrote a mystery series for slightly older children. Jed, Liza, and Bill, the three sleuths, solve family-related mysteries. For example, in *The Key to the Treasure* (1966) Grandpa tells them of an unsolved puzzle left by his grandfather, who was killed in the Civil War. Clues are provided in the form of coded notes, and readers will enjoy matching wits with Jed, Liza, and Bill to figure out the codes. Although some of the situations in the six mysteries are improbable, the action is fast-paced and the three children have enough individual personality to hold the reader's interest.

Throughout her career, Parish felt a strong commitment to encouraging children to read, a commitment clearly reflected in her books. P.R.

Park, Barbara

American author, b. 1947. Barbara Park, author of the Junie B. Jones series as well as numerous books of MIDDLE-GRADE FICTION, uses humor to deal with serious issues relevant to children. Subjects range widely and include divorce, remarriage, moving, sibling rivalry, death, Alzheimer's disease, and perceiving oneself as too tall, thin, fat, or smart.

But Park herself had a traditional childhood and has admitted that she was a class clown. Comic books were her favorite reading material, and she never considered writing as a career until she was almost thirty years old and the mother of two sons.

Since 1981, Park has published more than thirty books in three categories: the Junie B. Jones titles (easy CHAPTER BOOKS), longer books more appropriate for middle school readers, and a PICTURE BOOK. All focus on American children, kindergartners to eighth-graders. Each book presents a problem that a child might face, and humor is always present to entertain and make a serious issue easier to deal with.

A number of similarities are evident in Park's books. Most are told in the first person, in the voice of the main character. Readers feel that the character is actually addressing them because of Park's authentic, believable voice. In addition, most main characters in the books for older readers are boys.

Since 1991, Park has written eighteen books in the Junie B. Jones series. The character Junie B. is spontaneous and loud, and she has difficulty following rules; children enjoy reading about a character that gets into trouble. Titles in this popular series have appeared occasionally on the *New York Times* Best-Seller List.

In 1995, Park published the book that took her the longest to write, *Mick Harte Was Here*. Phoebe, the eighth-grade sister of Mick, explains on page one that her brother is dead as a result of a bicycle accident. It is one month after the accident, and in this short book she recounts life with, and now without, her brother. Often the book uses gentle humor, but the account is personal and sincere.

Having purchased her first typewriter in the 1980s, Park is now on her third computer. Considering the success of the Junie B. Jones series and the quality of *Graduation of Jake Moon* (2000), Park is still going strong. K.L.H.

Park, Linda Sue

Korean American author, b. 1960. The daughter of Korean immigrants who came to American after the Korean War, Linda Sue Park grew up outside Chicago. After earning degrees at Stanford University, Trinity College in Dublin, and the University of London, she wrote professionally for many years, as both a journalist and food critic. Eventually she turned to exploring her own heritage and Korean history in books for middle-grade readers: seventeenth-century Korea in *Seesaw Girl* (1999), fifteenth-century Korea in *Kite Fighters* (2000), and World War II in *When My Name Was Keoko* (2002).

In 2002 Park became the first Asian American writer to win the Newbery Medal for *A Single Shard* (2001). While researching her earlier books, she has become intrigued by the fact that during the twelfth century, Korea created the most beautiful pottery in the world, the magnificent celadon ware. Taking pride that such a small country could be the best at a craft, she wanted to let young readers know about the people and the time in which this happened. *A Single Shard* recounts the story of an impoverished ten-year-old orphan, Tree-ear, and his guardian, Crane-man. Eventually the orphan becomes an apprentice to a great potter and grows in mastery of the craft and in wisdom; by his courage, honor, and perseverance he achieves happiness. Park's unique focus for her novels and her sensibilities have made it possible, with only a few books to her name, for her to become one of the most important new voices to emerge in HISTORICAL FICTION for young readers at the beginning of the twenty-first century. A.S.

Parker, Robert Andrew

American illustrator, b. 1927. Robert Andrew Parker lives in a Connecticut farmhouse, and the walls of his large barn studio are lined with his art. Energetically working on several projects simultaneously, he has made clear that his many passions — travel and hiking, jazz, and family, as well as literature and art — spill over into his diverse creative work, including illustrations for dozens of children's books.

Parker, who was born in New Jersey and has lived in Seattle, St. Louis, and Chicago, began his travels early. Being part of a jazz-loving family, he became a proficient clarinet, sax, and drum player. While recuperating from a childhood illness in New Mexico, he started drawing, mostly Indian battles. His short experience in World War II and his exposure to the powerful war drawings of Otto Dix spurred him to draw more soldiers. Then he trained in art, in painting and printmaking at the Chicago Art Institute and, in New York, at Atelier 17. Influenced by the 1920s Stieglitz school, Charles Demuth, Max Beckmann, and Paul Klee, Parker went on to develop his own color-rich style. Parker was sent by *Fortune* magazine around the world to paint scenes such as Central American fruit plantations. He created art for the 1956 biographical film about Van Gogh (*Lust for Life*), opera sets, and album covers, including one for his favorite jazz musician, Thelonious Monk. He did drawings, lithographs, monoprints, and paintings. His art has been shown in several dozen one-man shows and hangs in many museums and private collections.

Parker still draws with the scribbly, energetic line he used at age ten, though his subject matter has expanded to include grim war scenes, voluptuous women in stories by Vladimir Nabokov, portraits, and landscapes. His George Grosz–like distortion, his Emil Nolde–like vivid colors, often in gouache or oil, show the influence of German expressionists whom he admired.

Parker has illustrated fifty children's books, including *The Trees Stand Shining* (1971), a volume of North American Indian POETRY edited by Hettie Jones. He has sensitively illustrated two poetry collections by William Cole. He produced accurately detailed ships and planes for *Battle in the Arctic Seas* (1976), written by THEO-

DORE TAYLOR. He has won prizes: *Pop Corn and Ma Goodness,* an imaginative story written by Edna Mitchell Preston, was a 1970 Caldecott Honor Book; *Liam's Catch,* written by Parker's first wife, Dorothy D. Parker, won an American Institute of Graphic Arts 1972 Book Show prize. It is the story of an Irish boy's opportunity to prove himself, watching from a lookout tower for the salmon to run. *The Whistling Skeleton,* Indian tales of the supernatural edited by JOHN BIERHORST, was a 1982 ALA Notable Book. *Cold Feet* (2000), written by Cynthia De Felice, won the Boston Globe–Horn Book Award in 2001.

Parker has skillfully modulated his style to suit the text. Sometimes he has chosen black and white watercolor, as he did for Richard Kennedy's touching tale of a widower sworn off fiddling, *Oliver Hyde's Dishcloth Concert* (1977). Other times he has begun dark and moved to warm colors, as in Cynthia De Felice's *The Dancing Skeleton* (1989), in which the stiff, idiosyncratic figures give way to the warm red fiddler furiously playing the parts of the skeleton. In other books Parker's love of music and jazz translates into vibrant rhythms, with Native American braves dancing or swans flying. He has also illustrated with etchings, as in *The Magician's Visit* (1993), a Passover tale retold by Barbara Goldin.

Parker, still drumming, biking, hunting in Ireland, hiking in Nepal, teaching, and lecturing, is also actively creating children's books. With his energetic interests and talents as a fine artist, he has produced an exciting body of work for young children. H.S.N.

Parnall, Peter

American author and illustrator, b. 1936. From the desert Southwest to the coastal Northeast, Peter Parnall's work explores the natural world. With stunning attention to detail, his more than eighty books survey the many complex relationships found in the wild.

Peter Parnall grew up in the Mojave Desert and the Big Bend country of Texas. This vast, open terrain and the wildlife he carefully observed influenced many works, especially those on which he and author Byrd Baylor have collaborated. They shared their talents in seven titles, three of which were Caldecott Honor Books: *The Desert Is Theirs* (1976), *Hawk, I'm Your Brother* (1976), and *The Way to Start a Day* (1978). Together, Parnall and Baylor have looked beyond the obvious to the quiet, simple beauty of the desert. Ten creatures, from the young jackrabbit to the old tortoise, speak to the reader in *Desert Voices* (1980). Black line drawings are shaded with only enough hints of color to capture the artist's focus. The result creates an interesting visual dichotomy, inviting readers to examine Parnall's chosen subject while reiterating the vastness of nature that often goes unnoticed. Such perspective also appears in the books written and illustrated solely by Parnall. In *Feet* (1988), for example, the youngest readers are invited on a "ground-up" tour of eighteen animals. Big feet, fast feet, thin, wet, and slow feet are the close-up illustrations set against a backdrop of subtle detail. If one looks closely, the rest of the animals to whom the feet belong can be found in Parnall's panoramas.

The influence of years spent on a farm along the rugged Maine coast is evident in a number of Parnall's books. In *Winter Barn* (1986) an ecosystem unto itself slowly evolves as the temperature drops below zero. Carefully, with great reverence and awe, Parnall has peeked into every corner to reveal the creatures who have taken refuge. Some, like the horses and mice, are yearlong residents, while others, including a bobcat and porcupines, seek warmth only in winter. While *Winter Barn* provides shelter to a variety of creatures, *Cats from Away* (1989) introduces generations of felines who, at one time or another, lived on Parnall's farm. There are Burl, Ives, Tigger, Cud, Blackie, and Thumbs, to name a few. All come from a place the author has referred to as "away," and most stay for a long time.

In addition to his PICTURE BOOKS, Parnall is

the author of several short, fictional CHAPTER BOOKS, including *Water Pup* (1993). When not working on books for young readers, Parnall pursues a number of other interests — riding, painting, and tending sheep. **B.A.M.**

Parrish, Maxfield

American illustrator, 1870–1966. Though the height of Maxfield Parrish's career was nearly one hundred years ago, his celebrated illustrations, with their intense colors and languid surrealism, seem strikingly contemporary. Christened Frederick Parrish by his parents, Parrish took his paternal grandmother's maiden name as his middle name when he began painting professionally, and eventually dropped his given name altogether. Encouraged in his artistic inclinations by his father, whose own artistic leanings had been stifled by a strict Quaker upbringing, Parrish always observed the world around him with an artist's eye. His letters home from the requisite trip abroad are filled with his impressions not only of the great cities he visited but also of the artists working in them and their art. His impatience in those letters with the conservatism of the European art world indicates his independence of mind.

While Parrish is best remembered today for his illustrations for children's books, during his lifetime he was renowned as a commercial artist and magazine illustrator. His commissions for commercial goods, the most famous of which was for Crane's Chocolates, brought his name to the attention of the American public. These commissions paved the way for a steady, lucrative income from the sale of color reproductions, and his famous "blue paintings" of the 1920s became common household items. The first children's book Parrish illustrated was L. FRANK BAUM's *Mother Goose in Prose* (1897). Its immediate success led to subsequent books, the most famous of which was Eugene Field's *Poems of Childhood* (1904). This is the first book in which Parrish's paintings were reproduced in full color, and it contains the famous illustration of "The Dinkey Bird," which depicts a nude youth on a swing, airborne against a deep blue mountain topped by a white-walled city, characteristic elements in Parrish's work.

Prior to illustrating *Poems*, Parrish illustrated editions of *The Golden Age* (1900) and *Dream Days* (1902), nostalgic stories of childhood by KENNETH GRAHAME, and his pictures for these works have been praised for their ability to capture and refine the mood set by the author. After *Poems*, his next book for children, *The Arabian Nights* (1909), edited by Nora Smith and Kate Douglas Wiggin, incorporates the sweeping architectural elements — magnificent staircases, towering pillars, huge urns — that were to become identified with Parrish's name. *Greek Mythology* (1910) and two collections of stories originally published by Nathaniel Hawthorne in 1852 and 1853, *The Wonder Book* and *Tanglewood Tales* (1910), contain illustrations Parrish had originally done for *Collier's* magazine. His final book for children was *The Knave of Hearts* (1925), a play by Louise Saunders. Glorious color and formal composition are the keynotes of this work.

In the 1930s, Parrish was able to leave all commissioned work behind him and concentrate on his first love, landscape painting. He did this until arthritis forced him to put down his paintbrush in 1962, at the age of ninety-one. While to the casual observer his illustrations for children's books seem to continue the romantic line of HOWARD PYLE, with whom he studied, and of N. C. WYETH, a closer look reveals his witty and unique use of traditional romantic subjects. Parrish used elements of heroic realism — mythic themes, voluminous drapery, vast vistas — and by rendering them in photographic detail in vivid colors, using several different techniques in one picture, he created a distinctly surrealistic, dreamlike quality. Parrish's style might well be called "heroic surrealism." He referred to his paintings as evoking "realism of impression, realism of mood of the moment, yes, but not realism of things." **S.G.K.**

Paterson, Katherine

American author, b. 1932. Katherine Paterson's powerful novels unveil humanity's most humble and truthful themes of personal growth. Realistic characters, usually outsiders, gain self-acceptance and the courage to accept everyday existence and its limitations by confronting difficult situations and sacrificing grandiose ideas about their futures. Their newfound self-realizations allow them to continue with their lives in hopeful, if not fully optimistic, anticipation of the future. Readers become passionate about Paterson's characters, accepting them as role models and referring to them as prototypes of literary personalities.

Philosophy and place are important to Paterson's work, evidence of the influence of her own life experience. Born in China to missionary parents, Paterson moved frequently during her childhood. She became a missionary in Japan after teaching for several years and receiving a master's degree in the English Bible. Returning to the United States to accept a fellowship and receive another master's degree, at Union Theological Seminary in New York, she met and married John Paterson. She and her husband, a Presbyterian minister, became parents to four children, two of whom are adopted.

While it is not generally viewed as didactic or proselytizing, Paterson's Christian theology pervades her work: an occasional religious zealot adds flavor to overriding themes of compassion, self-acceptance, personal strength in the face of adversity, and unconditional love. And, though some of Paterson's settings are countries on the other side of the globe, she is familiar with most of her locations from firsthand experience. With respect and great care in research, she placed her first three stories in eighteenth- and feudal twelfth-century Japan. Primarily noted for their suspense and the writer's craft, these works also contain characters as believable and fully realized as those in her contemporary settings.

The Master Puppeteer (1975), a National Book Award winner, is the most successful of these stories. The plot involves the intricacies of oper-
ating a Japanese puppet theater and a main character who discovers the reflection of life in art as he deals with a trying family situation amidst the chaos of civil strife. *The Sign of the Chrysanthemum* (1973) and *Of Nightingales That Weep* (1974), set in medieval Japan, have equally exciting stories. *Lyddie* (1991), set in early-nineteenth-century Lowell, Massachusetts, presents an independent and determined young female character and an eye-opening look at the labor conditions for mill workers, most of whom were women. Both *JIP, His Story* (1996) and *Preacher's Boy* (1999) use nineteenth-century Vermont towns as their settings. While many readers enjoy these historical works, a greater number are drawn to Paterson's contemporary novels, which offer more immediately involving issues. Each of Paterson's characters experiences a different process of self-realization, but each story is equally powerful. *Bridge to Terabithia* (1977) recounts both the friendship between a country boy, Jess, and an uprooted city girl, Leslie, and the story of how Jess comes to terms with Leslie's accidental death. In developing their touching friendship, Jess and Leslie invent the special kingdom of Terabithia. When Leslie is killed trying to reach their magical hideaway during a torrential downpour, Jess is overcome with grief and guilt. A realistic portrayal of the healing process shows him eventually accepting this tragedy and moving on by welcoming his younger, sometimes bothersome sister into the private place he had previously shared only with Leslie.

Another character who learns to accept her life is the inimitable Gilly Hopkins. In *The Great Gilly Hopkins* (1978) Paterson has provided moments of pure comedy through the manipulations and wisecracks of this sharp-tongued, precocious protagonist who willfully steers her own progression through a series of foster homes, keeping all intimate relationships at bay until the most unlikely character — the overweight, almost illiterate, "religious fanatic" foster mother, Maime Trotter — wins her love. For years, Gilly has fantasized about a reunion with her real mother, the "beautiful" Courtney; yet when it finally happens, Gilly learns that the flower-child mother who abandoned her still has no intention of staying around. Through Trotter, Gilly begins to realize that life is tough and "all that stuff about happy endings is lies" as she gains the strength to face life with the grandmother she has just met and who has volunteered to be responsible for her.

Like Gilly, Louise Bradshaw in Paterson's Newbery Medal–winning *Jacob Have I Loved* (1980) struggles to find a happy ending. In a serious, sophisticated novel that gets its name from the biblical passage "Jacob have I loved, but Esau have I hated," the self-pitying Louise takes years to overcome feelings of jealousy toward her favored twin sister. In the closing chapter, Louise, in her twenties, serves as a midwife at the birth of twins. After finding herself paying more attention to the weaker, younger child, a reflective Louise comes to a greater understanding of herself, and, finally, her feelings of resentment begin to fade.

Though some readers and critics have questioned the endings of Paterson's books — Leslie's death; Gilly's estrangement from the foster mother she's come to love; the final chapter of Louise's adult reflection — Paterson has maintained that she has done everything in her power to make the story live for the reader. Speaking of an intended reader, she has said, "She may not like how the story ends, but I want her to see that this ending is the inevitable one. I want her to want to keep reading, to wonder with a pounding heart how it will all come out; and then, when she comes to the final page, I want her to say: 'Of course! It had to be. No other ending was possible. Why didn't I realize it all along.'"

In addition to her masterly works of fiction, historical and contemporary, Paterson has written several collections of inspiring essays and speeches on writing books for children. She has won every major award for her work, including the Hans Christian Andersen Award. Whatever the genre, Paterson has made all her stories live in the imaginations of her readers. And, by laying bare the soul of her characters and revealing truths about the nature of humanity, she can gently extract emotion from even the most stoic reader. E.K.E.

Voices of the Creators

🖋 *Katherine Paterson*

Why do I write for children? This is not an easy question to answer. I don't know why I became a writer at all. I never meant to be a writer. I was already a writer and well past my thirtieth birthday before I realized that a writer was indeed what I wanted to be when I grew up.

I wrote as a child, but I certainly didn't plan to be a writer. I loved books, and I read a great deal, but I never imagined that I might write them. Actually, when I was nine, I had a dual fantasy life in which on some days I was the leader of a group of commandos saving the world from Axis domination, and on others I was the benevolent queen of the United States of America. Of course, I indulged in these grandiose fantasies because I was finding the real world a tough place to inhabit.

I do still have lots of childhood goblins that need exorcising. And now that I have been a parent and a writer as well as a child, I seem always to be on the child's side. But I know that children are not fair. They do not see their teachers and their parents objectively. They see only from their own limited vision. When I write for children, I try not only to be true to a child's point of view, but I try as well to give hints that the world is wider than it seems to a child, and that other people may be more complex and even more understanding and compassionate than the child character sees them to be.

For a writer to succeed in this attempt, however, demands the cooperation of a careful and perceptive reader. There are those who think that a writer for children should not ask for this level of wisdom from her readers. Maybe not. But I don't seem able to write in any other way, and I have been very fortunate in the readers who choose my books. A great number of them seem not only willing to dig below the surface, they seem eager to.

"I didn't catch on the first time I read it, but when I read it again . . ." is a refrain I hear surprisingly often. And, I must say, it is music to a writer's ears.

Although I became a writer for children more or less accidentally, I soon learned that I had stumbled into what was for me the world's best job — perhaps, as I say to my husband, the only job I will ever be able to keep.

Any freelance writer has the opportunity of choosing her own subjects and her own work methods and schedules, but I, as a writer for children, have an even more enviable situation. I know when I spend a year, two years, or more on a book, that I will be sending it to people who value books. I know that the book I have written will be carefully, even lovingly, edited and copyedited. If a book is to have illustrations, I know that a lot of thought will be given to selecting an appropriate illustrator. Whether the book is illustrated or not, a designer will make sure that its look will be satisfying. I have had books where jacket illustration after jacket illustration was rejected because it didn't reflect what my editor felt was the heart of the story. My publishing houses have known that it takes time for a children's book to find its readers, and they are willing to keep a book in print long enough for that to happen. I have friends who write novels for adults who find their books on a remainder table within less than six months of their original publication.

It's interesting how often people say to me, "Well, of course, your books aren't really for children" and think, thereby, that they have complimented me. Actually, my books are for anyone who is kind enough to read them. The great majority of those readers are, have been, and I profoundly hope will continue to be under the age of fourteen.

I got a letter once from a troubled child who poured out her anguish over her parents' divorce and her own subsequent behavior. "When I read *Gilly Hopkins*" she said, "I realized that you were the only person in the world who could understand how I feel." Poor child, I thought, can anyone understand your pain?

As much as we adults wish to spare children pain and so try to pretend to ourselves that they cannot feel as deeply as we do, they do hurt; they do fear; they do grieve. We who care for them must take these feelings seriously.

Why do I write for children? Because I'm practicing. Someday if I keep working at my craft, I may write a book worthy of a child — I may write a book worthy of the readers who have come to my books. 🐾

Paulsen, Gary

American author, b. 1939. In Gary Paulsen, young readers craving fast-paced action, harrowing escapes, and near-death experiences have found their savior. But these swift stories, so compelling to hungry readers, only serve as gateways to a literature that extends far beyond the realm of the average adventure novel. Paulsen's rich and powerful prose evokes the sights, sounds, and feelings of a wilderness setting while gently nudging the special issues of adolescence with sensitivity, integrity, and compassion. It is no wonder that his many fans return to his books again and again.

Although his main occupation is writing, Paulsen has at various times been a teacher, field engineer, soldier, actor, director, farmer, rancher, truck driver, trapper, professional archer, migrant farm worker, singer, and sailor. Born in Minneapolis and raised by a grandmother and several aunts, he was shuffled from school to school and met his father for the first time at age seven. Paulsen enjoyed hunting and trapping, but after he tried dogsledding he found he could no longer kill another animal. Dogs taught him about the "ancient and . . . beautiful bond" between humans and the natural world. This new passion for dogsledding soon found its way into several books, most notably the autobiographical *Woodsong* (1989). Like the most successful of his books, this documentation of Paulsen's experience running the famed Iditarod race has at its core a genuine awe for humanity's dependence on and alliance with the forces of nature.

A tale of strength, courage, and intelligence, Paulsen's acclaimed novel *Hatchet* (1987) has rapidly become one of the most popular adventure stories of all time. Written with the spare, evocative prose that has become the author's signature style, this brief tale documents the struggle of a troubled city boy to survive for two months in the Canadian wilderness, with only a hatchet to aid him. Through his ordeal, Brian Robeson gains an enduring respect for the forces of nature and a greater understanding of himself and those who play important roles in his life. Like many of Paulsen's most successful books, *Hatchet* combines elementary language with a riveting plot to produce a book both comprehensible and enjoyable for those children who frequently equate reading with frustration. Paulsen continued Brian's sagas in *Brian's Return* (1999) and *Brian's Winter* (1996).

Paulsen's young protagonists are often faced with difficult home environments in which parents are abusive or physically or emotionally absent. The ability of the young hero — usually a boy — to overcome his physical surroundings through some wilderness adventure correlates with a sense of self-development and the ability to understand, if not change, the emotional conflicts in his family. These honest and hopeful portrayals, combined with a low reading level, make the books ideal for reaching children at risk.

In addition to his YOUNG ADULT NOVELS, Paulsen is also known for his INFORMATION BOOKS on nature and sports. Using insight gained from experience, Paulsen's nature books often combine fact with personal anecdote to present a highly readable source of information, and they extend his novels' themes by addressing the survival skills of various animals such as moose, elk, buffalo, rabbits, and mice. His books on basketball, hockey, and even hot-air ballooning carefully cover the basics while also providing the little-known facts that are so appealing for children to master and share.

But it is in the fiction category that Paulsen's work has truly been hailed. Several of his novels have been named Newbery Honor Books, among them *Dogsong* (1985), *Hatchet* (1987), and *The Winter Room* (1989); he has been awarded the Regina Medal of the Catholic Library Association and the Margaret A. Edwards Award. In addition to his numerous books for children, Paulsen has written voluminously for adults, and he ranks among the most prolific writers in the nation. C.C.B.

Pearce, Philippa

British author, b. 1920. Recognized internationally for her complex, classic time FANTASY *Tom's Midnight Garden* (1958), which was awarded the British Library Association's prestigious Carnegie Medal, Philippa Pearce has written a number of novels and short stories that explore the ordinary experiences of memorable, solitary children who are often propelled by intense thoughts and secrets. The most compelling of her child characters is Tom Long from *Tom's Midnight Garden*, who has been sent to spend part of the summer with a distant aunt and uncle. Through two devices, a grandfather clock that strikes thirteen and an old woman's dreams of the past, Pearce connects two worlds: Tom's boring present and a Victorian-age garden. There Tom finds a friend in Hatty, another lonely child who is struggling to make a place for herself in an unsympathetic family, following the death of her parents. Suspense builds as Tom nears the end of his summer stay, trying desperately to understand the complexities of time in two worlds.

In *Minnow on the Say* (1955), which was published in the United States as *The Minnow Leads to Treasure*, young David Moss finds a canoe that has floated down-river during a storm. Reluctantly setting out to return it, he meets its owner, Adam Codling, who is determined to recover a legendary family treasure and save an old family home for his elderly aunt. The two boys join forces in what becomes their secret quest. This, Pearce's first novel, won a Carnegie Commendation, as have two of her other books, *The Shadow-Cage and Other Tales of the Supernatural* (1977) and *The Battle of Bubble and Squeak* (1978).

In *A Dog So Small* (1962), Ben Blewitt, the middle child in a family of seven, doesn't receive the real dog that his grandfather promised him as a birthday present. Disappointed, Ben retreats into a fantasy world where "a dog so small you can only see it with your eyes shut" becomes his constant companion. His obsession with the imaginary dog reaches its climax when Ben is hit by a car as he crosses a busy street with his eyes closed. While there is little plot or action, Pearce has engaged the reader with ordinary family vignettes and recognizably real dialogue.

Protagonist Kate Tranter, in *The Way to Sattin Shore* (1983), cuts school and bicycles many miles alone to find out about her father, who she previously assumed had died on the day she was born. In her quest to unravel the full truth, Kate excludes her only friend and involves her immediate family just when necessary and never with their full understanding. In the end, only her paternal grandmother shares the knowledge of what really happened.

Pearce's rich and precise language was developed and polished during years as a storyteller, scriptwriter, radio producer, and children's book editor. The mill house, garden, and countryside settings along the Say River, so vividly described in her work, hearken back to Pearce's own childhood. In many of her novels, Pearce has explored relationships between children and the elderly, often grandparents, and through Hatty in *Tom's Midnight Garden*, she also has explored the relationship between aging and the passage of time. Pearce does not provide readers with exact ages or physical descriptions of her fictional children, choosing rather to concentrate on the inner character of each.

Her short story collections, particularly *Lion at School and Other Stories* (1985), introduce other unique children and add to Pearce's reputation as one of the twentieth century's outstanding children's authors. G.W.R.

Peck, Richard

American author, b. 1934. Richard Peck is the renaissance man of contemporary young adult literature. Since he wrote *Don't Look and It Won't Hurt*, his first book, in 1972, Peck has been one of the most recognizable names,

one of the most dependable writers, and one of the most passionate advocates for teenagers. He has written in almost every genre: *Voices After Midnight* (historical, 1989), *Ghosts I Have Been* (horror, 1977), *Dreamland Lake* (MYSTERY, 1973), *Secrets of the Shopping Mall* (humor, 1979); and books that combine all these elements, such as *The Dreadful Future of Blossom Culp* (1983). Writing in the realistic genre, Peck has tackled some of the toughest problems that teenagers face: suicide, in *Remembering the Good Times* (1985); rape, in *Are You in the House Alone?* (1976); death, in *Close Enough to Touch* (1981); peer pressure, in *Princess Ashley* (1987); single parenting, in *Don't Look and It Won't Hurt* (1972); and family issues, in *Father Figure* (1978).

In addition, Peck has published essays, POETRY, adult novels, and short stories. He is a much-sought-after speaker and logs many miles each year visiting schools and libraries to meet his fans. His books regularly receive strong reviews and appear on the Young Adult Library Services Association's Best Books for Young Adults list. He received the Margaret A. Edwards Lifetime Achievement Award from *School Library Journal* and the Young Adult Library Services Association of the American Library Association for his body of work; his life and work are detailed in *Presenting Richard Peck* (1989), written by Donald Gallo, as part of Twayne's series on young adult authors.

Peck started writing late, not publishing his first novel until he was thirty-seven. Before that he was a teacher, and the influence shows heavily in his work. Peck's books often contain the central message of "think and act independently." All his characters face the challenge of trying to grow up. With wit, adolescent heart, and an easy-to-read writing style, Peck has written with compassion, an ear for true dialogue, and insight into the things that help teenagers in that difficult task. P.J.

In the 1990s Peck continued to publish stellar works notable for their diversity and overall excellence; he also began reaping long overdue literary honors.

Peck made his first entry into the field of SCI-
ENCE FICTION with *Lost in Cyberspace* (1995) and
The Great Interactive Dream Machine (1996), a
pair of novels depicting the fast-paced, humorous adventures of New York preppies Josh and
Aaron as they use their private school's computer to travel through space and time.

A frequent contributor to young adult anthologies ("Priscilla and the Wimps," a story
about middle school bullying and revenge, is a
classroom staple), Peck has expanded some of
his most memorable stories into full-length
works of fiction. "Shotgun Cheatham's Last
Night Above Ground" was originally written for
an anthology about guns, but its larger-than-life
protagonist proved so memorable that Peck created a series of tales about hard-edged Grandma
Dowdel and the two awed grandchildren, Joey
and Mary Alice, who visit her in rural Illinois
every summer between 1929 to 1935. *A Long Way
from Chicago* (1998) was a National Book Award
finalist and a Newbery Honor Book. A second
book about Grandma Dowdel, *A Year Down
Yonder* (2000), focuses on younger sister Mary
Alice, who spends an entire year with her grandmother during the height of the Depression. Just
as funny as its predecessor, but more moving
and cohesive, the book won the Newbery Medal.

With each new work, Peck continues to grow
in stature as one of today's most talented creators. P.D.S.

Peet, Bill

American author and illustrator, 1915–2002.
Ask any child from age five to eight about
his or her favorite authors, and it is very likely
that Bill Peet will make the list — with good reason. The creator of whimsical FANTASIES featuring a bevy of lifelike and lovable creatures, Peet
consistently produced the rare combination of
excellent storytelling with appealing, enduring
illustrations for over thirty years.

Born in Grandview, Indiana, William Bartlett
Peed (later changed to Peet) nurtured his childhood drawing talent and graduated from the

Illustration by Bill Peet from his book *The Wump World*
(1970).

John Herron Art Institute in Indianapolis. Left
to find employment in the midst of the Depression, he worked briefly at a greeting card company before heading west to California, where
he was recruited by Walt Disney as a sketch artist and continuity illustrator. Although he considered the position temporary, Peet remained
with Disney for twenty-seven years, eventually
becoming a screenwriter. His work helped produce beloved films such as *Fantasia, Sleeping
Beauty, Alice in Wonderland, Peter Pan,* and *101
Dalmatians.* With this background and a great
lack of recognition, it is no surprise that Peet
went on to create his own stories for children.
After several years of rejection, his first book,
Hubert's Hair-Raising Adventure, was published
in 1959. This tale of a haughty lion who accidentally loses his mane would be the first of a long
chain of successful books combining sketchy,
cartoonlike illustrations in full color, engaging
animal characters, and fast-paced stories of fantastical adventures delivered with warmth and
laugh-out-loud hilarity.

Often compared to DR. SEUSS for his whimsical creatures and fablelike tales, Peet is known
for his concise writing style, clever verse, and individualistic illustrations of animals and anthropomorphic machines. Working primarily with
pen-and-ink and crayon, he has created humor-

ous and highly expressive characters with a down-home flavor. Wide eyes, furrowed brows, and open mouths on animals and humans capture moments of near catastrophe that evolve into the high-intensity adventure and sheer fun bursting from every colorful page. Although his tales are always humorous and usually nonsensical, Peet has not sacrificed integrity and warmth, and his characters' plights often involve some universal difficulty such as fear, loneliness, or self-doubt, which they are able to overcome in a satisfactory manner. Stories featuring endearing characters that are either logical (a lion with "cage" fright, as in *Randy's Dandy Lions,* 1964) or loony (a pig whose spots resemble a world map, as in *Chester the Worldly Pig,* 1965) cannot help but draw the reader's attention and hold it straight to the conclusion.

Peet is one of the few authors who can successfully address world issues for young children, using humor to keep plots fresh and ease didacticism. In *Farewell to Shady Glade,* published in 1966 but still more than relevant today, he tackled the issue of urbanization from the point of view of a small band of meadow animals repeatedly uprooted by the great earthmoving machines that continue to pursue them. In contrast, *The Wump World* (1970) is an allegorical world of verdant pastures that is suddenly invaded by a band of intergalactic polluters who have destroyed their own planet and need a new one to ravage. These books, and others, are recommended by teachers and librarians as a means of introducing important, difficult concepts to young children.

Peet has thoroughly documented his life in his autobiography for children, *Bill Peet: An Autobiography.* Featuring an inviting, down-to-earth writing style and lavish black and white illustrations on every page, this volume has been sought after by fans of all ages since its publication in 1989 and serves as an excellent example of the caliber and style of his work as a whole. With humor, compassion, and an innate knowledge of just what details are important, Peet's life story is as fascinating as any fiction — a story that established him once and for all as not just

the creator of characters, but a grand teller of tales. C.C.B.

Perrault, Charles

French author, 1628–1703. The fairy tales written by the French aristocrat Charles Perrault have become such a part of our cultural lexicon that to consider him the "author" of tales such as "The Sleeping Beauty," "Little Red Riding-Hood," or "Cinderella" would seem almost on a par with naming the "author" of the Old Testament. The tales, first published in 1697, are by now an integral part of our collective childhood. Nearly every adult brought up in western Europe and the United States has heard of one or more of the eight tales; they are, in addition to the three above, "Tom Thumb" (or "Hop O' My Thumb"), "Bluebeard," "Puss in Boots," "The Fairies" (or "Diamonds and Toads"), and "Ricky of the Tuft."

Certainly, Perrault did not make up out of whole cloth the tales that bear his name. Prior to writing down the tales in *Histoires et contes du temps passé, avec des Moralités,* he had heard them from nurses, parents, and other storytellers or had read versions of the tales himself, perhaps in works such as the Italian Renaissance *Pentamerone,* written by Giambattista Basile. The book came to be known as *Les Contes de ma mère l'Oye,* in recognition of its sources in the traditional tales associated with Mother Goose, a personification of a village storyteller. The literary structure of the tales — the repetition, for instance, in "Little Red Riding-Hood" ("My, what big eyes you have, Grandmother!") or the gifts bestowed by the fairies on Sleeping Beauty, accomplishments prized by members of the court of Louis XIV — are all Perrault's own invention. It is in these embellishments that Perrault made the leap from collecting folklore to writing what has been termed the first "true literature for children." Prior to his collection of elegant fairy tales, most books written for children were intended solely to instruct, in keeping with the prevailing attitude that the primary

Illustration by Gustave Doré for "Little Red Riding Hood," from *Perrault's Fairy Tales* (1921; originally *Les Contes de Perrault, desins par Gustave Doré,* 1867), translated by A. E. Johnson.

value of children was as the adults they would become. The glorification of childhood for itself and the celebration of children for their innocence and proximity to nature and to God were ideas not fully realized until the Victorian era, a good hundred or so years away. Perrault's voice was a unique and prophetic one in children's literature.

Surely he sought to inculcate his young audience with moral character; thus, his stories always see evil punished and virtue rewarded, and each tale is completed by a moral in verse. "Bluebeard," one of the best-known, emphasizes the danger to young girls of succumbing to the blandishments of men. But any reader of the stories can see that Perrault's primary goal was to entertain. For example, the moral tacked on to "Puss in Boots" — that native cunning is better than inherited wealth — is completely irrelevant to the rollicking trickster humor of the tale. Perrault did write one tale, "The Princess," that carried heavy moral weight, but it is rarely re-

told. The true value of Perrault's contribution was not his moral instruction but his literary vision. S.G.K.

Petersham, Maud; Petersham, Miska

Maud: American author and illustrator, 1889–1971; Miska: American author and illustrator, 1888–1960. The Caldecott Medal–winning husband-and-wife team of Maud and Miska Petersham left a tremendous legacy to children through their distinguished books, which influenced the development of illustrated books for children in America. For more than thirty years, from the 1920s to the 1950s, they produced colorful, lively, sometimes tender, sometimes humorous PICTURE BOOKS that have charmed, delighted, entertained, and instructed several generations of young readers.

Maud Sylvia Fuller, a minister's daughter, grew up nourished by Bible stories, a parsonage life, and visits to her Quaker grandfather. After graduating from Vassar, she spent a year at art school in New York, where she met her future husband and lifelong collaborator. Miska Petersham, born Petrezselyem Mikaly, had left his native Hungary after graduation from the Budapest Academy of Art, immigrated to the United States in 1912, and become a naturalized citizen in "a country that I had dreamed of but never thought could really exist." After their marriage Miska left commercial art, and the couple devoted themselves entirely to children's books.

The Petershams' attractive illustrations for children's reading texts made them leaders in that field during the 1920s. At this time and throughout their career, they also illustrated trade books written by others. *Poppy Seed Cakes* (1924), written by Margery Clark, was a milestone for them and for children's books. A charming story for early readers with an Old World setting and flavor, it is illustrated in the colorful peasant style that came to be recognized as pure Petersham, and its decorative borders and endpapers show their feeling for good book design.

Miki (1929) is the first book the Petershams both illustrated and wrote, the first big, colored picture book printed in the United States, and the first of a tide of picture books set in a foreign land. Written for their six-year-old son, it portrays an imaginary trip to the land of his forebears. The Petershams visited Hungary in preparation for the book, and their passion for travel and the portrayal of authentic detail also led them to Palestine for *The Christ Child* (1931), the story of the Nativity as told by Matthew and Luke, which is illustrated in glowing watercolors that were reproduced in Germany. The use of watercolors represents a break from their customary use of lithography and resulted in what has been called "one of the most beautiful books for children ever made." *The Christ Child* is still in print. *Get-a-Way and Hary Janos* (1933) is illustrated in bright colors alternating with the grayed tones and shading in which Miska excelled. In this original story with great child appeal, toys from the Petershams' own collection were used as models.

The lavishly colored, detailed illustrations for the Petershams' series of informational storybooks, written between 1933 and 1939, set a new standard in nonfiction for children. A group of Old Testament tales rounded out their group of Bible stories. In the 1940s and 1950s the Petershams celebrated America's heritage in a number of books, including *An American ABC* (1941), a Caldecott Honor Book, and *The Rooster Crows: A Book of American Rhymes and Jingles,* which was awarded the Caldecott Medal in 1946 in the patriotic atmosphere prevalent during and after World War II.

The Petershams' weakness was in portraying the human face, whether strong-featured or doll-like. Two rhymes and their accompanying pictures of blacks were eliminated from the fourteenth printing of *The Rooster Crows* because they were considered offensive stereotypes. Two of their last books, *The Box with Red Wheels* (1949) and *The Circus Baby* (1950), continue to charm the youngest readers and listeners.

The Petershams' art and writing were infused with their backgrounds, their deep convictions and feelings, and their life together. Their joy, their sense of fun, their buoyant optimism, their respect for children and for all of life, and their response to beauty are reflected in all their work. As Maud Petersham herself said in an interview, "Anyone who knows our books knows us."

S.L.R.

Picture Books

In 1658, Comenius, a Moravian bishop and educator, produced what is considered the first picture book for children, *Orbis Sensualium Pictus* (Visible world). If today he could survey a well-stocked children's library, he would likely be bemused if not overwhelmed by the seemingly limitless choices available. Comenius's objective in adding illustrations to an informational text — for such was the *Orbis Pictus* — was "to stir up the attention . . . by sport, and a merry pastime." Today, nonfiction is only one of many genres formatted as picture books. These varied types can be loosely organized into at least five categories:

- *The "pure" or "true" picture book with little or no text:* Most ALPHABET BOOKS, COUNTING BOOKS, or concept books fit into this category.
- *The wordless book with no text:* These tell a story or impart information through a sequential arrangement of carefully designed illustrations.
- *The picture storybook and the picture* INFORMATION BOOK: In these books the illustrations are as integral to the content as the text is.
- *The illustrated book:* This category includes most books for beginning readers; these may have more text than pictures, but the pictures offer important interpretations of characters and situations, or, in the case of information books, extend or explain the factual material presented in the text. Sometimes the pictures may be simply decorative.
- *Toy and movable books (pop-up, lift-the-flap, pull-tabs, and so on):* Although usually designed for the very young, elements of these may be used, particularly in information books, for older readers. Their effectiveness depends on the quality of the paper engineering and the relationship between form and content.

Within each division are many variations. Some books with pictures span more than one category; that is, a concept book may also be a picture story; an alphabet book may provide information beyond letter and word identification; a folktale or poem may be designed in picture-story format; a movable or toy book may also be a story or information book.

Although there are remarkable achievements within these varied configurations, citations of the picture book as a unique art form usually refer to the exceptional combination of text and pictures found in the picture storybook. Alphabet, counting, or concept books may be acclaimed for graphic elegance, originality of execution, pedagogical applications — or all three — but in general, sequence and frequently even the text itself are predetermined. Spectacular results can be achieved despite the restrictions of these formats: consider MITSUMASA ANNO's pyrotechnical display of seemingly three-dimensional shapes in *Anno's Alphabet* (1975) or TOM FEELINGS's sculptured African figures in *Moja Means One: Swahili Counting Book* (1971), written by Muriel Feelings. They are not, however, picture storybooks. And when the text is substantial, as in Margaret Musgrove's *Ashanti to Zulu* (1976), illustrated by LEO and DIANE DILLON, the concept picture book moves toward the illustrated book category.

The wordless story — such as RAYMOND BRIGGS's *Snowman* (1978), remarkable for an almost ethereal blending of reality and fantasy — can be a tour de force for the illustrator, but the text changes with the interpretation of each "reader." While the "story line" may remain constant, the text does not. Toy and movable books may depend too heavily on kinesthetic effects, although a few author-illustrators, such as ERIC CARLE in *The Very Hungry Caterpillar* (1969), have successfully made the manipulation of physical form into an integral story element.

Folktales and FANTASY, like the alphabet, are set pieces for interpretation. Consequently, they can sometimes pose problems when translated into the picture book format. Most are illustrated stories in that the text can be read independently of the pictures. In many books, such as *Hansel and Gretel* (1984), retold by Rika Lesser and illustrated by PAUL O. ZELINSKY, the art adds new dimension to familiar materials. Sometimes, however, one wonders, particularly when yet another version of an old favorite appears, just how deep is that "cauldron of story" to which folklorists refer. Tales may be newly translated, as some are; they may be heavily edited, as some are; but the success of the folktale as picture-storybook text relies on the illustrator's and reteller's sense of pacing and editing so that the illustrations, like the voice of the true storyteller, offer a fresh, authentic interpretation rather than mere embellishment.

Original fantasy sets yet another trap. Adapting a text to the picture-storybook format may eradicate phrases that convey a distinct authorial tone; HANS CHRISTIAN ANDERSEN is particularly susceptible to such well-meaning but unfortunate efforts. Then there is Mother Goose, who has survived any number of attempts to adapt her unquenchable vivacity to showcase an illustrator's talents.

Despite its complex evolution, the history of the picture storybook is not very long. The idea of using pictures to complement instruction was devised by Comenius, but the concept of extending the meaning of the text beyond literal visualization belongs to the great nineteenth-century illustrator RANDOLPH CALDECOTT (1846–1886). Exemplified in his transformation of "Hey Diddle Diddle" (1882) into a story of star-crossed lovers, the interdependence of text and pictures is a fundamental element in the picture storybook. Marked by economy of line and a genuine sense of humor, Caldecott's illustrations are yardsticks against which others are measured. The printer Edmund Evans (1826–1905) also deserves mention for his pioneering work in the field of color printing, ensuring not only the beauty of Caldecott's work but also that of WALTER CRANE (1845–1915) and KATE GREENAWAY (1846–1901), both of whom had an enduring influence on children's book illustration. Crane envisioned text and illustrations as "an harmonious whole." Greenaway popularized the appealing view of childhood as quaint, charming, and unsullied. Later influential illustrators included L. LESLIE BROOKE (1862–1940) and the incomparable BEATRIX POTTER (1866–1943). Sized to fit children's small hands, Potter's books have texts so well composed that they could stand alone, but the accompanying meticulously executed illustrations drawn to the perspective of a small animal — or small child — add invaluable details that place the stories in particular seasons and locales. Like Caldecott, she set a high standard for the art of the picture storybook.

Until the late 1920s, the United States tended to celebrate the aesthetics of English or continental picture books as its standard. In addition to books by Brooke, Caldecott, Crane, Greenaway, and Potter, the work of French illustrator Maurice Boutet de Monvel (1851–1913), notably his *Jeanne d'Arc* (1896), beautifully printed and exquisitely composed, also exerted a strong influence on the formation of critical opinion.

Two other important English contributions to the art of the picture book were provided by William Nicholson (1872–1949). Nicholson's use of strong graphic elements in the *Square Book of Animals* (1899), with text by Arthur Waugh, was reflected in the design of C. B. Falls's *ABC* (1923), acclaimed as a significant accomplishment in American publishing for children. Even more important, perhaps, was Nicholson's devising of the "running text" for *Clever Bill* (1926), which completed the transformation of the illustrated story into the picture storybook. An important element in the overall design of these books, the term *running text* describes the division of sentences or paragraphs into short, precise units, which, when placed with interpretive illustrations, create a sense of movement and anticipation. Innately dynamic, this technique impels the reader to turn the pages.

By 1930, the conventions of the picture storybook had evolved: interdependence of words and pictures, expansion of text in pictures, precise text placed not as captions but as an integral element, and the concept of the book as a total design from casing to endpapers. For approximately thirty-five years, most illustrators attempted to codify the form, exploring its possibilities even as they adapted the conventions to their individual styles.

Some of the artists who became popular in the decades between 1930 and 1960 had emigrated from Europe to the United States: LUDWIG BEMELMANS, ROGER DUVOISIN, FEODOR ROJANKOVSKY, and TOMI UNGERER. All brought new visions and styles to picture book aesthetics, adding an international flair to American publishing. Others, like ROBERT MCCLOSKEY and GLEN ROUNDS, were more firmly grounded in American traditions. In contrast, WANDA GÁG, although born in the United States, drew upon the old-country customs of her immigrant family for inspiration. Still a classic, her *Millions of Cats* (1928) combines a memorable text with peasantlike illustrations in describing the adventures of the old man who, seeking a cat to keep himself and his wife company, encounters "Hundreds of cats, / Thousands of cats, / Millions and billions and trillions of cats." In black and white, not color, *Millions of Cats* has delighted millions of children. Its popularity confounds those who maintain that only a compelling palette guarantees success.

Similarly, ROBERT LAWSON's black and white illustrations for MUNRO LEAF's *Story of Ferdinand* (1936) — very different in style from Gág's — have also endured, despite efforts in the 1930s to squelch the book for what was perceived to be subversive pacifism. Ten years later, in December 1946, Jella Lepman, founder of the International Board of Books for Young People, would distribute thousands of cheaply produced copies to the children of war-ravaged Berlin.

Ferdinand also represented the felicitous blending of two talents, writer Leaf and illustrator Lawson. While such collaborations are not uncommon, many classic American picture storybooks from the first half of the century were conceived and executed individually: just a few examples are *And to Think That I Saw It on Mulberry Street* (1937), by DR. SEUSS; *Andy and the Lion* (1938), by JAMES DAUGHERTY; *Mike Mulligan and His Steam Shovel* (1939), by VIRGINIA LEE BURTON; *Make Way for Ducklings* (1941), by Robert McCloskey; and *In the Forest* (1944), by Marie Hall Ets. Of writers who worked with illustrators, MARGARET WISE BROWN, "the laureate of the nursery," was particularly fortunate in the varied talents of the artists with whom she worked, including Leonard Weisgard for *The Noisy Book* (1939) and Jean Charlot for *A Child's Good Night Book* (1943). RUTH KRAUSS was similarly successful in her collaboration with, among others, CROCKETT JOHNSON for *The Carrot Seed* (1945) and MAURICE SENDAK for *A Hole Is to Dig* (1952).

As picture books became a significant part of American publishing for children in the pre-1960s era, trends were established that would be further developed in the post-1960s decades. The nursery books of Margaret Wise Brown would find reflection in the deceptively simple BOARD BOOKS of ROSEMARY WELLS, featuring the long-suffering but always triumphant rabbit hero Max, who made his debut in 1979. Photography as illustration, anticipated in the 1940s and 1950s by the photographer Ylla, would find greater artistic expression in the work of TANA HOBAN. The wildly improbable cartoon visions of Dr. Seuss and the quirky talents of Gene Zion and MARGARET BLOY GRAHAM in *Dear Garbage Man* (1957) paved the way for *New Yorker* artists such as WILLIAM STEIG and JAMES STEVENSON. But, for the most part, the years from 1930 to the 1960s seem more continuum than revolution.

Then, in 1963, *Where the Wild Things Are* was published. In 1964, its creator, Maurice Sendak, received the Caldecott Medal. Perhaps it was content more than execution that made the book so much of a milestone and initially so controversial. The format is the cumulative expression of picture storybook conventions: pictures expanding text in the Caldecott tradition; the horizontal format and running text used by Nicholson; and quality of design and reproduction that would have pleased the nineteenth-century printer Evans. It is perhaps as close to the perfect picture storybook as an imperfect world allows. Then why the fuss? Perhaps because the vision of childhood presented is neither idealized nor nostalgic. When Max, the independent protagonist, tells his admonishing mother that he hates her, his imagination transforms his room into a wilderness and then populates it with monsterlike wild things over whom he comes to exert total command.

Whatever its magic, one fact is indisputable. With the publication of *Wild Things*, the modern era in children's books began. The picture storybook had received its ultimate codification.

After 1963, coinciding with societal and technological change, would come a period of expansion, exploration, and sometimes exploitation,
as seductively elaborate art would overwhelm
story or distract readers from weak texts. A
number of Sendak wannabes would produce
variations on his theme or style.

As for Sendak, he continued to exemplify the
trends of the late twentieth century in two additional picture storybooks that form a trilogy
with *Wild Things: In the Night Kitchen* (1970)
and *Outside over There* (1981). While all explore
children's psyches, each is different in style. *Wild
Things,* with its use of cross-hatching, recalls
nineteenth-century engraving; *Night Kitchen*
employs images from twentieth-century popular culture — films and comics; *Outside Over
There* is more painterly. Together they demonstrate three current approaches to children's
book illustration: traditional draftsmanship,
contemporary references, and fine art. Given
technological advances, illustrators can now be
less concerned with the strictures of the printing
process. The result is a dazzling array of techniques: from the stylized graphics of GERALD
McDERMOTT to the intricate collages of Jeannie
Baker; from the surrealistic perspectives of
CHRIS VAN ALLSBURG to the exquisitely rendered illustrations of BARBARA COONEY.

Should there be doubt that the picture storybook is a unique art form, one has only to examine books such as TOMIE dePAOLA's *Charlie
Needs a Cloak* (1974), a seamless blend of information and story, or *The Snowy Day* (1962), by
EZRA JACK KEATS, with its poetic simplicity, for
reassurance. While no art form can remain
blindly constant to conventions without becoming static, various critics have expressed concern
about a tendency to celebrate showmanship over
substance. Although many styles, techniques,
and subjects are possible, the picture book
works within a framework defined by form,
function, and audience. At the beginning of the
twenty-first century, we may be in danger of
confusing gilt with gold when we should perhaps be asking whether or not the emperor is
wearing clothes. M.M.B.

Pienkowski, Jan

Polish-born British illustrator and author, b.
1936. From a childhood spent moving to
different parts of Poland, then to Austria, Italy,
and finally England, Jan Pienkowski has remembered primarily visual images. The frost patterns
on the windowpanes of his family's house in
western Poland and the perversely beautiful fires
set during the 1944 German assault on Warsaw:
these memories manifest the designer's instinct
in his many books for children.

An ambivalent classics major but avid poster
maker at King's College, Cambridge, Pienkowski's pluck and artistic promise landed him a job
in the art department of a London advertising
agency upon graduation. A disdain for the
structure of office jobs led him to work that
much harder and succeed enormously as a freelance designer, which in turn led him to draw for
the BBC children's program *Watch!* and team
with Helen Nicoll, the show's director, to create
the Meg and Mog series of PICTURE BOOKS. Beginning with *Meg and Mog* in 1972, these stories
about a scraggly witch and her cat — sometimes
fat and sleepy, sometimes thin and supercharged
— establish the Pienkowski illustrative trademarks. Electric colors provide the background
and fill the interior of deceptively simple, bold
line drawings. Meg the witch, like other Pienkowski figures, is a glorified doodle, with dot
eyes, a line mouth, a ragged triangle dress, and
chaotic lines of hair. The placement of text often
corresponds visually with the activity at hand —
the words descending the stairs along with Meg,
for example — joining the illustrations to create
a self-contained, whimsical world. Pienkowski's
style of illustration has made him a natural success at concept books.

Numbers, Colors, Sizes, and *Shapes* (all published in 1973) and other titles entice and teach
the very young with saturated colors and basic,
clearly defined shapes. Another technique with
which Pienkowski has made a name for himself
is the silhouette. He began working with silhouettes when he discovered they allowed him to
universalize his characters — to let his readers,

whatever their race, imagine themselves into the pictures. The products of this discovery won him the Kate Greenaway Medal in 1972 for *The Kingdom Under the Sea,* a collection of eastern European fairy tales adapted by JOAN AIKEN, an author with whom he has collaborated on numerous books. Spidery and intricate, Pienkowski's fairyland scenes nevertheless exhibit his characteristic energy and sense of whimsy. In 1979 his energy ran wild to stupendous effect in his first pop-up book, *Haunted House.* This ghostly jamboree features not one but several spooky goings-on to a page, including the sound — generated by the opening and closing of the book — of someone or something sawing its way out of a crate. *Haunted House* won him another Kate Greenaway Medal, and successors such as *Robot* (1981), a futuristic postcard from space, and *Dinnertime* (1981), less busy than the first two but just as flamboyant, solidified his reputation for revitalizing the pop-up genre, the accomplishment for which he is best known in America. C.M.H.

Pilkey, Dav

A merican author and illustrator, b. 1966. Success has embraced Cleveland-born author and illustrator Dav Pilkey in spite of his sometimes troubled childhood. From his first book, *World War Won* (1987), to the thunderous popularity of his irreverent but fun Captain Underpants series, Pilkey has tackled dozens of children's book genres with personal flair. Each story shines with humor and compassion — two fundamentals that helped Pilkey survive his struggles with attention deficit disorder as a boy. Fellow students called Pilkey a class clown. Impatient teachers called him trouble. Even in high school, some educators told Pilkey that artists were "a dime a dozen" and that he'd never make a living by drawing pictures. Though those hurtful words haunted Pilkey during his school career, success has been a delightful way to prove them wrong.

As a freshman at Kent State University in Ohio in 1984, Pilkey drafted *World War Won* — a bear's tribute in rhyme to wisdom and peace. A year later, it won the Landmark Edition's National "Written and Illustrated by" Awards Contest for Students, ensuring Pilkey's destiny. Shortly after *World War Won* was published, Pilkey met author-illustrator CYNTHIA RYLANT, and they quickly became loyal friends. They moved to Oregon in 1990, where they live only blocks apart.

Three PICTURE BOOK series — Dragon; Big Dog, Little Dog; and Dumb Bunnies (with author Sue Denim) — contributed to Pilkey's snowballing popularity. But stand-alone titles such as *Dogzilla* (1993), *Kat Kong* (1993), and *Dog Breath: The Horrible Trouble with Hally Tosis* (1994), and his richly illustrated Caldecott Honor Book, *The Paperboy* (1996), prove that Pilkey can write with extraordinary grace and conscience.

In a different vein, Captain Underpants — the crown prince of potty-talk — debuted in 1999 with *The Adventures of Captain Underpants.* The ongoing tales of Harold and George (two misbehaving fourth-graders), their tighty-whities superhero friend, and their cranky principal engaged even the most reluctant young readers, rocketing Pilkey to children's book stardom. Designed with more cartoon content than text, these books have been blasted by some patrons of good taste. But children and childlike adults laugh out loud at Pilkey's crazy mix of high jinks, wordplay, and exaggerated comic art.

Pilkey doesn't see computer animation slipping into his portfolio. He likes to do his illustrations by hand. He also likes to laugh, stating that it's the driving force behind his literary creations. K.M.H.

Pinkney, Brian

A merican author and illustrator, b. 1961. Boys often emulate their fathers, making career decisions based on what they've seen. This is very true for Brian Pinkney, the son of illustrator JERRY PINKNEY; Brian enjoyed watching his father work. The younger Pinkney received a B.F.A. from the Philadelphia College of Art and an M.F.A. from the School of Visual Arts in New York City. While studying at the School of Visual Arts, Pinkney began experimenting with what was to become his favorite medium, scratchboard. In this technique, a white board is covered with black ink, then etched, or scratched, to reveal the white underneath. Pinkney has continued to experiment with this medium, adding color, generating movement and rhythm, to create his signature style of illustration.

Pinkney's career as a children's book illustrator began in the mid-1980s, when Pinkney illustrated books written by other writers. The first book that he both wrote and illustrated was *Max Found Two Sticks* (1994), which features Max, a drummer. He uses twigs to beat out the rhythm of the neighborhood around him, to express himself even though he doesn't feel like talking. When a real marching band rounds the corner, Max gets a surprise. Pinkney drew on his personal study of the martial arts in *JoJo's Flying Side Kick* (1995). The character JoJo overcomes her anxiety, earning a yellow belt in tae kwon do. Text and illustration combine to depict the child's turbulent emotions swirling to a triumphant conclusion. Pinkney's youthful experience on a newspaper route appears in *The Adventures of Sparrowboy* (1997). Pinkney's scratchboard technique creates a fantasy as the character Henry (AKA superhero Sparrowboy) delivers papers in an extraordinary way.

Pinkney has continued to illustrate works by other authors, winning many awards for his work. *The Faithful Friend* (1995), written by Robert San Souci, was selected as a Caldecott Honor Book. In this folktale from Martinique, friendship takes on new meaning when tested by creatures unleashed by a wizard. Double pages accommodate dark, moody scratchboard and oil illustrations.

Pinkney married Andrea Davis in 1991 and continued another family tradition. Like his father, who collaborated with his mother, Brian Pinkney has successfully collaborated with Andrea Davis Pinkney. Often their books focus on African American history and biography, including *Seven Days of Kwanzaa* (1993), *Mim's Christmas Jam* (2001), *Alvin Ailey* (1993), *Bill Pickett: Rodeo Ridin' Cowboy* (1996), and *Dear Benjamin Banneker* (1998). In each, Pinkney's illustrations add color, a vibrant contrast to the dark scratchboard, to highlight the movement and vigor of the subject. This technique is especially prominent in *Duke Ellington: The Piano Prince and His Orchestra* (1998), Pinkney's second Caldecott Honor Book. Swirls of color and line bring Ellington's era to life, creating a jazzy rhythm to counterpoint the cadenced, colloquial text. Black and white scratchboard illustrations enliven a new edition of LANGSTON HUGHES's 1932 POETRY collection, *The Dreamkeeper and Other Poems* (1994), another testament to the expressive power of Pinkney's carefully rendered illustration. M.B.S.

Pinkney, Jerry

American illustrator, b. 1939. Born in Philadelphia, Jerry Pinkney drew constantly and was recognized as a talented child in school. His parents encouraged him to pursue his talent. As a boy of about twelve, he sold newspapers at a stand, and because he was drawing between sales, he was noticed by a cartoonist, John Liney, who showed him some of the tools of his trade and became one of several mentors. The high school Pinkney attended had a commercial art program, and one of his teachers had a sign-painting business, so Pinkney was able to spend some after-school time gaining experience in several artistic skills. He won a scholarship to the Philadelphia Museum College of Art, where he studied for a number of years and where his technique was at odds with the abstract expressionism his teachers admired. He has stated that the artists who influenced him were Thomas Eakins, Charles White, ARTHUR RACKHAM, and Alan E. Cober.

A few years later, a designer led him to a job at a greeting card company, where he pursued his interest in the use of typography with illustration. He then became an illustrator-designer for a design studio and illustrated his first book, *The Adventures of Spider: A West African Folk Tale,* which was published in 1964. Pinkney later described the sensation of opening that book for the first time and knowing then that creating books was what he wanted to do. In an extensive biographical article in the *Horn Book Magazine,* Pinkney has extolled the marriage of art and design, emphasizing that text and art should work together on a page. He has said, "The book represents the ultimate in graphics." The pacing of narrative, the design, the drawing, and the typography are crucial elements.

He continued to illustrate a succession of folktales. When he illustrated *Kasho and the Twin Flutes* (1973), however, he stated that he began to "deal with getting some kind of emotion and more action in my figures instead of the people just being part of the composition." He began to take photographs of models reacting to one another, in order to record the movement between them. He illustrated MILDRED TAYLOR's 1975 novel, *Song of the Trees,* the first in her well-known books about the Logan family, using his own family as models. As he built up a body of work that included many African and African American characters, he realized that he "had something to contribute, especially in portraying black people." His realistic drawings of Cassie Logan and her family are synonymous with segregation for a generation of young readers.

His illustrations for *The Patchwork Quilt* (1985), a warm story of the members of an extended family who construct a quilt together, won a 1986 Coretta Scott King Award. He won the award again the next year for *Half a Moon and One Whole Star* (1986). In 1987 he illustrated *The Tales of Uncle Remus,* in which JULIUS LESTER retold Joel Chandler Harris's collection of folktales. Three more volumes of the highly acclaimed stories were published with his illustrations. *Mirandy and Brother Wind* (1988), a 1989 Caldecott Honor Book and a winner of the 1989 Coretta Scott King Award for illustration, celebrates African American culture in a PICTURE BOOK based on a cakewalk dance contest in the 1900s.

In the 1990s, Jerry Pinkney's work grew even stronger. *John Henry* (1994), a retelling of the legend, won the Boston Globe–Horn Book Award and was also a Caldecott Honor Book. Pinkney illustrated Julius Lester's *Sam and the Tigers: A New Telling of Little Black Sambo* (1996) and created a new version of HANS CHRISTIAN ANDERSEN's *The Ugly Duckling* (2000), another Caldecott Honor Book.

Pinkney has said that he likes to put a lot of information in his artwork. For this reason, research is important to him. In addition to his books for children, he has illustrated many limited-edition books of classic literature and has created commemorative stamps for the U.S. Postal Service. He has had many one-man shows and has spoken at colleges, universities, and museums. He is also associate professor of art at the University of Delaware and enjoys encouraging young artists. S.H.H.

Voices of the Creators

✣ Jerry Pinkney

I grew up in a small house in Philadelphia. One of six children, with two older brothers and one older sister, I was the middle child. I started drawing as far back as I can remember, at the age of four or five. My brothers drew, and in a way I was mimicking them. I found I enjoyed the act of putting marks on paper. It also gave me a way of creating my own space and quiet time, a way of expressing myself.

I attended an all-black elementary school. Because of the difficulty African American teachers had finding employment, Hill Elementary School attracted the best. I left there prepared and with a sense of who I was.

In first grade I had the opportunity to draw a large picture of a fire engine on the blackboard. When the drawing was finished, I was complimented and encouraged to draw more. The attention felt good, and I wanted more. I was not a terrific reader or an adept speller in my growing-up years. Drawing helped me feel good about myself.

My mother and father both supported me. My mother had a sixth sense about me and encouraged me to pursue my dreams. My dad was apprehensive about my pursuing art, but he was responsible for finding and enrolling me in after-school art classes.

There were mentors throughout my life. At age twelve I had a newspaper stand and would take a drawing pad to work with me, sketching people as they waited for a bus or trolley. John Liney, at that time the cartoonist of "Little Henry," would pass the newsstand on his way to his studio. He took notice of my drawing and invited me to visit his studio. There I learned about the possibility of making a living by creating pictures. What an eye opener! I visited John's studio often, and we became friends.

Roosevelt Junior High was an integrated school. I had many friends, white and black, at a time when there was little social mixing in school. At Roosevelt the spark for my curiosity about people was lit. This interest in and fascination with people of different cultures appear throughout my work.

My formal art training started at Dobbins Vocational High School, where I majored in commercial art. There I met my first African American artist and educator, Sam Brown. Upon graduation I received a scholarship to the Philadelphia Museum College of Art, where I studied in advertising and design.

When I left school, I freelanced in typography and hand lettering. In 1960 I had the opportunity to go to Boston and work for Rust Craft Greeting Cards. Along with my wife, Gloria Jean, and our first child, I moved to Boston. Boston provided good opportunities for me, because it was a publishing center. I was there at a time during which publishers were reconstructing their ideas about textbooks. The late 1960s and early 1970s brought about an awareness of the need for African American writers. Publishers sought out African American illustrators for this work. And there I was.

From the very beginning of my career in illus-trating books, research has been important. I do as much as possible on a given subject, whether it has anything directly to do with the project or not, so that I live the experience and have a vision of the people and the places. To capture a sense of realism for characters in my work, I use models that resemble as much as possible the people I want to portray. Gloria has been assisting me in finding the models. We keep a closet full of old clothes to dress up the models, and I have people act out the story. I take photos to aid me in better understanding body language and facial expressions. Once I have that photo as reference, I have freedom, because the more you know, the more you can be inventive.

In illustrating stories about animals, as with people, research is important. I keep a large reference file and have over a hundred books on nature and animals. The first step in envisioning a creature is for me to pretend to be that particular animal. I think about its size and the sounds it makes, how it moves, where it lives. When the stories call for anthropomorphic animals, I've used Polaroid photographs of myself posing as the animal characters.

Recently, I have been concentrating on doing books about people of color. As an African American artist doing black subject matter, I try to portray a sense of celebration, of self-respect and resilience, and also a sense of dignity.

It still amazes me how much the projects I have illustrated have given back to me — the personal as well as the artistic satisfaction. They have given me the opportunity to use my imagination to draw, to paint, and to travel through the voices of the characters in the stories — and above all else, to touch children. ✒

Pinkwater, Daniel

American author and illustrator, b. 1941. Daniel Manus Pinkwater has created numerous weird and whimsical stories that play upon the absurdity of reality. His books derive from an imagination that allows for fantasies such as a 266-pound chicken running loose and a blue moose helping in a kitchen. Yet children do not have to consider the logic of the story; they simply let go and follow "the fantastic Mr. Pinkwater," as he has been called.

Born in Memphis, Tennessee, Pinkwater grew up in Chicago and Los Angeles. At Bard College, he studied sculpture; later he moved to New York to pursue a career in fine arts. Currently, Pinkwater's humorous commentaries can be heard on National Public Radio's *All Things Considered.*

It was only after a trip to Africa that Pinkwater decided to illustrate a story — and he hasn't stopped since. His books embrace the ridiculous and rollick in the pleasure of it. Pinkwater's simple, cartoonlike illustrations have often been described as resembling children's art, yet his energetic lines effectively complement the droll and quirky text. Critics of his books accuse Pinkwater of relying on the absurd instead of creating a coherent plot. Others just don't appreciate his humor and desperately search for logic. When the stories are at their best, however, these concerns drop away, and their jocularity carries them to ludicrous new heights.

In *Blue Moose* (1975) Pinkwater shared a bizarre yet engaging tale of friendship between a chef and a moose. *The Hoboken Chicken Emergency* (1977) is a tall tale about Henrietta, a tall chicken, and Arthur, a little boy. Frightened by a dog, Henrietta runs loose in Hoboken; the loony adventure subsides with the affirmation of Arthur's love for his chicken. *Roger's Umbrella* (1982) explores the pure silliness of things as Pinkwater details the familiar foibles, illustrated by JAMES MARSHALL, of an untamed umbrella. In *Pickle Creature* (1979) a bumpy green being who savors raisins meets the tender Conrad in a supermarket and follows him home. This endearing tale wonderfully contrasts the apparently dull supermarket with the mysterious surprise within.

Two delightful insights into young boys' imaginations occur in *I Was a Second Grade Werewolf* (1983) and *Wempires* (1991). When Lawrence Talbot becomes a werewolf, he expects to see some changes in his life, but much to his dismay, nobody notices. Similar surprises occur when the young vampire discovers that real vampires, called "wempires," like to drink ginger ale instead of blood. *Guys from Space* (1989) relates the day's events as the young protagonists blast off to another planet. Like wempires, the guys from space enjoy simple pleasures such as root beer floats. The more realistic *Author's Day* (1993) presents the visit of a famous children's author to an enthusiastic classroom. Unfortunately, the excited children confuse Bramwell Wink-Porter with another author. Surely Pinkwater's fans would get it right, for he has captivated many with his straightforward text, odd sense of humor, and equally amusing illustrations.

Pinkwater's gang of offbeat characters and preposterous occurrences blend nicely with commonplace settings, forcing the reader to question reality — and then to laugh at it.

In recent years Pinkwater has become equally well known for the books he has chosen to review on National Public Radio's *Weekend Edition.* His enthusiasm for the books he loves is truly infectious. In a few short years, he has become the one review source able to create a *New York Times* bestseller based on his recommendation. C.M.H.

Poetry

The nonsense verse of the nineteenth century could be considered the beginnings of modern children's poetry. Prior to that, poetry written for children had been entirely religious, moralistic, or didactic in nature. Reacting to the hidebound conventions of the Victorian era, the zestful wordplay and subversive wit of writers such as EDWARD LEAR and LEWIS CARROLL caught the attention of children, and the influence of these writers has carried through the twentieth century and into the twenty-first. For much of the early part of the century, however, the poet whose work was most admired by critics was WALTER DE LA MARE. Although his poetry is not as widely known as it once was, it still has the power to move readers. *Peacock Pie*, first published in 1917, was reissued in 1989; his incomparable anthology, *Come Hither*, which contains more than five hundred traditional poems accompanied by his own insightful comments, was reissued in 1990.

The work of a handful of other children's poets from the first half of the century still appears in anthologies today. Harry Behn is chiefly remembered for his brief, deceptively simple verses that communicate his sense of wonder about the world. His contemporaries Aileen Fisher and Lilian Moore, who were also writing nature poems, continue to write verse. *Adam Mouse's Book of Poems* (1992) is a fine introduction for younger children to Lilian Moore's perfectly tuned lyric lines, where "Fireflies / Flash / Their cold glow" ("Fireflies") and a cricket makes "music / far into the / middle / of the soft summer / night" ("Fiddler"). The midcentury children's poet whose body of work surpasses all others, however, is DAVID MCCORD. The playful spontaneity that permeates his writing keeps it fresh. "Pickety Fence," with its inventive rhythms and sound effects, is a favorite with children. A prolific writer, McCord published hundreds of poems that vary widely in theme, subject matter, and emotional range. His first book of verse for children was *Far and Few* (1952). *All Small* (1986) is a collection made from the poet's previous books of appealing shorter poems.

During the 1960s, American poets began to explore new subjects, ones they felt drew a more accurate picture of their own time. Issues of war and peace, social injustice and racial prejudice, technology and urban life were addressed in children's poetry for the first time. They also began experimenting with new forms, such as free verse, concrete poetry, and the use of dialect. In *Poems to Solve* (1966) and *More Poems to Solve* (1971), May Swenson constructed clever riddle poems, visual patterns, and word puzzles. A new edition, which includes many selections from her previous books, has recently been published under the title *The Complete Poems to Solve* (1993). Another poet who adroitly manipulated

free verse forms is Eve Merriam. In *Finding a Poem* (1970) she commented wryly on modern technology and modern humanity. The concluding essay detailing the process of writing a poem offers some revealing insights into the creative process.

Also well regarded for his verbal craftsmanship, John Ciardi experimented with controlled vocabulary designed for beginning readers. *I Met a Man* (1961) and *You Read to Me, I'll Read to You* (1962), with their humorous easy-to-read riddles, make deft use of internal rhymes and puns. Along with Ciardi, Dennis Lee reintroduced some of the nonsense to poetry that had lost favor in the early part of the century. In *Alligator Pie* (1974) and *Garbage Delight* (1978) he adopted the speech patterns of children to create verses full of high-spirited energy, catchy rhymes, and repetitive phrasing. Another poet whose dancing rhythms and humorous twists and turns of phrase have attracted children is N. M. Bodecker. The playfulness of *Hurry, Hurry, Mary Dear! and Other Nonsense Poems* (1976) is reinforced by his black and white drawings. *Water Pennies and Other Poems* (1991), published posthumously and illustrated by Erik Blegvad, is a whimsical reverie on insects and other small creatures and contains some of the poet's finest lyric verses.

As the subject matter of children's poetry expanded in the 1960s to include a wider world, a new awareness of the country's cultural diversity led to the publication of a greater number of African American poets. One of the first books of poetry to describe the experience of urban African American children was Gwendolyn Brooks's *Bronzeville Boys and Girls* (1956), which adhered to standard language and poetic forms as it described young children in an essentially middle-class environment. The distinctive patterns of idiomatic black speech expressing a wider range of experience and emotions were heard in *Don't You Turn Back* (1969), a collection of poems by LANGSTON HUGHES that are accessible to children. That same year saw the publication of *Hold Fast to Dreams*, an anthology compiled by ARNA BONTEMPS, a distinguished poet in his own right. Arnold Adoff is another important anthologizer of poetry for and about African Americans. Eloise Greenfield's *Honey, I Love and Other Love Poems* (1978) reflects a child's love for her family and for life around her. Poems such as "Keepsake" and "Aunt Roberta" are profound in their unadorned emotional expression. In the later volumes *Nathaniel Talking* (1989) and *Night on Neighborhood Street* (1991), both illustrated by Jan Spivey Gilchrist, Greenfield again displayed a wealth of emotions and scenes from African American life in poetry that is realistic yet full of the nurturing spirit of community.

Voices from other cultures are being heard in increasing numbers as well. GARY SOTO's writings reflect the Latino experience in California. An example of the poetic sensibility of American Indians is found in the collection of prayers, lullabies, chants, and songs gathered by Hettie Jones in a fine book, *The Trees Stand Shining*. First published in 1971, it was reissued in 1993. James Berry's poems ring with the mellifluous cadences of the Caribbean.

Another positive development that grew out of the freedom of the 1960s was the flowering of lyric poetry in free verse form as poets searched for new and natural ways to express their thoughts and feelings. KARLA KUSKIN, intent on breaking down formalities, has frequently illustrated her books with her own line drawings. In *Near the Window Tree* (1975), her brief, imaginative poems are accompanied by her own notes describing her sources of inspiration. Siv Cedering Fox has created vivid imagery around bedtime themes such as sleeping, dreaming, and night fears in *The Blue Horse and Other Night Poems* (1979), the images reinforced by DONALD CARRICK's dreamy, gray-toned washes. Sylvia Cassedy's *Roomrimes: Poems* (1987), an alphabet of poems about rooms and other spaces, is noteworthy for its clever, unforced rhythms within an original conceptual framework. "Just what *is* it / in the closet / that I positively / hear?" asks the young narrator in "Closet." The poems are brief and easily accessible to children. Barbara Esbensen's *Who Shrank My Grandmother's House?* (1992) creates a new world of

discovery in ordinary objects. Her poetry sparkles with crisp images and sounds. In "Sand Dollar" this marine animal is transformed into money "spilled / from the green silk / pocket / of the sea." Of all those writing brief, unrhymed lyric verse for children, perhaps the most consistent in excellence was Valerie Worth, with her series of poems that first appeared in 1972. Using simple language in surprising ways, she celebrated the minutiae of everyday life. Poems like "Mice" and "Rags" can be enjoyed by adults and children in equal measure.

An undeniable impetus behind the increased interest in children's poetry in the past few decades has been the phenomenal popularity of SHEL SILVERSTEIN's two volumes, *Where the Sidewalk Ends* (1974) and *The Light in the Attic* (1974). Both books make impudent sport of children's fascination with the messy and the ridiculous. Second only to Silverstein in popularity is JACK PRELUTSKY. *The New Kid on the Block* (1984) and its companion volume, *Something Big Has Been Here* (1990), are full of puns and nonsense in the strong, unvarying beat and childlike language that characterize his work. His unerring sense of a child's notion of fun is nowhere more apparent than in his selections for the brief anthology *Poems of A. Nonny Mouse* (1989), complemented by the surrealistically outlandish illustrations of HENRIK DRESCHER, and its sequel, *A. Nonny Mouse Writes Again!* (1993), with illustrations by MARJORIE PRICEMAN.

Literary honors bestowed on books of poetry have earned them new cachet with adult readers as well as with children. NANCY WILLARD's *A Visit to William Blake's Inn* (1981), with its fanciful and mystical references, was the first volume of poetry to receive the Newbery Medal. In 1988 the same honor was accorded *Joyful Noise: Poems for Two Voices*, PAUL FLEISCHMAN's lyrical paean to the insect world, meant to be read by two people simultaneously or in alternating voices. "Cicadas" and "Fireflies" are notable among these triumphs of sound and harmony.

The highly visual treatment of poetry in an attempt to integrate art and text is a current publishing phenomenon. Narrative poems, with their strong element of story, adapt easily to this single-poem picture book format. Some recent examples include Ernest Thayer's classic "Casey at the Bat," which has been illustrated with droll wit by Wallace Tripp (1980) and by BARRY MOSER, whose more painterly style has produced a more elegant version (1988). The amusing possibilities inherent in Ogden Nash's "The Adventures of Isabel" have been impishly detailed by illustrator JAMES MARSHALL (1991).

Children are drawn to the illustrations in these books, but critics have raised questions about whether such illustrated editions stifle the imagination by eliminating the text's challenge to readers to create their own mental images. Works in which the words of the poet and the illustrations are universally agreed to complement and not detract from each other are the collaborations between Myra Cohn Livingston and Leonard Everett Fisher. *A Circle of Seasons* (1982), *Sky Songs* (1984), *Earth Songs* (1986), and *Space Songs* (1988) form a cycle of books celebrating the wonders of the world and the universe beyond. The artist's swirling abstract paintings evoke the spirit of the words with color and form rather than with concrete images. In like manner, ED YOUNG has suggested, rather than interpreted, the meaning of the lines in Robert Frost's narrative poem *Birches* (1988), with his muted impressionistic paintings. Barry Moser used ink and transparent watercolors on glossy black pages to evoke the spooky, mysterious nuances of Henry Treece's *The Magic Wood* (1992), with its hints of creatures hidden in the night forest.

Large general anthologies typifying the trend toward the more concrete, visual interpretation of poetry include *The Random House Book of Poetry for Children* (1983), profusely illustrated with color and black-and-white drawings by ARNOLD LOBEL, and *Sing a Song of Popcorn* (1988), illustrated by nine Caldecott Medal artists. Most anthologies today, however, are leaner and concentrate on specific themes, genres, ethnic groups, or audiences. Lillian Morrison, who began editing her series of thematic antholo-

gies in the 1950s, has continued to create noteworthy titles. *Rhythm Road* (1988) is a joyous, wide-ranging collection, pulsing with sounds and visual action in its graphics. Of the several anthologies compiled by Nancy Larrick, two outstanding titles were illustrated by Ed Young, *Cats Are Cats* (1988) and *Mice Are Nice* (1990). Editor William Cole's collections frequently take a humorous turn. One of the most recent is *A Zooful of Animals* (1992), with saucy illustrations by LYNN MUNSINGER reinforcing the absurdities in the verses. The collections compiled by LEE BENNETT HOPKINS appeal to a wide range of readers. *Surprises* (1984) contains short poems for beginning readers. *Side by Side: Poems to Read Together* (1988) is also a collection for younger children. Lilian Moore has edited *Sunflakes* (1992) for this same audience, illustrated by Jan Ormerod with beguiling children engaged in a variety of activities. X. J. KENNEDY, another accomplished poet, has compiled *Knock at a Star: A Child's Introduction to Poetry* (1982), a unique contribution to the current spate of anthologies with more than 150 entries, most of them infrequently anthologized and containing brief, conversational comments appealing to and easily understood by children.

The late twentieth century saw an increased interest in poetry for young adults. Preceding this trend, and foreshadowing it, was the appearance of *Reflections on a Gift of Watermelon Pickle* in 1966. Containing more than one hundred contemporary poems by writers such as William Jay Smith, Theodore Roethke, DONALD HALL, and Maxine Kumin, among others, the collection reflects the interests and moods of adolescents with incisive clarity. PAUL JANECZKO continues the effort to bring many modern poets to the attention of young adults in his carefully crafted anthologies. In *Poetspeak* (1983) sixty-two poets share their works and their comments about the writing process. *The Place My Words Are Looking For* (1990) does much the same for a slightly younger audience.

Brickyard Summer (1989) is a collection of Janeczko's own poems about growing up in a New England mill town. In *Judy Scuppernong*

(1990), Brenda Seabrooke has created a sensitive coming-of-age narrative in a series of poems revolving around one eventful summer in the lives of three girls growing up in Georgia. Another distinctly regional voice is heard in Jo Carson's *Stories I Ain't Told Nobody Yet* (1989), in which the poet speaks in the rough, eloquent voice of the people in her home mountains of Tennessee. These poems are as intimate and unconstrained as a conversation between old friends.

As the gradual shift of emphasis from print to electronic media makes young people more accepting of the new, the spontaneous, and the informal, poetry like Carson's seems to bring the form closer to its roots in oral tradition. In *This Same Sky: A Collection of Poems from Around the World* (1992), a book that cuts across language and culture, editor NAOMI SHIHAB NYE included a folk poem from Mali, translated by Judith Gleason, that typifies this bridge between the old and the new: "The beginning of the beginning rhythm / Is speech of the crowned crane; / The crowned crane says, 'I speak.' / The word is beauty." N.V.

Polacco, Patricia

American author and illustrator, b. 1944. Patricia Polacco's artistic and storytelling abilities, reflected in twenty highly praised books published within an eight-year span, brought her swiftly to the forefront of the picture book field. Her exceptional talents were clearly evident in her first book, *Meteor!* (1987), based on a childhood memory of a meteor landing in the yard of her grandparents' Michigan farm. Polacco's Michigan childhood and her Russian and Irish heritage have inspired many of her books. Her Russian grandmother is a dominant recurring character in her stories, but other family members and friends are also portrayed in *My Rotten Redheaded Older Brother* (1994), *The Bee Tree* (1993), *Picnic at Mudsock Meadow* (1992), *Some Birthday!* (1991), *Thunder Cake* (1990), *Casey at the Bat* (1988), and *Uncle Vova's Tree* (1988).

The autobiographical *The Keeping Quilt* (1988), with its story of how a family quilt is used as it is passed from generation to generation, further reflects Polacco's Russian Jewish heritage. But not all of Polacco's books are autobiographical. The fanciful *Babushka Baba Yaga* (1994) offers a sympathetic view of the legendary Russian witch, and *Rechenka's Eggs* (1988) features Ukrainian Easter eggs. Although preferring to write within her heritage, Polacco effectively explored aspects of contemporary Amish life in *Just Plain Fancy* (1990).

Some of Polacco's most touching stories focus on cross-cultural friendships. In *Mrs. Katz and Tush* (1992), an African American boy befriends an elderly Jewish woman, and Polacco celebrated her childhood friendship with a black family in *Chicken Sunday* (1992). Polacco, who has lived most of her life in Oakland, California, paid homage in *Tikvah Means Hope* (1994) to how her diverse neighbors supported each other during Oakland's devastating 1991 firestorm. But perhaps her most poignant portrayal of a cross-cultural friendship is in *Pink and Say* (1994), a story passed down on Polacco's father's side of the family. It tells of how her Yankee great-great-grandfather was rescued during a Civil War battle by a young black soldier before they were both captured and sent to the Confederate Andersonville Prison.

Polacco's stories are perfectly complemented by her distinctive style of art. She has used pencil, color marking pens, pastels, and acrylic paints to create bright, intense paintings set against a white background. The characters in her Russian-influenced stories wear clothing with multiple patterns and prints, giving those books a folk art quality. Sometimes faces and hands are left white, with expressive details sketched in with pencil. The autobiographical quality of some of Polacco's stories is heightened by the incorporation in her illustrations of framed family photographs. She has also incorporated reproductions of Russian icons in some of her books, reflecting not only her Russian heritage but her Ph.D. in art history.

Patricia Polacco may have begun her career as

a children's author-illustrator rather late in life, but she has shown no signs of slowing down and published a dozen books from 1995 to 2001, including *Thank You, Mr. Falker* (1998), about Polacco's difficulty in reading and her tribute to an important teacher, and *Betty Doll* (2001), a memoir about a doll created by Polacco's mother. P.O.B.

Politi, Leo

American author and illustrator, 1908–1996. Leo Politi's stories and illustrations demonstrate a quiet respect for children. Writing at a time when few authors noticed the country's cultural diversity, Politi was delighted by the many different children who lived around him in Los Angeles. A deeply religious man, he was also intrigued by the variety of celebrations they observed, from a Mexican Christmas procession or a Sicilian blessing of the fishing fleet to the Chinese New Year. His books reflect this multi-cultural nature of his world. He often integrated foreign words and phrases into his text, and several of his books were published in English and Spanish editions.

Politi was born in California to Italian immigrant parents but returned to Italy with his family when he was seven. At fifteen, he received a scholarship to the National Art Institute of Monza, near Milan, where he studied art for the next six years. He returned to California in 1931 and settled on Olvera Street in a Mexican section of Los Angeles. Here he struggled to earn his living as an artist and spent long hours drawing and painting the local people and street scenes. He finally began to achieve success in the early 1940s when he illustrated a series of books about California. The first book he both wrote and illustrated, *Pedro, the Angel of Olvera Street* (1946), was named a Caldecott Honor Book, as was *Juanita*, which he wrote in 1948, and in 1950 he received the Caldecott Medal for *Song of the Swallows*.

Politi's books convey an innocence, a naiveté, in which bad things work out in a loving and positive way. Peppe's father, for example, in *A Boat for Peppe* (1960) gets caught in a storm and his fishing boat does not return with the rest of the fleet. Although the picture shows the raging storm, Politi's words are reassuring. The fishermen urge Peppe to "keep faith." Then a rainbow appears, and when the sea is calm, they quickly find his father. In part, this idealized view of childhood stems from the era in which Politi was writing: during the 1940s and 1950s difficulties were often minimized in children's books.

Politi said that he felt a strong love for "people, animals, birds and flowers . . . for the simple, warm, and earthy things." This is particularly evident in his illustrations, which are filled with images of nature. Flowers, insects, and birds form decorative elements on each page. He used soft tones to create a gentle quality in his pictures. The dominant color themes in *Song of the Swallows* are muted greens and browns, highlighting the close relationship between the natural cycle of the swallows' arrival at the mission at Capistrano and the people. Yet the composition of his pictures creates a sense of vitality in spite of the quiet colors.

Later, he moved to a somewhat brighter palette. Piccolo, an organ grinder's monkey, escapes from his master and hides under a cable car in *Piccolo's Prank* (1965). The story is set in the center of Los Angeles, and the color scheme reflects the energy of the naughty monkey and of the city. Once again, Politi demonstrated his love for Los Angeles and its diverse neighborhoods and people, which provided him with a lifelong source of inspiration. P.R.

Potter, Beatrix

British author and illustrator, 1866–1943. Beatrix Potter's legacy to children's literature includes twenty-three small books and one longer collection of stories. Strict integrity to the nature of her animal characters, an ear for striking, precise language, and an eye for detail have made her stories perennial favorites since the early twentieth century. Potter insisted that her books, which address children intelligently and with humor, remain inexpensive and small enough to fit in a child's hands.

Potter grew up in a wealthy London family. Educated by governesses and isolated in a nursery much of the time, she kept a secret menagerie of pets. At various times these included rabbits named Benjamin and Peter, mice, newts, a frog, a tortoise, and a hedgehog named Mrs. Tiggy-winkle. She spent hours observing and painting her animals, immortalizing many of them later as characters in her books. Both Potter and her younger brother enjoyed drawing, although Potter did not care much for her art instructors and was mostly self-taught. Each summer, the family rented a large house or a castle in the Lake District or in Scotland where Potter sketched the country landscapes, many of which would become the settings for her books. Throughout her life, she had passionate interests to which she devoted her full concentration. With the benefit of her considerable intelligence and perfectionism, she excelled at each. In her twenties and early thirties, for example, she was fascinated by fossils and fungi, creating detailed paintings of the specimens she collected and conducting original research in mycology. It is during this period that she developed and refined her detailed dry-brush painting style.

With the success of *The Tale of Peter Rabbit* (1902), when she was thirty-six, Potter began concentrating on creating books, publishing two a year from 1902 to 1909. When the little books began to earn substantial royalties, she bought a farm in the Lake District, where she found excuses to spend more and more of her time, escaping from a stifling family situation. There, at the age of forty-seven, she married her solicitor, William Heelis. By then, her focus had begun to shift again, this time to land conservation, local antiques, and especially the breeding of Herdwick sheep, where she again achieved great success. Although she produced nine books between 1910 and 1930, her attention was divided, and the quality of those books is uneven. For the rest of her life, she was Mrs. Heelis — sheep

breeder, farmer, and landlord — and preferred to ignore her past success as Beatrix Potter. When she died in 1943, she left four thousand acres to the National Trust, including fifteen farms.

The Tale of Peter Rabbit, in which a young rabbit named Peter disobeys his mother, loses his way — and nearly loses his life — in Mr. McGregor's garden, and finally returns to the safety of home, is one of the great success stories of children's literature. It was first written in 1893 as an illustrated letter to Noel Moore, the five-year-old son of Potter's friend and former governess, while he was sick. Noel, like Peter, had three sisters at that time. When Potter tried to have it published, she was rejected by at least seven firms and eventually decided to print it in black and white at her own expense. It was not until the private edition was nearly complete that Frederick Warne and Company reconsidered its initial rejection and agreed to publish the story, provided that Potter repaint the illustrations in full color. Published by Warne in 1902, the book was an immediate success, selling 50,000 copies by the end of 1903. *Peter Rabbit* continues to sell at least 75,000 copies a year and has been translated into thirty languages.

Just why has *Peter Rabbit* been so successful? It contains, first, one of the oldest, simplest, and most compelling plots: separation from home, adventure, escape, return to home. This plot, occurring in favorite stories from Daniel Defoe's *Robinson Crusoe* to MAURICE SENDAK's *Where the Wild Things Are,* embodies the wishes and fears of every child. Then there is Peter. As a rabbit and a child, he is adventurous and timid, clever and incompetent, sweet and naughty. Both text and pictures show that Peter is not a boy thinly disguised as a rabbit, but a real animal who goes "lippity-lippity" when he walks and has powerful kicking hind legs, young large ears, and sensitive whiskers. Potter's understanding of animal anatomy, combined with her observations of animals in motion and her understanding of each animal's nature, are channeled into her characters so that readers believe instantly in the honesty and authenticity of her portrayals.

The Tailor of Gloucester (1903), Potter's own

favorite among her books, contains her only sympathetic human character. A Christmastime favorite for many families and for library story hours, it tells of a poor tailor who becomes ill before finishing the Lord Mayor's waistcoat. The mice in the tailor's shop take pity on him and finish all but the last buttonhole, despite the malicious meddling of the tailor's cat, Simpkin. Potter had heard this tale during a stay in Gloucester, though it was originally told as a fairy story. How much more appealing and sensible it becomes when the fairies are replaced by mice and a cat appears as their antagonist.

Some people have a mistaken impression of Beatrix Potter as the creator of cute animal characters in slightly sentimental stories. This could not be further from the truth. Some of her strongest characters are delightfully unsavory, like the foxy-whiskered gentleman in *The Tale of Jemima Puddleduck* (1908), Mr. Tod and Tommy Brock in *The Tale of Mr. Tod* (1912), and Samuel Whiskers, the rat, in *The Tale of Samuel Whiskers* (1908). The importance of the food chain is just below the surface of all her stories, and she always made it clear exactly what was most frightening to each animal. Surely any sentimentality is in the eye of the beholder.

She was also keenly aware of mischief and how much fun it can be, as in *The Tale of Two Bad Mice* (1904) and *The Tale of Samuel Whiskers.* These books give an occasional nod to proper behavior for the sake of the adults but leave children with no doubt that they are really about the joys of destructive behavior. Potter, who had been of necessity a proper, well-behaved child, intuitively understood the delight of breaking and entering, smashing dishes, and hiding from adults. In *Samuel Whiskers,* as in *The Tale of Tom Kitten* (1907) and *The Tale of Pigling Bland* (1913), the parents are portrayed as foolish and sometimes cruel, and the children, while disobedient, are only displaying natural behavior. Her young animals frequently shed their clothes, being more active and less concerned with appearances than their elders.

All of Beatrix Potter's books have remained in print continuously, to the delight of generations of readers. Despite the occasional dated turn of phrase, these books seem to appeal to children of any time because they are true to the nature of both children and the animals they portray. Potter's respect for children's integrity and intelligence and her intuitive understanding of childhood fears and delights are timeless.

L.R.

Powell, Randy

American author, b. 1956. Though many of his books concern athletes, Randy Powell should not be pigeonholed as a "sports novelist." Baseball, football, and tennis may play a role in his stories, but Powell's SPORTS STORIES are generally character-driven — his play-by-play commentary devoted not to sporting events but rather to complex relationships between teenagers and their friends, between boys and girls, between fathers and sons. As a result, he has created a body of work notable for its intelligence and incisive understanding of human dynamics.

The author was born in Seattle and lives there today with his wife and two sons. An athlete from an early age, Powell discovered an interest in writing during high school. After receiving a master's degree in education from the University of Washington, he began teaching at an alternative school for dropouts. Working with young adults, he began to write his own novel for teenagers. Published in 1988, *My Underrated Year* concerns Roger, a sophomore who hopes to be the star player on his school's football and tennis teams. But then a pair of athletic twins moves to town — Paul, a great running back, and Mary, a gifted tennis player — and eclipse Roger's role on both teams. In addition to some action-packed sports scenes, the novel includes a sympathetically insecure protagonist who must also contend with a new stepfather and romantic feelings for his new sports nemesis, Mary.

A most unlikely romance is at the core of Powell's next book, *Is Kissing a Girl Who Smokes like Licking an Ashtray?* (1992). Biff, an eighteen-year-old who's never had a date, spends much of his spring vacation chauffeuring a younger and wilder friend of the family, Heidi. This wild ride of a novel features verbal sparring that's sublimely humorous yet achingly poignant, as two opposites discover they have more in common than they think. Powell's gift for creating flawed but likable characters is also evident in *Dean Duffy* (1995), the story of a young man who always dreamed of a pro baseball career, but whose last seasons of high school are plagued by injuries and a batting slump. In the months after graduation, Dean begins a romance with a high school dropout and has an unexpected opportunity to try out for a college baseball scholarship. The novel's open ending (a literary technique Powell has employed in several books) is thought provoking.

The author has written some fine stories about ordinary kids in somewhat extraordinary circumstances: in *The Whistling Toilets* (1996) Stan coaches a national-ranked junior tennis champ, and *Tribute to Another Dead Rock Star* (1999) concerns a teenager whose rock star mother died of an overdose. Yet one of Powell's best books concerns the most ordinary of families, facing everyday joys and sorrows, and ultimately celebrating their unity. *Run If You Dare* (2001) mirrors the adolescent experiences of fourteen-year-old Gardner Dickinson with the midlife crisis of his father. Though the emotional journeys taken by father and son are universal, the characterizations, relationships, and dialogue are wonderfully specific to the Dickinson family, including a brief sex talk between Gardner and his dad, which is so natural and honest that readers will wonder why young adult fiction is rarely this direct and down to earth.

This naturalism is the hallmark of Powell's writing, which presents characters, emotions, and relationships that are sometimes complicated but always vividly real. P.D.S.

Prelutsky, Jack

American poet, b. 1940. For poetic creativity, accuracy, and appeal, there is no match for Jack Prelutsky. With a keen sensitivity to children's fears, pleasures, and funny bones, this prolific and gifted poet has delivered verses that are capable of converting the staunchest cries of "I hate poetry!" into a ceaseless clamoring for more. Possessing a restless spirit, Prelutsky tried a number of careers before settling on poetry. As a child in Brooklyn, New York, he was recognized as a gifted musician, a prodigy who was often paid to sing at various occasions and was even offered free lessons by the chorus master of New York's Metropolitan Opera, but he abandoned the idea of a singing career when he realized he might not become the best in the field. Success at other endeavors, including photography, pottery, folk singing, and drawing, was similarly forsaken. His talent for poetry was discovered by an editor at Macmillan to whom Prelutsky had submitted fanciful drawings with accompanying verse. The drawings were not accepted, but the verse was considered exceptional. Prelutsky was on his way. With over thirty volumes of poetry published since his debut in 1967, he has demonstrated a facility with words and images that has placed him among the best in his field.

Prelutsky is known for his irreverent style, technical versatility, and awareness of juvenile preferences, and his nonsensical subjects and surprise endings merit his audience's instant approval. While most of his volumes are composed of a brief series of verses centering around one overarching theme, his two most successful books, *The New Kid on the Block* (1984) and *Something Big Has Been Here* (1990), are larger volumes that address a vast array of topics both real and ridiculous. Ranked alongside SHEL SILVERSTEIN's *Where the Sidewalk Ends* and *The Light in the Attic* in terms of popularity and style, *The New Kid on the Block* has rapidly become a classic in the field of children's poetry. Its 107 verses have found a devoted readership in primary grade children, who are unable to resist unforgettable creatures such as the Slyne, the Gloopy Gloppers, and Baloney Belly Billy. But amusement is not the only theme here; Prelutsky's poems lend expression to the difficulties and frustrations of children, who recognize a true advocate in the voice behind the verse.

On a smaller scale, children in search of ghost

stories and other terrors find satisfaction in Prelutsky's several volumes of frightening poems, whose enticing covers and titles such as *Nightmares: Poems to Trouble Your Sleep* (1976) and *The Headless Horseman Rides Tonight* (1980) never fail to evoke a thrill. Similarly, several dozen marvelous monsters, with names like the Sneezy-Snoozer and the Nimpy-Numpy-Numpity, ooze, snarl, and otherwise cavort across the pages of *The Snopp on the Sidewalk* (1977) and *The Baby Uggs Are Hatching* (1982); in the same vein is the protagonist of *Awful Ogre's Awful Day* (2001). Aside from creating such fanciful creatures, Prelutsky has also been attuned to the basic subjects that children find most interesting, relevant, and fun. His subjects include dinosaurs, summer vacation, snow days, and the unpleasantness of going to bed, among many others, and he has also issued several holiday volumes for beginning readers.

In addition to his own writing, Prelutsky has translated several volumes of German and Swedish poetry into English. He has been compared with Ogden Nash, LEWIS CARROLL, and EDWARD LEAR, and critics have praised his rhythm, wit, and facility with words. Developing rhyming verse and standard metric schemes through carefully chosen onomatopoeic words and phrases, he has achieved a near-perfect structure that is especially rewarding when read aloud. A great crusader for the teaching and appreciation of poetry, Prelutsky is hailed for writing verse that attracts young readers to this long-stigmatized genre. C.C.B.

Preschool Books

Stories, rhymes, and lullabies have always been shared with young children. Mother Goose rhymes, fingerplays, and other ditties are standard in the nursery — and rightly so. The sound of language delights an infant. The rhythm and pattern of Mother Goose rhymes read or sung, for example, are magical for babies as they begin to absorb sounds and sights. The comfortable lap of a caring adult and a soothing voice add to the pleasure of sharing books. There is magic in books for young children.

Adults help children see, understand, and explore a spectrum of objects, activities, experiences, information, and ideas. Visual and verbal images combine in books for the young child to help them focus, empathize with others, vicariously experience emotions and activities, learn about their world, and perhaps most important, share all of this with a caring adult. As Dorothy Butler noted in *Babies Need Books* (1980), "It is not possible to gauge the width and depth of the increase in a child's grasp of the world that comes with books." It is possible, however, to make books available to all children — beginning with infants.

Adults who bring together children and their books must choose from a vast, sometimes overwhelming quantity. What books are likely to appeal to very young children? What makes a book appropriate for children? Children's book editor Louise Seaman Bechtel wrote in a 1941 *Horn Book Magazine* article that children need and enjoy books long before they reach five years, that they respond to the same age-old keys: "rhythm and laughter, the sense of climax, the magic of words."

Author-illustrator MARCIA BROWN wrote in *Lotus Seeds: Children, Pictures, and Books* (1986), "[It is] in their first books [that] children begin to form their taste for art and literature." Through early exposure to these books, children unconsciously develop an approach to their "visual world of order, rhythm, and interesting arrangements of color." Burton White, in *First Three Years of Life* (1990), contended that books with stiff pages "feed a baby's interest in hand-eye practice" and soon will "support the development of language, curiosity, and a healthy social life." Not only do books shared with young children stimulate intellectual development, but the pleasure of sharing these books is an early experience with other people — including authors and illustrators. The early work of psychologists such as Jean Piaget and Arnold Gesell continues to be refined, increasing our understanding of children's development and how they learn. However, it is still an elusive magic that we most seek in the growing pool of books for young children.

Publishers have responded to the demand for interesting but simple books for the youngest child. Since the early 1980s, books for the very young, often by well-known children's book illustrators and authors, have proliferated. About five thousand children's books were published in 1992.

Bright colors and clear shapes illustrate Max and Ruby's recognizable miniadventures on sturdy board pages. *Max's Bath, Max's Birthday, Max's Bedtime,* and *Max's Breakfast* (all 1985), written and illustrated by ROSEMARY WELLS, were perhaps the first BOARD BOOKS with action and characterizations as well as concepts understandable by the very young. These books, sized for small hands, remain appealing to children and to adults, who will recognize the subtle humor and nuance of character. In addition, since these books are also a tactile experience, felt and tasted by children, their rounded corners and small size allow for safe, independent handling.

My Daddy and I, I Make Music, and *My Doll Keshia* (all 1991), board books written by Eloise Greenfield and illustrated by Jan Spivey Gilchrist, simply relate the everyday activities of an African American child within the family. Small in size, with rounded corners, the books are realistically illustrated in wash and line. Adults appear less often as a multiracial cast of children engage in familiar activities in HELEN OXENBURY's *Tickle, Tickle, All Fall Down, Say Goodnight,* and *Clap Hands* (all 1987). Slightly larger in size, these board books provide ample white space to highlight engaging, well-defined watercolors that chronicle babies' joyful play.

Board books do not differ significantly from longer PICTURE BOOKS. Author-illustrator Helen Oxenbury has said about creating board books that she has strived to "keep the concepts extremely simple — objects and situations that very small children will recognize." Adults selecting such books for young children must also consider the simplicity of the concept, presentation, and format. Pleasing language, clear illus-

trations, and familiar objects and activities, all contained within sturdy books with rounded edges, encourage the youngest children to explore with and focus on their books.

Toddlers rapidly gain language, begin to manipulate ideas and deal with abstractions, start to pretend, and although they remain the vertex of their world, become social creatures. Books that present easy concepts or simple stories with concrete action, identifiable experiences, and recognizable characters will be relished by toddlers. Not only are such books developmentally appropriate, but also they can provoke memorable shared activity for both child and adult.

Most often, books that appeal to toddlers present familiar ideas and activities. Many adults still remember the cozy green bedroom created by MARGARET WISE BROWN in *Goodnight Moon* (1947). The simple, rhyming, evocative text is enriched and extended by CLEMENT HURD's uncluttered but satisfyingly detailed illustrations in striking, almost flat colors. *Goodnight Moon* is more than a bedtime story. It becomes a naming game as each object is examined again and again and as the familiar, such as the cow who jumped over the moon, is found and associations are made. The poetic, repetitive language of the simple text, when coupled with the dramatic flow of illustration, becomes unforgettable.

ANN JONAS chronicled a small boy's explorations in *Holes and Peeks* (1984) using minimal language and well-delineated, full-color illustrations. The child can see through peeks but not holes and remains frightened of the latter — until he gains a sense of control over them. Getting dressed can pose as many problems for young children as holes do. An awkward young bear cub, however, entertainingly overcomes the difficulties of appropriate attire in Shigeo Watanabe's *How Do I Put It On?* (1984). The softly lined and colored illustrations are childlike and appealing. Affection abounds in the families presented in VERA B. WILLIAMS's *"More More More," Said the Baby* (1990). Three families with young children live and play together, lovingly pictured in rich watercolors and a carefully crafted text.

These and other books that continue to appeal to young children are memorable because they demonstrate a respect for and understanding of the small child's world. They are remembered by adults, perhaps because the books help adults revisit, recall, and enjoy again earlier experiences. Through them, the everyday, creatively viewed, becomes magical.

Ideas or concepts, too, can create magic. Black and white photographs of objects common in a child's world effectively convey the notion of opposites in TANA HOBAN's *Push Pull Empty Full* (1972). A single word appears with a full-page photograph; its opposite appears on the facing page, thus clearly defining the concept in word and image. A child can count from one to ten in English and Swahili with *Moja Means One,* written by Muriel Feelings (1971). Though counting may be too abstract for younger children, the sounds are satisfying and the soft lines of TOM FEELINGS's monochromatic illustrations provide a respectful glimpse into another culture.

Many stories invite young children to participate in them and, like *Goodnight Moon,* incorporate patterns or objects to name. In *Spots, Feathers, and Curly Tails,* written and illustrated by NANCY TAFURI (1988), a partial picture (actually a very close-up view) accompanies a simple question such as "What has spots?" The entire animal — "A cow has spots" — appears on the next two-page spread. Crisp, cleanly lined, full-color illustrations of farm animals accompany the minimal, predictable text. Children are immediately drawn in as they eagerly respond to the text's questions.

Tafuri's interesting use of perspective enhances *Have You Seen My Duckling?* (1984), enabling young children to find the errant duckling, even when its mother cannot. Clear, appealing, and playful illustrations engage children in this satisfying, safe jaunt in which children (and the young duckling) are one step ahead of Mother.

Children look for the little black and white dog in *Where's Spot?* (1980) and the numerous other Spot books by ERIC HILL, as they lift flaps covering small surprises until Spot is found. Children eat through a week with *The Very Hungry Caterpillar* (1981), by ERIC CARLE, and feel the holes left by the caterpillar's munching spree. Brilliant color and stylized pictures bring the story to a satisfying conclusion when the caterpillar — no longer either hungry or small — emerges as a beautiful butterfly. In addition to their visual and verbal appeal, these books share an emotional appeal for young children. They are predictable though not contrived, and their texts and illustrations are satisfyingly complementary. The young child's world is rendered orderly and understandable through such books.

Many of the qualities of these books continue to appeal to the slightly older child, though the scope of books created specifically for them broadens in several important ways, reflecting their physical, mental, and emotional development and increasing experience. For example, as children grow more autonomous and their language becomes better developed, they enjoy dealing with increasingly abstract concepts in their explorations of their world. Children enjoy books of many kinds, but the qualities that render books exciting and give them the power to last are fairly consistent.

Books for very young children, including board books, are essentially picture books, books in which verbal and visual images work together to create a unified whole. And as Marcia Brown has recognized, "[A] picture book is somewhat related in its effects to that of a painting. The whole is greater than any of its parts, but all parts must relate directly to each other in harmony." To be fully savored, books for the very young, like paintings, must be shared. M.B.S.

Priceman, Marjorie

American illustrator, b. 1958. Marjorie Priceman's swirling, curvy watercolor paintings have graced more than twenty PICTURE BOOKS and POETRY anthologies. Priceman grew up on Long Island, New York, with a father who read "two-ton novels" and a mother who painted. Priceman herself cannot remember a time when she was not writing or drawing. She graduated from the Rhode Island School of Design and tried several artistic ventures, including magazine illustration and textile design.

With the encouragement of former professor DAVID MACAULAY, Priceman began illustrating children's books. She both wrote and illustrated her first book, *Friend or Frog* (1989), the story of a child who must find a new home for her pet frog. She saves it from humorous and disastrous turns of fate, such as becoming dinner for a zealous chef. The book's loose, flowing watercolor illustrations have become Priceman's signature. In her second book, *Rachel Fister's Blister* (1990)l, Priceman's romping illustrations perfectly match the text's strong rhyme and gentle, but quite silly, story.

Priceman has also illustrated poetry anthologies edited by JACK PRELUTSKY, including *A. Nonny Mouse Writes Again* (1993) and *For Laughing Out Louder: More Poems to Tickle Your Funnybone* (1995). In each collection, Priceman has captured the joy of the poetry with her sketchy, open paintings. She both wrote and illustrated *How to Make an Apple Pie and See the World* (1994). The book has delighted teachers with the amount of information it effortlessly presents; the imaginative lengths one child goes to in order to collect pie ingredients have pleased children and critics. *Zin Zin Zin, a Violin* (1995), the rhyming story of musicians who form an orchestra, was written by Lloyd Moss and earned recognition as a Caldecott Honor Book. In Priceman's swooping gouache paintings, players' elongated limbs and postures match the shape of their instruments.

Priceman's illustrated Elsa Okon Rael's reminiscences of Jewish life in the Lower East Side of Manhattan in the 1930s, in *What Zeesie Saw on Delancey Street* (1996) and *When Zaydeh Danced on Eldridge Street* (1997). Here her art is more formal and contained than her earlier work. The straight lines of the brownstones and the arches of the synagogue give symmetry to the pages.

Priceman's illustrations for Mary Ann Hoberman's *One of Each* (1997) also depart from her earlier style. Priceman has used both gouache and cut paper to good effect in this and subsequent books. The dog Oliver Tolliver, proud of his orderly life, is cut out of paper. The clean, sharp edges of the dog contrast with the soft painted backgrounds and help illuminate his rather rigid character traits. Whether using heavy gouache paint and cut paper (as in *Emaline at the Circus,* 1999) or thin, airy watercolor on white backgrounds (as in *Cousin Ruth's Tooth,* 1996), Priceman has developed character and tone with her loose, curved lines and energetic style. M.V.K.

Primavera, Elise

American illustrator and author, b. 1954. Elise Primavera had loved to draw as a child. When rheumatic fever confined her to bed for the entire summer at the end of fifth grade, she received three books on drawing to keep her occupied. But she wasn't convinced about being an artist yet. She had another love — horses.

When it came time for college, she wanted to ride full-time, but her parents insisted she try at least two years of school. They compromised: she attended art school and commuted home on the weekends to ride. What decided her career path was a visit to the Brandywine River Museum, where powerful paintings by HOWARD PYLE, N. C. WYETH, and Jessie Willcox Smith spoke to her, and she knew that she wanted to paint.

Primavera began her illustration career by doing freelance fashion illustration. She had earned a B.F.A. from Moore College of Art in 1976, but after a few years, she felt she wasn't being creatively challenged, and so she decided to delve into children's book illustration. In the summer of 1979 she put together a portfolio to show publishers and hit the streets of New York City. Her first break was a job to create a book jacket for Harper and Row; a PICTURE BOOK assignment followed a few months later — *Always Abigail* (1981), written by Joyce St. Peter.

Two years later, Primavera wrote and illustrated a story of her own, *Basil and Maggie*

(1983) — naturally, a story about a girl and a horse. She continued to illustrate stories by other authors as well as her own, gaining recognition for her spirited and humorous artwork for *Raising Dragons* (1998), written by Jerdine Nolen, as well as for three books Primavera wrote: *The Three Dots* (1993), *Plantpet* (1994), and the highly successful *Auntie Claus* (1999). The artwork for *Auntie Claus* took two years to complete, but Primavera's reward was the enthusiastic attention the book received; being featured in the holiday window display of Saks Fifth Avenue proved its popularity.

Often called "quirky," Primavera's style combines brightly colored pastels or subtle charcoals with opaque gouache and acrylic, to produce lively, imaginative creations. Her illustrations burst with exaggerated humor. In all of her projects, she has attempted to "make the most bizarre thing seem possible and real" — a special magic that engages and delights readers. J.C.

Provensen, Alice; Provensen, Martin

Alice: American author and illustrator, b. 1918; Martin: American author and illustrator, 1916–1987. As Aaron Copland's musical compositions draw heavily from the American experience, the Provensens' illustrations, with their deceivingly simplistic primitive style, their often limited palette, and their remarkable visual continuity, have a distinctive American flavor.

Both were born in Chicago, and during the Great Depression their families moved across the country, from town to town, in search of economic security. Both won scholarships to the Art Institute of Chicago. Both transferred to the University of California, Alice in Los Angeles and Martin in Berkeley. Both served an apprenticeship in the animation industry. Alice worked in the animation department of the Walter Lantz Studios, and Martin created storyboards for Walt Disney, working on films such as *Fantasia* and *Dumbo*. "No matter where we moved or how often," said the Provensens, "the libraries were safe havens for us. In the course of growing up, our paths must have crossed many times — in Chicago, in Los Angeles, in schools, in museums — but we did not meet until we were both working in the same animation studio during the Second World War. Now we often wonder if we couldn't have been sitting across from one another at one of those library tables so long ago." They married in 1944, moved to New York in 1945, and there began their work as children's book illustrators, creating over five hundred illustrations for *Fireside Book of Folksongs* (1947). In the early 1950s they traveled extensively in Europe, collecting material for illustrations and filling sketchbook upon sketchbook with drawings that provided a creative foundation for many of their early books, including *The Golden Bible: The New Testament* (1953) and *The Iliad and the Odyssey* (1956). They also bought a farm near Staatsburg, New York, and converted its barn into a studio. Maple Hill Farm, with its many animals and pastoral setting, became the backdrop for several of their books, including *The Year at Maple Hill Farm* (1978), *An Owl and Three Pussycats* (1981), and *Town and Country* (1985). The ornery goose, Evil Murdoch; cats Webster, Crook, and Fat Boy; Bashful the horse; and Goat Dear are among the many delightful characters cavorting across their well-designed pages. Drawing on their animation training, the Provensens used unique perspectives, color, creative hand lettering, and strong design to capture the reader and entice him or her to turn page after page. Children still delight in the escapades of the plucky Color Kittens from the Little Golden Book of the same name written by MARGARET WISE BROWN in 1949. In the Caldecott Medal winner *The Glorious Flight* (1983), the Provensens illuminated, literally and figuratively, the tale of Louis Blériot's triumphant flight across the English Channel.

In 1987 Martin Provensen died of a heart attack. He and Alice had spent over forty years creating beautiful PICTURE BOOKS for children. They maintained a happy collaboration, not unlike the medieval scribes and scriveners, passing sketches back and forth, critiquing, reworking "to find the right, the inevitable, pictures and words that say what we have to say." Alice Provensen persisted in their work. *The Buck Stops Here* (1990), her book of presidential history, continues the Provensen tradition of strong design and unique personal viewpoint.

M.B.B.

Pullman, Philip

British novelist and playwright, b. 1946. With the publication of *The Ruby in the Smoke* in England in 1985 (1987 in the United States), Philip Pullman, a former schoolteacher raised in Rhodesia, Australia, London, and Wales, launched his career as a writer of YOUNG ADULT NOVELS. Set in London during the Victorian era, the novel relates the adventures of Sally Lockhart, an inventive, courageous sixteen-year-old who finds herself caught in dangerous intrigue when she delves into the circumstances surrounding the death of the man she believed was her father. The setting is effectively realized in the engrossing tale, which begins a trilogy that continues with *The Shadow in the North* (1988), published in Great Britain in 1987 as *The Shadow in the Plate*, and *The Tiger in the Well* (1990). Sally's character develops as she grows older, falls in love, and becomes an unwed mother who runs her own financial consulting business. Over and over she displays her resourcefulness as she meets each new threat head-on.

The critically acclaimed novel *The Broken Bridge* (1990 Great Britain, 1992 U.S.), which focuses more on character, represents not a departure from Pullman's previous style, but an expansion of his technique. Ginny, a biracial teenager raised by her white father in a predominantly white community in Wales, seeks out the truth about her past and her parents and, with difficulty, adjusts to living with the brother she never knew she had. Pullman's depiction of Ginny's sense of alienation and search for identity provides universality and draws the reader into her life, while the tightly constructed plot

offers numerous surprises that ensure that readers of Pullman's HISTORICAL FICTION will not be disappointed with this modern novel.

At their best, Pullman's novels, daring and inventive, are page turners that immediately hook readers into the story and often introduce them to the Victorian age. His credits as a playwright include adaptations of Mary Shelley's *Frankenstein* and Alexandre Dumas's *The Three Musketeers* as well as original work.   A.E.D.

Pullman's greatest strength is his ability to weave complex and riveting plots that wrap the reader in suspense. Nowhere is this more apparent than in the three His Dark Materials books, in which he created a convincing world that has similarities to the known world while being quite different, fantastic, and mysterious. In Book I, *The Golden Compass* (1996), the orphan Lyra lives comfortably with the scholars of Oxford until two powerful visitors call on her. She begins a quest to rescue her kidnapped friend and starts a gripping, complex journey during which nothing is as it seems. The saga continues in *The Subtle Knife* (1997) when Will, who lives in our world, escapes pursuers by stepping through a window into another world. There he meets and joins forces with Lyra. As she carries the alethiometer, a device that identifies the truth and commands them to find Will's father, Will becomes a warrior bearing the Subtle Knife, another powerful amulet which can cut windows between worlds. The breathtaking pace of this multifaceted novel ends inconclusively. The story begins again immediately in the third and final volume of His Dark Materials, *The Amber Spyglass* (2000). It is perhaps the most complicated in the trilogy, attempting to resolve issues introduced in earlier books. While *The Amber Spyglass* does indeed tie up dangling threads, it also unravels many. It has been suggested that this is Pullman's retelling of *Paradise Lost*, presenting his own contentious view of the role of world religion. In his 1996 Carnegie Medal acceptance speech for *The Golden Compass*, Pullman said, "There are some themes, some subjects, too large for adult fiction; they can only be dealt with adequately in a children's book . . . There's more wisdom in a story than in volumes of philosophy." The epic proportions of the trilogy are worthy of discussion in terms of both content and structure.   M.B.S.

Pyle, Howard

American illustrator and author, 1853–1911. Considered by many to be the father of children's book illustration in America, Howard Pyle was developing his talents in the United States at the same time that WALTER CRANE, RANDOLPH CALDECOTT, and KATE GREENAWAY were becoming influential in England. Pyle did not have the advantage of working with printer Edmund Evans, and thus most of his work for children was in black and white rather than in color. Moreover, while his illustrations were beautifully composed and designed, his pictures were often single-page or partial-page illustrations that supplemented a long text rather than double-page drawings that interacted with the words in relatively brief passages, as did Crane's, Caldecott's, and Greenaway's. Yet Pyle's work was known and admired by these three, particularly Walter Crane, and Pyle contributed ideas and methods to the field of children's book illustration that still have important influence today.

Pyle was born and grew up in the Brandywine Valley in Wilmington, Delaware, and he remembered his childhood as an idyllic time that was centered on the wonderful old stone house he and his family lived in and on its garden, filled with profuse blooms and hidden wonders. His mother, who loved books and art, was a great influence on him, and both parents encouraged his talent for art, finally agreeing that he should be trained at a small art school in Philadelphia rather than attend college.

Because of problems with his father's leather business, Pyle spent several years after completing this training helping out in the family business. But in 1876 his mother sent an essay and sketches he had done while on vacation on Chincoteague Island to *Scribner's Magazine,* and

the editor accepted the article for publication, suggesting that Pyle come to New York to illustrate and write for periodicals. Once in New York Pyle sold his first painting to *Harper's Weekly,* a magazine that would continue to be an important venue for his work for many years. Indeed, the publisher of *Harper's Weekly* had assembled an exceptional group of professionals who were knowledgeable about illustration and trained in the newest methods of printing, and the House of Harper became an informal training ground for Pyle to learn every facet of the publishing process.

During his time in New York Pyle became more and more convinced that he wanted to write and illustrate books for children. He drew upon his vivid childhood memories to contribute stories to *St. Nicholas* magazine, and he read and studied many of the old folktales that he'd loved as a child, extending his reading to include less familiar tales from many nations. These folktales and the romances of his boyhood would become the central core of his work over his lifetime; although he is primarily remembered today for his contributions to illustration, he was a writer of some skill. Indeed, he has been compared to HANS CHRISTIAN ANDERSEN in the way his unique voice and imagination shaped his traditional folklore and FANTASY material.

After three years in New York, where he established himself with a reading public and a professional circle of fellow artists, Pyle returned to Wilmington in 1879. He illustrated two short children's books, *Yankee Doodle* (1881) and *The Lady of Shallott* (1881), both done in color in an experiment that sought to emulate the success of Edmund Evans's work in England. American printers, however, did not have Evans's skills, and the books were disappointing. Pyle returned to black and white illustrations with *The Merry Adventures of Robin Hood,* which he wrote and designed himself. This book, published in 1883, is generally considered Pyle's first children's book. Although the careful attention to book design that he insisted upon raised the cost of the book, eventually it was a great success. Even while he continued to illustrate for magazines,

Pyle's best love seems to have been writing and illustrating for children, and he went on to do thirteen more books for this audience. Among these were *Pepper and Salt* (1886) and *The Wonder Clock* (1887), collections of stories in the folktale tradition, and *Otto of the Silver Hand* (1888) and four volumes of the King Arthur legends, which were longer romances.

Influenced by the Arts and Crafts movement in England, Pyle's illustrations have the strong sense of line and composition that marked the work of many English artists of the same period, particularly Walter Crane. Yet Pyle became a master storyteller in pictures as well as words, and he never let his illustrations become fussy with decorative detail. His first works were wood engravings, but when halftone methods of printing were introduced, in which a continuous-tone image can be created by using a pattern of dots of varying sizes (as in newspaper photographs), he was able to achieve finer distinctions in tonal values. In all of these he exhibited a carefully restrained sense of drawing and composition. His lines had great strength as well as flowing movement, and he used the white spaces to create a balance in his pictures, just as he used lines to convey drama. His characters were real people with distinct personalities and emotions, and his illustrations lent important energy to the long printed text.

Pyle is notable not only for his contributions to children's literature but also for his dedicated teaching of illustration. He was dissatisfied with the formal methods of instruction then prevailing in most art schools, and he took a job teaching at Drexel Institute in Philadelphia, where he could expound upon his strong views about art and illustration. His courses were in great demand, and later he started a school in his backyard in Wilmington, where he taught promising students for free, charging only room and board. He believed that book illustration was the ground from which to produce painters, and his experience in publishing was invaluable to students like N. C. WYETH and Jessie Willcox Smith. Even more important, perhaps, were his ideas on illustration, which were at odds with many of the beliefs of the day. He felt that artists

needed to get beyond the stiff figures of the studio life class and let their figures and scenes come from the imagination rather than from a frozen pose. Believing in the importance of the overall design of the book, he helped his students learn how to integrate their illustrations into a whole. Pyle taught that the illustrator's role was to extend the text in personal ways rather than simply to reproduce what the text described. Through his many books and his teaching, Pyle made a contribution to children's literature that is acknowledged by readers and artists to this day. B.K.

R

Rackham, Arthur

British illustrator, 1867–1939. Of all those illustrators to follow in the footsteps of RANDOLPH CALDECOTT, WALTER CRANE, and KATE GREENAWAY, perhaps none had a greater sense of mystery and magic than Arthur Rackham. Yet Rackham had a conventional middle-class childhood, growing up near London as one of twelve children and training as an insurance clerk. Like Caldecott, he loved drawing from a young age and knew that he wanted someday to be an artist. He therefore studied nights at Lambeth School of Art while working by day for the Westminster Fire Office. Unlike Caldecott, however, Rackham's approach to his work was painstaking and methodical rather than spontaneous. He was just as careful in planning his training and his life; his move from clerk to illustrator took more than eight years. Rackham sold his first drawings to illustrated papers in London in 1891 when he was twenty-four, but he didn't leave the insurance office until 1893, when he was hired to work full-time as an illustrator for the *Westminster Budget*, a London newspaper. Rackham found the work there hard and later declared this period the worst time of his life. The newspaper's rigid schedules demanded quick sketches rather than the careful work Rackham preferred. Rackham also believed that photography was going to supplant illustration in newspapers, giving him anxiety over the future of his livelihood. The sheer volume of work required by the newspaper, however, provided him with valuable practice.

At the age of twenty-seven Rackham was given a commission for a travel book on the United States called *To the Other Side*. The success of this book was followed by other commissions, and although he had not yet achieved his unique and distinctive style, his work was good and in enough demand that in 1896 he was finally able to resign his job on the *Westminster Budget*. By the end of the nineteenth century, as he entered his thirties, he had illustrated nine books, among them Mary and Charles Lamb's *Tales from Shakespeare* (1899).

It may be that love was the catalyst that released Rackham's full artistic talents, for it was only in 1900, after meeting his future wife, painter Edyth Starkie, that he felt encouraged to follow his natural inclination to draw worlds of fantasy and magic. That same year he illustrated *The Fairy Tales from the Brothers Grimm* (1900), tales he remembered fondly from his own childhood, with one full-color illustration and ninety-nine drawings in black and white. This book was an overwhelming success and was reprinted twice. It was so popular that in 1909 he illustrated it again, this time with forty colored pictures and fifty-five in black and white. Rackham approached each picture in a similar manner, carefully drawing his subject in pencil until he was satisfied with the result and then inking over the pencil lines in India ink. For his color pictures he used transparent watercolors and laid down wash upon delicate wash. This technique gave his pictures an ethereal, otherworldly quality and was especially suited to the subjects of fantasy that he so loved.

During this time the process of photo separation and reproduction of original artwork had been refined, making it possible to print color illustrations much more easily, although each illustration had to be printed separately on special paper and pasted into the book. As a result, deluxe art book editions became highly prized in the years before World War I. Because he worked mostly in single-page illustration rather than in fully illustrated books, Rackham's style lent itself to this method of reproduction, and he benefited both financially and artistically. In 1905 Rackham contributed fifty-one illustrations to Washington Irving's *Rip Van Winkle*. When the original art was exhibited in London, almost all the paintings were sold, and a signed, limited edition of 250 copies was sold out even before the exhibition ended. His illustrations for J. M. Barrie's *Peter Pan in Kensington Gardens* (1906) enjoyed similar success and brought Rackham international fame.

Illustration by Arthur Rackham from *Alice's Adventures in Wonderland* (1907), by Lewis Carroll.

Despite his financial and professional success among collectors, Rackham never lost his quiet, unassuming manner, his love for magic, or his appeal to children. He firmly believed that children would benefit from the imaginative, the fantastic, and the playful in their art and in their books, and he showed the greatest respect for his child audience in all his works. In the thirty-three years that followed the publication of *Peter Pan in Kensington Gardens*, Rackham went on to illustrate other well-loved stories and enjoyed continued success. After World War I, however, the market for gift books declined, and the greatest demand for his books turned out to be in America rather than in England.

Throughout his career Rackham was not content to remain with a proven style but sought new artistic challenges, illustrating *Cinderella* (1919) and *The Sleeping Beauty* (1920) in silhouette and experimenting with line and color in *Irish Fairy Tales* (1920) and *The Tempest* (1926). He also had the courage to tackle works that were considered sacrosanct, illustrating *Alice in Wonderland* (1907) and *The Wind in the Willows* (1940). Rackham considered the opportunity to illustrate *The Wind in the Willows* a great gift, for he had been offered the original commission but had had to turn it down because of other commitments. He consulted with KENNETH GRAHAME's widow about the illustrations for the new edition and finally finished the book just weeks before his own death. Like his other work, the book is a fine example of his unique vision and his singular way with line and color. B.K.

Ransome, Arthur

British author, 1884–1967. Arthur Ransome's childhood summer holidays in northern England's Lake District led him, much later in his life, to write *Swallows and Amazons* (1930), the first of his popular twelve-book Swallows and Amazons series for children. His success was due at least in part to his vivid recollection of the ingredients of childhood happiness, but his own childhood was not all joyful. In school, he recalled, he was "extremely miserable." When he was thirteen, his father died and the family no longer vacationed at the lake, although in his twenties he spent some time there with a family who provided models for some of his fictional characters. Ransome's career as a journalist took him, among other places, to revolutionary Russia. There he met Trotsky's secretary, who later became his wife. The success of his first books enabled him to spend the rest of his life in the Lake District, where he continued the series, fulfilled at last.

"It seems to me," he wrote, "that in writing children's books I have the best of childhood over again and the best of being old as well." The best of childhood, he perceived, was the holidays, and in his books the characters are left alone to enjoy their holidays as they choose. Together they create their own adventures, on small sailboats, exploring an island, camping, seeking treasure, solving small mysteries. Group play is an important aspect of their adventures. The four older Walker children act out the roles of a traditional nuclear family, with patriarchal Captain John (ship's master) and maternal Susan (first mate) providing a secure environment in which their younger siblings, Able Seaman Titty and Ship's Boy Roger, can develop their own competence. Other children (and adults), such as the Blackett sisters, who are the Amazon pirates of the lake, and their fearsome/fun uncle, Captain Flint, sometimes take part in the group play, helping to shape the adventures. Like a father, Ransome is fond of all his characters. All have well-developed, individual personalities, and episodes are presented from their respective points of view. But he seems to have an especially strong attachment to dreamy, emotional Titty, who is not always able to distinguish between the real and the imagined and who draws the others into her fantasy world. Plausible experiences are amplified by the group imagination; once a fantasy has been developed (the little sailboat *Swallow* is a large sailing vessel, the *Amazon* is a pirate ship, there is a lost gold mine in the nearby hills, they are on an expedition to the North Pole), they all become serious about believing it. Occasionally, the children's adventures are exciting and even dangerous enough without the need for imaginative enhancement. For example, they are caught in a forest fire in *Pigeon Post* (1936), and they accidentally cross the English Channel in a fog while spending the night on an anchored sailboat in *We Didn't Mean to Go to Sea* (1937). Distinctive in Ransome's fiction is his attention to detail. His books unobtrusively provide a wealth of practical information about activities such as sailing, camping, prospecting, and signaling.

At the time of their publication in the 1930s and 1940s, the books were immensely popular. Today they are as well loved by a fewer number of readers who are still inspired by Ransome's warm, resourceful, energetic characters. D.C.

Raschka, Chris

American illustrator and author, b. 1959. Chris Raschka's bright colors and energetic characters have established him as one of today's foremost children's book creators. The son of history professors, Raschka was always drawing as a child. Though he majored in biology at Saint Olaf's College in Northfield, Minnesota, Raschka eventually parlayed his talent for illustration into editorial cartooning for a small newspaper. He eventually moved with his wife to New York City in order to gain more opportunities to illustrate children's books.

Raschka's love of jazz inspired his first PICTURE BOOK, *Charlie Parker Played Be-Bop* (1992). Breaking out of traditional picture book treatment of BIOGRAPHY, the book's loose narrative structure draws the reader into the cadence and rhythms of jazz music. Raschka's scraggly line drawings of Parker and his saxophone skillfully convey the spirit of the legendary musician rather than producing an exact replica of Parker's features. Bright colors and surreal landscapes — including marching lollipops, disembodied legs with dancing shoes, and jazzy birds — reflect the style of Raschka's subsequent books.

Raschka similarly jettisoned realism for a subjective style in order to capture the feelings and experiences of young children in *Yo! Yes?* (1993). This Caldecott Honor Book depicts the conversation of two young boys, one black and one white, who form a friendship. The joy of breaking through sadness and boredom is conveyed with a maximum of two words per page, mimicking the way young children sometimes communicate. Spare imagery and economic language focus the reader on the excitement of new friendship. A similar style pervades the companion volume, *Ring! Yo?* (2000), which follows the same two characters as they talk, argue, and then make up during the course of a perfectly depicted juvenile telephone call. Provided with only one side of the phone call, the reader must imagine the rest of the conversation. (An "explanation" is given at the end.)

Themes of loneliness and friendship are also explored in *like, likes, like* (1999), in which a cat is left alone by a group of animals who have all paired off. The cat wanders the countryside until he finds a friend: a fellow cat. *Waffle* (2001) continues the theme of the lonely outsider, with a different outcome. Instead of finding a friend, the title character discovers his special talents and strengths so he can quit "waffling."

Raschka has also illustrated work by other authors. His geometric backgrounds and traditional yet forward-looking drawings of children complement MARGARET WISE BROWN's posthumously published *Another Important Book* (1999). Swatches of patterned fabric added to paintings illuminate the POETRY collection *A Poke in the I* (2001), edited by PAUL JANECZKO. Raschka's handwriting and artwork bring to mind EZRA JACK KEATS's *The Snowy Day* in *Happy to Be Nappy* (1999), an ebullient celebration of African American girls and their hair. In all of Raschka's work, the bright, lively drawings and unique narrative style have an enduring appeal. E.M.A.

Raskin, Ellen

American author and illustrator, 1928–1984. Born in Milwaukee, Wisconsin, Ellen Raskin credited her inability to sing, dance, or play hopscotch to her love of reading: "Books were my escape; books were my friends."

Raskin graduated with a fine arts degree from the University of Wisconsin. She settled in New York City and began her career as a freelance commercial artist, designing and illustrating more than one thousand book jackets, for which she received fifteen major awards. Her entry into the world of children's literature began by illustrating the works of others. Her art can be seen in over a dozen books, whose subjects range from BIOGRAPHY, in *We Dickinsons: The Life of Emily Dickinson as Seen Through the Eyes of Her Brother Austin* (1965), to Greek legends, in *The King of Men* (1966); from mathematics, in *Probability: The Science of Chance* (1967), to POETRY, in *D. H. Lawrence: Poems Selected for Young People* (1967).

With her artist's eye and her perspective of the world — she felt her short stature allowed her to see as a child sees — she created books "consciously and proudly" for children. "I plan margins wide enough for hands to hold, typographic variations for eyes to rest, decorative breaks for minds to breathe. I want it to look like a wonderful place to be," said Raskin. The books that followed combined the same artistic vision, original stylized drawings, and offbeat, ironic sense of humor. The first book she both wrote and illustrated, *Nothing Ever Happens on My Block* (1966), was named Best Picture Book of the Year by the New York *Herald Tribune*. *Ghost in a Four-Room Apartment* (1969), chosen to represent the United States at the second Biennale of Illustrations in Czechoslovakia, provides a lesson in genealogy through cumulative, repetitive rhymes. *Franklin Stein* (1972) contrasts the blatant, yet consistent, red of the character Franklin with the ever-changing and mutable blues, greens, and whites of his relatives. *Who, Said Sue, Said Whoo?* (1973) is illustrated with a Rousseau-like charm and filled with nonsense rhymes. *Moose, Goose, and Little Nobody* (1974) blends repetitive text with acrobatic calligraphy in an elegant and witty way.

Raskin once asked herself, "Switching from commercial art to PICTURE BOOK is plausible, but what about from picture book to the novel?" The question was satisfactorily answered with the publication of Raskin's first full-length story. *The Mysterious Disappearance of Leon (I Mean Noel)* (1972) is crammed with word puzzles, zany characters, slapstick, and ingenious pictures created from letters and words. *Figgs and Phantoms* (1974), a Newbery Honor Book, chronicles the story of the Figg family's search for "Capri," their own personal paradise. Cryptic references to Velázquez, Gauguin, Schubert, Gilbert and Sullivan, Milton, Joseph Conrad, and William Blake provide Raskin with the opportunity to explore her own passions but may not be understood or appreciated by younger readers. In *The Tattooed Potato and Other Clues* (1975) budding artist Dickory Dock finds herself entangled in the mysterious world of Greenwich Village painter-detective Garson. Though the reader is entertained with nonsensical wordplay and rhyme, Raskin's story is more concerned with the idea of reality and illusion. "What I can teach you," Garson explains, is "how to observe . . . how to see through frills and facades . . . how to see through disguises." This book received the Mystery Writers of America's Edgar Allan Poe Special Award.

Raskin's last novel, *The Westing Game* (1978), received both the Newbery Medal and the Boston Globe–Horn Book Award. The book — the seemingly simple tale of an eccentric millionaire's will that sends his heirs off on a search for his murderer — combines Raskin's flair for word games, disguises, multiple aliases, and subterfuges with her love for the stock market, the game of chess, and her hometown. On being awarded the Newbery Medal, Raskin rejoiced in the fact that all her "beloved characters are alive and well and forevermore will be playing The Westing Game." The continued popularity of *The Westing Game* has assured the long life of heroine and puzzle-solver Turtle Wexler and her fellow heirs.

As Uncle Florence in *Figgs and Phantoms* says, "I dream of a gentle world, peopled with good people and filled with simple and good things. . . . From books I built my dreams; in books I found Capri." Through her picture books and novels, Raskin has allowed children and adults alike to find their own Capri.   M.I.A.

Rathmann, Margaret Crosby

American author and illustrator, b. 1953. Peggy Rathmann came to children's books after pursuing a variety of different interests. She grew up in St. Paul, Minnesota, one of five children. At first interested in becoming an anthropologist, she tried keeping scientific notes on her little brother but found herself inventing everything. This inventiveness has served her well in books that take a familiar plot and give it a dramatic, and always funny, new twist. Rathmann's first book, *Ruby the Copycat* (1991), garnered immediate attention, and Rathmann was named "Most Promising New Author" by *Publishers Weekly*. In the book a new girl in class, Ruby, hopes to make friends with the lovely Angela by copying every detail of Angela's life. The strong story, realistic resolution, and abundant details in both text and art are distinctive. Rathmann's palette of bright pinks, greens, and yellows, and her scratchy black ink outlines, fill the pages with movement.

Ruby the Copycat grew out of an assignment in a children's-book writing class at Otis Parsons School of Design; Rathmann's second book, *Bootsie Barker Bites* (1992), was written by Barbara Bottner, the instructor in that class. Rathmann's next book, *Goodnight Gorilla* (1994), garnered immediate critical and popular success. The almost wordless PICTURE BOOK about a gorilla who lets himself and his fellow zoo mates out so they can secretly accompany the zookeeper to his cozy house is as funny as it is original. Again, the unusually bright palette lets the reader know that this will be a romp instead of a more typical soothing bedtime story.

Officer Buckle and Gloria (1995), which won the Caldecott Medal, is the lively story of a police safety officer who makes his audiences snore until he is joined by a vivacious and naturally theatrical police dog, Gloria. The picture book is peppered with hilarious but very realistic details,

and Rathmann's sketchy, stylized figures pull the reader right into the story with their open, expressive facial expressions. Text and illustration are inseparable; the same symbiotic relationship exists between the protagonists — Gloria provides the pictures for Officer Buckle's text.

10 Minutes Til Bedtime (1998) provides a fresh approach to a very familiar subject. A child is joined in his bedtime countdown, which includes the usual bath and dental hygiene, by a tour group of hamsters. As in *Goodnight Gorilla* the text is almost nonexistent, but the story lies in adventures of scores of hamsters enjoying all the bedtime amenities, such as goldfish crackers and a bathtub large enough for water skiing. Once again, Rathmann's work is distinguished by her attention to detail, her understanding of the emotions and concerns of children, her outrageous sense of humor, and her vibrant art.

M.V.K.

Rawlings, Marjorie Kinnan

American author, 1896–1953. Marjorie Kinnan Rawlings discovered her literary voice in Florida, where she produced several classic works of American fiction. Although her best writing concerns rural regions, the author was born and raised in Washington, D.C., where her father was a patent attorney. Rawlings developed an early interest in writing and had a story published in the *Washington Post* at age eleven. She attended the University of Wisconsin in Madison, where she edited the school literary magazine and met her first husband. The author's early work experiences include writing publicity for the YWCA, editing a magazine, reporting for the Louisville *Courier-Journal* in Kentucky and the Rochester *Journal* in New York, and writing poetry for a newspaper syndicate.

In 1928 Rawlings left her husband and used an inheritance to purchase a seventy-two-acre orange grove in Cross Creek, in rural Florida. Rawlings immersed herself in the backwoods atmosphere, exploring nature and spending time with country people, who told her stories and took her hunting. Inspired by the locale, she began writing stories of rural life, including the classics "Jacob's Ladder" and "Gal Young Un."

Her first novel, *South Moon Under* (1933), which concerns the life of a Florida moonshiner, was followed by her masterpiece, *The Yearling* (1938), the story of twelve-year-old Jody Baxter, who lives in the Florida scrub country with his pragmatic mother and kindly, storytelling father. Rawlings beautifully described the natural setting and the poor yet proud families who reside there. Jody adopts an orphaned fawn, which is named Flag by the tragic, mystical Fodderwing, youngest son of the wild Forrester clan. During the course of one year, against a background that includes farming, hunting, a community feud, a weeklong rainstorm, Christmas, and many other events, Jody tames the fawn and the two grow to be close companions. But when Flag begins to trample and eat the family's crops, the yearling deer must be killed, and Jody runs away from his family. He soon returns home, with the newfound awareness that he is no longer a "yearling" himself; he has left childhood behind. Rawlings's evocative descriptions of rural Florida and its people make *The Yearling* regional fiction at its best, yet the novel is universal in its depiction of the human experience. The book was awarded the Pulitzer Prize and made into a 1946 motion picture starring Gregory Peck and Jane Wyman as Jody's parents. Although originally published for adults, it is now primarily read and enjoyed by children.

Rawlings wrote only one work expressly for children. Published posthumously, *The Secret River* (1955) is a timeless story about Calpurnia, an aspiring young poet who journeys from her Florida home to a secret river, where she catches some much-needed fish for her father to sell. Although the dialogue is occasionally sentimental, there is a magical quality to this gentle, allegorical tale, which was named a Newbery Honor Book. Among Rawlings's other works is the autobiographical *Cross Creek* (1942); actress Mary Steenburgen portrayed Rawlings in the 1983 film adaptation.

The last decade of the twentieth century marked a renewed interest in the life and writings of the author, suggesting that Rawlings's evocative stories of rural Florida will continue to be widely read and enjoyed in the twenty-first century. P.D.S.

Reid Banks, Lynne

British author, b. 1929. Lynne Reid Banks was born in London. During World War II, she was evacuated to Saskatchewan. After returning to England, she studied acting, hoping to become an actress, like her mother. After graduation from the Royal Academy of Dramatic Art in London and five years of work, however, she found she could not support herself in that career. She then worked as a journalist, becoming the first woman reporter on British television, and she was also a teacher on a kibbutz in Israel before she eventually became a full-time writer.

Reid Banks is known as a fine storyteller. Among her first works for adults is *The L-Shaped Room,* which was published in 1960. The protagonist, unmarried and pregnant, is turned out of her home by her angry father. The girl lives by herself in a small rented room, where an odd collection of neighbors extend their friendship to her. The book is widely read by young adults.

Her most popular books for children are those in a series that began with *The Indian in the Cupboard* (1981). In this fantasy, a magic cabinet, or cupboard, is used to bring to life a toy plastic figure of an American Indian. The tale is one of adventure, with life-and-death situations, spiced by the boys' fear of discovery as they enjoy the excitement of having such an important secret. The relationship drawn between friends — the arguments, the friendship — rings true and makes the fantasy element more believable. Although extremely popular, the book has been criticized for its stereotypical portrayal of American Indians. It has several sequels: *Return of the Indian* (1986), *The Secret of the Indian* (1989), *The Mystery of the Cupboard* (1993), and *The Key to the Indian* (1998).

Reid Banks's other works for children include

I, Houdini: The Autobiography of a Self-Educated Hamster (1988), a story of a conceited hamster who loves to escape from his cage and wreak havoc in the house where he lives with a family that includes three boys. *Melusine: A Mystery* (1989), a YOUNG ADULT NOVEL, is based on a twelfth-century French legend in which a young woman is condemned to change into the form of a snake. The chilling tale has elements of incest and murder. One of her books written for the adult market, *Dark Quartet: The Story of the Brontës,* was named an ALA Best Book for Young Adults in 1977. Reid Banks has also written books of history for adults and plays for stage, television, and radio. She has also acted in plays on the radio. Her flair for suspense and adventurous storytelling makes her stories compelling and popular. S.H.H.

Review Sources

Reviewing children's books seems a simple and common enough activity. Nearly every adult involved with children and children's reading acts as a children's book reviewer. In "Out on a Limb with the Critics" (*Horn Book Magazine*, 1970) Paul Heins wrote that "the very task of selection is, by its very nature, a task of criticism — of judgment." Thus, the teacher who selects books for a classroom and for particular students functions as a reviewer; the librarian, deciding which books to purchase and where to shelve them, performs as a reviewer; the bookseller choosing stock surely reviews children's books; and the parent who picks a book for bedtime reading becomes a reviewer.

And yet the term *book reviewing* connotes something more specific: a professional, insightful, informed viewpoint that can discern the strengths and weaknesses of a book's text and art and its potential to inform, entertain, or inspire. After all, adults often turn to published book reviews to steer them through the thousands of children's books published yearly and to help them choose the best possible books for specific children. For example, when Daniel Pinkwater discusses children's books on National Public Radio, one hears the voice of an articulate individual, an experienced reader, and a children's book author. His wonderfully quirky choices of children's books for dramatic read-aloud presentation on *All Things Considered* reflect his understanding of literacy merit. Like Pinkwater, a reviewer is trusted not only to be a better reader than most but also a reader willing to "step out on a limb" in evaluating new books.

What gauges of quality do reviewers use? How do they decide on a book's quality? In his May Hill Arbuthnot lecture (1971), critic John Rowe Townsend explained that some standards are decidedly book-centered, focused on literary value; others are child-centered and deal with "suitability to the child, popularity with the child, relevance to the child." Anita Silvey has described more complex process:

[When] writing a review . . . there's a committee that sits inside my head nattering away at me all the time. There's one member, the literary stylist, who may talk about the beauty of the writing, the quality of the artwork, how the book works as a piece of art. Next, the pragmatist gets in and says, "Yes, but what about an index? What school curriculum will this fit into?" The pragmatist is shortly followed by the populist, who says, "Will children read this? What children will read this? How popular will this book be?" There is the social scientist, or philosopher, who is arguing, "What does this book say to children? What values does it impart? What vision of life does it give?" (Hearne and Sutton, *Evaluating Children's Books: A Critical Look,* 1993)

Indeed, many reviews simultaneously explore literary value and merit and consider the potential audience and uses of the book. Taking a fundamentally formalist approach, they summarize the book: they describe its plot, characters, and setting; delineate its thematic concerns; classify it by genre; and end the short two hundred words with some kind of qualification or recommendation about the book's possible audience.

As a practical arm of publishing, children's book reviewing seldom provides lengthy, detailed analysis or the multiple interpretive lenses that critical essays may include. Instead, brevity and timeliness characterize the typical book review. To be a useful tool for the book-buying parent, teacher, or librarian, or to serve as a vehicle for promotion, the review must appear close on the heels of the book's publication. The tasks of selection, evaluation, and judgment dominate the reviewer's job. The best reviews are informed, clearly stated opinions about a particular book at a given time; they probably cannot and should not be objective. Don't the reviewer's knowledge of literature, the book's subject matter, and the needs of a certain audience challenge his or her objectivity? Isn't that a good thing? A passionate response to a book can relate far more about it than a lukewarm but balanced response. When skilled reviewers offer their unique personal responses to text or art, striking insights can result.

Virginia Woolf conceived of the perfect review as an exchange between the reviewer and the artist, enabling the artist to grow from the reviewer's experienced knowledge of literature. And reviewing can and does influence literary and visual art. It certainly affects editors and editorial decisions because reviews can sway sales — editor Dorothy Briley can recall a starred review that resulted in the paperback reprint of a book. And oddly enough, sometimes the books prominently advertised in a journal do not receive positive reviews in its pages. Despite concern that "wrong-headed reviewing" (Hearne and Sutton, *ECB*, 1993) can harm a book just as a starred review can promote it, Briley has found that "opinions expressed in reviews have influenced how books are put together" (Hearne and Sutton, *ECB*, 1993). Concrete changes in documentation, indexing, and labeling in children's information books and in the extraliterary material included in folktales have directly resulted from reviews.

Different publications offer different types of reviews of children's books. As an insider voice of the publishing industry, the children's section of *Publishers Weekly* reports information about sales figures, best-selling titles, licensing agreements, and marketing and publishing programs — a wider context for the magazine's reviews of children's books. The reviews themselves address bookstore buyers and individual customers (and many librarians refer to them as well), evaluating a book's literary merits as well as its potential popularity with its child audience. A staff of regular reviewers also contribute feature-length articles.

Also, the *New York Times Book Review* regularly includes children's books in its pages. This Sunday paper supplement includes only one or two signed pieces by invited reviewers of children's books. These writers may have expertise in children's literature or in a field related to the subject of the book. The publication also devotes expansive, informative special issues to the subject of children's books.

In addition to these two sources, five major journals (*School Library Journal, Booklist, Kirkus Reviews,* the *Bulletin of the Center for Children's Books,* and the *Horn Book Magazine*) traditionally have focused on the needs of public and school libraries, often including librarians on their editorial and reviewing staff. Each uses a "star system" to rank exemplary books. At various points in the publishing cycle, the journals declare their editorial policies regarding selection of books for review and the process by which a book can earn a star. Increasingly these journals make their print reviews available on line at password-restricted websites, and online bookstores, such as Amazon and Barnes and Noble, aggregate reviews by title. Thus, these five journals reach out to a wide array of children's book buyers, both traditional and new markets.

A monthly publication, *School Library Journal* has the highest circulation of these five journals. It attempts to review most, if not all, titles from major publishers, as well as significant contributions from small presses and samples of series books. It also reviews websites and multimedia releases. Its news articles focus on issues specific to librarians in schools and public libraries, such as funding resources, new technology, and strategies of delivering library service to students. The editorial staff employs hundreds of librarians from across the country as book reviewers.

In contrast, *Booklist,* the bimonthly publication of the American Library Association, depends on an in-house reviewing staff (supplemented by a small number of outside reviewers) and has a recommended-only policy that limits the number of books reviewed. *Booklist* reviews about half of the children's titles published each year, along with adult books, reference books, electronic reference tools, and audiovisual releases. Columns and feature articles include author interviews, thematic bibliographies, and essays about books and reading.

Kirkus Reviews also critiques books across genres, including children's books in every other issue. The journal contains only reviews of print books and no articles or essays. The children's book review editor works closely with a limited staff of contributing reviewers whose work is not signed. More than the other journals discussed here, *Kirkus Reviews* shows a consistency of prose style and literary judgment.

The *Bulletin of the Center for Children's Books* approaches that unity of voice because it depends on a small staff of reviewers, all located at the University of Illinois at Champaign-Urbana. Founded in 1945, the journal's roots in education and its belief in critical reading translate into reviews that not only describe and evaluate books but also indicate reading level and suggest possible curricular use. Each issue's front-page editorial discusses a single title at length and in depth. The journal exclusively reviews children's books, supplemented by information about professional reading and research.

The oldest of these journals, the *Horn Book Magazine,* was founded in 1924 as an extension of a children's bookstore and continues to work toward its original mission of "sounding the horn for good books for children." A small number of staff reviewers and a handful of guest reviewers complement an in-house editorial staff. The bimonthly magazine highlights about 20 percent of recently published children's books and significant paperback reprints. It also includes articles about children's literature and its practice and criticism, written by editors, teachers, librarians, booksellers, historians, and others. Provocative editorials comment on the state of and trends in contemporary children's books. The magazine staff works closely with the staff of *The Horn Book Guide,* a semiannual publication that reviews nearly all children's books published each year; therefore, a book not reviewed in the *Horn Book Magazine* will likely be reviewed in the *Guide.* Comprehensive and informative, the *Guide* uses a rating system of 1 (outstanding) through 6 (unacceptable). Its brief reviews are written by a variety of people who work with children. The extensive subject index and organization by genre and grade level demonstrate the usefulness of the *Guide.*

The use and study of children's literature reach across disciplines, and this trend in cross-curricular literary connections is also reflected in reviewing. *KLIATT* and *VOYA* (six issues per year each) are independent publications addressing library and educational needs. Containing only a handful of articles, each issue devotes pages to reviews of young adult reading materials across academic disciplines, including paperbacks and hardcovers, multimedia and print material. *BookLinks,* a bimonthly *Booklist* publication, also focuses on curriculum. Designed for teachers, librarians, library media specialists, booksellers, parents, and all adults interested in connecting children with high-quality books, each issue addresses a single theme in articles that pull together familiar and less well known, old and new children's books for different ages and across different genres.

The rise of independent children's bookstores in the mid-1980s did not shift book-buying trends away from the traditional base of school and library markets, but it did add parents as significant new buyers. The market has evolved again with the addition of children's departments in chain bookstores, and again with the advent of children's books in the wholesale price club; it will change again through the influence of e-books and the Internet. Journals such as *Five Owls* and *Riverbank Review* try to reach the new broadening audiences for children's literature. Instead of presenting a limited number of substantial reviews of new books of merit, these quarterlies provide more reviews that contain briefer information. *Five Owls* makes a special pitch to parents (but not exclusive of educators) in articles that share a thematic focus with annotated bibliographies. In aspiring to reach as many audiences as possible, *Riverbank Review* offers essays by children's book creators, reflections on working with children through literature, and a bookmark with brief annotations about ten great books on a particular topic.

Newspapers continue to be one of the most immediate, and most overlooked, venues for reviewing children's books. The *Washington Post* reviews a handful of children's books in Sunday's *Book World*. The *Times* and the *Post* may be the best known, but other city papers, such as the *Boston Globe* and the *Los Angeles Times*, and many small local papers value how children's books help develop an educated citizenship. C.M.M.

Rey, H. A.; Rey, Margret

H. A.: American illustrator, 1898–1977; Margret: American author, 1906–1996. Hans Augusto Rey combined an inquisitive mind and an extensive knowledge of natural sciences with a talent for expressive drawing and achieved an internationally recognized career as a creator and illustrator of PICTURE BOOKS for children and adults. Through the character of Curious George, the adventurous tailless monkey, he projected his own lively curiosity in the world around him and at the same time kept his stories within the realm of children's activities and comprehension. His books are rooted in his keen empathy with children and with their efforts to discover and try new things. Although Curious George began in England as a character named Zozo and is known in France as Fifi, his mischievous exploits in books such as *Curious George* (1941), *Curious George Takes a Job* (1947), *Curious George Rides a Bike* (1952), and *Curious*

George Goes to the Hospital (1966) are universal and have been translated into more than a dozen languages.

After laying out a rough dummy, Rey did the artwork for many of his books by making the color separations himself. His illustrations make vivid use of strong colors, often with an incisive black outline of objects and figures. They interplay on the page with the text and are full of action and humor. Rey gave his animals, such as George and Cecily G. (the giraffe in *Cecily G. and the Nine Monkeys,* 1942), individuality as characters, but their actions are informed by his precise knowledge of their anatomy.

During World War II, when toys and paper were scarce, Rey anticipated the flap books children enjoy today with a series of small-sized books, *Is Anybody at Home?* (1939), *How Do You Get There?* (1941), and *Where's My Baby?* (1943), in which the answers are hidden under flaps. His scientific knowledge and interest in stargazing prompted him to write and illustrate *The Stars: A New Way to See Them* (1952), a picture book for adults. Here his ability as an artist to see spaces and forms led him to try various connecting lines between the stars of a constellation until he had a shape that would make visual sense to the nonspecialist. He followed this with *Find the Constellations* (1954).

After World War I, in which he spent two years as a soldier in the German army, Rey studied languages, philosophy, and natural sciences at universities in Munich and Hamburg, and worked as a lithographer and illustrator. In the 1920s he lived in Brazil. There he met and married his wife, Margret, an artist and writer who was a partner in his work, often cowriting the texts for their books as well as creating stories of her own, such as *Pretzel* (1944), *Spotty* (1945), and *Whiteblack the Penguin Sees the World* (2000), for him to illustrate. He also used the pseudonym Uncle Gus. In 1936 the Reys moved to Paris, and several of his early picture books were published there. When the Nazis approached, the Reys fled on bicycles to Lisbon, eventually reaching New York via Rio de Janeiro in 1940. For many years they lived in Cambridge,

Illustration by H. A. Rey from his book *Curious George* (1941).

Massachusetts, and summered in New Hampshire.

After H. A. Rey's death in 1977, a series of books appeared with the text by Margret Rey and artwork by another artist working in Rey's style and using the Curious George character; the art lacked the quality of Rey's illustrations. Curious George remains, however, a recognized and beloved monkey who will continue to amuse and comfort children for years to come.

L.K.

Robinson, Barbara

American author, b. 1927. Many readers are first introduced to Barbara Robinson during the holiday season, when her book *The Best Christmas Pageant Ever* (1972) is read aloud in classrooms and libraries. Although she has written several other titles, including the sequel, *The Best School Year Ever* (1994), the author is best known for this perennial holiday favorite.

Robinson was born in Portsmouth, Ohio, and began writing as a child. She studied theater at Allegheny College, then worked in a library until she married. As a freelance writer, Robinson has sold fiction to a number of women's magazines, including *Ladies' Home Journal, McCall's,* and *Good Housekeeping.* Her first book, *Across from Indian Shore* (1962), was inspired by her interest in American Indians. It is the story of a boy who is friends with an aged Wampanoag princess. Robinson followed this novel with another Indian adventure, *Trace Through the Forest* (1965), and a rather didactic PICTURE BOOK, *The Fattest Bear in the First Grade* (1969).

The author's most popular book, *The Best Christmas Pageant Ever,* concerns the lying, stealing, cigar-smoking Herdman children, who are lured into church with the promise of treats and end up taking over the annual Christmas nativity program. This short, fast-paced novel contains laugh-out-loud humor that is slightly irreverent but never sacrilegious. The book's conclusion, in which the Herdmans come to appreciate Christmas, is moving but not saccharine. The nameless narrator represents the community's gradual, grudging respect for the Herdman family but plays no significant role in the story. Further, the six Herdman children are fairly interchangeable as characters. Nevertheless, the book is great fun and has also been adapted for the stage and produced as a television special.

Robinson developed *The Best Christmas Pageant Ever* from a story she had originally published in a women's magazine. She expanded another magazine story into *Temporary Times, Temporary Places* (1982), which tells of a teenage girl's first romance. This introspective, mature novel depicts fifteen-year-old Janet's crush on Eddie, then follows the relationship as they begin dating and eventually break up when Eddie starts seeing another girl. The conflicting emotions of young love are sensitively and honestly explored in this well-written novel. Robinson abandoned quiet introspection for broad comedy in *My Brother Louis Measures Worms and Other Louis Stories* (1988), a collection of interrelated stories about the Lawson family. Although narrator Mary Elizabeth Lawson is a rather indistinct character, her tales are filled with eccentric and colorful family members involved in zany situations, including her seven-year-old brother's experiences driving the family car.

Robinson's work demonstrates a talent for engaging the reader's emotions, whether she is poignantly writing about a first romance or provoking laughter with her humorous stories.

P.D.S.

Rockwell, Anne

American author and illustrator, b. 1934. Anne Rockwell has written and illustrated more than seventy books and collaborated with her husband, Harlow Rockwell, on over twenty more. Among them are PICTURE BOOKS, INFORMATION BOOKS for middle-grade readers, folktales, and folktale collections, including *The Three Bears and Fifteen Other Stories* (1975), a delightful collection of brightly illustrated tales. But her most significant contribution has been her information books for preschoolers. Characterized by simple text and vibrant, clear illustrations, these works capture the perspectives and interest of the youngest children.

Rockwell was born in Memphis, Tennessee, and spent her childhood in various parts of the United States. She developed an early interest in drawing and went on to study art at the Sculpture Center in New York City and at the Pratt Institute in Brooklyn. After the first of her three children was born, she began writing and illustrating children's books; her first, *Paul and Arthur Search for the Egg,* was published in 1964. Her books about transportation, including boats, cars, planes, trains, and trucks, are among her most popular. In each, a clearly delineated vehicle is depicted in context, with a peppy animal operator, and it starts with the familiar: on the title page of *Boats* (1982), a young bear heads to the bath with his toy boat; on the next page the same boat — now piloted by a bear — is accompanied by the simple text "Boats float." After introducing less familiar concepts, the text eventually returns to the boat of the first page.

Rockwell has presented a number of other concepts with books that feature Bear Child. *First Comes Spring* (1985) discusses seasons and seasonal activity with a nicely patterned structure. Each season is introduced with a picture of the world right outside Bear Child's house and with what Bear Child is wearing. The subsequent two-page spread shows bears doing all kinds of seasonal activity, and, on the next two pages, each activity is depicted and labeled — everything from making mud pies to putting screens on the windows.

Things That Go (1986) and *Things to Play With* (1988) help children classify and arrange their world. Each two-page spread describes an overall concept, such as "things that go in the air," and is illustrated with a dozen familiar and less familiar examples. Each "thing" is operated by an animal — with a pleasing absence of sex-role stereotyping — and is shown in use. The pages have enough activity to be exciting without being overwhelming.

Among the books that Rockwell has written with her husband are those in the My World series, which help young children feel comfortable with new ideas, such as baby sitters and being sick. The books maintain a young child's perspective by using a first-person narrative and providing details important to children. In *When I Go Visiting* (1984), the narrator talks about visiting his grandparents in the city: "I bring my bear so he won't be lonesome." Notable among Rockwell's works for older children are her books for beginning readers, which include simply colored illustrations and inventive, often funny, story lines.

Rockwell has approached her subjects with a deep understanding of early childhood and a light hand, helping children feel good about their growing mastery of the world around them. A.E.Q.

Rodgers, Mary

American novelist, b. 1931. The daughter of Richard and Dorothy Rodgers, Mary Rodgers was born in New York City. Following her education at Wellesley College in Massachusetts, she returned to New York where — like her composer father — she originated and wrote lyrics for several Broadway musicals, including *Once Upon a Mattress.* From 1957 to 1971, she worked as assistant producer of the New York Philharmonic's Young People's Concerts. Her musical scores for children include *Davy Jones' Locker* (1959) and *Pinocchio* (1973), both performed with the Bill Baird Marionettes, and *Young Mark Twain* (1964). She was also a contributing editor to the best-selling book and record *Free to Be . . . You and Me.*

But Rodgers is probably best known for her breakthrough novel, *Freaky Friday* (1972). "Since I had nothing to do but take care of five children, a nine-room apartment, an eleven-room house in the country, and show up once a month at the Professional Children's School Board of Trustees meeting, once a month at the Dramatist Guild Council meeting, and eight times at the A&P," she has said with the same wry wit that infuses her writing, "I thought I'd be delighted to write a children's book because I had all this extra time on my hands. (Between the hours of two and five A.M., I just loll around the house wondering how to amuse myself.)" The result was *Freaky Friday,* which became an ALA Notable Book and winner of numerous awards. The novel is about a thirteen-year-old who, the morning after an argument with her mother, is astonished when she awakens to find herself transformed. "You are not going to believe me," begins Annabel Andrews, "nobody in their right minds could *possibly* believe me, but it's true, really it is! *When I woke up this morning, I found I'd turned into my mother.*" At first overjoyed with the independence she had been fighting for all along, Annabel soon discovers what a damper adult responsibilities can put on one's fun. She also gains insight into how others — namely, the younger brother she calls Ape Face ("His real name is Ben") — view her.

Freaky Friday gained instant recognition and remains a highly successful, timeless story. It was followed by a sequel, *A Billion for Boris* (1974), a comedy of misadventures centered on Annabel's boyfriend and the problems he faces with his ec-

centric mother. In a third book, *Summer Switch* (1982), a sequel to both *Freaky Friday* and *A Billion for Boris,* Annabel's younger brother literally trades places with his dad.

All three novels deal with family and social issues such as freedom, manners, tidiness, sibling and parent-child relationships, and even bigotry. Through her spontaneous use of humor and offbeat, enduring plots, Rodgers has captured children in the throes of trying to comprehend the adult world surrounding them. C.S.

Rojankovsky, Feodor

Russian illustrator, 1891–1970. During the 1940s, Feodor Rojankovsky was one of the first European artists whose creative talents infused the field of American children's PICTURE BOOK illustration with a boldness of color and the vitality of fine, modern design. Often using crayon to create mood and texture, Rojankovsky imparted a childlike quality to much of his work, drawing simple, cheerful pictures of true-to-life animals and ordinary children.

About his youth, the Russian-born Rojankovsky remarked: "Two great events determined the course of my childhood. I was taken to the zoo and saw the most marvelous creatures on earth: bears, tigers, monkeys and reindeer; and, while my admiration was running high, I was given a set of color crayons." Passionate about nature and drawing, Rojankovsky honed skills and techniques that allowed him to matriculate at the Moscow Fine Arts Academy in 1912. His studies ended two years later with military service in World War I, followed by the Russian Revolution, in which he first began to illustrate Russian children's books.

After the war, Rojankovsky lived in Paris, where he worked for Domino Press, a small publishing firm owned by two American women. *Daniel Boone* (1931), Domino Press's first publication, was America's introduction to Rojankovsky's talent as an illustrator. Emblazoned with brilliant colors and an impeccable sense of design, *Daniel Boone* was hailed by

Anne Carroll Moore as "a unique first book in American history." The spirited lithographs spoke of Rojankovsky's affinity for the American frontier, and critics lauded him as a fine colorist. With unusual color schemes that combined red, yellow, purple, and green, the illustrations in *Daniel Boone* convey a liveliness and a daring befitting their subject.

Rojankovsky immigrated to America in 1941, where he joined the Artists and Writers Guild, then headed by Georges Duplaix. One year later, Duplaix arranged with Ursula Nordstrom, the gifted Harper juveniles editor, to publish Rojankovsky's *Tall Book of Mother Goose* (1942). Its elongated size — approximately five by twelve inches, ideal for presenting a great number of rhymes individually, each with its own illustration — was a new shape for Mother Goose books. Also new was the look of Rojankovsky's goose. Late-nineteenth-century collections often depicted a quaint, grandmotherly woman and her goose seated among dainty, well-behaved children, or a saccharine twosome in flight across the sky. Rojankovsky's goose, cheery and colorful, was without its human counterpart, and the children he pictured were just as natural and homely as the ones next door. His penchant for highly vibrant colors injected a gaiety into his remarkably unsentimental drawings.

Rojankovsky also illustrated some of the first Golden Books for Duplaix, founder of that imprint. In more than twenty Golden Books, Rojankovsky used color, realistic animals, and lively children; all three became his trademarks. *The Three Bears* (1948), a Little Golden Book Classic still in print, displays his trademarks with exceptional distinction: a peasant cottage filled with a riot of colors and a great deal of Russian folk art; three husky, auburn bears; and Goldilocks, whose braids are more red than blonde.

Equally respected in the trade book field, Rojankovsky's talent for observing and drawing nature enabled him to craft several other noteworthy titles; his illustrations for editor John Langstaff's *Frog Went A-Courtin'* earned him the Caldecott Medal in 1956. His choice of medium, crayon reinforced with pen-and-ink line, gave the drawings a rich grainy texture and conveyed a characteristic childlike quality that flawlessly matched the simplicity and the cheerfulness of the Scottish children's ballad.

When he died in 1970, Rojankovsky had illustrated more than one hundred children's books; his flair for color, his vision of design, and his love of nature have greatly enriched American picture books. S.L.S.

Rounds, Glen

American author and illustrator, b. 1906. Born in the Badlands of South Dakota, Glen Rounds was brought up on a ranch in Montana, so it is no surprise that his collection of work for children resonates with the vitality characteristic of the Western frontier.

Before and after attending the Kansas City Art Institute, Rounds held a number of jobs, including sign painter, textile designer, baker, and cowboy. He arrived in New York in 1930 and attended night school at the Art Students League. In 1935, with drawings in hand, he appeared on publishers' doorsteps around lunchtime; although many of the editors thought his work too coarse and wanted something more in the prevailing "slick and mannered" style of the day, he usually managed to get a good lunch.

It was not until 1936 that he became a full-time author and illustrator of children's books. He began his career by sketching and later, at an editor's suggestion, wrote his first story, *Ol' Paul, the Mighty Logger* (1936), to accompany his illustrations. In this first attempt at juvenile fiction, Rounds told the "true" account of Paul Bunyan. Testifying that he had previously worked for the giant logger, Rounds recounted ten tales about Bunyan, including how he built the Rockies. The rough black-and-white illustrations scattered throughout the chapters give a glimpse of the real West, the West that Bunyan created.

The Blind Colt (1941) tells the heart-warming story of how a blind colt survives life in the Badlands. In CHAPTER BOOK format, with straightforward text and simple black-ink sketches, Rounds captured the vitality of the young horse and how it manages to see by using its other senses.

Rounds is best known for his Whitey series, which stars the young cowboy, Whitey, and his cousin, Josie. With his humorous black-and-white illustrations, Rounds engaged the characters and the reader in adventures on a ranch. Critics and children alike have acclaimed these books because of their realistic depiction of Western life. He won the Lewis Carroll Shelf Award twice for *Wild Horses of the Red Desert* (1969) and *Stolen Pony* (1969).

In his old age, Rounds has continued to create books and to engage his young audience with his scraggly line. He has retold favorite songs in *Old MacDonald Had a Farm* (1989), *I Know an Old Lady Who Swallowed a Fly* (1990), and *Three Little Pigs and the Big Bad Wolf* (1992).

Throughout his career, Rounds has employed a variety of tools — pens, brushes, a house painter's brush — depending on the style he wanted to achieve. He has provided the world of children's literature with a vast collection of written and illustrated works — and an appealing array of heavily outlined, bowlegged characters.   J.M.

Rowling, J. K.

British author, b. 1965. A phenomenon in children's book publishing began in 1998 and continues to whirl around author Joanne K. Rowling and her books about the young wizard Harry Potter. The literary hoopla began in England, where *Harry Potter and the Sorcerer's Stone* (1998), Rowling's first novel, written when she was a young mother living on unemployment benefits, immediately hit the top of bestseller lists in England. Less than a year after it was published, the book, written for eight- to twelve-year-olds, won the British Book Awards Children's Book of the Year. It was sold to publishers in eight countries, including the United States.

The first four books of the series — *Harry Potter and the Sorcerer's Stone* (1998), *Harry Potter and the Chamber of Secrets* (1999), *Harry Potter and the Prisoner of Azkaban* (1999), and *Harry Potter and the Goblet of Fire* (2000) — have sold more than fifty million copies in the United States alone. Although the books have certainly delighted both adults and children, children themselves immediately took Harry and his stories to heart. It is easy to understand why. The stories are chock-full of the right ingredients: quirky and courageous characters, magic, humor, whimsical and bizarre settings, and a convincing blend of FANTASY and reality. And throughout, the narratives are woven with age-old themes of good and evil.

After twelve years of working shoulder to shoulder with her central character, Rowling "thinks one reason Harry's stories are so appealing is he has to accept adult burdens in his life, although he is a child. He is also an old-fashioned hero. What I mean by that is — there are enough human frailties in Harry that people of all ages identify with him, but he is also an honorable, admirable person."

The idea for Harry Potter's story came to the author when she was delayed on a train to London: "Harry as a character came fully formed, as did the idea for his sidekicks, the characters of Ron and Hermione. It started with Harry, then all these characters and situations came flooding into my head. It was an excitement I'd never known before." The characters arrived in 1990, but it took Rowling six years to develop the plot and write the book.

In *Harry Potter and the Sorcerer's Stone* Harry is orphaned in infancy and deposited on his aunt and uncle's doorstep. For ten years, Harry is raised in the household of his truly vile relatives; his bedroom is a closet under the stairs. But Harry is unique; he is a wizard. He is the surviving son of wizards who were killed by the evil sorcerer Lord Voldemort, and as a result of his ancestry he is blessed with enough common sense and tenacity to cope with his Muggle (nonmagical) relatives. An unassuming hero, he is oblivious to his own magical powers until a giant plucks him from the clutches of his nasty aunt and uncle and delivers him to Hogwarts School for Witchcraft and Wizardry.

Once at Hogwarts, his life changes forever. Harry begins to hone his magical skills and finds wonderful friends, as well as a few malcontents. As the story unfolds, readers realize Harry has a destiny to fulfill; he must rout out an evil within the depths of Hogwarts School. With the help of his pals, Hermione, Ron, and the giant Hagrid, along with the guidance of Head Wizard Dumbledore, Harry summons his courage and common sense to unearth an old enemy camped beneath the school building — Voldemort. The friends combine magical talents and send the odious sorcerer packing, at least temporarily, in a rousing, completely satisfying denouement.

In *Harry Potter and the Chamber of Secrets*, Harry returns to Hogwarts for his second year. His escapades are full of magic, genial ghosts, rivalries, eccentric teachers, and, once again, a sinister mystery lurking in the halls of Hogwarts. Rowling has used many of her trademark story ingredients to keep this tale zipping along, tapping into an engaging vein of fantasy peppered with humor, convoluted plots, a cast of idiosyncratic characters, and evil — which is kept at bay until Harry sorts out the skullduggery.

By the third installment of the Harry saga, the popularity of the books had become staggering. Children stood in lines for hours, waiting to buy *Harry Potter and the Prisoner of Azkaban*. All the basics remain in place in this book, though several new, colorful characters are introduced, and a tricky bit of time manipulation brings the tale to a delightful hair-raising climax. Most satisfying is the development of Harry himself, who squarely faces the violent deaths of his parents and becomes a stronger person and a more complex and endearing hero.

Most of the characters from the earlier books, beloved or bedeviled or both, return in *Harry Potter and the Goblet of Fire*– a fire that is almost extinguished by the book's sheer length, 734 pages. Devoted fans still follow the action to the end, although many subplots — including a preposterous, lengthy explanation of how Voldemort infiltrates Hogwarts — are distract-

ing. Themes of good and evil, courage, loyalty, friendship, and bigotry are expanded and have a powerful impact on Harry's spiritual and emotional odyssey as he comes of age.

Harry Potter is a publishing phenomena, unlike any seen in the United States. Some adults have wondered whether the public's attention and subsequent sales of the books result from the success factor itself, rather than the literary merit of Rowling's work. But clearly one of the most remarkable aspects of the Harry Potter craze is that children, even reluctant readers, have found sheer delight in reading the stories — time and again — for pleasure. Warner Brothers released a full-length feature film of Rowling's first volume in 2001, further fanning the enthusiasm of fans — who are just wild about Harry.

S.L.

Rylant, Cynthia

American author and poet, b. 1954. Through PICTURE BOOK texts, POETRY, short stories, and novels, Cynthia Rylant has demonstrated an inimitable ability to evoke the strongest of emotions through the simplest of words. For much of her writing, she has extracted experiences from her Appalachian childhood. Born in Hopewell, Virginia, Rylant lived in a small town in West Virginia with her grandparents from the time she was four until she was eight, while her mother attended nursing school. Though she has said she has never taken a creative writing class, it is apparent in her work that what she did study, especially during the early period of her life, was the language of the people around her and their amazing inner strength, despite financial or cultural impoverishment. In her work her characters re-create the unconditional love and acceptance she felt from family and those around her. Rylant has three degrees from three universities and has taught English at various universities in Ohio.

The impetus to write came from working at a library in the children's department, where she first discovered children's books, and from the birth of her son, Nathaniel. The images and reminiscences of her childhood began to appear with her first book, *When I Was Young in the Mountains* (1982), a peaceful, warm reflection of her days in Appalachia. More picture books followed, including *The Relatives Came* (1985), a visual and verbal depiction of a lovingly tumultuous visit from relatives, and *Appalachia: The Voices of Sleeping Birds* (1991), which has a text that flows like poetry and is subtitled after a passage by James Agee, one of Rylant's main influences. Both *When I Was Young in the Mountains* and *The Relatives Came* were Caldecott Honor Books.

In her short stories, Rylant has taken advantage of added room to flex her writing muscle, creating powerful images, such as those in *A Couple of Kooks: And Other Stories About Love* (1990). Not your typical collection of young adult love stories, these pieces show how Rylant can challenge herself as a writer by playing with perspective. The stories vary in points of view, ranging from that of a mentally challenged adult with a crush on a shopkeeper to a grandfather reflecting on love at his granddaughter's wedding. It is in the shorter form of picture books, poetry, and short stories that Rylant prefers to work, often perfecting in one sitting what becomes the published piece.

Though her novels may not come as easily, they do not falter in intensity but instead make her storytelling skill obvious. Her novels appear subdued on the surface, slow, almost silent, but their themes run deep, evoking emotions that much literature for children, or adults, does not dare stir. In *A Blue-eyed Daisy* (1985), we meet introverted Ellie, a girl on the verge of adolescence who lives with her family and alcoholic father in a small Appalachian coal-mining town; in *A Fine White Dust* (1986), a Newbery Honor Book, we are introduced to Pete, a young boy who becomes mesmerized by an itinerant preacher; and in *Missing May* (1992), we become involved in the search for the spirit of May by her husband, Ob, and her niece, Summer, who have grieved tremendously since her death.

In 1987 Rylant began the successful Henry and Mudge series of books, over twenty in number, in the EASY READER genre, about a charming character, Henry, and his big, affectionate dog, Mudge. The mild dramas of the domestic adventures of this dynamic duo emanate humor and warm emotion, and often leave the reader with a comforting, reassuring feeling of quietude. A strong sense of family underlies each story, while the action centers on episodes celebrating simple, everyday pleasures and experiences such as spring, Thanksgiving, snow, puddles, and grandmothers. Rylant's recognizable style brings an uncommonly poetic narrative to easy readers, making her texts resonate with the oral cadences of a storyteller and the natural rhythms of speech.

In her work, Rylant gives depth and dignity to a litany of quiet characters and sagaciously reflects on some of life's most confusing mysteries.   E.K.E.

S

Sabuda, Robert

American illustrator, b. 1965. Robert Sabuda had already illustrated several children's books when, in 1992, he was struggling to design a unique Christmas-themed book that did not copy holiday books already on the market. When friends suggested that the native of Pinckney, Michigan, consider creating a pop-up book, the idea appealed to him. Since he had grown up in a low-income household, Sabuda owned many Hallmark pop-up volumes, as they were some of the cheapest books for children on the market at the time. Drawing upon his memories of these books, as well as the work of innovators such as Czech artist Vojtech Kubasta, Sabuda taught himself the art of paper engineering. The result was an ALPHABET BOOK, *The Christmas Alphabet* (1994), a departure from traditional pop-up books in which pull-tabs and levers animate only a small part of the picture. *The Christmas Alphabet* established Sabuda's signature full-moving-image pop-up style. Rather than the usual full-color format, Sabuda's pop-up designs are intricately cut in pure white paper that emphasizes the details of the piece: a candle glimmers, a dove flies, and a gift, when opened, reveals the kitten inside.

He continued the Yuletide theme in *The 12 Days of Christmas* (1996). In Sabuda's hands, the book animates the traditional holiday song: four French hens move their necks to peek out of their cage, seven swans swim in a snow-flecked snow globe, eight maids a-milking jump off a cookie tray, and the eleven ladies dancing are ballerinas on a music box.

Sabuda's other notable pop-ups include *Cookie Count* (1997), *The Movable Mother Goose* (1999), and *ABC Disney* (1998), in which doors open to reveal full-color painted pictures of familiar Disney characters: Bambi slips on the ice and goes sprawling, the Queen of Hearts bellows while waving her flamingo croquet mallet, and Aladdin's genie pops out of his bottle in a cloud of swirling smoke.

One of Sabuda's greatest achievements is *The Wonderful Wizard of Oz: A Commemorative Pop-Up* (2000), which celebrates the centennial publication of the book by L. FRANK BAUM. Rather than drawing inspiration from the 1939 MGM film or creating an original look, Sabuda based his artwork on W. W. Denslow's original illustrations for the book. Sabuda's designs, with a Kansas cyclone that moves, a hot-air balloon that goes aloft, and a truly sinister castle of the Wicked Witch of the West, made *Oz* a critically acclaimed bestseller. That same year, he joined MAURICE SENDAK and ten other illustrators in *Brooklyn Pops Up*, a collaboration celebrating New York City's most populous borough.

Sabuda, who was trained at the Pratt Institute, has been just as successful when illustrating in other styles. His collages for Marguerite W. Davol's *The Paper Dragon* (1997) and his own *Saint Valentine* (1992) are impressive, while *Arthur and the Sword* (1995), which uses actual stained glass in the illustrations, is one of his finest efforts and proves that his artistic abilities extend well beyond the world of pop-up illustrations. E.M.A.

Sachar, Louis

American author, b. 1954. Louis Sachar's first novel, *Sideways Stories from Wayside School,* was published in 1979. He was inspired to write classroom stories while working as a teacher's aide to earn college credits after dropping a Russian class. The book contains thirty stories about a thirty-story school. It is full of intelligent, offbeat humor and kids who are familiar and yet a bit unreal. The book was accepted for publication the same week Sachar began law school. For the next six years Sachar wrote children's books while studying and later practicing law, until his books finally earned enough money for him to give up his law career.

Sachar has since written two more novels about the Wayside School, *Wayside School Is Falling Down* (1989) and *Wayside School Gets a Little Stranger* (1995), as well as *Sideways Arithmetic from the Wayside School* (1989) and *More Sideways Arithmetic from the Wayside School* (1994), in which Sachar's characters present his own unusual brand of mathematical puzzles. At Wayside School, ELF plus ELF equals FOOL, and MOTH plus TOOK equals HMMMM. Challenging and comical, the problems are perfectly matched with the witty surrealist tone of the Wayside School stories.

Many of Sachar's books have been popular among children and critics alike, including the touching and humorous *There's a Boy in the Girls' Bathroom* (1987), his Marvin Redpost series of early CHAPTER BOOKS, and one of his finest books, *Someday Angeline* (1983), about an exceptional eight-year-old who is alienated because of her intelligence. While Angeline's father, a trash collector, wants great things for her, all Angeline really wants is to go for a ride in his garbage truck. Angeline is an endearing character who values humor and friendship, and who is "in balance with the whole."

Not until 1998 did Sachar truly show the world the extent of his talent with the publication of the ambitious novel *Holes*, which won both the Newbery Medal and the National Book Award. The book was inspired by summer in Texas. After spending most of his life in temperate northern California, Sachar moved to Texas with his wife and daughter in 1991 and found the intense heat and long summers nearly unbearable. He sentenced the hero of *Holes*, Stanley Yelnats, to a stay at Camp Greenlake, a sort of desert prison for boys, after Stanley has been wrongly accused of stealing a pair of shoes. The boys at Camp Greenlake dig holes all day long under the hot desert sun. Unknowingly, they are digging for Kissing Kate Barlow's treasure, under the command of the wicked warden, a descendant of one of Kate's enemies. Woven into Stanley's tale is that of Kissing Kate and the town of Greenlake before it became a desert, as well as that of Stanley's own cursed ancestors. Every detail of the past plays into the events of the present, creating a flawless and entertaining puzzle that is solved marvelously at the end. More than any of Sachar's other books, *Holes* has a surreal quality to it. Every character is larger than life and yet grounded, human, and believable. Every turn of events is fantastic and yet inevitable.

Humor, quirky characters, a great sense of fun, and a true affection for young people and their idiosyncrasies mark Sachar's work. J.P.

Salisbury, Graham

American author, b. 1944. A single book can change a life. For Graham Salisbury, that book was Alex Haley's *Roots*. Salisbury grew up in Hawaii, where his ancestors had settled as missionaries in the early part of the nineteenth century. After a childhood spent exploring this tropical paradise, he worked as a deck hand on a

deep-sea fishing vessel, skippered a glass-bottom boat, and joined a rock band called Millennium. Even at thirty years of age and holding a degree from California State University, Salisbury had never read much more than what was required for school assignments. Then he read *Roots*, which changed him into a "voracious lifetime reader." This newfound love of reading inspired him to pursue both an interest in writing and an M.F.A. from Vermont College of Norwich University.

Salisbury's first YOUNG ADULT NOVEL, *Blue Skin of the Sea: A Novel in Stories* (1992), is notable for its exotic Hawaiian setting and its unusual structure. Eleven interrelated stories follow Sonny Mendoza from a water-fearing six-year-old in 1953 through his high school years in the mid-1960s. Along the way, the Portuguese-French protagonist tries to understand his enigmatic widowed father, deals with bullies, falls in love for the first time, and slowly grows in confidence and independence. Both the characters and the beautifully evoked setting — sandy beaches, rocky shorelines, "salt-thickened air" — linger in the reader's mind.

The author's subsequent books are also set in Hawaii and concern the growing-up experiences of island boys (or *Island Boyz*, as they are called in Salisbury's wide-ranging short story collection, published in 2002). A work of HISTORICAL FICTION, *Under the Blood-Red Sun* (1994) is the story of a Japanese American, Tomi Nakaji, who witnesses the attack on Pearl Harbor and whose life is forever altered by World War II as his father is interned, his mother loses her job, and family friendships change. This harrowing, richly observed novel won the Scott O'Dell Award for Historical Fiction.

Salisbury is also adept at working on a much smaller canvas, telling brief personal stories. Unfolding over the course of a single day, *Shark Bait* (1997) explores the universal themes of growing up, establishing personal identity, and sometimes substituting the immediate approbation of friends for the long-term respect of family. Narrated in a distinctive island voice by twelve-year-old Eric "Mokes" Chock, whose biggest fear is being known as a "daddy's boy," the novel is action-packed yet thoughtful, hard-edged yet sentimental. Another book that takes place within a brief period of time is *Lord of the Deep* (2001), in which a thirteen-year-old works on board his stepfather's fishing boat; a disturbing incident involving some charter fishermen causes Mikey's feelings for the older man to change from hero worship to grave disappointment. The subtle exploration of moral relativism is played out against an exciting and dramatic plot, making this one of the author's finest efforts.

Salisbury's multilayered stories feature sensitive, emotionally authentic portraits of adolescent boys, yet are fast-paced and dramatic enough to grab even reluctant readers. P.D.S.

Sandburg, Carl

American author, 1878–1967. Carl Sandburg is known for his celebration of the American spirit, and he embodied that spirit in his maverick approach to literature. His POETRY did not fit the accepted forms and did not deal with accepted poetic subjects; his biographical work did not have the expected footnotes; and his children's stories, which some consider his best work, were like nothing ever written. Everything he wrote was both lauded and scorned, and consensus has yet to be reached on his literary stature.

The son of Swedish immigrants, Sandburg spent most of his life in the Midwest. After fighting in Puerto Rico in the Spanish-American War, he attended college but did not graduate, preferring to get his education on the road. As he traveled through the United States, he took careful note of the vernacular and music of the people he met. He settled in Chicago and wrote for newspapers, raising three daughters with his wife, Lillian (sister of photographer Edward Steichen). He always wrote prolifically and became well known for his "performances," during which he might lecture, read his poetry, tell stories, and sing folk songs. Eventually, he was able to devote himself entirely to his writing at his family farm, making occasional public appearances, including the first address by a private citizen to a joint session of the houses of Congress.

Illustration by Maud and Miska Petersham for "How They Bring Back the Village of Cream Puffs When the Wind Blows It All Away," from *Rootabaga Stories* (1922), by Carl Sandburg.

Sandburg's straightforward poetry is accessible to a wide and diverse audience that includes children, so it is frequently included in anthologies of children's literature. Likewise, his children's BIOGRAPHY, *Abe Lincoln Grows Up* (1928), was not originally written for children but adapted from the first chapters of his monumental six-volume Lincoln biography, for which he had won a Pulitzer Prize. Only the collections *Rootabaga Stories* (1922), *Rootabaga Pigeons*

(1923), and *Potato Face* (1930) were written intentionally for children. He wrote these stories for his young daughters upon noticing that their scenery had little in common with that of traditional fairy tales. Sandburg's fairy tales take place not in ancient gnarly forests but in the "Rootabaga Country," which resembles the raw prairie, small towns, and farmland of Midwestern America in the early twentieth century. Instead of kings and woodcutters, his characters are whimsical exaggerations of Midwestern rural folks. And instead of fairy princesses and gossamer-winged sprites, corn fairies sew their overalls with corn silk and corn leaves between the corn rows, and potato bugs wear frying-pan hats. Each story is complete in itself, but they all are connected through their characters and settings. Sandburg's use of language here is poetic and playful; he chose his words and phrases for their sounds and their absurdity and made use of repetition, rhythmic cadences, and startling juxtapositions.

As a "nonsense" writer, he has been likened to English authors Rudyard Kipling (in his *Just So Stories*), LEWIS CARROLL, and EDWARD LEAR, but Sandburg's nonsense is clearly of the homespun American variety. His most enthusiastic fans have acknowledged that the selections in *Rootabaga Stories,* in their rollicking spontaneity, are uneven in quality, and some of the stories were probably better appreciated in their own time. Even so, many of them still hold enormous imaginative power and should not be lost to those readers of all ages who appreciate surrealism. D.C.

Say, Allen

Japanese American illustrator and author, b. 1939. Allen Say is widely hailed for his talent as both artist and author of books for children of many ages. Aside from showcasing an ever-developing illustrative technique that has garnered multiple awards, Say's work is noted for its gentle message of respect for the earth and for all peoples, its strong depiction of family, and its sensitivity to the similarities and differences between Eastern and Western cultures.

Born in 1937 in Yokohama, Japan, Say could not hide his love of drawing from his practical parents. At the age of twelve he apprenticed himself to the renowned Japanese cartoonist Noro Shinpei, who introduced him to both Eastern and Western drawing styles and impressed upon him the necessity of movement and fluidity in art. His tenure under Shinpei is documented in Say's critically acclaimed YOUNG ADULT NOVEL, *The Ink-Keeper's Apprentice* (1979). Say came to the United States at the age of sixteen and attended several art schools and universities before settling into a career in commercial illustration and photography. His cross-cultural upbringing and his early training under Shinpei are the greatest influences on his artistic style.

Say began publishing books for children in 1968. His early work, consisting mainly of pen and ink illustrations for Japanese folktales, was generally well received; however, true success came in 1982 with the publication of *The Bicycle Man.* Based on an incident in Say's life, the tale describes the appearance of two American soldiers at spring sports day in a post–World War II Japanese elementary school. The students and their families, at first alarmed by the appearance of the two men, are quickly charmed as one soldier demonstrates an uncanny ability to perform acrobatic stunts on a borrowed bicycle. The book is notable for the individuality of its characters, its subtlety and dramatic timing, and its thoughtful approach to emphasizing the similarities between two cultures. Say later returned to illustrating folktales with great success. *The Boy of the Three-Year Nap* (1988), written by Dianne Snyder, was selected as a 1989 Caldecott Honor Book and winner of the Boston Globe–Horn Book Award for best PICTURE BOOK. In this wry tale, a lazy boy concocts a plan to win the hand of a merchant's daughter and secure a life of leisure, only to have his clever and persistent mother manipulate events just enough that her son is compelled to work for his living. Say's illustrations, rendered in brush line and vibrant color, recall the work of traditional Japanese painters while incorporating humor through exaggerated gestures. They represented a significant break from the artist's early pen and ink style and won universal critical acclaim.

Since that time, Say's work has revolved around one or both of two distinct themes: the relationship between parent and child and the relationship between Asian and American peoples. A very successful combination of these themes appears in *Tree of Cranes* (1991), in which a young Japanese boy's American-born Japanese mother shares her reminiscences of Christmas by creating for him a special Christmas tree adorned with silver peace cranes. This beautifully crafted autobiographical story is also visually stunning; its soft, jewel-like paintings are filled with the glowing warmth of holiday candles and represent a more personal style than the vivid caricatures of *The Boy of the Three-Year Nap*. The same style resonates throughout *Tea with Milk* (1999) and *Grandfather's Journey* (1993), the Caldecott Medal winner, another intimate autobiographical portrait. With these three books, Say has taken the children of story, those of *The Bicycle Man, The Boy of the Three-Year Nap*, and the many folktales he has so successfully brought to Western readers, and made them real. His ability to thus successfully bridge two cultures is unparalleled. C.C.B.

Scarry, Richard

American illustrator and author, 1919–1994. Since the mid-1960s, Richard Scarry's books have provided hours of entertainment for young children, who eagerly pore over his outsize volumes, gazing at the cheerful faces of Busytown inhabitants such as Huckle Cat and Lowly Worm, Mr. Frumble and Mr. Fix-It, Miss Honey and Bugdozer. The books attract preschoolers and young readers with their colorful pages jam-packed with busy activity and hundreds upon hundreds of labeled objects, while brief texts, almost lost in the chaos, tell simple stories that often exhort gentle readers to be

kind, polite, helpful, and to brush their teeth and be good sports. The young recognize themselves in the ever-industrious characters, who enjoy going about the fascinating business of everyday life. And like children, Scarry's characters carry with them a clear sense of right and wrong — readers cheer along with Busytown whenever Sergeant Murphy catches Bananas Gorilla stealing his favorite yellow fruit from the grocer. International bestsellers, Scarry's numerous books have been translated into twenty-eight languages.

Scarry is not popular with everyone. Elitist attitudes about mass-market books have caused some to label Scarry's books as unimaginative carbon copies of each other, though a more accurate criticism might be that Scarry's brand of humor suits children more than it does adults. Slapstick appeals to the young, who find humor each day in their own slips, frequent bumps, spills, and goof-ups. Critics who have commented on the violence in his books — car wrecks, accidents, wild chases — fail to note that the only injuries are to someone's dignity. Scarry's deliberate use of anthropomorphic animals makes his books accessible to children of every color, but his lack of sensitivity regarding gender continues to be criticized. The early books depicted few females, and those that did appear were limited in their occupations and activities. Small improvements can be spotted in some of the later books: both mothers and fathers commute to work on the train; the term *firefighters* has replaced *firemen*; and boys learn to bake pies — though Mother Cat, sad to say, still can't change a tire.

Born in Boston, Massachusetts, Scarry attended the Boston Museum School from 1938 to 1941, completed a five-year stint in the army during World War II, and then moved to New York City to become a commercial artist. He began instead to illustrate children's books for Golden Press, and eleven years later started writing his own books. He found a successful formula with *Richard Scarry's Best Word Book Ever* (1963) and continued to reap the benefits of that discovery throughout his long career. Among the many titles that followed are perennial favorites such as *What Do People Do All Day?* (1968), *Richard Scarry's Best Mother Goose Ever* (1970), and *Richard Scarry's Busiest People Ever* (1976). J.M.B.

Schoenherr, John

American illustrator, b. 1935. Known for his black and white illustrations of nature stories and PICTURE BOOKS, John Schoenherr received new acclaim when his full-color paintings for *Owl Moon,* written by JANE YOLEN, won the 1988 Caldecott Medal. This award capped a career that has produced numerous paintings on wildlife subjects, illustrations for hundreds of SCIENCE FICTION book covers and magazine articles, and pictures for over forty children's books.

Schoenherr discovered early in life that he loved painting and at thirteen started to take art classes at the Art Students League in New York City. At the same time his interest in the natural world began to emerge, and he regularly visited local museums and zoos, observed displays and live animals, and sketched continually. He seriously considered becoming a biologist, but a high school science lab convinced him that he would prefer drawing live animals to dissecting dead ones. Graduating from Pratt Institute with the intention of being a painter of wildlife, he made his living by illustrating children's books and science fiction.

After moving his family from New York City to an old farmhouse in rural New Jersey, he turned increasingly to wildlife illustration, stimulated by the surrounding fields and woods and by the animals and scenes he encountered in his extensive travels. His black and white pictures showing humans and animals interacting with their environment grace the pages of award-winning books such as *Julie of the Wolves,* written by JEAN CRAIGHEAD GEORGE, which won the Newbery Medal in 1971, and the Newbery Honor Books *Rascal: A Memoir of a Better Era* (1963), written by Sterling North; *The Fox and the Hound* (1967), written by Daniel P. Mannix; and *Incident at Hawk's Hill* (1971), written by Allan W. Eckert. In the 1960s and 1970s, Schoenherr illustrated several picture books by Miska Miles, which also had strong nature themes. In the early 1980s, feeling limited by the demands of book illustration, he decided to devote himself exclusively to creating the dramatic, large wildlife paintings that expressed his own ideas.

His seven-year hiatus from illustration was ended by the arrival at his farm of an old friend, book editor Patricia Lee Gauch, who came bearing the spare poetic text of *Owl Moon,* a story about a girl and her dad who tramp through the snow on a moonlit night, calling for a great horned owl. Here was the kind of adventure that Schoenherr had actually shared with his own children, and he readily agreed to illustrate this story. With powerful watercolors, he captured the expectancy and excitement of the special nocturnal outing.

In 1991 he wrote and illustrated his own full-color picture book, *Bear,* a realistic account in which the dangers of a bear's coming of age are enhanced by dramatic scenes of the northern landscape. Still an avid traveler, photographer, and outdoorsman, Schoenherr continues to express his love of nature through wildlife paintings and illustrations for children's books.

H.G.N.

Schwartz, Alvin

American folklorist, 1927–1992. More than almost any other contemporary author, Alvin Schwartz single-handedly dusted off AMERICAN FOLKLORE archives and made this rich tradition come alive for young readers with his collections of wordplay, riddles, nonsense, scary stories, whoppers, tall tales, and folk poetry. A prolific author, Schwartz was able to appeal to a wide range of ages with his combination of extravagant humor and compelling material.

Born in Brooklyn, Schwartz grew up thinking

he would become either an archaeologist or a journalist. Though his interest in writing ultimately led to a career as a newspaper reporter and an author, the fascination of "digging out and understanding the unknown," he once recalled, remained with him for life. While his earlier writing focused on social issues and American institutions, his real interest was folklore. "I first became interested in folklore when I was a child," Schwartz explained, "but I had no idea that the games, songs, rhymes, and jokes I used or the tales I learned, or the customs we practiced were folklore. I also did not know that this material often was very old or that it was created by ordinary people like me, or that it survived simply and remarkably because one person told another."

With the success of *A Twister of Twists, a Tangler of Tongues: Tongue Twisters* (1972), Schwartz knew he was on the right track and pursued his passion. His reputation as a rigorous researcher and scholar was well earned. Schwartz combed library archives across the country and worked with leading folklorists to track down material. His favorite interview subjects included children and older people, and he routinely mined schoolyards, classrooms, camps, street corners, and country stores for sources. Frequently, his research took him across the country and sometimes involved translating material from other languages. It was not unusual for him to juggle several projects at once: "I overlap my work — sometimes I'm working on three things at once, and I do that for practical reasons. One of the reasons is that I 'block' or simply become very bored with what I am doing if I work with it too intensively."

His hard work and research translated into a high level of accuracy, careful source notations, and background information, but from his readers' point of view his books are just plain fun. The Noodle stories are light and funny, and his wordplay and riddle books offer "the kind of jokes that break up wise guys of nine or ten." With his collection of *Scary Stories to Tell in the Dark* (1981), Schwartz had a phenomenal success. Schwartz's collection developed from his research into stories on the theme of the unknown. As he saw it, some of the stories' appeal was as "self-chosen dares," in which readers explore, at arm's length, subject matter that intrigues or frightens them, in particular the idea of death. The stories were not gruesome, and the documented sources left readers pondering how much truth lived in the tales. Though he was reluctant to become a "scary-story specialist," Schwartz went on to write two more collections of scary stories. *In a Dark, Dark Room and Other Scary Stories* (1984) and *Ghosts! Ghostly Tales from Folklore* (1991) provided a deft combination of spookiness and humor that were designed to appeal to younger readers.

Shortly before his death, Schwartz published a collection of folk poems he had been researching for years, entitled *And the Green Grass Grew All Around* (1992). In keeping with his other collections, Schwartz continued to show his readers that authentic folklore has many forms. In this truly delightful collection, readers are treated to a selection of poems that are as amusing as they are diverse and original.

Schwartz left behind a huge legacy of folklore that might otherwise have never reached an audience of younger readers. C.L.

Schwartz, Amy

American author and illustrator, b. 1954. Amy Schwartz's illustrative trademarks in her own stories, as well as those she has created for other authors, are characters with soft, rounded, or elongated stuffed-doll shapes. All expression is contained in their eyes and mouths. Schwartz works in both pen and ink and in watercolor washes, sometimes combining media. By texturing her backgrounds with cross-hatching and dressing her two-dimensional people in uniquely patterned clothing, she has infused her illustrations with three-dimensional vitality.

In the PICTURE BOOKS she has created, for five- to eight-year-olds, Schwartz used inspiration founded on her family and ethnic background. Her first book was the whimsical FAN-TASY *Bea and Mr. Jones* (1982). Bea is bored with kindergarten; her father is equally disenchanted with corporate life. Deciding to change places, each confidently strides forth to meet the day: Bea in her father's suit, Mr. Jones in plaid slacks and sweater. The change works so well that Bea remains a successful executive, creating innovative advertising proposals, while Mr. Jones charms and entertains both kindergartners and teacher. The germ for the story came from Schwartz's curiosity about where her father went dressed in his suit and tie each workday and about what those serious-looking businessmen in Manhattan did all day.

Some of Schwartz's other works include the tale of spunky *Annabelle Swift, Kindergartner* (1988), based on a story that Schwartz's sister wrote as a teenager. Annabelle, happily confident that she will be the smartest kindergartner because her sister has prompted her with all the "right" answers, ends up embarrassing herself in class, but Schwartz exonerates her with true empathy. In *Oma and Bobo* (1987), she retold the story of the relationship between her dog and her grandmother. In this story, Oma overcomes her dislike of dogs in order to help Alice and Bobo win a blue ribbon at dog-obedience class. *Camper of the Week* (1991) asks how will Rosie, the Camper of the Week, reconcile her conscience when her friends are punished for putting worms in bully Bernice's bed and she, having secretly abetted them, goes unpunished? Two books, *Yossel Zissel and the Wisdom of Chelm* (1986) and *Mrs. Moskowitz and the Sabbath Candlesticks* (1983), stem from Schwartz's Jewish heritage. In the first, she adhered to Jewish folklore, creating an original tale about the simpletons of Chelm who are considered wise men. In the second, she showed how warm memories of the importance and comfort of Shabbat tradition motivate Mrs. Moskowitz to establish new memories in her new apartment. Humor abounds in Schwartz's adaptation of the Victorian "noodlehead" story *The Lady Who Put Salt in Her Coffee* (1989); in her *Mother Goose's Little Misfortunes* (1990),

which she wrote with her husband, Leonard Marcus; and in her rendition of *Old MacDonald* (1999).

Schwartz has admitted to being a voracious reader as a child. Her favorite pastime, next to reading, was drawing. She received a B.F.A. from the California College of Arts and Crafts in 1976 and has worked as a freelance illustrator, art teacher, and production assistant. She has received many awards for both stories and artwork. With warmth and gentle irony, Schwartz has insightfully and delightfully focused on creating individuals who surprise themselves when they win minor victories over everyday problems by tapping unsuspected inner resources.

S.R.

Science Fiction

What if there were a nuclear holocaust? What if we discovered life on another planet? What if we were able to recover DNA from an insect encased in amber and re-create dinosaurs? Science fiction books explore these and many other equally provocative topics. Science fiction is an imaginative literature, but it depicts plausible events, events that *might* happen. These events might not happen in our time or on our planet, but they are logical extrapolations from known facts. Science fiction writers take that which is known and imaginatively project themselves into the future to explore that which is unknown. Science fiction thus reflects the time period in which it is written more than does any other literature.

Science fiction is a recently developed genre. As Isaac Asimov, the late noted scientist and author, stated, "In fact, it is the only kind of literature that fits this age and no other, for there is no way in which it could exist until modern times." Though individual books by H. G. Wells, Jules Verne, and a few others could be classified as science fiction, the term *science fiction* was not coined until 1926, when a sufficiently large body of this type of writing had accumulated, warranting examination as a distinct genre.

Hugo Gernsback, often considered the father of science fiction, founded the pulp magazine *Amazing Stories* in 1926. He coined the term *science fiction* and kept his magazine going by reprinting stories by Wells and Verne in serial form. The Hugo Awards, given for science fiction writing, are named in his honor.

John Campbell Jr. founded the magazine known as *Astounding Science Fiction* in 1938. Campbell moved beyond reprints of Verne and Wells, demanding from his writers a level of sophistication in their work that went beyond what had been acceptable in earlier magazines. Early science fiction had focused predominantly on emerging technological developments and the wonders of science. Especially after the explosion of the atomic bomb in 1945, social science and the consideration of the moral dilemmas posed by science became a thematic mainstay. Campbell encouraged the writing of stories that explored the social impact of technology and the philosophy and value systems of society; he broadened science fiction to include social protest of politics, business, war, and religion. Campbell's writers influenced the course of the genre for the next fifty years. They included E. E. ("Doc") Smith, L. Sprague De Camp, Lester del Rey, Robert Heinlein, Theodore Sturgeon, and Isaac Asimov, among others. In the 1940s, many of these writers began to write for children as well as adults.

The emergence of science fiction for children or young adults can be traced to *The Angry Planet,* written by British writer John Keir Cross and published in 1946. The first American children's science fiction was *Rocket Ship Galileo,* written by Robert Heinlein and published in 1947. Heinlein followed this book with twelve junior novels, publishing one each year thereafter. They are some of his finest writing. Heinlein dominated the late 1940s, exemplifying the three major themes of the period: In *Rocket Ship Galileo,* good triumphs over evil, with evil represented by Nazi forces. The struggle between science and values is emphasized in *Beyond This Horizon* (1948). *Red Planet* (1949) extols the need for individualism.

The shift to social concerns continued in the 1950s. When the threat of Communism pervaded the American psyche, science fiction writers reflected society's concern, weaving the struggle between good and evil into their story lines, with evil now personified by Communists and the "good guys" by the Americans. Among the best of these books were Arthur C. Clarke's *Childhood's End* (1953) and Lester del Rey's *Step to the Stars* (1954) and *Mission to the Moon* (1956). Another major theme of the 1950s was the need for racial tolerance and commentary on racial intolerance. Though in earlier books this took the form of tolerance toward "aliens," it began to be more direct during this decade. Both Asimov in *Pebble in the Sky* (1950) and Heinlein in *The Last Planet* (1953) examined this theme. Heinlein also wrote a very moving and powerful plea for individualism and the need for racial tolerance in *Methuselah's Children* (1958), the story of a "family" of people who inherit longevity through genetic planning and of the envy that develops in the rest of society.

Upheaval was the byword of the 1960s. Society was in turmoil, and writers were trying to make sense of it all. Many authors wrote of the need for individualism in a society that inhibits it. In *Orphans of the Sky* (1964) Heinlein's four main characters try to raise themselves above the primitive level of the culture existing in the remnants of a starship. When their efforts are thwarted and their lives threatened, they leave the ship in search of a new planet on which to begin again.

The book that gave science fiction respectability in the field of children's literature was MADELEINE L'ENGLE's *A Wrinkle in Time* (1962), which won the prestigious Newbery Medal. Although rejected by many publishers, when finally published it caught the imagination of readers and remains a great favorite today. The strong characterization and intriguing plot make compelling reading. Focusing on the need to respect individual differences, L'Engle placed her characters in a struggle to defeat a world where everything is controlled by a computer.

JOHN CHRISTOPHER, a British writer, wrote

movingly of an alien invasion of Earth in which the Tripods have taken over and implant a Cap on every human at age fourteen, rendering the wearer helpless and little more than a robot. In his trilogy, *The White Mountains* (1967), *The City of Gold and Lead* (1967), and *The Pool of Fire* (1968), Christopher detailed the struggles of a few to escape Capping and to defeat the alien society. In 1988, in response to many readers' demands, Christopher returned to his story of the Tripods and provided a prequel, *When the Tripods Came.*

Another influential author of science fiction is ANDRÉ NORTON, who began publishing her works for children in 1952. She adopted her androgynous pseudonym to circumvent the 1950s prejudice that women could not write solid science fiction. Her works often broke barriers to discussing issues such as racial tolerance and the antiwar movement. Norton's book *Postmarked the Stars* (1969) was one of the first works of science fiction to recognize ecological concerns.

The 1970s were replete with *ism*s, social unrest, and a concern for ecology. Alarmed at television's pernicious hold on families, science fiction writers began to emphasize the need for an active, thinking society. With so many areas for concern and contemplation and with the growing appreciation of science fiction for children, the number of books published as well as the number of authors who wrote successfully increased. An outstanding example of the period's thoughtful and thought-provoking offerings is ROBERT C. O'BRIEN's Newbery Medal–winning *Mrs. Frisby and the Rats of NIMH* (1971), a highly popular exploration into the responsibilities attendant on intelligence and civilization.

The 1970s also saw the beginning of a continuing trend in which women writers began to be the most prolific and eminent in creating science fiction for youth. Among them were Kate Wilhelm, Vonda McIntyre, H. M. Hoover, Louise Lawrence, Pamela Sargent, Pamela Service, Wilanne Belden, and ANNE MCCAFFREY.

Anne McCaffrey's books about the inhabitants of the planet Pern were wildly successful with adults. Persuaded by editor Jean Karl, a successful writer of science fiction herself, to write stories about Pern for younger readers, McCaffrey produced *Dragonsong* (1976) and *Dragonsinger* (1977), beautifully written character studies of a young woman finding her place in an unaccepting society. There is adventure aplenty, but the focus is on the universal coming-of-age theme.

H. M. Hoover has written poignantly of the need for social harmony, acceptance of cultural differences, and concern about ecological matters. Her characters are strong. *The Delikon* (1977) has a unique beginning: "In the palace gardens were reflecting pools and an enclosure for tigers. Three children played in the garden; Alta was ten, Jason was twelve, and Varina was three hundred and seven." Varina is a Delikon, a member of an alien race that has conquered Earth, who has been transformed into human shape to serve as a teacher to humans. The book offers a fast-paced science fiction plot: alien beings, spaceships and aircars, war, and a race against time all combine to keep the reader turning pages rapidly. But it also goes far beyond this to explore both love and the conflicts that arise from cultural clashes. *Only Child* (1992) continues these themes. A young boy who has known life only on a spaceship visits a colonized planet and discovers that its sentient inhabitants are being destroyed. Cody's fight to expose and end this evil is both daring and thought-provoking.

Cultural conflict continued as an important theme in the 1980s. Monica Hughes wrote two stimulating novels, *Devil on My Back* (1984) and *The Dream Catcher* (1987), that examine the inherent evil of a rigid class system and the power of a computer gone amok. In *Moon–Flash* (1984), Patricia McKillip told of two youths who leave their primitive culture of Riverworld on a quest and discover a world that travels the stars. *The Moon and the Face* (1985) brings the two full circle, as they discover that even with their new technological knowledge, their roots remain in Riverworld.

The 1980s saw the publication of a number of

somber books about nuclear holocaust and its frightening aftermath of genetic mutation, fight for survival, and nuclear winter, in the tradition of O'Brien's *Z for Zachariah* (1975). In Robert Swindell's *Brother in the Land* (1984), three children struggle to survive in the weeks following a nuclear holocaust. Louise Lawrence portrayed the fates of three generations of one family following a nuclear war in *Children of Dust* (1985), which compares the loves of those who survived in a bunker living a constricted life with those who remained outside and became mutated. The most intriguing novel of the period, Whitley Strieber's *Wolf of Shadows* (1985), is told from the viewpoint of a wolf that survives nuclear destruction and the ensuing nuclear winter.

From the 1990s two powerful books stand out as models for the future. In *Eva* (1988), written by PETER DICKINSON, the title character wakes up in a hospital and realizes immediately that something is very wrong; she can't move and there are no mirrors in which she can see herself. She gradually learns the appalling truth: following a terrible accident, her brain has been transplanted into a chimpanzee's body. Dickinson's provocative and well-written story explores the social questions of overpopulation, the destruction of animal species, and the moral limits of science.

The second major work is *The Giver* (1993), written by Lois Lowry, winner of the 1994 Newbery Medal. She presented a Utopia, free from pain and poverty, racism and riots. But at what price? Through meticulous plotting, the reader is led on an inexorable march from comfort to horror, from Utopia to dystopia, revealing the ramifications of this "ideal" world through the eyes of one boy. Readers will be forced to confront their beliefs, and the implications will long echo in their minds.

In its short, dramatic history, science fiction has stimulated and provoked, satisfied and prodded. Those who write science fiction are on the cutting edge of knowledge and seek to share their vision of where that knowledge might lead. Science fiction has an important place in a well-rounded reader's library. M.J.G.

Scieszka, Jon

American author, b. 1954. Jon Scieszka has enterd classic fairy tales, turned them upside down, and exited with a smirk. What remains is hilarious buffoonery within his energetic yet sophisticated parodies.

Born in Flint, Michigan, and raised in a large family, Scieszka was educated at Albion College and received a master's degree from the writing program at Columbia University. As an elementary school teacher, Scieszka found inspiration for his lessons by rewriting fairy tales; the lessons, in turn, led him to write successful stories offering fresh perspectives on dusty old tales. Although publishers once thought them too sophisticated for children, Scieszka's stories now arouse endless laughter from an enchanted young audience.

His first book, *The True Story of the Three Little Pigs* (1989), is a delicious retelling of the famous tale. Narrator Alexander T. Wolf desperately defends his bad rap by arguing that he was framed. With prim spectacles and a proper bow tie, A. Wolf pleads that he was innocently borrowing a cup of sugar to bake a cake for dear granny, when he was suddenly seized by a case of the sneezes that left him huffing and puffing. Is he innocent? Perhaps not, yet this comic perspective sheds new light on the Big Bad Wolf. Scieszka challenged the GRIMM brothers as the frog character in *The Frog Prince, Continued* (1991) dares to ask what comes after "happily ever after." Plagued by the nagging princess, the Frog Prince can't help but wonder if he was happier as his original frog self before the day of the fateful kiss. As the satire plays out, the Frog Prince confronts familiar witches from "Sleeping Beauty," "Snow White," and "Hansel and Gretel." The tale finishes with a twist, but once again the Frog Prince and the princess live "happily ever after."

Scieszka has provided really funny books for the often overlooked middle reader with his Time Warp Trio series: *Knights of the Kitchen Table* (1991), *The Not-So-Jolly Roger* (1991), *The Good, the Bad, and the Goofy* (1992), *Your Mother*

Was a Neanderthal (1993), *See You Later, Gladiator* (2000), and *Sam Samurai* (2001). These easy-to-read, zany adventures take the trio — Joe, Sam, and Fred — back in time to face foes such as evil knights and burly pirates. Witty dialogue enlivens these bizarre tales.

Scieszka also is a master of the PICTURE BOOK format. *The Stinky Cheese Man and Other Fairly Stupid Tales* (1992), a Caldecott Honor Book, encapsulates all of Scieszka's wild and whimsical techniques of parody. The narrator, Jack, states that these stories "are almost Fairy Tales. But not quite." Individual tales such as "The Princess and the Bowling Ball," "Little Red Running Shorts," and "Cinderumpelstiltskin" capture Scieszka's original playfulness. Who would ever imagine that the ugly duckling would grow up to be a really ugly duck? Though his books are ageless, the traditional picture book audience would have to be familiar with the classic tales to thoroughly enjoy Scieszka's parodies. In *Math Curse* (1995) Scieszka adroitly explored math from the viewpoint of a child who starts to see everything as a math calculation. In *Baloney (Henry P.)* (2001), he created a character who is late for school and tells his tall tale in a multitude of languages — Finnish, Swahili, Latvian, Esperanto, Dutch, and Welsh.

One cannot discuss Scieszka's writing without mentioning the illustrations of LANE SMITH, who has shared the author's quest for the truly absurd. The unbreakable connection between text and illustration makes these hilarious picture books a complete and unified package. Scieszka's seriously silly characters, coupled with his genuinely goofy stories, are perfect for any reader who just wants to have fun. C.M.H.

Selden, George

American author, 1929–1989. George Selden Thompson, one of the best contemporary authors of animal FANTASY, crafts breezy, entertaining tales of pure imagination in which his brilliantly conceived animal characters often provide shrewd and subtly satiric glimpses into human behavior.

Thompson, who wrote under the name Selden, was born in Hartford, Connecticut. He attended the Loomis School in Windsor and in 1951 received his B.A. from Yale, where he was a contributor to the literary magazine. Selden was working as a freelance writer when his first book, *The Dog That Could Swim Under Water* (1956), was published. The adventures of a dog named Flossy Thompson reveal Selden's facility with fantasy and wit and his knack for inventiveness, distinguishing traits in all of his later work.

Selden eventually wrote more than fifteen books, but *The Cricket in Times Square* (1960), one of those rare works both critically applauded by adults and beloved by children, secured him a place of acclaim among writers of animal fantasy. The book has earned frequent comparisons with E. B. WHITE's *Charlotte's Web* for animal characters who are brought vividly to life and for its parallel themes of loyal and enduring friendship. Selden, a New Yorker, said of the creation of his best-known book, "One night I was coming home on the subway, and I did hear a cricket chirp in the Times Square subway station. The story formed in my mind within minutes." A devotee of opera, Selden wove his own love of melody into the engaging, urbane story of Chester, a musical cricket from Connecticut, and his streetwise friends Harry Cat and Tucker Mouse. The unlikely trio share a home in the Times Square subway station, where a boy named Mario Bellini and his family barely eke out a living from a newsstand. After the compassionate Chester befriends Mario, his operatic talents earn the cricket celebrity and salvage the Bellinis' failing business; but Chester, longing for the country, gives up his fame and returns home. *The Cricket in Times Square* was named a Newbery Honor Book in 1961. Eventually, the Cricket series grew to seven titles, including *Tucker's Countryside* (1969), *Chester Cricket's New Home* (1983), and *Harry Kitten and Tucker Mouse* (1986). Warm-hearted, beguiling pen and ink drawings by the well-loved American illustrator GARTH WILLIAMS accompany all of the Cricket stories.

Two BIOGRAPHIES of famous archaeologists, *Heinrich Schliemann: Discoverer of Buried Treasure* (1964) and *Sir Arthur Evans: Discoverer of Knossos* (1964), mesh Selden's talents as a writer with his lifelong interest in archaeology. Selden's other imaginative works, such as *The Garden Under the Sea* (1957) and *The Genie of Sutton Place* (1973), never achieved the enormous popularity of *Cricket.* Almost thirty-five years after his debut, the wise, compassionate, and irresistibly charming Chester Cricket and his friends continue to pay tribute to friendship and entertain legions of readers. For that noteworthy achievement alone, Selden's work will endure as a touchstone in the field of children's books.

C.S.

Sendak, Maurice

Amerikan artist and writer, b. 1928. In the early 1960s, Brian O'Doherty, then the art critic for the *New York Times,* called Maurice Sendak "one of the most powerful men in the U.S." because of his ability to "give shape to the fantasies of millions of children — an awful responsibility." It is a challenge Sendak has continued to meet in a career that has spanned four decades and has led to Sendak's creation of the texts and illustrations for more than seventy books, which have sold tens of millions of copies in more than a dozen languages. But though Max in his wolf suit and the monsters he tames in Sendak's classic *Where the Wild Things Are* (1963) have taken a permanent place in American popular culture and the global mythology of childhood, Sendak has confessed to being baffled by the acclaim his books have won. "It's amazing I've had success," he reflected, "because my books are so idiosyncratic and personal and striving for inner things rather than for outer things."

The "inner" subject that Sendak has explored in many of his books — and what he calls his

"obsession" as a writer and artist — is the FANTASIES that children create "to combat an awful fact of childhood." In accepting the prestigious Caldecott Medal for *Where the Wild Things Are,* Sendak explained this fact: "From their earliest years, children live on familiar terms with disrupting emotions. . . . They continually cope with frustration as best they can. And it is through fantasy that children achieve catharsis. It is the best means they have for taming Wild Things."

Before *Where the Wild Things Are* was published, Sendak had illustrated nearly fifty books written by others, many of them remarkable in their own right, like ELSE HOLMELUND MINARIK's Little Bear books, a memorable series of EASY READERS. Sendak's first major group of pictures appeared in *A Hole Is to Dig* (1952), RUTH KRAUSS's path-breaking collection of "first definitions" that children themselves had invented to describe their world. Buttons, one definition explained, are "to keep people warm"; others reasoned that "steps are to sit on," and rugs, of course, "are so dogs have napkins." To capture these fresh perceptions, Sendak set them dancing with dozens of small pen and ink drawings of children.

But these were not what Sendak described as the "all-American, white-toothed" children that were so common in children's books at the time. Instead, Sendak depicted the "hurdy-gurdy, fantasy-plagued kids" he remembered from the Brooklyn neighborhoods of the 1930s in which he spent his childhood, the son of immigrant Jewish parents who had left little villages in Poland to come to America just before World War I. These "little greenhorns just off the boat" that Sendak drew for *A Hole Is to Dig* effectively began the revolution in children's literature that Michael di Capua, one of Sendak's editors, has stated "turned the entire tide of what is acceptable, of what is possible to put in a children's-book illustration." Or, he might well have added, in a children's book as a whole.

Through the 1950s Sendak went on, like his favorite composer, Mozart, to play variations on the one theme that, he believes, runs throughout his books: "how kids get through a day, how they survive tedium, boredom, how they cope with anger, frustration." It is a subject close to his own experience in which he struggled through what he has called a "miserable" childhood. As a young boy, he was frequently ill, often desperately so — with measles, pneumonia, scarlet fever — and stuck indoors for weeks on end. But the positive effect of this isolation was that he was forced to develop his own imaginative resources; while his older siblings, Natalie and Jack, were out playing with the other kids, he "stayed home and drew pictures."

In *The Sign on Rosie's Door* (1960), Sendak gave this theme another variation when he introduced, as the book's main character, an eight-year-old girl named Rosie. Sendak had watched and sketched the real-life Rosie from the window of his family's Brooklyn apartment building during the summer of 1948. Recently graduated from high school, he was unemployed and trapped at home, all the while wishing he could be living across the river in Manhattan. He identified with Rosie: "She had the same problem that I had as a child in that she was stuck on a street that was probably inappropriate for her, but she'd have to make do. So, in a sense, she became the prototypical child of all my books." In fact, this "Fellini of 18th Avenue" transformed her daily task of survival into an art form, and herself into a superstar by creating elaborate dramas and movie scripts that she "hoaxed" the neighborhood kids into acting out with her.

Sendak's fascination with this child impresario and genius of improvisational play led him, in 1974, to do an animated television special about her ("Really Rosie, Starring the Nutshell Kids"), with music by another kid from Brooklyn, Carole King. And in 1981, he gave Rosie her ultimate star vehicle in the off-Broadway musical *Really Rosie*, which drew its characters from those who made their first appearance in Sendak's perennially popular boxed set of four small books, *The Nutshell Library* (1962). Among them were Johnnie, a little boy obsessed with lurid stories he picks up about kidnappings (as it happens, one of Sendak's own childhood fears), and Pierre, "who only could say 'I don't care.'" Then, of course, there is Rosie herself, who, by this time in her twenty-one-year career, can quip about how "you have to make peace with your crummy past."

Where the Wild Things Are, though, would be Sendak's breakthrough book. It was the first full-color PICTURE BOOK for which he both wrote the text and drew the pictures, and it took up, uncompromisingly and forcefully, one of those "inner things" that have continued to preoccupy Sendak's creative life. In Max, the tantrum-tossing wolf-child, Sendak portrayed what he regards as an ordinary but also "a very crucial point in a child's life," a dark moment when only a leap of faith into fantasy can help him find release from his rage.

Today, we are used to having around various furry, befanged descendants of the Wild Things — gobbling cookies, teaching the alphabet, or advising children about how they can cope with the dark. But when Sendak's monsters first appeared, they were revolutionary, unexpected creatures who had sprung out of the unconscious of a child. Ordinary children were not supposed to behave that way, at least not in the public pages of a picture book. Yet Sendak asked the reader to accept Max's behavior as just that — ordinary — and in doing so Sendak reminded us that the world of children's fantasies is one of their best-kept secrets. DR. SEUSS's *Cat in the Hat* had warned children about upsetting their parents by telling them what really went on "inside" while the adults were out. But Sendak let the cat out of the bag.

Other books that followed *Wild Things* took Sendak farther into the territory that the psychologist James Hillman has referred to as "the dark side of the bambino." *In the Night Kitchen* (1970) spins the reader through the surreal fantasy of a child's dream, like Alice into Wonderland or Dorothy into Oz. Mickey, the hero of this voyage into the unconscious, is popped into an oven by three giant, Oliver-Hardy bakers before he can escape in an airplane, which he fashions from dough, and fly off to find the missing ingredient for morning cake.

While the book is, in part, Sendak's homage to New York City and the movies of the 1930s that had so affected him as a child (among them Disney's early Mickey Mouse cartoons, *King Kong,* and Busby Berkeley's musicals), it was also a celebration of the primal, sensory world of childhood and an affirmation of its imaginative potency. The jubilant point that Sendak has made about our naked human nature continues to transcend the controversy that may arise as a result of Sendak's having let Mickey fall out of his bed and out of his pajamas across the pages of his adventure.

About ten years later, *Outside over There* (1981), the third book in what Sendak considers is his trilogy of works that deal specifically with that "inner" theme, took up the fantasy of a little girl, Ida, who is stuck looking after her baby sister. For an instant, Ida ignores the infant and plays her wonderhorn instead. In that brief moment, the baby is stolen by goblins and Ida must imagine a way to recover the infant. Sendak chose the late eighteenth century as the setting for the book, the time of the brothers Grimm (whose tales Sendak has illustrated in his 1973 collection, *The Juniper Tree,* done with translator Lore Segal) and of Sendak's favorite artist, Mozart. But though he placed the book in the past, Sendak again dealt with the complex emotional life of children in the present, as they try to cope with the mysteries of feeling through their fantasies.

Sendak believes that "his most unusual gift is that [his] child self seems still to be alive and well" and that he can continue to remain closely in touch with this source of creative energy. But there are some risks, he has noted: "Reaching back to childhood is to put yourself in a state of vulnerability again because being a child was to be so. But then all of living is so — to be an artist is to be vulnerable."

Sendak has continued to take these creative chances himself, beginning a second career in the 1980s as a designer for ballet and opera, gathering rave reviews for this new work that now ranges from Mozart's *Magic Flute* and Tchaikovsky's *Nutcracker* to a double bill of two short fantasy operas based on *Where the Wild Things Are* and another Sendak book, *Higglety-Pigglety Pop!* (1967). There also have been other book projects, including his powerful paintings for a hitherto unpublished Grimm's tale, *Dear Mili* (1988), and his spirited, playful drawings (reminiscent of those that began his career) for the children's folklore collected by IONA and PETER OPIE in *I Saw Esau* (1992).

Sendak has continued to draw on the rich interpretative possibilities of folk rhymes in *We Are All in the Dumps with Jack and Guy* (1993). The text for this work comes from two obscure Mother Goose rhymes whose meaning had puzzled Sendak, he reported, since the 1960s when he first came across them while working on a possible collection of NURSERY RHYMES. He was finally able to make sense of these verses when he saw that they could be used to illustrate the problem of the homeless, impoverished, violent conditions in which so many children today are forced to live. In the book that has emerged from this fusion of the archaic with his impassioned, contemporary vision, Sendak found the happiest ending that he could for his abandoned kids: in a world that is indifferent — indeed, hostile — to their needs, they end up taking care of one another. In the process they claim for themselves a moving, transcendent power — one based on compassion and community.

The 1990s offered Sendak other new directions for his creative drives, taking him to Hollywood, and back to the dramatic stage, as the founding force, with ARTHUR YORINKS, of the Night Kitchen Theater. The innovative national touring company has begun to produce original dramatic works by, among others, Yorinks and Sendak.

Though Sendak does not have any actual children, he has remained extremely close to those creative offspring who have appeared in his books. Every year, Sendak has reported, dozens of schools and children's groups ask him for permission to stage their own versions of *Where the Wild Things Are,* often with a girl playing

Max, a gender-breaking change in his text that has delighted him. And every year, he has said, he can hardly hold back the tears when "parents who were little people when I wrote the book present their children to me. And here are these new human beings with their eyes beaming, and they are again in wolf suits." J.O.C.

Voices of the Creators

🌿 Maurice Sendak

I was the youngest of three children growing up in Brooklyn, and when I got a book from my sister, about the last thing I did was read it. A book, to me, was for sniffing, poking, chewing, licking. The first real book I ever had was MARK TWAIN's *Prince and the Pauper,* illustrated by ROBERT LAWSON, whose work I still admire. I treasure that book, although I don't know if I ever actually read it.

Children have a sensuous approach to books. I remember one letter I received from a little boy who loved *Where the Wild Things Are.* Actually, I think the letter was written by the boy's mother, and he sent me a picture he had drawn. So I wrote him back and sent him a picture. Eventually, I received another letter, this time from his mother: "Jimmy liked your post card so much he ate it." That letter confirmed everything I'd ever suspected.

I seem to have been blessed, or cursed, with a vivid memory of childhood. This is not supposed to happen. According to Freud, there's a valve that shuts off the horrors of childhood to make room for the horrors of adolescence. I must have a leaky valve, because I have these torrential memories. From a career standpoint, I guess that's been a good thing. Socially, it's been nothing short of disaster.

I profited as a child from the dynamics of my family. My brother was a writer, and I was allowed to illustrate his stories. With alarming regularity, our home would be invaded by these galumphing people called relatives. My brother would be called upon to read his latest opus, and I would hold up illustrations that I had done on shirt cardboard.

I remember one story called "They Were Inseparable." It was about a brother and sister who loved each other so much that they planned to get married. You see, Freud never came to Brooklyn. At any rate, I could understand my brother's feelings. Our sister was very beautiful, in a Dolores del Rio way. But he must have had a hint that this would never work, because his story ended with a terrible accident in which the brother was permanently damaged. I did very well at illustrating the blood and bandages, but not nearly so well at creating the kissing scenes.

I was a sickly child and spent a lot of time looking out the window. There was a little girl across the street named Rosie, and I must have forty sketchpads filled with Rosie pictures and Rosie stories. She was incredible. She had to fight the other kids on the block for attention, and she had to be inventive. I remember one time, when she came up with the explosive line: "Did you hear who died?" Rosie started telling the kids that she had heard a noise upstairs — a noise like someone falling, furniture breaking, and gasping, choking sounds. She went to investigate, and her grandmother was on the floor. Rosie had to give her the kiss of life — twice. Her grandmother managed to whisper "Addio Rosie" before dying. While Rosie was talking, her grandmother came up the street, carrying groceries from the market. The kids waited until she had gone into the house before turning to Rosie with the request: "Tell us how your grandma died again."

Rosie's stories became the basis of *Really Rosie,* an animated film. Then ARTHUR YORINKS and I formed The Night Kitchen, a children's theater company, and we cast *Really Rosie* for the stage. Then we planned to collaborate on a production of *Peter Pan.*

J. M. Barrie left the copyright of the play with a children's hospital in London, so I visited the hospital to ask for permission to produce the work. While I was there, I visited some of the children. You might be surprised to learn that most of the children who are terminally ill know that they are. I was asked to go see a little girl who's dying. She had heard I was in the hospital, and since her favorite book was *Where the Wild Things Are,* she had asked to see me.

I sat down by her bed and started drawing. Before long, she was sitting so close to me that her face was practically on my elbow. She was saying "Put the horns on; put the teeth in" and ordering me about. She was wonderful and funny, and I drew very slowly to give her as much pleasure as possible. But after a while I became aware of something. I saw a look on her mother's face. The girl was engrossed in the drawing, and the mother was watching her child with a look that said "How can she be so cheerful and lively when we all know . . ." It was a puzzled, confused, lonely look. Suddenly, without glancing up, the girl reached out until her hand touched her mother's. Without looking, she took her mother's hand and squeezed it. Children know everything.

My books are written for and dedicated to children like Rosie and this little girl. Children who are never satisfied with condescending material. Children who understand real emotion and real feeling. Children who are not afraid of knowing emotional truth. 🦜

Series Books

They have been decried by critics and most librarians, but series books have always found a ready audience among young readers. A children's book series can be defined as a succession of related stories that usually focus on a continuing lead character. Perhaps the books should be termed "formula series" to distinguish them from *literary* works that also follow a continuing character through several volumes. LAURA INGALLS WILDER's Little House series and BEVERLY CLEARY's Ramona books have three-dimensional characterizations, thought-provoking themes, and high-quality writing that sets them far above the series label. The literary series is guided by an artistic vision, while the formula series seems to be driven by commercial considerations. Quantity, rather than quality, is the key for most formula series. Characteriza-

tion and thematic concerns are usually sacrificed for formulaic, plot-driven adventures and surface insights.

At the turn of the century, Horatio Alger was the foremost practitioner of formula series. His "rags to riches" story lines feature plucky, industrious boys who rise from humble beginnings to great success. Among his many series are Boys' Home, Rise in Life, and the Alger Series for Boys.

Laura Lee Hope directed her efforts at a somewhat younger audience when she began her Bobbsey Twins series in 1904. These overly sweet stories concern the mild adventures of two sets of twins in the same family, older siblings Nan and Bert, and their preschool counterparts, Flossie and Freddie. Like Alger's dated series, the Bobbsey Twins books are seldom read by contemporary children.

The various series produced by the Stratemeyer Literary Syndicate are among the best known of the twentieth century. Edward Stratemeyer created and wrote the initial volumes of the Nancy Drew series, the Hardy Boys series, and the Tom Swift series before assigning the bulk of the workload to commissioned writers for whom he provided detailed plots. Nancy Drew (written by "Carolyn Keene") and the Hardy Boys (written by "Franklin W. Dixon") are junior sleuths, noted for their exciting adventures and crime-solving techniques. Tom Swift stories were written by "Victor Appleton" and concern a scientific genius who uses his inventions for fighting crime and pursuing adventure.

Traditionally, series books have been published in inexpensive editions, so it is not surprising that the most popular series of the late twentieth century have been published in paperback. In 1982 Francine Pascal began the Sweet Valley High series, which focuses on teenage romance in a small-town school. The Baby-Sitters Club series by ANN M. MARTIN concerns a group of girls who work as baby sitters. The books on various periods in the American Girls series, published in both hardcover and paperback, are written by different authors, such as

Connie Porter and Valerie Tripp. The books are part of a marketing empire that produces expensive, well-made dolls representing girls from different historical eras, including the Civil War and World War II.

A huge number of series books were published in the twentieth century. Many, such as the Rover Boys series, the Elsie Dinsmore series, the Trixie Belden books, and Enid Blyton's Famous Five adventures, have faded from popularity. Some, like Nancy Drew, remain successful for decades. With prose that ranges from competent to downright awful, very few series books can be considered great literature. But these light, escapist books are appealing to children who find comfort in reading story after story about their favorite, familiar characters. P.D.S.

Seuss, Dr.

American author and illustrator, 1904–1991. Writing under the pseudonym "Dr. Seuss," Theodor Seuss Geisel was a publishing phenomenon, an author of unique nonsense books for children who gained unprecedented acclaim outside the children's book field. Two of his PICTURE BOOKS, *The Butter Battle Book* (1984) and *Oh, the Places You'll Go* (1990), broke records for the number of weeks they appeared on the *New York Times* adult best-seller list. Since 1937, his books have sold more than two hundred million copies and have been translated into some twenty languages as well as Braille. Yet Geisel never compromised his own artistic impulses, creating original, iconoclastic books that were at one time considered "too different" to be marketable.

Geisel's versatile creativity earned him three Academy Awards, including one for the animated cartoon "Gerald McBoing-Boing," and two Peabody Awards for the television specials "How the Grinch Stole Christmas" and "Horton Hears a Who," adapted from his children's books. His recognition within the children's book field was marked by two Caldecott Honor Books *McElligot's Pool* (1947) and *Bartholomew*

and the Oobleck (1949); in 1980 he was awarded the prestigious Laura Ingalls Wilder Award from the American Library Association for the body of his work.

Geisel was born in Springfield, Massachusetts, where his father was curator of public parks, including a small zoo. He spent much of his happy childhood with his father, learning about animals and storing that knowledge for the fantastic creatures that would later populate his picture books. In 1925 Geisel graduated from Dartmouth College, where he was editor of the school humor magazine — the first outlet for his freewheeling, zany humor. Geisel then attended Oxford University, intending to earn a Ph.D. in English literature; he found his studies "astonishingly irrelevant," however, and returned home. He soon found success — but not fulfillment — as an advertising illustrator and as a cartoonist for national magazines such as *Vanity Fair, The Saturday Evening Post,* and *Judge.*

A couplet he made up to the relentless pulse of an ocean liner's engines — "And that is a story that no one can beat / when I say that I saw it on Mulberry Street" — developed into Geisel's first children's book. In the cumulative tall tale *And to Think That I Saw It on Mulberry Street* (1937) a little boy's imagination transforms an ordinary horse and wagon into an increasingly outrageous parade of rajahs, elephants, brass bands, and magicians. The innovative, aggressively rhythmic *Mulberry Street* — the first of forty-six children's books written by Dr. Seuss — was reputedly turned down by twenty-eight publishers before it was finally accepted.

Mulberry Street was followed in 1938 by *The Five Hundred Hats of Bartholomew Cubbins,* an original Seussian fairy tale in which a hapless boy's hats keep reproducing as he doffs them, desperate to obey the mandate "Hats off to the King!" The story's traditional fairy tale structure contains pointed digs at pompous adults and spoiled children as well as the first glimmerings of Geisel's joyous experimentation with the English language.

Another beloved Seuss character was introduced in *Horton Hatches the Egg* (1940), about an elephant who agrees to sit on a bird's egg while the flighty, irresponsible mother takes a long vacation. Horton's brave constancy is rewarded when a tiny winged elephant hatches from the egg; his refrain, "I meant what I said, and I said what I meant / An elephant's faithful, one hundred percent," has become a classic line in children's literature. The sequel, *Horton Hears a Who!* (1954), finds the kind elephant doggedly protecting a complete microscopic world that exists on a speck of dust. The moral, "A person's a person, no matter how small," reflects Geisel's great respect for the world's underdogs — including its children.

During World War II, Geisel worked as a political cartoonist and as a filmmaker for the army (two of his wartime documentaries, *Hitler Lives!* and *Design for Death*, won Academy Awards). His concern for social and political issues found continuing outlets in many of his children's books, which explore topics such as the commercialization of Christmas, in *How the Grinch Stole Christmas* (1957); totalitarianism, in *Yertle the Turtle* (1958); pollution, in the ecological allegory *The Lorax* (1971); discrimination, in *The Sneetches and Other Stories* (1961); and nuclear disarmament, in *The Butter Battle Book* (1984).

Many of his books are simply celebrations of invention. Books such as *There's a Wocket in My Pocket* (1974), *Oh, the Thinks You Can Think* (1975), and *Oh, Say Can You Say* (1979) sparkle with wordplay and tongue twisters. Geisel's imagination ran rampant in extravaganzas such as *If I Ran the Zoo* (1950) or *On Beyond Zebra* (1955) with their impossible, fantastic, funny creatures and wildly imaginative situations.

Perhaps Geisel's greatest contribution to children's literature, however, came with the publication of *The Cat in the Hat* and its companions. In a 1954 article in *Life* magazine, novelist John Hersey decried the dullness of the "pallid primers" used in schools to teach reading, complaining that they featured "abnormally courteous, unnaturally clean boys and girls" that bored real children and discouraged them from learning to read. Geisel responded with *The Cat in the Hat*

(1957), published simultaneously as a trade book and a textbook; in it, Geisel used just 223 words to tell a decidedly unpallid story about what happened one rainy day when a completely conscienceless, mischievous, mayhem-making cat came to play. The book's open acceptance of children's misbehavior (subversive for that time), its wildly imaginative pictures and situation, and its spontaneous humor combined to give children a compelling incentive to read. *The Cat in the Hat* became the first of the Beginner Books, a division of Random House of which Geisel was president; seventeen more limited-vocabulary books followed, including the immensely popular *Green Eggs and Ham* (1960), which contained just fifty words — and, as one critic noted, "unlimited exuberance."

Although he received some criticism for a repetitive sameness of rhyme and illustration style, Dr. Seuss has remained a favorite of children of all ages — so beloved, in fact, that his name is "synonymous with laughter," according to critics May Hill Arbuthnot and Zena Sutherland. He gave children stories of great originality accompanied by pictures "characterized by a strange, wild grace, with their great heights and depths" and bright, clear colors. He inspired generations of children to explore the infinite possibilities of language and of their own imaginations.

The late Bennett Cerf, the publisher of the Dr. Seuss books, once said: "I've published any number of great writers, from William Faulkner to John O'Hara, but there's only one genius on my authors' list. His name is Ted Geisel." M.V.P.

Voices of the Creators

🌿 Dr. Seuss: An Interview

How do you get your ideas for books? This is the most asked question of any successful author. Most authors will not disclose their source for fear that other less successful authors will chisel in on their territory. However, I am willing to take a chance. I get all my ideas in Switzerland near the

Forka Pass. There is a little town called Gletch, and two thousand feet up above Gletch there is a smaller hamlet called Uber Gletch. I go there on the fourth of August every summer to get my cuckoo clock repaired. While the cuckoo is in the hospital, I wander around and talk to the people in the streets. They are very strange people, and I get my ideas from them.

How do you handle the nonsense words in translation? The books have been translated into about fifteen foreign languages. I have no idea how they handled it in the Japanese. Oddly enough, the Germanic and Nordic languages are much more successful for translating the nonsense words than the Romance languages are. Why that is, I don't know. The Germans will take a name like *Bartholomew Cubbins* and turn it into *Bartel Lugepros,* which I think is a very beautiful approximation.

Do your characters live with you all the time? Well, I hope not . . . If I were invited to a dinner party with my characters, I wouldn't show up.

Was your first book, And to Think That I Saw It on Mulberry Street (1937), *rejected by many publishers before it was accepted?* Twenty-seven or twenty-nine, I forget which. The excuse I got for all those rejections was that there was nothing on the market quite like it, so they didn't know whether it would sell.

How much has your own early childhood influenced your work? Not to a very great extent. I think my aberrations started when I got out of early childhood. My father, however, in my early childhood, did, among other things, run a zoo, and I used to play with the baby lions and the antelope and a few other things of that sort. Generally speaking, I don't think my childhood influenced my work. I think I skipped my childhood.

Do your ideas for books spring forth from free drawing you might be doing? Mine always start as a doodle. I may doodle a couple of animals; if they bite each other, it's going to be a good book. If you doodle enough, the characters begin to take over themselves — after a year and a half or so.

Sometimes you have luck when you are doodling. I did one day when I was drawing some trees. Then I began drawing elephants. I had a window that was open, and the wind blew the elephant on top of a tree. I looked at it and said, "What do you suppose that elephant is doing there?" The answer was: "He is hatching an egg." Then all I had to do was write a book about it. I have left that window open ever since, but it's never happened again.

How do you shut out the reality of the world when you're creating your books? Do nuclear weapons, cancer, unemployment, and pollution affect you? They're all there, but I look at them through the wrong end of the telescope. I change them in that way. ✥

Excerpt from the *Horn Book Magazine,* Vol. 65., pp. 582–588. © 1989 Glen Edward Sadler.

Shannon, David

American illustrator and author, b. 1959. "I've always liked to draw pictures, but it wasn't until I had completed a number of children's books that I realized that storytelling is what really interested me from the start." David Shannon was interested in art at a young age, and his parents encouraged him with a steady supply of materials. He made pictures prompted by the stories he was reading; in eighth or ninth grade he drew illustrations for *The Hobbit,* J. R. R. Tolkien's classic tale. In high school he knew he wanted art as his career, but not fine art; as a student at the Art Center College of Design in Pasadena, he realized that he could make a living at illustration.

In 1983, with his B.F.A. in hand, he headed to New York City with his portfolio, showing it to newspapers and magazines. He became a regular contributor to the *New York Times* op-ed section, which led to illustration work for the *New York Times Book Review.* A children's book editor spotted his work there and offered him the manuscript for Julius Lester's *How Many Spots Does a Leopard Have?* (1992). More manuscripts quickly followed. Shannon illustrated two more books published that same year: *The Rough-Face Girl* (1992), written by Rafe Martin, and *Encounter* (1992), written by Jane Yolen.

Encouraged to write his own stories, Shannon took his favorite sport (baseball), applied his dark illustrative style, and created an ominous parable in *How George Radbourn Saved Baseball* (1994). He has credited the book as his bridge between editorial work and children's books; it also earned him a New York Times Best Illustrated Book award. His next creation was *The Amazing Christmas Extravaganza* (1995), in which he depicted an over-the-top competition of holiday light displays. Brilliant colors and meticulous details spotlight the outrageous spectacle.

Shannon used realistic, full-color drawings to illustrate *The Bunyans* (1996), written by AUDREY WOOD. He conjured up the giant family with exaggerated perspectives and outsized scenes showing the Bunyans carving out the geological wonders of North America. But the book with which Shannon really made his mark emerged from his own childhood: *No, David!* (1998), a wildly popular Caldecott Honor Book. Shannon's mother had saved pictures that he drew when he was five, including a stick-figure boy doing things he's not supposed to; the words *No, David* appeared on every page because they were the only words Shannon could write. A sequel, *David Goes to School*, was published in 1999. In *A Bad Case of Stripes* (1998), Shannon put his pet, Fergus, a white West Highland terrier, into the story and the paintings.

Most notable about Shannon's acrylic illustrations is his use of color as a stylistic device to convey mood and tone, emphasize character development, and enhance the plot. Even the color palettes of his covers provide clues to the story inside — visually narrated with his vibrant, imaginative pictures. J.C.

Sharmat, Marjorie Weinman

American author, b. 1928. Marjorie Weinman Sharmat's first PICTURE BOOK, *Rex,* the story of a little boy who runs away from home to live with an elderly neighborhood man and pretends to be his dog, launched her career as a children's author in 1967. Her dream of becoming a writer arose tangentially from a childhood desire to become a detective. The eight-year-old Marjorie and a friend decided to incorporate and publish their surreptitious gleanings in a newspaper aptly named *The Snooper's Gazette,* but a lack of subscribers brought the paper to an untimely end. Undaunted and determined to become a writer, she went on to hone her craft on poetry, diaries, and school newspapers. In high school she followed her parents' encouragement and sent stories to national magazines, never letting her optimism be deterred by rejection slips. Because "it was practical," she majored in merchandising when she attended Westbrook Junior College in Portland, Maine, her hometown. Nevertheless, writing remained her love. Her first published works were a four-word advertising slogan for the W. T. Grant Company, a short story for adults, and an article about Yale, which merited assignment to the Yale Memorabilia Collection.

From the publication of *Rex* until 1982, Sharmat concentrated on books for preschool to middle school children. Among these are her I Can Read series and Easy Reader series, the most popular being the Nate the Great detective series, which began in 1972. Nate the Great is a nine-year-old pancake-eating sleuth who dresses in a trench coat and a Sherlock Holmes deer-stalker. He confidently and methodically goes about solving neighborhood mysteries with his faithful dog, Sludge. Within the limited vocabulary of this format, Sharmat has created a classic of her own. The stories are clever and witty, written in traditional deadpan detective style. A film of *Nate Goes Undercover* (1974) won a Los Angeles International Children's Film Festival Award. Among her stories about friendship, such as *Sophie and Gussie* (1973), *I'm Not Oscar's Friend Anymore* (1975), *Uncle Boris and Maude* (1979), *Mooch the Messy Meets Prudence the Neat* (1979), Sharmat has shown that ingenuity can resolve real and imagined wrongs that arise between friends with opposing personalities.

Memorable in her stories for older readers are those about sixth-grader Maggie Marmelstein, which include *Getting Something on Maggie Marmelstein* (1971). As this self-assured, dynamic, opinionated child faces daily trials, she finds that even perceived enemies can be loyal friends and that winning the battle can result in losing the war; tact and saving face are as important as being right. The Olivia Sharp, Agent for Secrets series follows a wealthy eleven-year-old's adventures as she either secures or uncovers secrets for her clients, while the Kids on the Bus series involves mysteries and clever problem solving for children seven to nine years old. Of less literary merit, although enjoyable recreational reading, are Sharmat's entertaining situation comedy young adult stories, such as *I Saw Him First* (1983) and *How to Meet a Gorgeous Guy* (1983). Many of Sharmat's books have been Junior Literary Guild selections and others have been chosen as Books of the Year by the Library of Congress, while several have been made into films for television.

In all her work, Sharmat has examined the entire gamut of children's emotions and fears with humor and understanding. She has done this successfully in over seventy books ranging from picture books through YOUNG ADULT NOVELS. S.R.

Shepard, E. H.

British illustrator, 1879–1976. Although Ernest Howard Shepard is best known as the illustrator of works by A. A. MILNE, the 1931 edition of KENNETH GRAHAME's *The Wind in the Willows* also helped establish him as one of the foremost illustrators of humorous books for children.

Shepard's mother, the daughter of a well-known watercolor artist, encouraged his early efforts and pointed him toward a career as an artist. She died when he was only ten, but Shepard's architect father continued to foster his son's artistic talent. By the time he was fifteen, Shepard had definitely decided that he would become an artist and, at age eighteen, was admitted to the Royal Academy Schools, where he met his future wife, Florence Chaplin. The Shepards had two children, Graham and Mary, and Mary followed in her father's footsteps, becoming an artist known for her illustrations for the Mary Poppins books.

Quite early in his career, Shepard began drawing for the magazine *Punch*. His association with that magazine gave him experience in depicting comic themes. He was particularly adept at exposing the humor lying just beneath the surface of a situation and was able to capture the subtlest expression with an economy of line. Although Shepard made color plates somewhat late in his career, he is chiefly known for his pen and ink illustrations, which are rich in detail and alive with the personalities of his characters. His expert use of this medium allowed him to create memorable scenes that capture a sense of place as well as a sense of character. Shepard's success as an illustrator was also due to an intuitive feel for motion in a picture, along with the elements of surprise and the unusual in his portrayal of characters. These attributes contribute to his success in capturing perfectly the childlike quality of Christopher Robin and the naiveté of Pooh in *Winnie-the-Pooh* (1926) and creating an unforgettable portrait of the witty but naughty Toad in *The Wind in the Willows*.

Shepard began his illustrations for *The Wind in the Willows* with great enthusiasm, though he had previously considered it a book that ought not to be illustrated. He had several meetings with Grahame, who showed him the nearby river that had inspired him to describe the lives of Mole, Badger, Rat, and Toad. Guided by Grahame's request that he treat these characters kindly, Shepard spent an afternoon beside the river with his sketchbook, searching for Rat's boathouse and examining the holes that were home to some of the animals and the meadows where Mole retired for the winter. Though Grahame did not live to see the finished work, he did express approval of the drafts that Shepard was able to show him. Later in his life, Shepard also tried his hand at writing, producing two autobiographies, *Drawn from Memory* (1957) and *Drawn from Life* (1961). He also wrote and illustrated two children's books, *Ben and Brock* (1965) and *Betty and Joe* (1966).

In all his work, Shepard encouraged readers to appreciate the humor in the stories he illustrated. Near the end of a long and immensely productive artistic life, Shepard received the Order of the British Empire in 1972, an honor he richly deserved for his contribution to the world of art and, in particular, to children's book illustration. D.L.M.

Shulevitz, Uri

Polish-born American author and illustrator, b. 1935. After living through the 1939 Warsaw blitz, young Uri Shulevitz wandered with his family for eight years, eventually settling in Paris and finally Israel. He moved to New York City as an adult, attended the Brooklyn Museum Art School, and in 1963 created his first PICTURE BOOK, *The Moon in My Room* (1963). Since then he has illustrated numerous folktales and FANTASIES as picture books and CHAPTER BOOKS, taught at several art schools, and published an invaluable resource called *Writing with Pictures: How to Write and Illustrate Children's Books* (1985).

In this profusely illustrated book, Shulevitz covered the technical aspects of creating a picture book and expounded his philosophies of writing and drawing, giving clear, concise examples: When conceiving a story idea, he first "writes" the story with pictures. Shulevitz believes that technique must be an "organic extension of content," and artistic style must suit each story's content and feeling. Detailed pen and ink drawings or stridently bright colors are equally within his grasp, but most of his books are done in watercolors or pen and ink. Later Shulevitz develops a text that does not repeat the pictorial details but expands story elements that cannot be told visually, an approach that leads to a tight blending of text and art.

Rain Rain Rivers (1969) displays Shulevitz's view that picture books are "closer to theater and film, silent films in particular, than to other kinds of books." After showing a girl in her room, the "camera" takes the reader through the city and into the countryside, all the way to the ocean. The artist also used the size and shape of the pictures to enhance the cinematic movement from close-up to expansive horizon. Shulevitz's characters tend to have a firm, sculpted appearance, and architecture, frequently the eastern European cities of his youthful travels, is often a strong presence in his pictures. Yet he has also mastered evocative landscapes, as in *Dawn* (1974), in which a spare Oriental influence can be seen as the simple story unfolds. From a soft-edged oval of nighttime blue, successive images gain light and clarity, revealing a mountain lake with two figures who wake in darkness and experience the dawn's sudden yellow-green illumination of their surroundings. The oval pictures with their soft edges keep the mood quiet until the color breaks forth, flowing off the page in the loud visual climax.

Shulevitz has won awards for *Dawn* and other books, including the Caldecott Medal for *The Fool of the World and the Flying Ship* (1968), a Russian folktale retold by ARTHUR RANSOME. This is a "story book" — in Shulevitz's definition — a book in which the text can stand alone. In his illustrations, Shulevitz added humor, details of the Russian landscape and architecture, even the sensation of flying a ship through the air. In this book, too, is evident the strong composition Shulevitz has considered necessary for excellent illustration. One's eye is always drawn back to the main element of the picture after it has discovered the secondary elements. Because of Shulevitz's thoughtful approach to illustration, his pictures have integrity, depth, and beauty. His child readers, he has said, are never far from his thoughts: "I try to suggest and evoke rather than state rigidly, in order to encourage the child to participate actively, filling in with his own imagination. This approach is based on the belief that my audience is intelligent and active rather than passive." S.S.

Silverstein, Shel

American author, illustrator, poet, and songwriter, 1932–1999. Born and raised in Chicago, Shel Silverstein said that he "couldn't play ball, couldn't dance, and the girls didn't want me. So I started to draw and write." While serving with U.S. forces in Japan and Korea in the 1950s, Silverstein was a cartoonist for the *Pacific Stars and Stripes*. A cartoonist for *Playboy* magazine, a composer, and a lyricist — one of his most famous songs was the Johnny Cash hit "A Boy Named Sue" — Silverstein was best known for his humorous poetry, innovative drawings, and allegorical stories.

The Giving Tree (1964), Silverstein's most successful book, was initially rejected by his future editor, who believed that "it was a nice book, but it would never sell." Despite an initial lack of interest, the book eventually brought Silverstein national acclaim. "Once there was a tree . . . and she loved a little boy," begins the simple tale, illustrated in graceful cartoon style and touched with sadness. As a small child, the boy plays in the shade of the tree, loving her as a friend; as he grows older, he begins to want more from the tree than just her love. She gives him her apples, her branches, and her trunk. When he returns as an old man, she can give him only her stump upon which to rest — she has nothing left to give him, but she is happy. While some interpret this story as a parable about giving and taking, loving and being loved, others see it as a "dressed-up version of the 'happy slave' myth" and a tale of "man's selfish plundering of the environment." The danger does exist that young readers will identify with the greedy, exploitative boy/man rather than with the generous, devoted tree.

The Missing Piece (1976) and its sequel, *The Missing Piece Meets the Big O* (1981), two books that revolve around simply drawn geometric shapes, have been accepted as tales of adaptation, growth, and the quest for self-fulfillment. In the first book, "it," a pie-shaped circle, searches for its missing piece only to realize that the piece isn't needed; in the sequel, it is the missing piece that arrives at the realization that it, too, can survive by itself. With just a few lines and circles, Silverstein anthropomorphized his inanimate objects, giving them individual personalities and human traits and allowing them to discover the gift of independence.

Silverstein's POETRY collections, *Where the Sidewalk Ends: The Poems and Drawings of Shel Silverstein* (1974) and the William Allen White Award winner *A Light in the Attic* (1981), provide a showcase for over 250 poems, some of which have been adapted from Silverstein's earlier song lyrics, and almost as many black-and-white line drawings. The poems, ranging from serious to silly, from philosophical to ridiculous, allow the reader or listener — the rhyme and rhythm of these nonsensical poems make them perfect for reading aloud — to discover Silverstein's greatest gift: his ability to understand the fears and wishes and silliness of children. From the list of frightening "whatifs" that plague children at night ("Whatif my parents get divorced?" "Whatif nobody likes me?") to Mrs. McTwitter, the baby sitter who actually sits on the baby, the poems are eerily attuned to the natural joy and playfulness of childhood. Allusions to belching, nose-picking, and the disruption of parental authority can be found in the poems, as can statements of friendship and tolerance: "We're all worth the same / When we turn off the light" and "I will not play at tug o' war / I'd rather play at hug o' war."

Silverstein said that he didn't believe in happy endings or magical solutions in children's books. Nevertheless, with his hilarious poetry, expressively simple drawings, and provocative fables, he succeeded in creating some magic of his own.

M.I.A.

Simon, Seymour

American author, b. 1931. From paper airplanes to optical illusions, from outer space to the ocean floor, from anatomy to computers, there are few subjects that award-winning science writer Seymour Simon hasn't covered in his more than 150 INFORMATION BOOKS for children.

Born and raised in New York City, Simon was fascinated with finding out about the world from an early age. He attended the Bronx High School of Science, earned a B.S. from City College in New York, and began teaching science in New York City public schools in 1955 while taking graduate courses in subjects as varied as psychology, philosophy, literature, and history. Frustrated by the lack of good science books for children to use in the classroom, Simon began his writing career in 1968 with *Animals in Field and Laboratory: Projects in Animal Behavior,* which contains ideas for experiments to help readers learn more about aspects of animal behavior such as communication and migration. He continued to write and teach until 1979, when he turned his attention to writing for children full-time.

Simon has drawn on his teaching experience in writing; his more than twenty years in the classroom are reflected in his ability to know what will interest children and to understand how to present new information in a straightforward and fascinating way. His books do not merely answer questions; rather, they teach children how to think about a problem and encourage them to become involved in discovering answers on their own. Simon took this approach because, he has said, "Many of the books I write are guidebooks to unknown territories."

Simon has written a number of outstanding series, including the Discovering books, which introduce readers to common and popular animals such as frogs, goldfish, and puppies; the Einstein Anderson fiction series, which features a whiz-kid sleuth; the Let's Try It Out series, which teaches readers about physical properties such as hot and cold and about how the heart and senses function; and photo-essays about animals, earth science, and the solar system. The photo-essays are Simon's most successful books, as the consistently spectacular photographs, accessible text, and strong, clear design work together to present mind-stretching concepts in a lively and engaging format.

His gift for clarity and for making the complex fathomable is what raises his books above the ordinary, often uninviting science book. In *Oceans* (1990), for example, Simon told readers that the amount of water in all the oceans on Earth is 1.5 quintillion tons. To most readers, this figure is probably difficult to grasp, but Simon put it in perspective: "That's 100 billion gallons

for each person in the world." The information is immediately much more manageable and useful.

His series of photo-essays about the planets also presents the unimaginable in language we can easily understand. In *Mars* (1987) Simon compared the size of that planet to Earth, saying that if Earth were hollow, seven planets the size of Mars could fit inside. Or from *Our Solar System* (1992), a companion to the Planets series: "If the sun were hollow, it could hold 1.3 *million* Earths." His animal photo-essays, such as *Whales* (1989), a New York Times Best Illustrated Book, combine fascinating facts and lively photographs to make beautiful and factual volumes.

For his contribution to children's science literature, Simon was awarded the Eva L. Gordon Award from the American Nature Society, and over one third of his books have been named Outstanding Science Trade Books for Children by the National Science Teachers Association and the Children's Book Council. Although he is no longer teaching in a classroom, Simon feels that as long as he continues to write, he won't ever really stop being a teacher. His books capture children's imaginations and encourage them to use science as a way to wonder and learn about the world. K.F.

Simont, Marc

French-born American illustrator, b. 1915. The prolific creator of pictures for nearly one hundred children's books over a span of six decades, Simont was born in Paris, France, to parents from the Catalonian region of Spain. His childhood was spent in France, Spain, and the United States. While the repeated relocations were detrimental to his schoolwork, traveling served to sharpen the observational skills that became so important to him as an artist — Simont has often claimed that how his teachers looked fascinated him more than what they said. As a young boy, Simont taught himself to draw by studying *El Ginesello,* a Spanish PICTURE BOOK, and drawing remained his foremost interest during his school years. While Simont never finished high school, he studied art at the Académie Julien and the Académie Ranson in Paris, as well as at New York's National Academy of Design. Despite his formal training, he considered his father, Joseph, a longtime illustrator for *L'Illustration* magazine, his most influential art teacher.

Before creating pictures for children's books, Simont painted portraits, designed visual aids, and produced work for magazines and advertising firms. Since providing the art for a collection of Scandinavian fairy tales in 1939, his work has consisted mainly of illustrating children's stories. While he has both written and illustrated a number of stories, it is Simont's illustrations for stories by well-known children's book authors, such as Meindert DeJong, Margaret Wise Brown, Charlotte Zolotow, Jean Fritz, David McCord, and Marjorie Weinman Sharmat, that form the bedrock of his success. The charming, soft charcoal pictures for Ruth Krauss's *The Happy Day* (1949), which capture the coziness of animals denned for winter and their joyful awakening at the first scent of spring, earned Simont a Caldecott Honor in 1950. In 1957 he was again honored when Janice May Udry's paean to trees, *A Tree Is Nice* (1955), was awarded the Caldecott Medal. Color-saturated pages alternate with loose-lined black and white drawings; Simont's watercolors perfectly complement the poetic simplicity of the text, allowing the reader room to engage in his or her own imaginative embroiderings about trees. In 2002 Simont's *The Stray Dog* earned a Caldecott Honor.

Other notable titles include *The Thirteen Clocks* (1951), *The Wonderful O* (1957), and *Many Moons*, written by James Thurber. *Many Moons* (1943), originally illustrated by Louis Slobodkin, won a Caldecott Medal in 1944, but Simont's 1990 reinterpretation adds fresh life through dreamy, elegant watercolor renderings of Thurber's richly imagined story of a princess who must have the moon to recover from an illness due to a "surfeit of raspberry tarts." Simont's inspired and invitingly humorous art

provides a brilliant foil for the wit, wordplay, and nonsense of these three much-loved tales, now considered contemporary classics.

Two books written by Karla Kuskin, *The Philharmonic Gets Dressed* (1982) and *The Dallas Titans Get Ready for Bed* (1986), also underscore Simont's strengths as an illustrator. The former is an antic, inside look at 105 members of the Philharmonic Orchestra as they bathe, dress, and prepare for an evening's performance; the latter is a hilarious locker-room peek at what goes on after a football team wins a big game. In both, Simont deftly rendered a large cast of characters of varied ages, genders, colors, and physiques with distinct personalities. Simple, almost cartoonlike drawings belie in style their richness of content as they convey humor, movement, and convincing emotion.

Whether painting scenes limpid with delicate watercolors and resonant with childlike sensibility or using sure brush strokes to capture characters brimming with life and humor, Simont has a remarkable ability to connect emotionally with the child reader. His visual interpretations of stories have ensured him a place as a much-loved illustrator in the world of children's books. C.S.

Singer, Isaac Bashevis

Polish-born American Yiddish author, 1904–1991. Isaac Bashevis Singer was awarded the Nobel Prize for Literature in 1978 for his stories drawn from Jewish life and traditions in the ghettos of eastern Europe prior to World War II. Most of these stories were written in Yiddish, the language of a vanished culture in which rabbis, thieves, merchants, and chedar boys existed side by side with imps, goblins, angels, and saints. In his stories for children, Singer distilled this culture into a microcosm where the mystical and fantastic become commonplace and everyday life assumes cosmic dimension.

Singer was brought up in a Hasidic household. His father was a rabbi, his mother the daughter of a rabbi, and the often-heated family discussions centered around topics such as whether or not proof of God's existence could better be found in the supernatural shrieking of dead geese or the stubborn pride of a Gentile washerwoman. The worldly and the other-worldly clashed continually in Singer's life, and he found the resolution to that conflict not in the religion of his father but in his own writing.

The stories in two of his best-known books for children illustrate the blending of the real and the imaginary that Singer made so resonant. Singer's first book for children, *Zlateh the Goat and Other Stories* (1966), a Newbery Honor Book illustrated by MAURICE SENDAK, is filled with tales of fools, magicians, witches, and saints. Yet the title story is an intensely realistic account of the love a young boy feels for his goat. Singer's National Book Award–winning *A Day of Pleasure: Stories of a Boy Growing Up in Warsaw* (1969) is a collection of autobiographical stories of a childhood saturated with wildly improbable events and characters in which the mysteries of the universe could be unlocked at any moment and heaven hung down very low.

Many critics of Singer's work are uneasy with the mix of "the mythic and the colloquial" in his work; others laud the way he "captured the poetic power of folktales" with "a quality of timelessness in the wisdom imparted and a feeling for the essence of human nature." Singer himself felt the importance of his work lay in its ability to entertain, to "intrigue the reader, uplift his spirit, give him the joy and escape that true art always grants." S.G.K.

Sis, Peter

C zechoslovakian-born American illustrator and author, b. 1949. Peter Sis came to the United States in 1982, and that act both changed his life and informs his work. He was born in Czechoslovakia and grew up in Prague in the 1950s and 1960s during the height of Soviet rule and has remembered the world outside his family's home as bleak and oppressive: "It's amazing, though, even within that very undesirable

world, we had time to play our games and have fun and everything as children do. So now, in retrospect, I think I had a wonderful childhood, mostly thanks to my parents." Sis's parents actively encouraged his artistic growth, actually giving the budding artist assignments with deadlines, creating an atmosphere of creative discipline that Sis has credited as one of the most powerful influences on his professional career. Once in formal art school, however, Sis found the lack of freedom of expression difficult: "It was very hard because there was really no space for fantasy or individuality." Despite this obstacle, Sis credited this academic experience with exposing him to the great European art traditions, traces of which can be seen in his pointillist, somewhat formal style.

Sis received his master's degree from the Academy of Applied Arts in Prague in 1974 and attended the Royal College of Art in London. When he arrived in the United States in 1982, he had found success in Europe as an artist and filmmaker and came to Los Angeles to do a film connected with the 1984 Olympics that were to be held there. When the Soviet-bloc countries withdrew from the games as the result of a political imbroglio, Sis remained behind. The isolation, loneliness, confusion, joy, and newfound freedom of the immigrant experience show up in his work again and again.

Sis was launched in his American career with the help of MAURICE SENDAK and began by illustrating works written by others, gaining praise for his ability to capture the story's mood and the writer's intent. His illustrations of SID FLEISCHMAN's work in particular garnered much critical attention, in books such as *The Whipping Boy* (1986), the Newbery Medal winner, and *The Scarebird* (1988). The first book that he both wrote and illustrated is *Rainbow Rhino* (1987), the story of a rhinoceros who lives on a vast plain ringed by mountains. The rhino climbs the mountains with three bird friends, leaving them behind one by one in a series of lovely new environments and collecting them all again when he heads home. The image of an isolated figure on a vast, empty expanse that is repeated throughout *Rainbow Rhino* has become a trademark of Sis's work.

In *Follow the Dream: The Story of Christopher Columbus* (1991), the tiny, determined figure of Columbus is repeatedly shown as dwarfed by the limitless sky, the trackless ocean, or a detailed map of the known world. Another theme that has intrigued Sis, the tension between confinement and freedom, is central to *An Ocean World* (1992), the poignant story of a baby whale who grows too large for the aquarium that holds her and is released to the ocean. Sis's 1992 book, *Komodo,* which won a Society of Illustrators Gold Medal, once again centers on a small figure in a large world. A young boy travels by boat with his family to see a Komodo dragon. The boy escapes the crush of tourists to explore on his own and is the only one to come face to face with the beast.

Sis's concept books, *Waving: A Counting Book* (1988), *Going Up! A Color Counting Book* (1989), and *Beach Ball* (1990), feature a solitary little girl amidst busy, detailed two-page spreads filled with visual puns and puzzles, another Sis hallmark.

The next ten years established Sis as one of the most important and creative illustrators of his era. His jackets graced J. R. R. TOLKIEN's *The Hobbit* (2001) and William Nicholson's *The Wing Singer* (2000) and *Slaves of Mastery* (2001). In the highly original *Tibet: Through the Red Box* (1998), he created compelling images for pages of his father's diary. In *Starry Messenger* (1997) he made the life story of Galileo attractive to adults and children alike. In one of his most childlike books, *Madelinka* (2000), he used a young girl's daily rounds of a city block to show the kinds of people and situations she encountered on a daily basis. During this time, Sis won a multitude of awards, including two Caldecott Honor awards for *Starry Messenger* and *Tibet.*

In his work for children, Sis has sought to foster the personal courage and creative freedom that have shaped his own life. "I think children should have choices, and I would like to participate in their growth," he has said. "It's sort of a civic responsibility, but it's also a romantic thing. I would like to re-create something from childhood — create something wonderful, some sort of magic." S.G.K.

Sleator, William

American author, b. 1945. William Sleator is acclaimed for his YOUNG ADULT NOVELS that explore scientific theories such as black holes, cloning, and time travel in an accessible manner.

Sleator was born in Maryland but grew up in University City, Missouri. Sleator's father was a college professor and his mother a physician. The author's volume of autobiographical stories, *Oddballs* (1993), presents an entertaining picture of life in an unconventional family, where the children are encouraged to pursue a variety of interests. Sleator's interests included playing the piano, composing music, and writing stories of the supernatural. He attended Harvard, planning to major in music, but graduated with a degree in English. He then spent time in London, studying musical composition and working as an accompanist with the Royal Ballet School. He continued to work with the Boston Ballet Company as a rehearsal pianist for much of his writing career.

Sleator's first book was *The Angry Moon* (1970), a retelling of a Tlingit Indian legend. This PICTURE BOOK received praise for the high quality of Sleator's writing and for BLAIR LENT's outstanding illustrations and was named a Caldecott Honor Book. The following year Sleator published his first young adult book. A gothic novel about an English schoolboy living in a haunted cottage, *Blackbriar* (1972) is based on the author's experiences in a similar English cottage. Sleator's gift for provoking shivers and maintaining suspense is evident in this first novel; subsequent novels have been even stronger due to tighter plotting and faster pacing. An early SCIENCE FICTION novel, *House of Stairs* (1974), is among Sleator's best. It is the story of five orphaned teenagers unknowingly participating in a psychological experiment. They live in a world without walls, ceilings, or floors. Their environment contains only endless stairways and a machine that dispenses food. Suspenseful and thought-provoking, this fascinating novel explores issues of conditioning, behavior modification, and survival.

Although Sleator has written a handful of books for younger readers, he is best known for his young adult science fiction, in which everyday teenagers stumble into extraordinary adventures. Barney, in *Interstellar Pig* (1984), finds himself playing a board game with his new neighbors and slowly comes to realize that they are aliens and the game has intergalactic consequences. In *The Green Futures of Tycho* (1981), a boy travels back and forth in time, ultimately meeting his own future self.

Sleator is greatly skilled at incorporating current scientific theories into his fiction, resulting in stories such as *Singularity* (1985), in which two brothers discover a time warp, and *The Boy Who Reversed Himself* (1986), which concerns travel to other dimensions. He is also extremely successful at setting tone in his novels. Some are bone-chilling throughout; others have a tongue-in-cheek quality behind the suspense.

A consistent weakness in Sleator's writing, however, is characterization. His protagonists seem to fall into two groups: blandly likable or downright disagreeable. And almost always, his teenagers behave and speak like children much younger than their stated ages. Nevertheless, Sleator has continued to show growth as a writer, and his skillful translation of scientific theories into entertaining fiction has resulted in an important body of work. P.D.S.

Slobodkina, Esphyr

Russian-born American illustrator, b. 1908. Amusing children for more than fifty years, Esphyr Slobodkina's *Caps for Sale* (1940) has become one of the most popular children's PICTURE BOOKS ever published. As an author and innovative illustrator of other notable titles, this prominent and multitalented painter, textile designer, and sculptor first entered the field of children's book publishing in the late 1930s, a time known as the golden age of the American picture book. Along with leading artists Leonard Weisgard and Charles Shaw, Slobodkina helped bring modern art to children's book illustrations.

Slobodkina, born in Siberia to a family with considerable artistic ability, was a frail child often confined to bed for lengthy periods; there she entertained herself with materials on hand and learned to cut out paper dolls and doilies. Immigrating to New York in 1928, Slobodkina brought with her a thorough knowledge of Russian modern art. She continued her schooling as an abstract artist for several years, observing the Russian influence on the American avant-garde movement during the post-Depression 1930s.

Early in 1938 a friend suggested that Slobodkina prepare a portfolio for another friend of his, a famous writer and editor of children's books: MARGARET WISE BROWN. Slobodkina resorted to her childhood pastime of cut-paper dolls as she constructed nineteen paper-collage storyboards for her portfolio. This paper doll technique favorably impressed Brown, and soon after the artist and editor's meeting, their first collaboration, *The Little Fireman* (1938), was published. The paper-collage originals, in brilliant, bold, and arbitrary colors, shared qualities of absolute flatness and simplicity. Slobodkina firmly asserted that using scissors enforced a "simplicity of line which cannot be achieved by a pen." She crafted the firemen with no countenances so that all children could easily identify with the characters. Slobodkina was in the vanguard of the cutout-collage method of illustration in American picture books, with many currently prominent illustrators following her example.

Although she illustrated the sequels, *The Little Farmer* (1948) and *The Little Cowboy* (1948), in collaboration with Brown, Slobodkina alone retold and illustrated in 1940 what proved to be her greatest success: *Caps for Sale*. A troop of monkeys relieves a napping street peddler of his stock of caps. Unwittingly, the peddler retrieves his goods as the amusing, imitative monkeys respond to his tantrum. Her inspiration for these illustrations was the late-nineteenth-century naive painter Henri Rousseau; this influence accounts for a mustachioed face on the peddler and mischievous faces on the monkeys. First published in just three primary colors, *Caps for Sale* improved its looks with a second edition in 1947. Slobodkina's subsequent palette of ocher, red, and robin's-egg blue watercolors softens her cutout collage technique. The highly repetitive and comic text possesses interactive qualities that encourage participation from even the very youngest of audiences: children mimic the furious antics of the flummoxed peddler and delight in retorting with the monkeys' laughably annoying "Tsz, tsz, tsz." Still in print, and with eight foreign-language editions, *Caps for Sale* is an enduring picture book classic.

Slobodkina's career in writing and illustrating children's books has also endured, as she created more than twenty titles in the ensuing four decades. And with the 1993 reissues of earlier books such as *The Little Fireman* and *The Wonderful Feast,* many of Slobodkina's picture books continue to enjoy popular and critical acclaim.

S.L.S.

Small, David

American author and illustrator, b. 1945. David Small was born and raised in Detroit, Michigan. The urban environment "made art and music all the more sweet in my [David Small's] life, more urgent, and more of a necessity," he has said. His artistic talent was evident from an early age and was encouraged by his mother, who had David take lessons at the Detroit Institute of Arts. After receiving an M.F.A. from Yale University, Small taught drawing and printmaking at the college level for fourteen years. When he lost his job due to cutbacks, he began a full-time career as a children's book illustrator. His first book, *Eulalie and the Hopping Head* (1982; reissued in 2001), was soon followed by *Imogene's Antlers* (1985). In *Imogene's Antlers,*

the title character wakes up one morning to find that she has sprouted antlers. The understated humor is revealed visually in what has become Small's trademark style. His illustrations, done in watercolor and pen and ink, create humor and emotion. The use of delicate line and great detail on carefully composed pages creates evocative characterization in interesting settings.

Small's style is perhaps most apparent in the books on which he collaborated with his wife, SARAH STEWART, including *The Library* (1995), *The Journey* (2001), and *The Gardener* (1997). The character Elizabeth Brown's passion for reading and book collecting ultimately creates the town's collection in *The Library,* told in light verse with much visual humor. *The Journey* documents an Amish farm girl's first trip to the city, chronicled by her journal entries and visually through meticulous watercolors. In *The Gardener,* a Caldecott Honor Book, Small's illustrations are coupled with letters from a child sent to live with her taciturn uncle in the city, where she creates a garden. Line, muted color, and varied perspectives effectively convey the Depression-era setting and the emotional impact of the story.

Small won the Caldecott Medal for *So You Want to Be President?* (2000), written by Judith St. George, an unusual glimpse into the presidency in text and illustration. Small's use of line and wash achieved the wry look of political cartoon satire. Small's illustrations, reproduced in black and white, illustrate RUSSELL HOBAN's *The Mouse and His Child* (1967, 2001). This new edition of a modern classic successfully communicates the drama and emotion of a multilayered novel and demonstrates the artist's adaptability and range. M.B.S.

Smith, Lane

American illustrator and author, b. 1959. Lane Smith created a sensation in the PICTURE BOOK world in 1989 with his illustrations for JON SCIESZKA's *The True Story of the Three Little Pigs.* This zany story, told from the wolf's point of view, is perfectly complemented by oil paintings of the bespectacled Alexander T. Wolf and his exploits. Scieszka and Smith's second picture book collaboration, *The Stinky Cheese Man and Other Fairly Stupid Tales* (1992), was also inventive in format, design, text, and illustration. This 1993 Caldecott Honor Book contains ten fractured fairy tales that are interrupted by Jack the Narrator and the screeching of Little Red Hen. Smith's dark palette and use of collage highlight the surreal nature of tales such as "The Princess and the Bowling Bowl" and "Little Red Running Shorts" (whose wolf will look familiar). Teachers delight in using these books to teach about point of view, parody, and book design.

Smith's first book, *The Halloween ABC* (1987), was just a set of spooky pictures until Eve Merriam composed equally creepy poems to match the mood of the pictures. Smith, a graduate of the Art Center College of Design in Pasadena, has written as well as illustrated some books in addition to his magazine, newspaper, and album cover illustration work. *The Big Pets* (1991) is a FANTASY in which children frolic with their huge pets in a dreamlike night world, and in *Glasses: Who Needs 'Em?* (1991), a ghoulish optometrist convinces a boy that he needs glasses. Both books feature Smith's complex process of using oil paints and acrylic sprays with collage and his characteristically bizarre-looking animals and people with their rows of tiny teeth. In his hilarious *The Happy Hocky Family* (1993), however, Smith used childlike drawings on brown paper to parody, with a relentlessly upbeat family and short, choppy sentences, the "Dick and Jane" readers. For *Math Curse* (1995), Smith provided a visually inventive and stunning design for the story of a young girl's problems with math; and for *Baloney (Henry P.)* (2001), he used computer graphics to create the world of a space alien.

Smith's books are groundbreaking works that have received much recognition. They have been influential in expanding the readership of picture books to older children and adults. Many baby boomers are thrilled to have books to share with their children that they enjoy as much — if not more — than their children do. Smith's books have also encouraged experimentation with book design. From the endpapers to the copyright notice to the author information on the dust jackets, surprises abound. His many fans continue to anticipate with glee every new book he publishes. P.O.B.

Voices of the Creators

Lane Smith

I like Funny Children's Books. There are a lot of fine, important books that teach us morals and good manners. But me, I like Funny. *The Stinky Cheese Man, James and the Giant Peach, The Happy Hocky Family.* Funny. I liked funny when I was a kid, and I like it now.

If not for the comical surrealism of Dr. Seuss or the understated humor of Charles Schulz, I would not have become hooked on reading at such an early age. Today I'm a big fan of FLORENCE PARRY HEIDE, JAMES MARSHALL, REMY CHARLIP, ROALD DAHL, Peter Neumeyer, MAURICE SENDAK, PETRA MATHERS, J. Otto Seibold, Vladimir Radunsky . . . (the list goes on). These folks really seem to know kids and what they like to read, not what they think kids should read.

I like Dark. Occasionally adults ask me, "Why is your work so dark?" When I was a child, I liked dark things. I liked the night. I liked being indoors with my family and listening to the sound the wind made outside. I liked the scratching of the clawlike branches against the roof. I liked thunderstorms. I liked building tents and castles out of blankets and chairs, then crawling in under them. I liked telling ghost stories. I liked Halloween.

When I wrote *The Big Pets,* a surreal nighttime journey of a little girl and her giant cat, I was expanding on my own childhood fantasies of slipping out into the night for fantastic adventures while always knowing there was a secure home base to come back to. It was essential that the paintings be mysterious, moody, and dark.

For the fairy tale books I've illustrated with JON

SCIESZKA, the palette had to be one of rich oil colors, the palette of the original fairy tales. If I had gone too light and cartoony, I would have taken the satiric edge off Jon's sly text.

I like Collage. I am always trying to include Found Bits to break up my illustrations and add another element of texture. A lot of the letters I get from kids acknowledge the collage pieces. Perhaps they relate it to their own school arts-and-crafts assignments. One boy appreciated Cousin Stinky's clothes made from fragments of novelty-joke-catalogue pages. He said, "It was my favorite part of *The Happy Hocky Family*. Cousin Stinky was funny and so were his pants."

I like and don't like Computer-Generated illustration. Some computer-generated work is inventive and truly unique, such as the work of J. Otto Seibold. But some is not so successful. The common criticism is "it looks too computery." I agree. Computer work can look cold or worse still — slick. But a computer is a tool like any other. It is only as good as the person using it. I use the computer as a collage tool.

I first paint my textures the traditional way — usually in oils. I then scan them into the computer and take it from there. The beauty of certain computer programs is that everything is on separate layers, so you can actually see where you've been and delete previous layers that you're not so excited about.

A few years ago, my work was tentative. I'd go so far with an illustration and then I'd stop, afraid that I might overwork it. Today I do a lot more experimentation. If it doesn't work out, I back up and erase layers. The first book that I did on the computer was *The Very Persistent Gappers of Frip*, written by George Saunders. My main objective was to do something moody and atmospheric and still very "painterly." With Jon Scieszka's *Baloney (Henry P.)* I was trying to achieve a graphic, retro, 1960s style that might not look out of place on a NASA brochure during the space race. Pinocchio, the Boy, was my visual homage to Golden Books and UPA cartoons with bright colors and geometric shapes. All of these were aided in some part by the computer, and I feel they are all consistent with my "traditional" painted work.

I like Good Design. Design is a crucial aspect of any children's books and sadly one that is often overlooked or taken for granted. A lot of children's books suffer from "cookie cutter" design. Luckily, I have ace designer, Molly Leach, to work with. In *Glasses, Who Needs 'Em?* Molly quickly involved the reader by designing the opening lines in the form of an eye chart, with the words shrinking down from oversize type to the point size used throughout the rest of the book.

A crucial element of the humor in *The Stinky Cheese Man* comes directly from the design. At one point the title character's malodorous vapor drifts up from the illustration to the text, resulting in type that actually wilts on the page. In another story, Jack the Narrator's "repeating" story shrinks smaller and smaller until it runs off the bottom of the book.

In *The Happy Hocky Family,* Molly used type reminiscent of MUNRO LEAF's instructional primers (*Health Can Be Fun, Manners Can Be Fun,* etc.), with certain words written in uppercase for emphasis. If she had designed these last sentences, they might look like this:

> I like READING kids' books.
> I like WRITING kids' books.
> I like ILLUSTRATING kids' books. ▨

Snicket, Lemony

American author, b. 1970. As a child, Daniel Handler sometimes threw books across the room. He couldn't abide the typical children's-book scenario of a plucky hero or heroine triumphing over adversity because he realized that being plucky didn't necessarily mean one would triumph over anything. So as an adult writing under the name Lemony Snicket, he has created compellingly subversive stories for young people that embody this pragmatic — some would say dark — worldview.

In Snicket's multivolume, mock-gothic A Series of Unfortunate Events, the three Baudelaire orphans — fourteen-year-old inventor Violet, twelve-year-old bibliophile Klaus, and baby

Sunny, whose sharp teeth and talent for biting have helped the children escape from several jams — are described as "intelligent, . . . charming, and resourceful" and having "pleasant facial features," though their lives have been "rife with misfortune, misery, and despair" since the deaths of their parents. At the start of each volume, the brazenly intrusive authorial voice advises readers to bypass the Baudelaires' woeful saga and seek out more pleasant reading material. These warnings, as intended, have had the reverse effect. Since *The Bad Beginning* appeared in 1999, the series has regularly occupied slots on the *New York Times* Children's Best-Seller List and been translated for publication in countries around the world.

Biographical information on the elusive Mr. Snicket, always shown in silhouette or from behind in author photographs, suggests he is forever on the run from unnamed foes, forwarding his manuscripts from the dismal environs where he conducts his Baudelaire research. Daniel Handler's whereabouts are much easier to track. Raised in San Francisco, he moved to New York City for five years after graduating from Wesleyan College in Connecticut. He published a novel for adults, *The Basic Eight* (1999), which prompted editors to approach him about writing for children, a pursuit he stubbornly resisted until he discovered a way to transform an abandoned manuscript for adults into A Series of Unfortunate Events.

As evil, inheritance-stealing Count Olaf tracks the Baudelaires to exaggeratedly awful places such as *The Miserable Mill* (2000), *The Austere Academy* (2000), *The Vile Village* (2001), and *The Hostile Hospital* (2001), readers are teased with intriguing questions. Who is Beatrice, the mysterious "darling, dearest, dead" person to whom Snicket dedicates each volume? What do the initials V. F. D. mean? All pieces gradually come together. The books' tone, as much as their suspense, has won them many faithful fans. Reading them is like being privy to an elaborate in-joke. The author has peppered his texts with literary references and whimsical definitions, purporting to inform his audience

about life as it is, not as it should be. The series respects its readers enough to admit what it presumes they already know: bad things happen to the best of us, and there isn't always much we can do about it.   C.M.H.

Snyder, Zilpha Keatley

American author, b. 1927. Whether she is writing a FANTASY of MIDDLE-GRADE FICTION or a realistic YOUNG ADULT NOVEL, there is a sense of magic and wonder in most of Zilpha Keatley Snyder's books.

Born in Lemoore, California, the author grew up in Ventura County, where she played fantasy games and read constantly. At an early age she determined that she would someday become a writer but, upon graduating from Whittier College, opted to teach instead. Although Snyder soon married, had children, and moved around the country with her husband as he attended school and served in the military, she always continued her teaching career, whether in California, New York, Washington, or Alaska. Teaching gave Snyder an understanding and appreciation for children that naturally found its way into her writing.

Recalling a childhood dream, she wrote her first book, a fantasy about a girl who uses a magic amulet to conjure up a herd of ponies. Accepted by the first editor who saw it, *Season of Ponies* was published in 1964. Snyder then quit teaching to write full-time and the following year published *The Velvet Room,* a Depression-era story of a homeless family finding work on a California fruit farm. Robin, the young protagonist, makes new friends and gains access to a mysterious book-filled room on a nearby estate. *The Velvet Room* is representative of many Snyder novels in its sure sense of setting, intriguing plot, evocative writing, and well-defined cast of characters. There is also a sense of magic and mystery hovering around the edges of the realistic story.

Although Snyder has written several books that deal directly with the supernatural, even her realistic novels seem to contain an elusive hint of magic. *The Egypt Game* (1967) concerns a group of children who play a highly imaginative game in the yard behind a junk shop. At the time of its publication, this inventive novel was unusual for its multicultural group of playmates; even now the book is somewhat daring for its matter-of-fact handling of a stalking child killer. *The Egypt Game* was named a Newbery Honor Book, as was Snyder's excellent *The Headless Cupid* (1971), the first of four books about the "Stanley Family," five stepbrothers and stepsisters who become involved in humorous, occasionally dangerous situations. Snyder received a third Newbery Honor designation for *The Witches of Worm* (1972), a spooky story about a girl who believes her cat is possessed by a witch.

In *The Changeling* (1970), a girl makes up a story about a place called "The Land of the Green Sky." Several years later, Snyder wrote *Below the Root* (1975), the first in a fantasy trilogy about Green-sky. This series, which continued with *And All Between* (1976) and *Until the Celebration* (1977), is intriguing but may not appeal to fans of the author's more realistic novels. Snyder's work is popular, but it is unfortunate that her best-known and most honored books were published rather early in her career. As good as those titles are, later books such as *Libby on Wednesdays* (1990), *And Condors Danced* (1987), and the beautifully written young adult novel *A Fabulous Creature* (1981) show an artist at the peak of her powers.

Snyder has written in a variety of genres, including POETRY, PICTURE BOOKS, and an adult gothic novel. In addition to her typically solid plots, three-dimensional characterizations, and rare ability to evoke mood, Snyder has matured in her handling of language. She continues creating books that linger in the imagination.

P.D.S.

Sobol, Donald J.

American author, b. 1924. Leroy Brown's vast reading background and keen memory have earned him the nickname "Encyclope-

dia." This boy detective cracks criminal cases for his police-chief father and helps neighborhood kids solve mysteries in a series of books that are exceptionally popular with intermediate readers. The author, Donald J. Sobol, was born and raised in New York City. After serving with the Army Corps of Engineers in World War II, he attended Oberlin College in Ohio, where he became interested in writing. He worked as a reporter for the *New York Sun* and the *Long Island Daily Press* before becoming a full-time writer. His children's books include HISTORICAL NOVELS, such as *The Lost Dispatch* (1958), which concerns an incident from the Civil War; a fictionalized biography, *The Wright Brothers of Kitty Hawk* (1961); and INFORMATION BOOKS, including *The First Book of Stocks and Bonds* (1963), which he wrote with his wife, Rose.

Encyclopedia Brown, Boy Detective was published in 1963 and followed by more than a score of volumes, including *Encyclopedia Brown Finds the Clues* (1966) and *Encyclopedia Brown Saves the Day* (1970). Each book contains ten plot-driven stories that the reader is invited to solve by using observation, deduction, and logic; Encyclopedia Brown's solutions are found at the end of each volume. Lacking literary pretensions, the stories have minimal characterization but are fast-moving and humorous, making them especially appealing to reluctant readers. Although each book follows a similar formula, there is enough diversity in subject matter and in the method of solving the individual cases that readers eagerly return to the shelves for another volume in order to again match wits with Encyclopedia Brown. P.D.S.

Soentpiet, Chris

American illustrator, b. 1970. Chris Soentpiet (pronounced soon-peet) creates realistic, meticulously rendered, luminous watercolors; influenced by an apparently unsettled, international early life, he authentically depicts diverse people in distinctive places and periods. After the death of both parents, eight-year-old Soentpiet and a twelve-year-old sister left their native Korea to live in Hawaii. Neither his adoptive father, an English-speaking Indonesian, nor his Dutch-Irish adoptive mother spoke Korean; the children did not know English. The couple moved with their four children and the two Korean adoptees to Oregon, where they later divorced. A high school art teacher in Oregon recognized Soentpiet's talent and helped him obtain a scholarship to the Pratt Institute in Brooklyn, New York. There he received a B.F.A. after studying commercial art and art education. Soentpiet took some of his own watercolors to a guest lecture at Pratt, given by children's book illustrator and watercolorist TED LEWIN. This encounter, and Lewin's recognition of Soentpiet's talent, changed the course of Soentpiet's career. He decided to eschew more lucrative commercial art in favor of using his skill and enthusiasm as a painter to create children's books.

Soentpiet wrote and illustrated *Around Town* (1994), a mostly visual jaunt through New York City in which watercolors capture the delight of a summer day in the city. Soentpiet says that his "books reflect my interest in people, history, and . . . culture."

To ensure cultural and historical accuracy, Soentpiet carefully has researched each project and then used models to ensure realism and consistency. In *More Than Anything Else* (1995), written by Marie Bradby, the illustrator researched period clothing for this spare, fictionalized account of Booker T. Washington. Viewers respond to the dramatic watercolors that use light to focus the eye and intensify the perspective. The large format of *Molly Bannaky* (1999), written by Alice McGill, is a satisfying forum for Soentpiet's vivid illustrations of the powerful story of an indentured English servant. Refusing to accept the mores of her time, Molly stakes claim to property, marries a slave, and becomes the grandmother of Benjamin Banneker, the mathematician, astronomer, and planner of Washington, D.C. The richly detailed watercolor illustrations bring England and colonial America to life while enhancing and augmenting the drama of the narrative. A similar theme is examined in Yin's *Coolies* (2001). Soentpiet's painstakingly detailed illustrations lend a cinematic quality to a grandmother's story of brothers who emigrated from China to work on America's transcontinental railroad.

Soentpiet's illustrations are as effective and authentic in tone and mood when created for contemporary stories. The beauty a young African American child finds in her gritty urban neighborhood is detailed in the meticulous illustrations in *Something Beautiful* (1998), written by Sharon Dennis Wyeth. In *Jin Woo* (2001), written by EVE BUNTING, the emotions of a family awaiting the arrival of their newest member are captured by what has become Soentpiet's signature style of illustration. Realistic, evocative watercolors use light and changing perspective to capture changing emotions through well-composed, focused illustrations.   M.B.S.

Soto, Gary

American author, b. 1952. Born and raised in Fresno, California, Gary Soto is a prize-winning poet and essayist who teaches at the University of California, Berkeley. *Baseball in April and Other Stories* (1990), Soto's first juvenile work, was highly acclaimed. Drawing on his memories of growing up Mexican American, Soto brought veracity and authenticity to these short stories about children and teenagers living in California's Central Valley. The stories tell vividly of the yearnings, disappointments, and joys of childhood and adolescence. In "The No-Blues Guitar," Fausto, guilt-ridden over a lie that brings him money for the guitar he desires, drops the cash in the collection plate at church and is later rewarded when his mother gives him his grandfather's old bass *guitarron*. Soto used small but telling details to give life to his characters: Alfonso's attempts to straighten his teeth leave him with pink and wrinkly thumbs; and Veronica, searching so long for her beloved Barbie doll's missing head, loses concentration and has to remind herself what she is looking for. Winner of the 1990 Beatty Award, the collection was named an ALA Best Book for Young Adults.

Already known for his adult POETRY, Soto

proved with *A Fire in My Hands: A Book of Poems* (1990) that he is also a young people's poet. In the foreword, the writer explains how, as a college student, he decided to give up geography to study poetry. Anecdotes precede each poem, and a concluding section answers questions young readers may have about Soto the poet and about the writing of poetry in general.

Those moved by the brief glimpses of people in Soto's short stories and poems can fully acquaint themselves with one of his characters in the novel *Taking Sides* (1991) and its sequel, *Pacific Crossing* (1992). In the first book, Lincoln Mendoza deals with racism when he and his mother move from the barrio to the suburbs and he is the only Latino on the school's basketball team. In the sequel, fourteen-year-old Lincoln is chosen to be an exchange student in Japan because of his interest in a Japanese martial art. The story is moving and humorous, as Lincoln, responding to his host family's questions, tries for the first time to express what his identity as a Mexican American means to him. Soto explored the problems of other Mexican American young adults in *Buried Onions* (1997) and *Petty Crimes* (1998).

Soto is also a perceptive writer for younger children, as evidenced by the brief novel *The Skirt* (1992). While tracing fourth-grader Miata's attempts to retrieve the *folklorico* skirt she has left on the school bus, the story highlights a family's success in combining old and new traditions. In *Too Many Tamales* (1993), a PICTURE BOOK, Soto told about a young girl who fears she has lost her mother's diamond ring while kneading the cornmeal for their holiday tamales. The amusing story presents a loving look at one middle-class family's Christmas celebration.

Glossaries are provided in most of Soto's books to define the Spanish words and phrases that are smoothly and naturally interjected throughout his writing. Though his characters are Mexican American, and many are economically disadvantaged, Soto's stories contain universal experiences of childhood that will be recognized by readers of every background. J.M.B.

Voices of the Creators

Gary Soto

For me, streets have always mattered. When I'm ready to write, ready to sit down, usually at our kitchen table, I conjure up inside my head an image of our old street in south Fresno, one that was torn down in the name of Urban Renewal at the beginning of the 1960s. It was, as one might imagine, a blighted area: a junk yard to the left of our house. Coleman Pickle across the street, a broom factory with its nightly *whack-whack* of straw taking shape and warehouses humming with machinery down the alley, and the almighty Sun-Maid Raisin factory in the distance. These are pictures that I take into my work, both in POETRY and prose, pictures that stir the past, which I constantly haunt with an inventory list. They muster up a power inside me, a delicious feeling of memory, imagination, and the willingness to care for the smallest of objects — shards of glass, taps on my shoes, a chicken claw that I worked like a lever, a bicycle part, and an inner tube I rolled from one end of the yard to the other. In short, all the raw and discarded elements of the world.

When I work, I divide up this world, this street that I speak of. In my book *A Summer Life*, I was able to part the memories in such a way that I didn't yawn over these simple objects. One object was the ceramic Buddha we kept on a stand near the telephone, a gold-splotched Buddha with a large belly and laughter on his face. My uncle "El Shorty" had brought him home from the Korean War. Just as I'm ready to write, it's not unusual for me to close my eyes for a moment and remember the Buddha and other symbols of childhood. I see people and things in their place, from my father, dead now, and an uncle, also dead, to our dusty-white house, the bean plants, the almond tree where I hung, ridiculously, by an army belt, the fishless pond, my uncle back from Korea sleeping in the sun porch. Nothing much happened. No one pushed ahead; no one got rich and jingled coins in his or her pockets. We leaned our sadness on fences, sat in twos or threes on porches. We all faced the street, that river of black asphalt embedded with bottle caps, and followed with a curious gaze every car that passed.

I spent my first six years running like a chicken from one dirt yard to another, and I can't think of a more curious or unadorned childhood. I kept busy running around, a flag of shirttail waving in the wind of my own doing. I was hot for action. I stole butt-faced plums from our neighbor on Van Ness Avenue. This was my favorite fruit. But when fall arrived and the turn of earth tugged at reddish leaves, my loyalty changed in favor of pomegranates, which I cracked like skulls on the curb, a sticky juice dripping from my chin. I was greedy for this fruit, treasure that glowed in the faintest light. Recently a young reader asked, "How come you have so many fruits in your poems?" I wanted to provide a large, complex metaphorical answer that would deepen my work. But I smiled and answered, "I'm a pig for fruit. Toss me an orange!"

How much memory is enough? How much can a writer siphon from the gorged heart of experience and yet have the heart still pump? If one cares about the mystery of childhood, then it's amazingly deep and long. The subjects come back again and again, sometimes effortlessly and sometimes with the stubbornness of a toad that won't leap. In one recollection from *A Summer Life,* I wrote about a handbrake. If I can reduce the narrative to a simple sentence, it's about my five-year-old self who discovers a discarded bicycle handbrake while looking about in an alley for something to do on a summer day. Its use? I tied the cable around my waist and raced about, whistling the sounds of an on-coming train. When I wanted to stop, I pulled on the lever, which worked like a chicken claw. I came to a stop in clouds of dust, blinked, and continued on, "the cable jumping on my waist, the lever shining with sunlight and God's forgiving stare."

It's these images from our old street that I take to the page, whether the subject is that street or another street from a time when I was older. It's these first images — these first losses when our street was leveled to the height of yellow weeds — that perhaps made me a writer. We lose family, deep friends, our place in childhood, and finally ourselves in the haunted end, when we'll lay on a rack of blackness in our graves. In short, as with other writers, I wish to restore these losses, first with private, closed-eyed moments in which I see our lives as they were, simple and full, and later in the shape of poems and prose, which may or may not live on the page. It depends on the luck we draw when I open my eyes, blink, look around, and take up a pencil. ❦

Adapted from an article that appeared in *CMLEA,* Fall 1992 (Vol. 16, No. 1).

Speare, Elizabeth George

American author, 1908–1994. Many writers of HISTORICAL FICTION for children are adept at crafting fairly authentic historical settings for their novels, but what separated Elizabeth George Speare from the vast majority of these writers was her ability to create complex, full-blooded characters within the historical setting.

Born and raised in Melrose, Massachusetts, the author began writing as a child. After a year at Smith College, Speare attended Boston University, where she received bachelor's and master's degrees. She then embarked on a teaching career in Massachusetts high schools, leaving the profession in 1936 when she married and moved to Connecticut. When her two children were in junior high school, Speare began writing articles for magazines such as *Woman's Day* and *Better Homes and Gardens.* One article, in which Speare retold an incident from Connecticut's past, appeared in *American Heritage* magazine and was later adapted for television.

Her first novel also had its origins in New England history. Speare came across a diary published in 1807 by a woman named Susanna Johnson, who, with her family, was taken prisoner by Native Americans and forced to walk from New Hampshire to Montreal, Canada, where they were held for ransom. Among the captives was Johnson's teenage sister, Miriam, but the narrative included scant information about her. Speare was intrigued by this character and began to imagine what life had been like for

ILLUSTRATED AMERICAN CLASSICS

The Witch of Blackbird Pond

ELIZABETH GEORGE SPEARE

ILLUSTRATED BY BARRY MOSER

Jacket illustration by Barry Moser for *The Witch of Blackbird Pond* (1958), by Elizabeth George Speare.

her. The resulting novel, *Calico Captive,* was published to great acclaim in 1957.

The following year, Speare published *The Witch of Blackbird Pond,* the story of sixteen-year-old Kit Tyler, born and raised in Barbados, who arrives in Connecticut to live with relatives in 1687. The impulsive, independent heroine feels constrained by the Puritans' way of life, and her restlessness leads to an accusation of witchcraft against her when she befriends an outcast Quaker woman. With its strong story and vivid characters, this portrait of colonial America was awarded the Newbery Medal, reportedly winning by a rare unanimous vote.

Three years later, Speare won a second Newbery Medal, for *The Bronze Bow* (1961), a novel set in Palestine at the time of Jesus. The protagonist is Daniel bar Jamin, a bitter Jewish youth seeking vengeance against the Romans. The novel contains wonderfully real characters, strong action, intrigue, and a scene in which

Daniel meets Jesus. Unlike the popular *The Witch of Blackbird Pond,* which has achieved near-classic status, *The Bronze Bow* has never been a widely read book, probably because of its remote setting and its religious content. Yet it is precisely these factors that underscore the book's greatness. Neither time nor distance prevents the author from bringing historical Palestine breathtakingly alive for modern readers. The religious material is handled with great delicacy: the author's presentation of Jesus is particularly masterful. *The Bronze Bow* is equal to, perhaps better than, *The Witch of Blackbird Pond.*

A nonfiction children's book, *Life in Colonial America,* and a historical novel for adults followed, but it was over twenty years before Speare's next work of fiction for children appeared. *The Sign of the Beaver,* based on the true story of a boy who spent the summer alone in colonial Maine, is vivid historical fiction and a compelling survival story. Speare once again received Newbery recognition when it was named a Newbery Honor Book. In 1989, Elizabeth George Speare won the Laura Ingalls Wilder Award for her fine body of work. Filled with memorable, strongly individualized characters and authentic details of setting, speech, and manners, Speare's work represents historical fiction at its best. P.D.S.

Spier, Peter

Dutch-American author and illustrator, b. 1927. Peter Spier's more than fifty PICTURE BOOKS cover a range of subjects that reveal both his pride in America and his childhood in Holland, where his lifelong love of boats and water began. His style is recognized for its descriptive black line drawings with color wash. While Spier has exceled at casual humor, he has not shied away from the harsher realities of the stories he has illustrated. This combination of humor and integrity seems to account for his success with both child and adult audiences.

Born in Amsterdam in 1927, Spier spent his

childhood in Broek-in-Waterland, a small village where boats passed by outside his window. His father was a well-known journalistic artist, and Spier grew up surrounded by books and exposed to current events, theater, and concerts. While in school, he considered careers in architecture, publishing, the navy, and the law, but at eighteen he enrolled in the Royal Academy of Art in Amsterdam. After art school, he joined the navy, where, he has said, "I liked the service a lot and almost signed on for a couple of decades. The discipline, the ships, the water, the people — everything about it pleased me." A job in publishing soon sent him to the United States, where he began his career as a children's book illustrator in 1953. In 1958 he became a U.S. citizen and married, later settling on Long Island, where he and his wife raised their two children.

Spier's earliest books, produced with color separations, use traditional, bright colors in pleasingly vivid combinations. His later books employ a lighter touch to show atmospheric effects of night and day, stormy skies, and other uses of a more refined palette. In all, he has illustrated close to one hundred books, though not all of them are children's picture books. His other work includes nonfiction for children and adults for Golden Books, Time-Life, and *Reader's Digest*. While Spier began his career by illustrating books by others, by the mid-1960s he was almost exclusively illustrating either his own writings or preexisting song texts. Many of his books are wordless, but when he wrote, he kept his texts as simple as possible. He has said, "Writing and drawing are two of the same art forms. What you say in the text, you no longer need to say in the pictures and vice versa. The ideal picture book doesn't need any text. I realize that this doesn't apply to all picture books. Some stories need to be told in words as well as in pictures." Spier has won several awards for his wordless or nearly wordless picture books and for his illustrated folk songs, among them the Caldecott Medal and the Lewis Carroll Shelf Award for *Noah's Ark* (1977); a Caldecott Honor for *The Fox Went Out on a Chilly Night* (1961); and the Boston Globe–Horn Book Award for illustration for *London Bridge Is Falling Down* (1967).

Spier spends about six months on each picture book. After sending a dummy to his publisher, he embarks on extensive research that includes quickly rendered sketches from life. In planning *The Erie Canal* (1970), he drove the length of the canal twice, stopping to draw frequently. Although his books appear to include pen and ink, he actually draws his final art in pencil, which the printer overexposes to print black. After his line drawings are photographed, Spier colors them on a light blue print. He has said, "I am integrally involved in every phase of production. I do my own mechanicals, spec type, paste-up, work with the printer and handle foreign rights."

Noah's Ark displays Spier's qualities at their apex. In this mostly wordless book, his palette is full of warm browns and sky blues, and he paid acute attention to pleasing juxtapositions of cool and warm colors. As the book progresses, the interiors become grayer and browner as the ark becomes dirtier. Both humans and animals are drawn with love and empathy mixed with humor, while the well-paced visual impact seesaws between pages full of detail to spreads of calm atmospheric beauty. The most rewarding aspect of the book comes from examining the details in the busy scenes inside the ark. Hundreds of small dramas occur involving interactions of the animals, the never-ending job of the humans to feed and clean up after the animals, and the overcrowding that begins almost immediately as the animals reproduce. Finally, the later spreads show an increasingly dark, gray-brown, dilapidated interior, giving way to the final spread, which uses colors not seen since the beginning of the book: spring-green fields with orange wheat, blue mountains, and, of course, the rainbow. Spier's books have been published in twenty-four languages and include a variety of subjects. Each book demonstrates his sense of fun, a consistently sharp yet benevolent eye, a confident color sense, and a gift for knowing which details are indispensable.

L.R.

Spinelli, Jerry

American author, b. 1941. In his many successful books for middle readers and young adults, Jerry Spinelli has proved that he has accomplished what is perhaps the most important aspect of writing for children: he has stayed in touch with childhood. With this gift he has produced a series of provocative stories that remain true to the language, the joys and sorrows, and the often difficult situations of children and young adults.

Spinelli and his wife, Eileen, also a writer of children's books, have seven children. Their lives and the author's own memories serve as inspiration for his lively tales, which focus on universal and sensitive issues — sibling rivalry, maturity, love, friendship, death, prejudice — while maintaining a balance through humorous dialogue and often comic situations. Many adults have objected to Spinelli's use of language, which allows young adult protagonists to refer to drinking, flatulence, and sexual situations and to use profanity, in order to be crude and inappropriate. Others, including his growing audience, appreciate the honesty of these characters and recognize in them a mirror of reality. Spinelli's early book *Space Station Seventh Grade* (1982) is chiefly the story of the irrepressible Jason Herkimer, who with an assortment of equally hormonal friends grapples with the difficult transitional period of seventh grade. In chapters organized under one-word titles such as "Hair," "Punishment," "Mothers," and "Girls," Spinelli tracked the ups and downs of Jason's year with a galloping hilarity sprinkled with reflection, and no topic is off limits. A sequel, *Jason and Marceline* (1986), probes the subject of relationships through earthy locker-room dialogue and adolescent escapades while successfully tackling the issues of male dominance and respect for women.

The most successful of Spinelli's works for middle-grade readers is *Fourth Grade Rats* (1991), a brief, lighthearted tale of a boy's struggle to make the transition into the fourth grade and to master requisite courageous tasks such as defying his mother and giving up his favorite lunchbox.

Content aside, all of the author's books demonstrate a true genius with words. Using a spare, evocative prose resplendent with imagery and metaphor to create narrative that often borders on the poetic, Spinelli can bring the most remote setting or situation to life. Nowhere is this more evident than in *Stargirl* (2000), a novel that introduces an amazing female protagonist, and the half-realistic, half-mythical tale *Maniac Magee* (1990), for which Spinelli was awarded both the Newbery Medal and the Boston Globe–Horn Book Award. The story of a homeless boy with extraordinary talents who takes on the very real issues of racial tension, illiteracy, and family strife, this novel represents a new direction for Spinelli and became a testament to the substantial and multifaceted abilities of this gifted writer. C.C.B.

Sports Stories

Sports make up an integral part of teenage life. Even for nonathletes, sports seem to dominate a school's social life, to determine its pecking order, and to define the cliques. It is no surprise, then, that sports stories have always been an important genre in young adult literature. Most young adult literature deals with the basic problems of adolescent development, such as building character. Sports, because they are about winning and losing, are about character building and about values. The heart of sports fiction isn't even about playing or winning the game, but about the heroes that sports create and the values that sports instill.

Such a hero is Roy Tucker. Tucker is the creation of the 1940s author John Tunis. Tucker is introduced in *The Kid from Tompkinsville* (1940) and patrols center field in several other novels. Tunis's books were quite successful at their original publication and were repackaged in the late 1980s for a new audience, one that was probably eager to escape the idea of the athlete as a millionaire superstar and return to a simpler time when only the game mattered. The details of the game are the strength of Tunis's work. He is a novelist but has a sportswriter's gift for making every crack of the bat sound authentic and even beautiful. His attention to the details of the game and the character that it builds made Tunis the forefather of contemporary young adult sports fiction.

After Tunis, there were many years without significant sports fiction. The genre was loaded down with collections of stories for girls, for boys, and about every sport. Books like John Carson's *The Coach Nobody Liked* (1960), Joe Archibald's *Right Field Rookie* (1967), and Tex Maule's *The Receiver* (1968) tried to recapture the Tunis touch. Writing about baseball and other sports, these authors worked the same field but just weren't in Tunis's league in terms of quality. Books by these authors and others during this period were often bogged down by formula elements, usually finding the athlete overcoming the odds to win the "big game."

Matt Christopher and Alfred Slote also began writing sports books in the 1960s, but for the preteen audience. While faults can be found in both authors' books, Christopher and Slote realized that sports are supposed to be fun and brought some of that feeling to their works. Christopher, in particular, wrote books that were just enjoyable to read — such as *The Team That Couldn't Lose* (1967) — in which he mixed a couple of characters, lots of action, and a likable and unheroic hero.

The breakthrough modern sports novel was very different from those of either Tunis or Christopher. ROBERT LIPSYTE's *The Contender* (1967) introduced a new hard edge to sports fiction. Early sports fiction was concerned primarily with what happened on the field, but the heart of *The Contender* took the action off the field and out of the ring. The boxing scenes are realistic yet also poetic as Lipsyte demonstrated his sportswriting skills. But as the title says, the book isn't just about being a winner or champion; it is about the importance of being a contender. In and out of the ring, Lipsyte's Alfred Brooks shows young readers the true meaning of being a hero.

With *The Contender* the sports story was transformed into what Jack Forman called the "sports metaphor novel." Writing in the *Horn Book Magazine,* Forman explained that this new breed of novel has "no formula, no uplifting moral, no climactic heroics, just the turbulence of adolescent life." Forman also pointed out that the focus of these novels is no longer the sport itself, but rather the character who just happens to have an interest in sports.

Another example of this trend was Robin Brancato's *Winning* (1977). In this novel the protagonist's life is shattered by a sports injury. Gary Madden is a high school football player left a quadriplegic from an accident during a game. Like Alfred Brooks, Gary has the goal no longer just to win but to survive with dignity. *Winning* is one of the few sports novels to deal with the often tragic consequences of violent high school athletics.

The other big 1970s breakthrough novels were those of R. R. Knudson, concerning female athlete Suzanne Hagen. Knudson is the Tunis of girls' sports fiction. She gets the characters and the action right as superwoman athlete Zan Hagen competes in several different sports in books like *Zanbanger* (1977). These titles opened the way for more realistic women's sports books. ROSEMARY WELLS's *When No One Was Looking* (1980) and CYNTHIA VOIGT's *Tell Me If the Lovers Are Losers* (1982) use sports — tennis and volleyball, respectively — as backdrops for novels looking at character building through athletics. A more recent trend in books like JERRY SPINELLI's *There's a Girl in My Hammerlock* (1991) and Paul Baczewski's *Just for Kicks* (1990) finds female athletes competing in boys' sports. Both novels are comic, yet the seriousness of the issue is also explored.

The 1980s brought a renewed interest in sports fiction. Paperback publishers attempted to create popular sports series, such as Bantam's

Varsity Coach and Ballantine's trio *Blitz, Rookies,* and *Hoops,* but the books failed to catch on. These books ignored the fact that sport is more than just a game: as Tunis proved in his novels, it is also beauty.

The 1980s also produced several powerful first novels by male writers, who used sports as a backdrop for complicated coming-of-age stories. In just a few years accomplished works such as *Vision Quest* (1980), written by Terry Davis; *Football Dreams* (1980), written by David Guy; *A Passing Season* (1982), written by Richard Blessing; *The Throwing Season* (1980), written by Michael French; *Juggling* (1982), written by Robert Lehrman; *Running Loose* (1983), written by CHRIS CRUTCHER; and *The Moves Make the Man* (1984), written by BRUCE BROOKS were all published. Covering a variety of sports, all these novels present a new kind of sports protagonist who uses sports as a method to achieve self-realization and sort out competing values: the biggest challenges are off the field.

But what makes these novels so successful as sports fiction is that the authors, like Tunis, get the details right. Brooks has written about basketball with the same grace and style that Tunis brought to the national pastime. While the actual amount of football played in *Running Loose* is minimal, Crutcher's writing brings the reader onto the field to feel the hits and catch the passes. Of all these writers, Crutcher has continued to use sports as his primary subject. Three of his later books, *Stotan!* (1986), *Crazy Horse Electric Game* (1987), and *Athletic Shorts* (1991) were all cited as Best Books for Young Adults, and deservedly so. In particular, the story collection *Athletic Shorts* merges the beauty of sportswriting à la Tunis with the modern realistic novel in a powerful fashion. During the same time, WALTER DEAN MYERS produced hard-hitting basketball novels such as *Hoops* (1981) and its sequel, *The Outside Shot* (1984), featuring African American characters. The books of Myers, Brooks, and Crutcher also place sports in a large societal perspective, addressing issues such as racism and the exploitation of athletes in high school and college.

Sports fiction has grown continually from the simple days of dime novels to the beauty of John Tunis, from the simple joy of Matt Christopher to the power and the glory of Chris Crutcher. The genre has evolved, following closely the evolution of young adult literature. As long as young adults are interested in sports, the literature will reflect this passion. In today's sports fiction, there are still winners and losers and heroes, but the heroes aren't perfect. They are human beings just like their readers, who are grappling with the same challenges of maturing, sorting out their values, and becoming contenders. P.J.

Stanley, Diane

Amerian author and illustrator, b. 1943. Born in Abilene, Texas, Diane Stanley grew up in New York City among writers, artists, actors, and musicians — friends of her mother, writer Fay Stanley. Diane Stanley and her mother read books together and even created their own, with Diane drawing the pictures to accompany her mother's stories.

Diane Stanley's path to illustrating award-winning PICTURE BOOKS, however, was a circuitous one. She developed her talent for drawing while attending Trinity University in San Antonio, Texas, and after graduating in 1965 with a B.A. in history and political science, she did postgraduate work at the University of Texas and the Edinburgh College of Art in Scotland. She began her career as a medical illustrator, thinking that her detailed, realistic drawing style was well suited to that type of work. It was, but Stanley discovered she wasn't. She obtained a master's degree in medical and biological illustration from Johns Hopkins University in 1970 and worked for some years as a medical illustrator, but she felt the field didn't offer her the freedom of creativity she had known as a child.

It wasn't until she was visiting libraries with her own children that she became interested in picture books and saw an opportunity to express herself creatively. After taking a year to compile a portfolio, she illustrated her first book, *The Farmer in the Dell* (1977), under the name Diane Zuromskis. Finally, she had found her niche, and she began to concentrate on illustrating children's books, primarily in gouache, an opaque watercolor, and on working in publishing as a graphic designer and an art director. *The Conversation Club* (1983) was the first book she both wrote and illustrated.

The illustrations in her early works are characteristically detailed and finely rendered, but it was with the publication of *Peter the Great* in 1986 that Stanley was able to employ her talents to their best advantage. She embarked on a series of picture book BIOGRAPHIES that combine accurate, exquisitely detailed illustrations and thoroughly researched stories of some of history's great men and women. The blending of art and text is masterful, as the illustrations and the story enhance each other. In *Peter the Great,* Stanley presented a brave reformer and leader who brought czarist Russia into the modern world. Her illustrations allow readers to see for themselves the contrasts between the old, archaic Russian society and modern eighteenth-century Europe with rich details in costume, architecture, and interiors. Complex issues are simplified in the text, but Stanley still managed to convey volumes about the man of vision and his times. *Shaka, King of the Zulus* (1988), written with her husband, Peter Vennema, is about another great leader, but one who ruled with brutal force and fear instead of concern about social reforms. Vennema and Stanley presented a thoughtful, unflinching portrait of this nineteenth-century South African military genius. As in all her books, Stanley maintained a keen sense of the overall design: from the intricate borders and the costumes to the use of full-color spreads to convey a sense of the awesome beauty of the African countryside, all the elements work together to give the reader a feel for the culture and times in which this story takes place. Other titles in this exceptional series include *Good Queen Bess: The Story of Elizabeth I of England* (1990), *Charles Dickens: The Man Who Had Great Expectations* (1993), *The Bard of Avon: The Story of William Shakespeare* (1993), and *Cleopatra* (1994), all written with Peter Vennema; *The Last Princess: The Story of Princess Ka'ialani of Hawai'i* (1991), written by Fay Stanley; and *Joan of Arc* (1998) and *Peter the Great* (1999).

Stanley's lively texts and sumptuous illustrations invite the reader to share adventures and encourage further study of the past. K.F.

Steig, William

American author and illustrator, b. 1907. William Steig has been deservedly praised for both his writing and his illustrating, receiving the Caldecott Medal for *Sylvester and the Magic Pebble* (1969), a Caldecott Honor for *The Amazing Bone* (1976), and two Newbery Honors for *Abel's Island* (1976) and *Doctor De Soto* (1982).

Steig grew up in the Bronx, where his father was a house painter and his mother a seamstress. He started painting at an early age. Among his influences, Steig credits the GRIMMS' fairy tales, Charlie Chaplin's movies, the Katzenjammer Kids, the opera *Hansel and Gretel,* and *Pinocchio.* He has said, "If I'd had it my way, I'd have been a professional athlete, a sailor, a beachcomber, or some other form of hobo, a painter, a gardener, a novelist, a banjo-player, a traveler, anything but a rich man." During the Depression, when his father could not find work, it was up to young Steig to support his family, which he did quite successfully by selling cartoons to the *New Yorker* and other magazines. He has published several volumes of these drawings, which are often enigmatic, thought-provoking doodles. Steig attended City College in New York for two years, then spent four years at the National Academy of Design. In the 1940s he began carving in wood, and his sculptures are in several museum collections. He came to children's books late, when he was sixty, at the suggestion of ROBERT KRAUS, a *New Yorker* colleague, and found immediate success. Since then he has written and illustrated more than twenty books and provided illustrations for eight more. He married his fourth wife in 1969 and has three children.

Describing his creative process, Steig has said, "I usually start a picture book by selecting a main character — donkey, mouse, or perhaps human. Then I decide what his or her occupation is and take it from there. I make a very rough dummy and afterward try to get the spontaneous quality of the rough drawings. . . . I like drawing, but not illustrating, because basically I'm a doodler. My best work is spontaneous and unconscious, as someone once pointed out, calling me a 'sublime doodler' — the best compliment I ever had." Once an idea is accepted by his editor, Steig will work quickly, taking about a week to write the text and a month to illustrate.

Steig's illustrations are instantly recognizable, as he has used a consistent style involving a fairly thick, sketchy black line with watercolor added loosely, often including stripes, polka dots, and flowered patterns in his characters' clothing and in the backgrounds. His prose has a forthright style, and he has used precise, often surprising language, which some adults fear is too challenging but which children love. He is serious about his characters and their situations. This is real life, even if it involves a mouse dentist or a donkey with a magic pebble, and the humor comes from the believable situations and characteristics the reader recognizes from his or her own experiences. In even his most fantastical stories, the problems his characters face are universal and their solutions are never didactic. Steig has said, "I feel this way: I have a position — a point of view. But I don't have to think about it to express it. I can write about anything and my point of view will come out. So when I am at work my conscious intention is to tell a story to the reader. All this other stuff takes place automatically."

Steig's books provide serious situations factually illustrated with familiar settings and characters with intensely real emotions. His humor, alternately silly and poignant, and his integrity regarding his characters and his readers should ensure his popularity for many years. L.R.

Voices of the Creators

✤ *William Steig*

I grew up in the Bronx. Lamplighters lit the old gas lamps; people sat on the stoops; gypsies wandered through the streets. Among the things that affected me most profoundly as a child were certain works of art: GRIMMS' fairy tales, Charlie Chaplin movies, Humperdinck's opera *Hansel and Gretel,* the Katzenjammer Kids, and *Pinocchio.* I can still remember the turmoil of emotions, the excitement, the fears, the delights, and the wonder with which I followed Pinocchio's adventures.

I didn't spend many years in school. I graduated from high school when I was fifteen and spent two years in the City College of New York where my biggest interest was not learning but playing — water polo. Then I went to the National Academy of Design. There was a time that I wanted to go to sea, and I had the necessary papers. If I'd had it my way, I'd have been a professional athlete, a sailor, a beachcomber, or some other form of hobo. When I was an adolescent, Tahiti was a paradise. I made up my mind to settle there someday. I was going to be a seaman, like Melville, but the Great Depression put me to work.

My father didn't want us to become laborers because we'd be exploited by businessmen, and he didn't want us to become businessmen because then we'd exploit the laborers. Since he couldn't afford to send us to school to become professionals, the arts were the only thing that remained. Now we were always poor. My father made six dollars a week and supported a family on that. Many years later came the Depression, and my father couldn't find work — nor could my brothers. My father said, "It is up to you to do something." So I started peddling cartoons. I flew out of the nest, with my family on my back.

I would have liked to become a writer. Since I had to make a living, I turned to cartooning. Cartooning is a kind of writing. I worked for a magazine called *Life* and a magazine called *Judge.* I started selling my pieces in 1930. The *New Yorker* was founded in 1925, so I felt I had come five years late. I'm not the oldest contributor, but the lengthiest.

I got into children's book writing by accident. ROBERT KRAUS, who was a colleague at the *New Yorker,* started a company, Windmill, and asked me to write a children's book. I actually even liked creating the color separations — the old method — because you have to imagine how the stuff is going to look. If you keep the color very simple, the results are usually good.

I like working on the longer books better because the process is more like writing. *The Real Thief* is my favorite. I enjoyed writing *Dominic,* my first long book. I read my wife, Jeanne, a bit from the book every night, and she encouraged me to go on.

My books always evolve from a character. I decide who the chief character is, and once I have made him, say, a dentist, the story is on its way. I do as little drawing as possible in the beginning; I imagine the character. I draw when I create the dummy; then when I illustrate, I try to get the spontaneous quality of the drawing in the dummy.

My best drawing doesn't appear anywhere, although it does occasionally in books. My biggest pleasure is just drawing. Sometimes I'm referred to as a doodler. I was flattered by someone's comment that "Steig is a sublime doodler." With illustration you have to repeat the same characters again and again, make sure they don't change. My unconscious is more intelligent than my conscious. I often ask myself, "What would be an ideal life?" I think an ideal life would be just drawing.

The child is the hope of humanity. If they are going to change the world, they have to start off optimistically. I wouldn't consider writing a depressing book for children. 🎨

This article is based on an interview with William Steig conducted by Anita Silvey in September 1992.

Steptoe, John

American illustrator and author, 1950–1989. The publication of John Steptoe's first book, *Stevie* (1969), commanded notice by the children's book world, first, because its creator was only nineteen, and second, because it depicted a black city child's experiences in simple, bulky illustrations and black dialogue, both unprecedented at that time. The title received instant recognition as an ALA Notable Book and garnered the Gold Medal from the Society of Illustrators, the Lewis Carroll Shelf Award, and other honors. Clearly, Steptoe not only achieved his desire to provide a book that black children would relate to, but reached children of all races.

Growing up in the Bedford-Stuyvesant section of Brooklyn, Steptoe was out of step with peer activities because he preferred to stay home to paint and draw. At sixteen he attended New York's High School of Art and Design but quit three weeks before finishing his senior year. Before that abrupt departure, a program at the Vermont Academy for minority artists provided the opportunity for Steptoe to apply his creative talent; three years later his first book was published.

Following *Stevie* came two more PICTURE BOOKS expressing the experience of black inner-city children, *Uptown* (1970) and *Train Ride* (1971), which formed the trilogy that established Steptoe's career and reputation. The births of his son and daughter were the next influences on his work. In *My Special Best Words* (1974) and *Daddy Is a Monster . . . Sometimes* (1980) were voiced the strong relationship between father and child. The foreboding, compact illustrations in *Stevie* were replaced with prismatic paintings in airier hues.

Published at an early age, Steptoe also died at an early age — thirty-nine. During his twenty years in children's book publishing, he wrote and illustrated eleven books and illustrated six books written by other authors. In the last phase of his work, he experimented with his style, reaching for new dimensions. For *The Story of Jumping Mouse: A Native American Legend* (1984), he used black-and-white pencil drawings to convey both the sensitivity and strength of light and dark. In *Mufaro's Beautiful Daughters: An African Tale* (1987), he added vivid coloration to his skillful patterns of light and dark, creating beautiful landscapes and beautiful people. Both books earned him Caldecott Honors, and *Mufaro* won a Boston Globe–Horn Book Honor Award.

The range of Steptoe's work embodies the growth of an illustrator: from densely formed shapes to delicately lined faces, from condensed composition to delicate, free-flowing lines. Throughout his books, Steptoe left readers with a specific image, message, and sensitivity, and a universal theme of self-pride in cultural heritage speaks loudly. Steptoe's interest in ethnic folk stories in his last years reinforced his belief in self-discovery through cultural esteem. In his acceptance speech for the Coretta Scott King Award for *Mother Crocodile* (1982), which he illustrated, he stated: "I'm gratified sometimes by the positive social effect my work may have had. But an effect comes after the aesthetic statement." His work has poignantly achieved both.

§ J.C.

Stevenson, James

American author and illustrator, b. 1929. While spending half his time contributing cartoons and features to the *New Yorker*, the prolific James Stevenson has created as many as five children's books each year, most of which he has both written and illustrated himself. With a devoted following for each of his careers and a long list of highly acclaimed and widely read books to his credit, Stevenson ranks among today's top PICTURE BOOK producers in both popularity and excellence.

Born in New York City, Stevenson graduated from Yale University in 1951 and spent several years in the U.S. Marines, followed by two years as a reporter for *Life* magazine. He joined the *New Yorker*'s art department in 1955, creating cartoon ideas for other artists, until writing aspirations drove him to begin reporting in addition to his artistic duties. By the time his first children's book, *If I Owned a Candy Factory*, was

released in 1968, he had already published three novels and a book of his own cartoons.

Stevenson is best known for his highly appealing picture books, which combine fast-moving stories with gentle humor and a keen interpretation of childhood. His illustrations, usually rendered in a cartoonlike style and often making use of the traditional frame sequences and dialogue bubbles, frequently give the impression of being breezy and effortless; however, through his careful use of line, Stevenson has provided his characters with a remarkable depth of emotion. Aside from many individual books centering on child-related themes such as fear, boredom, family issues, and holidays, Stevenson has developed several long-running series of popular books featuring a wide assortment of winsome characters. The best known of these series, launched with *Could Be Worse!* (1977) and continuing with *What's Under My Bed?* (1983), *Worse Than Willy* (1984), and more than ten additional titles, focuses on the imaginative and hilarious Grandpa, whose stories of youthful escapades with his brother Wainwright make for breathtaking, laugh-aloud reading. Stevenson's witty drawings, including the famous mustache apparently affixed to Uncle Wainey since his birth, double the appeal created by the books' already enjoyable texts. Other favorite series characters include Emma, the benevolent little witch who, from her debut in *Emma* (1985), has proven that she can easily foil her two less kindly witch colleagues in their hilarious attempts to outwit her; and The Worst, the crusty star of *The Worst Person in the World* (1978) and *The Worst Person's Christmas* (1991), a miserable grouch who somehow cannot escape his yearning for human interaction.

In a departure from his traditional style, Stevenson has also created a set of critically acclaimed autobiographical picture books, each featuring an episode from his youth. In addition to their subject matter, the books, including *When I Was Nine* (1986), *Higher on the Door* (1987), *July* (1990), and *Don't You Know There's a War On?* (1992), are distinguished from Stevenson's other work by their artistic style. Unlike his traditional watercolor washes enclosed by black line, here the artist has used only watercolors, creating a soft, blurred visual effect designed to emulate the hazy recollection of past events. This style, which Stevenson has called minimalist art, is designed to encourage readers to supply their own images from memory or imagination. In addition to his own writings, Stevenson has also illustrated books by authors such as JACK PRELUTSKY, CHARLOTTE ZOLOTOW, and Carol Otis Hurst, and has received several important awards, including the 1987 Christopher Award.

Stevenson has become a favorite with children everywhere because he can make them laugh, but his true gift lies beyond the humor. Whether the subject is a rainy day, a nightmare, or the terrible realities of war, Stevenson imbues it with a powerful understanding of children, of what is important and meaningful to them, and of how to fill even the most difficult situation with warmth, comfort, and joy. C.C.B.

Stewart, Sarah

American author, b. 1939. Sarah Stewart's first children's book, *The Money Tree* (1991), illustrated by DAVID SMALL, casts a droll and disapproving eye on the seductive power of greed. Its heroine, the iconoclastic Miss McGillicuddy, ultimately prefers the company of a cozy fire to that of a fat portfolio. Stewart hit full stride as a storyteller just four years later with the publication of *The Library* (1995). Presented as a series of spunky couplets, the story highlights one Elizabeth Brown, a tireless reader who's happiest when her nose is buried in a book. "She didn't like to play with dolls, she didn't like to skate," writes Stewart. "She learned to read quite early, and at an incredible rate." The story, based on the life of the late Mary Elizabeth Brown, a librarian, firmly establishes one of the tenets of Stewart's fictional terrain: to live a meaningful life, it's imperative to listen carefully to one's own heart. That topic is one that Stewart herself is no stranger to.

Stewart was born in Corpus Christi, Texas; two years later, her family moved to Fort Worth. When she was seven or eight, she began keeping a diary; writing and reading provided the extremely shy girl with a respite from her often-troubled family. After graduating from high school, Stewart attended Radcliffe College, Austin College, and then the University of Texas, studying philosophy and Latin. Stewart worked as a Head Start teacher, an ombudsman, a speechwriter, and at a number of odd jobs. Although she had been writing prose and poems for virtually her entire life, Stewart struggled to discover her true vocation. Looking back at those years, she has said, "I don't like to talk about my early life or my young life that much, because it was full of difficulty and missteps and errant paths — and a lot of failure."

A turning point in Stewart's life came in 1972, when she met David Small, then an assistant professor of art at the State University of New York at Fredonia. Stewart immediately recognized in Small, now an author and illustrator of children's books, a kindred spirit. Her relationship with Small, whom she married in 1980, finally enabled Stewart to affirm her talent as a writer. The couple now lives in Michigan, in a nineteenth-century house that sits on ten acres, beside a bend in the St. Joseph River.

Set in the America of the Depression era, *The Gardener* (1995), a Caldecott Honor Book, tells the story of Lydia Grace Finch, a "small, but strong" country girl who is sent to the city to live with her sourpuss uncle until her parents are able to find employment. Although the girl's green thumb eventually transforms her uncle's drab existence, most remarkable about Stewart's story are the internal changes that take place. Both the scrappy young girl and her uncle learn to love each other while remaining true to their own identities.

The Journey (2001) is the story of Hannah, a young Amish girl who leaves her quiet community and travels to Chicago to experience the alluring sights of a big city. Stewart's heartfelt text, presented as a week's worth of diary entries, enables even the most jaded reader to experience the all-too-familiar urban sights with a child's unencumbered sense of wonder.

At heart, Stewart's gently told stories are tales of personal discovery: revelations about individuals who possess the quiet courage to become their truest selves. Stewart's beautifully crafted sentences are also meditations on some of the poet and writer's deepest passions: her abiding love of reading and gardening and her admiration for tough-minded, tenderhearted women.

R.M.

Stolz, Mary

American author, b. 1920. Mary Stolz first won acclaim as a gifted writer of YOUNG ADULT NOVELS but later achieved equal success with her MIDDLE-GRADE FICTION and ANIMAL STORIES. The Boston-born author was raised in New York and attended the progressive Birch Wathen School, where her interests in reading and writing were encouraged. Later she was a student at Columbia University. Stolz always wanted to be a writer, but after leaving school, she sold books at Macy's, did secretarial work, married, and gave birth to a son. In the late 1940s, Stolz became ill for several months. Her physician suggested that she pursue an interest while recovering, so she began writing. The physician became her second husband; the manuscript, *To Tell Your Love,* was published in 1950. Stolz based the story on her own teenage years, and the resulting novel was praised as a sensitive depiction of first love. It was the first of many young adult books that the prolific author would write.

Stolz's young adult novels are mature, thought-provoking, and sensitive. Romance always plays a key role, usually as a catalyst for growth and change in the protagonist. The novels reflect their era and contain some sex-role stereotyping, but since the real focus is on the heroine's personal growth as a human being, there is also a modern sensibility that seems not at all dated. In light of the realism that young adult novels later achieved, Stolz's romances may now be considered cautious and chaste, but they cannot be described as immature. The typical Stolz protagonist is unusually intelligent and analytical; her conversations and opinions evoke the image of a thoughtful, eloquent college student rather than a fourteen- or fifteen-year-old girl. There is also realism in the unflinching way Stolz has presented her characters. One of her best books, *Because of Madeline* (1957), concerns a lower-class nonconformist who affects the lives of everyone she meets when she begins attending private school. Madeline is not particularly sympathetic, and many of the upper-class characters she encounters are presented as well intentioned but shallow. The characterizations are extremely perceptive in this stimulating novel about class and conformity.

Stolz has credited Ursula Nordstrom, the legendary Harper's editor, with providing writing guidance throughout much of her career, but Stolz herself can be credited with writing some of the most sophisticated young adult books of the 1950s, which paved the way for the "new realism" that arrived in the 1960s. During that new decade, Stolz continued to write the occasional young adult novel, but switched her main focus to early reader and middle-grade books. Her Barkham Street stories, particularly *The Bully of Barkham Street* (1963), are extremely popular, and her love of nature is evident in several animal tales, including *Cat Walk* (1983). Her outstanding middle-grade novel *The Noonday Friends,* concerning underprivileged Franny's friendship with a Puerto Rican girl, was named a Newbery Honor Book in 1966. An earlier Newbery Honor title was *Belling the Tiger* (1961), an enjoyable, if somewhat bland, tale about two mice. Stolz has written many other award-worthy novels, including *The Edge of Next Year* (1964), a haunting, poetic study of a family's recovery after the mother's accidental death, and the splendid time-travel FANTASY *Cat in the*

Mirror (1975). Stolz's work is notable for its diversity and general excellence. P.D.S.

Survival Stories

When children or adolescents are first introduced to literature, they are taught that conflict makes a story work. One such conflict is "man versus nature," which often shows up as the theme of survival stories. From the early days of literature with *Robinson Crusoe* (1719), written by Daniel Defoe, to Jack London's novels and stories, especially "To Build a Fire," the survival genre has been read, studied, and enjoyed by children and young adults over centuries. Unlike other genres, there is a timelessness to survival tales because of the basic conflict. They are also normally easy to read — the very nature of the tale means there will be few characters, lots of action and adventure, and the question: "Will this person survive?" Teens might also enjoy survival tales for deeper, more emotional reasons. Survival tales can be seen as a metaphor for adolescence itself: an endless series of obstacles for which teens are often unprepared and which leaves the teen, and many a parent, asking: "Will I survive?"

Although there are some survival stories with a female protagonist, such as the Newbery Medal winner *Julie of the Wolves* (1972), written by JEAN CRAIGHEAD GEORGE, most survival tales involve young men in danger. Reading interest surveys show that survival and adventure fiction is the most popular genre for teenage boy readers. A classical survival novel, Robb White's *Deathwatch* (1972) tells of a young man stalked in the wilderness by a crazed hunter. Although published as an adult title, *Deathwatch* has become a young adult staple and has been reprinted more than twenty-five times. Arthur Roth has written several survival novels, *The Iceberg Hermit* (1975) being his best. This work of HISTORICAL FICTION with a 1757 setting tells the story of a shipwreck survivor in the frozen north. *Snowbound* (1973), written by Harry Mazer, traps two unlikable characters in a car during a snowstorm. Mazer also wrote a Robinson Crusoe variation, *The Island Keeper* (1981), and a war story, *The Last Mission* (1979), with survival elements.

The island survival theme is explored in THEODORE TAYLOR's award-winning *The Cay* (1969), which tells of a young boy and an older black man stranded together. BROCK COLE's *The Goats* (1987) is a brilliant novel about two social misfits left on an island as part of a nasty prank. GARY PAULSEN in *Hatchet* (1986) has stranded his youthful protagonist in the Canadian north woods to fend for himself. *Hatchet* was an immediate sensation, earning rave reviews, being named as a Newbery Honor Book, and inspiring a sequel, *The River* (1991). P. J. Petersen has also written several books in this genre, and *Going for the Big One* (1986) has the best elements: teenage campers not only face nature's fury but also a "bad guy" drug dealer. Although many of these books are similar, with their stock settings of islands, mountains, and wilderness, there are enough differences in characters and challenges to make each one interesting.

Some authors have attempted to expand the genre even further. *Slake's Limbo* (1974), written by Felice Holman, tells a tale of urban survival as a thirteen-year-old boy makes a home for himself inside the New York City subway tunnels. Julian Thompson's *The Grounding of Group Six* (1983) presents radical new ways of telling a story, as Thompson's slam-bang, one-liner style is a far cry from the straight narrative of most survival tales. Finally, Art Spiegelman's *Maus* (1986) and *Maus II* (1991) examine Holocaust survival using comic-book storytelling. These acclaimed graphic novels demonstrate that while survival stories may be old and the theme basic to literature, enough new ways still exist to tell the tale.

Nonfiction survival books such as Piers Paul Read's *Alive* (1974) and Stephen Callahan's *Adrift* (1986) have proven popular, especially with older teenage readers. Part of the appeal, especially in a book like *Alive,* is the lurid elements and tactics people will take to survive. The survival theme doesn't just supply action, but also psychological insight. The theme is the undercurrent of horror and thriller fiction also popular with teens. Finally, most good young adult fiction is really a survival tale, not teens surviving against the elements so much as surviving through the changes and pain of growing up.

P.J.

T

Tabak, Simms

American illustrator and author, b. 1932. Simms Tabak came to PICTURE BOOKS from a background in graphic design. After graduating from the Music and Art High School in New York City and earning a bachelor's degree in fine arts at Cooper Union, Tabak worked as a designer for a variety of businesses, including CBS Records and the *New York Times*. He opened his own design studio in 1963 and illustrated his first children's book in 1964. His early work in illustration included a wide range of books, such as a collection of POETRY by John Travers Moore, *There's Motion Everywhere* (1970); a cookbook for adults; and Barbara K. Walker's collection of international humor, *Laughing Together: Giggles and Grins from Around the World* (1977). Many of these books introduce the round-faced, smiling, cartoonlike characters who would become familiar elements of Tabak's work. The most lasting of the picture books from Tabak's early career is Ann McGovern's, *Too Much Noise* (1967). The retelling of the traditional Jewish folktale is spare and understated. Tabak used equally simple illustrations,

allowing the story events to convey the hilarity of the situation.

Tabak is best known for his illustrations of humorous, simple stories and EASY READERS. His collaborations with Harriet Ziefert have been particularly successful because Tabak's rounded, simplified figures give life to Ziefert's equally simple texts. *Jason's Bus Ride* (1987) is typical of their books. Ziefert's text uses limited vocabulary to tell the story of a boy who rescues a dog. Tabak uses solid outlines and rounded shapes to convey a cheerful, sometimes humorous, but always comfortable world. In *Where Is My Baby?* (1994) bright colors and simple shapes attract toddlers. The book follows the successful formula in which the author poses a question and hides the answer behind a flap. Tabak's pen-and-ink and watercolor illustrations enhance the series of easy-reader riddle books written by Katy Hall and Lisa Eisenberg. Tabak has provided a literal interpretation of the riddle — essential for young readers depending on the picture to give word clues — but also added his own sly or outright silly details to the art.

Tabak is the first illustrator to receive Caldecott recognition for a "toy book," a book with die-cut holes throughout. Tabak's *There Was an Old Lady Who Swallowed a Fly* (1997), a Caldecott Honor Book, and *Joseph Had a Little Overcoat* (1999), winner of the Caldecott Medal, are the best kind of artistic descendants of a tradition that began with PETER NEWELL's *The Hole Book*, created in the early twentieth century. In Tabak's books the hole is an integral part of the story, not merely a gimmick. In *There Was an Old Lady Who Swallowed a Fly*, children can peek through the hole in the old lady's stomach and see the animal she just swallowed. This device is wonderfully funny, childlike, and just grotesque enough to suit the song. *Joseph Had a Little Overcoat* is a newly illustrated edition of a song Tabak first illustrated in 1978. The folk song is perfectly suited to the naive, childlike folk art, which includes both collage and die-cut elements. Die-cut windows show the progression of a wool coat as it wears out and is made into a scarf and eventually a button, and historical and religious details provide a setting in both time and place. Tabak's books are innovative, appealing to children, and true to their folk origins.

M.V.K.

Tafuri, Nancy

American illustrator, b. 1946. When Nancy Tafuri started illustrating PICTURE BOOKS, she provided the very youngest readers with a new, imaginative world of visual playfulness. *Will You Be My Friend?* (2000), *Where Did Bunny Go?* (2001), and Tafuri's 1984 Caldecott Honor Book, *Have You Seen My Duckling?* are representative of her distinctive artistic style. A master of visual storytelling, Tafuri has created illustrations in bright, flat colors that feature large, clearly limned characters set against accurate, intricately detailed backgrounds. Each picture, many of them two-page spreads, is the result of precise, often playful, placement of shapes on a page. Tafuri's books often feature simple hide-and-seek games, puzzles, and even visual jokes, which are scaled to the level of the picture book audience. The artist's visual ingenuity piques a child's interest, stimulates imagination, and encourages observation and discussion.

Tafuri studied illustration at the School of Visual Arts in New York City. While developing her portfolio, she and her husband opened a studio and began doing jacket illustrations for hardcover books. In 1981, Tafuri illustrated her first book, *The Piney Woods Peddler*, written by George Shannon. The text, a repetitive, cheerful rhyme, uses elements of traditional American swapping songs. The pictures are large and humorous, and their exaggerated style gives the book a folktale quality. Tafuri then illustrated *The Song* (1981), written by CHARLOTTE ZOLOTOW, and *If I Had a Paka* (1981), written by Charlotte Pomerantz, a book of poems that incorporates words and phrases from eleven languages. In 1983, Tafuri wrote and illustrated two books of her own; they were acclaimed critically for their imagination and child appeal. *All Year Long* is an artfully simple, artistically logical concept book explaining cycles — days of the week and months of the year; and *Early Morning in the Barn* (1983) follows three inquisitive baby chicks as they make their way around the farm, greeting other animals. Small children enjoy pointing to the easily recognizable barnyard friends and imitating the *moos, oinks, cheeps,* and *quacks* that constitute the book's text. The clever format used in *Spots, Feathers, and Curly Tails* (1988) is a favorite with preschoolers. A question and a clue is on one page: "What has spots?" The answer is found on the next: "A cow has spots."

Tafuri has spent much time working the sense into the pictures, as she feels too much print confuses younger readers. *The Ball Bounced* (1989) provides an imaginative example of the care she has taken in balancing the narrative and artwork. In only thirty-three words, Tafuri created a beguiling tale about a small boy whose random toss of a ball sends it on an adventure. Each page discloses the next tumble of the brilliant red, white, and blue ball. Young readers, who enjoy predictability, return repeatedly to this charming book.

Tafuri has illustrated a number of books written by other authors. *All Asleep* (1984), written by Charlotte Pomerantz, is a soothing combination of rhymes and pictures and a guaranteed soporific. Tafuri's stylized illustrations in Patricia Lillie's *Everything Has a Place* (1993) are equally as assuring to toddlers, who are just learning to bring order into a bewildering world. S.L.

Taylor, Mildred

American novelist, b. 1943. Mildred Taylor was born in Jackson, Mississippi. When she was a child, her father decided that he could not stand living in the segregated South any longer and left for Ohio, sending for his family three months later. Taylor grew up in Toledo but made return trips to the South with her family. During these travels, they reencountered segregationist signs such as those forbidding black people to drink from the same water fountains as whites, and, as they were not allowed to stay in hotels or motels, they had to drive straight through without stopping. Often, their car was stopped by police anyway, particularly because they drove expensive new cars with northern license plates. Such incidents later appeared in Taylor's books.

Taylor excelled in school but from an early age realized that the history books she read did not represent the dignity, the courage, and the achievements of the people she knew about from stories told in her family. She considers herself one in a line of these family storytellers and the one who put the words to paper. She tried and failed to become a published writer many times before entering a contest sponsored by the Council on Interracial Books for Children, with the story she told in *Song of the Trees,* which was published in 1975. In this book she introduced a vivid family of characters, most of whom were based on people in her own family. The Logans owned land in the South, as her family did. The main character, Cassie Logan, combined the feisty natures of her sister and an aunt, but Cassie's feelings were those of Mildred Taylor, who was a quieter child.

Taylor has stated that she wants children of all colors to walk in the shoes of the Logan family and understand the value system within the family. She has strived to convey how the strong black men and women she knew persevered, retained hope, and fought for what they believed in. She has recounted true incidents, such as beatings and near-lynchings, from real life.

Taylor's second book, *Roll of Thunder, Hear My Cry,* her best-known work, won the 1977 Newbery Medal from the American Library Association and was also a nominee for the 1977 National Book Award. The third book in the Logan series, *Let the Circle Be Unbroken,* was the winner of a Coretta Scott King Award in 1982. Additional books about the Logans followed: *The Friendship* was published in 1987; both *The Road to Memphis* and *Mississippi Bridge* were published in 1990; *The Well: David's Story* was released in 1995; and *The Land* appeared in 2001.

The Gold Cadillac (1987) is drawn from Taylor's childhood experiences during her family's first years in Toledo and in 1987 was named an Outstanding Book by the *New York Times,* an honor several of her other novels have earned.

Taylor is a graduate of the University of Toledo. After college she joined the Peace Corps and was sent to Ethiopia, where she taught English and history. After her return, she became a recruiter for the Peace Corps and received a master's degree in journalism from the University of Colorado. Before she became a full-time writer, she worked as a study-skills coordinator in a black education program she helped structure. Two documentaries have been produced about Taylor, including *Meet the Newbery Author: Mildred Taylor.*

Mildred Taylor's novels are excellently written, suspenseful stories of a strong, resourceful family. They serve to introduce readers, primarily children in elementary school, to the tragic history of injustice and violence against blacks in America. S.H.H.

Taylor, Sydney

American author, 1904–1978. Sydney Taylor began her career as an actress and professional dancer with the Martha Graham Dance Company. Also a student of dramatics, Taylor wrote, directed, and choreographed original plays in addition to writing books for children.

Taylor's native New York City provides the setting for the well-loved All-of-a-Kind Family series, which evolved from Taylor's own childhood on Manhattan's Lower East Side in the early 1900s. At the request of her daughter, Taylor finally began to record FAMILY STORIES about her adventures with her five sisters, and the All-of-a-Kind Family books were born. *All-of-a-Kind Family* (1951) introduces a close-knit family of five girls, ranging in age from four to twelve, Mama, and Papa, who operates a junk shop. It is a difficult life; money is hard-earned and precious, but there is no shortage of love in the girls' family. Mama is hardworking and wise, dispensing discipline and love with an even hand and a good deal of humor. Papa is the spiritual guide for the family, providing the foundation for a deep and abiding faith in Judaism. Joyous family celebrations, with the significance of each holiday often interpreted in a personal manner for a particular child, furnish an underlying theme throughout the series. Within the girls' extended family of relatives, friends, and neighbors there is a wonderful sense of community and vibrancy. In adventure after adventure, the girls come in contact with an engaging array of characters. In response to positive letters from children around the country about her first book, Taylor continued the saga with *More All-of-a-Kind Family* (1954), in which a much-awaited son, Charlie, is born; *All-of-a-Kind Family Uptown* (1958), which chronicles the family's move to the Bronx at the start of World War I; and *All-of-a-Kind Family Downtown* (1972), which records yet another move and a change in the family's financial status.

Taylor deftly established warm, congenial relationships between the sisters that are sustained through each volume, and skillfully developed characters so the reader gains a sense of the unique personality of each girl. The last book in the series, *Ella of All-of-a-Kind Family* (1978), focuses on one particular child as it follows Ella, the eldest, on her career as an aspiring singer. After being discovered, Ella joins a vaudeville troupe and, disillusioned after months of training and hard work, faces a difficult decision regarding her future. This book is of particular interest because the first stirrings of the women's movement are felt both by Ella, who must choose between the man she loves and her blossoming career, and by Henny, her younger sister, who faces an uphill battle for a class office against the boys in her class.

Taylor was honored for her work by the Jewish Book Council's National Jewish Book Award in 1951 for *All-of-a-Kind Family,* an award given for the work that "combines literary merit with an affirmative expression of Jewish values." She was also honored posthumously in 1979 by the Association of Jewish Libraries for her entire body of work. In addition to the series, Taylor's other books include *A Papa like Everyone Else*

(1966) and, for younger children, *Mr. Barney's Beard* (1961) and *The Dog Who Came to Dinner* (1965). Taylor's books may seem dated to the modern reader, yet they are still appreciated as a valuable retrospective of family life in the early part of the twentieth century. M.O'D.H.

Taylor, Theodore

American author, b. 1921. Theodore Taylor's earliest exposure to the printed word was an illustrated volume of Bible stories for children. His favorite tales, such as that of David and Goliath, were strong in action and adventure. Many years later, Taylor would be acclaimed for writing his own action-filled stories for children.

When he was thirteen years old, Taylor's family moved from Statesville, North Carolina, to Portsmouth, Virginia, where he soon acquired a job on the local newspaper, writing a column about high school sports. He continued his journalism career at the *Washington Daily News* as a copy boy, served as sports editor at two newspapers, and reported on the early space race for the *Orlando Sentinel-Star.* He has also worked as a merchant marine, press agent, and prizefighter manager. Taylor published two nonfiction books for adults before he entered the children's field with *People Who Make Movies* (1967), which was inspired by his own children's interest in the film industry. He has since written several INFORMATION BOOKS for young people, often focusing on World War II themes, as in *Air Raid — Pearl Harbor!* (1971). But Taylor is best known for writing fiction that is filled with vivid characterizations and strong action.

His first novel, *The Cay* (1969), is the story of eleven-year-old Phillip, who is shipwrecked on a Caribbean island with an elderly black sailor during World War II. Blinded by a torpedo attack, Phillip must overcome his prejudices and learn survival skills from Timothy, who teaches the boy how to hunt for food, signal for help, and weather a hurricane. The theme of racial harmony is powerfully explored in a series of suspenseful, tightly focused scenes. The book

Illustration by Sir John Tenniel from *Alice's Adventures in Wonderland* (1865), by Lewis Carroll.

has achieved great popularity among young readers but has also been a source of controversy. Amid charges that Timothy's background is underdeveloped, that his Creole dialect is undignified, and that his deference to the young white boy is offensive, Taylor was asked to relinquish the Jane Addams Book Award that the novel received in 1970. Much of the controversy seems unfounded, since Timothy is clearly the hero of the novel and functions as a teacher to Phillip throughout. His early subservience seems more a product of his historical era than a reflection of his own self-worth. Taylor addressed the subject of Timothy's past in a volume he has termed a "prequel-sequel." In alternating chapters, *Timothy of the Cay* (1993) parallels the story of Timothy's nineteenth-century youth with Phillip's post–World War II experiences.

Taylor has written other multivolume stories,

including a pair of books about Helen's blind dog, *The Trouble with Tuck* (1981) and *Tuck Triumphant* (1991), and a trilogy about a mysterious girl who is rescued from a shipwreck on the Outer Banks of North Carolina, *Teetoncey* (1974), *Teetoncey and Ben O'Neal* (1975), and *The Odyssey of Ben O'Neal* (1977). Taylor's other novels of adventure include *A Sailor Returns* (2001); *The Bomb* (1995); *Sniper* (1989), the story of a teenager guarding lions and tigers on his family's private nature preserve; and *The Weirdo* (1991), which concerns young people trying to protect wild bears in a North Carolina wildlife refuge. *Walking Up a Rainbow* (1986) is a rousing frontier story about an orphaned teenage girl, memorable for its colorful first-person narration.

A fine sense of dramatic action propels Taylor's fiction, making his fast-paced novels exciting and readable. P.D.S.

Tenniel, Sir John

British illustrator, 1820–1914. With the illustrations of only two children's books to his credit, Sir John Tenniel has nevertheless well earned his place as one of the great names in children's literature. His illustrations for Lewis Carroll's *Alice's Adventures in Wonderland* (1865) and *Through the Looking-Glass* (1872) have been termed the most perfect marriage of text and illustration in a children's book, with the illustrator's style complementing and expanding the scope of the author's story and, with time, becoming virtually inseparable from it.

Thought by many to have been the epitome of the Victorian gentleman, Tenniel was born the year before Queen Victoria ascended the throne and died on the eve of World War I, when the world order with which he had been so comfortable changed forever. In between, he lived a solid, steady life of respectability and satisfactory personal achievement, and his strong, literal artistic style captured and reflected his times. He was primarily a self-taught artist, having quit the Royal Academy School "in utter disgust of there being no teaching" and spent long hours at the British Museum and the Tower of London, studying and copying suits of armor and books on medieval costume. He hoped to make his living as a painter, and he viewed the illustrating work that came his way as incidental.

But in 1848 he was asked to illustrate *Aesop's Fables,* a retelling of AESOP by the Reverend Thomas James. The book met with wide success, and as a result he was invited to become the primary illustrator for *Punch,* a satirical magazine that set the political and social tone of the day. Tenniel's political cartoons for *Punch* form the other half of his enduring body of work, and they greatly influenced British political life for the half century he drew them. His early studies of knights and ladies loomed large in Tenniel's artistic vocabulary, as did his interest in animals (particularly lions and eagles) and his very Victorian love of whimsy, which frequently expressed itself in drawings of anthropomorphic animals: rabbits in waistcoats and fishes in knee breeches.

When Charles Dodgson, as Lewis Carroll, decided to publish the story about a little girl named Alice he had written for some of his young friends, he knew his own amateurish drawings would not do. He was taken with Tenniel's work in *Punch* and asked a mutual friend to introduce them. Thus began an extremely contentious, wearing, and ultimately fruitful collaboration. The two gentlemen met in 1864, and over the next eight years and through two books, they conducted a very courteous, highly restrained, but deadly serious battle over artistic control of Wonderland. Carroll had very definite ideas about how the illustrations for his books should look, having illustrated himself the first, unpublished version of *Alice,* called *Alice's Adventures Under Ground.* Tenniel felt himself to be little more than an employee of Carroll's, a position at which his independent nature balked. He had his own strong vision of the works, and occasionally, especially for the second book, Carroll incorporated his suggestions into the text. Carroll's mania for detail was matched only by Tenniel's, and the two drove each other to the ultimate reaches of patience with their competing fastidiousness.

The drawings were done in the manner of the day. This involved sketches followed by finished pen and ink drawings on paper; transferred by the artist onto wooden blocks, the drawings were then engraved by an engraver and handed over to a printer. It was a long, laborious process, with many opportunities for mistakes and misunderstandings. In fact, Tenniel and Carroll recalled the first printing of *Alice* because they felt it had been improperly printed, to the detriment of the illustrations. Ultimately, however, the two men produced books that have been celebrated for their beauty, wit, fantasy, and uncommon harmony between text and art. Tenniel diplomatically claimed, "It is a curious fact that with *Through the Looking-Glass* the faculty of making drawings for book illustrations departed from me," and he spent the rest of his career focused on his cartoons for *Punch.* When he died, a few days before his ninety-fourth birthday, his contemporaries mourned the passing of an era, along with the man who exemplified and captured it so well.   S.G.K.

Thomas, Jane Resh

American author, b. 1936. Jane Resh Thomas grew up in Kalamazoo, Michigan, and was taught to love two things from an early age: books and nature. Her mother was an avid reader and her father was an enthusiastic outdoorsman who often took his daughter fishing. Thomas also spent a great deal of time at her grandparents' nearby peach orchard and tree nursery, and thus was in her element both indoors and out. "I relied on books, as I did on nature," she has said, "not only to entertain but to sustain myself."

Thomas did not begin writing for children until after she had first trained and worked as a registered nurse and then returned to school to obtain her degree in English. From 1967 until 1980 she taught composition at the University of Minnesota, also working as a freelance writer for most of those years, and eventually went on to edit children's books as well. Thomas found that these ventures complemented one another and reinforced her philosophy of writing: draw from experience and write "what haunts you." Each of Thomas's books is, in some way, based on her own experiences and observations, which has enabled her to imbue characters with emotions that ring resonantly true.

Her first book for young readers was *Elizabeth Catches a Fish* (1977). The title character receives a fishing rod for her seventh birthday and looks forward to her first fishing trip with her father; clearly, the plot and setting were adapted from Thomas's own fond childhood memories. *The Comeback Dog* (1981) and its sequel, *Fox in a Trap* (1987), feature rural settings and a young boy who has an abiding respect for animals. In the first story, Daniel grapples with his emotional reactions after his beloved dog dies and he finds another that needs his help; in the second, he must find a way to express his objections to his uncle's love of hunting. In the poignant *Saying Goodbye to Grandma* (1988), Thomas depicted a young child attending the funeral of her grandmother, trying to make sense of the grief around her. Each story is invariably told with a well-crafted combination of gentle honesty and quiet wisdom.

Thomas has also made forays into the genres of multicultural literature, FANTASY, and NONFICTION. Her PICTURE BOOK *Lights on the River* (1994) depicts a Mexican family of migrant workers turning to a Christmas tradition for solace. In the author's note, Thomas stated, "I wrote this story more than forty years after seeing several migrant farm workers standing at the doorstep of the chicken coop where they were housed on a Michigan farm." *The Princess in the Pigpen* (1989) is a fantasy novel in which a young girl from seventeenth-century England is transported to a twentieth-century farm in Iowa, again drawing on Thomas's knowledge of farm life and of the emotions involved in finding oneself in unfamiliar circumstances. Finally, her incomparable portrait of Queen Elizabeth in *Behind the Mask: The Life of Elizabeth I* (1998) reveals Thomas's singular talent for research and her ability to bring fact and story into nearly flawless cooperation.

Thomas does not condescend to her reader, nor does she hold back. Whether crafting a fictional tale for very young readers or researching a longer work of nonfiction for the older end of the spectrum, Jane Resh Thomas has remained forever true to her word: she writes from her heart. H.F.R.

Thomas, Rob

American author, b. 1965. While working in Los Angeles for *Channel One,* a television news program shown in high school classrooms across the country, Rob Thomas began writing his first YOUNG ADULT NOVEL, *Rats Saw God* (1996). Thomas and his teenage narrator, Steven York, shared at least one thing in common. They both had recently moved from Texas to California, although, in Steve's case, the reason for the exodus wasn't a job but a failed relationship that had put his heart "through frappe, puree, and liquefy on a love blender." Throughout the book, which alternates between Steve's shell-shocked West Coast present and his painfully recalled Texas past, Thomas demonstrated a unique affinity with his audience. His biting wit, laden with pop culture references, figures prominently in this novel and his subsequent titles, all of which deal with teens pulled back and forth between cynicism and intense emotion.

Thomas has explored larger social issues alongside more typical young adult fare such as problem parents and tumultuous romance. A high school journalism teacher in Texas for five years, he no doubt encountered students like the ambitious Patrick Sheridan of *Satellite Down* (1998), who strives toward a career as an ace reporter. But Patrick's journalistic principles are challenged when he is selected to spend part of his senior year in Los Angeles as student anchor for the teen news show *Classroom Direct.* There he learns that good looks regularly win out over talent and hard work and that the news isn't as important to his employer as keeping sponsors and subscribers happy. Told from eight different perspectives, *Slave Day* (1997) points out the racist connotations of a suburban Texas high school's fundraising event, in which teachers and student council members are "sold" for a day to the highest student bidders. Thomas returned to this same high school in his short story collection *Doing Time: Notes from the Undergrad* (1997) to illuminate the complex, questionable motives and unexpected consequences surrounding the senior class's required community service projects. And in a novel for a somewhat younger audience, *Green Thumb* (1999), a science whiz narrator travels to a locale even more exotic than L.A. — the Amazon rain forest — for a lesson in environmental ethics, or rather a corrupt botanist's lack thereof.

In 1997, Thomas became a staff writer for the popular teen television drama *Dawson's Creek*. He has worked on other TV and movie projects, notably as the creator of the short-lived but critically admired series *Cupid*. Thomas also has frequently received e-mails from adoring teenage girls who mistakenly assume that he is the Rob Thomas who is the lead singer for the alt-rock band matchbox twenty. As the author's website notes, "the matchbox twenty Rob Thomas" was named one of *People* magazine's 50 Most Beautiful People, while he himself is *not* one of *People* magazine's 50 Most Beautiful People. He is, however, an author with an uncanny ability to speak in the voices of intelligent, observant teens deciding whether to actively participate in their lives or stick with a stance of disgusted detachment. C.M.H.

Thurber, James

American author, 1894–1961. Celebrated for his mordant sketches of contemporary life in the 1940s and 1950s, James Thurber's five works that have been classified as children's books show a lover of words at play. The books, starting with *Many Moons* (1943) and ending with *The Wonderful O* (1957), are filled with wordplay, allusions, rhymes, alliteration, snatches of song and poetry, wild flights of fancy that veer into the absurd, and — in the greatest departure from his work for adults — happy endings.

Many Moons is considered his best book for children, and it shows a tenderness and charm that his writing for adults does not. In its first incarnation, with illustrations by Louis Slobodkin, it won the Caldecott Medal for 1944. Slobodkin's illustrations emphasize the theatrical, light-opera quality of the tale, depicting a tiny and seemingly frail Princess Lenore nearly overwhelmed by the soaring castle surrounding her, making the solution to her problem all the more satisfying. MARC SIMONT reillustrated the story for reissue in 1990, putting the FANTASY of the piece on a more magical plane and calling forth a greater awareness of the King's love for his ill daughter. In *Many Moons* Thurber succeeded in corralling his acid wit and penchant for the absurd with a silken halter of sweetness and pure storytelling skill; in his subsequent books for children, he was less successful at controlling his natural pessimism. *The Great Quillow* (1944), *The White Deer* (1945), and *The Thirteen Clocks* (1950) are highly colored, extravagant fairy tales in which his wonderfully dark humor and basic disgust with the human race become more and more apparent. In his final children's book, *The Wonderful O,* the melancholy and sharpness that was a hallmark of his writing for adults overwhelms this slim tale of pirates who ban the letter *O* from the language of a small, mythical island.

Thurber's absurd view of his own childhood certainly influenced his writing for children. Born in Columbus, Ohio, the second of three boys in a "family of eccentrics," as he termed it, Thurber grew up amidst a large cast of unlikely characters. His father was a political animal whose employment in various appointed capacities lent an uncertain and peripatetic air to the Thurber household. His mother, Thurber wrote, was "an aspiring actress," and "deprived of a larger audience, the frustrated comedienne performed for whoever would listen." A childhood accident while playing "William Tell" with his brothers left Thurber with permanently impaired eyesight, which gradually deteriorated over his lifetime, eventually blinding him, a handicap that would cause him great pain, both physically and spiritually. Upon graduation from Ohio State University in 1919, he worked as a newspaper reporter in Columbus, Paris, and New York.

It was at a cocktail party in New York City in 1927 that he met E. B. WHITE and began the firm friendship (and sometime literary collaboration) that was to last the rest of his life. White introduced Thurber to Herbert Ross, founding editor of the *New Yorker,* which was then in its infancy. Ross hired Thurber as managing editor, and while Thurber was uncomfortable with executive authority and eventually demoted himself down to staff writer and then off the magazine entirely to become a contributing writer, he nevertheless had much to do with setting the tone and style that made the *New Yorker* such a literary high-water mark during its halcyon days.

Thurber's writing took many forms — all of them short. Essays, sketches, fables, satires, parables, FANTASIES, and reminiscences all share his bleak view of an overwhelming, chaotic world. But in the best of his writing for children, Thurber felt free to let good triumph over evil, love overcome hate, virtue gain its just reward, and hope hold fast. S.G.K.

Tolkien, J. R. R.

British scholar and writer, 1892–1973. John Ronald Reuel Tolkien's *The Hobbit or, There and Back Again* (1937), with illustrations by the author, is a captivating FANTASY with wide appeal for both children and adults. It concerns the quest of Bilbo Baggins, a comfort-loving, ordinary, and unambitious hero. The *New York Herald Tribune* awarded it a prize as the best book published for young children in the spring of 1938. That year, Tolkien's friend and colleague, C. S. LEWIS, wrote, "*The Hobbit* may well prove a classic." *The Hobbit,* in fact, has proved to be the most popular of all twentieth-century fantasies written for children. Tolkien

was so well grounded in ancient legend and saga, medieval literature, his own original languages, and philological study of the connections between language and literature, that there was, as Lewis said, "a happy fusion of the scholar's with the poet's grasp of mythology."

According to Tolkien, his stories "arose in the mind as 'given' things, and as they came, separately, so too the links grew . . . always I had the sense of recording what was already 'there,' somewhere, not of 'inventing.'" At a time when fairy stories were considered childish, Tolkien claimed in a 1939 lecture, "On Fairy-Stories," collected in *Tree and Leaf* (1964), that, "If fairy-story as a kind is worth reading at all it is worthy to be written for and read by adults." According to Tolkien, children were not a race or class apart from adults, but fellow humans of fewer experiences, and thus, usually, had less need for the fantasy, recovery, escape, and consolation provided by fairy stories. He had enjoyed fairy stories during his own childhood, but it was not until "the threshold of manhood," when his philological studies had made clear to him the connections between the origins of stories, language, and the creative human mind, that he developed a real taste for them. Fantasy, he said, is a natural human activity and is not in opposition to reason. We make or create from our imagination "because we are made; and not only made, but made in the image and likeness of a Maker." The storymaker is a successful sub-creator when his secondary world can be entered by the reader who is convinced by the inner consistency of the laws of that world that his experiences are "true." Later writers of fantasy for children, such as LLOYD ALEXANDER, SUSAN COOPER, ROBIN McKINLEY, and others, reflect some Tolkien influence.

As reprintings of *The Hobbit* continued, there followed many requests for more about hobbits. But it was not until seventeen years later that the long-awaited "sequel" finally appeared. It was *The Lord of the Rings* (1954–55), published in three volumes: Part I, "The Fellowship of the Ring"; Part II, "The Two Towers"; and Part III, "The Return of the King." Some of the delay was caused by the author's need to ensure that the geography, chronology, and nomenclature were perfectly consistent within the sequel; with its predecessor, *The Hobbit* (which required a revised edition, published in 1951); and with the foundation "history," a large body of unpublished original legends and many-layered mythologies of Elven lore of the "First Age of the World."

Since early adulthood, Tolkien had been engaged in the process of inventing variants, revising, and finely tuning integrations of this material, and he continued to do so until his death. (Much of this "history" was published posthumously as *The Silmarillion*, 1977, and additional volumes have appeared since the early 1980s, all edited by Christopher Tolkien, who had worked closely with his father.) When the first part of *The Lord of the Rings* appeared, C. S. Lewis again gave Tolkien's work generous praise: "This book is like lightning from a clear sky. To say that in it heroic romance, gorgeous, eloquent and unashamed, has suddenly returned at a period almost pathological in its anti-romanticism is inadequate . . . it makes . . . an advance or revolution: the conquest of new territory." In a short six weeks the first edition had sold out, demonstrating its popularity for a wide age range. Several years later, when a pirated paperback edition of *The Lord of the Rings* (and later an authorized one) became available, both works soared to the bestseller lists.

The sequels, similarly structured, share the time frame of "The Third Age of Middle-earth" and both are purported to have roots in the events of "The First Age"; but they differ in complexity and tone. The narrative tone is more relaxed and humorous in Bilbo's story, where there are occasional asides to children, and there are only a few fleeting glimpses of "the older matter." In *The Lord of the Rings*, however, Tolkien claimed that he was "discovering" the significance of these "glimpses" and expanding on their relation to his "Ancient histories." The primary link between the sequels is the Ring of Power, treacherously forged by Sauron to control Elven-kings, Dwarf-lords, and Mortal Men.

Central to a deeper understanding of Tolkien's life and mind are two short allegories, *Leaf by Niggle* (1947) and *Smith of Wooton Major* (1967). Both can be enjoyed by children, but in each case the stories have deeper meaning for adults. The first represents the author's fear of dying before he had completed *The Lord of the Rings*, and in the second the author recognized that the gift that permitted his visits to the land of faery must be relinquished and passed on to another generation. A humorous dragon story with more child appeal is *Farmer Giles of Ham* (1949). *The Adventures of Tom Bombadil* (1962) contains entertaining verses from "The Red Book," also the alleged source of *The Hobbit*. This collection, as well as *Bilbo's Last Song* (1974), is illustrated by Pauline Baynes, whose work greatly pleased Tolkien. *The Father Christmas Letters* (1976) and *Mr. Bliss* (1982) are both illustrated by the author and are evidence of his special joy in creating stories for his children.

The enormous popularity of Tolkien's work on American campuses during the 1960s may have slowed the academy's appreciation of his fiction. His academic reputation was well established. He had occupied two chairs as professor of Anglo-Saxon and professor of English language and literature, had lectured far more than was required, and had produced valued research publications. An authorized biography by Humphrey Carpenter (1977) and the appearance of Tolkien's letters (1981) stimulated academic attention. By the 1990s, his works had found their place in the canon of English literature and are now the subject of hundreds of critical and scholarly books, essays, dissertations, theses, and journal articles. He received many honors in the last two decades of his life, including honorary doctorates from University College, Dublin, and from Liège in 1954, and for his work in philology from Oxford University, in 1972. The same year he was awarded the Order of the British Empire. J. R. R. Tolkien's books have been translated into more than twenty-six languages and have reached annual worldwide sales of several million copies. E.C.H.

Travers, P. L.

British author, critic, and lecturer, 1899–1996. Pamela Lyndon Travers was as unwilling to "explain" herself as a writer as she was to explain the staunch and unbendable character for whom she is so well known — a British nanny in a 1930s household. *Mary Poppins* was published in 1934 and has since been translated into twenty-five languages and sold copies in the millions. It was the basis for a 1964 Disney film that had tremendous success despite its lack of favor with those loyal to the original book. Travers went on to write eight more books about Mary Poppins, including *Mary Poppins Comes Back* (1935), *Mary Poppins Opens the Door* (1943), *Mary Poppins in Cherry Tree Lane* (1982), and *Mary Poppins and the House Next Door* (1988). Critics have praised Travers for continuing to expand and explore her themes in the later books and for the enduring liveliness and unpredictability of her main character.

Mary Poppins has confounded critics over the years by being full of contradictions and impossible to characterize in a few simple words. She has been called stern, vain, proud, no-nonsense, unsentimental. She has the complete loyalty of her charges — Jane and Michael Banks and their younger brother and sister. In the series of episodes that make up *Mary Poppins,* she takes the children on adventures that both delight and amaze them. Whether she is gluing stars to the sky, having a tea party on the ceiling, or dancing under a full moon at the zoo, she leaves the children baffled and perplexed by her actions — never ceasing to deny that anything out-of-the-ordinary has taken place.

Travers drew her themes from a childhood rich in fairy tale and myth, a love of Shakespeare and the Bible, and later study of Eastern religion and philosophy. She grew up in Australia, daughter of an Irish father and a mother of Scottish and Irish descent. At eighteen, she traveled to England, determined to discover her roots — and made her home there. As a young woman she worked as a dressmaker, a dancer, an actress, and a reporter — first to help support her family in Australia after her father died and later to support herself in England, where she became established as a drama critic, travel essayist, and reviewer. She also wrote poetry and was taken under the wing of the Irish writer-editor George Russell, who published her work in the *Irish Statesman* and encouraged her literary growth and development for the rest of his life. Travers wrote several other children's books, including *I Go by Sea, I Go by Land* (1941), *The Fox at the Manger* (1962), and *Friend Monkey* (1971), as well as adult books — *Moscow Excursion* (1934) and *About the Sleeping Beauty* (1975). Although these titles haven't achieved the acclaim or success of the Mary Poppins books, they continued faithfully to explore the themes and ideas that intrigued their author.

In her writing Travers has a strongly mystical bent; she often said that she didn't create Mary Poppins at all; rather Mary Poppins found her way into Travers's consciousness and demanded that her story be told. Just as the character of Mary Poppins has continued to occupy the mind and writings of Travers over several decades, so the books have continued to be rediscovered by new generations of readers. **K.M.K.**

Tunis, Edwin

American artist and author, 1897–1973. "For the whole family" is a favorite catch phrase of overly optimistic publishers, but the term does, indeed, apply to the handsome social histories written and illustrated by Edwin Tunis. His books can be read by schoolchildren in the middle grades and enjoyed by history buffs long past their school years.

Born in Cold Spring Harbor, New York, and brought up in North Carolina (where he spent the first grade in a one-room schoolhouse), Maryland, and Delaware, Tunis developed a lifelong passion for American history and culture during his peripatetic early years. Trained at the

Maryland Institute of Art, he was an artist with a prodigious capacity for detail. His most ambitious undertaking, a mural depicting the history of spices, was 145 feet long, and two and a half years in the painting. The work required extensive research into ancient ships and prompted Tunis to write and illustrate his first book, *Oars, Sails, and Steam* (1952). Two other pictorial histories soon followed: *Wheels* (1955) and *Weapons* (1955).

Tunis proved to be as fine a writer as he was an artist. His books have an engaging, almost infectiously enthusiastic tone. They are simply written and astonishingly thorough. *Colonial Living* (1957) is representative of both his ambition and his skill. The subject is enormous: everyday living in seventeenth- and eighteenth-century America. From the fragile beachhead settlements to the highly structured society of Virginia at the dawn of the Revolutionary War, this is a vivid panorama of how the colonists really lived — what they ate, how they slept, how rich men tended their wigs, and how criminals were punished; the stuff of daily life is portrayed in simple prose and scores of finely crafted drawings.

Tunis's books were frequently favored by award committees. *Frontier Living* (1961), which tracks the manners and customs of American frontier life from the Revolutionary War through the nineteenth-century migrations, was a Newbery Honor Book. *Oars, Sails, and Steam* was chosen by the American Institute of Graphic Artists as one of their Fifty Books of the Year. *The Young United States: 1783–1830* (1969) was nominated for the National Book Award.

Like the topics they explore, Tunis's books are themselves of a time now long past. Few INFORMATION BOOKS for children look like this anymore. The illustrations are black and white; the design is simple and elegant. The texts, even in his PICTURE BOOKS, are long, helpfully broken down into topics, but not split by sidebars of historical oddities or trivia. His respect for history, and for his readers, distinguishes every page. A.Q.

Twain, Mark

American author, 1835–1910. Born Samuel Langhorne Clemens in Florida, Missouri, the youth who would become Mark Twain undertook careers as a printer, riverboat pilot, and prospector before turning to writing for his livelihood. First as a journalist and then as a writer of short stories, novels, and nonfiction, Twain was one of the nineteenth century's most successful writers. Since his death, young and adult readers around the world have continued to enjoy Twain's work, though the suitability of his writing for children has always been a subject of debate. In his own time Twain's work was attacked as too coarse for children; more recently, it has been criticized as too racist.

Perhaps the best explanation for Twain's reputation as a children's writer comes from Justin Kaplan's *Mr. Clemens and Mark Twain* (1966), a seminal biography that explores the split between Samuel Clemens, the man who strove for respectability and acceptance among America's eastern literary and social establishments, and Clemens's alter ego, Mark Twain, the earthy, funny, frontier-formed rough who loved attacking the hypocrisies of his era. Just as there is this split between Mr. Clemens and Mark Twain, there is a split between the fun-loving Mark Twain, much-loved children's author, and the dark Mark Twain, revered by adults — including many scholars — as one of the world's great literary geniuses.

As an author writing for adults, Twain imbued his works with irony and barbed social criticism that escapes most young readers, traits apparent even in such traditionally child-pleasing works as *The Prince and the Pauper* (1881), *The Adventures of Huckleberry Finn* (1884), and *A Connecticut Yankee in King Arthur's Court* (1889). Bitter disillusionment is another adult element that runs through Twain's work, dominating late-period writings such as "The Mysterious Stranger" (1898), *Mark Twain's Burlesque Autobiography* (1906), and "The War Prayer." Though Twain's works (with the exception of the notorious but insignificant *1601*, published in 1876) are not *adult* in the modern sense, they can include violence and language that many find inappropriate for children.

On the other hand, Twain's suitability as a children's author is attested to by his perennial popularity among young readers. Twain's marvelously accessible sense of humor — his sense of fun — has always been appreciated by the young. There is a nearly universal appeal to classic Twain humor, whether it is in the form of Tom Sawyer tricking his pals into paying for the honor of painting Aunt Polly's fence or of King Arthur's armored knights clanking to the rescue on their newly invented bicycles. Besides enjoying his sense of humor, young readers also appreciate the fact that Twain writes about children in a realistic way. Twain's best young characters are neither miniature adults nor stock symbols of innocence but rounded human beings. They are frequently in conflict with adult authority and can be, in turn, as disobedient, sweet, frightened, brave, serious, and playful as real children. It is the realistic completeness of Twain's child characters that makes them live long after the reading world has forgotten the countless one-dimensional children born of the dime-novel tradition that flourished during Twain's lifetime.

Twain's two greatest works featuring child characters are *The Adventures of Tom Sawyer* and *The Adventures of Huckleberry Finn*. Set in the fictional, pre–Civil War river town of St. Petersburg, *The Adventures of Tom Sawyer* (1875) is the story of a boy on the edge of adolescence, living a life that alternates between the restrictions imposed by the respectable adult-dominated society of St. Petersburg and the freedom offered by the Mississippi River wilderness surrounding the town. Acting out Everybody's fantasy, Tom gets to live wild on Jackson's Island, explore the labyrinths of McDougal's Cave, defeat the ominous Indian Joe, discover a treasure in gold, and woo Becky Thatcher, the girl of his puppy-love dreams. Tom also enjoys the sport of pulling practical jokes against enemies of the State of Boyhood such as the schoolteacher and the Sunday-school superintendent. Younger readers enjoy *The Adventures of Tom Sawyer* for its pranks and adventures of boyhood glory, but adults are more likely to appreciate the novel's nostalgic re-creation of the pleasures of boyhood. Twain's third-person narrative, detached and distant from the action, reinforces the nostalgic aspect of the novel, particularly when he bathed boyhood incidents in an irony that only adults can appreciate. Always a popular character, Tom would reappear in *The Adventures of Huckleberry Finn* as well as in two of Twain's least-satisfying books, *Tom Sawyer Abroad* (1894) and *Tom Sawyer, Detective* (1896). Twain also attempted to revive Tom in "Huck Finn and Tom Sawyer Among the Indians" and "Tom Sawyer's Conspiracy," two unpublished fragments.

Huckleberry Finn has attracted young readers who delight in Huck, the book's picaresque narrator, as well as his adventures. Huck's adventures are amusing and thrilling enough to hold the attention of young readers, while his journey down the Mississippi strikes a deeper chord by representing the delightful — and terrifying — possibilities inherent in any attempt to escape the tyranny of adult society. Besides attracting young readers, *The Adventures of Huckleberry Finn* has attracted debate over its suitability for children. Certainly its irony eludes many young readers, and the book's plot includes "unsuitable" elements such as theft, murder, running away from home, child abuse, human slavery, and mob violence. Furthermore, the text is spiced with dialect speech that many younger readers have trouble deciphering and contains language that many children and adults find offensive. The book's language has generated accusations of racism. These accusations have, in turn, generated hot denials from those readers who see the book as a testament to racial tolerance. Although there is no denying that some of Huck's words are racially offensive, he does, however, avow that he will "go to hell" rather than see his friend Jim remain enslaved. Despite this, the controversy over *Huckleberry Finn* continues to swirl like a Mississippi back eddy, just as the book itself continues to roll on with all the force of Huck's "monstrous big" river. Having appeared in over 850 editions published in some sixty-five languages, *The Adventures of Huckleberry Finn* remains a reading rite of passage for much of the literate world.

Twain's image as an author for children has been shaped not only by his own talent for writing about children but also by the various ways in which his works have been packaged. For years publishers have abridged, bowdlerized, and illustrated Twain's work expressly for the children's market. His work has also been packaged for children via feature films, television programs, stage plays, musicals, animated films, and comic books. Frequently, such child-oriented packaging has resulted in many freckle-faced and barefoot interpretations that omit or gloss over Twain's darker intentions.

As far as Twain's intentions go, his *Slovenly Peter*, a translation of a German fairy tale, is his only work indisputably intended for children alone, and it was not published until 1935. Twain's later attempts to revive the character of Tom Sawyer, as well as the largely forgotten *Personal Recollections of Joan of Arc* (1896), might be argued to have been intended for young readers, but it is clear Twain hoped they would be read by adults as well as children. On the other hand, his large body of nonfiction, including all of his immensely popular travel books, was not intended for young readers — though there is no reason a young adult reader could not enjoy the hilarious *Innocents Abroad* (1869) or the rousing *Roughing It* (1872). Similarly, popular novels such as *The Adventures of Huckleberry Finn, The Adventures of Tom Sawyer, The Prince and the Pauper,* and *A Connecticut Yankee in King Arthur's Court* were not written with children in mind — at least not exclusively so. It is largely these novels' enthusiastic appropriation by the young that has earned them their reputations as children's novels.

Despite LOUISA MAY ALCOTT's unfriendly recommendation that the coarse Mark Twain should not write for children, the fact is that most often Twain's intended audience was the entire family, not just its younger nor just its older members. Like all popular writers of his time and station, Twain tried (if not always successfully) to observe those nineteenth-century standards of taste and decorum that held that good writing should be fit for consumption by men, women, and children alike. So conscious of these standards was Twain that he willingly allowed his upright and proper wife, Olivia, to censor from his work anything that might prove offensive to young or old.

That Twain could successfully write for both young and old at the same time is as much a mark of his greatness as the fact that his work is as popular now, among both young and old, as it was when first published. And while the list of those who write for children but manage to appeal to adults is long, Twain is among the very few writers who have managed to find an audience of children without writing specifically for them. D.A.B.

U

Ungerer, Tomi

French-born American illustrator, b. 1931. His heroes are boa constrictors, bats, vultures, robbers, moon men, and octopi. His supporting cast is Dickensian. His style is both tender and satiric. His illustrations are both charming and frightening. He is not sweet. He is never pretty. He is, at the very least, JEAN DE BRUNHOFF and Eugène Ionesco, together, in one body.

Born in Strasbourg, France, Tomi Ungerer grew up in the shadow of death and poverty. His father, Theodor, died when Tomi was three years old. During the Depression, his mother was forced by economic hardship to move the family into her mother's home in nearby Colmar. The onslaught of World War II and the subsequent German occupation of Alsace formed a perilous and confusing backdrop for Ungerer: "My whole childhood was a schooling in relativity, in figuring out for myself who were the good guys and who were the bad." For three months, as the Allied Front moved over Colmar, Ungerer and his family lived in their cellar, bombs having destroyed their house. "There was plenty to see and remember," he has noted, "and my taste for the macabre certainly finds its roots there."

When the war ended, the disillusioned Ungerer set out on foot across Europe. Though he studied briefly at the École des Arts Décoratifs in Strasbourg, Ungerer has felt that the greater part of his education "came from travels through Europe, walking and hitchhiking, earning my way by odd jobs, and of course painting, drawing, and working in the graphic arts."

In 1956 Ungerer immigrated to the United States. Arriving in New York, he looked for work as a freelance illustrator. His first professional assignment came from *Sports Illustrated,* and soon after he received a children's book contract for *The Mellops Go Flying* (1957), the first of four humorous books about a resourceful pig family and their entertaining adventures. Among Ungerer's early improbable protagonists were Emile, the octopus; Adelaide, the flying kangaroo; and Rufus, the bat. Crictor, the clever boa constrictor, of the book by the same name, has earned, in children's eyes, the status of Babar and Curious George.

"I want to amuse myself and in the same process amuse children. I use a lot of satire because I find satire more digestible and I think it has less hypocrisy. Satire points out the foolish aspects of society and the absurdity," Ungerer has explained. In *The Beast of Monsieur Racine* (1971), an elderly gentleman befriends the beast who has been pilfering prize pears from his garden, only to find that the beast is actually two children in disguise. When the man in the moon, in *Moon Man* (1967), is jailed by the authorities after crash-landing on Earth, he wanes to his third quarter, slips through the bars, and escapes. A scientist, residing in a remote castle, launches him back into the air, where, his curiosity satiated, he remains "curled up in his shimmering seat in space." *The Three Robbers* (1962), graphically bold with dramatic color contrasts, is the story of three hoodlums converted to philanthropy by a young orphan. Only Ungerer would have robbers steal away a child named Tiffany. He elucidated the use of intense black in the book: "This book is really a book of darkness. It's a book of shadows. It reflects the fears I had as a child." Many of Ungerer's books, in the tradition of European fairy tales, offer darkly satiric details, both graphic and literal, which may appall adults' sensitivities, but children take gleeful delight in his sometimes gruesome humor.

Ungerer won the 1998 Hans Christian Andersen Award for illustration. He is also known for his sophisticated adult books and poster art. He can draw blood with an incisive stroke of his pen, but he also displays a keen understanding of, and affection for, the human condition. His *Moon Man* looks down on us all. M.B.B.

Vail, Rachel

American author, b. 1966. Born in New York City but raised in suburban New Rochelle, Rachel Vail had a youthful interest in dance, voice, magic, and various musical instruments. However, her main creative pursuit was acting, and besides performing in school and community theater, she also earned spending money working as a clown at children's parties. After graduating from Georgetown University, she worked in a variety of theater jobs, mostly backstage or in the box office. She has credited the experience of constructing believable characters for the stage for her ability to create unique fictional characters in her novels.

Her first book features one such character. *Wonder* (1991) is the story of Jessica's first year in junior high school. Trouble begins on the very first day when her best friend and five other girls arrive wearing matching outfits, derisively calling Jessica "Wonder" because her polka dot dress resembles the familiar Wonder Bread logo. Suddenly unpopular, the twelve-year-old tries a number of tactics to regain her self-confidence. Recalling the works of JUDY BLUME, this slice-of-suburban-life story features a likably insecure narrator, snappy dialogue, and a number of subplots, including Jessica's concern over her father's failing business and her crush on classmate Conor. Like its predecessor, *Do-Over* (1992) also focuses on a wide variety of everyday concerns — best friend problems, appearing in a school play, understanding the opposite sex — but this time the protagonist is male. Eighth-grader Whitman Levy, a classmate of Jessica's in *Wonder*, is also worried about his parents' separation, brought about by his father's affair with Whit's drama teacher. The mix of issues the protagonist must deal with, both large and small, gives the book verisimilitude, as does the contemporary, frank, and funny first-person narrative voice.

Vail moved in new directions with her next two novels. Though they also feature credible characters and insightful descriptions of complex human behavior and sudden moments of self-knowledge, they are written in different styles. *Ever After* (1994) is presented in diary entries as fourteen-year-old Molly records her crumbling friendship with Vicky, her neighbor on a small New England island. *Daring to Be Abigail* (1996) is composed of a series of letters that Abby writes from camp the summer she challenges herself to become a braver person. When Abby accepts a dare to play a particularly mean prank on an unpopular bunk mate, she learns some harsh truths about herself.

Although Vail has written a couple of PICTURE BOOKS, including the sophisticated *Over the Moon* (1998), her best books record the anxieties of girls just on the brink of adolescence. In the Friendship Ring series, a ring is passed back and forth between several seventh-grade friends as they shift allegiances, share a growing interest in boys, and in general, learn more about themselves and each other. The first three volumes (*if you only knew; please, please, please;* and *not that i care,* all 1998) were issued in both hardcover and paperback as CD-sized books with an eye-catching design; later entries were published in a more traditional paperback format. Though the books certainly had fans, they never achieved the popularity that many lesser, more formulaic series have enjoyed. Perhaps the usual readers of paperback romances were used to glossier, more superficial fare and didn't know what to make of these three-dimensional characters and Vail's keen ability to reveal their hearts and minds.

P.D.S.

Van Allsburg, Chris

American illustrator and author, b. 1949. The publication and subsequent success of Chris Van Allsburg's *The Polar Express* (1985) clearly established the illustrator-author as one of the premier creators of PICTURE BOOKS in twentieth-century children's literature. *The Polar Express,* immediately taken to heart by children and adults alike, was a phenomenon in children's publishing. It won the Caldecott Medal for illustration, appeared on the *New York Times* Best-Seller List, sold more than a million copies in its first five years of publication, and achieved the status of contemporary classic.

The story chronicles the adventures of a boy who boards the Polar Express, travels to the North Pole, meets Santa Claus, and is given a silver bell. Its sound can be heard only by those who believe in the impossible — that is, in Santa

Claus. Rich pastel illustrations, in blues and purples, are accompanied by a narrative that achieves an exceptional sense of story. The story appeals because Van Allsburg touches a universal chord — faith. The simple truth of the story is perceptively conveyed through a felicitous blend of pictures and narrative; the combination radiates with childlike wonder while reverberating with mysterious intensity.

Born in Grand Rapids, Michigan, Van Allsburg received his B.F.A. from the University of Michigan. He attended graduate school at the Rhode Island School of Design and received his M.F.A. in sculpture. In 1977, Van Allsburg's sculptures, described as "fastidiously crafted, surreal, enigmatic and whimsical," were exhibited in New York galleries. Originally, he began drawing as a casual diversion from sculpting, and his early black and white drawings contain elements of sculpture — heavy, solid forms, which appear to be built with even, controlled lines and architectural perspectives.

While *The Polar Express* unquestionably ranks as Van Allsburg's most popular book, it is only a part of his contribution to children's books. His first book, *The Garden of Abdul Gasazi* (1979), met with a variety of critical responses. The striking pointillistic graphite drawings were hailed as "intriguing and refreshing." The story, about a young boy pursuing a dog into the topiary gardens of the magician Gasazi, was labeled ominous and disquieting by some. The book won the Boston Globe–Horn Book Award for illustration; it was considered an auspicious beginning.

Van Allsburg has stated that stories begin as fragments of pictures in his mind. "Creating the story comes out of posing questions to myself. I call it the 'what if' and 'what then' approach. What if two bored children discover a board game? What then . . .?" That was the beginning of *Jumanji* (1981). As the protagonists, Judy and Peter, play the game, their house is transformed into a jungle — complete with a hungry lion, marauding monkeys, a menacing python, and an erupting volcano. The children know they must finish the game, and in a chaotic final moment all is set right when one player reaches the

end. Readers are spellbound by this cautionary adventure and delight in the final page when they witness the game being discovered by two more curious children. Masterly use of light and shadow and exaggerated changes of perspective create a bizarre and mythical world that leaves one wondering whether the adventure was real or imagined.

In *The Wreck of the Zephyr* (1983), a story about the disasters wrought by youthful pride, the artist left the dramatic tonal range of grays and black and white — characteristic of previous books — and burst into color. Using pastels, he created vibrant, luminous landscapes. The sharp delineation of figures and objects found in earlier work is more diffused here, imbuing the illustrations with a mysterious light.

This softening of line is carried into *The Mysteries of Harris Burdick* (1984), where richly shaded charcoal drawings intrigue and tantalize the imagination. The book is composed of fourteen illustrations, labeled with captions. Pictures range from whimsical to frightening, and are linked by unexplained elements or the supernatural. The book's enigmatic premise and the exquisite drawings, which speak eloquently without text, represent qualities that have become hallmarks of Van Allsburg's work.

Magic and the supernatural in *The Widow's Broom* (1993) are tempered by the practical, kindly nature of the widow, who assists a witch and is given her broom. Good versus evil is the theme, but the story bubbles with humor and affection when the protective magic broom and the widow become fast friends.

Van Allsburg's artistic style is often described as surrealistic fantasy. Van Allsburg has stated that he "is intrigued by a setting of a normal, everyday reality, where something strange or puzzling happens"; he also has enjoyed "creating impossible worlds." So it is not surprising that visual illusions, created by the dramatic use of scale and perspective, are a common thread running through his books. Also characteristic of Van Allsburg's illustrations are forms and figures that — to varying degrees — appear sculptured and frozen in time. But the breadth and sophistication in his style also allow for fluid, subtle nuances in human figures and detailed expressions, which reflect deeper psychological interpretations of character.

Whether executed in black and white or in color, Van Allsburg's illustrations never fail to fascinate the intellect, pique the senses, and emphasize the power of imagination. S.L.

Voices of the Creators

❧ Chris Van Allsburg

Over the years that have passed since my first book was published, a question I've been asked often is "Where do your ideas come from?" I've given a variety of answers to this question, such as "I steal them from the neighborhood kids" or "They are beamed to me from outer space."

It's not really my intention to be rude or smart-alecky. The fact is, I don't know where my ideas come from. Each story I've written starts out as a vague idea that seems to be going nowhere, then suddenly materializes as a completed concept. It almost seems like a discovery, as if the story were always there. The few elements I start out with are actually clues. If I figure out what they mean, I can discover the story that's waiting.

When I began thinking about what became *The Polar Express,* I had a single image in mind: a young boy sees a train standing still in front of his house one night. The boy and I took a few different trips on the train, but we did not, in a figurative sense, go anywhere. Then I headed north, and I got the feeling that this time I'd picked the right direction, because the train kept rolling all the way to the North Pole. At that point the story seemed literally to present itself. Who lives at the North Pole? Santa. When would the perfect time for a visit be? Christmas Eve. What happens on Christmas Eve at the North Pole? Undoubtedly, a ceremony of some kind, a ceremony requiring a child, delivered by a train that would have to be named the *Polar Express.*

These stray elements are, of course, merely events. A good story uses the description of events to reveal some kind of moral or psychological premise. I am not aware, as I develop a story, what the premise is. When I started the book, I thought I was writing about a train trip, but the story was actually about faith and the desire to believe in something. Creating books is an intriguing process. I know if I'd set out with the goal of writing a book about faith, I'd still be holding a pencil over a blank sheet of paper.

Santa Claus is our culture's only mythic figure truly believed in by a large percentage of the population. Most of the true believers are under eight years old, and that's a pity. The rationality we all embrace as adults makes believing in the fantastic difficult, if not impossible. Lucky are the children who know there is a jolly fat man in a red suit who pilots a flying sleigh. We should envy them. And we should envy the people who are so certain Martians will land in their back yard that they keep a loaded Polaroid camera by the back door. The inclination to believe in the fantastic may strike some as a failure in logic, but it's really a gift. A world that might have Bigfoot and the Loch Ness monster is clearly superior to one that does not.

The application of logical or analytical thought may be the enemy of belief in the fantastic, but it is not, for me, a liability in its illustration. When I conceived of the North Pole in the book, it was logic that insisted it be a vast collection of factories. I don't see this as a whim of mine or even as an act of imagination. How could it look any other way, given the volume of toys produced there every year?

I do not find that illustrating a story has the same quality of discovery as writing it. As I consider a story, I see it quite clearly. Illustrating is simply a matter of drawing something I've already experienced in my mind's eye. Because I see the story unfold as if it were on film, the challenge is deciding precisely which moment should be illustrated and from what point of view.

A fantasy of mine is a miraculous machine, a machine that could be hooked up to my brain and instantly produce finished art from the images in my mind. Conceiving something is only part of the creative process. Giving life to the conception is the other half. The struggle to master a medium, whether it's words, notes, paint, or marble, is the heroic part of making art. ❧

van Loon, Hendrik Willem

American writer and illustrator, 1882–1944. Born and raised in the Netherlands, Hendrik Willem van Loon immigrated to the United States in 1902. After graduating from Cornell University in 1905, he began his career as a journalist in Washington and later continued this profession in Russia. In 1911 he earned a doctorate in history from the University of Munich. Upon his return to the United States he taught at various colleges, continued his journalistic activity, and wrote books that received little attention.

In 1919 publisher Horace Liveright asked van Loon to write a series of eight history books for children. The first, *Ancient Man,* was published in 1920. Its success and the success of H. G. Wells's two-volume *Outline of History* (1920) gave Liveright the notion to have van Loon combine the ideas for the series into a single volume of history for children. The result, *The Story of Mankind* (1921), received fine reviews, sold well, and brought van Loon his first real measure of literary fame. In 1922 the book was the first recipient of the John Newbery Medal, given by the American Library Association for the most distinguished contribution to American children's literature. Van Loon's apparent delight in telling history, his exceptional ability to speak directly to his readers without condescension, and his lively storytelling style were all factors that made the book of interest to adults as well as to his intended child audience. Van Loon illustrated the book profusely, including a pictorial history at its end. For many years the book continued to sell well, and it was translated into several languages.

The Story of Mankind was not universally accepted, however, and several libraries chose not to purchase it, apparently because of van Loon's discussion of evolution. Today the book is seldom read and is subject to criticism because of racial and cultural slurs and because parts contain outdated information or interpretation despite van Loon's and later various publishers' updates to add later events. Despite these problems, with this book van Loon set a standard of what good INFORMATION BOOKS can do — engage the reader and impart their content in a lively fashion.

Following the success of *The Story of Mankind,* van Loon gave up teaching and turned his attention more fully to writing and illustrating. Among his other books for young readers are *The Story of the Bible* (1923), *Van Loon's Geography* (1932), several BIOGRAPHIES, and a few PICTURE BOOKS. In addition van Loon worked on three song books for children with Grace Castagnetta and illustrated other authors' books, such as Lucy Sprague Mitchell's *Here and Now Story Book* (1936). Besides the books he wrote for children, van Loon wrote many books for adults in the areas of history, the arts, biography, and autobiography. He also wrote magazine and newspaper articles, was associate editor of the Baltimore *Sun* in 1923–24, and was a prolific letter writer. In need of intellectual stimulation and change, van Loon moved often and sought out interesting people, but it is said he preferred to be the center of attention. He continued to lecture, often using the dramatic style that had engaged his college students. He also did radio commentary on arts and news events and during World War II broadcast to the Netherlands as part of the war effort.

In 1944 van Loon died of heart failure. Despite his success in several fields, it is *The Story of Mankind* that remains his best-known and most important contribution. B.J.P.

Viorst, Judith

American author and poet, b. 1931. Judith Viorst became well known first through her column in *Redbook,* which was witty, stylish, and self-deprecating. Her strong family orientation emerged in that forum and gracefully led her into writing children's books. Her books could win awards for title length alone: witness *My Mama Says There Aren't Any Zombies, Ghosts, Vampires, Creatures, Demons, Monsters, Fiends, Goblins, or Things* (1973). In this case her collaboration with illustrator Kay Chorao is a marriage of one clean, direct style with another, no excess baggage in either one. In *Alexander and the Terrible, Horrible, No Good, Very Bad Day* (1972), Viorst teamed with illustrator Ray Cruz in an effective partnership that carries poor Alex through a day of being ignored, harassed by his peers, and harshly judged.

Viorst always knew she would be a writer and has emphasized that her family provided inspiration and encouragement for her efforts. Born in Newark, she married political writer Milton Viorst in 1960. Both write at home, and Judith Viorst has said her husband encourages her efforts and provides constructive criticism. Viorst's writing began with odes to dead parents (who were still alive and annoyed, she has said), but it is Viorst's children whom she is writing about and writing for, even down to using their real names. She has three sons, Anthony, Nicholas, and Alexander, now grown, who have given her material for her work. She has said she wrote *I'll Fix Anthony* (1969) to reflect how her oldest son used to torment his brother Nick.

The Tenth Good Thing About Barney (1971) has become a classic in helping children deal with grief. In this book, the children in the family try to find positive things about their cat who has just died, from his value as a playmate to his worth as garden compost. *The Good-bye Book* (1988) is about a young boy who tries everything to talk his parents out of going out that evening — whining, threatening, begging — while they calmly get dressed through all of it. When the unfamiliar baby sitter arrives, the boy is pleasantly surprised to find a friendly teenage boy who may not be so bad after all.

Viorst's work is valued for her sensitivity to children and her slightly irreverent sense of humor, which can be appreciated by readers of any age. A.C.

Voigt, Cynthia

American author, b. 1942. In just over two decades — since 1981, when her first book, *Homecoming*, was published — this prolific writer has produced more than twenty books in a wide range of genres. Best known for her Crisfield novels — seven books set in a small town on Maryland's Eastern Shore that center around the Tillerman family and their friends — she has also written, among others, a gothic MYSTERY, *The Callendar Papers,* for which she won the 1984 Edgar Allan Poe Award for Best Juvenile Mystery; a medieval FANTASY, *Jackaroo* (1985), featuring a strong, swashbuckling heroine, and the sequels, *On Fortune's Wheel* (1990), *The Wings of a Falcon* (1993), and *Elske* (2000); a PICTURE BOOK, *Stories About Rosie* (1986); and several YOUNG ADULT NOVELS, including *Izzy, Willy-Nilly* (1986), about a "nice" teenager who loses a leg in an accident and must face her disability's effect on her life, and *When She Hollers* (1994), an intense novel about a girl's desperate attempt to put an end to her stepfather's sexual abuse.

Voigt's books are noted for their vivid descriptions, strong sense of place, memorable characters, and distinctive rhythm in both language and plot. A unique stylist, Voigt has often employed unorthodox punctuation or sentence structure to establish character or mood. Her settings — whether the real world of the Chesapeake Bay in the Crisfield novels or the imaginary feudal world of *Jackaroo* — are fully realized and convincing.

Born in Boston, Voigt decided in ninth grade that she wanted to become a writer. Following a long family tradition, her parents sent her to boarding school, Dana Hall in Wellesley, Massachusetts, an experience that Voigt says encouraged her independence. She attended Smith College in Northampton, graduating in 1963. After working for a time in New York City for a large advertising agency and earning her teaching accreditation at St. Michael's College (now the College of Santa Fe), Voigt eventually settled in Annapolis, Maryland, where she taught English for many years at the Key School, a small independent primary and secondary school. There she met Walter Voigt, whom she married in 1974; the Voigts have two children, Jessica and Peter.

It was while teaching fifth-graders at Key that Voigt discovered children's literature: "As a reader, I was delighted and excited. As a writer, it was as if somebody had opened a window for me, to show me a whole new landscape." Her flexible teaching schedule and the relaxed atmosphere of the school — she taught classes carrying her infant son in a Snugli — allowed her space to write.

She began working on *Tell Me If the Lovers Are Losers* (1982), a young adult novel that she has called an attempt to capture the tone and feeling of her years at college. One day while shopping she saw a car full of children left to wait alone in the parking lot. She asked herself what would happen if nobody ever came back for them, and the result was the first of Voigt's Crisfield novels, *Homecoming*. As she has said, "Writers only need to see the edges of a situation to be inspired to make it come alive." In *Homecoming* thirteen-year-old Dicey Tillerman, tough and resourceful, must take charge of her three younger siblings after the children's despairing mother, unable to cope with the overwhelming pressures in her life, abandons them in a shopping-center parking lot in Connecticut. In an odyssey down U.S. Route 1, Dicey leads James, Maybeth, and Sammy to Maryland in the hope of finding a home with their grandmother, whom they have never met. On the journey Dicey must not only struggle with their physical survival but also grapple with moral choices and fight for the Tillermans' survival as a family. *Dicey's Song*, winner of the 1983 Newbery Medal and the sequel to *Homecoming*, follows the Tillerman saga as the children begin tentatively to make a home for themselves with their eccentric Gram. The bonds grow tighter after their momma, who has been in a catatonic state in a Boston hospital, dies, and Dicey must learn how to reach out to people, hold on to those she loves, and let go when necessary. The book is a powerful and moving story of an unusual family.

A Solitary Blue, a 1984 Newbery Honor Book and a companion book to *Dicey's Song*, tells the story of Dicey's classmate and friend Jefferson Greene, who, almost irrevocably wounded by his manipulative mother's abandonment and betrayal, eventually finds himself through music, a new and honest relationship with his father, his

friendship with the Tillermans — and his gift for seeing the truth. Other Crisfield novels include *The Runner* (1985), which, centering on seventeen-year-old Bullet, Dicey's uncle, details the grim disintegration of the previous generation of the Tillerman family, and *Seventeen Against the Dealer* (1989), the final book about the Tillermans, in which Dicey's obsession with her long-dreamed-of boat-building business almost causes her to lose everything of importance to her. As the *Horn Book Magazine* said of *The Runner*, the book is "about connections — severed, denied, sustained, treasured," and indeed this human and deeply resonant theme is at the core of the entire Tillerman family saga. In addition, the books all reflect Voigt's love of music, the Eastern Shore landscape, and the waters of the Chesapeake Bay.

After many years of living in Maryland, Voigt and her family now make their home in Maine. Voigt has said that she has always considered herself a New Englander, and "real New Englanders live in Maine," which is the setting for *Tree by Leaf* (1988), a mystical novel exploring a twelve-year-old girl's communication with an omnipotent being, and *The Vandemark Mummy* (1991), an unusual — but accessible — mystery featuring Egyptian antiquities and classical languages.

In the late 1990s Voight began a series of novels featuring scheming classmates Mikey and Margalo. *Bad Girls* (1996) takes place over the course of fifth grade; *Bad, Badder, Baddest* (1997), in sixth; and *It's Not Easy Being Bad* (2001), in seventh. The books are unusual in their sympathetic portrayal of the trouble-making girls and in their treatment of school less as a place to learn than as backdrop for a series of power struggles.

In addition to her Newbery Awards, Voigt is the recipient of the 1989 ALAN Award, given by the Assembly on Literature for Adolescents by the National Council of Teachers of English, and of the 1995 Margaret A. Edwards Award in recognition of her outstanding contribution to literature for young adults. Voigt continues to challenge herself and her readers, breaking new ground with distinctive, original books. M.P.

Waber, Bernard

American author and illustrator, b. 1924. The best known of Bernard Waber's characters, Lyle, the lovable anthropomorphic crocodile, has delighted and won the hearts of readers since appearing in 1962 in *The House on East 88th Street.* The cartoon reptile has shared his madcap antics in a half-dozen PICTURE BOOKS, benefiting from Waber's adroit ability to blend fantasy and reality in credible and reasonable stories always beset with conflicts that parallel those of humans. Armed with a clear understanding of the anxieties, taunts, and humor that go hand in hand with childhood, Waber provides the readers of his more than twenty-four books with a mirror of their childhood experiences. From Arthur the anteater, to Legs the octopus, to a dog named Bernard, his protagonists lightheartedly cope with situations familiar to us all.

Waber, born in Philadelphia to immigrant parents, had a transient childhood. The failure of family businesses uprooted the Wabers frequently during the Depression, and they often moved just ahead of the bill collectors. With each move, young Bernard had two priorities — finding the neighborhood library and finding a movie theater — both significant elements in his survival kit. The youngest of four children, he was a constant recipient of hand-me-downs, the best being the books his siblings had read and loved. For Waber, the key to getting hooked on a book is its physical appearance and the opening paragraph. In his works, both are distinctive. His readers quickly turn the opening pages to discover who was making the "swish, swash, splash, swoosh" on East 88th Street and to discover Ira's conflict in *Ira Sleeps Over* (1972). In appealing to youngsters, Waber deliberately has made his books colorful and easily manipulated by small hands.

Waber's first job enhanced his ability to devise a plausible plot. Working in a movie theater after school at age eight stretched his imagination. His ushering duties allowed him only a glimpse at the final ten minutes of the big screen, so he began inventing plots: having seen only endings, he reconstructed the beginnings and the middles. This cinema background continues to help him create plots for young readers.

While his childhood drawings — copies of film star photos — didn't lead him directly to an art career, a tour of duty during World War II gave him a change of scenery and time to reflect on his future. He reconsidered his original plan of a career in finance, and when he returned from the service, he enrolled at the Philadelphia College of Art.

Illustration by Bernard Waber from his book *Lyle, Lyle, Crocodile* (1965).

With a degree in commercial art and newly married, he headed to New York City for a job in the promotions department of Condé Nast, publisher of several fashion magazines, where artists worked quickly to achieve a fresh and spontaneous effect. A whimsical style of drawing, developed while working for the fashion magazines, became embedded in his art.

Waber has claimed that a wastebasket became a necessity. He draws quickly and discards the "completed" product several times. His main characters, rendered in strong lines, appear within an environment resplendent with background details. Subtle watercolors, enhanced family portraits, patterned curtains, and significant details have become Waber's trademark in the homes into which he has invited his readers. His own home has become a memorial to the Primms and Lyle, a museum of crocodilia laden with artifacts sent by his readers and friends.

While Waber may not have been seeking a career creating children's books, several art directors who saw his portfolio told him his drawings were perfect for children's books. His own love of reading aloud to his three children encouraged him further, and his career was launched. *Lorenzo* (1961), his first book, was published after multiple rejections.

For over forty years, Waber has continued his anthropomorphic adventures. From Lyle's zoo escape to the relationship between an anteater and his mother, readers have been able to suspend their disbelief and casually accept the existence of his characters' situations. M.F.S.

Ward, Lynd

American graphic artist, illustrator, and author, 1905–1985. Lynd Kendall Ward was born in Chicago, son of Harry F. and Daisy Kendall Ward. Educated at Teachers College, Columbia University, he received his B.S. in 1926 with a major in fine arts. While in college Ward met May McNeer, a writer, and they married during graduation week. The Wards traveled to Germany where Lynd studied at the National Academy of Graphic Arts in Leipzig (1926–1927). Returning to the States, Lynd turned his talents to graphic arts and illustration while May McNeer embarked on her career as a children's author. They took great pleasure in working together. Ward illustrated several children's books written by his wife.

Childhood experiences influenced Lynd Ward's life and work. Lynd's father was a Methodist minister whose first ministry included Chicago's "back of the yards" neighborhood, its abject poverty, and the legendary Jane Addams. His family's lasting struggle to better the lot of abandoned people dominated Ward's conscience and his spirit. The code of conduct for children of a Methodist minister did not permit reading funny papers on Sunday. In this "extremity" young Lynd turned to books. A volume of Bible stories with little text but absorbing pictures became his favorite. His addiction had begun. Throughout Lynd's growing years the family spent summers in a log cabin on Lonely Lake in the Canadian wilderness. These summers nurtured his enduring respect and love for nature. His mature work reflects this childhood world.

Ward's career began in 1929 with his first book, *God's Man: A Novel in Woodcuts*. Five more books, engravings without words, established his reputation as a wood engraver. Not wishing to be relegated to one medium, Ward experimented with a variety of techniques for book illustration. He worked in watercolor, oil, lithography, in full color, and in black and white. His artistic versatility and his interest in children's books deepened as his career in illustration flourished.

An amazing collection of illustrations now poured from this inspired artist. His prodigious body of work includes more than two hundred books for children and adults. There is depth and variety of subject and style. Adult classics and scholarly editions stand beside children's fiction, BIOGRAPHY, and PICTURE BOOKS. Some enduring favorites are *The Biggest Bear* (1952), winner of the 1953 Caldecott Medal, the beloved tale of Johnny and his bear in which both story and cub grow dramatically through the humor and pathos of the illustrations; *The Silver Pony* (1973), a powerful wordless FANTASY of a boy and his magical pony, which won the Lewis Carroll Shelf Award and the Boston Globe–Horn Book Honor Award; *America's Ethan Allen* (1949), written by Stuart Holbrook and a 1950 Caldecott Honor Book; *The Cat Who Went to Heaven* (1930), written by Elizabeth Coatsworth and winner of the 1931 Newbery Medal; *Johnny Tremain* (1943), written by ESTHER FORBES and winner of the 1944 Newbery Medal; and *The Little Red Lighthouse and the Great Grey Bridge* (1942), written by Hildegarde Swift, a gentle story enlivened by Ward's winsome pictures. Among the many biographies written by his wife that Ward illustrated were *America's Abraham Lincoln* (1957) and *America's Mark Twain* (1962).

During his lifetime Ward was widely recognized for his distinguished contribution to children's literature. He clearly relished his life work as artist and illustrator. He believed that children's books offered great opportunities for "the best that artists can produce." In his Caldecott acceptance speech Ward opined that, more than any other artist he knew and "without punning," his life had been an open book, for "the things that I have learned are all there on the pages of the books on which I have worked." P.W.

Watson, Wendy

American author and illustrator, b. 1942. Wendy Watson was born in New Jersey but grew up in Putney, Vermont. Her cheerful, homey illustrations reflect this rural upbringing.

Watson attended Bryn Mawr College and studied drawing and painting at the National Academy of Design. After working as a book designer, she began illustrating children's books. She began by collaborating with her sister Clyde Watson, and they received much attention for their National Book Award nominee, *Father Fox's Pennyrhymes* (1971). This collection of rhymes, which were originally songs written by Clyde, are illustrated by Wendy with detailed, cartoonlike panels. The humorous, childlike verses are American Mother Goose rhymes, full of references to ginger beer, country fairs, and other bits of Americana. The pen-and-ink and watercolor illustrations of a large family of foxes depict the changing seasons of rural New England life and the chaos and warmth of family life.

Clyde and Wendy Watson followed this success with other collaborations, including the story of *Tom Fox and the Apple Pie* (1972) and another book of verse, *Catch Me and Kiss Me and Say It Again* (1978), both of which reflect the Watsons' love of family and an appreciation for the humor and details of childhood. The poems can be instantly memorized, and each is paired with a simple scene picturing toddlers throughout the day.

In addition to illustrating the work of others, Wendy Watson has written and illustrated her own PICTURE BOOKS and become recognized for her unpretentious stories and gentle humor. She created an inviting setting for *Tales for a Winter's Eve* (1988) in which Freddie Fox hurts a paw while skiing, and family and friends tell stories around the fire to ease his discomfort. Watson has brought to her children's books a heritage of folklore and an appreciation for old-fashioned pursuits.

Characters, as likely to be foxes as humans, are often dressed in overalls and sit around a hearth or collect sap for maple syrup. Children pinch their fingers while cracking nuts and tease each other with childlike insults.

In many of her illustrations, Watson has used cartoonlike balloons for her characters' speech, and she has encouraged her readers to pore over her illustrations by filling them with details not told in the text. Her honest, often wise stories and detailed country illustrations are full of joy and life. M.V.K.

Wells, Rosemary

American illustrator and author, b. 1943. Although best known for her PICTURE BOOKS about the inimitable rabbit Max and his older sister, Ruby, Rosemary Wells is a versatile storyteller with more than sixty books to her name, including ANIMAL STORIES, novels, BIOGRAPHIES, and retellings. Also a gifted illustrator, Wells began her career as an artist at the Museum School in Boston. There she was derided as no more than an illustrator, and she decided to leave school.

She worked first as an editor at Allyn and Bacon and later as an art designer at Macmillan in New York, where she presented the editor-in-chief with illustrations for a Gilbert and Sullivan song. This book became her first published work, *A Song to Sing, O!* (1968), and Wells has produced high-quality, award-winning books ever since.

From the beginning, her books have been lauded for their strong sense of humor and realism. Even when writing about mice or rabbits in human clothing, Wells can create very realistic interactions among siblings, parents, or neighbors. *Benjamin and Tulip* (1973) is a physically small book that tackles a large topic: bullies. Tulip beats up Benjamin each time he passes her. The two raccoons seem caught in their respective roles until Benjamin accidentally lands on Tulip when the two fall out of a tree. Benjamin, surprised into action, courageously confronts Tulip, and the two end up amiably sharing a squashed watermelon. Told with very few remarkably expressive words, the book succeeds through Wells's direct, funny approach to a perennial childhood problem. Tulip and Benjamin do not talk out their differences but act them out with watermelon juice dripping and overalls askew.

As with *Benjamin and Tulip,* much of the appeal of the Max books comes from Wells's gently rebellious approach to childhood. Her characters do not conform to adult ideals but rather act as human children. *Max's First Word, Max's New Suit, Max's Ride,* and *Max's Toys* (all 1979) were published simultaneously, the first funny BOARD BOOKS for very young children. Each brief book presents a complete interaction between Max, a toddler bunny, and his older sister, Ruby. (Wells has stated that the books were inspired by her own two daughters.) In each adventure, Ruby hopes to control Max, sure that she knows what is best for him. In *Max's First Word,* for example, Ruby is intent upon teaching Max words beyond "BANG," but Max reveals his strength of character and outsmarts his older sister. The books can be described as elementary concept books; bright art objects in vivid red, blue, and yellow; and early lessons in individuality. Most important, they express humor that is understandable to young children and hilarious to the adults asked to read the books again and again. Wells newly illustrated the Max board books in 1998 with slightly larger, more detailed illustrations. The signature humor and verve remained, and the publisher made both editions available.

In successive adventures, Max and Ruby grow older, and their adventures become more complex. *Max's Chocolate Chicken* (1989) tells of Max and Ruby's Easter egg hunt. In *Bunny Money* and *Bunny Cakes* (both 1997), Max and Ruby prepare for Grandma's birthday, looking for the perfect gift and making just the right cake. In these books the illustrations are created from pen-and-ink and watercolor. Max and Ruby, portrayed as squat, stylized rabbits, are sharply outlined in black. Wells used bright watercolors to fill in background, clothing, and setting. She developed character through minute changes in expression. Max's eyes and sly smile clearly express his feelings and motives.

Wells's interest in comic theater is evident in *Hazel's Amazing Mother* (1985), the story of a small badger who loses her way and is the victim of an attack by bullies. Hazel is saved by her mother, who literally flies to her rescue, blown by the wind and the power of love. This emotionally satisfying FANTASY was named a New York Times Best Illustrated Book of 1985. *Shy Charles* (1988), the tale of a shy mouse who eludes his parents' attempts to socialize him but does overcome his shyness in a crisis, won the Boston Globe–Horn Book Award. The trilogy *Voyage to the Bunny Planet* (1992) spins out fantasies in which small rabbits spend peaceful days filled with attention from parents and delicious food. In a three-book series, Edward, a young, timorous bear, is simply not ready for the challenges of school, a sleep-over, and a pool party in *Edward Unready for School, Edward's Overwhelming Overnight,* and *Edward in Deep Water* (all 1995). Wells created a character that struggles with being different in another way in *Yoko* (1998). Yoko, a Japanese American child depicted as a cat in Wells's characteristic style, is teased for bringing sushi to school for lunch until her wise teacher comes up with a satisfying resolution.

Wells's animated, often-humorous illustrations of animal children are ideal in her collaboration with folklorist IONA OPIE. *My Very First Mother Goose* (1996) and *Here Comes Mother Goose* (1999) present familiar and less well known nursery rhymes in a large format to be shared with children of all ages.

In contrast to her readily recognizable art, Wells has employed a spectrum of different styles as a writer. Many of her picture books are written in a spare, almost laconic style, while others include rich details and lyrical prose. *Waiting for the Evening Star* (1993), illustrated by SUSAN JEFFERS, is a quiet, historical picture book set on a Vermont farm in the early twentieth century. Wells is equally adept in writing biography. Mary Breckenridge, the extraordinary woman who started the Frontier Nursing Service in the Appalachian Kentucky, is deftly presented in *Mary On Horseback* (1999), with illustrations by Peter McCarty. *Tallchief: America's Prima Ballerina* (1999) is a powerful, well-crafted examination of the early life of the gifted musician and dancer, which Wells coauthored with Maria Tallchief herself; illustrations by Gary Kelly enhance the flow of the book.

Wells has also written YOUNG ADULT NOVELS, characterized by interwoven stories and faithful reproduction of the emotions of and interactions between adolescents. *The Fog Comes on Little Pig Feet* (1972), Wells's first novel, concerns a disaffected college dropout, a character based loosely on Wells herself. *The Man in the Woods* (1984) and *Through the Hidden Door* (1987) are both MYSTERIES peopled with highly realistic characters who struggle with ethical dilemmas. All in all, this highly skilled author and illustra-

tor has fashioned a fictional world in which both humor and individuality have saving powers.

M.V.K./M.B.S.

Voices of the Creators

🌿 Rosemary Wells

Many of the stories in my books come from our two children, Victoria and Beezoo. Ruby and Max are Victoria and Beezoo. They appeared on my drawing board in the summer of 1977. Victoria was then five and Beezoo nine months. Victoria had taken it upon herself to teach her baby sister about the world and dragged her, like a sack of flour, because she was too heavy to really carry, from object to object, shouting, "Table, Beezoo! say table, TA-BLE!" Beezoo did not cooperate at all and was always off in a world of her own.

Victoria tried to teach Beezoo how to get dressed — another complete failure, as Beezoo preferred to be undressed at all times. Victoria attempted to instruct vocabularyless Beezoo to share and not to take toys that didn't belong to her. This was like talking to the wind. Victoria took pride in wheeling Beezoo's stroller along the boardwalk. Beezoo had to be harnessed into it, with the zipper put on backward and pinned in four places, or she would immediately escape and crawl like a racing crab right into the ocean or the traffic or wherever danger lay.

These simple incidents from childhood are universal. The dynamics between older and younger sibling are also common to all families. What is funny is not the events, but Victoria's dogged insistence on leading Beezoo in the paths of righteousness and Beezoo's complete insouciance in the face of slightly skewed authority.

In part I wrote the BOARD BOOKS because there were no funny books around for very young children. But mostly I wrote them because the characters materialized on paper in front of me, under my hand, so to speak. The characters were alive; the stories were going on all around me. Other books come from other episodes in my life, in the children's lives. Victoria, in first grade, came home the day of the Christmas concert in bitter tears. She had selected a blouse and kilt to wear that morning. One of her classmates, Audrey, had told her she was supposed to wear a dress, not an everyday kilt. We patched up the day with conventional wisdom, but I used Audrey's remark as the basis for *Timothy Goes to School.*

Benjamin and Tulip was written before we had any children. It is partly a story of my best friend and me, wheeling our bicycles up a steep hill every day after school and being regularly ambushed by the boys who lived at the top of the hill. I changed the lead bully boy into Patty Gerardi, queen of the second grade, who was heard to say only two things in her career: "I'm captain," and "I'm gonna beat you up." I changed a boy to a girl here because a female bully was much funnier.

Once the story is there, the drawings just appear. I feel the emotion I want to show; then I let it run down my arm from my face, and it goes out the pencil. My drawings look as if they are done quickly. They are not. First they are sketched in light pencil, then nearly rubbed out, then drawn again in heavier pencil. What appears to be a confident, thick ink line is really a series of layers of tiny ink lines intensifying all day until the drawings are ready for color.

Most of my books use animals rather than children as characters. I draw animals more easily and amusingly than I do children. Animals are broader in range — age, race, time, and place — than children are. They also can do things in pictures that children cannot. All of my stories are written with deeply felt emotional content. Animals express this best most of the time for the same reason that a harpsichord expresses certain concertos better than an organ does. As I work on a book, I try to keep a few very simple things in mind. In order to stand up to hundreds of readings-aloud, a good PICTURE BOOK must be fresh, intelligent, and succinct. The words must spin out like song lyrics, and like song lyrics there must not be one syllable too many or too few.

We live in a curious time. Our people used to recognize that culture must enlighten as well as entertain. Now culture does one thing only. It sells via entertainment, and in so doing to children, the child's sense of privacy, individuality, and intellect is numbed. There is a vast market basket of merchandise aimed at the twenty-first-century consumer-child. In it I know only one commodity still able to enlighten as well as entertain. It is a children's book.

To hold a cutting edge in this cultural wasteland of products, many of which abet everything from attention deficiency to gang violence, a children's story must have great integrity and staying power. The hand of the artist — a little stained with paint around the fingernails — must be seen. The voice of the writer — passionate and idiosyncratic — must be heard. And whether it is through adventure or humor or pathos, the story and pictures must always touch the heart.

White, E. B.

American essayist, poet, and children's book author, 1899–1985. More than once, Elwyn Brooks White pretended ignorance of literary affairs. In fact, when one critic sent him an exhaustive scholarly exegesis of White's children's classic, *Charlotte's Web* (1952), the wry essayist, poet, and novelist replied, "It's good I did not know what in hell was going on. To have known might well have been catastrophic."

Actually, there can be little doubt about E. B. White's literary sophistication. He wrote virtually all his life, breaking into print for the first time in 1909 with a prize-winning poem in *Woman's Home Companion.* Eleven years later, at the university, White was elected editor of the *Cornell Daily Sun.* Having tried a stint at newspaper reporting and advertising, White, in 1925, submitted some short sketches to the newly founded *New Yorker* magazine. He joined the staff in 1926 and soon wrote for the magazine full-time, turning out countless pithy, ironical articles, squibs, and observations. Although, over the years, White contributed to other magazines as well, his primary allegiance for almost half a century was to the *New Yorker,* on which he left an indelible stamp. Playwright Marc

Connelly observed that it was White's distinctive style that "gave the steel and music to the magazine."

For children, however, White is of interest primarily as the author of three children's novels: *Stuart Little* (1945), *Charlotte's Web,* and *The Trumpet of the Swan* (1970). These do nothing to dispel the notion of White as a consummate stylist whose sentences put him clearly in the literary tradition of Henry David Thoreau and MARK TWAIN, and whose manuscripts testify to the infinite pains he took to research his materials and to hone his text.

As a novelist, White showed himself a deft deviser of plots, a keen observer of character, a virtuoso in the rendering of emotion — whether porcine or human. Few can read *Charlotte's Web* for the first time without shedding a tear at the death of the arachnid heroine. And, indeed, while making a commercial recording of the book, White himself choked as he read those elegiac words about Charlotte — "and no one was with her when she died" — so that the taping session had to be stopped.

But *Charlotte's Web* was not White's debut in the world of children's books. That honor goes to *Stuart Little,* the episodic, picaresque adventure story of a two-inch creature who, in White's words, "looks very much like a mouse," but who "obviously is not a mouse [but rather] a second son."

The story had been brewing with White for years as a disconnected series of bedtime tales for his nieces and nephews by the time it came to Harper. There, shepherded by the distinguished editor Ursula Nordstrom and felicitously illustrated by GARTH WILLIAMS, the book was eventually published — generally to high acclaim, but not without violent objection from the influential Anne Carroll Moore, head of the children's department of the New York Public Library, as well as from a number of librarians who objected to what was perceived as the hero's "monstrous birth."

The adventures of the Lilliputian hero are inherently funny — as he loosens stuck piano keys, fetches a ring from a drain, gets rolled up in a window shade, and sails a toy boat through a storm in Central Park. But quite beyond these surface amusements, the book sounds a resonant note as Stuart undertakes his quest for the beautiful bird, Margalo. And that quest, as White himself noted, "symbolizes the continuing journey that everybody takes — in search of what is perfect and unattainable. This is perhaps too elusive an idea to put into a book for children, but I put it in anyway."

It is, however, White's second book, *Charlotte's Web,* which has drawn the most widespread admiration. Essentially a pastoral comedy in which a little girl, Fern, saves the life of the runty thirteenth pig of a litter, the novel operates on two planes. On the first, we follow life in the barnyard, in which the animals converse with each other and empathically enter into the mercurial emotions of the pig, Wilbur. We meet the eponymous heroine, Charlotte, an articulate sophisticate, a lover of words, who — *by* the word, as it were — saves the life of Wilbur. On the second, we have the story of the little girl, Fern, richly rendered by White, memorably drawn by Garth Williams. It is the poignant story of a girl in one fleeting moment of her life. In the beginning she has an empathy for and understanding of the animals she loves; at the book's end, she has grown into a world of Ferris wheels, of boys — and will be, forever, beyond "childish things."

The book is resonant, lyrical, serious, profound. It is one of the very few books for young children that face, squarely, the subject of death. And above all it is celebratory. White called it "pastoral, seasonal . . . concerned with ordinary people," "a hymn to the barn, an acceptance of dung," a "story of friendship, life, death, salvation."

White's last book for children, *The Trumpet of the Swan,* published almost twenty years after *Charlotte,* is the unlikely tale of Louis, a mute trumpeter swan (named for Louis Armstrong), who compensates for his muteness by becoming a virtuoso player of a real trumpet. Louis is befriended by a young boy, Sam Beaver, a male counterpart to Fern of *Charlotte's Web,* with the significant difference that, at book's end, Sam remains loyal to the bird and, in a manner, keeps the faith.

White wrote the book in old age and under the impression that he was in financial need. As he had done with *Charlotte's Web*, he researched his material thoroughly — making inquiries about everything from the annual migration of trumpeter swans to the workings of the Swan Boats in the Boston Public Garden, and he wrote the text with the same scrupulous attention to detail. Nonetheless, with the striking exception of John Updike, who praised the author's "sense of the precious instinctual heritage represented by wild nature," most critics responded coolly to the implausible swan who flies through the world encumbered with a trumpet and a slate on which to write.

White has a firm place in American letters as a distinguished essayist, a man who expressed his wry view of the world in exquisitely chiseled sentences. Applying that same craft to three books for children, E. B. White has won a place in the hearts of the young forever.   P.F.N.

White, T. H.

British novelist, 1906–1964. Born in Bombay, India, Terence Hanbury White, known to his acquaintances as Tim, suffered an unhappy childhood and, for his entire life, had trouble escaping his deep loneliness. His manipulative mother vied for his undiluted love, and his parents fought bitterly and constantly until their divorce in 1920. The breakup of his family had a profound effect on White, who, from then on, felt a need to excel in all areas of life in order to feel secure. He earned first-class honors at Queens' College, Cambridge, and became head of the English department at Stowe School, but at age thirty he resigned to write full-time.

In 1938, after achieving some prominence as a writer of novels for adults, he published *The Sword in the Stone*, which was later revised and included as the first section of White's classic version of King Arthur's life, *The Once and Future King*, finished twenty years later. Inspired by Malory's *Morte d'Arthur*, *The Once and Future King* brings together the legend, White's vision of an ideal childhood, and his views on human interaction, particularly war.

In *The Sword in the Stone*, made into a motion picture in 1963 by Walt Disney Productions, the young Wart, a fosterling with no notion of his regal birth, receives special tutoring from Merlyn, who transforms him into a fish, a hawk, an ant, a goose, and a badger to teach him lessons about society and life. Without mincing words or leaving out unsavory details, the subsequent books relay the story of King Arthur's reign, Guenevere's devastating affair with Lancelot, Arthur's fatal seduction by his half sister, Morgause, and his relationship with Morgause's children — among them his son. With humor and wit, White delved into motivation and character as he retold the epic story, but threaded throughout is the serious theme of the futility of war. As a young king, Arthur sets out to create a new code of chivalry, in which knights fight for morality and truth rather than individual gain, but age and experience give him an understanding of the waste of war of any kind. White's personal perspective informs Arthur's growth in wisdom, and his own loneliness as a bachelor brings a keen understanding to Arthur's pain at his wife's betrayal. When White wrote *The Book of Merlyn*, which reunites Arthur with his magician teacher after his final defeat, he intended it to be the fifth book in the volume, but after much editing and arguing with his publishers, the piece was instead published posthumously as a separate book in 1972.

Mistress Masham's Repose (1946), White's other novel for children, also was inspired by a classic work of literature. Upon the premise that some of the Lilliputians from Swift's *Gulliver's Travels* ended up in England, White built a charming FANTASY, filled with details about life in miniature. Orphaned Maria finds the tiny community on an abandoned island on her estate and must prevent the Lilliputians' exploitation when their existence is discovered by Maria's evil guardians. The characters are delightfully drawn to illustrate the farce, showing off White's skill in stretching the boundaries of humor and caricature.

White's work received positive critical attention on both sides of the Atlantic. *The Once and Future King* inspired *Camelot,* the acclaimed and much beloved musical in which Julie Andrews and Richard Burton starred. Although disappointed by much in life, T. H. White left a lasting legacy. A.E.D.

Wiese, Kurt

American illustrator and author, 1887–1974. Kurt Wiese, one of the most prolific illustrators known in the field of American children's literature, illustrated over three hundred books during a highly respected career that spanned more than four decades. Best known for having illustrated MARJORIE FLACK's *Story About Ping* (1933) and Claire Huchet Bishop's timeless retelling of a Chinese folktale, *Five Chinese Brothers* (1938), Wiese was a versatile artist who imparted vitality, emotion, and a keen design sense to the variety of media in which he worked.

Published in the late 1920s and early 1930s, Wiese's first books were among the titles that established the genesis of the American PICTURE BOOK. Wiese worked for the three preeminent juvenile book editors of the time, Louise Seaman of Macmillan, May Massee of Doubleday, and Ernestine Evans of Coward-McCann. So productive was he that he had more books than any other artist published in the fall of 1930. Wiese and colleagues WANDA GÁG, Berta and Elmer Hader, and Lois Lenski were some of America's first prominent author-illustrators for children. Their creative talents shifted the focus of picture books from Europe to the United States.

Born and schooled in Germany, Wiese later lived in China for six years, Australia for five

years, and Brazil for four years. In 1927 a well-traveled Wiese arrived in America, looking for work. He soon found employment with *Collier's Weekly* and shortly afterward illustrated one of his first books for Louise Seaman. As one of twelve small picture books that constituted Macmillan's Happy Hour series, Wiese's *Three Little Kittens* (1928) contains innovative book design elements and lively lithographs, which launched his successful career.

In another of his notable picture books, *Liang and Lo* (1930), Wiese made new and exhilarating use of the interplay between two facing pages to picture the story of the young boy Liang and his newfound friend, Lo, who lives on a buffalo's back, and their encounter with a dragon. Knowledgeable in commercial color lithography, Wiese had a direct hand in creating his five-color illustrations for *Liang and Lo*. As a result, he achieved dramatic effects with color, making it serve both his drawings and the book's design.

Wiese's years in China also helped create his illustrations for *The Story About Ping*. Sincere and straightforward, Wiese's memorable pictures are a perfect match for Flack's words, rich with imagery, about the young Chinese duck who lives with his large extended family on a wise-eyed boat on the great Yangtze River. The resplendent lithographs, in predominant hues of yellow and blue, convey a cheerfulness touched by serenity, an appropriate mood that makes Ping's misadventure away from home palatable and universal to very young children. Developmentally significant to American picture books, *The Story About Ping* was one of the earliest collaborative efforts between a well-known writer and an accomplished illustrator. This important change in the making of picture books took hold, flourished, and came to fruition years later during the golden age of children's book publishing.

In spite of some criticism for his stereotypic depiction of the Chinese in *Five Chinese Brothers*, Wiese's choice of the long and narrow horizontal format, his animated two-color drawings of the clever brothers who possess unique magical powers, and the comic-strip feel imparted by the turning of the pages combine to make an exemplary picture book.

Among the several series of children's books Wiese illustrated were the tremendously popular Freddy, the Pig stories, written by WALTER R. BROOKS. Other noteworthy titles in Wiese's vast body of work include two Caldecott Honor Books that he wrote and illustrated, *You Can Write Chinese* (1945) and *Fish in the Air* (1948).

Wiese's global experience gave young American children some of their first glimpses of other cultures and countries in picture book form; his masterful, artistic interpretations of words have enlarged, enriched, and enchanted the children's book world. S.L.S.

Wiesner, David

American author and illustrator, b. 1956. Things in David Wiesner's books tend to "fly": from flying frogs to giant floating vegetables, his amusing inventiveness takes wing.

Born and raised in Bridgewater, New Jersey, Wiesner was known in school as "the kid who could draw." The youngest of five children, Wiesner had an artistic older sister and brother, so art supplies were abundant in the house. Ink bottles, tubes of paint, and boxes of pastels held an exotic appeal for him, and relatives always gave him art-related presents. His fascination with drawing and painting led him to copy all forms of illustration from comic books to reference books. In a history book he discovered dinosaurs, and the hazy but realistic black-and-white renditions, which he believed were actual photographs, became favorite subjects, which he drew over and over.

Wiesner's artistic pursuit led him to the Rhode Island School of Design and a B.F.A. in 1978. His first book contract came a year later, after he made the rounds of publishers. An editor offered him the manuscript for *Honest Andrew* (1980), an otter family story written by Gloria Skurzynski. The books that followed were a variety of fictional stories written by other people: Nancy Luenn's *The Ugly Princess* (1981) and Dennis Haseley's *Kite Flier* (1986). In 1987 Wiesner and his wife, Kim Kahng, retold *The Loathsome Dragon,* which he illustrated with watercolors. A year later he wrote and illustrated *Free Fall* (1988), a Caldecott Honor Book. In *Free Fall* the dream sequences are evoked, as Wiesner has described them, through a series of "metamorphosing landscapes through which the characters walk, float, fly and ride." The wordless adventure allows each reader to interpret the dream individually. In his next three books, Wiesner combined humor and creativeness with a playfulness and a wry use of perspective, which solidified into a detailed, imaginative style of telling stories with pictures. As flying appeared frequently as a motif in these books, Wiesner's illustrative style began to soar. Based on one of Wiesner's childhood experiences, *Hurricane* (1990) relates how two brothers share their fright during the storm and afterward, when they pretend a toppled tree is a jungle, a galleon, and a spaceship. Then came *Tuesday* (1991), in which an eerie flotilla of floating frogs flies through a sleeping town, leaving a lily-pad trail of suspicious doings. The subtleties and delightful humorous details in this PICTURE BOOK garnered the Caldecott Medal in 1992. In *June 29, 1999* (1992) Holly Evans's science project sends seedlings aloft into the ionosphere, creating skies filled with giant vegetables: lima beans loom over Levittown, artichokes advance on Anchorage, and parsnips pass by Providence. In *Sector 7* (1999), a Caldecott Honor Book, a factory in the sky generates whimsically shaped clouds. In Wiesner's most innovative book, *The Three Pigs* (2001), the old story becomes the platform for his homage to classic picture books and his own comical variation, when the pigs decide to walk out of the story. *The Three Pigs* received the Caldecott Medal in 2002.

In his picture books, Wiesner has visually explored the improbable with good humor and lively ingenuity. His hypothetical situations are the perfect beginning for his colorful, wittily depicted stretches of the imagination. J.C.

Wilder, Laura Ingalls

American author, 1867–1957. Laura Ingalls Wilder's Little House books chronicle life in the Midwest from 1870 to 1894. Written in the third person, with Wilder as principal protagonist, the books are rich in the social history that surrounds the effects of the Homestead Act and last phase of American westward expansion. Readers of the Little House books learn the intricacies of frontier house-building, agriculture, home economics, entertainment, schooling, and railroad and town building. In addition to Wilder's vivid descriptions of daily life in the pioneer era, her books recount the necessity of family solidarity versus an uncertain wilderness and the virtues of independent living far removed from government control.

Wilder's career as a children's author started in 1932, when at sixty-five she published her first book, *Little House in the Big Woods*. The book describes the Ingalls family's life in the forest near Pepin, Wisconsin, where the first two children, Mary and Laura, were born. The parents, Charles and Caroline Ingalls, were infected with the "go west" spirit of the post–Civil War period. They took their family to the area near Independence, Kansas, described in *Little House on the Prairie* (1935), but later returned north to Walnut Grove, Minnesota, in *On the Banks of Plum Creek* (1937). Wilder omitted two years from her saga (1876 to 1878) but resumed the story with her family's journey west to Dakota Territory in 1879 in *By the Shores of Silver Lake* (1939). *The Long Winter* (1940) and *Little Town on the Prairie* (1941) document homesteading and the building of the town of De Smet, South Dakota.

While the early books of the Little House series are written for middle-grade children, the later ones show a decidedly more complex plot structure and character development as Laura Ingalls enters young adulthood. The last of the series, *These Happy Golden Years* (1943), relates Laura's teaching career, courtship, and marriage to Almanzo Wilder in 1885. Chronologically, Wilder's second published book was *Farmer Boy* (1933), which is the story of her husband's boyhood near Malone, New York. The Wilder boys, Almanzo and Royal, reappear as homesteaders in the last four books, with Almanzo assuming the male protagonist role, in place of Pa Ingalls.

As farmers, Laura and Almanzo Wilder homesteaded near De Smet from 1885 to 1889. Their hardships with weather, disease, and other disasters make up the plot of *The First Four Years* (1971), published from an unpolished first draft fourteen years after Wilder's death. Its worth is largely informational, and it pales in comparison to the detailed, skillfully told earlier books in the series. The book introduces the only Wilder child to survive to adulthood, Rose (1886–1968). Rose Wilder Lane edited her mother's travel diary of her 1894 journey from South Dakota to Mansfield, Missouri, in *On the Way Home* (1962). The Wilders moved to the Missouri Ozarks, settling on Rocky Ridge Farm, which became the permanent family home. Laura Wilder's activities, in addition to her role as a farm wife, included the management of the Mansfield Farm Loan Association in the 1920s, numerous community betterment projects, and approximately fifteen years (1911–1926) as a country journalist. Wilder's essays, features, poetry, and interviews were printed regularly by the *Missouri Ruralist* and also appeared in *McCall's, Country Gentlemen,* and other regional publications. Some of these contributions are gathered in *A Little House Sampler* (1989).

Rose Wilder left the family farm for a more liberating career in business and journalism. Her influence on her mother's writing is evident in *West from Home* (1974), which consists of letters Wilder sent to her husband while visiting their journalist daughter in San Francisco in 1915. The Wilder-Lane writing collaboration has been examined with use of their manuscripts, letters, and the daughter's diaries.

In addition to her own work as a biographer, short story writer, foreign correspondent, and novelist, Lane successfully managed and promoted her mother's Little House books during the 1930s and 1940s. She alternated between tutor, publicist, intermediate agent, and editor through the twelve-year writing process of the Wilder titles. Wilder was accurate in later describing the books as truthful and autobiographical in content, but her daughter's skilled hand helped greatly in transforming memoir into compelling fiction. Editorial staff at Harper and Brothers found little need for revision on the Wilder manuscripts; essentially, that role was assumed by Lane, *sub rosa*.

The Little House books brought immediate accolades to their author; although none earned Newbery Medals, five were runners-up for that honor. The books enjoyed a grassroots popularity, and, because of their value as Americana, they quickly became entrenched in school curricula, where they show no signs of diminishing popularity. In 1993, a conservative estimate of Little House book printings topped forty million copies. They are also widely translated into foreign languages. Following World War II, the U.S. State Department ordered the translation of Wilder titles into German and Japanese for inclusion in education programs in those countries. The books have remained perennially popular in Japan. Although Wilder's meticulous, descriptive prose style diminishes the need for illustrations, GARTH WILLIAMS's 1953 drawings for the Little House series provide sensitive, graphic, and authentic art to enhance the author's words. His artwork replaced that of Helen Sewell and Mildred Boyle, which had appeared in earlier editions.

In 1954 the American Library Association created the Laura Ingalls Wilder Award, first to honor Wilder, and later to recognize creators of children's books whose cumulative work represents significant contributions to the field. Wilder was widely honored for her work during her lifetime and beyond. Libraries, schools, parks, highways, and streets bear her name. The settings of her books and her former homes are all preserved or memorialized. But Wilder's greatest tribute is the continued reading of her Little House books, which seem to cross all barriers of age, language, or nationality. Her life and writings make her perhaps the quintessential American pioneer. W.A.

Willard, Nancy

American author and poet, b. 1936. A writer of stories for adults as well as young people, Nancy Willard has enjoyed a reputation as an author with versatility, good humor, and, most of all, a gift for storytelling.

Born in Ann Arbor, she holds a B.A. and a Ph.D. from the University of Michigan and an M.A. from Stanford University.

Willard's books often deal with homey topics: family, food, the hearth. Her touch is loving and gentle, but she does not gloss over the anxieties of childhood or the essential sadness that is part of growing up. She is not limited, however, to the close to home, as demonstrated by her fascination with FANTASY and British poet William Blake, affinities she developed in childhood. Willard received the Newbery Medal for *A Visit to William Blake's Inn: Poems for Innocent and Experienced Travelers* (1981), a collection of poems illustrated by ALICE and MARTIN PROVENSEN, which exhibits Willard's talent for bringing the literary world to children in POETRY form. Her fantasy trilogy — *Sailing to Cythera and Other Anatole Stories* (1979), *The Island of the Grass King* (1979), and *Uncle Terrible: More Adventures of Anatole* (1982) — contains some of her best writing.

Willard's PICTURE BOOKS and illustrated books vary in look, as she has collaborated with different artists: Ilse Plume in *Night Story* (1986), TOMIE DEPAOLA in *Simple Pictures Are Best* (1977), David McPhail in *The Nightgown of the Sullen Moon* (1983), and Jane Dyer in *Cracked Corn and Snow Ice Cream: A Family Almanac* (1997). Angels often figure into the Willard formula, never more so than in *The High Rise Glorious Skittle Skat Roarious Sky Pie Angel Food*

Cake (1990), illustrated by Richard Jesse Watson, an enchanting story of a nine-year-old who wants Mom to have a heavenly birthday present.

Willard grew up in Michigan and spent summers at a cottage on a lake, the setting of her first book, *Sailing to Cythera,* sketching and making up stories with her sister. Encouraged by her parents to write and draw, Willard and her sister put out a little newspaper. To collect news, they visited neighbors, hoping for a newsworthy bit of gossip.

Willard is married to photographer Eric Lindbloom, and they have one son, James. A lecturer at Vassar, she lives in Poughkeepsie, New York. A.C.

Williams, Garth

American illustrator and author, 1912–1996. Garth Williams, best known as the illustrator of LAURA INGALLS WILDER's Little House books and E. B. WHITE's *Stuart Little* (1945) and *Charlotte's Web* (1952), illustrated more than eighty books and wrote seven PICTURE BOOKS, including *The Rabbit's Wedding* (1958), unintentionally controversial because of its depiction of the wedding of a black rabbit and a white rabbit.

Williams was born in New York City, but his family soon moved to a farm in New Jersey; his earliest memories of this time include riding with the farmer on his tractor. From there the family moved to Ontario and, in 1922, to England. His father was a cartoonist and his mother a landscape painter, and Williams said, "Everybody in my house was either painting or drawing, so I thought there was nothing else to do in life but make pictures." He attended the Westminster School of Art and went on to win a painting scholarship to the Royal College of Art; there he discovered sculpture. Williams's affinity for weight and texture in his illustrations seems to come from his sculpting. He applied for and received the British Prix de Rome, allowing him to study art in Italy, France, and Germany, where he met and married the first of his four wives. While driving an ambulance during World War II, he was wounded in the spine and went to the United States, where he continued to work for the war effort. In 1943 he began looking for work as an illustrator and cartoonist and was eventually accepted by the *New Yorker*. His first children's book illustrations appeared in *Stuart Little* in 1945, followed in 1946 by MARGARET WISE BROWN's *Little Fur Family,* which was bound in rabbit fur. This title began a collaboration with Brown that would eventually include eleven books.

When he worked with pen and ink, Williams combined a classical style of flowing lines and cross-hatching with humorous, loving depictions of his characters, as in the novels he illustrated for White, GEORGE SELDEN, and Margery Sharp. When he used pencil, as in RUSSELL HOBAN's *Bedtime for Frances* (1960) and Wilder's *Little House in the Big Woods* (1932) and the other books in this series, his lines are fewer and softer, yet still recognizable for the caring, understated facial expressions. Williams excelled at textures, particularly animal fur and the tall waving grasses in Wilder's books. When he worked with color, as in his picture books with Brown and JACK PRELUTSKY, he opted for deep colors to add warmth to his lines. About his animal drawings, he said, "I start with the real animal, working over and over until I can get the effect of human qualities and expressions and poses. I redesign animals, as it were."

Williams worked on the Little House books for nearly six years, meeting Wilder and traveling to the locations of all but one of her books. Though he was not the first illustrator for this series, his images quickly became the definitive ones. When he was approached about the job, he was uncertain about his ability to draw people. It is true that the faces and proportions of people in these books sometimes lack consistency, but Williams so closely matched the spirit of each character and setting that any flaws become irrelevant.

Williams's long career allowed him to work with some of the most respected children's authors. He is recognized for his uncanny ability to show realistic animals whose thoughts we can read because of their subtle human qualities, but he should be known equally well for his evocative yet solid settings for both animal fantasies and Wilder's realistic books. L.R.

Williams, Vera B.

American author and illustrator, b. 1927. A striking element in the award-winning books Vera Williams has created is the wealth of strong female characters. An active supporter of both peace and feminist issues, Williams has written about confident girls and women who live amicably with other people and with the environment. Also expressed in her books is the holistic philosophy taught at Black Mountain College in North Carolina, where Williams earned a degree in graphic art. Keenly aware of interdependence, her characters strive together toward goals — as families, neighbors, and friends. Most prominent in her stories, though, is the emphasis on people and simple pleasures rather than on money and material goods.

Williams, who was raised during the Depression, has told of families discovering beauty and joy in the simple things in life. *Three Days on a River in a Red Canoe* (1981), for example, describes a no-frills, but fun-filled, family vacation. When two young cousins are taken on a camping trip by their mothers, both knowledgeable campers and canoeists, they experience the inexpensive but rewarding adventure of the great outdoors. Another low-budget but exciting journey is described in *Stringbean's Trip to the Shining Sea* (1988), a joint effort created by the author-illustrator and her daughter, artist Jennifer Williams. This innovative book is an album of the post cards and pictures young Stringbean sends home while traveling by truck with his older brother from Kansas to the Pacific. The unpretentious descriptions of the trip are down-to-earth and authentically child-like. In *"More More More," Said the Baby: Three Love Stories* (1990), gentle vignettes depict toddlers having fun, not with fancy toys but with family — a father, mother, and grandmother — hugging, playing, and kissing. Exuberance and joy are depicted in this Caldecott Honor Book's lively art that depicts African American, Asian American, and Anglo-American children and adults. In *Amber Was Brave, Essie Was Smart* (2001) Williams told the story of two friends in poems, sketches, and full-color pictures.

The sincere enjoyment of simple things is also evident in the trio of books about Rosa and her mother and grandmother, a close-knit, working-class family. In the first, the Caldecott Honor Book *A Chair for My Mother* (1982), Rosa's mom, a waitress, needs a comfortable chair in which to relax after work, so daughter, mother, and grandmother save coins in a big jar until the long-awaited day when the jar is filled and the three can have the fun of shopping for the perfect chair. In *Something Special for Me* (1983) and *Music, Music for Everyone* (1984), Rosa discovers the pleasures of music. The art in these and Williams's other PICTURE BOOKS is unique and instantly recognizable. Multicultural communities and families people her stories, and spontaneity and energy — family love and deep joy — are all expressed in the brightly colored illustrations. When Williams utilizes borders, they serve as extensions of the story rather than mere decorations. Though her art is reminiscent of children's drawings and the appearance of her books is deceptively simple, together the pictures and stories evoke strong emotions that move both young and old readers. J.M.B.

Voices of the Creators

✿ *Vera B. Williams*

Those fairies that presided at my birth did not bring the gift of security. We had a struggle keeping jobs, family, and places to live. But I was given the promise that life, however rocky, would be an adventure. And just as my parents believed that material goods should be distributed equably, so they also believed in an equable distribution of culture and a chance at creative expression. Bread *and* roses. They found the free places where my sister and I might paint and sculpt, dance, and act. And that was a blessing, for I was a child with a lot to say. When people grew tired of my talking, I drew pictures. But then I had to tell about the pictures. Even with acting and dancing, I couldn't get it all told.

I still can't. Of course all stories aren't equally important to tell. I distinguish between natural and synthetic stories, by which I mean something about the depth from which a story springs. I admit it's a delight to make up stories and pictures, whatever their source. It flexes the muscles of the imagination. But it takes about a year for me to bring a book from its first shadowy glimmerings to a completed work in which each element is rooted in the tale to be told: type (sometimes hand lettering); paper; format; even the flaps and back cover. Naturally, I desire to embark only on projects with "serious consequences." But "serious" most certainly includes the colorful, playful, and humorous.

Take my book *Stringbean's Trip to the Shining Sea*. In it are the post cards and snapshots that Stringbean Coe and his brother Fred send home to their family from the long trip they make one summer in Fred's truck. I did this book with my adult daughter Jennifer Williams as co-illustrator. Despite rough spots, we shared the pleasure of a beguiling, childlike project creating stamps, picture post cards, post card-ese descriptions of places, including a restaurant in a cowboy boot. We could have gone on inventing cards and stamps for years. I had, in fact, no ending for the story for a long time. Yet something of deep importance to me was working its way.

Tied with a string in my drawer was a collection of post cards. I had sent them to my mother as I traveled across Canada in my late forties to make a canoe voyage down the Yukon River. She too had traveled through the West when she was young. I knew the snapshots of her trip well, and I wanted to provide her with a vicarious trip for her late years. My canoe trip led to my book *Three Days on a River in a Red Canoe*. But more important, it was a prelude to the main adventure of my fifties and sixties: creating PICTURE BOOKS. I well remember a day on the trip when I turned down a hike to stay in camp and wash up. But my real desire was to be left alone with myself as storyteller. I spent my time sketching equipment, making a storyboard.

I had had many adventures: parenthood, the organizing of a cooperative community and experimental school, arrests in antinuclear demonstrations, jobs as cook, baker, and teacher. I had been caught up in nature study, canoeing, and hiking — and love. But the time had come to fill that other promise of my childhood, to somehow tell my stories.

My mother died when I was on the threshold of this career. I had told her I was on my way to being an author-illustrator. She had said, "Hurry up! I'm not going to live much longer." After she died, I retrieved the post cards I had sent her. They became, in time, the mysterious engine of *Stringbean's Trip to the Shining Sea*. My mother used to call me Stringbean back when I was a skinny kid, driving her crazy with my need to report on everything. In the book, Stringbean finally gets to "tell" until he is content with it. He has had his say, but still he longs for his parents to hang on to his every word. And he looks forward to all those marvelous things he might yet do and see. For him it is a true trip to his own shining sea.

For me, its author and main character, it became a tightly condensed autobiography in which the enthusiasms of my or my daughter's life appear on the different cards — a great device for an autobiographical novel in forty-eight pages! I had been helped in this by a study of the post card tradition and its history. I saw that geography, history, personal events, and entertainment combined tidily on those little cards. I developed a friendly regard for the vanished writers and readers of the cards I read. Then, as I wrote my own cards, I began to feel that same affectionate bond with all the unknown readers-to-be of my and Jennifer's made-up cards. Now when I sign the book for people, I sometimes write, "Have your own wonderful trip to the shining sea." ✒

Wisniewski, David

American author and illustrator, b. 1953. Just when he was about to change careers, David Wisniewski received the phone call telling him that *Golem* (1996) had been awarded the Caldecott Medal. *Golem*, based on Jewish legend, is set in sixteenth-century Prague, where a rabbi brings to life a giant made of clay to defeat those who persecute the Jews. The dark, mysterious tale is made even more mesmerizing by the illustrator's signature style: cut-paper illustration. For this powerful tale, the artist used dark hues and powerful forms combined with precisely rendered detail. The author's note demonstrates not only Wisniewski's research but also his respect for the subject and the reader, also apparent in his Caldecott Medal acceptance speech: "Though demanding, making words and pictures fit and flow in narrative harmony is enormously satisfying. Few other professions are as metaphysical [as writing and illustrating]: the thoughts and images of one mind are transformed into a solid object which, when opened, conveys them to thousands of other minds. What a privilege . . . opportunity . . . responsibility!"

Wisniewski's early life and experiences well prepared him for a distinguished career as a writer and illustrator of children's books. The son of an American father serving in the U.S. Air Force, Wisniewski was born in England. The family traveled frequently, variously stationed in the United States, England, and Germany. Later, while studying drama at the University of Maryland, he met a clown from the Ringling Clown College, to which he applied and was accepted. Wisniewski later worked as a clown for Ringling Brothers Circus and Circus Vargas. His ability to perform and his interest in design led him to a work as a puppeteer. Also working as a puppeteer was Donna Harris, whom Wisniewski soon married. The couple ultimately started their own touring puppet company, the Clarion Shadow Theater. Cutting shadow puppets for theatrical presentations clearly influenced Wisniewsky's style of illustration. Used to great dramatic effect in his first book, *The Warrior and the Wise Man* (1989), the cut-paper illustrations set the tone for an original folktale of wisdom over physical force in twelfth-century Japan. Wisniewski depicted good and evil in cool greens and blues for the tenth-century Iceland in *Elfwyn's Saga* (1990). Ancient Mayan civiliza-

tion is depicted in the *Rain Player* (1991), featuring carefully crafted headdresses, temples, and lush jungles. The same style effectively portrays the rising leader of thirteenth-century West Africa in *Sundiata: Lion King of Mali* (1992) as well as the Pacific Northwest of the eighteenth century, where native people encounter Europeans in *The Wave of the Sea Wolf* (1994). Background notes are included in each book, citing sources as well as additional information.

Wisniewski's humor, verve, and sense of drama are evident in several very different books such as *The Secret Knowledge of Grown-ups* (1998) and *Tough Cookie* (1999). *Secret Knowledge* spoofs conspiracy theories by letting kids know what's *really* going on. *Tough Cookie* is a detective who lives with the crumbs at the bottom of the cookie jar. In both, cut-paper illustrations effectively convey pure zaniness combined with and respect for the reader. M.B.S.

Wittlinger, Ellen

American author, b. 1948. Ellen Wittlinger's first novel for young people, *Lombardo's Law* (1993), concerns a smart loner named Justine who discovers, to her surprise, that she is developing feelings for the eccentric boy who just moved in across the street. Though the plot may sound like standard romance fare, the book is distinguished by its insightful, multifaceted portrayals of the two principle characters and a refreshing twist to the tale: thirteen-year-old Mike is two years younger than Justine. This solid debut was followed by other YOUNG ADULT NOVELS with notably strong characterizations and edgy story lines.

An only child, Wittlinger was born and raised in Belleville, Illinois, where her parents ran a small grocery store. Though she worked at the store as a teenager, Wittlinger also developed a strong interest in the arts — particularly painting and drama. An art major at Millikin University in Decatur, she later focused on writing poetry and attended the famed University of Iowa

Writers' Workshop. Marriage took her to Massachusetts, where she started a family, published a volume of poetry, and had some plays produced. She also began working as a youth librarian, and as she discovered the field of young adult literature, she was motivated to write her own novel for teenagers.

Based on the positive response to *Lombardo's Law*, Wittlinger quit her library job and began writing full-time. Her next novel, *Noticing Paradise* (1995), is set in the Galapagos Islands and notable for employing two first-person narrators, Cat and Noah, who relate, in alternating chapters, a mystery involving disappearing tortoises as well as their own mysterious stirrings of first love.

Hard Love (1999) was Wittlinger's breakout novel. With some of the pages utilizing odd typefaces and graphics similar to those found in self-published "zines," the book draws immediate attention from readers. But even more intriguing is the cutting-edge story of John, a lonely sixteen-year-old who vents his frustrations over his parents' divorce in his own zine, and Marisol, another teenage zine publisher who describes herself as a "Puerto Rican Cuban Yankee Lesbian." Though the two outsiders form a deep friendship, John finds himself falling in love with a girl who cannot return his affections. The novel's trendy scenario, realistic characters and dialogue, and rueful blending of cynicism and poignancy captivated readers. *Hard Love* was selected as an Honor Book for the first Michael L. Printz Award.

Though Wittlinger's artistic, intelligent protagonists usually feel alienated — and sometimes even wear their isolation as a badge of honor — the author has also been realistic in depicting the pull toward conformity that these characters also experience. Justine is embarrassed to be seen in public with her younger male friend and even agrees to a date with a smarmy football player. John feels compelled to ask Marisol to the school prom. In *Razzle* (2001), teenage photographer Kenyon Baker becomes friends with an eccentric local girl, who serves as his artistic muse, but finds himself drawn to a more sophisticated and conventionally beautiful young woman.

All of Wittlinger's books, including *Gracie's Girl* (2000), a novel for younger readers, are written in the first-person voice. *What's in a Name?* (2000) employs ten first-person narratives in a collection of interrelated short stories told from the perspectives of, among others, a gay teenager, his athletic brother, and a foreign exchange student. These penetrating character studies, like her novels, demonstrate the author's ability to get into the heads of contemporary teens and explore their needs, insecurities, and inner conflicts with compassion and honesty.

P.D.S.

Wolff, Virginia Euwer

American writer, b. 1937. Virginia Euwer Wolff has brought to her YOUNG ADULT NOVELS a unique sensibility born of her Oregon woods upbringing; a love of nature, art, and music; and the experience of losing her father when she was a small child. Eschewing artistic ego, she takes artistic risks, producing five highly acclaimed novels, each of which challenges convention in form, style, or subject matter.

Wolff grew up on her family's fruit ranch in the Cascade Mountains, surrounded by natural beauty outside and culture inside: "the parlance in our home was of music and art and pets and harsh weather and love and Jesus." Wolff's father died when she was five, turning her world upside-down. At age eight, she began playing the violin — a passion that has sustained her all her life. After graduation from Smith College came marriage, two children, and a peripatetic life following her husband in the theater. Divorced in 1976, she returned to Oregon, taught high school English, and decided that she wanted to write.

Wolff's first young adult novel, *Probably Still Nick Swansen* (1988), is a compassionate, poignant story of a sixteen-year-old learning-disabled boy struggling not to let his limitations define who he is. Wolff has said that though she didn't know anyone like Nick, she identified with him: "Ineptitude is something that comes naturally to me. . . . I was totally absorbed in somebody who just doesn't get it as fast as other people do." In contrast, Wolff's second novel, *The Mozart Season* (1991), concerns a girl "who's up there with the best," a talented twelve-year-old violinist vying for first prize at a music competition — one of the few novels to portray, from an insider's point of view, the pressure-filled world of a young musician.

With *Make Lemonade* (1993), Wolff broke new ground: written in riveting, stream-of-consciousness free verse, it is also deliberately nonspecific in its presentation of setting and ethnicity. In a story that is simultaneously harrowing and uplifting, narrator LaVaughn, a bright, inner-city fourteen-year-old with aspirations for college, takes a job baby-sitting for uneducated, desperate teen mother Jolly and her two neglected children. Eventually they come to support each other and help each other toward a better life. Wolff has said that she wrote the novel in free verse "because that's the way I heard the voices. . . . I know mothers like Jolly have short attention spans. . . . I wanted to create something they could read." Indeed, *Make Lemonade,* so complex and yet so accessible, was chosen as an ALA Recommended Book for Reluctant Readers in addition to its many other accolades.

Bat 6 (1998) may be Wolff's most ambitious novel. With debatable success, Wolff used multiple narrators in her account of a single destructive incident during a much-anticipated championship girls' softball game in Oregon in 1949. All twenty-one sixth-grade girls on the two rival teams have a voice as they describe what happened between Shazam, whose mother instilled in her a hatred for the Japanese, and Aki, a Japanese American girl recently returned from the internment camps. The novel, which examines the cost of hatred, won the Jane Addams Peace Award in 1999.

Second in the Make Lemonade trilogy, *True Believer* (2001), again written in free verse, revisits LaVaughn, now fifteen and beginning the painful process of becoming an adult. She falls in love with a childhood friend, Jody. The journey the reader takes with LaVaughn is heart breaking but ultimately redemptive: though she is devastated by the discovery that Jody is gay, her capacity for love and her strength sustain her in the end. With its heart-stopping language and wrenching story, *True Believer* received the 2001 National Book Award for Young People's Literature. Wolff is currently working on the third book in the trilogy; her readers will await it eagerly, sure that it will reveal yet another facet of this remarkable writer. M.V.P.

Wood, Audrey; Wood, Don

Audrey: American author and illustrator, b. 1948; Don: American illustrator, b. 1945. Don and Audrey Wood are an acclaimed husband-and-wife author-and-illustrator team who have produced exuberant PICTURE BOOKS for young children. While Audrey has written and illustrated books on her own, Don has worked as an illustrator exclusively on his wife's texts.

Audrey has descended from a long line of artists that dates to the fifteenth century, but she has claimed to have broken the mold by being the first female working artist in the family. She was born in Little Rock, Arkansas, and raised with two younger sisters in a free-spirited childhood that included travel, intriguing people, and a broad exposure to the arts. She attended the Arkansas Art Center, an art and drama institute whose founders included her father and grandfather.

Don was brought up on a working farm in California's central San Joaquin Valley with little time to pursue his passion for art. After deciding to leave the family business and become an artist, Don graduated from the University of California at Santa Barbara in 1967 and received a master of fine arts degree from the California College of Arts and Crafts in 1969. He married Audrey the same year and worked at a number of jobs until, at his wife's request, he submitted sample drawings for a manuscript that she had written but not yet illustrated, and their success-ful collaboration was born.

The result of this merger, *Moonflute* (1980), was an admirable but flawed first effort. The lus-trous oil paintings demonstrate Don's mastery, yet they are somewhat static, and the text, while appropriately lyrical and dreamlike for this tale of an airborne nighttime journey, is a bit wordy. A more successful book is *The Napping House* (1984), named a New York Times Best Illustrated Book. In this cumulative tale about an unlikely heap of nappers, perfect for reading aloud at bedtime, Don's fresh, inventive style provides the perfect accompaniment to the rhythmic text that began as a melody in Audrey's head.

For Don, each book represents a particular artistic challenge with respect to dynamics of light and dark, point of view, perspective, or narrative slant. In *The Napping House,* Don's subtle, expert use of light brings the reader from the dim, blue glow of night to sunny, riotous color as day breaks.

The Woods have staged elaborate perfor-mances of their work for artistic inspiration and refinement at various points in the creative pro-cess. *King Bidgood's in the Bathtub* (1985), a Cal-decott Honor Book, demonstrates the Woods' collective sense of drama and reaps the benefits of this practice. *King Bidgood* resembles an ex-travagant opera about a robust king who refuses to leave his bath.

An admitted "fiddler and doer-over," Don has preferred oil because it is easily changed. His paintings for *Heckedy Peg* (1987), a tale based on an old English game, are reminiscent of the sixteenth-century Flemish masters. In *Piggies* (1991), a COUNTING BOOK, spare text spotlights the humorous antics of the frisky piggies as they cavort on colorful two-page spreads. *Elbert's Bad Word* (1988) is a satire of haughty high society upset by a particularly noxious, corporeal bad word. The Woods' fondness for the outrageous is apparent in their other collaborations — such as *I'm as Quick as a Cricket* (1998) and *The Tickle Octopus* (1994) — as well as in Audrey's light-hearted illustrations for *Tugford Wanted to Be Bad* (1983) and *Weird Parents* (1990), which she wrote and illustrated. The couple maintain a shared sense of fun while exploring each other's individuality for the perfect marriage of art and text. M.O'D.H.

Woodson, Jacqueline

American author, b. 1964. Writing about rough topics with a delicate touch, Jacque-line Woodson has emerged as a striking voice in contemporary fiction. Born in Columbus, Ohio, Woodson moved back and forth between South Carolina and New York as she was growing up. She became interested in writing in fifth grade, when she served as literary editor of a school magazine, but didn't see it as a possible career until she discovered the work of other African American authors, such as Toni Morrison and Rosa Guy. She has published an INFORMATION BOOK (*Martin Luther King, Jr., and His Birthday,* 1990), a PICTURE BOOK (*We Had a Picnic This Sunday Past,* 1997), and an adult novel (*Autobi-ography of a Family Photo,* 1994).

Her first children's book, *Last Summer with Maizon* (1990), concerns eleven-year-old best friends Margaret and Maizon who are separated when Maizon gets a scholarship to attend boarding school. Left alone in their Brooklyn neighborhood and grieving for her recently de-ceased father, Margaret is able to face her loneli-ness with the support of family and friends. A second book, *Maizon at Blue Hill* (1992), de-scribes Maizon's experiences as an African American trying to fit in at her nearly all-white school. The final volume in the trilogy, *Between Madison and Palmetto* (1993), takes place after Maizon has left boarding school and begins at-tending, with Margaret, a neighborhood school for the gifted. The girls are well characterized and their relationship rings true, even when the stories become overwhelmed with social prob-lems — such as Margaret's bulimia.

Most of Woodson's successive novels also concern social problems. In *The Dear One* (1991), the comfortable life of Afeni, an advan-taged twelve-year-old, is changed when a pregnant teenager from Harlem comes to stay with her family. Sexual abuse is the subject of *I Hadn't Meant to Tell You This* (1994), in which Marie, an African American girl, is entrusted with a secret by a white classmate, Lena. Two books deal with homosexuality: *From the Notebooks of Melanin Sun* (1995), in which a teenager's mother reveals she's a lesbian, and *The House You Pass on the Way* (1997), which concerns a fourteen-year-old biracial girl who becomes aware of her own same-sex desire when a female cousin arrives to spend the summer. This book, like most of the author's works, may be considered a novella, with brief chapters that sometimes read like prose poems creating a lyrical and emotional narrative through a collage of images.

Only when the author has tried to impose more of a traditional plot structure on her material does it feels artificial. *If You Come Softly* (1998) is a sensitively written story of a romance between an African American teenager and his white girlfriend, but the unexpected dramatic conclusion feels false and gives the book a truncated, rushed feeling. The same is true of *Lena* (1999), the sequel to *I Hadn't Meant to Tell You This*. As long as the story concerns the experiences of Lena and her younger sister as they run away from their abusive father, it remains credible and moving, but the conclusion, which tries to wrap things up too quickly and happily, feels contrived.

Woodson is at her best when writing on the experimental edge, crafting quietly powerful, emotionally intimate stories through a series of indelible images.   P.D.S.

Wyeth, N. C.

American illustrator, 1882–1945. HOWARD PYLE's most famous pupil and closest follower, Newell Convers Wyeth (known professionally by his initials) had an artistic personality quite distinct, in style and substance, from the Master's. Raised on a Massachusetts farm staked out by the Wyeths in 1730, he was a vigorous outdoorsman and a keen observer of na-

ture's contours and shadings. (His letters, otherwise banal, come alive in reference to "mellow, beseeching hills," to a large blue-black butterfly "lazying his way through the soft air.") The boy who drew horses and other real-life things became, at an art teacher's suggestion, a student of illustration. But the training, with its emphasis on cleverness and stunts, rankled; and when word reached Wyeth of Pyle's new school in the Brandywine Valley, he was an eager, anxious applicant. The ensuing interview was the pivotal event of Wyeth's life: though he sometimes criticized Pyle in later years and rued concentrating on illustration, Pyle remained the fountainhead of his aspirations, the impetus to "the *unattainable* in art."

Everything about the Pyle studio-school, then at full throttle, agreed with Wyeth: the summers at Chadds Ford on the Brandywine; the student camaraderie; the intense effort and inspired teaching; the manifest results. Spurred on by the advanced students' magazine work, Wyeth painted an oil in the flamboyant Wild West manner — a wild bronco, pitching and twisting to unseat his rider — and submitted it to the *Saturday Evening Post*; on February 21, 1903, Wyeth's first professional effort was the *Post*'s cover illustration, heralding a story by Western writer Emerson Hough, and the young artist, at twenty, was on his way.

The direction was plain. Further Western assignments led to a sketchbook-and-saddle trip through the Southwest, jointly sponsored by the *Post* and another Wyeth patron, *Scribner's Magazine*. Officially a student no longer, Wyeth stayed on at Wilmington, joining other professionals in the Pyle orbit. One slight adjustment remained. Wyeth's heart was in the gentle, historic Brandywine countryside, so like and unlike his beloved New England, and once married he settled permanently in Chadds Ford.

Through the World War I years Western illustration and magazine illustration flourished — boosted by full-color photographic reproduction — and Wyeth was swamped with assignments. By nature he was a painter of broadly rendered, richly colored and textured oils, not a linear artist like Pyle. With the advent of the four-color halftone process, Old Master paintings, reduced to the size of a printed page, came into wide circulation; Wyeth, in turn, made illustrations, on large canvases, that were indistinguishable from full-blown paintings. His compositions not only crackled with action (his mother once begged him for quieter scenes), but they made dramatic use of isolated figures, of light and shade, of odd, arresting angles. They had ambiguous depths. Pyle, who mastered every step in the transition from wood-engraved reproduction to halftone to full color, had also produced some memorable illustrations in oil; Wyeth, however, was to the medium born.

Full-color reproduction had an allure, as well, for publishers of children's books. The House of Scribner capitalized on its potential by launching a new series of elaborate reprint editions, Scribner Illustrated Classics. Wyeth's first contribution to the series was Robert Louis Stevenson's *Treasure Island* (1911). Printed on coated stock and tipped in, Wyeth's fourteen illustrations form a gallery of powerful images, from the explosive action of Billy Bones taking "one last tremendous cut" at the fleeing Black Dog to the doom-laden menace of Blind Pew, "tapping up and down the road in a frenzy."

Treasure Island was "a phenomenal success," as Wyeth wrote his mother, and a landmark in children's book publishing. Scribner's quickly commissioned Wyeth to illustrate Stevenson's *Kidnapped* (1913), putting the Illustrated Classics on a sure course, and other publishers weighed in with similar series, some of them virtually identical in appearance to the Scribner model. This stream of publication is hardly conceivable without Wyeth's affinity for romantic adventure. For the Scribner series he illustrated fourteen other titles, including *The Boy's King Arthur* (1917) and the two most popular Leatherstocking Tales of James Fenimore Cooper, *The Last of the Mohicans* (1919) and *The Deerslayer* (1924), as well as two additional Stevenson titles, *The Black Arrow* (1916) and *David Balfour* (1924). For Harper he illustrated MARK TWAIN's *Mysterious Stranger* (1916); for McKay, *Robin*

Illustration by N. C. Wyeth from *Treasure Island* (1911), by Robert Louis Stevenson.

Hood (1917) and *Rip Van Winkle* (1921); for Cosmopolitan, Arthur Conan Doyle's *White Company* (1922), Daniel Defoe's *Robinson Crusoe* (1920), and *Legends of Charlemagne* (1924); for Houghton Mifflin, two dubious choices, Henry Wadsworth Longfellow's *Courtship of Miles Standish* (1920) and Homer's *Odyssey* (1929). Sometimes Wyeth's contribution was crucial. Published for adults in 1925, James Boyd's Revolutionary War novel *Drums* became a children's book in the Scribner series with the addition — the added attraction — of illustrations by Wyeth, and MARJORIE KINNAN RAWLINGS's 1938 Pulitzer Prize winner, *The Yearling*, achieved instant children's-classic status the following year in the same fashion. Successful as interpretations or not, Wyeth's illustrations lent a glamour to classics that lured even indifferent readers and kept some of the titles in print for generations. Recently the best of the Scribner series, beginning with *Treasure Island*, have been reprinted in facsimiles of the first editions.

By the 1920s Wyeth had largely ceased doing

magazine illustration, switching for supplementary income — he was very well paid for his book work — to advertising design, calendar illustration, and other commercial art. Color prints of his famous illustrations, displayed in parlors and classrooms, provided still further exposure and income. Most gratifying to him were mural commissions, and in the 1930s he also fulfilled his yearning to paint easel pictures. His son Andrew, also a painter and a partial influence on his father, and others of the talented Wyeth brood were already renewing the Brandywine tradition.   B.B.

Wynne-Jones, Tim

Canadian writer and poet, b. 1948. Tim Wynne-Jones came to the writing of children's books sideways. He took fine arts degrees at York University and at the University of Waterloo, where he also studied to be an architect. A detour into book illustration and design led to writing, but it was only after the publication of two successful adult mystery novels that he sat down one morning and wrote *Zoom at Sea* (1983), the story of a cat who follows his seafaring Uncle Roy to an adventure on the dancing main.

Since his first appearance Zoom has starred in two more adventures, a trip to the North Pole in *Zoom Away* (1985) and a sojourn in ancient Egypt in *Zoom Upstream* (1992). The Zoom stories typify Wynne-Jones's strengths as a writer — the ability to shape a plot and pare it to its essentials, gentle child-centered humor, a palpable pleasure in words, and a musician's sense of rhythm and cadence.

The sense of music is also evident in Wynne-Jones's collection of POETRY, *Mischief City* (1986), a set of lively, celebratory poems in the first person: "Don't drink the bathwater! / Don't feed it to the cat. / Your sailboat's mucky / And poor rubber duck / He got stuck in the guck where he sat." The poems have been set to music and produced as a recording and as live theater.

Wynne-Jones's continuing interest in architecture can be seen in *The Builder of the Moon* (1988), his FANTASY adventure about David Finebloom, who travels to the moon on his homemade spaceship to answer the moon's plea for help. David's rebuilding of the moon, "course upon course, layer upon layer," can be seen as a metaphor for writing, or indeed any creative activity, and his confidence, competence, and pluck are typical of Wynne-Jones's child heroes. He has proven himself the master of the short story in collections such as *Some of the Kinder Planets* (1995), which won the Boston Globe–Horn Book Award, *The Book of Changes* (1995), and *Lord of the Fries* (1999).

There is a darker side to Wynne-Jones's writing, a side seen in his chilling adult novels. He plays with this darker, scary-story genre in *The Hour of the Frog* (1990), a single illustrated poem about the goings-on at the late-night frog hour: "Thlump. Thlump. He's at the foot of the stairs."

Wynne-Jones lives in the country with his wife, writer/calligrapher/director Amanda West Lewis, and their three children. When he is not writing novels, short fiction, PICTURE BOOKS, reviews, poems, or song lyrics, he sings with the local operetta company. Such versatility informs all Wynne-Jones's work, which, in its quirky humor and distinctive voice, reflects a mind of wide-ranging enthusiasms.   S.E.

Y

Yashima, Taro

Japanese American illustrator, 1908–1994. Artist and antifascist activist Taro Yashima, who was born as Jun Atsushi Iwamatsu, immigrated to America from Japan in 1939. He trained as an artist at the Japanese Imperial Art Academy and quickly received recognition for his work. However, he gave up any chance at formal success in Japan when he chose to openly criticize the government. He spent time in and out of jail before he and his wife escaped from Japan to America. His political ideology and experiences made up the material for his sophisticated illustrated autobiographies, *The New Sun* (1943) and *Horizon Is Calling* (1947).

Yashima's first book for children, *The Village Tree* (1953), was written to answer his young daughter's query about Yashima's own childhood in Japan. The book is a portrait of a time and a place — a time when children reveled in the entertainment provided them by a tree: "all sorts of bugs on the leaves, and places to play in the branches." The details of life are specific to Yashima's childhood Japanese village, yet universal. The expressionistic illustrations, done with sketchy black pencil outline and colored pencil shading, convey the feeling of the place.

Yashima began publishing for children during the postwar period when many Americans were fascinated with everything Japanese. *Crow Boy* (1953), a Caldecott Honor Book, is the story of a child isolated from his classmates because he is very different. He suffers for years at school until just before he is to leave the sixth grade. Then a new teacher discovers that Chibi has a tremendous knowledge of the outdoors. Chibi performs his "voices of crows" at a school talent show. The remarkable illustrations convey just how Chibi feels — as alone on the page, separated by a vast white space, as he is from his peers.

In all of his books Yashima uses light and line to convey meaning and emotion. After his success with *Crow Boy,* Yashima published other picture books, including several about his own daughter, Momo. *Umbrella* (1958), also a Caldecott Honor Book, is dedicated to Momo on her eighth birthday. It tells the story of a little girl who cannot wait to use her new umbrella and boots. When she finally christens the umbrella on a walk to nursery school, the narrator recalls that this is the first time the child makes the walk without holding her parent's hand — a milestone understood universally. In *Momo's Kitten* (1961), with his wife Mitsu Yashima, Yashima tells of his daughter's adoption of a stray cat and the subsequent family of kittens born to that cat. Yashima's other books include retellings of folktales, such as *Seashore Story* (1967), which earned a third Caldecott Honor, and *The Fisherman and the Goblet* (1971), written by Mark Taylor. In addition to illustrating, Yashima directed and taught at the Yashima Art Institute in Los Angeles.

Yashima's art reveals Japanese influence in his use of line and expressionist influence in his use of light and shadow. His texts are filled with details of sound and touch, and his paintings convey the sights and, most important, the feelings surrounding the events of childhood. M.V.K.

Yep, Laurence

American author, b. 1948. At age eighteen, Laurence Yep launched his writing career with the publication of a SCIENCE FICTION story, and his first novel, *Sweetwater* (1973), takes place on a planet called Harmony. Subsequently, his acclaimed works for children have spanned the genres from science fiction and FANTASY to realistic and HISTORICAL FICTION to collections of Chinese folktales. Yep's historical novels bring the Chinese and Chinese American cultures alive and brilliantly convey not only the settings but also the internal lives of the characters. Yep has introduced readers to life in China in *The Serpent's Children* (1984) and its sequel, *Mountain Light* (1985), which depict the struggles of Cassia and Foxfire, the children of a Chinese family in rebellion against the conquering Manchus.

Dragonwings (1975), which explores Yep's Chinese American heritage, garnered a Newbery Honor award as well as numerous other prizes. Moon Shadow is called to America, "the land of the Golden Mountain," to be with his father, Windrider, who dreamed that he was a dragon in a previous life and now wants to fly again —

this time in a handcrafted aeroplane. As the years pass, Moon Shadow learns not only that life in San Francisco at the turn of the century is more challenging and perilous than he had imagined but that his father can be unreasonable, proud, and full of a fighting spirit, as well as so driven by his passion to fly that he jeopardizes all that they possess and care for.

Similarly, Otter, in *Dragon's Gate* (1993), also a Newbery Honor Book, discovers the human side of his father and Uncle Foxfire, who are considered heroes back home in the Chinese village, when he joins them in the Sierra Nevada during the winter of 1867 on the construction site of the transcontinental railroad. Even as Otter and Moon Shadow grow in their understanding of their families, they gain experience in surviving in two cultures simultaneously, which is a common theme in much of Yep's fiction. *Child of the Owl* (1977), winner of the 1977 Boston Globe–Horn Book Award for fiction, details a young girl's growing awareness of her Chinese American background due to her grandmother's storytelling.

Having grown up in an African American neighborhood in San Francisco, Yep lacked a true understanding of Chinese traditions, so he began to record the stories his relatives told about their early experiences living in the United States. *The Star Fisher* (1991) is a fictionalized account of his mother's adolescence as a member of the only Asian family in a small West Virginia town.

In addition to writing historical and realistic fiction, Yep has composed several MYSTERIES, yet he has never lost his love of fantasy, and his fantasy novels have been well received by critics and readers. *Dragon of the Lost Sea* (1982), *Dragon Steel* (1985), *Dragon Cauldron* (1991), and *Dragon War* (1992) relay the adventures of a deposed Chinese dragon-princess named Shimmer and two children as they attempt to regain Shimmer's kingdom. Not only a much-respected creator of fiction, Yep has selected and retold Chinese folktales in *The Rainbow People* (1989) and *Tongues of Jade* (1991) and in PICTURE BOOKS such as *The Man Who Tricked a Ghost*

(1993); he has also edited a collection of Asian American fiction and POETRY entitled *American Dragons: Twenty-Five Asian American Voices* (1993).

By drawing from his own cultural inheritance, Yep has written exemplary CHINESE AMERICAN BOOKS FOR CHILDREN that introduce to all children and young adults specific eras of history and universal themes while providing for Chinese American readers a literature of their own. A.E.D.

Yolen, Jane

American author, b. 1939. With a confident writing style and inexhaustible imagination, Jane Yolen has proven herself one of the most prolific and diverse creators in the field of children's literature.

Born in New York City, Yolen spent her early years in Virginia and California but returned to New York, where she attended grade school and wrote the script, music, and lyrics for school plays. She continued to develop her writing and musical skills while attending high school in Connecticut and Smith College in Massachusetts. After graduation, she worked in publishing for several years, then settled in Massachusetts with her family and embarked on a full-time writing career.

Yolen's first book for children was *Pirates in Petticoats* (1963), a factual work about female pirates. Although she has continued to publish an occasional volume of nonfiction, including the biographical *Friend: The Story of George Fox and the Quakers* (1972), Yolen has concentrated on fiction and POETRY. She has published several volumes of verse, beginning with *See This Little Line?* in 1963 and including *How Beastly!: A Menagerie of Nonsense Poems* (1980) and *The Three Bears Rhyme Book* (1987). Although her PICTURE BOOKS include lighthearted narratives such as *No Bath Tonight* (1978), the story of Jeremy's attempts to avoid bathing, her best-known picture book texts are sensitive free-verse poems. *Owl Moon* (1987) received the Caldecott Medal for

JOHN SCHOENHERR's watercolor illustrations, but Yolen's story of a father and child walking in the woods on a winter night is equally masterful. *All the Secrets in the World* (1991), *Letting Swift River Go* (1992), and other prose poems are distinguished by their lyrical, evocative writing and the sense of wonder that imbues much of the author's work. Yolen's literary fairy tales, such as *The Girl Who Cried Flowers and Other Tales* (1974), combine traditional FANTASY motifs, including magic, giants, and animals transformed into human beings, with themes of death, kindness, and love to create memorable, original stories. With illustrator Mark Teague she created the extremely popular picture book *How Do Dinosaurs Say Goodnight?* (2000).

As Yolen's children grew, she extended her talents to writing books for young adults. *The Gift of Sarah Barker* (1981) is a HISTORICAL NOVEL about two teenagers who fall in love, although they belong to a celibate Shaker community. Their emerging sexuality is sensitively and tastefully explored, despite some unlikely plot twists. Yolen has sometimes included an implausible element of fantasy in her realistic fiction for older readers. This has a detrimental effect in *The Stone Silenus* (1984), which concerns a girl coping with her father's death, but works extremely well in *The Devil's Arithmetic* (1988), the moving story of a contemporary Jewish girl magically transported to a Nazi death camp. Yolen's first foray into young adult high fantasy was the well-received Pit Dragon trilogy, consisting of *Dragon's Blood* (1982), *Heart's Blood* (1984), and *A Sending of Dragons* (1987). Writing for a younger audience, she has published the humorous Commander Toad SCIENCE FICTION series, which includes *Commander Toad in Space* (1980).

Yolen has written well over a hundred books, has edited anthologies, continues to write stories and nonfiction for magazines, and oversees her own imprint of children's books for a major publishing house. Considering her prodigious output, Yolen's sure-handed writing is consistently high in quality and child appeal. An occasional volume may be considered slight or facile, but the majority are sensitive, poetic, and imaginative. P.D.S.

Yorinks, Arthur

American author, b. 1953. Arthur Yorinks has one of the most distinctive prose styles in children's literature. His PICTURE BOOK texts are spare, precise, and almost staccato in their rhythm. He favors short phrases and ironic turns of plot. No matter where his stories are set, his characters speak in the clipped cadence of New Yorkers. They are often a bit world-weary, nagged by unfulfillment, and eager for whatever transforming miracle comes their way.

Brought up in suburban New York, Yorinks was a teenager when he found himself drawn to picture books, especially the work of TOMI UNGERER, WILLIAM STEIG, and above all, MAURICE SENDAK. At sixteen, he appeared on Sendak's doorstep, handed his somewhat-taken-aback idol some manuscripts, and began an unlikely friendship. Sendak later introduced Yorinks to RICHARD EGIELSKI, setting into motion a long and successful collaboration. Yorinks later collaborated with his hero William Steig in *Arthur Yorinks's The Flying Latke* (1999).

Yorinks and Egielski are best known for *Hey, Al* (1986), for which Egielski won the 1987 Caldecott Medal: "Al, a nice man, a quiet man, a janitor," lives with Eddie, his ambitious dog. When an exotic bird flies into their minuscule apartment and offers them a new life in a terrific place, Eddie is ready to take flight immediately and Al soon concurs. They are ferried up to a lush island in the sky, where all at first is bliss, until they discover its too-high price. They then make a harrowing retreat to the city, where they happily discover that "Paradise lost is sometimes Heaven found."

As in much of Yorinks's work, there are no children anywhere. The predicament is adult and so are many of the longings — for release from dreary work, escape from a dreary home. Yet there is also an offhand and childlike acceptance of the magical in this very earthbound fantasy. Dogs talk, birds do too, and men can sprout wings. The central dilemma is common to readers of any age. When push comes to shove, what matters most? How much are you willing to give up for your dreams? The story provokes and challenges while at the same time offering considerable comfort. Maybe heaven really is close to home.

Yorinks's inspirations come from many sources, including, a bit unexpectedly, Franz Kafka's *Metamorphosis*. In *Louis the Fish* (1980), also illustrated by Egielski, a third-generation butcher is profoundly unhappy with his lot in life. Poor Louis loathes meat but loves fish. He is obsessed by them. And one morning, miraculously, he becomes one and finally finds bliss. For "after a hard life, Louis was a happy fish."

Idiosyncratic and often unabashedly strange, Yorinks's picture books are neither cozy nor sweet, but they are kindhearted and knowing, providing their own perspective on the measure of a life well lived.   A.Q.

Young, Ed

American illustrator and author, b. 1931. Mice, elephants, wolves, and rabbits are among the many animals brought vividly to life by PICTURE BOOK illustrator Ed Young, whose career began with lunch-hour sketches at New York's Central Park Zoo. A former architecture student, Young switched to art, graduating from the Art Center College of Design in Los Angeles before moving to New York to work in advertising. While working, he continued to take art and design classes at Pratt Institute in Brooklyn and was urged by friends who saw his animal sketches to try illustrating children's books. When Young illustrated *The Mean Mouse and Other Mean Stories* (1962), written by Janice May Udry, he expected it to be his first and last book, but it won an American Institute of Graphic Arts award and launched a career that has resulted in over fifty books, including a few he wrote himself.

Born in Tientsin, China, Young spent his childhood in Shanghai and attended high school in Hong Kong before moving to the United States in 1951, where he has lived since. He has illustrated numerous stories set in his native China, including the Caldecott Honor Book *The Emperor and the Kite* (1967), edited by JANE YOLEN, and his own folktale retelling, the Caldecott Medal winner *Lon Po Po: A Red Riding Hood Story from China* (1989). Skilled in the use of a variety of media, Young is also skilled in choosing the best medium with which to illustrate a particular story; one example is the ancient Chinese paper-cutting technique used in *The Emperor and the Kite*, which perfectly suits the poetic beauty of Yolen's narrative. In *Lon Po Po*, Young's illustrations reveal his interest in the panel art found in a number of cultures. The drawings are split into sections that give the art the appearance of Chinese decorative panels; however, strong color and dramatic angles transform the art, giving it a thoroughly contemporary look.

Young has illustrated many tales from lands other than China, among them *Seven Blind Mice* (1992), another Caldecott Honor Book. In Young's version of the Indian fable, blind mice make humorously incorrect judgments about an object they encounter; only the seventh mouse, who examines the entire object, guesses rightly that it is an elephant — the moral is "Knowing in part may make a fine tale, but wisdom comes from seeing the whole." Another moral — "A change in circumstances can make the strong weak and the weak strong" — is illustrated in Young's rendition of *The Lion and the Mouse* (1979), the AESOP fable of the small creature who promises to one day repay the lion if he will spare him. A Jataka tale adapted by RAFE MARTIN, *Foolish Rabbit's Big Mistake* (1985), is a version of the Chicken Little story. Young's large, brightly colored illustrations in the amusing tale differ from his earlier art, much of which resembles Indian miniatures. The striking and powerful figures — in one case, a lion's paw fills an entire two-page spread — add impact to the story by placing readers at the center of the drama.

The stories, folktales, fables, and myths

Young has illustrated impart simple but significant truths about people and the world. The age-old technique of using ANIMAL STORIES to teach spiritual lessons has been given new life by this versatile and talented artist.   J.M.B.

Voices of the Creators

🞲 *Ed Young*

I read a fable about a naturalist who was visiting a farm and was surprised to find an eagle feeding among the chickens. The farmer said, "Since I raised it from the beginning and fed it chicken feed, it never learned to fly or act as an eagle." "Still," insisted the naturalist, "it has the heart of an eagle and can surely learn to fly." They put the eagle on a tall fence so that he could stretch his wings and fly. The eagle was confused. Seeing the chickens feeding, he gladly jumped down to join them again. Undeterred, the following day the naturalist took the eagle up on the roof of a house and urged him again, saying, "You are an eagle. Stretch forth your wings and fly!" But the eagle was afraid of the unknown and jumped down once more with the chickens. Still determined, the naturalist rose early the third day and took the eagle to a high mountain. There he raised the eagle high above his head, saying, "You are an eagle. King of all birds. Stretch out your wings and fly!" The eagle began to tremble. Slowly he stretched his wings. At last, with a triumphant cry, he soared into the heavens.

I identify myself with that eagle in many ways. Because of ill health, I was kept home an additional year before my schooling. When I did go to school, everyone in my class was a head shorter than me. I sat in the rear of the classroom, where there were plenty of distractions for all my school years in Shanghai and, later, in Hong Kong. It was not great for my self-esteem — as the oldest and the biggest student in class, I was not also the smartest. I had no incentive to excel and whiled my time away, drawing or simply daydreaming. Heaven only knows how I managed to graduate from high school, and it was even more puzzling

that I was admitted by an accredited college in the United States.

As my parents were still in communist China, my guardian uncle in Hong Kong took me aside before I embarked on the boat to America. "You will soon be on your own, Ed. If there is something in you to make your life a success, this is now your chance. This opportunity may not come your way again." I took stock of myself and was surprised to find that all the years of drawing and playing were considered wasted time in a world of measurable assets, of which I had none. So, once I landed in the United States, I took up every avenue of menial work offered to me — janitorial jobs, pot- and dishwasher, paper cutter, houseboy, cook, busboy, bellhop, waiter, soda jerk — with a great sense of newness and adventure far beyond the expectation of my superiors. In my studies I saw that architecture was not exactly where my strength lay. So, against the advice of my advisers at the University of Illinois, I transferred into a professional art school in Los Angeles. In another three years, I began my career, focused totally on success. Although I was proud of my skills in what I call "the art of visual persuasion," I was not pleased with the advertising world — in which the norm is to exploit the public. It was then I received word from my father behind the Bamboo Curtain. Although the letter was addressed to all his offspring, I suspected that he had my new profession in mind: "You may put down as rule number one that life is not rich, not real, unless you partake of life with your fellowmen. A successful life and a happy life is one measured by how much you have accomplished for others and not one measured by how much you have done for yourself." I understood then that to realize my potential as an artist was subservient to my worth as a human being. To be truly successful, I needed to find a place where my work would also inspire others to fuller and happier lives. Luckily my enthusiasm about nature led me into the world of children's literature.

I also began my study of tai chi chuan with a Chinese master, who cured a knee injury I had had for many years. With him I also returned to Chinese calligraphy. The brush exercise was done by sitting squarely on a stool and drawing equally spaced horizontal and vertical lines with a thin brush on newsprint paper with the least amount of tension in my arms and body. He told stories of how, as a boy, he did this with diluted ink on newspaper, gradually darkening the spaces in between strokes until each sheet was completely covered with crisscross lines. Every morning his desk would be filled by stacks of blackened paper. As I practiced and thought I was improving with each executed line, I noticed that the lines were actually correcting something in me. Although I had not resisted work in the United States, I now realize that it is not just labor, but a love of labor that opens our innermost potential.

I wish to share with everyone my father's words about success and my teacher's brush lesson: work can, in fact, be the rooftop from which we launch ourselves to higher places. 🐛

Young Adult Novels

In 1967 and 1968 three books were published that established the form of literature we now term the realistic young adult novel or the problem novel — S. E. HINTON's *The Outsiders* (1967), PAUL ZINDEL's *The Pigman* (1968), and ROBERT LIPSYTE's *The Contender* (1967).

Though these three novels clearly set the young adult novel on a new path, they did not just appear ex nihilo. They were an outgrowth of the twenty-year post–World War II period when authors such as Henry Gregor Felsen and Maureen Daly directed their storytelling talents exclusively to the American adolescent. Felsen's *Hot Rod* (1950) and Daly's *Seventeenth Summer* (1942), for example, were involving and inspiring junior novels geared to the narrow and very special interests of adolescents as seen by authors who reflected society's stereotypical views of teenagers. For one thing, they believed that boys will be boys — and girls will be girls; novels for males were about cars and sports, and those for females were about dates and dances. The world in which the teen characters lived seldom extended further than the home and the high school, and the plots dealt with the challenges the teen protagonists faced within this limited, white, middle-class environment.

While even the best of these novels were often didactic, they created sharply etched, highly individual characters with whom teen readers could easily identify. And, for the first time, they treated adolescents as entities with social and psychological needs separate from those of children.

During this same postwar period, another phenomenon took place that influenced the development of what we now call the young adult realistic novel. A small number of provocative novels, put out by trade publishers for adult audiences, filtered down slowly to the more sophisticated teen readers who found the junior novels too limiting and too remote from their everyday lives. These stories — such as J. D. Salinger's *Catcher in the Rye* (1951), William Golding's *The Lord of the Flies* (1955), and John Knowles's *A Separate Peace* (1959) — all possessed coming-of-age themes and youthful protagonists whose relationships with peers and the outside adult world highlighted moral and social concerns ignored by junior novels.

By 1967 the teenagers of the 1960s had witnessed the assassination of a youthful, popular president and had seen the hopeful promises of the Great Society and of the newly created Peace Corps dissipate as a result of an uncertain war in Southeast Asia. They had also witnessed the bravery of many of their older brothers and sisters in Martin Luther King Jr.'s campaign of nonviolent civil disobedience against segregation laws, and they had seen the violent reactions to it. Television was thrusting the turbulence of the outside world into the relatively confined world of teenagers that Felsen and Daly had so effectively portrayed in their novels. In addition, rock music had matured into a creative form of expression that communicated the needs and aspirations of American teenagers in the 1960s. Fewer and fewer teen readers believed that the worlds created by Felsen and Daly had any relevance to their own worlds.

It is therefore not surprising that the young

adult novel would try to reflect some of the changes taking place then. Like the junior novels of the post–World War II period, *The Outsiders, The Pigman,* and *The Contender* were about teenagers and were directed exclusively to teen readers. And like the earlier stories, they attempted to deal with the social and psychological needs of the adolescent: social identity, personal identity, peer relationships, independence from family, and social responsibility. But the milieu had changed — radically. Bolstered by the surprising success of Salinger's, Golding's, and Knowles's novels among teen readers and influenced by the fast-moving and intrusive political and cultural events of the 1960s, Hinton, Zindel, and Lipsyte moved the center of their fictional setting from the family and the school to places beyond — the street, the community, and the adult world.

In *The Outsiders,* S. E. Hinton wrote about a socially stratified high school society based not on personality differences but on socioeconomic backgrounds. The conflicts between the Socs and the Greasers were different from the ethnically stratified gangs of *West Side Story* (also written in the early 1960s) and from later stories dealing with youth gangs in the 1970s and 1980s. In *The Outsiders* one group (the Socs) represent the establishment and one (the Greasers) represent the "outsiders"; the Greasers' lifestyle, clothing, and families' socioeconomic background set them apart from the middle-class mainstream of the high school. Into this stratified setting, Hinton interjected highly individualistic teen characters who get caught up in a gang fight, with tragic consequences. Likewise, in Paul Zindel's *The Pigman,* tragic consequences result from the attempt of two disaffected teens to exploit the goodwill of a lonely old man whose wife has recently died. Here, however, the focus is not on what happens when teenagers are prisoners of social strata, but what happens when teenagers focus on satisfying their immediate needs at the expense of what they are doing to others. And with a more positive outcome, Robert Lipsyte's *The Contender* mixes the themes of personal success and social

responsibility in a racially stratified setting that itself creates pressures on a young and talented black would-be boxer.

The realistic young adult novel also parted company with the post–World War II junior novel in its refusal to accept gender pigeonholes. *The Pigman,* for example, has coequal protagonists — a boy and a girl who share the successes and the failures of their ill-fated relationship with Mr. Pignati. And, although *The Outsiders* is about boys, S. E. Hinton is female — and the story appeals equally to both genders of teen readers.

The characters in most post–World War II junior novels were white, Protestant, and middle class. The realistic young adult novel changed all that by developing characters with a wide variety of ethnic, racial, and religious backgrounds. The major characters in *The Contender* are black, Italian, and Jewish — representing an accurate microcosm of New York City, where the story takes place.

As these three novels quickly found acceptance with teen readers, more books followed that built on the strengths of this new genre. John Donovan's *I'll Get There. It Better Be Worth the Trip* (1969) deals with a teenager, raised by his grandmother, who is forced to live with his alcoholic mother in New York City. Vera and Bill Cleaver's *Where the Lilies Bloom* (1969) — and its sequel, *Trial Valley* (1977) — relates the story of a gritty and tenacious Appalachian teenager, orphaned with her younger brothers and sisters, who struggles to keep her family together under adverse conditions. Glendon Swarthout's *Bless the Beasts and the Children* (1970) creates a bond between five "misfit" children at a summer camp and a herd of hunted buffalo. *Go Ask Alice* (1971), published as a true diary of a runaway girl's involvement with street drugs and prostitution, is actually a fictionalized account based on a true story; the book shocked parents, teachers, and librarians because it was about a white, middle-class girl who, thirty years before, could have been the lead character of *Seventeenth Summer.*

Following the lead of the above-mentioned novels, other authors published books, but many did not meet the high standards established by Hinton, Zindel, and Lipsyte. In these inferior stories, fully developed characters became predictable stereotypes, imaginative writing and critical examination became clichés and pieties, and original plots were turned into derivative story lines. Even the later stories of Zindel, Hinton, and Lipsyte, all of whom wrote other novels in the 1970s, are vulnerable to these criticisms. But the 1970s also saw the publication of perhaps the most discussed and controversial young adult novel of the century — ROBERT CORMIER's *The Chocolate War* (1974). It is an intriguing, gripping, and tightly written story dealing with a variation of "the outsider" theme: what happens when a lone teenager in a private school refuses to sell boxes of chocolate. When the teenager says no, he bucks not only the morally bankrupt leadership of the school, led by power-hungry, cynical Brother Leon, but also the intense and violent peer pressure of the established school gang that has been co-opted by the school administration to enforce its dictates. The reason why the novel was so controversial was not the cynicism of the school nor the violence of the gang but the story's pessimistic ending and ostensible message. "Don't disturb the universe," the physically beaten and spiritually drained teen rebel tells his one remaining friend. Parents, teachers, librarians, and even a few teen readers assailed this message of defeatism, but Cormier and his defenders claimed the novel was a description of the real world, not a prescription for passivity. *The Chocolate War*'s controversial ending, however, highlights a major feature of realistic young adult novels: like the best of adult fiction, the novels end celebrating the human spirit or depicting the depths of human depravity. *The Chocolate War* indicated that teenagers were no longer going to be protected from the dark side of life.

Nonetheless, many of these books emphasize the light at the end of the tunnel, often with humor and wit. Three of WALTER DEAN MYERS's most popular novels — *The Young Landlords* (1979), *Motown and Didi* (1984), and *It Ain't All for Nothin'* (1978) — are about young teens in Harlem who transform their bleak inner-city environment into successful business projects, overcome their disruptive family lives while making close friends and falling in love, and turn street problems into adventurous challenges. M. E. KERR's *Dinky Hocker Shoots Smack* (1972) parodies a mother who tries to do good for others but neglects her overweight daughter, and her *If I Love You, Am I Trapped Forever?* (1973) humorously shows the surprise and confusion of the self-proclaimed "most popular" boy in school when an unlikely nonconformist newcomer challenges his leadership role. RICHARD PECK, a former high school teacher, wrote many successful novels about personal and social problems teens face, but three of his most popular stories — *The Ghost Belonged to Me* (1975), *Ghosts I Have Been* (1977), and *The Dreadful Future of Blossom Culp* (1983) — revolve around an unforgettable character named Blossom Culp, whose encounters with ghosts and other unworldly forms of life create some of the most down-to-earth and humorous situations in young adult fiction. Peck's imaginative satire of suburban life in *Secrets of the Shopping Mall* (1979) and his parody of beauty pageants in *Representing Super Doll* (1974) reflect the realistic novel's concern with societal issues even as it tries to entertain its intended teen readership.

Between 1967 and the late 1970s, the realistic novel constituted the mainstream of young adult literature. A serious challenge to the realistic novel's dominant position arose in the second half of the 1970s because of a decision by publishers to package fiction for teenagers in genre series in order to appeal to the interests and enthusiasms of young adult readers. This change in publishing strategy was a result of a variety of factors: the increasing success of the juvenile and young adult paperback market in retail bookstores; the influence of television and movies on what teens read; the realization that many teens were graduating from high school unable to read at the twelfth-grade level; and the success of the "hi-low" (high-interest, low-reading-level) books packaged for this increasingly large group of young problem readers. However, although the genre packages that the publishers developed — such as "Sweet Valley High," "Sweet Dreams," "Wildfire," and "Confidentially Yours" — were initially profitable for publishers, they did not adversely affect the influence of the realistic novel. In fact, it could be argued that the realistic novel co-opted the genre stories.

The genre of SPORTS NOVELS, for example, combines sports action with predictable characters, who exist largely to make baskets, score touchdowns, or hit home runs — and to leave readers with hackneyed homilies and positive feelings. However, in the late 1970s and the 1980s when the genre packages were flourishing, well-written and provocative realistic novels with teen characters involved actively in sports were published for young adults. The function of the sports action, however, was not to drive the plot but rather to serve as a metaphor for the real action of the story that was taking place off the playing field. *Juggling* (1982), by David Lehrman; *Football Dreams* (1982), by David Guy; *A Passing Season* (1982), by Richard Blessing; *The Moves Make the Man* (1984), by BRUCE BROOKS; and *Running Loose* (1983), by CHRIS CRUTCHER are five of the best such stories, all of which feature teenagers whose athletic pursuits parallel their life away from sports.

It is a far cry from the formula-driven saccharine plots of "Sweet Dreams" and "Wildfire," but many quality realistic young adult novels published during this same period deal with teen romance. Robert Lipsyte's *Jock and Jill* (1982) mixes broad humor, a dash of politics, some sports action, and a lot of romance into a novel about love under even the most improbable of circumstances. JUDY BLUME's *Forever . . .* (1975) sketches a sexual love affair between two innocent teenagers that emphasizes the humor of sexual activity and the impermanence of love. Harry Mazer's *The Girl of His Dreams* (1987) — a sequel to *The War on Villa Street* (1978) — is about a young high-school graduate who dreams of the perfect girl to meet. *Annie on My Mind* (1982), by Nancy Garden, sensitively portrays a teen lesbian relationship that parallels the physical and emotional aspects of teen heterosexual relationships. In all of these novels about love, romance is used as a backdrop in order to develop a rich, entertaining, unpredictable story peopled with colorful, complex, unstereotypical teen characters to whom teen readers can easily relate.

In addition to enriching literature published specifically for young adult readers, the realistic young adult novel has raised the standards and broadened the parameters of all the fiction teenagers read. By successfully fighting the battles to tear down subject taboos and by introducing sophisticated literary devices and techniques such as foreshadowing, metaphors and similes, irony and allegory, and alternate first-person narratives and omniscient third-person narratives, the realistic novel has paved the way for the quality contemporary adult novel to be considered desirable reading material for young adults. Among the more prominent of these novels are Ernest Gaines's *A Gathering of Old Men* (1983), Chaim Potok's *The Chosen* (1967) and *My Name Is Asher Lev* (1972), James Baldwin's *If Beale Street Could Talk* (1974), and William Wharton's *Birdy* (1979), all of which were published originally for adult audiences. It is largely because of the influences of the successful realistic young adult novel that serious fiction has gained such a wide readership among teenagers.

During the early 1990s, one young Los Angeles novelist has emerged whose work promises to push the young adult novel into a very new direction. In four novels — *Weetzie Bat* (1989), *Witch Baby* (1990), *Cherokee Bat and the Goat Guys* (1991), and *Missing Angel Juan* (1993) — FRANCESCA LIA BLOCK has created a cast of memorable teen characters whose lives reflect a bizarre mixture of campy fairy-tale and punk reality. Her interconnected short novels are told in a richly lyrical and often allusive prose that portrays Block's sensitive but alienated adolescents as they make their way through L.A.'s often eerie and very real fantasyland.

What about the future of the realistic young adult novel? Rock music changed the direction of American popular music irrevocably in the 1950s and 1960s; although it has undergone changes of form and style since then, the core of the music is what it was at its birth. No one can safely predict the shape it will take in the next decade. Similarly, the realistic young adult novel changed young adult literature irrevocably in the 1960s. Although it has changed forms and extended in many directions since then, it is as strong and influential as ever. It has made young adult literature honest, and it has kept the teen-age reader honest. And the realistic young adult novel will probably continue to be the main-stream force in young adult literature, as long as it reflects life in a truthful way and keeps faith with the young adult's needs and aspira-tions. J.F.

Z

Zelinsky, Paul O.

American illustrator, b. 1953. Paul O. Zelinsky was born in Evanston, Illinois. His father, a college professor, taught in various places, so the family moved often; Zelinsky, forced to make new friends, found that his pre-dilection for drawing made him the "class artist" wherever he lived. When he was in high school, he learned printmaking and made etchings and linoleum cuts to illustrate stories and poems that others wrote. In college, he was introduced to children's books in a class taught by author-illustrator MAURICE SENDAK on the history and making of children's books. He graduated from Yale University in 1974 and received an M.F.A. degree in painting from Tyler School of Art in 1976.

Zelinsky's first PICTURE BOOK was Boris Zhitkov's *How I Hunted the Little Fellows* (1979),

a Russian story that allowed him to research late-nineteenth-century Russian interiors. He then illustrated a novel by AVI, *The History of Helpless Harry: To Which Is Added a Variety of Amusing and Entertaining Adventures* (1980), which was set in 1845. He was pulled ahead to the current century with *Ralph S. Mouse* (1982), his first assignment to illustrate a novel by BEVERLY CLEARY. Cleary's Newbery Medal–winning *Dear Mr. Henshaw* came next, in 1983. These books brought Zelinsky's work to the at-tention of the widest possible audience in the field of books for children, so that when his magnificent *Hansel and Gretel* appeared in 1984, many adults in the children's book field knew his name. Rich paintings with details redolent of a more romantic and a more rustic time limn the familiar tale of two children who best a witch. The book was named a Caldecott Honor Book by the American Library Association, as was his *Rumpelstiltskin* (1986). The latter was ex-hibited in an American Institute of Graphic Art-ists show, as were several others of his books, and was also named a Bratislava Biennale se-lection by the International Board on Books for Young People. Zelinsky won the Caldecott Medal for his lush illustrations for a GRIMM story, *Rapunzel* (1997).

A completely different picture book style is used in *The Maid and the Mouse and the Odd-Shaped House* (1981), which is based on a late-nineteenth-century "tell-and-draw" story de-signed to be created on a school blackboard, with each child adding to the picture. Zelinsky's mastery of book design is evident in this decep-tively simple, whimsical, and clever book. The book was chosen by judges to appear in the *Horn Book Magazine* "Graphic Gallery" as an ex-ample of admirable illustration and design crite-ria, and it was a New York Times Best Illustrated Children's Book of 1981. Another picture book, *The Story of Mrs. Lovewright and Purrless Her Cat* (1985), is a story by Lore Segal, illustrated to full comic effect. It too was named a New York Times Best Illustrated Children's Book. In one of his most brilliant books, Anne Isaac's *Swamp Angel* (1994), which received a Caldecott Honor award, Zelinsky re-created American folk art and primitive American painting to illustrate the tall tale of a great woodswoman of Tennessee.

Zelinsky is capable of humor and an almost cartoonish style as in *Mrs. Lovewright* and of geometrically drawn, clean lines and innovative design as in *The Maid and the Mouse*. He can paint sumptuous pictures for traditional tales, such as the forest scenes and the gingerbread house in *Hansel and Gretel*, with lush detail and intricate composition. Clearly, this artist is capable of completely changing his approach to design and his style of illustration with practically every book and with repeated success. S.H.H.

Voices of the Creators

🕸 *Paul O. Zelinsky*

I fell short in my art school training because I never quite believed in Quality of Edge or Color Relationship as a painting's only reason for being; I was, and still am, happier trying to put these abstract qualities in the service of something else, such as a story.

Every story is a different experience, carries its own feelings and associations. When I read a story to illustrate it, I want to capture the feelings — grab them and hold on, because they can be fleeting — and figure out how to make pictures that support and intensify them. This problem demands abstract solutions (a quality of line, a kind of space, a color relationship), which often means playing with new and different media: pencil, pastel, oils, on paper, canvas, drafting film, wood. But increasingly, I spend time just thinking about the feelings in the story.

Often these feelings come to me as a sort of flavor. I know that when I call up my earliest memories, what I remember seeing and hearing is accompanied by a flavorlike sense of what it felt like to be *there* and see *that*. It is usually a wonderful sense, belonging to the whole experience, the way the smell of a room can become the whole experience of the room. Some years ago I was

reading my daughter a Babar book for the second or third time when suddenly an illustration (of the monkeys' tree houses) sparked a lost memory. It was simply the memory of that same page, but as I had seen it as a young child. Not only did the crudeness of the drawing fall away in this child's-eye view, and the sketchy detail blossom into something incredible, but the whole scene was enveloped in a kind of air, had a particular quality. Suddenly I could breathe, smell, and taste this world. So, too, with each new text I take on, I want to grasp what its taste is, and bring it out in the pictures.

When I first learned the song "The Wheels on the Bus" I knew I wanted to illustrate it someday (I was well out of kindergarten and already illustrating books). My literal mind immediately suggested a book where the bus's moving parts would really move. But what should the pictures look like? The song reminded me a little of bubble gum: it was sweet and bouncy. The pictures needed plenty of rhythm, and the sense of sinking your teeth into something. I thought thick oil paint might give that chewy feeling. And the palette of colors I eventually came up with does, I think, give some of the same kind of pleasure as sweets do. There was also a physical pleasure in the laying down of paint and the way colored pencil lines would sometimes plow through the wet oils. Altogether the flavor is strong and full of energy. I hope the pictures are more nutritious, though, than bubble gum.

Lore Segal's marvelous ear for language gave *The Story of Mrs. Lovewright and Purrless Her Cat* a tangy quality. I think perhaps of dill pickles, which are sour, deliciously flavorful, and somehow unintentionally funny. Looking for ways to make these feelings visual, I saw all stretched-out shapes and sharp angles. (Not how a pickle looks, certainly, but how I think the *taste* of a pickle would look.) Mrs. Lovewright was so uncomfortable a person — a chilly woman, trying vainly to make things cozy by cuddling with an unwilling cat. The drawings were in colored pencil; its line has a fittingly edgy quality, unlike, say, watercolor.

I used watercolor as well as opaque watercolor and pastels for Mirra Ginsburg's good-night book,

The Sun's Asleep Behind the Hill. This chantlike text seems to breathe the smells of a summer night. Soft and darkening by degrees, the watercolor pictures took on a filmy haze of color, consisting of pastels rubbed onto the thumb and smeared over the paper. The best pictures were done while house-sitting for friends in the country, where night came on slowly and I was alone to sense the changes of color and the sounds and smells in the air. That was an attempt to bring some real-life experience into the illumination of a text. Drawing *Rumpelstiltskin* was an effort to create a purely imagined world. It called for a sort of perfect beauty: smooth surfaces placed in a clear light, reminiscent of the paintings of the Northern Renaissance. These were painted in many transparent layers of carefully applied oil paint, and I worked out my own version of the technique. I would have liked to paint what it's like on the inside of a jewel — bright and still, perhaps with no smell at all.

It seems I give myself the task with every book of inventing a new way of working toward a different effect. Three-quarters of the way through each project, I wonder why it has taken so very long before the drawing started to flow. It is hard to remember after the fact how much trial and error — and error and error — go into the earliest stage of the work of illustrating: sensing the flavor of a text, and figuring out how to capture it for the eyes. 🏮

Zemach, Margot

American illustrator and author, 1931–1989. Since the publication of *A Small Boy Is Listening* (1959), a collaboration with Harve Zemach, Margot Zemach has ranked among the finest of contemporary children's book illustrators. Zemach's strong graphic language — animated drawings, comic high spirits, and impeccable design — inform all her work.

Zemach was born in Los Angeles. Her mother was an actress and her stepfather a dancer and choreographer, thespian influences that helped Zemach prepare for her future ca-

reer. As Zemach detailed in *Self-Portrait: Margot Zemach* (1978), "When there is a story I want to tell in pictures, I find my actors, build the sets, design the costumes and light the stage . . . when the book closes, the curtain comes down."

Pursuing her childhood ambition to become an artist, Zemach studied at the Los Angeles County Art Institute and other Los Angeles art schools. After receiving a Fulbright scholarship, she attended the Vienna Academy of Fine Arts. There she met Harvey Fischstrom, a fellow Fulbright student who became her husband and collaborator, using the name Harve Zemach. Zemach's early career was characterized by collaborations with Harve as storyteller. These joint productions include *Nail Soup: A Swedish Folk Tale Retold* (1964), *Salt: A Russian Tale* (1965), and *Too Much Nose: An Italian Tale* (1967). These tales, like much of Zemach's work, resonate with a distinct European sensibility. Zemach's tenure abroad, first in Vienna and later in Italy, Denmark, and England, imbued her work with an understanding of, and appreciation for, other cultures.

Using the folktale as a vehicle, Zemach's portrayal of human foibles and absurdities is recognizable for its comic warmth and clear-eyed yet sympathetic vision of humanity. Zemach's human comedy is fully developed in *The Judge: An Untrue Tale* (1969), a Caldecott Honor Book, in which a lusty cast of characters are successively imprisoned for attempting to warn a judge that "a horrible thing is coming this way, creeping closer day by day." *Duffy and the Devil: A Cornish Tale* retells the Rumpelstiltskin story. The lazy girl Duffy bargains with the devil to do all her knitting, with the proviso that at the end of three years he'll take her away unless she can guess his name. Rich with the authentic flavor of England, the book won the 1974 Caldecott Medal. Both books burst with antic wit, robust line drawing, and incandescent color.

After Harve's death in 1974, Zemach continued to interpret and revitalize tales from traditional sources, including the brothers GRIMM. With the exception of *Jake and Honeybunch Go to Heaven* (1981), an adaptation of an African

American folktale disparaged for promoting stereotypes, Zemach's work has won wide critical acclaim. Besides illustrating nine ALA Notable Children's Books, Zemach herself was twice selected as a United States candidate for the Hans Christian Andersen Award, honoring the body of an artist's work. Zemach's matchless talent for creating graphic interpretations — whether explosively energetic, broadly comic, or purposely understated — brought exuberant new life to a varied body of stories. Margot Zemach died of Lou Gehrig's disease. C.L.S.

Zindel, Paul

American author, b. 1936. Pulitzer Prize–winning author of the brilliant, emotionally devastating play *The Effect of Gamma Rays on Man-in-the-Moon Marigolds* (1965), Paul Zindel was first inspired to write novels by CHARLOTTE ZOLOTOW, an editor who had seen the play and recognized the enormous potential of this talented writer. His first YOUNG ADULT NOVEL, *The Pigman* (1968), is the story of John and Lorraine, two high school students who befriend a lonely old man, with disastrous consequences. Funny, poignant, and believable, *The Pigman* firmly established Zindel's reputation as a major author of literature for adolescents, and it is considered a classic in the field of realistic teenage novels.

Zindel grew up on Staten Island. His parents were divorced when he was young, and he had an unhappy childhood, characterized by poverty and isolation. Zindel has documented many of his childhood and teenage experiences in his autobiography for young people, *The Pigman and Me* (1991). As an adult he spent ten years as a chemistry teacher. His early experiences and his firsthand knowledge of teenagers and life in a public high school are reflected in his work. Staten Island serves as the backdrop for most of his novels, although they could easily be set anywhere in suburban America. His books are generally written in the first person, and he has captured the teenage vernacular with amazing accuracy. His characters are troubled teenagers, trying to cope with real-life problems in a hostile world.

In *My Darling, My Hamburger* (1969), Zindel's second novel, a beautiful and intelligent young woman named Liz becomes pregnant in her senior year of high school. How she and her boyfriend, Sean, and their two best friends, Dennis and Maggie, cope with the catastrophic effects of an unwanted pregnancy is a subject young people still find relevant more than twenty years after the book's first publication. Yvette and Dewey, the unlikely protagonists of *I Never Loved Your Mind* (1970), seem to be polar opposites. Although they are both high school dropouts, Dewey is a beer-guzzling cynic and Yvette an idealistic vegetarian. The story of this mismatched couple's attempts to love each other is an insightful, if depressing, commentary on the sense of alienation many teenagers feel when confronted with the emptiness at the heart of our materialistic culture.

Many of Zindel's books, including *The Pigman* and its sequel, *The Pigman's Legacy* (1980), *Confessions of a Teenage Baboon* (1977), and *A Begonia for Miss Applebaum* (1989), center on the relationship between teenagers and one remarkable, sympathetic adult. *Confessions of a Teenage Baboon* is the story of a lonely boy dominated by his mother, a kleptomaniacal private nurse. When Chris and his mother go to live with Lloyd Dipardi, a middle-aged alcoholic, Chris takes some important steps forward in achieving independence from his mother and taking responsibility for himself. In *A Begonia for Miss Applebaum* Henry and Zelda learn invaluable lessons about the meaning of life and love when they become the companions of their beloved science teacher, a woman dying of cancer.

Zindel has been criticized for frequently portraying the parents of his characters in an extremely negative light. But as Zindel himself has written, "Kids don't like to admit how strong an influence parents have on them, and it's natural to have to reject them . . . in order to find themselves." The enduring popularity of Zindel's novels is testimony to his ability to speak directly to adolescents.   K.T.

Zolotow, Charlotte

American author, b. 1915. A Virginian who attended the University of Wisconsin before coming to New York, Charlotte Zolotow would have attained professional distinction had she been only a writer of PICTURE BOOKS or only an editor, but she has made signal contributions in both areas. She is the author of more than seventy picture books. Unusual in their laser-beam perception of a child's emotions, they are written with a deceptive simplicity that is in fact polished prose.

Zolotow's first book, *The Park Book* (1944), was published by Harper when she was an assistant to children's book editor Ursula Nordstrom; Zolotow in fact wrote it in response to Nord-

strom's encouragement. Nordstrom was one of a legendary group of pioneer editors in the field of children's literature; Zolotow has credited her as the major influence in her writing and editing career and has pointed out that it was from this mentor that she learned to differentiate between her role as an author and her role as an editor.

Some of Zolotow's writing is in verse, and often her prose has a poetic quality. Almost all her picture books are explorations of personal relationships cast in story form and given depth by humor and tenderness. *The Storm Book* (1953), illustrated by MARGARET BLOY GRAHAM, and *Mr. Rabbit and the Lovely Present* (1963), illustrated by MAURICE SENDAK (and one of the author's few fanciful tales), were Caldecott Honor Books.

In *The Hating Book* (1969) a small girl learns that it may not always be easy to be a friend but that it's worth the effort. Two books about parent-child relationships, *When I Have a Little Girl*

Illustration by Helen Craig from *The Bunny Who Found Easter* (1959), by Charlotte Zolotow.

(1965) and *When I Have a Little Boy* (1967, originally published under the title *When I Have a Son*), express children's plans for their own future progeny, plans that do not include having to take piano lessons (boy) and not being allowed to eat snow (girl). There weren't many people taking a stand against stereotyped sex roles in children's books in 1972, but in her quiet way Charlotte Zolotow struck a blow for common sense in *William's Doll,* the story of a boy who wanted a doll so he could practice being a father.

Zolotow's understanding of children's emotional needs and problems and her ability to express them at a young child's level of comprehension, leavened with a gentle, affectionate humor, have made her one of the major contemporary writers of realistic books for young children. She has edited books for older readers with courage and percipience and has produced two excellent anthologies for adolescent readers, *Early Sorrows: Ten Stories of Youth* (1986) and *An Overpraised Season: Ten Stories of Youth* (1973).

Zolotow became editorial director of Harper Junior Books in 1976, and in 1981 was appointed vice president of Harper and Row. Six years later she resigned these positions to become editorial consultant to Harper Junior Books and editorial director of her own imprint, Charlotte Zolotow Books. In 1986 she received the University of Minnesota's Kerlan Award for "her singular attainments in the creation of children's literature." The University of Mississippi presented her, in 1990, with the Silver Medallion, awarded annually for the body of an author's or an artist's work, and in 1991 the American Library Association adopted a resolution acknowledging "her far-reaching contribution to children's literature." Z.S.

Zwerger, Lisbeth

Austrian illustrator, b. 1954. In 1990 Lisbeth Zwerger was awarded the Hans Christian Andersen Award for lifetime achievement and contribution to the field of children's literature. Just sixteen years earlier, she had dropped out of art school, frustrated and disillusioned. None of her teachers had encouraged the art of illustration nor felt it was a worthwhile endeavor. Around the same time, Zwerger met an English artist, John Rowe, who later became her husband. They lived in Vienna, where Zwerger had grown up, and struggled to support themselves as artists. At one point, Rowe showed Zwerger a book of illustrations by ARTHUR RACKHAM. This was a turning point for Zwerger, who found in Rackham's work both the inspiration and the direction she had lost.

She began to illustrate stories and to sell individual pieces, and eventually her work caught the eye of an Austrian publisher, who gave her a contract for her first book, *The Strange Child* (1984), written by E. T. A. Hoffman. Zwerger has now illustrated more than fifteen books, all fairy tales, folktales, or classic stories such as O. Henry's *Gift of the Magi* (1982), Oscar Wilde's *Selfish Giant* (1984), and Charles Dickens's *A Christmas Carol* (1988). Although Zwerger's artwork is immediately recognizable, she acknowledges her great debt to Rackham and other English illustrators. Accustomed to working in black and white, she has used a very limited palette in her earlier work, such as *Thumbeline* (1980), *The Swineherd* (1982), and *The Nightingale* (1984). Her characterization was superb, as seen in the ghostlike witch of *Hansel and Gretel* (1979) and the simple and informal portrayal of Marie in *The Nutcracker* (1987).

During her developmental years, Zwerger concentrated on composition, technique, and accuracy of detail. Her backgrounds were open and vague — almost dreamlike — creating a wonderful dramatic contrast. The reader's eye focuses immediately on her characters and on significant objects in a scene.

While her pictures have elegance and an often breathtaking beauty, Zwerger has also shown respect for great storytellers; her art never overwhelms the story. Over the years, she has added more color to her work, as in Heinz Janisch's *Till Eugenspiegel's Merry Pranks* (1990), in which the pictures are gay and light compared with her earlier work and are framed in handsome decorative borders, and in her 1992 collection *Hans Christian Andersen Fairy Tales,* which includes "The Sandman" and "The Naughty Boy" along with old favorites such as "The Princess and the Pea" and "The Emperor's New Clothes."

Zwerger has said that the most difficult task for her now is choosing material to illustrate; at first she gravitated toward childhood favorites, but later she tired of traditional fairy tale endings, which often seemed sexist or overly moralistic. Her work has continued to be published in Austria; in addition, she is published in more than sixteen other countries, and her work has been exhibited worldwide. Zwerger has been honored several times at the Bologna International Children's Book Fair, at the Biennial of Illustrators at Bratislava, and by library organizations and literary publications in the United States. She is among the best illustrative artists to have emerged in this century. K.M.K.

Notes on the Contributors

Born and raised in Springfield, Massachusetts (also the hometown of Dr. Seuss), **Edward M. Aycock** received his master's degree in library and information science from Rutgers University. He lives in New York City.

Mara Ilyse Amster's work has been published in *Engaging Feminism: Students Speak Up and Speak Out.*

After working for several years as a library-media specialist in Lexington, Massachusetts, **Lois F. Anderson** now lives in Chapel Hill, North Carolina.

William Anderson, an educator and author, specializes in American studies and children's literature. He has written several books about Laura Ingalls Wilder and helped establish the historical sites and memorials at "Little House" book locales.

Barbara Bader is a former editor and juvenile editor of *Kirkus Reviews* and the author of *American Picturebooks from Noah's Ark to the Beast Within.*

Donald A. Barclay is assistant director of the Houston Academy of Medicine, Texas Medical Library. He has published in the areas of children's literature, the literature of the American West, and library science.

Mary Brigid Barrett, writer and illustrator, is the author of *Snow Baby, Mud Baby, Leaf Baby,* and *Day Care Days.*

Barbara M. Barstow is a children's librarian. The coauthor of *Beyond Picture Books: A Guide to First Readers,* she is actively involved in both the Association for Library Service to Children and the United States Board on Books for Young People.

Christine C. Behr was the children's librarian at the Wayland Public Library in Wayland, Massachusetts, and a regular reviewer for the *Horn Book Guide.*

Jane Botham was coordinator of children's services for Milwaukee, Wisconsin.

Susan Boulanger served as editor for *Children's Books and Their Creators.*

Jennifer M. Brabander is a graduate of the Simmons College Center for the Study of Children's Literature and serves as senior editor for the *Horn Book Guide.*

Paula Overland Brandt is the coordinator of the Curriculum Laboratory in the College of Education at the University of Iowa, Iowa City.

Beverly J. Braun is the resource director of the Nonprofit Support Center in Santa Barbara, California.

Susan A. Burgess is a Westwood, Massachusetts, children's literature consultant and Framingham (Massachusetts) State College graduate faculty educator.

Constance Burns is a librarian and reviewer. She holds a master's in library science from Simmons College and a master's in art for New England studies from the University of Southern Maine.

Former coordinator of the Curriculum Library at Framingham (Massachusetts) State College, **Mary Mehlman Burns**, a former children's librarian and secondary school teacher, teaches about, lectures on, and reviews books for children.

Margaret Bush, associate professor of library science at Simmons College, has also been a longtime children's librarian, book reviewer, and selector of science books for *The Elementary School Library Collection.*

Marie C. Campbell, a children's book editor in Canada, wrote her M.A. thesis on L. M. Montgomery's Emily of New Moon trilogy.

Dudley B. Carlson served as head of children's services in Princeton, New Jersey.

Betty Carter, professor of children's and young

adult literature at Texas Woman's University, is the coauthor of *Nonfiction for Young Adults.*

John O. Cech, writer and scholar, is the author of *Angels and Wild Things: The Archetypal Poetics of Maurice Sendak* and the children's books *My Grand-mother's Journey* (1991), *First Snow, Magic Snow* (1992), and *Django* (1994). He teaches children's literature at the University of Florida in Gainesville.

Barbara A. Chatton is an associate professor at the University of Wyoming, the author of *Using Poetry Across the Curriculum: A Whole Language Approach,* and the coauthor of *Blurring the Edges: Integrated Curriculum Through Writing and Children's Literature.*

Bill W. Clark is a freelance writer who obtained a master's degree in technical and professional writing from Northeastern University. He writes about natural history, computers, and hiking.

Andrea Cleghorn, a journalist and former children's book editor for the *Boston Herald,* is the author of *Rosie's Place.*

Julie Cummins was the coordinator of children's services for the New York Public Library for thirteen years and was the editor in chief of *School Library Journal.* She plays an active leadership role in the American Library Association.

Donnelyn Curtis was a reference–information technology librarian at New Mexico State University in Las Cruces.

Ann-Marie Davis is a freelance writer.

Former managing editor of the *Horn Book Guide,* **Anne E. Deifendeifer** holds a master's degree in children's literature from Simmons College.

A university professor and school district administrator in Madison, Wisconsin, **Eliza T. Dresang** provides literary leadership through speaking, writing, and research. She has served on the Newbery and Caldecott Award committees.

Mary Beth Dunhouse is currently coordinator of special projects and collections at the Boston Public Library. A graduate of the Center for the Study of Children's Literature at Simmons College, she is active in the Association for Library Service to Children and the New England Round Table of Children's Librarians.

Eden K. Edwards has worked in a children's bookstore and reviewed for the *Horn Book Guide.* She currently works in children's book publishing.

Barbara Elleman is the past editor of ALA's *Book-list* and the founder of *Book Links.* She is professor emeritus of children's literature at Marquette University.

Sarah Ellis is a Vancouver writer, librarian, and storyteller. She writes a regular column on Canadian children's books for the *Horn Book Magazine.*

Librarian **Ellen G. Fader** reviews for *School Library Journal.* She has been on the Newbery Medal Committee twice and has served as a Boston Globe–Horn Book Award judge.

Katherine Flynn has worked as an editor for Morrow Junior Books. She is executive editor of the *Horn Book Guide.*

Jack Foreman is a reviewer of young adult books and the author of *Presenting Paul Zindel.*

A parent, critic, and children's bookseller, **Sheila McMorrow Geraty** received her master's degree from Simmons College's Center for the Study of Children's Literature.

Bernie Goedhart reviews children's literature for the *Montreal Gazette* and, as a bibliophile in her own right, has a particular passion for picture books.

Carol Goldenberg has designed many award-winning books for children. Formerly art director for a major children's book publisher, she is now a freelance designer and consultant living in Newton, Massachusetts.

M. Jean Greenlaw is Regents Professor at the University of North Texas. She is an author of professional and trade books, a critic, and a recipient of the Arbuthnot Award.

Kelly Milner Halls is a Washington-based freelance writer. Her work has regularly appeared in *Booklist, Book Links,* the *Children's Writer's & Illustrator's Market, Writer's Digest,* the *Chicago Tribune,* the *Washington Post,* the *Denver Post,* and many other publications.

Karen Harris, professor of library science and confirmed bibliophile, has written extensively about books and children in fortuitous combinations.

Crystal Haynes-Smith specializes in African-American children's books.

Karen Lee Henning received a B.A. from Ursinus College in 1969 and has since worked as a secondary English teacher and K–12 school librarian. She currently lives in the rural Northeast Kingdom of Vermont.

Christine M. Heppermann is a columnist and reviewer for the *Horn Book Magazine* as well as a contributing editor for *Riverbank Review of Books for Young Readers.*

Maryclare O'Donnell Himmel contributed essays to *The Sixth Book of Junior Authors and Illustrators* and *Twentieth-Century Young Adult Writers.*

Peggy Hogan is a former teacher, children's bookstore manager, and marketing manager for a children's book publisher.

Elizabeth C. Hoke, coordinator of children's services, Montgomery County (Maryland) Public Libraries (1979–1989), served on ALA, Newbery, Caldecott, Batchelder, and Notable Books committees and has coordinated many Montgomery College Children's Literature Celebrations.

Sally Holmes Holtze, who served as series editor of the H. W. Wilson Company's Junior Authors volumes, wrote *Presenting Norma Fox Mazer* and also writes for film (*Meet the Author: Louisa May Alcott*).

Lyn Littlefield Hoopes is the author of several picture books, including *Wing a Ding* and *My Own Home.* She teaches creative writing to elementary school children.

Johnathan Hunt teaches fifth grade at Golden View Elementary in San Ramon, California.

Elizabeth Hurd served as coordinator of children's services for Greensboro, North Carolina.

Anne Irish was the owner of Pooh Corner Bookstore in Madison, Wisconsin. She has been president of the Association of Booksellers for Children and a reviewer for the *Horn Book Guide.*

An expert in children's and young adult literature, **Cyrisse Jaffee** has been a trade book editor, librarian, and lecturer. The author of many reviews and articles, she is currently a freelance editor, writer, and book consultant in the Boston area.

J. Alison James writes novels and translates children's books from Swedish and German.

Karen Jameyson, a former managing editor of the *Horn Book Magazine,* moved to Australia in 1989. A critic and reviewer, she also worked for the *New South Wales School Magazine.*

Patrick Jones is a former youth services librarian and the author of *Connecting Young Adults and Libraries, Do the Right Thing: Best Practices for Serving Young Adults in School and Public Libraries,* and many articles on young adult library services and literature.

Barbara Kiefer is associate professor at Teachers College, Columbia University, where she teaches courses in children's literature and reading.

Lee Kingman lives in Gloucester, Massachusetts, has written books for children and young adults, edited books about art and writing in children's literature, and been a director of The Horn Book, Inc.

Karen M. Klockner is a children's book editor who has been on the staff of Little, Brown and Orchard Books. She currently freelances from her home in Shaker Heights, Ohio.

Maeve Visser Knoth works part time as a children's librarian for the San Mateo County Library System in California, teaches a course in children's literature at Lesley University, and is a former reviewer for the *Horn Book Magazine.*

Sarah Guille Kvilhaug holds a master's degree in children's literature and is a freelance writer specializing in children's literature.

Starr LaTronica is the youth services manager of the Four County Library System in Vestal, New York. She has served on the Newbery and Caldecott committees and chaired the 2003 Newbery Committee.

Retired Sonoma County Schools librarian **Mildred Lee** works as a library consultant when not traveling to see the world she found in books. She lives in Santa Rosa, California.

Deborah M. Locke holds a master's degree in children's literature from Simmons College, has chaired Maine's Intellectual Freedom Committee, and reviews books on tape for *AudioFile.*

Stephanie Loer, children's book commentator for the *Boston Globe,* has written several guides about teaching children to read.

Claudia Logan is a freelance writer.

Leonard S. Marcus is the author of *Margaret Wise Brown: Awakened by the Moon; Dear Genius: The Letters of Ursula Nordstrom; A Caldecott Celebration;* and *Side by Side.*

Rick Margolis is an editor for *School Library Journal.* He fell in love with children's books when he turned thirty.

Barbara A. Marinak is a founder and past president of the Children's Literature Council of Pennsylvania. She enjoys reviewing for a number of publications.

Jill P. May is professor of literacy and languages at Purdue University, where she teaches courses in children's literature. She wrote *Films and Filmstrips for Language Arts* and *Lloyd Alexander* (1991) and edited *Children and Their Literature.*

Juliana McIntyre worked for several publishers and the *Horn Book Magazine.*

Amy J. Meeker is a freelance writer living in the Boston area.

Associate director and assistant professor at the Simmons College Center for the Study of Children's Literature, **Cathryn M. Mercier** chaired the 2001 Boston Globe–Horn Book Award Committee and has served on the Caldecott, Newbery, and Sibert committees. She reviews children's and young adult books for *Five Owls* and has written the professional reading column for the *Horn Book Magazine.*

Bobbi Miller earned her master of arts in children's literature from Simmons College and her M.F.A. in writing for children from Vermont College. As a writer, she has published short stories, reviews, and articles and is currently completing several books.

Sara Miller was director of the children's department at the public library in White Plains, New York, and an instructor of children's and young adult literature at Manhattanville College. She is pursuing an M.F.A. in writing for children at Vermont College.

Dianne L. Monson, professor emerita of the University of Minnesota, has served as president of the United States Board on Books for Young People.

Helen Green Neuburg is a former teacher and school director and a cofounder of the Cheshire Cat Bookstore.

Helen Snell Neumeyer, former children's book editor and teacher of grades K through graduate school, has written and edited several language arts texts.

Peter F. Neumeyer is a professor, writer, and reviewer. He has published more than ten books for children and adults, and his *Annotated Charlotte's Web* was published in 1994.

Martha V. Parravano is executive editor of the *Horn Book Magazine.*

Bette J. Peltola, professor emerita at the University of Wisconsin in Milwaukee, chaired the 1975 Newbery and Caldecott Awards Committee and the 1988 Caldecott Award Committee.

Jamie Pittel holds an M.F.A. in writing for children from Vermont College. She works as a children's librarian in Cambridge, Massachusetts, and writes fiction for young adults.

Amy E. Quigley is a librarian, writer, and reviewer.

Anne Quirk has worked for a number of children's

book publishers and is the associate publisher and marketing director of the *Horn Book Magazine.*

Sandra Ray holds a master's degree in children's literature from Simmons College.

Patricia Riley has master's degrees in writing for children, children's literature, and social work. She reviews books and teaches about writing children's books.

Lolly Robinson, an artist, is the designer and production manager of the *Horn Book Magazine.*

Hannah F. Rodgers holds an M.A. in children's literature from Simmons College and is pursuing an M.F.A. in writing for children at Vermont College. She works in children's book publishing and resides in Boston.

Sarah L. Rueter, a Boston-area librarian long involved with children's books, has served as chair of the Boston Globe–Horn Book Award Committee.

Grace W. Ruth is children's book selection specialist for the San Francisco Public Library. She chaired the 1988 and 1989 ALA Notable Children's Books and 1995 Caldecott Award committees.

Maria B. Salvadore, former coordinator of children's services for the Washington, D.C., Public Library, works as a specialist and consultant in children's literature and literacy for organizations such as PBS, RIF, and Catholic Charities. An active member of ALA, she serves on its council and the Notable Children's Books Committee.

Sheryl Lee Saunders is the author of *Look — and Learn!* and *The Author Visit Handbook.*

A freelance children's literature reviewer, **Suzy Schmidt** is coauthor of *Abraham Lincoln* and a contributor to *From Sea to Shining Sea: A Treasury of American Folklore and Folk Songs.*

Dr. Isabel Schon, founding director of the Center for the Study of Books in Spanish for Children and Adolescents at California State University, San Marcos, has written extensively about books for and about Latino young readers.

Leda Deirdre Schubert is a consultant for the Vermont Department of Education. She has served on the Caldecott and Arbuthnot committees and has taught, written, and reviewed children's books.

A content research editor and freelance writer, **Carolyn L. Shute** has taught courses on children's literature in the United States and Canada. She holds a master's degree in children's literature from Simmons College.

Martha F. Sibert, who has master's degrees in children's literature and writing for children, is a book reviewer and former children's coordinator for a public library system.

Phyllis Sidorsky was the librarian for National Cathedral School in Washington, D.C.

Peter D. Sieruta grew up in Detroit. A frequent contributor to reference books about children's and young adult literature, he is a reviewer for the *Horn Book Magazine* and the author of *Heartbeats and Other Stories.*

Editor in chief of the *Horn Book Magazine* from 1985 to 1995, **Anita Silvey** teaches, lectures, and writes about children's and young adult books.

A 1981 graduate of Simmons College Center for the Study of Children's Literature, **Cooki Slone** was the children's book reviewer for the *Middlesex News* in Framingham, Massachusetts.

Jill A. Smilow, a consultant in the field of children's literature, has been professionally associated with the *Horn Book Magazine*, Scholastic, Inc., Candlewick Press, and the Massachusetts Corporation for Educational Telecommunications.

Emily Smith received an undergraduate degree from the University of North Carolina at Chapel Hill and an M.F.A. in writing for children from Vermont College.

Henrietta M. Smith, professor emerita, University of South Florida, Tampa, teaches storytelling and children's literature. She is particularly interested in research related to literature and the African-American child.

John Warren Stewig, a professor of children's literature at the University of Wisconsin, Milwaukee, is past president of the Wisconsin and the National Council of Teachers of English. He served as a member of the Caldecott Committee and as its chair in 1998. The author of fourteen books for teachers and librarians, he is also the author of nine picture books.

Jewell Stoddard, a bookseller in the Washington, D.C., area, was co-owner of the Cheshire Cat Book Store and a member of the 1994 Caldecott Committee.

Zena Sutherland, professor emerita, University of Chicago, is the author of *Children and Books* and was an editor for *Saturday Review* and *Bulletin of the Center for Children's Books.*

Katrin Tchana has been an avid reader of children's literature for twenty-seven years. She works as a teacher and writer.

Formerly an editor of children's books, **Nancy Vasilakis** is currently librarian at the Tower School in Marblehead, Massachusetts.

Caroline Ward is the youth services coordinator at the Ferguson Library in Stamford, Connecticut. She served as chairperson of the 1990 Newbery Committee.

A dedicated bookseller in the Chicago area, **Pat Wroclawski** was an original member of the Association of Booksellers for Children, taught children's literature at National-Louis University, and writes a book review column.

Illustration Credits

Index